P9-ELT-011

FUNDAMENTALS OF INVESTING

FUNDAMENTALS OF INVESTING

SEVENTH EDITION

Lawrence J. Gitman
San Diego State University

Michael D. Joehnk
Arizona State University

An Imprint of Addison Wesley Longman, Inc.

Reading, Massachusetts • Menlo Park, California • New York • Harlow, England
Don Mills, Ontario • Sydney • Mexico City • Madrid • Amsterdam

Executive Editor: Denise Clinton
Acquisitions Editor: Julie Zasloff
Development Editor: Ann Torbert
Senior Production Supervisor: Nancy Fenton
Marketing Manager: Jennifer Chapelle
Project Coordination, Text Design, Art Studio, and Electronic Page Makeup:
Thompson Steele Production Services
Cover Designer: Regina Hagen
Cover Image: © 1998 PhotoDisc, Inc.
Print Buyer: Sheila Spinney
Printer and Binder: RR Donnelley & Sons Company
Cover Printer: Lehigh Press Lithographers

For permission to use copyrighted material, grateful acknowledgment is made to the copyright holders on pp. C-1–C-2, which are hereby made part of this copyright page.

Library of Congress Cataloging-in-Publication Data

Gitman, Lawrence J.
Fundamentals of Investing / Lawrence J. Gitman, Michael D. Joehnk. — 7th ed.
p. cm.
Includes bibliographical references (p.).
ISBN 0-321-02106-1 (alk. paper)
1. Investments. 2. Investments—Problems, exercises, etc.
I. Joehnk, Michael D. II. Title.
HG4521.G547 1998
332.67'8—dc21 98-8175
CIP

Please visit our Web site at http://hepg.aw.com

45678910—DOW—010099

Reprinted with corrections, December 1998

Brief Contents

Detailed Contents

Investing in Action:

Take a Deep Breath and Don't Panic 281

Investing in Action:

Here's a TIP: Look Before You Leap 316

The Dream Factory on Wall Street 325

CHAPTER 9 BOND VALUATION AND ANALYSIS 343

CHAPTER 10 PREFERRED STOCK AND CONVERTIBLE SECURITIES 381

Part Four Derivative Securities 415

CHAPTER 14 Real Estate and Other Tangible Investments 543

CHAPTER 15 Tax-Advantaged Investments 586

PREFACE

"Market Hits New High." How many times have investors read this headline or heard this market report over the course of the last few years? The performance of the stock market has been *the* major story in the financial press recently and has had a widespread impact on investors, investment vehicles, and the investment environment in general. The golden glow of the stock market has changed the way many people view the activity of investing; some have even suggested that the financial community has overcome the inevitability of dips in the business cycle. Yet many remain wary of the possibility of market tremors, such as that in October 1997, and some even fear the financial equivalent of a seismic "big one." In the midst of the market euphoria on the one hand and prophecies of a market collapse on the other stands the individual investor wondering what to believe and what to do with his or her investment funds.

This textbook, *Fundamentals of Investing,* seventh edition, reflects the realities of today's changing investment environment—from new investment vehicles, techniques, and strategies to regulations and taxes. The book serves investors who wish to develop and monitor their own investment portfolios actively. It meets the needs of professors and students in the first course in investments offered at colleges and universities, junior and community colleges, professional certification programs, and continuing education courses. Focusing both on individual securities and on portfolios of securities, *Fundamentals of Investing* explains how to implement investment goals in light of risk–return tradeoffs. A conversational tone and liberal use of examples guide students through the material and demonstrate important points.

Key Features of the Seventh Edition

Using information gathered from both academicians and practicing investment professionals, plus feedback from adopters, the seventh edition reflects the realities of today's investment environment. At the same time, it provides a structured framework for successful teaching and learning.

Comprehensive and Integrated Learning System

Learning Goals at the beginning of each chapter are the central feature of our proven teaching/learning system. Each Learning Goal is tied by a special icon to the associated first-level head in the text, and these goals are restated and reviewed, point by point, at the chapter's end. To support these Learning Goals, Concepts in Review questions appear at the end of each section of the chapter (positioned before the next first-level head) and allow students to test their understanding of each section before moving on to the next section of the chapter. In addition, each goal is keyed to the end-of-chapter discussion questions, problems, cases, and selected supplements.

By focusing on the Learning Goals, students will know what material they need to learn, where they can find it in the chapter, and whether they've mastered it by the end of the chapter. In addition, instructors can build lectures and assignments around the Learning Goals.

Clear Focus on the Individual Investor

Today, about one out of every three adult Americans owns stock either directly or indirectly (through mutual funds). The focus of *Fundamentals of Investing* has always been on the individual investor. This focus on the individual investor gives students the information they need to plan, implement, and manage a successful investment program. It also provides students with a solid foundation on which subsequent courses can develop an understanding of the advanced concepts, tools, and techniques used by institutional investors and money managers.

Timely Topics

Various issues and developments constantly reshape financial markets and investment vehicles. We have revised virtually all topics to take into account changes in the investment environment that have occurred since the previous edition was published. To retain the text's timeliness, we also expanded coverage of certain topics, including online sources of investment information, derivatives, new forms of IRAs, and international diversification. These discussions provide students with a realistic understanding of the investment arena. In addition, we have added various Internet linkages to guide students to sites that will provide current data, information, and decision models.

Globalization

As a result of the growing globalization of securities markets, *Fundamentals of Investing* continues to stress the global aspects of investing. We initially look at the growing importance of international markets, investing in foreign securities—indirectly or directly, international investment performance, and the risks of investing internationally. In later chapters, popular international investment opportunities and strategies are described as part of the coverage of each specific type of investment vehicle. This integration of international topics helps students understand the importance of maintaining a global focus when planning, building, and managing an investment portfolio. Global topics are highlighted by inclusion of a globe icon .

Comprehensive yet Flexible Organization

The text provides a firm foundation for learning by first describing the overall investment environment, including the concepts of risk and return. It then examines each of the popular investment vehicles—common stocks, bonds, preferred stocks, convertible securities, options, futures, mutual funds, real estate and other tangibles, and tax-advantaged investments. The final section of the book focuses on investment administration—constructing, managing and controlling portfolios of the popular investment vehicles discussed in earlier chapters. Although the first and last parts of the the textbook are best covered at the start and end of the course, respectively, instructors can cover particular investment vehicles in just about any sequence.

We organized each chapter according to a decision-making perspective, and we have been careful always to point out the pros and cons of the various vehicles and strategies that we present. With this information, individual investors can select the investment actions that are most consistent with their objectives. In addition, we've illustrated investment vehicles and strategies in such a way that students learn the decision-making implications and consequences of each investment action they contemplate. The comprehensive yet flexible nature of the book enables instructors to customize it to their own course structure and teaching objectives.

Specific Content Changes by Chapter

- *Chapter 1,* on the role and scope of investments, has been shortened to provide a "quick start out of the blocks." It retains an overview of types of investments, the investment process, and investment vehicles—essential information that serves as a foundation on which to build understanding in subsequent chapters. Discussion of the steps in investing has been moved to Chapter 3. The overview of the textbook has been omitted. We have inserted marginal annotations that explain the book's pedagogical features to improve students' understanding of these important features as they appear.

- *Chapter 2,* on investment markets and transactions, contains expanded and updated coverage of international investment performance and foreign securities and a significantly updated discussion of stockbrokers that includes online as well as full-service and discount brokers. We also added discussion of the use of alternative dispute resolution processes to reduce conflicts between investors and their brokers.

- *Chapter 3,* on investment planning and information, now begins with a streamlined discussion of investment planning. The chapter reflects tax updates consistent with the Taxpayer Relief Act of 1997. The revised discussion of short-term investments now precedes updated and streamlined discussions of types and sources of investment information and advice and market averages and indexes, which now have a more global focus.

- *Chapter 4,* on measuring investment return and risk, emphasizes the actual rather than the approximate yield—an approach now used throughout the textbook. The chapter includes a boxed discussion of deflation and its risks. The discussions of various aspects of risk, including beta and CAPM, have been clarified and streamlined.

- *Chapter 5,* on common stock investments, contains updated information on market performance through the third quarter of 1997, including a discussion of the 1997 market "stumble," which triggered the use of the circuit breakers installed after the 1987 crash. The chapter also now contains discussion of stock spin-offs, the effects of currency movements in international investing, and the Russian stock market. Finally, the chapter has been streamlined, primarily to eliminate duplication of material on buying and selling stocks.

- *Chapter 6,* on analytical dimensions of stock selection, now includes more coverage of the impact that growth in earnings has on share prices, as it introduces the reader to PEG which relates a firm's P/E ratio to its rate of growth in earnings.

- *Chapter 7,* on stock valuation and investment decisions, has been updated throughout and now emphasizes the use of IRR procedures to measure stock returns, rather than approximate yield—which has been dropped.

- *Chapter 8,* on bond investments, includes updated information on market performance through 1997. It also has new material on Treasury inflation-indexed bonds (TIPs), asset-backed bonds, crossover bonds, and taxable munis.

- *Chapter 9,* on bond valuation and analysis, now focuses more clearly on the term structure of interest rates and the pricing of bonds. It also discusses a barbell bond investment strategy.

- *Chapter 10,* on preferred stock and convertible securities, has been thoroughly updated to reflect the latest market trends. An example is new coverage of monthly income preferred stock (MIPS) and convertible bonds.

- *Chapter 11,* on options, now includes more coverage of Dow Jones-linked products, such as the DJ index options, which are some of the hottest vehicles in the market. The chapter also includes discussion of customizing convertible bonds and using index options to protect a portfolio

- *Chapter 12,* on commodities and financial futures, also introduces the reader to the new Dow Jones futures contracts and notes the difference between these contracts and other traditional equity index contracts, like the S&P 500; also included is discussion of arbitrage trading and the triple-witching day.

- *Chapter 13,* on mutual funds, has been revised and updated to reflect growth in this form of investment in the last few years. Coverage now includes discussion of "funds of funds" and information on reading prospectuses and on single-country index funds (WEBS).

- *Chapter 14,* on real estate and other tangible investments, includes an updated discussion of the state of real estate markets, applies the latest revisions of the tax laws, and demonstrates the calculation of actual yield for real estate investment. The example of real estate valuation has been revised to fully reflect the impact of the Taxpayer Relief Act of 1997 on cash flows. The discussion of other tangible investments is also thoroughly revised and streamlined.

- *Chapter 15,* on tax-advantaged investments, has been thoroughly updated to reflect the latest tax laws, particularly the Taxpayer Relief Act of 1997, and related investment strategies and vehicles. The discussions of 401(k) and Keogh plans have been revised and updated, and the discussion of IRAs has been thoroughly reworked to reflect the impact of the new tax law on them, including the creation of Roth IRAs and Education IRAs.

- *Chapter 16,* on portfolio construction, includes a revised section on the effectiveness, methods, and benefits of international diversification. The discussion of traditional versus modern portfolio theory is streamlined and improved.

- *Chapter 17,* on portfolio management and control, has been updated to focus more clearly on the evaluation and assessment of portfolio performance and the methods for timing portfolio transactions.

Pedagogical Features

This textbook has long been recognized for its numerous pedagogical features designed to help students focus their study of investments. Among the useful features it includes are Learning Goals, a marginal glossary, *Investing in Action* boxed readings, Concepts in Review questions, Internet linkages, Investor Facts, and varied end-of-chapter materials.

LG 1 Learning Goals

Each chapter begins with six Learning Goals, labeled with numbered icons (noted at left of head), that clearly state the concepts and materials to be covered. The Learning Goal icons are tied to first-level headings, are reviewed point by point at the chapter's end, and are keyed to end-of-chapter discussion question, problems, and cases.

Alongside the chapter's Learning Goals at the beginning of each chapter is a brief vignette that features a real-world company or event and ties it to the chapter topic.

Marginal Glossary

New terms are set in boldface type and defined when first introduced in the text. In addition, each term appears with its definition in the text margin, to facilitate student learning and review. The page numbers on which these entries appear within the text are noted in boldface in the book's index, to make it easy to find these definitions.

Investing in Action

Each chapter features two boxed essays, called *Investing in Action,* that describe real-life investing situations or events. Although we have revised and retained a few of the most popular from the previous edition, the majority are new. These high-interest boxes, which have been written specifically for this textbook, demonstrate concepts introduced in the text and enliven the students' reading at a level consistent with their abilities.

Concepts in Review

Concepts in Review questions appear at the end of each section of the chapter (positioned before the next first-level heading) and are marked with a special design element. As students progress through the chapter, they can test their understanding of each concept, tool, or technique before moving on to the next section within the chapter. In this edition we have added Concepts in Review questions related to the *Investing in Action* boxes. These questions help to integrate the key concepts in the boxes with the text material.

Internet Linkages

The growth of the Internet and its increasing usage in college coursework has impelled us to add several types of Internet linkages in the seventh edition. The first is Internet interlineals—inserts following the Concepts in Review at the ends of key text sections. These inserts refer students to Web sites related to the topic covered in the section. In addition, each chapter ends with Home Page Exercises, which are described under the heading End-of-Chapter Materials later in the Preface. The third Internet linkage is the textbook's Home Page (at **hepg.aw.com**), which offers a wide variety of informational resources for students and instructors. This resource is described in more detail in the Supplemental Materials section of the Preface.

We feel certain that the inclusion of these rich Internet linkages in the seventh edition of the textbook adds further real-world flavor and a timely source of useful information for both students and instructors.

Investor Facts

Each chapter also contains two to three Investor Facts—brief sidebar items that give an interesting statistic or cite an unusual investment experience. The facts and figures in these boxes are intended to stimulate student interest and motivate further thought. For example, the Investor Fact on page 70 demonstrates the impact of taxes on the amount of money you would accumulate by making annual $2,000 deposits into an account that earns 8% annual interest over 30 years. The Investor Fact on page 578 uses an example of an item auctioned from Jacqueline Kennedy's estate to demonstrate the impact of celebrity on the value of collectibles.

End-of-Chapter Materials

A number of important elements at the end of each chapter reinforce the concepts, tools, and techniques described in the chapter and help students review and integrate chapter content.

Summary Each summary lists the chapter's key concepts and ideas, which correspond directly to the six numbered Learning Goals presented at the beginning of the chapter. The Learning Goal icons precede each summary item, which begins with a boldfaced restatement of the learning goal.

Discussion Questions A handful of thought-provoking Discussion Questions, keyed to the Learning Goals, are included at the end of each chapter. They guide students to integrate, investigate, and analyze the key concepts presented in the chapter. Many questions require that students apply the tools and techniques presented in the chapter to investment information they have obtained, and then make a recommendation with regard to a specific investment strategy or vehicle. These project-type questions are far broader than the Concepts in Review questions included within the chapter.

Problems A set of 8 to 15 Problems is included at the end of each chapter except Chapter 1. The Problems, keyed to the Learning Goals, vary in complexity and scope and thus ensure professors a wide choice of assignable materials. A CD-ROM symbol appears next to the Problems that can be solved using the *Fundamentals of Investing CD-ROM,* described in detail below.

Case Problems Two Case Problems, keyed to the Learning Goals, encourage students to use higher-level critical thinking skills: to apply techniques presented in the chapter, to evaluate alternatives, and to recommend how an investor might solve a specific problem.

Home Page Exercises The Home Page Exercises section—new in the seventh edition—consists of two parts. The first is a brief statement of how and where the chapter topic is covered and where it may be found on the Internet, with additional sites listed as resources for student exploration. Next come the Exercises, which require students to obtain data, information, or computational assistance from particular Web sites in order to answer questions or solve simple problems. These Web sites are linked through our textbook Home Page at **hepg.aw.com**. Frederick P. Schadler of East Carolina University is the author of this feature.

Supplemental Materials

We recognize the key role of a complete and creative package of materials to supplement a basic textbook. We believe that the following materials, offered with the seventh edition, will enrich the investments course for both students and instructors.

The *Fundamentals of Investing CD-ROM*

Included with each new copy of the book is the *Fundamentals of Investing CD-ROM,* which was revised and improved for this edition by Kathryn E. Coates and David Geis of KDC Software Solutions. The purpose of the CD-ROM is to perform the calculation of virtually all of the formulas, ratios, and valuation procedures presented in the book. The CD-ROM is user-friendly and fully interactive. More than a problem solver, it also enhances the student's understanding of the investment process. The CD-ROM is keyed to all applicable text discussions and end-of-chapter and ancillary materials with a disk symbol . Detailed instructions for using the disk are printed on the back left endpaper and in a help file contained on the CD-ROM.

Fundamentals of Investing Home Page

The textbook's Home Page (at **hepg.aw.com**) offers a rich variety of informational resources for students and instructors. Visitors to the site will find links to related sites mentioned in the interlineals at the ends of text sections; links to sites mentioned in the Home Page Exercises at the ends of chapters; interviews with investors, who share their investing philosophies and their successes or failures; readings on various topics; additional material beyond the normal scope of the first-level investments course; information on more investors' resources; and a calculator keystrokes manual.

Study Guide

The student review manual, *Study Guide to Accompany Fundamentals of Investing, Seventh Edition,* prepared by Karin B. Bonding, of the McIntire School at the University of Virginia and CFA, President of Capital Markets Institute, Inc., Ivy, Virginia has been completely revised. Each chapter of the *Study Guide* contains a chapter summary, a chapter outline, and a programmed self-test that consists of true-false and multiple-choice questions. Following the self-test are problems with detailed solutions and, where appropriate, calculator key strokes showing use of the calculator to solve certain problems. All elements are similar in form and content to those found in the book.

Instructor's Manual

Written by the text authors, with the assistance of Kumar Venkataraman of Arizona State University, the *Instructor's Manual* contains chapter outlines; a list of major topics discussed in each chapter; detailed chapter reviews; answers to all Concepts in Review questions, Discussion Questions, and Problems; solutions to the Case Problems; and ideas for outside projects. Instructions for outside projects are printed on separate sheets, for ease in duplicating them for classroom distribution.

Test Bank

Revised for the seventh edition by Susan Mason, the *Test Bank* now includes a substantial number of new questions. Each chapter now contains at least 15 true-false questions, at least 40 multiple-choice questions, and several problems and short-essay questions. The *Test Bank* is also available in Test Generator Software (TestGen-EQ with QuizMaster-EQ for Windows). Fully networkable, this software is available for Windows and Macintosh. TestGen-EQ's friendly graphical interface enables instructors to easily view, edit, and add questions; export questions to create tests; and print tests in a variety of fonts and forms. Search and sort features let the instructor quickly locate questions and arrange them in a preferred order. QuizMaster-EQ automatically grades the exams, stores results on disk, and allows the instructor to view or print a variety of reports.

PowerPoint Transparency Slides

To facilitate classroom presentations, PowerPoint slides of key text images are available for Windows and Macintosh. A PowerPoint viewer is provided for use by those who do not have the full software program.

Acknowledgments

Many people gave their generous assistance during the initial development and the revisions of *Fundamentals of Investing*. The expertise, classroom experience, and general advice of both colleagues and practitioners have been invaluable. Reactions and suggestions from students throughout the country—comments we especially enjoy receiving—sustained our belief in the need for a fresh, informative, and teachable investments text.

A few individuals provided significant subject matter expertise in the initial development of the book. They are Terry S. Maness of Baylor University, Arthur L. Schwartz, Jr., of the University of South Florida at St. Petersburg, and Gary W. Eldred. Their contributions are greatly appreciated. In addition, Addison Wesley Longman obtained the advice of a large group of experienced reviewers. We appreciate their many suggestions and criticisms, which have had a strong influence on various aspects of this volume. Our special thanks go to the following people, who reviewed all or part of the manuscripts for the previous six editions of the book.

M. Fall Ainina
Gary Baker
Harisha Batra
Richard B. Bellinfante
Cecil C. Bigelow
Paul Bolster
A. David Brummett
Gary P. Cain
Gary Carman
Daniel J. Cartell
P. R. Chandy
David M. Cordell
Timothy Cowling
Robert M. Crowe
Richard F. DeMong
Clifford A. Diebold
James Dunn
Betty Marie Dyatt
Steven J. Elbert
Thomas Eyssell
Frank J. Fabozzi
Robert A. Ford
Chaim Ginsberg
Joel Gold
Brian Grinder
Harry P. Guenther
Mahboubul Hassan
Gay Hatfield
Elizabeth Hennigar
Robert D. Hollinger
Sue Beck Howard
Roland Hudson, Jr.
A. James Ifflander
Donald W. Johnson
Ravindra R. Kamath
Bill Kane
Daniel J. Kaufmann, Jr.
Nancy Kegelman
David S. Kidwell
Phillip T. Kolbe
Sheri Kole
Thomas M. Krueger
George Kutner
Robert T. LeClair
Larry A. Lynch
Weston A. McCormac
David J. McLaughlin
Keith Manko
Timothy Manuel
Kathy Milligan
Warren E. Moeller
Homer Mohr
Majed R. Muhtaseb
Joseph Newhouse
Joseph F. Ollivier
John Park
Ronald S. Pretekin
Stephen W. Pruitt
William A. Richard
Linda R. Richardson
William A. Rini
Roy A. Roberson
Edward Rozalewicz
William J. Ruckstuhl
Gary G. Schlarbaum
Keith V. Smith
Harold W. Stevenson
Nancy E. Strickler
Glenn T. Sweeney
Phillip D. Taylor
Robert C. Tueting
Howard E. Van Auken
John R. Weigel
Peter M. Wichert
Glenn A. Wilt, Jr.
John C. Woods
Richard H. Yanow

The following people provided extremely useful reviews and input to the seventh edition:

Paul J. Bolster, *Northeastern University*

Thomas M. Krueger, *University of Wisconsin–La Crosse*

Chun I. Lee, *Texas Southern University*

Larry A. Lynch, *Roanoke College*

Thomas Patrick, *College of New Jersey*

David Russo, *SUNY, Empire State College*

Pat R. Stout, *College of DuPage*

Amir Tavakkol, *Kansas State University*

Wenyuh Tsay, *University of Texas at Arlington*

Because of the wide variety of topics covered in the book, we called upon many experts for advice. We thank them and their firms for allowing us to draw on their insights and awareness of recent developments, to ensure that the text is as current as possible. In particular, we want to mention Russell L. Block, San Diego, California; George Ebenhack, Oppenheimer & Co., Los Angeles, California; Richard Esposito, Prana Investments, Inc., New York; Dennis P.

Hickman, La Jolla, California; N. Arthur Hulick, Investment Planning and Management, Scottsdale, Arizona; Mike Iacampo, Donaldson, Lufkin, & Jenrette, Los Angeles, California; Martin P. Klitzner, Sunrise Capital Partners, Del Mar, California; Douglas R. Lempereur, Templeton Global Bond Managers, Ft. Lauderdale, Florida; David M. Love, Kenmar Institutional Investment Management, Rancho Santa Fe, California; Robert Luck, CFA, Association for Investment Management and Research (AIMR), Charlottesville, Virginia; David H. McLaughlin, Chase Investment Counsel Corp., Charlottesville, Virginia; Michael R. Murphy, Sceptre Investment Counsel, Toronto, Ontario, Canada; Mark S. Nussbaum, PaineWebber, La Jolla, California; John Richardson, Northern Trust Bank of Arizona, Phoenix, Arizona; Pat Rupp, IDS, Inc., Dayton, Ohio; Richard Russell, Dow Theory Letters, La Jolla, California; Mike Smith, Economic Analysis Corporation, Los Angeles, California; Eric Sorenson, Salomon Bros., Inc., New York; Barbara Walchli, First Interstate Capital Management, Scottsdale, Arizona; Fred Weaver, Great Western Bank, Phoenix, Arizona; and Lynn Yturri, BancOne Arizona, Phoenix, Arizona.

We greatly appreciate the support of our colleagues at San Diego State University and Arizona State University. Special thanks to attorney Robert J. Wright of Wright & Wright, CPAs, San Diego, and to Vaughn Armstrong of Washington State University–Vancouver for their help in revising and updating the many tax discussions, and to Professor Christopher M. Korth of Western Michigan University for his help in "internationalizing" the text. Thanks also to Professor Frank Griggs of Grand Valley State University for his ideas on strengthening the material on the P/E approach to stock valuation and to Professor Albert J. Fredman of California State University, Fullerton, for his help in preparing the material on closed-end mutual funds. We also thank Frederick P. Schadler for authoring the Internet linkages and Home Page Exercises, Karin Bonding for her useful feedback and for revising the *Study Guide,* Susan Mason for revising and updating the *Test Bank,* and Kumar Venkataraman for revising and updating the *Instructor's Manual.* Special thanks to Stuart Weiss of Stuart Weiss Business Writing, Inc., Portland, Oregon, for his work in preparing chapter vignettes, *Investing in Action* boxes, and Investor Facts. Our thanks also go to Kaye Coates and David Geis of KDC Software Solutions for developing the *Fundamentals of Investing CD-ROM.*

The staff of Addison Wesley Longman, particularly Julie Zasloff and Denise Clinton, contributed their creativity, enthusiasm, and commitment to this textbook. Freelance development editor Ann Torbert, production editor Elinor Stapleton of Thompson Steele Production Services, and Nancy Fenton of Addison Wesley Longman warrant special thanks for shepherding the project through the development and production stages. Without their care and concern, the text would not have evolved into the teachable and interesting text we believe it to be.

Finally, our wives, Robin and Charlene, and our children, Jessica and Zachary, and Chris and Terry and his wife, Sara, played important roles by providing support and understanding during the book's development, revision, and production. We are forever grateful to them, and we hope that this edition will justify the sacrifices required during the many hours we were away from them working on this book.

Lawrence J. Gitman
Michael D. Joehnk

Part One

The Investment Environment

CHAPTER 1

THE ROLE AND SCOPE OF INVESTMENTS

LEARNING GOALS

After studying this chapter, you should be able to:

LG 1 Understand the meaning of the term *investment.*

LG 2 Review the factors commonly used to differentiate among various types of investments.

LG 3 Describe the structure of and participants in the investment process and the types of investors.

LG 4 Discuss the principal types of investment vehicles, including short-term vehicles, common stock, and fixed-income securities.

LG 5 Describe derivative securities, the most popular derivatives (options and futures), and mutual funds.

LG 6 Describe other kinds of popular investment vehicles: real estate, tangibles, and tax-advantaged investments.

Twenty years ago, most people had very little daily exposure to the investment world. Perhaps the only reminder was hearing a ten-second announcement on the radio about the fortunes of the Dow Jones Industrial Average that day. Today, radio stations specialize in business and investing coverage. Cable TV channels like CNNfn and CNBC are all about business. You can't pass a newsstand without seeing headlines that scream, "Ten Stocks to Buy Now!" or "The Hottest Mutual Funds." Besides the *Wall Street Journal*, you can subscribe to *Investor's Business Daily, Barron's, Money, Smart Money, Kiplinger's Personal Finance Magazine,* and dozens more publications dedicated to investing. Also, some of the best sites on the Internet are devoted to the topic, as the *Investing in Action* box on page 4 explains.

In short, the world of investments has come center stage in American life. Studying this textbook will help you to understand this increasingly important subject and to make the most of your financial resources. This first chapter sets the stage for an in-depth look at investing that will be presented throughout the book. It introduces the types of investments that are available, the structure of the investment process, and the key investment vehicles. Becoming familiar with various investment alternatives and developing realistic investment plans should greatly increase your chance of achieving financial success.

Investments and the Investment Process

LG 1 LG 2 LG 3

Note: The Learning Goals shown at the beginning of the chapter are keyed to text discussions using these icons.

investment
any vehicle into which funds can be placed with the expectation that it will generate positive income and/or preserve or increase its value.

If you have ever deposited money in a savings account, you already have at least one investment to your name. An **investment** is simply any vehicle into which funds can be placed with the expectation that they will generate positive income and/or that their value will be preserved or increased. The rewards, or returns, from investing are received in either of two basic forms: current income or increased value. For example, money invested in a bank savings account provides current income in the form of periodic interest payments. Similarly, buying a piece of raw land is an investment, because the land is expected to increase in value between the time it is purchased and the time it is sold. Is cash placed in a simple (no-interest) checking account an investment? No, because it fails both tests of the definition—it does not provide any type of added income, nor does its value increase. (In fact, the value of the cash in a checking account is likely to decrease, because it is eroded over time by inflation.) We begin our study of investments by looking at types of investments and at the structure of the investment process.

Types of Investments

When you invest, the organization in which you invest—whether it is a company or a government entity—offers you an expected future benefit in exchange for the current use of your funds. Organizations compete for the use of your funds, and the one that will get your investment dollars is the one that offers a benefit you judge to be better than any competitor offers. However, different investors judge desirable benefits differently. As a result, investments of every type are available, from "sure things" such as earning 3% interest on your bank savings account, to the possibility of tripling your money fast by investing in raw land adjacent to a planned interstate highway. What investments you choose will depend on a combination of your resources, your goals, and your personality. The various types of investments can be differentiated on the basis of a number of factors. Let's look at the differences in the paragraphs that follow.

Securities or Property

securities
investments that represent evidence of debt or ownership or the legal right to acquire or sell an ownership interest.

property
investments in real property or in tangible personal property.

Investments that represent evidence of debt or ownership (of a business or other assets) or the legal right to acquire or sell an ownership interest (in a business or other assets) are called **securities.** The most frequently used types of securities are stocks, bonds, and options. **Property,** on the other hand, consists of investments in real property or tangible personal property. *Real property* is land, buildings, and that which is permanently affixed to the land. *Tangible personal property* includes items such as gold, artwork, antiques, and other collectibles. In this book we will focus primarily on securities.

Direct or Indirect

direct investment
investment in which an investor directly acquires a claim on a security or property.

indirect investment
investment made in a *portfolio,* or group of securities or properties.

portfolio
collection of securities or properties, typically constructed to meet one or more investment goals.

A **direct investment** is one in which an investor directly acquires a claim on a security or property. If you buy a stock, a bond, a parcel of real estate, or a rare coin in order to earn income or preserve value, you have made a direct investment. An **indirect investment** is an investment made in a **portfolio,** or collection of securities or properties, typically constructed to meet one or more investment goals. You may purchase a share of a *mutual fund,* which gives you a claim on a fraction of the entire portfolio rather than on the security of a single firm.

Debt, Equity, or Derivative Securities

debt
funds lent in exchange for interest income and the promised repayment of the loan at a given future date.

Usually, an investment represents either a debt or an equity interest. **Debt** represents funds lent in exchange for interest income and the promised repayment of the loan at a given future date. When you buy a debt instrument like a

INVESTING IN ACTION

Checking Out the Web for Hot Investment Sites

Noah Tratt is the epitome of today's financial entrepreneur: He's 27 years old, and he loves computers as well as investing. A few months ago, he cashed in stock he had accumulated while working at Microsoft, lined up some financial backers in Seattle, and launched a new investment Web site, the Daily Rocket. Tratt uses state-of-the-art tools and a dash of multimedia to provide a package of data and analysis.

Tratt is in the right place at the right time. Finance and investing have melded into one of the most successful categories on the Internet. Getting financial information online has become so popular that entrepreneurs like Tratt face increasing competition, often from surprising places . . . such as his former employer: Microsoft has swooped into the world of online financial information with an offering of its own called Microsoft Investor.

The pace of change on the Internet is staggering. Just a few years ago, investors got excited by the debut of the first site to offer stock quotes. Today's investment sites provide much more sophisticated information. Some of it is the kind of material that Wall Street investment firms used to buy for thousands of dollars a year. Nowadays, the standard offerings include corporate balance sheets and income statements, profit projections, up-to-the-minute press releases, and news stories tailored to the user's interests. Chat rooms, once rare, are popping up all over, and electronic links to other sites have proliferated. E-mail alerts about news related to specific stocks are everywhere, and some nifty tools are available to help investors select companies that have attractive characteristics.

The upshot is that the individual investor has at his or her fingertips information that used to be reserved for such institutional investors as banks and insurance companies. This means that the playing field has leveled somewhat in favor of the "little investor." People no longer need to call their brokers to find out how their stocks are doing. They don't have to wait a month to get a company's annual report. The more computer-savvy among them can assemble enough information on their own to make informed investment decisions.

It's no wonder, then, that the online brokerage industry is booming. The low cost of executing trades online has allowed newcomers like E*Trade and AmeriTrade to charge rock-bottom commissions. According to Forrester Research, online brokerage accounts will grow from 3 million in 1997 to 14 million by 2002. These services charge a fraction of the commissions charged by major national brokerage firms such as Merrill Lynch and Paine Webber.

Can the computer completely replace investment professionals such as stockbrokers and financial planners? It can replace only the bad ones. After all, having access to a lot of information without knowing how to use it wisely can be dangerous. The computer is a wonderful tool, but it will never replace human judgment and experience.

Note: Two *Investing in Action* boxes per chapter describe real-life investing situations or elaborate on innovative investment vehicles. These high-interest boxes have been written for this textbook, with student readers in mind. Concept review questions in the chapter are related to material in these boxes.

bond, in effect you lend money to the issuer, who agrees to pay you a stated rate of interest over a specified period of time, at the end of which the original sum will be returned.

equity
ongoing ownership in a specific business or property.

Equity represents ongoing ownership in a specific business or property. An equity investment may be held by title to a specific property or as a security. The most popular type of equity security is *common stock.*

derivative securities
securities that are structured to exhibit characteristics similar to those of an underlying security or asset and that derive their value from the underlying security or asset.

Derivative securities are neither debt nor equity. They derive their value from and have characteristics similar to those of an underlying security or asset. *Options* are an example: An investor essentially buys the opportunity to sell or buy another security or asset at a specified price during a given period of time. Options and other derivative security investments, though not so common as debt and equity investments, have grown rapidly in popularity during recent years.

Low or High Risk

risk
the chance that an investment's value or return will be less than its expected value or return.

Investments are sometimes differentiated on the basis of risk. As used in finance, **risk** refers to the chance that the value or return on an investment will be less than its expected value or return. In other words, risk is the chance that an investment will earn less than expected. The broader the range of possible values or returns associated with an investment, the greater its risk.

Investors are confronted with a continuum of investments that range from low to high risk. Although each type of investment vehicle has a basic risk characteristic, the actual level of risk depends on the specific vehicle. For example, stocks are generally believed to be more risky than bonds. However, it is not difficult to find high-risk bonds that are in fact more risky than the stock of a financially sound firm such as IBM or McDonald's. *Low-risk investments* are those considered safe with regard to the receipt of a positive return. *High-risk investments* are considered speculative: their levels of income and future value are highly uncertain. Simply stated, **speculation** offers highly uncertain earnings and future value, so it is high-risk investment. Of course, because of this greater risk, the returns associated with speculation are expected to be greater. Both investment and speculation differ from gambling, which involves merely playing games of chance. In this book we will use the term *investment* for both investment and speculation.

speculation
the purchase of high-risk investment vehicles that offer highly uncertain earnings and future value.

Short- or Long-Term

short-term investments
investments that typically mature within 1 year.

long-term investments
investments with maturities of longer than a year or with no maturity at all.

The life of an investment can be described as either short- or long-term. **Short-term investments** typically mature within 1 year. **Long-term investments** are those with longer maturities or perhaps, like common stock, with no maturity at all. As will become clear later, it is not unusual to find investors matching the maturity of an investment to the period of time over which they wish to invest their funds.

Domestic or Foreign

Note: Discussions of international investing are highlighted by this icon.

domestic investments
debt, equity, and derivative securities and property of U.S.-based companies.

foreign investments
debt, equity, and derivative securities and property of foreign-based companies.

As recently as 10 to 15 years ago, individuals invested almost exclusively in purely **domestic investments:** the debt, equity, and derivative securities and property of U.S.-based companies. Today, these same investors routinely also look for **foreign investments**—both direct and indirect—that might offer more attractive returns or lower risk than purely domestic investments. Because of the ready availability of information on foreign companies and the ease and relatively low cost of making foreign investments, many individuals now actively invest in foreign securities. All aspects of foreign investing are therefore routinely considered throughout this book.

The Structure of the Investment Process

financial institutions
organizations that channel the savings of governments, businesses, and individuals into loans or investments.

financial markets
forums in which suppliers and demanders of funds make financial transactions.

The investment process is the mechanism for bringing together *suppliers* of extra funds with *demanders* who need funds. Suppliers and demanders are most often brought together through a financial institution or a financial market. (Occasionally—especially in property transactions such as real estate—buyers and sellers deal directly with one another.) **Financial institutions** are organizations that channel the savings of governments, businesses, and individuals into loans or investments. Banks and insurance companies are financial institutions. **Financial markets** are forums in which suppliers and demanders of funds make financial transactions, often through intermediaries. They include securities, commodities, and foreign exchange markets.

The dominant financial market in the United States consists of the *securities markets,* which include stock markets, bond markets, and options markets. Similar markets exist in most major economies throughout the world. Their common feature is that the price of an investment vehicle at any point in time results from an equilibrium between the forces of supply and demand. As new information about returns, risk, inflation, world events, and so on becomes available, the changes in the forces of supply and demand may result in a new equilibrium or *market price.* Financial markets streamline the process of bringing together suppliers and demanders of funds, and they allow transactions to be made quickly and at a fair price. They also publicize security prices.

Figure 1.1 diagrams the investment process. Note that the suppliers of funds may transfer their resources to the demanders through financial institutions, through financial markets, or in direct transactions. As the broken line shows, financial institutions can participate in financial markets as either suppliers or demanders of funds. The characteristics of the dominant financial market—the securities markets—will be discussed in greater detail in Chapter 2.

FIGURE 1.1
The Investment Process

Note that financial institutions participate in the financial markets as well as transfer funds between suppliers and demanders. Although the arrows go only from suppliers to demanders, for some transactions (e.g., the sale of a bond), the principal amount borrowed by the demander from the supplier (the lender) is eventually returned.

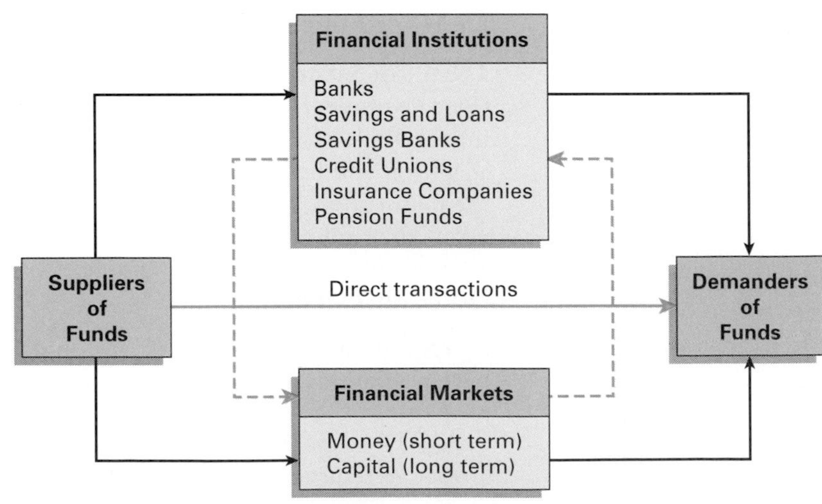

Participants in the Investment Process

Government, business, and individuals are the three key participants in the investment process. Each may act as a supplier and a demander of funds. Funds must be available to qualified individuals and to government and business for the economy to grow and prosper. If individuals began suddenly hiding their excess funds under floorboards rather than putting them in financial institutions or investing them in the financial markets, then government, business, and other individuals in need of funds would have difficulty obtaining them. As a result, government spending, business expansion, and consumer purchases would decline, and economic activity would be greatly retarded.

Government All levels of government—federal, state, and local—require vast sums of money. Some goes to finance *capital expenditures:* long-term projects related to the construction of public facilities such as schools, hospitals, public housing, and highways. Usually the financing for such projects is obtained by issuing various types of long-term debt securities. Another demand for funds comes from *operating needs*—the money required to keep the government running. At the federal level, for example, these funds are used to pay employee and other costs associated with national defense, education, public works, welfare, Social Security, Medicare, and so on, as well as interest on the national debt. These operating costs are usually paid from tax revenue and fee collections. However, when operating expenditures exceed government revenues (a common outcome for the federal government) or when there is a timing mismatch between government receipts and payments, the government borrows funds—typically by issuing short-term debt securities.

Occasionally, governments are also suppliers of funds. If a state has temporarily idle cash, it may make a short-term investment to earn a positive return, rather than just hold these resources in a checking account. In general, though, government is a *net demander of funds;* that is, it demands more funds than it supplies. The financial activities of governments, both as demanders and suppliers of funds, significantly affect the behavior of financial institutions and financial markets.

Note: Marginal Investor Facts offer interesting or entertaining tidbits of information.

INVESTOR FACT

AMERICANS LOVE STOCKS—At year-end 1996, the American public owned $7.3 trillion worth of stock, either directly or indirectly (through mutual funds). That represented 31.1% of total household financial assets, which also include savings accounts, money market funds, and bonds. In the past half-century, that percentage was higher only once—in 1968. The lowest percentage occurred in 1982, when just 12.8% of total household financial assets were invested in the stock market.

Business Most business firms require large sums of money to support operations. Like government, business has both long- and short-term financial needs. On the long-term side, businesses seek funds to build plants, acquire equipment and facilities, and develop products. Their short-term needs center on obtaining funds to finance inventory and accounts receivable and to meet other operating costs. Businesses issue a wide variety of debt and equity securities to finance these needs.

Businesses also supply funds when they have excess cash. In fact, many large business firms have sophisticated cash-management operations and are major purchasers of short-term securities. But like government, business firms in general are *net demanders of funds.*

Individuals You might be surprised to learn that the individual investor's role in the investment process is significant. Most individuals are more aware of their need to borrow than they are of the ways in which they put money into the financial system. They frequently demand funds in the form of loans to finance the acquisition of property—typically automobiles and houses. Yet, in fact, the activities of individual investors help to satisfy the net demands of government and business for funds in a variety of ways: They place funds in savings accounts, buy debt or equity instruments, buy insurance, make retirement plan contributions, or purchase various types of property. Although the individual demand for funds seems great, individuals as a group are *net suppliers of funds:* They put more funds into the financial system than they take out.

Types of Investors

individual investors
investors who manage their own funds.

When we refer to individuals in the investment process, we do so to differentiate households from government and business. We can further characterize the participation of individuals in the investment process in terms of who manages the funds. **Individual investors** manage their personal funds in order to achieve their financial goals. The individual investor usually concentrates on earning a return on idle funds, building a source of retirement income, and providing security for his or her family. As the *Investing in Action* box on page 9 discusses, "Generation Xers" appear to be saving and investing more than their parents. The sole activity of many individual investors involves selecting the investment vehicles to be included in their employer retirement plan or individual portfolio.

institutional investors
investment professionals paid to manage other people's money.

Individuals with large sums of money to invest and those who lack the time or expertise to make investment decisions often employ **institutional investors**—investment professionals who are paid to manage other people's money. They trade large volumes of securities for individuals, businesses, and governments. Institutional investors include financial institutions (e.g., banks, life insurance companies, mutual funds, and pension funds), large nonfinancial corporations, and in some cases professional investors. Financial institutions invest large sums in order to earn a significant return for their customers. For example, a life insurance company invests its premium receipts to earn returns that will permit payments to policyholders or beneficiaries.

Both individual and institutional investors apply similar fundamental principles. However, institutional investors generally invest larger sums of money on behalf of others and therefore are often more sophisticated in both investment knowledge and investment methods. The information presented in this textbook is aimed primarily at individual investors; it represents only the first step toward developing the expertise needed to qualify as an institutional investor.

Note: The review questions at the end of each text section encourage you, before you move on, to test your understanding of the material you've just read.

CONCEPTS IN REVIEW

1.1 Define the term *investment* and explain why individuals invest.

1.2 According to the *Investing in Action* box on page 4 about investment sites on the Web, can the computer replace investment professionals? Why or why not?

1.3 Differentiate among the following types of investments and cite an example of each: (a) securities versus property investments; (b) direct versus indirect investments; (c) debt, equity, and derivative securities; and (d) short-term investments versus long-term investments.

INVESTING IN ACTION

Twentysomethings Aren't Slacking on Personal Savings

Despite warnings about the solvency of Social Security, U.S. families as a group aren't squirreling away money for the future: Their saving rate for retirement is just 4% of their household income. But according to a survey by the Employee Benefit Research Institute (EBRI), members of Generation X—those in their twenties and early thirties—are doing a far better job of saving than their baby boomer parents. The survey shows that 65% of Gen Xers say they've already begun investing for retirement. And 19% say they've already stashed away more than $50,000. By contrast, only a third of those aged 50 and older have saved that much, even with a 20-year head start.

How could this be? For one thing, baby boomers who've been in the work force for more than 20 years can still remember when retirement meant a gold watch, a Social Security check, and payments for life from the company. Many of them are counting on such pensions to carry them through. In addition, baby boomers are often squeezed by the expenses of putting children through college and caring for elderly parents.

But those who are entering the work force in the 1990s face a different situation than their parents did—one that forces them to give more thought to their financial futures. First, loyalty to one company is rare. The old stigma against job hopping is mostly a memory, because employers have shown that they are no longer reluctant to lay off employees for an improved bottom line. Second, Social Security payments are a diminishing fraction of what it takes to retire. A $20,000 annual benefit, even upwardly adjusted for inflation, is hardly enough to make ends meet in old age. Third, fewer companies offer a fixed pension payment at retirement. The result: today's new generation of workers realize that they have to look out for themselves.

Additionally, many young people have yet to take on the financial obligations of home ownership and parenthood. Salaries can therefore be allocated to current expenditures and to long-term savings. The savings rates of Generation Xers will probably suffer when added family expenses hit.

The shift to 401(k) retirement plans—corporate America's increasingly popular employee benefit—may also be spurring Generation Xers to save. These plans allow employees to put away up to $10,000 of their salary each year into an account that grows without immediate taxation. Companies make it less painful to invest by deducting the money from employee paychecks. The benefits of investing for the long term make such early savings decisions especially valuable.

Still, the Gen Xers' thrift isn't enough to shore up the nation's dismal savings rate. According to the EBRI, three-fourths of all workers have no idea how much they'll need to save for retirement. The implications are ominous for those retirees who haven't socked away enough money by the time they reach age 65. But at least young adults are headed in the right direction. And maybe, 50 years from now, when they're reminiscing about the Spice Girls' greatest hits, they won't have to worry about whether a Social Security check is going to arrive on time.

1.4 Define the term *risk* and explain how risk is used to differentiate among investments.

1.5 What are *foreign investments* and what role do they play today for the individual investor?

1.6 Describe the structure of the overall investment process. Define and explain the role played by *financial institutions* and *financial markets.*

1.7 Classify the role of (a) government, (b) business, and (c) individuals as net suppliers or net demanders of funds. Discuss the impact of each on the investment process.

1.8 According to the *Investing in Action* box on page 9, why are Generation Xers taking charge of their own financial futures?

1.9 Differentiate between *individual investors* and *institutional investors.*

Note: Addresses of additional information sources that can be found on the Internet are interspersed, at the ends of major sections, throughout the chapter.

http://hepg.aw.com

American Century Investments provides access to educational material on investing. Once at the site, follow the *Learning About Investing* and *General Information* links to find educational information on stocks, bonds, mutual funds, and other investment terms.

www.americancentury.com

Investment Vehicles

LG 4 LG 5 LG 6

A wide variety of investment vehicles are available to individual investors. Each investment vehicle has different maturities or lives, costs, return and risk characteristics, and tax considerations. We devote the bulk of this book—Chapters 5 through 15—to describing the characteristics, special features, returns and risks, and possible investment strategies that can be used with vehicles available to the individual investor. Here we will introduce the various investment outlets and give a brief overview of each. Table 1.1 summarizes the information presented in this section.

TABLE 1.1 Overview of Investment Vehicles

Type	Description	Examples	Where Covered in This Book
Short-term vehicles	Savings instruments with lives of 1 year or less. Used to warehouse idle funds and to provide liquidity.	Deposit accounts	Ch. 3
		U.S. Treasury bills (T-bills)	Ch. 3
		Certificates of deposit (CDs)	Ch. 3
		Commercial paper	Ch. 3
		Banker's acceptances	Ch. 3
		Money market mutual funds	Ch. 3
		Series EE savings bonds	Ch. 3
Common stock	Equity investment vehicles that represent ownership in a corporation.		Chs. 5–7
Fixed-income securities	Investment vehicles that offer a fixed periodic return.	Bonds	Chs. 8, 9
		Preferred stock	Ch. 10
		Convertible securities	Ch. 10
Derivative securities	Securities that are neither debt nor equity but are structured to exhibit the characteristics of the underlying securities or assets from which they derive their value.	Options	Ch. 11
		Futures	Ch. 12
Mutual funds	Companies that raise money from sale of shares and invest in and professionally manage a diversified portfolio of securities.		Ch. 13
Other popular investment vehicles	Various other investment vehicles that are widely used by investors.	Real estate	Ch. 14
		Tangibles	Ch. 14
		Tax-advantaged investments	Ch. 15

Short-Term Vehicles

short-term vehicles
savings instruments that usually have lives of 1 year or less.

Short-term vehicles include savings instruments that usually have lives of 1 year or less. Short-term vehicles generally carry little or no risk. Often such instruments are used to "warehouse" idle funds and earn a return while suitable long-term vehicles are being evaluated. They are also popular among conservative investors, who may use short-term vehicles as a primary investment outlet. The most important of these are various types of deposit accounts, U.S. Treasury bills (T-bills), certificates of deposit (CDs), commercial paper, banker's acceptances, money market mutual funds, and Series EE savings bonds.

liquidity
the ability of an investment to be converted into cash quickly and with little or no loss in value.

In addition to their "warehousing" function and their use by conservative investors, short-term vehicles provide **liquidity**—they can be converted into cash quickly and with little or no loss in value. Provision for liquidity is an important part of any financial plan. As a rule of thumb, financial planners often suggest that anywhere from 3 to 6 months' worth of after-tax income should be held in short-term vehicles to meet unexpected needs or to take advantage of attractive opportunities.

Common Stock

common stock
equity investment representing ownership in a corporation; each share represents a fractional ownership interest in the firm.

Common stock is an equity investment that represents ownership in a corporation. Each share of common stock represents a fractional ownership interest in the firm. For example, one share of common stock in a corporation that has 10,000 shares outstanding would represent 1/10,000 ownership interest. Next to short-term vehicles and home ownership, common stock is the most popular form of investment vehicle.

dividends
periodic payments made by corporations to their stockholders.

capital gains
the amount by which the sale price of an asset exceeds its purchase price.

The return on common stock investment comes from either of two sources: **dividends,** which are periodic payments made by the corporation to its shareholders from its current and past earnings, and **capital gains,** which result from selling the stock at a price above that originally paid. For example, say you purchased a single share of M and N Industries common stock for $40 per share. During the first year you owned it, you received $2.50 per share in cash dividends; at the end of the year, you sold the stock for $44 per share. If we ignore the costs associated with buying and selling the stock, you earned $2.50 in dividends and $4 in capital gains ($44 sale price − $40 purchase price).

Fixed-Income Securities

fixed-income securities
investment vehicles that offer a fixed periodic return.

Fixed-income securities are a group of investment vehicles that offer a fixed periodic return. Some forms offer contractually guaranteed returns; others have specified, but not guaranteed, returns. Because of their fixed returns, fixed-income securities tend to be popular investments during periods of high interest rates when investors seek to "lock in" high returns. The key forms of fixed-income securities are bonds, preferred stock, and convertible securities.

bonds
long-term debt instruments (IOUs), issued by corporations and governments, that offer a known interest return plus return of the bond's *face value* at maturity.

Bonds

Bonds are the long-term debt instruments—IOUs—of corporations and governments. A bondholder has a contractual right to receive a known interest return, plus return of the bond's *face value*—the stated value given on the certificate—at maturity (typically 20 to 40 years). If you purchased a $1,000 bond paying 9% interest in semiannual installments, you would expect to be paid $45 (i.e., 9% × ½ year × $1,000) every 6 months; at maturity you would receive the $1,000 face value of the bond. An investor may be able to buy or sell a bond prior to maturity. As with common stock, a wide range of return–risk combinations is available to the bond investor.

Preferred Stock

preferred stock
ownership interest in a corporation; has a stated dividend rate, payment of which is given preference over common stock dividends of the same firm.

Like common stock, **preferred stock** represents an ownership interest in a corporation. Unlike common stock, preferred stock has a stated dividend rate; payment of this dividend is given preference over common stock dividends of the same firm. Preferred stock has no maturity date. Investors typically purchase it for the dividends it pays, but it may also provide capital gains.

Convertible Securities

convertible security
a fixed-income obligation (bond or preferred stock) with a feature permitting conversion into a specified number of shares of common stock.

A **convertible security** is a special type of fixed-income obligation (bond or preferred stock) with a feature permitting the investor to convert it into a specified number of shares of common stock. Convertible bonds and convertible preferreds provide the fixed-income benefit of a bond (interest) or preferred stock (dividends) while offering the price-appreciation (capital gain) potential of common stock.

Derivative Securities

As noted earlier, *derivative securities* derive their value from that of an underlying security or asset. They typically possess high levels of risk, because they usually have uncertain returns or unstable market values. Because of their above-average risk, these vehicles also have high levels of expected return. The key derivative securities are options and futures.

Options

options
securities that give the investor an opportunity to sell or buy another security or property at a specified price over a given period of time.

Options are securities that give the investor an opportunity to sell or buy another security or property at a specified price over a given period of time. Most often, options are purchased in order to take advantage of an anticipated decrease or increase in the price of common stock. However, the purchaser of an option is not guaranteed any return and could even lose the entire amount invested because the option does not become attractive enough to use. Aside from their speculative use, options are sometimes used to protect existing investment positions against losses. Three common types of options are *puts* and *calls, rights,* and *warrants,* which we will discuss in detail in Chapter 11.

Futures

futures
legally binding obligations stipulating that the sellers of such contracts will make delivery and the buyers of the contracts will take delivery of a specified commodity or financial instrument at some specific date in the future, at a price agreed on at the time the contract is sold.

Futures are legally binding obligations stipulating that the sellers of such contracts will make delivery and the buyers of the contracts will take delivery of a specified commodity or financial instrument at some specific date in the future, at a price agreed on at the time the contract is sold. Examples of commodities sold by contract include soybeans, pork bellies, platinum, and cocoa. Examples of financial futures are contracts for Japanese yen, U.S. Treasury securities, interest rates, and stock indexes. Trading in commodity and financial futures is generally a highly specialized, high-risk proposition.

INVESTOR FACT

EXPLODING FUNDS!—In 1970 there were 361 mutual funds investing in stocks and bonds in the United States. Ten years later, the number was still less than 500. By 1989, however, the number of mutual funds had nearly quintupled, to 2,253. Then, during just the next 7 years, the number of funds more than doubled—to 5,305. The U.S. mutual fund industry controls assets totalling more than $4.0 trillion.

Mutual Funds

mutual fund
a company that raises money from sale of its shares and invests in and professionally manages a diversified portfolio of securities.

money market mutual funds
mutual funds that invest solely in short-term investment vehicles.

A company that raises money from sale of its shares and invests in and professionally manages a diversified portfolio of securities is called a **mutual fund.** Investors in the fund own an interest in the fund's portfolio of securities. All mutual funds issue and repurchase shares of the fund as demanded at a price that reflects the value of the portfolio at the time the transaction is made. **Money market mutual funds,** mentioned earlier as short-term investment vehicles, are mutual funds that invest solely in other short-term vehicles.

Other Popular Investment Vehicles

Various other investment vehicles are also widely used by investors. The most common are real estate, tangibles, and tax-advantaged investments.

Real Estate

real estate
entities such as residential homes, raw land, and income property.

The term **real estate** refers to entities such as residential homes, raw land, and a variety of forms of income property, including warehouses, office and apartment buildings, and condominiums. As a result of generally increasing values and favorable tax treatments since World War II, real estate was a popular investment vehicle through the 1970s and much of the 1980s. Although its popularity waned during the early-to-mid 1990s, improved economic conditions during the mid-1990s have resulted in a resurgence in the popularity of real estate. Historically, the appeal of real estate investment stemmed from the fact that it offered returns in the form of rental income, tax write-offs, and capital gains that were not available from alternative investment vehicles.

Tangibles

tangibles
investment assets, other than real estate, that can be seen or touched.

Tangibles are investment assets, other than real estate, that can be seen or touched. They include gold and other precious metals, gemstones, and collectibles such as coins, stamps, artwork, and antiques. These assets are purchased as investments in anticipation of price increases. During the ownership period, some may also provide the investor with psychological or esthetic enjoyment.

Tax-Advantaged Investments

Because of provisions in the federal tax law, some investment vehicles offer certain tax advantages over others. For example, interest received on most municipal bonds is not taxed at all, and taxation on income from money put aside in certain retirement accounts is deferred until the money is actually taken out of the account. Because the federal income tax rate for an individual can be as high as 39.6%, many investors look for **tax-advantaged investments**—investment vehicles and strategies for legally reducing one's tax liability. With these, they find that their after-tax rates of return can be far higher than with conventional investments.

tax-advantaged investments investment vehicles and strategies for legally reducing one's tax liability.

CONCEPTS IN REVIEW

1.10 Discuss the role of short-term vehicles in an individual's investment plans. Why is a provision for *liquidity* important?

1.11 What is *common stock* and what are its two sources of potential return?

1.12 Briefly define and differentiate among the following investment vehicles. Which offer fixed returns? Which are derivative securities? Which offer professional investment management?

a. Bonds
b. Preferred stock
c. Convertible securities
d. Options
e. Futures
f. Mutual funds
g. Real estate
h. Tangibles
i. Tax-advantaged investments

http://hepg.aw.com

The *Wise Investor Resource Center* link at The Montgomery Funds Web site will lead you to a glossary of terms that can be used to review the definitions of many of the securities listed in this section.

www.montgomeryfunds.com

Summary

Note: The Summary restates the chapter's Learning Goals and reviews the key points of information related to each goal.

LG 1 **Understand the meaning of the term *investment*.** An investment is any vehicle into which funds can be placed with the expectation that they will generate positive income and/or that their value will be preserved or will increase. The rewards from investing are received either as current income or as increased value.

LG 2 **Review the factors commonly used to differentiate among various types of investments.** Some investment vehicles are securities; others are forms of property. Some investments are made directly, others indirectly. An investment can be a debt, an equity, or a derivative security such as an option. It can possess risk ranging from very low to extremely high. An individual can invest in either short-term or long-term vehicles. Today, individual investors have ready access to foreign as well as domestic investments.

LG 3 **Describe the structure of and participants in the investment process and the types of investors.** The investment process is structured around financial institutions and financial markets that bring together suppliers and demanders of funds. The dominant financial market in the United States is the securities markets for stocks, bonds, and options. The participants in the investment process are government, business, and individuals. Of these groups, only individuals are net suppliers of funds. Investors can be either individual investors or institutional investors.

LG 4

Discuss the principal types of investment vehicles, including short-term vehicles, common stock, and fixed-income securities. A broad range of investment vehicles is available. Short-term vehicles have low risk. They are used to earn a return on temporarily idle funds, to serve as a primary investment outlet of conservative investors, and to provide liquidity. Common stocks offer dividends and capital gains. Fixed-income securities—bonds, preferred stock, and convertible securities—offer fixed periodic returns with some potential for gain in value.

LG 5

Describe derivative securities, the most popular derivatives (options and futures), and mutual funds. Derivative securities are high risk, high expected-return vehicles. The key derivatives are options and futures. Options offer the investor an opportunity to buy or sell another security or property at a specified price over a given period of time. Futures are contracts between a seller and a buyer for delivery of a specified commodity or financial instrument, at a specified future date, at an agreed-on price. Mutual funds are popular investment vehicles that allow investors conveniently to buy or sell interests in a professionally managed, diversified portfolio of securities.

LG 6

Describe other kinds of popular investment vehicles: real estate, tangibles, and tax-advantaged investments. Other popular investment vehicles include real estate—residential homes, raw land, and a variety of forms of income property. Tangibles such as gold and other precious metals, gemstones, and collectibles interest some investors, as do tax-advantaged investments, which reduce one's tax liability and thereby increase the after-tax rate of return.

Case Problem 1.1 *Investments or Golf?*

LG 1 LG 2 LG 3 LG 4 LG 5 LG 6

Note: Two Case Problems appear at the end of every chapter. They ask you to apply what you have learned in the chapter to a hypothetical investment situation. Also, in all chapters after Chapter 1, Discussion Questions and Problems precede the Case Problems. All end-of-chapter assignment materials are keyed to the chapter learning goals.

Judd Read and Judi Todd, senior accounting majors at a large midwestern university, have been good friends since high school. Each has already found a job that will begin after graduation. Judd has accepted a position as an internal auditor in a medium-sized manufacturing firm. Judi will be working for one of the major public accounting firms. Each is looking forward to the challenge of a new career and to the prospect of achieving success both professionally and financially.

Judd and Judi are preparing to register for their final semester. Each has one free elective to select. Judd is considering taking a golf course offered by the physical education department, which he says will help him socialize in his business career. Judi is planning to take a basic investments course. Judi has been trying to convince Judd to take investments instead of golf. Judd believes he doesn't need to take investments, because he already knows what common stock is. He believes that whenever he has accumulated excess funds, he can invest in the stock of a company that is doing well. Judi argues that there is much more to it than simply choosing common stock. She feels that exposure to the field of investments would be more beneficial than learning how to play golf.

QUESTIONS

a. Explain to Judd the structure of the investment process and the economic importance of investing.

b. List and discuss the other types of investment vehicles with which Judd is apparently unfamiliar.

c. Assuming that Judd already gets plenty of exercise, what arguments would you give to convince Judd to take investments rather than golf?

Case Problem 1.2 Evaluating Molly Porter's Investment Plan

LG 4 LG 5

Molly Porter's husband, Vance, was recently killed in an airplane crash. Fortunately, he had a sizable amount of life insurance, the proceeds of which should provide Molly with adequate income for a number of years. Molly is 33 years old and has two children, David and Phyllis, who are 6 and 7 years old, respectively. Although Molly does not rule out the possibility of marrying again, she feels it is best not to consider this when making her financial plans. In order to provide adequate funds to finance her children's college education as well as her own retirement, Molly has estimated that she needs to accumulate $400,000 within the next 15 years. If she continues to teach school, she believes sufficient excess funds will be available each year (salary plus insurance proceeds minus expenses) to permit her to achieve this goal. She plans to make annual deposits of these excess funds into a money market mutual fund, which is currently earning 6 percent interest.

QUESTIONS

a. In view of Molly's long-term investment goals, assess her choice of a money market mutual fund as the appropriate investment vehicle.

b. What alternative investment vehicles might Molly consider?

c. If you were Molly, given your limited knowledge of investments, in what vehicles would you invest the excess funds? Explain.

Home Page Exercises

Note: Home Page Exercises section—new to the seventh edition—directs you to even more financial and investment resources on the Internet. In addition, several exercises in each chapter give you the opportunity to practice finding investment information at selected Web sites.

http://hepg.aw.com **Keyword: Invest**

Investing is a topic of potential interest to just about every adult. The widespread necessity and popularity of investing means that many people want to share and or seek information related to the specific investment topic in which they are interested. The World Wide Web is tailor-made for this sharing of information. At the end of every chapter in this book, we provide information about Web sites that offer information related to the chapter topic. For example, the following Web sites are a few of the general information sources that can be used to learn more about investing.

Web Address	*Primary Investment Focus*
www.aaii.com	Educational material on stocks, bonds, mutual funds, and portfolios
www.kiplinger.com	Articles about investing and investments
www.nylcare.com/viewer/wsh-nyl/mainstay/ie.html	General information about investing and its benefits
www.troweprice.com	A mutual fund company whose site also contains general investment information under the *Mutual Fund Information* and *Getting Started* icons

Also included in this section are exercises that guide you to specific sites and ask you to search out certain information there.

All of the sites mentioned in the Home Page Exercises section can be accessed either directly at the addresses shown or through our textbook's Web page at **hepg.aw.com,** which offers links to these sites. The material available on the home page is divided into chapters that parallel the chapters in the textbook. There, in addition to links to the Web addresses cited in the chapter, you will find interviews with investors and other related information that supplements the material in the textbook.

W1.1. This chapter introduces many of the different types of assets that are available for individual investors. The following five sites provide information on certain investment assets. Go to each of the five sites and write a brief description of the type of asset or assets on which information can be found at that site.

www.cme.com

www.frbsf.org

www.resicom.com

www.quote.com

www.publicdebt.treas.gov

W1.2. Given the many investment choices available, it is sometimes difficult for investors to narrow down the selections. This task is eased somewhat by two types of information: (1) knowing your risk tolerance as an investor and (2) determining the *asset allocation mix* that is best for you—that is, how best to divide your resources among various investment alternatives. Go to the following site and read about your risk tolerance level. Then complete and print out the questionnaire on the type of investor you are, and determine your asset allocation strategy from the table provided.

www.deferred-comp.com/investment.htm

CHAPTER 2 INVESTMENT MARKETS AND TRANSACTIONS

LEARNING GOALS

After studying this chapter, you should be able to:

LG 1 Describe the basic types of securities markets and the characteristics of organized exchanges and the over-the-counter market.

LG 2 Discuss the third and fourth markets, trading hours, regulation, and the general conditions of securities markets.

LG 3 Review the importance, performance, investment procedures, and risks associated with investing globally in foreign securities.

LG 4 Explain the role of stockbrokers in security transactions—services provided, selection, opening an account, account types, and transaction sizes.

LG 5 Describe the basic types of orders (market, limit, and stop-loss), transaction costs, and the legal aspects of investor protection.

LG 6 Understand long purchases and the motives, regulations, procedures, and calculations involved in making margin transactions and short sales.

Stockbroker, money manager, investment banker, trader, market maker, regulator, international financier—the investment markets offer booming career opportunities for college graduates with backgrounds in finance. Virtually every community in the United States has a stock brokerage firm. Some graduates work at national brokerage firms, buying and selling stocks and bonds for individual and corporate clients. Others work at regional or local firms that focus on companies in that region. Budding stockbrokers are given training in investments and sales techniques. Most communities also have money management firms—companies that invest (rather than sell stocks and bonds) for clients. Typically, a graduate begins such a career as an analyst, studying the firms that issue stocks and bonds to assess their attractiveness as investments. Many of the top careers in finance tend to be based in the larger U.S. financial centers such as New York, Chicago, and San Francisco.

In this chapter, we will study the markets, the exchanges, the transactions, and the regulations that surround financial careers. Our purpose in presenting these topics is to make you a more intelligent investor whether you choose a career in finance or not.

Securities Markets

LG 1 LG 2

Securities markets are forums that allow suppliers and demanders of *securities* to make financial transactions. They permit such transactions to be made quickly and at a fair price. In this section we will look at the various types of markets, their organization, their regulation, and their general behavior.

securities markets
forums that allow suppliers and demanders of *securities* to make financial transactions; include both the *money market* and the *capital market.*

money market
market in which short-term securities are bought and sold.

capital market
market in which long-term securities such as stocks and bonds are bought and sold.

Types of Securities Markets

Securities markets may be classified as either money markets or capital markets. In the **money market,** short-term securities are bought and sold. In the **capital market,** transactions are made in longer-term securities such as stocks and bonds. In this book we will devote most of our attention to the capital market, through which stock, bond, options, futures, and mutual fund investments can be made. Capital markets can be classified as either primary or secondary, depending on whether securities are initially being sold by their issuing company or by intervening owners.

The Primary Market

primary market
market in which *new issues* of securities are sold to the public.

initial public offering (IPO)
the first public sale of a company's stock.

Securities and Exchange Commission (SEC)
federal agency that regulates securities offerings and markets.

public offering
the sale of a firm's securities to the general public.

rights offering
an offer of shares of stock to existing stockholders on a pro rata basis.

private placement
the sale of new securities directly to selected groups of investors, without SEC registration.

investment banker
financial intermediary that purchases new securities from the issuing firm at an agreed-on price and resells them to the public.

underwriting
the role of the investment banker in bearing the risk of reselling at a profit the securities purchased from an issuing corporation at an agreed-on price.

underwriting syndicate
a group formed by an *investment banker* to spread the financial risk associated with underwriting new securities.

selling group
a large number of brokerage firms that join and accept responsibility for selling a certain portion of a new security issue.

The market in which *new issues* of securities are sold to the public is the **primary market.** It is the market in which the proceeds of sales go to the issuer of the securities. In 1997, 629 companies offered their stock for sale in the primary market. The main vehicle in the primary market is the **initial public offering (IPO)**—the first public sale of a company's stock. Before securities can be offered for public sale, the issuer must register them with and obtain approval from the **Securities and Exchange Commission (SEC).** This federal regulatory agency must confirm both the adequacy and the accuracy of the information provided to potential investors before a security is publicly offered for sale. In addition, the SEC regulates the securities markets.

To market its securities in the primary market, a firm has three choices: (1) a **public offering,** in which the firm offers its securities for sale to the general public; (2) a **rights offering,** in which the firm offers shares to existing stockholders on a pro rata basis; or (3) a **private placement,** in which the firm sells new securities directly, without SEC registration, to selected groups of investors, such as insurance companies and pension funds.

Most public offerings are made with the assistance of an **investment banker**—a financial intermediary (such as Salomon Brothers or Goldman Sachs) that specializes in selling new security issues. The main activity of the investment banker is **underwriting.** This process involves purchasing the security issue from the issuing firm at an agreed-on price and bearing the risk of reselling it to the public at a profit. The investment banker also provides the issuer with advice about pricing and other important aspects of the issue.

In the case of very large security issues, the investment banker brings in other bankers as partners to form an **underwriting syndicate,** and thus spread the financial risk associated with buying the entire issue from the issuer and reselling the new securities at a profit to the public. The originating investment banker and the syndicate members put together a **selling group,** normally made up of themselves and a large number of brokerage firms. Each member of the selling group accepts the responsibility for selling a certain portion of the issue and is paid a commission on the securities it sells. The selling process for a large security issue is depicted in Figure 2.1.

FIGURE 2.1
The Selling Process for a Large Security Issue

The investment banker hired by the issuing corporation may form an underwriting syndicate. The underwriting syndicate buys the entire security issue from the issuing corporation at an agreed-on price. The underwriter then has the opportunity (and bears the risk) of reselling the issue to the public at a profit. Both the originating investment banker and the other syndicate members put together a selling group to sell the issue on a commission basis to investors.

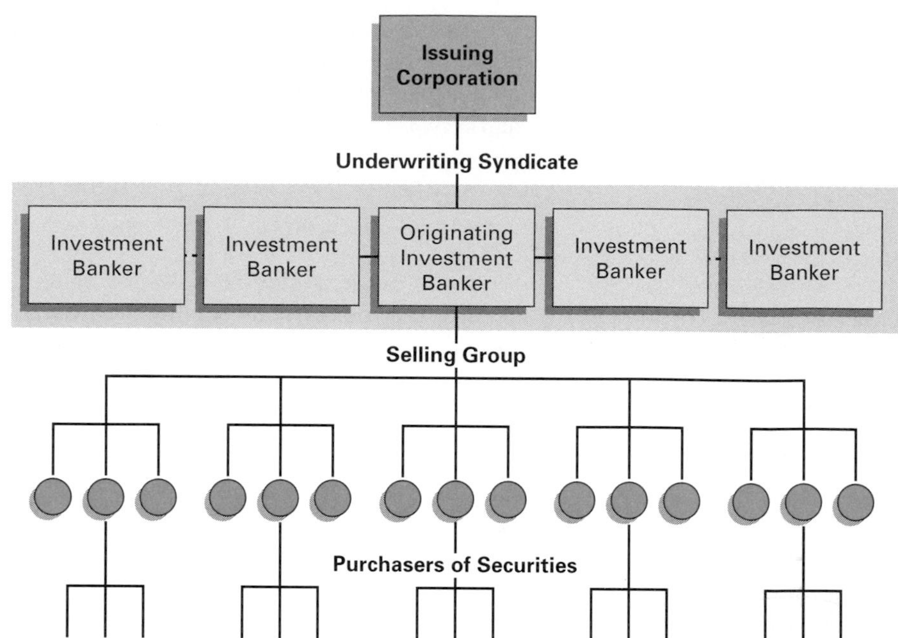

INVESTOR FACT

EDGAR TAKES A BIG BYTE— The SEC allows companies to file disclosures electronically. Its "EDGAR" site on the Internet recently had a big meal when Morgan Stanley filed a 10,200-page disclosure report. (A typical filing is about 42 pages.) Morgan Stanley said the filing included appraisals on 104 real estate properties. The electronic version probably saved Morgan Stanley and the underwriting syndicate thousands of dollars in printing and postal charges.

The relationships among the participants in this process can also be seen in the so-called *tombstone announcements* of new security issues. An announcement for the Florida Panthers' (hockey team) 1997 common stock offering is shown in Figure 5.3 (on page 176 of Chapter 5). The layout of the announcement indicates the roles of the various participating firms. Isolated firm names or a larger typeface differentiates the underwriter and the underwriting syndicate from the selling group. (In the figure, the key participants in the offering are labeled in the margin at the right.)

Compensation for underwriting and selling services typically comes in the form of a discount from the sale price of the securities. For example, an investment banker may pay the issuing firm $24 per share for stock that will be sold for $26 per share. The investment banker may then sell the shares to members of the selling group for $25.25 per share. In this case, the original investment banker earns $1.25 per share ($25.25 sale price – $24 purchase price), and the members of the selling group earn 75 cents for each share they sell ($26 sale price – $25.25 purchase price). Although some primary security offerings are directly placed by the issuer, the majority of new issues are sold through public offering using the mechanism just described.

Secondary Markets

secondary market
the market in which securities are traded *after they have been issued.*

The market in which securities are traded *after they have been issued* is the **secondary market,** or the *aftermarket.* The secondary market exists because some purchasers of securities already issued may wish to sell them and others may wish to buy them. In the secondary market, unlike the primary market, the corporation whose securities are traded is not involved in the transaction. Instead, money and securities are exchanged between investors; the seller exchanges securities for cash paid by the buyer. The secondary market gives security purchasers *liquidity*. It also provides a mechanism for continuous pricing of securities to reflect their value at each point in time, on the basis of the best information then available.

organized securities exchanges centralized institutions in which transactions are made in securities already outstanding.

over-the-counter (OTC) market widely scattered telecommunications network through which transactions are made in both *initial public offerings (IPOs)* and securities already outstanding.

Included among secondary markets are the various organized securities exchanges and the over-the-counter market. **Organized securities exchanges** are centralized institutions in which the forces of supply and demand for securities already outstanding are brought together. The **over-the-counter (OTC) market,** on the other hand, is a widely scattered telecommunications network through which transactions are made in both *initial public offerings (IPOs)* and securities already outstanding. Organized securities exchanges are auction markets in which price is determined by the flow of buy and sell orders. The over-the-counter markets use a quote system in which negotiation and dealer quotes determine the price. Because popular investment vehicles are traded both on the organized exchanges and in the over-the-counter market, individual investors are likely to make transactions in both of these markets.

Organized Securities Exchanges

Securities traded on organized securities exchanges account for about 59% of the total *dollar volume* of domestic shares traded. All trading at a given exchange is carried out in one place (for example, the New York Stock Exchange on Wall Street) and under a broad set of rules by persons who are members of that exchange. The best-known exchanges on which stock and bond transactions are made are the New York Stock Exchange (NYSE) and the American Stock Exchange (AMEX), both located in New York City. They account for approximately 90% and 2%, respectively, of the total annual dollar volume of shares traded on organized U.S. exchanges. Other domestic exchanges include *regional exchanges*, such as the Chicago Stock Exchange and the Pacific Stock Exchange. Regional exchanges deal primarily in securities with regional or local appeal. Together, the regional exchanges account for about 8% of the annual dollar share volume on organized U.S. exchanges. In addition, *foreign stock exchanges* list and trade shares of firms in their own foreign markets. Separate domestic exchanges exist for options trading and trading in futures. Here we will consider the basic structure, rules, and operations of each of these organized domestic securities exchanges. (Foreign exchanges are discussed later.)

The New York Stock Exchange

Most organized securities exchanges are modeled after the New York Stock Exchange (NYSE), the dominant organized exchange. In order to be a member, an individual or firm must own or lease a "seat" on the exchange. The word *seat* is used only figuratively, because members trade securities standing up. The majority of seat holders are brokerage firms, and each typically owns more than one seat. The largest brokerage firm, Merrill Lynch Pierce Fenner & Smith, Inc., owns over 20 of the 1,366 seats on the NYSE.

Firms such as Merrill Lynch designate officers to occupy seats. Only such designated individuals are permitted to make transactions on the floor of the exchange. Membership is often divided into broad classes based on the members' activities. Although the majority of members make purchase and sale

TABLE 2.1 NYSE Member Activities

Type of Member	Approximate Percentage of Total Membership*	Primary Activities
A. Make transactions for customers		
Commission brokers	52%	Make purchase and sale transactions of stocks and bonds as requested by customers.
Bond brokers	2	Commission brokers who make only bond transactions for customers.
B. Make transactions for other members		
Specialists	29	Make a continuous, fair, and orderly market in the one or more issues assigned to them. Also make purchase and sale transactions of less than 100 shares (odd lots) for members of the exchange.
Floor brokers ("two-dollar brokers")	10	Execute orders for other brokers who are unable to do so because of excessive market activity.
C. Make transactions for their own account		
Registered traders	4	Purchase and sell securities for their own accounts. Must abide by certain regulations established to protect the public.

*Because approximately 3% of the members are inactive, the percentages given total to only 97%.

transactions on behalf of their customers, some members specialize in making transactions for other members or for their own account. Table 2.1 classifies and briefly describes member activities. You can see that commission brokers and specialists perform the majority of the activities on the exchange.

Trading Activity Trading is carried out by members on the floor of the organized exchanges. The largest—the floor of the NYSE—is an area about the size of a football field. Its operation is typical of the various exchanges (though details vary). On the NYSE floor are 18 trading posts. Certain stocks are traded at each of the posts. (Bonds and less active stocks are traded in an annex.) All trades are made on the floor of the exchange by members of the exchange. Around the perimeter are telephones and electronic equipment used to transmit buy and sell orders from brokers' offices to the exchange floor and back again once an order has been executed.

All transactions on the floor of the exchange are made through an auction process. The goal is to fill all buy orders at the lowest price and to fill all sell orders at the highest price. The price is determined by the flow of buy and sell orders. The actual auction takes place at the post where the particular security is traded. Members interested in purchasing a given security publicly negotiate a transaction with members interested in selling that security. The job of the **specialist**—an exchange member who specializes in making transactions in one or more stocks—is to buy or sell (at specified prices) in order to provide a continuous, fair, and orderly market in those securities assigned to her or him.

specialist
stock exchange member who specializes in making transactions in one or more stocks.

Listing Policies To have its shares listed on an organized stock exchange, a firm must file an application and meet certain listing requirements. Currently, over 2,900 firms, accounting for about 3,300 stocks (common and preferred) and 2,100 bond issues, are listed on the NYSE. Some firms are listed on more than one exchange; they are said to have **dual listing.**

dual listing
listing of a firm's shares on more than one exchange.

The New York Stock Exchange has the most stringent listing requirements. In order to be eligible for listing on the NYSE, a firm must have at least 2,000 stockholders owning 100 or more shares. It must have a minimum of 1.1 million shares of publicly held stock; earnings of at least $15 million over the previous 3 years, with no loss in the previous 2 years; and a minimum of $100 million in stockholders' equity. A foreign company must have earnings of at least $100 million over the previous 3 years, with at least $25 million in each of the previous 2 years. The firm also must pay a listing fee. Once a firm's securities have been accepted for listing, it must meet the requirements of the federal Securities and Exchange Commission (SEC), which regulates certain aspects of listed securities. If listed firms do not continue to meet specified requirements, they may be **de-listed** from the exchange.

de-listed
removed from listing on an organized stock exchange.

The American Stock Exchange

The American Stock Exchange (AMEX) is the second largest organized U.S. securities exchange in terms of the number of listed companies. In terms of dollar volume of trading, the AMEX is actually smaller than the two largest regional exchanges—the Chicago and the Pacific. Its organization and its procedures are similar to those of the NYSE, except that its listing requirements are not as stringent. In mid-1998 the AMEX merged with the National Association of Securities Dealers (NASD)—the backbone of the over-the-counter market—and like the OTC became a subsidiary of the NASD Market Holding Company. There are approximately 660 seats on the AMEX, with about 900 listed stocks and 85 (corporate) listed bonds.

Regional Stock Exchanges

Each of the regional exchanges typically lists the securities of 100 to 500 companies. As a group, these exchanges handle about 8% of the dollar volume of all shares traded on organized U.S. exchanges. The best-known regional exchanges are the Chicago, Pacific (co-located in Los Angeles and San Francisco), Philadelphia, Boston, and Cincinnati exchanges. Most are modeled after the NYSE, but their membership and listing requirements are considerably more lenient.

It is not uncommon for the regional exchanges to list securities that are also listed on the NYSE or the AMEX. This dual listing is often done to enhance a security's trading activity. In addition, a number of the regional exchanges, along with the NYSE, the AMEX, and the over-the-counter market, are linked together through an electronic communications network—the *Intermarket Trading System (ITS)*—that allows brokers and other traders to make transactions at the best prices.

Options Exchanges

Options allow their holders to sell or to buy another security or property at a specified price over a given period of time. Securities options are listed and traded on the Chicago Board Options Exchange (CBOE), as well as on the AMEX, the NYSE, the Pacific Stock Exchange, and the Philadelphia Stock Exchange. The dominant options exchange is the CBOE. Usually, an option to sell or buy a given security is listed on only one of the options exchanges, although dual listing does sometimes occur. Options exchanges deal only in security options; options to sell or buy property are not traded in this marketplace, but rather result from private transactions made directly between sellers and buyers.

Futures Exchanges

Futures are contracts that guarantee the delivery of a specified commodity or financial instrument at a specific future date at an agreed-on price. The dominant exchange on which commodity and financial futures are traded is the Chicago Board of Trade (CBT). There are a number of other futures exchanges, some of which specialize in certain commodities and financial instruments rather than the broad spectrum listed on the CBT. The largest of these exchanges are the New York Mercantile Exchange, the Chicago Mercantile Exchange, the Deutsche Terminboerse, the London International Financial Futures Exchange, the New York Coffee, Sugar & Cocoa Exchange, the New York Cotton Exchange, the Kansas City Board of Trade, and the Minneapolis Grain Exchange.

The Over-the-Counter Market

The *over-the-counter (OTC) market* is not a specific institution; rather, it is another way of trading securities. The OTC market is the result of an intangible relationship among sellers and purchasers of securities, who are linked by a telecommunications network. It accounts for about 41% of the total dollar volume of domestic shares traded. The prices at which securities are traded in the OTC market are determined by using a quote system that involves negotiation and dealer quotes. The actual process, which is described later, depends on the general activity of the security.

A *numerical* majority of stocks are traded over the counter, as are most government and corporate bonds. Of the over 35,000 issues traded over the counter, about 6,400 have an active market in which transactions take place frequently. A numerical majority of all corporate bonds, some of which are also listed on the NYSE, are traded in the OTC market. Securities traded in this market are sometimes called *unlisted securities.*

INVESTOR FACT

NEW ISSUES—In 1997, new U.S. stock issues totaled $39.25 billion, about 20% below 1996's record $50 billion in new equity financing.

New Issues and Secondary Distributions

secondary distributions
the public sales of large blocks of previously issued securities held by large investors.

To create a continuous market for unlisted securities, the OTC market also provides a forum in which initial public offerings (IPOs), both listed and unlisted, are sold. If they are listed, subsequent transactions are made on the appropriate organized securities exchange; unlisted securities continue to trade in the OTC market. **Secondary distributions**—the public sales of large blocks of previously issued securities held by large investors—are also made in the OTC market to minimize the potentially negative effects of such transactions on the price of listed securities. These transactions are forms of third- or fourth-market trades, which we will describe in a moment.

The Role of Dealers

dealers
traders who "make markets" by offering to buy or sell certain over-the-counter securities at stated prices.

The market price of OTC securities results from a matching of supply and demand for securities by traders known as **dealers.** Each dealer "makes markets" in certain securities by offering to buy or sell them at stated prices. Thus, unlike the organized exchanges (where the buyer and seller of a security are brought together by a broker), the OTC market links a buyer or seller with a dealer. That is, the second party to an OTC transaction is always a dealer. For example, a dealer making a market in Raco Enterprises might offer to buy shares from investors at $29.50 and sell shares to other investors at $31. The **bid price** is the highest price offered by the dealer to purchase a given security; the **ask price** is the lowest price at which the dealer is willing to sell a given security. Because more than one dealer frequently makes a market in a given security, dealers compete. Buyers and sellers attempt to find and negotiate the best price—lowest buy price or highest sell price—when making OTC market transactions. The dealer makes a profit from the spread between the bid price and the ask price.

bid price
the highest price offered by a dealer to purchase a given security.

ask price
the lowest price at which a dealer is willing to sell a given security.

Nasdaq

OTC dealers are linked with the sellers and purchasers of securities through the **Nasdaq (National Association of Securities Dealers Automated Quotation) system.** Nasdaq is an automated system that provides up-to-date bid and ask prices on about 6,400 selected, highly active OTC securities. It enables buyers and sellers to locate one another easily. Not all OTC securities are listed on Nasdaq, however. To trade in securities not quoted on Nasdaq, buyers and sellers must find each other through references or through known dealers in the securities involved.

Nasdaq (National Association of Securities Dealers Automated Quotation) system
an automated system that provides up-to-date bid and ask prices on certain selected, highly active OTC securities.

About 4,400 of the Nasdaq stocks are included in the **Nasdaq National Market.** These are stocks that meet certain qualification standards relative to financial size, performance, and trading activity. Transactions in stocks on this list are reported more quickly (immediately) and in more detail (similar to NYSE and AMEX trades) than non–Nasdaq National Market transactions are. Their more detailed quotations are isolated from other OTC stocks when published in the financial press. The *Investing in Action* box on page 26 indicates that in spite of heated competition between Nasdaq and the NYSE, the NYSE currently dominates the world.

Nasdaq National Market
a list of Nasdaq stocks meeting certain qualification standards relative to financial size, performance, and trading activity.

Third and Fourth Markets

The **third market** is the name given to over-the-counter transactions made in securities listed on the NYSE, the AMEX, or one of the other organized exchanges. It exists to serve the needs of large institutional investors, such as mutual funds, pension funds, and life insurance companies, by allowing them to make large transactions at a reduced cost. These transactions are typically handled by firms or dealers that are not members of an organized securities exchange. For bringing together large buyers and sellers, dealers charge commissions below those charged for making similar transactions on the associated securities exchange. Institutional investors are thus often able to realize sizable savings in brokerage commissions as well as to have minimal impact on the price of the transaction.

third market
over-the-counter transactions made in securities listed on the NYSE, AMEX, or other organized exchange.

The **fourth market** is the name given to transactions made directly between large institutional buyers and sellers of securities. Unlike third-market transactions, fourth-market transactions bypass the dealer. But in order to find a suitable seller or buyer, an institution may hire a firm to facilitate the transaction.

fourth market
transactions made directly between large institutional buyers and sellers of securities.

INVESTING IN ACTION

The New York Stock Exchange Dominates the World

You've built a company from scratch somewhere in Europe or Asia, and you want to sell shares to the public. Where do you want to be listed? London? Tokyo? Perhaps. But it's the New York Stock Exchange, located at 11 Wall Street in downtown Manhattan, not in London or Tokyo, where many of the world's leading companies want their stocks listed.

Although Tokyo and London have enjoyed periods in the last 15 years when their stature as financial centers was rising at the expense of New York, the NYSE is now benefiting from the swing in the balance of power toward New York as the world's most important financial center.

To be sure, the U.S. stock market's superior performance during much of the 1990s has had a lot to do with the desire of foreign companies to be listed on the New York Stock Exchange. Indeed, in 1997, one out of every four new listings on the NYSE was a foreign company, and such listings have almost tripled in the past 5 years. The NYSE's international roster is led by companies from Britain, Canada, Chile, and Mexico.

However, the NYSE's global ambitions are hampered by its own stringent requirements, as well as by slow progress in developing international accounting standards acceptable to the U.S. Securities and Exchange Commission and other countries. As a result, the NYSE is also looking to boost membership from competing U.S. exchanges where accounting is not an issue. It is also attracting a record number of Nasdaq transfers, including such high-profile technology companies as America Online and Gateway 2000.

The NYSE is also in hot pursuit of U.S. initial public offerings, where Nasdaq has long reigned supreme. Until 1983, only three IPOs had been launched on the NYSE. Since then, over 700 companies have gone public on the NYSE. In 1996, it had 117 IPOs, up from 74 the prior year. In comparison, Nasdaq had 730 IPOs in 1996.

The NYSE's international prestige is a selling point for Nasdaq companies that are considering a switch to the "Big Board." America Online's CEO, Stephen M. Case, says moving to the NYSE was about improving the company's "global profile" as it pushes into new markets in Europe and Asia. Despite high-profile defections, however, Nasdaq still boasts many of the leading technology companies, many of whom have a strong sense of loyalty to a market that took them when NYSE would not. Nasdaq listing fees are also far lower than those of the NYSE.

Meanwhile, business is booming on the NYSE. Membership prices are skyrocketing. Memberships, called seats, allow firms to trade on the floor of the NYSE. Seat prices hit an all-time high in 1997, when one sold for $2 million, up 38% from the high price in 1996. No wonder: The bull market has sent volume to a daily average topping 500 million shares, handled without a hitch by the NYSE's trading system. In late 1997, the NYSE took billion-share trading days in stride.

In the war between the exchanges, the winner will be the trading system that offers the greatest efficiency, the best service, and the most liquidity at the lowest price. But there are other winners, too: the companies that will get fairer and more open markets for the trading of their stocks, and the investors, both big and small, who will get the most for their investment dollars.

Trading Hours of Securities Markets

Both the organized U.S. exchanges and Nasdaq recently expanded their trading hours beyond the traditional session (9:30 A.M. to 4:00 P.M. Eastern time) to compete more effectively with foreign securities markets, in which investors can execute trades when U.S. markets are closed. In mid-1991, the NYSE added two short electronic trading sessions that begin after the 4:00 P.M.

closing bell. The first, from 4:15 to 5:00 P.M., trades stocks at that day's closing prices via a computer-matching system. Transactions occur only if a match can be made, and they are handled on a first-come, first-served basis. The second session lasts from 4:00 to 5:15 P.M. and allows institutional investors to trade large blocks of stock valued at $1 million or more. Since their inception, the NYSE has experienced growing interest in both sessions.

Nasdaq began its own expanded-hours electronic trading session in January 1992. Called *Nasdaq International*, it runs from 3:30 A.M. (when the London Exchange opens) to 9:00 A.M. Eastern time, half an hour before the start of regular trading sessions in U.S. markets. Because it lists NYSE stocks as well as other U.S. equities and has less stringent disclosure requirements than other markets, Nasdaq International is designed to attract traders from both the New York and London exchanges. The Pacific Stock Exchange also conducts an after-hours trading session, from 4:00 to 4:50 P.M. Eastern time. Unlike the NYSE and Nasdaq, the Pacific Stock Exchange's after-hours session is run on an auction basis. It continues to make markets, rather than trading electronically at fixed prices. Other U.S. markets are expected eventually to expand their hours as well.

These actions represent the first steps toward the development of 24-hour global trading of securities, both electronically and at auction through organized exchanges. Actually, large institutional investors are already able to trade securities after hours (from 4:00 P.M. to 9:30 A.M. Eastern time) through *Instinet*, a private electronic trading system owned by Reuters, the British communications conglomerate. This system facilitates *fourth-market* transactions in about 10,000 U.S. and European stocks. In addition, in 1992 the Chicago Board of Trade and the Chicago Mercantile Exchange for competitive reasons established *Globex*. It is a computerized electronic trading system that creates a 24-hour global marketplace in which options and futures listed on those exchanges can be traded at times when the exchanges are closed. Some people believe that Globex could become the model for the 24-hour global stock exchange of the future. Many experts expect longer trading sessions to be used primarily by institutional investors but question their value for the average individual investor.

Regulation of Securities Markets

Securities laws are passed to protect investors and to meet the needs of the financial marketplace as it grows in both size and complexity. A number of state and federal laws require that adequate and accurate disclosure of information be made to investors. Such laws also regulate the activities of participants in the securities markets. State laws that control the sale of securities within state borders are commonly called "blue sky laws" because they are intended to prevent investors from being sold nothing but "blue sky." These laws typically establish procedures for regulating both security issues and sellers of securities doing business within the state. As part of this process, most states have a regulatory body, such as a state securities commission, that is charged with the enforcement of the related state statutes. However, the most important securities laws, briefly summarized below, are those enacted by the federal government.

Securities Act of 1933

Congress passed the *Securities Act of 1933* to ensure full disclosure of information about new security issues and prevent a stock market collapse similar to that of 1929–1932. The act requires the issuer of a new security to file with the Securities and Exchange Commission (SEC) a registration statement containing information about the new issue. The firm cannot sell the security until the SEC approves the registration statement, a process that usually takes about 20 days.

prospectus
a portion of a security registration statement that details the key aspects of the issue, the issuer, and its management and financial position.

red herring
a preliminary prospectus made available to prospective investors after a registration statement's filing but before its approval.

One portion of the registration statement, called the **prospectus,** details the key aspects of the issue, the issuer, and its management and financial position. During the waiting period between the statement's filing and its approval, a preliminary prospectus is made available to prospective investors. It is often called a **red herring** because a notice printed in red on the front cover indicates the tentative nature of the offer. If the statement is approved, the new security issue can be offered for sale. If the registration statement is found to be fraudulent, the SEC will reject the issue and may also sue the directors and others responsible for the misrepresentation. The cover of the preliminary prospectus describing the 1998 stock issue of Playtex Products is shown in Figure 2.2. Note the red herring printed vertically on its left edge.

FIGURE 2.2
Cover of a Preliminary Prospectus for a Stock Issue

Some of the key factors related to the 1998 stock issue by Playtex Products are summarized on the cover of its 51-page preliminary prospectus. Note that the type printed vertically on the left edge is normally red: a *red herring.* (Source: Playtex Products, Inc., April 23, 1998, p. 1.)

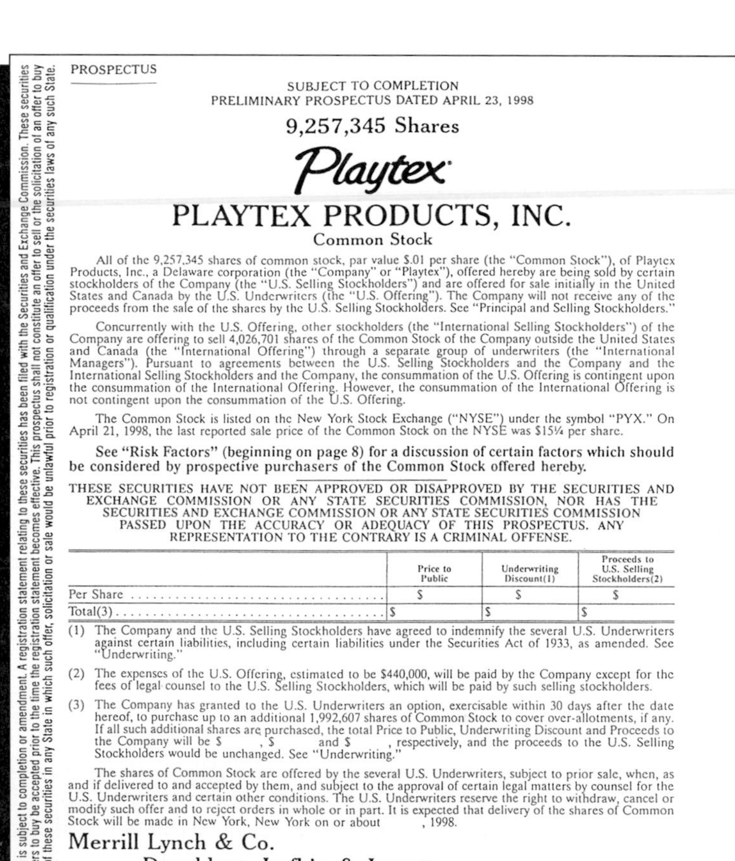

Information contained herein is subject to completion or amendment. A registration statement relating to these securities has been filed with the Securities and Exchange Commission. These securities may not be sold nor may offers to buy be accepted prior to the time the registration statement becomes effective. This prospectus shall not constitute an offer to sell or the solicitation of an offer to buy nor shall there be any sale of these securities in any State in which such offer, solicitation or sale would be unlawful prior to registration or qualification under the securities laws of any such State.

PROSPECTUS

SUBJECT TO COMPLETION
PRELIMINARY PROSPECTUS DATED APRIL 23, 1998

9,257,345 Shares

Playtex

PLAYTEX PRODUCTS, INC.

Common Stock

All of the 9,257,345 shares of common stock, par value $.01 per share (the "Common Stock"), of Playtex Products, Inc., a Delaware corporation (the "Company" or "Playtex"), offered hereby are being sold by certain stockholders of the Company (the "U.S. Selling Stockholders") and are offered for sale initially in the United States and Canada by the U.S. Underwriters (the "U.S. Offering"). The Company will not receive any of the proceeds from the sale of the shares by the U.S. Selling Stockholders. See "Principal and Selling Stockholders."

Concurrently with the U.S. Offering, other stockholders (the "International Selling Stockholders") of the Company are offering to sell 4,026,701 shares of the Common Stock of the Company outside the United States and Canada (the "International Offering") through a separate group of underwriters (the "International Managers"). Pursuant to agreements between the U.S. Selling Stockholders and the Company and the International Selling Stockholders and the Company, the consummation of the U.S. Offering is contingent upon the consummation of the International Offering. However, the consummation of the International Offering is not contingent upon the consummation of the U.S. Offering.

The Common Stock is listed on the New York Stock Exchange ("NYSE") under the symbol "PYX." On April 21, 1998, the last reported sale price of the Common Stock on the NYSE was $15¼ per share.

See "Risk Factors" (beginning on page 8) for a discussion of certain factors which should be considered by prospective purchasers of the Common Stock offered hereby.

THESE SECURITIES HAVE NOT BEEN APPROVED OR DISAPPROVED BY THE SECURITIES AND EXCHANGE COMMISSION OR ANY STATE SECURITIES COMMISSION, NOR HAS THE SECURITIES AND EXCHANGE COMMISSION OR ANY STATE SECURITIES COMMISSION PASSED UPON THE ACCURACY OR ADEQUACY OF THIS PROSPECTUS. ANY REPRESENTATION TO THE CONTRARY IS A CRIMINAL OFFENSE.

	Price to Public	Underwriting Discount(1)	Proceeds to U.S. Selling Stockholders(2)
Per Share	$	$	$
Total(3)	$	$	$

(1) The Company and the U.S. Selling Stockholders have agreed to indemnify the several U.S. Underwriters against certain liabilities, including certain liabilities under the Securities Act of 1933, as amended. See "Underwriting."

(2) The expenses of the U.S. Offering, estimated to be $440,000, will be paid by the Company except for the fees of legal counsel to the U.S. Selling Stockholders, which will be paid by such selling stockholders.

(3) The Company has granted to the U.S. Underwriters an option, exercisable within 30 days after the date hereof, to purchase up to an additional 1,992,607 shares of Common Stock to cover over-allotments, if any. If all such additional shares are purchased, the total Price to Public, Underwriting Discount and Proceeds to the Company will be $, $ and $, respectively, and the proceeds to the U.S. Selling Stockholders would be unchanged. See "Underwriting."

The shares of Common Stock are offered by the several U.S. Underwriters, subject to prior sale, when, as and if delivered to and accepted by them, and subject to the approval of certain legal matters by counsel for the U.S. Underwriters and certain other conditions. The U.S. Underwriters reserve the right to withdraw, cancel or modify such offer and to reject orders in whole or in part. It is expected that delivery of the shares of Common Stock will be made in New York, New York on or about , 1998.

Merrill Lynch & Co.
Donaldson, Lufkin & Jenrette
Securities Corporation
Goldman, Sachs & Co.
Morgan Stanley Dean Witter
PaineWebber Incorporated
Salomon Smith Barney

The date of this Prospectus is , 1998.

As an investor, you should realize that approval of the registration statement by the SEC does not mean the security is a good investment; it merely indicates that the facts presented in the statement appear to reflect the firm's true position.

Securities Exchange Act of 1934

The *Securities Exchange Act of 1934* formally established the SEC as the agency in charge of administering federal securities laws. The act gave the SEC the power to regulate the organized securities exchanges and the over-the-counter market by extending disclosure requirements to outstanding securities. It required the stock exchanges as well as the stocks traded on them to be registered with the SEC.

As a result of this act, the SEC covers the organized exchanges and the OTC market, their members, brokers and dealers, and the securities traded in these markets. Each of these participants must file reports with the SEC and must periodically update them. The act has been instrumental in providing adequate disclosure on issues that are traded in the secondary markets. The 1934 act, which has been amended several times over the years, and the Securities Act of 1933, remain the key pieces of legislation that protect participants in the securities markets.

INVESTOR FACT

DYED IN THE (GREEN AND GOLD) WOOL—In 1997 the Green Bay Packers sold a stock offering to finance stadium improvements. The prospectus for the offering acknowledged in capital letters: "IT IS VIRTUALLY IMPOSSIBLE" for investors ever to make a profit on the stock. In addition, the stock will pay no dividends and cannot be sold. Then why buy it? If you have to ask, you're not a Packers fan!

Maloney Act of 1938

The *Maloney Act of 1938*, an amendment to the Securities Exchange Act of 1934, provided for the establishment of trade associations to self-regulate the securities industry. Since its passage, only one such trade association, the National Association of Securities Dealers (NASD), has been formed. NASD members include nearly all of the nation's securities firms that do business with the public. The NASD, operating under SEC supervision, establishes standardized procedures for securities trading and ethical behavior, monitors and enforces compliance with these procedures, and serves as the industry spokesperson. Membership in the NASD allows member firms to make transactions with other member firms at rates below those charged to nonmembers. Today, any securities firms that are not members of the NASD must agree to be supervised directly by the SEC. Because the SEC can revoke the NASD's registration, it has the same power over this organization as over the exchanges. In addition to its self-regulatory role, the NASD has greatly streamlined the functioning of the over-the-counter market by creating Nasdaq.

Investment Company Act of 1940

The *Investment Company Act of 1940* was passed to protect those purchasing investment company shares. An *investment company* is one that obtains funds by selling its shares to numerous investors and uses the proceeds to purchase securities. The dominant type of investment company is the *mutual fund* (which is discussed in detail in Chapter 13). The Investment Company Act of 1940 established rules and regulations for investment companies and formally authorized the SEC to regulate their practices and procedures. It required the investment companies to register with the SEC and to fulfill certain disclosure requirements. The act was amended in 1970 to prohibit investment companies from paying excessive fees to their advisers and from charging excessive commissions to purchasers of company shares.

Investment Advisers Act of 1940

The *Investment Advisers Act of 1940* was passed to protect investors against potential abuses by *investment advisers*—persons hired by investors to advise them about security investments. It requires that advisers disclose all relevant information about their backgrounds, conflicts of interest, and so on, as well as about any investments they recommend. The act requires advisers to register and file periodic reports with the SEC. A 1960 amendment extended the SEC's powers to permit inspection of the records of investment advisers and to revoke the registration of advisers who violate the act's provisions. *This act does not provide any guarantee of competence on the part of advisers;* it merely helps to protect the investor against *fraudulent and unethical practices* by the adviser.

Securities Acts Amendments of 1975

In 1975 Congress amended the securities acts to require the SEC and the securities industry to develop a competitive national system for trading securities. As a first step, the SEC abolished fixed-commission schedules, thereby providing for negotiated commissions. (Commissions are discussed in more detail later in this chapter.) A second action was establishment of the *Intermarket Trading System (ITS)*. Today, this electronic communications network links nine markets, including the NYSE, the AMEX, major regional exchanges, and the Nasdaq market, and trades over 4,000 eligible issues. This system allows trades to be made across these markets wherever the network shows a better price for a given issue.

Insider Trading and Fraud Act of 1988

insider trading
the illegal use of material *nonpublic* information about a company to make profitable securities transactions.

The 1980s were a decade of general economic prosperity and rapidly rising stock prices. As typically happens during periods of excess in the financial markets, the decade also witnessed a takeover and buyout mania that spawned a host of speculators intent on profit. Many times these speculators operated without regard for the legality of their actions. Although the tactics varied, many of the illegal gains were achieved through insider-trading practices. **Insider trading** involves using private information to make profitable securities transactions. It is both illegal and unethical. The *Insider Trading and Fraud Act of 1988* defined an insider as one who possesses material *nonpublic* information, and it established penalties for insider trading. Insiders are typically a company's directors, officers, major shareholders, bankers, investment bankers, accountants, or attorneys. Of course, insiders are not legally prohibited from trading the firm's shares once private information becomes public. To allow it to monitor insider trades, the SEC requires corporate insiders to file monthly reports detailing all transactions made in the company's stock.

The prosecution and conviction of a number of high-profile insiders during the 1980s and early 1990s created a body of case law that more clearly defines illegal and unethical acts. The definition of the term *insider,* which originally referred only to a company's employees, directors, and their relatives, was expanded to include anyone who obtains private information about a company. Recent legislation substantially increased the penalties for insider trading and gave the SEC greater power to investigate and prosecute claims of illegal insider-trading activity.

ethics
standards of conduct or moral judgment.

Clearly, the many insider-trading cases of the 1980s and early 1990s heightened the public's awareness of **ethics**—standards of conduct or moral judgment—in business. The financial community is continuing to develop and enforce ethical standards that will motivate market participants to adhere to laws and regulations. Although it is indeed difficult to enforce ethical standards, it appears that opportunities for abuses in the financial markets are being reduced, thereby providing a more level playing field for all investors.

General Market Conditions: Bull or Bear

bull markets
favorable markets normally associated with rising prices, investor optimism, economic recovery, and government stimulus.

bear markets
unfavorable markets normally associated with falling prices, investor pessimism, economic slowdown, and government restraint.

Conditions in the securities markets are commonly classified as "bull" or "bear," depending on whether securities prices are rising or falling over time. Changing market conditions generally stem from changes in investor attitudes, changes in economic activity, and government actions aimed at stimulating or slowing down economic activity. **Bull markets** are favorable markets normally associated with rising prices, investor optimism, economic recovery, and government stimulus. **Bear markets** are unfavorable markets normally associated with falling prices, investor pessimism, economic slowdown, and government restraint. Since late 1990, the stock market has been bullish primarily as a result of low inflation, improving trade balances, shrinking budget deficits, and economic recovery.

In general, investors experience higher (or positive) returns on common stock investments during a bull market. However, some securities are bullish in a bear market or bearish in a bull market. Of course, during bear markets many investors invest in vehicles other than securities to obtain higher and less risky returns. Market conditions are difficult to predict and usually can be identified only after they exist. Sources of information that can be used to assess market conditions are described in Chapter 3 and applied to the analysis and valuation of common stock in Chapters 6 and 7.

CONCEPTS IN REVIEW

2.1 Differentiate between each of the following pairs of words:
   a. *Money market* and *capital market*
   b. *Primary market* and *secondary market*
   c. *Organized securities exchanges* and *over-the-counter (OTC) market*

2.2 Briefly describe the role of the investment banker in underwriting a public offering. Differentiate among the terms *public offering, rights offering,* and *private placement.*

2.3 For each of the items in the left-hand column, select the most appropriate item in the right-hand column. Explain the relationship between the items matched.

a. AMEX	1. Trades unlisted securities
b. CBT	2. Futures exchange
c. NYSE	3. Options exchange
d. Boston Stock Exchange	4. Regional stock exchange
e. CBOE	5. Second largest organized U.S. exchange
f. OTC	6. Has the most stringest listing requirements

2.4 Explain how the *over-the-counter market* works. Be sure to mention dealers, bid and ask prices, Nasdaq, and the Nasdaq National Market. What role does this market play in initial public offerings (IPOs) and secondary distributions? What are the third and fourth markets?

2.5 According to the *Investing in Action* box on page 26, what are two key reasons why companies wish to be listed on the New York Stock Exchange? What will ultimately determine the winner in the war between the exchanges?

2.6 Briefly describe the key rules and regulations that resulted from each of the following securities acts:
   a. Securities Act of 1933
   b. Securities Exchange Act of 1934
   c. Maloney Act of 1938
   d. Investment Company Act of 1940
   e. Investment Advisers Act of 1940
   f. Securities Acts Amendments of 1975
   g. Insider Trading and Fraud Act of 1988

2.7 Differentiate between a *bull market* and a *bear market.*

http://hepg.aw.com

To get insight into how the secondary markets work, you can go right to the source of the action. Exchange-traded securities are covered at the Web location of the New York Stock Exchange and the OTC markets are explained at the NASD site. At the NASD site, follow the *Profile, The Nasdaq Market,* and the *How it Works* links.

www.nyse.com/public/thenyse/1b/1bix.htm

www.nasd.com

Globalization of Securities Markets

diversification
the inclusion of a number of different investment vehicles in a portfolio to increase returns or reduce risk.

Today investors, issuers of securities, and securities firms look beyond the markets of their home countries to find the best returns, lowest costs, and best international business opportunities. The basic goal of most investors is to earn the highest return with the lowest risk. This outcome is achieved through **diversification**—the inclusion of a number of different investment vehicles in a portfolio to increase returns or reduce risk. The investor who includes foreign investments in a portfolio can greatly increase the potential for diversification by holding (1) a wider range of industries and securities, (2) securities traded in a larger number of markets, and (3) securities denominated in different currencies. The smaller and less diversified an investor's home market is, the greater the potential benefit from prudent international diversification. However, even investors from the United States and other highly developed markets can benefit from global diversification.

Advances in technology and communications, together with the elimination of many political and regulatory barriers, allow investors to make cross-border securities transactions with relative ease. More and more financial markets are opening and becoming integrated with the rest of the world's markets. Both investors and seekers of funds can view the world's markets as available to them. In short, globalization of the securities markets is enabling investors to seek out opportunities to profit from rapidly expanding economies throughout the world. Here, we consider the growing importance of international markets, ways to invest in foreign securities, and the risks of investing internationally.

Growing Importance of International Markets

Organized securities exchanges now operate in more than 30 countries worldwide. They are located not only in the major industrialized nations such as Japan, Great Britain, Canada, and Germany but also in emerging economies such as Brazil, Chile, India, South Korea, Malaysia, Mexico, Taiwan, and Thailand. The top four organized securities markets worldwide (based on 1997 dollar volume) are the New York, London, Tokyo, and Paris stock exchanges. Other important foreign exchanges include Frankfurt, Osaka, Toronto, Montreal, Sydney, Hong Kong, Zurich, and Taiwan. The European stock markets are expected to take on additional importance with economic integration of the European Union (EU), which is expected to be complete in 2002. Among the EU's major goals are the development of a central capital market, a central bank, and a single currency unit—the *euro*—for the 15 countries that are currently members. The market capitalization of the combined EU markets now represents a market competitive with New York and Tokyo.

Bond markets too have become global, and more investors than ever before regularly purchase government and corporate fixed-income securities in foreign markets. The United States dominates the international government bond market; it is followed by Japan, Germany, and Great Britain.

International Investment Performance

A primary motive for investing overseas is the lure of high returns. In fact, only once since 1980 did the United States finish number one among the major stock markets of the world. For example, in 1997 investors would have earned higher returns in such markets as France, Germany, Mexico, Russia, and the United Kingdom than in the United States. During that year the stock price index for France increased by 29.5%, that for Germany by 47.1%, that for Mexico by 54.9%, that for Russia by 125.9%, and that for the United Kingdom by 24.7%, compared to a 22.6% increase in the U.S. stock price index. Of course, foreign securities markets tend to be more risky than U.S. markets. A market with high returns in one year may not do so well in the next year.

Investors can compare activity on U.S. and foreign exchanges by following market indexes that track the performance of those exchanges. For instance, the Dow Jones averages and the Standard & Poor's indexes are popular measures of the U.S. markets, and indexes for more than 20 different stock markets are available. (We'll discuss indexes in more detail in Chapter 3.) Most of the major indexes, trading activity in selected stocks on major foreign exchanges, and currency exchange rates are reported daily in the *Wall Street Journal* and regularly in other financial publications. Also, the *Wall Street Journal*'s "World Stock Markets" section (of Part C) frequently compares the performance of the U.S. exchanges with that of selected foreign markets.

Investing in Foreign Securities

Foreign security investments can be made either indirectly or directly. One form of *indirect* investment is the purchase of shares of a U.S.-based multinational with substantial foreign operations. Many U.S.-based multinational firms, such as Exxon, IBM, Citicorp, Dow Chemical, Coca-Cola, Colgate-Palmolive, and Hewlett-Packard, receive more than 50% of their revenues from overseas operations. By investing in the securities of such firms, an investor can achieve a degree of international diversification. Another form of indirect foreign investment can be achieved by purchasing shares in a mutual fund that invests primarily in foreign securities. Both of these types of indirect foreign securities investment transactions are made in a conventional fashion through a stockbroker, as explained later in this chapter and in Chapter 13, which is devoted to mutual funds.

Direct investment in foreign companies can be achieved in three ways: by purchasing securities on foreign exchanges, by buying securities of foreign companies that are traded on U.S. exchanges, or by buying *American Depositary Receipts (ADRs)*. The first way—purchasing securities on foreign exchanges—involves additional risks because the securities are not traded in U.S. dollars. This approach is not for the timid or inexperienced investor. The *Investing in Action* box on page 35 describes a relatively new opportunity, for example, to invest directly in the stocks of Russian companies.

Because each country's exchange has its own regulations and procedures, investors must be prepared to cope not only with currency exchange (dollars to pesos, for example) but also with varying degrees of market regulation and efficiency and with different securities exchange rules, transaction procedures, accounting standards, tax laws, and language barriers. These transactions are best handled either through brokers at major Wall Street firms with large international operations or through major banks, such as Bankers Trust and Citicorp, that have special units to handle foreign securities transactions. Brokers at these firms provide information and advice and make foreign security transactions for their clients. Investors can alternatively deal with foreign broker–dealers, but such an approach is more complicated and more risky.

Yankee bonds
dollar-denominated debt securities issued by foreign governments or corporations and traded in U.S. securities markets.

The second form of direct investment is to buy the securities of foreign companies that are traded on both organized and over-the-counter exchanges. These securities are issued by large, well-known foreign companies. Stocks of companies such as Alcan, Gucci, Seagram, and Singer trade directly on U.S. exchanges. In addition, **Yankee bonds,** dollar-denominated debt securities issued by foreign governments or corporations and traded in U.S. securities markets, are traded on organized exchanges and in the over-the-counter market in the United States. Transactions in foreign securities that are traded on U.S. exchanges are handled in the same way as exchange-traded domestic securities.

American Depositary Receipts (ADRs)
dollar-denominated negotiable receipts for the stocks of foreign companies that are held in the vaults of banks in the companies' home countries.

Finally, foreign stocks are also traded on U.S. exchanges in the form of **American Depositary Receipts (ADRs),** which are dollar-denominated negotiable receipts for the stocks of foreign companies that are held in the vaults of banks in the companies' home countries. Today, nearly 1,200 ADRs representing about 40 different home countries are traded on U.S. exchanges. About one-fourth of them are actively traded. Included are ADRs of well-known companies such as Daimler-Benz, Sony, Toyota, Unilever, and Volvo. ADRs trade in the same way as standard domestic securities. ADRs are further discussed in Chapter 5.

INVESTING IN ACTION

Investing in Russia Remains a Rowdy Game

In 1993 there was no stock market in Russia. President Boris N. Yeltsin had just defeated the Communist Party hard-liners. Industrial output was collapsing and inflation was rampant. Russians with money were smuggling billions of dollars out of the country. There were no stock exchanges, no corporate earnings reports, and almost no earnings.

But there was stock. Under Mr. Yeltsin's privatization program, shares in thousands of former government-owned enterprises were auctioned off or given to workers and managers. Most people thought these shares were worthless. Instead, Russian stock is red hot. Six years after the collapse of the Soviet Union, Russia's stock market tripled between early 1996 and late 1997. Moscow's top hotels are swarming with Western bankers, brokers, and deal makers. The money pouring into Russian stocks has come overwhelmingly from foreign investment funds whose investors are from Wall Street, London, Hong Kong, and elsewhere.

The boom has been driven by two factors: a conviction that Mr. Yeltsin's economic changes are making Russia safe for capitalism, and the lure of cheap assets. Russian companies control some of the world's biggest oil reserves, its largest supplier of natural gas, its biggest nickel and platinum mines, and thousands of factories. Yet the combined stock value of Russia's 50 largest companies is about the same as the value of Coca-Cola.

By any measure, investing in Russia is not for the faint-hearted. Russia's economy is still bleak. Growth is essentially zero; industrial output has only begun to stabilize after 5 years of decline. Outside the glitter of Moscow, Russia remains a land of poverty. Russian companies are in a shocking state of disrepair, needing either billions of dollars in reconstruction or outright demolition. Many managers have brazenly looted assets or ceded control to organized crime. Only a few companies report audited financial results. Many stocks trade so rarely that it can take weeks to buy or sell them. And like many former communist countries, Russia has had its share of blatant fraud and pyramid schemes.

Many Russian companies, though, offer real opportunities. The country's most actively traded stock is Unified Energy System, Russia's main electric utility. During a stretch of 1997, the stock soared nearly 600% after the company reported a modest profit. But those revenues include several hundred million dollars in unpaid customer bills, and investors don't yet know how much the company will be able to collect. Another big company is Avto Vaz, which makes 70% of all cars in Russia. Its cars roll out of the factory with an average of 42 defects apiece and are widely loathed by Russian consumers. Yet the stock climbed tenfold between mid-1996 and mid-1997. Although Russia remains too wild for most mutual funds or institutional investors such as insurance companies, its sheer size and recent performance have made it impossible to ignore.

Risks of Investing Internationally

Investing abroad is not without pitfalls. In addition to the usual risks involved in making any security transaction, you must consider the risks associated with doing business in a particular foreign country. Changes in trade policies, labor laws, and taxation may affect operating conditions for the country's firms. The government itself may not be stable. Therefore, when making investments in foreign markets, you must watch similar environmental factors in each foreign country. That is, of course, more difficult than at home because of your lack of familiarity with the foreign economic and political environments, as well as the number of countries involved.

U.S. securities markets are generally viewed as highly regulated, efficient, and reliable. This is not always the case in foreign markets, many of which lag substantially behind the United States in both operations and regulation. Some countries place various restrictions on foreign investment. In Korea, Brazil, and Thailand, for example, mutual funds are the only way for foreigners to invest; Mexico has a two-tier market, with some securities restricted to foreigners. Some countries make it difficult for foreigners to get their funds out, and many impose taxes on dividends. For example, Swiss taxes are about 20% on dividends paid to foreigners. In addition, accounting standards vary from country to country. These differences in accounting practices can affect the apparent profitability, conceal other attractive assets (e.g., hidden reserves and undervalued assets that are permitted in many countries), and fail to disclose other risks. As a result, it is difficult to compare fairly the financial performances and positions of firms operating in different foreign countries. Other difficulties include illiquid markets and an inability to obtain reliable investment information because of a lack of reporting requirements.

Furthermore, international investing involves securities denominated in foreign currencies, so trading profits and losses are affected not only by a security's price changes but also by changes in currency exchange rates. The values of the world's major currencies fluctuate with respect to each other on a daily basis, and the relationship between two currencies at a specified date is called the **currency exchange rate.** On November 26, 1997, the currency exchange rate for the French franc (Ff) and the U.S. dollar (US$) was expressed as follows:

currency exchange rate
the relationship between two currencies at a specified date.

US$ 1.00 = Ff 5.89

Ff 1.00 = US$ 0.170

On that day, you would have received 5.89 French francs for every $1. Conversely, each French franc was worth $0.170.

Changes in the value of a particular foreign currency with respect to the US$—or any other currency—are called *appreciation* and *depreciation.* For example, on May 26, 1998, the Ff/US$ exchange rate was 5.94; in 6 months, the French franc had *depreciated* relative to the dollar (and the dollar *appreciated* relative to the franc). On May 26, it took more francs to buy $1 (5.94 versus 5.89), so each franc was worth less in dollar terms ($0.168 versus $0.170). Had the French franc instead *appreciated* (and the dollar *depreciated* relative to the franc), each franc would have been worth more in dollar terms.

currency exchange risk
the risk caused by the varying exchange rates between the currencies of two countries.

Currency exchange risk is the risk caused by the varying exchange rates between the currencies of two countries. For example, assume that on November 26, 1997, you bought 100 shares of a French stock at 100 Ff per share, held it for 6 months, and then sold it for its original purchase price of 100 French francs. The following table summarizes these transactions:

Date	Transaction	Number of Shares	Price in Ff	Value of Transaction Ff	Exchange Rate Ff/US$	Value in US$
11/26/97	Purchase	100	100	10,000	5.89	$1,697.79
5/26/98	Sell	100	100	10,000	5.94	$1,683.50

Although you realized the original purchase price in French francs, in dollar terms the transaction resulted in a loss of $14.29 ($1,697.79 – $1,683.50).

The value of the stock in dollars decreased because the French franc was worth less—had depreciated—relative to the dollar. Therefore, investors in foreign securities must be aware that the value of the foreign currency in relation to the dollar can have a profound effect on returns from foreign security transactions.

CONCEPTS IN REVIEW

2.8 Why is globalization of securities markets an important issue today? How have international investments performed in recent years?

2.9 Describe how foreign security investments can be made, both indirectly and directly. Describe the risks of investing internationally, particularly *currency exchange risk.*

2.10 According to the *Investing in Action* box on page 35, what Russian assets might be of particular interest to investors? What are the risks of investing in Russian stocks?

Making Securities Transactions

LG 4 LG 5

Understanding how the securities markets are structured, how they function, and their global dimension is only the first step in developing a sound investment program. You must also understand the procedures required to make transactions. In this section we will look at the role of stockbrokers, the basic types of orders that can be placed, the costs of making investment transactions, and investor protection.

The Role of Stockbrokers

stockbrokers
individuals licensed by stock exchanges to facilitate transactions between buyers and sellers of securities.

Stockbrokers—also called *account executives, investment executives,* and *financial consultants*—act as intermediaries between buyers and sellers of securities. They typically charge a commission for facilitating these securities transactions. Stockbrokers must be licensed by the exchanges on which they place orders and must abide by the ethical guidelines of the exchanges and the SEC. Stockbrokers work for the brokerage firms that own seats on the organized securities exchanges, and members of the securities exchange execute orders transmitted to them by the brokers in the various sales offices. For example, the largest U.S. brokerage firm, Merrill Lynch, transmits orders for listed securities from its offices in most major cities throughout the country to the main office of Merrill Lynch and then to the floor of the stock exchanges (NYSE and AMEX), where they are executed. Confirmation of the order is sent back to the broker placing the order, who then relays it to the customer. This process can be carried out in a matter of minutes with the use of sophisticated telecommunications networks. As noted later, personal computers and the Internet have opened up new ways of making security transactions.

Orders for over-the-counter securities are transmitted by the brokerage firm to *market makers,* who are dealers in the OTC market specializing in that security. The Nasdaq system, along with the available information on who makes markets in certain securities, enables brokers to execute orders in OTC securities. Normally, OTC transactions can be executed rapidly, because market makers maintain inventories of the securities in which they deal. Although the procedure for executing orders on organized exchanges may differ from that in the OTC market, an investor always places orders with his or her broker in the same manner.

Brokerage Services

The primary activity of stockbrokers involves executing clients' purchase and sale transactions at the best possible price. Brokerage firms will hold the client's security certificates for safekeeping; the stocks kept by the firm in this manner are said to be held in **street name.** Because the securities are issued in the brokerage house's name and held in trust for the client (rather than issued in the client's name), they can be transferred at the time of sale without the client's signature. Street name is actually a common way of buying securities, because many investors do not want to be bothered with handling and safekeeping stock certificates. In such cases, the brokerage firm records the details of the client's transaction and keeps track of his or her investments through a series of bookkeeping entries. Dividends and notices received by the broker are forwarded to the client who owns the securities.

street name
stock certificates issued in the brokerage house's name but held in trust for its client, who actually owns them.

Stockbrokers also offer clients a variety of other services. For example, the brokerage firm normally provides free information about investments. Quite often, the firm has a research staff that periodically issues analyses of economic, market, industry, or company behavior and makes recommendations to buy or sell certain securities. As a client of a large brokerage firm, you can expect to receive regular bulletins on market activity and possibly a recommended investment list. You will also receive a statement describing your transactions for the month and showing commission and interest charges, dividends and interest received, and detailed listings of your current holdings.

INVESTOR FACT

TOO MUCH PAPERWORK—Wasn't the computer supposed to cut down on paperwork? Tell that to the stock brokerage firms and mutual fund companies that send you monthly and year-end statements, confirmations of buy and sell orders, newsletters, and so on. What can you throw away? Keep your most recent brokerage statements and the year-end documents (which you'll need to prepare your tax filings). Check over the monthly statements to make sure they're correct—and then toss them when the next month's statements come.

Today most brokerage firms will invest surplus cash left in a customer's account in a money market mutual fund, allowing the customer to earn a reasonable rate of interest on these balances. Such arrangements help the investor earn as much as possible on temporarily idle funds. Most brokerage offices also have electronic equipment that provides up-to-the-minute stock price quotations and world news. Price information can be obtained by consulting the *ticker* (a lighted screen that displays all NYSE, AMEX, and regional exchange security transactions as they occur) or by keying into a computer system that provides a capsulized description of almost all securities and their prices. World news, which can significantly affect the stock market, is obtained from a wire service subscribed to by the brokerage office. Finally, most offices have a reference library available for use by clients.

Selecting a Stockbroker

It is crucial to select a stockbroker who understands your investment goals and who can effectively assist you in pursuing these goals. If you choose a broker whose own disposition toward investing is similar to yours, you should be able to establish a solid working relationship. You should also consider the cost and types of services available from the firm with which the broker is affiliated. The broker you select should be the person you believe best understands your investment goals and will provide the best service at the lowest possible cost to you. She or he should make you aware of investment possibilities that are consistent with your objectives and attitude toward risk.

It is probably wise to ask friends or business associates to recommend a broker. However, it is not important—and often not even advisable—to know your stockbroker personally. A strictly business relationship eliminates the possibility that social concerns will interfere with the achievement of your investment goals. This does not mean that your broker's sole interest should be commissions. Responsible brokers do not engage in **churning**—that is, causing excessive trading of their clients' accounts to increase commissions. Churning is both illegal and unethical under SEC and exchange rules. However, it is often difficult to prove.

churning
an illegal and unethical act by a broker to increase commissions by causing excessive trading of clients' accounts.

Investors who wish merely to make transactions and are not interested in obtaining the full array of brokerage services available from so-called **full-service brokers** should consider either a *discount broker* or an *online broker.* **Discount brokers** merely make transactions for customers: They charge low commissions and provide little or no research information or investment advice. The investor calls a toll-free number to initiate a transaction, and the discount broker confirms the transaction by phone or return mail. Discount brokers that charge the lowest commissions and provide virtually no services are commonly referred to as *deep discounters.* **Online brokers** (also called *Internet brokers* and *electronic brokers*) are typically *deep-discount brokers* through which investors can execute trades electronically online. This is typically accomplished through one of the commercial online services (such as America Online and CompuServe) or through the Internet. The investor merely accesses the online broker's Web site to open an account, review the commission schedule, or see a demonstration of the available transactional services and procedures. Confirmation of electronic trades can take as little as 10 seconds, and most occur within 1 minute. The rapid growth of online investors, particularly among affluent, young investors who enjoy surfing the Web, is expected to cause most brokerage firms to offer online trading, probably through subsidiaries, within the next few years. The rapidly growing volume of business done by discount and online brokers attests to their success. Today, many banks and savings institutions are making discount and online brokerage services available to their depositors who wish to buy stocks, bonds, mutual funds, and other investment vehicles. Some of the major full-service, discount, and online brokers are listed in Table 2.2.

full-service broker
broker who, in addition to facilitating transactions, provides clients with a full array of brokerage services.

discount broker
broker who charges low commissions to make transactions for customers but provides little or no research information or investment advice.

online broker
typically a *deep-discount broker* through which investors can execute trades electronically online through a commercial service or on the Internet. (Also called *Internet broker* and *electronic broker.*)

TABLE 2.2 Major Full-Service, Discount, and Online Brokers

Type of Broker		
Full-Service	Discount	Online
A.G. Edwards	Charles Schwab	Accutrade
Dean Witter	Fidelity Brokerage Services	AmeriTrade
Merrill Lynch	Jack White & Company	DLJ Direct
Paine Webber	Kennedy, Cabot & Co.	E* Trade
Prudential Securities	Olde	e. Schwab
Smith Barney	Quick & Reilly	Net Investor

Opening an Account

To open an account, the customer must fill out various documents that establish a legal relationship between the customer and the brokerage firm. A signature card and a personal data card provide the information needed to identify the client's account. The stockbroker must also have a reasonable understanding of a client's personal financial situation in order to assess his or her investment goals—and to be sure that the client can pay for the securities purchased. Instructions regarding the transfer and custody of securities must be given to the broker. If the customer wishes to borrow money to make transactions, a *margin account* (described below) must be established. If the customer is acting as a trustee or an executor or is a corporation, additional documents are required. No laws or rules prohibit an investor from having accounts with more than one stockbroker. Many investors establish accounts at different firms to obtain the benefit and opinions of a diverse group of brokers and to reduce the cost of making purchase and sale transactions.

Types of Accounts

A number of different types of accounts can be established with a stockbroker. We will briefly consider several of the more popular types.

custodial account
the brokerage account of a minor; requires a parent or guardian to be part of all transactions.

Single or Joint A brokerage account may be either single or joint. *Joint accounts* are most common between husband and wife or parent and child. The account of a minor (a person less than 18 years of age) is a **custodial account,** in which a parent or guardian must be part of all transactions. Regardless of which form of account is maintained, the name(s) of the account holder(s) and an account number are used to identify the account.

cash account
a brokerage account in which a customer can make only cash transactions.

margin account
a brokerage account in which the customer has been extended borrowing privileges by the brokerage firm.

Cash or Margin A **cash account,** the more common type, is one in which the customer can make only cash transactions. Customers can initiate cash transactions via phone or online and are given three business days in which to transmit the cash to the brokerage firm. The firm is likewise given three business days in which to deposit the proceeds from the sale of securities in the customer's cash account.

A **margin account** is an account in which a creditworthy customer has been extended borrowing privileges by the brokerage firm. By leaving securities with the firm to be held as collateral, the customer is permitted to borrow a prespecified proportion of the purchase price. The brokerage firm will, of course, charge the customer a specified rate of interest on borrowings. (More discussion of margin trading is included later in this chapter.)

wrap account
a brokerage account in which customers with large portfolios pay a flat annual fee that covers the cost of a money manager's services and the commissions on *all* trades.

Wrap The **wrap account** allows brokerage customers with large portfolios (generally $100,000 or more) to shift stock-selection decisions conveniently to a professional money manager, either in-house or independent. In return for a flat annual fee equal to between 2% and 3% of the portfolio's total asset value, the brokerage firm helps the investor select a money manager, pays the manager's fee, and executes the money manager's trades. Of course, the investor's overall goals are initially communicated to the manager. Wrap accounts are appealing for a number of reasons other than convenience. Because the annual fee in most cases covers commissions on *all* trades, the chance of the broker churning the account is virtually eliminated. In addition, the broker monitors the manager's performance and provides the investor with detailed reports, typically quarterly.

Odd-Lot or Round-Lot Transactions

odd lot
less than 100 shares of stock.

round lot
100-share units of stock or multiples thereof.

Stock transactions can be made in either odd or round lots. An **odd lot** consists of less than 100 shares of a stock; a **round lot** is a 100-share unit or multiple thereof. You would be dealing in an odd lot if you bought, say, 25 shares of stock but in a round lot if you bought 200 shares. A trade of 225 shares would be a combination of an odd lot and two round lots.

Because transactions in odd lots require either additional processing by the brokerage firm or the assistance of a specialist, an added fee—known as an *odd-lot differential*—is tacked on to the normal commission charge, driving up the costs of these small trades. Small investors in the early stages of their investment programs are primarily responsible for odd-lot transactions.

Basic Types of Orders

Different types of orders are used in making security transactions. The type placed normally depends on the investor's goals and expectations. The three basic types of orders are the market order, the limit order, and the stop-loss order.

Market Order

market order
an order to buy or sell stock at the best price available when the order is placed.

An order to buy or sell stock at the best price available when the order is placed is a **market order.** It is generally the quickest way to have orders filled, because market orders are usually executed as soon as they reach the exchange floor or are received by the dealer. Because of the speed with which market orders are executed, the buyer or seller of a security can be sure that the price at which the order is transacted will be very close to the market price prevailing at the time the order was placed.

Limit Order

limit order
an order to buy at or below a specified price or to sell at or above a specified price.

An order to buy at or below a specified price or to sell at or above a specified price is known as a **limit order.** When a limit order is placed, the broker transmits it to a specialist dealing in the security. The specialist makes a notation in his or her book, indicating the number of shares and price of the limit order. The order is executed as soon as the specified market price (or better) exists and all other orders with precedence—similar orders received earlier, buy orders at a higher specified price, or sell orders at a lower specified price—have been satisfied. The limit order can be placed as one of the following:

1. A *fill-or-kill order,* which if not immediately executed is canceled.
2. A *day order,* which if not executed is automatically canceled at the end of the day.
3. A *good-'til-canceled (GTC) order,* which generally remains in effect for 6 months unless executed, canceled, or renewed.

Assume, by way of example, that you place a limit order to buy 100 shares of a stock currently selling at 30½ (security market terminology for $30.50) at a limit price of $30. Once the specialist has cleared all similar orders received before yours, and once the market price of the stock has fallen to $30 or less, the order is executed. It is possible, of course, that your order might expire (if it is not a GTC order) before the stock price drops to $30.

Although a limit order can be quite effective, it can also keep you from making a transaction. If, for instance, you wish to buy at $30 or less and the stock price moves from its current $30.50 price to $42 while you are waiting, you have missed the opportunity to make a profit of $11.50 per share ($42 − $30.50). Had you placed a market order to buy at the best available price ($30.50), the profit of $11.50 would have been yours. Limit orders for the sale of a stock are also disadvantageous when the stock price closely approaches, but does not attain, the minimum sale price limit before dropping substantially. Generally speaking, limit orders are most effective when the price of a stock is known to fluctuate greatly, because there is then a better chance that the order will be executed.

Stop-Loss Order

stop-loss (stop) order
an order to sell a stock when its market price reaches or drops below a specified level; can also be used to buy stock when its market price reaches or rises above a specified level.

An order to sell a stock when its market price reaches or drops below a specified level is called a **stop-loss** or **stop order.** Stop-loss orders are *suspended orders* that are placed on stocks and activated when and if a certain price is reached. The stop-loss order is placed on the specialist's book and becomes active once the stop price has been reached. Like limit orders, stop-loss orders are typically day or GTC orders. When activated, the stop order becomes a *market order* to sell the security at the best price available. Thus it is possible for the actual price at which the sale is made to be well below the price at which the stop was initiated. These orders are used to protect investors against the adverse effects of a rapid decline in share price.

For example, assume you own 100 shares of Ballard Industries, which is currently selling for $35 per share. Because you believe the stock price could decline rapidly at any time, you place a stop order to sell at $30. If the stock price does in fact drop to $30, the specialist will sell the 100 shares at the best price available at that time. If the market price declines to $28 by the time your stop-loss order comes up, you will receive less than $30 per share. Of course, if the market price stays above $30 per share, you will have lost nothing as a result of placing the order, because the stop order will never be initiated. Often investors will raise the level of the stop as the price of the stock rises; such action helps to lock in a higher profit when the price is increasing.

Stop orders can also be placed to *buy* a stock, although they are far less common than sell orders. For example, an investor may place a stop order to buy 100 shares of MJ Enterprises, currently selling for $70 per share, once its price rises to, say, $75—the stop price. These orders are commonly used either to limit losses on short sales (discussed later) or to buy a stock just as its price begins to rise.

To avoid the risk of the market moving against you when your stop order becomes a market order, you can place a *stop-limit order,* rather than a plain stop order. This is an order to buy or sell stock at a given price or better once a stipulated stop price has been met. For example, in the Ballard Industries example, had a stop-limit order been in effect, then when the market price of Ballard dropped to $30, the broker would have entered a limit order to sell your 100 shares at $30 a share *or better.* Thus, there would be no risk of getting less than $30 a share for your stock—*unless the price of the stock kept right on falling*. In that case, as is true for any limit order, you might miss the market altogether and end up with stock worth much less than $30. Even though the stop order to sell was triggered (at $30), the stock will *not* be sold, with a limit order, if it keeps falling in price.

Transaction Costs

Making transactions through brokers or dealers is considerably easier for investors than it would be to negotiate directly, trying to find someone who wants to buy that which they want to sell (or vice versa). To compensate the broker for executing the transaction, investors pay transaction costs, which are usually levied on both the purchase and the sale of securities. When making investment decisions, you must consider the structure and magnitude of transaction costs, because they affect returns.

fixed-commission schedules
fixed brokerage commissions that typically apply to small transactions.

negotiated commissions
brokerage commissions agreed on by the client and the broker as a result of their negotiations.

Since the passage of the Securities Acts Amendments of 1975, brokers have been permitted to charge whatever commission they deem appropriate. Most firms have established **fixed-commission schedules** that apply to small transactions, the ones most often made by individual investors. An example of such a schedule for a full-service broker is given in Table 2.3. On large institutional transactions, **negotiated commissions**—commissions mutually agreed on by the client and broker—are frequently used. Negotiated commissions are also available to individual investors who maintain sizable accounts—typically above $50,000.

The commission structure varies depending on the type of security and the type of broker. The basic commission structures for various types of securities are described in subsequent chapters. The commissions charged on transactions of different size, shown in Table 2.4, clearly demonstrate varying transactions costs among full-service, discount, and online brokers.

Obviously, discount brokers charge substantially less than full-service brokers for the same transaction. However, most discounters charge a minimum

TABLE 2.3 A Schedule of Brokerage Commissions Paid in Common Stock Transactions

Share Price	Number of Shares: 5	10	25	50	100	200	500
$ 1	$35.00	$35.00	$35.00	$35.00	$35.00	$ 35.00	$ 59.81
5	35.00	35.00	35.00	35.00	35.00	44.90	101.13
10	35.00	35.00	35.00	35.00	35.92	66.77	129.73
25	35.00	35.00	35.00	37.52	58.71	103.63	225.03
35	35.00	35.00	35.00	45.79	70.15	132.11	284.83
50	35.00	35.00	37.26	58.18	84.77	168.00	354.60
75	35.00	35.00	47.58	72.48	88.52	175.97	434.33
100	35.00	35.00	57.91	84.23	88.52	175.97	438.33
125	35.00	37.10	65.06	87.99	88.52	175.97	438.33
150	35.00	41.22	72.21	87.99	88.52	175.97	438.33

Source: A major full-service brokerage house. (These commissions are, of course, subject to change; also, some brokers/dealers may charge more than the indicated commission, others less.)

TABLE 2.4 Comparative Commissions: Full-Service, Discount, and Online Brokers

	Size of Stock Transaction				
Type of Broker	$3,000 (100 shares at $30)	$5,000 (500 shares at $10)	$10,000 (1,000 shares at $10)	$15,000 (300 shares at $50)	$25,000 (500 shares at $50)
Typical full-service broker	$65	$130	$240	$235	$355
Typical discount broker	$40	$60	$80	$60	$80
Discount broker commissions as percentage of full-service broker commissions	61%	46%	33%	25%	22%
Typical online broker	$20	$20	$20	$20	$20
Online broker commissions as percentage of full-service broker commissions	31%	15%	8%	9%	6%

fee to discourage small orders. For example, Charles Schwab, the nation's largest discounter, charges a minimum fee of about $40 for any stock transaction. The savings from the discounter are substantial: Depending on the size and type of transaction, the discount broker can typically save investors between 30% and 80% of the commission charged by the full-service broker. Further savings can be realized, as shown in Table 2.4, by using an online broker to make transactions electronically. Some online brokers require minimum balances of $5,000 to $10,000 and offer broker trading for an additional fee of $5 to $15 per order. Online brokerage fees vary from about $8 to $40 per order, but many are fixed regardless of the number of shares or dollar value of the order. The basic online brokerage service is purely transactional—contact with a broker, advice, and research assistance generally can be obtained only at a higher price. Investors must weigh the added commissions they pay a full-service broker against the value of the advice they receive, because the amount of available advice is the only major difference among the discount, the online, and the full-service broker.

Investor Protection: SIPC and Arbitration

Although most investment transactions take place safely, it is important for you to know what protection you have if things don't go smoothly. As a client, you are protected against the loss of the securities or cash held by your broker. The **Securities Investor Protection Corporation (SIPC)**, a nonprofit membership corporation, was authorized by the *Securities Investor Protection Act of 1970* to protect customer accounts against the consequences of financial failure of the brokerage firm. The SIPC currently insures each customer's account for up to $500,000, with claims for cash limited to $100,000 per customer. Note that SIPC insurance does not guarantee that the dollar value of the securities will be recovered; it guarantees only that the securities themselves will be returned. Some brokerage firms also insure certain customer

Securities Investor Protection Corporation (SIPC)
a nonprofit membership corporation, authorized by the federal government, that insures each brokerage customer's account for up to $500,000, with claims for cash limited to $100,000 per customer.

accounts for amounts in excess of the required $500,000 of SIPC insurance. Certainly, in light of the diversity and quality of services available among brokerage firms, you should carefully consider your choice of a firm as well as of an individual broker.

The SIPC provides protection in case your brokerage firm fails. But what happens if your broker gave you bad advice and, as a result, you lost a lot of money on an investment? Or what if you feel your broker is churning your account, the illegal but difficult-to-prove act of causing excessive trading of your account in order to increase commissions? In either case, the SIPC won't help. It's not intended to insure you against bad investment advice or churning. Instead, if you have a dispute with your broker, the first thing you should do is discuss the situation with the managing officer at the branch where you do business. If that doesn't do any good, then contact the firm's compliance officer and the securities commission in your home state.

mediation
an informal, voluntary dispute resolution process in which a customer and a broker agree to a *mediator,* who facilitates negotiations between them to resolve the case.

arbitration
a formal dispute resolution process in which a customer and a broker present their argument before a panel, which then decides the case.

If you still don't get any satisfaction, you can use litigation (judicial methods in the courts) to resolve the dispute. Alternative dispute resolution processes that may avoid litigation include *mediation* and *arbitration.* **Mediation** is an informal, voluntary approach in which you and the broker agree to a *mediator,* who then facilitates negotiations between the two of you to resolve the case. The mediator acts as a facilitator and does not impose a solution on you and the broker. The NASD and securities-related organizations encourage investors to mediate disputes rather than arbitrate them, because mediation can reduce costs and time for both investors and brokers. If mediation is not pursued or if it fails, you may have no choice but to take the case to **arbitration,** a formal process whereby you and your broker present the two sides of the argument before an arbitration panel. The panel then decides the case. Many brokerage firms require you to resolve disputes by *binding arbitration;* in this case, you don't have the option to sue. You must accept the arbitrator's decision, and in most cases you cannot go to court to review your case. Before you open an account, check whether the brokerage agreement contains a binding-arbitration clause.

Settling securities disputes through mediation or arbitration rather than litigation has advantages and disadvantages. Mediation and arbitration proceedings typically cost less and are resolved more quickly than litigation. Until recently, however , the brokerage agreements that required investors to submit to binding arbitration also specified the use of securities industry arbitration panels, which were often composed entirely of persons with relationships to the securities industry. As a result of pressure from the SEC and a 1990 court decision in New York state, many investors now have the option of using either securities industry panels or independent arbitration panels such as those sponsored by the American Arbitration Association (AAA), which are considered more sympathetic toward investors. In addition, only one of the three arbitrators on a panel can be connected with the securities industry.

Probably the best thing you can do to avoid the need to mediate, arbitrate, or litigate with your broker is to use care when selecting him or her, understand the financial risks involved in the broker's recommendations, carefully evaluate the advice he or she offers, and continuously monitor the volume of transactions that he or she recommends and executes. Clearly, it is much less costly to choose the right broker initially than to incur later the financial and emotional costs of having chosen a bad one.

CONCEPTS IN REVIEW

2.11 Describe the types of services offered by brokerage firms, and discuss the criteria for selecting a suitable stockbroker.

2.12 Briefly differentiate among the following types of brokerage accounts:
a. Single or joint
b. Custodial
c. Cash
d. Margin
e. Wrap

2.13 Differentiate among a *market order*, a *limit order*, and a *stop-loss order.* What is the rationale for using a stop-loss order rather than a limit order?

2.14 In what two ways are commissions typically charged by brokers for executing their clients' transactions? Differentiate between the services and costs associated with full-service, discount, and online brokers.

2.15 What protection does the Securities Investor Protection Corporation (SIPC) provide securities investors? How are *mediation* and *arbitration* procedures used to settle disputes between investors and their brokers?

http://hepg.aw.com

Trading securities online is fast becoming a popular way of trading. Most online trading services are currently provided by discount brokerage firms. If you decide to trade online, which firm is right for you? Check out the procedure for selecting an online broker at the CyberInvesting site. Follow the *Brokers* link.

www.cyberinvest.com

Basic Types of Transactions

LG 6

An investor can make a number of basic types of security transactions. Each type is available to those who meet certain requirements established by various government agencies as well as by brokerage firms. Although the various types of transactions can be used in a number of ways to meet investment objectives, we describe only the most popular use of each transaction here. The three most common types of transaction are the long purchase, margin trading, and short selling.

Long Purchase

long purchase
a transaction in which investors buy securities in the hope that they will increase in value and can be sold at a later date for profit.

The **long purchase** is a transaction in which investors buy securities in the hope that they will increase in value and can be sold at a later date for profit. The object, then, is to buy low and sell high. A long purchase is the most common type of transaction. Each of the basic types of orders that we have described can be used with long transactions. Because investors generally expect the price of a security to rise over the period of time they plan to hold it, their return comes from any dividends or interest received during the ownership period, *plus* the difference (capital gain) between the price at which they sell the security and the price paid to purchase it. This return, of course, is reduced by the transaction costs.

Ignoring any dividends (or interest) and transaction costs, we can illustrate the long purchase by a simple example. After studying various aspects of Varner Industries, you are convinced that its common stock, which currently sells for $20 per share, will increase in value over the next few years. On the basis of your analysis, you expect the stock price to rise to $30 per share within 2 years. You place a limit order and buy a round lot (100 shares) of Varner for $20. If the stock price rises to, say, $40 per share, you will profit from your long purchase; if it drops below $20 per share, you will experience a loss on the transaction. Obviously, one of the major motivating factors in making a long transaction is an expected rise in the price of the security.

Margin Trading

margin trading
the use of borrowed funds to purchase securities; magnifies returns by reducing the amount of capital that the investor must put up.

Security purchases do not have to be made on a cash basis; borrowed funds can be used instead. This activity is referred to as **margin trading,** and it is used for one basic reason: to magnify returns. As peculiar as it may sound, the term *margin* refers to the amount of equity (stated as a percentage) in an investment, or the amount that is *not* borrowed. If an investor uses 75% margin, for example, it means that 75% of the investment position is being financed with the person's own capital and the balance (25%) with borrowed money. Margin purchases must be approved by a broker. The brokerage firm then lends the purchaser the needed funds and retains the purchased securities as collateral. It is important to recognize that margin purchasers must pay a specified rate of interest on the amount they borrow.

margin requirement
the minimum amount of equity that must be a margin investor's own funds; set by the Federal Reserve Board.

The Federal Reserve Board ("the Fed"), which governs our banking system, sets the **margin requirement,** specifying the minimum amount of equity that must be the margin investor's own funds. The margin requirement for stocks has been at 50% for some time. By raising and lowering the margin requirement, the Fed can depress or stimulate activity in the securities markets.

A simple example will help to clarify the basic margin transaction. Assume you wish to purchase 70 shares of common stock, which is currently selling for $63.50 per share. With the prevailing margin requirement of 50%, you need put up only $2,222.50 in cash ($63.50 per share × 70 shares × 0.50). The remaining $2,222.50 will be lent to you by your brokerage firm. You will, of course, have to pay interest on the amount you borrow, plus the applicable brokerage fees. With the use of margin, investors can purchase more securities than they could afford on a strictly cash basis. In this way, investors can magnify their returns (as demonstrated in a later section).

Although margin trading can lead to increased returns, it also presents substantial risks. One of the biggest is that the issue may not perform as expected. If this occurs, no amount of margin trading can correct matters. Margin trading can only *magnify* returns, not *produce* them, and if the security's return is negative, margin trading magnifies that loss. Because the security being margined is always the ultimate source of return, *choosing the right securities is critical to this trading strategy.*

Essentials of Margin Trading

Margin trading can be used with most kinds of securities. It is regularly used, for example, with both common and preferred stocks, most types of bonds, options, warrants, futures, and mutual funds. It is not normally used with tax-exempt municipal bonds, because the interest paid on such margin loans is not deductible for income tax purposes. Since mid-1990, it has been possible to use margin on certain foreign stocks and bonds that meet prescribed criteria and appear on the Fed's "New List of Foreign Margin Stocks." For simplicity, we will use common stock as the vehicle in our discussion of margin trading.

financial leverage
the use of debt financing to magnify investment returns.

Magnified Profits and Losses With an investor's equity serving as a base, the idea of margin trading is to employ **financial leverage**—the use of debt financing to magnify investment returns. Here is how it works: Suppose you have $5,000 to invest and are considering the purchase of 100 shares of stock at $50 per share because you feel the stock in question will go up in price. If you do not margin, you can buy outright 100 shares of the stock (ignoring brokerage commissions). However, if you margin the transaction—for example, at 50%—you can acquire the same $5,000 position with only $2,500 of your own money. This leaves you with $2,500 to use for other investments or to buy on margin another 100 shares of the same stock. Either way, by margining you will reap greater benefits from the stock's price appreciation.

The concept of margin trading is more fully illustrated in Table 2.5. An unmargined (100% equity) transaction is depicted, along with the same transaction using various margins. Remember that the margin rates (e.g., 65%) indicate the investor's equity in the investment. When the investment is

TABLE 2.5 The Effect of Margin Trading on Security Returns

	Without Margin (100% Equity)	With Margins of 80%	65%	50%
Number of $50 shares purchased	100	100	100	100
Cost of investment	$5,000	$5,000	$5,000	$5,000
Less: borrowed money	0	1,000	1,750	2,500
Equity in investment	$5,000	$4,000	$3,250	$2,500
A. Investor's position if price rises by $30 to $80/share				
Value of stock	$8,000	$8,000	$8,000	$8,000
Less: cost of investment	5,000	5,000	5,000	5,000
Capital gain	$3,000	$3,000	$3,000	$3,000
Return on investor's equity (capital gain/ equity in investment)	60%	75%	92.3%	120%
B. Investor's position if price falls by $30 to $20/share				
Value of stock	$2,000	$2,000	$2,000	$2,000
Less: cost of investment	5,000	5,000	5,000	5,000
Capital loss	$3,000	$3,000	$3,000	$3,000
Return on investor's equity (capital loss/ equity in investment)*	(60%)	(75%)	(92.3%)	(120%)

*With a capital loss, return on investor's equity is *negative*.

unmargined and the price of the stock goes up by $30 per share (see Table 2.5, part A), the investor enjoys a very respectable 60% rate of return. However, observe what happens when margin is used: The rate of return shoots up as high as 120%, depending on the amount of equity in the investment. This is so because the gain is the same ($3,000) *regardless of how the transaction is financed.* Clearly, as the investor's equity in the investment *declines* (with lower margins), the rate of return *increases* accordingly.

Three facets of margin trading become obvious from the table: (1) The price of the stock will move in whatever way it is going to regardless of how the position is financed. (2) The lower the amount of the investor's equity in the position, *the greater the rate of return* the investor will enjoy when the price of the security rises. (3) *The loss is also magnified* (by the same rate) when the price of the security falls (see Table 2.5, part B).

Advantages and Disadvantages of Margin Trading A magnified return is the major advantage of margin trading. The size of the magnified return depends on both the price behavior of the security being margined and the amount of margin being used. Another, more modest benefit of margin trading is that it allows for greater diversification of security holdings, because investors can spread their capital over a greater number of investments.

The major disadvantage of margin trading, of course, is the potential for magnified losses if the price of the security falls. Another disadvantage is the cost of the margin loans themselves. A **margin loan** is the official vehicle through which the borrowed funds are made available in a margin transaction. All margin loans are made at a stated interest rate, which depends on prevailing market rates and the amount of money being borrowed. This rate is usually 1% to 3% above the **prime rate**—the lowest interest rate charged the best business borrowers; for large accounts, it may be at the prime rate. The loan cost, which must be paid by the investor, will increase daily, reducing the level of profits (or increasing losses) accordingly.

margin loan
vehicle through which borrowed funds are made available, at a stated interest rate, in a margin transaction.

prime rate
the lowest interest rate charged the best business borrowers.

Making Margin Transactions

To execute a margin transaction, an investor must establish a **margin account.** It is opened with a minimum of $2,000 in equity, in the form of either cash or securities. The broker will retain any securities purchased on margin as collateral for the loan.

margin account
a brokerage account for which margin trading is authorized.

The margin requirement established by the Federal Reserve Board sets the minimum amount of equity for margin transactions. Investors need not execute all margin transactions by using exactly the minimum amount of margin; they can use more than the minimum if they wish. Moreover, it is not unusual for brokerage firms and the major exchanges to establish their own margin requirements, which are more restrictive than those of the Federal Reserve. There are basically two types of margin requirements: initial margin and maintenance margin.

Initial Margin The minimum amount of equity that must be provided by the investor *at the time of purchase* is the **initial margin.** It is used to prevent overtrading and excessive speculation. Generally, it is this margin requirement that investors refer to when discussing margin trading. All securities that can be margined have specific initial requirements, which can be changed at the

initial margin
the minimum amount of equity that must be provided by a margin investor *at the time of purchase.*

TABLE 2.6 Initial Margin Requirements for Various Types of Securities (December 1997)

Security	Minimum Initial Margin (Equity) Required
Listed common and preferred stock	50%
OTC stocks traded on Nasdaq National Market	50%
Convertible bonds	50%
Corporate bonds	30%
U.S. Treasury bills, notes, and bonds	8% of principal
Other federal government issues	10% of principal
Federal-government-guaranteed issues	15% of principal
Options	Option premium plus 20% of market value of underlying stock
Futures	2% to 10% of the value of the contract

discretion of the governing authorities. Table 2.6 shows initial margin requirements for various types of securities. The more stable investment vehicles, such as Treasury issues, generally have substantially lower margin requirements and therefore offer greater opportunities to magnify returns. OTC stocks traded on the Nasdaq National Market can be margined like listed securities; all other OTC stocks are considered to have no collateral value and therefore *cannot be margined.*

As long as the margin in an account remains at a level equal to or greater than prevailing initial requirements, the investor may use the account in any way he or she wants. However, if the value of the investor's holdings declines, the margin in his or her account will also drop. In this case, the investor will have what is known as a **restricted account,** one whose equity is less than the initial margin requirement. It does not mean that the investor must put up additional cash or equity, but as long as the account is restricted, the investor may not make further margin purchases and must bring the margin back to the initial level when securities are sold.

restricted account
a margin account whose equity is less than the initial margin requirement; the investor may not make further margin purchases and must bring the margin back to the initial level when securities are sold.

Maintenance Margin The absolute minimum amount of margin (equity) that an investor must maintain in the margin account at all times is the **maintenance margin.** When an insufficient amount of maintenance margin exists, an investor will receive a **margin call.** This call gives the investor a short period of time (perhaps 72 hours) to bring the equity up to the initial margin. If this is not done, the broker is authorized to sell enough of the investor's margined holdings to bring the equity in the account up to this standard.

maintenance margin
the absolute minimum amount of margin (equity) that an investor must maintain in the margin account at all times.

margin call
notification of the need to bring the equity of an account whose margin is below the maintenance level up to the initial margin level or have margined holdings sold to reach this point.

The maintenance margin protects both the brokerage house and investors: Brokers avoid having to absorb excessive investor losses, and investors avoid being wiped out. The maintenance margin on equity securities is currently 25%. It rarely changes, although it is often set slightly higher by brokerage firms for the added protection of brokers and customers. For straight debt securities like Treasury bonds, there is no official maintenance margin except that set by the brokerage firms themselves.

Note: Key financial topics offer opportunities for additional study to enhance learning. A CD-ROM icon appears next to topics covered in the tutorials that are featured on the FOI Student CD-ROM.

debit balance
the amount of money being borrowed in a margin loan.

The Basic Margin Formula

The amount of margin is always measured in terms of its relative amount of equity, which is considered the investor's collateral. A simple formula can be used with all types of *long purchases* to determine the amount of margin in the transaction at any given point. Basically, only two pieces of information are required: (1) the prevailing market value of the securities being margined, and (2) the **debit balance,** which is the amount of money being borrowed in the margin loan. Given this information, we can compute margin according to Equation 2.1:

Equation 2.1

$$\text{Margin} = \frac{\text{value of securities} - \text{debit balance}}{\text{value of securities}}$$

Equation 2.1a

$$= \frac{V - D}{V}$$

To illustrate the use of this formula, consider the following example. Assume you want to purchase 100 shares of stock at $40 per share at a time when the initial margin requirement is 70%. Because 70% of the transaction must be financed with equity, the balance (30%) can be financed with a margin loan. Therefore, you will borrow 0.30 × $4,000, or $1,200; this, of course, is the debit balance. The remainder ($4,000 – $1,200 = $2,800) represents your equity in the transaction. In other words, equity is represented by the numerator ($V - D$) in the margin formula.

What happens to the margin as the value of the security changes? If over time the price of the stock moves to $65, the margin is then:

$$\text{Margin} = \frac{V - D}{V} = \frac{\$6{,}500 - \$1{,}200}{\$6{,}500} = .815 = \underline{\underline{81.5\%}}$$

Note that the margin (equity) in this investment position has risen from 70% to 81.5%. *When the price of the stock goes up, the investor's margin also increases.*

On the other hand, *when the price of the security goes down, so does the amount of margin.* For instance, if the price of the stock in our illustration drops to $30 per share, the new margin is only 60% [($3,000 – $1,200) ÷ $3,000]. In that case, we would be dealing with a *restricted account,* because the margin level would have dropped below the prevailing initial margin.

Finally, note that although our discussion has been couched largely in terms of *individual transactions,* the same margin formula is used with *margin accounts.* The only difference is that we would be dealing with input that applies to the account as a whole—the value of *all securities* held in the account and the *total amount* of margin loans.

Return on Invested Capital

When assessing the return on margin transactions, you must take into account the fact that you put up only part of the funds. Therefore, you are concerned with the *rate of return* earned on only the portion of the funds that you provided. Using both current income received from dividends or interest and total interest paid on the margin loan, we can apply Equation 2.2 to determine the return on invested capital from a margin transaction:

Equation 2.2

$$\text{Return on invested capital from a margin transaction} = \frac{\text{total current income received} - \text{total interest paid on margin loan} + \text{market value of securities at sale} - \text{market value of securities at purchase}}{\text{amount of equity at purchase}}$$

This equation can be used to compute either the expected or the actual return from a margin transaction. To illustrate: Assume you want to buy 100 shares of stock at \$50 per share because you feel it will rise to \$75 within 6 months. The stock pays \$2 per share in annual dividends (though with the 6-month holding period, you will receive only half of that amount, or \$1 per share). You are going to buy the stock with 50% margin and will pay 10% interest on the margin loan. Therefore, you are going to put up \$2,500 equity to buy \$5,000 worth of stock that you hope will increase to \$7,500 in 6 months. Because you will have a \$2,500 margin loan outstanding at 10% for 6 months, you will pay \$125 in total interest costs (\$2,500 × 0.10 × 6/12 = \$125). We can substitute this information into Equation 2.2 to find the expected return on invested capital from this margin transaction:

$$\text{Return on invested capital from a margin transaction} = \frac{\$100 - \$125 + \$7{,}500 - \$5{,}000}{\$2{,}500} = \frac{\$2{,}475}{\$2{,}500} = .99 = \underline{\underline{99\%}}$$

Keep in mind that the 99% figure represents the rate of return earned over a 6-month holding period. If you wanted to compare this rate of return to other investment opportunities, you could determine the transaction's annualized rate of return by multiplying by 2 (the number of 6-month periods in a year). This would amount to 198% (99% × 2 = 198%).

Uses of Margin Trading

pyramiding
the technique of using paper profits in margin accounts to partly or fully finance the acquisition of additional securities.

excess margin
more equity than is required in a margin account.

Margin trading is most often used in one of two ways. As we have seen, one of its uses is to magnify transaction returns. The other major margin tactic is called pyramiding, which takes the concept of magnified returns to its limits. **Pyramiding** uses the paper profits in margin accounts to partly or fully finance the acquisition of additional securities. This allows such transactions to be made at margins below prevailing initial margin levels, and sometimes substantially so. In fact, with this technique it is even possible to buy securities with no new cash at all; rather, they can all be financed entirely with margin loans. The reason is that the paper profits in the account lead to **excess margin,** more equity in the account than required. For instance, if a margin account holds \$60,000 worth of securities and has a debit balance of \$20,000, it is at a margin level of 66⅔% [(\$60,000 – \$20,000) ÷ \$60,000]. This account would hold a substantial amount of excess margin if the prevailing initial margin requirement were only 50%.

The principle of pyramiding is to use the excess margin in the account to purchase additional securities. The only constraint, and the key to pyramiding, is that when the additional securities are purchased, the investor's margin account must be at or above the prevailing required initial margin level. Remember that it is the account, not the individual transactions, that must meet the minimum standards. If the account has excess margin, the investor can use it to build up security holdings. Pyramiding can continue as long as there are additional paper profits in the margin account and as long as the margin level exceeds the prevailing initial requirement when purchases are made. The tactic is somewhat complex but is also profitable, especially because it minimizes the amount of new capital required in the investor's account.

In general, margin trading is simple, but it is also risky. Risk is primarily associated with potential price declines in the margined securities. A decline in prices can result in a *restricted account.* If prices fall enough to cause the actual margin to drop below the maintenance margin, the resulting *margin call* will force the investor to deposit additional equity into the account almost immediately. In addition, losses (resulting from the price decline) are magnified in a fashion similar to that demonstrated in Table 2.5, part B. Clearly, the chance of a margin call and the magnification of losses make margin trading more risky than nonmargined transactions. Margin should be used only by investors who fully understand its operation and appreciate its pitfalls.

Short Selling

Short selling is used when a decline in security prices is anticipated. This technique enables investors to profit from falling security prices. However, as we shall see, it could formerly be used to *protect* investors from falling security prices. Almost any type of security can be "shorted": Common and preferred stocks, all types of bonds, convertible securities, options, warrants, and listed mutual funds can all be sold short. In practice, though, the short-selling activities of most investors are limited almost exclusively to common stock and to options.

Essentials of Short Selling

short selling
the sale of borrowed securities, their eventual repurchase by the short seller, and their return to the lender.

Short selling is generally defined as the practice of selling borrowed securities. Unusual as it may sound, selling borrowed securities is (in most cases) legal and quite common. Short sales start when securities that have been borrowed from a broker are sold in the marketplace. Later, when the price of the issue has declined, the short seller buys back the securities, which are then returned to the lender. A short seller must make an initial equity deposit with the broker subject to rules similar to those for margin trading. The deposit plus the proceeds from sale of the borrowed shares assures the broker that sufficient funds are available to buy back the shorted securities at a later date, even if their price increases. Short sales, like long and margin transactions, require investors to work through a broker.

Making Money When Prices Fall Making money when security prices fall is what short selling is all about. Like their colleagues in the rest of the investment world, short sellers are trying to make money by buying low and selling

TABLE 2.7 The Mechanics of a Short Sale

Step 1—Short sale initiated:	
100 shares of borrowed stock are *sold* at $50/share:	
Proceeds from sale to investor	$5,000
Step 2—Short sale covered:	
Later, 100 shares of the stock are *purchased* at $25/share and returned to broker from whom stock was borrowed:	
Cost to investor	2,500
Net profit	$2,500

high. The only difference is that they reverse the investment process: They start the transaction with a sale and end it with a purchase.

Table 2.7 shows how a short sale works and how investors can profit from such transactions. (For simplicity, we ignore transaction costs.) That transaction results in a net profit of $2,500 as a result of an initial sale of 100 shares of stock at $50 per share (step 1) and subsequent covering (purchase) of the 100 shares for $25 per share (step 2). The amount of profit or loss generated in a short sale depends on the price at which the short seller can buy back the stock. Short sellers earn profit only when the proceeds from the sale of the stock are greater than the cost of buying it back.

Who Lends the Securities? Acting through their brokers, short sellers obtain securities from the brokerage firm or from other investors. Of the two, brokers are the principal source of borrowed securities. As a service to their customers, they lend securities held in the brokers' portfolios or in *street name* accounts. It is important to recognize that when the brokerage firm lends street name securities, it is lending the short seller the securities of other investors. Individual investors typically do not pay fees to the broker for the privilege of borrowing the shares and, as a result, do not earn interest on the funds they leave on deposit with the broker.

Advantages and Disadvantages The major advantage of selling short is, of course, the chance to profit from a price decline. The key disadvantage of many short-sale transactions is that the investor faces limited return opportunities, along with high risk exposure. The price of a security can fall only so far (to a value of or near zero), yet there is really no limit to how far such securities can rise in price. (Remember, a short seller is hoping for a price *decline;* when a security goes *up* in price, a short seller loses.) For example, note in Table 2.7 that the stock in question cannot possibly fall by more than $50, yet who is to say how high its price can go?

A less serious disadvantage is that short sellers never earn dividend (or interest) income. In fact, short sellers owe the lender any dividends (or interest) paid while the transaction is outstanding. That is, if a dividend is paid during the course of a short-sale transaction, the short seller must pay an equal amount to the lender of the stock. (The mechanics of these payments are taken care of automatically by the short seller's broker.)

Uses of Short Selling

Investors short sell primarily to seek speculative profits when the price of a security is expected to drop. Because the short seller is betting against the market, this approach is subject to a considerable amount of risk exposure. The actual procedure works as explained earlier and demonstrated in Table 2.7. Note that had you been able to sell the stock at $50/share and later repurchase it at $25/share, you would have generated a profit of $2,500 (ignoring dividends and brokerage commissions). However, if the market had instead moved against you, all or most of your $5,000 investment could have been lost.

shorting-against-the-box
a conservative hedging technique used to protect existing security profits by following a profitable long purchase with a short sale of an equivalent number of the same shares. The *Taxpayer Relief Act of 1997,* effective June 8, 1997, eliminated the benefits of this strategy.

Before the effective date of June 8, 1997, for the *Taxpayer Relief Act of 1997*, short sales were commonly used to *hedge*, or protect, existing security profits. Called **shorting-against-the-box,** this conservative technique was initiated after an investor generated a profit in an earlier long purchase by selling short an equivalent number of the same shares. An investor who already owned, say, 100 shares of stock (the long transaction) would short an equal number of shares of stock in the same company. The investor would then have two positions—one long and one short—both involving the same number of shares. By doing this, he or she was able to protect the profit until the *next* tax year. This strategy no longer works, because the new tax law recognizes the gain when you sell the borrowed shares rather than when the short sale is later covered.

CONCEPTS IN REVIEW

2.16 What is a *long purchase?* What expectation underlies such a purchase? What is *margin trading,* and what is the key reason why it is sometimes used as part of a long purchase?

2.17 How does margin trading magnify profits and losses? What are the key advantages and disadvantages of margin trading?

2.18 Describe the procedures and regulations associated with margin trading. Be sure to explain *restricted accounts,* the *maintenance margin,* and the *margin call.* Define the term *debit balance,* and describe the common uses of margin trading.

2.19 What is the primary motive for short selling? Describe the basic short-sale procedure. Why must the short seller make an initial equity deposit?

2.20 Describe the key advantages and disadvantages of short selling. How are short sales used to earn speculative profits? What is *shorting-against-the-box,* and why does it no longer work?

http://hepg.aw.com

In placing buy and sell orders, investors must be aware of the type of order they are placing, as well as of the cost of any accounts opened and trades made. Discover Brokerage provides an example of the types of costs that can be encountered. These costs are at the address listed here; the *Tutorial and Tips* link leads to a glossary of trading terms and conditions.

www.lombard.com/cgi-bin/Help/fees

Summary

LG 1

Describe the basic types of securities markets and the characteristics of organized exchanges and the over-the-counter market. Short-term investment vehicles are traded in the money market; longer-term securities, such as stocks and bonds, are traded in the capital market. The organized securities exchanges are auction markets. They include the New York Stock Exchange (NYSE), the American Stock Exchange (AMEX), regional stock exchanges, foreign stock exchanges, and other specialized exchanges. The organized exchanges act as secondary markets in which existing securities are traded. The over-the-counter (OTC) market acts as a primary market in which initial public offerings (IPOs) are made, and it also handles secondary trading in unlisted securities. It is a dealer market in which negotiation and dealer quotes, often obtained through its automated system, Nasdaq, determine price.

LG 2

Discuss the third and fourth markets, trading hours, regulation, and the general conditions of securities markets. Over-the-counter transactions in listed securities are made in the third market, and transactions directly between large institutional buyers and sellers are made in the fourth market. Recently, some U.S. exchanges have expanded their trading hours in order to compete more effectively with foreign markets. The securities markets are regulated by the federal Securities and Exchange Commission (SEC) and by state commissions. The key federal laws regulating the securities industry are the Securities Act of 1933, the Securities Exchange Act of 1934, the Maloney Act of 1938, the Investment Company Act of 1940, the Investment Advisers Act of 1940, the Securities Acts Amendments of 1975, and the Insider Trading and Fraud Act of 1988. Market conditions are commonly classified as "bull" or "bear," depending on whether securities prices are generally rising or falling.

LG 3

Review the importance, performance, investment procedures, and risks associated with investing globally in foreign securities. Today securities markets must be viewed globally. Foreign security investments can be made indirectly by buying shares of a U.S.-based multinational with substantial foreign operations or by purchasing shares of a mutual fund that invests primarily in foreign securities. Direct foreign investment can be achieved by purchasing securities on foreign exchanges, by buying securities of foreign companies that are traded on U.S. exchanges, or by buying American Depositary Receipts (ADRs). International investments can enhance returns, but they entail added risk, particularly currency exchange risk.

LG 4

Explain the role of stockbrokers in security transactions—services provided, selection, opening an account, account types, and transaction sizes. Stockbrokers intermediate between buyers and sellers of securities, and they provide a variety of other client services. An investor should select a stockbroker who has a compatible disposition toward investing and whose firm offers the desired services at competitive costs. Brokerage services vary among full-service, discount, and online brokers. A variety of types of brokerage accounts, such as single, joint, custodial, cash, margin, and wrap, may be established. An investor can make odd-lot transactions (less than 100 shares) or round-lot transactions (100 shares or multiples thereof). An added fee is typically charged on odd-lot transactions.

LG 5

Describe the basic types of orders (market, limit, and stop-loss), transaction costs, and the legal aspects of investor protection. A market order is an order to buy or sell stock at the best price available. A limit order is an order to buy at a specified price or below or to sell at a specified price or above. Stop-loss orders become market orders as soon as the minimum sell price or the maximum buy price is hit. Limit and stop-loss orders can be placed as fill-or-kill orders, day orders, or good-'til-canceled (GTC) orders. On small transactions, most brokers have fixed-commission schedules; on larger transactions, they will negotiate commissions. Commissions also vary by type of security and type of broker: full-service, discount, or online broker. The Securities Investor Protection Corporation (SIPC) insures customers' accounts against the brokerage firm's failure. To avoid litigation, mediation and arbitration procedures are frequently employed to resolve disputes between investor and broker. These disputes typically concern the investor's belief that the broker either gave bad advice or churned the account.

LG 6

Understand long purchases and the motives, regulations, procedures, and calculations involved in making margin transactions and short sales. Most investors make long purchases—buy low, sell high—in expectation of price increases. Many investors establish margin accounts to use borrowed funds to enhance their buying power. The Federal Reserve Board establishes the margin requirement—the minimum investor equity in a margin transaction, both initially and during the margin transaction. The return on invested capital in a margin transaction is magnified; that is, positive returns *and* negative returns are larger than in a comparable unmargined transaction. Paper profits can be used to pyramid a margin account by investing its excess margin. The risks of margin trading are the chance of a restricted account or margin call and the consequences of magnification of losses due to price declines.

Short selling is used when a decline in security prices is anticipated. It involves selling borrowed securities with the expectation of earning a profit by repurchasing them at a lower price in the future. To execute a short sale, the investor must make an initial equity deposit with the broker, similar to what is done in margin trading. The investor borrows the shares from the broker. The major advantage of selling short is the chance to profit from a price decline. The disadvantages of selling short are the limited return opportunities in spite of the high risk of unlimited loss potential and the fact that short sellers never earn dividend (or interest) income. Short selling is used primarily to seek speculative profits from an anticipated decline in share price. The Taxpayer Relief Act of 1997 eliminated its use as a conservative hedging technique to protect earned profits by shorting-against-the-box.

Discussion Questions

LG 1

Q2.1. Why do you think some large, well-known companies such as Apple Computer, Intel, and Microsoft are traded on the Nasdaq National Market rather than listed and traded on a major organized exchange such as the NYSE (for which they easily meet the listing requirements)? Discuss the pros and cons of listing on a major organized exchange.

LG 1 LG 2 LG 3

Q2.2. On the basis of the current structure of the world's financial markets and your knowledge of the NYSE and OTC, describe the key features, functions, and problems faced by a single global market (exchange) on which transactions can be made in all securities of all of the world's major companies. Discuss the likelihood of such a market developing.

LG 4

Q2.3. Prepare a checklist of questions and issues you would use when shopping for a stockbroker. Describe both the ideal broker and the ideal brokerage firm, given your investment goals and disposition. Discuss the pros and cons of using a full-service rather than a discount or online broker.

LG 5 LG 6

Q2.4. Describe how a conservative and an aggressive investor might use, if at all, each of the following types of orders and types of transactions as part of their investment programs. Contrast these two types of investors in view of these preferences.

a. Types of orders
   (1) Market
   (2) Limit
   (3) Stop-loss

Note: The Discussion Questions at the end of the chapter ask you to analyze and synthesize information on the key concepts, tools, and techniques presented in the chapter.

b. Types of transactions
   (1) Long purchase
   (2) Margin
   (3) Short sale

Problems

 LG 3

P2.1. In each of the following cases, calculate the price of one share of the foreign stock measured in US$.

a. A Belgian stock priced at 9,000 Belgian francs (Bf) when the exchange rate is 35.3 Bf/US$
b. A French stock priced at 700 French francs (Ff) when the exchange rate is 5.60 Ff/US$
c. A Japanese stock priced at 1,350 yen (¥) when the exchange rate is 125 ¥/US$

 LG 3

Note: The Problems at the end of the chapter offer opportunities for calculation using the tools and techniques learned in the chapter. A CD-ROM icon appears next to problems that can be solved using the Fundamentals of Investing software, packaged with the book.

P2.2. Lola Paretti purchased 50 shares of BMW, a German stock traded on the Frankfurt Exchange, for 500 marks (DM) per share exactly 1 year ago, when the exchange rate was 1.60 DM/US$. Today the stock is trading at 530 DM per share, and the exchange rate is 1.30 DM/US$.

a. Did the DM depreciate or appreciate relative to the US$ during the past year? Explain.
b. How much in US$ did Lola pay for her 50 shares of BMW when she purchased them a year ago?
c. How much in US$ can Lola sell her BMW shares for today?
d. Ignoring brokerage fees and taxes, how much profit (or loss) in US$ will Lola realize on her BMW stock if she sells it today?

LG 4 LG 5

P2.3. Al Cromwell places a market order to buy a round lot of Thomas, Inc., common stock, which is traded on the NYSE and is currently quoted at $50 per share. Ignoring brokerage commissions, how much money would Cromwell probably have to pay? If he had placed a market order to sell, how much money would he receive? Explain.

LG 4 LG 5

P2.4. Imagine that you have placed a limit order to buy 100 shares of Sallisaw Tool at a price of $38, though the stock is currently selling for $41. Discuss the consequences, if any, of each of the following:

a. The stock price drops to $39 per share 2 months before cancellation of the limit order.
b. The stock price drops to $38 per share.
c. The minimum stock price achieved before cancellation of the limit order was $38.50, and when canceled the stock was selling for $47.50 per share.

LG 5

P2.5. If you place a stop-loss order to sell at $23 on a stock currently selling for $26.50 per share, what is likely to be the minimum loss you will experience on 50 shares if the stock price rapidly declines to $20.50 per share? Explain. What if you had placed a stop-limit order to sell at $23, and the stock price tumbled to $20.50?

LG 6

P2.6. Elmo Inc.'s stock is currently selling at $60 per share. For each of the following situations (ignoring brokerage commissions), calculate the gain or loss realized by Maureen Katz if she makes a round-lot transaction.

a. She sells short and repurchases the borrowed shares at $70 per share.
b. She takes a long position and sells the stock at $75 per share.
c. She sells short and repurchases the borrowed shares at $45 per share.
d. She takes a long position and sells the stock at $60 per share.

 LG 6

P2.7. Assume an investor buys 100 shares of stock at $50 per share, putting up a 70% margin.

a. What is the debit balance in this transaction?
b. How much equity capital must the investor provide to make this margin transaction?
c. If the stock rises to $80 per share, what is the investor's new margin position?

 LG 6

P2.8. Jerri Kingston bought 100 shares of stock at $80 per share using an initial margin of 60%. Given a maintenance margin of 25%, how far does the stock have to drop before Ms. Kingston faces a margin call? (Assume there are no other securities in the margin account.)

 LG 6

P2.9. An investor buys 200 shares of stock selling at $80 per share, using a margin of 60%. The stock pays annual dividends of $1 per share, and a margin loan can be obtained at an annual interest cost of 8%. Determine what return on invested capital the investor will realize if the price of the stock increases to $104 within 6 months. What is the annualized rate of return on this transaction?

 LG 6

P2.10. Marlene Bellamy purchased 300 shares of Writeline Communications stock at $55 per share using the prevailing minimum initial margin requirement of 50%. She held the stock for exactly 4 months and sold it without any brokerage costs at the end of that period. During the 4-month holding period, the stock paid $1.50 per share in cash dividends. Marlene was charged 9% annual interest on the margin loan. The minimum maintenance margin was 25%.

a. Calculate the initial value of the transaction, the debit balance, and the equity position on Marlene's transaction.
b. For each of the following share prices, calculate the actual margin percentage and indicate whether Marlene's margin account would have excess equity, be restricted, or be subject to a margin call.
   (1) $45
   (2) $70
   (3) $35
c. Calculate the dollar amount of (1) dividends received and (2) interest paid on the margin loan during the 4-month holding period.
d. Use each of the following sale prices at the end of the 4-month holding period to calculate Marlene's annualized rate of return on the Writeline Communications stock transaction.
   (1) $50
   (2) $60
   (3) $70

LG 6

P2.11. Not long ago, Dave Edwards bought 200 shares of Almost Anything, Inc., at $45 per share; he bought the stock on margin of 60%. The stock is now trading at $60 per share, and the Federal Reserve has recently lowered initial margin requirements to 50%. Dave now wants to do a little pyramiding and buy another 300 shares of the stock. What's the minimum amount of equity he'll have to put up in this transaction?

LG 6

P2.12. Calculate the profit or loss per share realized on each of the following short-sale transactions.

Transaction	Stock Sold Short at Price/Share	Stock Purchased to Cover Short at Price/Share
A	$75	$83
B	30	24
C	18	15
D	27	32
E	53	45

LG 6

P2.13. Charlene Hickman expected the price of Bio International shares to drop in the near future in response to the expected failure of its new drug to pass FDA tests. As a result she sold short 200 shares of Bio International at 27½. How much would Charlene earn or lose on this transaction if she repurchased the 200 shares 4 months later at each of the following prices per share?

a. 24¾ b. 25⅛
c. 31¼ d. 27

Case Problem 2.1 Dara's Dilemma: Hold, Sell, or . . . ?

LG 4 LG 5

As a result of her recent divorce, Dara Simmons, a 40-year-old mother of two teenage children, received 400 shares of Casinos International common stock. The stock is currently selling for $54 per share. After a long discussion with a friend who is an economist with a major commercial bank, Dara believes that the economy is turning down and a bear market is likely. With the aid of her stockbroker, Dara has researched Casinos International's current financial situation and finds that the future success of the company may hinge on the outcome of pending court proceedings on the firm's application to open a new floating casino on a nearby river. If the permit is granted, it seems likely that the firm's stock will experience a rapid increase in value, regardless of economic conditions. On the other hand, if the permit is not granted, the stock value is likely to be adversely affected.

Dara felt, on the basis of the available information, that the price of Casinos was likely to fluctuate a great deal over the near future. Her first reaction was to sell the stock and invest the money in a safer security, such as a high-rated corporate bond. At the same time, she felt that this impulse might be overly pessimistic. She realized that if Casinos had its floating casino application granted, she would make a killing on the stock. As a final check before making any decision, Dara talked with her accountant, who suggested that for tax purposes it would be best to delay the sale of the stock for an additional 4 months. After making a variety of calculations, the accountant indicated that the consequences of selling the stock now at $54 per share would be approximately equivalent to receiving $48 per share any time after the 4-month period had elapsed.

Dara felt that following four alternatives were open to her:

Alternative 1: Sell now at $54 per share and use the proceeds to buy high-rated corporate bonds.

Alternative 2: Keep the stock and place a limit order to sell the stock at $60 per share.

Alternative 3: Keep the stock and place a stop-loss order to sell at $45 per share.

Alternative 4: Hold the stock for an additional 4 months before making any decision.

QUESTIONS

a. Evaluate each of these alternatives. On the basis of the limited information presented, recommend the one you feel is best.

b. If the stock price rises to $60, what will happen under alternatives 2 and 3? Evaluate the pros and cons of these outcomes.

c. If the stock price drops to $45, what will happen under alternatives 2 and 3? Evaluate the pros and cons of these outcomes.

d. In light of the rapid fluctuations anticipated in the price of Casinos stock, how might Dara use a stop-limit order to sell to reduce the risk associated with the stock? What is the cost of such a strategy? Explain.

Case Problem 2.2 *Ravi Dumar's High-Flying Margin Account*

LG 6

Ravi Dumar is a stockbroker who lives with his wife, Sasha, and their five children in Milwaukee, Wisconsin. Ravi firmly believes that the only way to make money in the market is to follow an aggressive investment posture—for example, to use margin trading. In fact, Ravi himself has built a substantial margin account over the years. He currently holds $75,000 worth of stock in his margin account, though the debit balance in the account amounts to only $30,000. Recently, Ravi uncovered a stock that, on the basis of extensive analysis, he feels is about to take off. The stock, Running Shoes (RS), currently trades at $20 per share. Ravi feels it should soar to at least $50 within a year. RS pays no dividends, the prevailing initial margin requirement is 50%, and margin loans are now carrying an annual interest charge of 10%. Because Ravi feels so strongly about RS, he wants to do some pyramiding by using his margin account to purchase 1,000 shares of the stock.

QUESTIONS

a. Discuss the concept of pyramiding as it applies to this investment situation.

b. What is the present margin position (in percent) of Ravi's account?

c. Ravi buys the 1,000 shares of RS through his margin account (bear in mind that this is a $20,000 transaction).

1. What will the margin position of the account be after the RS transaction if Ravi follows the prevailing initial margin (50%) and uses $10,000 of his money to buy the stock?
2. What if he uses only $2,500 equity and obtains a margin loan for the balance ($17,500)?
3. How do you explain the fact that the stock can be purchased with only 12.5% margin when the prevailing initial margin requirement is 50%?

d. Assume that Ravi buys 1,000 shares of RS stock at $20 per share with a minimum cash investment of $2,500 and that the stock does take off and its price rises to $40 per share in a year.

1. What is the return on invested capital for this transaction?
2. What return would Ravi have earned if he had bought the stock without margin—if he had used all his own money?

e. What do you think of Ravi's idea to pyramid? What are the risks and rewards of this strategy?

Home Page Exercises

http://hepg.aw.com Keyword: Invest

After reading this chapter, you know how an investor goes about buying and selling securities and are acquainted with the operating characteristics of the various markets—primary, secondary, capital, and money markets—where securities are traded. Most investors complete their trading in the secondary markets. Prices in these markets change rapidly throughout the day. The Web is very effective at providing the investor with timely information about the current price of an asset. It also provides up-to-the-minute data on how the overall market is doing for a particular type of asset, such as stocks or bonds. The following Web sites offer important and timely information about the major U.S secondary markets.

Web Address	*Primary Investment Focus*
www.nasdaq.com	Information about the National Association of Securities Dealers Automated Quotation (Nasdaq) system and price quotations
www.nyse.com	Historical, regulatory, and listing information about the New York Stock Exchange (NYSE)
www.amex.com	Price quotes and other information about companies listed on the American Stock Exchange (AMEX)
www.cboe.com	Educational information about the Chicago Board Options Exchange (CBOE), including products and prices
www.chicagostockex.com	Historical and listing information on the Chicago Stock Exchange

W2.1. Go to the Nasdaq Web site, whose address is listed below, and obtain the latest bid price, ask price, and change in price from the preceding day for Intel Corporation and for Microsoft Corporation.

www.nasdaq.com

W2.2. Many consider the New York Stock Exchange the premier U.S. equity market. To be listed on the NYSE, a firm must meet very stringent financial criteria. Go to the home page for the NYSE; find and list the minimum quantitative requirements for a firm to qualify for listing on the NYSE. You can obtain this information by following first the *Listed Companies* icon and then the *Domestic Listing Standards and Procedures* icon.

www.nyse.com

W2.3. Securities markets are among the most tightly regulated industries in the country. The objective of many regulations is consumer protection. Investors who encounter behavior or practices that they believe are outside the law should begin by discussing the matter with their financial adviser. If they need to go further with the inquiry, the next move is generally to contact the authority in their state that is responsible for security regulations. The Securities and Exchange Commission has a listing of what organization to contact within each state. Go to the SEC's home page and find the appropriate contact for your state. Once you reach the SEC home page, follow the *Investor Assistance and Complaints* icon to locate this information.

www.sec.gov

Investment Planning and Information

Chapter 3

The Motley Fool

In Elizabethan days, the motley fool was the court jester who wore multicolored garb. Fools were the only people who could get away with telling the King or Queen the truth. The Motley Fool Web site (**www.motleyfool.com**) was created by two English majors who studied more Shakespeare than they studied investments when in college but who are now in the business of offering investment advice. David and Tom Gardner talk to their readers in a straightforward manner. They ask investors to think for themselves, giving them the tools to do so. Meanwhile, their Motley Fool Portfolio, put together by a couple of guys wearing silly hats, consistently stacks up well against the market professionals. The Motley Fool's strategy for beginners is (1) learn the rudiments of investment research, (2) pay down debt before beginning, (3) start with mutual funds that mimic the major stock indexes, and (4) invest in stocks you expect to hold for a long time.

In this chapter, you'll learn about the role of investment plans and the sources of information you need to make investment decisions. Most of this is serious and straightforward. But as The Motley Fool has shown, some aspects of investing can also be fun.

Learning Goals

After studying this chapter, you should be able to:

LG 1 Describe the steps in the investing process, particularly establishing investment goals, and cite fundamental personal tax considerations.

LG 2 Discuss investing over the life cycle and investing in different economic environments.

LG 3 Understand the role, popular types, key features, and suitability of short-term investment vehicles available for meeting liquidity needs.

LG 4 Identify the types and major sources of investment information.

LG 5 Evaluate sources of electronic and online investment information, the use of investment advisers, and the role of investment clubs.

LG 6 Explain the characteristics, interpretation, and uses of the commonly cited stock and bond market averages and indexes.

Making Investment Plans

LG 1 LG 2

The process of investing should be guided by well-developed plans and can be carried out by following a logical progression of steps. It is important that your plans take into account the impact of taxes on investment returns and be responsive to your stage in the life cycle and to the changing economic environment.

Steps in Investing

Investing can be conducted in various ways. One approach is a haphazard, "seat of the pants" method in which actions are taken on a strictly intuitive basis. Another approach—exactly opposite to the first—is to rely on plans carefully developed to achieve specific goals. Evidence suggests that the more logical approach usually results in better returns. The serious investor should therefore first establish a set of overall financial goals and then develop and execute an investment program consistent with those goals.

Following is a brief overview of the steps in investing that will help to set the stage for the more detailed discussion of the concepts, tools, and techniques presented throughout the book.

Step 1: Meeting Investment Prerequisites

Before investing, you must make certain that the *necessities of life* are adequately provided for. This category includes funds for housing, food, transportation, taxes, and clothing. In addition, a pool of easily accessible funds should be established for meeting emergency cash needs. Funds for this purpose are typically held in some form of liquid, short-term investment vehicle. (*Note:* Meeting liquidity needs is discussed later in this chapter.)

Another prerequisite is adequate protection against the losses that could result from death, illness or disability, damage to property, or a negligent act. Protection against such risks can be acquired through life, health, property, and liability insurance. (*Note:* Detailed information with regard to meeting life insurance needs is available on this text's Web site—**hepg.aw.com.**)

Planning for adequate retirement income can also be viewed as an investment prerequisite. Achieving this goal may partially depend on the success of one's investment program. At the very least, you need to establish certain retirement goals before setting specific investment goals.

Step 2: Establishing Investment Goals

investment goals
the financial objectives that one wishes to achieve by investing.

Once you have satisfied the prerequisites and set clearly defined financial goals, you must establish *investment goals.* **Investment goals** are the financial objectives you wish to achieve by investing in any of a wide range of potential investment vehicles. Clearly, your investment goals will determine the types of investments you will make. Common investment goals include

1. *Accumulating Retirement Funds.* Accumulating funds for retirement is the *single most important reason for investing.* Too often, people tend to rely heavily on Social Security and employers for retirement funds. It is of the utmost importance to review the amounts that can realistically be expected from these sources and to decide, on the basis of your retirement goals, *whether they will be adequate to meet your needs.* If they are not, they must be supplemented through your own investment program. The earlier in life

you assess your retirement needs, the greater your chance of accumulating sufficient funds to meet them.

2. *Enhancing Current Income.* Investments enhance current income by earning dividends or interest. Retirees frequently choose investments offering *high current income at low risk.* The idea of a retired person "clipping coupons"—collecting interest—from high-yield bonds is a fair description of what most senior citizens *should* be doing at that point in their lives.

3. *Saving for Major Expenditures.* Families often put aside money over the years to accumulate the funds needed to make major expenditures. The most common of these are the down payment on a home, education, a "once in a lifetime" vacation, and capital to start a business. The appropriate types of investment vehicles depend on the purpose and the amount of money needed. For purposes such as the down payment on a home or a child's education, for example, much less risk should be tolerated than for other goals. The attainment of such basic goals should not, if possible, be placed in jeopardy.

4. *Sheltering Income from Taxes.* As will be explained in Chapter 15, federal income tax law allows certain noncash charges to be deducted from specified sources of income, thereby reducing the amount of final taxable income. Obviously, if a person can avoid (or defer) paying taxes on the income from an investment, he or she will have more funds left for reinvestment.

INVESTOR FACT

WOULD YOU RATHER CALL A BROKER OR A DENTIST?—A *Worth* magazine/Roper survey of Americans' attitudes toward money revealed that 28% ranked making the wrong choice with a large investment a major cause of anxiety, ahead of such well-known fears as being audited by the IRS and speaking in public.

Step 3: Adopting an Investment Plan

investment plan
a written document describing how funds will be invested and specifying the target date for achievement of each investment goal and the amount of tolerable risk.

Once your general goals have been established, you should adopt an **investment plan**—a written document describing how funds will be invested. A series of supporting investment goals can be developed for each long-term goal. For each goal, specify the target date of achievement and the amount of tolerable risk. Generally, the more important the financial objective, the lower the risk that should be assumed. Suppose, for example, one long-run goal is to accumulate \$80,000 in cash by the end of 10 years. That goal could be spelled out in the investment plan as a plan to accumulate \$80,000 in cash by investing in a portfolio evenly divided between low-risk and speculative stocks providing a total return of 10% per year. The more specific you can be in your statement of investment goals, the easier it will be to establish an investment plan consistent with your goals. The *Investing in Action* box on page 66 describes the role of professional financial planners in helping their clients formulate investment goals and plans.

Step 4: Evaluating Investment Vehicles

Once you have your investment goals and plan laid out, you next must evaluate investment vehicles in terms of your investment goals by assessing each vehicle's potential return and risk. This process typically involves *valuation,* the use of measures of return and risk to estimate the perceived worth of an investment vehicle. (Chapter 4 offers a general discussion of the procedures for measuring these key dimensions of potential investments. Subsequent chapters focus on the valuation of specific vehicles.)

Step 5: Selecting Suitable Investments

You now gather additional relevant information and use it to select specific investment vehicles consistent with your goals. The best investments may not

INVESTING IN ACTION

A Bull Market for Financial Planners

They come from such fields as accounting, insurance, law, and stock brokerage. Their mission: helping their clients invest money. Welcome to the booming financial planning profession.

Why is financial planning a growth industry? With the Dow Jones Industrial Average multiplying by a factor of 10 in the past 15 years, Americans have bigger investment portfolios than ever before. As Social Security and corporate pension plans diminish in dollar value in relation to what it costs to retire, the average person has more responsibility to invest wisely. Many former accountants, insurance consultants, lawyers, and stockbrokers have found that their services as financial planners are much in demand.

A good financial planner can assess your current financial position and tell you how to reach your financial goals. Many planners also double as money managers, investing your nest egg in stocks, bonds, and mutual funds. Obviously, hiring a financial planner entails placing a great deal of authority and responsibility in his or her hands. That's why you want to be very careful when you hire one.

Unlike practitioners of many other professions, such as accounting and law, financial planners needn't pass rigorous examinations to practice their craft. They can simply open an office and call themselves financial planners. True, there are professional organizations that financial planners can choose to become affiliated with. These include the International Association of Financial Planning, the Institute of Certified Financial Planners, the American Society of Chartered Life Underwriters & Chartered Financial Consultants, and the National Association of Personal Financial Advisors. Exams offered by these and other organizations bring various professional certifications, such as Certified Financial Planner (CFP) and Chartered Financial Consultant (ChFC). But as in other professions, certification is no guarantee of competence, integrity, or honesty. To find a financial planner, then, your best bet is to ask people whom you respect to recommend a financial planner and then to interview two or three planners before making up your mind. Ask about their education and training, and talk to their clients.

Financial planners are compensated in two ways: fees and commissions. *Fee-only planners* charge either a flat fee or an hourly rate to create a personalized financial plan for you. If they implement the plan by managing your investment portfolio, they also collect a fee, usually 1% of the dollar amount that you've entrusted to them. *Commission-only planners* charge you nothing for advice but receive commissions on the products—insurance policies, stocks, bonds, mutual funds, etc.—that they sell you. The advantage of the commission-only planner is that you pay only when you make an investment. The disadvantage is a built-in conflict of interest: Your planner may be more interested in selling you products than in giving you objective advice.

If you're a traditional college student in your late teens or early twenties, you're probably not personally in the market for a financial planner. But if you are an older student—or if your parents are struggling to send you to college, pay their living expenses, and plan for their own retirement—then enlisting the counsel of a good financial planner might be a wise investment.

be those that simply maximize return; other factors, such as risk and tax considerations, may also be crucial. For example, to receive maximum annual dividends, you might purchase the common stock of a firm expected to pay high dividends. However, if the firm whose stock you purchased goes bankrupt, you could lose the money. The stock of a firm that pays lower dividends but with less risk of bankruptcy might have been a better choice. Careful selection of investment vehicles that are consistent with established goals and offer acceptable levels of return, risk, and value is essential to successful investing.

Step 6: Constructing a Diversified Portfolio

Selecting suitable investments includes choosing vehicles in such a way that investment goals can be achieved and return, risk, and investment values are optimized. To do this, you will assemble an investment *portfolio* that meets one or more investment goals. For example, an investment portfolio might contain common stock, government bonds, and short-term investments. *Diversification,* the inclusion of a number of different investment vehicles, is fundamental to constructing an effective portfolio. By *diversifying* in this way, investors are able to earn higher returns or be exposed to less risk than if they limit their investments to just one or two vehicles. *Diversification* is the financial term for the age-old advice "Don't put all your eggs in one basket."

Step 7: Managing the Portfolio

Once a portfolio has been constructed, you should measure and evaluate its actual behavior in relation to expected performance. If the investment results are not consistent with your objectives, you may need to take corrective action. Such action usually involved selling certain investments and using the proceeds to acquire other vehicles for the portfolio. Portfolio management therefore involves monitoring the portfolio and restructuring it as dictated by the actual behavior of the investments.

Considering Personal Taxes

Besides carefully developing plans for achieving your specific investment goals, it's also important to consider the tax consequences associated with various investment vehicles and strategies. A knowledge of the tax laws can help you reduce taxes and thereby increase the amount of after-tax dollars available for achieving your investment goals. Because tax laws are complicated and subject to frequent revision, we present only the key concepts and their applications to popular investment transactions.

Basic Sources of Taxation

The two major types of taxes are those levied by the federal government and those levied by state and local governments. The federal *income tax* is the major form of personal taxation. Federal rates currently range from 15 to 39.6% of taxable income.

State and local taxes vary from area to area. Some states have income taxes that range as high as 15% or more of income. Some cities, especially large East Coast cities, also have local income taxes that typically range between 1% and 5% of income. In addition to income taxes, state and local governments rely heavily on sales and property taxes as a source of revenue. Although sales taxes vary from state to state, most are between 3% and 7%. Property taxes are levied on real estate and personal property, such as automobiles, boats, and furniture. These taxes vary from community to community.

Income taxes at the federal, state, and local levels have the greatest impact on security investments, whose returns are in the form of dividends, interest, and increases in value. Property taxes can have a sizable impact on real estate and other forms of property investment.

Types of Income

The income of individuals used to be classified simply as either ordinary or capital gain (or loss). That classification changed with the *Tax Reform Act of 1986*. One of the major revisions of the sweeping 1986 tax law was the creation of *three basic categories of income,* devised to reduce or eliminate the tax-advantaged treatment of certain types of investments.

1. *Active income,* consisting of everything from wages and salaries to bonuses, tips, pension income, and alimony. Active income is made up of income earned on the job as well as most other forms of *noninvestment* income.

2. *Portfolio income,* comprising earnings generated from various types of investment holdings. This category of income covers most (but not all) types of investments, from savings accounts, stocks, bonds, and mutual funds to options and futures. For the most part, portfolio income consists of interest, dividends, and capital gains (the profit on the sale of an investment).

3. *Passive income,* a special category of income composed chiefly of income derived from real estate, limited partnerships, and other forms of tax-advantaged investments.

The key feature of these categories is that they limit the amount of deductions (write-offs) that can be taken, particularly with regard to portfolio and passive income. Specifically, the amount of allowable deductions associated with portfolio and passive income is *limited to the amount of income derived from these two sources.* For example, if you had a total of $380 in portfolio income for the year, you could deduct no more than $380 in investment-related interest expense. For deduction purposes, the portfolio and passive income categories cannot be mixed or combined with each other or with active income. *Investment-related expenses can be used only to offset portfolio income,* and (with a few exceptions) *passive investment expenses can be used only to offset the income from passive investments.*

Ordinary Income Regardless of whether it's classified as active, portfolio, or passive, ordinary income—after certain computations—is taxed at one of five rates: 15, 28, 31, 36, or 39.6%. There is one structure of tax rates for taxpayers who file *individual* returns and another for those who file *joint* returns with a spouse. Table 3.1 shows the tax rates and income brackets for these two filing categories. Note that the rates are *progressive;* taxpayers with taxable income above a specified amount are taxed at a higher rate.

An example will demonstrate how ordinary income is taxed. Consider the Ellis sisters, Joni and Cara. Both are single. Joni's taxable income is $18,000; Cara's is $36,000. Using Table 3.1, we can calculate their taxes as follows:

Joni:
$(0.15 \times \$18{,}000) = \underline{\underline{\$2{,}700}}$

Cara:
$(0.15 \times \$24{,}650) + [.28 \times (\$36{,}000 - \$24{,}650)]$
$= \$3{,}698 + \$3{,}178 = \underline{\underline{\$6{,}876}}$

The progressive nature of the federal income tax structure can be seen by the fact that although Cara's taxable income is only twice that of Joni, her income tax is more than 2.5 times Joni's.

TABLE 3.1 Tax Rates and Income Brackets for Individual and Joint Returns (1997)

	Taxable Income	
Tax Rates	Individual Returns	Joint Returns
15%	$0 to $24,650	$0 to $41,200
28%	$24,651 to $59,750	$41,201 to $99,600
31%	$59,751 to $124,650	$99,601 to $151,750
36%	$124,651 to $271,050	$151,751 to $271,050
39.6%	Over $271,050	Over $271,050

capital gain
the amount by which the proceeds from the sale of a capital asset *exceed* its original purchase price.

Capital Gains and Losses A *capital asset* is property owned and used by the taxpayer for personal reasons, pleasure, or investment. The most common types are securities and real estate, including one's home. A **capital gain** represents the amount by which the proceeds from the sale of a capital asset *exceed* its original purchase price. The amount of any capital gain realized is added to other sources of income, and the total is taxed at the rates given in Table 3.1, but the *maximum tax rate on the capital gain is 28% for assets held for more than 1 year but not over 18 months, and 20% (or 10% if the taxpayer is in the 15% tax bracket) for assets held more than 18 months.*

For example, imagine that James McFail, a single person who has other taxable income totaling $45,000, sold at $12 per share 500 shares of stock that he purchased 2 years earlier for $10 per share. The total capital gain on this transaction was $1,000 [500 shares × ($12/share − $10/share)]. Thus McFail's taxable income would total $46,000, which puts him in the 28% tax bracket (see Table 3.1). Because the $1,000 capital gain resulted from an asset that was held for more than 18 months, and because James is in the 28% tax bracket, the capital gain would be taxed at the maximum rate of 20%. His total tax would be calculated as follows:

Ordinary income ($45,000)	
(0.15 × $24,650) + (0.28 × [$45,000 − $24,650]) =	$9,395.50
Capital gain ($1,000)	
(0.20 × $1,000) =	200.00
Total tax	$9,595.50

James' total tax would be $9,595.50. Had his other taxable income been below $24,650 (i.e., in the 15% bracket), the $1,000 capital gain would have been taxed at 10% rather than 20%. Had James held the asset for more than 1 year but less than 18 months, his $1,000 capital gain would have been taxed at the 28% rate. Had the asset been held for less than 1 year, the $1,000 gain would have been taxed as ordinary income, which in James's case would also result in a 28% rate.

Capital gains are appealing to investors because they are not taxed until actually realized. For example, if you own a stock originally purchased for $50 per share that at the end of the tax year has a market price of $60 per share, you have a "paper gain" of $10 per share. This *paper,* or *unrealized, gain* is not taxable, because you still own the stock. *Only realized gains are taxed.* If you sold the stock for $60 per share during the tax year, you would have a realized—and therefore taxable—gain of $10 per share.

capital loss
the amount by which the proceeds from the sale of a capital asset are *less than* its original purchase price.

net losses
the amount by which capital losses exceed capital gains; up to $3,000 of net losses can be applied against ordinary income in any year.

A **capital loss** results when a capital asset is sold for *less than* its original purchase price. Before taxes are calculated, all gains and losses must be netted out. Up to $3,000 of **net losses** can be applied against ordinary income in any year. Losses that cannot be applied in the current year may be carried forward and used to offset future income, subject to certain conditions.

Investments and Taxes

tax planning
the development of strategies that will defer and minimize an individual's level of taxes over the long run.

The opportunities created by the tax laws make tax planning important in the investment process. **Tax planning** involves looking at your earnings, both current and projected, and developing strategies that will defer and minimize the level of taxes. The tax plan should guide your investment activities in such a way that over the long run you will achieve maximum after-tax returns for an acceptable level of risk. For example, from a tax point of view, capital gains are appealing to many investors. The fact that these gains are not taxed until actually realized allows the investor to defer tax payments on them as well as control the timing of these payments. However, investments that are likely to lead to capital gains income generally have higher risk than those that provide only current investment income. Therefore, the choice of investment vehicles cannot be made solely on the basis of the timing and possible reduction of tax payments. The levels of return and risk need to be viewed in light of their tax effects. *It is the after-tax return and associated risk that should be considered.*

INVESTOR FACT

UNCLE SAM TAKES HIS CUT—If you were to invest $2,000 per year for 30 years, then you would accumulate about $227,000 at the end of the period, assuming an 8% average compounded annual return *and no taxation.* However, if you were to invest the same amount of money in a taxable account, then you would accumulate only $146,000, assuming you're in the 31% federal income tax bracket. Because of the impact of compounding, the taxed account accumulates 36% less money than the tax-free account.

Tax plans should also reflect the form in which one wants to receive returns—current income, capital gains, or tax-advantaged income. One common strategy is to claim losses as soon as they occur and to delay profit taking. Such an approach allows you to benefit from the tax deductibility of a loss and to delay having to claim income from gains. Tax planning, which is usually done in coordination with an accountant, tax expert, or tax attorney, is most common among individuals with high levels of income ($100,000 or more annually). Yet sizable savings can result for investors with lower incomes as well. Chapter 15 will present further information on tax strategies and tax-advantaged investments.

Investing over the Life Cycle

Investors tend to follow different investment philosophies as they move through different stages of the life cycle. Generally speaking, most investors tend to be more aggressive when they're young and more conservative as they grow older. Typically, investors move through the following investment stages:

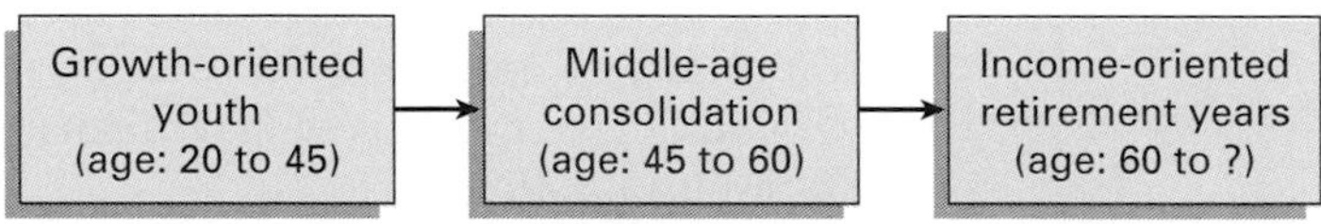

Most young investors, in their twenties and thirties, tend to prefer growth-oriented investments that stress *capital gains* rather than current income. Often young investors don't have much in the way of investable funds, so capital gains are viewed as the quickest (if not necessarily the surest) way to build up investment capital. Such investors tend to favor growth-oriented and speculative vehicles, particularly high-risk common stocks, options, and futures.

As investors approach the middle-age consolidation stage of life (the mid-forties), family demands and responsibilities such as educational expenses and retirement contributions become more important, and the approach to investing changes. Thus the whole portfolio goes through a transition to *higher-quality securities*. Low risk growth and income stocks, preferred stocks, convertibles, high-grade bonds, and mutual funds are all widely used at this stage in life.

Finally, investors approach their retirement years. Preservation of capital and current income become the principal concerns. A secure, high level of income is paramount, and capital gains are viewed as merely a pleasant, occasional by-product of investing. The investment portfolio now becomes *highly conservative*, consisting of low-risk income stocks, high-yielding government bonds, quality corporate bonds, bank certificates of deposit (CDs), and other money market investments. At this stage, investors reap the rewards of a lifetime of saving and investing.

Investing in Different Economic Environments

Despite the government's arsenal of weapons for moderating economic swings, numerous changes are sure to occur in the economy during your lifetime of investing. At all stages of the life cycle, your investment program must be flexible enough to allow you to recognize and react to changing economic conditions. The first rule of investing is to know *where* to put your money; the second is to know *when* to make your moves. The first question is easier to deal with, because it involves matching the risk and return objectives of your investment plan with the available investment alternatives. For example, if you're a seasoned investor who can tolerate the risk, then speculative stocks may be right for you. On the other hand, if you're a novice who wants a fair return on your capital, perhaps you should consider a good growth-oriented mutual fund. Unfortunately, although stocks and growth funds may do well when the economy is expanding, they can turn out to be disasters at other times. This leads to the second, and more difficult, question: What effect do economic and market conditions have on investment returns?

The question of when to invest is difficult because it deals with *market timing*. The fact is that most economists and most professional money managers—not to mention most investors—cannot predict the peaks and troughs in the economy or stock market with much consistency. It's a lot easier to get a handle on the *current state* of the economy/market. That is, knowing whether the economy/market is in a state of expansion or decline is considerably different from being able to pinpoint when it's about to change course. Thus, for our purposes, we can define **market timing** as the process of identifying the current state of the economy/market and assessing the likelihood of its continuing on its present course.

market timing
the process of identifying the current state of the economy/market and assessing the likelihood of its continuing on its present course.

As an investor, it's best to confine your assessment of the market to three distinct conditions: (1) a state of recovery or expansion, (2) a state of decline or recession, or (3) uncertainty as to the direction of its movement. These different stages are illustrated in Figure 3.1. It's easy to see when things are moving up (recovery/expansion) or when they're moving down (decline/recession). The difficulty comes with the peaks and troughs. At those points, you don't know whether the market will continue in its current direction, up or

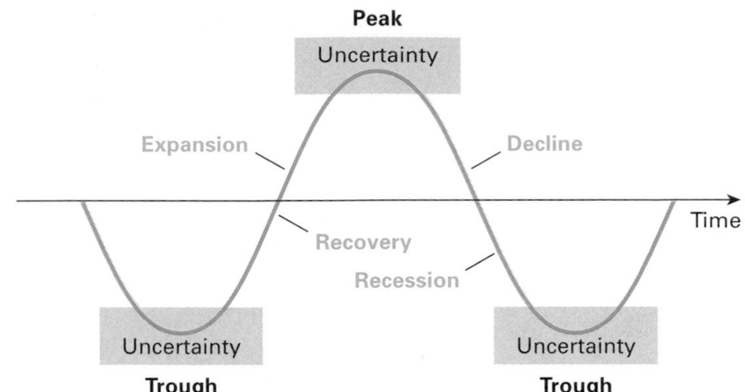

FIGURE 3.1
Different Stages of an Economic/Market Cycle

The economic/market cycle shows three different conditions: (1) a state of recovery/expansion, (2) a state of decline/recession, and (3) uncertainty as to the direction in which the economy/market is going to move (shown by the shaded areas).

down, or whether it will change direction. That is why these areas in the figure are shaded, depicting *uncertainty.* How you will respond to these conditions depends on whether your investments are in stocks, bonds, or real estate and other tangible investments.

Stocks and the Business Cycle

Common stocks and other equity-related securities (e.g., convertible securities, stock options, stock index futures, and stock mutual funds) are highly responsive to conditions in the economy. Economic conditions are described generically as the *business cycle.* The business cycle reflects the current status of a variety of economic variables, including GDP (gross domestic product), industrial production, personal disposable income, the unemployment rate, and more. A strong economy is reflected in an expanding business cycle. When business is good and profits are up, stocks react by increasing in value and return. Growth-oriented and speculative stocks tend to do especially well in strong markets, as, to a lesser extent, do low-risk and income-oriented stocks. In contrast, when economic activity is declining, the values and returns on common stocks tend to be off as well.

Bonds and Interest Rates

Bonds and other forms of fixed-income securities (e.g., preferred stocks and bond funds) are highly sensitive to movements in interest rates. In fact, interest rates are the single most important variable in determining bond price behavior and returns to investors. Because interest rates and bond prices move in opposite directions (as will be explained in Chapters 8 and 9), rising interest rates are unfavorable for outstanding bonds already held in an investor's portfolio. Of course, high interest rates enhance the attractiveness of new bonds because they offer high returns.

Real Estate, Other Tangible Investments, and Inflation

Real estate and other tangible investments, including gold and other precious metals, gemstones, and collectibles such as artwork and antiques, are generally more responsive to the *rate of inflation* than to anything else. Housing prices and the prices of commodities like coffee, oil, meat, corn, and sugar are components of the consumer price index (CPI). *When consumer prices start to rise, the returns on real estate and other tangible investments start to go up as well.* But when inflation comes back down to more normal levels, returns on real estate and other tangible investments also decline.

CONCEPTS IN REVIEW

3.1 What should an investor first establish before developing and executing an investment program? List and briefly describe each of the seven steps involved in investing.

3.2 What are four common investment goals?

3.3 According to the *Investing in Action* box on page 66, what is the safest way to choose a financial planner? What professional certifications would you look for in a planner?

3.4 Define and differentiate among the following, and explain how each is related to federal income taxes.
- a. Active income
- b. Portfolio and passive income
- c. Capital gain
- d. Capital loss
- e. Tax planning

3.5 Describe the differing investment philosophies typically applied during each of the following stages of an investor's life cycle.
- a. Youth (ages 20 to 45)
- b. Middle age (ages 45 to 60)
- c. Retirement years (age 60 on)

3.6 Describe the four stages of the economic/market cycle, and discuss the impact of this cycle on each of the following forms of investment.
- a. Stocks
- b. Bonds
- c. Real estate and other tangible investments

http://hepg.aw.com

Financial planning is too important to leave to luck. The Web is extremely useful in helping investors establish their investment plans. The Wall Street City Web site has an interactive program that helps investors develop these plans. Visit the following address to learn more about planning.

www.tscn.com/wsc/Macroworld_Planning.html

liquidity
the ability to convert an investment into cash quickly and with little or no loss in value.

Meeting Liquidity Needs: Investing in Short-Term Securities

LG 3

Once you have developed your investment plan, you should ensure that you have adequate liquidity. This provision is an important part of an investment plan and a prerequisite to implementing the plan's long-term goals. **Liquidity** as used here refers to the ability to convert an investment into cash quickly and with little or no loss in value. A checking account is highly liquid. Stocks and bonds are not liquid, because there is no definite assurance that you will be able to sell the securities at a price equal to or greater than their purchase price.

The Role of Short-Term Securities

Short-term securities are an important part of most savings and investment programs. They generate income—which can be quite high during periods of high interest rates. However, their primary function is to provide a pool of reserves that can be used for emergencies or simply to accumulate funds for some specific purpose. When viewed as part of an investment portfolio, short-term securities are usually held as a *temporary*, highly liquid investment until something better comes along. Some individuals choose to hold short-term securities because they simply are more comfortable with these vehicles. In fact, this approach has had considerable merit during periods of economic (and investment) instability, such as those experienced during the 1970s and early 1980s. Regardless of your motives for holding short-term securities, you should evaluate them in terms of their risk and return, just as you would longer-term securities.

Determining Interest on Short-Term Securities

discount basis
a method of earning interest on a security by purchasing it at a price below its redemption value; the difference is the interest earned.

bond equivalent yield (BEY)
the annual percentage rate that would be earned on a short-term security sold at a discount if it were purchased today at its current price and held to its maturity.

Short-term investments earn interest in one of two ways. Some investments, such as savings accounts, pay a *stated rate of interest*. In this case, you can easily find the interest rate—it's the stated rate on the account. Alternatively, interest is earned on short-term investments on a **discount basis.** This means that the security is purchased at a price below its redemption value, and the difference is the interest earned. U.S. Treasury bills (T-bills), for example, are issued on a discount basis.

It is desirable, of course, to be able to compare a vehicle with a stated rate of interest to one sold on a discount basis. To do that, the return on a discount basis can be expressed as a **bond equivalent yield (BEY).** The BEY is the annual percentage rate that you would earn on a short-term security sold at a discount if it were purchased today at its current price and held to its maturity. The following equation gives the BEY:

Equation 3.1

$$\text{Bond equivalent yield on a discount security} = \left(\frac{365}{\text{number of days to maturity}}\right) \times \left(\frac{\text{redemption value} - \text{current price}}{\text{current price}}\right)$$

Equation 3.1a

$$BEY = \left(\frac{365}{n}\right) \times \left(\frac{R - P}{P}\right)$$

To illustrate, suppose you buy for \$9,905 a T-bill that can be redeemed for \$10,000 at the end of 91 days. The total interest on this security is \$95 (redemption value − current price), and its bond equivalent yield (BEY) is

$$\begin{aligned} BEY &= \left(\frac{365}{91}\right) \times \left(\frac{\$10{,}000 - \$9{,}905}{\$9{,}905}\right) \\ &= (4.011) \times (.0096) \\ &= \underline{\underline{0.0385, \text{ or } 3.85\%}} \end{aligned}$$

The T-bill's BEY of 3.85% would be comparable to the stated annual rate of interest of 3.85% on an investment such as a savings account.

Risk Characteristics

Short-term investments are generally considered low in risk. Their primary risk results from the *loss of potential purchasing power* that occurs when the rate of return on these investments falls short of the inflation rate. Unfortunately, this has often been the case with such vehicles as *passbook savings accounts,* the traditional bank savings accounts that generally pay a low rate of interest and have no minimum balance. Most other short-term investments have averaged, over long periods of time, rates of return that are about equal to, or maybe slightly higher than, the average inflation rate.

The *risk of default*—nonpayment—is virtually nonexistent with short-term investment vehicles. The principal reason is that the primary issuers of most short-term securities are highly reputable institutions, such as the U.S. Treasury, large banks, and major corporations. Furthermore, deposits in commercial banks, savings and loans, savings banks, and credit unions are insured for up to $100,000 per account by government agencies. Finally, because the value of short-term investments does not change much in response to changing interest rates, exposure to capital loss is correspondingly low. These securities have short maturities (often measured in days and never exceeding a year), and the shorter the maturity of an issue, the less volatile its market price.

Advantages and Disadvantages of Short-Term Investments

As noted, the major advantages of short-term investments are their high liquidity and low risk. Most are available from local financial institutions and can be readily converted to cash with minimal inconvenience. Finally, because the returns on most short-term investments vary with inflation and market interest rates, investors can readily capture higher returns as rates move up. On the negative side, when interest rates go down, returns drop as well.

Although a decline in market rates has undesirable effects on most short-term vehicles, perhaps their biggest disadvantage is their relatively low return. Because these securities are generally so low in risk, you can expect the returns on short-term investments to average less than the returns on long-term investments.

Popular Short-Term Investment Vehicles

Over the past 25 years or so, short-term investment vehicles, particularly for individual investors of modest means, have proliferated. Saving and investing in short-term securities is no longer the easy task it once was, when the decision for most people amounted to whether funds should be placed in a passbook savings account at a local bank or in Series E government savings bonds. Today, even some checking accounts pay interest on idle balances. Along with the dramatic increase in investment alternatives has come greater sophistication in short-term investment management. Short-term vehicles can be used as secure investment outlets for the long haul or as a place to hold cash until a longer-term outlet for the funds is found.

In the material that follows, we will first examine each of the major short-term investment deposits and vehicles. Then we will briefly look at several ways in which these deposits/securities can be used in an investment portfolio.

passbook savings account
a savings account, offered by banks, that generally pays a low rate of interest and has no minimum balance.

NOW (negotiated order of withdrawal) account
a bank checking account that pays interest; has no legal minimum balance, but many banks impose their own.

money market deposit accounts (MMDAs)
a bank deposit account with limited check-writing privileges; has no legal minimum balance, but many banks impose their own.

central asset account
a comprehensive deposit account that combines checking, investing, and borrowing activities; it automatically "sweeps" excess balances into short-term investments and borrows to meet shortages.

U.S. Treasury bills (T-bills)
obligations of the U.S. Treasury, sold on a discount basis, and having varying short-term maturities; regarded as the safest of all investments.

Note that all the *deposit accounts* we discuss are issued by commercial banks, savings and loans (S&Ls), savings banks, and credit unions; often we will simply use the term *bank* to refer to any one or all of these financial institutions and not necessarily to commercial banks alone.

Deposit Accounts

Banks offer investors several forms of deposit accounts that pay interest on account balances. Four such accounts are **passbook savings accounts, NOW (negotiated order of withdrawal) accounts, money market deposit accounts (MMDAs),** and **central asset accounts.** Some of the distinguishing features of these accounts are summarized in Table 3.2. The first two—passbook savings accounts and NOW accounts—are primarily used as savings vehicles; they provide the individual investor with a highly liquid pool of funds that can be accessed easily to meet scheduled as well as unexpected expenditures. The second two—MMDAs and central asset accounts—are more likely to be used for investment purposes, to earn a reasonably competitive short-term return while maintaining sufficient liquidity to meet unexpected needs and seize attractive investment opportunities.

U.S. Treasury Bills

For many years, before recent market innovations, **U.S. Treasury bills (T-bills)** were the key short-term investment for those with sufficient funds to meet the rather high minimum investment requirement. T-bills are obligations of the U.S. Treasury issued as part of its ongoing process of funding the national debt. T-bills are sold on a discount basis in minimum denominations of $10,000, with $1,000 increments thereafter. They are issued with 3-month (13-week or 91-day), 6-month (26-week or 182-day), and 1-year maturities. The 3- and 6-month bills are issued at auction every Monday (for delivery on the following Thursday), and there is an auction for 1-year bills approximately every 4 weeks.

Purchasing T-Bills You can purchase T-bills *directly* (through participation in the weekly Treasury auctions) or *indirectly* (through local commercial banks, securities dealers, or brokers who buy bills for investors on a commission basis). You also can purchase outstanding Treasury bills in the secondary market through banks or brokers. The biggest advantage of the secondary market is that you have a much wider selection of maturities to choose from, ranging from less than a week to as long as a year.

It is relatively simple to buy T-bills directly. All you need to do is submit a tender offer to the nearest Federal Reserve Bank or branch, specifying both the amount and the maturity of T-bills desired. (Tender forms can be obtained by writing the Bureau of the Public Debt, Department N, Washington, DC 20239–1500, or by calling 202-874-4000.) The Treasury tries to accommodate individual investors through its noncompetitive bidding system, which most people use because of its simplicity. In essence, all noncompetitive tender offers are awarded T-bills at a price equal to the average of all the accepted competitive bids. Thus you are assured of buying bills in the quantity desired, while obtaining the benefits of an open auction system—all without going through the hassle of a competitive bid. Note, though, that T-bills bought directly through noncompetitive bidding are meant to be held to maturity;

TABLE 3.2 Distinguishing Features of Interest-Paying Deposit Accounts

Type of Account	Brief Description*	Minimum Balance	Interest Rate	Federal Insurance
Passbook savings account	Savings accounts offered by banks. Used primarily for convenience or if investors lack sufficient funds for other short-term vehicles.	Typically none	2%–6% depending on economy	Yes, up to $100,000 per deposit.
NOW (negotiated order of withdrawal) account	Bank checking account that pays interest on balances.	No legal minimum, but often set at $500 to $1,000	At or near passbook rates	Yes, up to $100,000 per deposit.
Money market deposit account (MMDA)	Bank deposit account with limited check-writing privileges.	No legal minimum, but often set at about $2,500	Typically about 1% above passbook rate	Yes, up to $100,000 per deposit.
Central asset account	Deposit account at bank, brokerage house, mutual fund, or insurance company that combines checking, investing, and borrowing. Automatically "sweeps" excess balances into short-term investments and borrows to meet shortages.	Typically $5,000 to $20,000	Similar to MMDAs	Yes, up to $100,000 per deposit in banks. Varies in other institutions.

*The term *bank* refers to commercial banks, savings and loans (S&Ls), savings banks, and credit unions.

they should not be purchased by investors who may want to trade them. It is difficult and time-consuming to sell them in the aftermarket.

bank discount yield (BDY)
the rate at which T-bills are quoted in the financial media; represents the annualized percentage discount (redemption value − current price) at which the T-bill can be currently purchased.

Calculating T-Bill Yields Treasury bill rates are quoted in the *Wall Street Journal* and other major financial media at the **bank discount yield (BDY).** This is the annualized percentage discount (redemption value − current price) at which the T-bill can be currently purchased. Equation 3.2 gives the formula for the BDY.

Equation 3.2

$$\text{Bank discount yield} = \left(\frac{360}{\text{number of days to maturity}}\right) \times \left(\frac{\text{redemption value} - \text{current price}}{\text{redemption value}}\right)$$

Equation 3.2a

$$BDY = \left(\frac{360}{n}\right) \times \left(\frac{R - P}{R}\right)$$

Substituting the data for the T-bill discussed earlier into Equation 3.2, we get a bank discount yield of

$$BDY = \left(\frac{360}{91}\right) \times \left(\frac{\$10{,}000 - \$9{,}905}{\$10{,}000}\right)$$
$$= (3.956) \times (.0095)$$
$$= \underline{\underline{0.0376, \text{ or } 3.76\%}}$$

Equation 3.3 can be used to convert a BDY to the *bond equivalent yield (BEY),* which (as noted earlier) is the annual percentage rate earned by purchasing the T-bill today at its current price and holding it to maturity:

Equation 3.3

$$\text{Bond equivalent yield} = \frac{365 \times \text{bank discount yield}}{360 - \left(\text{bank discount yield} \times \text{number of days to maturity}\right)}$$

Equation 3.3a

$$BEY = \frac{365 \times BDY}{360 - (BDY \times n)}$$

Substituting the T-bill data into Equation 3.3, we get a bond equivalent yield of

$$BEY = \frac{365 \times .0376}{360 - (.0376 \times 91)}$$

$$= \frac{13.72}{356.58}$$

$$= \underline{\underline{0.0385, \text{ or } 3.85\%}}$$

Note that the 3.85% BEY is the same value calculated for the T-bill in Equation 3.1, which arrived at the BEY using the bond's price data rather than its bank discount yield (BDY). In this case the T-bill, which is quoted at an annualized bank discount yield (BDY) of 3.76%, will provide the investor with a bond equivalent yield (BEY), or annual percentage rate, of 3.85%.

Evaluating T-bills A particularly attractive feature of T-bills is that they are *exempt from state and local income taxes,* which in some areas can be as high as 20%. Federal taxes are not due until the interest is actually received at maturity (the same is true for CDs and commercial paper). Because they are issued by the U.S. Treasury, T-bills are regarded as the safest, though generally the lowest-yielding, of all investments. Furthermore, there is a highly active secondary market for Treasury bills (other than those bought through noncompetitive bidding), so they can easily be sold if you need the cash.

Certificates of Deposit

certificates of deposit (CDs) savings instruments in which funds must remain on deposit for a specified period; withdrawals prior to maturity incur interest penalties.

Certificates of deposit (CDs) differ from the deposit accounts discussed earlier in that funds must remain on deposit for a specified period, which can range from 7 days to a year or more. Although it is possible to withdraw funds prior to maturity, an interest penalty (equal to 31–90 days of interest, depending on the original maturity of the CD) usually makes withdrawal costly. Banks today are free to offer any rate and maturity on these securities. The interest rate on them is fixed over their stated maturity. A wide variety of CDs are offered by most banks and thrift institutions, and these vehicles go by an equally wide variety of names.

CDs are convenient to buy and hold, and all offer attractive and highly competitive returns plus federal insurance protection. The decision whether to invest in a CD or in a more liquid short-term investment vehicle, such as a MMDA or a T-bill, generally depends on the length of the holding period and interest rate expectations. Uncertain holding periods and expected interest rate increases would favor MMDAs and T-bills; certain holding periods and expected interest rate declines would favor CDs.

brokered CDs
certificates of deposit sold by stockbrokers; offer slightly higher yields than other CDs and typically can be sold prior to maturity without incurring a penalty.

CDs can also be purchased from stockbrokers, in the form of **brokered CDs.** The brokerage house looks around the country for the highest yield it can get, buys these CDs, and then resells them to its clients. In essence, a bank issues the CDs, and the brokerage house places them with the investing public. There's usually no commission to pay, because the broker earns its commission from the issuing bank. The minimum denomination is usually $1,000.

Brokered CDs are attractive for two reasons: First, they can be sold prior to maturity without incurring a penalty, because the brokerage firms maintain active secondary markets. Of course, there are no guarantees, and the market prevails: If rates go up, the relative value of a CD falls, and its return will decline if it is sold prior to maturity. Second, brokered CDs may provide higher yields—frequently ¼ to ¾ of a percent higher—than those available from a local bank. But because a broker can always get higher yields by selling CDs issued by troubled financial institutions, it is best to buy *only those brokered CDs that are issued by a federally insured institution.*

Commercial Paper

commercial paper
short-term, unsecured promissory notes (IOUs) issued by corporations with very high credit standings.

Commercial paper is short-term, unsecured promissory notes (IOUs) issued by corporations with very high credit standings. These notes are typically sold by firms in need of short-term loans. Although sometimes issued in denominations as small as $25,000 or $50,000, most commercial paper is initially sold in multiples of $100,000. Typical maturities range from a few days up to 270 days, the maximum maturity that does not require registration with the Securities and Exchange Commission (SEC). Because the secondary market for commercial paper is limited, most investors hold commercial paper to maturity. Commercial paper is rated as to its quality by independent agencies. Its yield is comparable to the rate of return earned on large-denomination CDs. A popular strategy is to buy high-rated paper with a maturity that closely matches the desired investment horizon.

Typically, only larger institutions deal directly in commercial paper, because of its large denominations. Most individual investors who obtain commercial paper do so from a bank or broker, who will "break down" the paper and sell the investor a small portion. However, you can generally earn returns competitive with commercial paper by purchasing CDs, which have a fixed maturity like commercial paper but in addition have federal insurance protection.

Banker's Acceptances

banker's acceptances
short-term, low-risk investment vehicles arising from bank guarantees of business transactions; are sold at a discount from their face value and generally provide yields slightly below those of CDs and commercial paper.

Banker's acceptances arise from short-term credit arrangements used by business firms to finance transactions, most often involving firms in foreign countries or with unknown credit capacities. Typically, an importer's bank agrees to pay its foreign supplier on behalf of the importer, who is contractually obligated to repay the bank within the 3 to 6 months it takes to receive and sell the merchandise involved in the transaction. The importer's bank may either hold the acceptance to maturity or sell it at a discount to obtain immediate cash. An investor who buys a banker's acceptance is therefore promised payment of its face value by the importer at the specified future date. As a result of its sale, the banker's acceptance becomes a marketable security. The initial maturities of banker's acceptances are typically between 30 and 180 days, 90 days being most common. If the importer fails to pay the amount due at maturity, the bank is liable for the payment. Because of this, banker's acceptances, which typically have a minimum denomination of $100,000, are low-risk securities with good secondary markets. The yields on banker's acceptances are generally slightly below those of CDs and commercial paper; they can usually be purchased through a bank or stockbroker.

Money Market Mutual Funds

money market mutual fund (MMMF)
a mutual fund that pools the capital of a large number of investors and uses it to invest exclusively in high-yielding, short-term securities.

A **money market mutual fund** (MMMF) is simply a mutual fund that pools the capital of a large number of investors and uses it to invest exclusively in high-yielding, short-term securities, such as Treasury bills, large certificates of deposit, and commercial paper. Because such securities are sold in denominations of $10,000 to $1 million (or more), most small investors cannot purchase them individually. The MMMF makes these vehicles, which very often offer the highest short-term returns, available to even small investors. Shares of MMMFs can be purchased (through brokers and investment dealers or directly from the fund) in initial amounts as small as $500 to $1,000, although $1,000 to $5,000 is a more typical amount. MMMFs provide convenient and easy access to funds through check-writing privileges; the nice feature of this privilege is that you continue to earn interest while the check is being cleared through the banking system. Almost every major brokerage firm has a money fund of its own; hundreds more are unaffiliated with a specific brokerage firm.

The returns on money funds amount to what fund managers are able to earn from their investment activity in various short-term securities. Thus, the returns rise and fall with money market interest rates. As Figure 3.2 shows, these are *highly volatile* rates that cause investor yields to vary accordingly. The returns on MMMFs are closely followed in the financial media. In fact, the current yields on about 750 of the largest taxable funds are reported every Thursday in the *Wall Street Journal,* and the yields on other large funds are reported regularly in most major newspapers (see Figure 3.3). Note in this case that not only are yields reported, but so are average maturities and total assets.

We will describe mutual funds more fully in Chapter 13; however, several characteristics of money funds should be noted here. One concern of many investors is safety. Though they are not federally insured, MMMFs have been virtually free of even the threat of failure for as long as they have existed. Default risk is almost zero, because the securities the funds purchase are very low in risk to begin with and diversification by the funds lowers risk even more. Despite this remarkable safety record, it is impossible to say with certainty that MMMFs are as risk-free as federally insured deposits. In the event of a massive financial crisis, they probably are not. On the other hand, the amount of extra risk might be viewed as so minimal as to be easily offset by a slightly higher yield. This is a choice you must make within your own risk–return framework.

FIGURE 3.2
The Behavior of Short-Term Market Rates over Time

The yields on marketable short-term securities (such as Treasury bills) are highly unstable. They therefore have a dramatic effect on returns to investors in money funds and other short-term vehicles (like MMDAs).

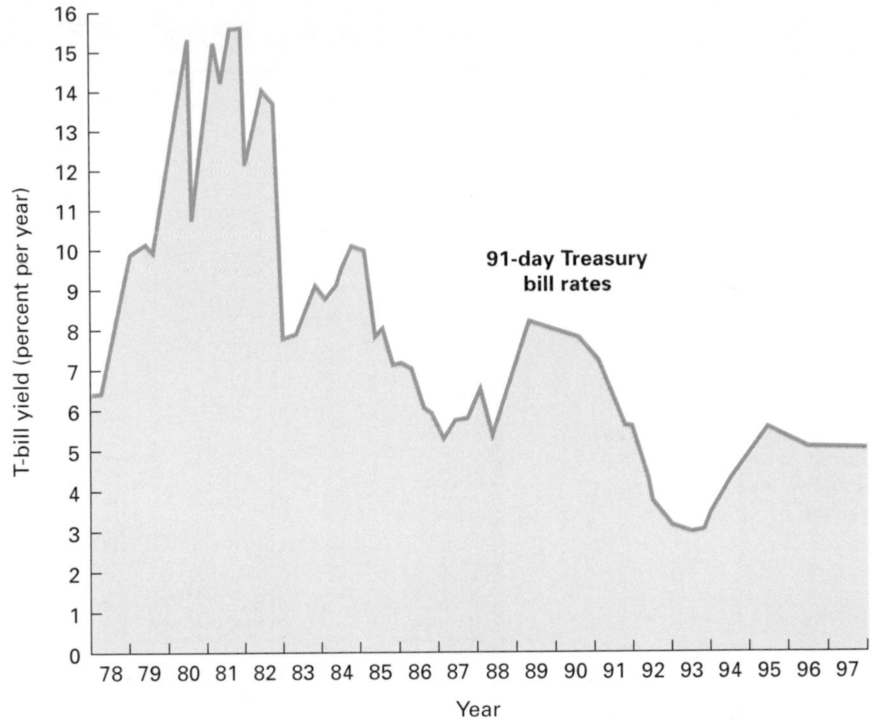

government securities money funds
money market mutual funds that confine their investments to Treasury bills and other short-term securities issued by the U.S. government and its agencies.

Government securities money funds were established to meet investor concerns for safety. These funds effectively eliminate any risk of default by confining their investments to Treasury bills and other short-term securities issued by the U.S. government and its agencies. They are like standard MMMFs in all other respects except for slightly lower yields (which is the price you pay for the higher quality).

tax-exempt money fund
a money market mutual fund that limits its investments to tax-exempt municipal securities with very short (30 to 90 days) maturities.

In addition to standard money market mutual funds and government securities money funds, there are over 400 tax-exempt money funds. The **tax-exempt money fund** limits its investments to tax-exempt municipal securities with very short (30 to 90 days) maturities. Except for this feature, they are like the standard money market funds. Because their income is free from federal (and some state) income tax, they yield less than standard, fully taxable money funds do. They appeal predominantly to investors in the higher tax brackets for whom the lower tax-free yield is better than the after-tax return they could earn on standard money funds. The current yields on most major tax-exempt money funds are separately reported every Thursday in the *Wall Street Journal* and in other major newspapers.

Series EE Savings Bonds

Series EE savings bonds
savings bonds issued by the U.S. Treasury and sold at banks and through payroll deduction plans, in varying denominations, at 50% of face value; pay a variable rate of interest tied to U.S. Treasury security market yields and calculated every 6 months in May and November.

Series EE savings bonds are the well-known savings bonds that have been available for decades. You may have been given some by thrifty (or patriotic) relatives on birthdays or other special occasions. (First issued in 1941, they used to be called Series E bonds.) EE bonds are often purchased through payroll deduction plans. Although issued by the U.S. Treasury, they are quite different from T-bills. In fact, perhaps their only similarity to the latter is

FIGURE 3.3
Published Yield Information on Major Money Market Mutual Funds

Data on money funds are widely quoted in the financial press. Here we see that the information includes the portfolios' average maturity (in days), the 7-day average of the annualized yield currently available, and the total assets in the portfolio measured in millions of dollars. (Source: *Wall Street Journal,* April 16, 1998, p. C15. Reprinted by permission of the *Wall Street Journal.* © Dow Jones & Company, Inc., 1998. All rights reserved.)

MONEY MARKET MUTUAL FUNDS

The following quotations, collected by the National Association of Securities Dealers Inc., represent the average of annualized yields and dollar-weighted portfolio maturities ending Wednesday, April 15, 1998. Yields don't include capital gains or losses.

Fund	Avg. Mat.	7 Day Yield	Assets
Money Market:			
AALMny	57	4.77	241
AARP HQ	38	4.73	477
AAdMileP	41	4.59	66
AAdvGovP	38	4.71	83
AAdvMMPlat	41	4.71	596
AFD ExRsv A	24	4.34	83
AFD ExResB	24	3.84	81
AIM MM C	17	4.65	339
AIM MMA	17	4.58	302
ARK GvIn II	32	5.13	91
ARK MMIn II	61	5.26	92
ARKMM A	61	5.30	240
ARKUSG A	32	5.15	1164
ARKUST A	27	4.92	273
ARKUST R	27	4.69	36
AccUSGov	60	4.93	49
ActAsGv	64	4.88	736
ActAsMny	69	5.17	11854
Advantus a	39	5.24	57
AetnaAdvs	59	5.22	164
Aetna Sel	59	5.22	274
AlexBwn	44	4.96	2965
AlxBTr	51	4.68	805
AlgerMM	12	4.77	161
AlliaGenMu	19	2.96	152
AlliaGov	50	4.59	147
AlliMMass	46	2.71	21
AlliaPrime	69	4.65	3870
Alli TrResv	53	4.42	731
AlliaCpRs	78	4.67	7016
AliaGvR	57	4.59	4570

Fund	Avg. Mat.	7 Day Yield	Assets
FstAmTrObD	42	5.01	3541
FstAmerInstit	41	5.25	4905
FstAmerInv	41	5.00	874
FstAmPrObD	41	5.10	445
FstAmTxFrOb	40	3.06	39
FstAmTrObA p	42	4.91	74
FstAmTrObC	42	5.16	1225
FirstChCshRvS	53	5.14	99
FirstChUSTrRvS	75	4.94	69
FirstCshRsvIII	44	5.06	56
FtInvCs	34	4.89	144
First Muni	30	3.29	39
FstOmahaGv	63	4.83	99
FirPrTreasTr	72	4.74	225
FirPrTreasIn	72	4.34	54
First USGv	37	5.22	87
First USTrs	39	5.10	11
FsrInstMn	45	5.26	1224
FsrMM	51	5.01	254
FsrUSGovt	54	4.89	198
FsrUST	61	4.78	71
FlexInst	64	5.40	539
FlexFd	64	5.27	156
Fortis A	57	4.77	140
ForumDAT Obl	3	5.50	57
ForumDATrs	29	4.95	57
Founders	24	4.68	89
FountSComP Inv	40	5.04	36
FountSGvResInv	42	4.98	158
FountSGv	42	4.98	189
FountSCPTr	40	5.04	389
FountSTO	35	5.20	738

Fund	Avg. Mat.	7 Day Yield	Assets
PBHG CshRes	54	4.91	98
PIMCO MM	47	5.23	36
PcfCptlCshAs	30	4.99	377
PcfCptlUSTrs	21	4.95	143
PcHrzTO H	57	5.12	36
PcHrzGvHor	30	5.41	52
PfCapUST SS	21	4.70	151
PcHrzGvPH	30	5.09	152
PcHrzPr	46	5.18	2537
PcHrzTr	36	5.06	302
PcHrzTO PH	57	4.80	207
PW PACE	73	5.19	25
PW Cash	45	5.10	5666
PW RMA	79	5.06	11315
PW RM US	61	4.94	1269
PW Retr	66	4.87	4252
ParkTrInvA	28	4.93	235
ParkPrInvA	50	4.88	211
ParkPrInst	50	4.98	729
ParkTrInst	28	5.03	340
ParkUS C	38	4.93	190
ParkUSInvA	38	4.83	193
PegCM S	37	5.17	1081
PegCM I	37	5.42	901
PegMM I	56	5.25	1543
PegMI A	55	2.92	29
PegMuni I	59	3.18	610
PegMuniMgtI	46	3.29	297
PegMuniMgtS p	46	3.04	69
PegTreas I	36	5.17	796
PegTPCM S	50	4.79	275
PegTPCM I	50	5.04	80
PegTrsMgtS p	32	5.02	246
PegGovCM I	37	5.29	729
PegGovC S	37	5.06	441
PerfrmTrCsr	54	4.98	107
PerfrmTrInst	54	5.23	335
PhoenixA	54	4.94	164

Fund	Avg. Mat.	7 Day Yield	Assets
BROHSv	57	3.16	74
BRPASv	28	3.00	226
BRVAInst	37	3.50	63
BR PA Instl	28	3.30	285
BR PA Invest	28	2.84	114
Boston1784 TaxFr	54	3.29	1057
Bradfd Muni	50	2.94	177
CRTTaxEx	40	2.96	792
CalMuCsIs	45	3.40	44
CalDalyA	35	2.75	204
CalMuCs	45	3.15	315
CalTF	40	3.10	119
ClvTF CA	22	3.48	340
CalvTxFr	26	3.49	1455
CardTx	80	3.50	65
CashActTrst	31	2.87	385
CshResourceCA p	36	2.76	96
CashEq	33	3.12	419
CsTrIIMun	50	3.05	294
CshTrMuni	47	2.85	653
Centn NY	63	2.81	56
Centn CA	46	2.72	223
CentenTx	62	3.10	1940
ChVistaCA	51	3.02	55
ChVistaCT	51	2.85	44
ChVistaNJ	56	2.76	26
ChVista NY	42	3.07	1163
ChVistaTF	47	3.17	691
ChVistaTF Pre	47	3.23	133
ChVista TFI	47	3.50	252
CitFCATFR	51	3.03	264
CitFCTTFR	55	3.05	168
CitFITxFrR	59	3.53	129
CitFNYTFR	49	3.08	1123
CitFTxFrR	59	3.13	541
ConnDlyA	51	2.85	169
Core TFY	60	3.11	139
CCRTxF	40	2.99	114

that they are sold on a discount basis and are exempt from state and local income taxes.

accrual-type securities
securities for which interest is paid when the bond is cashed, on or before maturity, rather than periodically over the life of the bond.

Series EE bonds are **accrual-type securities,** which means that interest is paid when the bond is cashed, on or before maturity, rather than periodically over the life of the bond. The purchase price of all denominations is 50% of the face value. Thus a $100 bond costs $50 and will be worth $100 at maturity. Series EE bonds are backed by the full faith and credit of the U.S. government and can be replaced without charge in case of loss, theft, or destruction. They can be purchased at banks or other thrift institutions or through payroll deduction plans. They are issued in denominations of $50 through $10,000. A person is limited to maximum annual Series EE bond purchases of $15,000 (i.e., $30,000 face value).

The actual maturity date on EE bonds is unspecified because they pay a variable rate of interest. The higher the rate of interest being paid, the shorter the period of time it takes for the bond to *accrue* from its discounted purchase price to its face value. On May 1, 1997, new rules for savings bonds went into effect. The rate of interest paid on EE bonds is 90% of the average 5-year Treasury security market yields for the preceding 6 months. All EE bonds held from 6 months to 5 years—bonds can be redeemed any time after the first 6 months—are penalized by forfeiting the last 3 months of interest earned. Interest rates are calculated every 6 months (in May and November) and change in accordance with prevailing Treasury security market yields. You can obtain current rates on Series EE bonds from your bank or simply by calling 800-487-2663. (*Note:* For bonds purchased after May 1, 1997, the rate for the 6-month period ending October 31, 1998, was 5.06%.) Interest is credited every 6 months and compounds semiannually.

In addition to being exempt from state and local taxes, Series EE bonds provide an appealing tax twist: *Investors need not report the interest earned on their federal tax returns until the bonds are redeemed.* Although interest can be reported annually (this might be done, for example, if the bonds are held in the name of a child who has limited interest income), most investors choose to defer reporting the interest. In effect, this means the funds are being reinvested at an after-tax rate equal to the bond's current interest rate. Another attractive tax feature allows partial or complete tax avoidance of EE bond earnings when proceeds are used to pay education expenses (such as college tuition) for the bond purchaser, a spouse, or other IRS-defined dependent. To qualify the purchaser must be age 24 or older and must, after December 31, 1997, have adjusted gross income below $52,250 for single filers and $78,350 for married couples. (The maximum income levels are adjusted annually.)

What's more, it is even possible to defer the tax shelter *beyond* the redemption date of your Series EE bond. You can extend your tax shelter if, instead of cashing in the bonds, you exchange them for Series HH bonds. HH bonds, unlike EE bonds, are issued at their full face value and pay semiannual interest at the current fixed rate of 4%. Series HH bonds can be obtained only through the exchange of Series E or Series EE bonds, have an initial 10-year maturity and can be extended for an additional 10 years, and are available in denominations of $500 to $10,000. If you exchange your EE bonds for HH bonds, the accumulated interest on the Series EE bonds remains free of federal income tax for a while longer, because you will not have to pay the tax on those interest earnings until the HH bonds reach maturity (up to 20 years) or until you cash *them* in. Thus, in contrast to their predecessors, today's Series EE bonds not only represent a safe and secure form of investment but also provide highly competitive yields and offer attractive tax incentives.

Investment Suitability

Deposit accounts and short-term securities are widely used by individuals as both savings and investment vehicles. They are used to build up or maintain a desired level of savings that will be readily available when and if the need arises—in essence, to provide *safety and security.* In this case, high yield is less important than safety, liquidity, and convenience. Passbook savings accounts, NOW accounts, and Series EE savings bonds are the most popular savings vehicles.

Yield is often just as important as liquidity when short-term vehicles are used for *investment purposes.* However, because the objective is different, the securities tend to be used much more aggressively as investments than in savings programs. Most investors will hold at least a part of their portfolio in short-term, highly liquid securities, if for no other reason than to be able to act on unanticipated investment opportunities. Some investors, in fact, may as a matter of practice devote all or most of their portfolios to such securities. They do so in the belief that these investments provide attractive rates of return for the risk, because they are unfamiliar with other investment vehicles, or simply because they do not wish to devote the time necessary to managing their portfolios.

One of the most common uses of short-term securities as investment vehicles is as temporary outlets—either to warehouse funds until an attractive permanent investment can be found or to sit on the sidelines in times of unsettled or undesirable market conditions. For example, if you have just sold some stock but do not have a suitable long-term investment alternative, you might place the proceeds in a money fund until you find a longer-term use for them. Or if you feel that interest rates are about to rise sharply, you might sell your long-term bonds and use the proceeds to buy T-bills. The high-yielding securities—like MMDAs, CDs, commercial paper, banker's acceptances, and money funds—are generally preferred for use as part of an investment program, as are central asset accounts at major brokerage firms.

To decide which securities are most appropriate for a particular situation, you need to consider such issue characteristics as availability, safety, liquidity, and yield. Though all the investments we have discussed satisfy the basic liquidity demand, they do so to varying degrees. A NOW account is unquestionably the most liquid of all, because you can write as many checks as you wish and for any amount. A certificate of deposit, on the other hand, is not so liquid, because early redemption involves an interest penalty. Table 3.3 summarizes the key characteristics for most of the short-term investments discussed here. The letter grade assigned the investments for each characteristic reflects an estimate of the investment's quality in that area. For example, MMMFs rate only a B+ on liquidity, because withdrawals must usually be made in a minimum amount of $250 to $500 depending on the fund. NOW accounts, on the other hand, are somewhat better in this respect, because a withdrawal can be for any amount. Yields are self-explanatory, although you should note that if an investment scores lower on availability, safety, or liquidity, it will generally offer a higher yield.

TABLE 3.3 A Scorecard for Short-Term Accounts and Securities

Savings or Investment Vehicle	Availability	Safety	Liquidity	Yield (Average Rate)*
Passbook savings account	A+	A+	A	C– (2.0%)
NOW account	A–	A+	A+	F (1.5%)
Money market deposit account (MMDA)	B	A+	A	B– (2.0%)
Central asset account	B–	A	A+	C– (2.2%)
U.S. Treasury bill (91-day)	B–	A++	A–	A– (5.0%)
Certificate of deposit (3-month, large denomination)	B	A+	C	A (5.4%)
Commercial paper (90-day)	B–	A–	C	A (5.5%)
Banker's acceptance (90-day)	B–	A	B	A– (5.4%)
Money market mutual fund (MMMF); standard and government security funds	B	A/A+	B+	B (5.1%)
Series EE savings bond	A+	A++	C–	B+ (5.1%)

*The average rates reflect representative or typical rates that existed in early 1998.

CONCEPTS IN REVIEW

3.7 What makes an asset liquid? Why hold liquid assets? Would 100 shares of IBM stock be considered a liquid investment? Explain.

3.8 Explain the characteristics of short-term investments with respect to both purchasing power and default risk.

3.9 Briefly describe the key features and differences among the following deposit accounts.
- a. Passbook savings account
- b. NOW account
- c. Money market deposit account
- d. Central asset account

3.10 Define, compare, and contrast the following short-term investments.
- a. U.S. Treasury bills
- b. Certificates of deposit
- c. Commercial paper
- d. Banker's acceptances
- e. Money market mutual funds
- f. Series EE savings bonds

http://hepg.aw.com

Short-term rates change frequently, and the Web is probably the easiest way to get up-to-the-minute returns. Data Broadcasting Corporation provides current rates on U.S. Treasury securities, including Treasury bills, notes, and bonds. Check out the current rate on 3-month, 6-month, and 1-year T-bills.

www.dbc.com/cgi-bin/htx.exe/newsroom/bel_tres.html

Types and Sources of Investment Information

LG 4 LG 5

Once you have developed your investment plans and have met your liquidity needs, you can begin searching for the right investments. You should start by examining investment information of various kinds in order to formulate expectations of the risk–return behaviors of potential investments. The remainder of this chapter describes the investment information that will help guide you in putting your investment plan into action and monitoring the results. In this section we consider the key types and sources of investment information, and in the final section we focus on market averages and indexes.

descriptive information
factual data on the past behavior of the economy, the market, the industry, the company, or a given investment vehicle.

analytical information
available current data in conjunction with projections and recommendations about potential investments.

Investment information can be either descriptive or analytical. **Descriptive information** presents factual data on the past behavior of the economy, the market, the industry, the company, or a given investment vehicle. **Analytical information** presents available current data in conjunction with projections and recommendations about potential investments. The sample page from *Value Line* included in Figure 3.4 provides both descriptive and analytical information on Hewlett-Packard. Items that are primarily descriptive are keyed with a D; analytical items are noted with an A. Examples of descriptive information are the company's capital structure and monthly stock price ranges for the past 13 years. Examples of analytical information are rank for timeliness and estimated average price range for the next 3 to 5 years.

Some forms of investment information are free; others must be purchased individually or by annual subscription. Free information can be obtained from newspapers, magazines, and brokerage firms, and more can be found in public, university, and brokerage firm libraries. Alternatively, you can

FIGURE 3.4 A Report Containing Descriptive and Analytical Information

This report—*Value Line's* full-page report on Hewlett-Packard from January 23, 1998—contains both descriptive (marked *D*) and analytical (marked *A*) information. (Source: Adapted from *The Value Line Investment Survey, Ratings and Reports,* Edition 7, January 23, 1998, p. 1096. © Value Line Publishing, Inc.)

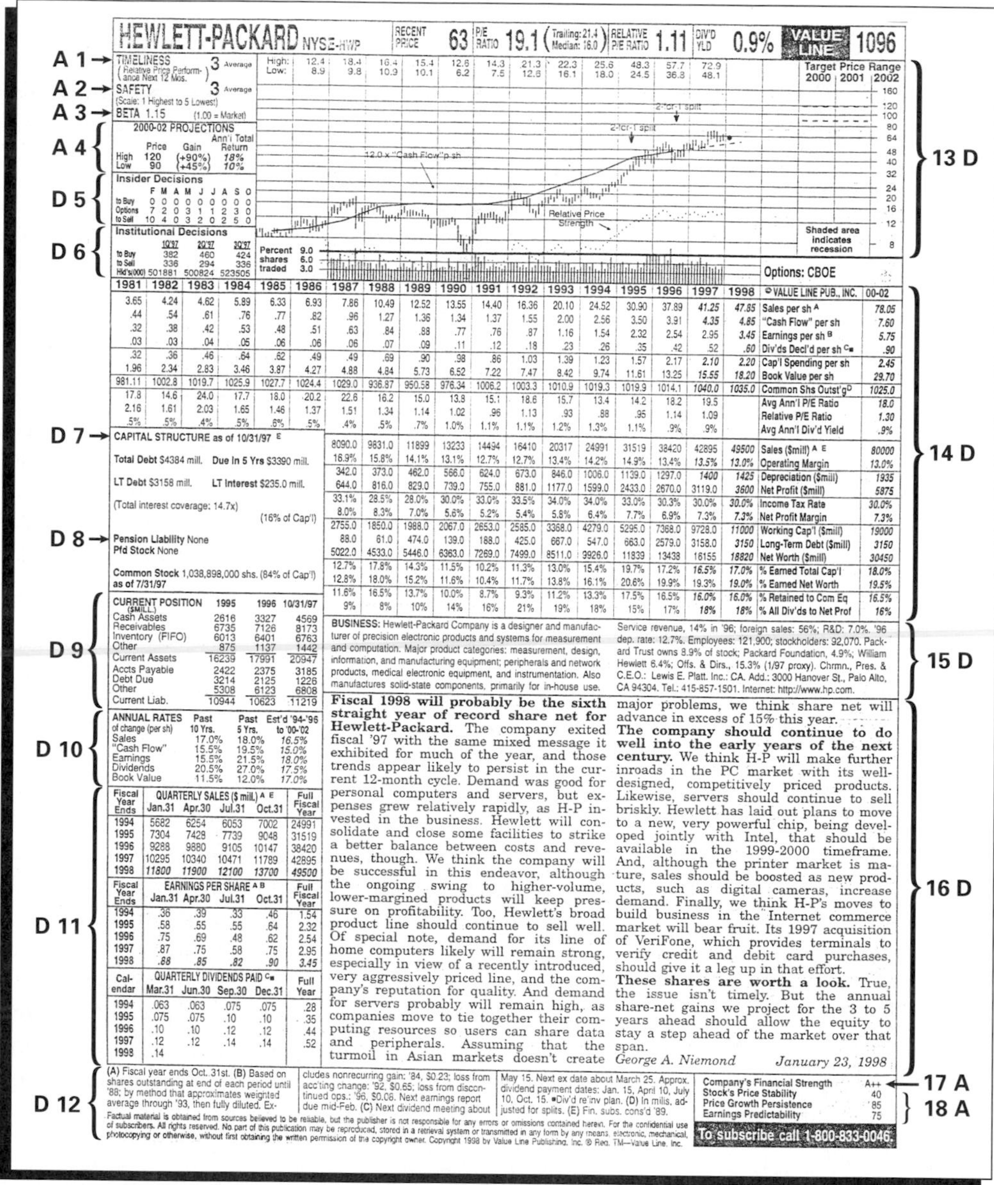

HEWLETT-PACKARD NYSE-HWP | RECENT PRICE 63 | P/E RATIO 19.1 (Trailing: 21.4 / Median: 16.0) | RELATIVE P/E RATIO 1.11 | DIV'D YLD 0.9% | VALUE LINE 1096

A 1 → TIMELINESS 3 Average (Relative Price Performance Next 12 Mos.)
A 2 → SAFETY 3 Average (Scale: 1 Highest to 5 Lowest)
A 3 → BETA 1.15 (1.00 = Market)

A 4 — 2000-02 PROJECTIONS

	Price	Gain	Ann'l Total Return
High	120	(+90%)	18%
Low	90	(+45%)	10%

D 5 — Insider Decisions

	F	M	A	M	J	J	A	S	O
to Buy	0	0	0	0	0	0	0	0	0
Options	7	2	0	3	1	1	2	3	0
to Sell	10	4	0	3	2	0	2	5	0

D 6 — Institutional Decisions

	1Q'97	2Q'97	3Q'97
to Buy	382	460	424
to Sell	336	294	336
Hld's(000)	501881	500824	523505

	1986	1987	1988	1989	1990	1991	1992	1993	1994	1995	1996	1997
High:	12.4	18.4	16.4	15.4	12.6	14.3	21.3	22.3	25.6	48.3	57.7	72.9
Low:	8.9	9.8	10.9	10.1	6.2	7.5	12.6	16.1	18.0	24.5	36.8	48.1

1981	1982	1983	1984	1985	1986	1987	1988	1989	1990	1991	1992	1993	1994	1995	1996	1997	1998	© VALUE LINE PUB., INC.	00-02
3.65	4.24	4.62	5.89	6.33	6.93	7.86	10.49	12.52	13.55	14.40	16.36	20.10	24.52	30.90	37.89	41.25	47.85	Sales per sh A	78.05
.44	.54	.61	.76	.77	.82	.96	1.27	1.36	1.34	1.37	1.55	2.00	2.56	3.50	3.91	4.35	4.85	"Cash Flow" per sh	7.60
.32	.38	.42	.53	.48	.51	.63	.84	.88	.77	.76	.87	1.16	1.54	2.32	2.54	2.95	3.45	Earnings per sh B	5.75
.03	.03	.04	.05	.06	.06	.06	.07	.09	.11	.12	.18	.23	.26	.35	.42	.52	.60	Div'ds Decl'd per sh C■	.90
.32	.36	.46	.64	.62	.49	.49	.69	.90	.98	.86	1.03	1.39	1.23	1.57	2.17	2.10	2.20	Cap'l Spending per sh	2.45
1.96	2.34	2.83	3.46	3.87	4.27	4.88	4.84	5.73	6.52	7.22	7.47	8.42	9.74	11.61	13.25	15.55	18.20	Book Value per sh	29.70
981.11	1002.8	1019.7	1025.9	1027.7	1024.4	1029.0	936.87	950.58	976.34	1006.2	1003.3	1010.9	1019.3	1019.9	1014.1	1040.0	1035.0	Common Shs Outst'g D	1025.0
17.8	14.6	24.0	17.7	18.0	20.2	22.6	16.2	15.0	13.8	15.1	18.6	15.7	13.4	14.2	18.2	19.5		Avg Ann'l P/E Ratio	18.0
2.16	1.61	2.03	1.65	1.46	1.37	1.51	1.34	1.14	1.02	.96	1.13	.93	.88	.95	1.14	1.09		Relative P/E Ratio	1.30
.5%	.5%	.4%	.5%	.6%	.5%	.4%	.5%	.7%	1.0%	1.1%	1.1%	1.2%	1.3%	1.1%	.9%	.9%		Avg Ann'l Div'd Yield	.9%
						8090.0	9831.0	11899	13233	14494	16410	20317	24991	31519	38420	42895	49500	Sales ($mill) A E	80000
						16.9%	15.8%	14.1%	13.1%	12.7%	12.7%	13.4%	14.2%	14.9%	13.4%	13.5%	13.0%	Operating Margin	13.0%
						342.0	373.0	462.0	566.0	624.0	673.0	846.0	1006.0	1139.0	1297.0	1400	1425	Depreciation ($mill)	1935
						644.0	816.0	829.0	739.0	755.0	881.0	1177.0	1599.0	2433.0	2670.0	3119.0	3600	Net Profit ($mill)	5875
						33.1%	28.5%	28.0%	30.0%	33.0%	33.5%	34.0%	34.0%	33.0%	30.3%	30.0%	30.0%	Income Tax Rate	30.0%
						8.0%	8.3%	7.0%	5.6%	5.2%	5.4%	5.8%	6.4%	7.7%	6.9%	7.3%	7.3%	Net Profit Margin	7.3%
						2755.0	1850.0	1988.0	2067.0	2653.0	2585.0	3368.0	4279.0	5295.0	7368.0	9728.0	11000	Working Cap'l ($mill)	19000
						88.0	61.0	474.0	139.0	188.0	425.0	667.0	547.0	663.0	2579.0	3158.0	3150	Long-Term Debt ($mill)	3150
						5022.0	4533.0	5446.0	6363.0	7269.0	7499.0	8511.0	9926.0	11839	13438	16155	18820	Net Worth ($mill)	30450
						12.7%	17.8%	14.3%	11.5%	10.2%	11.3%	13.0%	15.4%	19.7%	17.2%	16.5%	17.0%	% Earned Total Cap'l	18.0%
						12.8%	18.0%	15.2%	11.6%	10.4%	11.7%	13.8%	16.1%	20.6%	19.9%	19.3%	19.0%	% Earned Net Worth	19.5%
						11.6%	16.5%	13.7%	10.0%	8.7%	9.3%	11.2%	13.3%	17.5%	16.5%	16.0%	16.0%	% Retained to Com Eq	16.5%
						9%	8%	10%	14%	16%	21%	19%	18%	15%	17%	18%	18%	% All Div'ds to Net Prof	16%

14 D

D 7 → CAPITAL STRUCTURE as of 10/31/97 E

Total Debt $4384 mill. Due In 5 Yrs $3390 mill.
LT Debt $3158 mill. LT Interest $235.0 mill.
(Total interest coverage: 14.7x) (16% of Cap'l)

D 8 → Pension Liability None
Pfd Stock None

Common Stock 1,038,898,000 shs. (84% of Cap'l) as of 7/31/97

D 9 —

CURRENT POSITION ($MILL.)	1995	1996	10/31/97
Cash Assets	2616	3327	4569
Receivables	6735	7126	8173
Inventory (FIFO)	6013	6401	6763
Other	875	1137	1442
Current Assets	16239	17991	20947
Accts Payable	2422	2375	3185
Debt Due	3214	2125	1226
Other	5308	6123	6808
Current Liab.	10944	10623	11219

D 10 —

ANNUAL RATES of change (per sh)	Past 10 Yrs.	Past 5 Yrs.	Est'd '94-'96 to '00-'02
Sales	17.0%	18.0%	16.5%
"Cash Flow"	15.5%	19.5%	15.0%
Earnings	15.5%	21.5%	18.0%
Dividends	20.5%	27.0%	17.5%
Book Value	11.5%	12.0%	17.0%

D 11 —

Fiscal Year Ends	QUARTERLY SALES ($ mill.) A E Jan.31	Apr.30	Jul.31	Oct.31	Full Fiscal Year
1994	5682	6254	6053	7002	24991
1995	7304	7428	7739	9048	31519
1996	9288	9880	9105	10147	38420
1997	10295	10340	10471	11789	42895
1998	11800	11900	12100	13700	49500

Fiscal Year Ends	EARNINGS PER SHARE A B Jan.31	Apr.30	Jul.31	Oct.31	Full Fiscal Year
1994	.36	.39	.33	.46	1.54
1995	.58	.55	.55	.64	2.32
1996	.75	.69	.48	.62	2.54
1997	.87	.75	.58	.75	2.95
1998	.88	.85	.82	.90	3.45

Cal-endar	QUARTERLY DIVIDENDS PAID C■ Mar.31	Jun.30	Sep.30	Dec.31	Full Year
1994	.063	.063	.075	.075	.28
1995	.075	.075	.10	.10	.35
1996	.10	.10	.12	.12	.44
1997	.12	.12	.14	.14	.52
1998	.14				

BUSINESS: Hewlett-Packard Company is a designer and manufacturer of precision electronic products and systems for measurement and computation. Major product categories: measurement, design, information, and manufacturing equipment; peripherals and network products, medical electronic equipment, and instrumentation. Also manufactures solid-state components, primarily for in-house use. Service revenue, 14% in '96; foreign sales: 56%; R&D: 7.0%. '96 dep. rate: 12.7%. Employees: 121,900; stockholders: 92,070. Packard Trust owns 8.9% of stock; Packard Foundation, 4.9%; William Hewlett 6.4%; Offs. & Dirs., 15.3% (1/97 proxy). Chrmn., Pres. & C.E.O.: Lewis E. Platt. Inc.: CA. Add.: 3000 Hanover St., Palo Alto, CA 94304. Tel.: 415-857-1501. Internet: http://www.hp.com.

15 D

Fiscal 1998 will probably be the sixth straight year of record share net for Hewlett-Packard. The company exited fiscal '97 with the same mixed message it exhibited for much of the year, and those trends appear likely to persist in the current 12-month cycle. Demand was good for personal computers and servers, but expenses grew relatively rapidly, as H-P invested in the business. Hewlett will consolidate and close some facilities to strike a better balance between costs and revenues, though. We think the company will be successful in this endeavor, although the ongoing swing to higher-volume, lower-margined products will keep pressure on profitability. Too, Hewlett's broad product line should continue to sell well. Of special note, demand for its line of home computers likely will remain strong, especially in view of a recently introduced, very aggressively priced line, and the company's reputation for quality. And demand for servers probably will remain high, as companies move to tie together their computing resources so users can share data and peripherals. Assuming that the turmoil in Asian markets doesn't create major problems, we think share net will advance in excess of 15% this year.

The company should continue to do well into the early years of the next century. We think H-P will make further inroads in the PC market with its well-designed, competitively priced products. Likewise, servers should continue to sell briskly. Hewlett has laid out plans to move to a new, very powerful chip, being developed jointly with Intel, that should be available in the 1999-2000 timeframe. And, although the printer market is mature, sales should be boosted as new products, such as digital cameras, increase demand. Finally, we think H-P's moves to build business in the Internet commerce market will bear fruit. Its 1997 acquisition of VeriFone, which provides terminals to verify credit and debit card purchases, should give it a leg up in that effort.

These shares are worth a look. True, the issue isn't timely. But the annual share-net gains we project for the 3 to 5 years ahead should allow the equity to stay a step ahead of the market over that span.

George A. Niemond *January 23, 1998*

16 D

D 12 — (A) Fiscal year ends Oct. 31st. (B) Based on shares outstanding at end of each period until '88; by method that approximates weighted average through '93, then fully diluted. Excludes nonrecurring gain: '84, $0.23; loss from acc'ting change: '92, $0.65; loss from discontinued ops.: '96, $0.08. Next earnings report due mid-Feb. (C) Next dividend meeting about May 15. Next ex date about March 25. Approx. dividend payment dates: Jan. 15, April 10, July 10, Oct. 15. ■Div'd re'inv plan. (D) In mills, adjusted for splits. (E) Fin. subs. cons'd '89.

Company's Financial Strength	A++
Stock's Price Stability	40
Price Growth Persistence	85
Earnings Predictability	75

← 17 A
} 18 A

1. **Rank for timeliness (price performance in next twelve months)—from 1 (highest) to 5 (lowest)**
2. **Rank for long-term safety—1 (highest) down to 5 (lowest)**
3. **Beta (the stock's sensitivity to market fluctuation—NYSE average = 1.00)**
4. **Estimated average price range—3–5 years ahead**
5. **Insider decisions**
6. **Institutional decisions**
7. **Company's capital structure**
8. **Pension liability**
9. **Working capital**
10. **Growth rates**
11. **Quarterly sales, earnings, dividends—actual past, estimated future**
12. **Footnotes—including estimated constant dollar earnings, dividend payment dates.**
13. **Monthly price ranges—past 13 years and value line (cash flow line)**
14. **Statistical milestones—on a per share basis and a company basis—historical past and estimated future**
15. **Brief summary of company's business**
16. **Critique—of recent developments and prospects**
17. **Company's financial strength**
18. **Important indices of quality**

subscribe to services that provide periodic reports summarizing the investment outlook and recommending certain actions. Such services cost money, but locating, reading, and analyzing free information all cost time. Thus it is necessary to evaluate the worth of potential information: For example, paying $40 for information that increases your return by $27 would not be economically sound. The larger your investment portfolio, the easier it is to justify information purchases, because their benefit can usually be applied to a number of investments.

Types of Information

Investment information can be divided into five types, each concerned with an important aspect of the investment process.

1. *Economic and current event information* includes background as well as forecast data related to economic, political, and social trends, on a domestic as well as a global basis. Such information provides a basis for assessing the environment in which decisions are made.

2. *Industry and company information* includes background as well as forecast data on specific industries and companies. Investors use such information to assess the outlook in a given industry or specific company. Because of its company orientation, it is most relevant to stock, bond, or options investments.

3. *Information on alternative investment vehicles* includes background and predictive data for various forms of real estate and other tangible investments as well as for securities other than stocks, bonds, and options—such as futures.

4. *Price information* includes current price quotations on certain investment vehicles, particularly securities. These quotations are commonly accompanied by statistics on the recent price behavior of the vehicle.

5. *Information on personal investment strategies* includes recommendations on investment strategies or specific purchase or sale actions. In general, this information tends to be educational or analytical rather than descriptive.

Sources of Information

A complete listing of the sources of each type of investment information is beyond the scope of this book. Our discussion considers the most common sources of information on economic and current events, industries and companies, and prices.

Economic and Current Event Information

It is clearly important for investors to stay abreast of major economic and current events. An awareness of events should translate into better investment decisions. Popular sources of economic and current event information include financial journals, general newspapers, institutional news, business periodicals, government publications, and special subscription services.

Wall Street Journal
a daily business newspaper, published regionally; the most popular source of financial news.

Barron's
a weekly business newspaper; a popular source of financial news.

Financial Journals The ***Wall Street Journal*** is the most popular source of financial news. It is published daily Monday through Friday in a number of locations around the country; European and Asian editions are also published. In addition to giving daily price quotations on thousands of investment vehicles, it reports world, national, regional, and corporate news. The first page of the third section of the *Journal* usually contains a column, "Your Money Matters," that addresses personal finance issues and topics.

A second popular source of financial news is ***Barron's,*** which is published weekly. *Barron's* generally offers lengthier articles on a variety of topics of interest to individual investors. Probably the most popular column in *Barron's* is Alan Abelson's "Up & Down Wall Street," which provides a critical and often humorous assessment of major developments affecting the stock market and business. Current price quotations and a summary of statistics on a range of investment vehicles also are included.

Investor's Business Daily, a third national business newspaper, is published daily Monday through Friday. It is similar to the *Wall Street Journal* but contains more detailed price and market data. Other sources of financial news are the *Commercial and Financial Chronicle,* the *Financial Times,* and the *Journal of Commerce.*

General Newspapers Another popular source of financial news is *USA Today,* the national newspaper published daily Monday through Friday. Each issue contains a "Money" section (Section B) devoted to business and personal financial news and to current security price quotations and summary statistics.

Local newspapers are still another convenient source of financial news. In most large cities, the daily newspaper devotes at least a few pages to financial and business news. Major metropolitan newspapers such as the *New York Times* and the *Los Angeles Times* provide investors with a wealth of financial information. Most major newspapers contain stock price quotations for major exchanges, price quotations on stocks of local interest, and a summary of the major stock market averages and indexes.

Institutional News The monthly economic letters of the nation's leading banks, such as BankAmerica (based in Charlotte, North Carolina), Northern Trust (Chicago), and Wells Fargo (San Francisco), provide useful economic information. To keep customers abreast of important news developments, most brokerage firms subscribe to a number of wire services such as the Dow Jones, Bloomberg Financial Services, AP (Associated Press), and UPI (United Press International). Access to these services is best obtained through a stockbroker.

Business Periodicals Business periodicals vary in scope. Some present general business and economic articles, others cover securities markets and related topics, and still others focus solely on specific industries or property investments. Regardless of the subject matter, most business periodicals present descriptive information, and some also include analytical information. They rarely offer recommendations.

General business and economic articles are presented in the business sections of general-interest periodicals such as *Newsweek, Time,* and *U.S. News & World Report.* A number of strictly business- and finance-oriented periodicals are also available. These include *Business Week, Fortune, Business Month,* and *Nation's Business.*

Securities and marketplace articles can be found in a number of financial periodicals. The most basic, commonsense articles appear in *Forbes, Kiplinger's Personal Finance Magazine, Money, Smart Money,* and *Worth. Forbes,* published every 2 weeks, is the most investment-oriented. Each January it publishes an "Annual Report on American Industry," which compares the growth and performance of key industries over the past 5 years. In August of each year, *Forbes* also publishes a comparative evaluation of mutual funds. *Kiplinger's Personal Finance Magazine, Money, Smart Money,* and *Worth* are published monthly and contain articles on managing personal finances and on investments.

Other periodicals aimed at the sophisticated investor are listed and described in the Investor's Resources section on our Web site at **hepg.aw.com.**

Government Publications A number of government agencies publish economic data and reports useful to investors. A broad view of the current and expected state of the economy can be found in the annual *Economic Report of the President.* This document reviews and summarizes economic policy and conditions and includes data on important aspects of the economy. The *Federal Reserve Bulletin,* published monthly by the Board of Governors of the Federal Reserve System, and periodic reports published by each of the 12 Federal Reserve District Banks provide articles and data on various aspects of economic and business activity. A useful Department of Commerce publication is the *Survey of Current Business.* Published monthly, it includes indicators and data related to economic and business conditions. A good source of financial statement information on all manufacturers, broken down by industry and asset size, is the *Quarterly Financial Report for Manufacturing Corporations,* published jointly by the Federal Trade Commission and the Securities and Exchange Commission.

Special Subscription Services For those who want additional insights into business and economic conditions, special subscription services are available. These reports include business and economic forecasts and give notice of new government policies, union plans and tactics, taxes, prices, wages, and so on. One popular service is the *Kiplinger Washington Letter,* a weekly publication that provides a wealth of economic information and analyses.

Industry and Company Information

Of special interest to investors is information on particular industries and companies. Often, after choosing an industry in which to invest, the investor will want to analyze specific companies. General articles related to the activities of specific industries can be found in trade publications such as *Chemical Week, American Banker, Computer, Oil and Gas Journal,* and *Public Utilities Fortnightly.* More specific popular sources are discussed below.

stockholders' (annual) report
a report published yearly by a publicly held corporation; contains a wide range of information, including financial statements for the most recent period of operation.

Stockholders' Reports An excellent source of data on an individual firm is the **stockholders',** or **annual, report** published yearly by publicly held corporations. These reports contain a wide range of information, including financial statements for the most recent period of operation, along with summarized statements for several prior years. These reports are free and may be obtained from the companies themselves or from brokers. A sample page from Hewlett-Packard's 1997 stockholders' report is shown in Figure 3.5.

FIGURE 3.5
A Page from a Stockholders' Report

The first page of Hewlett-Packard's report quickly acquaints the investor with the key information on the firm's operations over the past year, in tabular and graphical form. (Source: *Hewlett-Packard 1997 Annual Report.* Palo Alto, California: Hewlett-Packard, 1998, p. 1.)

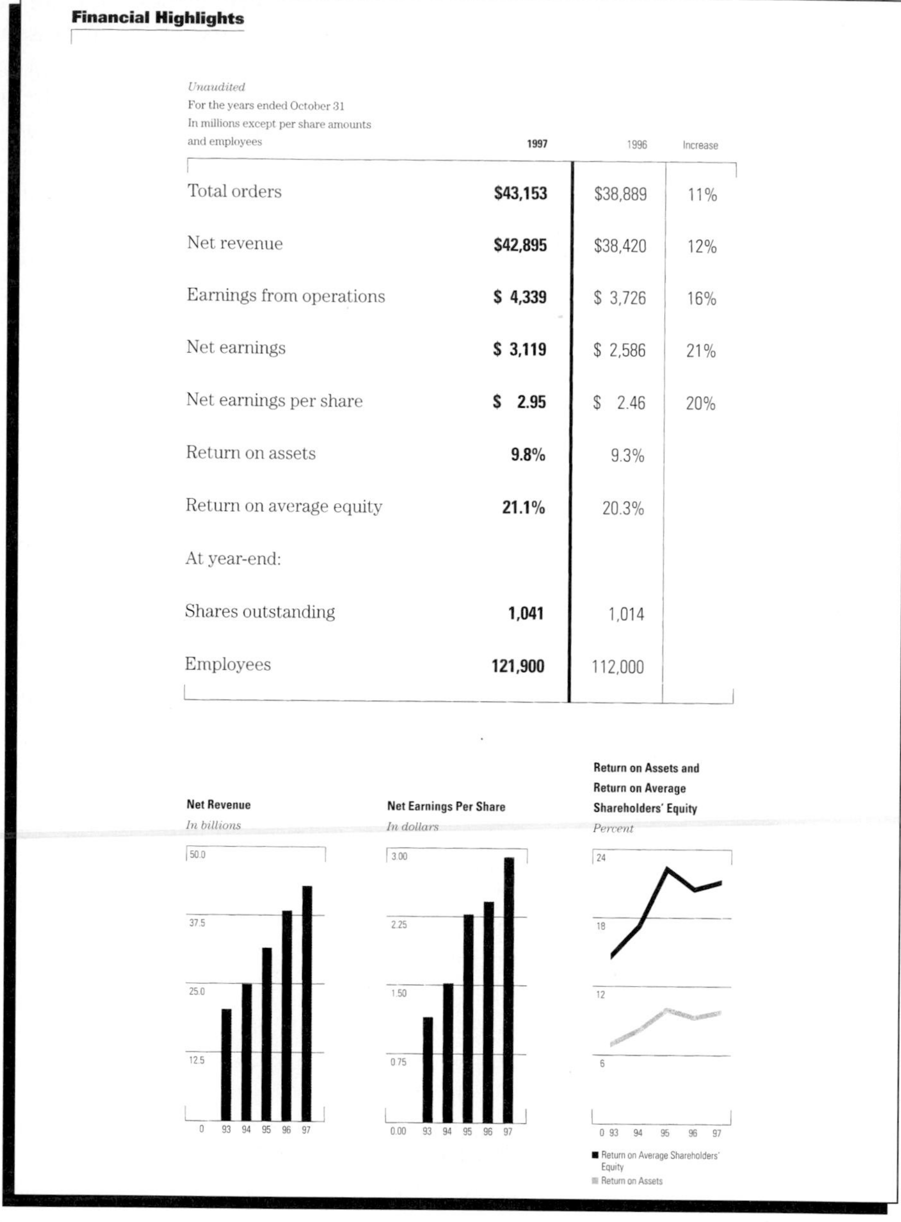

Financial Highlights

Unaudited
For the years ended October 31
In millions except per share amounts and employees

	1997	1996	Increase
Total orders	$43,153	$38,889	11%
Net revenue	$42,895	$38,420	12%
Earnings from operations	$ 4,339	$ 3,726	16%
Net earnings	$ 3,119	$ 2,586	21%
Net earnings per share	$ 2.95	$ 2.46	20%
Return on assets	9.8%	9.3%	
Return on average equity	21.1%	20.3%	
At year-end:			
Shares outstanding	1,041	1,014	
Employees	121,900	112,000	

Form 10-K
a statement that must be filed with the SEC by all firms having securities listed on an organized exchange or traded in the Nasdaq National Market.

In addition to the stockholders' report, many serious investors review a company's **Form 10-K,** a statement that firms with securities listed on an organized exchange or traded in the Nasdaq National Market must file with the SEC.

Comparative Data Sources A number of useful sources of comparative data, typically broken down by industry and firm size, are available for use in analyzing the financial conditions of companies. Among these sources are Dun & Bradstreet's *Key Business Ratios,* Robert Morris and Associates' *Annual Statement Studies,* the *Quarterly Financial Report for Manufacturing Corporations* (cited above), and the *Almanac of Business and Industrial*

Financial Ratios. The data provided by these sources, which are typically available in public and university libraries, are used as a benchmark for evaluating the financial outcomes and conditions of a company.

Subscription Services A variety of subscription services provide data on specific industries and companies. Today, many of these services are available on computer diskette or CD-ROM with accompanying software, and much of the information is available over the Internet. See the Investor's Resources section on our Web site at **hepg.aw.com.** Generally, a subscriber pays a basic fee that entitles him or her to information periodically published by the service. In addition to the basic service, you can purchase other services that provide information of greater depth or range. The major subscription services provide both descriptive and analytical information, but they generally do not make recommendations. Most investors, rather than subscribing to these services, gain access to them through their stockbrokers or a large public or university library.

Standard & Poor's Corporation (S&P)
publisher of a large number of financial reports and services, including *Corporation Records* and *Stock Reports.*

Moody's Investor Services
publisher of a variety of financial reference manuals, including *Moody's Manuals.*

Value Line Investment Survey
one of the most popular subscription services used by individual investors; subscribers receive three basic reports.

The dominant subscription services are those offered by Standard & Poor's Corporation, Moody's Investor Services, and Value Line. **Standard & Poor's Corporation** (S&P) offers a large number of different financial reports and services. Five of the most popular services are briefly summarized in Table 3.4. **Moody's Investor Services** publishes a variety of materials. Five of its most popular services are also briefly described in Table 3.4. The ***Value Line Investment Survey*** is one of the most popular subscription services used by individual investors. Its subscribers receive the three basic reports briefly described in Table 3.4.

back-office research reports
brokerage firm's analyses of and recommendations on investment prospects; made available on request at no cost to existing and potential clients.

Brokerage Reports Brokerage firms often make available to their clients reports from the various subscription services. They also provide clients with prospectuses for new security issues and *back-office research reports.* As noted in Chapter 2, a *prospectus* is a document that describes in detail the key aspects of the issue, the issuer, and its management and financial position. The cover of the prospectus describing the 1998 stock issue of Playtex Products was shown in Chapter 2, in Figure 2.2 on page 28. **Back-office research reports** include the brokerage firm's analyses of and recommendations on prospects for the securities markets, specific industries, or specific securities. Usually a brokerage firm publishes lists of securities classified by its research staff as either "buy" or "sell." Brokerage research reports are available on request at no cost to existing and potential clients.

investment letters
provide, on a subscription basis, the analyses, conclusions, and recommendations of experts in securities investment.

Investment Letters **Investment letters** provide, on a subscription basis, the analyses, conclusions, and recommendations of experts in securities investment. Some letters concentrate on specific types of securities, whereas others are concerned solely with assessing the economy or securities markets. Among the more popular investment letters are *Bob Nurock's Advisory,* the *Dick Davis Digest, Dines Letter, Dow Theory Letters,* the *Growth Stock Outlook, Professional Tape Reader,* the *Prudent Speculator,* and *Street Smart Investing.* The more popular ones are generally issued monthly or weekly and usually cost from $75 to $400 a year. Advertisements for many of these investment letters can be found in *Barron's* and in various business periodicals. The *Hulbert Financial Digest,* which monitors the performance of investment letters, is an excellent source of objective information on investment letters.

TABLE 3.4 Most Popular Offerings of the Most Dominant Subscription Services

Subscription Service Offerings	Coverage	Frequency of Publication
Standard & Poor's Corporation		
Corporation Records	Detailed descriptions of publicly traded securities of over 10,000 public corporations.	Annually with updates throughout the year
Stock Reports (sample shown in Figure 6.2, page 240)	Summary of financial history, current finances, and future prospects for thousands of companies.	Annually with updates throughout the year
Stock Guide	Statistical data and analytical rankings of investment desirability for major stocks.	Monthly
Bond Guide	Statistical data and analytical rankings of investment desirability for major bonds.	Monthly
The Outlook	Analytical articles with investment advice on the market, industries, and securities.	Weekly magazine
Moody's Investor Services		
Moody's Manuals	Eight reference manuals—*Bank and Finance, Industrial, International, Municipal and Government, OTC Industrial, OTC Unlisted, Public Utility,* and *Transportation.* Contain a wealth of historical and current financial, organizational, and operational data on major firms.	Annually with biweekly updates
Handbook of Common Stocks	Provides financial information on over 1,000 common stocks.	Quarterly
Dividend Record	Recent dividend announcements and payments by thousands of companies.	Twice weekly, with annual summary
Bond Survey	Assesses bond market conditions and new offerings.	Weekly
Bond Record	Price and interest rate behavior of thousands of bonds.	Monthly
Value Line Investment Survey		
Includes three reports:	Covers 1,700 of the most widely held stocks.	Weekly
1. *Summary and Index*	Current ratings for each stock.	
2. *Ratings and Reports* (sample shown in Figure 3.4)	Full-page report including financial data, descriptions, analysis, and ratings for each of about 130 stocks	
3. *Selection and Opinion*	Selected investment, business, and stock market prospects, and advice on investment strategy.	

Price Information

quotations
price information about various types of securities, including current price data and statistics on recent price behavior.

Price information about various types of securities is contained in their **quotations,** which include current price data and statistics on recent price behavior. Price quotations are readily available for actively traded securities. The most up-to-date quotations can be obtained from a stockbroker. Some brokerage offices have equipment that allows customers to key into a computer terminal to obtain quotations. Another automated quotation device found in most brokerage offices is the *ticker,* a lighted screen on which stock transactions made

TABLE 3.5 Ticker Symbols for Some Well-Known Companies

Company	Symbol	Company	Symbol
Aluminum Co. of America	AA	Mobil Corporation	MOB
AT&T	T	Netscape	NSCP
Coca-Cola	KO	Nike	NKE
Disney (Walt)	DIS	Pepsico, Inc.	PEP
Eastman Kodak	EK	Procter & Gamble	PG
Ford Motor	F	Quaker Oats	OAT
General Electric	GE	Reebok	RBK
General Motors	GM	Sears, Roebuck	S
Hewlett-Packard	HWP	Starbucks	SBUX
International Business Machines	IBM	Texas Instruments	TXN
McDonald's Corp.	MCD	Upjohn	UPJ
Microsoft	MSFT	Wendy's International	WEN
Merrill Lynch	MER	Xerox Corporation	XRX

on the NYSE, AMEX, and regional exchanges are consolidated and reported as they occur. Cable TV subscribers in many areas can watch the ticker at the bottom of the screen on certain channels, including CNN.fn, CNN Headline News, and MSNBC. The ticker symbols for some well-known companies are listed in Table 3.5. Access to price information via personal computers is also available on a fee basis through a variety of online services.

Investors can easily find the prior day's security price quotations in the published news media, both nonfinancial and financial. The major source of security price quotations is the *Wall Street Journal,* which presents quotations for each previous business day's activities in all major markets. (Actual price quotations will be demonstrated and discussed as part of the coverage of specific investment vehicles in later chapters.)

Electronic and Online Investment Information

Today, many investors use their personal computers to obtain current, often up-to-the-minute, investment information provided on diskette, on CD-ROM, online, or from the Internet. Accompanying these data sets is software that can be used to access and, in many cases, analyze the data in a variety of ways. For example, the *Media General Standard Data Diskette* contains financial data on 7,000 companies and is revised monthly.

A more popular approach to obtaining investment information is online either directly from the data service, such as *Dow Jones News/Retrieval,* or through one of the established online services, such as America Online, CompuServe, or the Internet. All of these online services are accessed by personal computer via a modem. Often the online service subscriber must pay extra for an "extended" or "premium" service that includes particular investment/financial data. For example, CompuServe subscribers can access stock quotes, a variety of stock databases, selected SEC filings, corporate insider-trading information, and articles from more than 800 periodicals. (Except for delayed stock quotes, all of these CompuServe offerings entail an hourly surcharge.) *Dow Jones News/Retrieval* is a popular online service that provides stock quotes, extensive financial data, and same-day access to the *Wall Street*

INVESTOR FACT

GOOD TIP OR CYBER-SCAM?—Investor bulletin boards on the Internet offer open forums in which investors can ask questions, offer advice, or simply read what others have written. Alas, with the push of a few keys, con artists can also reach a wide audience to peddle dubious stocks and get-rich-quick schemes. Therefore, don't buy stocks you haven't researched, and don't assume that people using the bulletin board have *your* best interests in mind. After all, as the editor of *Boardwatch Magazine* says, "If you see a tip, it may be from one of the top brokers in the country, or it could be from an 11-year-old kid."

Journal and *Barron's* articles. In addition to databases and analysis software, the major online services—America Online and CompuServe—and the Internet provide access to online trading facilities that allow subscribers to execute orders through a discount broker.

An obvious advantage of electronic and online services is convenience—having data at one's fingertips. Another advantage is currency: Investment analysis requires considerable amounts of economic and financial information, and the more current it is, the better. However, as is true of investment information from any source, one needs to be aware of the potential for high-tech fraud.

Most electronic and online investment information services have a basic monthly charge that may cover a specified number of hours' usage beyond which additional hourly charges are levied. Charges also sometimes vary depending on the time of day the service is accessed. Additional charges are frequently imposed for access to certain premium services that may include specified or expanded databases, analytical software, advisory services, or order execution facilities. In addition, some of the more specialized online services, like *Dow Jones News/Retrieval,* charge a one-time start-up fee. Of course, upon initiation of these services, subscribers are given a user's guide that describes the procedures for access, how to obtain help, the services available, and the associated fees. The growing use of online services as a source of both investment information and software is expected to accelerate as investors become more familiar and comfortable with them, as their accessibility and offerings expand, and as their costs moderate. Clearly, investment information is an important vehicle on the expanding information highway.

Using Investment Advisers

investment advisers
individuals or firms that provide investment advice—typically for a fee.

Although numerous sources of financial information are available, many investors have neither the time nor the expertise to analyze it and make decisions on their own. Instead, they turn to an investment adviser. **Investment advisers** are individuals or firms that provide investment advice—typically for a fee.

The Adviser's Product

The "product" provided by investment advisers ranges from broad general advice to detailed specific analyses and recommendations. The most general form of advice is a newsletter published by the adviser. These letters offer general advice on the economy, current events, market behavior, and specific securities. Investment advisers also provide complete investment evaluation, recommendation, and management services.

Regulation of Advisers

As pointed out in Chapter 2, the Investment Advisers Act of 1940 ensures that investment advisers make full disclosure of information about their backgrounds, about conflicts of interest, and so on. The act requires professional advisers to register and file periodic reports with the SEC. A 1960 amendment permits the SEC to inspect the records of investment advisers and to revoke the registration of those who violate the act's provisions. However, financial planners, stockbrokers, bankers, lawyers, and accountants who provide investment advice *in addition to their main professional activity* are not regulated by the act. Many states have also passed similar legislation, requiring investment advisers to register and to abide by the guidelines established by the state law.

Be aware that the federal and state laws regulating the activities of professional investment advisers *do not guarantee competence.* Rather, they are intended to protect the investor against fraudulent and unethical practices. It is important to recognize that, at present, *no law or regulatory body controls entrance into the field.* Therefore, investment advisers range from highly informed professionals to totally incompetent amateurs. Advisers possessing a professional designation are usually preferred because they have completed academic courses in areas directly or peripherally related to the investment process. Such designations include CFA (Chartered Financial Analyst), CIC (Chartered Investment Counselor), CFP (Certified Financial Planner), ChFC (Chartered Financial Consultant), CLU (Chartered Life Underwriter), and CPA (Certified Public Accountant). Brief descriptions of these certifications are included in the Investor's Resources section on our Web site at **hepg.aw.com.**

The Cost and Use of Investment Advice

Professional investment advice typically costs between ¼ of 1% and 3% annually of the amount of money being managed. For large portfolios, the fee is typically in the range of ¼ to ¾ of 1%. For small portfolios (less than $100,000), an annual fee ranging from 2% to 3% of the amount of funds managed would not be unusual. These fees generally cover complete management of a client's money, excluding any purchase or sale commissions. The cost of periodic investment advice not provided as part of a subscription service could be based on a fixed-fee schedule or quoted as an hourly charge for consultation.

Some investment advisory services are better than others. More expensive services do not necessarily provide better advice. It is best to study carefully the track record and overall reputation of an investment adviser before purchasing his or her services. Not only should the adviser have a good performance record, but he or she also should be responsive to the investor's personal goals.

Investment Clubs

investment club
a legal partnership through which a group of investors are bound to a specified organizational structure, operating procedures, and purpose, which is typically to earn favorable long-term returns from moderate-risk investments.

Another way to obtain investment advice—and experience—is to join an investment club. This route can be especially useful for those of moderate means who do not want to incur the cost of an investment adviser. An **investment club** is a legal partnership binding a group of investors (partners) to a specified organizational structure, operating procedures, and purpose. The goal of most clubs is to earn favorable long-term returns by making investments in vehicles of moderate risk.

Investment clubs are usually formed by a group of individuals with similar goals who wish to pool their knowledge and money to create a jointly owned and managed portfolio. Certain members are responsible for obtaining and analyzing data on a specific investment vehicle or strategy. At periodic meetings, the members present their findings and recommendations, which are discussed and further analyzed by the membership. The group decides whether the proposed vehicle or strategy should be pursued. Most clubs require members to make scheduled contributions to the club's treasury, thereby providing for periodic increases in the pool of investable funds. Although most clubs concentrate on investments in stocks and bonds, they are occasionally formed to invest in real estate, options, or futures. The *Investing in Action* box on page 97 describes some college-based investment clubs and some key principles of investment clubs.

Membership in an investment club provides an excellent way for the novice investor to learn the key aspects of portfolio construction and investment management, while (one hopes) earning a favorable return on funds. The National Association of Investors Corporation (NAIC), a nonprofit organization of more than 570,000 individual investors and 32,000 investment clubs, publishes a variety of useful materials and also sponsors regional and national meetings. (A free information package on how to start an investment club can be obtained by writing NAIC, P.O. Box 220, Royal Oak, MI 48068, or by calling 248–583–6242.)

CONCEPTS IN REVIEW

3.11 Differentiate between *descriptive information* and *analytical information.* How might one logically assess whether the acquisition of investment information or advice is economically justified?

3.12 What popular financial business periodicals would you use to follow the financial news? General news? Business news?

3.13 Briefly describe the following sources of company information and indicate the types of information they provide.
  a. Stockholders' report
  b. Comparative data sources
  c. *Standard & Poor's Stock Reports*
  d. *Moody's Handbook of Common Stocks*

3.14 List and briefly describe the subscription services and types of information available from:
  a. Standard & Poor's Corporation
  b. Moody's Investor Services
  c. *Value Line Investment Survey*

3.15 Briefly describe the content and source of each of the following types of information.
  a. Prospectuses
  b. Back-office research reports
  c. Investment letters
  d. Price quotations

3.16 What role does electronic and online investment information play for many individual investors? Briefly describe the types of such information currently available.

3.17 Describe the services that professional *investment advisers* perform, how they are regulated, and the cost of investment advice.

3.18 What benefits does an *investment club* offer the small investor? According to the *Investing in Action* box on page 97, why do investment clubs regularly outperform the market and the pros?

INVESTING IN ACTION

Investment Clubs: Coming to a Location Near You

Most college seniors take along resumés when they go to job interviews. How would you like to take a six-figure investment portfolio with you to show potential employers?

That's what some students at Lafayette College in Easton, Pennsylvania, are able to do. Lafayette College enables its students to become involved in investment clubs, where groups of students meet once a month to pool their funds and invest in the stock market. Campus investment clubs have been around for decades, but they grew increasingly popular during the 1990s bull market. You'll find investment clubs at schools as varied as Bryn Mawr, Brigham Young, UCLA, and the California Institute of Technology.

The clubs are usually financed by alumni, and about half the clubs are managed by students who are working on M.B.A. degrees. The Lafayette fund is run by undergraduates who are majoring in a variety of disciplines. "Our club is inclusive and we like to focus on students who may know less about the market," said Donald R. Chambers, a professor of finance at Lafayette and the club's faculty adviser. Recently, 75% of the fund was invested in stocks, 20% in bonds, and 5% in a money market fund. At various times, the portfolio has held stocks in America Online, Coca-Cola, Dell Computer, Dow Chemical, and Ford Motor. The portfolio also produces dividends from stocks and interest from bonds and the money market fund. The students use the money for investment club expenses such as financing an annual day trip to Wall Street. Some of the club's money is donated to the college to help buy library books and to help prospective minority students to visit the campus.

Although the club provides a great social outlet, the members are dead serious. The students do their investing homework—interviewing brokers, reading stock brokerage research, surfing the Web for information about investments, and using software provided in the college's investment course to analyze investments. Students give 15-minute presentations during the meetings, defending their investment ideas to the rest of the club.

The investment club concept has been around for decades—mostly off campus. Thousands of off-campus clubs are affiliated with the National Association of Investors Corporation (NAIC), a Michigan-based nonprofit organization that provides education and training to its thousands of members. One such club, the Beardstown Ladies Investment Club, has even written a best-selling book in which the members, mostly retired women, offered their investment advice. According to the NAIC, investment clubs regularly beat the stock market and professional money managers. The reason: Investment clubs buy stocks for the long term instead of trying to make a quick buck.

Generally, the NAIC has four principles of investing: (1) Invest regularly, without trying to "time" the market. Very few professional money managers can pick the optimal time to get in or get out of the market, and most don't even try. (2) Reinvest dividends. When you receive a dividend from a stock, you can put it in your pocket and spend it on something, or you can reinvest the money for more profits. (3) Invest in growth companies. Over the years, companies with growing sales and profits do better in the stock market, particularly if you have a long-term view. (4) Diversify. Don't put all your eggs in one basket.

http://hepg.aw.com

There are a multitude of information sources. The two sites listed here provide various types of up-to-date specific and general information about personal investing.

www.bloomberg.com

www.forbes.com

Understanding Market Averages and Indexes

LG 6

The investment information we have discussed helps investors understand when the economy is moving up or down and how individual investments have performed. Additionally, this and other information can be used to formulate expectations about future investment performance. It is also important to know whether market behavior is favorable or unfavorable. The ability to interpret various market measures should help you to select and time investment actions.

A widely used way of assessing the behavior of securities markets is to study the performance of market averages and indexes. These measures allow you conveniently to (1) gauge general market conditions, (2) compare your portfolio's performance to that of a large diversified (market) portfolio, and (3) study market cycles, trends, and behaviors in order to forecast future market behavior. Here we discuss key measures of stock and bond market activity; in later chapters we discuss averages and indexes associated with other forms of investments.

Stock Market Averages and Indexes

Stock market averages and indexes are used to measure the general behavior of stock prices over time. Although the terms *average* and *index* tend to be used interchangeably when people discuss market behavior, technically they are different types of measures. **Averages** reflect the arithmetic average price behavior of a representative group of stocks at a given point in time. **Indexes** measure the current price behavior of a representative group of stocks in relation to a base value set at an earlier point in time.

averages
numbers used to measure the general behavior of stock prices by reflecting the arithmetic average price behavior of a representative group of stocks at a given point in time.

indexes
numbers used to measure the general behavior of stock prices by measuring the current price behavior of a representative group of stocks in relation to a base value set at an earlier point in time.

Averages and indexes provide a convenient method of capturing the general mood of the market. They also can be compared at different points in time to assess the relative strength or weakness of the market. Current and recent values of the key averages and indexes are quoted daily in the financial news, in most local newspapers, and on many radio and television news programs. Figure 3.6, a version of which is published daily in the *Wall Street Journal,* provides a summary and statistics on the major stock market averages and indexes. Let's look at the key averages and indexes listed there.

The Dow Jones Averages

Dow Jones & Company, publisher of the *Wall Street Journal,* prepares five stock averages. The most popular is the **Dow Jones Industrial Average (DJIA),** which is made up of 30 stocks selected for total market value and broad public ownership. The group consists of high-quality industrial stocks whose behaviors are believed to reflect overall market activity. The box within Figure 3.7 lists the stocks currently included in the DJIA. Occasionally, a merger, bankruptcy, or extreme lack of activity causes a particular stock to be dropped from the average. In that case, a new stock is added, and the average is readjusted so that it continues to behave in a manner consistent with the immediate past.

Dow Jones Industrial Average (DJIA)
a stock market average made up of 30 high-quality industrial stocks selected for total market value and broad public ownership and believed to reflect overall market activity.

The value of the DJIA is calculated each business day by substituting the *closing share prices* of each of the 30 stocks in the average into the following equation:

FIGURE 3.6
Major Stock Market Averages and Indexes

The "Stock Market Data Bank" summarizes the key indexes and includes statistics showing the change from the previous day, the annual change, and the year-to-date change. (Source: *Wall Street Journal,* April 16, 1998, p. C2.)

STOCK MARKET DATA BANK 4/15/98

MAJOR INDEXES

†12-MO HIGH	†12-MO LOW		DAILY HIGH	DAILY LOW	CLOSE	NET CHG	% CHG	†12-MO CHG	% CHG	FROM 12/31	% CHG
DOW JONES AVERAGES											
9162.27	6658.60	**30 Industrials**	9162.27	9083.55	9162.27	+ 52.07	+ 0.57	+ 2482.40	+ 37.16	+ 1254.02	+ 15.86
3661.90	2467.74	**20 Transportation**	3662.45	3591.01	3661.90	+ 71.82	+ 2.00	+ 1194.16	+ 48.39	+ 405.40	+ 12.45
291.18	209.47	**15 Utilities**	288.40	286.91	287.89	+ 0.06	+ 0.02	+ 74.85	+ 35.13	+ 14.82	+ 5.43
2951.65	2099.72	**65 Composite**	2951.65	2923.98	2951.65	+ 26.52	+ 0.91	+ 851.86	+ 40.57	+ 344.28	+ 13.20
1062.76	716.79	**DJ Global US**	1061.94	1054.82	1061.32	+ 3.63	+ 0.34	+ 340.97	+ 47.33	+ 138.98	+ 15.07
NEW YORK STOCK EXCHANGE											
583.17	399.40	**Composite**	582.77	579.46	582.77	+ 1.46	+ 0.25	+ 181.02	+ 45.06	+ 71.58	+ 14.00
719.90	506.55	**Industrials**	716.11	711.35	716.11	+ 3.09	+ 0.43	+ 206.94	+ 40.64	+ 85.73	+ 13.60
388.87	249.07	**Utilities**	377.77	374.77	376.77	− 0.55	− 0.15	+ 124.18	+ 49.16	+ 41.58	+ 12.40
537.19	365.83	**Transportation**	531.59	525.29	531.58	+ 6.11	+ 1.16	+ 165.75	+ 45.31	+ 65.33	+ 14.01
576.63	358.98	**Finance**	576.78	573.68	575.43	− 1.20	− 0.21	+ 213.65	+ 59.06	+ 79.47	+ 16.02
STANDARD & POOR'S INDEXES											
1122.70	760.37	**500 Index**	1119.90	1112.24	1119.32	+ 3.57	+ 0.32	+ 355.79	+ 46.60	+ 148.89	+ 15.34
1306.33	895.42	**Industrials**	1293.45	1283.86	1292.82	+ 5.90	+ 0.46	+ 393.58	+ 43.77	+ 171.44	+ 15.29
249.41	180.93	**Utilities**	246.00	244.96	245.75	− 0.18	− 0.07	+ 61.53	+ 33.40	+ 9.94	+ 4.22
377.09	248.04	**400 MidCap**	377.26	374.48	377.09	+ 2.61	+ 0.70	+ 125.62	+ 49.95	+ 43.72	+ 13.11
203.97	135.14	**600 SmallCap**	203.97	202.93	203.97	+ 1.04	+ 0.51	+ 66.70	+ 48.59	+ 22.81	+ 12.59
240.50	162.51	**1500 Index**	240.21	238.67	240.11	+ 0.87	+ 0.36	+ 76.76	+ 46.99	+ 31.31	+ 15.00
NASDAQ STOCK MARKET											
1863.26	1203.95	**Composite**	1866.92	1843.03	1863.26	+ 20.23	+ 1.10	+ 652.99	+ 53.95	+ 292.91	+ 18.65
1233.66	798.65	**Nasdaq 100**	1238.21	1213.12	1231.36	+ 18.24	+ 1.50	+ 432.71	+ 54.18	+ 240.56	+ 24.28
1414.11	971.06	**Industrials**	1382.70	1373.66	1382.70	+ 12.18	+ 0.89	+ 385.92	+ 38.72	+ 161.67	+ 13.24
1945.34	1410.15	**Insurance**	1949.62	1926.43	1945.34	+ 10.30	+ 0.53	+ 530.57	+ 37.50	+ 147.39	+ 8.20
2287.67	1354.88	**Banks**	2288.47	2264.93	2287.67	+ 12.90	+ 0.57	+ 928.61	+ 68.33	+ 204.45	+ 9.81
783.78	486.38	**Computer**	787.99	777.69	783.78	+ 13.65	+ 1.77	+ 297.40	+ 61.15	+ 165.12	+ 26.69
392.46	198.06	**Telecommunications**	393.27	390.03	392.31	+ 1.78	+ 0.46	+ 187.67	+ 91.71	+ 85.71	+ 27.95
OTHERS											
747.19	541.20	**Amex Composite**	742.46	739.86	742.46	+ 2.60	+ 0.35	+ 185.95	+ 33.41	+ 57.85	+ 8.45
590.88	398.62	**Russell 1000**	590.18	586.46	589.84	+ 1.94	+ 0.33	+ 188.54	+ 46.98	+ 76.05	+ 14.80
487.12	335.85	**Russell 2000**	487.12	484.81	487.12	+ 2.31	+ 0.48	+ 146.88	+ 43.17	+ 50.10	+ 11.46
622.47	421.23	**Russell 3000**	621.94	618.22	621.64	+ 2.14	+ 0.35	+ 197.62	+ 46.61	+ 78.59	+ 14.47
506.31	365.36	**Value-Line**(geom.)	506.34	504.15	506.31	+ 2.16	+ 0.43	+ 136.35	+ 36.86	+ 51.96	+ 11.44
10683.76	7198.92	**Wilshire 5000**	...	...	10683.76	+ 42.53	+ 0.40	+ 3440.77	+ 47.50	+ 1385.57	+ 14.90

†-Based on comparable trading day in preceding year.

Equation 3.4

$$\text{DJIA} = \frac{\begin{matrix}\text{closing share price} \\ \text{of stock 1}\end{matrix} + \begin{matrix}\text{closing share price} \\ \text{of stock 2}\end{matrix} + \cdots + \begin{matrix}\text{closing share price} \\ \text{of stock 30}\end{matrix}}{\text{DJIA divisor}}$$

The value of the DJIA is merely the sum of the closing share prices of the 30 stocks included in it, divided by a "divisor." For example, on April 15, 1998, the sum of the closing prices of the 30 industrials was 2299.73, which when divided by the divisor of 0.251 resulted in a DJIA value of 9162.27 (i.e., 2299.73 ÷ 0.251). The purpose of the divisor is to adjust for any stock splits, company changes, or other events that have occurred over time, thereby allowing the DJIA to be used to make time-series comparisons.

Because the DJIA results from summing the prices of the 30 stocks, higher-priced stocks tend to affect the index more than lower-priced stocks do. For example, a 5% change in the price of a $50 stock (i.e., $2.50) has less impact on the index than a 5% change in a $100 stock (i.e., $5.00). In spite of this and other criticisms leveled against the DJIA, it remains the most widely cited stock market indicator.

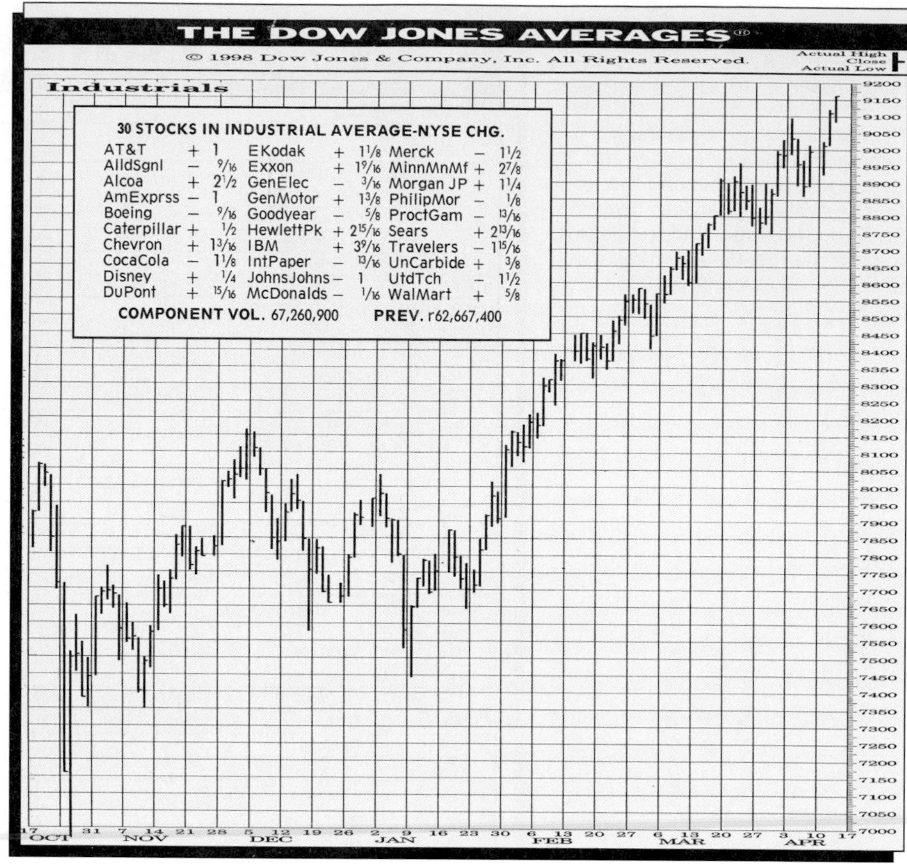

FIGURE 3.7
The DJIA from October 17, 1997, to April 15, 1998

From mid-October through mid-November 1997 the stock market was somewhat bearish. As measured by the DJIA, it moved from over 8000 to below 7000, a decline of over 12%. During the following 90 days, the market was somewhat sideways, with the DJIA fluctuating around 7800. Beginning in mid-February 1998, the ongoing bull market continued its rapid rise with the DJIA breaking through 9100 in mid-April 1998. This represented a 1000-point, or over 12%, gain in 60 days. (Source: *Wall Street Journal,* April 16, 1998, p. C4. Reprinted by permission of the *Wall Street Journal.* © Dow Jones & Company, Inc., 1998. All rights reserved.)

The actual value of the DJIA is meaningful only when compared to earlier values. For example, the DJIA on April 15, 1998, closed at 9162.27. This value is meaningful only when compared to the previous day's closing value of 9110.20. Many people mistakenly believe that one DJIA "point" equals $1 in the value of an average share; actually, one point currently translates into about 0.84 cents in average share value. Figure 3.7 shows the DJIA over the 6-month period October 17, 1997, to April 15, 1998. Beginning in mid-October 1997, the DJIA declined through mid-November 1997, was sideways through mid-February 1998, and then rapidly increased through April 15, 1998.

The four other Dow Jones averages are the transportation, utilities, composite, and global–U.S. The *Dow Jones Transportation Average* is based on 20 stocks, including railroads, airlines, freight forwarders, and mixed transportation companies. The *Dow Jones Utilities Average* is computed using 15 public utility stocks. The *Dow Jones 65 Stocks Composite Average* is made up of the 30 industrials, the 20 transportations, and the 15 utilities. The *Dow Jones Global–U.S. Index* is a market-weighted index—companies with large total market values have the most effect on the index's movement—that reflects 80% of the total market value for nine specific economic sectors. The base value of the index is 100, which is its value on June 30, 1982. Like the DJIA, each of the other Dow Jones averages is calculated to allow for continuity of the average over time. The transportation, utilities, 65 stocks composite, and global–U.S. averages are often cited in the financial news along with the DJIA, as shown in Figure 3.6.

Standard & Poor's Indexes

Standard & Poor's indexes true indexes that measure the current price of a group of stocks relative to a base having an index value of 10.

Standard & Poor's Corporation, another leading financial publisher, publishes six major common stock indexes. One often cited S&P index is the 500 stock composite index. Unlike the Dow Jones averages, **Standard & Poor's indexes** are true indexes. They are calculated each business day by substituting the *closing market value of each stock* (closing price × number of shares outstanding) into the following equation:

Equation 3.5

$$\text{S\&P Index} = \frac{\begin{array}{c}\text{current closing}\\\text{market value}\\\text{of stock 1}\end{array} + \begin{array}{c}\text{current closing}\\\text{market value}\\\text{of stock 2}\end{array} + \cdots + \begin{array}{c}\text{current closing}\\\text{market value}\\\text{of last stock}\end{array}}{\begin{array}{c}\text{base period}\\\text{closing market}\\\text{value of stock 1}\end{array} + \begin{array}{c}\text{base period}\\\text{closing market}\\\text{value of stock 2}\end{array} + \cdots + \begin{array}{c}\text{base period}\\\text{closing market}\\\text{value of last stock}\end{array}} \times 10$$

The value of the S&P index is found by dividing the sum of the market values of all stocks included in the index by the market value of the stocks in the base period and then multiplying the resulting quotient by 10, the base value of the S&P indexes. Most indexes are calculated in a similar fashion; the main differences lie in the stocks included in the index, the base period, and the base value of the index. For example, on April 15, 1998, the ratio of the closing market values of the S&P 500 composite stocks to the 1941–1943 base-period closing market values was 111.932, which when multiplied by the base value of the S&P index of 10 results in an index value of 1119.32 (as shown in Figure 3.6).

Certain of the S&P indexes contain many more shares than the Dow averages do, and all of them are based on *market values* rather than *share prices.* Therefore, many investors feel that the S&P indexes provide a more broad-based and representative measure of general market conditions than the Dow averages do. Although some technical computational problems exist with these indexes, they are widely used—frequently as a basis for estimating the "market return," an important concept that will be introduced in Chapter 4.

Like the Dow averages, the S&P indexes are meaningful only when compared to values in other time periods or the 1941–1943 base-period value of 10. For example, the April 15, 1998, value of the S&P 500 stock composite index of 1119.32 means that the market values of the stocks in the index increased by a factor of 111.93 (1119.32 ÷ 10) since the 1941–1943 period. The April 15, 1998, market value of the stocks in the index was 1.47 times the lowest index value of 760.37 in the preceding 365-day period (1119.32 ÷ 760.37), or an increase of 47%.

The eight major common stock indexes published by Standard & Poor's are as follows: the *industrials index,* made up of the common stock of 400 industrial firms; the *transportation index,* which includes the stock of 20 transportation companies; the *utilities index,* made up of 40 public utility stocks; the *financials index,* which contains 40 financial stocks; the *composite index* (described above), which consists of the total of 500 stocks that make up the industrials, transportation, utilities, and financials indexes; the *midcap index,* made up of the stocks of 400 medium-sized companies; the *smallcap index,* made up of 600 small-sized companies; and the *1500 index,* which includes all stocks in the composite, midcap, and smallcap indexes. The S&P midcap, smallcap, and 1500 indexes are the newest. Their popularity results from strong investor interest in the stocks of medium-sized and small-sized companies. Like the Dow averages, many of the S&P indexes are frequently quoted in the financial news, as shown in Figure 3.6.

Although the Dow Jones averages and S&P indexes tend to behave in a similar fashion over time, their day-to-day magnitude and even direction (up or down) can differ significantly, because the Dows are averages and the S&Ps are indexes.

NYSE, AMEX, and Nasdaq Indexes

Three indexes are based on the daily results of the New York Stock Exchange (NYSE), the American Stock Exchange (AMEX), and the National Association of Securities Dealers Automated Quotation (Nasdaq) system. Each reflects the movement of stocks listed on its exchange. The **NYSE composite index** includes all of the 2,800 or so stocks listed on the "Big Board." The base of 50 reflects the December 31, 1965, value of stocks listed on the NYSE. In addition to the composite index, the NYSE publishes indexes for industrials, utilities, transportation, and finance subgroups. The behavior of the NYSE industrial index is normally similar to that of the DJIA and the S&P 500 indexes.

NYSE composite index
measure of the current price behavior of the stocks listed on the NYSE.

The **AMEX index** reflects the price of all shares traded on the American Stock Exchange, relative to a base of 100 set at August 31, 1973. Although it does not always closely follow the S&P and NYSE indexes, the AMEX index tends to move in the general direction they do.

AMEX index
measure of the current price behavior of the stocks listed on the AMEX.

The **Nasdaq indexes** reflect over-the-counter market activity. They are based on a value of 100 set at February 5, 1971. The most comprehensive of the Nasdaq indexes is the *OTC composite index,* which is calculated using the 6,400 or so domestic common stocks traded on the Nasdaq system. Also important is the *Nasdaq 100,* which includes the top 100 nonfinancial companies listed on Nasdaq. The other five commonly quoted Nasdaq indexes are the *industrials,* the *insurance,* the *banks,* the *computer,* and the *telecommunications indexes.* Although their degrees of responsiveness may vary, the Nasdaq indexes tend to move in the same direction at the same time as the other major indexes.

Nasdaq indexes
measures of current price behavior of securities sold OTC.

Value Line Indexes

Value Line publishes a number of stock indexes constructed by equally weighting the price of each stock included. This is accomplished by considering only the percentage changes in stock prices. This approach eliminates the effects of differing market price and total market value on the relative importance of each stock in the index. The **Value Line composite index** includes the approximately 1,700 stocks in the *Value Line Investment Survey* that are traded on the NYSE, AMEX, and OTC market. The base of 100 reflects the June 30, 1961, stock prices. In addition to its composite index, Value Line publishes indexes for *industrials, rails,* and *utilities.*

Value Line composite index
stock index that reflects the percentage changes in share price of about 1,700 stocks, relative to a base of 100.

Other Averages and Indexes

In addition to the major indexes just described, a number of others are available. The **Wilshire 5000 index,** published by Wilshire Associates, Inc., is reported daily in the *Wall Street Journal.* It represents the total dollar value (in billions of

Wilshire 5000 index
measure of the total dollar value of 5,000 actively traded stocks, including all those on the NYSE and the AMEX in addition to active OTC stocks.

dollars) of 5,000 actively traded stocks, including all those on the NYSE and the AMEX in addition to active OTC stocks. Frank Russell Company, a pension advisory firm, publishes three primary indexes. The *Russell 1000* includes the 1,000 largest companies, the *Russell 2000* includes 2,000 small-sized companies, and the *Russell 3000* includes the 3,000 largest U.S. companies. *Barron's* publishes a *50-Stock Average.* The *New York Times* publishes its own average, which is similar to the Dow Jones averages. Moody's Investor Services prepares market indicators for a variety of groupings of common stock.

In addition, the *Wall Street Journal* publishes a number of global and foreign stock market indexes in Section C under "World Stock Markets." Included are Dow Jones averages for countries in the Americas, Europe, Africa, Asia, and the Pacific that (except for the U.S. averages) are based on a value of 100 set at December 31, 1991. More than 20 foreign stock market indexes and the Morgan Stanley Indexes are also given for major countries, including a *World Index* and the *Europe/Australia/Far East (EAFE) Index.* Each index is calculated in local currencies and based on a value of 100 set at December 31, 1969. Like the purely domestic averages and indexes, these averages and indexes measure the general price behavior of the stocks that are listed and traded in the given market. Useful comparisons of the market averages and indexes over time and across markets are often made to assess both trends and relative strengths of foreign markets throughout the world.

Bond Market Indicators

A number of indicators are available for assessing the general behavior of the bond markets. A "Bond Market Data Bank" that includes a wealth of return and price index data for various types of bonds and various domestic and foreign markets is published daily in the *Wall Street Journal.* However, there are not nearly so many indicators of *overall* bond market behavior as there are of stock market behavior. The key measures of overall U.S. bond market behavior are bond yields, the Dow Jones bond averages, and the New York Stock Exchange bond statistics.

Bond Yields

bond yield
summary measure of the total return an investor would receive on a bond if it were purchased at its current price and held to maturity; reported as an annual rate of return.

A **bond yield** is a summary measure of the total return an investor would receive on a bond if it were purchased at its current price and held to maturity. Bond yields are reported as annual rates of return. For example, a bond with a yield of 8.50% will provide its owner with a total return from periodic interest and capital gain (or loss) that would be equivalent to an 8.50% annual rate of earnings on the amount invested, if the bond were purchased at its current price and held to maturity.

Typically, bond yields are quoted for a group of bonds that are similar with respect to type and quality. For example, *Barron's* quotes the yields on the Dow Jones bond averages of 10 utilities, 10 industrials, and 20 bond composites, as well as for specified grades of corporate bonds. In addition, like the *Wall Street Journal,* it quotes numerous other bond indexes and yields, including those for Treasury and municipal bonds. Similar bond yield data are also available from S&P, Moody's, and the Federal Reserve. Like stock market averages and indexes, bond yield data are especially useful when viewed over time.

Dow Jones Bond Averages

Dow Jones bond averages mathematical averages of the closing prices for groups of utility, industrial, and composite bonds.

The **Dow Jones bond averages** include a utility, an industrial, and a composite bond average. Each average reflects the simple mathematical average of the *closing prices,* rather than yields, for each group of bonds included. The utility bond average is based on the closing prices of 10 utility bonds, the industrial bond average is based on the closing prices of 10 industrial bonds, and the composite bond average is based on the closing prices of 10 utility and 10 industrial bonds.

Like bond price quotations, the bond averages are presented in terms of the percentage of face value at which the bond sells. For example, the April 15, 1998, Dow Jones 20 bond composite average of 105.17 indicated that, on average, bonds were on the day reported selling for 105.17% of their face or maturity value. For a $1,000 bond, the average price of an issue would equal about $1,051.70. The Dow Jones bond averages are published daily in the *Wall Street Journal* and summarized weekly in *Barron's*. Similar bond market indexes, prepared primarily by leading investment bankers such as Merrill Lynch, Lehman Brothers, and Salomon Brothers, are also published daily in the *Wall Street Journal* and summarized weekly in *Barron's*.

NYSE Bond Statistics

The New York Stock Exchange is the dominant organized exchange on which bonds are traded. Thus certain summary statistics on daily bond-trading activity on the NYSE provide useful insight into the behavior of the bond markets in general. These statistics include the number of issues traded; the number that advanced, declined, or remained unchanged; the number of new April 15, 1998, 237 domestic issues were traded; 86 advanced, 87 declined, and 64 remained unchanged. Of the issues traded, 3 achieved a new price high for the year, and 6 fell to new price lows. Total sales volume was $14,410,000. NYSE bond statistics are published daily in the *Wall Street Journal* and summarized weekly in *Barron's*.

CONCEPTS IN REVIEW

3.19 Describe the basic philosophy and use of stock market *averages* and *indexes.* Explain how the behavior of an average or index can be used to classify general market conditions as bull or bear.

3.20 List each of the major averages or indexes prepared by (a) Dow Jones & Company and (b) Standard & Poor's Corporation. Indicate the number and source of the securities used in calculating each average or index.

3.21 Briefly describe the composition and general thrust of each of the following indexes.

a. NYSE composite index
b. AMEX index
c. Nasdaq indexes
d. Value Line composite index
e. Wilshire 5000 index

3.22 Discuss each of the following as they are related to assessing bond market conditions.
  a. Bond yields
  b. Dow Jones bond averages
  c. NYSE bond statistics

http://hepg.aw.com

Whether one is interested in stocks or bonds, the Web makes it easy to keep in touch with the latest indexes. At the CNBC site, follow *The Investor Toolkit* to find both stock and bond market indexes.

www.cnbc.com

Summary

LG 1 **Describe the steps in the investing process, particularly establishing investment goals, and cite fundamental personal tax considerations.** Investing is a process that should be driven by well-developed plans established to achieve specific goals. It involves a logical set of steps, which include meeting investment prerequisites, establishing investment goals, adopting an investment plan, evaluating investment vehicles, selecting suitable investments, constructing a diversified portfolio, and managing the portfolio. Investment goals determine the types of investments made. Common investment goals include accumulating retirement funds, enhancing current income, saving for major expenditures, and sheltering income from taxes.

The tax consequences associated with various investment vehicles and strategies must also be considered. The key dimensions are ordinary income, capital gains and losses, and tax planning.

LG 2 **Discuss investing over the life cycle and investing in different economic environments.** The actual investment vehicles selected are affected by both the investor's stage in the life cycle and economic/market cycles. Younger investors tend to prefer growth-oriented investments that stress capital gains, but as they age they move to higher-quality securities, and as they approach retirement they become even more conservative. The stage of the economy—(1) recovery or expansion, (2) decline or recession, or (3) uncertainty as to direction of movement—both current and expected, also affects investment choice. The investor's response to economic conditions depends on the types of investment vehicles held.

LG 3 **Understand the role, popular types, key features, and suitability of short-term investment vehicles available for meeting liquidity needs.** Investment goals and plans must ensure adequate liquidity. Liquity needs can be met by investing in various short-term securities. These securities can earn interest at a stated rate or on a discount basis. They typically have low risk; the primary risk results from a potential loss in purchasing power. Numerous short-term investment vehicles are available from banks, brokerage firms, and the government. Their suitability depends on the investor's attitude toward availability, safety, liquidity, and yield.

LG 4 **Identify the types and major sources of investment information.** Investment information, descriptive or analytical, includes information about the economy and current events, industries and companies, and alternative investment vehicles, as well as price information and personal investment strategies. It can be obtained from financial journals, general newspapers, institutional news, business periodicals, government publications, special subscription services, stockholders' reports, comparative data sources, brokerage reports, investment letters, price quotations, and electronic and online sources.

LG 5 **Evaluate sources of electronic and online investment information, the use of investment advisers, and the role of investment clubs.** Online data services and databases provide PC-based and Internet access to both current and historical investment information. There are a variety of different types of investment advisers, who charge an annual fee ranging from 0.25% to 3% of the amount being managed and are often regulated by federal and state law. Investment clubs provide individual investors with investment advice and help them gain investing experience.

LG 6 **Explain the characteristics, interpretation, and uses of the commonly cited stock and bond market averages and indexes.** Investors commonly rely on stock market averages and indexes to stay abreast of market behavior. The most often cited are the Dow Jones averages, which include the Dow Jones Industrial Average (DJIA). Also widely followed are the Standard & Poor's indexes, the NYSE composite index, the AMEX index, the Nasdaq indexes, and the Value Line indexes. Numerous other averages and indexes, including a number of global and foreign market indexes, are regularly published in financial publications.

Bond market indicators are most often reported in terms of average bond yields and average prices. The Dow Jones bond averages are among the most popular. A wealth of return and price index data is also available for various types of bonds and various domestic and foreign markets. Both stock and bond market statistics are published daily in the *Wall Street Journal* and summarized weekly in *Barron's*.

Discussion Questions

LG 1 LG 2 Q3.1. Assume that you are 35 years old, are married with two young children, are renting a condo, and have an annual income of $70,000. Use the following questions to guide your preparation of a rough investment plan consistent with these facts.

a. What are your key investment goals?
b. How might personal taxes affect your investment plans? Use current tax rates to assess their impact.
c. How might your stage in the life cycle affect the types of risk you might take?
d. What impact might the current economic environment have on the investment vehicles you choose?
e. Can you realistically expect to achieve the goals you specified in part (a)?

LG 3 Q3.2. What role, if any, will short-term investments play in your portfolio? Why? Complete the following table for the short-term investments listed. Find their yields in a current issue of the *Wall Street Journal,* and explain which, if any, you would include in your investment portfolio.

Savings or Investment Vehicle	Minimum Balance	Yield	Federal Insurance	Method and Ease of Withdrawing Funds
a. Passbook savings account	None		Yes	In person or through teller machines; very easy
b. NOW account				Unlimited check-writing privileges
c. Money market deposit account (MMDA)				
d. Central asset account				
e. U.S. Treasury bill				
f. Certificate of deposit (CD)				

Savings or Investment Vehicle	Minimum Balance	Yield	Federal Insurance	Method and Ease of Withdrawing Funds
g. Commercial paper				
h. Banker's acceptance				
i. Money market mutual fund (MMMF)				
j. Series EE savings bond	Virtually none			

LG 4 LG 5

Q3.3. During 1997, the common stock of an innovative Internet-based bookseller—Amazon.com—was initially sold. Gather appropriate information from relevant sources to assess the following with an eye toward investing in Amazon.com.

a. Economic conditions and the key current events during the immediate past 12 months
b. Information on the status and growth—past and future—of the bookselling industry and specific information on Amazon.com and its major competitors
c. Brokerage reports and analysts' recommendations with respect to Amazon.com
d. A history of the past and recent dividends and price behavior of Amazon.com, which is traded on the Nasdaq National Market
e. A recommendation with regard to the advisability of investing in Amazon.com

LG 5

Q3.4. Survey the market and identify the most popular online services that offer investment information. For each of these services, compile a list of the types of investment information, decision models, advisory services, and order execution services it provides. Also catalog the costs, if any, of obtaining these services. Then compare the services on a benefit–cost basis, and choose and justify the online service you would subscribe to, given your investment plans.

LG 6

Q3.5. Gather and evaluate relevant market averages and indexes over the past 6 months to assess recent stock and bond market conditions. Describe the conditions in each of these markets. Using recent history, coupled with relevant economic and current event data, forecast near-term market conditions. On the basis of your assessment of market conditions, would you recommend investing in stocks, in bonds, or in neither at this point in time? Explain the reasoning underlying your recommendation.

Problems

LG 1 LG 2

P3.1. Sonia Gomez, a 45-year-old widow, wishes to accumulate $250,000 over the next 15 years to supplement her retirement programs that are being funded by her employer and the federal government. She expects to earn an average annual return of about 8% by investing in a low-risk portfolio containing about 20% short-term securities, 30% common stock, and 50% bonds.

Sonia currently has $31,500 that at an 8% annual rate of return will grow to about $100,000 at the end of 15 years (found using time-value techniques that will be described in Chapter 4). Her financial adviser indicated that for every $1,000 Sonia wishes to accumulate at the end of 15 years, she will have to make an annual investment of $36.83. (This amount is also calculated on the basis of an 8% annual rate of return using the time-value techniques that are described in Chapter 4.) Sonia plans to accumulate needed funds by making equal, annual, end-of-year investments over the next 15 years.

a. How much money does Sonia need to accumulate by making equal, annual, end-of-year investments to reach her goal of $250,000?
b. How much must Sonia deposit annually to accumulate at the end of year 15 the sum calculated in part (a)?

LG 1

P3.2. During 1997, the Allens and the Zells both filed joint tax returns. The Allens' taxable income was $130,000, and the Zells had total taxable income of $65,000 for the tax year ended December 31, 1997.
a. Using the federal tax rates given in Table 3.1, calculate the taxes for both the Allens and the Zells.
b. Calculate and compare the ratio of the Allens' to the Zells' taxable income and the ratio of the Allens' to the Zells' taxes. What does this demonstrate about the federal income tax structure?

LG 3

P3.3. A short-term investment vehicle with a $10,000 redemption value and 182 days to maturity can be purchased at its current price of $9,700.
a. Use Equation 3.1 to find the security's bond equivalent yield (BEY).
b. What effect would a drop in the current price to $9,600 have on the BEY calculated in part (a)? Why?

LG 3

P3.4. A Treasury bill (T-bill) with a $10,000 redemption value and 91 days to maturity can currently be purchased for $9,800.
a. Use Equation 3.2 to find the T-bill's bank discount yield (BDY).
b. What effect would the fact that the T-bill has 182 days to maturity have on the BDY calculated in part (a)? Why?

LG 3

P3.5. Chaim Begin is considering the purchase of a Treasury bill that has a bank discount yield (BDY) of 5.74% and has 182 days until it matures to its $10,000 redemption value.
a. Use Equation 3.3 to find the bond equivalent yield (BEY) of this T-bill.
b. What effect would a drop in the BDY to 5.10% have on the BEY calculated in part (a)? Why?

LG 3

P3.6. The O'Sheas are considering a short-term investment that has a redemption value of $50,000 at the end of 120 days. The investment can be purchased at a current price of $48,700.
a. Use Equation 3.1 to find the bond equivalent yield (BEY) on the O'Sheas' proposed investment.
b. Use Equation 3.2 to find the bank discount yield (BDY) on the proposed investment.
c. Use Equation 3.3 to convert the bank discount yield (BDY) found in part (b) to a bond equivalent yield (BEY).
d. Compare the comment on the values for BEY found in parts (a) and (c).

LG 4 LG 5

P3.7. Bill Shaffer estimates that if he does 10 hours of research using data that will cost $75, there is a good chance that he can improve his expected return on a $10,000 one-year investment from 8% to 10%. Bill feels that he must earn at least $10 per hour on the time he devotes to his research.
a. Find the cost of Bill's research.
b. By how much (in dollars) will Bill's return increase as a result of the research?
c. On a strict economic basis, should Bill perform the proposed research?

LG 6

P3.8. Imagine that the Mini-Dow Average (MDA) is based on the closing prices of five stocks. The divisor used in the calculation of the MDA is currently 0.765. The closing prices for each of the five stocks in the MDA today and exactly a year ago, when the divisor was 0.790, are given in the table at the top of the following page.

Stock	Closing Stock Price	
	Today	One Year Ago
Ace Computers	$ 65	$74
Coburn Motor Company	37	34
National Soap & Cosmetics	110	96
Ronto Foods	73	72
Wings Aircraft	96	87

a. Calculate the MDA today with that of a year ago.
b. Compare the values of the MDA calculated in part (a) and describe the apparent market behavior over the last year. Was it a *bull* or a *bear* market?

LG 6

P3.9. The SP-6 index (a fictitious index) is used by many investors to monitor the general behavior of the stock market. It has a base value set equal to 100 at January 1, 1970. The closing market values for each of the six stocks included in the index are given for three dates.

Stock	Closing Market Value of Stock		
	June 30, 1999 (Thousands)	January 1, 1999 (Thousands)	January 1, 1970 (Thousands)
1	$ 430	$ 460	$240
2	1,150	1,120	630
3	980	990	450
4	360	420	150
5	650	700	320
6	290	320	80

a. Calculate the value of the SP-6 index both on January 1, 1999, and on June 30, 1999, using the data presented here.
b. Compare the values of the SP-6 index calculated in part (a) and relate them to the base index value. Would you describe the general market condition during the 6-month period January 1 to June 30, 1999, as a *bull* or a *bear* market?

LG 6

P3.10. Carla Sanchez wishes to develop an average or index that can be used to measure the general behavior of stock prices over time. She has decided to include six closely followed, high-quality stocks in the average or index. She plans to use August 15, 1975, her birthday, as the base and is interested in measuring the value of the average or index on August 15, 1996, and August 15, 1999. She has found the closing prices for each of the six stocks, A through F, at each of the three dates and has calculated a divisor that can be used to adjust for any stock splits, company changes, and so on that have occurred since the base year, which has a divisor equal to 1.00.

Stock	Closing Stock Price		
	August 15, 1999	August 15, 1996	August 15, 1975
A	$46	$40	$50
B	37	36	10
C	20	23	7
D	59	61	26
E	82	70	45
F	32	30	32
Divisor	0.70	0.72	1.00

Note: The number of shares of each stock outstanding has remained unchanged at each of the three dates. Therefore, the closing stock prices will behave identically to the closing market values.

a. Using the data given in the table, calculate the market *average*, using the same methodology used to calculate the Dow averages, at each of the three dates—the fifteenth of August 1975, 1996, and 1999.
b. Using the data given in the table and assuming a base index value of 10 on August 15, 1975, calculate the market *index*, using the same methodology used to calculate the S&P indexes, at each of the three dates.
c. Use your findings in parts (a) and (b) to describe the general market condition—*bull* or *bear*—that existed between August 15, 1996, and August 15, 1999.
d. Calculate the percentage changes in the average and index values between August 15, 1996, and August 15, 1999. Why do they differ?

Case Problem 3.1 *Preparing Carolyn Bowen's Investment Plan*

LG 1 LG 2

Carolyn Bowen, who just turned 55, is a widow currently employed as a receptionist for the Xcon Corporation, where she has worked for the past 20 years. She is in good health, lives alone, and has two grown children. A few months ago, her husband, who was an alcoholic, died of liver disease. Although at one time a highly successful automobile dealer, Carolyn's husband left her with only their home and the proceeds from a $75,000 life insurance policy. After she paid medical and funeral expenses, $60,000 of the life insurance proceeds remained. In addition to the life insurance proceeds, Carolyn has $37,500 in a savings account, which she had secretly built over the past 10 years. Recognizing that she is within 10 years of retirement, Carolyn wishes to use her limited resources to develop an investment program that will allow her to live comfortably once she retires.

Carolyn is quite superstitious. After consulting with a number of psychics and studying her family tree, she feels certain she will not live past 80. She plans to retire at either 62 or 65, whichever will better allow her to meet her long-run financial goals. After talking with a number of knowledgeable individuals—including, of course, the psychics—Carolyn estimates that to live comfortably, she will need $45,000 per year, before taxes, once she retires. This amount will be required annually for each of 18 years if she retires at 62 or for each of 15 years if she retires at 65. As part of her financial plans, Carolyn intends to sell her home at retirement and rent an apartment. She has estimated that she will net $112,500 if she sells the house at 62 and $127,500 if she sells it at 65. Carolyn has no financial dependents and is not concerned about leaving a sizable estate to her heirs.

If Carolyn retires at age 62, she will receive from Social Security and an employer-sponsored pension plan a total of $1,359 per month ($16,308 annually); if she waits until age 65 to retire, her total retirement income will be $1,688 per month ($20,256 annually). For convenience, Carolyn has already decided that to convert all her assets at the time of retirement into a stream of annual income, she will at that time purchase an annuity by paying a single premium. The annuity will have a life just equal to the number of years remaining until her 80th birthday. Because Carolyn is uncertain as to the actual age at which she will retire, she obtained the following interest factors from her insurance agent in order to estimate the annual annuity benefit provided for a given purchase price.

Life of Annuity	Interest Factor
15 years	11.118
18 years	12.659

The yearly annuity benefit can be calculated by dividing the factors into the purchase price. Carolyn plans to place any funds currently available into a savings account paying 6% compounded annually until retirement. She does not expect to be able to save or invest any additional funds between now and retirement. To calculate the future value of her savings, she will need to multiply the amount of money currently available to her by one of the following factors, depending on the retirement age being considered.

Retirement Age	Time to Retirement	Future-Value Interest Factor
62	7 years	1.504
65	10 years	1.791

QUESTIONS

a. Assume that Carolyn places currently available funds in the savings account. Determine the amount of money Carolyn will have available at retirement once she sells her house if she retires at (1) age 62 and (2) age 65.

b. Using the results from question (a) and the interest factors given above, determine the level of annual income that will be provided to Carolyn through purchase of an annuity at (1) age 62 and (2) age 65.

c. With the results found in the preceding questions, determine the total annual retirement income Carolyn will have if she retires at (1) age 62 and (2) age 65.

d. From your findings, do you think Carolyn will be able to achieve her long-run financial goal by retiring at (1) age 62 or (2) age 65? Explain.

e. Evaluate Carolyn's investment plan in terms of her use of a savings account and an annuity rather than some other investment vehicles. Comment on the risk and return characteristics of her plan. What recommendations might you offer Carolyn? Be specific.

Case Problem 3.2 *A Rich Uncle—The Perezes' Good Fortune*

LG 3 LG 4

Angel and Marie Perez own a small pool hall located in southern New Jersey. They enjoy running the business, which they have owned for nearly 3 years. Angel, a retired professional pool shooter, saved for nearly 10 years to buy this business, which he and his wife own free and clear. The income from the pool hall is adequate to allow Angel, Marie, and their two children, Mary (age 10) and José (age 4), to live comfortably. Although lacking formal education beyond the 10th grade, Angel has become an avid reader. He enjoys reading about current events and personal finance, particularly investing. He especially likes *Money*, from which he has gained numerous ideas for better managing their finances. Because of the long hours required to run the business, Angel can devote 3 to 4 hours a day (on the job) to reading.

Recently, Angel and Marie were notified that Marie's uncle had died and left them a portfolio of stocks and bonds having a current market value of $300,000. They were elated to learn of their good fortune but decided it would be best not to change their lifestyle as a result of this inheritance. Instead, they want their newfound wealth to provide for their children's college education as well as their own retirement. They decided that, like their uncle, they would keep these funds invested in stocks and bonds. Angel felt that in view of this, he needed to acquaint himself with the securities currently in the portfolio. He knew that if he were to manage the portfolio himself, he would have to stay abreast of the securities markets as well as the economy in general. He also realized he would need to follow each security in the portfolio and continuously evaluate possible alternative securities that could be substituted as conditions warranted. Because Angel had plenty of time in which to follow the market, he strongly believed that, with proper information, he could manage the portfolio. Given the amount of money involved, Angel was not too concerned with the information costs; rather, he wanted the best information he could get at a reasonable price.

QUESTIONS

a. Explain what role the *Wall Street Journal* and/or *Barron's* might play in meeting Angel's needs. What other general sources of economic and current event information would you recommend to Angel? Explain.

b. How might Angel be able to use the services of Standard & Poor's Corporation, Moody's Investor Services, and the *Value Line Investment Survey* to acquaint himself with securities in the portfolio? Indicate which, if any, of these services you would recommend, and why.

c. Explain to Angel the need to find a good stockbroker and the role the stockbroker could play in providing information and advice.

d. Describe the services and sources of investment advice available to Angel. Would you recommend that he hire an adviser to manage the portfolio? Explain the potential costs and benefits of such an alternative.

e. Give Angel a summary prescription for obtaining information and advice that will help to ensure the preservation and growth of the family's newfound wealth.

Home Page Exercises

http://hepg.aw.com **Keyword: Invest**

One of the most important aspects of making an investment is having high-quality current information. To buy a common stock or a corporate bond without adequate information about both the firm and the financial asset is to set oneself up for possible financial loss. As this chapter indicated, there are a multitude of sources of investment information on economic and current events, industries and companies, and prices of the market as a whole and of individual securities in particular. The World Wide Web allows free and immediate access to information previously available just to professionals, or for a hefty fee. The following Web addresses take you to some locations where financial and qualitative data can be obtained on selected financial assets.

Web Address	*Primary Investment Focus*
www.zacks.com	Selected financial and descriptive information on companies
www.hoovers.com	Selected financial and descriptive information on companies
www.valueline.com	Selected financial and descriptive information on companies
www.pathfinder.com	Access to summaries of feature articles published by *Money, Fortune, Time,* and several other magazines
reality.sgi.com/rchiang_esd/ Invest-Research.html	Links to other Web sites that offer historical information and projections

W3.1. Unless you are a do-it-yourself investor, you will probably seek the advice of a professional adviser at some point. Although professional licensing is not required for financial planners, it is wise to know the qualifications and credentials of anyone you hire as an adviser. One highly regarded qualification is certification as a Certified Financial Planner (CFP). The Web site for the Certified Financial Planning Board provides information on the requirements for obtaining the CFP designation. List the requirements that an adviser must meet to earn CFP certification.

www.cfp-board.org

W3.2. The Dow Jones Industrial Average (DJIA) is probably the most widely followed and quoted stock market measure in the world. To understand its importance, one needs to know the names of the firms that make up this average. From the Web page listed here, obtain the names of the 30 firms in the DJIA. Also, for the date shown in the listing, find out which firm exhibited the largest percentage increase and the largest percentage decrease in its price from the preceding day's close.

cbs.marketwatch.com/data/dbcfiles/dowt.htx

W3.3. The *Value Line Investment Survey* is among the most popular and widely used financial resources. Value Line is probably best known for its Timeliness Ranking, Safety Ranking, and Financial Strength Rating. Go to Value Line's home page to find the definition of the following four terms: (a) timeliness, (b) safety ranking, (c) financial strength rating, and (d) beta.

www.valueline.com/learn.html

CHAPTER 4 Investment Return and Risk

Learning Goals

After studying this chapter, you should be able to:

LG 1 Review the concept of return, its components, its importance, and the forces that affect the investor's level of return.

LG 2 Discuss the time value of money and the calculations involved in finding the future value of various types of cash flows.

LG 3 Explain the concept of present value, the procedures for calculating present values, and the use of present value in determining whether an investment is satisfactory.

LG 4 Describe real, risk-free, and required returns and the computation and application of holding period return, yield (internal rate of return), and growth rates.

LG 5 Discuss the key sources of risk and the two components of risk: diversifiable and nondiversifiable risk.

LG 6 Understand the risk of a single asset, beta and the capital asset pricing model (CAPM), and how they can be used to assess the risk–return characteristics of investment vehicles.

The Coca-Cola Company

When you go shopping for a computer, a sound system, or clothing, you typically go to the store and sample the merchandise. When you invest in the stock of a company, what can you sample? For one thing, you could reach the company's Web site, where you'd find corporate news and financial data. Let's say you did that with Coca-Cola by going to **www.cocacola.com.** You would read that the company's earnings per share rose 19% in 1997 compared to 1996, and you would see that the company was in great financial shape.

What is harder to find out is what risks are associated with owning the stock. For that, you might search in the business press for articles about the company, and you might try to get your hands on investment research. In the case of Coca-Cola, you would find that some analysts wonder whether the company's stock, trading at about $68 per share, is too expensive in relation to 1997 earnings per share of $1.67—more than 40 times earnings. In addition, the company does a lot of business in Asia, where many currencies have recently been devalued.

Chapter 4 explains the concepts of return and risk, which are the essence of any investment decision.

The Concept of Return

LG 1

return
the level of profit from an investment—that is, the reward for investing.

Investors are motivated to invest in a given vehicle by its expected return. The **return** is the level of profit from an investment—that is, the reward for investing. Suppose, for example, you have $1,000 in an insured savings account paying 5% annual interest and a business associate asks you to lend her that much money. If you lend her the money for 1 year, at the end of which she pays you back, your return will depend on the amount of interest you charge. If you make an interest-free loan, your return will be zero. If you charge 5% interest, your return will be $50 (0.05 × $1,000). Because you are already earning a safe 5% on the $1,000, it seems clear that to equal that return you should charge your associate a minimum of 5% interest.

Some investment vehicles guarantee a return; others do not. For example, the $1,000 deposited in an insured savings account at a large bank can be viewed as a certain return. The $1,000 loan to your business associate might be less certain: What is your return if she runs into financial difficulty? Assume that she can repay you only $850. In this case, your return will be minus $150 ($850 − $1,000), or minus 15% ($150 ÷ $1,000). Thus the size of the expected return is one important factor in choosing a suitable investment.

Components of Return

The return on an investment may come from more than one source. The most common source is periodic payments such as dividends or interest. The other source of return is appreciation in value—the gain from selling an investment vehicle for more than its original purchase price. We will call these two sources of return *current income* and *capital gains* (or *capital losses*), respectively.

Current Income

current income
usually cash or near-cash that is periodically received as a result of owning an investment.

Current income may take the form of dividends from stocks, interest received on bonds, rent received from real estate, and so on. To be considered income, it must be received in the form of cash or be readily convertible into cash. For our purposes, **current income** is usually cash or near-cash that is periodically received as a result of owning an investment.

Using the data in Table 4.1, we can calculate the current income from investments A and B—both purchased for $1,000—over a 1-year period of ownership. Investment A would provide current income of $80, investment B $120. On the basis of the current income received over the 1-year period, investment B seems preferable. Of course, the market value of the invested funds may have changed, so it would be premature to declare now which investment is better.

Capital Gains (or Losses)

The second dimension of return is concerned with the change, if any, in the market value of an investment. Investors pay a certain amount for an investment, from which they expect to receive not only current income but also the return of the invested funds sometime in the future. As we noted in Chapter 3, the amount by which the proceeds from the sale of an investment exceed its original purchase price is called a *capital gain*. If an investment is sold for less than its original purchase price, a *capital loss* results.

TABLE 4.1 Profiles of Two Investments

	Investment A	Investment B
Purchase price (beginning of year)	$1,000	$1,000
Cash received		
1st quarter	$ 10	$ 0
2nd quarter	20	0
3rd quarter	20	0
4th quarter	30	120
Total current income (for year)	$ 80	$ 120
Sale price (end of year)	$1,100	$ 960

total return the sum of the current income and the capital gain (or loss) earned on an investment over a specified period of time.

Let's calculate the capital gain or loss of investments A and B in Table 4.1. For investment A, a capital gain of $100 ($1,100 sale price − $1,000 purchase price) is realized over the 1-year period. In the case of investment B, a $40 capital loss ($960 sale price − $1,000 purchase price) results. Combining the capital gain (or loss) with the current income (calculated in the preceding section) gives the **total return** on each investment:

Return	Investment A	Investment B
Current income	$ 80	$120
Capital gain (loss)	100	(40)
Total return	$180	$ 80

In terms of the total return earned on the $1,000 investment over the 1-year period, investment A is superior to investment B.

The use of *percentage returns* is generally preferred to the use of dollar returns because percentages allow direct comparison of different sizes and types of investments. Stated as a percentage of the initial investment, an 18% return ($180 ÷ $1,000) was earned on investment A, whereas B yielded only an 8% return ($80 ÷ $1,000). Although at this point investment A appears preferable, differences in risk as well as certain tax factors might cause some investors to prefer B. (We will see why later in this chapter.)

Why Return Is Important

Return is a key variable in the investment decision: It allows us to compare the actual or expected gains provided by various investments with the levels of return we need to be fairly compensated for the risks involved. For example, you would be satisfied with an investment that earns 12% if you needed it to earn only 10%. You would not be satisfied with a 10% return if you needed a 14% return. Return can be measured in a historical sense, or it can be used to formulate future expectations.

Historical Performance

Although most people recognize that future performance is not guaranteed by past performance, they would agree that past data often provide a meaningful basis for formulating future expectations. A common practice in the investment world is to look closely at the historical performance of a given vehicle when formulating expectations about its future. Because interest rates and other measures of financial return are most often cited on an annual basis, evaluation of past investment returns is typically done on the same basis. Consider the data for a hypothetical investment presented in Table 4.2. Two aspects of these data are important. First, we can determine the average level of return generated by this investment over the past 10 years. Second, we can analyze the trend in this return. As a percentage, the average total return (column 6) over the past 10 years was 8.10%. Looking at the yearly returns, we can see that after the negative return in 1990, 4 years of positive and generally increasing returns occurred before the negative return was repeated in 1995. From 1996 through 1999, positive and increasing returns were again realized.

Expected Return

expected return
the return an investor thinks an investment will earn in the future.

In the final analysis, it's the future that matters when we make investment decisions; **expected return** is a vital measure of performance. It's what you think the investment will earn in the future (in terms of current income and capital gains) that determines what you should be willing to pay for it. To see how, let's return to the data in Table 4.2. Looking at the historical return figures in the table, an investor would note the increasing trend in returns from 1996 through 1999. But to project future returns, we need insights into the investment's prospects. If the trend in returns seems likely to continue, an expected return in the range of 12% to 15% for 2000 or 2001 would seem reasonable. On the other hand, if future prospects seem poor, or if the investment is subject to cycles, an expected return of 8% to 9% may be a more reasonable estimate. Over the past 10 years, the investment's returns have cycled from 1 poor year (1990 and 1995) to 4 years of increasing return (1991–1994 and 1996–1999). We might therefore expect low returns in 2000 to be followed by increasing returns in the 2001–2004 period.

TABLE 4.2 Historical Investment Data for a Hypothetical Investment

		Market Value (Price)			Total Return	
Year	(1) Income	(2) Beginning of Year	(3) End of Year	(4) (3) − (2) Capital Gain	(5) (1) + (4) ($)	(6) (5) ÷ (2) (%)*
1990	$4.00	$100	$ 95	−$ 5.00	−$ 1.00	− 1.00%
1991	3.00	95	99	4.00	7.00	7.37
1992	4.00	99	105	6.00	10.00	10.10
1993	5.00	105	115	10.00	15.00	14.29
1994	5.00	115	125	10.00	15.00	12.00
1995	3.00	125	120	− 5.00	− 2.00	− 1.60
1996	3.00	120	122	2.00	5.00	4.17
1997	4.00	122	130	8.00	12.00	9.84
1998	5.00	130	140	10.00	15.00	11.54
1999	5.00	140	155	15.00	20.00	14.29
Average	$4.10			$ 5.50	$ 9.60	8.10%

*Percent return on beginning-of-year market value of investment.

Level of Return

The level of return achieved or expected from an investment will depend on a variety of factors. The key factors are internal characteristics and external forces.

Internal Characteristics

Certain characteristics of an investment affect its level of return. Examples include the type of investment vehicle, the quality of management, the way the investment is financed, and the customer base of the issuer. For example, the common stock of a large, well-managed, completely equity-financed plastics manufacturer whose major customer is IBM would be expected to provide a level of return different from that of a small, poorly managed, largely debt-financed clothing manufacturer whose customers are small specialty stores. As we will see in later chapters, assessing internal factors and their impact on return is one important step in analyzing potential investments.

External Forces

External forces such as Federal Reserve actions, shortages, war, price controls, and political events may also affect the level of return. None of these are under the control of the issuer of the investment vehicle. Because investment vehicles are affected differently by these forces, it is not unusual to find two vehicles with similar internal characteristics offering significantly different returns. As a result of the same external force, the expected return from one vehicle may increase, whereas that of another decreases. Likewise, the economies of various countries respond to external forces in different ways.

inflation
a period of generally rising prices.

deflation
a period of generally declining prices.

Another external force is the *general level of price changes,* either up—**inflation**—or down—**deflation**. Inflation tends to have a positive impact on certain types of investment vehicles, such as real estate, and a negative impact on others, such as stocks and fixed-income securities. Rising interest rates, which normally accompany increasing rates of inflation, can significantly affect returns. Depending on which actions, if any, the federal government takes to control inflation, its presence can increase, decrease, or have no effect on investment returns. Furthermore, the return on each *type* of investment vehicle exhibits its own unique response to inflation. As the *Investing in Action* box on page 119 demonstrates, moderate deflation positively affects consumers and investors, but greater deflation poses some threat to them.

CONCEPTS IN REVIEW

4.1 Explain what is meant by the *return* on an investment. Differentiate between the two components of return—current income and capital gains (or losses).

4.2 What role do historical performance data play in estimating the expected return from a given investment? Discuss the key factors affecting investment returns—internal characteristics and external forces.

4.3 What are the causes of deflation, according to the *Investing in Action* box on page 119? In your opinion, how likely is the threat of deflation in the near future?

INVESTING IN ACTION

The Threat of Deflation

In many areas of life—college tuition being a notable exception—prices are coming down. The computer you're using today may have cost $1,500, but it is probably cheaper and more powerful than the model you might have purchased 2 years ago. Items ranging from TV sets and household appliances to long-distance phone calls and auto loans also have become less expensive. According to Merrill Lynch, the core consumer price index (CPI), which excludes food and energy prices, declined at an annual rate of 2.2% during the third quarter of 1997, the steepest drop on record.

That's the American way: Competition makes products and services cheaper and better. But *deflation*—an environment in which a dollar buys more goods and services, not fewer—is *not* typically American. The CPI typically measures inflation, not deflation. Most of us have never experienced falling prices. Then why do some analysts now see deflation as a possible threat?

One reason is the global shift to capitalism by once-socialist countries. In capitalist societies, companies that hope to increase market share typically must do so by cutting costs, and a key way to do that is by investing in more efficient production capacity. Increased production in low-wage economies such as China, Latin America, and Eastern Europe wouldn't matter much if each country operated behind closed doors, but the trend is toward free trade.

Thanks to a building binge throughout Asia, continuing economic expansion in the United States, and recovering economies in Europe, production everywhere is running ahead of consumption. Today, for the first time in years, there is worldwide overcapacity in many industries, from semiconductors to autos. The result: The global economy may well be heading into a new era of deflation as supply exceeds demand and prices fall.

But rapid deflation can do enormous damage very quickly. The Great Depression of the 1930s was exactly this sort of deflationary spiral. From 1929 to 1933, prices fell by 10% annually, and companies went under because they couldn't pay bills with meager profits. The banking system was devastated as collateral used to secure loans depreciated, and the stock market went into a deep swoon that was ended only by World War II.

True, such a bleak scenario doesn't exist today. Deflation in the United States is modest, and investors can be winners in such an environment. Stock prices rally when interest rates and raw material prices drop, cutting corporate borrowing and operating costs. If wages remain under control, corporate profits rise, driving stock prices higher. But in a serious deflationary environment, there would be a glut of inventory that has to be sold, driving prices down. This pressure on prices would make profits decline or become losses.

Thus, although moderate deflation is a pleasant environment for consumers, the risk of plunging prices poses some threat to the stock market and the U.S. economy, as it did earlier in this century.

The Time Value of Money*

Imagine that at age 25, you begin making annual cash deposits of $1,000 into a savings account that pays 5% annual interest. After 40 years, at age 65, you will have made deposits totaling $40,000 (40 years × $1,000 per year). Assuming you made no withdrawals, what do you think your account balance will be—$50,000? $75,000? $100,000? The answer is none of the above; your $40,000 will have grown to nearly $121,000! Why? Because the time value of money allows the deposits to earn interest that is compounded over the

*This section presents the fundamental concepts and techniques of time value of money. Those who have already mastered these important materials may wish to skip this discussion and continue at the heading "Determining a Satisfactory Investment" on page 127.

time value of money
the fact that as long as an opportunity exists to earn interest, the value of money is affected by the point in time when the money is expected to be received.

40 years. **Time value of money** refers to the fact that as long as an opportunity exists to earn interest, the value of money is affected by the point in time when the money is expected to be received.

Because opportunities to earn interest on funds are readily available, *the sooner you receive a return on a given investment, the better.* For example, two investments each requiring a $1,000 outlay and each expected to return $100 interest over a 2-year holding period are *not necessarily* equally desirable. Assuming that the base value of each investment remains at $1,000, if the first investment returns $100 at the end of the first year and the second investment returns the $100 at the end of the second year, the first investment is preferable. This is because the $100 interest earned by investment 1 could be *reinvested to earn more interest* while the $100 in interest from investment 2 is still accruing at the end of the first year. Therefore, you should not fail to consider time-value concepts when making investment decisions.

Interest: The Basic Return to Savers

interest
the "rent" paid by a borrower for use of the lender's money.

A savings account at a bank is one of the most basic forms of investment. The saver receives interest in exchange for placing idle funds in an account. **Interest** can be viewed as the "rent" paid by a borrower for use of the lender's money. The saver will experience neither a capital gain nor a capital loss, because the value of the investment (the initial deposit) will change only by the amount of interest earned. For the saver, the interest earned over a given time frame is that period's current income.

Simple Interest

simple interest
interest paid only on the initial deposit for the amount of time it is held.

#yrs * Interest * $

The income paid on such vehicles as certificates of deposit (CDs), bonds, and other forms of investment that pay interest is most often calculated using the **simple interest** method: Interest is paid only on the initial deposit for the amount of time it is held. For example, if you held a $100 initial deposit in an account paying 6% interest for 1½ years, you would earn $9 in interest (1½ × 0.06 × $100) over this period. Had you withdrawn $50 at the end of half a year, the total interest earned over the 1½ years would be $6, because you would earn $3 interest on $100 for the first half-year (½ × 0.06 × $100) and $3 interest on $50 for the next full year (1 × 0.06 × $50).

true rate of interest (or return)
the actual rate of interest earned.

Using the simple interest method, the stated rate of interest is the **true rate of interest (or return)**, which is the actual rate of interest earned. In the foregoing example, the true rate of interest is 6%. Because the interest rate reflects the rate at which current income is earned regardless of the size of the deposit, it is a useful measure of current income.

Compound Interest

compound interest
interest paid not only on the initial deposit but also on any interest accumulated from one period to the next.

Compound interest is paid not only on the initial deposit but also on any interest accumulated from one period to the next. This is the method usually used by savings institutions. When interest is compounded annually over a single year, compound and simple interest calculations provide similar results; in this case, the stated interest rate and the true interest rate are equal. The data in Table 4.3 illustrate compound interest. In this case, the interest earned

TABLE 4.3 Savings Account Balance Data (5% interest compounded annually)

Date	(1) Deposit (Withdrawal)	(2) Beginning Account Balance	(3) 0.05 × (2) Interest for Year	(4) (2) + (3) Ending Account Balance
1/1/98	$1,000	$1,000.00	$50.00	$1,050.00
1/1/99	(300)	750.00	37.50	787.50
1/1/00	1,000	1,787.50	89.38	1,876.88

each year is left on deposit rather than withdrawn. The $50 of interest earned on the $1,000 initial deposit during 1998 becomes part of the beginning (initial) balance on which interest is paid in 1999, and so on. *Note that the simple interest method is used in the compounding process;* that is, interest is paid only on the initial balance held during the given time period.

When compound interest is used, the stated and true interest rates are equal *only* when interest is compounded annually. In general, *the more frequently interest is compounded at a stated rate, the higher the true rate of interest.* The interest calculations for the deposit data in Table 4.3, assuming that interest is compounded semiannually (twice a year), are shown in Table 4.4. The interest for each 6-month period is found by multiplying the beginning (initial) balance for the 6 months by half of the stated 5% interest rate (see column 3 of Table 4.4). We can see that larger returns are associated with more frequent compounding: Compare the end-of-2000 account balance of $1,876.88 calculated in Table 4.3 at 5% compounded annually with the end-of-2000 account balance of $1,879.19 calculated in Table 4.4 at 5% compounded semiannually. Clearly, with semiannual compounding, the true rate of interest is greater than the 5% rate associated with annual compounding. The true rates of interest associated with a 5% stated rate and various compounding frequencies are shown in Table 4.5.

continuous compounding interest calculation in which interest is compounded over the smallest possible interval of time.

Continuous compounding, which is compounding over the smallest possible interval of time, results in the maximum true rate of interest that can be achieved with a given stated rate of interest. The data in Table 4.5 show that the more frequently interest is compounded, the higher the true rate of

TABLE 4.4 Savings Account Balance Data (5% interest compounded semiannually)

Date	(1) Deposit (Withdrawal)	(2) Beginning Account Balance	(3) .05 × 1/2 × (2) Interest for 6 Months	(4) (2) + (3) Ending Account Balance
1/1/98	$1,000	$1,000.00	$25.00	$1,025.00
7/1/98		1,025.00	25.63	1,050.63
1/1/99	(300)	750.63	18.77	769.40
7/1/99		769.40	19.24	788.64
1/1/00	1,000	1,788.64	44.72	1,833.36
7/1/00		1,833.36	45.83	1,879.19

TABLE 4.5 True Rate of Interest for Various Compounding Frequencies (5% stated rate of interest)

Compounding Frequency	True Rate of Interest	Compounding Frequency	True Rate of Interest
Annually	5.000%	Monthly	5.120%
Semiannually	5.063	Weekly	5.125
Quarterly	5.094	Continuously	5.127

interest. Because of the impact that differences in compounding frequencies have on return, you should evaluate the true rate of interest associated with various alternatives before making a deposit.

Future Value: An Extension of Compounding

future value
the amount to which a current deposit will grow over a period of time when it is placed in an account paying compound interest.

Future value is the amount to which a current deposit will grow over a period of time when it is placed in an account paying compound interest. Consider a deposit of $1,000 that is earning 8% (0.08 in decimal form) compounded annually. The following calculation yields the future value of this deposit at the end of 1 year.

Equation 4.1

$$\text{Future value at end of year 1} = \$1{,}000 \times (1 + 0.08) = \underline{\underline{\$1{,}080}}$$

If the money were left on deposit for another year, 8% interest would be paid on the account balance of $1,080. Thus, at the end of the second year, there would be $1,166.40 in the account. This $1,166.40 would represent the beginning-of-year balance of $1,080 plus 8% of the $1,080 ($86.40) in interest. The future value at the end of the second year would be calculated as follows:

Equation 4.2

$$\text{Future value at end of year 2} = \$1{,}080 \times (1 + 0.08) = \underline{\underline{\$1{,}166.40}}$$

INVESTOR FACT

THE POWER OF COMPOUND INTEREST— Retirement may seem to you a long way off. But the power of compound interest is a persuasive argument to start saving now. If you socked away $2,000 per year for the next 8 years only, and you earned 10% per year on that investment, you would have more than $475,000 after 40 years on a $16,000 investment. Yes, you can wait—but it will cost you money in the long run. Time is your biggest investment ally.

To find the future value of the $1,000 at the end of year *n*, the procedure illustrated above would be repeated *n* times. Future values, like present values (discussed later), can be determined either mathematically or by using a financial calculator, a computer, or appropriate financial tables. Here we use tables of future-value interest factors. A complete set of these tables is included in Appendix A, Table A.1; a portion of that table is shown in Table 4.6.

The factors in Table 4.6 represent the amount to which an initial $1 deposit would grow for various combinations of periods (typically years) and interest rates. For example, a dollar deposited in an account paying 8% interest and left there for 2 years would accumulate to $1.166. Using the future-value interest factor for 8% and 2 years (1.166), we can find the future value of an investment (deposit) that can earn 8% over 2 years by *multiplying* the amount invested (or deposited) by the appropriate interest factor. In the case of $1,000 left on deposit for 2 years at 8%, the resulting future value is $1,166 (1.166 × $1,000), which agrees (except for a slight rounding difference) with the value calculated in Equation 4.2.

TABLE 4.6 Future-Value Interest Factors for One Dollar

	Interest Rate					
Period	5%	6%	7%	8%	9%	10%
1	1.050	1.060	1.070	1.080	1.090	1.100
2	1.102	1.124	1.145	1.166	1.188	1.210
3	1.158	1.191	1.225	1.260	1.295	1.331
4	1.216	1.262	1.311	1.360	1.412	1.464
5	1.276	1.338	1.403	1.469	1.539	1.611
6	1.340	1.419	1.501	1.587	1.677	1.772
7	1.407	1.504	1.606	1.714	1.828	1.949
8	1.477	1.594	1.718	1.851	1.993	2.144
9	1.551	1.689	1.838	1.999	2.172	2.358
10	1.629	1.791	1.967	2.159	2.367	2.594

Note: All table values have been rounded to the nearest thousandth; thus calculated values may differ slightly from the table values.

A few points with respect to the table of future-value interest factors should be emphasized.

1. The values in the table represent factors for determining the future value of one dollar at the *end* of the given year.
2. As the interest rate increases for any given year, the future-value interest factor also increases. Thus the higher the interest rate, the greater the future value.
3. Note that for a given interest rate, the future value of a dollar increases with the passage of time.
4. The future-value interest factor is always greater than 1. Only if the interest rate were zero would this factor equal 1, and the future value would therefore equal the initial deposit.

Future Value of an Annuity

annuity
a stream of equal cash flows that occur at equal intervals over time.

ordinary annuity
an annuity for which the cash flows occur at the *end* of each period.

An **annuity** is a stream of equal cash flows that occur at equal intervals over time. Receiving $1,000 per year at the end of each of the next 8 years is an example of an annuity. The cash flows can be *inflows* of returns earned from an investment or *outflows* of funds invested (deposited) to earn future returns. Investors are sometimes interested in finding the future value of an annuity. Their concern is typically with what's called an **ordinary annuity**—one for which the cash flows occur at the *end* of each period. (We will concern ourselves only with this type of annuity.) Here we simplify our calculations by using tables of these factors for an annuity. A complete set of these tables is included in Appendix A, Table A.2. A portion is shown in Table 4.7.

The factors in Table 4.7 represent the amount to which annual end-of-year deposits of $1 would grow for various combinations of periods (years) and interest rates. For example, a dollar deposited at the end of each year for 8 years into an account paying 6% interest would accumulate to $9.897. Using the future-value interest factor for an 8-year annuity earning 6% (9.897), we can find the future value of this cash flow by *multiplying* the annual investment

TABLE 4.7 Future-Value Interest Factors for a One-Dollar Annuity

	Interest Rate					
Period	5%	6%	7%	8%	9%	10%
1	1.000	1.000	1.000	1.000	1.000	1.000
2	2.050	2.060	2.070	2.080	2.090	2.100
3	3.152	3.184	3.215	3.246	3.278	3.310
4	4.310	4.375	4.440	4.506	4.573	4.641
5	5.526	5.637	5.751	5.867	5.985	6.105
6	6.802	6.975	7.153	7.336	7.523	7.716
7	8.142	8.394	8.654	8.923	9.200	9.487
8	9.549	9.897	10.260	10.637	11.028	11.436
9	11.027	11.491	11.978	12.488	13.021	13.579
10	12.578	13.181	13.816	14.487	15.193	15.937

Note: All table values have been rounded to the nearest thousandth; thus calculated values may differ slightly from the table values.

(deposit) by the appropriate interest factor. In the case of $1,000 deposited at the end of each year for 8 years at 6%, the resulting future value is $9,897 (9.897 × $1,000).

Present Value: An Extension of Future Value

present value
the *value today* of a sum to be received at some future date; the inverse of future value.

Present value is the inverse of future value. That is, rather than measuring the value of a present amount at some future date, **present value** expresses the *current value of a future sum.* By applying present-value techniques, we can calculate the *value today* of a sum to be received at some future date.

discount rate
the annual rate of return that could be earned currently on a similar investment; used when finding present value; also called *opportunity cost.*

When determining the present value of a future sum, we are answering the basic question "How much would have to be deposited today into an account paying y% interest in order to equal a specified sum to be received so many years in the future?" The applicable interest rate when we are finding present value is commonly called the **discount rate** (or *opportunity cost*). It represents the annual rate of return that could be earned currently on a similar investment.

The basic present-value calculation is best illustrated using a simple example. Imagine that you are offered an opportunity that will provide you, 1 year from today, with exactly $1,000. If you could earn 8% on similar types of investments, how much is the most you would pay for this opportunity? In other words, what is the present value of $1,000 to be received 1 year from now discounted at 8%? Letting x equal the present value, we can use Equation 4.3 to describe this situation:

Equation 4.3

$$x \times (1 + 0.08) = \$1,000$$

Solving Equation 4.3 for x, we get:

Equation 4.4

$$x = \frac{\$1,000}{(1 + 0.08)} = \underline{\underline{\$925.93}}$$

Thus the present value of $1,000 to be received 1 year from now, discounted at 8%, is $925.93. In other words, $925.93 deposited today into an account paying 8% interest will accumulate to $1,000 in 1 year. To check this conclusion, *multiply* the future-value interest factor for 8% and 1 year, or 1.080 (from Table 4.6), by $925.93. The result is a future value of $1,000 (1.080 × $925.93).

The calculations involved in finding the present value of sums to be received in the distant future are more complex than for a 1-year investment. Here we use tables of present-value interest factors to simplify these calculations. A complete set of these tables is included in Appendix A, Table A.3; a portion of Table A.3 is shown in Table 4.8. The factors in the table represent the present value of $1 associated with various combinations of periods (years) and discount (interest) rates. For example, the present value of $1 to be received 1 year from now discounted at 8% is $0.926. Using this factor (0.926), we can find the present value of $1,000 to be received 1 year from now at an 8% discount rate by *multiplying* it by $1,000. The resulting present value of $926 (0.926 × $1,000) agrees (except for a slight rounding difference) with the value calculated in Equation 4.4.

Another example may help clarify the use of present-value tables. The present value of $500 to be received 7 years from now, discounted at 6%, is calculated as follows:

$$\text{Present value} = 0.665 \times \$500 = \underline{\underline{\$332.50}}$$

The 0.665 represents the present-value interest factor for 7 years discounted at 6%.

A few points with respect to the table of present-value interest factors should be emphasized.

1. The present-value interest factor for a single sum is always less than 1; only if the discount rate were zero would this factor equal 1.
2. The higher the discount rate for a given year, the smaller the present-value interest factor. In other words, the greater your opportunity cost, the less you have to invest today in order to have a given amount in the future.

TABLE 4.8 Present-Value Interest Factors for One Dollar

	Discount (Interest) Rate					
Period	5%	6% ↓	7%	8% ↓	9%	10%
→ 1	.952	.943	.935	.926	.917	.909
2	.907	.890	.873	.857	.842	.826
3	.864	.840	.816	.794	.772	.751
4	.823	.792	.763	.735	.708	.683
5	.784	.747	.713	.681	.650	.621
6	.746	.705	.666	.630	.596	.564
→ 7	.711	.665	.623	.583	.547	.513
8	.677	.627	.582	.540	.502	.467
9	.645	.592	.544	.500	.460	.424
10	.614	.558	.508	.463	.422	.386

Note: All table values have been rounded to the nearest thousandth; thus calculated values may differ slightly from the table values.

3. The further in the future a sum is to be received, the less it is worth at present.
4. At a discount rate of 0%, the present-value interest factor always equals 1; therefore, in such a case the future value of a sum equals its present value.

The Present Value of a Stream of Returns

In the preceding paragraphs, we illustrated the technique for finding the present value of a single sum to be received at some future date. Because the returns from a given investment are likely to be received at various future dates rather than as a single lump sum, we also need to be able to find the present value of a *stream of returns*. A stream of returns can be viewed as a package of single-sum returns; it may be classified as a mixed stream or an annuity. A **mixed stream** of returns is one that exhibits no special pattern. As noted earlier, an *annuity* is a stream of equal periodic returns. Table 4.9 shows the end-of-year returns illustrating each of these types of patterns. To find the present value of each of these streams (measured at the *beginning* of 1999), we must calculate the total of the present values of the individual annual returns. Because shortcuts can be used for an annuity, calculation of the present value of each type of return stream is illustrated separately.

mixed stream
a stream of returns that, unlike an annuity, exhibits no special pattern.

Present Value of a Mixed Stream

To find the present value of the mixed stream of returns given in Table 4.9, we must find and then total the present values of the individual returns. Assuming a 9% discount rate, calculation of the present value of the mixed stream is as shown (using present-value interest factors) in Table 4.10. The resulting present value of $187.77 represents the amount today (*beginning* of 1999) invested at 9% that would provide the same returns as those shown in column 1 of Table 4.10. Once the present value of each return is found, the values can be added, because each is measured at the same point in time—the beginning of 1999.

Present Value of an Annuity

The present value of an annuity can be found in the same way as the present value of a mixed stream. Fortunately, however, there are simpler approaches. Here we use tables of present-value interest factors for annuities to simplify

TABLE 4.9 Mixed and Annuity Return Streams

	Returns	
Year	Mixed Stream	Annuity
1999	$30	$50
2000	40	50
2001	50	50
2002	60	50
2003	70	50

TABLE 4.10 Mixed-Stream Present-Value Calculation

Year	(1) Return	(2) 9% Present-Value Interest Factor	(3) (1) × (2) Present Value
1999	$30	.917	$ 27.51
2000	40	.842	33.68
2001	50	.772	38.60
2002	60	.708	42.48
2003	70	.650	45.50
		Present value of stream	$187.77

Note: Column (1) values are from Table 4.9. Column (2) values are from Table 4.8 for a 9% discount rate and 1 through 5 periods (years).

these calculations. A complete set of these tables is included in Appendix A, Table A.4; a portion of Table A.4 is shown in Table 4.11. The factors in the table represent the present value of a $1 annuity associated with various combinations of periods (years) and discount (interest) rates. For example, the present value of $1 to be received at the end of each year for the next 5 years discounted at 9% is $3.890. Using this factor, we can find the present value of the $50, 5-year annuity (given in Table 4.9) at a 9% discount rate by *multiplying* the annual return by the appropriate interest factor. The resulting present value is $194.50 (3.890 × $50).

Determining a Satisfactory Investment

satisfactory investment
an investment whose present value of benefits (discounted at the appropriate rate) *equals or exceeds* the present value of its costs.

Techniques for assessing the time value of money can be used to determine an acceptable investment. Ignoring risk at this point, a **satisfactory investment** would be one for which the present value of benefits (discounted at the appropriate rate) *equals or exceeds* the present value of its costs. Because the cost (or purchase price) of the investment would be incurred initially (at time zero),

TABLE 4.11 Present-Value Interest Factors for a One-Dollar Annuity

	Discount (Interest) Rate					
Period	5%	6%	7%	8%	9% ↓	10%
1	.952	.943	.935	.926	.917	.909
2	1.859	1.833	1.808	1.783	1.759	1.736
3	2.723	2.673	2.624	2.577	2.531	2.487
4	3.546	3.465	3.387	3.312	3.240	3.170
→ 5	4.329	4.212	4.100	3.993	3.890	3.791
6	5.076	4.917	4.767	4.623	4.486	4.355
7	5.786	5.582	5.389	5.206	5.033	4.868
8	6.463	6.210	5.971	5.747	5.535	5.335
9	7.108	6.802	6.515	6.247	5.995	5.759
10	7.722	7.360	7.024	6.710	6.418	6.145

Note: All table values have been rounded to the nearest thousandth; thus calculated values may differ slightly from the table values.

TABLE 4.12 Present Value Applied to an Investment

Year	(1) Income	(2) 8% Present-Value Interest Factor	(3) (1) × (2) Present Value
1999	$ 90	.926	$ 83.34
2000	100	.857	85.70
2001	110	.794	87.34
2002	120	.735	88.20
2003	100	.681	68.10
2004	100	.630	63.00
2005	1,200	.583	699.60
		Present value of income	$1,175.28

the cost and its present value are viewed as one and the same. The three possible benefit–cost relationships and their interpretations follow:

1. If the present value of the benefits *just equals the cost,* you would earn a rate of return equal to the discount rate.
2. If the present value of benefits *exceeds the cost,* you would earn a rate of return greater than the discount rate.
3. If the present value of benefits *is less than the cost,* you would earn a rate of return less than the discount rate.

It should be clear that *you would prefer only those investments for which the present value of benefits equals or exceeds its cost*—situations 1 and 2. In these cases, the rate of return would be equal to or greater than the discount rate.

The information in Table 4.12 demonstrates the application of present value to investment decision making. Assuming an 8% discount rate, we can see that the present value (at the beginning of 1999) of the income (returns) to be received over the assumed 7-year period (year-end 1999 through year-end 2005) is $1,175.28. If the cost of the investment (beginning of 1999) were any amount less than or equal to the $1,175.28 present value, it would be acceptable. At that cost, a rate of return equal to at least 8% would be earned. At a cost above the $1,175.28 present value, the investment would not be acceptable. At that cost, the rate of return would be less than 8%. Clearly, in this case it would be preferable to find an alternative investment with a present value of benefits that equals or exceeds its cost.

CONCEPTS IN REVIEW

4.4 What is the *time value of money?* Explain why an investor should be able to earn a positive return.

4.5 Define, discuss, and contrast the following terms.

a. Interest
b. Simple interest
c. Compound interest
d. True rate of interest (or return)

4.6 When interest is compounded more frequently than annually at a stated rate, what happens to the *true rate of interest?* Under what condition would the stated and true rates of interest be equal? What is *continuous compounding?*

4.7 Describe, compare, and contrast the concepts of future value and present value. Explain the role of the discount rate (or opportunity cost) in the present-value calculation.

4.8 What is an *annuity?* How can calculation of the future value of an annuity be simplified? What about the present value of an annuity?

4.9 What's a *mixed stream* of returns? Describe the procedure used to find the present value of such a stream.

4.10 What is a *satisfactory investment?* When the present value of benefits exceeds the cost of an investment, what is true of the rate of return earned by the investor relative to the discount rate?

http://hepg.aw.com

The Web even provides sites that will do the time-value-of-money mathematics for you. Click on the *Calculator* link at the following address to do some calculations.

www.datachimp.com

Measuring Return

LG 4

Thus far, we have discussed the concept of return in terms of its two components (current income and capital gains), its importance, and the key factors that affect the level of return (internal characteristics and external forces). These discussions intentionally oversimplified the computations usually involved in determining the historical or expected return. To compare returns from different investment vehicles, we need to apply a consistent measure. Such a measure must somehow incorporate time value of money concepts that explicitly consider differences in the timing of investment income and capital gains (or losses). It must also allow us to place a current value on future benefits. Here we will look at several measures that enable us to assess and compare alternative investment vehicles effectively. First, we will define and consider the relationships among various rates of return.

Real, Risk-Free, and Required Returns

required return
the rate of return an investor must earn on an investment to be fully compensated for its risk.

Rational investors will choose investments that fully compensate them for the risk involved. The greater the risk, the greater the return required by investors. The return that fully compensates for an investment's risk is called the **required return.** To understand better the required returns on which investors focus, it is helpful to consider their makeup. The required return on any investment i consists of three basic components: the real rate of return, an expected inflation premium, and a risk premium, as noted in Equation 4.5.

Equation 4.5

$$\text{Required return on investment } i = \text{real rate of return} + \text{expected inflation premium} + \text{risk premium for investment } i$$

Equation 4.5a

$$r_i = r^* + IP + RP_i$$

real rate of return
the rate of return that could be earned in a perfect world where all outcomes were known and certain—where there was no risk.

The **real rate of return** is the rate of return that could be earned in a perfect world where all outcomes were known and certain—where there was no risk. In such a world, the real rate of return would create an equilibrium between the supply of savings and the demand for funds. The real rate of return changes with changing economic conditions, tastes, and preferences. Historically, it has been relatively stable and in the range of 1% to 2%. For convenience, we'll assume a real rate of return of 2%.

expected inflation premium
the average rate of inflation expected in the future.

risk-free rate
the rate of return that can be earned on a risk-free investment; the sum of the real rate of return and the expected inflation premium.

The **expected inflation premium** represents the average rate of inflation expected in the future. By adding the expected inflation premium to the real rate of return, we get the **risk-free rate**—the rate of return that can be earned on a risk-free investment, most commonly a 3-month U.S. Treasury bill. This rate is shown in Equation 4.6.

Equation 4.6

$$\text{Risk-free rate} = \begin{matrix}\text{real rate}\\ \text{of return}\end{matrix} + \begin{matrix}\text{expected inflation}\\ \text{premium}\end{matrix}$$

Equation 4.6a

$$R_F = r^* + IP$$

To demonstrate, a real rate of return of 2% and an expected inflation premium of 4% would result in a risk-free rate of return of 6%.

risk premium
a return premium that reflects the issue and issuer characteristics associated with a given investment vehicle.

The required return can be found by adding to the risk-free rate a **risk premium,** which varies depending on specific issue and issuer characteristics. *Issue characteristics* are the type of vehicle (stock, bond, etc.), its maturity (2 years, 5 years, infinity, etc.), and its features (voting/nonvoting, callable/noncallable, etc.). *Issuer characteristics* are industry and company factors such as the line of business and financial condition of the issuer. Together, these factors cause investors to require a risk premium above the risk-free rate.

Substituting the risk-free rate, R_F, from Equation 4.6a, into Equation 4.5a for the first two terms to the right of the equal sign ($r^* + IP$), we get Equation 4.7.

Equation 4.7

$$\begin{matrix}\text{Required return}\\ \text{on investment } i\end{matrix} = \begin{matrix}\text{risk-free}\\ \text{rate}\end{matrix} + \begin{matrix}\text{risk premium}\\ \text{for investment } i\end{matrix}$$

Equation 4.7a

$$r_i = R_F + RP_i$$

For example, if the required return on IBM common stock is 11% when the risk-free rate is 6%, investors require a 5% risk premium (11% − 6%) as compensation for the risk associated with common stock (the issue) and IBM (the issuer). Later in this chapter, the relationship between the risk premium and required returns is further developed. Next, we consider the specifics of return measurement.

Holding Period Return

The return to a *saver* is the amount of current income (interest) earned on a given deposit. However, the amount "invested" in a savings account is not subject to change in value, as it is for investments such as stocks, bonds, mutual funds, and real estate. Because we are concerned with a broad range of investment vehicles, most of which have some degree of marketability, we need a measure of return that captures both periodic benefits and changes in value. One such measure is *holding period return.*

holding period
the period of time over which one wishes to measure the return on an investment vehicle.

The **holding period** is the period of time over which one wishes to measure the return on an investment vehicle. When comparing returns, be sure to use holding periods of the same length. For example, comparing the return on a stock over the 6-month period ended December 31, 1998, with the return on a bond over the 1-year holding period ended June 30, 1998, could result in a poor investment decision. To avoid this problem, you should define the holding period and consistently apply or annualize it to create a standard. And when comparing the returns from alternative investment vehicles, you should use similar periods in time.

Understanding Return Components

realized return
current income actually received by an investor during a given period.

paper return
a return that has been achieved but not yet realized by an investor during a given period.

Earlier in this chapter we identified the two components of investment return: current income and capital gains (or losses). The portion of current income received by the investor during the period is a **realized return.** Most but not all current income is realized. (Accrued interest on taxable zero-coupon bonds is treated as current income for tax purposes but is *not* a realized return until the bond is sold or matures.) Capital gains returns, on the other hand, are realized *only* when the investment vehicle is actually sold at the end of the holding period. Until the vehicle is sold, the capital gain is merely a **paper return.** For example, the capital gain return on an investment that increases in market value from $50 to $70 during a year is $20. For that capital gain to be realized, you would have to have sold the investment for $70 at the end of that year. An investor who purchased the same investment but plans to hold it for another 3 years would also have experienced the $20 capital gain return during the year specified, although he or she *would not have realized the gain in terms of cash flow.* However, *despite the fact that the capital gains return may not be realized during the period over which the total return is measured, it must be included in the return calculation.*

A second point to recognize about returns is that *both* the current income and the capital gains component *can* have a negative value. Occasionally, an investment may have negative current income, which means that you may be required to pay out cash to meet certain obligations. This situation is most likely to occur in various types of property investments. For example, an investor may purchase an apartment complex, and the rental income, because of poor occupancy, may be inadequate to meet the payments associated with its operation. In such a case, the investor would have to pay the deficit in operating costs, and such a payment would represent negative current income. A capital loss can occur on *any* investment vehicle: Stocks, bonds, options, futures, mutual funds, real estate, and gold can all decline in market value over a given holding period.

Computing the Holding Period Return (HPR)

holding period return (HPR)
the total return earned from holding an investment for a specified holding period (usually 1 year or less).

The **holding period return** (HPR) is the total return earned from holding an investment for a specified period of time (the holding period). *This measure is customarily used with holding periods of 1 year or less.* (We'll explain why later.) It represents the sum of current income and capital gains (or losses) achieved over the holding period, divided by the beginning investment value. The equation for HPR is

Equation 4.8

$$\text{Holding period return} = \frac{\begin{matrix}\text{current income} \\ \text{during period}\end{matrix} + \begin{matrix}\text{capital gain (or loss)} \\ \text{during period}\end{matrix}}{\text{beginning investment value}}$$

Equation 4.8a

$$\text{HPR} = \frac{C + CG}{V_0}$$

where

Equation 4.9

$$\begin{matrix}\text{Capital gain (or loss)} \\ \text{during period}\end{matrix} = \begin{matrix}\text{ending investment} \\ \text{value}\end{matrix} - \begin{matrix}\text{beginning investment} \\ \text{value}\end{matrix}$$

Equation 4.9a

$$CG = V_n - V_0$$

The HPR equation provides a convenient method for either measuring the total return realized or estimating the total return expected on a given investment. For example, Table 4.13 summarizes the key financial variables for four investment vehicles over the past year. The total current income and capital gain or loss for each during the holding period are given in the lines labeled (1) and (3), respectively. The total return over the year is calculated, as shown in line (4), by adding these two sources of return. Dividing the total return value [line (4)] by the beginning-of-year investment value [line (2)], we find the holding period return, given in line (5). Over the 1-year holding period, the common stock had the highest HPR (12.25%), and the savings account had the lowest (6%). As these calculations show, all we need to find the HPR is beginning- and end-of-period investment values, along with the value of current income received by the investor during the period. Note that if the current income and capital gain (or loss) values in lines (1) and (3) of Table 4.13 had been drawn from a 6-month rather than a 1-year period, the HPR values calculated in line (5) would have been *the same.*

TABLE 4.13 Key Financial Variables for Four Investment Vehicles

	Investment Vehicle			
	Savings Account	Common Stock	Bond	Real Estate
Cash received				
1st quarter	$15	$10	$ 0	$0
2nd quarter	15	10	70	0
3rd quarter	15	10	0	0
4th quarter	15	15	70	0
(1) Total current income	$60	$45	$140	$0
Investment value				
End-of-year	$1,000	$2,200	$ 970	$3,300
(2) Beginning-of-year	1,000	2,000	1,000	3,000
(3) Capital gain (loss)	$ 0	$ 200	($ 30)	$ 300
(4) Total return [(1) + (3)]	$ 60	$ 245	$ 110	$ 300
(5) Holding period return [(4) ÷ (2)]	6.00%	12.25%	11.00%	10.00%

Holding period return can be negative or positive. HPRs can be calculated with Equation 4.8 using either historical data (as in the preceding example) or forecast data.

Using the HPR in Investment Decisions

The holding period return is easy to use in making investment decisions. Because it considers both current income and capital gains relative to the beginning investment value, it tends to overcome any problems that might be associated with comparing investments of different size. If we look only at the *total returns* calculated for each of the four investments in Table 4.13 [line (4)], the real estate investment appears best, because it has the highest total return. However, the real estate investment would require the largest dollar outlay ($3,000). The holding period return offers a *relative comparison*, by dividing the total return by the amount of the investment. Comparing HPRs, we find the investment alternative with the *highest return per invested dollar:* the common stock's HPR of 12.25%. Because the return per invested dollar reflects the efficiency of the investment, the HPR provides a logical method for evaluating and comparing the investment returns.

Yield: The Internal Rate of Return

An alternative way to define a satisfactory investment is in terms of the compounded annual rate of return it earns. Why do we need an alternative to the HPR? Because *HPR fails to consider the time value of money.* Although the holding period return is useful with investments held for 1 year or less, it is generally inappropriate for longer holding periods. Sophisticated investors typically do not use HPR when the time period is greater than 1 year. Instead, they use a present-value-based measure, called **yield** or **internal rate of return,** to determine the compounded annual rate of return earned on investments held for longer than one year. The yield on an investment can also be defined as the discount rate that produces a present value of benefits just equal to its cost.

yield (internal rate of return) the compounded annual rate of return earned by a long-term investment; the discount rate that produces a present value of the investment's benefits that just equals its cost.

Once the yield has been determined, acceptability can be decided. If the yield on an investment is *equal to or greater than the required return,* then the investment is acceptable. An investment with a yield *below the required return* is unacceptable; it fails to compensate the investor adequately for the risk involved.

The yield on an investment providing a single future cash flow is relatively easy to calculate. The yield on an investment providing a stream of future cash flows generally involves more time-consuming calculations. Note that many hand-held financial calculators as well as computer software programs are available for simplifying these calculations.

Yield for a Single Cash Flow

Some investments, such as U.S. savings bonds, stocks paying no dividends, zero-coupon bonds, and gold, are made by paying a fixed amount up front to purchase them. The investor expects them to provide *no periodic income,* but rather a single—and, the investor hopes, large—future cash flow at maturity or when the investment is sold. The yield on investments expected to provide a single future cash flow can be estimated using either future-value or present-value interest factors. Here we will use the present-value interest factors given in Appendix A, Table A.3.

To illustrate the yield calculation, assume you wish to find the yield on an investment costing \$1,000 today and expected to be worth \$1,400 at the end of a 5-year holding period. We can find the yield on this investment by solving for the discount rate that causes the present value of the \$1,400 to be received 5 years from now to equal the initial investment of \$1,000. The first step involves dividing the present value (\$1,000) by the future value (\$1,400), which results in a value of .714. The second step is to find in the table of present-value interest factors the 5-year factor that is closest to .714. Referring to the abbreviated present-value table (see Table 4.8), we find that for 5 years the factor closest to .714 is .713, which occurs at a 7% discount rate. Therefore, the yield on this investment is about 7%. (The precise value found using a financial calculator is 6.96%.) If you require a 6% return, this investment is acceptable (7% expected return ≥ 6% required return).

Yield for a Stream of Income

Investment vehicles such as income-oriented stock, bonds, and income properties typically provide the investor with a *stream of income.* The yield for a stream of income (returns) is generally more difficult to estimate. The most accurate approach is based on searching for the discount rate that produces a present value of income just equal to the cost of the investment.

If we use the investment in Table 4.12 and assume that its cost is \$1,100, we find that the yield must be greater than 8%, because at an 8% discount rate, the present value of income is greater than the cost (\$1,175.28 vs. \$1,100). The present values at 9% and 10% discount rates are calculated in Table 4.14. If we look at the present values of income calculated at the 9% and 10% rates (\$1,117.61 and \$1,063.08, respectively), we see that the yield on the investment must be somewhere between 9% and 10%. At 9% the present value is too high, and at 10% it's too low. Somewhere in between we'll end up with a present value of \$1,100. The discount rate that causes the present value of income to be closer to the \$1,100 cost is 9%, because it is only \$17.61 away from \$1,100. At the 10% rate, the present value of income is \$36.92 away from the \$1,100. (The precise yield value found using a financial calcu-

TABLE 4.14 Yield Calculation for a \$1,100 Investment

Year	(1) Income	(2) 9% Present-Value Interest Factor	(3) (1) × (2) Present Value at 9%	(4) 10% Present-Value Interest Factor	(5) (1) × (4) Present Value at 10%
1999	\$ 90	.917	\$ 82.53	.909	\$ 81.81
2000	100	.842	84.20	.826	82.60
2001	110	.772	84.92	.751	82.61
2002	120	.708	84.96	.683	81.96
2003	100	.650	65.00	.621	62.10
2004	100	.596	59.60	.564	56.40
2005	1,200	.547	656.40	.513	615.60
	Present value of income		\$1,117.61		\$1,063.08

lator is 9.32%.) Thus, if you require an 8% return on the investment, it is clearly acceptable.

Interest on Interest: The Critical Assumption

The critical assumption underlying the use of yield as a return measure is an ability to earn a return equal to the yield on *all income* received from the investment during the holding period. This concept can best be illustrated with a simple example. Suppose you buy a $1,000 U.S. Treasury bond that pays 8% annual interest ($80) over its 20-year maturity. Each year you receive $80, and at maturity the $1,000 in principal is repaid. There is no loss in capital, no default; all payments are made right on time. But if you are unable to *reinvest* the $80 annual interest receipts, you end up earning only 5%—rather than 8%—on this investment.

Figure 4.1 shows the elements of return on this investment to demonstrate the point. If you *don't reinvest* the interest income of $80 per year, you'll end up on the 5% line; you'll have $2,600—the $1,000 principal plus $1,600 interest income ($80/year × 20 years)—at the end of 20 years. (The yield on a single cash flow of $1,000 today that will be worth $2,600 in 20 years is about 5%.) To move to the 8% line, you have to earn 8% on the annual interest receipts. If you do, you'll have $4,661—the $1,000 principal plus the $3,661 future value of the 20-year $80 annuity of interest receipts invested at 8% [$80/year × 45.762 (the 8%, 20-year factor from Table A.2)]—at the end of 20 years. (The yield on a single cash flow of $1,000 today that will be worth $4,661 in 20 years is 8%.) The future value of the investment would be $2,061 greater ($4,661 − $2,600) with interest on interest than without reinvestment of the interest receipts.

reinvestment rate
the rate of return earned on interest or other income received from an investment over the relevant investment horizon.

From this illustration, it should be clear that because you started out with an 8% investment, *you have to earn that same rate of return when reinvesting your income.* The rate of return you start with, in effect, is the required, or minimum, **reinvestment rate**—the rate of return earned on interest or other

FIGURE 4.1
Earning Interest on Interest

If you invested in a $1,000, 20-year bond with an 8% coupon, you would have only $2,600 at the end of 20 years if you *did not reinvest* the $80 annual interest receipts—only about a 5% rate of return. If you *reinvested* the interest at the 8% interest rate, you would have $4,661 at the end of 20 years—an 8% rate of return. To achieve the calculated yield of 8%, you must therefore be able to earn interest on interest at that rate.

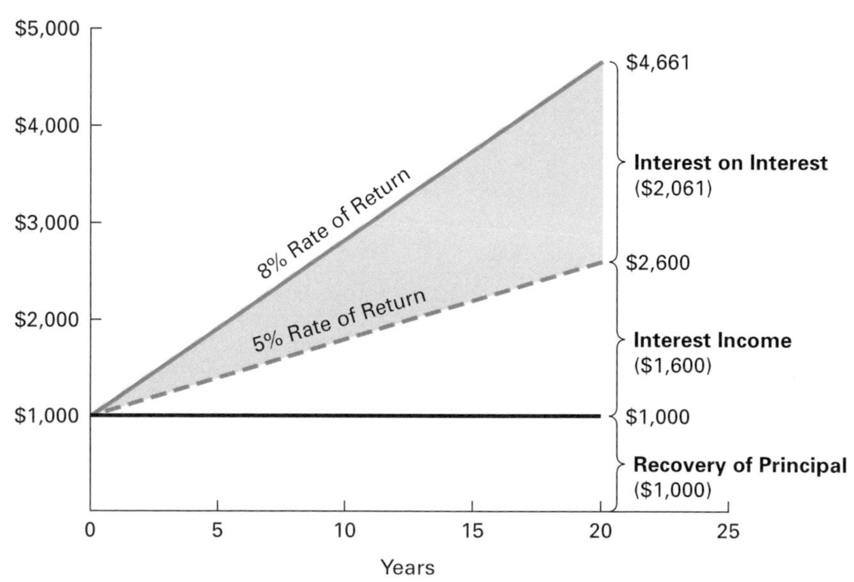

income received over the relevant investment horizon. By putting your current income to work at this rate, you'll earn the rate of return you set out to. If you fail to do so, your return will decline accordingly. Even though a bond was used in this illustration, the same principle applies to any other type of investment vehicle. The earning of interest on interest is what the market refers to as a **fully compounded rate of return.** It's an important concept: You can't start reaping the full potential from your investments until you start earning a fully compounded rate of return on them.

fully compounded rate of return
the rate of return that includes interest earned on interest.

As long as periodic investment income is involved, the reinvestment of that income and earning interest on interest are matters that have to be dealt with. In fact, *interest on interest is a particularly important element of return for investment programs that involve a lot of current income.* In contrast to capital gains, the individual investor has to reinvest the current income. (With capital gains, the investment vehicle itself is automatically doing the reinvesting.) It follows, therefore, that for investment programs that lean toward income-oriented securities, interest on interest—and the continued reinvestment of income—play an important role in the investment success achieved.

Finding Growth Rates

In addition to finding compounded annual rates of return, we frequently need to find the **rate of growth**—the compounded annual rate of change in the value of a stream of income, particularly dividends or earnings. Here we describe a simple technique for estimating growth rates that relies on the use of the present-value interest factors presented in Table A.3. The technique can best be demonstrated with an example.

rate of growth
the compounded annual rate of change in the value of a stream of income.

Imagine that you wish to find the rate of growth for the dividends given in Table 4.15. The year numbers in the table show that 1990 is viewed as the base year (year 0) and that the subsequent years, 1991–1999, are considered years 1 through 9, respectively. Although 10 years of data are presented in Table 4.15, they represent only 9 years of growth, because the value for the earliest year must be viewed as the initial value at time zero. To find the growth rate, we first divide the dividend for the earliest year (1990) by the dividend for the latest year (1999). The resulting quotient is .700 ($2.45 ÷ $3.50); it represents the value of the present-value interest factor for 9 years. To find the compound annual dividend growth rate, we find the discount rate in Table A.3 (Appendix A, page A-8) associated with the factor closest to .700 for 9 years. Looking across year 9 in Table A.3 shows that the factor for 4%

TABLE 4.15 Dividends Per Share

Year	Year Number	Dividends per Share	Year	Year Number	Dividends per Share
1990	0	$2.45	1995	5	$3.15
1991	1	2.60	1996	6	3.20
1992	2	2.80	1997	7	3.20
1993	3	3.00	1998	8	3.40
1994	4	3.20	1999	9	3.50

is .703—very close to the .700 value. Therefore, the growth rate of the dividends in Table 4.15 is approximately 4%. (The precise value found using a financial calculator is 4.04%.) The use of growth rates, which are often an important input to the common stock valuation process, is explored in greater detail in Chapter 7.

CONCEPTS IN REVIEW

4.11 Define the following terms and explain how they are used to find the risk-free rate of return and the required rate of return for a given investment.
   a. *Real rate of return*
   b. *Expected inflation premium*
   c. *Risk premium* for a given investment

4.12 What is meant by the *holding period,* and why it is advisable to use holding periods of equal length when comparing alternative investment vehicles? Define the *holding period return (HPR)* and explain for what length holding periods it is typically used.

4.13 Define *yield* or *internal rate of return* and explain when it is appropriate to use yield rather than the HPR to measure the return on an investment.

4.14 Explain why you must earn 10% on *all* income received from an investment during its holding period in order for its yield actually to equal the 10% value you've calculated.

4.15 Explain how either the present value (of benefits vs. cost) or the yield measure can be used to find a *satisfactory investment.* Given the following data, indicate which, if any, of these investments is acceptable. Explain your findings.

	Investment		
	A	B	C
Cost	$200	$160	$500
Appropriate discount rate	7%	10%	9%
Present value of benefits	—	$150	—
Yield	8%	—	8%

Risk: The Other Side of the Coin

LG 5

risk
the chance that the actual return from an investment may differ from what is expected.

risk–return tradeoff
the relationship between risk and return, in which investments with more risk should provide higher returns, and vice versa.

Thus far, our primary concern in this chapter has been return. However, we cannot consider return without also looking at **risk**, the chance that the actual return from an investment may differ from what is expected. The risk associated with a given investment is directly related to its expected return. In general, the broader the range of possible returns associated with a given investment, the greater its risk, and vice versa. Put another way, riskier investments should provide higher levels of return. Otherwise, what incentive is there for an investor to risk his or her capital? In general, investors attempt to minimize risk for a given level of return or to maximize return for a given level of risk. This relationship between risk and return, called the **risk–return tradeoff,** will be discussed later in the chapter. Here we examine the key sources of risk and its two components.

Sources of Risk

The risk associated with a given investment vehicle may result from a combination of a variety of possible sources. A prudent investor considers how the major sources of risk, discussed below, might affect potential investment vehicles. Of course, as discussed in Chapter 2, *currency exchange risk* should also be considered when investing internationally.

Business Risk

business risk
the degree of uncertainty associated with an investment's earnings and the investment's ability to pay the returns owed investors.

In general, **business risk** is concerned with the degree of uncertainty associated with an investment's earnings and the investment's ability to pay interest, principal, dividends, and any other returns owed investors. For example, a business firm may experience poor earnings and, as a result, fail to pay investors fully. In this case, business owners may receive no return if earnings are not adequate to meet obligations. Debtholders, on the other hand, are likely to receive some—but not necessarily all—of the amount owed them, because of the preferential treatment legally accorded to debt.

Much of the business risk associated with a given investment vehicle is related to its kind of business. For example, the business risk of a public utility common stock differs from that of a high-fashion clothing manufacturer or a parcel of commercial real estate. Generally, investments in similar kinds of firms or properties have similar business risk, although differences in management, costs, and location can cause varying levels of risk.

Financial Risk

financial risk
the degree of uncertainty of payment attributable to the mix of debt and equity used to finance a firm or property; the larger the proportion of debt financing, the greater this risk.

The degree of uncertainty of payment attributable to the mix of debt and equity used to finance a firm or property is **financial risk.** The larger the proportion of debt used to finance a firm or property, the greater its financial risk. Debt financing obligates the firm to make interest payments as well as to repay the debts, thus increasing the firm's risk. These fixed-payment obligations must be met before the distribution of any earnings to the owners of such firms or properties. Inability to meet obligations associated with the use of debt could result in business failure and in losses for bondholders as well as stockholders and owners.

Purchasing Power Risk

purchasing power risk
the chance that changing price levels in the economy (inflation or deflation) will adversely affect investment returns.

The chance that changing price levels within the economy (inflation or deflation) will adversely affect investment returns is **purchasing power risk.** Specifically, this risk is the chance that generally rising prices (inflation) will reduce *purchasing power*—the amount of a given commodity that can be purchased with a dollar. For example, if last year a dollar would buy three candy bars, an increase in the price of a candy bar to 50 cents would mean that only two candy bars could be bought with the same dollar today. In periods of declining price levels (deflation), the purchasing power of the dollar increases.

In general, investments whose values move with general price levels have low purchasing power risk and are most profitable during periods of rising prices. Those that provide fixed returns have high purchasing power risk and are most profitable during periods of declining price levels or low inflation. The returns on real and tangible personal property investments, for example, tend to move with the general price level, whereas returns from deposit accounts and bonds do not.

Interest Rate Risk

interest rate risk
the chance that changes in interest rates will adversely affect a security's value.

Securities are especially affected by interest rate risk; this is particularly true for those securities that offer purchasers a fixed periodic return. **Interest rate risk** is the chance that changes in interest rates will adversely affect a security's value. The interest rate changes themselves result from changes in the general relationship between the supply of and the demand for money. As interest rates change, the prices of many securities fluctuate: They typically decrease with increasing interest rates and increase with decreasing interest rates. As we will see in greater detail in Chapters 8, 9, and 10, the prices of fixed-income securities (bonds and preferred stock) drop when interest rates rise. They thus provide purchasers with the same rate of return that would be available at prevailing rates. The opposite occurs when interest rates fall: The return on a fixed-income security is adjusted downward to a competitive level by an upward adjustment in its market price.

A second, more subtle aspect of interest rate risk is associated with reinvestment of income received from an investment. As noted in our earlier discussion of interest on interest, only if you can earn the initial rate of return on income received from an investment can you achieve a *fully compounded rate of return* equal to the initial rate of return. In other words, if a bond pays 8% annual interest, you must be able to earn 8% on the interest received during the bond's holding period in order to earn a fully compounded 8% rate of return over that period. This same aspect of interest rate risk applies to reinvestment of the proceeds received from a bond or other investment at its maturity or sale.

A final aspect of interest rate risk is related to investing in short-term securities such as T-bills, certificates of deposit, commercial paper, and banker's acceptances (discussed in Chapter 3). Some investors include these securities in their portfolios rather than investing in long-term securities. Investors face the risk that when short-term securities mature, their proceeds may have to be invested in lower-yielding, new short-term securities. By initially making a long-term investment, you can lock in a return for a period of years, rather than face the risk of declines in short-term interest rates. Clearly, when interest rates are declining, the returns from a short-term security investment strategy are adversely affected. On the other hand, interest rate increases have a positive impact on such a strategy. The chance that interest rates will decline is therefore the interest rate risk of a short-term security investment strategy.

Most investment vehicles are subject to interest rate risk. Although fixed-income securities are most directly affected by interest rate movements, they also affect other long-term vehicles such as common stock and property. *Generally, the higher the interest rate, the lower the value, and vice versa.*

Liquidity Risk

liquidity risk
the risk of not being able to liquidate an investment conveniently and at a reasonable price.

The risk of not being able to liquidate an investment conveniently and at a reasonable price is called **liquidity risk.** The liquidity of a given investment vehicle is an important consideration for an investor. In general, investment vehicles traded in *thin markets,* where demand and supply are small, tend to be less liquid than those traded in *broad markets.*

One can generally sell an investment vehicle merely by significantly cutting its price. However, to be liquid, an investment must be easily sold *at a reasonable price*. For example, a security recently purchased for $1,000 would not be viewed as highly liquid if it could be quickly sold only at a greatly reduced price, such as $500. Vehicles such as stocks and bonds of major companies listed on the New York Stock Exchange are generally highly liquid; others, such as an isolated parcel of raw land, are not.

Tax Risk

tax risk
the chance that Congress will make unfavorable changes in tax laws, driving down the after-tax returns and market values of certain investments.

The chance that Congress will make unfavorable changes in tax laws is known as **tax risk.** The greater the chance that such changes will drive down the after-tax returns and market values of certain investments, the greater the tax risk. Undesirable changes in tax laws include elimination of tax exemptions, limitation of deductions, and increases in tax rates. During recent years, Congress has passed numerous changes in tax laws. One of the most significant was the Tax Reform Act of 1986, which contained provisions that reduced the attractiveness of many investment vehicles, particularly real estate and other tax shelters. More recently, the *Taxpayer Relief Act of 1997* reduced the maximum rate applicable to capital gains realized on assets held more than 18 months. Clearly, this change benefits investors and does not represent the unfavorable consequences of tax risk. Though virtually all investments are vulnerable to increases in tax rates, certain tax-advantaged investments, such as municipal and other bonds, real estate, and natural resources, generally have greater tax risk.

Market Risk

market risk
risk of decline in investment returns because of market factors independent of the given security or property investment.

Market risk is the risk that investment returns will decline because of market factors independent of the given security or property investment. Examples include political, economic, and social events, as well as changes in investor tastes and preferences. Market risk actually embodies a number of different risks: purchasing power risk, interest rate risk, and tax risk.

The impact of market factors on investment returns is not uniform; both the degree and the direction of change in return differ among investment vehicles. For example, legislation placing restrictive import quotas on Japanese goods may result in a significant increase in the value (and therefore the return) of domestic automobile and electronics stocks. Essentially, market risk is reflected in the *price volatility* of a security—the more volatile the price of a security, the greater its perceived market risk.

Event Risk

event risk
risk that comes from a largely (or totally) unexpected event that has a significant and usually immediate effect on the underlying value of an investment.

Event risk occurs when something happens to a company or property that has a sudden and substantial impact on its financial condition. Event risk goes beyond business and financial risk. It does not necessarily mean the company or market is doing poorly. Instead, it involves a largely (or totally) unexpected event that has a significant and usually immediate effect on the underlying value of an investment. An example of event risk is the 1997 withdrawal of Redux, the "fen" in the popular fen-phen prescription diet-drug combination, in response to evidence suggesting it may damage heart valves. The stock of American Home Products—the drug's producer—was quickly and negatively affected. Event risk can take many forms and can affect all types of investment vehicles. Fortunately, its impact tends to be isolated in most cases. For instance, the stocks of only a small number of companies were affected by the withdrawal of Redux.

Components of Risk

diversifiable (unsystematic) risk
the portion of an investment's risk that results from uncontrollable or random events and can be eliminated through diversification.

nondiversifiable (systematic) risk
the inescapable portion of an investment's risk attributable to forces that affect all investments and therefore are not unique to any given vehicle.

total risk
the sum of an investment's nondiversifiable risk and diversifiable risk.

The risk of an investment consists of two components: diversifiable and nondiversifiable risk. **Diversifiable risk,** sometimes called **unsystematic risk,** results from uncontrollable or random events, such as labor strikes, lawsuits, and regulatory actions. Such risk affects various investment vehicles differently. It represents the portion of an investment's risk that can be eliminated through diversification. **Nondiversifiable risk,** also called **systematic risk,** is attributed to forces such as war, inflation, and political events that affect all investments and therefore are not unique to a given vehicle. The sum of nondiversifiable risk and diversifiable risk is called **total risk.**

Equation 4.10

$$\text{Total risk} = \text{nondiversifiable risk} + \text{diversifiable risk}$$

Any intelligent investor can virtually eliminate or reduce diversifiable risk by holding a diversified portfolio of securities. Studies have shown that, on average, by carefully selecting 8 to 15 securities for a portfolio, investors can eliminate most diversifiable risk. Therefore, *the only relevant risk is nondiversifiable risk*. Nondiversifiable risk is inescapable. Each security has its own unique level of nondiversifiable risk, which we can measure, as we'll show later. (The concept of diversification and its implications are fully developed in Chapter 16 on portfolio construction.)

CONCEPTS IN REVIEW

4.16 Define *risk.* Explain what we mean by the *risk–return tradeoff.* What happens to the required return as risk increases? Explain.

4.17 Define and briefly discuss each of the following sources of risk.
- a. Business risk
- b. Financial risk
- c. Purchasing power risk
- d. Interest rate risk
- e. Liquidity risk
- f. Tax risk
- g. Market risk
- h. Event risk

4.18 Briefly define and give examples of each of the following components of total risk. Which is the relevant risk, and why?
- a. Diversifiable risk
- b. Nondiversifiable risk

http://hepg.aw.com

Vanguard has a series of education modules that beginning individual investors especially find useful. The modules cover a variety of investment topics. Risk is one of the topics covered, and one of the modules dealing with risk is at the address shown here.

www.vanguard.com/educ/module2/m2_2_2.html

Measuring and Assessing Risk

LG 6

Most people have at some time in their lives asked themselves how risky some anticipated course of action is. In such cases, the answer is usually a subjective judgment, such as "not very" or "quite risky," which may or may not help in decision making. In finance, we are able to quantify the measurement of risk, which improves comparisons between investments and enhances decision making. Here we consider the measurement and assessment of risk: the risk of a single asset; beta, a popular measure of risk; the capital asset pricing model (CAPM), which uses beta to estimate return; and the assessment of risk associated with a potential investment and the steps by which return and risk can be combined in the decision process.

Risk of a Single Asset

The risk or variability of both single assets and portfolios of assets can be measured statistically. Here we focus solely on the risk of single assets. We first consider standard deviation, an absolute measure of risk, and then consider the coefficient of variation, a relative measure of risk.

Standard Deviation: An Absolute Measure of Risk

standard deviation, *s*
a statistic used to measure the dispersion (variation) of returns around an asset's average or expected return.

The most common single indicator of an asset's risk is the **standard deviation, *s***, which measures the dispersion (variation) of returns around an asset's average or expected return. The formula is

Equation 4.11

$$\text{Standard deviation} = \sqrt{\frac{\sum_{i=1}^{n}\left(\text{return for outcome } i - \text{average or expected return}\right)^2}{\text{total number of outcomes} - 1}}$$

Equation 4.11a

$$s = \sqrt{\frac{\sum_{i=1}^{n}(r_i - \bar{r})^2}{n-1}}$$

Consider two competing investments—A and B—described in Table 4.16. Note that both investments earned an average return of 15% over the 6-year period 1994–1999. Reviewing the returns shown for each investment in light

TABLE 4.16 Returns on Investments A and B

	Rate of Return	
Year	Investment A	Investment B
1994	15.6%	8.4%
1995	12.7	12.9
1996	15.3	19.6
1997	16.2	17.5
1998	16.5	10.3
1999	13.7	21.3
Average	15.0%	15.0%

TABLE 4.17 Calculation of Standard Deviations of Returns for Investments A and B

Investment A

Year (i)	(1) Return, r_i	(2) Average Return, $\bar{r}$	(3) (1) − (2) $r_i - \bar{r}$	(4) $(3)^2$ $(r_i - \bar{r})^2$
1994	15.6%	15.0%	.6%	0.36%
1995	12.7	15.0	−2.3	5.29
1996	15.3	15.0	.3	0.09
1997	16.2	15.0	1.2	1.44
1998	16.5	15.0	1.5	2.25
1999	13.7	15.0	−1.3	1.69
				$\sum_{i=1}^{6} (r_i - \bar{r})^2 = 11.12$

$$s_A = \sqrt{\frac{\sum_{i=1}^{6} (r_i - \bar{r})^2}{n-1}} = \sqrt{\frac{11.12}{6-1}} = \sqrt{2.224} = \underline{\underline{1.49\%}}$$

Investment B

Year (i)	(1) Return, r_i	(2) Average Return, $\bar{r}$	(3) (1) − (2) $r_i - \bar{r}$	(4) $(3)^2$ $(r_i - \bar{r})^2$
1994	8.4%	15.0%	−6.6%	43.56%
1995	12.9	15.0	−2.1	4.41
1996	19.6	15.0	4.6	21.16
1997	17.5	15.0	2.5	6.25
1998	10.3	15.0	−4.7	22.09
1999	21.3	15.0	6.3	39.69
				$\sum_{i=1}^{6} (r_i - \bar{r})^2 = 137.16$

$$s_B = \sqrt{\frac{\sum_{i=1}^{6} (r_i - \bar{r})^2}{n-1}} = \sqrt{\frac{137.16}{6-1}} = \sqrt{27.432} = \underline{\underline{5.24\%}}$$

of their 15% averages, we can see that the returns for investment B vary more from this average than the returns for investment A do.

The standard deviation provides a quantitative tool for assessing and comparing investment risk. Table 4.17 demonstrates the calculation of the standard deviations, s_A and s_B, for investments A and B, respectively. Evaluating the calculations, we can see that the standard deviation of 1.49% for the returns on investment A is, as expected, considerably below the standard deviation of 5.24% for investment B. The greater absolute dispersion of investment B's return, reflected in its larger standard deviation, indicates that B is the more risky investment. Of course, these values are absolute measures based on *historical* data. There is no assurance that the risks of these two investments will remain the same in the future.

coefficient of variation, *CV* a statistic used to measure the *relative* dispersion of an asset's returns; it is useful in comparing the risk of assets with differing average or expected returns.

Coefficient of Variation: A Relative Measure of Risk

The **coefficient of variation, *CV*,** is a measure of the *relative* dispersion of an asset's returns.It is useful in comparing the risk of assets with differing average or expected returns. Equation 4.12 gives the formula for the coefficient of variation.

Equation 4.12

$$\text{Coefficient of variation} = \frac{\text{standard deviation}}{\text{average or expected return}}$$

Equation 4.12a

$$CV = \frac{s}{\bar{r}}$$

As for the standard deviation, the higher the coefficient of variation, the greater the risk.

Substituting into Equation 4.12a the standard deviation values (from Table 4.17) and the average returns (from Table 4.16) for investments A and B results in coefficients of variation for A and B of 0.099 (1.49% ÷ 15%) and 0.349 (5.24% ÷ 15%), respectively. Investment B has the higher coefficient of variation and, as expected, has more relative risk than investment A. Because both investments have the same average return, the coefficient of variation in this case has not provided any more information than the standard deviation.

The real utility of the coefficient of variation is in comparing investments that have *different* expected returns. For example, assume you want to select the less risky of two alternative investments—X and Y. The average return, the standard deviation, and the coefficient of variation for each of these investments are as follows:

Statistics	Investment X	Investment Y
(1) Average return	12%	20%
(2) Standard deviation	9%*	10%
(3) Coefficient of variation [(2) ÷ (1)]	0.75	0.50*

* Preferred investment using the given risk measure.

If you compared the investments solely on the basis of their standard deviations, you would prefer investment X, because it has a lower standard deviation than investment Y (9% vs. 10%). However, by comparing the coefficients of variation of the investments, you can see that you would be making a serious error in choosing investment X over investment Y, because the *relative* dispersion, or risk, of the investments, as reflected in the coefficient of variation, is lower for Y than for X (0.50 vs. 0.75). Clearly, using the coefficient of variation to compare investment risk is effective because it also considers the relative size, or average return, of each investment.

Beta: A Popular Measure of Risk

beta
a measure of *nondiversifiable,* or *market, risk* that indicates how the price of a security responds to market forces; found by relating the historical returns for a security to the *market returns,* the historical returns for the market.

During the past 35 years much theoretical work has been done on the measurement of risk and its use in assessing returns. The two key components of this theory are *beta,* which is a measure of risk, and the *capital asset pricing model (CAPM),* which relates the risk measured by beta to the level of required or expected return. First we will look at **beta,** a number that measures *nondiversifiable, or market, risk.* That is, beta indicates how the price of a security responds to market forces. The more responsive the price of a security is to changes in the market, the higher that security's beta. Beta is found by

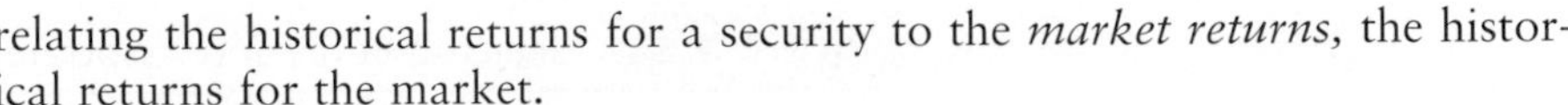

relating the historical returns for a security to the *market returns*, the historical returns for the market.

market return
the average return on all (or a large sample of) stocks, such as those in Standard & Poor's 500 stock composite index.

Market return is the average return for all (or a large sample of) stocks. The average return on all stocks in the Standard & Poor's 500 stock composite index or some other broad stock index is commonly used to measure market return. Although betas for actively traded securities can be obtained from a variety of sources, it is important to understand their derivation, interpretation, and use.

Deriving Beta

The relationship between a security's return and the market return, and its use in deriving beta, can be demonstrated graphically. Figure 4.2 plots the relationship between the returns of two securities—C and D—and the market return. Note that the horizontal (x) axis measures the market returns and the vertical (y) axis measures the individual security's returns. The first step in deriving beta is plotting the coordinates for the market return and the security return at various points in time. Such annual market return and security return coordinates are shown in Figure 4.2 for security D for the years 1992 through 1999 (the years are noted in parentheses). For example, in 1999 security D's return was 20% when the market return was 10%. By use of statistical techniques, the "characteristic line" that best explains the relationship between security-return and market-return coordinates is fit to the data points. *The slope of this line is beta.* The beta for security C is about 0.80, and for security D it is about 1.30. Security D's *steeper characteristic line slope*

FIGURE 4.2
Graphical Derivation of Beta for Securities C and D

Betas can be derived graphically by plotting the coordinates for the market return and security return at various points in time and using statistical techniques to fit the "characteristic line" to the data points. The slope of the characteristic line is beta. For securities C and D, beta is found to be 0.80 and 1.30, respectively.

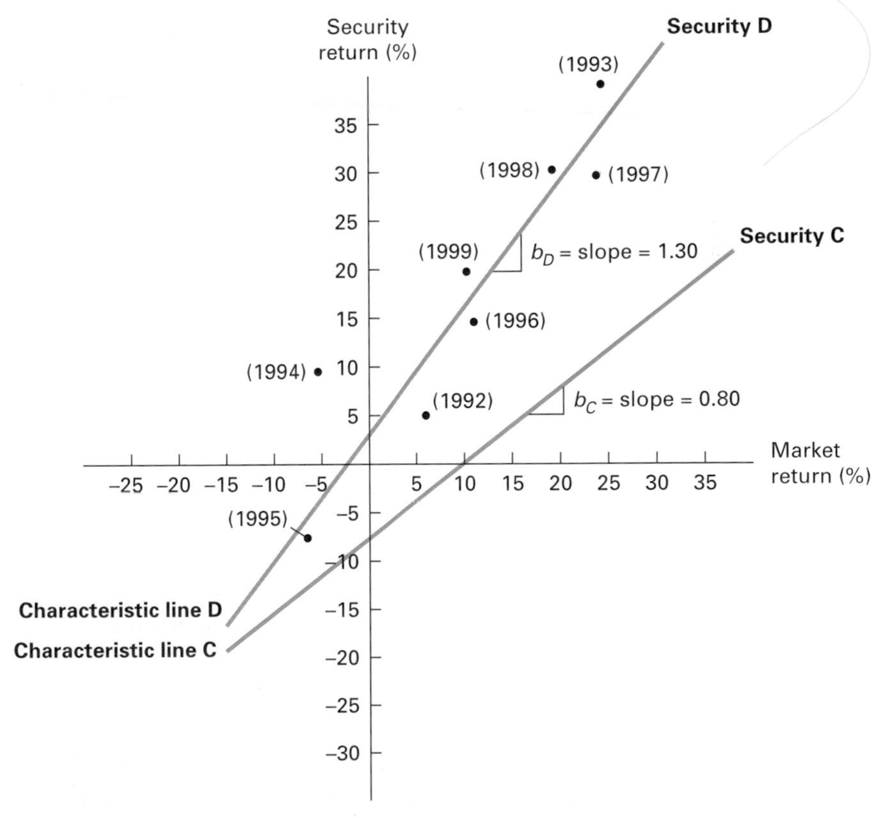

TABLE 4.18 Selected Betas and Associated Interpretations

Beta	Comment	Interpretation*
2.00	Move in same direction as the market	Twice as responsive as the market
1.00		Same response or risk as the market
0.50		Only half as responsive as the market
0		Unaffected by market movement
−0.50	Move in opposite direction from the market	Only half as responsive as the market
−1.00		Same response or risk as the market
−2.00		Twice as responsive as the market

*A stock that is twice as responsive as the market will experience a 2% change in its return for each 1% change in the return of the market portfolio. The return of a stock that is half as responsive as the market will change by ½ of 1% for each 1% change in the return of the market portfolio.

indicates that its return is more responsive to changing market returns: It has a higher beta and therefore is more risky.

Interpreting Beta

The beta for the overall market is considered to be 1.00. All other betas are viewed in relation to this value. Table 4.18 shows some selected beta values and their associated interpretations. As you can see, betas can be positive or negative, though nearly all betas are positive. The positive or negative sign preceding the beta number merely indicates whether the stock's return changes in the *same direction as the general market* (positive beta) or in the *opposite direction* (negative beta). Most stocks have betas that fall between 0.50 and 1.75. Listed here, for illustration purposes, are the actual betas for some popular stocks, as reported by *Value Line* on April 17, 1998:

Stock	Beta	Stock	Beta
American Greetings	1.00	B. F. Goodrich	1.05
Atlantic Richfield	0.70	Hawaiian Electric	0.70
Bank of Boston	1.25	Hewlett-Packard	1.15
Briggs & Stratton	0.85	LSI Logic	1.70
Cincinnati Bell	0.90	Maytag	1.15
Compaq Computer	1.55	Microsoft	1.10
Disney	0.95	Quaker Oats	0.70
Dow Chemical	0.95	Southwestern Energy	0.75
Ford Motor	1.00	Timberland	1.35
General Electric	1.20	Xerox	1.10

INVESTOR FACT

MUTUAL FUNDS HAVE BETAS TOO—Mutual funds consider beta a big selling point. For example, Pegasus Intrinsic Value Fund has a beta of 0.45. In October 1997, when the S&P 500 stock composite index was down 3.4%, the fund dropped just 1.6%. The next month, when the S&P 500 rose 4.2%, Pegasus Intrinsic Value rose 1.3%. "We're not so flashy," says Chris Gassen, the fund's portfolio manager, in explaining the fund's response to changes in the market. "But that is the performance our investors are looking for over time."

Many large brokerage firms, as well as subscription services like *Value Line*, publish betas for a broad range of securities. The ready availability of security betas has enhanced their use in assessing investment risks. *In general, the higher the beta, the riskier the security.* The importance of beta in planning and building portfolios of securities will be discussed in greater detail in Chapter 16.

Using Beta

Individual investors will find beta useful in assessing market risk and understanding the impact the market can have on the return expected from a share of stock. Beta reveals how a security responds to market forces. For example, if the market is expected to experience a 10% *increase* in its rate of return over the next period, we would expect a stock with a beta of 1.50 to experience an *increase* in return of approximately 15% (1.50 × 10%) over the same period. Because the beta of this particular stock is greater than 1.00, it is more volatile than the market as a whole.

For stocks that have positive betas, increases in market returns result in increases in security returns. Unfortunately, decreases in market returns are likewise translated into decreasing security returns—and this is where the risk lies. In the preceding example, if the market is expected to experience a 10% *decrease,* then a stock with a beta of 1.50 should experience a 15% *decrease* in its return. Because the stock has a beta of greater than 1.00, it is more responsive than the market, either up or down.

Stocks that have betas less than 1.00 are, of course, less responsive to changing returns in the market. They are therefore considered less risky. For example, a stock with a beta of 0.50 will experience an increase or decrease in its return of about half that in the market as a whole. Thus, if the market went down by 8%, such a stock would probably experience only about a 4% (0.50 × 8%) decline.

Here are some important points to remember about beta:

1. Beta measures the nondiversifiable, or market, risk of a security.
2. The beta for the market is 1.00.
3. Stocks may have positive or negative betas; nearly all are positive.
4. Stocks with betas greater than 1.00 are more responsive to changes in market return—and therefore more risky—than the market. Stocks with betas less than 1.00 are less risky than the market.
5. Because of its greater risk, the higher a stock's beta, the greater should be its level of expected return, and vice versa.

The CAPM: Using Beta to Estimate Return

capital asset pricing model (CAPM) model that uses beta, the risk-free rate, and the market return to help investors define the required return on an investment; it formally links the notions of risk and return.

About 35 years ago, finance professors William F. Sharpe and John Lintner developed a model that uses beta to link formally the notions of risk and return. Called the **capital asset pricing model (CAPM),** it was developed to explain the behavior of security prices and to provide a mechanism whereby investors can assess the impact of a proposed security investment on their portfolio's risk and return. We can use the CAPM to understand the basic risk–return tradeoffs involved in various types of investment decisions. The CAPM can be viewed both as an equation and as a graph.

The Equation

With beta, b, as the measure of nondiversifiable risk, the capital asset pricing model defines the required rate of return on an investment as follows:

Equation 4.13

$$\text{Required return on investment } i = \text{risk-free rate} + \left[\text{beta for investment } i \times \left(\text{market return} - \text{risk-free rate}\right)\right]$$

Equation 4.13a

$$r_i = R_F + [b_i \times (r_m - R_F)]$$

where

r_i = the required return on investment *i*, given its risk as measured by beta

R_F = the risk-free rate of return; the return that can be earned on a risk-free investment

b_i = beta coefficient, or index of nondiversifiable risk, for investment *i*

r_m = the market return; the average return on all securities (typically measured by the average return on all securities in the Standard & Poor's 500 stock composite index or some other broad stock market index)

The equation shows that *as beta increases, the required return for a given investment increases.*

Application of the CAPM can be demonstrated with the following example. Assume you are considering security Z with a beta (b_Z) of 1.25 at a time when the risk-free rate (R_F) is 6% and the market return (r_m) is 10%. Substituting these data into the CAPM equation, Equation 4.13a, we get:

$$r_z = 6\% + [1.25 \times (10\% - 6\%)] = 6\% + [1.25 \times 4\%]$$
$$= 6\% + 5\% = \underline{\underline{11\%}}$$

You should therefore expect—indeed, require—an 11% return on this investment as compensation for the risk you have to assume, given the security's beta of 1.25. If the beta were lower, say 1.00, the required return would be lower:

$$r_z = 6\% + [1.00 \times (10\% - 6\%)] = 6\% + 4\% = \underline{\underline{10\%}}$$

If the beta were higher, say 1.50, the required return would be higher:

$$r_z = 6\% + [1.50 \times (10\% - 6\%)] = 6\% + 6\% = \underline{\underline{12\%}}$$

Clearly, the CAPM reflects the positive mathematical relationship between risk and return, because the higher the risk (beta), the higher the required return.

The Graph: The Security Market Line (SML)

security market line (SML)
the graphical depiction of the capital asset pricing model; reflects the investor's required return for each level of nondiversifiable risk, measured by beta.

When the capital asset pricing model is depicted graphically, it is called the **security market line (SML)**. Plotting the CAPM, we would find that the SML is, in fact, a straight line. For each level of nondiversifiable risk (beta), the SML, like the CAPM, reflects the required return the investor should earn in the marketplace.

The CAPM at a given point in time can be plotted by simply calculating the required return for a variety of betas. Of course, at the given point in time, the risk-free rate and the market return would be constant. For example, as we saw earlier, using a 6% risk-free rate and a 10% market return, the required return is 11% when the beta is 1.25. Increase the beta to 2.00, and the required return equals 14% (6% + [2.00 × (10% − 6%)]). Similarly, we can find the required return for a number of betas and end up with the following combinations of risk (beta) and required return:

Risk (beta)	Required Return (percent)
0.0	6
0.5	8
1.0	10
1.5	12
2.0	14
2.5	16

Plotting these values on a graph (with beta on the horizontal axis and required returns on the vertical axis) would yield a straight line like the one in Figure 4.3. It is clear from the SML that as risk (beta) increases, so does the required return, and vice versa.

INVESTOR FACT

NO FREE LUNCH—For the decade ended December 31, 1997, the U.S. stock market, as measured by the Standard & Poor's 500 stock composite index, produced an average annual return of 18.05%, excluding dividends. In contrast, the U.S. taxable bond market produced an average annual return of 8.64%. Because bonds are considered a more conservative investment than stocks, the difference in performance is a good demonstration of the risk–return tradeoff.

Assessing Risk

Techniques for quantifying the risk of a given investment vehicle will, however, be of little use if you are unaware of your feelings toward risk. Investors must somehow relate the risk perceived in a given vehicle not only to the expected return but also to their own dispositions toward risk. The individual investor typically tends to seek answers to these questions: "Is the amount of perceived risk worth taking to get the expected return?" "Can I get a higher return for the same level of risk or a lower risk for the same level of return?" A look at the general risk–return characteristics of alternative investment vehicles and the question of an acceptable level of risk will help shed light on the nature of risk evaluations.

FIGURE 4.3
The Security Market Line (SML)

The security market line clearly depicts the tradeoff between risk and return. At a beta of 0, the required return is the risk-free rate of 6%; at a beta of 1.0, the required return is the market return of 10%. Given these data, the required return on an investment with a beta of 1.25 is 11%.

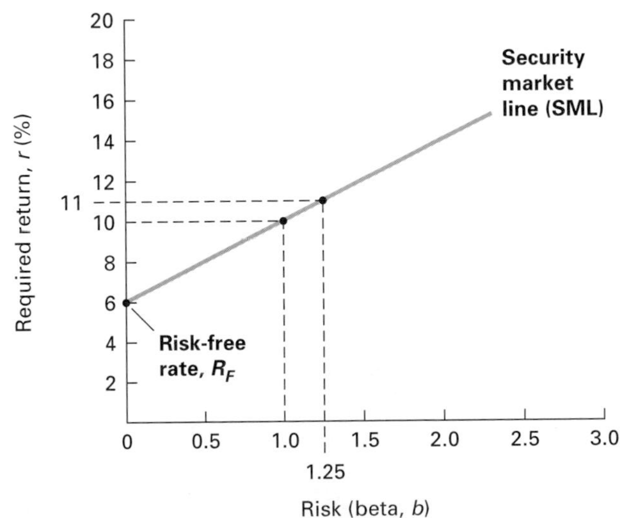

Risk–Return Characteristics of Alternative Investment Vehicles

A wide variety of risk–return behaviors are associated with each type of investment vehicle. Some common stocks offer low returns and low risk; others offer high returns and high risk. In general, though, the risk–return characteristics of the major investment vehicles can be depicted as shown in Figure 4.4. Of course, a broad range of risk–return behaviors exists for specific investments of each type. In other words, once the appropriate type of vehicle has been selected, the investor must still decide which specific security or property to acquire.

An Acceptable Level of Risk

risk-indifferent
describes an investor who does not require a change in return as compensation for greater risk.

risk-averse
describes an investor who requires greater return in exchange for greater risk.

risk-seeking
describes an investor who will accept a lower return in exchange for greater risk.

Because of differing investor preferences, it is impossible to specify a general acceptable level of risk. The three basic risk preference behaviors (risk-indifferent, risk-averse, and risk-seeking) are depicted graphically in Figure 4.5. As risk goes from x_1 to x_2 on the graph, the required return does not change for the **risk-indifferent** investor: In essence, no change in return would be required as compensation for the increase in risk. For the **risk-averse** investor, the required return increases for an increase in risk. Because they shy away from risk, these investors require higher expected returns to compensate them for taking greater risk. For the **risk-seeking** investor, the required return decreases for an increase in risk. Theoretically, because they enjoy risk, these investors are willing to give up some return to take more risk. *Most investors are risk-averse: For a given increase in risk, they require an increase in return.* Note that the security market line (SML) in Figure 4.3 on page 149 clearly depicts the risk-averse behavior of investors who require increasing returns, r, for increased levels of nondiversifiable risk as measured by beta, b. This risk-averse behavior is also depicted in Figure 4.4.

Of course, the amount of return required by each investor for a given increase in risk differs depending on the investor's degree of risk aversion (reflected in the slope of the line). Investors generally tend to be conservative rather than aggressive when accepting risk. Of course, the more aggressive an investor you are (the farther to the right you operate on the risk-averse line),

FIGURE 4.4
Risk–Return Tradeoffs for Various Investment Vehicles

A risk–return tradeoff exists such that for a higher risk one expects a higher return, and vice versa. Low-risk–low-return investment vehicles include U.S. government securities and savings accounts. High-risk–high-return vehicles include real estate and other tangible investments, options, and futures.

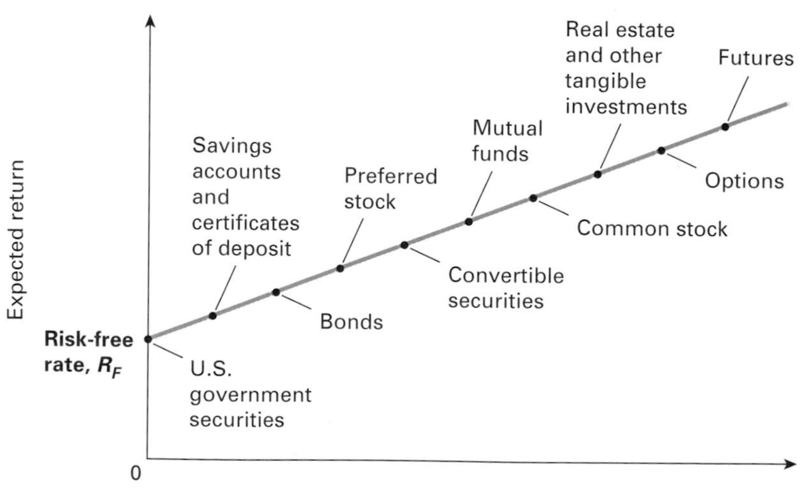

FIGURE 4.5
Risk Preferences

The risk-indifferent investor requires no change in return for a given increase in risk. The risk-averse investor requires an increase in return for a given risk increase. The risk-seeking investor gives up some return for more risk. The majority of investors are risk-averse.

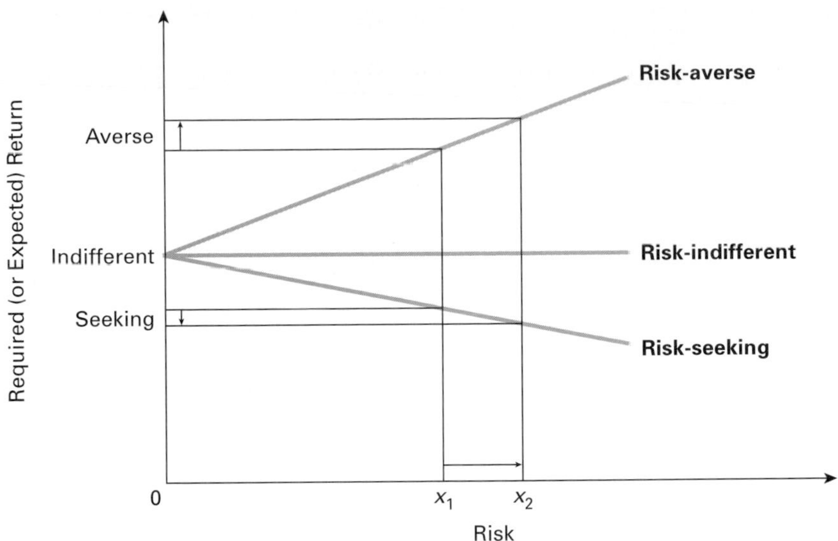

the greater your tolerance for risk, and the greater your required return. To get a feel for your own risk-taking orientation, read the *Investing in Action* box on page 152.

Steps in the Decision Process: Combining Return and Risk

Investors should take the following steps that combine return and risk when deciding among alternative investments.

1. Using historical or projected return data, estimate the expected return over a given holding period. Use yield (or present-value) techniques to make sure you give the time value of money adequate consideration.

2. Using historical or projected return data, assess the risk associated with the investment. Subjective risk assessment, use of the standard deviation or coefficient of variation of returns, and use of beta (for securities) are the primary approaches available to the individual investor.

3. Evaluate the risk–return behavior of each alternative investment to make sure that the return expected is reasonable given the level of risk. If other vehicles with lower (or equal) levels of risk provide equal (or greater) returns, the investment is not acceptable.

4. Select the investment vehicles that offer the highest returns associated with the level of risk you are willing to take. Because most investors are risk-averse, they acquire lower-risk vehicles and therefore receive lower investment returns. As long as you get the highest return for the acceptable level of risk, you have made a "good investment."

Probably the most difficult step in this process is assessing risk. Aside from return and risk considerations, other factors, such as taxes, liquidity, and portfolio considerations, affect the investment decision. We will look at these in later chapters.

INVESTING IN ACTION

How Much Investment Risk Can You Handle?

An effective investment plan is based on a balance between the risks you are willing to take and the returns you need to achieve your goals. The conservative investor saving for retirement or college funding might want to buy only "safe" investments such as bank CDs or U.S. Treasury bills. Historically, though, these fixed-rate investments have barely kept pace with inflation, and taxes lessen returns even further. On the other hand, the stock market—a riskier choice—has far outperformed other investments over the long run. Many financial experts advise having at least 30% to 40% of your portfolio in equities (some suggest even 50% to 75%) if you want to accumulate assets over the long term (more than five to ten years).

The key to risk taking is to determine your personal level of risk tolerance—how comfortable you feel with the volatility of your investments. Understanding your risk tolerance will prevent you from taking more risk than you can handle and will reduce the likelihood that you will panic and abandon your plan midstream.

One way to assess your risk tolerance is to ask yourself how much you could lose on your investments over a 1-year period and still stick to your plan. In general, investors with low risk tolerance can withstand annual losses of no more than 5%, those with moderate tolerance can withstand losses of 6% to 15%, and those with high tolerance will accept losses of 16% to 25%.

The following quiz can help you evaluate your personal capacity for risk.

What Is Your Investment Risk Tolerance?

1. Which best describes your feelings about investing?
   a. "Better safe than sorry."
   b. "Moderation in all things."
   c. "Nothing ventured, nothing gained."

2. Which is the most important to you as an investor?
   a. Steady income
   b. Steady income and growth
   c. Rapid price appreciation

3. You won! Which prize would you select?
   a. $4,000 in cash
   b. A 50% chance to win $10,000
   c. A 20% chance to win $100,000

4. The stocks in your retirement account have dropped 20% since last quarter. The market experts are optimistic. What would you do?
   a. Transfer out of stocks to avoid losing more.
   b. Stay in stocks and wait for them to come back.
   c. Shift more money into stocks. If they made sense before, they're a bargain now.

5. The stocks in your retirement account have suddenly gone up 20%. You have no more information. What would you do?
   a. Transfer out of stocks and lock in my gains.
   b. Stay in stocks, hoping for more gains.
   c. Transfer more money into stocks. They might go higher.

6. Would you borrow money to take advantage of a good investment opportunity?
   a. Never
   b. Maybe
   c. Yes

7. How would you characterize yourself as an investor?
   a. Conservative
   b. Moderate risk taker
   c. Aggressive

How to determine your score:

Each (a) answer is worth 1 point. Each (b) is worth 2 points. Each (c) is worth 3 points. Add them up to find your total score.

7–11 points: a conservative investor
12–16 points: a moderate risk taker
17–21 points: an aggressive investor

CONCEPTS IN REVIEW

4.19 Briefly describe each of the following measures of risk or variability, and explain their similarity. Under what circumstances is each preferred when comparing the risk of competing investments?
   a. Standard deviation
   b. Coefficient of variation

4.20 Explain what is meant by *beta*. What is the relevant risk measured by beta? What is the *market return*? How is the interpretation of beta related to the market return?

4.21 What range of values does beta typically exhibit? Are positive or negative betas more common? Explain.

4.22 What is the *capital asset pricing model (CAPM)?* What role does beta play in it? How is the *security market line (SML)* related to the CAPM?

4.23 Differentiate among the three basic risk preferences: risk-indifferent, risk-averse, and risk-seeking. Explain which of these behaviors best describes most investors.

4.24 Judging by the results when you took the quiz in the *Investing in Action* box on page 152, what is your personal tolerance for investment risk? Using the graph in Figure 4.4, determine what investment vehicles might be appropriate for your level of risk tolerance.

4.25 Describe the steps involved in the investment decision process. Be sure to mention how returns and risks can be evaluated together to determine the group of reasonable or acceptable investments from which the final selection can be made.

Summary

LG 1 **Review the concept of return, its components, its importance, and the forces that affect the investor's level of return.** Return is the reward for investing. The total return provided by an investment includes current income and capital gains (or losses). Return is commonly calculated on a historical basis and then used to project expected returns. The level of return depends on internal characteristics and external forces, which include the general level of price changes.

LG 2 **Discuss the time value of money and the calculations involved in finding the future value of various types of cash flows.** Because investors have opportunities to earn interest on their funds, the time value of money must be considered when evaluating investment returns. Interest can be applied using either the simple interest method or the compound interest method. The more frequently interest is compounded at a stated rate, the higher the true rate of interest. The future value of a present sum or an annuity can be found using compound interest concepts.

LG 3 **Explain the concept of present value, the procedures for calculating present values, and the use of present value in determining whether an investment is satisfactory.** The present value of a future sum is the amount that would have to be deposited today, into an account earning interest at a given rate, to accumulate the specified future sum. The present value of streams of future returns can be found by adding the present values of the individual returns. When the stream is an annuity, its present value can be more simply calculated. A satisfactory investment is one for which the present value of its benefits equals or exceeds the present value of its costs.

LG 4 **Describe real, risk-free, and required returns and the computation and application of holding period return, yield (internal rate of return), and growth rates.** The required return on an investment is the rate of return an investor must earn to be fully compensated for the investment's risk. It represents the sum of the real rate of return and the expected inflation premium, which together represent the risk-free rate, and the risk premium for the investment. The risk premium varies depending on issue and issuer characteristics. The holding period return (HPR) is the return earned over a specified period of time. It is frequently used to compare returns earned in periods of 1 year or less.

Yield or internal rate of return is the compounded annual rate of return earned on investments held for more than 1 year. If the yield is greater than or equal to the required return, the investment is acceptable. Implicit in the use of yield is an ability to earn a return equal to the calculated yield on *all* income received from the investment during the holding period. Present-value techniques can be used to find a rate of growth—the compounded annual rate of change in the value of a stream of income, particularly dividends or earnings.

LG 5 **Discuss the key sources of risk and the two components of risk: diversifiable and nondiversifiable risk.** Risk is the chance that the actual return from an investment will differ from what is expected. The total risk associated with a given investment vehicle may result from a combination of sources: business, financial, purchasing power, interest rate, liquidity, tax, market, and event risk. The two basic components of total risk are diversifiable (unsystematic) and nondiversifiable (systematic) risk; nondiversifiable risk is the relevant risk.

LG 6 **Understand the risk of a single asset, beta and the capital asset pricing model (CAPM), and how they can be used to assess the risk–return characteristics of investment vehicles.** The risk of both single assets and portfolios of assets can be measured statistically on an absolute basis by the standard deviation and on a relative basis by the coefficient of variation. Beta can be used to measure the nondiversifiable, or market, risk associated with a security investment. It is derived from the historical relationship between a security's return and the market return. The capital asset pricing model (CAPM), which can be depicted graphically as the security market line (SML), relates risk (as measured by beta) to return. The CAPM reflects increasing required returns for increasing risk.

There is a tradeoff between risk and return. Generally, each type of investment vehicle displays certain risk–return characteristics. Most investors are risk-averse: In exchange for a given increase in risk, they require an increase in return. The investment decision involves estimating the return and risk of each alternative investment and then selecting those that offer the highest returns associated with the level of risk the investor is willing to take.

Discussion Questions

LG 1 Q4.1. Choose a publicly traded company that has been listed on a major exchange or in the over-the-counter market for at least 5 years. Use any data source of your choice to find the annual cash dividend, if any, paid by the company in each of the immediately past 5 calendar years. Also find the closing price of the stock at the end of each of the immediately preceding 6 years.

a. Calculate the return for each of the five 1-year periods.
b. Graph the returns on a set of year (x-axis)–return (y-axis) axes.

c. On the basis of the graph in part (b), estimate the return for the coming year, and explain your answer.

LG 2 LG 3

Q4.2. Estimate the amount of cash you will need each year over the next 20 years to live at the standard you desire. Also estimate the rate of return you can reasonably expect to earn annually, on average, during that 20-year period.

a. How large a single lump sum would you need today to provide the annual cash required to allow you to live at the desired standard over the next 20 years? (*Hint:* Be sure to use the appropriate discount rate.)
b. Would the lump sum calculated in part (a) be larger or smaller if you could earn a higher return during the 20-year period? Explain.
c. If you had the lump sum calculated in part (a) but decided to delay your planned retirement in 20 years for another 3 years, how much extra cash would you have accumulated over the 3-year period if you could invest it to earn a 7% annual rate of return?

LG 4 LG 5 LG 6

Q4.3. Choose three NYSE-listed stocks and maintain a record of their dividend payments, if any, and closing prices each week over the next 6 weeks.

a. At the end of the 6-week period, calculate the 1-week holding period returns (HPRs) for each stock for each of the 6 weeks.
b. For each stock, average the six weekly HPRs calculated in part (a) and compare them.
c. Use *Value Line* to find the beta for each of the three stocks, and compare and discuss their relative risk–return behaviors over the 6-week period.
d. On the basis of your findings in part (c), did the stock perform as expected (higher risk–higher return) over the 6-week period? What explanations can you suggest for any discrepancies?

LG 4 LG 5 LG 6

Q4.4. Access appropriate government and economic data at your public or university library to obtain current estimates of the real rate of return and the expected inflation premium. Also find the current market return. Find both the most recent holding period return and the beta (from *Value Line*) for each of the following stocks.

1. General Motors (autos)
2. Compaq (computers)
3. ENOVA (utilities)
4. Kroger (groceries)
5. Paine Webber (financial services)

a. Use the appropriate data you have gathered to estimate the current risk-free rate.
b. Find the required return for each of the five stocks, using the capital asset pricing model (CAPM) and the relevant values gathered earlier and calculated in part (a).
c. Discuss, compare, and contrast the relative risks and returns for each of the five stocks.

LG 4 LG 5 LG 6

Q4.5. Find the current risk-free rate and market return. Use *Value Line* to find current betas for each of the companies listed on page 146.

a. Compare, contrast, and comment on the current betas in light of the April 17, 1998, betas given in the chapter for each of the companies.
b. Do you think the betas should remain the same over time? What might cause them to change, even in a stable economic environment?
c. Use the current betas and the capital asset pricing model (CAPM) to estimate each stock's required return.
d. Compare and discuss your findings in part (c) with regard to the specific business that each company is in.

Problems

LG 1 **P4.1.** How much would an investor earn on a stock purchased 1 year ago for \$63 if it paid an annual cash dividend of \$3.75 and had just been sold for \$67.50? Would the investor have experienced a capital gain? Explain.

LG 1 **P4.2.** Assuming you purchased a share of stock for \$50 one year ago, sold it today for \$60, and during the year received three dividend payments totaling \$2.70, calculate
a. Current income
b. Capital gain (or loss)
c. Total return
(1) In dollars
(2) As a percentage of the initial investment

LG 1 **P4.3.** Consider the historical data given in the accompanying table.
a. Calculate the total return (in dollars) for each year.
b. Indicate the level of return you would expect in 2000 and in 2001.
c. Comment on your forecast.

		Market Value (Price)	
Year	Income	Beginning	Ending
1995	\$1.00	\$30.00	\$32.50
1996	1.20	32.50	35.00
1997	1.30	35.00	33.00
1998	1.60	33.00	40.00
1999	1.75	40.00	45.00

LG 2 **P4.4.** For each of the savings account transactions in the accompanying table, calculate the following:
a. End-of-year account balance (assume that the account balance at December 31, 1998, is zero).
b. Annual interest, using 6% simple interest and assuming all interest is withdrawn from the account as it is earned.
c. True rate of interest, and compare it to the stated rate of interest. Discuss your finding.

Date	Deposit (Withdrawal)	Date	Deposit (Withdrawal)
1/1/99	\$5,000	1/1/01	2,000
1/1/00	(4,000)	1/1/02	3,000

LG 2 **P4.5.** Using the appropriate table of interest factors found in Appendix A, calculate:
a. The future value of a \$300 deposit left in an account paying 7% annual interest for 12 years.
b. The future value at the end of 6 years of an \$800 annual end-of-year deposit into an account paying 7% annual interest.

LG 2 **P4.6.** For each of the following initial investment amounts, calculate the future value at the end of the given investment period if interest is compounded annually at the specified rate of return over the given investment period.

Investment	Investment Amount	Rate of Return	Investment Period
A	\$ 200	5%	20 years
B	4,500	8	7
C	10,000	9	10
D	25,000	10	12
E	37,000	11	5

 LG 2

P4.7. For each of the following annual deposits into an account paying the stated annual interest rate over the specified deposit period, calculate the future value of the annuity at the end of the given deposit period.

Deposit	Amount of Annual Deposit	Interest Rate	Deposit Period
A	$ 2,500	8%	10 years
B	500	12	6
C	1,000	20	5
D	12,000	6	8
E	4,000	14	30

 LG 2

P4.8. If you could earn 9% on similar-risk investments, what is the least you would accept at the end of a 6-year period, given the following amounts and timing of your investment?

a. Invest $5,000 as a lump sum today.
b. Invest $2,000 at the end of each of the next 5 years.
c. Invest a lump sum of $3,000 today and $1,000 at the end of each of the next 5 years.
d. Invest $900 at the end of years 1, 3, and 5.

 LG 3

P4.9. For each of the following investments, calculate the present value of the future sum, using the specified discount rate and assuming the sum will be received at the end of the given year.

Investment	Future Sum	Discount Rate	End of Year
A	$ 7,000	12%	4
B	28,000	8	20
C	10,000	14	12
D	150,000	11	6
E	45,000	20	8

 LG 3

P4.10. A Florida State savings bond can be converted to $1,000 at maturity 8 years from purchase. If the state bonds are to be competitive with U.S. savings bonds, which pay 6% interest compounded annually, at what price will the state's bonds sell, assuming they make no cash payments prior to maturity?

 LG 3

P4.11. Find the present value of each of the following streams of income, assuming a 12% discount rate.

A		B		C	
End of Year	Income	End of Year	Income	End of Year	Income
1	$2,200	1	$10,000	1–5	$10,000/yr
2	3,000	2–5	5,000/yr	6–10	8,000/yr
3	4,000	6	7,000		
4	6,000				
5	8,000				

 LG 3

P4.12. Consider the streams of income given in the table at the top of page 158.

a. Find the present value of each income stream, using a 15% discount rate.
b. Compare the calculated present values and discuss them in light of the fact that the undiscounted total income amounts to $10,000 in each case.

End of Year	Income Stream A	Income Stream B
1	$ 4,000	$ 1,000
2	3,000	2,000
3	2,000	3,000
4	1,000	4,000
Totals	$10,000	$10,000

LG 3

P4.13. For each of the following investments, calculate the present value of the annual end-of-year returns at the specified discount rate over the given period.

Investment	Annual Returns	Discount Rate	Period
A	$ 1,200	7%	3 years
B	5,500	12	15
C	700	20	9
D	14,000	5	7
E	2,200	10	5

LG 3

P4.14. Using the appropriate table of interest factors found in Appendix A, calculate:

a. The present value of $500 to be received 4 years from now, using an 11% discount rate.

b. The present value of the following end-of-year income streams, using a 9% discount rate and assuming it is now the beginning of 2000.

End of Year	Income Stream A	Income Stream B
2000	$80	$140
2001	80	120
2002	80	100
2003	80	80
2004	80	60
2005	80	40
2006	80	20

LG 2 LG 3

P4.15. Terri Allessandro has an opportunity to make any of the following investments. The purchase price, the amount of its lump-sum future value, and its year of receipt are given below for each investment. Terri can earn a 10% rate of return on investments similar to those currently under consideration. Evaluate each investment to determine whether it is satisfactory and make an investment recommendation to Terri.

Investment	Purchase Price	Future Value	Year of Receipt
A	$18,000	$30,000	5
B	600	3,000	20
C	3,500	10,000	10
D	1,000	15,000	40

LG 2 LG 3

P4.16. Kent Weitz wishes to assess whether the two investments shown at the top of page 159 are satisfactory. Use his required return (discount rate) of 17% to evaluate each investment. Make an investment recommendation to Kent.

	Investment	
	A	B
Purchase price	$13,000	$8,500
End of Year	Income Stream	
1	$ 2,500	$4,000
2	3,500	3,500
3	4,500	3,000
4	5,000	1,000
5	5,500	500

LG 4

P4.17. Given a real rate of interest of 3%, an expected inflation premium of 5%, and risk premiums for investments A and B of 3% and 5%, respectively, find:

a. The risk-free rate of return, R_F.

b. The required returns for investments A and B.

LG 4

P4.18. Calculate the holding period return (HPR) for the following two investment alternatives. Which, if any, of the return components is likely not to be realized if you continue to hold each of the investments beyond 1 year? Which vehicle would you prefer, assuming they are of equal risk? Explain.

	Investment Vehicle	
	X	Y
Cash received		
1st quarter	$ 1.00	$ 0
2nd quarter	1.20	0
3rd quarter	0	0
4th quarter	2.30	2.00
Investment value		
End of year	$29.00	$56.00
Beginning of year	30.00	50.00

LG 4

P4.19. Assume you invest $5,000 today in an investment vehicle that promises to return $9,000 in exactly 10 years.

a. Use the present-value technique to estimate the yield on this investment.

b. If a minimum return of 9% is required, would you recommend this investment?

LG 4

P4.20. Use the appropriate present-value interest factor table to estimate the yield to the nearest 1% for each of the following investments.

Investment	Initial Investment	Future Value	End of Year
A	$ 1,000	$ 1,200	5
B	10,000	20,000	7
C	400	2,000	20
D	3,000	4,000	6
E	5,500	25,000	30

LG 4

P4.21. Rosemary Santos must earn a return of 10% on an investment that requires an initial outlay of $2,500 and promises to return $6,000 in 8 years.

a. Use present-value techniques to estimate the yield on this investment to the nearest 1%.

b. On the basis of your finding in part (a), should Rosemary make the proposed investment? Explain.

LG 4

P4.22. Use the appropriate present-value interest factors to estimate the yield to the nearest 1% for each of the following two investments.

	Investment	
	A	B
Initial Investment	$8,500	$9,500
End of Year	Income	
1	$2,500	$2,000
2	2,500	2,500
3	2,500	3,000
4	2,500	3,500
5	2,500	4,000

LG 4

P4.23. Elliott Dumack must earn a minimum rate of return of 11% to be adequately compensated for the risk of the following investment.

Initial Investment	$14,000
End of Year	Income
1	$ 6,000
2	3,000
3	5,000
4	2,000
5	1,000

a. Use present-value techniques to estimate the yield on this investment to the nearest 1%.
b. On the basis of your finding in part (a), should Elliott make the proposed investment? Explain.

LG 4

P4.24. Assume the investment that generates income stream B in Problem P4.14 can be purchased at the beginning of 2000 for $1,000 and sold at the end of 2006 for $1,200. Estimate the yield for this investment to the nearest 1%. If a minimum return of 9% is required, would you recommend this investment? Explain.

LG 4

P4.25. For each of the following streams of dividends, estimate (to the nearest 1%) the compound annual rate of growth between the earliest year for which a value is given and 1999.

	Dividend Stream		
Year	A	B	C
1990		$1.50	
1991		1.55	
1992		1.61	
1993		1.68	$2.50
1994		1.76	2.60
1995	$5.00	1.85	2.65
1996	5.60	1.95	2.65
1997	6.40	2.06	2.80
1998	7.20	2.17	2.85
1999	8.00	2.28	2.90

LG 6

P4.26. The historical returns for two investments—A and B—are summarized in the accompanying table for the period 1995 to 1999. Use the data to answer the questions that follow.

	Investment	
	A	B
Year	Rate of Return	
1995	19%	8%
1996	1	10
1997	10	12
1998	26	14
1999	4	16
Average	12%	12%

a. On the basis of a review of the return data, which investment appears to be more risky? Why?
b. Calculate the standard deviation and the coefficient of variation for each investment.
c. On the basis of your calculations in part (b), which investment is more risky? Compare this conclusion to your observation in part (a).
d. Does the coefficient of variation provide better risk comparison than the standard deviation in this case? Why or why not?

LG 6

P4.27. Imagine you wish to estimate the betas for two investments, A and B. In this regard, you have gathered the following return data for the market and for each of the investments over the past 10 years, 1990–1999.

	Historical Returns		
		Investment	
Year	Market	A	B
1990	6%	11%	16%
1991	2	8	11
1992	−13	−4	−10
1993	−4	3	3
1994	−8	0	−3
1995	16	19	30
1996	10	14	22
1997	15	18	29
1998	8	12	19
1999	13	17	26

a. On a set of market return (x-axis)–investment return (y-axis) axes, use the data to draw the characteristic lines for investments A and B on the same set of axes.
b. Use the characteristic lines from part (a) to estimate the betas for investments A and B.
c. Use the betas found in part (b) to comment on the relative risks of investments A and B.

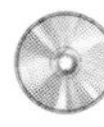

LG 6

P4.28. A security has a beta of 1.20. Is this security more or less risky than the market? Explain. Assess the impact on the required return of this security in each of the following cases.

a. The market return increases by 15%.
b. The market return decreases by 8%.
c. The market return remains unchanged.

LG 6

P4.29. Assume the betas for securities A, B, and C are as shown here.

Security	Beta
A	1.40
B	0.80
C	−0.90

a. Calculate the change in return for each security if the market experiences an increase in its rate of return of 13.2% over the next period.
b. Calculate the change in return for each security if the market experiences a decrease in its rate of return of 10.8% over the next period.
c. Rank and discuss the relative risk of each security on the basis of your findings. Which security might perform best during an economic downturn? Explain.

LG 6

P4.30. Use the capital asset pricing model (CAPM) to find the required return for each of the following securities in light of the data given.

Security	Risk-Free Rate	Market Return	Beta
A	5%	8%	1.30
B	8	13	0.90
C	9	12	−0.20
D	10	15	1.00
E	6	10	0.60

LG 6

P4.31. The risk-free rate is currently 7%, and the market return is 12%. Assume you are considering the following investment vehicles with the betas noted.

Investment Vehicle	Beta
A	1.50
B	1.00
C	0.75
D	0
E	2.00

a. Which vehicle is most risky? Least risky?
b. Use the capital asset pricing model (CAPM) to find the required return on each of the investment vehicles.
c. Draw the security market line (SML), using your findings in part (b).
d. On the basis of your findings in part (c), what relationship exists between risk and return? Explain.

Case Problem 4.1 *Solomon's Decision*

LG 2 LG 3 LG 4

Dave Solomon, a 23-year-old mathematics teacher at Xavier High School, recently received a tax refund of $1,100. Because Dave doesn't currently need this money, he decided to make a long-term investment. After surveying a large number of alternative investments costing no more than $1,100, Dave isolated two that seemed most suitable to his needs. Each of the investments cost $1,050 and was expected to provide income over a 10-year period. Investment A provided a relatively certain stream of income, whereas Dave was a little less certain of the income provided by investment B. From his search for suitable alternatives, Dave found that the appropriate discount rate for a relatively certain investment was 12%. Because he felt a bit uncomfortable with an investment like B, he estimated that such an investment would have to provide a return at least 4% *higher* than investment A. Although Dave planned to reinvest funds returned from the investments in other vehicles providing similar returns, he wished to keep the extra $50 ($1,100 – $1,050) invested for the full 10 years in a savings account paying 5% interest compounded annually. As he makes his investment decision, Dave has asked for your help in answering the questions that follow the expected return data for these investments.

	Expected Returns			Expected Returns	
Year	A	B	Year	A	B
2000	$150	$100	2005	$ 150	$350
2001	150	150	2006	150	300
2002	150	200	2007	150	250
2003	150	250	2008	150	200
2004	150	300	2009	1,150	150

QUESTIONS

a. Assuming that investments A and B are equally risky and using the 12% discount rate, apply the present-value technique to assess the acceptability of each investment and to determine the preferred investment. Explain your findings.

b. Recognizing that investment B is more risky than investment A, reassess the two alternatives, applying a 16% discount rate to investment B. Compare your findings relative to acceptability and preference to those found for question (a).

c. From your findings in questions (a) and (b), indicate whether the yield for investment A is above or below 12% and whether that for investment B is above or below 16%. Explain.

d. Use the present-value technique to estimate, to the nearest 1%, the yield on each investment. Compare your findings and contrast them with your response to question (c).

e. From the information given, which, if either, of the two investments would you recommend that Dave make? Explain your answer.

f. Indicate to Dave how much money the extra $50 will have grown to by the end of 2009, given that he makes no withdrawals from the savings account.

Case Problem 4.2 *The Risk–Return Tradeoff: Molly O'Rourke's Stock Purchase Decision*

LG 4 LG 5 LG 6

Over the past 10 years, Molly O'Rourke has slowly built a diversified portfolio of common stock. Currently, her portfolio includes 20 different common stock issues and has a total market value of $82,500. Molly is at present considering the addition of 50 shares of one of two common stock issues—X or Y. To assess the return and risk of each of these issues, she has gathered dividend income and share price data for both over each of the last 10 years (1990 through 1999). Molly's investigation of the outlook for these issues suggests that each will, on average, tend to behave in the future just as it has in the past. She therefore believes that the expected return can be estimated by finding the average holding period return (HPR) over the past 10 years for each of the stocks.

Molly plans to use betas to assess the risk and required return of each stock. Her broker, Jim McDaniel, indicated that the betas for stocks X and Y are 1.60 and 1.10, respectively. In addition, currently the risk-free rate is 7% and the market return is 10%. The historical dividend income and stock price data collected by Molly are given in the accompanying table.

	Stock X			Stock Y		
		Share Price			Share Price	
Year	Dividend Income	Beginning	Ending	Dividend Income	Beginning	Ending
1990	$1.00	$20.00	$22.00	$1.50	$20.00	$20.00
1991	1.50	22.00	21.00	1.60	20.00	20.00
1992	1.40	21.00	24.00	1.70	20.00	21.00
1993	1.70	24.00	22.00	1.80	21.00	21.00
1994	1.90	22.00	23.00	1.90	21.00	22.00
1995	1.60	23.00	26.00	2.00	22.00	23.00
1996	1.70	26.00	25.00	2.10	23.00	23.00
1997	2.00	25.00	24.00	2.20	23.00	24.00
1998	2.10	24.00	27.00	2.30	24.00	25.00
1999	2.20	27.00	30.00	2.40	25.00	25.00

QUESTIONS

a. Determine the holding period return (HPR) for each stock in each of the preceding 10 years. Find the expected return for each stock, using the approach specified by Molly.

b. Use the HPRs and expected return calculated in question (a) to find both the standard deviation and the coefficient of variation of the HPRs for each stock over the 10-year period 1990 to 1999.

c. Use your findings to evaluate and discuss the return and risk associated with stocks X and Y. Which stock seems preferable? Explain.

d. Use the capital asset pricing model (CAPM) to find the required return for each stock. Compare this value with the average HPRs calculated in question (a).

e. Compare and contrast your findings in questions (c) and (d). What recommendations would you give Molly in light of the investment decision currently under consideration? Explain why Molly is better off using beta, rather than either a subjective approach or the standard deviation or coefficient of variation, to assess investment risk.

Home Page Exercises

http://hepg.aw.com **Keyword: Invest**

Risk and return are two common themes that run through all aspects of finance. As an investor, you need to know how to calculate return, including both historical and expected returns. It is also important to be aware of your personal risk tolerance and of the potential return you can earn by accepting this risk: the risk–return tradeoff. The Web is a valuable source of objective measures for discovering or clarifying an investor's tolerance for risk. It also has excellent sources of data for obtaining or calculating historical returns. The following Web sites offer information related to risk and return.

Web Address	*Primary Investment Focus*
www.wsrn.com	Links to reports and other information on companies and other investment information
www.streeteye.com	Links to reports and other information on companies and other investment information
investor.msn.com/contents.asp	Under its *Research Central* icon, offers access to price and volume data on stocks on a daily, weekly, monthly, or yearly basis

W4.1. "A picture is worth a thousand words." This saying holds true in many situations, and it certainly applies to investing. At the address shown here, access and print out a chart showing the historical return for the past year for Iomega Corporation and for Wal-Mart Corporation. Discuss the similarities and differences between the return patterns observed over the past year for these two firms.

www.investools.com/cgi-bin/charts.pl/

W4.2. Knowing your personal tolerance for risk is vital for putting together an acceptable portfolio. Answer the risk tolerance questionnaire at each of the two sites listed here to derive an objective measurement of your risk tolerance. Discuss any differences you find between the results of the two questionnaires.

advisor.wsaccess.com/edprofile.htm

www.npcgroup.com/risk.htm

W4.3. Knowledge of historical returns is useful for forming expectations of future returns. Look at the Web address listed here and collect the following information for stocks, T-bills, and T-bonds.

www.stern.nyu.edu/~adamodar/New_Home_Page/datafile/histret.html

a. Average arithmetic return from 1926 to 1997, 1962 to 1997, and 1987 to 1997.
b. Average internal rate of return from 1926 to 1997, 1962 to 1997, and 1987 to 1997.
c. Average risk premium (market return − risk-free rate) on stock during 1926–1997, 1962–1997, and 1987–1997.

Part Two

Investing in Common Stock

CHAPTER 5 COMMON STOCK INVESTMENTS

LEARNING GOALS

After studying this chapter, you should be able to:

LG 1 Explain the investment appeal of common stocks and why individuals like to invest in them.

LG 2 Describe stock returns from a historical perspective and gain an appreciation of how current returns measure up to historical standards of performance.

LG 3 Discuss the basic features of common stocks, including issue characteristics, stock quotations, and transaction costs.

LG 4 Understand the different kinds of common stock values.

LG 5 Discuss common stock dividends, types of dividends, and dividend reinvestment plans.

LG 6 Describe various types of common stocks, including foreign stocks, and note the different ways in which stocks can be used as investment vehicles.

Intel Corp.

Investing in common stocks is about taking educated risks. It is also about receiving returns—sometimes spectacular ones. In 1971 a company called Intel sold its stock to the public at $23.50 per share. The company was unprofitable and virtually unknown. That year, though, the company made technological history by introducing the world's first microprocessor, the "brains" that control a computer's central processing of data. Today Intel is a major supplier to the computing industry of chips, boards, systems, and software. And its original investors have been handsomely rewarded: A purchase of 100 shares at $23.50 per share in 1971 grew to 15,188 shares, worth more than $2 million, by the end of 1996—a return of nearly one thousand times the initial investment.

In hindsight, it looks so easy. But in fact, investors who put their money at risk need to learn as much as possible about each company they consider and the industry in which it operates. They also need to know how to analyze and interpret the information they gather. This chapter looks at common stocks and introduces some of the key concepts and principles of investing in these complex but potentially rewarding securities.

What Stocks Have to Offer

LG 1 LG 2

The basic investment attribute of common stocks is that they enable investors to participate in the profits of the firm. Every shareholder is a part owner of the firm and, as such, is entitled to a piece of the firm's profit. This claim on income is not without limitations, however, because common stockholders are really the **residual owners** of the company. That is, they are entitled to dividend income and a share of the company's earnings only after all other corporate obligations have been met. Equally important, as residual owners, holders of common stock have no guarantee that they will ever receive any return on their investment. The challenge, of course, is to find stocks that will provide the kind of return you're looking for. As anyone who has ever purchased stock can attest, that's no easy task, for there are literally thousands of actively traded stocks to choose from.

residual owners
owners/stockholders of a firm, who are entitled to dividend income and a prorated share of the firm's earnings only after all the firm's other obligations have been met.

The Appeal of Common Stocks

Common stocks are a popular form of investing, used by millions of individual investors. Their popularity stems in large part from the fact that they offer investors an opportunity to tailor their investment programs to meet individual needs and preferences. Given the size and diversity of the stock market, it's safe to say that no matter what the investment objective, there are common stocks to fit the bill. For retired people and others living on their investment holdings, stocks provide a way of earning a steady stream of current income (from the dividends they produce). For investors less concerned about current income, common stocks can serve as the basis for long-run accumulation of wealth. With this strategy, stocks are used very much like a savings account: Investors buy stock for the long haul as a way to earn not only dividends but also a steady flow of capital gains. These investors recognize that stocks have a tendency to go up in price over time, and they simply position themselves to take advantage of that fact. Indeed, it is this potential for capital gains that is the real draw for most investors. Whereas dividends can provide a steady stream of income, the big returns come from capital gains. And few securities can match common stocks when it comes to capital gains.

Putting Stock Price Behavior in Perspective

Given the underlying nature of common stocks, when the market is strong, investors can generally expect to benefit from steady price appreciation. A good example is the performance of 1996, when the market, as measured by the Dow Jones Industrial Average (DJIA), went up some 26%. When the market falters, however, so do investor returns. The most dramatic example is the hair-raising market of 1987. In that year, stock prices had shot up almost 30% in the first 6 months, only to experience a terrible crash on October 19. That day was not just another bad day in the market—it was the *worst* day in the market's history. Stock prices, as measured by the DJIA, fell 508 points on volume of over 600 million shares. The day set a number of records, including the largest point drop, the largest 1-day volume of shares traded, and the largest percentage decline (23%), almost twice the previous single-day record.

Ten years later, almost to the day, it happened again. On October 27, 1997, the DJIA dropped 554 points (a new record) on volume of 685 million

INVESTOR FACT

SO, WHAT'S IN A BEAR?—We all know a bear market occurs when stock prices are falling. But not all falling markets end up as bears. A **routine decline** signifies a drop of *5% or more* in the Dow Jones Industrial Average. They typically occur a few times a year. A **correction** is a drop of *10% or more* in the Dow; a recent one occurred in October 1997. Finally, there's a **bear market**—a term reserved for severe market declines of *20% or more*. Though they normally occur every 3 to 4 years, the 1990s have been mostly bear-free.

shares (also a record). In percentage terms, however, the market ended the day down just over 7%, which wasn't even close to the record. (The 7% decline was the 12th-largest in percentage terms.) And unlike the 1987 crash, this one didn't last long: The market recovered all of its losses *within 2 weeks,* and within 2 months the October decline was little more than a memory. In stark contrast, it took over 2½ years for the market to recover from the 1987 crash.

Fortunately, days such as October 19, 1987, and October 27, 1997, are the exceptions rather than the rule. More often than not, the stock market offers attractive returns, rather than just risk and wild price volatility. Take a look at Figure 5.1, which shows the behavior of the market over the 16-year period from 1982 through the third quarter of 1997. This market run, which began in August 1982, has seen the Dow soar more than 10-fold, making it one of the biggest market advances of all time. Among its many achievements, the thing that makes this market stand out is the extent to which it has moved in a relatively short period of tme. That is, the Dow has gone from less than 1,000 points to over 8,000 (through 1997)—and most of that advance has occurred in the last 5 or 6 years. Movements of the magnitude seen on October 27, 1997, are hard to comprehend calmly, especially to those who remember the feelings of fear and uncertainty associated with much smaller changes in earlier years. But 100- or 200-point swings are not the same when the DJIA is at 7,000 or 8,000 as when the market was trading at the 2,000 or 3,000 level—which was happening not many years ago.

Look again at Figure 5.1. Note the two lines on the graph. The top one tracks the actual behavior of the Dow; the lower one follows the same performance, except on a logarithmic ("log") scale that shows the *rate of change* in the market instead of absolute values. Clearly, rather than showing a market that's going through the roof, the second line shows a strong market that's moving up at a relatively stable pace. Whether the market can continue to do so for much longer remains to be seen. The one thing we know for sure is that

FIGURE 5.1
The Great Bull Market of 1982–1997

One of the greatest bull markets ever began on August 12, 1982, with the Dow at 777, and has continued for more than 15 years. It was strong enough to survive two market crashes (one in 1987 and another in 1997) and one mild recession/bear market (in 1990). Indeed, this bull has had only one down year (1990), as it has charged to a high of over 8,000 on the Dow (so far).

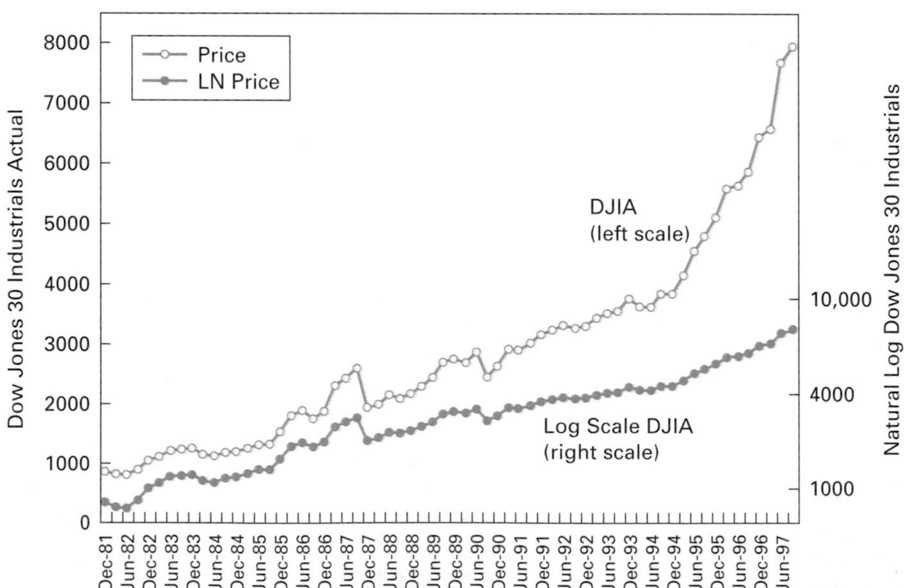

the market has been very good to investors for the past 15 years. And so long as earnings remain strong and interest remains low, there's no reason the market can't continue to climb.

From Stock Prices to Stock Returns

Our discussion so far has centered on *stock prices,* but what's even more important to investors is *stock returns,* which take into account not only price behavior but also dividend income. Table 5.1 uses the DJIA to show annual market returns over the 50-year period from 1948–1997. In addition to total returns, market performance is broken down into the two basic sources of return: dividends and capital gains. These figures, of course, reflect the *general behavior of the market as a whole,* not necessarily that of *individual* stocks. Think of them as the return behavior on a well-balanced portfolio of common stocks.

The numbers show a market that, over the past 50 years, has provided annual returns ranging from a low of −21.45% (in 1974) to a high of +48.28% (in 1954). Breaking down the returns into dividends and capital

TABLE 5.1 Annual Returns in the Stock Market, 1948–1997 (returns based on performance of the DJIA)

Year	Rate of Return from Dividends	Rate of Return from Capital Gains	Total Rate of Return	Year	Rate of Return from Dividends	Rate of Return from Capital Gains	Total Rate of Return
1997	1.68%	23.22%	24.90%	1972	3.16%	14.58%	17.74%
1996	2.03	26.01	28.04	1971	3.47	6.11	9.58
1995	2.27	33.45	35.72	1970	3.76	4.82	8.58
1994	2.75	2.14	4.89	1969	4.24	−15.19	−10.95
1993	2.65	13.72	16.37	1968	3.32	4.27	7.59
1992	3.05	4.17	7.22	1967	3.33	15.20	18.53
1991	3.00	20.32	23.32	1966	4.06	−18.94	−14.88
1990	3.90	−4.34	−0.44	1965	2.95	10.88	13.83
1989	3.74	26.96	30.70	1964	3.57	14.57	18.14
1988	3.67	11.85	15.52	1963	3.07	17.00	20.07
1987	3.67	2.26	5.93	1962	3.57	−10.81	−7.24
1986	3.54	22.58	26.12	1961	3.11	18.71	21.82
1985	4.01	27.66	31.67	1960	3.47	−9.34	−5.87
1984	5.00	−3.74	1.26	1959	3.05	16.40	19.45
1983	4.47	20.27	24.74	1958	3.43	33.96	37.39
1982	5.17	19.60	24.77	1957	4.96	−12.77	−7.81
1981	6.42	−9.23	−2.81	1956	4.60	2.27	6.87
1980	5.64	14.93	20.57	1955	4.42	20.77	25.19
1979	6.08	4.19	10.27	1954	4.32	43.96	48.28
1978	6.03	−3.15	2.88	1953	5.73	−3.77	1.96
1977	5.51	−17.27	−11.76	1952	5.29	8.42	13.71
1976	4.12	17.86	21.98	1951	6.07	14.37	20.44
1975	4.39	38.32	42.71	1950	6.85	17.63	24.48
1974	6.12	−27.57	−21.45	1949	6.39	12.88	19.27
1973	4.15	−16.58	−12.43	1948	6.49	−2.13	4.36

Note: Total return figures are based on both dividend income *and* capital gains (or losses); all figures are compiled from DJIA performance information, as obtained from *Barron's* and the *Wall Street Journal;* 1997 figures are through the third quarter (September 30th) of the year.

TABLE 5.2 Holding Period Returns in the Stock Market, 1948–1997

Holding Periods	Average Annual Returns	Cumulative Returns	Amount to Which $10,000 Will Grow
5 yr.: 1993–97	21.5%	164.9%	$ 26,492.75
10 yr: 1988–97	18.1	426.6	52,656.74
15 yr: 1983–97	17.8	1,070.0	117,000.44
25 yr: 1973–97	12.8	1,950.5	205,048.58
50 yr: 1948–97	12.1	30,868.5	3,096,852.58
The 1990s: 1990–97	13.3	248.8	34,875.56
The 1980s: 1980–89	17.2	390.5	49,049.80
The 1970s: 1970–79	5.3	67.9	16,792.04
The 1960s: 1960–69	5.2	66.0	16,602.04
The 1950s: 1950–59	18.0	421.7	52,171.33

Note: Average annual return figures are fully compounded returns and assume that all dividend income *and* capital gains are automatically reinvested. All figures compiled from DJIA performance information, as obtained from *Barron's* and the *Wall Street Journal;* 1997 data through third quarter.

gains reveals that the big returns (or losses) come from capital gains. Overall, as Table 5.2 shows, *stocks provided average annual returns of around 12% over the full 50-year period.* And if you look at just the last 5 to 10 years, you'll find average returns have been more like 18% to 20%! In fact, over the last 15 years (1983–1997), stocks have produced an average annual return of nearly 18%—clearly, this market for most of the past 15 years has been anything *but* average.

Keep in mind that the numbers represent market performance; *individual* stocks can and often do perform quite differently. At least, the averages give us a benchmark against which we can assess current stock returns and our expectations. For example, if a return of 10% to 12% can be considered a good long-term estimate for stocks, then *sustained* returns of 18% to 20% should definitely be viewed as extraordinary. (These higher returns are possible, of course, but to get them, investors must either take on a lot more risk or hope that this incredible market goes on for another 10 or 15 years.) Likewise, long-run stock returns of only 6% to 8% should be viewed as substandard performance. If that's the best you think you can do, then you probably should stick with bonds or CDs, where you'll earn almost as much with much less risk.

The Pros and Cons of Stock Ownership

One reason why stocks are so appealing to investors is the substantial return opportunities they offer. As we just saw, stocks generally provide attractive, highly competitive returns over the long haul. Indeed, common stock returns compare very favorably to alternative investment outlets such as long-term corporate bonds and U.S. Treasury securities. For example, over the 50-year period from 1948 through 1997, high-grade corporate bonds averaged annual returns of around 6%—*about half that of common stocks.* Although long-term bonds sometimes outperform stocks on a year-by-year basis (as they did in the mid-1980s, when interest rates were falling), the opposite is true far more often than not; that is, stocks outperform bonds, and usually by a wide margin. The main reason is that with equity securities, stockholders are entitled to participate fully in the residual profits of the firm. When the company prospers, so do investors—in the form of rising share prices (capital gains). And because stocks can be counted on to provide, over most periods, returns that exceed annual inflation rates, these securities also make ideal inflation hedges. Indeed, since 1982, stocks have done quite well against inflation. And it's very likely, so long as inflation rates remain at reasonably low levels of 3% to 4% (or less), that stocks will continue to produce attractive inflation-adjusted returns.

Stocks offer other benefits as well: They are easy to buy and sell, and the transaction costs are modest. Moreover, price and market information is widely disseminated in the news and financial media. A final advantage of stock ownership is that the unit cost of a share of common is usually within the reach of most individual investors. Unlike bonds, which carry minimum denominations of at least $1,000, and some mutual funds that have fairly hefty minimum requirements, common stocks present no such investment hurdles. Instead, most stocks today are priced at less than $75 a share—and any number of shares, no matter how few, can be bought or sold.

There are also some *disadvantages* to common stock, risk being perhaps the most significant. Stocks are subject to a number of different types of risk, including business and financial risk, purchasing power risk, market risk, and possibly event risk. All of these can adversely affect a stock's earnings and dividends, its price appreciation, and, of course, the rate of return earned by an investor. Even the best of stocks possess elements of risk that are difficult to overcome, because company earnings are subject to many factors, including government control and regulation, foreign competition, and the state of the economy. Because such factors affect sales and profits, they also affect the

FIGURE 5.2
The Current Income of Stocks and Bonds

Clearly, the level of current income (dividends) paid to stockholders falls far short of the amount of interest income paid to bondholders.

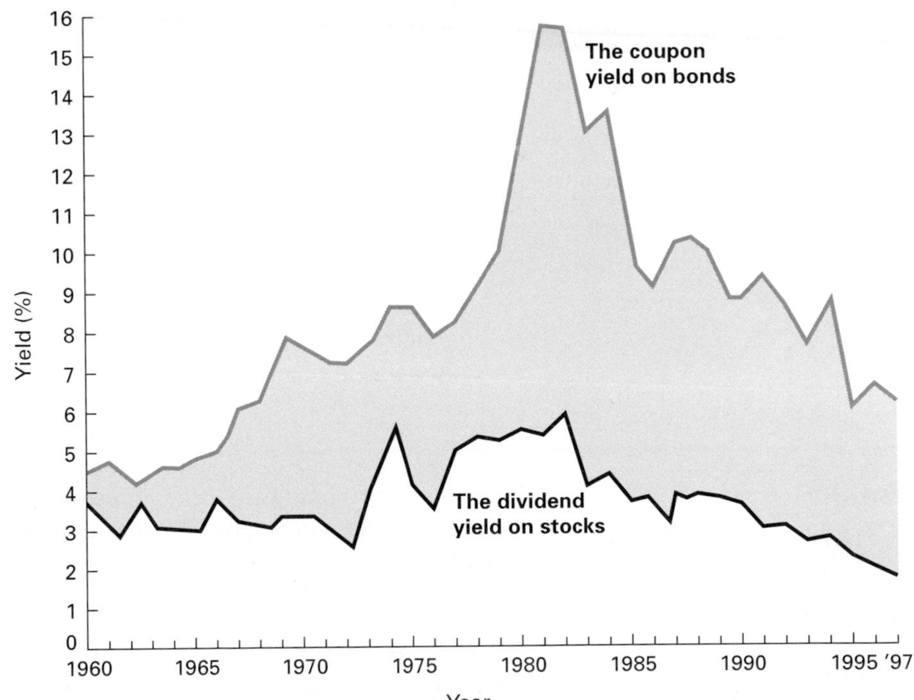

price behavior of the stock and possibly even dividends. All of this leads to another disadvantage: The earnings and general performance of stocks are subject to wide swings, so it is difficult to value common stocks and consistently select top performers. The selection process is complex because so many elements go into formulating expectations of how the price of the stock will perform in the future. In other words, not only is the future outcome of the company and its stock uncertain, but the evaluation and selection process itself is far from perfect.

A final disadvantage of stocks is the sacrifice of current income. Several types of investments—bonds, for instance—not only pay higher levels of income but do so with much greater certainty. Figure 5.2 (page 173) compares the dividend yield of common stocks with the coupon yield of bonds. It shows how the spread in current income has behaved over time and reveals the degree of sacrifice common stock investors make. Although the spread has improved a bit lately, common stocks have a long way to go before they catch up with the *current income levels* available from other investment vehicles.

CONCEPTS IN REVIEW

5.1 What is a *common stock?* What is meant by the statement that holders of common stock are the *residual owners* of the firm?

5.2 What are two or three of the major investment attributes of common stocks?

5.3 Briefly describe the behavior of the U.S. stock market over the past 10 to 15 years, paying special attention to the market that started in August 1982.

5.4 How important are dividends as a source of return? What about capital gains? Which is more important to total return? Which causes wider swings in total return?

5.5 What are some of the advantages *and* disadvantages of owning common stock? What are the major types of risk to which stockholders are exposed?

http://hepg.aw.com

There are many reasons why you may want to have part of your portfolio in common stocks. One of the main reasons is the inflation protection that equities provide because of their historically high average return. See what Prudential Securities has to say about investing in equities.

www.prusec.com/in_stock.htm

Basic Characteristics of Common Stocks

LG 3 LG 4

equity capital
evidence of ownership position in a firm, in the form of shares of common stock.

Each share of common stock represents equity (ownership) in a company. Indeed, it's this equity position that explains why common stocks are often referred to as *equity securities* or **equity capital.** Every share entitles the holder to an equal ownership position and participation in the corporation's earnings and dividends, an equal vote, and an equal voice in management. Together, the common stockholders own the company, and the more shares an investor owns, the bigger his or her ownership position. Common stock has no maturity date—it remains outstanding indefinitely.

Common Stock as a Corporate Security

Though all corporations "issue" common stock of one type or another, the shares of many, if not most, corporations are never traded, because the firms either are too small or are family-controlled. The stocks of interest to us in this book are **publicly traded issues**—the shares that are readily available to the general public and which are bought and sold in the open market. The firms issuing such shares range from giants like AT&T and IBM to much smaller regional or local firms, whose securities are traded either over the counter (OTC) or on one of the regional exchanges. The market for publicly traded stocks is enormous: The value of all actively traded listed and OTC stocks in 1997 was over *$9 trillion.*

publicly traded issues
shares of stock that are readily available to the general public and are bought and sold in the open market.

Shares of common stock can be issued in several different ways. The most widely used procedure today is the **public offering,** whereby the corporation, working with an underwriter, offers the investing public a certain number of shares of its stock at a certain price. Figure 5.3 shows an announcement for such an offering. In this case Florida Panthers Holdings, the owners of the NHL Florida Panthers hockey team, sold nearly 6.8 million shares of stock at a price of $19.25 a share.

public offering
an offering to sell to the investing public a set number of shares of a firm's stock at a specified price.

New shares of stock can also be issued using what is known as a **rights offering.** In a rights offering, existing stockholders are given the first opportunity to buy the new issue and can purchase new shares in proportion to their current ownership position. For instance, if a stockholder currently owns 1% of a firm's stock and the firm issues 10,000 additional shares, the rights offering will give that stockholder the opportunity to purchase 1% (or 100 shares) of the new issue. The net result of a rights offering is the same as that of a public offering: The firm ends up with more equity in its capital structure, and the number of shares outstanding increases.

rights offering
an offering of a new issue of stock to existing stockholders, who may purchase new shares in proportion to their current ownership position.

Perhaps one of the most creative ways of bringing new issues to the market is through a **stock spin-off.** Basically, a spin-off occurs when a company gets rid of one of its subsidiaries or divisions, as Quaker Oats did when it spun off its Fisher-Price subsidiary. But the company doesn't just sell the subsidiary to some other firm; rather, it creates a new stand-alone company and then distributes all the stock in that company, via a spin-off, to its existing stockholders. Thus every Quaker Oats shareholder received a certain (prorated) number of shares in the newly created, and now publicly traded, Fisher-Price company. Actually, there have been hundreds of stock spin-offs in the last 10 years or so—some of the more notable ones being the spin-off of Lucent Technologies by AT&T, the spin-off of Allstate by Sears, and the Payless ShoeSource spin-off by May Department Stores. Normally, companies execute stock spin-offs if they believe the subsidiary is no longer a good fit, or if they feel they've become too diversified and want to focus on their core products. Not surprisingly, as discussed in the *Investing in Action* box on page 177, such spin-offs often work very well for investors, too.

stock spin-off
conversion of one of a firm's subsidiaries to a stand-alone company by distribution of stock in that new company to exisiting shareholders.

Stock Splits

Companies can also increase the number of shares outstanding by executing a **stock split.** In declaring a split, a firm merely announces that it will increase the number of shares outstanding by exchanging a specified number of new shares for each outstanding share of stock. For example, in a 2-for-1 stock split, two new shares of stock are exchanged for each old share; in a 3-for-2 split, three

stock split
a maneuver in which a company increases the number of shares outstanding by exchanging a specified number of new shares of stock for each outstanding share.

FIGURE 5.3 An Announcement of a New Stock Issue

Did you ever have the urge to own a piece of a big-league sports team? That's exactly what investors were able to do in 1997, when this issue came to market. Here, the National Hockey League's Florida Panthers sold some 6.8 million shares of stock to the public and in the process raised more than $125 million in new capital. (Source: Courtesy of Donaldson, Lufkin & Jenrette.)

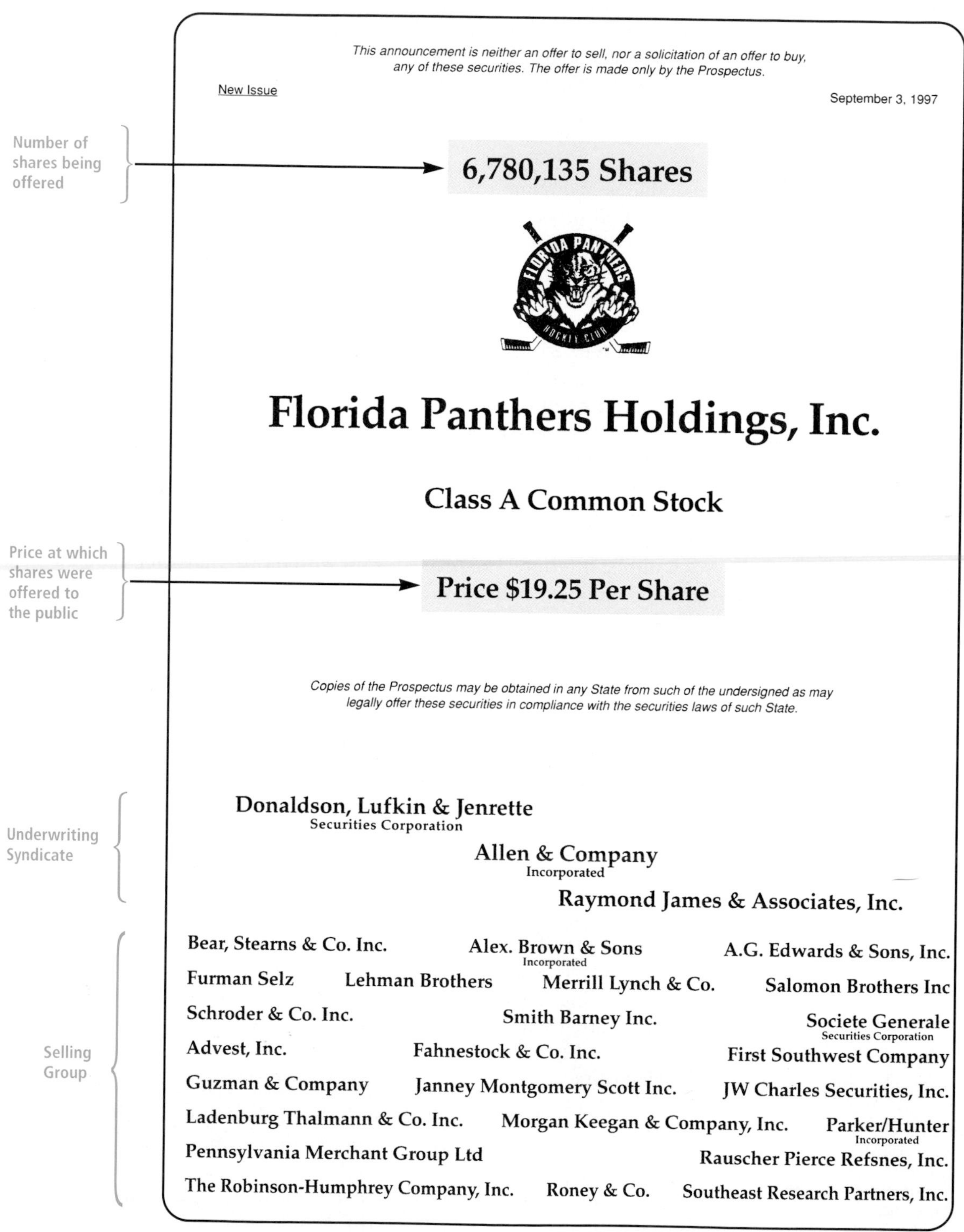
This announcement is neither an offer to sell, nor a solicitation of an offer to buy, any of these securities. The offer is made only by the Prospectus.

New Issue

September 3, 1997

6,780,135 Shares

Florida Panthers Holdings, Inc.

Class A Common Stock

Price $19.25 Per Share

Copies of the Prospectus may be obtained in any State from such of the undersigned as may legally offer these securities in compliance with the securities laws of such State.

Donaldson, Lufkin & Jenrette
Securities Corporation

Allen & Company
Incorporated

Raymond James & Associates, Inc.

Bear, Stearns & Co. Inc. Alex. Brown & Sons Incorporated A.G. Edwards & Sons, Inc.
Furman Selz Lehman Brothers Merrill Lynch & Co. Salomon Brothers Inc
Schroder & Co. Inc. Smith Barney Inc. Societe Generale Securities Corporation
Advest, Inc. Fahnestock & Co. Inc. First Southwest Company
Guzman & Company Janney Montgomery Scott Inc. JW Charles Securities, Inc.
Ladenburg Thalmann & Co. Inc. Morgan Keegan & Company, Inc. Parker/Hunter Incorporated
Pennsylvania Merchant Group Ltd Rauscher Pierce Refsnes, Inc.
The Robinson-Humphrey Company, Inc. Roney & Co. Southeast Research Partners, Inc.

INVESTING IN ACTION

Stock Spin-offs Often Perform Better Than Their Parents

The breakup of AT&T introduced the average investor to the world of stock spin-offs, where a company sheds divisions and creates "infant companies." If you owned shares in AT&T in 1983, then you got fractions of shares in seven spin-offs, the Baby Bells. The fractional shares were a nuisance at the time, but those who held on to them were well rewarded: The babies outperformed their parent over the next several years.

Once considered unusual, stock spin-offs have become a popular way to restructure a company. In recent years, many of them have scored big gains in the stock market after starting life on their own. Recent winners include Earthgrains, a baking company shed by Anheuser Busch; Dean Witter/Discover, which was purged by Sears and then merged with Morgan Stanley in early 1997; and CBS, which was spun off by Westinghouse in late 1997. More recently, PepsiCo spun off its underperforming restaurant operations—Pizza Hut, KFC, and Taco Bell—into a new company called Tricon Global Restaurants. The jury is still out on that one.

Investors have also discovered spin-offs, so there are fewer bargains available today. J.P. Morgan, the big New York bank, studied the performance of spin-offs that have occurred since the beginning of 1995 and compared them to those that occurred in the prior 10 years. The result: The latest crop isn't beating the overall stock market by as much as the earlier group. Post-1995 spin-offs topped the S&P 500 Index by an average of 2.6 percentage points in their first 18 months, whereas the pre-1995 collection beat the index by 18.5 percentage points.

The market performance of spin-offs initially is "underwhelming" because it takes time for firms to adjust to being on their own. Furthermore, Wall Street securities analysts find analyzing them more trouble than it's worth. A typical analyst might be following 20 companies. When a spin-off comes along, the analyst must either assess a new company with no earnings history or wait 9 months to a year for the company to develop a track record. Many analysts prefer to wait, so their firm doesn't buy until time passes.

But there are several factors in favor of spin-offs. For one thing, the companies being shed generally aren't the parent's best divisions. This often turns out to be a plus, because the new managers of the company, spurred on by incentives such as stock options, generally find ways to improve financial performance. The managers no longer take orders from the bureaucracy, so they become more entrepreneurial. These factors also make spin-offs attractive acquisition targets.

Some analysts like to distinguish between "pure spin-offs," like Tricon, which immediately land in the hands of Pepsi shareholders, and "carve-outs," like Lucent, in which the parent company (AT&T) first sells a percentage interest in a division, next establishes a market for the securities, and finally distributes the rest of the company to stockholders. Either way, spin-offs remain an intriguing investment opportunity.

new shares are exchanged for every two shares outstanding. A stockholder who owned 200 shares of stock before a 2-for-1 split automatically becomes the owner of 400 shares; the same investor would hold 300 shares if there had been a 3-for-2 split.

Stock splits are used when a firm wants to enhance its stock's trading appeal by lowering its market price. Normally, the firm gets the desired result, because the price of the stock tends to fall in close relation to the terms of the split (unless the stock split is accompanied by a big increase in the level of dividends). Thus, using the ratio of the number of old shares to new, we can expect a \$100 stock, for example, to trade at or close to \$50 after a 2-for-1 split. Specifically, dividing the original price of \$100 a share by the ratio of new shares to old (2/1), we have \$100 ÷ 2/1 = \$100 ÷ 2 = \$50. That same \$100 stock would trade at about \$67 after a 3-for-2 split—that is, \$100 ÷ 3/2 = \$100 ÷ 1.5 = \$67. (A variation of the stock split, known as a stock dividend, will be discussed later in this chapter.)

Treasury Stock

treasury stock
shares of stock that have been sold and subsequently repurchased by the issuing firm.

Instead of increasing the number of shares outstanding, corporations sometimes find it desirable to *reduce* the number of shares in the hands of the investing public by buying back their own stock. Generally speaking, firms repurchase their own stocks when they view them as undervalued in the marketplace. When that happens, the company's own stock becomes an attractive investment candidate. Those firms that can afford to do so will purchase their stock in the open market by becoming investors, like any other individual or institution. When these shares are acquired, they become known as **treasury stock.** Technically, treasury stocks are simply shares of stock that have been issued and subsequently repurchased by the issuing firm. Treasury stocks are kept by the corporation and can be used for mergers and acquisitions, to meet employee stock option plans, or as a means of paying stock dividends—or the shares can simply be held in treasury for an indefinite time.

The impact of these share repurchases—or *buybacks,* as they're sometimes called—is really not clear. Generally speaking, the feeling seems to be that if the buyback plan is substantial (involving a significant number of shares), the stockholder's equity position and claim on income will increase. This result is likely to benefit stockholders to the extent that such action has a positive effect on the market price of the stock. However, it has also been suggested that buybacks are too often used merely as a way to prop up the price of an overvalued stock.

Classified Common Stock

classified common stock
common stock issued by a company in different classes, each of which offers different privileges and benefits to its holders.

For the most part, all the stockholders in a corporation enjoy the same benefits of ownership. Occasionally, though, a company will issue different classes of common stock, each of which entitles the holder to different privileges and benefits. These issues are known as **classified common stock.** Hundreds of publicly traded firms have created such stock classes. Even though issued by the same company, each class of common stock is different and has its own value.

Classified common stock is customarily used to denote either different voting rights or different dividend obligations. For instance, class A could be used to designate nonvoting shares, and class B would carry normal voting rights. Or the class A stock would receive no dividends, whereas class B would receive regular cash dividends. Notable for its use of classified stock is the Ford Motor Company, which has two classes of stock outstanding: Class A stock is owned by the investing public, and class B stock is owned by the Ford family and their trusts or corporations. The two classes of stock share equally in the dividends, but class A stock has one vote per share and the voting rights of the class B stock are structured to give the Ford family a 40% absolute control of the company. Similar types of classified stock are used at the Washington Post, Dillards Department Stores, Dow Jones & Co., Nike, and

Berkshire Hathaway. Regardless of the specifics, whenever there i one class of common stock outstanding, investors should take determine the privileges, benefits, and limitations of each class.

Buying and Selling Stocks

Whether buying or selling stocks, investors should be familiar with the way stocks are quoted and with the costs of executing common stock transactions. Certainly, keeping track of *current prices* is an essential element in the buy-and-sell decisions of investors. They are the link in the decision process that lets the investor decide when to buy or sell a stock; they also help investors monitor the market performance of their security holdings. Similarly, *transaction costs* are important because of the impact they can have on investment returns. Indeed, the costs of executing stock transactions can sometimes consume most (or all) of the profits from an investment. These costs should not be taken lightly.

Reading the Quotes

Investors in the stock market have come to rely on a highly efficient information system that quickly disseminates market prices to the public. The stock quotes that appear daily in the financial press are a vital part of that information system. To see how price quotations work and what they mean, consider the quotes that appear daily (Monday through Friday) in the *Wall Street Journal.* As we'll see, these quotes give not only the most recent price of each stock but also a great deal of additional information.

Some NYSE stock quotes are presented in Figure 5.4—let's use the Disney quotations for purposes of illustration. These quotes were published in the *Wall Street Journal* on Wednesday, September 10, 1997. They describe the trading activity that occurred the day before, which in this case was Tuesday, September 9. A glance at the quotations shows that stock prices are expressed in either eighths or sixteenths of a dollar, where each eighth of a point is worth 12½ cents and a sixteenth amounts to half that much, or 6¼ cents. (Note that this pricing system is subject to change at any time. There is considerable pressure to quote and price stocks in dollars and cents, as we do most other products.) Other information is also conveyed in a stock quote:

- The first two columns, labeled "Hi" and "Lo," show the highest and lowest prices at which the stock sold during the past 52 weeks; note that Disney traded between 85⅛ and 55⅝ during the preceding 52-week period.

- Listed to the right of the company's name is its *stock symbol;* Disney goes by the three-letter abbreviation DIS. These stock symbols are the abbreviations used on the *market tapes* seen in brokerage offices and on various TV networks to identify specific companies. Every common stock (or mutual fund) has a unique three- to five-letter symbol that distinguishes it from any other security and is used to execute market trades.

- The figure listed after the stock symbol is the annual cash dividend paid on each share of stock, which here amounts to 53 cents. This is followed by the stock's dividend yield (0.7% for Disney) and its price/earnings (P/E) ratio. Note that Disney was trading at 28 times earnings.

FIGURE 5.4 Stock Quotations

Shown in this figure are the quotations for a small sample of stocks traded on the NYSE; these quotes provide a summary of the transactions that occurred on one day. (Source: *Wall Street Journal,* September 10, 1997.)

52 Weeks Hi	52 Weeks Lo	Stock	Sym	Div	Yld %	PE	Vol 100s	Hi	Lo	Close	Net Chg
25 1/8	22 7/8	DetEd QUIDS26	DTA	1.91	7.7	...	175	25	24 7/8	24 7/8	− 1/8
25 5/8	24	DetEd dep pfF			...	...	3	25 1/8	25 1/8	25 1/8	...
25 7/8	24 3/4	DetEd QUIDS	DTD	2.13	8.3	...	4	25 5/8	25 9/16	25 5/8	+ 1/8
25	18 1/4	Dtsche Tel ADR	DT	.35p	...	...	456	20 7/8	20 9/16	20 3/4	− 1/8
40 1/4	32	DevDivrsRlty	DDR	2.52	6.4	21	158	39 1/4	39 1/8	39 1/4	...
27 1/16	24 3/4	DevDivrsRlty pf	A	2.38	9.1	...	84	26 1/4	26	29 23/128	− 1/16
27	24 3/8	DevDivrsRlty pfB		2.36	9.0	...	47	26 3/16	26	26 3/16	...
30 3/8	18 3/8	DeVry	DV		...	38	366	26 5/8	26 3/8	26 1/2	− 1/4
40 3/16	28 3/4	Dexter	DEX	.96	2.5	17	573	38 3/8	38 1/16	38 1/16	− 3/16
39 5/8	25	DiagnstPdt	DP	.48	1.6	21	83	29 3/8	29	29 5/16	− 1/8
17 3/4	11 1/2	DialCp	DL	.32	1.8	54	1506	17 9/16	17 1/4	17 5/16	...
57 3/8	25 3/8	DmndOffshr	DO	.14e	.2	...	6146	57 3/8	56 1/16	56 15/16	+ 13/16
50 5/8	28	Diebold	DBD	.50	1.0	31	904	49 3/16	48 3/4	49	+ 1/8
47 13/16	25	DigitalEqp	DEC		...	64	10734	44 11/16	43 15/16	43 15/16	− 7/8
25 7/8	24	DigitalEqp pfA		2.22	8.6	...	161	25 13/16	25 11/16	25 11/16	− 1/16
42 3/4	28	Dillards	DDS	.16	.4	20	4631	42 9/16	41 3/4	42 9/16	+ 1/16
21 1/8	12 3/4	DimeBcp	DME	.08e	.4	20	2928	20 1/16	19 7/8	20 1/16	− 1/16
26 3/4	17 7/8	Dimon	DMN	.60	2.4	14	955	25 1/2	24 13/16	25 3/16	+ 3/16
5 1/8	1 5/8	CG Dina	DIN		...	...	8637	5 7/8	4 15/16	5 3/4	+ 15/16
3 15/16	1 3/8	CG Dina L	DINL		...	...	3025	4 1/4	3 1/2	4 3/16	+ 5/8
49 1/4	18 5/8	Disco	DXO		...	...	105	45 1/2	45 1/8	45 1/8	− 5/8
26 1/2	12 7/8	DiscountAuto	DAP		...	28	266	22 3/16	21 9/16	22 1/8	+ 5/16
85 1/8	55 5/8	Disney	DIS	.53	.7	28	9220	79 1/8	77 7/16	78 1/2	+ 5/8
44 1/2	30 7/8	DoleFood	DOL	.40	1.0	23	881	42	41	41 15/16	+ 15/16
45 1/2	21 19/32	DirGen	DG	.20	.5	39	1510	44 3/4	43 3/4	43 3/4	− 1/4
18 1/8	13 1/2	DomainEngy	OXD		...	...	547	17 7/8	16 3/4	17 7/8	+ 3/8
30 15/16	17 3/4	DomSprmkt	DFF		...	...	355	27	26 13/16	26 7/8	− 1/8
69 15/16	31	DonLufJen	DLJ	.50	.8	13	441	63 3/4	62 15/16	63 3/4	+ 9/16
26	24 5/8	DLJ CapTr pf		2.11	8.2	...	73	25 7/8	25 3/4	25 13/16	− 1/16
27 1/4	17	Doncasters	DCS		...	...	127	26 7/8	26 9/16	26 7/8	+ 1/8
25 1/2	8 7/8	DonnaKrn	DK		...	dd	685	13 1/16	12 15/16	13	− 1/16
41 3/4	29 3/8	Donnelly	DNY	.80f	2.1	25	3674	39 1/4	38 3/4	38 15/16	− 1/16
23	13 3/4	Donnelly	DON	.40	1.8	22	368	22 7/8	22 1/4	22 1/4	− 1/2
73 3/8	41 7/8	Dover	DOV	.76f	1.1	18	4204	68 5/16	67 3/8	68 1/8	− 1/4

- High and low prices for previous 52 weeks
- Company name
- Stock symbol used to identify company
- Annual dividends per share for past 12 months
- Dividend yield (dividends as percent of share price)
- Price/earnings ratio: $\left(\frac{\text{market price}}{\text{earnings per share}}\right)$
- Share volume, in hundreds
- High and low prices for the day
- Closing (final) price for the day—this is also the price used to compute dividend yield and the P/E ratio
- Net change in price from previous day

- The daily volume follows the P/E ratio: The sales numbers are listed in lots of 100 shares, so the figure 9220 means that 922,000 shares of Disney stock were traded on September 9.

- The next three entries, in the "Hi," "Lo," and "Close" columns, contain the highest, lowest, and last (closing) prices at which the stock sold on the day in question.

- Finally, as the last ("Net Change") column shows, Disney closed up ⅝ of a point (or at 62½ cents a share) on September 9, which means the stock closed ⅝ of a point lower, at 77⅞, the day before (September 8).

The same basic quotation system is used for AMEX stocks and for *some* OTC stocks. Actually, for quotation purposes, OTC stocks can be divided into two groups: Nasdaq National Market issues and other OTC stocks. The National Market stocks are those of major, actively traded companies; *they are quoted just like NYSE issues.* Other OTC stocks either are quoted in highly abbreviated form (as in the case of Nasdaq Small Cap issues) or are listed on the basis of their *bid* and *ask* prices.

Transaction Costs

Common stock can be bought and sold in round or odd lots. A *round lot* is 100 shares of stock or multiples thereof. An *odd lot* is a transaction involving less than 100 shares. The sale of 400 shares of stock would be a round-lot transaction; the sale of 75 shares would be an odd-lot transaction. Trading 250 shares of stock would involve a combination of two round lots and an odd lot.

An investor incurs certain transaction costs when buying or selling stock. In addition to some modest transfer fees and taxes paid by the *seller,* the major cost is the brokerage fee paid—by both *buyer and seller*—at the time of the transaction. As a rule, brokerage fees amount to about 1% to 5% of most transactions—though they can go much higher, particularly for very small trades. This is so because the purchase or sale of odd lots requires the assistance of a specialist known as an *odd-lot dealer.* This usually results in an *odd-lot differential* of 12.5 to 25 cents per share, which is tacked on to the normal commission charge, driving up the costs of these small trades. Indeed, the relatively high cost of an odd-lot trade makes it better to deal in round lots whenever possible.

Common Stock Values

The worth of a share of common stock can be described in a number of ways. Terms such as *par value, book value, market value,* and *investment value* are all found in the financial media. Each designates some accounting, investment, or monetary attribute of the stock in question.

Par Value

par value
the stated, or face, value of a stock.

The term **par value** refers to the stated, or face, value of a stock. It is not really a measure of anything, and except for accounting purposes, it is relatively useless. In many ways, par value is a throwback to the early days of corporate law, when it was used as a basis for assessing the extent of a stockholder's legal liability. Because the term has little or no significance for investors, many stocks today are issued as no-par or low-par stocks—that is, they may have par values of only a penny or two.

Book Value

book value
the amount of stockholders' equity in a firm; equals the amount of the firm's assets minus the firm's liabilities and preferred stock.

Book value, another accounting measure, represents the amount of stockholders' equity in the firm. As we will see in the next chapter, it is commonly used in security analysis and stock valuation. Book value indicates the amount of stockholder funds used to finance the firm; it is calculated by subtracting the firm's liabilities and preferred stock from its assets. Let's assume that a corporation has $10 million in assets, owes $5 million in various forms of short- and long-term debt, and has $1 million worth of preferred stock outstanding. The book value of this firm would be $4 million. This amount can be converted to a per-share basis—*book value per share*—by dividing it by the number of common shares outstanding. For example, if this firm has 100,000 shares of common stock outstanding, then its book value per share is $40. As a rule, most stocks have market prices that are above their book values.

market value
the prevailing market price of a security.

INVESTOR FACT

MARKET MUSCLE—The total market value of a company—defined as the stock price multiplied by the number of shares outstanding—is a measure of what investors think a company is worth. In 1998, General Electric topped the list with a market value, or "market capitalization," of nearly $260 billion—more than the value of the whole Singapore stock market. Some other big-cap companies are Microsoft ($200 billion), Coca-Cola ($175 billion), Exxon ($158 billion), and Merck ($154 billion).

Market Value

Market value is one of the easiest stock values to determine; it is simply the prevailing market price of an issue. In essence, market value indicates how the market participants as a whole have assessed the worth of a share of stock. By multiplying the market price of the stock by the number of shares outstanding, we can also find the market value of the firm itself—or what is known as the firm's *market capitalization*. For example, if a firm has 1 million shares outstanding and its stock trades at $50 per share, the company has a market value (or "market cap") of $50 million. Because investors are always interested in an issue's market price, the market value of a share of stock is generally of considerable importance to stockholders as they formulate their investment policies and programs.

investment value
the amount that investors believe a security should be trading for, or what they think it's worth.

Investment Value

Investment value is probably the most important measure for a stockholder. It indicates the worth investors place on the stock—in effect, what they think the stock *should* be trading for. Determining a security's investment worth is a complex process based on expectations of the return and risk behavior of a stock. Any stock has two potential sources of return: annual dividend payments and the capital gains that arise from appreciation in market price. In establishing investment value, investors try to determine how much money they will make from these two sources and then use that estimate as the basis for formulating the return potential of the stock. At the same time, they try to assess the amount of risk to which they will be exposed by holding the stock. Such return and risk information helps them place an investment value on the stock. This value represents the *maximum* price an investor should be willing to pay for the issue. Investment value is the major topic in Chapter 7.

CONCEPTS IN REVIEW

5.6 What is a *stock split?* How does a stock split affect the market value of a share of stock? Do you think it would make any difference (in price behavior) if the company also changed the dividend rate on the stock? Explain.

5.7 The *Investing in Action* box on page 177 discusses *stock spin-offs.* Explain how a stock spin-off works. Are they of any value to investors? Explain.

5.8 Define and differentiate between the following pairs of terms.

a. *Treasury stock* vs. *classified stock*
b. *Round lot* vs. *odd lot*
c. *Par value* vs. *market value*
d. *Book value* vs. *investment value*

5.9 What is an *odd-lot differential* and does it really add to the cost of buying and selling stocks? How can you avoid odd-lot differentials? Which of the following transactions would involve an odd-lot differential?

a. Buy 90 shares of stock
b. Sell 200 shares of stock
c. Sell 125 shares of stock

Common Stock Dividends

LG 5

In 1997, American corporations paid out over $250 billion in dividends. Yet, in spite of these numbers, dividends still don't seem to get any respect, and many investors, particularly younger ones, often put very little value on dividends. That's unfortunate, because dividend income is one of the two basic sources of return to investors. And although dividends are subject to higher taxes than long-term capital gains, they're also far *less risky.* That is, the stream of annual dividends is far more predictable than the capital gains that may or may not occur in the future. Let's take a closer look at this important source of income and examine several procedural aspects of the corporate dividend decision.

The Dividend Decision

By paying out dividends, typically on a quarterly basis, companies share with their stockholders the profits they earn. Actually, the question of how much to pay in dividends is decided by a firm's board of directors. The directors evaluate the firm's operating results and financial condition to determine whether dividends should be paid and, if so, in what amount. If the directors decide to pay dividends, they also establish several important payment dates. In this section we'll look at the corporate and market factors that go into the dividend decision; this information is helpful in assessing the dividend potential of a stock. Then we'll briefly explain the payment dates.

Corporate Versus Market Factors

When the board of directors assembles for a regular dividend meeting, it weighs a variety of factors in making the dividend decision. First, the board looks at the firm's earnings. For even though a company does not have to show a profit to pay dividends, profits still are considered a vital link in the dividend decision. With common stocks, the annual earnings of a firm are usually measured and reported in terms of **earnings per share (EPS)**. Basically, EPS translates total corporate profits into profits on a per-share basis and provides a convenient measure of the amount of earnings available to stockholders. Earnings per share is found by using the following simple formula:

earnings per share (EPS)
the amount of annual earnings available to common stockholders, as stated on a per-share basis.

Equation 5.1

$$\text{EPS} = \frac{\text{net profit after taxes} - \text{preferred dividends}}{\text{number of shares of common stock outstanding}}$$

For example, if a firm reports a net profit of $1.25 million, pays $250,000 in dividends to preferred stockholders, and has 500,000 shares of common outstanding, it has an EPS of $2—that is, ($1,250,000 – $250,000)/500,000. Note in Equation 5.1 that preferred dividends are subtracted from profits, since they must be paid before any monies can be made available to common stockholders.

Now, while profits are being assessed, the board also looks at the firm's growth prospects. Probably some of the firm's present earnings will be needed for investment purposes and to help finance expected growth. The board also considers the firm's cash position to make sure it has sufficient liquidity to meet a cash dividend of a given size. Finally, the board wants to ensure that it is meeting all legal and contractual constraints (e.g., the firm may be subject to a loan agreement that legally limits the amount of dividends it can pay).

After looking at internal matters, the board considers certain market effects and responses. Most investors feel that if a company is going to retain earnings rather than pay them out in dividends, it should exhibit proportionately higher growth and profit levels. The market's message is clear: If the firm is investing the money wisely and at a high rate of return, fine; otherwise, pay a larger portion of earnings out in the form of dividends. Moreover, to the extent that different types of investors tend to be attracted to different types of firms, the board must make every effort to meet the dividend expectations of its shareholders. For example, income-oriented investors are attracted to firms that generally pay high dividends; failure to meet those expectations can lead to disastrous results—a sell-off of the firm's stock—in the marketplace.

Some Important Dates

Let's assume the directors decide to declare a dividend. They then must indicate the date of payment and other important dates associated with the dividend. Normally, the directors issue a statement to the press indicating their dividend decision, along with the pertinent dividend payment dates. These statements are widely quoted in the financial media. Typical of such releases are the dividend news captions depicted in Figure 5.5.

date of record
the date on which an investor must be a registered shareholder of a firm to be entitled to receive a dividend.

payment date
the actual date on which the company will mail dividend checks to shareholders (also known as the *payable date*).

ex-dividend date
three business days before the date of record; determines whether one is an official shareholder of a firm and thus eligible to receive a declared dividend.

Three dates are particularly important to the stockholder: date of record, ex-dividend date, and payment date. The **date of record** is the date on which the investor must be a registered shareholder of the firm to be entitled to a dividend. These stockholders are often referred to as *holders of record*. When the board specifies the date of record, all investors who are official stockholders of the firm as of the close of business on that date will receive the dividends that have just been declared. The **payment date,** also set by the board of directors, generally follows the date of record by a week or two. It is the actual date on which the company will mail dividend checks to holders of record. (Note that in the dividend news reported in Figure 5.5, this date is called the *payable date*.)

Because of the time needed to make bookkeeping entries after a stock is traded, the stock will sell on an ex-dividend basis for three business days prior to the date of record. That is, the **ex-dividend date** will dictate whether you were an official shareholder and therefore eligible to receive the declared dividend. If you sell a stock *on or after* the ex-dividend date, you receive the dividend. If you sell before this date, the new shareholder will receive the recently declared dividend.

FIGURE 5.5
Important Dates and Data About Dividends

The dividend actions of corporations are big news in the financial community. This news release, taken from the *Wall Street Journal,* provides timely information about cash and stock dividends, as well as stocks that have gone ex-dividend. Note that there's even information about recent stock splits. (Source: *Wall Street Journal,* September 12, 1997.)

CORPORATE DIVIDEND NEWS

Dividends Reported September 11

Company	Period	Amt.	Payable date	Record date
REGULAR				
Alden (John) Finl	Q	.12	10–20–97	9–30
Alum Co Amer	Q	.25	11–25–97	11– 7
Alum Co Amer$3.75pf	Q	.93¾	1– 1–98	12–12
Amer Explor depshC	Q	.56¼	9–30–97	9–22
Atlantic Energy	Q	.38½	10–15–97	9–22
Birmngham Util	Q	.15	9–30–97	9–23
Brown Group Inc	Q	.25	10– 1–97	9–22
Canwest Glbl Communicatn	S	b.12½	10–15–97	9–30
Commercial Federal	Q	.07	10–14–97	9–30
CmnwlthEd $1.90pf	Q	.47½	11– 1–97	9–30
CmnwlthEd $2.00pf	Q	.50	11– 1–97	9–30
CmnwlthEd $7.24pf	Q	1.81	11– 1–97	9–30
CmnwlthEd $8.38pf	Q	2.09½	11– 1–97	9–30
CmnwlthEd $8.40pf	Q	2.10	11– 1–97	9–30
CmnwlthEd $2.425pf	Q	.60⅝	11– 1–97	9–30
CmnwlthEd pfB	Q	2.10	11– 1–97	9–30
Dow Chemical	Q	.87	10–30–97	9–30
Enhance Finl Svcs	Q	.11	9–26–97	9–22
First Essex Bncp	Q	.12	10–15–97	9–30
1st Leesport Bncp	Q	.13	10–15–97	10– 1
First Union RE Inv pfA	Q	.52½	10–30–97	9–30
Franklin Resources	Q	.09	10–15–97	9–30
Hollinger Intl A	Q	.10	10–15–97	10– 1
Hollinger Intl PRIDES	Q	.2377	11– 1–97	10–15
Hubbell Inc clA	Q	.29	10–10–97	9–22
Hubbell Inc clB	Q	.29	10–10–97	9–22
Idaho Power Co	Q	.46½	11–20–97	10–24
Kaneb Svcs adjpfA	Q	.22	9–30–97	9–22
LSB Bncshs NC	Q	.11	10–15–97	10– 1
Mid Ocean Ltd ClA	Q	.75	10– 9–97	9–22
Oilgear Co	Q	.10	10–10–97	9–30
Owosso Corp	Q	.09	10–23–97	10– 6
Pep Boys ManMoeJk	Q	.06	10–27–97	10–13
Plenum Publishing	Q	.31	10– 8–97	9–26
Pulte Corp	Q	.06	1– 1–98	12–12
Rouge Industries Inc ClA	Q	.03	10–24–97	10–10
Rowe Furniture	Q	.02½	10–10–97	9–19
Royal Bk Canada	Q	b.39	11–24–97	10–27
Spartech Corp	Q	.05	10– 9–97	9–25
Spieker Props pfB	Q	.59	9–30–97	9–19
Storage USA Inc	Q	.60	10–14–97	9–26
Trinity Indus	Q	.17	10–31–97	10–15
Unicom Corp	Q	.40	11– 1–97	9–30
Unitil Corp	Q	.33½	11–14–97	10–31
WashingtonPost clB	Q	1.20	11– 7–97	10– 3
Westco Bancorp	Q	.15	10–14–97	9–30
IRREGULAR				
Debt Strategies Fd	M	h0.0828	r9–30–97	9–18
r-Revised payable date.				
First M&F Corp	Q	.22	9–30–97	9–22
Monterey Resources	Q	.15	10–23–97	9–30
FUNDS · REITS · INVESTMENT COS · LPS				
American Genl Hospitality	Q	n.42¾	10–30–97	10–15
n-Increased amount.				
Chelsea GCA Rlty	Q	.63	10–20–97	9–30
Evans Withy Resid	Q	.38	10–10–97	9–26
Excel Realty Trust 8.5pfA	Q	.53⅛	10–15–97	10– 1
Excel Realty Trust	Q	.50	10–15–97	10– 1
Fedl Rlty Invst Tr	Q	n.43	10–15–97	9–25
n-Increased amount.				
First Union RE	Q	.11	10–30–97	9–30
Fortis Securities	M	n.063	10–15–97	9–25
n-Increased amount.				
Grove Property Trust	Q	.16	10–17–97	9–30
Humphrey Hosp Tr	Q	.19	11– 3–97	9–24
Prospect StrHiIncO	M	.03½	9–30–97	9–23
Prudential Utility A	Q	h.077	9–19–97	9–16
Prudential Utility B	Q	h.057	9–19–97	9–16
Prudential Utility Z	Q	h.083	9–19–97	9–16
Ramco-Gershenson Props	Q	.42	10–21–97	9–30
SouthrnCo Cap TrIII quips	Q	.484⅜	9–30–97	9–15
Spieker Props	Q	.47	10–20–97	9–30
STOCK				
1st West VA Bncp		c	10–27–97	10– 1
c-Correction; s-3-for-2 stock split.				
Fluke Corp		s	10–15–97	9–26
s-2-for-1 stock split.				
Granite Bdcstng pf		6.375%	10– 1–97	9–15
Movado Group Inc		s	9–29–97	9–19
s-3-for-2 stock split.				

INCREASED

Company	Period	Amounts New	Amounts Old	Payable date	Record date
Consumers Water Co	Q	.30½	.30	11–25–97	11–10
Independ Bk Mass	Q	.09	.08	10–11–97	9–26
InterWest Bancorp	Q	.16	.15	10–10–97	9–22
Maryland Fedl Bncp	Q	c.21	.20	9–19–97	9– 5
c-Corrected amount.					

Stocks Ex-Dividend September 15

Company	Amount
20th Century Indus	.05
Amer Bankers Insur	s
s-2-for-1 stock split.	
BMC Industries	.015
CV REIT	.29
Carolina P&L $5pf	1.25
Gabelli Conv Secs	.12
Gabelli Equity Tr	.25
Green Mountain Pwr	.27½
JamesRiver depsh L	.87½
JamesRiver depsh O	.515⅝
LongIslandLght pfB	1.25
LongIslandLighting	.44½
LongIslandLght pfE	1.08¾
Medtronic Inc	s
s-2-for-1 stock split.	
One LibertyProp pf	.40
One LibertyProps	.30
One Valley Bancorp	s
s-5-for-4 stock split.	
PugetSond7.45%pfII	.465⅝
PugetSond8.5%pfIII	.53⅛
Raymond (J) Finl	.08
RoyDutchPete	t.643
Telefonos Mex serL	t.43¾
True North Commun	.15
Waste Management	.17
Willamette Indus	s
s-2-for-1 stock split.	
Witco Corp	.28

t-Approximate U.S. dollar amount per American Depositary Receipt/Share before adjustment for foreign taxes.

* * *

To see how this all works, consider the following sequence of events. On June 3, the board of directors of Cash Cow, Inc., declares a quarterly dividend of 50 cents a share to holders of record on June 18, with checks to be mailed on June 30. The calendar below shows these various dividend dates. Thus, if you owned 200 shares of the stock on June 12, you'd receive a check in the mail sometime after June 30 in the amount of $100.

June

S	M	T	W	T	F	S
	1	2	3	4	5	6
7	8	9	10	11	12	13
14	15	16	17	18	19	20
21	22	23	24	25	26	27
28	29	30				

Declaration date (3)
Date of record (18)
Ex-dividend date (15)
Payment date (30)

Unfortunately, unlike long-term capital gains, which are subject to a maximum tax rate of 20%, the IRS views cash dividends as *ordinary income* and therefore subject to normal tax rates (of anywhere from 15% to 39.6%). Thus, unless you held the stock in some type of tax-sheltered account (such as an IRA or Keogh account), you would incur a tax liability (of as much as 39.6%) with each dividend check you receive.

Types of Dividends

cash dividend
payment of a dividend in the form of cash.

stock dividend
payment of a dividend in the form of additional shares of stock.

Normally, companies pay dividends in the form of cash, though sometimes they do so by issuing additional shares of stock. The first type of distribution is known as a **cash dividend;** the latter is called a **stock dividend.** Occasionally, dividends are paid in still other forms, such as a *stock spin-off,* which we discussed earlier in this chapter, or perhaps even samples of the company's products. But dividends in the form of either cash or stock remain by far the most popular, so let's take a closer look at them.

Cash or Stock

More firms use *cash dividends* than any other type of dividend payment procedure. A nice by-product of cash dividends is that *they tend to increase over time, as companies' earnings grow.* The average annual increase in dividends is around 5% to 7%, though that rate of growth has dropped off a bit in recent years. Such a tendency appeals to investors because a steady stream of dividends—even better, a *steadily increasing* stream of dividends—acts to shore up stock returns in soft markets.

dividend yield
a measure that relates dividends to share price and puts common stock dividends on a relative (percentage) rather than absolute (dollar) basis.

A convenient way of assessing the amount of dividends received is to measure the stock's **dividend yield.** Basically, dividend yield is a measure of common stock dividends on a relative (percentage) basis rather than on an absolute (dollar) basis. Dividend yield, in effect, indicates the rate of current income earned on the investment dollar. It is computed as follows:

Equation 5.2

$$\text{Dividend yield} = \frac{\text{annual dividends received per share}}{\text{current market price of the stock}}$$

Thus a company that annually pays $2 per share in dividends to its stockholders, and whose stock is trading at $40, has a dividend yield of 5%.

dividend payout ratio
the portion of earnings per share (EPS) that a firm pays out as dividends.

To put dividend yield into perspective, it is often helpful to look at a company's **dividend payout ratio.** By definition, the payout ratio describes that portion of earnings per share (EPS) that is paid out as dividends. It is computed as follows:

Equation 5.3

$$\text{Dividend payout ratio} = \frac{\text{dividends per share}}{\text{earnings per share}}$$

Thus a company would have a payout ratio of 50% if it had earnings of $4 a share and paid annual dividends of $2 a share. Although stockholders like to receive dividends, they normally do not like to see payout ratios over 60% to 70%. Payout ratios that high are difficult to maintain and may lead the company into trouble.

Occasionally, a firm may declare a *stock dividend* instead of (or in addition to) a cash dividend. A stock dividend simply means that the dividend is paid in additional shares of stock. For instance, if the board declares a 10% stock dividend, each shareholder receives 1 new share of stock for each 10 shares currently owned.

Although they seem to satisfy the needs of some investors, *stock dividends really have no value,* because they represent the receipt of something already owned. The market responds to such dividends by adjusting share prices according to the terms of the stock dividend. Thus, in the example above, a 10% stock dividend normally leads to a decline of around 10% in the share price of the stock. As a result, the market value of your shareholdings after a stock dividend is likely to be the same as it was before the stock dividend. You may have more shares, but each share has a lower market price. There is, however, one bright spot in all this: Unlike cash dividends, these dividends are not taxed *until the stocks are actually sold.*

Dividend Reinvestment Plans

dividend reinvestment plans (DRIPs)
plans in which shareholders have cash dividends automatically reinvested into additional shares of the firm's common stock.

Want to have your cake and eat it too? Well, when it comes to dividends, there is a way to do just that. All you have to do is participate in a **dividend reinvestment plan (DRIP)**. Essentially, these are corporate-sponsored programs whereby shareholders can have some or all of their cash dividends automatically reinvested into additional shares of the company's common stock. (Similar reinvestment programs are offered by mutual funds, which we'll discuss in Chapter 13, and by some brokerage houses, such as Merrill Lynch and Fidelity.) The basic investment philosophy at work here is that *if the company is good enough to invest in, it's good enough to reinvest in.* As Table 5.3 demonstrates, such an approach can have a tremendous impact on your investment position over time. Today more than 1,000 companies (including

TABLE 5.3 Cash or Reinvested Dividends?

Situation: Buy 100 shares of stock at $25 a share (total investment $2,500); stock currently pays $1 a share in annual dividends. Price of the stock increases at 8% per year; dividends grow at 5% per year.

Investment Period	Number of Shares Held	Market Value of Stock Holdings	Total Cash Dividends Received
		Take Dividends in Cash	
5 years	100	$ 3,672	$ 552
10 years	100	5,397	1,258
15 years	100	7,930	2,158
20 years	100	11,652	3,307
		Full Participation in Dividend Reinvestment Plan (100% of cash dividends reinvested)	
5 years	115.59	$ 4,245	$ 0
10 years	135.66	7,322	0
15 years	155.92	12,364	0
20 years	176.00	20,508	0

most major corporations) offer dividend reinvestment plans, and each one provides investors with a convenient and inexpensive way to accumulate capital. Stocks in most DRIPs are acquired free of any brokerage commissions, and most plans allow *partial participation*. That is, rather than committing all of their cash dividends to these plans, participants may specify a portion of their shares for dividend reinvestment and receive cash dividends on the rest. Some plans even sell stocks to their DRIP investors at below-market prices—often at discounts of 3% to 5%. In addition, most plans will credit fractional shares to the investor's account, and many will even allow investors to buy additional shares of the company's stock. For example, once enrolled in Motorola's plan, investors can purchase up to $5,000 worth of the company's stock each quarter.

Shareholders can join dividend reinvestment plans simply by sending a completed authorization form to the company. (Generally, it takes about 30 to 45 days for all the paperwork to be processed.) Once you're in, the number of shares you hold will begin to accumulate with each dividend date. There is a catch, however: Even though these dividends take the form of additional shares of stock, taxes must be paid on them *as though they were cash dividends*. Don't confuse these dividends with stock dividends—*reinvested dividends are taxable as ordinary income in the year they're received*, just as though they had been received in cash.

CONCEPTS IN REVIEW

5.10 Briefly explain how the dividend decision is made. What corporate and market factors are important in deciding whether, and in what amount, to pay dividends?

5.11 Why is the *ex-dividend date* important to stockholders? If a stock is sold *on* the ex-dividend date, who receives the dividend—the buyer or the seller? Explain.

5.12 What is the difference between a *cash dividend* and a *stock dividend?* Which would be more valuable to you? How does a stock dividend compare to a stock split? Is a 200% stock dividend the same as a 2-for-1 stock split? Explain.

5.13 What are *dividend reinvestment plans* and what benefits do they offer to investors? Are there any disadvantages?

http://hepg.aw.com

Purchasing stock directly from companies without using a broker has increased in recent years. This trend will probably continue as acceptance of trading on the Web increases. Netstock Direct provides a wealth of information on direct stock purchase plans (DSPs) and dividend reinvestment plans (DRIPs).

www.netstockdirect.com

Types and Uses of Common Stock

LG 6

Common stocks appeal to investors because they offer the potential for everything from current income and stability of capital to attractive capital gains. The market contains a wide range of stock, from the most conservative to the highly speculative. Generally, the kinds of stocks that investors seek will depend on their investment objectives and investment programs. We will examine several of the more popular types of common stocks here, as well as the various ways such securities can be used in different types of investment programs.

Types of Stocks

As an investor, one of the things you'll want to understand is the market system used to classify common stock. This is so because a stock's general classification reflects not only its fundamental source of return but also the quality of the company's earnings, the issue's susceptibility to market risks, the nature and stability of its earnings and dividends, and even the susceptibility of the stock to adverse economic conditions. Such insight is useful in selecting stocks that will best fit your overall investment objectives. Among the many different types of stocks, blue chips, income stocks, growth stocks, speculative stocks, cyclical stocks, defensive stocks, mid-cap stocks, and small-cap stocks are the most common. We will now look at each of these to see what they are and how they might be used.

Blue-Chip Stocks

blue-chip stocks
financially strong, high quality stocks with long and stable records of earnings and dividends.

Blue chips are the cream of the common stock crop: They are stocks that are unsurpassed in quality and have a long and stable record of earnings and dividends. **Blue-chip stocks** are issued by large, well-established firms that have impeccable financial credentials. These companies hold important, often leading positions in their industries and frequently set the standards by which other firms are measured. Not all blue chips are alike, however. Some provide consistently high dividend yields; others are more growth oriented. Good examples of blue-chip growth firms are Merck, Hewlett-Packard, Abbott Labs, Coca-Cola, Federal Home Loan Mortgage Corp., and Wal-Mart Stores. (Some basic operating and market information about Wal-Mart stock, as obtained from the introductory part of a typical *S&P Stock Report,* is shown in the accompanying exhibit.) Examples of high-yielding blue chips include such companies as American Home Products, Philip Morris, General Mills, Atlantic Richfield, and JCPenney.

Blue chips are particularly attractive to investors who are looking for quality investment outlets that offer decent dividend yields and respectable growth potential. Many use them for long-term investment purposes and, because of their relatively low risk, as a way of obtaining modest but dependable rates of return on the investment dollar. Blue chips are popular with a large segment of the investing public and, as a result, are often relatively high in price, especially when the market is unsettled and investors become more quality-conscious.

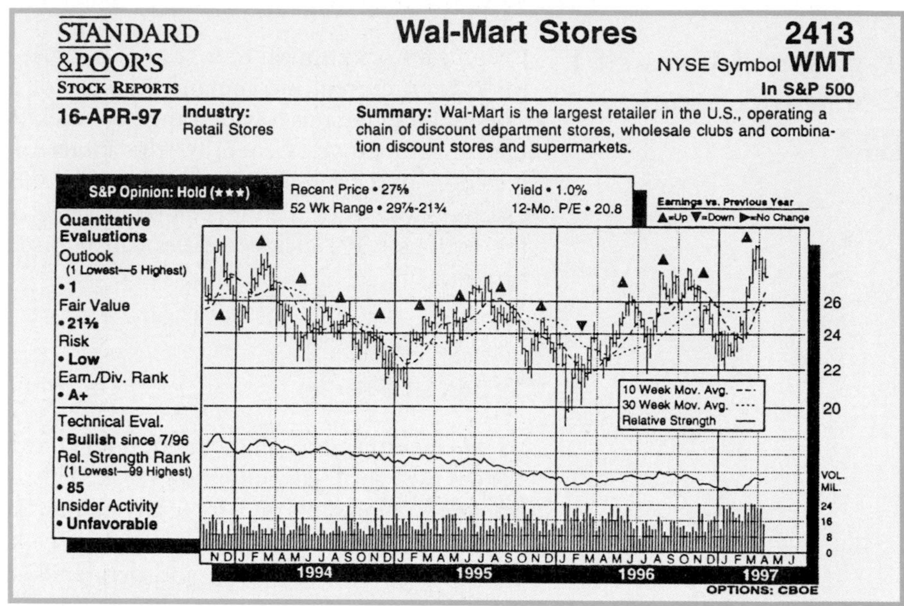

Income Stocks

income stocks
stocks with long and sustained records of paying higher-than-average dividends.

Some stocks are appealing simply because of the dividends they pay. This is the case with **income stocks**—issues that have a long and sustained record of regularly paying higher-than-average dividends. Income stocks are ideally suited for those who seek a relatively safe and high level of current income from their investment capital. But there's more: Holders of income stocks (unlike bonds and preferred stocks) can expect the dividends they receive to increase regularly over time. Look at Consolidated Edison (of New York), for example. It paid dividends of $1.48 a share in 1987; 10 years later, in 1997, it was paying almost 45% more: $2.12 a share. Percentage-wise, that's a big jump in dividends, and it's something that can have quite an impact on total return.

The major disadvantage of income stocks is that some of them may be paying high dividends because of limited growth potential. Indeed, it's not unusual for income securities to exhibit only low or modest rates of growth in earnings. This does not mean that such firms are unprofitable or lack future prospects. Quite the contrary: Most firms whose shares qualify as income stocks are highly profitable organizations with excellent future prospects. A number of income stocks are among the giants of American industry, and many are also classified as quality blue chips. Many public utilities, such as PacifiCorp, Duke Power, Boston Edison, Brooklyn Union Gas, Energy West, and Potomac Electric Power, are found in this group, as are phone company stocks (e.g., Ameritech and U.S. West) and selected industrial and financial issues, such as Texaco, Dow Chemical, H&R Block, Chrysler, Bank One, and CoreStates Financial. By their nature, income stocks are not exposed to a great deal of business and market risk. They are, however, subject to a fair amount of interest rate risk.

Growth Stocks

growth stocks
stocks that experience high rates of growth in operations and earnings.

Shares that have experienced, and are expected to continue experiencing, consistently high rates of growth in operations and earnings are known as **growth stocks.** A good growth stock might exhibit a *sustained* rate of growth in earn-

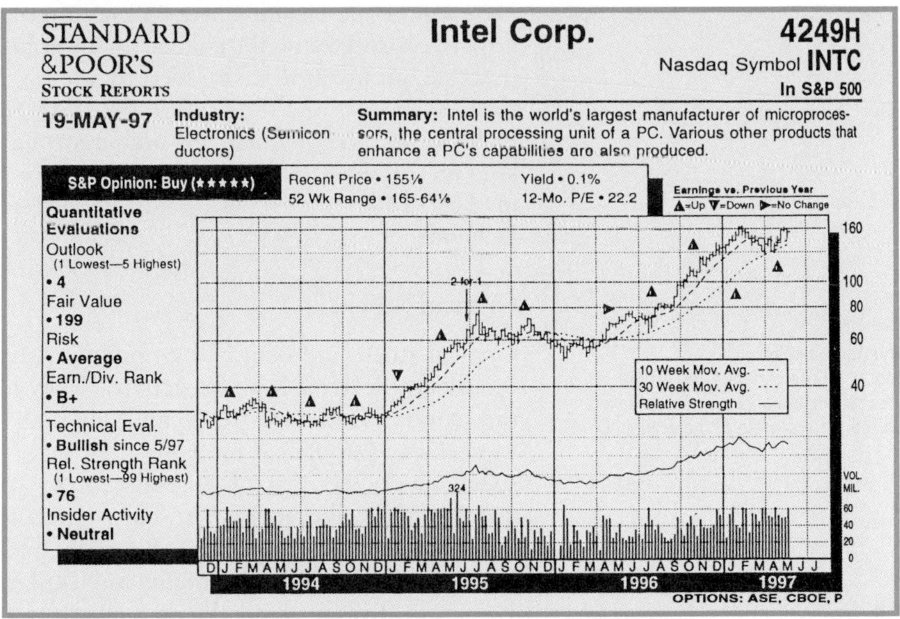

ings of 15% to 18% a year over a period when common stocks, on average, are experiencing growth rates of only 6% to 8%. Generally speaking, established growth companies combine steady earnings growth with high returns on equity. In addition, they have high operating margins and plenty of cash flow to service their debt. Microsoft, Boeing, Franklin Resources, Motorola, Sun Microsystems, Amgen, Home Depot, and Intel (shown here) are all prime examples of growth stocks. As this list suggests, some growth stocks also rate as blue chips and provide quality growth, whereas others represent higher levels of speculation.

Growth stocks normally pay little or nothing in the way of dividends, so their payout ratios seldom exceed 15% to 20% of earnings. Rather, all or most of the profits are reinvested in the company and used to help finance rapid growth. Thus the major source of return to investors is price appreciation. Growth shares generally appeal to investors who are looking for attractive capital gains rather than dividends and who are therefore willing to assume a higher element of risk.

Speculative Stocks

speculative stocks
stocks that offer the potential for substantial price appreciation, usually because of some special situation, such as new management or the introduction of a promising new product.

Shares that lack sustained records of success but still offer the potential for substantial price appreciation are known as **speculative stocks.** Perhaps investors' hopes are spurred by a new management team that has taken over a troubled company or by the introduction of a promising new product. Other times, it's the hint that some new information, discovery, or production technique will favorably affect the growth prospects of the firm and inflate the price of the stock. Speculative stocks are a special breed of securities, and they enjoy a wide following, particularly when the market is bullish.

Generally speaking, the earnings of speculative stocks are uncertain and highly unstable. These stocks are subject to wide swings in price, and they usually pay little or nothing in dividends. On the plus side, speculative stocks such as Aspect Telecommunications, Sierra Semiconductors, Granite Broadcasting,

National Home Health Care, Players International, and Petco offer attractive growth prospects and the chance to "hit it big" in the market. To be successful, however, an investor has to identify the big-money winners before the rest of the market does and the price of the stock is driven up. Speculative stocks are highly risky; they require not only a strong stomach but also a considerable amount of investor know-how. They are used to seek capital gains, and investors often trade in and out of these securities aggressively as the situation demands.

Cyclical Stocks

cyclical stocks
stocks whose earnings and overall market performance are closely linked to the general state of the economy.

Cyclical stocks are issued by companies whose earnings are closely linked to the general level of business activity. They tend to reflect the general state of the economy and to move up and down as the business cycle moves through its peaks and troughs. Companies that serve markets tied to capital equipment spending on the part of business, or to consumer spending for big-ticket, durable items like houses and cars, typically head the list of cyclical stocks. Examples include Caterpillar, Premark International, Coachman Industries, Echlin, Harnischfeger, Raychem, and Timken.

Cyclical stocks generally do well when the economy is moving ahead, but they tend to do *especially well* when the country is in the early stages of a recovery. They are, however, perhaps best avoided when the economy begins to weaken. Because their prices have a tendency to move with the level of economic activity, they are probably most suitable for investors who are willing to trade in and out of these issues as the economic outlook dictates and who can tolerate the accompanying exposure to risk.

Defensive Stocks

defensive stocks
stocks that tend to hold their own, and even do well, when the economy starts to falter.

Sometimes it is possible to find stocks whose prices will remain stable or even increase when general economic activity is tapering off. These securities are known as **defensive stocks,** because they tend to be less affected by downswings in the business cycle than the average issue. Defensive stocks include the shares of many public utilities, as well as industrial and consumer goods companies that produce or market such staples as beverages, foods, and drugs. An excellent example of a defensive stock is Bandag; this recession-resistant company is the world's leading manufacturer of rubber used to retread tires. Other examples are Checkpoint Systems, a manufacturer of antitheft clothing security clips; Union Corp., a debt collection company; and WD-40, the maker of that famous all-purpose lubricant. Perhaps the best known of all defensive stocks, particularly in inflationary periods, are gold mining shares; these stocks blossom when inflation becomes a serious problem. Defensive shares are commonly used by more aggressive investors. For the most part, such investors tend to "park" their funds temporarily in defensive stocks while the economy remains soft, or until the investment atmosphere improves.

Mid-Cap Stocks

A stock's size is based on its market value—or, more commonly, on what is known as its *market capitalization* (the market price of the stock times the number of shares outstanding). Generally speaking, the U.S. stock market can be broken into three segments, as measured by a stock's market "cap":

small-cap	less than \$750 million
mid-cap	\$750 million to \$3–\$4 billion
large-cap	more than \$3–\$4 billion

The large-cap stocks are the real biggies—the AT&Ts, GMs, and Exxons of the investment world. Although there are far fewer large-cap stocks than any other size, these companies account for about 60% of the total market value of all U.S. equities. But as the saying goes, bigger isn't necessarily better. And nowhere is that statement more accurate than in the stock market. Indeed, *both* the small-cap and mid-cap segments of the market tend to outperform the large stocks over time.

mid-cap stocks
medium-sized stocks, generally with market values of less than \$3 to \$4 billion but more than \$750 million.

Mid-cap stocks are a special breed, and offer investors some attractive return opportunities. They provide much of the sizzle of small-stock returns, without all the price volatility. (We'll look at small-cap stocks soon.) At the same time, because mid-caps are fairly good-sized companies and many of them have been around for a long time, they offer some of the safety of the big, established stocks. Among the ranks of the mid-caps are such well-known companies as Starbucks, Wendy's International (shown here), Chris-Craft Industries, Fisher Scientific, Lone Star Steakhouse, and Apollo Group, in addition to some not-so-well-known names. Although these securities offer a nice alternative to large stocks without the drawbacks and uncertainties of small-caps, they probably are most appropriate for investors who are willing to tolerate a bit more risk and price volatility.

One type of mid-cap stock that is particularly interesting is the so-called *baby blue chip*. Also known as "baby blues," these companies have all the characteristics of a regular blue chip *except size*. Like their larger counterparts, baby blues have rock-solid balance sheets, with only modest levels of debt, and long histories of steady profit growth. For the most part, they've been able to secure niches in fast-growing specialty markets. Some of these companies, in fact, have been posting gains in annual earnings for 30 to 40 years in a row. Baby blues

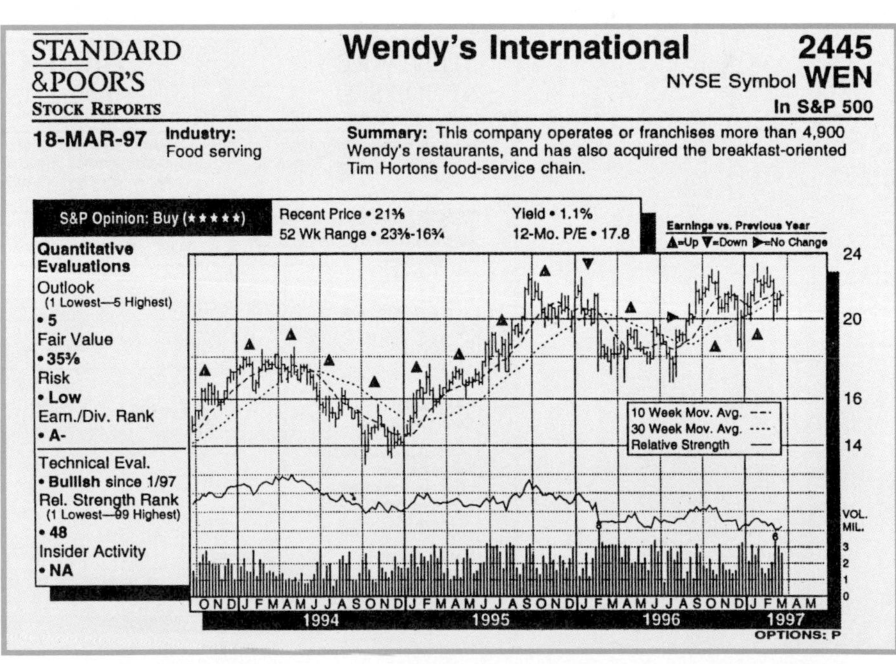

normally pay a modest level of dividends, but like most mid-caps, they tend to emphasize growth. Thus they're considered ideal for investors seeking quality long-term growth. Some well-known baby blues are Tootsie Roll, Pall Corp., Reynolds & Reynolds, Hormel, RPM, and Wallace Computer Service.

Small-Cap Stocks

small-cap stocks
stocks that generally have market values of less than \$500–\$750 million but can offer above-average returns.

Some investors consider small companies to be in a class by themselves in terms of attractive return opportunities. And in many cases, this has turned out to be true. Known as **small-cap stocks,** these companies generally have annual revenues of less than \$250 million. Because of their size, spurts of growth can have dramatic effects on their earnings and stock prices. ShowBiz Pizza Time, Mail Boxes Etc., Boston Celtics (the NBA basketball team), Ben & Jerry's, Earl Scheib, and Alaska Air (shown here) are some of the better-known small-cap stocks. Although some small-caps (like Alaska Air) are solid companies with equally solid financials, that's not the case with most of them. Indeed, because many of these companies are so small, they don't have a lot of stock outstanding, and their shares are not widely traded. In addition, small-company stocks have a tendency to be "here today and gone tomorrow." Although some of these stocks may hold the potential for high returns, investors should also be aware of the very high risk exposure that comes with many of them.

A special category of small-company stock is the so-called *initial public offering (IPO)*. Most IPOs are small, relatively new companies that are going public for the first time. (Prior to their public offering, these stocks were privately held and *not* publicly traded.) Like other small-cap stocks, IPOs are attractive because of the substantial—sometimes phenomenal—capital gains that investors can earn. Of course, there's a catch: In order to stand a chance of buying some of the better, more attractive IPOs, you need to be either a big-time trader or a preferred client of the broker. Otherwise, the only IPOs you will be offered are the ones the big guys don't want—which should tell you something about that particular IPO. More often than not, the small individual

STANDARD &POOR'S STOCK REPORTS

Alaska Air Group **46**

NYSE Symbol **ALK**

In S&P MidCap 400

24-MAR-97 **Industry:** Air Transport

Summary: ALK operates two passenger airlines: Alaska Airlines, the leading carrier between Alaska and the lower 48 states, and Horizon Air, which serves smaller cities in the Northwest.

S&P Opinion: Accumulate (★★★★) Recent Price • 27 52 Wk Range • 30¾-19⅛ Yield • Nil 12-Mo. P/E • 10.2

Quantitative Evaluations
Outlook (1 Lowest—5 Highest) • **3−**
Fair Value • **27½**
Risk • **Average**
Earn./Div. Rank • **B-**

Technical Eval. • **Bullish** since 9/96
Rel. Strength Rank (1 Lowest—99 Highest) • **95**
Insider Activity • **NA**

Earnings vs. Previous Year ▲=Up ▼=Down ▶=No Change

10 Week Mov. Avg. 30 Week Mov. Avg. Relative Strength

30 25 20 15 VOL. (000) 1200 800 400 0 2951 3491

O N D J F M A M J J A S O N D J F M A M J J A S O N D J F M A M J J A S O N D J F M A M
1994 1995 1996 1997

OPTIONS: ASE

investor gets a chance to buy a new issue only after it's been driven way up in price and the initial investors start bailing out, taking their profits with them. Surprisingly, this may take only a few hours or days to occur. If you're not in on the first day, the odds are that your returns will be mediocre, at best. It's an open secret on Wall Street that when it comes to hot IPOs, most individual investors stand little chance of even playing the game, much less winning.

Without a doubt, IPOs are extremely high-risk investments, with the odds stacked against the investor. Because there's no market record to rely on, these stocks should be used only by investors who know what to look for in the company and who can tolerate substantial exposure to risk. IPOs tend to flourish when the market heats up, and they very definitely are faddish, their ranks often dominated by trendy retail outlets, food chains, and high-tech firms.

Investing in Foreign Stocks

One of the most dramatic changes in our financial markets in the 1980s was the trend toward globalization. Indeed, globalization has become the buzzword of the 1990s, and nowhere is that more evident than in the world equity markets. Consider, for example, that in 1970 the U.S. stock market accounted for fully *two-thirds of the world market.* In essence, our stock market was twice as big as all the rest of the world's stock markets *combined.* That's no longer true: In 1997, the U.S. share of the world equity market had dropped to just over 40%.

Today the world equity markets are dominated by six countries, which together account for about 75% of the total market:

	Approximate Market Value (1997)
United States	$9.1 trillion
Japan	2.0 trillion
United Kingdom/ Britain	1.8 trillion
Germany	735 billion
France	590 billion
Canada	510 billion

The United States is still the biggest player and is one of only three countries with trillion-dollar stock markets. In addition to these six, another dozen or so markets are also regarded as major world players. Among the markets in this second tier are Switzerland, Australia, Italy, the Netherlands, Hong Kong, Spain, and Singapore. Finally, a number of relatively small, emerging markets—like South Korea, Mexico, Malaysia, Portugal, Thailand, and Russia—are beginning to make their presence felt. Clearly, the landscape has changed a lot in the last 20 years, and there's every reason to believe—with the historic changes taking place in Eastern Europe and the former communist bloc—that even greater changes lie ahead.

Although it is clear that the U.S. market dominates in terms of sheer size—as well as in the number of listed companies (about 8,500 of them)—that still leaves unanswered a very important question: How has the U.S. equity market performed in comparison to the rest of the world's major stock markets? Not

TABLE 5.4 Comparative Annual Returns in the World's Major Equity Markets, 1980–1997

	Annual Total Returns (in U.S. dollars)								
	Australia	Canada	France	Germany	Japan	Switzerland	United Kingdom	United States	Rank**
1997*	18.9%	20.7%	37.0%	47.3%	−7.3%	45.8%	33.2%	24.9%	5th
1996	5.9	20.6	12.1	23.1	−6.5	29.0	16.4	28.0	2nd
1995	15.4	17.6	13.3	16.6	−0.5	45.2	23.3	35.7	2nd
1994	1.4	−5.1	−7.3	3.1	21.4	30.0	−4.4	4.9	3rd
1993	33.4	17.4	19.6	34.8	23.9	41.7	19.0	16.4	8th
1992	−6.1	−4.6	5.2	−2.1	−26.0	26.0	14.0	7.2	3rd
1991	35.8	12.1	18.6	8.7	9.0	16.8	16.0	23.3	2nd
1990	−16.2	−12.2	−13.3	−8.8	−35.9	−5.1	10.4	−0.4	2nd
1989	10.8	25.2	37.6	48.2	2.3	28.0	23.1	30.7	3rd
1988	38.2	17.9	37.1	19.8	35.4	5.8	4.1	15.5	6th
1987	9.5	14.8	−13.9	−24.6	41.0	−9.2	35.2	5.9	5th
1986	45.0	10.8	79.9	36.4	101.2	34.7	27.7	26.1	7th
1985	21.1	16.2	84.2	138.1	44.0	109.2	53.4	31.7	6th
1984	−12.4	−7.1	4.8	−5.2	17.2	−11.1	5.3	1.2	4th
1983	55.2	32.4	33.2	23.9	24.8	19.9	17.3	24.7	5th
1982	−22.2	2.6	−4.2	10.5	−0.6	2.9	9.0	24.8	1st
1981	−23.8	−10.1	−28.5	−10.3	15.7	−9.5	−10.2	−2.8	2nd
1980	54.7	21.6	−2.0	−10.7	30.4	−7.8	42.0	20.6	5th
	Average Annual Returns Over Extended Holding Periods								
5 years									
1993–97	14.5%	13.8%	14.0%	24.0%	5.4%	38.1%	16.8%	21.5%	
1988–92	10.4	6.8	15.3	11.5	−6.5	13.6	13.3	13.9	
1983–87	21.2	12.7	31.8	23.5	43.0	22.2	26.8	17.3	
10 years									
1988–97*	12.4	10.2	14.7	17.6	−0.7	25.3	15.1	18.1	
Decades									
1990–97*	9.7	7.6	9.6	14.0	−4.9	27.6	15.5	13.3	
1980–89	13.9	11.6	17.6	16.3	28.6	12.2	19.3	17.2	
18 years									
1980–97*	12.0	9.8	14.0	15.2	12.5	18.8	17.6	16.6	

Note: Total return = coupon income + capital gain (or loss) + profit (or loss) from changes in currency exchange rates.

*1997 data through third quarter (September 1997).

**"Rank " shows how U.S. returns ranked among the listed major markets (e.g., in 1994, the United States ranked third out of the 8 markets listed in the table).

Source: International returns obtained from Morgan Stanley Capital International and Templeton International; U.S. returns based on DJIA.

too well, unfortunately. Table 5.4 provides a summary of total annual returns (in U.S. dollars), for the 18-year period from 1980 through 1997, for eight of the world's largest equity markets. Note that the United States finished first only once (in 1982), and in 9 of those 18 years, the U.S. equity markets finished in the bottom half of the distribution. But keep in mind that *those returns are in U.S. dollars* and, as the *Investing in Action* box on page 197 reveals, a good deal of that performance is due to the behavior of *currency exchange rates* and not the markets themselves. Indeed, the U.S. stock market is one of the strongest and best performing in the world! Still, the fact remains that when both markets and currencies are combined, some very rewarding opportunities are available to U.S. investors willing to invest in foreign securities.

INVESTING IN ACTION

Currencies: In International Investing, They Can Make You or Break You

There are many good reasons to invest overseas: Capitalism is spreading around the world like wildfire. Economic growth in many developing areas dwarfs U.S. growth. Computers and advances in telecommunications have made it easier to trade in other countries. Accounting practices have improved, as many foreign companies have realized that they must make extensive financial disclosures—beyond their normal comfort level—if they want to attract U.S. investors. Finally, investing overseas is an excellent way to diversify a portfolio, because economies around the world generally move independently. If the U.S. stock market stalls, foreign markets may be booming.

Yet even given these advantages and opportunities around the world, it's difficult to believe that an investor in international stocks can consistently outperform his or her U.S. counterpart. For example, take a look at the graph below: Foreign stocks appear to have outperformed American equities between 1985 and 1995. That is, foreign stock returns, when measured in U.S. dollars, produced a 470% return compared to the 412% return produced by U.S. stocks. But what the numbers don't show is the impact of a weakening U.S. dollar. *If you exclude the currency factor, then U.S. stocks dwarfed the performance of their overseas counterparts:* Instead of a 470% return, foreign stocks returned 193%.

A favorable currency movement for a U.S. investor in a foreign market is a weakening dollar. This is because money that's invested overseas is typically converted to a local currency and then later converted back to dollars. If the dollar is weakening, then the local currency can buy more dollars when the money is converted later.

It's important to separate investing in foreign markets from currency risk. Indeed, some money managers remove the currency risk through complex hedging strategies. But these strategies cost money to implement, and many are loath to employ them and thereby miss any *favorable* currency movements that occur.

In contrast, a stronger dollar is bad news for U.S. investors, because the local currency later buys fewer dollars. In the mid-1990s, the U.S. dollar strengthened against most currencies. For example, over the 3-year period ending March 1997, the U.S. stock market produced average annual returns of about 22%. The Mexican stock market produced an average annual return of 17% in local-currency terms. However, in terms of U.S. dollars, the average annual return in Mexico was a very poor 12%. The reason: The dollar strengthened against the peso.

Indeed, not too many stock markets outperformed the U.S. in dollar terms. The ones that did—among them Egypt, Russia, Turkey, and Zimbabwe—were coming from very low base values. And many of these markets carried risks well beyond currency risk, such as the stability of their governments, that we don't worry about in the United States.

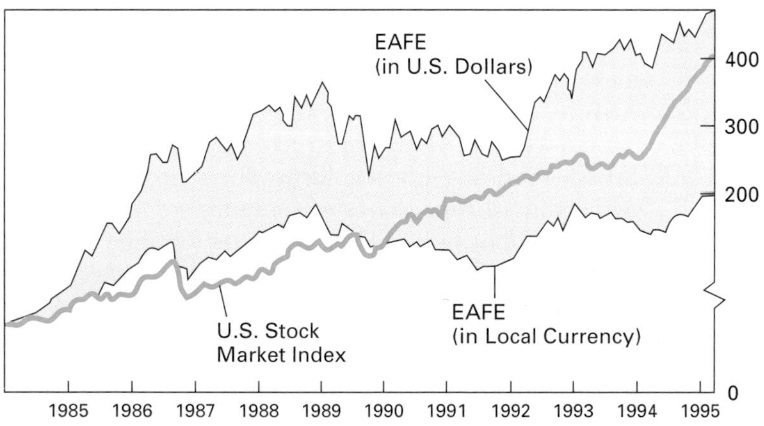

Source: Data Morgan Stanley Capital International

Going Global: Direct Investments or ADRs

Basically, there are two ways to invest in foreign stocks: One way is to do it through direct investments and the other is through ADRs. (We'll discuss a third way—international mutual funds—in Chapter 13.) Without a doubt, the most adventuresome way is to *buy shares directly in foreign markets.* Investing directly is *not* for the uninitiated, however. You have to know what you're doing and must be prepared to tolerate a good deal of market risk. Although most major U.S. brokerage houses are set up to accommodate investors interested in buying foreign securities, there are still many logistical problems to be faced. To begin with, you have to cope with currency fluctuations and changing foreign exchange rates. As we'll see, these can have a dramatic impact on your returns. But that's just the start: You also have to deal with a different set of regulatory and accounting standards. The fact is that most foreign markets, even the bigger ones, are not so closely regulated as U.S. exchanges. Investors in foreign markets thus have to put up with insider trading and other practices that can cause wild swings in market prices. Furthermore, accounting standards are often much looser, making detailed information about a company's financial condition and operating results a lot harder to come by. Finally, there are the obvious language barriers, tax problems, and general "red tape" that all too often plague international transactions. There's no doubt that the returns from direct foreign investments can be substantial, but so can the obstacles placed in your way.

Fortunately, there is an easier way to invest in foreign stocks, and that is to buy *American Depositary Receipts (ADRs)*—or *American Depositary Shares,* as they're sometimes called. As we saw in Chapter 2, ADRs are negotiable instruments, each ADR representing a specific number of shares in a specific foreign company. (Actually, the number of shares held can range from a fraction of a share to 20 shares or more.) ADRs are great for individual investors who want foreign stocks but don't want the hassles that usually come with them. That's because American Depositary Receipts are bought and sold on American markets just like stocks in U.S. companies—and their prices are quoted in U.S. dollars, not British pounds, Japanese yen, or German marks. Furthermore, dividends are paid in dollars. Although there are about 350 foreign companies *whose shares are directly listed on U.S. exchanges* (over 200 of which are Canadian), most foreign companies are traded in this country as ADRs. Indeed, shares of about 1,000 companies, from more than 40 countries, are traded as ADRs on the NYSE, AMEX, and Nasdaq/OTC markets.

To see how ADRs are structured, take a look at Cadbury Schweppes, the British food and household products firm. Each Cadbury ADR represents ownership of four shares of Cadbury stock. These shares are held in a custodial account by a U.S. bank (or its foreign correspondent), which receives dividends, pays any foreign withholding taxes, and then converts the net proceeds to U.S. dollars, which it passes on to investors. Other foreign stocks that can be purchased as ADRs include Sony, Daimler-Benz, Elf Aquitaine, Cathay Pacific Airways, Glaxo Wellcome, Nestlé's, Shanghai Petrochemicals, and Nintendo. You can even buy ADRs on Russian companies, such as Vimpel-Communications, a Moscow-based cellular phone company whose shares trade (as ADRs) on the NYSE!

INVESTOR FACT

FROM RUSSIA, WITH LOVE— Want to buy Russian stocks? Well, now you can buy them right on the New York Stock Exchange. Among the big ones are Unified Energy Systems (ticker symbol EESR), the primary national electric utility, and LUKoil (LKOH), Russia's largest oil company. Perhaps you want to buy a diversified portfolio of Russian shares. In that case, Templeton Russia Fund (TRF) or the Morgan Stanley Russia & New Europe Fund (RNE) might be for you. But be prepared for volatility, especially if the country's leader falls ill.

Putting Returns in a Global Perspective

Whether an investor is buying foreign stocks directly or through ADRs, the whole process of global investing is a bit more complex and more risky than domestic investing. For when investing globally, *the investor has to pick not only the right stock but also the right market.* Basically, foreign stocks are valued much the same way as American stocks. Indeed, the same variables that drive U.S. share prices (earnings, dividends, etc.) also drive stock values in foreign markets. On top of this, each market reacts to its own set of economic forces (inflation, interest rates, the level of economic activity, etc.), which sets the tone of the market. At any given time, therefore, some markets are performing better than others. The challenge facing global investors is to be in the right market at the right time. As with American stocks, foreign shares produce the same two basic sources of stock returns: dividends and capital gains (or losses).

But with global investing, there is a third variable—*currency exchanger-ates*—that plays an important role in defining returns to U.S. investors. As the U.S. dollar becomes weaker or stronger relative to a foreign currency, the returns to U.S. investors from foreign stocks increase or decrease accordingly. Essentially, in a global context, total return to U.S. investors in foreign securities is defined as follows:

Equation 5.4

$$\frac{\text{Total return}}{\text{(in U.S. dollars)}} = \frac{\text{current income}}{\text{(dividends)}} + \frac{\text{capital gains}}{\text{(or losses)}} \pm \frac{\text{changes in currency}}{\text{exchange rates}}$$

Because current income and capital gains are in the "local currency" (the currency in which the foreign stock is denominated, such as the German mark or the Japanese yen), we can shorten the total return formula to:

Equation 5.5

$$\begin{matrix}\text{Total return} \\ \text{(in U.S. dollars)}\end{matrix} = \begin{matrix}\text{returns from current} \\ \text{income and capital gains} \\ \text{(in local currency)}\end{matrix} \pm \begin{matrix}\text{returns from} \\ \text{changes in currency} \\ \text{exchange rates}\end{matrix}$$

Thus, the two basic components of total return are *those generated by the stocks themselves* (dividends plus change in share prices) and *those derived from movements in currency exchange rates.*

Employing the same two basic components noted above in Equation 5.5, we can compute total return in U.S. dollars by using the following holding period return (HPR) formula, as modified for changes in currency exchange rates.

Equation 5.6

$$\begin{matrix}\text{Total return} \\ \text{(in U.S. dollars)}\end{matrix} = \left[\frac{\begin{matrix}\text{ending value of} \\ \text{stock in foreign} \\ \text{currency}\end{matrix} + \begin{matrix}\text{amount of dividends} \\ \text{received in} \\ \text{foreign currency}\end{matrix}}{\begin{matrix}\text{beginning value of stock} \\ \text{in foreign currency}\end{matrix}} \times \frac{\begin{matrix}\text{exchange rate} \\ \text{at } \textit{end} \text{ of} \\ \text{holding period}\end{matrix}}{\begin{matrix}\text{exchange rate} \\ \text{at } \textit{beginning} \text{ of} \\ \text{holding period}\end{matrix}}\right] - 1.00$$

where the "exchange rate" represents *the value of the foreign currency in U.S. dollars*—that is, how much one unit of the foreign currency is worth in U.S. money.

Note that because this is a (modified) HPR formula, it is best used over investment periods of 1 year or less. Also, because it is assumed that dividends are received at the same exchange rate as the ending price of the stock, this equation provides only an *approximate* measure of return—though a fairly close one. Essentially, the first component of Equation 5.6 provides returns on the stock, in local currency, and the second element accounts for the impact of changes in currency exchange rates.

To see how this formula works, consider an American investor who buys several hundred shares of Petrofina, a large Belgium petroleum and chemical company that trades on the Brussels stock exchange. The investor paid a price *per share* of 9,140 Belgium francs (Bf) for the stock, at a time when the exchange rate between the U.S. dollar and the Belgium franc (U.S.\$/Bf) was \$0.0307, which means the Bf was worth a little more than 3 cents. Put another way, this exchange rate amounts to 32.55 Bf per U.S. dollar, so 1 U.S.\$/32.55 Bf = \$0.0307. The stock paid *annual* dividends of 275 Bf per share, and at the end of the year it was trading at 9,500 Bf per share, when the U.S.\$/Bf exchange rate was \$0.0336 (which is equivalent to 29.75 Bf per U.S. dollar). The stock clearly went up in price, so the investor must have done all right. To find out just what kind of return this investment generated (in U.S. dollars), we'll have to use Equation 5.6.

$$\begin{aligned}\text{Total return (in U.S. dollars)} &= \left[\frac{9{,}500 + 275}{9{,}140} \times \frac{\$0.0336}{\$0.0307}\right] - 1.00\\ &= [1.0695 \times 1.0945] - 1.00\\ &= [1.1705] - 1.00\\ &= \underline{\underline{17.05\%}}\end{aligned}$$

Actually, at a return of 17.05%, the investor seems to have done quite well. However, as it turns out, *most of this return was due to currency movements, not to the behavior of the stock*. Look at just the first part of the equation: It shows the return (in local currency) *earned on the stock* from dividends and capital gains—that is, 1.0695 − 1.00 = 6.95%. Thus the stock itself produced a return of less than 7%, and all the rest—more than 10% (i.e., 17.05 − 6.95)—came from the change in currency values. In this case, the value of the U.S. dollar went down relative to the Belgian franc and thus added to the return.

As we've just seen, exchange rates can have a dramatic impact on investor returns. They can convert mediocre returns or even losses into very attractive returns—and vice versa. There's really only one thing that determines whether the so-called *currency effect* is going to be positive or negative, and that's the behavior of the U.S. dollar relative to the currency in which the foreign security is denominated. In essence, *a stronger dollar has a negative impact on total returns to U.S. investors, and a weaker dollar has a positive impact.* Thus, other things being equal, the best time to be in foreign securities is when the dollar is *falling,* because that *adds* to returns to U.S. investors. Of course, the greater the amount of fluctuation in the currency exchange rate, the greater the impact on total returns. The challenge facing global investors, therefore, is to find not only the best-performing foreign stock(s) but also the best-performing foreign currencies. That means you want *the value of both the for-*

eign stock and the foreign currency to go up over your investment horizon. And this rule applies both to direct investment in foreign stocks and to the purchase of ADRs (because even though ADRs are denominated in dollars, their quoted prices vary with ongoing changes in currency exchange rates).

Alternative Investment Strategies

Basically, common stocks can be used (1) as a "storehouse" of value, (2) as a way to accumulate capital, and (3) as a source of income. Storage of value is important to all investors; nobody likes to lose money. However, some investors are more concerned about it than others and therefore rank safety of principal first in their stock selection criteria. These investors are more quality-conscious and tend to gravitate toward blue chips and other nonspeculative shares. Accumulation of capital, in contrast, is generally an important goal to those with long-term investment horizons. These investors use the capital gains and/or dividends that stocks provide to build up their wealth. Some use growth stocks for such purposes, others do it with income shares, and still others use a little of both. Finally, some investors use stocks as a source of income. To them, a dependable flow of dividends is essential. High-yielding, good-quality income shares are usually the preferred investment vehicle for these people.

Individual investors can use a number of different *investment strategies* to reach one or more of their investment goals. These include buy-and-hold, high income, quality long-term growth, aggressive stock management, and speculation and short-term trading. The first three strategies appeal to investors who consider storage of value important. Depending on the temperament of the investor and the time he or she has to devote to an investment program, any of the strategies might be used to accumulate capital. In contrast, the high-income strategy is the logical choice for those using stocks as a source of income.

Buy-and-Hold

Buy-and-hold is the most basic and certainly one of the most conservative of all investment strategies. The objective is to place money in a secure investment outlet (safety of principal is vital) and watch it grow over time. High-quality stocks that offer attractive current income and/or capital gains are selected and held for extended periods—perhaps as long as 10 to 15 years. This strategy is often used to finance future retirement plans, to meet the educational needs of children, or simply as a convenient way to accumulate capital over the long haul. Generally, investors pick out a few good stocks and then invest in them on a regular basis for long periods of time, until either the investment climate or corporate conditions change dramatically.

Not only do buy-and-hold investors regularly add fresh capital to their portfolios (many treat them like savings plans), but most also plow the income from annual dividends back into the portfolio and reinvest in additional shares (often through dividend reinvestment plans). Long popular with so-called *value-oriented investors,* this approach is used by quality-conscious individuals who are looking for competitive returns over the long haul.

High Income

Individual investors often use common stocks to seek high levels of current income. Common stocks are viewed as desirable outlets for such purposes not only because of their current yields but also because their *dividend levels tend to increase over time*. Safety of principal and stability of income are vital, and capital gains are of secondary importance. Quality income shares are the popular investment medium for this kind of strategy. Because of the high yields available from many income shares, some investors adopt this strategy simply as a way of earning high (and relatively safe) returns on their investment capital. More often, however, high-income strategies are used by those who are trying to supplement their income and plan to use the added income for consumption purposes, such as a retired couple supplementing their retirement benefits with income from stocks.

Quality Long-Term Growth

This strategy is *less conservative* than either of the first two in that it seeks capital gains as the primary source of return. A fair amount of trading takes place with this approach, most of which is confined to quality growth stocks (including baby blues and other mid-caps) that offer attractive growth prospects and the chance for considerable price appreciation. Dividends are not ignored, however, because a number of growth stocks also pay dividends, which many growth-oriented investors consider *an added source of return*. But even with dividend-paying growth stocks, this strategy still emphasizes capital gains as the principal way to earn the big returns. The approach involves a greater element of risk, because of its heavy reliance on capital gains. Therefore, a good deal of diversification is often used. Long-term accumulation of capital is the most common reason for using this approach, but compared to the buy-and-hold tactic, the investor aggressively seeks a bigger payoff by doing considerably more trading and assuming more market risk.

A variation of this investment theme—one that combines quality long-term growth with high income—is the so-called *total-return approach* to investing. Though solidly anchored in long-term growth, this approach also considers dividend income as a viable and important source of return—one that should be sought after, rather than relegated to an after-thought or treated as merely a pleasant by-product. In essence, with the total return approach, investors seek attractive long-term returns from *both* dividend income *and* capital gains. These investors hold both income stocks and growth stocks in their portfolios, or they may hold stocks that provide both dividends and capital gains (in which case, the investor doesn't necessarily look for high-yielding stocks, but rather for stocks that offer the potential for *high rates of growth in their dividend streams*). Like their counterparts who employ high-income or quality long-term growth strategies, these investors are very concerned about quality. Indeed, about the only thing that separates these investors from high-income and quality long-term growth investors is that to them, what matters is not so much the *source of return* as the *amount of return*. For this reason, total-return investors seek the most attractive returns wherever they can find it—be it from a growing stream of dividends or from appreciation in the price of a stock.

Aggressive Stock Management

Aggressive stock management also uses quality issues but seeks attractive rates of return through a fully managed portfolio—that is, one in which the investor aggressively trades in and out of various stocks in order to achieve eye-catching returns, primarily from capital gains. Blue chips, growth stocks, mid-caps, and cyclical issues are the primary investment vehicles; more aggressive investors might even consider small-cap stocks, foreign shares, and ADRs.

This approach is somewhat similar to the quality long-term growth strategy, but it involves considerably more trading, and the investment horizon is generally much shorter. For example, rather than waiting 2 or 3 years for a stock to move, an aggressive stock trader would go after the same investment payoff in 6 months to a year. Timing security transactions and turning investment capital over fairly rapidly are both key elements of this strategy. These investors try to stay fully invested in stocks when the market is bullish, and when it weakens, they often shift to a more defensive posture by putting a big chunk of their money into defensive stocks or even into cash and other short-term debt instruments. This strategy has obvious and substantial risks, and it also places real demands on the individual's time and investment skills, but the rewards can be equally substantial.

Speculation and Short-Term Trading

Speculation and short-term trading characterize the least conservative of all investment strategies, especially when carried to the extreme. The sole investment objective is capital gains, and if the objective can be achieved in 2 weeks, so much the better. Although such investors confine most of their attention to speculative or small-cap stocks, they are not averse to using foreign shares (especially those found in so-called *emerging markets*) or other forms of common stock if these offer attractive short-term capital gains opportunities. Many speculators find that information about the industry or company is much less important than market psychology or the general tone of the market itself. It is a process of constantly switching from one position to another as new investment opportunities unfold. Because the strategy involves so much risk, many transactions yield little or no profit, or even substantial losses. The hope is, of course, that when one does hit, it will be in a big way, and returns will be more than sufficient to offset losses. This strategy obviously requires considerable knowledge, time, and—perhaps most important—the psychological and financial fortitude to withstand the shock of financial losses.

CONCEPTS IN REVIEW

5.14 Define and briefly discuss the investment merits of each of the following.

a. *Blue chips*
b. *Income stocks*
c. *Mid-cap stocks*
d. *American Depositary Receipts*
e. *IPOs*

5.15 Why do most income stocks offer only limited capital gains potential? Does this mean the outlook for continued profitability is also limited? Explain.

5.16 With all the securities available in this country, why would a U.S. investor want to buy foreign stocks? Briefly describe the two ways in which a U.S. investor can buy stocks in a foreign company. As an American investor, which approach would you prefer? Explain.

5.17 The effects of currency exchange rates on market returns were discussed in the *Investing in Action* box on page 197. Can currency exchange rates have an impact on security returns? Explain. How do returns in the U.S. stock market stack up to returns in foreign markets once currency exchange rates are factored out?

5.18 Which investment approach (or approaches) do you feel would be most appropriate for a quality-conscious investor? Explain. How about someone who is willing to tolerate a good deal of risk?

http://hepg.aw.com

This section describes how stocks may be classified into subcategories on the basis of certain characteristics. At the site listed here, Prudential Securities provides some additional information on these classifications.

www.prusec.com/classstk.htm

Summary

LG 1 **Explain the investment appeal of common stocks and why individuals like to invest in them.** Common stocks have long been a popular investment vehicle, largely because of the attractive return opportunities they provide. From current income to capital gains, there are common stocks available to fit just about any investment need.

LG 2 **Describe stock returns from a historical perspective and gain an appreciation of how current returns measure up to historical standards of performance.** Historically, stocks have provided investors with annual returns of around 10% to 15%. These returns consist of both dividends and capital gains. Of course, higher returns may be possible over shorter periods of time and for those willing to assume a greater amount of risk.

LG 3 **Discuss the basic features of common stocks, including issue characteristics, stock quotations, and transaction costs.** Common stocks are a form of equity capital, with each share representing partial ownership of a company. Publicly traded stock can be issued via public offering or through a rights offering to existing stockholders. Companies can also increase the number of shares outstanding through a stock split. To reduce the number of shares of stock in circulation, companies can buy back shares, which are then held as treasury stock. Occasionally, a company issues different classes of common stock, known as classified common stock.

LG 4 **Understand of the different kinds of common stock values.** There are several ways to calculate the value of a share of stock, ranging from book value, which represents accounting value, to market and investment values, which are most important to investors. These latter two represent what the stock is or should be worth.

LG 5 **Discuss common stock dividends, types of dividends, and dividend reinvestment plans.** Companies often share their profits by paying out cash dividends to stockholders. Such actions are normally taken only after carefully considering a variety of corporate and market factors. Sometimes companies declare stock dividends rather than, or in addition to, cash dividends. Many firms that pay cash dividends have dividend reinvestment plans, whereby shareholders can have cash dividends automatically reinvested in the company's stock.

LG 6

Describe various types of common stocks, including foreign stocks, and note the different ways in which stocks can be used as investment vehicles. The type of stock selected depends on an investor's needs and preferences. In today's market, the investor has a full range of stocks to choose from, including blue chips, income stocks, growth stocks, speculative issues, cyclicals, defensive shares, mid-cap stocks, small-cap stocks, and initial public offerings. In addition, U.S. investors can buy the common stocks of foreign companies either directly on foreign exchanges or on U.S. markets as American Depositary Receipts (ADRs). Generally speaking, common stocks can be used as a storehouse of value, as a way to accumulate capital, and as a source of income. Different investment strategies—buy-and-hold, high income, quality long-term growth, aggressive stock management, and speculation and short-term trading—can be followed to achieve these objectives.

Discussion Questions

LG 2

Q5.1. Look at the record of stock returns in Tables 5.1 and 5.2, particularly the return performance during the 1970s, 1980s, and 1990s.

a. How would you compare the returns during the 1970s with those produced in the 1980s? How would you characterize market returns so far during the decade of the nineties (1990–1997). Is there anything that stands out about this market?

b. Considering the average annual returns that have been generated over *holding periods* of 5 years or more, what rate of return do you feel is typical for the stock market in general? Is it unreasonable to expect this kind of return, on average, in the future? Explain.

LG 3

Q5.2. Assume that the following quote for the Alpha Beta Corp. (a NYSE stock) was obtained from the Thursday, April 10, issue of the *Wall Street Journal*.

254	150½	AlphaBet	ALF	6.00	3.1	15	755	194¼	189	189⅛	−3⅞

Given this information, answer the following questions.

a. On what day did the trading activity occur?

b. At what price did the stock sell at the end of the day on Wednesday, April 9?

c. What are the highest and lowest prices at which the stock sold on the date quoted?

d. What is the firm's price/earnings ratio? What does that indicate?

e. What is the last price at which the stock traded on the date quoted?

f. How large a dividend is expected in the current year?

g. What are the highest and the lowest prices at which the stock traded during the latest 52-week period?

h. How many shares of stock were traded on the day quoted?

i. How much, if any, of a change in stock price took place between the day quoted and the immediately preceding period? What did the stock close at on the immediately preceding day?

LG 4

Q5.3. Listed below are three pairs of stocks. Look at each pair and select the security you would like to own, given that you want to *select the one that's worth more money.* Then, *after* you make all three of your selections, use the *Wall Street Journal* or some other source to find the latest market value of the two securities in each pair.

a. 50 shares of Berkshire Hathaway (stock symbol BRKA) or 150 shares of Coca-Cola (stock symbol KO). (Both are listed on the NYSE.)

b. 100 shares of WD-40 (symbol WDFC—a Nasdaq National Market issue) or 100 shares of Nike (symbol NKE—a NYSE stock).

c. 150 shares of Wal-Mart (symbol WMT) or 50 shares of Sears (symbol S). (Both are listed on the NYSE.)

How many times did you pick the one that was worth more money? Did the price of any of these stocks surprise you? If so, which one(s)? Does the price of a stock represent its value? Explain.

LG 6

Q5.4. Assume that a wealthy individual comes to you looking for investment advice. She is in her early forties and has $250,000 to put into stocks. She wants to build up as much capital as she can over a 15-year period and is willing to tolerate a "fair amount" of risk.

a. What types of stocks do you think would be most suitable for this investor? Come up with at least three different types of stocks and briefly explain the rationale for each.
b. Would your recommendations change if you were dealing with a smaller amount of money—say, $50,000? What if the investor were more risk-averse? Explain.

LG 6

Q5.5. Identify and briefly describe the three sources of return to U.S. investors in foreign stocks. How important are currency exchange rates, and, with regard to currency exchange rates, when is the best time to be in foreign securities?

a. Listed below are exchange rates (for the beginning and end of a hypothetical 1-year investment horizon) for three currencies: the British pound (B£), Australian dollar (A$), and Mexican peso (Mp).

	Currency Exchange Rates at	
Currency	Beginning of Investment Horizon	End of One-Year Investment Horizon
British pound (B£)	1.55 U.S.$ per B£	1.75 U.S.$ per B£
Australian dollar (A$)	1.35 A$ per U.S.$	1.25 A$ per U.S.$
Mexican peso (Mp)	0.10 U.S.$ per Mp	0.08 U.S.$ per Mp

From the perspective of an American investor holding a foreign (British, Australian, or Mexican) stock, which of the above changes in currency exchange rates would have a positive effect on returns (in U.S. dollars) and which would have a negative effect?

b. ADRs are denominated in U.S. dollars. Are their returns affected by currency exchange rates? Explain.

LG 6

Q5.6. Briefly define each of the following types of investment programs, and note the kinds of stock (blue chips, speculative stocks, etc.) that would best fit with each.

a. A buy-and-hold strategy
b. A high-income portfolio
c. Long-term total return
d. Aggressive stock management

Problems

P5.1. An investor owns some stock in General Refrigeration & Cooling. The stock recently underwent a 5-for-2 stock split. If the stock was trading at $50 per share just before the split, how much is each share most likely selling for right after the split? If the investor owned 200 shares of the stock before the split, how many shares would she own afterward?

LG 4

P5.2. The Kracked Pottery Company has total assets of $2.5 million, total short- and long-term debt of $1.8 million, and $200,000 worth of 8% preferred stock outstanding. What is the firm's total book value? What would its book value per share amount to if it had 50,000 shares of common stock outstanding?

LG 5

P5.3. The W. C. Fields Beverage Company recently reported net profits after taxes of $15.8 million. It has 2.5 million shares of common stock outstanding and pays preferred dividends of $1 million per year.

a. Compute the firm's earnings per share (EPS).
b. Assuming that the stock currently trades at $60 per share, determine what the firm's dividend yield would be if it paid $2 per share to common stockholders?
c. What would the firm's dividend payout ratio be if it paid $2 a share in dividends?

LG 4 LG 5

P5.4. Consider the following information about Associated Industries, Inc.

Total assets	$240 million
Total debt	$115 million
Preferred stock	$25 million
Common stockholders' equity	$100 million
Net profits after taxes	$22.5 million
Number of preferred stock outstanding	1 million shares
Number of common stock outstanding	10 million shares
Preferred dividends paid	$2/share
Common dividends paid	$0.75/share
Market price of the preferred stock	$30.75/share
Market price of the common stock	$25.00/share

Use this information to find

a. The company's book value
b. Its book value per share
c. The stock's earnings per share (EPS)
d. The dividend payout ratio
e. The dividend yield on the common stock
f. The dividend yield on the preferred stock

LG 5

P5.5. Angus Brewmeister owns 200 shares of Consolidated Glue. The company's board of directors recently declared a cash dividend of 50 cents a share payable April 18 (a Wednesday) to shareholders of record on March 22 (a Thursday).

a. How much in dividends, if any, will Angus receive if he *sells* his stock on March 20?
b. Assume Angus decides to hold on to the stock rather than sell it. If he belongs to the company's dividend reinvestment plan, how many new shares of stock will he receive if the stock is currently trading at 40 and the plan offers a 5% discount on the share price of the stock? (Assume that all of Angus's dividends are diverted to the plan.) Will Angus have to pay any taxes on these dividends, given that he is taking them in stock rather than cash?

LG 5

P5.6. Southwest Investments Corp. has the following 5-year record of earnings per share.

Year	EPS
1994	$1.40
1995	2.10
1996	1.00
1997	3.25
1998	0.80

Which of the following procedures would produce the greater amount of dividends to stockholders over this 5-year period?

a. Paying out dividends at a fixed payout ratio of 40% of EPS
b. Paying out dividends at the fixed rate of $1 per share

LG 4 LG 5

P5.7. Using the resources available at your campus or public library, select three common stocks (pick any three you like), and determine the latest book value per share, earnings per share, dividend payout ratio, and dividend yield for each. (Show all your calculations.)

LG 4 LG 5

P5.8. In January 1993, an investor purchased 800 shares of Engulf & Devour, a rapidly growing high-tech conglomerate. Over the 5-year period from 1993 through 1997, the stock turned in the following dividend and share price performance.

Year	Share Price at Beginning of Year	Dividends Paid During Year	Share Price at End of Year
1993	$42.50*	$0.82	$ 54.00
1994	54.00	1.28	74.25
1995	74.25	1.64	81.00
1996	81.00	1.91	91.25
1997	91.25	2.30	128.75

*Investor purchased stock in 1993 at this price.

a. On the basis of this information, find the *annual* holding period returns for 1993 through 1997. (*Hint:* See Chapter 4 for the HPR formula.)
b. Use the return information in Table 5.1 to evaluate the investment performance of this stock. How do you think Engulf & Devour stacks up against the market? Would you consider this a good investment? Explain.

LG 6

P5.9. George Robbins considers himself to be a pretty aggressive investor. At the present time, he's thinking about investing in some foreign securities; in particular, he's looking at two stocks: (1) Löwenbräu, the famous German beer maker, and (2) Ciba-Geigy, the big Swiss pharmaceutical firm.

Löwenbräu, which trades on the Frankfurt Exchange, is currently priced at 2,400 German marks (Dm) per share and pays annual dividends of 25 Dm per share. Robbins expects the stock to climb to 2,700 Dm within a period of 12 months. The current exchange rate is 1.58 Dm/U.S.$, but that's expected to rise to 1.75 Dm/U.S.$. The other company, Ciba-Geigy, trades on the Zurich Exchange and is currently priced at 715 Swiss francs (Sf) per share. The stock pays annual dividends of 15 Sf per share, and its share price is expected to go up to 760 Sf within a year. At current exchange rates, one Sf is worth $0.75 U.S., but that's expected to go to $0.85 by the end of the 1-year holding period.

a. *Ignoring the currency effect,* which of the two stocks promises the higher total return (in its local currency)? Based on this information, which of the two stocks looks like the better investment?
b. Now, which of the two stocks has the better total return, *in U.S. dollars?* Did currency exchange rates affect their returns in any way? Do you still want to stick with the same stock you selected in part (a)? Explain.

Case Problem 5.1 *Sara Decides to Take the Plunge*

LG 1 LG 6

Sara Thomas is a child psychologist who has built up a thriving practice in her hometown of Phoenix, Arizona. Her practice has been so lucrative, in fact, that over the past several years she has been able to accumulate a substantial sum of money. She has worked long and hard to be successful, but she never imagined anything like this. Fortunately, success has not spoiled Sara. Still single, she keeps to her old circle of friends. One of her closest friends is Terry Jenkins, who happens to be a stockbroker. Sara sees a lot of Terry, who has acted as her financial adviser.

Not long ago, Sara attended a seminar on investing in the stock market. Since then she's been doing some reading about the market, and she has concluded that keeping all of her money in low-yielding savings accounts really doesn't make any sense. As a result, Sara has decided to move part of her money to stocks. One evening, Sara told Terry about her decision and explained that she had found several stocks that she thought looked "sort of interesting." She described them as follows:

- *North Atlantic Swim Suit Company.* This highly speculative stock pays no dividends. Although the earnings of NASS have been a bit erratic, Sara feels that its growth prospects have never been brighter—"what with more people than ever going to the beaches the way they are these days," she says.

- *Town and Country Computer.* This is a long-established computer firm that pays a modest dividend yield (of about 2½%). It is considered a quality growth stock. From one of the stock reports she read, Sara understands that it offers excellent long-term growth and capital gains potential.

- *Southeastern Public Utility Company.* This income stock pays a nice dividend yield of around 5%. Although it's a solid company, it has limited growth prospects because of its location.

- *International Gold Mines, Inc.* This stock has performed quite well in the past, especially when inflation has become a problem. Sara feels that if it can do so well in inflationary times, it will do even better in a strong economy. Unfortunately, the stock has experienced wide price swings in the past and pays almost no dividends.

QUESTIONS

a. What do you think of the idea of Sara keeping "substantial sums" of money in savings accounts? Would common stocks make better investments than savings accounts? Explain.

b. What is your opinion of the four stocks Sara has described? Do you think they are suitable for her investment needs? Explain.

c. What kind of common stock investment program would you recommend for Sara? What investment objectives do you think she should set for herself, and how can common stocks help her achieve her goals?

Case Problem 5.2 *Dave Starts Looking for Yield*

LG 5 LG 6

Dave Peterson is a commercial artist who makes a good living by doing freelance work—mostly layouts and illustrations for local ad agencies and major institutional clients (such as large department stores). Dave has been investing in the stock market for some time, buying mostly high-quality growth stocks. He has been seeking long-term growth and capital appreciation and feels that with the limited time he has to devote to his security holdings, high-quality issues are his best bet. He has become a bit perplexed lately with the market, disturbed that some of his growth stocks aren't doing even as well as many good-grade income shares. He therefore decides to have a chat with his broker, Al Fried.

During the course of their conversation, it becomes clear that both Al and Dave are thinking along the same lines. Al points out that dividend yields on income shares are indeed way up and that, because of the state of the economy, the outlook for growth stocks is not particularly bright. He suggests that Dave seriously consider putting some of his money into income shares to capture the high dividend yields that are available. After all, as Al says, "the bottom line is not so much where the payoff comes from as how much it amounts to!" They then talk about a high-yield public utility stock, Hydro-Electric Light and Power. Al digs up some forecast information about Hydro-Electric and presents it to Dave for his consideration:

Year	Expected EPS	Expected Dividend Payout Ratio
1998	$3.25	40%
1999	3.40	40
2000	3.90	45
2001	4.40	45
2002	5.00	45

The stock currently trades at $60 per share, and Al thinks that within 5 years it should be trading at a level of $75 to $80. Dave realizes that in order to buy the Hydro-Electric stock, he will have to sell his holdings of CapCo Industries—a highly regarded growth stock that Dave is disenchanted with because of recent substandard performance.

QUESTIONS

a. How would you describe Dave's present investment program? How do you think it fits him and his investment objectives?

b. Consider the Hydro-Electric stock.

1. Determine the amount of annual dividends Hydro-Electric can be expected to pay over the years 1998 to 2002.
2. Compute the total dollar return that Dave will make from Hydro-Electric if he invests $6,000 in the stock and all the dividend and price expectations are realized.
3. If Dave participates in the company's dividend reinvestment plan, how many shares of stock will he have by the end of 2002, and what will they be worth if the stock trades at $80 on December 31, 2002? Assume that the stock can be purchased through the dividend reinvestment plan at a net price of $50 a share in 1998, $55 in 1999, $60 in 2000, $65 in 2001, and $70 in 2002. Use fractional shares, to two decimals, in your computations. Also, assume that, as in part (b), Dave starts with 100 shares of stock and all dividend expectations are realized.

c. Would Dave be going to a different investment strategy if he decided to buy shares in Hydro-Electric? If the switch is made, how would you describe his new investment program? What do you think of this new approach, and is it likely to lead to more trading on Dave's behalf? If so, can you reconcile that with the limited amount of time he has to devote to his portfolio?

Home Page Exercises

http://hepg.aw.com **Keyword: Invest**

The text discussed dividends as a source of common stock returns, the features of dividends, and important dividend-related dates. It also covered how to purchase common stock through dividend reinvestment plans and how to invest in foreign companies' common stock through American Depositary Receipts (ADRs). When many people think of investments, they think common stocks. The allure of common stocks is enticing and exciting. There are several ways of referring to the value of common stock, such as market value, book value, and par value, and there are many types, such as treasury stock and classified stock. You need to understand these features before undertaking any investment in stocks. You also need to understand dividends as a source of common stock returns. The Web provides easy and quick access to information sources, such as those sites listed here, on common stocks. Without the Web, many investors would have to pay for this information or invest valuable time seeking out hard-copy sources.

Web Address	*Primary Investment Focus*
www.bankofny.com/adr	Educational material on the definition and trading of ADRs, along with a listing of all ADRs in the U.S. markets
www.ipocentral.com	Information about recent and upcoming initial public offerings
www.marketguide.com/ MGI/PRODUCTS/	Company profiles, some ratios, and market quotes

W5.1. After arriving at the home page for Delta Airlines at the address listed here, use the pull-down menu to select "All about Delta index"; then click *Annual Report* to get the company's financial statements. Using the financial statements for the latest year-end for Delta, obtain the par value of Delta's common stock, the number of shares of common stock issued, the amount and number of shares of treasury stock, the book value per share of common stock, and the amount of dividends Delta paid per share. Does Delta have any classified stock?

www.delta-air/res/

W5.2. Often, initial public offerings of common stock lead to abnormally high returns shortly after issuance. From a list provided on the Web site here, find a firm whose listing indicates that it went public as close to a year ago as possible. (That is, look at firms whose listing matches the current month.) Calculate the holding period return on that stock from the time of issuance through the current date.

www.ipocentral.com/features/aftermkt.html

CHAPTER 6

Analytical Dimensions of Stock Selection

Learning Goals

After studying this chapter, you should be able to:

LG 1 Discuss the security analysis process, including its goals and functions.

LG 2 Appreciate the purpose and contributions of economic analysis.

LG 3 Describe industry analysis and note how it is used.

LG 4 Demonstrate a basic understanding of fundamental analysis and why it is used.

LG 5 Calculate a variety of financial ratios and describe how financial statement analysis is used to gauge the financial vitality of a company.

LG 6 Use various financial measures to assess a company's performance, and explain how the insights derived form the basic input for the valuation process.

The Walt Disney Company

Just about everywhere you look there is a product or service created by a company that issues stock. Indeed, Ben & Jerry's Homemade, Citicorp, Dell Computer, Disney, Ford, McDonald's, Wal-Mart, and so on, all sell products and services that have become part of our national landscape. Acquaintance with a company's products is certainly helpful in deciding whether to buy its stock, but it shouldn't be the only thing you consider. In his 1996 letter to shareholders, Michael Eisner, CEO of The Walt Disney Company, listed various successful Disney products. Twelve pages later in the annual report, a chart indicated a much more salient fact: Since 1986, Disney's stock price had grown at a 22% compound annual rate. In comparison, the S&P 500 Index grew at a 15% annual rate. To put it another way: $1,000 invested in Disney stock in 1986 was worth $7,265 a decade later, whereas $1,000 invested in the stock market as a whole was worth just $4,113.

In this, the first of two chapters on security analysis, we will introduce some of the techniques and procedures used to evaluate stocks like Disney—keeping in mind that it is often the intangibles of a company that make its stock perform well.

Security Analysis

LG 1

The obvious motivation for investing in stocks is to watch your money grow. Consider, for example, the case of the computer software company Oracle Corp. If an investor had put $2,500 into Oracle stock when it first went public in March 1984, that investment would have soared to over a quarter-million dollars by June 1997. Not bad for a 13-year period of time—indeed, that's not bad for a lifetime! Unfortunately, for every story of great success in the market, there are dozens more that don't end so well. Most of the disasters can be traced to bad timing, greed, poor planning, or failure to use common sense in making investment decisions. Although these chapters on stock investments cannot offer the keys to sudden wealth, they do provide sound principles for formulating a successful long-range investment program. The techniques described are quite traditional; they are the same (proven) methods that have been used by millions of investors to achieve attractive rates of return on their capital.

Principles of Security Analysis

security analysis
the process of gathering and organizing information and then using it to determine the value of a share of common stock.

intrinsic value
the underlying or inherent value of a stock, as determined through fundamental analysis.

Security analysis consists of gathering information, organizing it into a logical framework, and then using the information to determine the inherent or intrinsic value of a common stock. That is, given a rate of return that's compatible to the amount of risk involved in a proposed transaction, **intrinsic value** provides a measure of the underlying worth of a share of stock. It provides a standard for helping you judge whether a particular stock is undervalued, fairly priced, or overvalued. The entire concept of stock valuation is based on the belief that all securities possess an intrinsic value that their current market or trading value must approach over time.

In investments, the question of value centers on return. In particular, a satisfactory investment candidate is one *that offers a level of expected return commensurate with the amount of risk involved.* That is, there's a *desired or minimum rate of return* that you should be able to earn on an investment, and that rate varies with the amount of risk you have to assume. As a result, not only must an investment candidate be profitable, it must be *sufficiently* profitable—in the sense that you'd expect it to generate a return that's high enough to offset the perceived exposure to risk.

If you could have your way, you'd probably like to invest in something that offers complete preservation of capital, along with sizable helpings of current income and capital gains. The problem, of course, is finding such a security. One approach is to buy whatever strikes your fancy. A more rational approach is to use security analysis to look for promising investment candidates. Security analysis addresses the question of *what to buy* by determining what a stock *ought to be worth.* Presumably, an investor will buy a stock *only if its prevailing market price does not exceed its worth*—that is, its intrinsic value. Ultimately, intrinsic value depends on several factors:

1. Estimates of the stock's future cash flows (the amount of dividends you expect to receive over the holding period and the estimated price of the stock at time of sale)
2. The discount rate used to translate these future cash flows into a present value
3. The amount of risk embedded in achieving the forecasted level of performance

Traditional security analysis usually takes a "top-down" approach: It begins with economic analysis and then moves to industry analysis and finally to fundamental analysis. *Economic analysis* is concerned with assessing the general state of the economy and its potential effects on security returns. *Industry analysis* deals with the industry within which a particular company operates, how the company stacks up against the major competitors in the industry, and the general outlook for that industry. *Fundamental analysis* looks in depth at the financial condition and operating results of a specific company and the underlying behavior of its common stock. In essence, it looks at the "fundamentals of the company"—at the company's investment decisions, the liquidity of its assets, its use of debt, its profit margins and earnings growth, and ultimately at the future prospects of the company and its stock. Fundamental analysis is closely linked to the notion of intrinsic value, because it *provides the basis for projecting a stock's future cash flows*. A key part of this analytical process is *company analysis,* which takes a close look at the actual financial performance of the company. Such analysis is not meant simply to provide interesting tidbits of information about how the company has performed in the past; rather, it's done to *help investors formulate expectations about the future performance of the company and its stock*. Make no mistake about it: In the field of investments, it's the future that matters. But in order to understand the future prospects of the firm, an investor should have a good handle on the company's current condition and its ability to produce earnings. And that's just what company analysis does: It helps investors predict the future by looking at the past and determining how well the company is situated to meet the challenges that lie ahead.

Who Needs Security Anaylsis in an Efficient Market?

The concept of security analysis in general and fundamental analysis in particular is based on the assumption that investors are capable of formulating reliable estimates of a stock's future behavior. Fundamental analysis operates on the broad premise that some securities may be mispriced in the marketplace at any given point in time. Further, fundamental analysis assumes that, by undertaking a careful analysis of the inherent characteristics of each of the firms in question, it is possible to distinguish those securities that are correctly priced from those that are not.

To many, those two assumptions of fundamental analysis seem reasonable. However, there are others who just don't accept the assumptions of fundamental analysis. These are the so-called *efficient market* advocates. They believe that the market is so efficient in processing new information that securities trade very close to or at their correct values (proper prices) at all times. Thus, they argue, it is virtually impossible to outperform the market on a consistent basis. In its strongest form, the *efficient market hypothesis* asserts (1) that securities are rarely, if ever, substantially mispriced in the marketplace and (2) that no security analysis, however detailed, is capable of identifying mispriced securities with a frequency greater than that which might be expected by random chance alone. Is the efficient market hypothesis correct? Is there a place for fundamental analysis in modern investment theory? Interestingly, most financial theorists and practitioners would answer yes to both of these questions.

The solution to this apparent paradox is really quite simple. Basically, fundamental analysis is of value in the selection of alternative investment vehicles for two important reasons. First, financial markets are as efficient as they are because a large number of people and powerful financial institutions invest a great deal of time and money in analyzing the fundamentals of most widely held investments. In other words, markets tend to be efficient— and securities tend to trade at or near their intrinsic values—simply because a great many people have done the research necessary to determine just what their intrinsic values should be. Second, although the financial markets are generally quite efficient, they are by no means perfectly efficient. Pricing errors are inevitable, and those individuals who have conducted the most thorough studies of the underlying fundamentals of a given security are the most likely to profit when errors do occur. We will study the ideas and implications of efficient markets in some detail in Chapter 7. For now, however, we will assume that traditional security analysis is useful in identifying attractive equity investments.

CONCEPTS IN REVIEW

6.1 Identify the three major parts of security analysis and explain why security analysis is important to the stock selection process.

6.2 What is *intrinsic value,* and how does it fit into the security analysis process?

6.3 How would you describe a satisfactory investment vehicle? How does security analysis help in identifying investment candidates?

6.4 Would there be any need for security analysis if we operated in an efficient market environment? Explain.

Economic Analysis

LG 2

If we lived in a world where economic activity had absolutely no effect on the stock market or on security prices, we could avoid studying the economy altogether. The fact is, of course, that we do not live in such a world. Rather, stock prices are heavily influenced by the state of the economy and by economic events. As a rule, stock prices tend to move up when the economy is strong, and they retreat when the economy starts to soften. Of course, it's not a perfect relationship, but it is a powerful one.

The reason why the economy is so important to the market is simple: The overall performance of the economy has a significant bearing on the performance and profitability of the companies that issue common stock. As the fortunes of the issuing firms change with economic conditions, so do the prices of their stocks. Of course, not all stocks are affected in the same way or to the same extent. Some sectors of the economy, like food retailing, may be only mildly affected by the economy; others, like the construction and auto industries, are often hard hit when times get rough. The nearby *Investing in Action* box details the effects of just one economic condition—unemployment—on the markets.

economic analysis
a study of general economic conditions that is used in the valuation of common stock.

Economic analysis—a general study of the economy—should not only give an investor a grasp of the *underlying nature of the economic environment* but also enable him or her to assess the *current state of the economy* and formulate

INVESTING IN ACTION

Taking Stock of the Economy

There has often been an inverse relationship between the health of the economy and the markets. A case in point: the unemployment rate. As the 1990s percolated along, the U.S. unemployment rate fell lower and lower. In October 1997, the jobless rate fell to 4.7%, its lowest level in 24 years. According to the U.S. Labor Department, employers added 284,000 jobs to payrolls during the month. The job gains were spread across most industries, and factory output posted its biggest 1-month increase in more than 7 years.

The strong economy was a major issue in 1997's off-year elections. It's one reason (in addition to the lower crime rate) why Rudolph Gulliani was easily re-elected to a second term as mayor of New York City. It's also why President Clinton had a 60% approval rating during much of the first 2 years of his second term. Most Americans love the effects of a strong economy, and so do most politicians.

But on Wall Street, a great economy can cause volatility. Often, a drop in the unemployment rate can mean a plunge in the Dow Jones Industrial Average on a given day. The reason: Investors hate inflation, and full employment exerts upward pressure on wages. Essentially, if everybody's working, then they can demand raises. During October 1997, the average hourly wage jumped six cents, or 0.5%, to $12.41. Investors in stocks also hate inflation because it is generally followed by higher interest rates. The combination of higher wages and higher interest rates eventually translates into lower corporate profits.

The Federal Reserve Board, which manages the economy by raising or lowering short-term interest rates, uses the strength of the economy generally—one element of which is unemployment—as a factor in determining what to do about interest rates. In late 1997 the Fed, though concerned about wage pressures, kept interest rates on an even keel because of the financial turmoil in Asia and its uncertain impact on the U.S. economy.

Another reason for the Fed's hands-off stance was that plunging unemployment had not yet made much of an impact on the inflation rate. Investors can worry all they want, but they don't truly get scared until the Consumer Price Index starts to head upward. Instead, it has been falling. Besides, U.S. wages are just one component of the inflation rate. So many goods sold in the United States are made in other parts of the world where wages are much lower. That includes computers, shoes, sound systems, clothing, and automobiles. No wonder, then, that despite U.S. unemployment being at its lowest level since 1974, U.S. inflation was at its lowest level since 1964.

Until falling unemployment and wage pressures have a significantly greater impact on the inflation rate, the good news that comes out of the Labor Department is likely to cause only momentary jitters on Wall Street.

expectations about its *future course*. It can go so far as to include a detailed examination of each sector of the economy, or it may be done on a very informal basis. Regardless of how it is performed, however, the purpose—from a security analysis perspective—is always the same: to establish a sound foundation for the valuation of common stock.

Economic Analysis and the Business Cycle

Economic analysis sets the tone for security analysis. If the economic future looks bleak, you can probably expect most stock returns to be equally dismal. If the economy looks strong, stocks should do well. As we saw in Chapter 3,

business cycle
an indication of the current state of the economy, reflecting changes in total economic activity over time.

the behavior of the economy is captured in the **business cycle,** which reflects changes in total economic activity over time. Two widely followed measures of the business cycle are gross domestic product and industrial production. *Gross domestic product* (GDP) represents the market value of all goods and services produced in a country over the period of a year. *Industrial production,* in contrast, is a measure (it's really an index) of the activity/output in the industrial or productive segment of the economy. Normally, GDP and the index of industrial production move up and down with the business cycle.

Key Economic Factors

Several parts of the economy are especially important because of the impact they have on total economic activity. These include

Government fiscal policy:
Taxes
Government spending
Debt management

Monetary policy:
Money supply
Interest rates

Other factors:
Inflation
Consumer spending
Business investments
Foreign trade and foreign exchange rates

Government fiscal policy tends to be expansive when it encourages spending—when the government reduces taxes and/or increases the size of the budget. Similarly, monetary policy is said to be expansive when money is readily available and interest rates are relatively low. An expansive economy also depends on a generous level of spending by consumers and business concerns. These same variables moving in a reverse direction can have a contractionary (recessionary) impact on the economy, as for example, when taxes and interest rates increase or when spending by consumers and businesses falls off.

The impact of these major forces filters through the system and affects several key dimensions of the economy. The most important of these are industrial production, corporate profits, retail sales, personal income, the unemployment rate, and inflation. For example, a strong economy exists when industrial production, corporate profits, retail sales, and personal income are moving up and unemployment is down. Thus, when conducting an economic analysis, an investor should keep an eye on fiscal and monetary policies, consumer and business spending, and foreign trade *for the potential impact they have on the economy.* At the same time, he or she must stay abreast of the level of industrial production, corporate profits, retail sales, personal income, unemployment, and inflation *in order to assess the state of the business cycle.*

To help you keep track of the economy, Table 6.1 provides a brief description of some key economic measures. These economic statistics are compiled by various government agencies and are widely reported in the financial media. (Most of the reports are released monthly.) Take time to read carefully

TABLE 6.1 Keeping Track of the Economy

To sort out the confusing array of figures that flow almost daily from Washington, D.C., and to help you keep track of what's happening in the economy, here are some of the most important economic measures and reports to watch.

- **Gross domestic product.** This broadest measure of the economy's performance replaces the old "GNP" measure. Issued every three months by the Commerce Department, it is an estimate of the total dollar value of all the goods and services produced in this country. Movements in many areas of the economy are closely related to changes in GDP, so it is a good analytic tool. In particular, watch the annual rate of growth or decline in "real" or "constant" dollars. This number eliminates the effects of inflation and thus measures the actual volume of production. Remember, though, that frequent revisions of GDP figures sometimes change the picture of the economy.
- **Industrial production.** Issued monthly by the Federal Reserve Board, this index shows changes in the physical output of America's factories, mines, and electric and gas utilities. The index tends to move in the same direction as the economy, which makes it a good guide to business conditions between reports on GDP. Detailed breakdowns of the index give a reading on how individual industries are faring.
- **Leading indicators.** This boils down to one number, which summarizes the movement of a dozen statistics that tend to predict—or "lead"—changes in the GDP. The monthly index, issued by the Commerce Department, includes such things as layoffs of workers, new orders placed by manufacturers, changes in the money supply, and the prices of raw materials. If the index moves in the same direction for several months, it's a fairly good sign that total output will move the same way in the near future.
- **Personal income.** A monthly report from the Commerce Department, this shows the before-tax income received by people in the form of wages and salaries, interest and dividends, rents, and other payments such as Social Security, unemployment compensation, and pensions. As a measure of individuals' spending power, the report helps explain trends in consumer buying habits, a major part of total GDP. When personal income rises, it often means that people increase their buying. But note a big loophole: Excluded are the billions of dollars that change hands in the so-called underground economy—cash transactions that are never reported to tax or other officials.
- **Retail sales.** The Commerce Department's monthly estimate of total sales at the retail level includes everything from cars to bags of groceries. Based on a sample of retail establishments, the figure gives a rough clue to consumer attitudes. It can also indicate future conditions: A long slowdown in sales can lead to cuts in production.
- **Money supply.** A measure of the amount of money in circulation as reported weekly by the Federal Reserve. Actually, there are three measures of the money supply: *M1,* which is basically currency, demand deposits, and NOW accounts; *M2,* the most widely followed measure, which equals M1 plus savings deposits, money market deposit accounts, and money market mutual funds; and *M3,* which is M2 plus large CDs and a few other less significant types of deposits/transactions. Reasonable growth in the money supply, as measured by M2, is thought necessary to accommodate an expanding economy. Such growth should have a positive impact on the economy—*unless* the money supply is growing too rapidly. A rapid rate of growth in money is considered inflationary; in contrast, a sharp slowdown in the growth rate is viewed as recessionary.
- **Consumer prices.** Issued monthly by the Labor Department, this index shows changes in prices for a fixed market basket of goods and services. The most widely publicized figure is for all urban consumers. A second, used in labor contracts and some government programs, covers urban wage earners and clerical workers. Both are watched as a measure of inflation, but many economists believe that flaws cause them to be wide of the mark.
- **Producer prices.** This monthly indicator from the Labor Department shows price changes of goods at various stages of production, from crude materials such as raw cotton to finished goods like clothing and furniture. An upward surge may mean higher consumer prices later. The index, however, can miss discounts and may exaggerate rising price trends. Watch particularly changes in the prices of finished goods. These do not fluctuate as widely as the prices of crude materials and thus are a better measure of inflationary pressures.
- **Employment.** The percentage of the work force that is involuntarily out of work is a broad indicator of economic health. But another monthly figure issued by the Labor Department—the number of payroll jobs—may be better for spotting changes in business. A decreasing number of jobs is a sign that firms are cutting production.
- **Housing starts.** A pickup in the pace of housing starts usually follows an easing of credit conditions—the availability and cost of money—and is an indicator of improvement in economic health. This monthly report from the Commerce Department also includes the number of new building permits issued across the country, an even earlier indicator of the pace of future construction.

about the various economic measures and reports cited in Table 6.1. When you understand the behavior of these statistics, you can make your own educated guess as to the current state of the economy and where it's headed.

Developing an Economic Outlook

Conducting an economic analysis involves studying fiscal and monetary policies, inflationary expectations, consumer and business spending, and the state of the business cycle. Often investors do this on a fairly informal basis. As they form their economic judgments, many rely on one or more of the popular published sources (e.g., the *Wall Street Journal, Barron's, Fortune,* and *Business Week*) as well as on periodic reports from major brokerage houses. These sources provide a convenient summary of economic activity and give investors a general feel for the condition of the economy.

Once you have developed a general economic outlook, you can use the information in one of two ways. One approach is to construct an economic outlook and then consider where it leads in terms of possible areas for further analysis. For example, suppose you uncover information that strongly suggests the outlook for business spending is very positive. On the basis of such an analysis, you might want to look more closely at capital goods producers, such as machine tool manufacturers, as investment candidates. Similarly, if you feel that because of the sweeping changes that have taken place in Eastern Europe and what used to be the USSR, U.S. government defense spending is likely to drop off substantially, you might want to avoid the stocks of major defense contractors.

A second way to use information about the economy is to consider specific industries or companies and ask, "How will they be affected by expected developments in the economy?" Take an investor with an interest in *apparel stocks*. Because of the nature of the business (durable fashion goods), these stocks are susceptible to changing economic conditions. Especially important here is the level of discretionary consumer spending: Normally such spending tends to accelerate when the economy picks up steam and slackens when the economy slows down. In this instance, our imaginary investor would first want to assess the current state of the business cycle. Using that insight, he would then formulate some expectations about the future of the economy and the potential impact it holds for the stock market in general and apparel stocks in particular. (Table 6.2 shows how some of the more important economic variables can affect the behavior of the stock market. It should be clear that the market is not immune to the economy but, rather, reacts to different economic forces in different ways.) Our imaginary investor has to determine how the economy may affect particular segments of the market—in this case, apparel stocks. To see how this might be done, let's assume that the economy has just entered the recovery stage of the business cycle. Employment is starting to pick up, inflation and interest rates have dropped to their lowest levels in years, both GDP and industrial production have experienced sharp increases in the past two quarters, and Congress is putting the finishing touches on a major piece of legislation that would lead to reduced taxes. More important, because the economy now seems to be in the early stages of a recovery, it should strengthen in the future, and both personal income and consumer spending should increase. All of these predictions should be good

TABLE 6.2 Economic Variables and the Stock Market

Economic Variable	Potential Effect on the Stock Market
Real growth in GDP	Positive impact—it's good for the market.
Industrial production	Continued increases are a sign of strength, which is good for the market.
Inflation	Detrimental to stock prices. Higher inflation leads to higher interest rates and lower price/earnings multiples and generally makes equity securities less attractive.
Corporate profits	Strong corporate earnings are good for the market.
Unemployment	A downer—an increase in unemployment means business is starting to slow down.
Federal deficit	May be positive for a depressed economy but can lead to inflation in a stronger economic environment and therefore have a negative impact.
Weak dollar	Often the result of big trade imbalances, a weak dollar has a negative effect on the market because it makes our markets less attractive to foreign investors. On the other hand, it also makes our products more affordable in overseas markets and therefore can have a positive impact on our economy.
Interest rates	Another downer—rising rates tend to have a negative effect on the market for stocks.
Money supply	Moderate growth can have a positive impact on the economy and the market. Rapid growth, however, is inflationary and therefore detrimental to the stock market.

news for the producers of men's and women's apparel, because a good deal of their sales and an even larger portion of their profits depend on the level of consumer income and spending. In short, our investor sees an economy that appears to be in good shape and set to become even stronger, the consequences of which are favorable not only for the market but for apparel stocks as well.

Note that these conclusions were reached by relying on sources no more sophisticated than *Barron's* or *Business Week*. In fact, about the only "special thing" this investor did was to pay careful attention to those economic forces that are particularly important to the apparel industry (e.g., personal income). The economic portion of the analysis, in effect, has set the stage for further evaluation by indicating what type of economic environment to expect in the near future. The next step is to narrow the focus a bit and conduct the industry phase of the analysis.

However, before we continue with our analysis, it is vital to clarify further the relationship that normally exists between the stock market and the economy. In particular, as we just saw, the economic outlook is used to get a handle on the market and to direct investors to developing industry sectors. Yet it is important to note that changes in stock prices normally occur *before* the actual forecasted changes become apparent in the economy. To go a bit further, we can say the current trend of stock prices is frequently used to help *predict* the course of the economy itself. The apparent conflict here can be resolved somewhat by noting that because of this relationship, it is even more important to derive a reliable economic outlook and to be sensitive to underlying economic changes that may mean the current outlook is becoming dated.

Investors in the stock market tend to look into the future to justify the purchase or sale of stock. If their perception of the future is changing, stock prices are also likely to be changing. Therefore, watching the course of stock prices as well as the course of the general economy can make for more accurate investment forecasting.

CONCEPTS IN REVIEW

6.5 Describe the general concept of *economic analysis.* Is this type of analysis necessary, and can it really help the individual investor make a decision about a stock? Explain.

6.6 According to the *Investing in Action* box on page 216, who or what is it that manages the economy, and what is the key mechanism used to do so? What is the relationship between the employment rate and inflation?

6.7 Why is the business cycle so important to economic analysis? Does the business cycle have any bearing on the stock market?

6.8 Briefly describe each of the following:
a. Gross domestic product
b. Leading indicators
c. Money supply
d. Producer prices

6.9 What effect, if any, does inflation have on common stocks?

http://hepg.aw.com

You do not have to be a trained economist to evaluate economic conditions. What is important is that you know the *current* state of the economy. An excellent source of up-to-date economic indicators is provided at the following Web site.

www.whitehouse.gove/fsbr/esbr.html

Industry Analysis

LG 3

Have you ever thought about buying oil stocks, or autos, or chemicals? How about conglomerates or electric utility stocks? Looking at securities in terms of industry groupings is a popular way of viewing stocks and is widely used by both individual and institutional investors. This is a sensible approach because stock prices are influenced by industry conditions. The level of demand in an industry and other industry forces set the tone for individual companies. Clearly, if the outlook is good for an industry, then the prospects are likely to be strong for the companies that make up that industry.

Key Issues

industry analysis
study of industry groupings that looks at the competitive position of a particular industry in relation to others and identifies companies that show particular promise within an industry.

The first step in **industry analysis** is to establish the competitive position of a particular industry *in relation to others,* for, as Figure 6.1 indicates, not all industries perform alike. The next step is to identify companies *within the industry* that hold particular promise. This sets the stage for a more thorough

FIGURE 6.1
A Look at the Stock Performance of Key Industry Groups

In searching for value, an early step is to look at the big picture: *industry-group trends.* The data shown here present a broad overview of 30 key industries from Standard & Poor's list of 104 industry groups. Each of these groups has its own market index that measures the performance of stocks within that group. As is apparent, some industries simply do much better than others, at least over certain time periods. (Source: 1997 *Analyst's Handbook,* Standard & Poor's Corporation.)

	Stock Price Index		Change in Index		
	12/31/92	12/31/97	1 Year	3 Years	5 Years
S & P 500 Industrials	435.71	970.43	31.00%	111.30%	122.72%
Aerospace	429.54	1245.03	1.60%	116.83%	189.85%
Airlines	264.97	520.31	68.10%	168.56%	96.37%
Automobiles	155.34	335.43	27.10%	59.55%	115.93%
Beverages (Alcoholic)	371.13	549.48	2.10%	49.46%	48.06%
Beverages	1413.08	3815.08	28.80%	146.23%	169.98%
Broadcast Media	5540.23	12639.29	64.40%	75.86%	128.14%
Building Materials	280.36	460.57	19.80%	86.56%	64.28%
Chemicals	194.87	463.71	20.20%	96.52%	137.96%
Communication Equip. Mfgr.	77.78	190.12	29.60%	125.55%	144.43%
Computers Systems	106.61	354.73	45.50%	155.29%	232.74%
Electric Utilities	76.78	91.49	19.20%	37.99%	19.16%
Electrical Equipment	1151.34	3337.86	38.50%	150.84%	189.91%
Electronics (Semiconductors)	117.09	544.01	7.40%	160.54%	364.61%
Entertainment	1842.44	3501.53	45.00%	74.87%	90.05%
Foods	853.14	1686.22	40.50%	102.77%	97.65%
Homebuilding	88.27	132.65	58.10%	100.74%	50.28%
Hospital Management	57.77	129.95	12.80%	42.66%	124.94%
Hotel-Motel	186.34	583.01	39.20%	93.39%	214.56%
Household Furnishings	475.11	817.65	43.50%	53.53%	72.10%
Leisure	166.45	151.23	30.20%	−10.11%	−9.14%
Natural Gas	360.13	781.04	15.10%	104.05%	116.88%
Oil: Domestic	575.41	907.66	15.50%	54.69%	57.74%
Oil: International	350.47	757.47	20.70%	85.53%	116.13%
Publishing	1748.13	3540.14	45.00%	77.14%	102.51%
Restaurant	283.57	505.21	6.60%	55.76%	78.16%
Retail: Drug Chains	176.02	481	53.10%	169.86%	173.26%
Retail: Food Chains	559.67	1037.61	28.70%	85.19%	85.40%
Telephone	293.52	552.52	34.60%	87.56%	88.24%
Textile: Apparel Mfgrs.	278.25	312.9	6.50%	58.52%	12.45%
Tobacco	1367.37	2289.61	19.30%	116.43%	67.45%

analysis of individual companies and securities. Analyzing an industry means looking at such things as its makeup and basic characteristics, the key economic and operating variables that drive industry performance, and the outlook for the industry. The investor will also want to keep an eye out for specific companies that appear well situated to take advantage of industry conditions. Companies with strong market positions should be favored over those with less secure positions. Such dominance confers the ability to maintain pricing leadership and suggests that the firm will be in a position to enjoy economies of scale and low-cost production. Market dominance also enables a company to support a strong research and development effort, thereby helping it secure its leadership position for the future.

Normally, an investor can gain valuable insight about an industry by seeking answers to the following questions:

1. *What is the nature of the industry?* Is it monopolistic, or are there many competitors? Do a few set the trend for the rest?

2. *To what extent is the industry regulated?* Is it regulated (e.g., public utilities)? If so, how "friendly" are the regulatory bodies?

3. *What role, if any, does labor play in the industry?* How important are labor unions? Are there good labor relations within the industry? When is the next round of contract talks?

4. *How important are technological developments?* Are any new developments taking place, and what impact are potential breakthroughs likely to have?

5. *Which economic forces are especially important to the industry?* Is demand for the industry's goods and services related to key economic variables? If so, what is the outlook for those variables? How important is foreign competition to the health of the industry?

6. *What are the important financial and operating considerations?* Is there an adequate supply of labor, material, and capital? What are the capital spending plans and needs of the industry?

growth cycle
a reflection of the amount of business vitality that occurs within an industry (or company) over time.

The preceding questions can sometimes be answered in terms of an industry's **growth cycle,** which reflects the vitality of the industry over time. In the first phase—*initial development*—investment opportunities are usually not available to most investors. The industry is new and untried, and the risks are very high. The second stage is *rapid expansion,* during which product acceptance is spreading and investors can foresee the industry's future more clearly. At this stage, economic variables have little to do with the industry's overall performance. Investors will be interested in investing almost regardless of the economic climate. This is the phase that is of substantial interest to investors, and a good deal of work is done to find such opportunities. Unfortunately, most industries do not experience rapid growth for long. Instead, they eventually slip into the category of *mature growth,* which is the third stage and the one most influenced by economic developments. In this stage, expansion comes from growth of the economy. It is a slower source of overall rate of growth than that experienced in stage 2. In stage 3, the long-term nature of the industry becomes apparent. Industries in this category include defensive ones, like food and apparel, and cyclical industries, like autos and heavy equipment. The last phase is either *stability* or *decline.* In the decline phase, demand for the industry's products is diminishing, and companies are leaving the industry. Investment opportunities at this stage are almost nonexistent, unless the investor is seeking only dividend income.You would obviously want to avoid this stage. However, few really good companies ever reach this final stage because they continually bring new products to the market and, in so doing, remain at least in the mature growth phase.

Developing an Industry Outlook

Industry analysis can be conducted by individual investors themselves or, as is more often the case, with the help of published industry reports such as the popular S&P *Industry Surveys*. These surveys cover all the important economic, market, and financial aspects of an industry, providing commentary as well as vital statistics. Other widely used sources of industry information include brokerage house reports and various write-ups in the popular financial media.

Let's resume our example of the imaginary investor who is thinking about buying apparel stocks. Recall from our prior discussion that the economic phase of the analysis suggested a strong economy for the foreseeable future—one in which the level of personal disposable income would be expanding. Now the investor is ready to focus on the apparel industry. A logical starting point is to assess the expected industry response to forecasted economic developments. Demand for the product and industry sales would be especially important. The industry is made up of many large and small competitors, and although it is unregulated, the industry is labor-intensive, and labor unions are an important force. Thus our investor may want to look closely at these factors and especially at their potential effect on the industry's cost structure. Also important would be the outlook for imported fashion goods and foreign competition.

Industry analysis yields an understanding of the nature and operating characteristics of an industry, which can then be used to form judgments about the prospects for industry growth. Let's assume that our investor, by using various types of published reports, has examined the key elements of the apparel industry and has concluded that it is indeed well positioned to take advantage of the improving economy. Apparel demand should increase, and although profit margins may tighten a bit, the level of profits should move up smartly, providing a healthy growth outlook. Several companies within this industry stand out, but one looks particularly attractive: MarCor Industries, a moderately sized but rapidly growing producer of medium- to high-priced apparel for men and women. Everything about the economy and the industry looks favorable, so our investor decides to study MarCor more closely.

CONCEPTS IN REVIEW

6.10 What is *industry analysis,* and why is it important?

6.11 Identify and briefly discuss several aspects of an industry that are important to its behavior and operating characteristics. Note especially how economic issues fit into industry analysis.

6.12 What are the four stages of an industry's growth cycle? Which of these stages offers the biggest payoff to investors? Which stage is most influenced by forces in the economy?

http://hepg.aw.com

You should know the main characteristics of any industry in which you may invest. To get an in-depth view of any industry, you need to read publications that people in the industry read and rely on for information. The automobile industry offers one example of the availability of this detailed information on the Web.

www.aiada.org/pubs/iad/iad.htm

fundamental analysis
the in-depth study of the financial condition and operating results of a firm.

Fundamental Analysis

LG 4 LG 5 LG 6

Fundamental analysis is the study of the financial affairs of a business for the purpose of better understanding the nature and operating characteristics of the company that issued the common stock. In this part of the chapter, we will deal with several aspects of fundamental analysis. We will examine the general concept of fundamental analysis, introduce the several types of financial statements that provide the raw material for this phase of the analytical process, describe the key financial ratios widely used in company analysis, and conclude with an interpretation of those financial ratios.

The Concept

Fundamental analysis rests on the belief that *the value of a stock is influenced by the performance of the company that issued the stock.* If a company's prospects look strong, the market price of its stock is likely to reflect that and be bid up. However, the value of a security depends not only on the return it promises but also on the amount of its risk exposure. Fundamental analysis captures these dimensions and conveniently incorporates them into the valuation process. It begins with a historical analysis of the financial strength of a firm: the so-called *company analysis* phase. Using the insights obtained, along with economic and industry figures, an investor can then formulate expectations about the future growth and profitability of a company.

In the historical (or company analysis) phase, the investor studies the financial statements of the firm to learn the strengths and weaknesses of the company, identify any underlying trends and developments, evaluate operating efficiencies, and gain a general understanding of the nature and operating characteristics of the firm. The following points are of particular interest:

1. The competitive position of the company
2. Its composition and growth in sales
3. Profit margins and the dynamics of company earnings
4. The composition and liquidity of corporate resources (the company's asset mix)
5. The company's capital structure (its financing mix)

The historical phase is in many respects the most demanding and the most time-consuming. Most investors, however, have neither the time nor the inclination to conduct such an extensive study, so they rely on published reports for the needed background material. Fortunately, individual investors have a variety of sources to choose from, including the reports and recommendations of major brokerage houses, the popular financial media, and financial subscription services like S&P and *Value Line,* not to mention a whole array of computer-based software and online financial services. These are all valuable sources of information, and the paragraphs that follow are not intended to replace them. Yet to be an intelligent investor, it is important to understand fully the content and implications of such financial reports and, ultimately, to make your own judgment about the company and its stock.

Financial Statements

Financial statements are a vital part of company analysis, because they enable investors to develop an opinion about the operating results and financial condition of a firm. Three types of financial statements are used in company analysis: the balance sheet, the income statement, and the statement of cash flows. The first two statements are essential to carrying out basic financial analysis (in particular, to compute many of the financial ratios). The third statement—the cash flow statement—is used to assess the cash/liquidity position of

INVESTOR FACT

NO THANKS, WE'LL PASS—Most companies today use long-term debt as a major source of financing. That's not true in all cases, however. Some big, well-known companies get along just fine without it or use very little of it. Among them are MicroAge, Intel, AutoZone, and Liz Claiborne, all of whom have capital structures made up of less than 3% in long-term debt. And some firms do even better: Microsoft, Wm. Wrigley, Medtronic, and Estee Lauder, for example, have less than 1% long-term debt in their capital structures.

the firm. Company statements are prepared on a quarterly basis (these are *abbreviated* statements, compiled for each 3-month period of operation) and again at the end of each calendar year or *fiscal year* (a 12-month period the company has defined as its operating year, which may or may not end on December 31). Annual financial statements must be fully verified by independent certified public accountants (CPAs), filed with the U.S. Securities and Exchange Commission, and distributed on a timely basis to all stockholders in the form of annual reports. By themselves, corporate financial statements are a most important source of information to the investor; when used with financial ratios and in conjunction with fundamental analysis, they become even more powerful.

The Balance Sheet

balance sheet
a financial summary of a firm's assets, liabilities, and shareholders' equity at a single point in time.

The **balance sheet** is a statement of the company's assets, liabilities, and shareholders' equity. The *assets* represent the resources of the company (the things the company owns), the *liabilities* are its debts, and *equity* is the amount of stockholders' capital in the firm. A balance sheet may be thought of as a summary of the firm's assets balanced against its debt and ownership positions *at a single point in time* (on the last day of the calendar or fiscal year, or at the end of the quarter). To balance, the total assets must equal the total amount of liabilities and equity. A typical balance sheet is illustrated in Table 6.3. It shows the comparative 1997–1998 figures for MarCor Industries, the apparel firm our investor is interested in analyzing. Note that although the MarCor name is fictitious, the financial statements are not—*they are the actual financial statements of a real company*. Some of the entries have been slightly modified for pedagogical purposes, but these tables accurately depict what real financial statements look like and how they're used in financial statement analysis.

The Income Statement

income statement
a financial summary of the operating results of a firm covering a specified period of time, usually 1 year.

The **income statement** provides a financial summary of the operating results of the firm. It is a summary of the amount of revenues generated over a period of time, the cost and expenses incurred over the same period, and the company's profits (obtained by subtracting all costs and expenses, including taxes, from revenues). Unlike the balance sheet, the income statement covers activities that have occurred over the course of time, or for a given operating period. Typically, this period extends no longer than a fiscal or calendar year. Table 6.4 shows MarCor Industries' income statements for 1997 and 1998. Note that these annual statements cover operations for the 12-month period ending on December 31, which corresponds to the date of the balance sheet. The income statement indicates how successful the firm has been in using the assets listed on the balance sheet. That is, management's success in operating the firm is reflected in the profit or loss the company generates during the year.

The Statement of Cash Flows

statement of cash flows
a financial summary of a firm's cash flow and other events that caused changes in the company's cash position.

The **statement of cash flows** provides a summary of the firm's cash flow and other events that caused changes in the cash position. A relatively new report, first required in 1988, it is also one of the most useful, because it shows how the company is doing in generating cash. The fact is, a company's reported earnings may bear little resemblance to the firm's cash flow. For whereas profits

TABLE 6.3 Corporate Balance Sheet

MarCor Industries
Comparative Balance Sheet
December 31
($ in thousands)

	1998	1997
Assets		
Current assets		
Cash and short-term investments	$ 7,846	$ 16,279
Accounts receivable	105,400	102,889
Inventories	164,356	159,238
Prepaid expenses	1,778	16,279
Total current assets	$279,380	$278,697
Long-term assets		
Land	$ 1,366	$ 1,317
Buildings	13,873	13,889
Furniture, fixtures, and equipment	75,717	73,199
Leasehold improvements	49,412	50,209
Gross long-term assets	$140,368	$138,614
Less: Accumulated depreciation	(85,203)	(80,865)
Net long-term assets	$ 55,165	$ 57,749
Other assets	$ 4,075	$ 4,108
Total assets	$338,620	$340,554
Liabilities and Stockholders' Equity		
Current liabilities		
Notes payable	$ 2,000	$ 11,500
Current maturities	4,831	1,090
Accounts payable and accrued expenses	68,849	69,696
Taxes on earnings	3,806	3,119
Other accrued taxes	5,460	4,550
Total current liabilities	$ 84,946	$ 89,955
Long-term debt		
Long-term debt, less current maturities	$ 83,723	$ 91,807
Stockholders' equity		
Common shares, $2.50 par value	$ 21,787	$ 21,777
Capital surplus	10,068	10,028
Retained earnings	138,096	126,987
Total stockholders' equity	$169,951	$158,792
Total liabilities and stockholders' equity	$338,620	$340,554

are simply the difference between revenues and the accounting costs that have been charged against them, *cash flow is the amount of money a company actually takes in as a result of doing business.*

Table 6.5 presents the 1997–1998 statement of cash flows for MarCor Industries. Note that this report brings together items from *both* the balance sheet and the income statement to show how the company obtained its cash and how it used this valuable liquid resource. The statement is broken into three parts, the most important of which is the first one, labeled "Cash from Operations." It's important because it captures the *net cash flow from operations*—the line highlighted on the statement. This is what is generally meant by the term *cash flow;* it represents the amount of cash generated by the company and available for investment and financing activities.

TABLE 6.4 Corporate Income Statement

MarCor Industries
Income Statement
Fiscal Year Ended December 31
($ in thousands)

	1998	1997
Net sales	$606,610	$567,986
Other income	6,792	6,220
Interest income	1,504	895
Total revenues	$614,906	$575,101
Cost of goods sold	$337,322	$354,424
Selling, administrative, and other operating expenses	205,864	194,419
Interest expense	5,765	5,523
Total costs and expenses	$588,951	$554,366
Earnings before taxes	$ 25,955	$ 20,735
Taxes on earnings	7,950	5,230
Net earnings (net profit after taxes)	$ 18,005	$ 15,505
Earnings per share	$ 4.74	$ 4.08
Number of common shares outstanding (in thousands)	3,800	3,800

Note that MarCor's 1998 cash flow from operations was nearly $19 million—way up from the year before. However, because the company spent more on its investments and financing activities than it took in, its actual cash position declined by some $8.4 million. That change is shown near the bottom of the statement, in the line labeled "Net Increase (Decrease) in Cash." A high (and preferably increasing) cash flow means the company has plenty of money to pay dividends, service debt, and finance growth. In addition, you'd like to see the firm's cash position increase over time because of the positive impact that has on the company's liquidity and its ability to meet operating needs in a prompt and timely fashion.

Key Financial Ratios

To see what accounting statements really have to say about the financial condition and operating results of the firm, it is necessary to turn to *financial ratios.* Such ratios are useful because they provide a different perspective on the financial affairs of the firm—particularly with regard to the balance sheet and income statement—and thus expand the information content of the company's financial statements. Ratios lie at the very heart of company analysis. Indeed, company analysis as a system of information would be incomplete without this key ingredient.

ratio analysis
the study of the relationships between financial statement accounts.

Ratio analysis is the study of the relationships between various financial statement accounts. Each measure relates one item on the balance sheet (or income statement) to another, or, as is more often the case, a balance sheet account to an operating (income statement) element. In this way, the investor looks not so much at the absolute size of the financial statement accounts as

TABLE 6.5 Statement of Cash Flows

MarCor Industries
Statement of Cash Flows
For the Year Ended December 31
($ in thousands)

	1998	1997
Cash from operations		
Net earnings	$18,005	$15,505
Depreciation and amortization	8,792	8,202
Other noncash charges	560	54
Increase (decrease) in current assets	(7,296)	(21,696)
Increase (decrease) in current liabilities	(1,268)	3,041
Net cash flow from operations	$18,793	$ 5,106
Cash from investing activities		
Acquisitions of property, plant, and equipment—net	($ 6,685)	($ 4,686)
Net cash flow from investing activities	($ 6,685)	($ 4,686)
Cash from financing activities		
Proceeds from long-term borrowing	—	$ 7,950
Reduction in long-term debt, including current maturities and early retirements	($11,825)	(1,240)
Payment of dividends on common stock	(8,626)	(7,287)
Net cash flow from financing activities	($20,451)	($ 557)
Net increase (decrease) in cash	($ 8,433)	($ 157)
Cash and short-term investments at beginning of period	$16,279	$16,436
Cash and short-term investments at end of period	$ 7,846	$16,279

at the liquidity, activity, and profitability of the firm. However, as the accompanying *Investing in Action* box suggests, to get the most from ratio analysis, you must have a good understanding of the uses and limitations of the financial statements themselves.

The most significant contribution of financial ratios is that they enable an investor to assess the firm's past and present financial condition and operating results. The mechanics of ratio analysis are actually quite simple: Selected information is obtained from annual financial statements and used to compute a set of ratios, which are then compared to historical and/or industry standards to evaluate the financial condition and operating results of the company. When historical standards are used, the company's ratios are compared and studied from one year to the next. Industry standards, in contrast, involve a comparison of a particular company's ratios to the performance of other companies in the same line of business. And, remember, the reason we're doing all this is to *develop information about the past that can be used to get a handle on the future.* It's only from a thorough understanding of a company's past performance that an investor can forecast its future with some degree of accuracy. For example, even if sales have been expanding rapidly over the past few years, an investor must carefully assess the reasons for the growth before naively assuming that past growth-rate trends will continue into the future. Such insights are obtained from financial ratios and financial statement analysis.

INVESTING IN ACTION

The Ten Commandments of Financial Statement Analysis

Individuals must pass a test before obtaining a driver's license, but investors don't need to pass any type of test before trying to use financial statements as part of their investment analyses. Yet analyzing financial statements requires at least as much knowledge and skill as driving an automobile. Perhaps each financial statement should contain a warning to potential users, similar to those found on many products. As a starter, the warning might include these ten commandments:

1. **Thou shalt not use financial statements in isolation.** Instead, use them with other available information, such as data on economy-wide conditions and industrywide conditions.

2. **Thou shalt not use financial statements as the only source of firm-specific information.** There are many other sources of information about the company. Consider, for example, financial periodicals and analysts' reports.

3. **Thou shalt not avoid reading footnotes, which are an integral part of financial statements.** Financial statements cannot be reasonably analyzed without reading and understanding the footnotes.

4. **Thou shalt not focus on a single number.** Financial statements are not designed to be reduced to a single number. Net income is not intended to be the number that summarizes all the information relevant to an investment decision. A user must analyze growth and leverage, among other factors, as well as profitability.

5. **Thou shalt not overlook the implications of what is read.** It is not sufficient simply to know that a company is a high-growth or highly leveraged firm; one must also know that such characteristics typically imply higher risk as well.

6. **Thou shalt not ignore events subsequent to the financial statements.** Financial statements are not forecasts of the future; rather, they report the financial condition of the company as of year-end. They do not capture the effects of events that occur after year-end. They thus become increasingly out of date as the year progresses.

7. **Thou shalt not overlook the limitations of financial statements.** Financial statements report only a specified set of events, not all events or all possible financial effects of a single event. Financial statements do not generally represent estimates of the market values of the reported assets and liabilities, nor do they reflect changes in the market values of those assets and liabilities.

8. **Thou shalt not use financial statements without adequate knowledge.** Investors should be sufficiently competent to read, understand, and analyze financial statements.

9. **Thou shalt not shun professional help.** If unwilling or unable to attain adequate knowledge, the investor should defer to someone who does have this ability, such as a financial analyst or a professional money manager.

10. **Thou shalt not take unnecessary risks.** If unwilling or unable to obtain professional help, the investor should undertake investments where investment risk is minimal or where analysis of financial statements is not an issue.

liquidity measures
financial ratios concerned with a firm's ability to meet its day-to-day operating expenses and satisfy its short-term obligations as they come due.

Financial ratios can be divided into five groups: (1) liquidity, (2) activity, (3) leverage, (4) profitability, and (5) common stock, or market, measures. Using the 1998 figures from the MarCor financial statements (Tables 6.3 and 6.4), we will now identify and briefly discuss some of the widely used measures in each of these five categories.

Measuring Liquidity

Liquidity is concerned with the firm's ability to meet its day-to-day operating expenses and satisfy its short-term obligations as they come due. Of major concern is whether a company has adequate cash and other liquid assets on hand to service its debt and operating needs in a prompt and timely fashion. A general overview of a company's liquidity position can often be obtained from two simple measures: current ratio and net working capital.

Current Ratio One of the most commonly cited of all financial ratios, the *current ratio* is computed as follows

Equation 6.1

$$\text{Current ratio} = \frac{\text{current assets}}{\text{current liabilities}}$$

In 1998, MarCor Industries had a current ratio of

$$\text{Current ratio for MarCor} = \frac{\$279,380}{\$84,946} = \underline{\underline{3.29}}$$

This figure indicates that MarCor had $3.29 in short-term resources to service every dollar of current debt. This is a fairly high number and, by most standards, would be considered very strong.

Net Working Capital Though technically not a ratio in the formal sense of the word, net working capital is nonetheless often viewed as such. Actually, *net working capital is an absolute measure of liquidity* and indicates the dollar amount of equity in the working capital position of the firm. It is the difference between current assets and current liabilities. For 1998, the net working capital position for MarCor Industries amounted to

Equation 6.2

$$\text{Net working capital} = \text{current assets} - \text{current liabilities}$$

$$\text{For MarCor} = \$279,380 - \$84,946 = \underline{\underline{\$194,434}}$$

A net working capital figure that approaches the $200 million mark is substantial (for a company this size) and suggests that the liquidity position of this firm is good—so long as it is not made up of slow-moving and obsolete inventories and/or past-due accounts receivable.

Activity Ratios

activity ratios
financial ratios that are used to measure how well a firm is managing its assets.

Measuring general liquidity is only the beginning of the analysis, for we must also assess the composition and underlying liquidity of key current assets and evaluate how effectively the company is managing these assets. **Activity ratios** compare company sales to various asset categories in order to measure how well the company is utilizing its assets. Three of the most widely used activity ratios deal with accounts receivable, inventory, and total assets.

Accounts Receivable Turnover A glance at most financial statements will reveal that the asset side of the balance sheet is dominated by just a few accounts that make up 80% to 90%, or even more, of total resources. Certainly, this is the case with MarCor, where, as you can see in Table 6.3, three entries (accounts receivable, inventory, and net long-term assets) accounted for about 95% of total assets in 1998. Most firms invest a significant amount of capital in accounts receivable, and for this reason they are viewed as a crucial corporate resource. *Accounts receivable turnover* is a measure of how these resources are being managed. It is computed as follows:

Equation 6.3

$$\text{Accounts receivable turnover} = \frac{\text{annual sales}}{\text{accounts receivable}}$$

$$\text{For MarCor} = \frac{\$606{,}610}{\$105{,}400} = \underline{\underline{5.76}}$$

In essence, this turnover figure indicates the kind of return the company is getting from its investment in accounts receivable. Other things being equal, the higher the turnover figure, the more favorable it is. In 1998, MarCor turned its receivables over about 5.8 times; put another way, each dollar invested in receivables supported, or generated, $5.76 in sales.

Inventory Turnover Another important corporate resource—and one that requires a considerable amount of management attention—is inventory. Control of inventory is important to the well-being of a company and is commonly assessed with the *inventory turnover* measure:

Equation 6.4

$$\text{Inventory turnover} = \frac{\text{annual sales}}{\text{inventory}}$$

$$\text{For MarCor} = \frac{\$606{,}610}{\$164{,}356} = \underline{\underline{3.69}}$$

Again, the more mileage (sales) the company can get out of its inventory, the better the return on this vital resource. A figure of 3.69 for MarCor reveals its goods were bought and sold out of inventory about 3.7 times a year. Generally, the higher the turnover figure, the less time an item spends in inventory and, thus, the better the return the company is able to earn from funds tied up in inventory.

Total Asset Turnover *Total asset turnover* indicates how efficiently assets are being used to support sales. It is calculated as follows:

Equation 6.5

$$\text{Total asset turnover} = \frac{\text{annual sales}}{\text{total assets}}$$

$$\text{For MarCor} = \frac{\$606{,}610}{\$338{,}620} = \underline{\underline{1.79}}$$

Note in this case that MarCor is generating about $1.80 in revenues from every dollar invested in assets. This is a fairly high number and is important because it has a direct bearing on corporate profitability. The principle at work here is much like the return to an individual investor: Earning $100 from a $1,000 investment is far more desirable than earning the same $100 from a $2,000 investment. A high total asset turnover figure suggests that corporate resources are being well managed and that the firm is able to realize a high level of sales (and, ultimately, profits) from its asset investments.

Leverage Measures

leverage measures
financial ratios that measure the amount of debt being used to support operations and the ability of the firm to service its debt.

Leverage deals with the firm's different types of financing and indicates the amount of debt being used to support the resources and operations of the company. The amount of indebtedness within the financial structure and the ability of the firm to service its debt are major concerns in leverage analysis. There are two widely used leverage ratios: The first, the debt-equity ratio, measures the *amount of debt* being used by the company, and the second, times interest earned, assesses how well the company can *service its debt.*

Debt-Equity Ratio A measure of leverage, or the relative amount of funds provided by lenders and owners, the *debt-equity ratio* is computed as follows:

Equation 6.6

$$\text{Debt-equity ratio} = \frac{\text{long-term debt}}{\text{stockholders' equity}}$$

$$\text{For MarCor} = \frac{\$83{,}723}{\$169{,}951} = \underline{\underline{0.49}}$$

Because highly leveraged firms (those that use large amounts of debt) run an increased risk of defaulting on their loans, this ratio is particularly helpful in assessing a stock's risk exposure. The 1998 debt-equity ratio for MarCor is reasonably low (at 49%) and shows that most of the company's capital comes from its owners. Stated another way, this figure means there was only 49 cents of debt in the capital structure for every dollar of equity.

Times Interest Earned *Times interest earned* is a so-called coverage ratio and measures the ability of the firm to meet its fixed interest payments. It is calculated as follows:

Equation 6.7

$$\text{Times interest earned} = \frac{\text{earnings before interest and taxes}}{\text{interest expense}}$$

$$\text{For MarCor} = \frac{\$25{,}955 + \$5{,}765}{\$5{,}765} = \underline{\underline{5.50}}$$

The ability of the company to meet its interest payments (which, with bonds, are fixed contractual obligations) in a timely and orderly fashion is an important consideration in evaluating risk exposure. MarCor's times interest earned ratio indicates that the firm has about $5.50 available to cover every dollar of interest expense. As a rule, a coverage ratio of 6 to 7 times earnings is considered pretty strong. There's usually little concern until the measure drops to something less than 2 or 3 times earnings.

Measuring Profitability

profitability measures
financial ratios that measure a firm's returns by relating profits to sales, assets, or equity.

Profitability is a relative measure of success. Each of the various profitability measures relates the returns (profits) of a company to its sales, assets, or equity. There are three widely used profitability measures: net profit margin, return on assets, and return on equity.

Net Profit Margin This is the "bottom line" of operations. *Net profit margin* indicates the rate of profit from sales and other revenues. It is computed as follows:

Equation 6.8

$$\text{Net profit margin} = \frac{\text{net profit after taxes}}{\text{total revenues}}$$

$$\text{For MarCor} = \frac{\$18{,}005}{\$614{,}906} = \underline{\underline{2.9\%}}$$

The net profit margin looks at profits as a percent of sales (and other revenues). Because it moves with costs, it also reveals the type of control management has over the cost structure of the firm. Note that MarCor had a net profit margin of 2.9% in 1998—that is, the company's return on sales was roughly 3 cents on the dollar. Although this is a bit below average for U.S. corporations in general, a net profit margin of nearly 3% is good (i.e., above average) for a fashion apparel firm.

Return on Assets As a profitability measure, *return on assets (ROA)* looks at the amount of resources needed to support operations. Return on assets reveals management's effectiveness in generating profits from the assets it has available—and *is perhaps the single most important measure of return.* It is computed as follows:

Equation 6.9

$$\text{ROA} = \frac{\text{net profit after taxes}}{\text{total assets}}$$

$$\text{For MarCor} = \frac{\$18{,}005}{\$338{,}620} = \underline{\underline{5.3\%}}$$

In the case of MarCor Industries, the company earned 5.3% on its asset investments in 1998. A return of 5.3% is certainly not spectacular, but for an apparel stock, it's not too bad—indeed, as we'll soon see, it's actually above average. As a rule, you'd like to see a company maintain as high an ROA as possible, because the higher the ROA, the more profitable the company.

Return on Equity A measure of the overall profitability of the firm, *return on equity (ROE)* is closely followed by investors because of its direct link to the profits, growth, and dividends of the company. Return on equity—or return on investment (ROI), as it's sometimes called—measures the return to the firm's stockholders by relating profits to shareholder equity:

Equation 6.10

$$\text{ROE} = \frac{\text{net profit after taxes}}{\text{stockholders' equity}}$$

$$\text{For MarCor} = \frac{\$18{,}005}{\$169{,}951} = \underline{\underline{10.6\%}}$$

ROE shows the annual payoff to investors, which in the case of MarCor amounts to nearly 11 cents for every dollar of equity. Generally speaking, look for a high or increasing ROE; in contrast, watch out for a falling ROE that could spell trouble later on.

Breaking Down ROA and ROE

Both ROA and ROE are important measures of corporate profitability. But to get the most from these two measures, we have to break them down into their component parts. ROA, for example, is made up of two key components: the firm's net profit margin and its total asset turnover. Thus, rather than using Equation 6.9 to find ROA, we can use the following expanded format:

Equation 6.11

$$\text{ROA} = \text{net profit margin} \times \text{total asset turnover}$$

Using the net profit margin and total asset turnover figures that we computed (Equations 6.8 and 6.5, respectively), we can find MarCor's 1998 ROA.

$$\text{ROA} = 2.9\% \times 1.79 = \underline{\underline{5.2\%}}$$

Small rounding errors account for the difference between the number computed here and the one computed earlier (5.2% here vs. 5.3% in Equation 6.9).

Why use the expanded version of ROA? *The major reason is that it shows you what's driving company profits.* As an investor, you want to know if ROA is moving up (or down) because of improvements (or deteriorations) in the company's profit margin and/or its total asset turnover. Ideally, you'd like to see ROA moving up (or staying high) because the company does a good job of managing *both* its profits and its assets.

Just as ROA can be broken into its component parts, so too can the return on equity (ROE) measure. Actually, ROE is nothing more than an extension of ROA; it introduces the company's financing decisions into the assessment of profitability. That is, the expanded ROE measure indicates the extent to which financial leverage (or "trading on the equity") can increase return to stockholders. The use of debt in the capital structure, in effect, means that *ROE will always be greater than ROA.* The question is how much greater. Rather than using the abbreviated version of ROE in Equation 6.10, we can compute ROE as follows:

Equation 6.12

$$\text{ROE} = \text{ROA} \times \text{equity multiplier}$$

where

$$\text{Equity multiplier} = \frac{\text{total assets}}{\text{total stockholders' equity}}$$

To find ROE according to Equation 6.12, we first have to find the equity multiplier.

$$\text{Equity multiplier for MarCor} = \frac{\$338{,}620}{\$169{,}951} = 1.99$$

Now we can find the 1998 ROE for MarCor as follows:

$$\text{ROE} = 5.3\% \times 1.99 = \underline{\underline{10.6\%}}$$

Here we can see that the use of debt (the equity multiplier) has magnified—in this case, doubled—returns to stockholders.

Alternatively, we can expand Equation 6.12 still further by breaking ROA in the equation *into its component parts*. In that case, we could compute ROE as

Equation 6.13

$$\begin{aligned} \text{ROE} &= \text{ROA} \times \text{equity multiplier} \\ &= (\text{net profit margin} \times \text{total asset turnover}) \times \text{equity multiplier} \end{aligned}$$

$$\text{For MarCor} = 2.9\% \times 1.79 \times 1.99 = \underline{\underline{10.6\%}}$$

This expanded version of ROE is especially helpful, because it enables investors to assess the company's profitability in terms of three key components: net profit margin, total asset turnover, and financial leverage. In this way, an investor can determine whether ROE is moving up simply because the firm is employing more debt, which isn't necessarily beneficial, or because of the way it is managing its assets and operations, which certainly does have positive long-term implications. To stockholders, ROE is a critical measure of performance (and thus merits careful attention) because of the impact it has on growth and earnings—both of which, as we'll see in Chapter 7, play vital roles in the stock valuation process.

Common Stock Ratios

common stock (market) ratios financial ratios that convert key information about a firm to a per-share basis.

There are a number of **common stock**, or so-called **market ratios,** that convert key bits of information about the company to a per-share basis. They are used to assess the performance of a company for stock valuation purposes. These ratios tell the investor exactly what portion of total profits, dividends, and equity is allocated to each share of stock. Popular common stock ratios include earnings per share, price/earnings ratio, dividends per share, dividend yield, payout ratio, and book value per share. We examined two of these measures in Chapter 5 (earnings per share and dividend yield); let's look now at the other four.

Price/Earnings Ratio This measure is an extension of the earnings-per-share ratio and is used to determine how the market is pricing the company's common stock. The *price/earnings (P/E) ratio* relates the company's earnings per share (EPS) to the market price of its stock.

Equation 6.14

$$\text{P/E} = \frac{\text{market price of common stock}}{\text{EPS}}$$

To compute the P/E ratio, it is necessary first to calculate the stock's EPS. Using the earnings-per-share equation from the previous chapter, we see that the EPS for MarCor Industries in 1998 was

$$\text{EPS} = \frac{\text{net profit after taxes} - \text{preferred dividends}}{\text{number of common shares outstanding}}$$

$$\text{For MarCor} = \frac{\$18{,}005 - \$0}{3{,}800} = \underline{\underline{\$4.74}}$$

INVESTOR FACT

JAPAN'S GROWLING BEAR—The 1990s have been a tough time for investors in Japanese stocks, which are in the midst of a prolonged bear market. The Japanese economy stalled as nearby Asian countries produced lower-cost goods. And now, Asia's financial crisis is hurting Japanese banks, which are major lenders to the area. But another big problem in Japan has been sky-high price/earnings ratios. For example, Mitsubishi, a maker of electrical equipment, recently sold at a P/E multiple of 157. Even in a depressed market, investors find the stock overpriced. After all, in 1997 the average P/E was a bit over 20 times in the U.S. and about 25 in Europe.

In this case, the company's profits of $18 million translate into earnings of $4.74 for *each share* of outstanding common stock. Given this EPS figure and the stock's current market price (assume it is currently trading at 48½), we can use Equation 6.14 to determine the P/E ratio for MarCor Industries.

$$\text{P/E} = \frac{\$48.50}{\$4.74} = \underline{\underline{10.2}}$$

In effect, the stock is currently selling at a multiple of about 10 times its 1998 earnings. Price/earnings multiples are widely quoted in the financial press and are an essential part of many stock valuation models. Other things being equal, you'd like to find stocks with *rising P/E ratios,* because higher P/E multiples usually translate into higher future stock prices and better returns to stockholders. But even though you'd like to see them going up, you also want to *watch out for* P/E ratios that become too high (relative either to the market or to what the stock has done in the past). That's because when this multiple gets too high, it may be a signal that the stock is becoming overvalued (and may be due for a fall).

One way to assess the P/E ratio is to compare it to the company's rate of growth in earnings. The market has developed a measure of this comparison called the **PEG ratio.** Basically, it looks at the latest P/E relative to the 3- to 5-year rate of growth in earnings (where the earnings growth can be all historical—the last 3 to 5 years—or perhaps part historical and part forecasted earnings). The PEG ratio is computed as

PEG ratio
a financial ratio that relates a stock's price/earnings multiple to the company's rate of growth in earnings.

Equation 6.15

$$\text{PEG ratio} = \frac{\text{stock's P/E ratio}}{\text{3- to 5-year growth rate in earnings}}$$

For example, MarCor Industries had a P/E in 1998 of 10.2 times earnings; if earnings for the past 5 years had been growing at an average annual rate of, say, 9.8%, then its PEG ratio would be

$$\text{For MarCor} = \frac{10.2}{9.8} = \underline{\underline{1.04}}$$

A PEG ratio this close to 1.0 is certainly reasonable and suggests that the company's P/E is not out of line with the earnings growth of the firm. In fact, the idea is to *look for stocks that have PEG ratios that are equal to or less than one.* In contrast, a high PEG means the stock's P/E has outpaced its growth in earnings and, if anything, the stock is probably "fully valued." Some investors, in fact, won't even look at stocks if their PEGs are too high—say, more than 1.5 or 2.0. At the minimum, PEG is probably something you would want to look at, because it is certainly not unreasonable to expect some correlation between a stock's P/E and its rate of growth in earnings.

Dividends per Share The principle here is the same as for EPS: to translate total common dividends paid by the company into a per-share figure. (*Note:* If it is not on the income statement, the amount of dividends paid to common stockholders can be found on the statement of cash flows—Table 6.5.) *Dividends per share* is measured as follows.

Equation 6.16

$$\text{Dividends per share} = \frac{\text{annual dividends paid to common stock}}{\text{number of common shares outstanding}}$$

$$\text{For MarCor} = \frac{\$8{,}626}{3{,}800} = \underline{\underline{\$2.27}}$$

For fiscal 1998 MarCor Industries paid out dividends of $2.27 per share—at a quarterly rate of about 57 cents per share. As we saw in the preceding chapter, we can also relate dividends per share to the market price of the stock to determine its present *dividend yield:* $2.27 ÷ $48.50 = 4.7%.

Payout Ratio Another important dividend measure is the dividend *payout ratio.* It indicates the amount of earnings paid out to stockholders in the form of dividends. Well-managed companies try to maintain *target payout ratios.* Thus, if earnings are going up over time, so will dividends. The payout ratio is calculated as follows:

Equation 6.17

$$\text{Payout ratio} = \frac{\text{dividends per share}}{\text{earnings per share}}$$

$$\text{For MarCor} = \frac{\$2.27}{\$4.74} = \underline{\underline{0.48}}$$

For MarCor Industries in 1998, dividends accounted for about 48% of earnings. Traditionally, that's been fairly typical of corporate payout ratios. That is, most companies that pay dividends tend to pay out somewhere between 40% and 60% of earnings. However, payout ratios have been declining in recent years, because firms have been retaining more of their earnings or using them for other purposes. Even so, a payout of nearly 50% could still be appropriate for a firm like MarCor, and such payouts are common in the apparel industry.

Although low dividend payout ratios are certainly not a cause for concern (indeed, they're common among growth companies), the same cannot be said of companies that have high payout ratios. In particular, once the payout ratio reaches 70% to 80% of earnings, extra care should be taken. A payout ratio that high is often an indication that the company will not be able to maintain its current level of dividends. That generally means that dividends will have to be cut back to more reasonable levels—and if there's one thing the market doesn't like, it's cuts in dividends.

Book Value per Share The last common stock ratio is *book value per share,* a measure that deals with stockholders' equity. Actually, book value is simply another term for equity (or net worth); it represents the difference between total assets and total liabilities. Book value per share is computed as follows:

Equation 6.18

$$\text{Book value per share} = \frac{\text{stockholders' equity}}{\text{number of common shares outstanding}}$$

$$\text{For MarCor} = \frac{\$169{,}951}{3{,}800} = \underline{\underline{\$44.72}}$$

Presumably, a stock should sell for *more* than its book value (as MarCor does). If not, it could be an indication that something is seriously wrong with the company's outlook and profitability.

A convenient way to relate the book value of a company to the market price of its stock is to compute the *price-to-book-value ratio.*

Equation 6.19

$$\text{Price-to-book-value} = \frac{\text{market price of common stock}}{\text{book value per share}}$$

$$\text{For MarCor} = \frac{\$48.50}{\$44.72} = \underline{\underline{1.08}}$$

Widely used by investors, this ratio shows how aggressively the stock is being priced. Most stocks have a price-to-book-value ratio of more than 1.0—which simply indicates that the stock is selling for more than its book value. In fact, in strong bull markets, it's not uncommon to find stocks trading at two or three—or even four or five—times their book values. On the other hand, a price-to-book ratio of only 1.08, like MarCor's, is often viewed (especially by so-called value investors) as a sign that the stock is reasonably priced relative to its underlying asset base.

Interpreting the Numbers

Rather than compute all the financial ratios themselves, most investors rely on published reports for such information. Many large brokerage houses and a variety of financial services firms publish such reports, an example of which is given in Figure 6.2. These reports provide a good deal of vital information in a convenient and easy-to-read format; best of all, they relieve investors of the chore of computing the financial ratios themselves. (Similar information is also available from some of the computer online services, as well as from various software providers.) Even so, you, as an investor, must be able to evaluate this published information. To do that, you need not only a basic understanding of financial ratios but also some standard of performance, or benchmark, against which you can assess trends in company performance.

Basically, two types of performance standards are used in financial statement analysis: historical and industry. With *historical standards,* various financial ratios and measures are run on the company for a period of 3 to 5 years (or longer) to assess developing trends in the company's operations and financial condition. That is, are they improving or deteriorating, and where do the company's strengths and weaknesses lie? *Industry standards,* in contrast, enable the investor to compare the financial ratios of the company with comparable firms or with the average results for the industry as a whole. Here, attention centers on determining the relative strength of the firm with respect to its competitors. Using MarCor Industries, we'll see how both of these standards of performance can be used to evaluate and interpret financial ratios.

Using Historical and Industry Standards

Take a look at Table 6.6. It provides a summary of historical data and average industry figures (for the latest year) for most of the ratios we have discussed. By carefully evaluating these ratios, we should be able to draw some basic

FIGURE 6.2
An Example of a Published Report with Financial Statistics

This and similar reports are widely available to investors and play an important part in the security analysis process. (Source: Standard & Poor's *NYSE Reports,* April 23, 1997.)

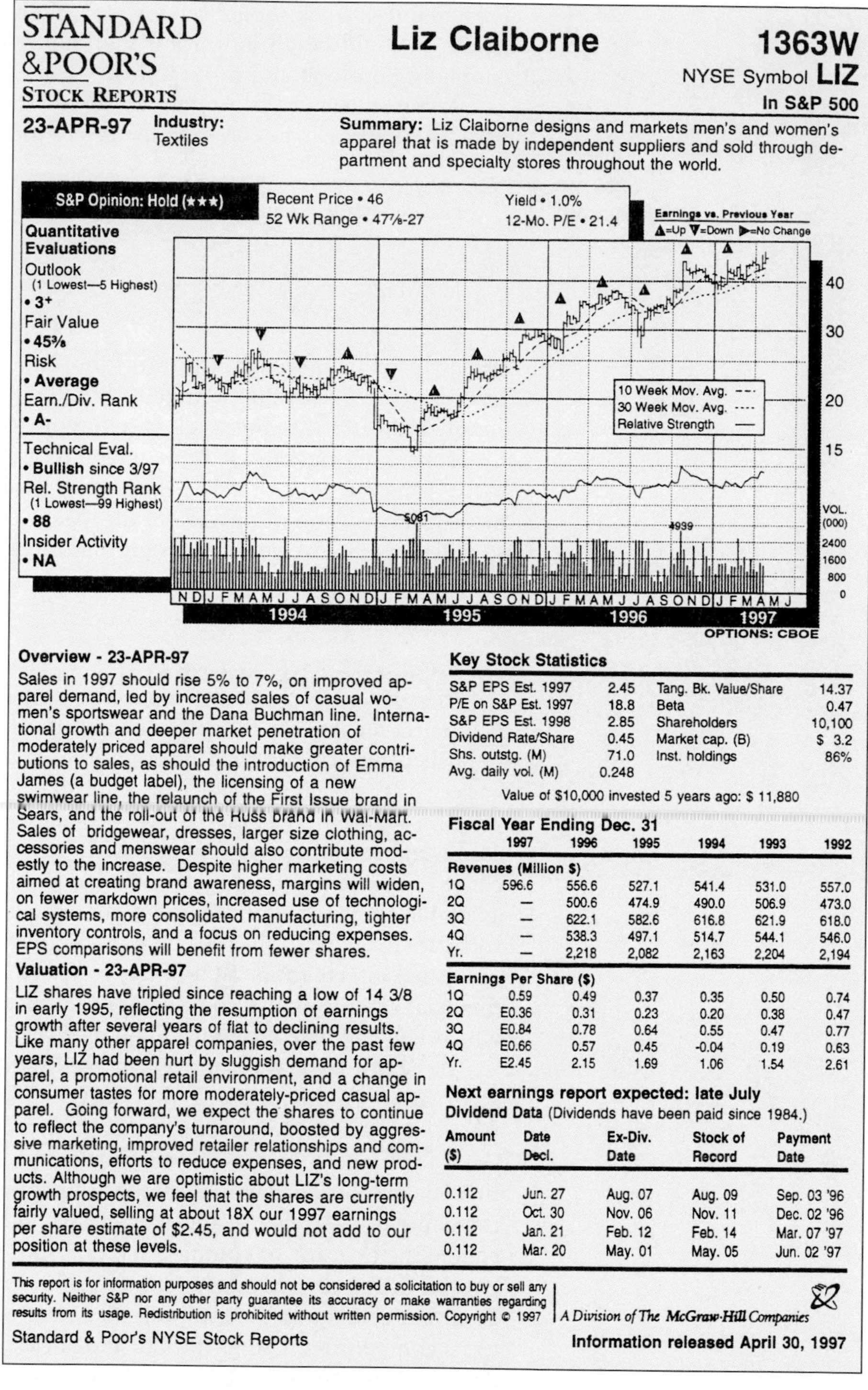

STANDARD &POOR'S STOCK REPORTS

Liz Claiborne **1363W**

NYSE Symbol **LIZ**

In S&P 500

23-APR-97 **Industry:** Textiles

Summary: Liz Claiborne designs and markets men's and women's apparel that is made by independent suppliers and sold through department and specialty stores throughout the world.

S&P Opinion: Hold (★★★) Recent Price • 46 52 Wk Range • 47⅞-27 Yield • 1.0% 12-Mo. P/E • 21.4

Quantitative Evaluations
Outlook (1 Lowest—5 Highest) • 3+
Fair Value • 45⅜
Risk • **Average**
Earn./Div. Rank • **A-**

Technical Eval. • **Bullish** since 3/97
Rel. Strength Rank (1 Lowest—99 Highest) • **88**
Insider Activity • **NA**

Overview - 23-APR-97

Sales in 1997 should rise 5% to 7%, on improved apparel demand, led by increased sales of casual women's sportswear and the Dana Buchman line. International growth and deeper market penetration of moderately priced apparel should make greater contributions to sales, as should the introduction of Emma James (a budget label), the licensing of a new swimwear line, the relaunch of the First Issue brand in Sears, and the roll-out of the Russ brand in Wal-Mart. Sales of bridgewear, dresses, larger size clothing, accessories and menswear should also contribute modestly to the increase. Despite higher marketing costs aimed at creating brand awareness, margins will widen, on fewer markdown prices, increased use of technological systems, more consolidated manufacturing, tighter inventory controls, and a focus on reducing expenses. EPS comparisons will benefit from fewer shares.

Valuation - 23-APR-97

LIZ shares have tripled since reaching a low of 14 3/8 in early 1995, reflecting the resumption of earnings growth after several years of flat to declining results. Like many other apparel companies, over the past few years, LIZ had been hurt by sluggish demand for apparel, a promotional retail environment, and a change in consumer tastes for more moderately-priced casual apparel. Going forward, we expect the shares to continue to reflect the company's turnaround, boosted by aggressive marketing, improved retailer relationships and communications, efforts to reduce expenses, and new products. Although we are optimistic about LIZ's long-term growth prospects, we feel that the shares are currently fairly valued, selling at about 18X our 1997 earnings per share estimate of $2.45, and would not add to our position at these levels.

Key Stock Statistics

S&P EPS Est. 1997	2.45	Tang. Bk. Value/Share	14.37
P/E on S&P Est. 1997	18.8	Beta	0.47
S&P EPS Est. 1998	2.85	Shareholders	10,100
Dividend Rate/Share	0.45	Market cap. (B)	$ 3.2
Shs. outstg. (M)	71.0	Inst. holdings	86%
Avg. daily vol. (M)	0.248		

Value of $10,000 invested 5 years ago: $ 11,880

Fiscal Year Ending Dec. 31

	1997	1996	1995	1994	1993	1992
Revenues (Million $)						
1Q	596.6	556.6	527.1	541.4	531.0	557.0
2Q	—	500.6	474.9	490.0	506.9	473.0
3Q	—	622.1	582.6	616.8	621.9	618.0
4Q	—	538.3	497.1	514.7	544.1	546.0
Yr.	—	2,218	2,082	2,163	2,204	2,194
Earnings Per Share ($)						
1Q	0.59	0.49	0.37	0.35	0.50	0.74
2Q	E0.36	0.31	0.23	0.20	0.38	0.47
3Q	E0.84	0.78	0.64	0.55	0.47	0.77
4Q	E0.66	0.57	0.45	-0.04	0.19	0.63
Yr.	E2.45	2.15	1.69	1.06	1.54	2.61

Next earnings report expected: late July

Dividend Data (Dividends have been paid since 1984.)

Amount ($)	Date Decl.	Ex-Div. Date	Stock of Record	Payment Date
0.112	Jun. 27	Aug. 07	Aug. 09	Sep. 03 '96
0.112	Oct. 30	Nov. 06	Nov. 11	Dec. 02 '96
0.112	Jan. 21	Feb. 12	Feb. 14	Mar. 07 '97
0.112	Mar. 20	May. 01	May. 05	Jun. 02 '97

Standard & Poor's NYSE Stock Reports **Information released April 30, 1997**

conclusions about the financial condition, operating results, and general financial health of the company. By comparing the financial ratios contained in Table 6.6, we can make the following observations about MarCor:

TABLE 6.6 Comparative Historical and Industry Ratios

	Historical Figures for MarCor Industries				Industry Averages for the Apparel Industry in 1998
	1995	1996	1997	1998	
Liquidity measures:					
Current ratio	3.05	2.86	3.10	3.29	2.87
Activity measures:					
Receivables turnover	5.22	4.87	5.52	5.76	8.00
Inventory turnover	3.10	2.98	3.57	3.69	3.75
Total asset turnover	1.75	1.65	1.67	1.79	1.42
Leverage measures:					
Debt-equity ratio	0.52	0.56	0.58	0.49	0.89
Times interest earned	4.65	4.50	4.75	5.50	3.35
Profitability measures:					
Net profit margin	3.6%	3.0%	2.7%	2.9%	2.5%
Return on assets	6.3%	4.9%	4.6%	5.3%	3.9%
Return on equity	11.8%	8.6%	9.8%	10.6%	8.9%
Common stock measures:					
Earnings per share	$4.67	$ 4.15	$ 4.08	$ 4.74	$ 2.86
Price/earnings ratio	9.50	10.90	11.20	10.20	10.10
Dividend yield	4.90%	4.20%	4.20%	4.70%	3.9%
Payout ratio	47.0%	46.0%	47.0%	48.0%	45.5%
Price-to-book-value ratio	1.07	1.15	1.09	1.08	1.05

1. We see a modest improvement in MarCor's already strong *liquidity position,* as the current ratio remains well above the industry standard.

2. The *activity measures* show that although receivables and inventory turnover are improving, they still remain below industry standards. Accounts receivable turnover appears to be especially out of line—almost 40% below normal. Unless there is an operating or economic explanation for this, a lot of excess (nonproductive) resources seem to be tied up in accounts receivable, costing the firm millions of dollars a year in profits. The inventory position, in contrast, has improved. Though still a bit below average, it certainly does not appear to be much of a problem. Finally, total asset turnover is up from last year and continues well above average.

3. The *leverage position* of MarCor Industries seems well controlled: The company tends to use a lot less debt in its financial structure than the average firm in the apparel industry. The payoff for this judicious use of debt comes in the form of a coverage ratio well above average.

4. The *profitability picture* for MarCor is equally attractive; the profit margin, return on assets, and ROE are all improving and remain well above the industry norm.

In summary, our analysis suggests that, with the possible exception of accounts receivable, this firm is fairly well managed and highly profitable. The results of this are reflected in *common stock ratios* that are consistently equal or superior to industry averages.

Looking at the Competition

In addition to analyzing a company historically and relative to the average performance of the industry, it's also advisable to evaluate the firm relative to two or three of its major competitors. A lot can be gained by seeing how a company stacks up against its competitors and by determining whether it is, in fact, well positioned to take advantage of unfolding developments. Table 6.7 offers an array of comparative financial statistics for MarCor and three of its major competitors. (This type of firm-specific data can generally be obtained from industry surveys similar to those put out by S&P and others—or, again, from various software providers.)

As the data show, MarCor Industries is fully capable of holding its own against other leading producers in the industry. Indeed, in virtually every category, MarCor's numbers are about equal or superior to any one of its three major competitors. It may be smaller than a couple of the firms, but it outperforms them in profit margins and growth rates. Equally important, MarCor is a lot less leveraged than the other manufacturers—a real plus in a highly volatile industry. Yet even with its low financial leverage, it is able to maintain a highly attractive ROE. Tables 6.6 and 6.7 suggest that MarCor Industries is a solid, up-and-coming business that's been able to make a real name for itself in a highly competitive industry; the company has certainly

TABLE 6.7 Comparative Financial Statistics: MarCor Industries and Its Major Competitors

(All figures are for year-end 1998 or for the 5-year period ending in 1998; $ in millions)

Financial Measure	MarCor Industries	Regatta Group	Holbrook Industries	Bellwood, Inc.
Total assets	$338.6	$568.6	$231.9	$469.4
Long-term debt	$ 53.7	$124.8	$ 41.5	$128.1
Stockholders' equity	$170.0	$196.9	$103.7	$200.2
Stockholders' equity as a % of total assets	50.2%	34.6%	44.7%	42.6%
Total revenues	$614.9	$807.5	$505.9	$808.0
Net earnings	$ 18.0	$ 14.5	$ 10.6	$ 12.4
Net profit margin	2.9%	1.8%	2.1%	1.5%
5-year growth rates in:				
Total assets	8.9%	10.2%	8.6%	5.6%
Total revenues	8.8%	9.5%	9.0%	3.5%
Net earnings	9.8%	8.1%	7.5%	5.6%
Dividends	10.8%	N/A	8.0%	6.0%
Total asset turnover	1.79×	1.42×	2.18×	1.73×
Debt-equity ratio	0.49	0.74	0.60	0.84
Times interest earned	5.50×	2.65×	4.67×	2.26×
ROA	5.30%	4.10%	5.20%	4.50%
ROE	10.60%	6.70%	8.50%	9.20%
Price/earnings ratio	10.20×	10.20×	13.60×	12.90×
PEG ratio	1.04	1.26	1.81	2.32
Payout ratio	48.00%	N/A	58.80%	67.00%
Dividend yield	4.70%	N/A	4.30%	6.25%
Price-to-book-value ratio	1.08	1.07	0.95	1.17

done well in the past and appears to be well managed today. Our major concern at this point (and the topic of the first part of Chapter 8) is whether MarCor will continue to produce above-average returns to investors.

CONCEPTS IN REVIEW

6.13 What is *fundamental analysis?* Does the performance of a company have any bearing on the value of its stock? Explain.

6.14 Why do investors bother to look at the historical performance of a company when future behavior is what really counts? Explain.

6.15 What is *ratio analysis?* Describe the contribution of ratio analysis to the study of a company's financial condition and operating results.

6.16 In the *Investing in Action* box on page 230, which of the 10 "commandments" listed there do you feel is most important? Explain. Why is it important to carefully review footnotes when analyzing a company's financial statements?

6.17 Contrast historical standards of performance with industry standards. Briefly note the role of each in analyzing the financial condition and operating results of a company.

http://hepg.aw.com

One key to good fundamental analysis is the quantity and quality of financial information. Knowing what other analysts are thinking is also beneficial. Streetnet offers free access to financial statements and to the earnings projections of professional analysts. At its home page, click on *Free Research Reports.*

www.streetnet.com

Summary

LG 1 **Discuss the security analysis process, including its goals and functions.** Success in buying common stocks is largely a matter of careful security selection and investment timing. Security analysis helps the investor make the crucial selection decision by approximating the intrinsic value (or underlying worth) of a stock.

LG 2 **Appreciate the purpose and contributions of economic analysis.** Economic analysis evaluates the general state of the economy and its potential effects on security returns. Its purpose is to characterize the future economic environment the investor will face, and is used to set the tone for the security analysis process.

LG 3 **Describe industry analysis and note how it is used.** In industry analysis, the investor focuses on the activities of one or more industries. Especially important are how the competitive position of a particular industry stacks up against others and which companies within an industry hold particular promise.

LG 4 **Demonstrate a basic understanding of fundamental analysis and why it is used.** Fundamental analysis looks closely at the financial and operating characteristics of the company—at its competitive position, its sales and profit margins, its asset mix, its capital structure, and, eventually, its future prospects. A key aspect of this analytical process is company analysis, which involves an in-depth study of the financial condition and operating results of the company.

LG 5 **Calculate a variety of financial ratios and describe how financial statement analysis is used to gauge the financial vitality of a company.** The company's balance sheet, income statement, and statement of cash flows are all used in company analysis. An essential part of this analysis is financial ratios, which expand the perspective and information content of financial statements. There are five broad categories of financial ratios—liquidity, activity, leverage, profitability, and market (common stock) ratios. All involve the study of relationships between financial statement accounts.

LG 6 **Use various financial measures to assess a company's performance, and explain how the insights derived form the basic input for the valuation process.** In order to evaluate financial ratios properly, it is necessary to base the analysis on historical and industry standards of performance. Whereas historical standards are used to assess developing trends in the company, industry benchmarks enable the investor to see how the firm stacks up against competitors.

Discussion Questions

LG 2 Q6.1. Economic analysis is generally viewed as an integral part of the "top-down" approach to security analysis. In this context, identify each of the following and note how each would probably behave in a strong economy.

a. Fiscal policy
b. Interest rates
c. Industrial production
d. Retail sales
e. Producer prices

LG 1 LG 2 Q6.2. As an investor, what kind(s) of economic information would you look for if you were thinking about investing in the following?

a. An airline stock
b. A cyclical stock
c. An electrical utility stock
d. A building materials stock
e. An aerospace firm, with heavy exposure in the defense industry

LG 5 Q6.3. Match the specific ratios in the left-hand column with the category in the right-hand column to which it belongs.

a. Inventory turnover	1. Profitability ratios
b. Debt-equity ratio	2. Activity ratios
c. Current ratio	3. Liquidity ratios
d. Net profit margin	4. Leverage ratios
e. Return on assets	5. Common stock ratios
f. Total asset turnover	
g. Price/earnings ratio	
h. Times interest earned	
i. Price-to-book-value ratio	
j. Payout ratio	

Problems

 LG 5

P6.1. Assume you are given the following abbreviated financial statements.

	($ in millions)
Current assets	$150.0
Fixed and other assets	200.0
Total assets	$350.0
Current liabilities	$100.0
Long-term debt	50.0
Stockholders' equity	200.0
	$350.0
Common shares outstanding	10 million shares
Total revenues	$500.0
Total operating costs and expenses	435.0
Interest expense	10.0
Income taxes	20.0
Net profits	$ 35.0
Dividends paid to common stockholders	$ 10.0

On the basis of this information, calculate as many liquidity, activity, leverage, profitability, and common stock measures as you can. (*Note:* Assume the current market price of the common stock is $75/share.)

 LG 6

P6.2. The Amherst Company has net profits of $10 million, sales of $150 million, and 2.5 million shares of common stock outstanding. The company has total assets of $75 million and total stockholders' equity of $45 million; it pays $1 per share in common dividends, and the stock trades at $20 per share. Given this information, determine

a. Amherst's earnings per share (EPS)
b. Amherst's book value per share *and* price-to-book-value ratio
c. The firm's price/earnings (P/E) ratio
d. The company's net profit margin
e. The stock dividend payout ratio *and* its dividend yield
f. The stock's PEG ratio, given that the company's earnings have been growing at an average annual rate of 7.5%.

 LG 5

P6.3. Sunbelt Solar Products produces $2 million in profits from $28 million in sales and has total assets of $15 million.

a. Calculate SSP's total asset turnover and compute its net profit margin.
b. Find the company's ROA, ROE, and book value per share, given that SSP has a total net worth of $6 million and 500,000 shares of common stock outstanding.

 LG 5 LG 6

P6.4. Financial Learning Systems has 2.5 million shares of common stock outstanding and 100,000 shares of preferred stock (the preferred pays annual cash dividends of $5 a share, and the common pays annual cash dividends of 25 cents a share). Last year, the company generated net profits (after taxes) of $6,850,000. The company's balance sheet shows total assets of $78 million, total liabilities of $32 million, and $5 million in preferred stock. The firm's common stock is currently trading in the market at $45 a share.

a. Given the preceding information, find the stock's earnings per share, price/earnings ratio, and book value per share.
b. What will happen to the price of the stock if earnings per share rises to $3.75 and the P/E ratio stays where it is? What will happen if EPS *drops* to $1.50 and the P/E ratio doesn't change?

c. What will happen to the price of the stock if EPS rises to $3.75 and the P/E ratio jumps to 25 times earnings?
d. What will happen if *both* EPS and the P/E ratio *drop*—to $1.50 and 10 times earnings, respectively?
e. Comment on the effect that EPS and the P/E ratio have on the market price of the stock.

 LG 5

P6.5. The Shasta Flower Farm has total assets of $10 million, an asset turnover of 2.0 times, and a net profit margin of 15%.
a. What is Shasta's return on assets?
b. Find Shasta's ROE, given that 40% of the assets are financed with stockholders' equity.

 LG 5

P6.6. Find the EPS, P/E ratio, and dividend yield of a company that has 5 million shares of common stock outstanding (the shares trade in the market at $25), earns 10% after taxes on annual sales of $150 million, and has a dividend payout ratio of 35%. At what rate would the company's net earnings be growing if the stock had a PEG ratio of 2.0?

 LG 5

P6.7. Using the resources available at your campus or public library, select any common stock you like and determine as many of the profitability, activity, liquidity, leverage, and market ratios as you can; compute the ratios for the latest available fiscal year. (*Note:* Show your work for all calculations.)

 LG 4 LG 5 LG 6

P6.8. Listed below are six pairs of stocks. Pick *one of these pairs* and then, using the resources available at your campus or public library, comparatively analyze the two stocks to determine which is fundamentally stronger and holds more promise for the future. Compute (or obtain) as many ratios as you see fit. As part of your analysis, obtain the latest S&P and/or *Value Line* reports on both stocks, and use them for added insights about the firms and their stocks.
a. Wal-Mart vs. Kmart
b. J. M. Smucker vs. Campbell Soup
c. IBM vs. Intel
d. H&R Block vs. Crown Cork & Seal
e. Liz Claiborne vs. Hartmarx
f. General Dynamics vs. Weyerhaeuser

 LG 4 LG 5 LG 6

P6.9. Listed here are the 1997 and 1998 financial statements for Oasis Marine Motors, a major manufacturer of topline outboard motors.

Balance Sheets ($ in thousands)

Assets	December 31, 1998	December 31, 1997
Current assets:		
Cash and cash equivalents	$ 56,203	$ 88,942
Accounts receivable, net of allowances	20,656	12,889
Inventories	29,294	24,845
Prepaid expenses	5,761	6,536
Total current assets	$111,914	$133,212
Property, plant and equipment, at cost	137,273	85,024
Less: Accumulated depreciation and amortization	(50,574)	(44,767)
Net fixed assets	$ 86,699	$ 40,257
Other assets:	105,327	51,001
	$303,940	$224,470

Balance Sheets ($ in thousands)

Liabilities and Shareholders' Equity

	December 31, 1998	December 31, 1997
Current liabilities:		
Notes and accounts payable	28,860	4,927
Dividends payable	1,026	791
Accrued liabilities	20,976	16,780
Total current liabilities	$ 50,862	$ 22,498
Noncurrent liabilities:		
Long-term debt	$ 40,735	$ 20,268
Shareholders' equity:		
Common stock	7,315	7,103
Capital in excess of par value	111,108	86,162
Retained earnings	93,920	88,439
Total shareholders' equity	$212,343	$181,704
	$303,940	$224,470
Average number of common shares outstanding	10,848,000	10,848,000

Income Statements ($ in thousands)

Liabilities and Shareholders' Equity

	For the Year Ended December 31, 1998	For the Year Ended December 31, 1997
Net sales	$259,593	$245,424
Cost of goods sold	133,978	127,123
Gross margin	$125,615	$118,301
Operating expenses:	72,098	70,368
Earnings from operations	$ 53,517	47,933
Other income (expense), net	4,193	3,989
Earnings before income taxes	$ 57,710	$ 51,922
Provision for income taxes	22,268	19,890
Net earnings	$ 35,442	$ 32,032
Cash dividends ($.35 and $.27 per share)	3,769	2,947
Average price per share of common stock (in the fourth quarter of the year)	$ 74.25	$ 80.75

a. On the basis of the information provided, calculate the following financial ratios for 1997 and 1998.

	Oasis Marine Motors 1997	Oasis Marine Motors 1998	Industry Averages (for 1998)
Current ratio			2.36
Total asset turnover			1.27
Debt-equity ratio			10.00
Net profit margin			9.30
ROA			15.87
ROE			19.21
EPS			1.59
P/E ratio			19.87
Cash dividend yield			.44
Payout ratio			.26
Price-to-book-value			6.65

b. Considering the financial ratios you computed, along with the industry averages, how would you characterize the financial condition of Oasis Marine Motors? Explain.

LG 5 LG 6

P6.10. The following summary financial statistics were obtained from the 1994 Oasis Marine Motors (OMM) annual report.

	1994 ($ in millions)
Net sales	$179.3
Total assets	$136.3
Net earnings	$ 20.2
Shareholders' equity	$109.6

a. Use the profit margin and asset turnover to compute the 1994 ROA for OMM. Now introduce the equity multiplier to find ROE.
b. Obtain the same summary financial information from the *1998* OMM financial statements (see Problem 6.9), and use it to compute the 1998 ROA and ROE. Use the same procedures to calculate these measures as you did in part (a).
c. On the basis of your calculations, describe how *each* of the components contributed to the change in OMM's ROA and ROE between 1994 and 1998. Which component(s) contributed the most to the change in ROA? Which contributed the most to the change in ROE?
d. Generally speaking, do you think that these changes are fundamentally healthy for the company?

Case Problem 6.1 *Some Financial Ratios Are Real Eye-Openers*

LG 5 LG 6

Jack Simms is a resident of Brownfield, Texas, where he is a prosperous rancher and businessman. He has also built up a sizable portfolio of common stock, which, he believes, is due to the fact that he thoroughly evaluates each stock he invests in. As Jack says, "Y'all can't be too careful about these things! Anytime I'm fixin' to invest in a stock, you can bet I'm gonna learn as much as I can about the company." Jack prefers to compute his own ratios even though he could easily obtain various types of analytical reports from his broker at no cost. (In fact, Billy Bob Smith, his broker, has been volunteering such services for years.)

Recently, Jack has been keeping an eye on a small chemical issue. This firm, South Plains Chemical Company, is big in the fertilizer business—which, not by coincidence, is something Jack knows a lot about. Not long ago, he received a copy of the firm's latest financial statements (summarized here) and decided to take a closer look at the company.

Balance Sheet
($ Thousands)

Cash	$1,250		
Accounts receivable	8,000	Current liabilities	$10,000
Inventory	12,000	Long-term debt	8,000
Current assets	$21,250	Stockholders' equity	12,000
Fixed and other assets	8,750		
Total	$30,000	Total	$30,000

Income Statement
($ Thousands)

Sales	$50,000
Cost of goods sold	25,000
Operating expenses	15,000
Operating profit	$10,000
Interest expense	2,500
Taxes	2,500
Net profit	$ 5,000

Notes: Dividends paid to common stockholders ($ in thousands)	$1,250
Number of common shares outstanding	5 million
Recent market price of the common stock	$25

QUESTIONS

a. Compute the following ratios, using the South Plains Chemical Company figures.

	Latest Industry Averages		Latest Industry Averages
Liquidity		*Common Stock Ratios*	
a. Net working capital	N/A	l. Earnings per share	$2.00
b. Current ratio	1.95	m. Price/earnings ratio	20.0
		n. Dividends per share	$1.00
Activity		o. Dividend yield	2.5%
c. Receivables turnover	5.95	p. Payout ratio	50.0%
d. Inventory turnover	4.50	q. Book value per share	$6.25
e. Total asset turnover	2.65	r. Price-to-book-value ratio	6.4
Leverage			
f. Debt-equity ratio	0.45		
g. Times interest earned	6.75		
Profitability			
h. Operating ratio	85.0%		
i. Net profit margin	8.5%		
j. Return on assets	22.5%		
k. ROE	32.2%		

b. Compare the company ratios you prepared to the industry figures. What are the company's strengths? What are its weaknesses?

c. What is your overall assessment of South Plains Chemical? Do you think Simms should continue with his evaluation of the stock? Explain.

Case Problem 6.2 Doris Looks at an Auto Issue

LG 2 LG 3 LG 5

Doris Wise is a young career woman; she lives in Chicago, where she owns and operates a highly successful modeling agency. Doris manages her modest but rapidly growing investment portfolio, made up mostly of high-grade common stocks. Because she's young and single and has no pressing family requirements, Doris has invested primarily in stocks that offer the potential for attractive capital gains. Her broker recently recommended one of the auto issues and sent her some literature and analytical reports to study. Among the reports was one prepared by the brokerage house she deals with; it provided an up-to-date look at the economy, an extensive study of the auto industry, and an equally extensive review of several auto companies (including the one her broker recommended). She feels strongly about the merits of security analysis and believes it is important to spend time studying a stock before making an investment decision.

QUESTIONS

a. Doris tries to stay informed about the economy on a regular basis. At the present time, most economists agree that the economy, now well into the third year of a recovery, is healthy, with industrial activity remaining strong. What other information about the economy do you think Doris would find helpful in evaluating an auto stock? Prepare a list—and be specific. Which three items of economic information (from your list) do you feel are most important? Explain.

b. In relation to a study of the auto industry, briefly note the importance of each of the following.

1. Auto imports
2. The United Auto Workers union
3. Interest rates
4. The price of a gallon of gas

c. A variety of financial ratios and measures are provided about one of the auto companies and its stock. These are incomplete, however, so some additional information will have to be computed. Specifically, we know

Net profit margin	15%
Total assets	$25 billion
Earnings per share	$3.00
Total asset turnover	1.5
Net working capital	$3.4 billion
Payout ratio	40%
Current liabilities	$5 billion
Price/earnings ratio	12.5

Given this information, calculate

1. Sales
2. Net profits after taxes
3. Current ratio
4. Market price of the stock
5. Dividend yield

Home Page Exercises

http://hepg.aw.com **Keyword: Invest**

The value of a stock is affected by more than the fundamental financial condition and operating results of the issuing corporation. Corporations operate as part of a larger industry and as an even smaller part of the economy. Factors or trends that affect the corporation's industry or the economy at large are reflected in the asset's value (its price). This chapter presented the types of economic and industry information needed for thorough security analysis. If, as the saying goes, the language of business is accounting, then the language of investments is ratios. Ratios encapsulate the meaning in what would otherwise be just a bunch of formally organized numbers. The following Web sites provide information for economic, industry, or firm-specific analysis.

Web Address	*Primary Investment Focus*
www.marketguide.com	Company ratios and industry links
www.moodys.com	Economic commentary
www.vanguard.com	Economic commentary and data
www.reportgallery.com	A library of annual reports

W6.1. A strong economy and favorable industry conditions are meaningless if the fundamental financial condition and operating results of a corporation are weak. Locate The GAP's financial statements at the Web site here and calculate as many liquidity, activity, leverage, profitability, and common stock measures as you can.

www.gap.com

W6.2. Monetary policy, a key economic factor, is set at meetings of the Federal Open Market Committee. The minutes of this meeting recount the committee's discussion of economic trends and the actions it takes in response to those trends. The Web sites of the various Federal Reserve Banks contain links to the minutes of the most recent meeting (they become available several weeks after each meeting). Find the Web site of the Federal Reserve Bank of Atlanta at the address here, and follow instructions to find the link to the latest minutes. List the 12 attending members of the Federal Open Market Committee.

www.frbatlanta.org

Select *Economics.*

Select *Monetary policy.*

Select *FOMC Minutes.*

Select the latest minutes available (they are listed by date).

To go directly to minutes:

www.bog.frb.fed.us/fomc/minutes/19971216.htm

CHAPTER 7 Stock Valuation and Investment Decisions

Learning Goals

After studying this chapter, you should be able to:

LG 1 Explain the role that a company's future plays in the stock valuation process and develop a forecast of a stock's expected cash flow.

LG 2 Discuss the concepts of intrinsic value and required rates of return and note how they are used.

LG 3 Determine the underlying value of a stock using the dividend valuation model, as well as other present-value-based stock valuation models.

LG 4 Explain the role that the price/earnings ratio plays in defining a stock's price behavior and how the P/E multiple can be used in the stock valuation process.

LG 5 Describe the key attributes of technical analysis, including some popular measures and procedures used to assess the market.

LG 6 Discuss the idea of random walks and efficient markets and note the challenges these theories hold for the stock valuation process.

Wells Fargo

They used to be sleepy investments, the kind that Grandpa owned along with the telephone company and the local electric utility. But banks today are one of the hottest investments on Wall Street. Over the past several years, Congress has deregulated the banking industry, allowing banks to do business across state lines and to merge with other banks across the country. By merging, banks can create economies of scale, doing more business with less overhead. One beneficiary of this merger trend is San Francisco–based Wells Fargo, which has been gobbling up banks in California and other parts of the West. Meanwhile, Wells Fargo stock had doubled in 3 years, so that at the end of 1997, the stock, at \$339 a share, was selling at about 32 times earnings, a 50% premium over the stock market as a whole. Then, in 1998, Wells Fargo entered into a megamerger with Norwest banks (of Minneapolis) that boosted the value of the stock even more—to nearly \$370 a share at the time the merger was announced.

This chapter looks in detail at the question of a stock's worth. It shows how to develop estimates from the expected returns of a company's stock, which help explain why investors are willing to pay premiums for some companies and why other companies fall out of favor.

Valuation: Obtaining a Standard of Performance

LG 1 LG 2

stock valuation
the process by which the underlying value of a stock is established on the basis of its forecasted risk and return performance.

Obtaining a standard of performance that can be used to judge the investment merits of a share of stock is the underlying purpose of **stock valuation.** A stock's intrinsic value furnishes such a standard because it indicates the future risk and return performance of a security. The question of whether and to what extent a stock is under- or overvalued is resolved by comparing its current market price to its intrinsic value. At any given point in time, the price of a share of common stock depends on investor expectations about the future behavior of the security. If the outlook for the company and its stock is good, the price will probably be bid up. If conditions deteriorate, the price of the stock will probably go down. Let's look now at the single most important issue in the stock valuation process: *the future.*

Valuing a Company and Its Future

Thus far, we have examined several aspects of security analysis, including economic and industry analysis, as well as the historical (company) phase of fundamental analysis. It should be clear, however, that it's *not the past* that's important but *the future.* The primary reason for looking at past performance is to gain insight about the future direction of the firm and its profitability. Granted, past performance provides no guarantees about future returns, but it can give us a good idea of company strengths and weaknesses. For example, it can tell us how well the company's products have done in the marketplace, how the company's fiscal health shapes up, and how management tends to respond to difficult situations. In short, the past can reveal how well the company is positioned to take advantage of the things that may occur in the future.

Because *the value of a stock is a function of its future returns,* the investor's task is to use available historical data to project key financial variables into the future. In this way, you can assess the future prospects of the company and the expected returns from its stock. We are especially interested in dividends and price behavior.

Forecasted Sales and Profits

The key to our forecast is, of course, the future behavior of the *company,* and the most important aspects to consider in this regard are the outlook for sales and the trend in the net profit margin. One way to develop a sales forecast is to assume that the company will continue to perform as it has in the past and simply extend the historical trend. For example, if a firm's sales have been growing at the rate of 10% per year, then assume they will continue at that rate of growth. Of course, if there is some evidence about the economy, industry, or company that suggests a faster or slower rate of growth, the forecast should be adjusted accordingly. More often than not, this "naive" approach will be about as effective as more complex techniques.

Once the sales forecast has been generated, we can shift our attention to the net profit margin. We want to know what kind of return on sales we can expect. A naive estimate can be obtained simply by using the average profit margin that has prevailed for the past few years; again, this should be adjusted to account for any unusual industry or company developments. For most individual investors, valuable insight about future revenues and earnings can be obtained from industry or company reports put out by brokerage houses, advisory services (e.g., *Value Line*), and the financial media (e.g., *Forbes*).

Given a satisfactory sales forecast and estimate of the future net profit margin, we can combine these two pieces of information to arrive at future earnings.

Equation 7.1

$$\text{Future after-tax earnings in year } t = \text{estimated sales for year } t \times \text{net profit margin expected in year } t$$

The "year t" notation in the equation simply denotes a given calendar or fiscal year in the future. It can be next year, the year after that, or any other year in which we are interested. Let's say that in the year just completed, a company reported sales of $100 million, and it is estimated that revenues will grow at an 8% annual rate, while the net profit margin should amount to about 6%. Thus estimated sales next year will equal $108 million ($100 million × 1.08), and with a 6% profit margin, we should see earnings next year of

$$\text{Future after-tax earnings next year} = \$108 \text{ million} \times 0.06 = \underline{\underline{\$6.5 \text{ million}}}$$

Using this same process, we would then estimate sales and earnings *for all other years* in our forecast period.

Forecasted Dividends and Prices

At this point, we have an idea of the future earnings performance of the company—assuming, of course, that our expectations and assumptions hold up. We are now ready to evaluate the effects of this performance on returns to common stock investors. Given a corporate earnings forecast, we need three additional pieces of information:

1. An estimate of future dividend payout ratios
2. The number of common shares that will be outstanding over the forecast period
3. A future price/earnings (P/E) ratio

For the first two variables, unless we have evidence to the contrary, we can simply project the firm's recent experience into the future and assume that these estimates will hold for the forecast period. Payout ratios are usually fairly stable, so there is little risk in using a recent average figure. (Or, if a company follows a fixed-dividend policy, we could use the latest dividend rate in our forecast.) At the same time, it is generally safe to assume that the number of common shares outstanding will hold at the latest level or perhaps increase at some moderate rate of growth that's reflective of the past.

INVESTOR FACT

U.S. STOCKS: STILL A BARGAIN?—As the U.S. stock market continued to climb during the 1990s, concerns grew about the P/E ratio of the Standard & Poor's 500 Index. True, the S&P 500 Index was selling at 24 times 1997 earnings, historically high for the U.S. But compared to what? In Europe, the Swiss stock market was selling at nearly 38 times earnings. Japan's stock market had a P/E ratio of 54. The cheapest stock market was oil-rich Venezuela, selling at just 9 times earnings.

Getting a Handle on the P/E Ratio The only really thorny issue in this whole process is coming up with an estimate of the future P/E ratio, a figure that has considerable bearing on the future price behavior of the stock. Generally speaking, the P/E ratio is a function of several variables:

1. The growth rate in earnings
2. The general state of the market

3. The amount of debt in a company's capital structure
4. The current and projected rate of inflation
5. The level of dividends

As a rule, higher P/E ratios can be expected with higher rates of growth in earnings, an optimistic market outlook, and lower debt levels (less debt means less financial risk).

The link between the inflation rate and P/E multiples is a bit more complex. Generally speaking, as inflation rates rise, so do bond interest rates, which, in turn, causes required returns on stocks to rise (in order for stock returns to remain competitive with bond returns)—and higher required returns on stocks mean lower stock prices and lower P/E multiples. On the other hand, declining inflation (and interest) rates normally translate into higher P/E ratios and stock prices. We can also argue that a high P/E ratio should be expected with high dividend payouts. In practice, however, most companies with high P/E ratios have *low dividend payouts.* The reason: Earnings growth tends to be more valuable than dividends, especially in companies with high rates of return on equity.

A useful starting point for evaluating the P/E ratio is the *average market multiple,* which is simply the average P/E ratio of stocks in the marketplace. The average market multiple indicates the general state of the market and gives us an idea of how aggressively the market, in general, is pricing stocks. Other things being equal, the higher the P/E ratio, the more optimistic the market. Table 7.1 lists S&P price/earnings multiples for the past 37 years and shows that market multiples do tend to move over a fairly wide range.

TABLE 7.1 Average Market P/E Multiples 1961–1997

Year	Market Multiples (Average S&P P/E Ratio)	Year	Market Multiples (Average S&P P/E Ratio)
1961	22.4	1980	9.1
1962	17.2	1981	8.1
1963	18.7	1982	10.2
1964	18.6	1983	12.4
1965	17.8	1984	10.0
1966	14.8	1985	13.7
1967	17.7	1986	16.3
1968	18.1	1987	15.1
1969	15.1	1988	12.2
1970	16.7	1989	15.6
1971	18.3	1990	15.5
1972	19.1	1991	26.2
1973	12.2	1992	22.8
1974	7.3	1993	21.3
1975	11.7	1994	17.0
1976	11.0	1995	17.4
1977	8.8	1996	20.7
1978	8.3	1997	24.0
1979	7.4		

Source: Average year-end multiples derived from Standard & Poor's *Index of 500 Stocks* and its *Statistical Service—Security Price Index Record,* various issues. Listed P/Es are all year-end (December) figures, except 1997, which is as of the end of the third quarter.

relative P/E multiple
the measure of how a stock's P/E behaves relative to the average market multiple.

With the market multiple as a benchmark, the investor can evaluate a stock's P/E performance relative to the market. That is, you can calculate a **relative P/E multiple** by dividing a stock's P/E by the market multiple. For example, if a stock currently has a P/E of 25 and the market multiple is 15, the stock's relative P/E is 25/15 = 1.67. Looking at the relative P/E, the investor can quickly get a feel for how aggressively the stock has been priced in the market and what kind of relative P/E is normal for the stock. Other things being equal, a high relative P/E is desirable; the higher this measure, the higher the stock will be priced in the market. But watch out for the downside: High relative P/E multiples can also mean more price volatility. (Similarly, we can use average *industry* multiples to get a feel for the kind of P/E multiples that are standard for a given industry and then use that information, along with market multiples, to assess or project the P/E for a particular stock.)

Now we can generate a forecast of what the stock's *future* P/E will be over the anticipated *investment horizon*—that is, the period of time over which we expect to hold the stock. For example, with the existing P/E multiple as a base, an *increase* might be justified if you believe the *market multiple* will increase (as the market tone becomes more bullish) and the *relative P/E* is likely to increase also.

Estimating Earnings per Share So far we've been able to come up with an estimate for the dividend payout ratio, the number of shares outstanding, and the price/earnings multiple. We're now ready to forecast the stock's future earnings per share (EPS). That can be done as follows:

Equation 7.2

$$\text{Estimated EPS in year } t = \frac{\text{future after-tax earnings in year } t}{\text{number of shares of common stock outstanding in year } t}$$

As you can see, Equation 7.2 simply converts aggregate or total corporate earnings to a per-share basis by relating company (forecasted) profits to the expected number of shares outstanding. Though this approach works quite effectively, some investors would rather by-pass the projection of aggregate sales and earnings and instead *concentrate on earnings from a per-share basis right from the start.* That can be done by looking at the major forces that drive earnings per share: ROE and book value. Quite simply, by employing these two variables, we can define earnings per share as follows:

Equation 7.3

$$\text{EPS} = \text{ROE} \times \text{book value per share}$$

This formula will produce exactly the same results as the standard EPS equation shown first in Chapter 5 (Equation 5.1) and then again in Chapter 6. The major advantage of this form of the equation is that it allows the investor to assess the extent to which EPS is influenced by the company's book value position and (especially) its ROE. As we saw in the previous chapter, ROE is a key financial measure, because it captures the amount of success the firm is having in managing its assets, operations, and capital structure. And as we see here, ROE not only is important in defining overall corporate profitability but also plays a crucial role in defining a stock's EPS.

To produce an estimated EPS using Equation 7.3, the individual investor would go directly to the two basic components of the formula and try to get a handle on their future behavior. In particular, what kind of growth is expected in the firm's book value per share, *and* what's likely to happen to the company's ROE? In the vast majority of cases, ROE is really the driving force, so it's important to produce a good estimate of that variable. Investors often do that by breaking ROE into its component parts—margin, turnover, and the equity multiplier (see Equation 6.13 in Chapter 6). Once the investor has projected ROE and book value per share, these figures can be plugged into Equation 7.3 to produce estimated EPS. The bottom line is that, one way or another (using the approach reflected in Equation 7.2 or that in Equation 7.3), the investor has to arrive at a forecasted EPS number that he or she is comfortable with. When that's been done, it's a pretty simple matter to use the forecasted payout ratio to estimate dividends per share.

Equation 7.4

$$\begin{matrix}\text{Estimated dividends} \\ \text{per share in year } t\end{matrix} = \begin{matrix}\text{estimated EPS} \\ \text{in year } t\end{matrix} \times \begin{matrix}\text{estimated} \\ \text{payout ratio}\end{matrix}$$

The last item is the future price of the stock, which can be determined as

Equation 7.5

$$\begin{matrix}\text{Estimated share price} \\ \text{at end of year } t\end{matrix} = \begin{matrix}\text{estimated EPS} \\ \text{in year } t\end{matrix} \times \begin{matrix}\text{estimated P/E} \\ \text{ratio}\end{matrix}$$

Putting It All Together We've seen the various components that go into our estimates of future dividends and share prices. Now, to see how they all fit together, let's continue with the example we started above. Using the aggregate sales and earnings approach, if the company had 2 million shares of common stock outstanding and that number was expected to hold in the future, then given the estimated earnings of $6.5 million that we computed earlier, the firm should generate earnings per share (EPS) next year of

$$\begin{matrix}\text{Estimated EPS} \\ \text{next year}\end{matrix} = \frac{\$6.5 \text{ million}}{2 \text{ million}} = \underline{\underline{\$3.25}}$$

This result, of course, would be equivalent to the firm having a projected ROE of, say, 15% and an estimated book value per share of $21.67. According to Equation 7.3, those conditions would also produce an estimated EPS of $3.25 (i.e., 0.15 × $21.67). Anyway, using this EPS figure, along with an estimated payout ratio of 40%, we see that dividends per share next year should equal

$$\begin{matrix}\text{Estimated dividends} \\ \text{per share next year}\end{matrix} = \$3.25 \times .40 = \underline{\underline{\$1.30}}$$

Of course, if the firm adheres to a *fixed-dividend policy,* this estimate may have to be adjusted to reflect the level of dividends being paid. For example, if the company has been paying annual dividends at the rate of $1.25 per share *and is expected to continue doing so for the near future,* then estimated dividends should be adjusted accordingly (i.e., use $1.25/share). Finally, if it has been estimated that the stock should sell at 17.5 times earnings, then a share of stock in this company should be trading at a price of about 56⅞ by the *end* of next year.

$$\text{Estimated share price at the end of next year} = \$3.25 \times 17.5 = \underline{\underline{\$56.88}}$$

Actually, we are interested in the price of the stock at the end of our anticipated investment horizon. Thus the 56⅞ figure would be appropriate if we had a 1-year horizon. However, if we had a 3-year holding period, we would have to extend the EPS figure for 2 more years and repeat our calculations with the new data. As we shall see, *the estimated share price is important because it has embedded in it the capital gains portion of the stock's total return.*

Developing an Estimate of Future Behavior

Using MarCor Industries, we can illustrate the forecasting procedures we discussed above with a concrete example. Recall from Chapter 6 that an assessment of the economy and the apparel industry was positive and that the company's operating results and financial condition looked strong, both historically and relative to industry standards. Because everything looks favorable for MarCor, we decide to take a look at the future prospects of the company and its stock. Assume we have chosen a 3-year investment horizon, because we believe (from earlier studies of economic and industry factors) that the economy and the market for apparel stocks will start running out of steam near the end of 2001 or early 2002.

Selected historical financial data are provided in Table 7.2. They cover a 6-year period (ending with the latest, 1998, fiscal year) and will provide the basis for much of our forecast. The data in the table reveal that except for 1993 (which was an "off" year for MarCor), the company has performed at

TABLE 7.2 Selected Historical Financial Data, MarCor Industries

	1993	1994	1995	1996	1997	1998
Total assets (millions)	$220.9	$240.7	$274.3	$318.2	$340.5	$338.6
Debt-equity ratio	53%	51%	52%	56%	58%	49%
Total asset turnover	1.72×	1.81×	1.75×	1.65×	1.67×	1.79×
Net sales (millions)	$397.9	$435.6	$480.0	$525.0	$568.0	$606.6
Annual rate of growth in sales*	−5.7%	9.5%	10.2%	9.4%	8.2%	6.8%
Interest and other income (millions)	$ 6.3	$ 6.0	$ 6.8	$ 7.7	$ 7.1	$ 8.3
Net profit margin	1.1%	2.0%	3.6%	3.0%	2.7%	2.9%
Payout ratio	97.0%	45.0%	47.0%	46.0%	47.0%	48.0%
Price/earnings ratio	8.3×	12.8×	9.5×	10.9×	11.2×	10.2×
Number of common shares outstanding (millions)	3.2	3.2	3.7	3.8	3.8	3.8

*Annual rate of growth in sales = change in sales from one year to the next divided by the level of sales in the base (or earliest) year; for 1994, the annual rate of growth in sales equaled 9.5% = (1994 sales − 1993 sales)/1993 sales = ($435.6 − $397.9)/$397.9 = 0.095.

a fairly steady pace and has been able to maintain a respectable rate of growth. Our economic analysis suggests that the economy is about to pick up, and our research (from Chapter 6) indicates that the industry and company are well situated to take advantage of the upswing. Therefore, we conclude that the rate of growth in sales should increase in 1999 to about 9.5%. After a modest amount of pent-up demand is worked off, the rate of growth in sales should then drop to about 9% in 2000 and stay there through 2001.

The essential elements of the financial forecast for 1999, 2000, and 2001 are provided in Table 7.3. Highlights of the key assumptions and the reasoning behind them follow.

- *Net profit margin.* Various published industry and company reports suggest a comfortable improvement in earnings, so we decide to use a profit margin of 3.0% in 1999, followed by an even better 3.2% in 2000. Finally, because of some capacity problems prominently mentioned in one of the reports, we project a drop in the margin in 2001 back to 3.0%.

- *Common shares outstanding.* Our assessment indicates that the company will be able to handle the growth in assets and meet its financing needs without issuing any new common stock. Therefore, the common shares outstanding remain at 3.8 million throughout the forecast period.

- *Payout ratio.* We assume that the dividend payout ratio will hold at around 50% of earnings, as it has for most of the recent past—with the notable exception of 1993.

- *P/E ratio.* Primarily on the basis of expectations of improved growth in revenues and earnings, we are projecting a P/E multiple that will gradually rise from its present level of 10 times earnings to roughly 11 times earnings in

TABLE 7.3 Summary Forecast Statistics, MarCor Industries

	Latest Actual Figures (Fiscal 1998)	Average for the Past 5 Years (1994–1998)	Forecasted Figures		
			1999	2000	2001
Annual rate of growth in sales	6.8%	9.8%	9.5%	9.0%	9.0%
Net sales (millions)	$606.6	N/A*	$664.2**	$724.0**	$789.2**
+ Interest and other income (millions)	$ 8.3	$ 7.2	$ 7.2	$ 7.2	$ 7.2
= Total revenue (millions)	$614.9	N/A	$671.4	$731.2	$796.4
× Net profit margin	2.9%	2.8%	3.0%	3.2%	3.0%
= Net after-tax earnings (millions)	$ 18.0	N/A	$ 20.1	$ 23.4	$ 24.0
÷ Common shares outstanding (millions)	3.8	3.7	3.8	3.8	3.8
= Earnings per share	$ 4.74	N/A	$ 5.29	$ 6.16	$ 6.32
× Payout ratio	48.0%	39.0%	50.0%	50.0%	55.0%
= Dividends per share	$ 2.27	$ 1.75	$ 2.65	$ 3.08	$ 3.48
Earnings per share	$ 4.74	N/A	$ 5.29	$ 6.16	$ 6.32
× P/E ratio	10.20	10.92	10.50	10.75	11.00
= Share price at year end	$ 48.50	N/A	$ 55.50	$ 66.25	$ 69.50

*N/A: Not applicable.

**Forecasted sales figures: Sales from *preceding* year × growth rate in sales = growth in sales; then growth in sales + sales from preceding year = forecast sales for the year. For example, for 2000: $664.2 × .09 = $59.5 + $664.2 = $724.0 million.

2001. Although this is a fairly conservative increase in the P/E, when it is coupled with the hefty growth in EPS, the net effect will be a big jump in the projected price of MarCor stock.

Table 7.3 also shows the sequence involved in arriving at forecasted dividends and price behavior.

1. The company dimensions of the forecast are handled first. These include sales and revenue estimates, net profit margins, net earnings, and the number of shares of common stock outstanding. Note that after-tax earnings are derived according to the procedure described earlier in this chapter.

2. Next we estimated earnings per share, following the procedures established earlier.

3. The bottom line of the forecast is, of course, the returns in the form of dividends and capital gains that the investor can expect from a share of MarCor stock, given that the assumptions about net sales, profit margins, earnings per share, and so forth hold up. We see in Table 7.3 that dividends should go up by about $1.21 per share over the next 3 years (from $2.27 to an expected $3.48) and that the price of a share of stock should appreciate by more than 40%, rising from its latest price of $48.50 to $69.50 in 2001. We now have an idea of what the future cash flows of the investment are likely to be and are in a position to establish an intrinsic value for MarCor Industries stock.

The Valuation Process

valuation
process by which an investor uses risk and return concepts to determine the worth of a security.

Valuation is a process by which an investor determines the worth of a security using the risk and return concepts introduced in Chapter 4. This formal process can be applied to any asset that produces a stream of cash flow—a share of stock, a bond, a piece of real estate, or an oil well. To establish the value of an asset, the investor must determine certain key inputs, including the amount of future cash flows, the timing of these cash flows, and the rate of return required on the investment. In terms of common stock, the essence of valuation is to determine what the stock *ought to be worth,* given estimated returns to stockholders (future dividends and price behavior) and the amount of potential risk exposure. Toward this end, we employ various types of stock valuation models, the end product of which represents the elusive intrinsic value we have been seeking. That is, the stock valuation models determine either an *expected rate of return* or the *intrinsic worth of a share of stock,* which in effect represents the stock's "justified price." In this way, we obtain a standard of performance, based on future stock behavior, that can be used to judge the investment merits of a particular security.

If the computed rate of return equals or exceeds the yield the investor feels is warranted or if the justified price (intrinsic worth) is equal to or greater than the current market price, then the stock under consideration is considered a worthwhile investment candidate. Note especially that a security is considered acceptable even if its yield simply *equals* the required rate of return or if its intrinsic value simply *equals* the current market price of the stock. There is nothing irrational about such behavior. In either case, the security meets the minimum standards you've established (it is giving you the rate of return you wanted).

However, remember this about the valuation process: Even though valuation plays an important part in the investment process, there is *absolutely no assurance* that the actual outcome will be even remotely similar to the forecasted behavior. The stock is still subject to economic, industry, company, and market risks that could well negate *all* your assumptions about the future. Security analysis and stock valuation models are used not to guarantee success but to help investors better understand the return and risk dimensions of a proposed transaction.

Required Rate of Return

required rate of return the return necessary to compensate an investor for the risk involved in an investment.

One of the key elements in the stock valuation process is the **required rate of return.** Generally speaking, the amount of return required by an investor should be related to the level of risk that must be assumed in order to generate that return. In essence, the required return provides a mechanism whereby the investor establishes a level of compensation compatible with the amount of risk involved in an investment. Such a standard helps the investor determine whether the expected return on a stock (or any other security) is satisfactory. Because you don't know for sure what the cash flow of an investment will be, you should expect to earn a rate of return that reflects this uncertainty. Thus the greater the perceived risk, the more you should expect to earn. As we saw in Chapter 4, this is basically the notion behind the *capital asset pricing model* (CAPM).

Recall that using the CAPM, we define a stock's required return as

Equation 7.6

$$\frac{\text{Required}}{\text{rate of return}} = \frac{\text{risk-free}}{\text{rate}} + \left[\frac{\text{stock's}}{\text{beta}} \times \left(\frac{\text{market}}{\text{return}} - \frac{\text{risk-free}}{\text{rate}}\right)\right]$$

The required input for this equation is readily available: You can obtain a stock's beta from *Value Line* or S&P's *Stock Reports,* the risk-free rate is basically the average return on Treasury bills for the past year or so, and a good proxy for the market return is the average stock returns over the past 10 to 15 years (like the data reported in Table 5.1).

In the CAPM, the risk of a stock is captured by its beta. For that reason, the required return on a stock increases (or decreases) with increases (or decreases) in its beta. As an illustration of the CAPM at work, consider MarCor's stock, which has a beta of 1.10. Given that the risk-free rate is 5% and the market return is 13%, this stock would have a required return of

$$\text{Required return} = 5\% + [1.10 \times (13\% - 5\%)] = \underline{\underline{13.8\%}}$$

This return—let's round it to 14%—can now be used in a stock valuation model to assess the investment merits of a share of stock.

As an alternative, or perhaps even in conjunction with the CAPM, you could take a more subjective approach to finding required return. For example, if your assessment of the historical performance of the company had uncovered wide swings in sales and earnings, you could conclude that the stock is subject to a good deal of business risk. Also important is market risk, as measured by a stock's beta. A valuable reference point in arriving at a measure of risk is the rate of return available on less risky but competitive investment vehicles. For example, you could use the rate of return on long-term

Treasury bonds or high-grade corporate issues as a starting point in defining your desired rate of return. That is, starting with yields on long-term, low-risk bonds, you could adjust such returns for the levels of business and market risk to which you believe the common stock is exposed.

To see how these elements make up the desired rate of return, let's go back to MarCor Industries. Assume that it is now early 1999 and rates on Treasury bonds are hovering around 8%. Given that our analysis thus far has indicated that the apparel industry in general and MarCor in particular are subject to a "fair" amount of business risk, we would want to adjust that figure upward—probably by around 2 or 3 points. In addition, with its beta of 1.10, we can conclude that the stock carries some market risk. Thus we should increase our base rate of return even more—say, by another 3 points. That is, starting from a base (Treasury bond) rate of 8%, we tack on 3% for the company's added business risk and another 3% for the stock's market risk. We conclude that an appropriate required rate of return for an investment in MarCor Industries common stock is around 14%. Note that this figure of 14% is almost the same as what we would obtain from the CAPM using a beta of 1.1, a risk-free rate of 5%, and a market return of 13% (as in Equation 7.6). The fact that the two numbers are so close shouldn't be surprising. If they're carefully (and honestly) done, the CAPM and the subjective approach should yield similar results. Whichever procedure is used, the required rate of return stipulates the minimum return you should expect to receive from an investment. To accept anything less means you'll fail to be fully compensated for the risk you must assume.

CONCEPTS IN REVIEW

7.1 What is the purpose of stock valuation? What role does *intrinsic value* play in the stock valuation process?

7.2 Are the expected future earnings of the firm important in determining a stock's investment suitability? Discuss how these and other future estimates fit into the stock valuation framework.

7.3 Can the growth prospects of a company affect its price/earnings multiple? Explain. How about the amount of debt a firm uses? Are there any other variables that affect the level of a firm's P/E ratio?

7.4 What is the *market multiple,* and how can it help in evaluating a stock's P/E? Is a stock's *relative P/E* the same thing as the market multiple? Explain.

7.5 In the stock valuation framework, how can you tell whether a particular security is a worthwhile investment candidate? What roles does the required rate of return play in this process? Would you invest in a stock if all you could earn was a rate of return that equaled your required return? Explain.

http://hepg.aw.com

As noted in this section, one of the hardest tasks for an investor is to come up with a projection of a firm's earnings and P/E ratio. One of the best-known Web sites for getting estimates from professional analysts is that of Zacks Investment Research. At the site, select the *Free Research* option.

www.zacks.com

Stock Valuation Models

LG 3 LG 4

Take a look in the market and you'll discover that investors employ a number of different stock valuation models. Though they all may ultimately be aimed at the future cash benefits of the security, their approaches to valuation are nonetheless considerably different. Take, for example, those investors who search for value in a company's financials—by keying in on such factors as book value, debt load, return on equity, and cash flow. These are the so-called *value investors*, who rely as much on historical performance as on earnings projections to identify undervalued stock. Then there are the *growth investors*, who concentrate solely on growth in earnings. To them, though past growth is important, the real key lies in projected earnings—that is, in finding companies that are going to produce big earnings, along with big price/earnings multiples, in the future. Whereas value investors tend to buy and hold for the long haul, growth investors do not hesitate to dump their holdings at the first sign of trouble. The value and growth approaches to stock valuation are popular with many individual as well as institutional investors. And more often than not, investors tend to prefer one approach over the other. That is, they tend to be *either* value investors *or* growth investors. For although there are some similarities in these two approaches, as the accompanying *Investing in Action* box suggests, there are also some real differences.

There are still other models that use variables like dividend yield, price-to-sales ratios, abnormally low P/E multiples, and even company size as key elements in the decision-making process. For purposes of our discussion here, we'll focus on several stock valuation models that are both theoretically sound and widely used by the investment community. In one form or another, these models use the required rate of return, along with expected cash flows from dividends and/or the future price of the stock, to derive the intrinsic value of an investment. Let's begin with a procedure known as the dividend valuation model.

The Dividend Valuation Model

In the valuation process, the intrinsic value of any investment equals the *present value of the expected cash benefits*. For common stock, this amounts to the cash dividends received each year plus the future sale price of the stock. Another way to view the cash flow benefits from common stock is to assume that the dividends will be received over an infinite time horizon—an assumption that is appropriate so long as the firm is considered a "going concern." Seen from this perspective, *the value of a share of stock is equal to the present value of all the future dividends it is expected to provide over an infinite time horizon.*

Although a stockholder can earn capital gains in addition to dividends by selling a stock for more than he or she paid for it, from a strictly theoretical point of view, what is really being sold is the right to all remaining future dividends. Thus, just as the *current* value of a share of stock is a function of future dividends, the *future* price of the stock is also a function of future dividends. In this framework, the *future* price of the stock will rise or fall as the outlook for dividends (and the required rate of return) changes. This approach, which holds that the value of a share of stock is a function of its future dividends, has come to be known as the **dividend valuation model** (DVM).

dividend valuation model (DVM)
a model that values a share of stock on the basis of the future dividend stream it is expected to produce; its three versions are zero-growth, constant-growth, and variable-growth.

INVESTING IN ACTION

Value vs. Growth—Which Camp Are You In?

The professional stock pickers on Wall Street specialize in a lot of ways. Some focus on small-cap stocks. Some only look at foreign shares. And there's another way they tend to specialize: They're either value investors or growth investors.

A growth investor is willing to pay premium prices for companies with above-average growth in sales and earnings. In contrast, the value investor wants to go to the discount rack and buy cheap stocks that are out of favor or are being ignored by Wall Street. Sometimes, growth stocks as a whole outperform value stocks. And vice versa.

Growth stocks tend to do well when overall economic growth is sluggish. For example, let's say the U.S. economy grows only an average of 2% in the years 1998–2000. Investors saw that as a distinct possibility in early 1998, as the Asian financial crisis threatened to choke off growth of the global economy. What stocks shined? Drug stocks, for one. Why? They're able to grow consistently at a greater rate than the overall U.S. economy. Their profits are likely to grow faster than those of the average U.S. company, too. The reason they've been growing so well is that they've got lots of new products in the pipeline. In addition, the Food & Drug Administration, which had long been a sluggish bureaucracy when it came to approving new therapies, has been streamlined and is acting more quickly. Because drug companies promised double-digit profit growth in a single-digit world, investors have been willing to pay more than 30 times earnings for many of these stocks.

But even growth managers aren't willing to overpay for the privilege of higher sales and earnings. In mid-1997, Coca-Cola was selling at nearly 40 times earnings, yet its profits were not projected to grow more than 20%. The stock was hovering around $70 a share when the company announced that earnings were going to be disappointing. The stock tumbled to $55 within a few weeks. Indeed, many growth managers temper their enthusiasm for a stock by describing their style as "growth, but at a reasonable price."

The value investors on Wall Street believe that it's better to find a stock down on its luck and buy it at a discount—as long as there is a potential catalyst on the horizon to push up the stock price. The classic value stock of the mid-1990s was IBM, which was selling at about 10 times earnings for a few years. The stock was cheap, and for good reason: The company had staked its future on huge mainframe computers, but the world was moving toward the PC, which was becoming increasingly powerful. Value investors in IBM believed that the company had the strength to reposition itself into PCs as well as to move into technology consulting for large corporations. A new chief executive officer was brought in as the catalyst, and he achieved exactly that.

Growth and value investors are each quite passionate about their craft. But you don't have to take sides. Both styles have their place in a diversified portfolio.

There are three versions of the dividend valuation model, each based on different assumptions about the future rate of growth in dividends; they are (1) *the zero-growth model,* which assumes that dividends will not grow over time; (2) *the constant-growth model,* which is the basic version of the dividend valuation model and assumes that dividends will grow by a fixed/constant rate over time; and (3) *the variable-growth model,* in which the rate of growth in dividends varies over time.

Zero Growth

The simplest way to picture the dividend valuation model is to assume that you're dealing with a stock that has a fixed stream of dividends. In other words, dividends stay the same year in and year out, and they're expected to do so in the future. Under such conditions, the value of a zero-growth stock is simply *the capitalized value of its annual dividends.* To find the capitalized value, just divide annual dividends by the required rate of return, which in effect acts as the capitalization rate. That is,

Equation 7.7

$$\text{Value of a share of stock} = \frac{\text{annual dividends}}{\text{required rate of return}}$$

For example, if a stock paid a (constant) dividend of \$3 a share and you wanted to earn 10% on your investment, you would value the stock at \$30 a share (\$3/0.10 = \$30).

As you can see, the only cash flow variable that's used in this model is the fixed annual dividend. Given that the annual dividend on this stock never changes, does that mean the price of the stock never changes? Absolutely not! For as the capitalization rate—that is, the required rate of return—changes, so will the price of the stock. Thus, if the capitalization rate goes up to, say, 15%, then the price of the stock will fall to \$20 (\$3/0.15). Although this may be a very simplified view of the valuation model, it's actually not as far-fetched as it may appear. As we'll see in Chapter 10, this is basically the procedure used to price *preferred stocks* in the marketplace.

Constant Growth

The zero-growth model is a good beginning, but it does not take into account a growing stream of dividends, which is more likely to be the case in the real world. That is, rather than assume no growth in dividends, the standard and more widely recognized version of the dividend valuation model assumes that dividends will grow over time at a specified rate. Under this variation of the model, the value of a share of stock is still considered to be a function of its future dividends, but in this case such dividends are expected to grow forever (to infinity) at a constant rate of growth, *g*. Accordingly, the value of a share of stock can be found as follows:

Equation 7.8

$$\text{Value of a share of stock} = \frac{\text{next year's dividends}}{\text{required rate of return} - \text{constant rate of growth in dividends}}$$

Equation 7.8a

$$V = \frac{D_1}{k - g}$$

where

D_1 = annual dividends expected to be paid *next* year (the first year in the forecast period)

k = the discount rate, or capitalization rate (which defines the required rate of return on the investment)

g = the annual rate of growth in dividends, which is expected to hold constant to infinity

This model succinctly captures the essence of stock valuation: *Increase* the cash flow (through D or g) and/or *decrease* the required rate of return (k), and the value of the stock will *increase.*

The constant-growth DVM should not be used with just any stock. Rather, *it is best suited to the valuation of mature companies* that hold established market positions—companies with strong track records that have reached the "mature" stage of growth. This means that you're probably dealing with large-cap (or perhaps even some mature mid-cap) companies that have demonstrated an ability to generate steady rates of growth year in and year out. The growth rates may *not be identical* from year to year, but they tend to move within such a small range that they are seldom far off the average rate. These are companies that have established dividend policies, particularly with regard to the payout ratio, and fairly predictable growth rates in earnings and dividends. Thus, to use the constant-growth DVM on such companies, all that's required is some basic information about the stock's *current* level of dividends and the expected rate of growth in dividends, g.

One popular and fairly simple way to find the dividend growth rate is to look at the *historical* behavior of dividends and, if they are in fact growing at a relatively constant rate, then assume that they'll continue to grow at (or near) that average rate for the future. You can get historical dividend data in a company's annual report, from online computer services, or from publications like *Value Line*. Given this stream of dividends, you can use basic present-value arithmetic to find the average rate of growth. Here's how: Take the level of dividends, say, 10 years ago and the level that's being paid today. Of course, dividends today will be (much) higher than they were 10 years ago, so, using your calculator or computer, find the present value discount rate that equates the (higher) dividend today to the level paid 10 years earlier. When you find that, you've found the growth rate, because in this case, the *discount rate is the average rate of growth in dividends*. (See Chapter 4 for a detailed discussion of how to use present value to find growth rates.)

Once you've determined the dividend growth rate, g, you can find next year's dividend, D_1, as $D_0 \times (1 + g)$, where D_0 equals the actual (current) level of dividends. Let's say that in the latest year Sweatmore Industries paid \$2.50 a share in dividends. If you expect these dividends to grow at the rate of 6% a year, you can find next year's dividends as follows: $D_1 = D_0\,(1 + g) = \$2.50\,(1 + .06) = \$2.50\,(1.06) = \$2.65$. The only other information you need is the capitalization rate, or required rate of return, k. (Note that k must be greater than g for the constant-growth model to be mathematically operative.)

To see this dividend valuation model at work, consider a stock that currently pays an annual dividend of \$1.75 a share. Let's say that by using the present-value approach described above, you find that dividends are growing at a rate of 8% a year and you expect they will continue to do so into the future. In addition, you feel that because of the risks involved, the investment should carry a required rate of return of 12%. Given this information, you can use Equation 7.8 to price the stock. That is, given $D_0 = \$1.75$, $g = 0.08$, and $k = 0.12$, it follows that

$$\text{Value of a share of stock} = \frac{D_0\,(1+g)}{k-g} = \frac{\$1.75\,(1.08)}{0.12 - 0.08} = \frac{\$1.89}{0.04} = \underline{\underline{\$47.25}}$$

If you want to earn a 12% return on this investment, then according to the constant-growth dividend valuation model, you should pay no more than \$47.25 a share for this stock.

Note that with this version of the DVM, *the price of the stock will increase over time* so long as k and g don't change. This occurs because the cash flow from the investment will increase with time as dividends grow. To see how this happens, let's carry our example further. Recall that $D_0 = \$1.75$, $g = 8\%$, and $k = 12\%$; on the basis of this information, we found the current value of the stock to be \$47.25. Now look what happens to the price of this stock if k and g don't change:

Year	Dividend	Stock Price*
(Current year) 0	\$1.75	\$47.25
1	1.89	51.00
2	2.04	55.00
3	2.20	59.50
4	2.38	64.25
5	2.57	69.50

*As determined by the dividend valuation model, given $g = 0.08$, $k = 0.12$, and D_0 = dividend level for any given year.

As you can see in this table, the price of the stock *in the future* can also be found by using the standard dividend valuation model. To do this, we simply redefine the appropriate level of dividends. For example, to find the price of the stock in year 3, we use the expected dividend in the third year, \$2.20, and increase it by the factor $(1 + g)$; thus the stock price in year 3 = $D_3 \times (1 + g)/(k - g)$ = \$2.20 × (1 + 0.08)/(0.12 − 0.08) = \$2.38/0.04 = \$59.50. Of course, if future expectations about k or g do change, the *future price* of the stock will change accordingly. Should that occur, an investor could use the new information to decide whether to continue to hold the stock.

Variable Growth

Although the constant-growth dividend valuation model is an improvement over the zero-growth model, it still has some shortcomings, one of the most obvious of which is the fact that it does not allow for any changes in expected growth rates. To overcome this problem, we can use a form of the DVM that allows for *variable rates of growth* over time. Essentially, the *variable-growth dividend valuation model* derives, in two stages, a value based on future dividends and the future price of the stock (which price is a function of all future dividends to infinity). The variable-growth version of the model finds the value of a share of stock as follows:

Equation 7.9

$$\text{Value of a share of stock} = \begin{array}{c}\text{present value of}\\ \text{future dividends}\\ \text{during the initial}\\ \text{variable-growth period}\end{array} + \begin{array}{c}\text{present value of the price}\\ \text{of the stock at the end of}\\ \text{the variable-growth period}\end{array}$$

Equation 7.9a

$$V = (D_1 \times PVIF_1) + (D_2 \times PVIF_2) + \cdots + (D_v \times PVIF_v) + \left(PVIF_v \times \frac{D_v(1 + g)}{k - g}\right)$$

where

D_1, D_2, etc. = future annual dividends

$PVIF_t$ = present value interest factor, as specified by the required rate of return for a given year t (Table A.3 in the Appendix)

v = number of years in the initial variable-growth period

Note that the last element in this equation is the standard constant-growth dividend valuation model, which is used to find the price of the stock at the end of the initial variable-growth period.

This form of the DVM is appropriate for companies that are expected to experience variable rates of growth for a period of time—perhaps for the first 3 to 5 years, or more—and then settle down to a constant (average) growth rate thereafter. This, in fact, is the growth pattern of many companies, so the model has considerable application in practice. Finding the value of a stock using Equation 7.9 is actually a lot easier than it looks. All you need do is follow these steps:

1. Estimate annual dividends during the initial variable-growth period and then specify the constant rate, g, at which dividends will grow after the initial period.

2. Find the present value of the dividends expected during the initial variable-growth period.

3. Using the constant-growth DVM, find the price of the stock at the end of the initial growth period.

4. Find the present value of the price of the stock (as determined in step 3); note that the price of the stock is discounted at the same PVIF as the last dividend payment in the initial growth period, because the stock is being priced (per step 3) at the end of this initial period.

5. Add the two present-value components (from steps 2 and 4) to find the value of a stock.

To see how this works, let's apply the variable-growth model to MarCor Industries. Let's assume that dividends will grow at a variable rate for the first 3 years (1999, 2000, and 2001); after that, the annual rate of growth in dividends is expected to settle down to 8% and stay there for the foreseeable future. We can use the dividend projections we prepared (for 1999–2001) in Table 7.3, along with our required rate of return (formulated earlier) of 14%. Table 7.4 shows the variable-growth DVM in action. As we can see in the table, the value of MarCor stock, according to the variable-growth DVM, is just under $49.25 a share. In essence, that's the maximum price you should be willing to pay for the stock if you want to earn a 14% rate of return.

Defining the Expected Growth Rate

Mechanically, application of the DVM is really quite simple. It relies on just three key pieces of information: future dividends, future growth in dividends, and a required rate of return. But this model is not without its difficulties, and certainly one of the most difficult (and most important) aspects of the DVM is *specifying the appropriate growth rate,* g, *over an extended period of time.*

TABLE 7.4 Using the Variable-Growth DVM to Value MarCor Stock

Step

1. Projected annual dividends: (see Table 7.3)

1999	\$2.65
2000	\$3.08
2001	\$3.48

Estimated annual rate of growth in dividends, *g*, for 2002 and beyond: 8%

2. Present value of dividends—using a required rate of return, *k*, of 14%—during the initial variable growth period:

Year	Dividends	×	PVIF (k = 14%)	=	Present Value
1999	\$2.65		.877		\$2.32
2000	3.08		.769		2.37
2001	3.48		.675		2.35
				Total	\$7.04 (to step 5)

3. Price of the stock at the end of the initial growth period:

$$P_{2001} = \frac{D_{2002}}{k - g} = \frac{D_{2001} \times (1 + g)}{k - g} = \frac{\$3.48 \times (1.08)}{0.14 - 0.08} = \frac{\$3.75}{0.06} = \underline{\underline{\$62.50}}$$

4. Discount the price of the stock (as computed above) back to its present value, at k = 14%.

$$PV(P_{2001}) = \$62.50 \times PVIF_{14\%,\, 3\text{ yr}} = \$62.50 \times 0.675 = \underline{\underline{\$42.19}} \text{ (to step 5)}$$

5. Add the present value of the initial dividend stream (step 2) to the present value of the price of the stock at the end of the initial growth period (step 4).

Value of MarCor stock = \$7.04 + \$42.19 = \$49.23

Whether an investor is using the constant-growth or the variable-growth version of the dividend valuation model, the growth rate, *g*, is a crucial element in the DVM and has an enormous impact on the value derived from the model. Indeed, the DVM is *very sensitive* to the growth rate being used, because it affects both the model's numerator and its denominator. Accordingly, coming up with the proper growth rate is worth considerable effort.

As we saw earlier in this chapter, we can choose the growth rate from a strictly historical perspective—by using present value to find the past rate of growth—and then use it (or something close) in the DVM. Although that technique might work fine with the constant-growth model, it has some obvious shortcomings for use with the variable-growth DVM. One procedure widely used in practice is to define the growth rate, *g*, according to the following equation:

Equation 7.10

$$g = \text{ROE} \times \text{the firm's retention rate, } rr$$

where

$$rr = 1 - \text{dividend payout ratio}$$

Both variables in Equation 7.10 (ROE and *rr*) are *directly related to the firm's rate of growth,* and both play key roles in defining a firm's future growth.

The *retention rate* represents the percentage of the firm's profits that are plowed back into the company. Thus if the firm pays out 35% of its earnings in dividends (i.e., it has a dividend payout ratio of 35%), then it has a retention rate of 65%: $rr = 1 - 0.35 = 0.65$. The retention rate, in effect, is an indication of the amount of capital that is flowing into the company to finance its growth. Other things being equal, the more money that's being retained in the company, the higher the rate of growth. The other component of Equation 7.10 is the familiar return on equity. Clearly, the more the company can earn on its retained capital, the higher the growth rate.

Let's look at some numbers to see how this actually works. For example, if a company retained, on average, about 80% of its earnings and generated an ROE of around 15%, you'd expect it to have a growth rate of

$$g = \text{ROE} \times rr = 0.15 \times 0.80 = \underline{\underline{12\%}}$$

Actually, the growth rate will probably be a bit more than 12%, because Equation 7.10 ignores financial leverage, which in itself will magnify growth. But at least the equation gives you a good idea what to expect. Or it can serve as a starting point in assessing past and future growth. That is, you can use Equation 7.10 to compute expected growth and then assess the two key components of the formula (ROE and *rr*) to see whether they're likely to undergo major changes in the future. If so, then what impact is the change in ROE and/or *rr* likely to have on the growth rate, *g*? The idea is to take the time to study the forces (ROE and *rr*) that drive the growth rate, because the DVM itself is so sensitive to the rate of growth being used. Employ a growth rate that's too high and you'll end up with an intrinsic value that's way too high also. The downside to that, of course, is that you may end up buying a stock that you really shouldn't.

Alternatives to the DVM

The variable-growth approach to stock valuation is fairly compatible with the way most people invest. That is, unlike the underlying assumptions in the standard dividend valuation model (which employs an infinite investment horizon), most investors have a holding period that seldom exceeds 5 to 7 years. Under such circumstances, *the relevant cash flows are future dividends and the future selling price of the stock.*

There are some alternatives to the DVM that use comparable cash flow streams to value stock. One is the so-called *dividends-and-earnings approach,* which in many respects is quite similar to the variable-growth DVM. Another is the *P/E approach,* which builds the stock valuation process around the stock's price/earnings ratio. Let's now take a closer look at both of these, as well as a technique that arrives at the expected return on the stock (in percentage terms) rather than a (dollar-based) "justified price."

A Dividends-and-Earnings Approach

As we saw in the variable-growth DVM, the value of a share of stock is a function of the amount and timing of future cash flows and the level of risk that must be taken on to generate that return. A stock valuation model has been developed that conveniently captures the essential elements of expected risk and return and does so in a present-value context. The model is

Equation 7.11

$$\text{Present value of a share of stock} = \text{present value of future dividends} + \text{present value of the price of the stock at date of sale}$$

Equation 7.11a

$$V = (D_1 \times PVIF_1) + (D_2 \times PVIF_2) + \cdots + (D_N \times PVIF_N) + (SP_N \times PVIF_N)$$

where

D_t = future annual dividend in year t

$PVIF_t$ = present-value interest factor, specified at the required rate of return (Table A.3 in the Appendix)

SP_N = estimated share price of the stock at date of sale, year N

N = number of years in the investment horizon

dividends-and-earnings (D&E) approach
stock valuation approach that uses projected dividends, EPS, and P/E multiples to value a share of stock.

This is the so-called **dividends-and-earnings (D&E) approach** to stock valuation. Note its similarities to the variable-growth DVM: It's also present-value-based, and its value is also derived from future dividends and the expected selling price of the stock. The big difference between the two procedures revolves around how the future price of the stock is determined. That is, whereas the variable-growth approach uses future dividends to price the stock, the D&E approach employs projected earnings per share and estimated P/E multiples—the same two variables that drive the price of the stock in the market. Its major advantages are that it is a bit more flexible than the DVM and is a lot easier to understand and apply. Using the D&E valuation approach, the investor's attention is directed toward projecting future dividends and share price behavior over a defined, finite investment horizon, much as we did for MarCor in Table 7.3.

Especially important in the D&E approach is finding a viable P/E multiple that can be used to project the future price of the stock. This is a critical part of this stock valuation process, because of the major role that capital gains (and therefore the estimated price of the stock at its projected date of sale) play in defining the level of security returns. Using market or industry P/Es as benchmarks, the investor will try to establish a multiple that he or she feels the stock will trade at in the future. Couple this number with projected earnings per share and you have an estimate of what the stock should sell for in the future. Like the growth rate, g, in the DVM, the P/E multiple is the single most important (and most difficult) variable to project in the present-value model. Using this input, along with estimated future dividends, this present-value-based stock valuation model generates a *justified price* based on estimated returns. This intrinsic value represents the price you should be willing to pay for the stock, given its expected dividend and price behavior, and assuming you want to realize a return that is equal to or greater than your required rate of return (as found by using the CAPM or some other more subjective approach).

To see how this procedure works, consider once again the case of MarCor Industries. Let's return to our original 3-year investment horizon. Given the forecasted annual dividends and share price from Table 7.3, along with a 14% required rate of return, we can see that the value of MarCor stock is

$$\text{Present value of a share of MarCor stock} = (\$2.65 \times 0.877) + (\$3.08 \times 0.769) + (\$3.48 \times 0.675) + (\$69.50 \times 0.675)$$
$$= \$2.32 + \$2.37 + \$2.35 + \$46.92$$
$$= \underline{\underline{\$53.96}}$$

You'll note that compared to the variable-growth DVM, this model produces a slightly higher intrinsic value ($53.96 vs. $49.23, as computed in Table 7.4). This difference, of course, is due to the higher share price we're projecting here ($69.50), compared to the one we ended up with in the DVM ($62.50). All the other variables are basically the same. In any event, the present-value figure computed here means that with the projected dividend and share price behavior, we would realize our desired rate of return *only* if we were able to buy the stock at around $54 a share. Because MarCor Industries is currently trading at $48.50, we can conclude that the stock at present is an attractive investment vehicle. That is, because we can buy the stock at something less than its computed intrinsic value, we'll be able to earn our required rate of return—so long as dividends, EPS, and P/E projections hold up.

Determining Expected Return

Sometimes investors find it more convenient to deal in terms of expected return rather than a dollar-based justified price. This is no problem, nor is it necessary to sacrifice the present-value dimension of the stock valuation model to achieve such an end. That's because expected return can be found by using the (present-value-based) *internal rate of return (IRR)* procedure first introduced in Chapter 4. This approach to stock valuation uses forecasted dividend and price behavior, along with the *current market price* of the stock, to arrive at the fully compounded rate of return you can expect to earn from a given long-term investment.

To see how a stock's expected return is computed, let's look once again at MarCor Industries. Using the 1999–2001 information from Table 7.3, along with the stock's current price of $48.50, we can determine MarCor's expected return by finding the discount rate that equates the future stream of benefits from the investment (i.e., the future annual dividends and future price of the stock) to its current market price. In other words, find the discount rate that produces a present value of future benefits equal to the price of the stock, and you have the IRR, or expected return on that stock. Here's how it works: Using the MarCor example, we know that the stock is expected to pay per-share dividends of $2.65, $3.08, and $3.48, respectively, over each of the next 3 years. At the end of that time, we hope to sell the stock for $69.50. Given that the stock is currently trading at $48.50, we're looking for the discount rate that will produce a present value (of the future annual dividends and stock price) equal to $48.50. That is,

$$(\$2.65 \times PVIF_1) + (\$3.08 \times PVIF_2) + (\$3.48 \times PVIF_3) + (\$69.50 \times PVIF_3) = \$48.50$$

We need to solve for the discount rate—or the present-value interest factors (PVIFs)—in this equation. Through a process of "hit and miss" (with the help of a personal computer or hand-held calculator), you'll find that if you use an interest factor of 18.3%, the present value of the future cash benefits from this investment will equal exactly $48.50. That, of course, is our expected return. Thus MarCor can be expected to earn a fully compounded annual return of about 18%, assuming that the stock can be bought at $48.50, is held for 3 years (during which time investors receive indicated annual dividends), and then is sold for $69.50 at the end of the 3-year period. When compared to its 14% *required rate of return*, the 18.3% *expected return* makes MarCor look like a pretty good investment candidate.

The Price/Earnings (P/E) Approach

price/earnings (P/E) approach stock valuation approach that tries to find the P/E ratio that's most appropriate for the stock; this ratio, along with estimated EPS, is used to determine a reasonable stock price.

One of the problems with the stock valuation procedures that we've looked at is that they are fairly mechanical (i.e., mathematical) and involve a good deal of "number crunching." Although such an approach is fine with a lot of stocks, it just doesn't work well with others. Fortunately, there is an alternative that is more intuitive in approach. That alternative is the **price/earnings** (or **P/E) approach** to stock valuation.

The P/E approach is a favorite of professional security analysts and, along with the dividend valuation model, is widely used in practice. It's relatively simple to use (mechanically, anyway), because it's based on the standard P/E formula first introduced in Chapter 6 (Equation 6.14). There we showed that a stock's P/E is equal to its market price divided by the stock's EPS. Using this equation and solving for the market price of the stock, we have

Equation 7.12

$$\text{Stock price} = \text{EPS} \times \text{P/E ratio}$$

Equation 7.12 basically captures the P/E approach to stock valuation. That is, given an estimated EPS figure, *you decide on a P/E ratio that you feel is appropriate for the stock. Then you use it in Equation 7.12 to see what kind of price you come up with and how that compares to the stock's current price.*

Actually, this approach is no different from what's used in the market every day. It shows what investors are willing to pay for one dollar of earnings: The higher the multiple, the better investors feel about the company and its future prospects. Look at the stock quotes in the *Wall Street Journal;* they include the stock's P/E and show what investors are willing to pay for earnings. Essentially, the *Journal* relates the company's earnings per share for the *last* 12 months (known as *trailing earnings*) to the latest price of the stock. In practice, however, investors buy stocks not for their past earnings but for their *expected future earnings.* Thus, in Equation 7.12, it's customary to *use forecasted EPS for next year.*

As you might expect, the key concern of the investor using this approach to stock valuation is the stock's P/E ratio. Indeed, a good deal of the investor's time is spent in coming up with an appropriate P/E ratio. Fortunately, though, it's not as big a problem as it may at first appear, for the P/E ratio can be derived directly from the constant-growth dividend valuation model. That is, by dividing both sides of the constant-growth DVM by expected earnings per share for next year, E_1, we get an equation that defines a stock's P/E:

Equation 7.13

$$\text{Price/earnings ratio} = \frac{\text{next year's (expected) dividend payout ratio}}{\text{required rate of return} - \text{the expected rate of growth in dividends}}$$

Equation 7.13a

$$P_0/E_1 = \frac{D_1/E_1}{k - g}$$

It is important to note that in Equation 7.13, the P/E ratio is defined as the *current* price of the stock, P_0, relative *to next year's* expected EPS, or E_1. This is a common way of looking at the P/E ratio—and is, in fact, the standard for the P/E stock valuation approach. Also note that we are using the *dividend payout ratio* (D_1/E_1) in the numerator of the equation. Of course, because both the dividends and earnings variables are next year's estimates, we are using the *expected payout ratio,* rather than the current dividend payout. And that's fine, because just as the standard dividend valuation model uses an estimate of next year's dividend, it's only appropriate that the P/E version of the model use an estimate of next year's dividend payout ratio.

According to Equation 7.13, we can see that a stock's P/E ratio is determined by three factors: (1) the investor's required rate of return, k; (2) the expected rate of growth in dividends (or earnings), g; and (3) the expected dividend payout ratio. All of these variables are important, but the P/E ratio, and consequently the forecasted price of the stock, is perhaps most sensitive to the first two, k and g. Let's take an example. Assume that the appropriate required rate of return is 12%, earnings (and dividends) are expected to grow at a 6% rate for the foreseeable future, and the firm is expected to pay out 60% of its earnings as dividends. According to Equation 7.13, this should result in a P/E of around 10 times earnings. That is

$$P/E = \frac{0.60}{0.12 - 0.06} = \frac{0.60}{0.06} = \underline{\underline{10}}$$

Using an expected EPS of \$3.50 results in a stock price of \$3.50 × 10 = \$35 a share. Now look what happens when the growth rate drops to 4%:

$$P/E = \frac{0.60}{0.12 - 0.04} = \frac{0.60}{0.08} = \underline{\underline{7.5}}$$

or when the required return increases to 14%:

$$P/E = \frac{0.60}{0.14 - 0.06} = \frac{0.60}{0.08} = \underline{\underline{7.5}}$$

In either case, the P/E drops to 7.5 times earnings, and the price of the stock also drops, to \$3.50 × 7.5 = \$26.25. Thus if the growth rate is expected to drop or if the required return goes up (with higher perceived risk), the net effect is a *lower P/E* and therefore a *lower stock price.* Such behavior is totally predictable, however; you'd expect the price of a stock (and therefore its P/E ratio) to have strong ties to earnings growth and the (perceived) riskiness of the investment.

To implement the P/E approach, the first thing the investor has to do is come up with a forecasted EPS. In the early part of this chapter, we saw how this might be done (see, for instance, Equation 7.3). Given the forecasted EPS, the next task is to evaluate the variables that drive the P/E ratio. Most of that assessment is intuitive. For example, as we have seen, the investor would try to determine the stock's expected payout ratio, required rate of return (potential risk exposure), and rate of growth in earnings or dividends (perhaps by using something like Equation 7.10). The P/E ratio so obtained might then be adjusted a bit to account for the perceived state of the market and/or anticipated changes in the rate of inflation. Along with estimated EPS, we now have the P/E we need to compute (via Equation 7.12) the price at which the stock should be trading. By comparing that targeted price to the current market price of the stock, we can decide whether the stock is a good buy. For example, we would consider the stock undervalued and therefore a good buy if the computed price of the stock were more than its market price.

An alternative way of using this stock valuation approach is to isolate the stock's latest P_0/E_1 ratio and look at the expectations embedded in that ratio. For example, given an *estimated* EPS and the *current* market price of the stock, what kind of growth rate, payout ratio, and so on are implied by the latest P_0/E_1 ratio? If, on the whole, these estimates seem reasonable, then the stock is probably being fairly valued in the market and should be considered a viable investment candidate.

CONCEPTS IN REVIEW

7.6 In general, according to the *Investing in Action* box on page 264, do value investors want to pay premium or discount prices for the stocks they buy? What prices (premium or discount) do growth investors want to pay? What is the relationship between growth stocks and the economy?

7.7 Briefly describe the *dividend valuation model* and the three different ways this model can be used. Explain how CAPM fits into the *variable-growth DVM.*

7.8 What is the difference between the variable-growth dividend valuation model and the *dividends-and-earnings approach* to stock valuation? Which of these two would you prefer? Explain.

7.9 How would you go about finding the *expected return* on a stock? Note how such information would be used in the stock selection process.

7.10 Briefly describe the *P/E approach* to stock valuation and note how this approach differs from the variable-growth DVM.

7.11 Explain how risk fits into the stock valuation process. Note especially its relationship to the investment return of a security.

http://hepg.aw.com

Several of the widely known stock valuation models were presented in this section. There also are a number of proprietary valuation models that will never be seen in textbooks. One such model is the Value Point Analysis Model, which is available to the public at Investor Education Services. Try it out.

www.eduvest.com

Technical Analysis

LG 5

How many times have you turned on the TV or radio and in the course of the day's news heard a reporter say, "The market was up 47 points today" or "The market remained sluggish in a day of light trading"? Such comments reflect the importance of the stock market itself. The market is important because of the role it plays in determining the price behavior of common stocks. In fact, some experts believe the market is so important that studying it should be the major, if not the only, ingredient in the stock selection process. These experts argue that much of what is done in security analysis is useless because it is the *market* that matters, not individual companies. Others argue that studying the stock market is only one element in the security analysis process and is useful in helping the investor time decisions.

technical analysis
the study of the various forces at work in the marketplace and their effect on stock prices.

Analyzing the stock market is known as **technical analysis** and involves a study of the various forces at work in the marketplace itself. For some investors, it's another piece of information to use when deciding whether to buy, hold, or sell a stock; for others, it's the only input they use in their investment decisions; and for still others, technical analysis, like fundamental analysis, is regarded as a big waste of time. Here we will assume that technical analysis does have some role to play in the investment decision process. Accordingly, we will examine the major principles of market analysis, as well as some of the techniques used to assess market behavior.

Principles of Market Analysis

Analyzing market behavior dates back to the 1800s, when there was no such thing as industry or company analysis. Detailed financial information simply was not made available to stockholders, let alone the general public. There were no industry figures, balance sheets, or income statements to study, no sales forecasts to make, and no earnings-per-share data or price/earnings multiples. About the only thing investors could study was the market itself. Some investors used detailed charts in an attempt to monitor what large market operators were doing. These charts were intended to show when major buyers were moving into or out of particular stocks and to provide information that could be used to make profitable buy-and-sell decisions. The charts centered on stock price movements, because it was believed that these movements produced certain "formations" that indicated when the time was right to buy or sell a particular stock. The same principle is still applied today: Technical analysts argue that internal market factors, such as trading volume and price movements, often reveal the market's future direction long before the cause is evident in financial statistics.

If the behavior of stock prices were completely independent of market movements, market studies and technical analysis would be useless. But we have ample evidence that stock prices do, in fact, tend to move with the market. Studies of stock betas have shown that as a rule, anywhere from 20% to 50% of the price behavior of a stock can be traced to market forces. When the market is bullish, stock prices in general can be expected to behave accordingly. When the market turns bearish, most issues are affected.

Stock prices, in essence, react to various forces of supply and demand that are at work in the market. After all, it's the *demand* for securities and the *supply* of funds in the market that determine whether we're in a bull or a bear market. So long as a given supply-and-demand relationship holds, the market will remain strong (or weak). When the balance begins to shift, however, future prices can be expected to change as the market itself changes. Thus, more than anything else, technical analysis is intended to monitor the pulse of the supply and demand forces in the market and to detect any shifts in this important relationship.

Measuring the Market

If assessing the market is a worthwhile endeavor, then we need some sort of tool or measure to do it. Charts are popular with many investors because they provide a visual summary of the behavior of the market and the price movements of individual stocks. As an alternative or supplement to *charting*, however, some investors prefer to study various market statistics, such as the volume of trading, the amount of short selling, and the buying and selling patterns of small investors (odd-lot transactions). This approach is based on the idea that by assessing some of the key elements of market behavior, investors can gain valuable insights into the general condition of the market and, perhaps, where it's headed over the next few months. Normally, several of these measures are used together, either in an informal way or more formally as a series of complex ratios and measures, such as 200-day moving averages or buy-sell ratios. Although there are many market measures—or *technical indicators*, as they are called—we will confine our discussion to the most closely followed technical indicators: (1) market volume, (2) breadth of the market, (3) short interest, (4) odd-lot trading, and (5) relative price levels. After we've discussed each of these, we'll take a look at charting.

Market Volume

Market volume is an obvious reflection of the amount of investor interest. Volume is a function of the supply of and demand for stocks and indicates underlying market strengths and weaknesses. The market is considered *strong* when volume goes up in a rising market or drops off during market declines. In contrast, it is considered *weak* when volume rises during a decline or drops off during rallies. For instance, the market would be considered strong if the Dow Jones Industrial Average went up by, say, 108 points while market volume was heavy. Investor eagerness to buy or sell is felt to be captured by market volume figures. The financial press regularly publishes volume data, so investors can conveniently watch this important technical indicator. An example of this and other vital market information is shown in Figure 7.1.

INVESTOR FACT

PICKING A WINNER—Is the Super Bowl a predictor of market performance? Many people think so. Indeed, a most unusual but highly successful market adage holds that if a team from the National Football Conference (or one that was originally in the NFL, like Indianapolis or Pittsburgh) wins the Super Bowl, the stock market is in for a good year. For whatever reason, it's been right 28 out of the last 31 Super Bowls—a remarkable 90% rate. Super Bowl XXXII, by the way, was won by the Denver Broncos, an AFC team; that means 1998 should have been a down year for stocks. So, how did the market do in 1998?

Breadth of the Market

Each trading day, some stocks go up in price and others go down; in market terminology, some stocks *advance* and others *decline*. The breadth-of-the-market indicator deals with these advances and declines. The idea behind it is actually quite simple: So long as the number of stocks that advance in price on a given day exceeds the number that decline, the market is considered strong. The extent of that strength, however, depends on the spread between the number of advances and declines. For example, if the spread narrows so that the number of declines starts to approach the number of advances, market

FIGURE 7.1
Some Market Statistics

Individual investors can obtain all sorts of technical information at little or no cost from brokerage houses, investment services, and the popular financial media. Here, for example, is a sample of information from the *Wall Street Journal.* Note that a variety of information about market volume, new highs and lows, number of advancing and declining stocks, and market averages is available from this one source. (Source: *Wall Street Journal,* November 12, 1997, p. C4.)

STOCK MARKET DATA BANK 11/11/97

MAJOR INDEXES

†12-MO HIGH	†12-MO LOW		DAILY HIGH	DAILY LOW	CLOSE	NET CHG	% CHG	†12-MO CHG	% CHG	FROM 12/31	% CHG
DOW JONES AVERAGES											
8259.31	6266.04	30 Industrials	7599.74	7518.21	7558.73	+ 6.14	+ 0.08	+ 1292.69	+ 20.63	+ 1110.46	+ 17.22
3368.33	2216.85	20 Transportation	3156.69	3140.34	3148.87	+ 5.86	+ 0.19	+ 927.11	+ 41.73	+ 893.20	+ 39.60
247.99	209.47	15 Utilities	245.11	243.00	244.64	+ 1.53	+ 0.63	+ 10.43	+ 4.45	+ 12.11	+ 5.21
2620.84	1977.29	65 Composite	2482.31	2465.55	2474.60	+ 4.91	+ 0.20	+ 490.26	+ 24.71	+ 448.77	+ 22.15
929.94	681.02	DJ Global-US	880.47	872.48	876.14	+ 1.92	+ 0.22	+ 187.44	+ 27.22	+ 175.58	+ 25.06
NEW YORK STOCK EXCHANGE											
514.21	380.85	Composite	487.79	483.77	485.66	+ 0.79	+ 0.16	+ 99.48	+ 25.76	+ 93.36	+ 23.80
643.81	480.94	Industrials	611.17	605.96	608.32	+ 1.45	+ 0.24	+ 120.54	+ 24.71	+ 113.94	+ 23.05
310.70	247.87	Utilities	301.94	299.08	301.94	+ 2.86	+ 0.96	+ 44.14	+ 17.12	+ 42.03	+ 16.17
481.05	341.87	Transportation	453.56	451.40	452.17	− 0.27	− 0.06	+ 104.24	+ 29.96	+ 99.87	+ 28.35
493.08	339.08	Finance	461.87	456.50	457.92	− 2.19	− 0.48	+ 116.74	+ 34.22	+ 106.75	+ 30.40
STANDARD & POOR'S INDEXES											
983.12	720.98	500 Index	928.29	919.63	923.78	+ 2.65	+ 0.29	+ 194.22	+ 26.62	+ 183.04	+ 24.71
1146.82	847.68	Industrials	1083.16	1073.33	1078.53	+ 4.70	+ 0.44	+ 221.70	+ 25.87	+ 208.56	+ 23.97
211.44	180.93	Utilities	207.84	206.06	207.78	+ 1.72	+ 0.83	+ 5.70	+ 2.82	+ 8.97	+ 4.51
339.84	247.16	400 MidCap	320.24	317.59	318.24	− 1.11	− 0.35	+ 67.92	+ 27.13	+ 62.66	+ 24.52
192.48	134.54	600 SmallCap	180.80	179.50	180.44	− 0.29	− 0.16	+ 40.74	+ 29.16	+ 34.96	+ 24.03
212.04	155.37	1500 Index	200.14	198.34	199.19	+ 0.40	+ 0.20	+ 42.06	+ 26.77	+ 39.38	+ 24.64
NASDAQ STOCK MARKET											
1745.85	1201.00	Composite	1596.38	1580.52	1584.86	− 5.86	− 0.37	+ 328.33	+ 26.13	+ 293.83	+ 22.76
1148.21	783.92	Nasdaq 100	1020.17	1006.65	1010.96	− 0.58	− 0.06	+ 216.87	+ 27.31	+ 189.60	+ 23.08
1414.11	971.06	Industrials	1276.52	1264.16	1266.47	− 7.73	− 0.61	+ 168.28	+ 15.32	+ 156.84	+ 14.13
1884.02	1383.61	Insurance	1780.84	1769.33	1777.19	+ 9.82	+ 0.56	+ 393.58	+ 28.45	+ 311.76	+ 21.27
1977.59	1221.13	Banks	1919.81	1911.61	1915.59	+ 1.44	+ 0.08	+ 694.46	+ 56.87	+ 642.13	+ 50.42
732.03	478.25	Computer	650.67	642.77	644.90	− 0.31	− 0.05	+ 145.63	+ 29.17	+ 126.11	+ 24.31
312.80	198.06	Telecommunications	295.19	289.90	291.86	− 2.57	− 0.87	+ 78.69	+ 36.91	+ 75.95	+ 35.18
OTHERS											
721.90	541.20	Amex Composite*	683.26	679.12	680.43	− 0.04	− 0.01	+ 106.62	+ 18.58	+ 108.09	+ 18.89
518.94	382.40	Russell 1000	490.78	486.34	488.35	+ 0.89	+ 0.18	+ 100.75	+ 25.99	+ 94.60	+ 24.03
465.21	335.85	Russell 2000	435.87	432.47	433.43	− 1.97	− 0.45	+ 87.30	+ 25.22	+ 70.82	+ 19.53
551.24	407.16	Russell 3000	520.89	516.34	518.37	+ 0.61	+ 0.12	+ 106.76	+ 25.94	+ 98.93	+ 23.59
477.08	365.15	Value-Line(geom.)	449.49	446.87	447.98	− 0.49	− 0.11	+ 81.61	+ 22.28	+ 72.66	+ 19.36
9486.69	6998.62	Wilshire 5000	...	...	8925.59	+ 8.26	+ 0.09	+ 1857.96	+ 26.29	+ 1727.30	+ 24.00

†-Based on comparable trading day in preceding year. *-Replaced previous index eff. 1/02/97.

MOST ACTIVE ISSUES

NYSE	VOLUME	CLOSE	CHANGE
Compaq	7,696,500	61 7/16	+ 1/4
BayNtwk	6,668,000	29 3/8	− 3/4
Caterpillar	4,960,200	48 3/16	− 2
DuPont	4,013,400	60 1/2	+ 2
EKodak	3,954,700	62 3/16	− 4 1/16
TelcmBrslrs	3,928,600	93 1/4	− 2 3/4
Seagram	3,843,600	33	+ 1/8
ColumHCA	3,661,900	30 15/16	+ 7/8
TexInstr	3,426,400	106 1/4	− 2 1/8
HewlettPk	3,385,700	59 9/16	− 15/16
DialCp	3,279,200	19	+ 11/16
WestnDigitl	3,187,000	21 1/4	− 1/2
GenElec	3,097,200	67 3/8	+ 3/8
GTE	3,077,600	45 1/4	+ 3/8
Boeing	2,965,900	46 1/4	− 3/8
NASDAQ			
WorldCom	23,497,200	30 1/4	− 3/4
MCI	19,863,500	41 1/2	.....
AppldMatl	12,148,100	31 1/8	− 1 1/4
Intel	10,479,400	76 1/4	+ 1 1/8
3ComCp	9,563,300	35 1/8	− 15/16
DellCptr	9,175,200	76 3/16	+ 9/16
CiscoSys	6,593,400	80 5/8	− 1 3/16
QuantumCp	6,407,200	27 7/16	− 7/8
Centocor	6,305,700	41 9/16	− 1 9/16
EricsnTel	4,961,500	42 5/8	− 1 7/8
SunMicrsys	4,689,300	33 11/16	− 7/8
PairGainTch	4,652,600	24 1/8	− 3 15/16
Microsoft	4,626,700	130 5/8	+ 7/16
AMEX			
SPDR	3,212,400	92 13/32	+ 1/32
NaborsInd	1,165,000	43 7/32	− 31/32
JTS Cp	1,044,300	9/16	+ 1/16
ViacomB	1,003,200	32 3/16	+ 1 3/8
XCL Ltd	952,600	9/16	+ 1/32

DIARIES

NYSE	TUES	MON	WK AGO
Issues traded	3,412	3,426	3,421
Advances	1,336	1,459	1,537
Declines	1,486	1,431	1,385
Unchanged	590	536	499
New highs	54	64	110
New lows	44	40	17
zAdv vol (000)	199,073	178,459	309,051
zDecl vol (000)	215,629	259,686	210,261
zTotal vol (000)	434,605	463,421	537,138
Closing tick[1]	+463	+390	+326
Closing Arms[2] (trin)	.97	1.48	.76
zBlock trades	9,323	9,337	10,944
NASDAQ			
Issues traded	5,743	5,741	5,732
Advances	1,789	2,020	1,979
Declines	2,281	2,185	2,238
Unchanged	1,673	1,536	1,515
New highs	75	72	113
New lows	60	45	34
Adv vol (000)	177,167	198,483	293,231
Decl vol (000)	324,982	358,816	299,511
Total vol (000)	567,564	589,742	631,088
Block trades	8,392	8,314	8,746
AMEX			
Issues traded	733	755	743
Advances	262	302	307
Declines	310	301	271
Unchanged	161	152	165
New highs	14	19	12
New lows	9	13	7
zAdv vol (000)	8,633	7,263	15,587
zDecl vol (000)	7,821	13,105	9,104
zTotal vol (000)	20,470	23,095	28,279
Comp vol (000)	27,447	31,167	34,949
zBlock trades	n.a.	410	529

strength is said to be deteriorating. Similarly, the market is considered weak when the number of declines repeatedly exceeds the number of advances. The principle behind this indicator is that the number of advances and declines reflects the underlying sentiment of investors. When the mood is optimistic, for example, look for advances to outnumber declines. Again, information on advances and declines is published daily in the financial press.

Short Interest

short interest
the number of stocks sold short in the market at any given time; a technical indicator believed to indicate future market demand.

When investors anticipate a market decline, they sometimes sell a stock short —that is, they sell borrowed stock. The number of stocks sold short in the market at any given point in time is known as the **short interest.** The more stocks that are sold short, the higher the short interest. Because all short sales must eventually be "covered" (the borrowed shares must be returned), a short sale in effect ensures *future demand for the stock*. Thus the market is viewed optimistically when the level of short interest becomes relatively high by historical standards. The logic is that as shares are bought back to cover outstanding short sales, the additional demand will push stock prices up. The amount of short interest on the NYSE, the AMEX, and Nasdaq's National Market is published monthly in the *Wall Street Journal* and *Barron's*. Figure 7.2 shows the type of information that's available.

Keeping track of the level of short interest can indicate future market demand, but it can also reveal *present* market optimism or pessimism. Short selling is usually done by knowledgeable investors, and a significant buildup or decline in the level of short interest is thought to reveal the sentiment of sophisticated investors about the current state of the market or a company. For example, a significant shift upward in short interest is believed to indicate pessimism concerning the *current* state of the market, even though it may signal optimism with regard to *future* levels of demand.

Odd-Lot Trading

A rather cynical saying on Wall Street suggests that the best thing to do is just the opposite of whatever the small investor is doing. The reasoning behind this is that as a group, small investors are notoriously wrong in their timing of investment decisions: The investing public usually does not come into the market in force until after a bull market has pretty much run its course, and it does not get out until late in a bear market. Although its validity is debatable (especially in view of the current market environment), this is the premise behind a widely followed technical indicator and is the basis for the **theory of contrary opinion.** This theory uses the amount and type of odd-lot trading as an indicator of the current state of the market and pending changes. Because many individual investors deal in transactions of less than 100 shares, the combined sentiments of this type of investor are supposedly captured in these odd-lot figures. The idea is to see what odd-lot investors are doing "on balance." So long as there is little or no difference in the spread between the volume of odd-lot purchases and sales, the theory of contrary opinion holds that the market will probably continue pretty much along its current line (either up or down). But when the balance of odd-lot purchases and sales begins to change dramatically, it may be a signal that a bull or bear market is about to end. For example, if the amount of odd-lot purchases starts to exceed odd-lot sales by an ever widening margin, it may suggest that speculation on

theory of contrary opinion
a technical indicator that uses the amount and type of odd-lot trading as an indicator of the current state of the market and pending changes.

FIGURE 7.2
Short Interest in the NYSE and the AMEX

The amount of short selling in the market is closely watched by many investment professionals and individual investors. The summary report shown here provides an overview of the extent to which stocks are being shorted in the NYSE and the AMEX. In addition to summary statistics, this monthly report lists all stocks that have been sold short and the number of shares shorted. (Source: *Wall Street Journal,* October 22, 1997, p. C18.)

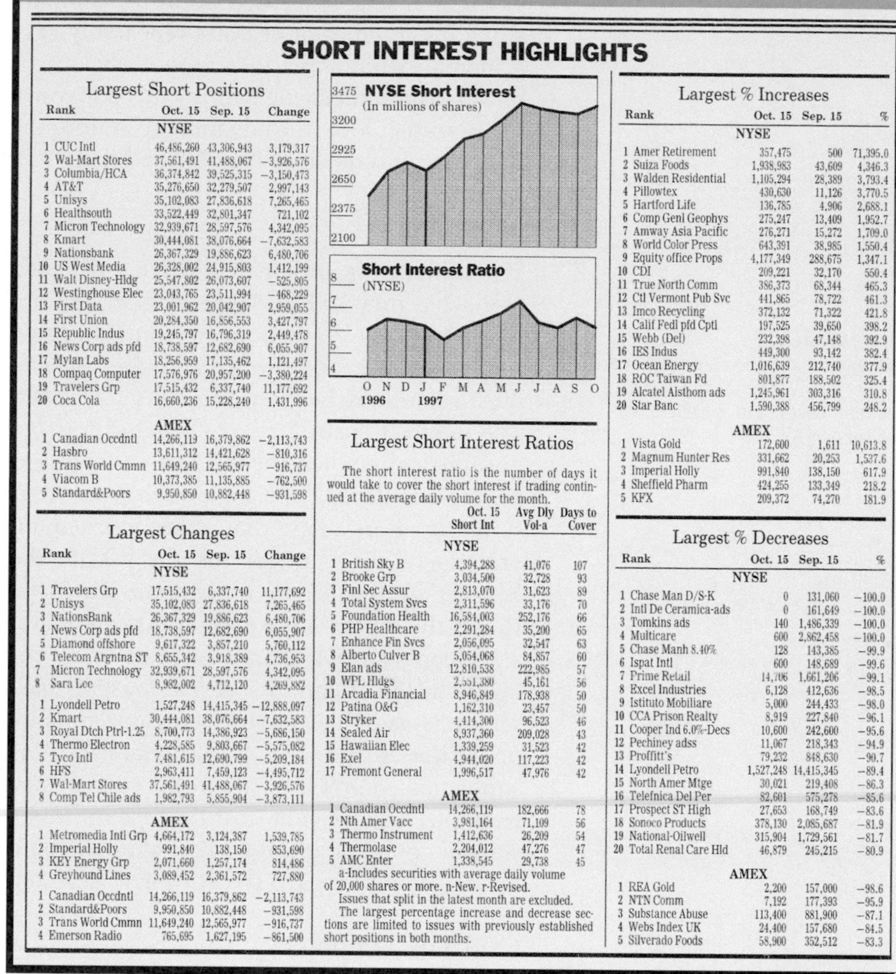

SHORT INTEREST HIGHLIGHTS

Largest Short Positions

Rank	Oct. 15	Sep. 15	Change
NYSE			
1 CUC Intl	46,486,260	43,306,943	3,179,317
2 Wal-Mart Stores	37,561,491	41,488,067	−3,926,576
3 Columbia/HCA	36,374,842	39,525,315	−3,150,473
4 AT&T	35,276,650	32,279,507	2,997,143
5 Unisys	35,102,083	27,836,618	7,265,465
6 Healthsouth	33,522,449	32,801,347	721,102
7 Micron Technology	32,939,671	28,597,576	4,342,095
8 Kmart	30,444,081	38,076,664	−7,632,583
9 Nationsbank	26,367,329	19,886,623	6,480,706
10 US West Media	26,328,002	24,915,803	1,412,199
11 Walt Disney-Hldg	25,547,802	26,073,607	−525,805
12 Westinghouse Elec	23,043,765	23,511,994	−468,229
13 First Data	23,001,962	20,042,907	2,959,055
14 First Union	20,284,350	16,856,553	3,427,797
15 Republic Indus	19,245,797	16,796,319	2,449,478
16 News Corp ads pfd	18,738,597	12,682,690	6,055,907
17 Mylan Labs	18,256,959	17,135,462	1,121,497
18 Compaq Computer	17,576,976	20,957,200	−3,380,224
19 Travelers Grp	17,515,432	6,337,740	11,177,692
20 Coca Cola	16,660,236	15,228,240	1,431,996
AMEX			
1 Canadian Occdntl	14,266,119	16,379,862	−2,113,743
2 Hasbro	13,611,312	14,421,628	−810,316
3 Trans World Cmmn	11,649,240	12,565,977	−916,737
4 Viacom B	10,373,385	11,135,885	−762,500
5 Standard&Poors	9,950,850	10,882,448	−931,598

Largest Changes

Rank	Oct. 15	Sep. 15	Change
NYSE			
1 Travelers Grp	17,515,432	6,337,740	11,177,692
2 Unisys	35,102,083	27,836,618	7,265,465
3 NationsBank	26,367,329	19,886,623	6,480,706
4 News Corp ads pfd	18,738,597	12,682,690	6,055,907
5 Diamond offshore	9,617,322	3,857,210	5,760,112
6 Telecom Argntna ST	8,655,342	3,918,389	4,736,953
7 Micron Technology	32,939,671	28,597,576	4,342,095
8 Sara Lee	8,982,002	4,712,120	4,269,882
1 Lyondell Petro	1,527,248	14,415,345	−12,888,097
2 Kmart	30,444,081	38,076,664	−7,632,583
3 Royal Dtch Ptrl-1.25	8,700,773	14,386,923	−5,686,150
4 Thermo Electron	4,228,585	9,803,667	−5,575,082
5 Tyco Intl	7,481,615	12,690,799	−5,209,184
6 HFS	2,963,411	7,459,123	−4,495,712
7 Wal-Mart Stores	37,561,491	41,488,067	−3,926,576
8 Comp Tel Chile ads	1,982,793	5,855,904	−3,873,111
AMEX			
1 Metromedia Intl Grp	4,664,172	3,124,387	1,539,785
2 Imperial Holly	991,840	138,150	853,690
3 KEY Energy Grp	2,071,660	1,257,174	814,486
4 Greyhound Lines	3,089,452	2,361,572	727,880
1 Canadian Occdntl	14,266,119	16,379,862	−2,113,743
2 Standard&Poors	9,950,850	10,882,448	−931,598
3 Trans World Cmmn	11,649,240	12,565,977	−916,737
4 Emerson Radio	765,695	1,627,195	−861,500

Largest Short Interest Ratios

The short interest ratio is the number of days it would take to cover the short interest if trading continued at the average daily volume for the month.

	Oct. 15 Short Int	Avg Dly Vol-a	Days to Cover
NYSE			
1 British Sky B	4,394,288	41,076	107
2 Brooke Grp	3,034,500	32,728	93
3 Finl Sec Assur	2,813,070	31,623	89
4 Total System Svcs	2,311,596	33,176	70
5 Foundation Health	16,584,003	252,176	66
6 PHP Healthcare	2,291,284	35,200	65
7 Enhance Fin Svcs	2,056,095	32,547	63
8 Alberto Culver B	5,054,068	84,857	60
9 Elan ads	12,810,538	222,985	57
10 WPL Hldgs	2,551,380	45,161	56
11 Arcadia Financial	8,946,849	178,938	50
12 Patina O&G	1,162,310	23,457	50
13 Stryker	4,414,300	96,523	46
14 Sealed Air	8,937,360	209,028	43
15 Hawaiian Elec	1,339,259	31,523	42
16 Exel	4,944,020	117,223	42
17 Fremont General	1,996,517	47,976	42
AMEX			
1 Canadian Occdntl	14,266,119	182,666	78
2 Nth Amer Vacc	3,981,164	71,109	56
3 Thermo Instrument	1,412,636	26,209	54
4 Thermolase	2,204,012	47,276	47
5 AMC Enter	1,338,545	29,738	45

a-Includes securities with average daily volume of 20,000 shares or more. n-New. r-Revised.
Issues that split in the latest month are excluded.
The largest percentage increase and decrease sections are limited to issues with previously established short positions in both months.

Largest % Increases

Rank	Oct. 15	Sep. 15	%
NYSE			
1 Amer Retirement	357,475	500	71,395.0
2 Suiza Foods	1,938,983	43,609	4,346.3
3 Walden Residential	1,105,294	28,389	3,793.4
4 Pillowtex	430,630	11,126	3,770.5
5 Hartford Life	136,785	4,906	2,688.1
6 Comp Genl Geophys	275,247	13,409	1,952.7
7 Amway Asia Pacific	276,271	15,272	1,709.0
8 World Color Press	643,391	38,985	1,550.4
9 Equity office Props	4,177,349	288,675	1,347.1
10 CDI	209,221	32,170	550.4
11 True North Comm	386,373	68,344	465.3
12 Ctl Vermont Pub Svc	441,865	78,722	461.3
13 Imco Recycling	372,132	71,322	421.8
14 Calif Fedl pfd Cptl	197,525	39,650	398.2
15 Webb (Del)	232,398	47,148	392.9
16 IES Indus	449,300	93,142	382.4
17 Ocean Energy	1,016,639	212,740	377.9
18 ROC Taiwan Fd	801,877	188,502	325.4
19 Alcatel Alsthom ads	1,245,961	303,316	310.8
20 Star Banc	1,590,388	456,799	248.2
AMEX			
1 Vista Gold	172,600	1,611	10,613.8
2 Magnum Hunter Res	331,662	20,253	1,537.6
3 Imperial Holly	991,840	138,150	617.9
4 Sheffield Pharm	424,255	133,349	218.2
5 KFX	209,372	74,270	181.9

Largest % Decreases

Rank	Oct. 15	Sep. 15	%
NYSE			
1 Chase Man D/S-K	0	131,060	−100.0
2 Intl De Ceramica-ads	0	161,649	−100.0
3 Tomkins ads	140	1,486,339	−100.0
4 Multicare	600	2,862,458	−100.0
5 Chase Manh 8.40%	128	143,385	−99.9
6 Ispat Intl	600	148,689	−99.6
7 Prime Retail	14,706	1,661,206	−99.1
8 Excel Industries	6,128	412,636	−98.5
9 Istituto Mobiliare	5,000	244,433	−98.0
10 CCA Prison Realty	8,919	227,840	−96.1
11 Cooper Ind 6.0%-Decs	10,600	242,600	−95.6
12 Pechiney adss	11,067	218,343	−94.9
13 Proffitt's	79,232	848,630	−90.7
14 Lyondell Petro	1,527,248	14,415,345	−89.4
15 North Amer Mtge	30,021	219,408	−86.3
16 Telefnica Del Per	82,601	575,278	−85.6
17 Prospect ST High	27,653	168,749	−83.6
18 Sonoco Products	378,130	2,085,687	−81.9
19 National-Oilwell	315,904	1,729,561	−81.7
20 Total Renal Care Hld	46,879	245,215	−80.9
AMEX			
1 REA Gold	2,200	157,000	−98.6
2 NTN Comm	7,192	177,393	−95.9
3 Substance Abuse	113,400	881,900	−87.1
4 Webs Index UK	24,400	157,680	−84.5
5 Silverado Foods	58,900	352,512	−83.3

the part of small investors is starting to get out of control—an ominous signal that the final stages of a bull market may be at hand.

Relative Price Levels

Whereas market volume, short-interest positions, and odd-lot trading are of interest to many investors, others are concerned more about market prices in general. To them, the question is not so much what's driving the market as how pricey the market is getting. Many professional traders track prices in the market by jointly monitoring three measures of overall market performance: (1) the *market P/E multiple,* (2) the *market's price-to-book-value ratio,* and (3) its *dividend yield.* In a sense, these measures provide yardsticks about *the relative value* of stocks and, as such, capture underlying price pressures in the market. For example, a large upward move in overall market prices will cause the market P/E and price-to-book-value ratios to move up and the dividend yield to move down. The idea is that if prices are going up, they should be doing so because of healthy growth in corporate earnings, stockholders' equity, and dividends—not because of unbridled investor speculation. If prices suddenly go down, it's also helpful to understand why, in order to decide what

INVESTING IN ACTION

Take a Deep Breath and Don't Panic

What do you do when the market plunges? While it's tempting to think about getting out, it usually doesn't make much sense to sell your stocks right after the market takes a big hit. After all, if you were happy with the market when the Dow Jones Industrial Average hit a peak of 8,259 on August 6, 1997, why wouldn't you love stocks when they're a thousand points cheaper—as they were in October 1997?

But if you're inclined to panic, here are some suggestions:

1. Don't call your broker or mutual fund company. Instead, call a friend. Think it through. Do you think the economy has suddenly changed and stocks are really overvalued? At times of market turmoil, remember that you're investing for the long term. This isn't your rent money, or at least it shouldn't be. This is your retirement money—or your college fund for the kids. Twenty years from now, no one will remember a day like October 27, 1997. If this really upsets you and you're losing sleep, then maybe you should lighten up on stocks. But don't do it on a bad day in the market.

2. Use the turmoil as an opportunity to rebalance your portfolio among stocks, bonds, and cash. When stocks fall, your portfolio could suddenly be too light on stocks. Instead of 65% stocks, 20% bonds, and 15% cash, it's now 50% stocks, 30% bonds, and 20% cash. You might want to sell some bonds or use some of your money market funds to buy more stocks.

3. Identify stocks or mutual funds that performed particularly badly during this time of market volatility. Put a checkmark next to their names. When the market recovers, you might consider selling some of those shares. After all, an investment that performs poorly in a time of stress could be a bad long-term investment as well.

Historically, the U.S. stock market has consistently posted 10% to 12% annual returns since the Great Depression of the late 1920s. Yes, there have been some bad stretches, such as the early 1970s, when the market was battered by inflation, energy shortages, and the political turmoil of Watergate. But for investors who were patient and who had a long-term time horizon, the stock market has provided excellent returns. This is especially true since 1982, when the Dow Jones Industrial Average bottomed at 777.

Today, the prospects for U.S. stocks still look bright. Inflation, which erodes the value of all financial assets, is virtually nonexistent. Interest rates are low, which means that investors have few attractive alternatives outside the stock market. The U.S. economy is growing steadily, unemployment is low, and worker productivity is excellent. The federal budget deficit is likely to be a surplus in fiscal 1998. The average investor as well as the seasoned pro can see that the U.S. stock market is an attractive place to be. And that's why the stock market in recent years has bounced back quickly from some truly frightening days.

to do in response. The accompanying *Investing in Action* box offers some suggestions—other than to panic.

Using these three measures, technical analysts have developed historical standards of performance that are felt to reflect normal market behavior. These standards are not designed to pinpoint market swings or indicate how deep or how long a bear (or bull) market will last. Rather, they are meant to offer signals that historically have pointed out zones of extreme over- or undervaluation. That is, these relative price measures point out when the market appears to be moving into danger zones (on the upside) or toward significant buying opportunities (on the downside). Generally speaking, it's felt that the market is starting to overheat and prices, in general, are getting too high when the market P/E (on the S&P 500) moves under above 20 times earnings, the market's average price-to-book-value ratio goes above 2 to 2.5, and the average dividend yield drops below 2 or 3%. On the other hand, it's felt that stocks have proved to be bargains when the market P/E drops to 10 or less, the price-to-book-value ratio starts getting close to 1.0, and dividend yield rises above 5% or 6%. As a point of reference, in late 1997 the market (as represented by the S&P 500) had an average P/E ratio of over 20 times earnings, an average price-to-book-value ratio of 2.49, and a dividend yield of 1.72%. The first two measures were definitely on the high side and getting pretty close to the danger zone, whereas the average dividend yield was clearly a source of concern. However, the low dividend yield may be more a reflection of the current state of thinking in corporate America than an indication of a potential problem. That is, over the past few years, companies have been systematically moving to lower dividend rates and using other, more tax-efficient ways of rewarding investors. Keeping track of the market's P/E, price-to-book-value ratio, and dividend yield is fairly easy, because this information is regularly reported in the *Wall Street Journal, Barron's,* and a number of other sources.

Using Technical Analysis

Investors have a wide range of choices with respect to technical analysis. They can use the charts and complex ratios of the technical analysts, or they can, more informally, use technical analysis just to get a general sense of the market. In the latter case, market behavior itself is not as important as the implications such market behavior can have on the price performance of a particular common stock. Thus technical analysis might be used in conjunction with fundamental analysis to determine the proper time to add a particular investment candidate to one's portfolio. Some investors and professional money managers, in fact, look at the technical side of a stock *before* doing any fundamental analysis. If the stock is found to be technically sound, then they'll look at its fundamentals; if not, they'll look for another stock. For these investors, the concerns of technical analysis are still the same: *Do the technical factors indicate that this might be a good stock to buy?*

Most investors rely on published sources, such as those put out by brokerage firms, to obtain necessary technical insights, and they often find it helpful to use several different approaches. For example, an investor might follow market P/Es, dividend yields, and price-to-book values and at the same time keep track of information on market volume and breadth of the market. Such information provides the individual investor with a convenient and low-cost way of staying abreast of the market. Certainly, trying to determine the right (or best) time to get into the market is a principal objective of technical analysis—and one of the major pastimes of many investors.

Charting

charting
the activity of charting price behavior and other market information and then using the patterns these charts form to make investment decisions.

Charting is perhaps the best-known activity of the technical analyst. Technicians—analysts who believe it is chiefly (or solely) supply and demand forces that establish stock prices—use various types of charts to plot the behavior of everything from the Dow Jones Industrial Average to the share price movements of individual listed and OTC stocks. Also, just about every kind of technical indicator is charted in one form or another. Figure 7.3 shows a typical stock chart; in this case, the price behavior of Liz Claiborne has been plotted, along with a variety of supplementary information. Charts are popular because they provide a visual summary of activity over time and, perhaps more important, because (in the eyes of technicians, at least) they contain valuable information about developing trends and the future behavior of the market and/or individual stocks. Chartists believe price patterns evolve into *chart formations* that provide signals about the future course of the market or a stock. We will now briefly review the practice of charting, including popular types of charts, chart formations, and investor uses of charts.

bar chart
the simplest kind of chart, where share price is plotted on the vertical axis and time on the horizontal axis; stock prices are recorded as vertical bars showing high, low, and closing prices.

Bar Charts

The simplest and probably most widely used type of chart is the **bar chart.** Market or share prices are plotted on the vertical axis, and time is plotted on the horizontal axis. This type of chart derives its name from the fact that prices

FIGURE 7.3 A Stock Chart

This chart for Liz Claiborne contains information about the daily price behavior of the stock, along with the stock's relative strength, its trading volume, and several other pieces of supplementary data. (Source: "A Stock Chart—Liz Claiborne." Courtesy of Daily Graphs. Graph reprinted with permission from Daily Graphs, Inc., 12655 Beatrice Street, Los Angeles, CA 90066. Phone: 800-472-7429 or 310-448-6843.)

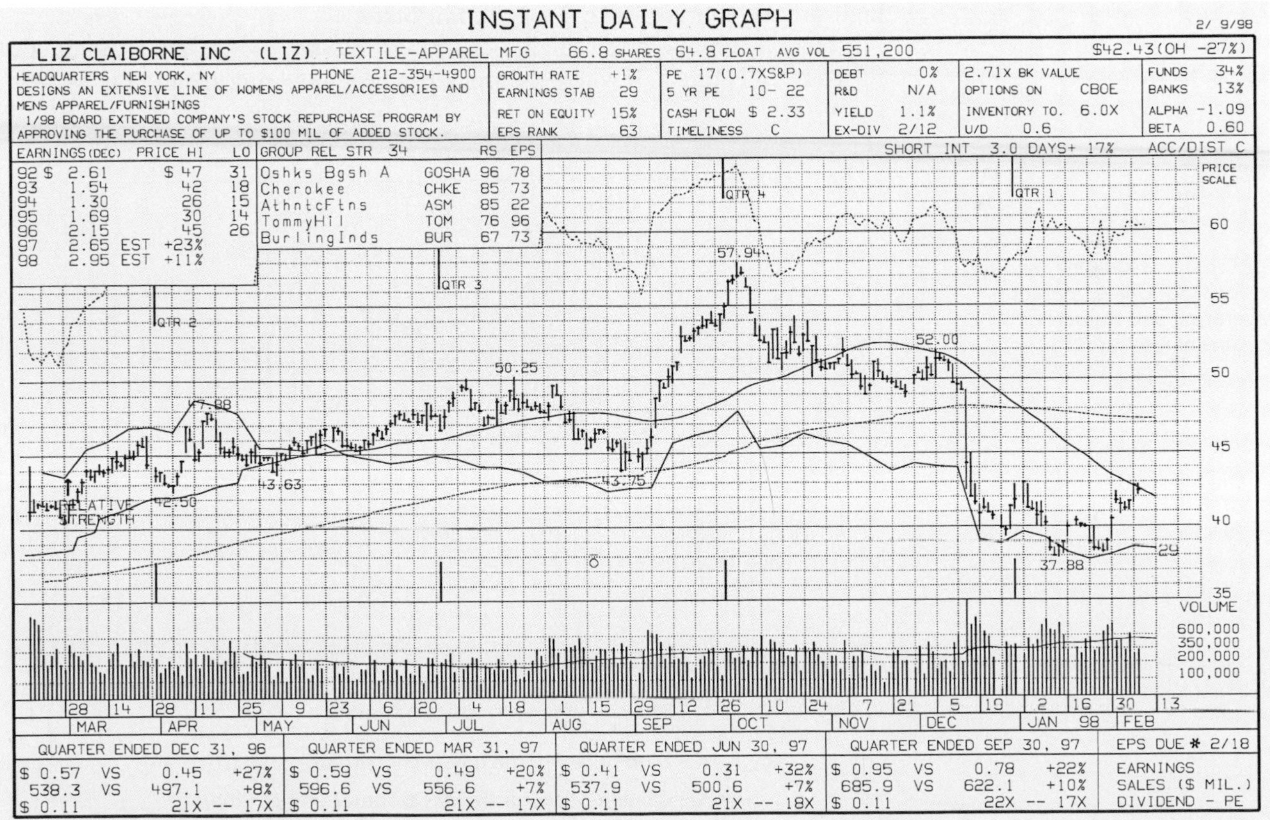

are recorded as vertical bars that depict high, low, and closing prices. A typical bar chart is shown in Figure 7.4. Note that on December 31, this particular stock had a high price of 29, had a low of 27, and closed at 27½. Because these charts contain a time element, technicians frequently plot a variety of other pertinent information on them. For example, volume is often put at the base of bar charts (see the Liz Claiborne chart in Figure 7.3).

Point-and-Figure Charts

point-and-figure charts charts used to keep track of emerging price patterns by plotting significant price changes with *X*s and *O*s but with no time dimension used.

Point-and-figure charts are used strictly to keep track of emerging price patterns. Because there is no time dimension on them, they are *not* used for plotting technical measures. In addition to the time feature, point-and-figure charts are unique in two other ways: First, only *significant* price changes are recorded on these charts. That is, prices have to move by a certain minimum amount—usually at least a point or two—before a new price level is recognized. Second, price *reversals* show up only after a predetermined change in direction occurs. Normally, only closing prices are charted, though some point-and-figure charts use all price changes during the day. An *X* is used to denote an increase in price, an *O* a decrease.

Figure 7.5 shows a common point-and-figure chart. In this case, the chart employs a 2-point box, which means that the stock must move by a minimum of 2 points before any changes are recorded. The chart can cover a span of 1 year or less if the stock is highly active. Or it can cover a number of years if the stock is not very active. As a rule, low-priced stocks are charted with 1-point boxes, moderately priced shares with increments of 2 to 3 points, and high-priced securities with 3- to 5-point boxes.

Here is how point-and-figure charts work: Suppose we are at point A on the chart in Figure 7.5, where the stock has been hovering around the $40–$41

FIGURE 7.4
A Bar Chart

Bar charts are widely used to track stock prices, market averages, and numerous other technical measures.

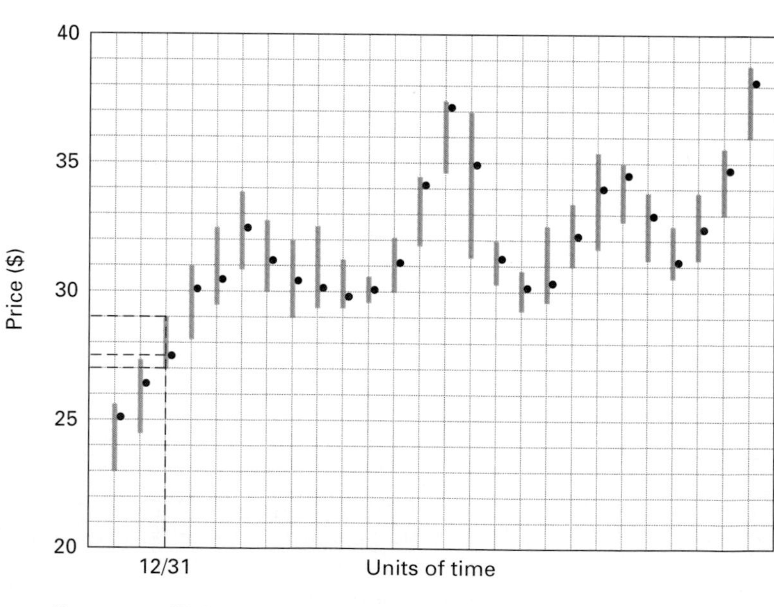

FIGURE 7.5
A Point-and End Figure Chart

Point-and figure charts are unusual because they have no time dimension. Rather, a column of Xs is used to reflect a general upward drift in prices, and a column of Os is used when prices are drifting downward.

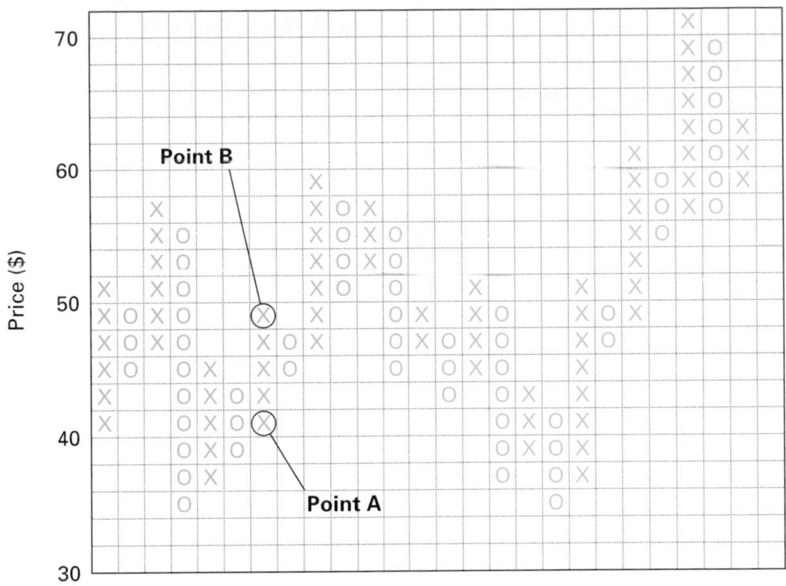

mark for some time. Assume, however, that it just closed at 42⅛. Now, because the minimum 2-point movement has been met, the chartist would place an X in the box immediately *above* point A. The chartist would remain with this new box as long as the price moved (up or down) within the 2-point range of 42 to 43⅞. Although the chartist follows *daily* prices, a new entry is made on the chart only after the price has changed by a certain minimum amount and moved into a new 2-point box. We see that from point A, the price generally moved up over time to nearly $50 a share. At that point (indicated as point B on the chart), things began to change as a reversal set in. That is, the price of the stock began to drift downward and in time moved out of the $48–$50 box. This reversal prompts the chartist to change columns and symbols, by moving one column to the right and recording the new price level with an O in the $46–$48 box. The chartist will continue to use Os as long as the stock continues to close on a generally lower note.

Chart Formations

The information that charts supposedly contain about the future course of the market (or of a stock) is thought by some to be revealed in chart *formations*. That is, chartists believe that in response to certain supply and demand forces, emerging price patterns will result in various types of formations that historically have indicated that certain types of market behavior are imminent. If you know how to interpret charts (which, by the way, is no easy task), you can see formations building and recognize buy and sell signals. These chart formations are often given some pretty exotic names: *head and shoulders, falling wedge, scallop and saucer, ascending triangle,* and *island reversal,* for example.

Figure 7.6 shows four formations. The patterns form "support levels" and "resistance lines" that, when combined with the basic formations, yield buy and sell signals. Panel A is an example of a *buy* signal, which occurs when prices break out above a resistance line after a particular pattern has been formed. In contrast, when prices break out below a support level, as they do at

FIGURE 7.6
Some Popular Chart Formations

To chartists, each of these formations has meaning about the future course of events.

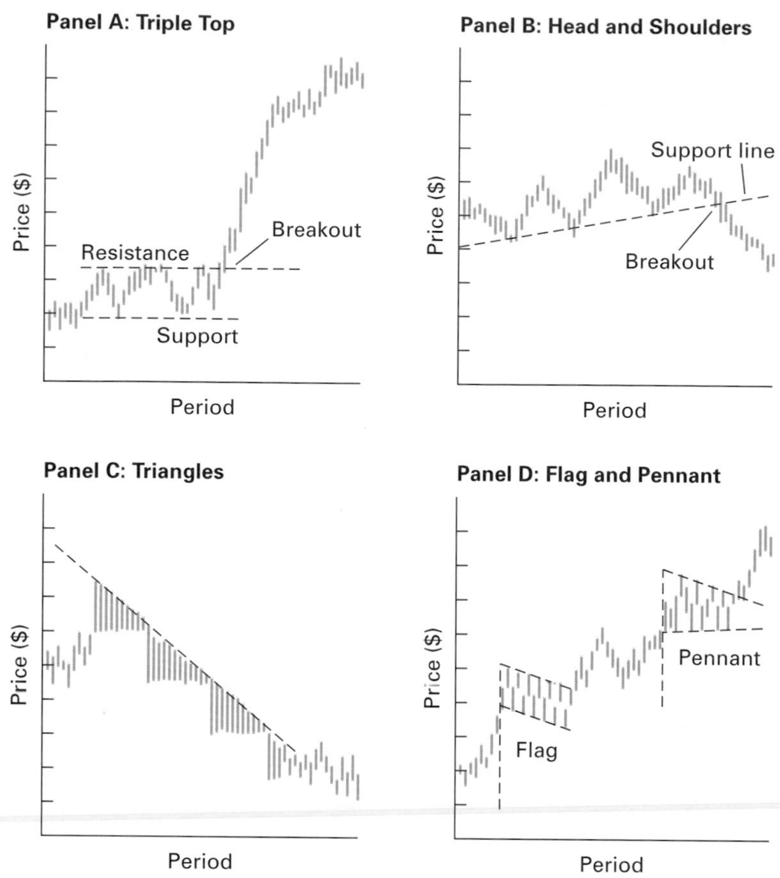

the end of the formation in panel B, a *sell* signal is said to occur. Supposedly, a sell signal means everything is in place for a major drop in the market (or in the price of a share of stock), and a buy signal indicates that the opposite is about to occur. Unfortunately, one of the major problems with charting is that the formations rarely appear as neatly and cleanly as those in Figure 7.6. Rather, identifying and interpreting them often demands considerable imagination.

Investor Uses

Charts are nothing more than tools used by market analysts and technicians to assess conditions in the market and/or the price behavior of individual stocks. Unlike other types of technical measures, charting is seldom done on an informal basis. Either you chart because you believe in its value, or you don't chart at all. A chart by itself tells you little more than where the market or a stock has been. But to a chartist, those price patterns yield formations that, along with things like resistance lines, support levels, and breakouts, tell them what to expect in the future. Chartists believe that history repeats itself, so they study the historical reactions of stocks (or of the market) to various formations and devise trading rules based on these observations. It makes no difference to chartists whether they are following the market or an individual stock, because *it is the formation that matters*, not the issue being plotted. The value of charts lies in knowing how to "read" them and how to respond to the signals they are said to give about the future. A long-standing debate (some would call it a feud) still rages on Wall Street regarding the merits of charting. Although a large segment of investors and investment professionals may scoff at it, to avid chartists, charting is no laughing matter.

CONCEPTS IN REVIEW

7.12 What is the purpose of *technical analysis?* Explain how and why it is used by technicians; note how it can be helpful in timing investment decisions.

7.13 Can the market really have a measurable effect on the price behavior of individual securities? Explain.

7.14 What are some reactions to a market plunge recommended by the *Investing in Action* box on page 281?

7.15 What is a stock chart? What kind of information can be put on charts, and what is the purpose of charting?
   a. What is the difference between a *bar chart* and a *point-and-figure chart?*
   b. What are chart formations, and why are they important?

http://hepg.aw.com

Basic technical analysis is used by many—if not most—professional investors. Even so, few analysts understand the detailed methods behind the analysis. To learn more about this challenging approach to security selection, you can read the book *Technical Analysis from A to Z,* starting on the following Web page.

www.equis.com/free/index.html

Random Walks and Efficient Markets

LG 6

random walk hypothesis
the theory that stock price movements are unpredictable, so there's no way to know where prices are headed.

If a drunk were abandoned in an open field at night, where would you begin to search for him the next morning? The answer, of course, is the spot where the drunk was left the night before, because there's no way to predict where he will go. To some analysts, stock prices seem to wander about in a similar fashion. Observations of such erratic movements have led to a body of evidence called the **random walk hypothesis.** Its followers believe that price movements are unpredictable and therefore security analysis will not help to predict future market behavior. This hypothesis obviously has serious implications for much of what we have discussed in the last two chapters.

A Brief Historical Overview

To describe stock prices as a random walk suggests that price movements cannot be expected to follow any type of pattern or, put another way, that price movements are independent of one another. In order to find a theory for such behavior, researchers developed the concept of efficient markets. Basically, the idea behind an efficient market is that the market price of securities always fully reflects available information and that it is difficult, therefore, if not impossible, to outperform the market consistently by picking "undervalued" stocks.

INVESTOR FACT

WHAT A DIFFERENCE A DAY MAKES—Most professional money managers know that trying to time the market just doesn't pay. Consider, for example, the fact that if you had been fully invested in stocks every day from January 1, 1986, through December 31, 1995, you would have earned a return of 14.8%. However, had you been in the market for *all but the 30 best days,* your total return would have dropped to a dismal 4.8%! Imagine, just 1% of the trading days accounted for 68% of the return.

Random Walks

The first evidence of random price movements dates back to the early 1900s. During that period, statisticians noticed that commodity prices seemed to follow a "fair game" pattern; that is, prices seemed to move up and down randomly, giving no advantage to any particular trading strategy. Although a few studies on the subject appeared in the 1930s, thorough examination of the randomness in stock prices did not begin until 1959. From that point on, particularly through the decade of the 1960s, the random walk issue was one of the most keenly debated topics in stock market literature. The development of high-speed computers has helped researchers compile convincing evidence that stock prices do, in fact, come very close to a random walk.

Efficient Markets

Given the extensive random walk evidence, market researchers were faced with another question: What sort of market would produce prices that seem to fluctuate randomly? Such behavior could be the result of investors who are irrational and make investment decisions on whim. However, it has been argued much more convincingly that investors are not irrational; rather, random price movements are evidence of highly efficient markets.

efficient market
a market in which securities reflect all possible information quickly and accurately.

An **efficient market** is one in which securities fully reflect all possible information quickly and accurately. The concept holds that investors incorporate all available information into their decisions on the price at which they are willing to buy or sell. At any point in time, then, the current price of a security incorporates all information. Additionally, the current price not only reflects past information, such as might be found in company reports, financial newspapers, and magazine articles, but also includes information about events that have been announced but haven't occurred yet, like a forthcoming dividend payment. Furthermore, the current price reflects *predictions* about future information: Investors, in their zeal to beat the competition, actively forecast important events and incorporate those forecasts into their estimate of the correct price. Obviously, because of the keen competition among investors, when new information becomes known, the price of the security adjusts quickly. This adjustment is not always perfect. Sometimes it is too large and at other times too small, but on average it balances out and is correct. The new price, in effect, is set after investors have fully assessed the new information.

Why Should Markets Be Efficient?

Active markets, such as the New York Stock Exchange, are efficient—they are made up of many rational, highly competitive investors who react quickly and objectively to new information. Investors, searching for stock market profits, compete vigorously for new information and do extremely thorough analyses. The **efficient markets hypothesis** (EMH), which is the basic theory describing the behavior of such a market, has several tenets:

efficient markets hypothesis (EMH)
basic theory of the behavior of efficient markets, in which there are a large number of knowledgeable investors who react quickly to new information, causing securities prices to adjust quickly and accurately.

1. There are many knowledgeable investors actively analyzing, valuing, and trading any particular security. No one of these individual traders alone can affect the price of any security.

2. Information is widely available to all investors at approximately the same time, and this information is practically "free."
3. Information on events, such as labor strikes, industrial accidents, and changes in product demand, tends to occur randomly.
4. Investors react quickly and accurately to new information, causing prices to adjust quickly and, on average, accurately.

For the most part, the securities markets do, in fact, exhibit these characteristics.

Levels of Market Efficiency

The efficient markets hypothesis is concerned with information—not only the type and source of information, but also the quality and speed with which it is disseminated among investors. It is convenient to discuss the EMH in three cumulative categories or forms: past prices only, past prices *plus* all other public data, and, finally, past prices and public data *plus* private information. Together, these three ways of looking at information flows in the market represent three forms of the EMH: the weak, semi-strong, and strong forms.

Weak Form

weak form (EMH)
form of the EMH holding that past data on stock prices are of no use in predicting future prices.

The **weak form of the EMH** holds that past data on stock prices are of no use in predicting future price changes. If prices follow a random walk, price changes over time are random. Today's price change is unrelated to yesterday's or to that of any other day, just as each step by a drunkard is unrelated to previous steps. If new information arrives randomly, then prices will change randomly.

A number of people have asserted that it is possible to profit from "runs" in a stock's price. They contend that when a stock's price starts moving up, it will continue to move up for a period of time, developing a momentum. If you can spot a run, then, on the basis of past prices alone, you can develop a trading strategy that will produce a profit. The results from much careful research suggest that, indeed, momentum in stock prices does exist, and if investors quickly trade at the beginning of the run, large profits can be made. But there's a problem: In addition to spotting a run right off the bat (no easy task), an investor would have to make numerous trades, and when commissions are factored in, the only person who makes a profit is the broker. Many other trading rules have been tested to determine whether profits can be made by examining past stock price movements, and there is very little, if any, evidence that a trading rule *based solely on past price data* can outperform a simple buy-and-hold strategy.

Semi-Strong Form

semi-strong form (EMH)
form of the EMH holding that abnormally large profits cannot be consistently earned using publicly available information.

The **semi-strong form of the EMH** holds that abnormally large profits cannot be consistently earned using publicly available information. This information includes not only past price and volume data but also data such as corporate earnings, dividends, inflation, and stock splits. The semi-strong information set includes all of the information publicly considered in the weak form, *as well as all other information publicly available.* Tests of the semi-strong form of the EMH are basically concerned with the speed at which information is disseminated to investors. The overall conclusions of research tests support the position that stock prices adjust very rapidly to new information and therefore support the semi-strong form of the EMH—but there are still some unanswered questions.

Most tests of semi-strong efficiency have examined how a stock price changes in response to an economic or financial event. A famous early study involved stock splits. A stock split does not change the value of a company, so the value of the stock should not be affected by a stock split. Although the research indicated that there are sharp increases in the price of a stock *before* a stock split, the changes after the split are random. Investors cannot gain by purchasing stocks on or after the announcement of a split; they would have to purchase before the split to earn abnormal profits. By the time the stock split is announced, the market has already incorporated any favorable information associated with the split into the price.

Other studies have examined the impact of major events on stock prices. The overwhelming evidence indicates that stock prices react within minutes, if not seconds, to any important new information. Certainly, by the time an investor reads about the event in the newspaper, the stock price has almost completely adjusted to the news. Even hearing about the event on the radio or television usually allows too little time to react and complete the transaction in time to make an abnormal profit.

Strong Form

strong form (EMH)
form of the EMH that holds that there is no information, public or private, that allows investors to earn abnormal profits consistently.

The **strong form of the EMH** holds that there is no information, public or private, that allows investors to earn abnormal profits consistently. It states that stock prices immediately adjust to any information, even if it isn't available to every investor. This extreme form of the EMH has not received universal support.

One type of private information is the kind obtained by corporate insiders, such as officers, directors, or other privileged individuals within a corporation. They have access to valuable information about major strategic and tactical decisions the company makes. They also have detailed information about the financial state of the firm that may not be available to other shareholders. Corporate insiders may legally trade shares of stock in their own company, if they report the transactions to the Securities and Exchange Commission (SEC) each month. This information is then made public, usually within several weeks. It should not be surprising to learn that most studies of corporate insiders find that they consistently earn abnormally large profits when they sell their company stock. They are able to sell their stock holdings before major announcements are made to the public and can thereby profit from the stock price adjustment that comes quickly after important news is released.

Other market participants occasionally have inside—nonpublic—information that they obtained *illegally*. With this information, they can gain an unfair advantage that permits them to earn an excess return. Clearly, those who trade securities on the basis of illegal inside information have an unfair and illegal advantage. Empirical research has confirmed that those with such inside information do indeed have an opportunity to earn an excess return.

Possible Implications

The concept of an efficient market holds serious implications for investors. In particular, it could have considerable bearing on traditional security analysis and stock valuation procedures and on the way stocks are selected for investment purposes. There are, in fact, some who contend that rather than trying to beat the market, investors should spend less time analyzing securities and more time on such matters as reducing taxes and transaction costs, eliminating unnecessary risk, and constructing a widely diversified portfolio that is compatible with the investor's risk temperament. Make no mistake about it: *Even in an efficient market, all sorts of return opportunities are available.* But to proponents of efficient markets, the only way to increase returns is to invest in a portfolio of higher-risk securities.

Implications for Technical Analysis

The most serious challenge the random walk evidence presents is to technical analysis. If price fluctuations are purely random, charts of past prices are unlikely to produce significant trading profits. In a highly efficient market, shifts in supply and demand occur so rapidly that technical indicators simply measure after-the-fact events, with no implications for the future. If markets are less than perfectly efficient, however, information may be absorbed slowly, producing gradual shifts in supply and demand conditions—and profit opportunities for those who recognize the shifts early. Although the great bulk of evidence supports a random walk, many investors follow a technical approach because they believe it improves their investment results.

Implications for Fundamental Analysis

Many strict fundamental analysts were at first pleased by the random walk attack on technical analysis. Further development of the efficient markets concept, however, was not so well received: In an efficient market, it's argued, prices react so quickly to new information that not even security analysis will enable investors to realize consistently superior returns on their investments. Because of the extreme competition among investors, security prices are seldom far above or below their justified levels, and fundamental analysis thus loses much of its value. The problem is not that fundamental analysis is poorly done; on the contrary, it is done all too well! As a result, so many investors, competing so vigorously for profit opportunities, simply eliminate the opportunities before other investors can capitalize on them.

So Who Is Right?

Some type of fundamental analysis probably has a role in the stock selection process, for even in an efficient market, there is no question that stock prices reflect a company's profit performance. Some companies are fundamentally strong and others fundamentally weak, and investors must be able to distinguish between the two. Thus some time can profitably be spent in evaluating a company and its stock to determine, not if it is undervalued, but whether it is fundamentally strong.

The level of investor return, however, is more than a function of the fundamental condition of the company; the level of risk exposure is also important. We saw earlier that fundamental analysis can help assess potential risk exposure and identify securities that possess risk commensurate with the return they offer. The extent to which the markets are efficient is still subject to considerable debate. At present, there seems to be a growing consensus that although the markets may not be *perfectly* efficient, evidence suggests that they are at least *reasonably* efficient.

In the final analysis, it is the individual investor who must decide on the merits of fundamental and technical analysis. Certainly, a large segment of the investing public believes in security analysis, even in a market that may be efficient. What is more, the principles of stock valuation—that promised return should be commensurate with exposure to risk—are valid in any type of market setting.

CONCEPTS IN REVIEW

7.16 What is the *random walk hypothesis,* and how does it apply to stocks? What is an *efficient market?* How can a market be efficient if its prices behave in a random fashion?

7.17 Explain why it is difficult, if not impossible, to outperform an efficient market consistently.

a. Does that mean that high rates of return are not available in the stock market?
b. How can an investor earn a high rate of return in an efficient market?

7.18 What are the implications of random walks and efficient markets for technical analysis? For fundamental analysis? Do random walks and efficient markets mean that technical analysis and fundamental analysis are useless? Explain.

http://hepg.aw.com

The degree of efficiency of the financial markets, especially the stock markets, will be debated for many years to come. Most of the information on the Web about efficient markets starts off "nice and easy" but quickly leads to more technical discussions. The Web page included here is one educational site that presents some interesting observations *against* the idea that the markets are efficient.

www.investorhome.com/anomaly.htm

Summary

LG 1 **Explain the role a company's future plays in the stock valuation process and develop a forecast of a stock's expected cash flow.** The final phase of security analysis involves an assessment of the investment merits of a specific company and its stock. The focus here is on formulating expectations about the company's future prospects and the potential risk and return behavior of the stock. In particular, we would like to get some idea of what the stock's future earnings, dividends, and share prices look like, because that's ultimately the basis of our return.

LG 2 **Discuss the concepts of intrinsic value and required rates of return and note how they are used.** Information such as projected sales, forecasted earnings, and estimated dividends are important in establishing the intrinsic value of a stock—which is a measure, based on expected return performance and risk exposure, of what the stock ought to be worth. A key element is the investor's required rate of return, which is used to define the amount of return that should be earned on the investment given the stock's perceived exposure to risk. The more risk in the investment, the more return one should require.

LG 3 **Determine the underlying value of a stock using the dividend valuation model, as well as other present-value-based stock valuation models.** A number of stock valuation procedures are in use today, including the dividend valuation model, which derives the value of a share of stock from the stock's future growth in dividends. Another popular valuation procedure is the dividends-and-earnings approach, which uses a finite investment horizon to derive a present-value-based "justified price." Sometimes investors find it more convenient to deal in terms of expected returns than in dollar-based justified prices; that's no problem, because it's easy to find the fully compounded rate of return by solving for the discount rate in the present-value-based stock valuation model.

LG 4 **Explain the role that the price/earnings ratio plays in defining a stock's price behavior and how the P/E multiple can be used in the stock valuation process.** The price/earnings (P/E) multiple is one of the most important determinants of stock performance and has a direct bearing on the price behavior of a share of stock: Other things being equal, as the P/E ratio moves up (or down), so does the price of the stock. It's a key variable in determining the amount of capital gains a stock is capable of producing and, as a result, has a substantial impact on defining a stock's return potential. In fact, it's the centerpiece of the so-called P/E approach, which uses a stock's price/earnings ratio to determine whether the stock is fairly valued.

LG 5 **Describe the key attributes of technical analysis, including some popular measures and procedures used to assess the market.** Technical analysis is another phase of the analytical process; it deals with the behavior of the stock market itself and the various economic forces at work in the marketplace. A number of tools can be used to assess the state of the market, including market measures like volume of trading, breadth of the market, short-interest positions, odd-lot trading, and relative price levels. In contrast, other investors like to use charting to assess the condition of everything from the overall market to specific stocks.

LG 6 **Discuss the idea of random walks and efficient markets and note the challenges these theories hold for the stock valuation process.** In recent years, the whole notion of both technical and fundamental analysis has been seriously challenged by the random walk and efficient market hypotheses. Indeed, considerable evidence indicates that stock prices do move in a random fashion. The efficient market hypothesis is an attempt to explain *why* prices behave randomly. The idea behind an efficient market is that available information about the company and/or its stock is always fully reflected in the price of securities, so investors should *not* expect to outperform the market consistently.

Discussion Questions

LG 1 LG 2 LG 3

Q7.1. Using the resources available at your campus or public library, select a company from *Value Line* that would be of interest to you. (*Hint:* Pick a company that's been publicly traded for at least 10 to 15 years, and avoid public utilities, banks, and other financial institutions.) Obtain a copy of the latest *Value Line* report on your chosen company. Using the historical and forecasted data reported in *Value Line,* along with one of the valuation techniques described in this chapter, calculate the maximum (i.e., justified) price you'd be willing to pay for this stock. Use the CAPM to find the required rate of return on your stock. (For the purposes of this problem, use a market rate of return of 12%, and for the risk-free rate, use the latest 3-month Treasury bill rate.)

a. How does the justified price you computed above compare to the latest market price of the stock?
b. Would you consider the stock you've valued to be a worthwhile investment candidate? Explain.

LG 5 Q7.2. Briefly define each of the following, and note the conditions that would suggest the market is technically strong.

a. Breadth of the market
b. Short interest
c. The market's price-to-book ratio
d. Theory of contrary opinion
e. Head and shoulders

LG 6 Q7.3. A lot has been written and said about the concept of an *efficient market*. Although you may or may not believe the markets are efficient, it's probably safe to say that there are some of your classmates who believe the markets may be efficient and others who believe they are not. Let's have a debate to see whether we can resolve this issue (at least among ourselves). Pick a side, either for or against efficient markets, and then develop your "ammunition." Be prepared to discuss these three aspects:

a. Exactly what is an efficient market, and do such markets really exist?
b. Are stock prices always (or nearly always) correctly set in the market? If so, does that mean there's little opportunity to find undervalued stocks?
c. Can you find any reason(s) to use fundamental and/or technical analysis in your stock selection process? If not, how would you go about selecting stocks?

Problems

LG 1 P7.1. An investor estimates that next year's sales for Gilt Edge Products should amount to about $75 million. The company has 2.5 million shares outstanding, generates a net profit margin of about 5%, and has a payout ratio of 50%. All figures are expected to hold for next year. Given this information, compute

a. Estimated net earnings for next year
b. Next year's dividends per share
c. The expected price of the stock (assuming the P/E ratio is 12.5 times earnings)
d. The expected holding period return (latest stock price: $15/share)

LG 2 P7.2. Charlene Lewis is thinking about buying some shares of Education, Inc., at $50 per share. She expects the price of the stock to rise to $75 over the next 3 years, during which time she also expects to receive annual dividends of $5 per share.

a. What is the intrinsic worth of this stock, given a 10% required rate of return?
b. What is its expected return?

LG 3 P7.3. Amalgamated Something-or-Other, Inc., is expected to pay a dividend of $1.50 in the coming year. The required rate of return is 16%, and dividends are expected to grow at 7% per year. Using the dividend valuation model, find the intrinsic value of the company's common shares.

LG 3 P7.4. Assume you've generated the following information about the stock of Bufford's Burger Barns: The company's latest dividends of $4 a share are expected to grow to $4.32 next year, to $4.67 the year after that, and to $5.04 in year 3. In addition, the price of the stock is expected to rise to $77.75 in 3 years.

a. Use the dividends-and-earnings model and a required rate of return of 15% to find the value of the stock.
b. Use the IRR procedure to find the stock's expected return.

c. Given that dividends are expected to grow indefinitely at 8%, use a 15% required rate of return and the dividend valuation model to find the value of the stock.

d. Assume dividends in year 3 actually amount to \$5.04, the dividend growth rate stays at 8%, and the required rate of return stays at 15%. Use the dividend valuation model to find the price of the stock at the end of year 3. [*Hint:* In this case, the value of the stock will depend on dividends in year 4, which equal $D_3 \times (1 + g)$.] Do you note any similarity between your answer here and the forecasted price of the stock (\$77.75) given in the problem? Explain.

LG 3

P7.5. Let's assume that you're thinking about buying some stock in U.S. Electronics. So far in your analysis, you've uncovered the following information: The stock pays annual dividends of \$2.50 a share (and that's not expected to change within the next few years—*nor are any of the other variables*); it trades at a P/E of 12 times earnings and has a beta of 1.15; in addition, you plan on using a risk-free rate of 7% in the CAPM, along with a market return of 14%. You would like to hold the stock for 3 years, at the end of which time you think EPS will peak out at about \$7 a share. Given that the stock currently trades at \$55, use the IRR approach to find this security's expected return. Now use the present-value (dividends-and-earnings) model to put a price on this stock. Does this look like a good investment to you? Explain.

LG 3

P7.6. The price of Consolidated Everything is now \$75, and the company pays no dividends. Ms. Bossard expects the price 3 years from now to be \$100 per share. Should Ms. B. buy Consolidated E. if she desires a 10% rate of return? Explain.

LG 3

P7.7. This year, Southwest Light and Gas (SWL&G) paid its stockholders an annual dividend of \$3 a share. A major brokerage firm recently put out a report on SWL&G stating that, in its opinion, the company's annual dividends should grow at the rate of 10% per year for each of the next 5 years and then level off and grow at the rate of 6% a year thereafter.

a. Use the variable-growth DVM and a required rate of return of 12% to find the maximum price you should be willing to pay for this stock.

b. Redo the SWL&G problem in part (a), except this time assume that after year 5, dividends stop growing altogether (for year 6 and beyond, $g = 0$). Use all the other information given to find the stock's intrinsic value.

c. Contrast your two answers and comment on your findings. How important is growth to this valuation model?

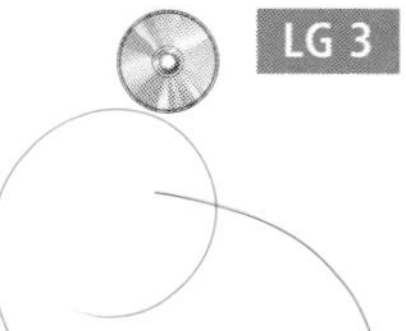
LG 3

P7.8. Assume there are three companies that in the past year paid exactly the same annual dividend of \$2.25 a share. In addition, the future annual rate of growth in dividends for each of the three companies has been estimated as follows:

Buggies-Are-Us	Steady Freddie, Inc.	Gang Buster Group	
$g = 0\%$	$g = 6\%$	Year 1	\$2.53
(i.e., dividends	(for the	2	\$2.85
are expected	foreseeable	3	\$3.20
to remain at	future)	4	\$3.60
\$2.25/share)		Year 5 and beyond: $g = 6\%$	

Assume also that as the result of a strange set of circumstances, these three companies all have the same required rate of return ($k = 10\%$).

a. Use the appropriate DVM to value each of these companies.

b. Comment briefly on the comparative values of these three companies. What is the major cause of the differences among these three valuations?

 LG 3

P7.9. Fast-Buck Company's stock sells at a P/E ratio of 14 times earnings; it is expected to pay dividends of $2 per share in each of the next 5 years and to generate an EPS of $5 per share in year 5. Using the dividends-and-earnings model and a 12% discount rate, compute the stock's justified price.

 LG 3

P7.10. A particular company currently has sales of $250 million; these are expected to grow by 20% next year (year 1). For the year after next (year 2), the growth rate in sales is expected to equal 10%. Over each of the next 2 years, the company is expected to have a net profit margin of 8%, to have a payout ratio of 50%, and to maintain the number of shares of common stock outstanding at 15 million shares. The stock always trades at a P/E ratio of 15 times earnings, and the investor has a required rate of return of 20%. Given this information:

a. Find the stock's intrinsic value (its justified price).
b. Use the IRR approach to determine the stock's expected return, given that it is currently trading at $15 per share.
c. Find the holding period returns for this stock for year 1 and for year 2.

 LG 2  LG 3

P7.11. Assume a major investment service has just given Oasis Electronics its highest investment rating, along with a strong buy recommendation. As a result, you decide to take a look for yourself and to place a value on the company's stock. Here's what you find: This year, Oasis paid its stockholders an annual dividend of $3 a share, but because of its high rate of growth in earnings, its dividends are expected to grow at the rate of 12% a year for the next 4 years and then to level out at 9% a year. So far, you've learned that the stock has a beta of 1.80, the risk-free rate of return is 6%, and the expected return on the market is 11%. Using the CAPM to find the required rate of return, put a value on this stock.

  LG 3

P7.12. Consolidated Software doesn't currently pay any dividends but is expected to start paying dividends in 4 years. That is, Consolidated will go 3 more years without paying any dividends, and then it's expected to pay its first dividend (of $3 per share) in the fourth year. Once the company starts paying dividends, it's expected to continue to do so. The company is expected to have a dividend payout ratio of 40% and to maintain a return on equity of 20%. Given a required rate of return of 15%, what is the maximum price you should be willing to pay for this stock today?

  LG 3

P7.13. Assume you obtain the following information about a certain company:

Total assets	$50,000,000
Total equity	$25,000,000
Net income	$ 3,750,000
EPS	$5.00 per share
Dividend payout ratio	40%
Required return	12%

Use the constant-growth DVM to place a value on this company's stock.

 LG 4

P7.14. You're thinking about buying some stock in Astro Corporation and want to use the P/E approach to value the shares. So far, you've estimated that next year's earnings should come in at about $4.00 a share and that the company should pay dividends of $2.40 a share next year. The company has been experiencing growth in earnings (and dividends) of about 6% per year, and this is expected to hold for the foreseeable future.

a. Given that you feel a 12% required rate of return is appropriate for this security, what's the maximum price you should be willing to pay for the stock?
b. Given the information supplied above, if this stock is currently trading at $48 a share, what is its P_0/E_1 ratio? Given a 12% required rate of return and

a 60% payout ratio, what growth rate is embedded in this P_0/E_1 ratio? Do you think that growth rate is reasonable, given the past growth rates noted in the problem? Explain.

LG 4

P7.15. AviBank Plastics has an ROE of 16%, its book value per share *next year* is expected to rise to $20 per share, it has a dividend payout ratio of 40% (which is expected to hold in the future), and the stock has a 12% required rate of return. Use the P/E approach to set a value on this stock.

Case Problem 7.1 Chris Looks for a Way to Invest His Newfound Wealth

LG 1

Chris Norton is a young Hollywood writer who is well on his way to television superstardom. After writing several successful television specials, he was recently named the head writer for one of TV's top-rated sitcoms. Chris fully realizes that his business is a fickle one and, on the advice of his dad and manager, has decided to set up an investment program. Chris will earn about a half-million dollars this year. Because of his age, income level, and desire to get as big a bang as possible from his investment dollars, he has decided to invest in speculative, high-growth stocks.

Chris is currently working with a respected Beverly Hills broker and is in the process of building up a diversified portfolio of speculative stocks. The broker recently sent him information on a hot new issue. She advised Chris to study the numbers and, if he likes them, to buy as many as 1,000 shares of the stock. Among other things, corporate sales for the next 3 years have been forecasted to be as follows:

Year	Sales (in millions)
1	$22.5
2	35.0
3	50.0

The firm has 1.2 million shares of common stock outstanding (they are currently being traded at 62½ and pay no dividends). It has been running a phenomenal net profit rate of 20%, and its stock has been trading at a P/E ratio of around 25 times earnings (which is a bit on the high side, even for a stock like this). All these operating characteristics are expected to hold in the future.

QUESTIONS

a. Looking first at the stock:
   1. Compute the company's net profits and EPS for each of the next 3 years.
   2. Compute the price of the stock 3 years from now.
   3. Assuming that all expectations hold up and that Chris buys the stock at 62½, determine his expected return on this investment.
   4. What risks is he facing by buying this stock? Be specific.
   5. Should he consider the stock a worthwhile investment candidate? Explain.

b. Now, looking at Chris's investment program in general:
   1. What do you think of his investment program? What do you see as its strengths and weaknesses?
   2. Are there any suggestions you would make?
   3. Do you think Chris should consider adding foreign stocks to his portfolio? Explain.

Case Problem 7.2 *An Analysis of a High-Flying Stock*

LG 3 LG 5

Glenn Wilt is a recent university graduate and a security analyst with the Kansas City brokerage firm of Lippman, Brickbats, and Shaft. Wilt has been following one of the hottest issues on Wall Street, C&I Construction Supplies, a company that has turned in an outstanding performance lately and, even more important, has exhibited excellent growth potential. It has 5 million shares outstanding and pays a nominal annual dividend of 25 cents per share. Wilt has decided to take a closer look at C&I to see whether it still has any investment play left. Assume the company's sales for the past 5 years have been as follows:

Year	Sales (in millions)
1994	$10.0
1995	12.5
1996	16.2
1997	22.0
1998	28.5

Wilt is concerned with the future prospects of the company, not its past. As a result, he pores over the numbers and generates the following estimates of future performance:

Expected net profit margin	12%
Estimated annual dividends per share	25¢
Number of common shares outstanding	No change
P/E ratio at the end of 1999	35
P/E ratio at the end of 2000	50

QUESTIONS

a. Determine the average annual rate of growth in sales over the past 5 years.

1. Use this average growth rate to forecast revenues for next year (1999) and the year after that (2000).
2. Now determine the company's net earnings and EPS for each of the next 2 years (1999 and 2000).
3. Finally, determine the expected future price of the stock at the end of this 2-year period.

b. Because of several intrinsic and market factors, Wilt feels that 20% is a viable figure to use for a desired rate of return.

1. Using the 20% rate of return and the forecasted figures you came up with in question a, compute the stock's justified price.
2. If C&I is currently trading at $25 per share, should Wilt consider the stock a worthwhile investment candidate? Explain.

c. The stock is actively traded on the AMEX and enjoys considerable market interest. Recent closing prices follow.

1. Prepare a point-and-figure chart of these prices (use a 1-point system—that is, make each box worth $1).
2. Discuss how these and similar charts are used by technical analysts.
3. Cite several other types of technical measures, and note how they might be used in the analysis of this stock.

Recent Price Behavior: C&I Construction Supplies			
14 (8/15/98)	18½	20	17½
14¼	17½	20¼	18½
14⅞	17½	20¼	19¾
15½	17¼	20⅛	19½
16	17	20	19¼
16	16¾	20¼	20
16½	16½	20½	20⅞
17	16½	20¾	21
17¼	16⅛	20	21¾
17½	16¾	20	22½
18	17⅛	20¼	23¼
18 (9/30/98)	17¼	20	24
18½	17¼	19½	24¼
18½	17¼ (10/31/98)	19¼	24⅛
18¾	17¾	18¼ (11/30/98)	24¾
19	18¼	17½	25
19⅛	19¼	16¾	25½
18⅞	20½	17	25½ (12/31/98)

Home Page Exercises

http://hepg.aw.com **Keyword: Invest**

Much analysis is devoted to the study of the market. Even more analysis is performed for each security traded on the market. Investors in individual stocks expect the total return on the stock to meet or exceed their required return. Forming expectations for total return requires the investor to derive some estimate of future cash flows. These cash flows include both dividend income and capital gains from price appreciation. Information on both dividends and earnings is needed to derive an intrinsic value. Investors can benefit from the work done by investment specialists. As the sites listed here demonstrate, a great deal of information from investment specialists is readily available on the World Wide Web.

Web Address	*Primary Investment Focus*
www.businessweek.com	Market indexes and charts
www.libertyresearch.com	Technical charts of the 30 DJIA stocks
www.viwes.com/invest/shorts/top20/index.html	Tables of short interest on common stocks
www.timely.com	Quotes and technical charts on indexes and companies

W7.1. Forecasting earnings per share often involves subjective assumptions about future performance. A detailed analysis of past performance can be time-consuming at best and limited at worst. Estimates of future earnings per share, calculated by investment experts who have access to the most current and relevant financial information, are available on the Web for most publicly traded corporations. Look at the the Web site listed here and use information you find there to answer the following questions.

www.e-analytics.com

Select *Weekly earnings announcements.*

Input ticker symbol DOL.

Select *Equity.*

a. What are the earnings estimates for Dole Foods? List the earnings estimates for (1) the current fiscal year and (2) the next fiscal year.

b. Also calculate the firm's P/E ratio using each of the earnings estimates.
c. Compare these P/E ratios with the current P/E found in the *Wall Street Journal.*

W7.2. Many investors and theorists believe that market movement is the most important predictor of a security's future price. Various market indexes are typically used to approximate market return. Using information found at the Web site here, list the current market level, the last change, and the last update for the following major market indexes: (a) Dow Jones Industrial Average, (b) Nasdaq Composite, (c) S&P 500, and (d) Russell 2000.

www.cnnfn.com
Select *Markets.*
Select *US Stockmarkets.*

W7.3. This chapter presented various dividend valuation models. Which model is the best predictor of a particular company's common stock price depends on which model's assumptions most closely match the characteristics of the company. At the Web site listed here, find historical dividend information for Sara Lee Corporation, and use it to do the analysis that follows.

www.saralee.com/financial/stock/t1.htm

a. Calculate the historical growth rate in dividends from 1992 through 1997.
b. Use this growth rate in the constant growth dividend valuation model to calculate the intrinsic value of Sara Lee's common stock. For the required return, use 13%.
c. Compare the results of this model with the actual price of Sara Lee's common stock. Does the constant growth model appear to be an appropriate valuation model for Sara Lee stock? Discuss your answer.

Part Three

Investing in Fixed-Income Securities

CHAPTER 8 BOND INVESTMENTS

LEARNING GOALS

After studying this chapter, you should be able to:

LG 1 Explain the basic investment attributes of bonds and the appeal they hold as investment vehicles.

LG 2 Describe the essential features of a bond and distinguish among different types of call, refunding, and sinking-fund provisions.

LG 3 Describe the relationship between bond prices and yields, and explain why some bonds are more volatile than others.

LG 4 Identify the different types of bonds and the kinds of investment objectives these fixed-income securities can fulfill.

LG 5 Discuss the global nature of the bond market and the difference between dollar-denominated and non-dollar-denominated foreign bonds.

LG 6 Describe the role that bond ratings play in the market and the quotation system used with various types of bonds.

Mobil

The oil industry is one of the world's most capital-intensive businesses, requiring billions of dollars worth of equipment for exploration and production of natural resources. One of the largest oil companies is Mobil, which searches for oil and natural gas throughout the world. Much of Mobil's equipment is financed through the issuance of long-term bonds. Mobil's 1996 annual report indicates that the company has outstanding long-term debt of $4.45 billion. The company lists about 20 different debt issues that is has in place throughout the world.

Because Mobil is such a strong company, investors in its bonds are fairly confident that the debt will be paid. Mobil, of course, must pay investors interest on these bonds, but because it has a strong credit rating, it doesn't have to pay as high an interest rate as some other companies.

As you'll see in this chapter, investors in bonds such as Mobil's have to consider credit quality, interest rates, length of maturity, and other factors when deciding whether to invest in these securities.

Why Invest in Bonds

LG 1

bonds
publicly traded long-term debt securities, whereby the issuer agrees to pay a fixed amount of interest over a specified period of time and to repay a fixed amount of principal at maturity.

For many years, bonds were viewed as rather dull investments that produced current income and little else. No longer is this true; instead, bonds today are viewed as highly competitive investment vehicles that offer the potential for attractive returns. **Bonds** are publicly traded, long-term debt securities; they are issued in convenient denominations and by a variety of borrowing organizations, including the U.S. Treasury, various agencies of the U.S. government, state and local governments, and corporations. Bonds are often referred to as *fixed-income securities* because the debt-service obligations of the issuers are fixed. That is, the issuing organization agrees to pay a fixed amount of interest periodically and to repay a fixed amount of principal at maturity.

Like any other type of investment vehicle, bonds provide investors with two kinds of income: (1) They provide a generous amount of current income, and (2) they can often be used to generate substantial amounts of capital gains. The current income, of course, is derived from the interest payments received over the life of the issue. Capital gains, in contrast, are earned whenever market interest rates fall. A basic trading rule in the bond market is that *interest rates and bond prices move in opposite directions.* When interest rates rise, bond prices fall, and when rates drop, bond prices move up. Thus it is possible to buy bonds at one price and to sell them later at a higher price. Of course, it is also possible to incur a capital loss, should market rates move against you. Taken together, the current income and capital gains earned from bonds can lead to attractive investor returns.

Bonds are also a versatile investment outlet. They can be used conservatively by those who primarily (or exclusively) seek high current income, or they can be used aggressively by those who go after capital gains. Although bonds have long been considered attractive investments for those seeking current income, it is only since the advent of volatile interest rates that they have also been recognized as outstanding trading vehicles. Investors found that, given the relation of bond prices to interest rates, the number of profitable trading opportunities increased substantially as wider and more frequent swings in interest rates began to occur.

In addition, certain types of bonds can be used for tax shelter: Municipal obligations are perhaps the best known in this regard, but as we'll see later in this chapter, Treasury and certain federal agency issues also offer some tax advantages. Finally, because of the general high quality of many bond issues, they can also be used for the preservation and long-term accumulation of capital. With quality issues, not only do investors have a high degree of assurance that they'll get their money back at maturity, but the stream of interest income is also highly dependable.

Putting Bond Market Performance in Perspective

The bond market is driven by interest rates. In fact, *the behavior of interest rates is the single most important force in the bond market.* These rates determine not only the amount of current income investors will make but also the amount of capital gains (or losses) bondholders will incur. It's not surprising, therefore, that bond market participants follow interest rates closely and that bond market performance is generally portrayed in terms of market interest rates.

Figure 8.1 provides a look at bond interest rates over the 36-year period from 1961 to 1997. It shows that from a state of relative stability, interest

FIGURE 8.1
The Behavior of Interest Rates Over Time—1961–1997*

From an era of relative stability, bond interest rates rose dramatically and became far more volatile. The net result was that bond yields not only became highly competitive with the returns offered by other securities, but also provided investors with attractive capital gains opportunities. (1997 yields through the third quarter: September 1997.)

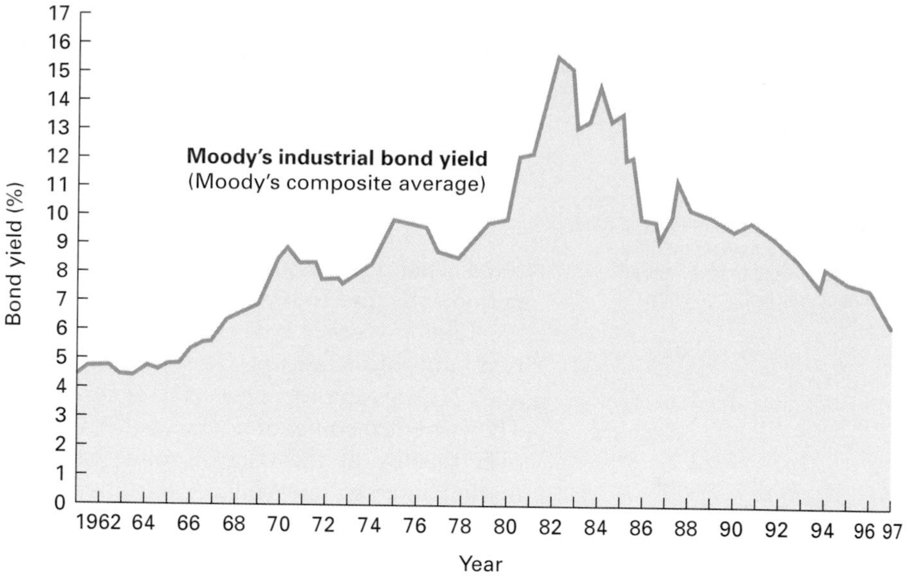

rates took off in the latter half of the 1960s, and over the course of the next 15 years, the rates paid on high-grade bonds almost tripled. Indeed, interest rates rose from the 4% to 5% range in the early 1960s to over 16% by 1982. But then rates dropped sharply, and by 1986 they were back to the single-digit range once again. Thus, after a protracted bear market, bonds abruptly reversed course, and the strongest bull market on record occurred from 1982 to early 1987 (the bond market is considered *bearish* when market interest rates are high or rising, *bullish* when rates are low or falling). Even though interest rates did move back up for a short time in 1987–1988, they quickly retreated, and by 1993 interest rates were down to a level not seen in over a quarter-century! In fact, by 1993 short-term securities, like Treasury bills and bank certificates of deposit, were yielding *less than 3%*, and long Treasury bonds were down to *under* 6%. Unfortunately, rates bottomed out in late 1993 and rose sharply in 1994, as the economy started to move into high gear. But even that didn't last long, as interest rates once again headed down: By the end of the third quarter of 1997, they were under 6½% and still falling.

As with stocks, *total returns* in the bond market are made up of current income and capital gains (or losses). Not surprisingly, because rising rates mean falling prices, the drawn-out bear market in bonds meant depressing returns for bondholders. For investors just entering the market, the higher market yields were welcomed, because they meant higher levels of interest income. *But for those already holding bonds,* the implications were much different, as returns fell way *below* expectations and, in many cases, resulted in outright losses.

Table 8.1 shows year-end market yields and total annual returns for high-grade corporate bonds for the 36-year period from 1961 through 1997. Note how bond returns started to slip in 1965, as market yields began to climb; in fact, from 1965 to 1981, there were no fewer than 8 years when average returns were negative. In contrast, look what happened over the 15-year period from 1982 through 1997 (third quarter), when rates were in a general

TABLE 8.1 Historical Annual Yields and Returns in the Bond Market: 1961–1997
(Yields and returns based on performance of high-grade corporate bonds)

Year	Year-End Bond Yields*	Total Rates of Return**	Year	Year-End Bond Yields*	Total Rates of Return**
1997*	7.16%	11.62%	1978	9.32%	−0.07%
1996	7.43	1.40	1977	8.50	1.71
1995	6.86	27.20	1976	8.14	18.65
1994	8.64	−5.76	1975	8.97	14.64
1993	7.31	13.19	1974	8.89	−3.06
1992	8.34	9.39	1973	7.79	1.14
1991	8.58	19.91	1972	7.41	7.26
1990	9.61	6.86	1971	6.48	11.01
1989	9.18	16.23	1970	6.85	18.37
1988	9.81	10.70	1969	7.83	−8.09
1987	10.33	−0.27	1968	6.62	2.57
1986	9.02	19.85	1967	6.30	−4.95
1985	10.63	30.90	1966	5.55	0.20
1984	12.05	16.39	1965	4.79	−0.46
1983	12.76	4.70	1964	4.46	4.77
1982	11.55	43.80	1963	4.46	2.19
1981	14.98	−0.96	1962	4.34	7.95
1980	13.15	−2.62	1961	4.56	4.82
1979	10.87	−4.18			

*Year-end bond yields are for (S&P) AA-rated corporate (industrial and utility) bonds; 1997 yields and returns through third quarter (September) 1997.

**Total return figures are based on interest income as well as capital gains (or losses).

Sources: Annual yields derived from Standard & Poor's S&P *Trade and Security Statistics;* total return figures from Ibbotson and Sinquefield, *Stocks, Bonds, Bills, and Inflation: Historical Returns (1926–1997).*

state of decline: We had only 2 years of negative returns (in 1987 and again in 1994), whereas double-digit returns (of 10.7% to 43.8%) occurred in no fewer than 10 of the 15 years. Clearly, the 1982–1997 period was not a bad time to be in bonds.

To see how market yields and bond returns interact over time, compare the bond yield and bond return columns in Table 8.1. Note that when yields go one way, returns go the other. For example, in 1980, market yields went way up, but total returns fell to −2.62%. In contrast, 2 years later, in 1982, it was market yields that plunged, and total returns were a whopping 43.8%—a standard of performance that holds up well even against stocks.

Table 8.2 contains return performance over various holding periods of 5 to 36 years. These figures demonstrate the type of long-term returns possible from bonds and show that *average annual returns of around 8% to 10% on high-grade issues are not out of the question.* Although such performance may lag behind that of stocks (which it should, in light of the reduced exposure to risk), it really isn't bad. The big question facing bond investors, however, is what kind of returns they will be able to produce over the next 10 to 12 years. The 1980s and early 1990s were very good for bond investors. But that market was driven by falling interest rates, which in turn produced hefty capital gains and outsize returns. Whether or not market interest rates will (or even can) continue on that path is doubtful. Most market observers, in fact, caution against expecting abnormally high (double-digit) rates of return over the next 10 or so years. Indeed, some market pros even go so far as to

TABLE 8.2 Holding Period Returns in the Bond Market: 1961–1997*

		Average Annual Returns*	Cumulative Total Returns	Amount to Which a $10,000 Investment Will Grow over Holding Period
5 years:	1993–97*	9.5%	53.6%	$ 15,357.20
10 years:	1988–97*	11.0	176.9	27,695.88
15 years:	1983–97*	11.9	428.1	52,808.32
25 years:	1973–97*	9.5	845.2	94,520.93
36 years:	1961–97*	7.8	1,342.4	144,239.65
The 1960s:	1960–69	1.7	18.1	11,809.13
The 1970s:	1970–79	6.2	83.1	18,305.73
The 1980s:	1980–89	13.0	240.2	34,022.87
The 1990s:	1990–97*	10.4	115.3	21,526.72

*Average annual return figures are fully compounded returns and are based on interest income as well as capital gains (or losses); all 1997 data through third quarter (September) 1997.

Sources: Annual yields derived from Standard & Poor's S&P *Trade and Security Statistics;* total return figures from Ibbotson and Sinquefield, *Stocks, Bonds, and Inflation: Historical Returns (1926–1997).*

question whether bonds should have *any place at all* in an investment portfolio. They reason that if interest rates have bottomed out, then bonds won't have much to offer investors (other than relatively low returns). But that view ignores one of the key roles of bonds: *the element of stability they introduce to a portfolio.* Besides, what's so bad about generating fully compounded returns of 8% or 9%, over extended periods of time, from a traditionally low-risk investment vehicle?

Exposure to Risk

Like any other type of investment vehicle, fixed-income securities should be viewed in terms of their risk and return. Generally speaking, bonds are exposed to five major types of risks: interest rate risk, purchasing power risk, business/financial risk, liquidity risk, and call risk.

- **Interest Rate Risk.** Interest rate risk is the number one source of risk to fixed-income investors, because *it's the major cause of price volatility in the bond market.* In the case of bonds, interest rate risk translates into market risk: The behavior of interest rates, in general, affects *all* bonds and cuts across *all* sectors of the market—even the U.S. Treasury market. When market interest rates rise, bond prices fall, and vice versa. And as interest rates become more volatile, so do bond prices.

- **Purchasing Power Risk.** Purchasing power risk accompanies inflation. During periods of mild inflation, bonds do pretty well, because their returns tend to outstrip inflation rates. Purchasing power risk really heats up when inflation takes off, the way it did in the late 1970s; when that happens, bond yields start to lag behind inflation rates. The reason: You have a fixed coupon rate on your bond, so even though market yields are rising with inflation, your return is locked in for the long haul.

• **Business/Financial Risk.** This is basically the risk that the *issuer will default on interest and/or principal payments*. Also known as *credit risk*, business/financial risk has to do with the quality and financial integrity of the issuer; the stronger the issuer, the less business/financial risk there is to worry about. This risk doesn't even exist for some securities (e.g., U.S. Treasuries), whereas for others (corporate and municipal bonds), it's a very important consideration.

• **Liquidity Risk.** Liquidity risk is the risk that a bond will be difficult to unload if you want or have to sell it. In certain sectors of the market, this is a far bigger problem than a lot of investors realize. For even though the U.S. bond market is enormous, the market is chiefly over-the-counter in nature, and much of the activity occurs in the primary/new-issue market. Therefore, with the exception of the Treasury market and a good deal of the agency market, relatively little trading is done in the secondary markets, particularly with corporates and municipals.

• **Call Risk.** Call risk, or *prepayment risk*, is the risk that a bond will be "called"—that is, retired—long before its scheduled maturity date. Issuers are often given the opportunity to prepay their bonds, and they do so by calling them in for prepayment. (We'll examine call features later in this chapter.) When issuers call their bonds, the bondholders end up getting cashed out of the deal and have to find another place for their investment funds—and there's the problem. Because bonds are nearly always called for prepayment after interest rates have taken a big fall, comparable investment vehicles just aren't available. Thus the investor has to replace a high-yielding bond with a much lower-yielding issue. Being able to prepay a bond might be great for the issuer, but from the bondholder's perspective, a called bond means not only a disruption in the investor's cash flow but also a sharply reduced rate of return.

CONCEPTS IN REVIEW

8.1 What appeal do bonds hold for individual investors? Give several reasons why bonds make attractive investment outlets.

8.2 How would you describe the behavior of market interest rates and bond returns over the last 30–35 years? Do swings in market interest rates have any bearing on bond returns? Explain.

8.3 Identify and briefly describe the five types of risk to which bonds are exposed. What is the most important source of risk for bonds in general? Explain.

http://hepg.aw.com

Bonds, like any investment asset, have their own risk and return features. Just about every investor needs to carry bonds in his or her portfolio at one time or another. *SmartMoney* has a primer that discusses the risks and returns associated with investing in bonds.

www.smartmoney.com/si/tools/onebond

Essential Features of a Bond

LG 2 LG 3

A *bond* is a negotiable, long-term debt instrument that carries certain obligations (including the payment of interest and the repayment of principal) on the part of the issuer. Because bondholders, unlike the holders of common stock, are only lending money to the issuer, they are not entitled to an ownership position or to any of the rights and privileges that go along with it. But bondholders (as well as bond issuers) do have a number of well-defined rights and privileges that together help define the essential features of a bond. We'll now take a look at some of these more important features. As you will see, when it comes to bonds, it's especially important to know what you're getting into; *many seemingly insignificant features (like a bond's coupon or maturity) can have dramatic effects on its price behavior and investment return.*

Bond Interest and Principal

coupon
feature on a bond that defines the amount of annual interest income.

principal
on a bond, the amount of capital that must be paid at maturity.

In the absence of any trading, a bond investor's return is limited to fixed interest and principal payments. That's because bonds involve a fixed claim on the issuer's income (as defined by the size of the periodic interest payments) and a fixed claim on the assets of the issuer (equal to the repayment of principal at maturity). As a rule, bonds pay interest every 6 months. There are exceptions, however; some issues carry interest payment intervals as short as a month, and a few as long as a year. The amount of interest due is a function of the **coupon,** which defines the annual interest income that will be paid by the issuer to the bondholder. For instance, a $1,000 bond with an 8% coupon pays $80 in interest annually—generally in the form of two $40 semiannual payments. The **principal** amount of a bond, also known as an issue's *par value,* specifies the amount of capital that must be repaid at maturity. For example, there is $1,000 of principal in a $1,000 bond.

Of course, debt securities regularly trade at market prices that differ from their principal (or par) values. This occurs whenever an issue's coupon differs from the prevailing market rate of interest. That is, the price of the issue changes inversely with interest rates until its yield is compatible with the prevailing market yield. Such behavior explains why a 7% issue carries a market price of only $825 in a 9% market. The drop in price from its par value of $1,000 is necessary to raise the yield on this bond from 7% to 9%. In essence, the new, higher yield is produced in part from annual coupons and in part from capital gains, as the price of the issue moves from $825 back to $1,000 at maturity.

Maturity Date

maturity date
the date on which a bond matures and the principal must be repaid.

Unlike common stock, all debt securities have limited lives and will expire on a given date in the future, the issue's **maturity date.** Although a bond carries a series of specific interest payment dates, the principal is repaid only once: on or before maturity. Because the maturity date is fixed (and never changes), it not only defines the life of a new issue but also denotes the amount of time remaining for older, outstanding bonds. Such a life span is known as an issue's *term to maturity.* For example, a new issue may come out as a 25-year bond, but 5 years later, it will have only 20 years remaining to maturity.

term bond
a bond that has a single, fairly lengthy maturity date.

serial bond
a bond that has a series of different maturity dates.

note
a debt security originally issued with a maturity of 2 to 10 years.

Two types of bonds can be distinguished on the basis of maturity: term and serial issues. A **term bond** has a single, fairly lengthy maturity date and is the most common type of issue. A **serial bond** has a series of different maturity dates, perhaps as many as 15 or 20, within a single issue. For example, a 20-year term bond issued in 1995 has a single maturity date of 2015, but that same issue as a serial bond might have 20 annual maturity dates that extend from 1996 through 2015. At each of these annual maturity dates, a certain portion of the issue would come due and be paid off. Maturity is also used to distinguish a *note* from a *bond*. That is, a debt security that's originally issued with a maturity of 2 to 10 years is known as a **note,** whereas a *bond* technically has an initial term to maturity of more than 10 years. In practice, notes are often issued with maturities of 5 to 7 years, whereas bonds normally carry maturities of 20 to 30 years or more.

Call Features—Let the Buyer Beware!

call feature
feature that specifies whether and under what conditions the issuer can retire a bond prior to maturity.

Consider the following situation: You've just made an investment in a high-yielding, 25-year bond. Now all you have to do is sit back and let the cash flow in, right? Well, perhaps. Certainly, that will happen for the first several years. However, if market interest rates drop, it's also likely that you'll receive a notice from the issuer that the bond is being *called*. This means that the issue is being retired before its maturity date. There's really nothing you can do but turn in the bond and invest your money elsewhere. It's all perfectly legal because every bond is issued with a **call feature,** which stipulates whether and under what conditions a bond can be called in for retirement prior to maturity.

Basically, there are three types of call features:

1. A bond can be *freely callable,* which means that the issuer can prematurely retire the bond at any time.
2. A bond can be *noncallable,* which means that the issuer is prohibited from retiring the bond prior to maturity.
3. The issue could carry a *deferred call,* which means that the issue cannot be called until after a certain length of time has passed from the date of issue. In essence, the issue is noncallable during the deferment period and then becomes freely callable thereafter.

Obviously, in our illustration above, either the high-yielding bond was issued as a freely callable security or it became freely callable with the end of its call deferment period.

Call features are placed on bonds *for the benefit of the issuers.* They're used most often to replace an issue with one that carries a lower coupon, and the issuer benefits by realizing a reduction in annual interest cost. Thus, when market interest rates undergo a sharp decline, as they did in 1982–1986 and again in 1991–1993, bond issuers retire their high-yielding bonds (by calling them in) and replace them with lower-yielding obligations. *The net result is that the investor is left with a much lower rate of return than anticipated.*

call premium
the amount added to a bond's par value and paid to investors when a bond is retired prematurely.

call price
the price the issuer must pay to retire a bond prematurely; equal to par value plus the call premium.

In a halfhearted attempt to compensate investors who find their bonds called out from under them, a **call premium** is tacked onto a bond and paid to investors, along with the issue's par value, at the time the bond is called. The sum of the par value plus call premium represents the issue's **call price,** which is the amount the issuer must pay to retire the bond prematurely. As a general rule, call premiums usually equal about 8 to 12 months' interest at the earliest date of call and then become systematically smaller as the issue nears maturity. Using this rule, the initial call price of a 9% bond could be as high as $1,090, where $90 represents the call premium.

refunding provisions
provisions that prohibit the premature retirement of an issue from the proceeds of a lower-coupon refunding bond.

In addition to call features, some bonds may also carry **refunding provisions,** which are much like call features except that they prohibit just one thing: the premature retirement of an issue from the proceeds of a lower-coupon refunding bond. For example, a bond could come out as freely callable but *nonrefundable* for 5 years; in this case, the bond would probably be sold by brokers as a *deferred refunding issue,* with little or nothing said about its call feature. The distinction is important, however; it means that a nonrefunding or deferred refunding issue *can still be called and prematurely retired for any reason other than refunding.* Thus, an investor could face a call on a high-yielding (nonrefundable) issue if the issuer has the cash to retire the bond prematurely.

Sinking Funds

sinking fund
a provision that stipulates the amount of principal that will be retired annually over the life of a bond.

Another provision that's important to investors is the **sinking fund,** which stipulates how a bond will be paid off over time. This provision applies only to term bonds, of course, because serial issues already have a predetermined method of repayment. Not all (term) bonds have sinking-fund requirements, but for those that do, a sinking fund specifies the annual repayment schedule that will be used to pay off the issue; it indicates how much principal will be retired each year. Sinking-fund requirements generally begin 1 to 5 years after the date of issue and continue annually thereafter until all or most of the issue is paid off. Any amount not repaid (which might equal 10% to 25% of the issue) would then be retired with a single "balloon" payment at maturity. Unlike a call or refunding provision, generally no call premium exists with sinking-fund calls; instead, bonds are normally called for sinking-fund purposes at par.

Secured or Unsecured Debt

senior bonds
secured debt obligations, backed by a legal claim on specific property of the issuer.

mortgage bonds
senior bonds secured by real estate.

collateral trust bonds
senior bonds backed by securities owned by the issuer but held in trust by a third party.

equipment trust certificates
senior bonds secured by specific pieces of equipment; popular with transportation companies such as airlines.

first and refunding bonds
bonds secured in part with both first and second mortgages.

junior bonds
debt obligations backed only by the promise of the issuer to pay interest and principal on a timely basis.

A single issuer may have a number of different bonds outstanding at any given point in time. In addition to coupon and maturity, one bond can be differentiated from another by the type of collateral behind the issue. Issues can be either junior or senior. **Senior bonds** are secured obligations, which are backed by a legal claim on some specific property of the issuer. Such issues would include **mortgage bonds,** which are secured by real estate; **collateral trust bonds,** which are backed by financial assets owned by the issuer but held in trust by a third party; **equipment trust certificates,** which are secured by specific pieces of equipment (e.g., boxcars and airplanes) and are popular with railroads and airlines; and **first and refunding bonds,** which are basically a *combination* of first mortgage and junior lien bonds (i.e., the bonds are secured in part by a first mortgage on some of the issuer's property and in part by second or third mortgages on other properties). (Note that first and refunding bonds are *less secure* than, and should *not* be confused with, straight first-mortgage bonds.)

Junior bonds, on the other hand, are backed only by the promise of the issuer to pay interest and principal on a timely basis. There are several classes

debenture
an unsecured (junior) bond.

subordinated debentures
unsecured bonds whose claim is secondary to other debentures.

income bonds
unsecured bonds requiring that interest be paid only after a specified amount of income is earned.

of unsecured bonds, the most popular of which is known as a **debenture.** Figure 8.2 shows the announcement of a debenture bond that was issued in 1997. Note that even though there was no collateral backing up this obligation, the issuer—Ford Motor Company—was able to sell $500 million worth of these securities at an interest rate of just 7.7%. And, no, the date is not a typo: These bonds do not come due until the year 2097—a maturity of *100 years.* **Subordinated debentures** are also used; these issues have a claim on income secondary to other debenture bonds. **Income bonds,** the most junior of all, are unsecured debts requiring that interest be paid only after a certain amount of income is earned. With these bonds, there is no legally binding requirement to meet interest payments on a timely or regular basis so long as a specified amount of income has not been earned. These issues are similar in many respects to *revenue bonds* found in the municipal market.

FIGURE 8.2
Announcement of a New Corporate Bond Issue

This $500 million bond was issued by Ford Motor Co. in 1997 and is secured by nothing more than the good name of the company. These unsecured debenture bonds carry a coupon of 7.70%. There is nothing unusual about that except that this is a *100-year* bond that won't mature until 2097. Over the next century, if the bond isn't called in prior to maturity, Ford will pay out over $3.8 *billion* in interest on this issue. And as far as principal is concerned, if inflation runs at a meager 2.5% per year, an original investment of $1,000 in this bond will be "worth" only about $85 in 2097 dollars—about what it will probably cost to buy a fancy dinner for two! (Source: *Wall Street Journal,* September 10, 1997, p. C2.)

This announcement is neither an offer to sell nor a solicitation of an offer to buy any of these securities. The offering is made only by the Prospectus Supplement and the related Prospectus.

New Issue

$500,000,000

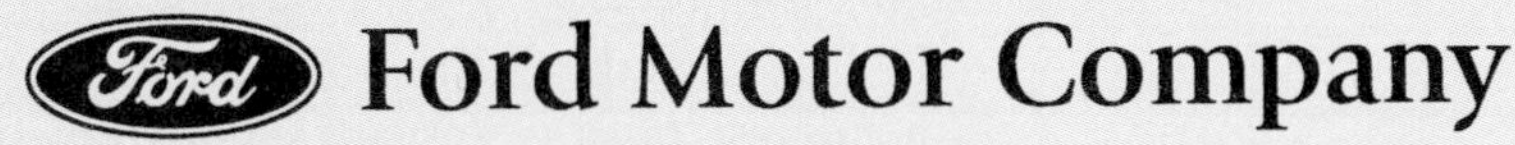

7.70% Debentures due 2097
Interest payable May 15 and November 15

Price 98.591%
Plus accrued interest, if any, from May 13, 1997

Copies of the Prospectus Supplement and the related Prospectus may be obtained from the undersigned in any State in which this announcement is circulated, and where such securities may lawfully be offered.

Bear, Stearns & Co. Inc.
Chase Securities Inc.
Goldman, Sachs & Co.
Lehman Brothers
Morgan Stanley & Co.
Incorporated

INVESTOR FACT

HERE'S SOME TOE-TAPPING COLLATERAL FOR YOU—Talk about unusual collateral for a bond, how about the future album sales of rock star David Bowie! It happened in 1997, when the rock legend came out with a $55 million, 10-year bond issue that was secured by the future royalties he's expected to earn on his early albums. And just like his albums, these "Bowie Bonds" were quickly snapped up by investors.

Principles of Bond Price Behavior

The price of a bond is a function of its coupon, its maturity, and the movement of market interest rates. The relationship of bond prices to market interest rates is captured in Figure 8.3. Basically, the graph reinforces the *inverse relationship* that exists between bond prices and market rates: *Lower* rates lead to *higher* bond prices. Figure 8.3 also shows the difference between premium and discount bonds. A **premium bond** is one that sells for more than its par value. A premium results whenever market interest rates drop below the coupon rate on the bond. A **discount bond,** in contrast, sells for less than par; the discount is the result of market rates being greater than the issue's coupon rate. Thus, the 10% bond in Figure 8.3 trades as a premium bond when market rates are at 8%, but as a discount bond when rates are at 12%.

premium bond
a bond with a market value in excess of par; occurs when interest rates drop below the coupon rate.

discount bond
a bond with a market value lower than par; occurs when market rates are greater than the coupon rate.

When a bond is first issued, it is usually sold to the public at a price that equals or is very close to its par value. Likewise, when the bond matures—some 15, 20, or 30 years later—it will once again be priced at its par value. But what happens to the price of the bond in between is of considerable interest to most bond investors. In this regard, we know that the extent to which bond prices move depends not only on the *direction* of change in interest rates but also on the *magnitude* of such change; the greater the moves in interest rates, the greater the swings in bond prices.

However, bond price volatility also varies according to the coupon and maturity of an issue. That is, bonds with *lower coupons* and/or *longer maturities* respond more vigorously to changes in market rates and therefore undergo sharper price swings. (Note in Figure 8.3 that for a given change in interest rates—e.g., from 10% to 8%—the largest change in price occurs when the bond has the greatest number of years to maturity.) Therefore, if a *decline* in interest rates is anticipated, an investor should seek lower coupons and longer maturities (this will maximize capital gains). When interest rates move

FIGURE 8.3
The Price Behavior of a Bond

A bond will sell at its par value so long as the prevailing market interest rate remains the same as the bond's coupon—in this case, 10%. However, when market rates drop (or rise), bond prices move up (or down). As a bond approaches its maturity, the price of the issue moves toward its par value *regardless* of the level or prevailing interest rates.

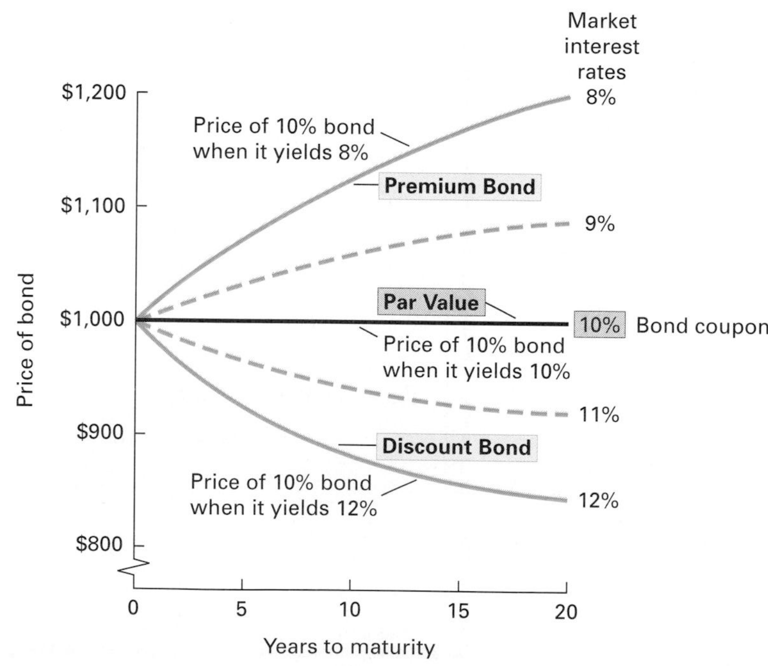

up, the investor should do just the opposite: seek high coupons with short maturities. This choice will minimize price variation and act to preserve as much capital as possible.

Actually, of the two variables, the *maturity* of an issue has the greater impact on price volatility. For example, look what happens to the price of an 8% bond when market interest rates rise by 1, 2, or 3 percentage points:

	Change in the Price of an 8% Bond When Interest Rates Rise by:		
Bond Maturity	1 Percentage Point	2 Percentage Points	3 Percentage Points
5 years	−4.0%	−7.7%	−11.2%
25 years	−9.9%	−18.2%	−25.3%

For purposes of this illustration, we assume the changes in interest rate occur "instantaneously," so the maturities remain fixed, at 5 or 25 years. Given the computed price changes, it's clear that the shorter (5-year) bond offers a lot more price stability. Such a behavioral trait is universal with all fixed-income securities. This is a very important feature, because it means that if you want to reduce your exposure to capital loss or, more to the point, to lower the amount of price volatility in your bond holdings, then just *shorten your maturities*.

CONCEPTS IN REVIEW

8.4 Can issue characteristics (such as coupon and call features) affect the yield and price behavior of bonds? Explain.

8.5 What is the difference between a *call feature* and a *sinking-fund provision?* Briefly describe the three different types of call features. Can a bond be freely callable but nonrefundable?

8.6 What is the difference between a *premium bond* and a *discount bond?* What three attributes are most important in determining an issue's price volatility?

http://hepg.aw.com

Like many aspects of investing, bonds have their own jargon. Knowledge of the terminology of bonds leads to a better understanding of their features and of bonds as investment alternatives. Click on *Glossary* at the following Web address to learn more about bonds than you ever thought possible.

www.bondsonline.com/bondprofindex.html

The Market for Debt Securities

LG 4 LG 5

Thus far, our discussion has dealt with basic bond features; we now shift our attention to a review of the market in which these securities are traded. The bond market is chiefly over-the-counter in nature, because listed bonds represent only a small portion of total outstanding obligations. And the bond market is far more price-stable than the stock market. Granted, interest rates (and therefore bond prices) do move up and down and have been volatile in recent times, but when bond price activity is measured on a daily basis, it is remarkably stable. There are two things about the bond market that stand out—it's big, and it has been growing at a rapid clip. From a $250 billion market in 1950, it has grown to the point where the amount of bonds outstanding in this country in early 1998 stood at some $12 *trillion!* That makes the bond market bigger than the U.S. stock market, although the gap is narrowing.

Major Market Segments

There are issues available in today's bond market to meet almost any investment objective and to suit just about any type of investor. As a matter of convenience, the bond market is normally separated into four major segments, according to type of issuer: Treasury, agency, municipal, and corporate. As we shall see, each sector has developed its own issue and operating features, as well as its own trading characteristics.

Treasury Bonds

"Treasuries" (or "governments," as they are sometimes called) are a dominant force in the fixed-income market, and if not the most popular type of bond, they certainly are the best known. In addition to T-bills (a popular short-term debt security discussed in Chapter 3), the U.S. Treasury also issues notes and bonds, as well as *inflation-indexed bonds,* the newest type of Treasury security, introduced in January 1997. All Treasury obligations are of the highest quality because they are all backed by the "full faith and credit" of the U.S. government. This feature, along with their liquidity, makes them very popular with individual and institutional investors both here and abroad. Indeed, the market for U.S. Treasury securities is the biggest and most active in the world. *Every day,* more than $150 billion worth of Treasury obligations change hands, as these securities are traded in all the major markets of the world, from New York to London to Tokyo. That's three-quarters of a *trillion* dollars in bond trades *every week.* To put that number in perspective, in an average week, the NYSE trades about $150 to $200 billion worth of stock.

Treasury notes
U.S. Treasury debt securities that are issued with maturities of 10 years or less.

Treasury bonds
U.S. Treasury debt securities that are issued with maturities of more than 10 years—usually with 30-year maturities.

Treasury notes carry maturities of 2 to 10 years, whereas **Treasury bonds** have maturities of more than 10 years and up to 30 years. Note that although technically T-bonds can carry just about any maturity that exceeds 10 years, *most are issued today with 30-year maturities.* Treasury notes and bonds are sold in $1,000 denominations (except 2- to 3-year notes, which are sold in $5,000 minimums). Interest income is subject to normal federal income tax but *is exempt from state and local taxes.* The Treasury issues its notes and bonds at regularly scheduled auctions, the results of which are widely reported by the financial media (see Figure 8.4). It's through this auction process that the Treasury establishes the initial yields and coupons on the securities it issues. All government notes and bonds (including the inflation-adjusted bonds) are issued as *noncallable* securities. In fact, the last time the U.S. Treasury issued callable bonds was in 1984; until then, most Treasury bonds carried long-term call deferments, under which the bonds became freely callable during the last 5 years of the issue's life. There are still some deferred-call Treasuries outstanding, but they're easy to pick out, because the deferred-call features are a specific part of the bond listing system. For example, a 10% issue of 2005–10 signifies that this Treasury bond has a maturity date of 2010 and a deferred-call feature that extends through 2005.

FIGURE 8.4 The Reported Results of a Treasury Note Auction

Treasury auctions are closely followed by the financial media; here, the results of a 5-year Treasury note auction are reported. These auctions are highly competitive; the amount of bids submitted generally far exceeds the size of the issue, so the spread between the highest and lowest bids is quite small—sometimes as small as 2 basis points, or 2/100 of 1%. (Source: *Wall Street Journal,* November 26, 1997.)

Here are details of yesterday's 5-year note auction:

All bids are awarded at a single price at the market-clearing yield. Rates are determined by the difference between that price and the face value.

5-YEAR NOTES

Applications	$32,774,586,000	The amount of bids submitted
Accepted bids	$11,002,576,000	Size of the issue—the amount of bids accepted
Bids at market-clearing yield accepted	40%	
Accepted noncompetitively	$311,076,000	The amount of noncompetitive bids submitted (and accepted)
Auction price (rate)	99.918 (5.769%)	The average price and yield (rate) on the issue
Interest rate	5 3/4%	The coupon that the issue will carry, which is set after the auction
CUSIP number	912827303	

The notes are dated November 30, 1997, will be issued December 1, 1997, and mature November 30, 2002.

Treasury inflation-indexed bonds (TIPS)
a type of Treasury security that provides protection against inflation by adjusting investor returns for the annual rate of inflation.

As noted above, the newest form of Treasury security is the **Treasury inflation-indexed bond.** They're also known as **TIPS,** which stands for "Treasury inflation-protection securities." These securities offer investors the opportunity to stay ahead of inflation by periodically adjusting their returns for any inflation that has occurred. That is, if inflation is running at an annual rate of, say, 3%, then at the end of the year, the par (or maturity) value of your bond will increase by 3%. (Actually, the adjustments to par value are done every 6 months.) Thus the $1,000 par value will grow to $1,030 at the end of the first year. If the 3% inflation rate continues for the second year, the par value will once again move up, this time from $1,030 to $1,061 (or $1,030 × 1.03). Unfortunately, the coupons on these securities are set very low, because they're meant to provide investors with so-called *real (inflation-adjusted) returns.* Thus one of these bonds might carry a coupon of only 3.5% at a time when regular T-bonds were paying, say, 6.5% or 7%. But there's an advantage even to this: The actual size of *the coupon payment will increase over time as the par value on the bond goes up.* For investors who are concerned about inflation protection, these securities may be just the ticket. But as the accompanying *Investing in Action* box suggests, these securities are a lot more complex than the traditional Treasury bond.

Agency Bonds

agency bonds
debt securities issued by various agencies and organizations of the U.S. government.

Agency bonds are debt securities issued by various agencies and organizations of the U.S. government, such as the Federal Home Loan Bank, the Federal Farm Credit Banks, and the Government National Mortgage Association. For

INVESTING IN ACTION

Here's a TIP: Look Before You Leap

Bondholders look at inflation like Superman looks at kryptonite. Superman weakens when faced with the dreaded substance and would die if exposed to it for long. Bondholders weaken when inflation heats up because it causes bond prices to buckle and fixed payments to lose their purchasing power. Some people have the mistaken impression that they can't lose money investing in Treasury bonds. But they can—not because the government can't pay, but because bond prices fall in a rising inflationary environment. Now, the U.S. government wants investors to buy its bonds without fearing inflation, so in 1997, Uncle Sam created TIPS, Treasury inflation-protected securities.

Here's how TIPS work: The government issues a 10-year bond with a $1,000 face value that pays, say 3% interest, or $30 per year—and that rate stays fixed for the life of the issue. But if the consumer price index rises, *so does the face amount of the bond.* For example, because the CPI rose 1.7% in 1997, the new face amount was adjusted up to $1,000 × 1.017 = $1,017. Therefore, in 1998, the annual interest payment would be $30.51 (3% of $1,017). When the TIPS mature in 10 years, the investor gets the inflation-adjusted face value at that time, which could be as much as $2,000 if inflation really takes off. A lot can change over a decade, but inflation looks pretty tame these days. As one professional investor puts it, buying TIPS now is like buying flood insurance during a drought.

Are TIPS a good deal or not? They certainly are for the government, which is able to pay 3% interest instead of an inflation-adjusted premium like 6% or 7%. Taxpayers should like that too, because it helps keep government interest payments down. And, unlike the case with conventional fixed-income securities, the investor doesn't have to worry about the Treasury bond's value plummeting if inflation heats up.

Take a look at what happens to a conventional bond if inflation is rekindled beyond the implied inflation premium (in this case, 3%). Investors get 6% per year, or $60, no matter what happens to the level of prices. In 10 years, that $1,000 principal will certainly have less purchasing power than it does today. It might be able to buy just $700 worth of goods. In addition, rising inflation generally means rising interest rates. In the marketplace, conventional bond prices fall when interest rates rise. Therefore, an investor who wishes to sell a conventional bond prior to maturity is likely to take a loss if interest rates are higher than when the bond was purchased.

TIPS protect investors from such erosion in bond prices. TIPS are not so great, however, if inflation stays dormant, because the investors are getting only 3% on their money. You could get that kind of interest at your local bank, and you don't need to lock up your money nearly as long as you do with TIPS.

There's one other downside to TIPS: *taxes.* Investors have to pay a tax on the increasing face value of their bonds—$17 in the first year in the foregoing example. That may not seem like much, but the government doesn't actually pay out the increase in the bond's face value until maturity. Thus you end up paying taxes on income you've earned but don't have in hand. For that reason, TIPS probably make the most sense for individual retirement accounts (IRAs) and other tax-sheltered retirement accounts. TIPS are also a good idea for investors who want to allocate a portion of their assets to income-generating securities *and* don't want to worry that inflation will erode their value. But the tradeoff for that protection is significant: loss of about half the income.

the most part, though these securities are the closest things to Treasuries, they are not obligations of the U.S. Treasury and technically should not be considered the same as a Treasury bond. An important feature of agency bonds is that they usually provide yields that are comfortably above the market rates for Treasuries; thus they offer investors a way to increase returns with little or no real difference in risk.

TABLE 8.3 Characteristics of Popular Agency Issues

Type of Issue	Minimum Denomination	Initial Maturity	Tax Status*		
			Federal	State	Local
Federal Farm Credit Banks	$ 1,000	13 months to 15 years	T	E	E
Federal Home Loan Bank	10,000	1 to 20 years	T	E	E
Federal Land Banks	1,000	1 to 10 years	T	E	E
Farmers Home Administration	25,000	1 to 25 years	T	T	T
Federal Housing Administration	50,000	1 to 40 years	T	T	T
Federal Home Loan Mortgage Corp.** ("Freddie Macs")	25,000	18 to 30 years	T	T	T
Federal National Mortgage Association** ("Fannie Maes")	25,000	1 to 30 years	T	T	T
Government National Mortgage Association** (GNMA—"Ginnie Maes")	25,000	12 to 40 years	T	T	T
Student Loan Marketing Association	10,000	3 to 10 years	T	E	E
Tennessee Valley Authority (TVA)	1,000	5 to 50 years	T	E	E
U.S. Postal Service	10,000	25 years	T	E	E
Federal Financing Corp.	1,000	1 to 20 years	T	E	E

*T = taxable; E = tax-exempt
**Mortgage-backed securities.

There are basically two types of agency issues: government-sponsored and federal agencies. Although there are only six government-sponsored organizations, the number of federal agencies exceeds two dozen. To overcome some of the problems in the marketing of many relatively small federal agency securities, Congress established the Federal Financing Bank to consolidate the financing activities of all federal agencies. (As a rule, the generic term *agency* is used to denote both government-sponsored and federal agency obligations.)

Selected characteristics of some of the more popular agency bonds are presented in Table 8.3. As the list of issuers in the table indicates, most of the government agencies that exist today were created to support either agriculture or housing. Although agency issues are not direct liabilities of the U.S. government, a few of them actually do carry government guarantees and therefore effectively represent the full faith and credit of the U.S. Treasury. But even those issues that do not carry such guarantees are highly regarded in the marketplace. They are all viewed as *moral obligations* of the U.S. government, so it's highly unlikely that Congress would ever allow one of them to default. Also, like Treasury securities, agency issues are normally noncallable or carry lengthy call deferment features. One final point: Since 1986 *all new agency (and Treasury) securities* have been issued in *book entry form.* This means that no certificate of ownership is issued to the buyer of the bonds; rather, the buyer receives a "confirmation" of the transaction, and his or her name is entered in a computerized logbook, where it remains as long as the security is owned. Many experts believe that in the not-too-distant future, all security transactions will be handled in this way.

municipal bonds
debt securities issued by states, counties, cities, and other political subdivisions; most of these bonds are tax-exempt (free of federal income tax on interest income).

Municipal Bonds

Municipal bonds are the issues of states, counties, cities, and other political subdivisions, such as school districts and water and sewer districts. This is a trillion-dollar market today, and it's the only segment of the bond market

general obligation bonds
municipal bonds backed by the full faith, credit, and taxing power of the issuer.

revenue bonds
municipal bonds that require payment of principal and interest only if sufficient revenue is generated by the issuer.

municipal bond guarantees
guarantees from a party other than the issuer that principal and interest payments will be made in a prompt and timely manner.

INVESTOR FACT

HELPING CAL RIPKIN WITH HIS STREAK—Who knows? If it hadn't been for taxable munis, Cal Ripkin might have hurt himself on Astroturf and not been able to set the record for consecutive baseball games played. Instead, taxable munis helped finance beautiful Camden Yards, Baltimore's state-of-the-art ballpark. A taxable muni sounds like a contradiction. Aren't all municipal bonds tax-free? No, they're not. Taxable munis pay interest to bondholders, who in turn *pay federal income tax on that interest.* Taxable munis exist to fund public projects that also benefit the private sector—in this case, baseball owners. Congress created them in the mid-1980s to help finance these types of projects but decided that investors shouldn't get a tax break to bankroll entrepreneurs. In contrast, tax-free munis finance projects such as schools, hospitals, and water/sewer systems that benefit the public at large.

that's dominated by individual investors: About two-thirds of all municipal bonds are held by individuals. (There are few tax incentives for institutional investors to hold these securities.) These bonds are often issued as *serial obligations,* which means that the issue is broken into a series of smaller bonds, each with its own maturity date and coupon.

Municipal bonds ("munis") are brought to the market as either general obligation or revenue bonds. **General obligation bonds** are backed by the full faith, credit, and taxing power of the issuer. **Revenue bonds,** in contrast, are serviced by the income generated from specific income-producing projects (e.g., toll roads). Although general obligations used to dominate the municipal market, the vast majority of munis today come out as revenue bonds (accounting for about 70% to 75% of the new issue volume).

The distinction between a general obligation bond and a revenue bond is important for a bondholder, because the issuer of a revenue bond is obligated to pay principal and interest *only if a sufficient level of revenue is generated.* (If the funds aren't there, the issuer does not have to make payment on the bond.) General obligation bonds, however, are required to be serviced in a prompt and timely fashion irrespective of the level of tax income generated by the municipality. Obviously, revenue bonds involve a lot more risk than general obligations, and because of that, they provide higher yields. Regardless of the type, municipal bonds are customarily issued in $5,000 denominations.

A somewhat unusual aspect of municipal bonds is the widespread use of **municipal bond guarantees.** With these guarantees, a party other than the issuer assures the bondholder that principal and interest payments will be made in a prompt and timely manner. The third party, in essence, provides an additional source of collateral in the form of insurance, placed on the bond at the date of issue, that is nonrevocable over the life of the obligation. As a result, bond quality is improved. The three principal insurers are the Municipal Bond Investors Assurance Corporation (MBIA), the American Municipal Bond Assurance Corporation (AMBAC), and the Financial Guaranty Insurance Co. (FGIC). These guarantors will normally insure any general obligation or revenue bond as long as it carries an S&P (Standard & Poor's) rating of triple-B or better. (*Note:* We'll explore bond ratings in more detail later in this chapter.) Municipal bond insurance results in higher ratings (usually triple-A) and improved liquidity, because these bonds are generally more actively traded in the secondary markets. Insured bonds are especially common in the revenue market, and insurance markedly boosts the attractiveness of these issues. Whereas an uninsured revenue bond lacks certainty of payment, a guaranteed issue is very much like a general obligation bond because the investor knows that principal and interest payments will be made on time.

Tax Advantages Without a doubt, the thing that makes municipal securities unique is the fact that, in most cases, their interest income is exempt from federal income taxes. This is why these issues are known as *tax-free,* or *tax-exempt,* bonds. Normally, the obligations are also exempt from state and local taxes *in the state in which they were issued.* For example, a California issue is free of California tax if the bondholder lives in California, but its interest income is subject to state tax if the investor resides in Arizona. Note, however, that *capital gains on municipal bonds are not exempt from taxes.*

TABLE 8.4 Taxable Equivalent Yields for Various Tax-Exempt Returns

Taxable Income*			Tax-Free Yield							
Joint Returns ($000)	Individual Returns ($000)	Federal Tax Bracket	5%	6%	7%	8%	9%	10%	12%	14%
$0–$41.2	$0–$24.6	15%	5.88	7.06	8.24	9.41	10.59	11.76	14.12	16.47
$41.2–$99.6	$24.6–$59.7	28	6.94	8.33	9.72	11.11	12.50	13.89	16.67	19.44
$99.6–$151.7	$59.7–$124.6	31	7.25	8.70	10.15	11.59	13.04	14.49	17.39	20.29
$151.7–$271.0	$124.6–$271.0	36	7.81	9.38	10.94	12.50	14.06	15.63	18.75	21.88
$271.0 and above	$271.0 and above	39.6	8.28	9.93	11.59	13.25	14.90	16.56	19.87	23.18

*Taxable income and federal tax rates effective January 1, 1998.

Individual investors are the biggest buyers of municipal bonds, and tax-free yield is certainly a major draw. Table 8.4 shows what a taxable bond would have to yield to equal the net yield of a tax-free bond. *It demonstrates how the yield attractiveness of municipals varies with an investor's income level.* Clearly, the higher the individual's tax bracket, the more attractive municipal bonds become. Generally speaking, an investor has to be in one of the higher federal tax brackets (i.e., 31% to 39.6%) before municipal bonds offer yields that are truly competitive with fully taxable issues. This is so because municipal yields are substantially lower than those available from fully taxable issues (such as corporates); and unless the tax effect is sufficient to raise the yield on a municipal to a figure that equals or surpasses taxable rates, it obviously doesn't make much sense to buy municipal bonds.

taxable equivalent yield
the return a fully taxable bond would have to provide to match the after-tax return of a lower-yielding, tax-free municipal bond.

We can determine the level of return a fully taxable bond would have to provide in order to match the after-tax return of a lower-yielding, tax-free issue by computing what is known as a municipal's **taxable equivalent yield.** This measure can be calculated according to the following simple formula:

Equation 8.1

$$\text{Taxable equivalent yield} = \frac{\text{yield of municipal bond}}{1 - \text{federal tax rate}}$$

For example, if a certain municipal offered a yield of 6.5%, then an individual in the 39.6% tax bracket would have to find a fully taxable bond with a yield of 10.76% (i.e., 6.5%/0.604 = 10.76%) to reap the same after-tax returns as the municipal.

Note, however, that Equation 8.1 considers *federal taxes only.* As a result, the computed taxable equivalent yield applies only to certain situations: (1) to states that have no state income tax, (2) to situations where the investor is looking at an out-of-state bond (which would be taxable by the investor's state of residence), or (3) where the investor is comparing a municipal bond to a Treasury (or agency) bond—in which case *both* the Treasury and the municipal bonds are free from state income tax. Under any of these conditions, the only tax that's relevant is federal income tax, so using Equation 8.1 is appropriate.

But what if the investor is comparing an in-state bond to, say, a corporate bond? In this case, the in-state bond would be free from both federal and state taxes, but the corporate bond would not. As a result, Equation 8.1 could not be used. Instead, the investor should use a form of the equivalent yield formula that considers *both* federal and state income taxes:

Equation 8.2

$$\text{Taxable equivalent yield for both federal and state taxes} = \frac{\text{municipal bond yield}}{1 - \left[\text{federal tax rate} + \text{state tax rate}\left(1 - \text{federal tax rate}\right)\right]}$$

When both federal and state taxes are included in the calculations, the net effect is to *increase* the taxable equivalent yield. Of course, the size of the increase depends on the level of state income taxes; in a high-tax state like California, for example, the impact can be substantial. Return to the 6.5% municipal bond introduced above: If a California resident in the maximum federal and state tax brackets (39.6% and 11%, respectively) were considering a corporate issue, she would have to get a yield of 12.09% on the corporate to match the 6.5% yield on the California bond:

$$\text{Taxable equivalent yield for both federal and state taxes} = \frac{6.5}{1 - [.396 + .11(1 - .3960]}$$

$$= \frac{6.5}{1 - [.396 + .066]}$$

$$= \underline{\underline{12.09\%}}$$

This yield compares to a taxable equivalent yield of 10.76% when only federal taxes were included in the calculation. That's a difference of more than one full percentage point—certainly *not* an insignificant amount.

Corporate Bonds

The major nongovernmental issuers of bonds are corporations. The market for corporate bonds is customarily subdivided into four segments: *industrials* (the most diverse of the groups), *public utilities* (the dominant group in terms of volume of new issues), *rail and transportation bonds,* and *financial issues* (banks, finance companies, etc.). Not only is there a full range of bond quality available in the corporate market, but there's also a wide assortment of different types of bonds, ranging from first-mortgage obligations to convertible bonds (which we'll examine in Chapter 10), debentures, subordinated debentures, senior subordinated issues, capital notes (a type of unsecured debt issued by banks and other financial institutions), and income bonds. Interest on corporate bonds is paid semiannually, and sinking funds are fairly common. The bonds usually come in $1,000 denominations and are issued on a term basis with a single maturity date. Maturities usually range from 25 to 40 years or more, and many corporates, especially the longer ones, carry call deferment provisions that prohibit prepayment for the first 5 to 10 years. Corporate issues are popular with individuals because of their relatively attractive yields.

Although most corporates fit the general description above, one that does not is the *equipment trust certificate,* a security issued by railroads, airlines, and other transportation concerns. The proceeds from equipment trust certificates are used to purchase equipment (e.g., jumbo jets and railroad engines) that serves as the collateral for the issue. These bonds are usually issued in serial form and carry uniform annual installments throughout. They normally carry maturities that range from 1 year to a maximum that seldom exceeds 15 to 17 years. An attractive feature of equipment trust certificates is that despite a near-perfect payment record that dates back to pre-Depression days, these issues generally offer above-average yields to investors.

Specialty Issues

In addition to the basic bond vehicles described above, investors can also choose from a number of *specialty issues*—bonds that possess unusual issue characteristics. For the most part, these bonds have coupon or repayment provisions that are out of the ordinary. Most are issued by corporations, although they are being used increasingly by other issuers as well. Four of the most actively traded specialty issues today are zero-coupon bonds, mortgage-backed securities (including collateralized mortgage obligations, or CMOs), asset-backed securities, and high-yield junk bonds. All four of these rank as some of the most popular bonds on Wall Street. Let's now take a closer look at each of these specialty issues.

Zero-Coupon Bonds

zero-coupon bonds
bonds with no coupons that are sold at a deep discount from par value.

As the name implies, **zero-coupon bonds** have no coupons. Rather, these securities are sold at a deep discount from their par values and then increase in value over time at a compound rate of return so that at maturity, they are worth much more than their initial investment. Other things being equal, the cheaper the zero-coupon bond, the greater the return an investor can earn: For example, a 6% bond might cost $420, and an issue with a 10% yield only $240.

Because they don't have coupons, these bonds do not pay interest semiannually; in fact, they pay *nothing* to the investor until the issue matures. As strange as it might seem, this feature is the main attraction of zero-coupon bonds. Because there are no interest payments, investors do not have to worry about reinvesting coupon income twice a year. Instead, the fully compounded rate of return on a zero-coupon bond is virtually guaranteed at the rate stated when the issue was purchased. For example, in late 1997, U.S. Treasury zero-coupon bonds with 20-year maturities were available at yields of around 6.25%. Thus, for less than $300, you could buy a bond that would be worth more than three times that amount, or $1,000, at maturity in 20 years. Best of all, you would be *locking in* a 6.25% compound rate of return on your investment for the full 20-year life of the issue.

The foregoing advantages notwithstanding, zeros have some serious disadvantages. One is that if rates do move up over time, you won't be able to participate in the higher return (you'll have no coupon income to reinvest). In addition, zero-coupon bonds are subject to tremendous price volatility: If market rates climb, you'll experience a sizable capital loss as the prices of zero-coupons plunge. (Of course, if interest rates *drop,* you'll reap enormous capital gains if you hold long-term zeros; indeed, such issues are unsurpassed in capital gains potential.) A final disadvantage is that the IRS has ruled that zero-coupon bondholders must report interest as it is accrued, even though no interest is actually received. For this reason, most fully taxable zero-coupon bonds should either be used in tax-sheltered investments, such as Individual

Retirement Arrangements (IRAs), or be held by minor children who are 14 or older and likely to be taxed at the lowest rate, if at all.

Treasury Strips (Strip-Ts) zero-coupon bonds created from U.S. Treasury securities.

Zeros are issued by corporations, municipalities, and federal agencies. You can even buy U.S. Treasury notes and bonds in the form of zero-coupon securities—they're known as **Treasury Strips,** or **Strip-Ts,** for short. Actually, the Treasury does *not* issue zero-coupon bonds but, instead, *allows government securities dealers to take regular coupon-bearing notes and bonds in stripped form,* which can then be sold to the public as zero-coupon securities. Essentially, the coupons are stripped from the bond, repackaged, and then sold separately as zero-coupon bonds. For example, a 20-year Treasury bond has 40 semiannual coupon payments, plus one principal payment; these 41 cash flows can be repackaged and sold as 41 different zero-coupon securities, with maturities that range from 6 months to 20 years. Because they sell at such large discounts, Treasury Strips are often sold in minimum denominations (par values) of $10,000—but with their big discounts, that means you probably will pay only $2,800 or $2,900 for $10,000 worth of 20-year Strip-Ts, depending on their yields. Because there's an active secondary market for Treasury Strips, investors can get in and out of these securities with ease just about anytime they want. Strip-Ts offer the maximum in issue quality, a full array of different maturities, and an active secondary market—all of which helps explain why these securities are so popular.

Mortgage-Backed Securities

mortgage-backed bond a debt issue secured by a pool of home mortgages; issued primarily by federal agencies.

Simply put, a **mortgage-backed bond** is a debt issue that is secured by a pool of residential mortgages. An issuer, such as the Government National Mortgage Association (GNMA), puts together a pool of home mortgages and then issues securities in the amount of the total mortgage pool. These securities, known as *pass-through securities* or *participation certificates,* are usually sold in minimum denominations of $25,000. Though their maturities can go out as far as 30 years, the average life of one of these issues is generally much shorter (perhaps as short as 8 to 10 years) because so many of the pooled mortgages are paid off early.

As an investor in one of these securities, you hold an undivided interest in the pool of mortgages. When a homeowner makes a monthly mortgage payment, that payment is essentially passed through to you, the bondholder, to pay off the mortgage-backed bond you hold. Although these securities come with normal coupons, *the interest is paid monthly rather than semiannually.* Actually, the monthly payments received by bondholders are, like mortgage payments, made up of both principal and interest. Because the principal portion of the payment represents return of capital, it is considered tax-free. The interest portion, however, is subject to ordinary state and federal income taxes.

Mortgage-backed securities are issued primarily by three federal agencies. Although there are some state and private issuers—mainly big banks and S&Ls—agency issues dominate the market and account for 90% to 95% of the activity. The major agency issuers of mortgage-backed securities (MBSs) are

- *Government National Mortgage Association (GNMA).* Known as Ginnie Mae, it is the oldest and largest issuer of MBSs.
- *Federal Home Loan Mortgage Corporation (FHLMC).* Known as Freddie Mac, it was the first to issue pools containing conventional mortgages. Stock in FHLMC is publicly owned and traded on the NYSE.

- *Federal National Mortgage Association (FNMA).* Known as Fannie Mae, it's the newest agency player and the leader in marketing seasoned/older mortgages. Its stock is also publicly owned and traded on the NYSE.

One of the problems with mortgage-backed securities is that they are *self-liquidating investments;* a portion of the monthly cash flow to the investor is repayment of principal. Thus the investor is always receiving back part of the original investment capital, and at maturity there is *no* big principal payment. To counter this problem, a number of *mutual funds* were formed that invest in mortgage-backed securities *but* automatically and continually reinvest the capital/principal portion of the cash flows. Mutual fund investors therefore receive only the interest from their investments and are thus able to preserve their capital.

Collateralized Mortgage Obligations Loan prepayments are another problem with mortgage-backed securities. In fact, it was in part an effort to defuse some of the prepayment uncertainty in standard mortgage-backed securities that led to the creation of **collateralized mortgage obligations,** or **CMOs.** Normally, as pooled mortgages are prepaid, *all* bondholders receive a prorated share of the prepayments. The net effect is to reduce sharply the life of the bond. A CMO, in contrast, divides investors into classes (formally called "tranches," which is French for "slice"), depending on whether they want a short-term, intermediate-term, or long-term investment. Now, although interest is paid to all bondholders, *all principal payments* go first to the shortest class until it is fully retired; then the next class (tranche) in the sequence becomes the sole recipient of principal; and so on until the last tranche is retired.

collateralized mortgage obligation (CMO)
mortgage-backed bond whose holders are divided into classes based on the length of investment desired; principal is channeled to investors in order of maturity, with short-term classes first.

Basically, CMOs are *derivative securities* created from traditional mortgage-backed bonds, which are placed in a trust; participation in this trust is then sold to the investing public in the form of CMOs. The net effect of this transformation is that CMOs look and behave very much like any other bond: They offer predictable interest payments and have (relatively) predictable maturities. However, although they carry the same triple-A ratings and implicit U.S. government backing as the mortgage-backed bonds that underlie them, CMOs represent a quantum leap in complexity. Some types of CMOs can be as simple and safe as Treasury bonds, but others can be far more volatile—and risky—than the standard MBSs they're made from. That's because when putting CMOs together, Wall Street performs the financial equivalent of gene splicing: Investment bankers isolate the interest and principal payments from the underlying MBSs and then rechannel them to a number of different tranches. It's not issue quality or risk of default that's the problem here, but rather prepayment, or call, risk—all the bonds will be paid off; it's just a matter of when. Different types of CMO tranches have different levels of prepayment risk. The overall risk in a CMO cannot exceed that of the underlying mortgage-backed bonds, so in order for there to be some CMO tranches with very little (or no) prepayment risk, others have to endure a lot more. The net effect is that while some CMO tranches are low in risk, others are extremely volatile. Unfortunately, CMOs became so complex and so exotic that nobody, not even professional money managers, knew what they were getting into. When market interest rates shot way up in 1994, CMO investors took huge losses and, in the process, lost much of their appetite for these securities. Of course, the mortgage market still exists today, but investors are no longer so interested in the "exotics"; instead, their attention has shifted back to plain vanilla MBSs or to simpler, less exotic (i.e., less risky) CMOs.

Asset-Backed Securities

securitization
the process of transforming bank lending vehicles such as mortgages into marketable securities.

asset-backed securities (ABS)
securities similar to mortgage-backed securities that are backed by a pool of bank loans, leases, and other assets.

The creation of mortgage-backed securities and CMOs quickly led to the development of a new market technology—the process of **securitization,** whereby various bank lending vehicles are transformed into marketable securities, much like a mortgage-backed security. Investment bankers are now selling billions of dollars of pass-through securities, known as **asset-backed securities** (or **ABS,** for short), which are backed by pools of auto loans and credit card bills (two of the principal types of collateral that back these securities), as well as computer leases, hospital receivables, small business loans, truck rentals, and even royalty fees. These securities, which were first introduced in the mid-1980s, are created when an investment banker bundles up some type of debt-linked asset (such as loans, receivables, and other forms of credit) and then sells investors—via asset-backed securities—the right to receive all or a part of the future payments made on that debt. For example, GMAC, the financing arm of General Motors, is a regular issuer of collateralized *auto loan* securities. When it wants to get some of its car loans off its books, GMAC takes the monthly cash flow from a pool of auto loans and pledges them to a new issue of bonds, which are then sold to investors. In similar fashion, *credit card receivables* are regularly used as collateral for these bonds (indeed, they represent the biggest segment of the ABS market), as are *home equity loans,* the second-biggest type of ABS.

Investors are drawn to ABSs for a number of reasons. One is the relatively *high yields* they offer; another is their *short maturities,* which often extend out no more than 3 to 5 years; a third is the *monthly, rather then semiannual, principal/interest payments* that accompany many of these securities. Also important to investors is their *high credit quality.* That's due to the fact that most of these deals are backed by generous credit protection. For example, the securities are often overcollateralized, which means that the pool of assets backing the bonds may be 25% to 50% larger than the bond issue itself. For whatever reason, about 75% of the ABSs outstanding have received the highest credit rating possible (triple-A) from the leading agencies. All of these factors explain why this market is growing so rapidly. From less than $10 billion outstanding in 1987, the asset-backed market had grown by 1997 to over $175 billion. Over $100 billion of this amount is centered in the three major forms of collateral—credit card receivables, home equity loans, and auto loans—but the rest of the market is anything but traditional; it seems that just about anything can be securitized, from trade receivables and aircraft loans to taxi medallions and lottery winnings. Indeed, as the accompanying *Investing in Action* box reveals, the only real limitation on this rapidly growing market appears to be the imagination and creativity of Wall Street.

Junk Bonds

junk bonds
high-risk securities that have low ratings but produce high yields.

Junk bonds, or *high-yield bonds,* as they're also called, are highly speculative securities that have received low, sub-investment-grade ratings (typically Ba or B) from such bond rating organizations as Moody's and Standard & Poor's. These bonds are issued primarily by corporations and, increasingly, by munic-

INVESTING IN ACTION

The Dream Factory on Wall Street

The richest people in the world used to be those who produced tangible products such as automobiles, buildings, and factory equipment—things you can touch. Now the richest people are inventing things you can't touch but can trade. Such Wall Street inventions enable investors to trade a billion shares of stock on the New York Stock Exchange in one day and let small, growing companies borrow money in the form of junk bonds. In the 1990s, one of the great inventions has been something called securitization. Securitization takes an asset that a small group of people previously could collect, such as movie profits, and turns it into a piece of paper that can be bought and sold by a broader audience. During the past decade, financial wizards have figured out how to turn the mundane into securities that can be traded. Home mortgages, auto loans, credit card receivables, lottery winnings, and even a rock star's earnings (page 312) are among the streams of income that have been "securitized" and sold on Wall Street. Dubbed "asset-backed bonds," this industry is proving that Wall Street can—and will—securitize anything.

The concept of securitization is really about pooling risks. If a Third World country borrows money from a bank, the country has to pay the bank an interest rate that reflects, in part, the risk that the country's economy or political structure might fail. But if the country is able to get together with a dozen other countries with the same needs, then the combined interest rate might be lower, because the risk of nonpayment has been diluted. Indeed, that's essentially how Citibank is lending money to such emerging markets as Latin America and Eastern Europe.

These same commercial banks are also taking their corporate loans and turning them into a new type of bond, called collateralized loan obligations (CLOs). Investors are essentially buying a piece of a bank's broad loan portfolio without taking the risk of buying a loan of an individual company. Any time you can lower risk while keeping the same rate of return, you come out ahead. Another hot product is the collateralized bond obligation (CBO), which is created by pooling dozens of junk-bond securities. A CBO can specialize in higher-quality junk or in offerings that are ready to default at any minute. Once again, the advantage is the pooled risk that a diversified portfolio offers to investors.

Aircraft leases, taxicab medallions, Italian cemetery revenues, money-grams from Mexican workers in the United States to relatives back home, and even yet-to-be-released Disney films—anything that produces a stream of cash flow can and will be turned into a traded security at a brokerage firm near you.

ipalities as well. Junk bonds generally take the form of *subordinated debentures*, which means the debt is unsecured and has a low claim on assets. These bonds are called "junk" because of the high risk of loss associated with them: The companies that issue them use excessive amounts of debt in their capital structures, and their ability to service that debt is subject to considerable doubt. Probably the most unusual type of junk bond is something called a **PIK-bond.** PIK stands for *payment in kind* and means that rather than paying the bond's coupon in cash, the issuer can make annual interest payments in the form of additional debt. This "financial printing press" usually goes on for 5 or 6 years, after which time the issuer is supposed to start making interest payments in real money.

PIK-bond
a payment-in-kind junk bond that gives the issuer the right to make annual interest payments in new bonds rather than in cash.

Traditionally, the term *junk bond* was applied to the issues of troubled companies, which might have been well rated when first issued but slid to low ratings through corporate mismanagement, heavy competition, or other factors. That all changed during the 1980s, when the vast majority of junk bonds originated not with troubled companies but with a growing number of mature (fairly well-known) firms that used enormous amounts of debt to finance takeovers and buyouts. These companies would change overnight from investment-grade firms to junk as they piled on debt to finance a takeover—or the threat of one. (Wall Street refers to these firms as "fallen angels.")

Why would any rational investor be drawn to junk bonds? The answer is simple: They offer very high yields. Indeed, in a typical market, relative to investment-grade bonds, you can expect to pick up anywhere from 2.5 to 5 percentage points in added yield. In late 1997, for example, investors were getting around 9% or 10% yields on junk bonds, compared to 7% or 8% on investment-grade corporates. Obviously, *such yields are available only because of the correspondingly higher exposure to risk*. However, as we saw earlier in this chapter, there's more to bond returns than yield alone: The *returns* you end up with don't always correspond to the *yields* you went in with. Junk bonds are subject to a good deal of risk, and their prices are unstable. Indeed, unlike investment-grade bonds, whose prices are closely linked to the behavior of market interest rates, junk bonds tend to behave more like stocks. As a result, the returns you actually end up with are highly unpredictable. Accordingly, only investors who are thoroughly familiar with the risks involved, and who are comfortable with such risk exposure, should use these securities.

A Global View of the Bond Market

Globalization has hit the bond market, just as it has the stock market, and investors who are taking advantage of it are loving it. Foreign bonds have caught on with American investors because of their high yields and attractive returns. Indeed, some market observers feel that, as more of these securities find their way to the portfolios of U.S. investors, foreign bonds will be to the 1990s what junk bonds were to the 1980s. There are risks with foreign bonds, of course, but high risk of default (which is so prevalent with junk bonds) is *not* one of them. Instead, the big risk with foreign bonds has to do with the impact that currency fluctuations can have on returns in U.S. dollars.

By year-end 1997, the total value of the world bond market reached some $27 trillion. The United States has the biggest debt market, accounting for about 45% of the total. Far behind us is Japan, with about 23% of the world market, followed by Germany (at 13%), then France, Italy, the United Kingdom, and Canada. Together, these seven countries account for nearly 90% of the world bond market.

Although the United States today accounts for less than half of the available fixed-income securities, that percentage is sure to decline in the future as foreign markets continue to expand. Therefore, by investing solely in the U.S. fixed-income markets, an investor is excluding not only half of the investment possibilities worldwide but, more important, the faster growing half. Also, as Table 8.5 reveals, investors in U.S. bonds are missing out on some pretty attractive returns. (The results reported in the table are *total returns in U.S. dollars* and include coupon income, capital gains or losses, and the effects of changes in currency exchange rates.) In fact, over the 18-year period from 1980 through 1997, the U.S. market provided the highest annual return just twice (once in 1982, and again in 1997). A lot of the difference between U.S.

TABLE 8.5 Comparative Annual Returns in the World's Major Bond Markets

	Annual Total Returns (in U.S. Dollars)							
	Australia	Canada	France	Germany	Italy	Japan	U.K.	U.S.
1997	−7.3%	4.8%	−7.0%	−8.9%	−2.3%	4.3%	10.4%	11.6%
1996	19.4	11.6	5.0	−0.1	30.4	−6.1	17.8	1.4
1995	15.0	23.3	27.7	26.6	21.4	10.5	17.0	27.2
1994	6.2	−9.9	4.6	9.1	2.1	8.5	−1.7	−7.8
1993	16.2	11.4	13.1	7.3	14.0	27.1	19.5	13.2
1992	−0.1	−0.5	4.6	6.2	−14.4	11.3	−3.9	9.4
1991	24.3	21.5	13.4	9.8	15.1	23.4	12.8	19.9
1990	16.3	7.2	22.4	14.8	28.8	7.2	31.3	6.9
1989	5.1	16.1	8.9	5.6	15.5	−14.6	−3.7	16.2
1988	29.8	18.9	2.2	−6.6	−1.0	2.6	2.5	10.7
1987	29.1	10.4	27.6	28.6	14.2	41.4	47.7	−0.3
1986	17.1	19.5	34.4	38.4	88.6	36.4	13.8	19.8
1985	−13.2	34.0	53.1	41.8	37.5	36.8	38.6	30.9
1984	4.9	1.1	6.6	1.4	21.9	2.3	−12.4	16.4
1983	0.5	1.9	−0.4	−7.7	15.1	12.3	8.1	4.7
1982	15.0	1.4	5.3	16.5	11.5	3.6	28.8	43.8
1981	−7.1	−4.7	−18.8	−8.8	−25.0	8.4	−18.8	−0.9
1980	−19.0	−1.6	−11.0	−10.3	−11.8	24.0	31.2	−2.6
	Average Annual Returns Over Extended Holding Periods							
5 years:								
1993–97	9.5%	7.7%	8.1%	6.2%	12.5%	6.5%	12.3%	8.5%
1988–92	14.5	12.3	10.1	5.7	7.7	5.2	8.7	12.5
1983–87	6.7	12.7	22.8	18.8	33.0	24.8	17.1	13.8
10 years:								
1988–97	11.9	10.0	9.1	5.9	10.1	5.8	10.5	10.5
15 years:								
1980–97	7.6	8.7	9.4	8.0	12.2	11.6	12.4	11.6

Note: Total return = coupon income + capital gain (or loss) + profit (or loss) from changes in currency exchange rates.
Source: International returns obtained from JP Morgan Goverment Bond Index/Total Return (U.S. Dollars).

and foreign returns in the bond market is due, of course, to the impact of currency exchange rates. Still, the fact remains that from an international perspective, better returns to U.S. investors are usually available to those willing to go offshore.

U.S.-Pay Versus Foreign-Pay Bonds

There are several different ways to invest in foreign bonds (*excluding* foreign bond mutual funds, which we'll examine in Chapter 13). From the perspective of a U.S. investor, foreign bonds can be divided into two broad categories on the basis of the currency in which the bond is denominated: *U.S.-pay* (or dollar-denominated) bonds and *foreign-pay* (or non-dollar-denominated) bonds. All the cash flows—including purchase price, maturity value, and coupon income—from dollar-denominated foreign bonds are in U.S. dollars, whereas the cash flows from nondollar bonds are designated in a foreign currency or in a basket of foreign currencies, such as the European Currency Unit (ECU).

Yankee bonds
bonds issued by foreign governments or corporations but denominated in dollars and registered with the SEC.

Eurodollar bonds
foreign bonds denominated in dollars but not registered with the SEC, thus restricting sales of new issues.

Dollar-Denominated Bonds Dollar-denominated foreign bonds are of two types: Yankee bonds and Eurodollar bonds. **Yankee bonds** are issued by foreign governments or corporations or by so-called supernational agencies, like the World Bank and the InterAmerican Bank. These bonds are issued and traded in the United States; they're registered with the SEC, and all transactions are in U.S. dollars. Buying a Yankee bond, then, is really no different from buying any other U.S. bond: These bonds are traded on U.S. exchanges and our OTC market, and *because everything is in dollars, there's no currency exchange risk to deal with.* The bonds are generally very high in quality (which is not surprising, given the quality of the issuers) and offer highly competitive yields to investors.

Eurodollar bonds, in contrast, are issued and traded outside the United States. They are denominated in U.S. dollars, but they are not registered with the SEC, which means underwriters are legally prohibited from selling new issues to the U.S. public. (Only "seasoned" Eurodollar issues can be sold in this country.) The Eurodollar market today is dominated by foreign-based investors (though that is changing) and is primarily aimed at institutional investors.

Foreign-Pay Bonds From the standpoint of U.S. investors, foreign-pay international bonds encompass all those issues denominated in some currency other than dollars. These bonds are issued and traded overseas and are not registered with the SEC. Examples are German government bonds, which are payable in deutsche marks; Japanese bonds, issued in yen; and so forth. When investors speak of *foreign bonds,* it's this segment of the market that most are thinking of. *These bonds are subject to changes in currency exchange rates,* which in turn can dramatically affect total returns to U.S. investors. The returns on foreign-pay bonds are a function of three things: (1) the level of coupon (interest) income earned on the bonds; (2) the change in market interest rates, which determine the level of capital gains (or losses); and (3) the behavior of currency exchange rates. The first two variables are the same as those that drive bond returns in this country and are, of course, just as important to foreign bonds as they are to domestic bonds. Thus, if you're investing overseas, you still want to know where yields are today and where they're headed; it's really the third variable that separates the return behavior of dollar-denominated from foreign-pay bonds.

We can assess returns from foreign-pay bonds by employing the same (modified) holding period return formula first introduced in our discussion of foreign stock returns. (See Equation 5.6 on page 199.) For example, assume an American investor purchased a German government bond, in large part because of the attractive 10% coupon it carried. If the bond was bought at par and market rates fell over the course of the year, the security itself would have provided a return in excess of 10%, because the decline in rates would have provided some capital gains to the investor. However, if the deutsche mark fell relative to the dollar, the total return (in U.S. dollars) could have actually ended up at a lot less than 10%, depending on what happened to the U.S. $/D-mark exchange rate. To find out exactly how this investment turned out, all you'd have to do is use Equation 5.6 and make a few (very minor) modifications to it (e.g., use interest income in place of dividends received). Like foreign stocks, foreign-pay bonds can pay off from both the behavior of the security and the behavior of the currency. As Table 8.5 shows, that combination, in many cases, means superior returns to U.S. investors. Knowledgeable investors also find these bonds attractive not only because of their competitive returns but also because of the positive diversification effects they have on bond portfolios.

CONCEPTS IN REVIEW

8.7 Briefly describe each of the following types of bonds: (a) *Treasury bonds,* (b) *agency issues,* (c) *municipal securities,* and (d) *corporate bonds.* Note some of the major advantages and disadvantages of each.

8.8 Briefly define each of the following and briefly note how they might be used by fixed-income investors: (a) *zero-coupon bonds,* (b) *CMOs,* (c) *junk bonds,* and (d) *Yankee bonds.*

8.9 According to the *Investing in Action* box on page 316, why would investors be interested in TIPS? Why would the U.S. Treasury issue such a security? What are the advantages and disadvantages of this security from the investor's point of view?

8.10 What are the special tax features of (a) Treasury securities, (b) agency issues, and (c) municipal bonds?

8.11 According to the *Investing in Action* box on page 325, what are CLOs and CBOs? What is the central idea behind securitization?

8.12 Identify the 6 or 7 biggest bond markets in the world. How important is the U.S. bond market relative to the rest of the world?

8.13 What's the difference between dollar-denominated and non-dollar-denominated (or foreign-pay) bonds? Briefly describe the two major types of U.S.-pay bonds. Can currency exchange rates affect the total return of U.S.-pay bonds? Of foreign-pay bonds? Explain.

http://hepg.aw.com

Of the many types of bonds available, one of the least understood is mortgage-backed securities. Arcturus Management, Inc., offers a good explanation of the benefits and historical behavior of these bond issues.

www.arcturus.com/pres.html

Trading Bonds

LG 6

In large part as a result of the perceived safety and stability of bonds, many individual investors view bond investing as a relatively simple process. Such thinking, however, can often lead to unsatisfactory results, even losses. The fact is that not all bonds are alike, and picking the right security for the time is just as important for bond investors as it is for stock investors. Indeed, success in the bond market demands a thorough understanding not only of the different types of bonds but also of the many technical factors that drive bond yields, prices, and returns—things like call features, refunding provisions, and the impact that coupon and maturity can have on bond price volatility. Also, because bond ratings are so important to a smooth-running bond market, investors should become thoroughly familiar with them. Let's take a look at these ratings and at the quotation system used for bonds.

Bond Ratings

bond ratings
letter grades that designate investment quality and are assigned to a bond issue by rating agencies.

Bond ratings are like grades: A letter grade that designates its investment quality is assigned to an issue on the basis of extensive, professionally conducted financial analysis. Ratings are widely used and are an important part of the municipal and corporate bond markets, where issues are regularly evaluated and rated by one or more of the rating agencies. Even some agency issues, like the Tennessee Valley Authority (TVA), are rated, though they always receive ratings that confirm the obvious—that the issues are prime grade. The two largest and best-known rating agencies are Moody's and Standard & Poor's; two lesser known but still important bond-rating agencies are Fitch Investors Service and Duff & Phelps.

How Ratings Work

Every time a large new issue comes to the market, it is analyzed by a staff of professional bond analysts to determine default risk exposure and investment quality. (A fee, usually ranging from $1,000 to $15,000 and paid by the issuer or the underwriter of the securities, is charged for rating each corporate bond.) The financial records of the issuing organization are thoroughly worked over and its future prospects assessed. Although the specifics of the actual credit analysis conducted by the rating agencies change with each issue, several major factors enter into most bond ratings. With a corporate issue, for example, these factors include an analysis of the issue's indenture provisions, an in-depth study of the firm's earning power (including the stability of its earnings), a look at the company's liquidity and how it is managed, a study of the company's relative debt burden, and an in-depth exploration of its coverage ratios to determine how well it can service both existing debt and any new bonds that are being contemplated or proposed. As you might expect, the firm's financial strength and stability are very important in determining the appropriate bond rating. Indeed, although there is far more to setting a rating than cranking out a few financial ratios, a strong relationship exists between the operating results and financial condition of the firm and the rating its bonds receive. Generally, the higher ratings are associated with more profitable companies that rely *less* on debt as a form of financing, are more liquid, have stronger cash flows, and have no trouble servicing their debt in a prompt and timely fashion.

Table 8.6 lists the various ratings assigned to bonds by each of the two major services. In addition to the standard rating categories noted in the table, Moody's uses numerical modifiers (1, 2, or 3) on bonds rated double-A to B, and S&P uses plus (+) or minus (−) signs on the same rating classes to show relative standing within a major rating category. For example, A+ (or A1) means a strong, high A rating, whereas A− (or A3) indicates that the issue is on the low end of the A rating scale. Except for slight variations in designations (Aaa vs. AAA), the meanings and interpretations are basically the same. Note that the top four ratings (Aaa through Baa, or AAA through BBB) des-

TABLE 8.6 Bond Ratings

Moody's	S&P	Definition
Aaa	AAA	*High-grade investment bonds.* The highest rating assigned, denoting extremely strong capacity to pay principal and interest. Often called "gilt edge" securities.
Aa	AA	*High-grade investment bonds.* High quality by all standards but rated lower primarily because the margins of protection are not quite as strong.
A	A	*Medium-grade investment bonds.* Many favorable investment attributes, but elements may be present that suggest susceptibility to adverse economic changes.
Baa	BBB	*Medium-grade investment bonds.* Adequate capacity to pay principal and interest but possibly lacking certain protective elements against adverse economic conditions.
Ba	BB	*Speculative issues.* Only moderate protection of principal and interest in varied economic times. (This is one of the ratings carried by junk bonds.)
B	B	*Speculative issues.* Generally lacking desirable characteristics of investment bonds. Assurance of principal and interest may be small; this is another junk-bond rating.
Caa	CCC	*Default.* Poor-quality issues that may be in default or in danger of default.
Ca	CC	*Default.* Highly speculative issues, often in default or possessing other market shortcomings.
C		*Default.* These issues may be regarded as extremely poor in investment quality.
	C	*Default.* Rating given to income bonds on which no interest is paid.
	D	*Default.* Issues actually in default, with principal or interest in arrears.

Source: Moody's *Bond Record* and Standard & Poor's *Bond Guide.*

ignate *investment-grade* bonds. Such ratings are highly coveted by issuers; they indicate financially strong, well-run companies. The next two ratings (Ba/B or BB/B) are reserved for junk bonds. These ratings mean that although *the principal and interest payments on the bonds are still being met in a prompt and timely fashion,* the risk of default is relatively high, because the issuers generally lack the financial strength that backs investment-grade issues. (Sometimes the Caa1/CCC+ category is counted as part of the junk category, although technically the C rating class is meant to designate bonds that are already in default or are getting very close to it.) Most of the time, Moody's and S&P assign identical ratings. Sometimes, however, an issue carries two different ratings. These **split ratings** are viewed simply as "shading" the quality of an issue one way or another. For example, an issue might be rated Aa by Moody's but A or A+ by S&P.

split ratings
different ratings given to a bond issue by the two major rating agencies.

Also, just because a bond is given a certain rating at the time of issue doesn't mean it will keep that rating for the rest of its life. Ratings change as the financial condition of the issuer changes. In fact, all rated issues are reviewed on a regular basis to ensure that the assigned rating is still valid. Many issues carry a single rating to maturity, but it is not uncommon for ratings to be revised up or down during the life of the issue. As you might expect, the market responds to rating revisions by adjusting bond yields accordingly. For example, an upward revision (e.g., from A to AA) causes the market yield on the bond to drop, as a reflection of the bond's improved quality. One final point: Although it may appear that the firm is receiving the rating, it is actually the *issue* that receives it. As a result, a firm's different issues can have different ratings. The senior securities, for example, might carry one rating and the junior issues another, lower rating.

> **INVESTOR FACT**
>
> BETTING ON AN UPGRADE—"You say *potayto* and I say *potawto,*" as the old song goes. It turns out that some corporate bonds appear to be of investment-grade quality to one credit rating agency but look like junk to another. Such bonds—which are given a low *investment-grade* rating by one agency and a lower *junk bond* rating by another—are known as crossover bonds, and they are proving to be popular with investors. For one thing, they usually pay higher interest rates than a purely investment-grade bond, because one rating agency thinks the credit risk is greater. But they also offer investors the opportunity for capital appreciation. The reason: Often, the rating agency that called the bond junk eventually upgrades its credit rating, making the bond more valuable.

What Ratings Mean

Most bond investors pay close attention to agency ratings, because they can affect not only potential market behavior but comparative market yields as well. Specifically, the higher the rating, the lower the yield of an obligation, other things being equal. For example, whereas an A-rated bond might offer a 7.5% yield, a comparable triple-A issue would probably yield something like 7%. Furthermore, investment-grade securities are far more interest-sensitive and tend to exhibit more uniform price behavior than junk bonds and other lower-rated issues. Perhaps most important, *bond ratings serve to spare individual investors the drudgery of evaluating the investment quality of an issue on their own.* Large institutional investors often have their own staff of credit analysts who independently assess the creditworthiness of various corporate and municipal issuers; individual investors, in contrast, have little if anything to gain from conducting their own credit analysis. After all, credit analysis is time-consuming and costly, and it demands a good deal more expertise than the average individual investor possesses. Most important, the ratings are closely adhered to by a large segment of the bond investment community, in large part because it has been shown that *the rating agencies themselves do a remarkably good job of assessing bond quality.* Thus individual investors can depend on assigned agency ratings as a viable measure of the creditworthiness of the issuer and an issue's risk of default. A word of caution is in order, however: Bear in mind that bond ratings are intended to measure only an issue's *default risk,* which has no bearing whatsoever on an issue's exposure to *market risk.* Thus if interest rates increase, even the highest-quality issues go down in price, subjecting investors to capital loss and market risk.

Reading the Quotes

One thing you quickly learn in the bond market is that transactions are not always as easy to conduct as they may seem. In the first place, many bonds have relatively "thin" markets, which means that not a lot of trading goes on; indeed, some issues may trade only five or ten bonds a week, and many have no secondary market at all. There are, of course, numerous high-volume issues, but even so, you should pay particularly close attention to an issue's trading volume—especially if you're looking for lots of price action and need prompt order executions. In addition, it's not always easy to obtain current information on bond prices and other market developments. That's because most bonds trade in over-the-counter markets, which are somewhat specialized, rather than on centralized exchanges; the financial pages provide little information on general market activity and even less on particular securities. Indeed, daily price quotes are widely available on only a few of the thousands of publicly traded corporate and municipal bonds. Finally, investors often have to look to both brokers and bankers to complete transactions. The reason is that most brokerage houses tend to confine their activities to new issues and to secondary market transactions of listed Treasury obligations, agency issues, and corporate bonds; commercial banks, in contrast, are still the major dealers in municipal bonds and are active in Treasury and agency securities as well.

Except for municipal issues (which are usually quoted in terms of the yield they offer), bonds are quoted on the basis of their dollar prices. Such quotes are always interpreted as a *percent of par.* Thus a quote of 97½ does not mean $97.50 but, instead, means that the issue is trading at 97.5% of the par value of the obligation. In the bond market, it's assumed that we're dealing with bonds that have par values of $1,000—or some multiple thereof. Accordingly, a quote of 97½ translates into a dollar price of $975. (With bond quotes, 1 point = $10, and ⅛ of a point = $1.25.) As can be seen in the bond quotes in Figure 8.5, one quotation system is used for corporate bonds and another for governments. (Treasuries and agencies are quoted the same.)

Corporate Bond Quotes

current yield
measure of the annual interest income a bond provides relative to its current market price.

To understand the system used with corporate bonds, look at the AT&T issue highlighted in Figure 8.5. The group of numbers immediately following the company name (which is often highly abbreviated) gives the coupon and the year in which the bond matures; thus, the "8⅛ 22" means that this particular bond carries an 8⅛% annual coupon and will mature in the year 2022. The next column, labeled "Curr Yld," provides the *current yield*—in this case, 7.8%—being offered by the issue at its *current market price.* **Current yield** is a measure of the amount of annual interest income a bond provides relative to its prevailing market price. It is found by dividing annual coupon income by the closing price of the issue. In many respects, it is equivalent to the dividend yield measure used with stocks. We'll look at this bond valuation measure in more detail in Chapter 9. The next entry in the AT&T quote in Figure 8.5 is the "Vol" column, which shows the actual number of bonds traded. In this case, 65 bonds were traded on the day of the quotes. The last two columns provide the bond's closing price for the day and the net change in the closing price. Thus the bond's closing (or last) price was 104¾, which was down a quarter of a point (−¼) from its last close. In dollars, that means the bond traded at $1,047.50, which was $2.50 lower than its previous close. Note that corporate bonds are usually quoted in eighths of a point (for that matter, so are munis), although as we'll see, that's not the case with Treasury and agency bonds.

Government Bond Quotes

In contrast to corporates (and munis), U.S. government bonds (which include Treasuries as well as agency issues) are listed in thirty-seconds of a point. With government bonds, the figures to the right of the colon (:) indicate the number of thirty-seconds in the fractional bid or ask price. For example, look at the bid price of the highlighted 10¾% Treasury issue; observe that it is being quoted at 129:19 (bid). Translated, that means the bond is being quoted at 129¹⁹⁄₃₂, or 129.594% of par. Thus if you wanted to buy, say, $15,000 worth of this issue, you would have to pay $19,439 ($15,000 × 1.29594). Actually, the amount would be more than that after dealer spreads and other transaction costs were tacked on. Here's an example of a bond that is trading at a big premium (some 29 percent *above* its par value), in large part because market interest rates have fallen well below the bond's coupon.

Treasury (and agency) bond quotes include not only the coupon (see the "Rate" column of the Treasury quotes) but also the year and *month* of maturity. Note also that when there's more than one date in the maturity column (e.g., see the 13⅞% Treasury bond, which shows a maturity of 2006–11), it's the *second* figure that indicates the issue's maturity date; the first one shows

FIGURE 8.5 Price Quotations for Corporate and Government Bonds

Both corporate and Treasury bonds are quoted as a percent of their par values, but note that corporate bonds are quoted in eighths of a point, whereas Treasuries are quoted in thirty-seconds. Also observe that both coupon and maturity play vital roles in the quotation system. (Source: *Wall Street Journal,* November 21, 1997.)

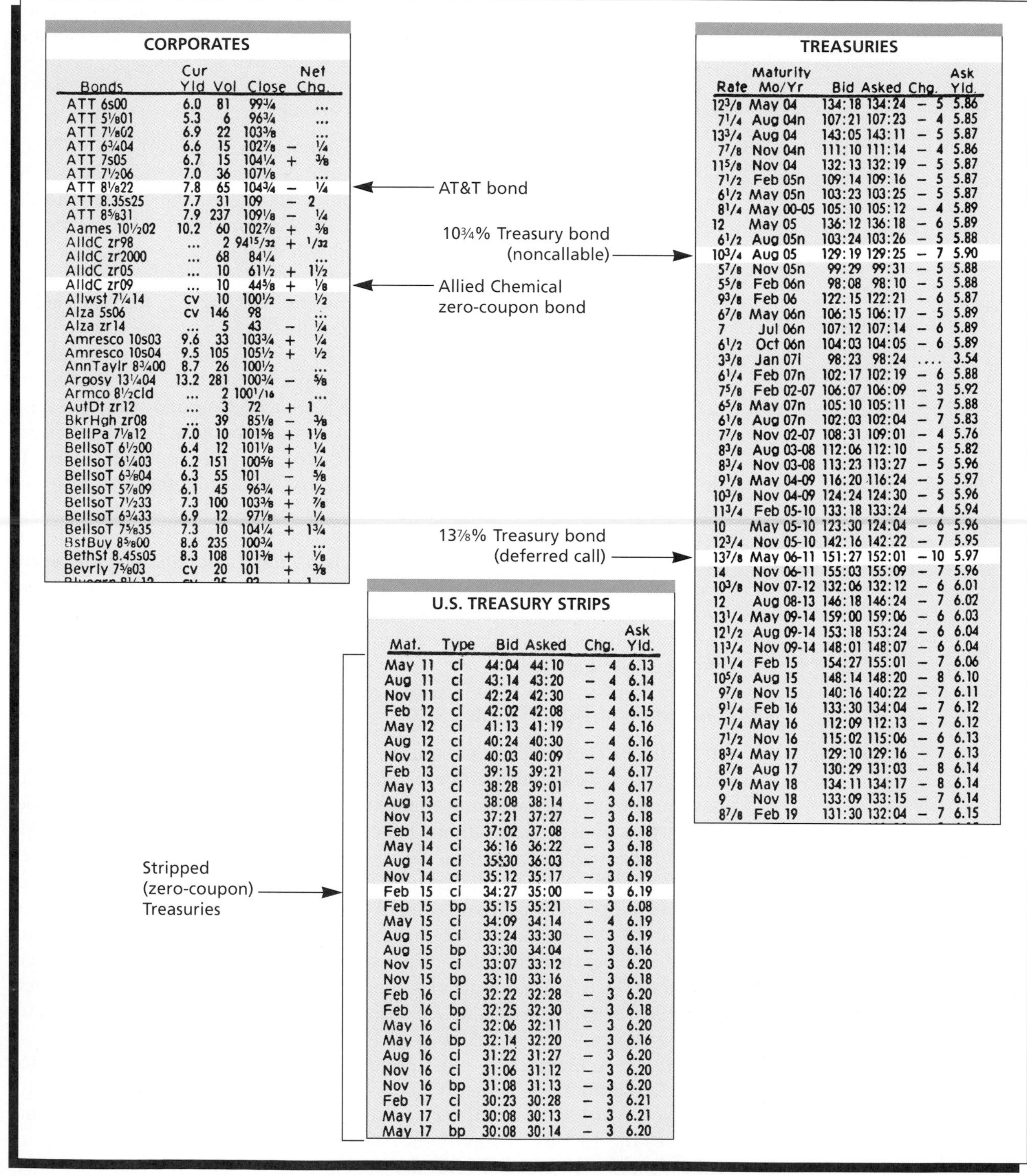

CORPORATES

Bonds	Cur Yld	Vol	Close	Net Chg.
ATT 6s00	6.0	81	99¾	...
ATT 5⅛01	5.3	6	96¾	...
ATT 7⅛02	6.9	22	103⅜	...
ATT 6¾04	6.6	15	102⅞	− ¼
ATT 7s05	6.7	15	104¼	+ ⅜
ATT 7½06	7.0	36	107⅛	...
ATT 8⅛22	7.8	65	104¾	− ¼
ATT 8.35s25	7.7	31	109	− 2
ATT 8⅝31	7.9	237	109⅛	− ¼
Aames 10½02	10.2	60	102⅞	+ ⅜
AlldC zr98	...	2	94 15/32	+ 1/32
AlldC zr2000	...	68	84¼	...
AlldC zr05	...	10	61½	+ 1½
AlldC zr09	...	10	44⅝	+ ⅛
Allwst 7¼14	cv	10	100½	− ½
Alza 5s06	cv	146	98	...
Alza zr14	...	5	43	− ¼
Amresco 10s03	9.6	33	103¾	+ ¼
Amresco 10s04	9.5	105	105½	+ ½
AnnTaylr 8¾00	8.7	26	100½	...
Argosy 13¼04	13.2	281	100¾	− ⅝
Armco 8½cld	...	2	100 1/16	...
AutDt zr12	...	3	72	+ 1
BkrHgh zr08	...	39	85⅛	− ⅜
BellPa 7⅛12	7.0	10	101⅝	+ 1⅛
BellsoT 6½00	6.4	12	101⅛	+ ¼
BellsoT 6¼03	6.2	151	100⅝	+ ¼
BellsoT 6⅜04	6.3	55	101	− ⅝
BellsoT 5⅞09	6.1	45	96¾	+ ½
BellsoT 7½33	7.3	100	103⅜	+ ⅞
BellsoT 6¾33	6.9	12	97⅛	+ ¼
BellsoT 7⅝35	7.3	10	104¼	+ 1¾
BstBuy 8⅝00	8.6	235	100¾	...
BethSt 8.45s05	8.3	108	101⅜	+ ⅛
Bevrly 7⅝03	cv	20	101	+ ⅜

TREASURIES

Rate	Maturity Mo/Yr	Bid	Asked	Chg.	Ask Yld.
12⅜	May 04	134:18	134:24	− 5	5.86
7¼	Aug 04n	107:21	107:23	− 4	5.85
13¾	Aug 04	143:05	143:11	− 5	5.87
7⅞	Nov 04n	111:10	111:14	− 4	5.86
11⅝	Nov 04	132:13	132:19	− 5	5.87
7½	Feb 05n	109:14	109:16	− 5	5.87
6½	May 05n	103:23	103:25	− 5	5.87
8¼	May 00-05	105:10	105:12	− 4	5.89
12	May 05	136:12	136:18	− 6	5.89
6½	Aug 05n	103:24	103:26	− 5	5.88
10¾	Aug 05	129:19	129:25	− 7	5.90
5⅞	Nov 05n	99:29	99:31	− 5	5.88
5⅝	Feb 06n	98:08	98:10	− 5	5.88
9⅜	Feb 06	122:15	122:21	− 6	5.87
6⅞	May 06n	106:15	106:17	− 5	5.89
7	Jul 06n	107:12	107:14	− 6	5.89
6½	Oct 06n	104:03	104:05	− 6	5.89
3⅜	Jan 07I	98:23	98:24	....	3.54
6¼	Feb 07n	102:17	102:19	− 6	5.88
7⅝	Feb 02-07	106:07	106:09	− 3	5.92
6⅝	May 07n	105:10	105:11	− 7	5.88
6⅛	Aug 07n	102:03	102:04	− 7	5.83
7⅞	Nov 02-07	108:31	109:01	− 4	5.76
8⅜	Aug 03-08	112:06	112:10	− 5	5.82
8¾	Nov 03-08	113:23	113:27	− 5	5.96
9⅛	May 04-09	116:20	116:24	− 5	5.97
10⅜	Nov 04-09	124:24	124:30	− 5	5.96
11¾	Feb 05-10	133:18	133:24	− 4	5.94
10	May 05-10	123:30	124:04	− 6	5.96
12¾	Nov 05-10	142:16	142:22	− 7	5.95
13⅞	May 06-11	151:27	152:01	− 10	5.97
14	Nov 06-11	155:03	155:09	− 7	5.96
10⅜	Nov 07-12	132:06	132:12	− 6	6.01
12	Aug 08-13	146:18	146:24	− 7	6.02
13¼	May 09-14	159:00	159:06	− 6	6.03
12½	Aug 09-14	153:18	153:24	− 6	6.04
11¾	Nov 09-14	148:01	148:07	− 6	6.04
11¼	Feb 15	154:27	155:01	− 7	6.06
10⅝	Aug 15	148:14	148:20	− 8	6.10
9⅞	Nov 15	140:16	140:22	− 7	6.11
9¼	Feb 16	133:30	134:04	− 7	6.12
7¼	May 16	112:09	112:13	− 7	6.12
7½	Nov 16	115:02	115:06	− 6	6.13
8¾	May 17	129:10	129:16	− 7	6.13
8⅞	Aug 17	130:29	131:03	− 8	6.14
9⅛	May 18	134:11	134:17	− 8	6.14
9	Nov 18	133:09	133:15	− 7	6.14
8⅞	Feb 19	131:30	132:04	− 7	6.15

U.S. TREASURY STRIPS

Mat.	Type	Bid	Asked	Chg.	Ask Yld.
May 11	ci	44:04	44:10	− 4	6.13
Aug 11	ci	43:14	43:20	− 4	6.14
Nov 11	ci	42:24	42:30	− 4	6.14
Feb 12	ci	42:02	42:08	− 4	6.15
May 12	ci	41:13	41:19	− 4	6.16
Aug 12	ci	40:24	40:30	− 4	6.16
Nov 12	ci	40:03	40:09	− 4	6.16
Feb 13	ci	39:15	39:21	− 4	6.17
May 13	ci	38:28	39:01	− 4	6.17
Aug 13	ci	38:08	38:14	− 3	6.18
Nov 13	ci	37:21	37:27	− 3	6.18
Feb 14	ci	37:02	37:08	− 3	6.18
May 14	ci	36:16	36:22	− 3	6.18
Aug 14	ci	35:30	36:03	− 3	6.18
Nov 14	ci	35:12	35:17	− 3	6.19
Feb 15	ci	34:27	35:00	− 3	6.19
Feb 15	bp	35:15	35:21	− 3	6.08
May 15	ci	34:09	34:14	− 4	6.19
Aug 15	ci	33:24	33:30	− 3	6.19
Aug 15	bp	33:30	34:04	− 3	6.16
Nov 15	ci	33:07	33:12	− 3	6.20
Nov 15	bp	33:10	33:16	− 3	6.18
Feb 16	ci	32:22	32:28	− 3	6.20
Feb 16	bp	32:25	32:30	− 3	6.18
May 16	ci	32:06	32:11	− 3	6.20
May 16	bp	32:14	32:20	− 3	6.16
Aug 16	ci	31:22	31:27	− 3	6.20
Nov 16	ci	31:06	31:12	− 3	6.20
Nov 16	bp	31:08	31:13	− 3	6.20
Feb 17	ci	30:23	30:28	− 3	6.21
May 17	ci	30:08	30:13	− 3	6.21
May 17	bp	30:08	30:14	− 3	6.20

when the bond becomes freely callable. Thus the 13⅞% bond matures in May 2011, and it carries a call deferment provision that extends through May 2006. In contrast, a Treasury note or bond with a single maturity date, such as the 10¾% bond of August 2005, indicates that the issue is *noncallable.* Unlike corporates, these bonds are quoted in bid/ask terms, where the bid price signifies what the bond dealers are willing to pay for the securities (which is how much you can sell them for), and the ask price is what the dealers will sell the bonds for (which is what you have to pay to buy them). Again, keep in mind that these bid/ask prices ignore transaction costs. When transaction costs are factored in, you'll end up getting *less* than the quoted price when you sell and paying *more* than the quoted price when you buy. This is especially true in the Treasury, agency, and municipal markets, where (secondary market) trades of, say, $25,000 or less can involve transactions costs of as much as *1% to 5%* of the amount traded. Finally, note that the "Yld" column with Treasuries is not the current yield of the issue but rather the bond's *promised yield-to-maturity.* Promised yield-to-maturity is basically a fully compounded measure of return that captures both current income and capital gains or losses. (We'll examine yield-to-maturity in Chapter 9.)

Quotes on Zero-Coupon Bonds

Also highlighted in both the corporate and Treasury quotes are some zero-coupon bonds. Look at the Allied Chemical ("AlldC") bonds in the corporate column; these are all zero-coupon bonds. Such bonds are easy to pick out because they're identified by a *zr* in place of their coupons. For instance, note the highlighted Allied Chemical bond; the *zr09* tells you the issue is a zero-coupon bond that matures in 2009. Zeros are even easier to pick out in the Treasury quotes, because they're all listed under the heading "U.S. Treasury Strips." As we discussed earlier in this chapter, the Treasury creates these securities by "stripping" the coupons from their bond issues and selling them separately from the principal. Thus the principal and interest *cash flows* can be sold on their own. (Look at the Strips quotes: A *ci* behind the maturity date means the issue is made up of coupon/interest cash flow, whereas a *bp* means it is made up of bond principal.) Regardless of whether they're corporates or stripped Treasuries, the prices of most zeros are quite low compared to regular coupon bonds; this is particularly true for longer maturities. Thus the quoted price of 44⅝ for the highlighted Allied Chemical issue is *not* a misprint; rather, it means you could buy this bond for $446.25 (or 44.625% of par) and in the year 2009 receive $1,000 in return. Likewise, you could buy the (highlighted) Feb-15 stripped Treasury for just $350 (or 35.00% of par) and in 2015 receive a payment of $1,000 on your investment, which would provide you with a fully compounded return of 6.19%.

CONCEPTS IN REVIEW

8.14 What are *bond ratings,* and how can they affect investor returns? What are *split ratings?*

8.15 From the perspective of an individual investor, what good are bond ratings? Do bond ratings provide any indication of the amount of market risk embedded in a bond? Explain.

8.16 Bonds are said to be quoted "as a percent of par." What does that mean? What is 1 point worth in the bond market?

8.17 Why should an aggressive bond trader be concerned with the trading volume of a particular issue?

http://hepg.aw.com

If investors plan to hold their bond investments until maturity, the risk most relevant to them is the probability of default. The Web makes it easier than ever to keep abreast of changes in bond ratings. Moody's Investors Service is one of the premier companies that provide default ratings.

www.Moodys.com

Summary

LG 1 **Explain the basic investment attributes of bonds and the appeal they hold as investment vehicles.** Bonds are publicly traded debt securities that provide investors with two types of income: (1) current income and (2) capital gains. Current income is derived from the coupon (interest) payments received over the life of the issue, whereas capital gains can be earned whenever market interest rates fall. In addition to their yields and returns, bonds can also be used to shelter income from taxes and for the preservation and long-term accumulation of capital.

LG 2 **Describe the essential features of a bond and distinguish among different types of call, refunding, and sinking-fund provisions.** All bonds carry some type of coupon, which specifies the annual rate of interest to be paid by the issuer. In addition, bonds have predetermined maturity dates—some bonds carry a single maturity date (e.g., term bonds), and others have a series of maturity dates (e.g., a serial issue). Every bond is issued with some type of call feature, be it freely callable, noncallable, or deferred callable. Call features spell out whether an issue can be prematurely retired and, if so, when. Some bonds (temporarily) prohibit the issuer from paying off one bond with the proceeds from another by including a refunding provision, and others are issued with sinking-fund provisions, which specify how a bond is to be paid off over time.

LG 3 **Describe the relationship between bond prices and yields, and explain why some bonds are more volatile than others.** The price behavior of a bond depends on the issue's coupon and maturity and on the movement in market interest rates. When interest rates go down, bond prices go up, and vice versa. However, the extent to which bond prices move up or down depends on the coupon and maturity of an issue. Bonds with lower coupons and/or longer maturities generate larger price swings.

LG 4 **Identify the different types of bonds and the kinds of investment objectives these fixed-income securities can fulfill.** The bond market is divided into four major segments: Treasuries, agencies, municipals, and corporates. Treasury bonds are issued by the U.S. Treasury and are virtually default-free. Agency bonds are issued by various political subdivisions of the U.S. government and make up an increasingly important segment of the bond market. Municipal bonds are issued by state and local governments in the form of either general obligation or revenue bonds. Corporate bonds make up the major nongovernment sector of the market and are backed by the assets and profitability of the issuing companies. Generally speaking, Treasuries are attractive because of their high quality, agencies and corporates because of the added returns they provide, and munis because of the tax shelter they offer.

LG 5 **Discuss the global nature of the bond market and the difference between dollar-denominated and non-dollar-denominated foreign bonds.** There's growing investor interest in foreign bonds—particularly foreign-pay securities—because of the highly competitive yields and returns they offer. Foreign-pay bonds cover all those issues that are denominated in some currency other than dollars. These bonds have an added source of return: currency exchange rates. In addition, there are dollar-denominated foreign bonds—Yankee bonds and Eurodollar bonds—which have no currency exchange risk because they are issued in U.S. dollars.

LG 6 **Describe the role that bond ratings play in the market and the quotation system used with various types of bonds.** Municipal and corporate issues are regularly rated for bond quality by independent rating agencies. A rating of Aaa indicates an impeccable record; lower ratings, such as A or Baa, indicate less protection for the investor. As with all investments, the returns required of lower-quality instruments generally are higher than those required of high-quality bonds. The bond market also has its own quotation system, wherein bonds are quoted as a percent of par. Thus 1 point in the bond market represents $10, not $1 as in the stock market.

Discussion Questions

LG 1

Q8.1. Using the bond returns in Tables 8.1 and 8.2 as a basis of discussion:

a. Compare the returns during the 1970s to those produced in the 1980s. How do you explain the differences?

b. How's the market doing so far in the 1990s? How does the performance in this decade compare to that in the 1980s and 1970s? Explain.

c. What do you think would be a fair rate of return to expect from bonds in the future? Explain.

LG 4

Q8.2. Identify and briefly describe each of the following types of bonds.

a. Agency bonds
b. Municipal bonds
c. Zero-coupon bonds
d. Junk bonds
e. Foreign bonds
f. Collateralized mortgage obligations (CMOs)

What type of investor do you think would be most attracted to each?

LG 1 LG 4

Q8.3. "Treasury securities are guaranteed by the U.S. government; therefore, there is no risk in the ownership of such bonds." Briefly discuss the wisdom (or folly) of this statement.

LG 4 LG 5

Q8.4. Select the security in the left-hand column that best fits the investor desire described in the right-hand column.

a. 5-year Treasury note	1. Lock in a high coupon yield.
b. A bond with a low coupon and a long maturity	2. Accumulate capital over a long period of time.
c. Yankee bond	3. Generate a monthly income.
d. Insured revenue bond	4. Avoid a lot of price volatility.
e. Long-term Treasury Strips	5. Generate tax-free income.
f. Noncallable bond	6. Invest in a foreign bond.
g. CMO	7. Go for the highest yield available.
h. Junk bond	8. Invest in a pool of credit-card receivables.
i. ABS	9. Go for maximum price appreciation.

LG 6

Q8.5. Using the quotes in Figure 8.5, answer the following questions.

a. What's the dollar (bid) price of the Feb–17 Treasury Strip bond, and when does it mature?

b. What's the current yield on the Feb–17 Treasury Strip issue?
c. Which is higher priced: the AT&T 7⅛–02 or the 7½% U.S. Treasury of Nov–16? (Use ask prices.) Both bonds carry roughly the same coupons. Why don't they sell for about the same price?
d. What's the dollar (ask) price of the 14% U.S. Treasury of Nov 06–11? Why is that issue priced so high? When does it mature?
e. Contrast the call feature on the 12½% Aug 09–14 Treasury bond with the 9¼% Feb–16 Treasury issue.
f. Which bond was more actively traded, the AT&T 7½–06 or the Bell South Telephone (BellsoT) 6¼–03?
g. Which of the following bonds has the highest current yield, the Ann Taylor 8¾–00, the U.S. Treasury 13¼% of Aug–04 or the U.S. Treasury Strip of Nov–17? Which one has the lowest current yield? Which one would produce the most dollar amount of annual interest income (per $1,000 par bond)?

Problems

LG 6 P8.1. A 6%, 15-year bond has 3 years remaining on a deferred call feature (the call premium is equal to 1 year's interest). The bond is currently priced in the market at $850. What is the issue's current yield?

LG 4 P8.2. An investor is in the 28% tax bracket and lives in a state with no income tax. He is trying to decide which of two bonds to purchase. One is a 7½% corporate bond that is selling at par, and the other is a municipal bond with a 5¼% coupon that is also selling at par. If all other features of these two bonds are comparable, which should the investor select? Why? Would your answer change if this were an *in-state* municipal bond and the investor lived in a place with high state income taxes? Explain.

LG 4 P8.3. Sara Thomas is a wealthy investor who's looking for a tax shelter. Sara is in the maximum (39.6%) federal tax bracket, and she lives in a state with a very high state income tax (she pays the maximum of 11½% in state income tax). Sara is currently looking at two municipal bonds, both of which are selling at par. One is a double-A-rated *in-state* bond that carries a coupon of 6⅜%, and the other is a double-A-rated *out-of-state* bond that carries a 7⅛% coupon. Her broker has informed her that comparable fully taxable corporate bonds are currently available with yields of 9¾%; alternatively, long Treasuries are now available at yields of 9%. She has $100,000 to invest, and because all the bonds are high-quality issues, she wants to select the one that will give her maximum after-tax returns.

a. Which one of the four bonds should she buy?
b. Rank the four bonds (from best to worst) in terms of their taxable equivalent yields.

LG 6 P8.4. Which of the following three bonds offers the highest current yield?

a. A 9½%, 20-year bond quoted at 97¾
b. A 16%, 15-year bond quoted at 164⅝
c. A 5¼%, 18-year bond quoted at 54

LG 6 P8.5. Assume that an investor pays $850 for a long-term bond that carries a 7½% coupon. Over the course of the next 12 months, interest rates drop sharply, and as a result, the investor sells the bond at a price of $962.50.

a. Find the current yield that existed on this bond at the beginning of the year. What was it by the end of the 1-year holding period?
b. Determine the holding period return on this investment. (See Chapter 4 for the HPR formula.)

LG 1

P8.6. In early January 1994, an investor purchased $30,000 worth of some single-A-rated corporate bonds; the bonds carried a coupon of 8⅞% and mature in 2011. The investor paid 94⅛ when she bought the bonds, and over the 5-year period from 1994 through 1998, the bonds were priced in the market as follows:

	Quoted Prices		
Year	Beginning of the Year	End of the Year	Year-End Bond Yields
1994	94⅛	100⅝	8.82%
1995	100⅝	102	8.70
1996	102	104⅝	8.48
1997	104⅝	110¼	8.05
1998	110¼	121⅛	7.33

Coupon payments were made on schedule throughout the 5-year period.

a. Find the annual holding period returns for 1994 through 1998. (See Chapter 4 for the HPR formula.)
b. Use the return information in Table 8.1 to evaluate the investment performance of this bond. How do you think it stacks up against the market? Explain.

LG 5

P8.7. Letticia Garcia is an aggressive bond investor and is currently thinking about investing in a foreign (non-dollar-denominated) government bond. In particular, she's looking at a German government bond that matures in 15 years and carries a 9½% coupon. The bond has a par value of 10,000 D-marks and is currently trading at 110 (i.e., at 110% of par).

Letticia plans to hold the bond for a period of 1 year, at which time she thinks it will be trading at 117½—she's anticipating a sharp decline in German interest rates, which explains why she expects bond prices to move up. The current exchange rate is 1.58 D-marks/U.S. $, but she expects that to fall to 1.25 D-marks/U.S. $. Use the foreign investment return formula introduced in Chapter 5 (Equation 5.6) to answer the questions below.

a. *Ignoring the currency effect,* find the bond's total return (in its local currency).
b. Now find the total return on this bond *in U.S. dollars.* Did currency exchange rates affect the return in any way? Do you think this bond would make a good investment? Explain.

Case Problem 8.1 *Frank and Lucille Develop a Bond Investment Program*

LG 4 LG 6

Frank and Lucille Lasnicka, along with their two teenage sons, Lou and Lamar, live in Jenks, Oklahoma. Frank works as an electronics salesman, and Lucille is a personnel officer at a local bank; together they earn an annual income of around $75,000. Frank has just learned that his recently departed rich uncle has named him in his will to the tune of some $250,000 after taxes. Needless to say, the Lasnickas are elated. Frank intends to spend $50,000 of his inheritance on a number of long-overdue family items (e.g., some badly needed remodeling of their kitchen and family room, the down payment on a new Porsche Boxster, and braces to correct Lamar's overbite); he wants to invest the remaining $200,000 in various types of fixed-income securities.

Frank and Lucille have no unusual income requirements or health problems. Their only investment objectives are that they want to achieve some capital appreciation and they want to keep their funds fully invested for a period of at least 20 years. They would rather not have to rely on their investments as a source of current income but want to maintain some liquidity in their portfolio just in case.

QUESTIONS

a. Describe the type of bond investment program you think the Lasnickas should follow. In answering this question, give appropriate consideration to both return and risk factors.

b. List several different types of bonds that you would recommend for their portfolio, and briefly indicate why you would recommend each.

c. Using a recent issue of the *Wall Street Journal* or *Barron's*, construct a $200,000 bond portfolio for the Lasnickas. Use real securities and select any eight bonds (or notes) you like, given the following ground rules:

1. The portfolio must include at least one Treasury, one agency, and one corporate bond.
2. No more than 5% of the portfolio can be in short-term U.S. Treasury bills.
3. Ignore all transaction costs (i.e., invest the full $200,000) and assume all securities have par values of $1,000 (though they can be trading in the market at something other than par).
4. Use the latest available quotes to determine how many bonds/notes/bills you can buy.

d. Prepare a schedule listing all the securities in your recommended portfolio. *Use a form like the one shown here,* and include the information it calls for on each security in the portfolio.

Security Issuer-Coupon-Maturity	Latest Quoted Price	Number of Bonds Purchased	Amount Invested	Annual Coupon Income	Current Yield
Example: U.S. Treas - 8½%-'05	96⁸⁄₃₂	25	$ 24,062	$ 2,125	8.83%
1.					
2.					
3.					
4.					
5.					
6.					
7.					
8.					
Totals	—		$200,000	$	%

e. *In one brief paragraph,* note the key investment attributes of your recommended portfolio and the investment objectives you hope to achieve with it.

Case Problem 8.2 The Case of the Missing Bond Ratings

LG 6

A lot goes into a bond rating, but it's probably safe to say that there's nothing more important in determining a bond's rating than the underlying financial condition and operating results of the company issuing the bond. Generally speaking, a variety of financial ratios are used to assess the financial health of a firm, and just as financial ratios can be used in the analysis of common stocks, they can be used in the analysis of bonds—a process we refer to as *credit analysis*. In credit analysis, attention is directed toward the basic liquidity and profitability of the firm, the extent to which the firm employs debt, and the ability of the firm to service its debt.

The following financial ratios are often helpful in carrying out such analysis: (1) current ratio, (2) quick ratio, (3) net profit margin, (4) return on total capital, (5) long-term debt to total capital, (6) owners' equity ratio, (7) pretax interest coverage, and (8) cash flow to total debt. The first two ratios measure the liquidity of the firm, the next two its profitability, the following two the debt load, and the final two the ability of the firm to service its debt load. (For ratio 5, the *lower* the ratio, the better; for all the others, the *higher* the ratio, the better.) The following table lists each of these ratios for six different companies.

A Table of Financial Ratios

(All ratios are real and pertain to real companies.)

Financial Ratio	Company 1	Company 2	Company 3	Company 4	Company 5	Company 6
1. Current ratio	1.13 ×	1.39 ×	1.78 ×	1.32 ×	1.03 ×	1.41 ×
2. Quick ratio	0.48 ×	0.84 ×	0.93 ×	0.33 ×	0.50 ×	0.75 ×
3. Net profit margin	4.6%	12.9%	14.5%	2.8%	5.9%	10.0%
4. Return on total capital	15.0%	25.9%	29.4%	11.5%	16.8%	28.4%
5. Long-term debt to total capital	63.3%	52.7%	23.9%	97.0%	88.6%	42.1%
6. Owners' equity ratio	18.6%	18.9%	44.1%	1.5%	5.1%	21.2%
7. Pretax interest coverage	2.3 ×	4.5 ×	8.9 ×	1.7 ×	2.4 ×	6.4%
8. Cash flow to total debt	34.7%	48.8%	71.2%	20.4%	30.2%	42.7%

Notes: Ratio (2)—Whereas the current ratio relates current assets to current liabilities, the quick ratio considers only the most liquid current assets (cash, short-term securities, and accounts receivable) and relates them to current liabilities.
Ratio (4)—Relates pretax profit to the total capital structure (long-term debt + equity) of the firm.
Ratio (6)—Shows the amount of stockholders' equity used to finance the firm (stockholders' equity ÷ total assets).
Ratio (8)—Looks at the amount of corporate cash flow (from net profits + depreciation) relative to the total (current + long-term) debt of the firm.
The other four ratios are as described in Chapter 6.

QUESTIONS

a. Three of these companies have bonds that carry investment-grade ratings, and the other three companies carry junk-bond ratings. Judging by the information in the table, which three companies have the investment-grade bonds and which three the junk bonds? Briefly explain your selections.

b. One of these six companies is a AAA-rated firm and one is B-rated. Identify those two companies. Briefly explain your selection.

c. Of the remaining four companies, one carries a AA rating, one carries an A rating, and two are BB-rated. Which companies are they?

Home Page Exercises

http://hepg.aw.com **Keyword: Invest**

Loans are the most common type of regular financing for business and government. Investors have the opportunity to lend to some of the largest companies in the world through the purchase of bonds. Investors also help to finance part of the massive debt incurred by both federal and state governments. Information on bond investing is not so plentiful as the information that can be found on stocks. In spite of this relative paucity of information, the Web offers some interesting and useful information on bond investments.

Web Address	*Primary Investment Focus*
www.publicdebt.treas.gov/ bpd/bpdindex.htm#speindex	A wealth of information about all types of U.S. Treasury debt
www.bradynet.com	Dedicated totally to bonds, particularly strong in emerging markets
www.standardandpoors.com	Primarily information on bond ratings and other S&P services
www.dcrco.com	Primarily information on bond ratings and other Duff and Phelps services
www.moneyline.com/ mlc_bond.html	Descriptive information on municipal, Treasury, and agency bonds
www.psa.com	The Bond Market Association home page with links to bond Web sites

W8.1. Because the total debt of the U.S. Treasury exceeds $5 trillion, the Treasury must issue new debt on a regular schedule. Go to the following address and determine how often and when the U.S. Treasury issues its bills, notes, and bond

www.public.debt.treas.gov.of/ofpatsec.htm

W8.2. Knowledge of the probability of default is one of the most important inputs into the decisions investors make about which bonds to purchase. Moody's Investors Services is one of the best-known default-rating agencies. At Moody's Web address, find three issues that most recently have undergone changes in bond ratings. What bond ratings were changed and why?

www.Moodys.com/cgi-bin/pr.exe

Bond Valuation and Analysis

CHAPTER 9

Black & Decker

Black & Decker is one of the nation's largest and most successful manufacturers. Over the years, the company has acquired many smaller companies, often financing the acquisitions with long-term bonds. For example, as of December 31, 1997, the company had $250 million worth of debt paying 6.625% due in the year 2000. It also had $500 million in notes paying 7.5% due in 2003 and $250 million in notes paying 7% due in 2006. However, because of the relatively large amount of debt on its balance sheet, Black & Decker is rated only BBB− by Standard & Poor's Corporation. That is the lowest "investment-grade" rating issued by S&P. If the company's financial position were to weaken, then S&P could downgrade the bonds into the "junk" category, and the market price of Black & Decker bonds would react accordingly (it would go down).

As we'll see in this chapter, a number of factors determine a bond's price, including credit quality and the general level of interest rates. Investors must evaluate these factors when deciding whether the market value of a bond will provide the kind of return they need.

Learning Goals

After studying this chapter, you should be able to:

LG 1 Explain the behavior of market interest rates and identify the forces that cause interest rates to move.

LG 2 Describe the term structure of interest rates and note how these so-called yield curves can be used by investors.

LG 3 Gain an understanding of how bonds are valued in the marketplace.

LG 4 Describe the various measures of yield and return, and explain how these standards of performance are used in the bond valuation process.

LG 5 Understand the basic concept of duration, how it can be measured, and its use in the management of bond portfolios.

LG 6 Discuss various bond investment strategies and the different ways these securities can be used by investors.

The Behavior of Market Interest Rates

LG 1 LG 2

You will recall from Chapter 4 that rational investors try to earn a return that fully compensates them for risk. In the case of bondholders, that required return (r_i) has three components: the real rate of return (r^*), an expected inflation premium (IP), and a risk premium (RP). Thus the required return on a bond can be expressed by the following equation:

Equation 9.1

$$r_i = r^* + IP + RP$$

The real rate of return and inflation premium are external economic factors, and together they equal the risk-free rate (R_F). Now, to find the required return, we need to consider the unique features and properties of the bond issue itself; we can do this by adding the bond's risk premium to the risk-free rate. A bond's risk premium (RP) will take into account key issue and issuer characteristics, including such variables as the type of bond, maturity, call features, and bond rating. These three components (r^*, IP, and RP) then work together to determine interest rate levels at a given point in time.

Because interest rates have such a significant bearing on bond prices and yields, they are closely monitored by both conservative and aggressive investors. Interest rates are important to conservative investors because one of their major objectives is to lock in high yields. Aggressive traders also have a stake in interest rates because their investment programs are often built on the capital gains opportunities that accompany major swings in rates.

Keeping Tabs on Market Interest Rates

yield spreads
differences in interest rates that exist in various sectors of the market.

Just as there is no single bond market but a series of different market sectors, so too there is no single interest rate that applies to all segments of the market. Rather, each segment has its own, unique level of interest rates. Granted, the various rates tend to drift in the same direction over time and to follow the same general pattern of behavior, but it's also common for **yield spreads** (or interest rate differentials) to exist in the various market sectors. We can summarize the more important market yields and yield spreads as follows:

1. Municipal bonds usually carry the lowest market rates because of the tax-exempt feature of these obligations. As a rule, their market yields are about two-thirds those of corporates. In the taxable sector, Treasuries have the lowest yields (because they have the least risk), followed by agencies and then corporates, which provide the highest returns.

2. Issues that normally carry bond ratings (e.g., municipals or corporates) generally display the same behavior: The lower the rating, the higher the yield.

3. There is generally a direct relationship between the coupon an issue carries and its yield: Discount (low-coupon) bonds yield the least, and premium (high-coupon) bonds yield the most.

4. In the municipal sector, revenue bonds yield more than general obligation bonds.

5. Bonds that are freely callable generally provide the highest returns, at least at date of issue; these are followed by deferred call obligations and then by noncallable bonds, which yield the least.

6. As a rule, bonds with long maturities tend to yield more than short issues. However, this rule does not hold all the time; sometimes, such as in early 1989, short-term yields exceed the yields on long-term bonds.

The preceding list can be used as a general guide to the higher-yielding segments of the bond market. For example, income-oriented municipal bond investors might do well to consider certain high-quality revenue bonds as a way to increase yields; and investors who like to stick to high-quality issues might select agency bonds, rather than Treasuries, for the same reason.

As an investor, you should pay close attention to interest rates and yield spreads, and try to stay abreast not only of the current state of the market but also of the *future direction in market rates.* For example, if you are a conservative (income-oriented) investor and think that rates have just about peaked, that should be a clue to try to lock in the prevailing high yields with some form of call protection (e.g., buy bonds—like Treasuries or double-A-rated utilities—that are noncallable or still have lengthy call deferments). In contrast, if you're an aggressive bond trader who thinks rates have peaked (and are about to drop), that should be a signal to buy bonds that offer maximum price appreciation potential (e.g., low-coupon bonds that still have a long time before they mature). Clearly, in either case, the *future direction of interest rates is important!*

But how does a bond investor formulate such expectations? Unless you have considerable training in economics, you will probably have to rely on various published sources. Fortunately, a wealth of such information is available. Your broker is an excellent source for such reports, as are investor services such as Moody's and Standard & Poor's. Finally, there are widely circulated business and financial publications—like the *Wall Street Journal, Forbes, Business Week,* and *Fortune*—that regularly address the current state and future direction of market interest rates. One of the best of these is illustrated in Figure 9.1. Make no mistake about it, predicting the future direction of interest rates is not easy. However, by taking the time to read some of these publications and reports regularly and carefully, you, too, can keep track of the behavior of interest rates and at least get a handle on what experts predict is likely to occur in the near future—say, over the next 6 to 12 months, perhaps even longer.

What Causes Rates to Move?

Although the subject of interest rates is a complex economic issue, we do know that certain forces are especially important in influencing the general behavior of market rates. Serious bond investors should make it a point to become familiar with the major determinants of interest rates and try to monitor those variables—at least informally.

And in that regard, perhaps no variable is more important than *inflation.* Changes in the inflation rate (or even expectations about the future course of inflation) have a direct and pronounced effect on market interest rates and have been a leading cause of wide swings in interest rates. Clearly, if expectations are for inflation to slow down, then market interest rates should fall as well. To gain an appreciation of the extent to which interest rates are linked to inflation, take a look at Figure 9.2. Note that as inflation drifts up, so do

FIGURE 9.1 A Popular Source of Information About Interest Rates and the Credit Markets

The "Credit Markets" column, which appears every day in the *Wall Street Journal,* provides a capsule view of current conditions and future prospects in the bond market. Note that on this particular day, a good deal of the article was devoted to falling inflation, problems in the Asian markets, and municipal bonds. (Source: *Wall Street Journal,* November 19, 1997.)

CREDIT MARKETS

Bond Prices Slip Despite News of Low Inflation; Pittsburgh Sells Munis in Cyberspace Offering

By Brian Blackstone
And Kim Frick
Dow Jones Newswires

NEW YORK – Bond prices ended slightly lower, as profit-taking and continued concerns about events in Asia negated the impact of favorable inflation news here.

Meanwhile, Pittsburgh sold $70 million of general-obligation bonds in what underwriters said was the first municipal-bond auction via a limited-access Internet site. Pittsburgh's bonds were among $2 billion in municipal securities brought to market yesterday.

In trading, the benchmark 30-year Treasury bond fell 3/32 point, or 93.75 cents, for a bond with a $1,000 face value, to end at 100 22/32. Its yield rose to 6.066% from 6.059% late Monday, as bond yields move inversely to prices.

Treasurys gained early in the session after the Labor Department said consumer prices, either including or excluding food and energy, rose a moderate 0.2% last month. The gains, which were in line with forecasts, suggested that inflation remained subdued at the consumer level despite indications that labor markets remained tight amid brisk economic growth.

But the bond market quickly reversed course. Traders cited profit-taking and concerns that Japan's government may sell some U.S. government securities as part of an effort to boost its stock market and support troubled financial institutions.

"It felt like people's game plan was that if there was a weak CPI, they were going to take profits," said Hugh Whelan, vice president of the fixed-income group at Aeltus Investment Management. "We got as-expected numbers, and [the market] sold anyway," he added.

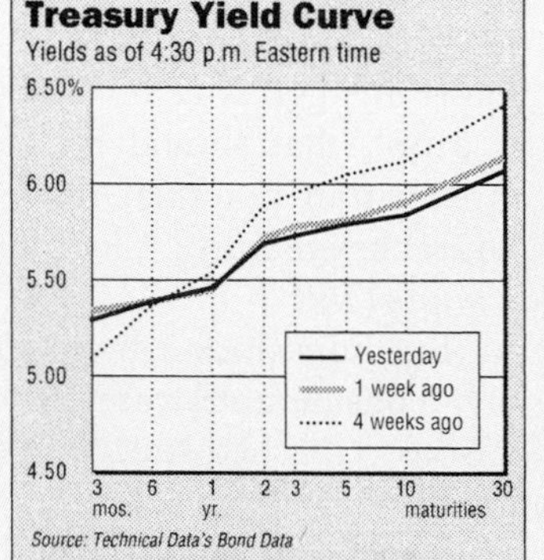

YIELD COMPARISONS

Based on Merrill Lynch Bond Indexes, priced as of midafternoon Eastern time.

	11/18	11/17	–52 Week– High	Low
Corp.-Govt. Master	6.13%	6.12%	7.02%	6.03%
Treasury 1-10yr	5.78	5.77	6.65	5.66
10+ yr	6.15	6.15	7.26	6.15
Agencies 1-10yr	6.19	6.19	7.08	6.04
10+ yr	6.42	6.43	7.56	6.32
Corporate				
1-10 yr High Qlty	6.26	6.26	7.18	6.12
Med Qlty	6.54	6.54	7.39	6.36
10+yr High Qlty	6.79	6.79	7.75	6.68
Med Qlty	7.07	7.07	8.05	6.98
Yankee bonds(1)	6.78	6.77	7.51	6.55
Current-coupon mortgages (2)				
GNMA 6.50%	6.79	6.78	7.93	6.72
FNMA 6.50%	6.84	6.83	7.87	6.80
FHLMC6.50%	6.85	6.83	7.88	6.81
High-yield corporates	8.49	8.49	9.65	8.29
Tax-Exempt Bonds				
7-12-yr G.O. (AA)	4.78	4.78	5.32	4.59
12-22-yr G.O. (AA)	5.19	5.19	5.87	5.02
22+yr revenue (A)	5.37	5.37	6.01	5.27

Note: High quality rated AAA-AA; medium quality A-BBB/Baa; high yield, BB/Ba-C.

(1) Dollar-denominated, SEC-registered bonds of foreign issuers sold in the U.S. (2) Reflects the 52-week high and low of mortgage-backed securities indexes rather than the individual securities shown.

real-estate investment trust was reduced in size and needed to offer a fatter yield than first advertised – a sign investors might be reluctant to buy up new high-yield bond supply in the wake of the Asian financial crisis and volatile U.S. equities markets.

"The calendar is way too deep," bemoaned Sandy Rufenacht, a portfolio manager at Janus Capital Corp. "Everyone has had a good year" and high-yield investor response so far this week shows a lack of desire for taking any new risks.

"Clearly, there are a few diamonds in the rough" in the calendar and "those deals will get done," predicted Melissa Weiler, a portfolio manager at California-based Trust Co. of the West. The others might have to try again in January, she added.

Mortgage Securities

Mortgage-backed securities closed 1/32 to 2/32 lower, despite heavy buying by underwriters accumulating collateral as a base for new structured mortgage deals.

While the market weakened, traders reported about $1 billion of demand for Fannie Mae 6.5% and 7% pass-throughs from dealers putting together new real estate mortgage investment conduit issues. Most of the Remic-driven buying took place Monday and yesterday, traders said.

The new structured deals haven't yet been publicly announced.

Although Remic issuance is humming along, some investors like Patrick Miner at Mutual of Omaha don't find planned amortization class, or PAC, securities particularly tempting at the moment. PACs are commonly created when underwriters put together structured deals. Recently Mr. Miner has stopped buying PACs because of their unappealing pricing.

interest rates. On the other hand, a drop in inflation is matched by a similar decline in interest rates.

In addition to inflation, there are at least five other important economic variables that can significantly affect the level of interest rates:

1. *Changes in the money supply.* An increase in the money supply pushes rates down (as it makes more funds available for loans), and vice versa. This

FIGURE 9.2
The Impact of Inflation on the Behavior of Interest Rates

The behavior of interest rates has always been closely tied to movements in the rate of inflation. What changed in the early 1980s, however, was the spread between inflation and interest rates. Whereas a spread of roughly 3 points was common in the past, it has held at about 5 to 6 percentage points since 1982.

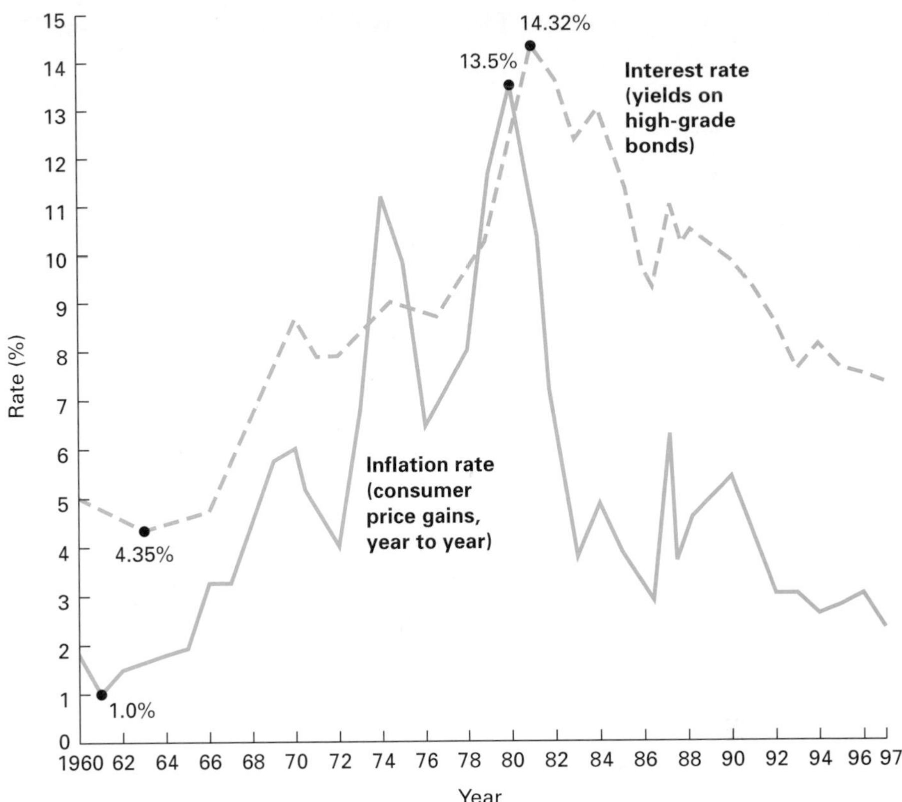

is true only up to a point, however. If the growth in the money supply becomes excessive, it can lead to inflation, which, of course, means higher interest rates.

2. *The size of the federal budget deficit.* When the U.S. Treasury must borrow large amounts to cover the budget deficit, the increased demand for funds exerts an upward pressure on interest rates. That's why bond market participants view the prospect of a balanced (or "near-balanced") federal deficit so favorably. That is, as the federal budget deficit declines/disappears, so will a lot of the pressure on bond interest rates (which brings with it the potential for falling market rates).

3. *The level of economic activity.* Businesses need more capital when the economy expands. This need increases the demand for funds, and rates tend to rise. During a recession, economic activity contracts, and rates typically fall.

4. *Policies of the Federal Reserve.* Actions of the Federal Reserve to control inflation also have a major effect on market interest rates. For example, when the Fed wants to slow real (or perceived) inflation, it usually does so by driving up interest rates, as it did seven times during 1994. Unfortunately, such actions can also have the nasty side effect of slowing down business activity as well.

5. *The level of interest rates in major foreign markets.* Today, investors look beyond national borders for investment opportunities. If rates in major foreign markets rise, that puts pressure on rates in the United States to rise as well; if they don't rise, foreign investors may be tempted to dump their dollars, as they did in 1992, to buy high-yielding foreign securities.

The Term Structure of Interest Rates and Yield Curves

term structure of interest rates
the relationship between the interest rate or rate of return (yield) on a bond and its time to maturity.

yield curve
a graph that represents the relationship between a bond's term to maturity and its yield at a given point in time.

Although many factors affect the behavior of market interest rates, one of the most popular and widely studied is *bond maturity.* The relationship between interest rates (yield) and time to maturity for any class of similar-risk securities is called the **term structure of interest rates.** This relationship can be depicted graphically by a **yield curve,** which relates a bond's *term* to maturity to its *yield* to maturity at a given point in time. A particular yield curve exists for only a short period of time; as market conditions change, so do the yield curve's shape and location.

Types of Yield Curves

Two different types of yield curves are illustrated in Figure 9.3. By far, the most common type is curve 1, the *upward-sloping* curve. It indicates that yields tend to increase with longer maturities. The longer a bond has to go to maturity, the greater the potential for price volatility and the risk of loss. Investors, therefore, require higher risk premiums to induce them to buy the longer, riskier bonds. Occasionally, the yield curve takes the *inverted,* or downward-sloping, shape shown in curve 2, where short-term rates are higher than long-term rates. This generally results from actions by the Federal Reserve to curtail inflation by driving short-term interest rates way up. In addition to these, there are two other types of yield curves that appear from time to time: the *flat* yield curve, when rates for short- and long-term debt are essentially the same, and the *humped* yield curve, when intermediate-term rates are the highest.

Plotting Your Own Curves

Yield curves are constructed by plotting the yields for a group of bonds that are similar in all respects but maturity. Treasury securities (bills, notes, and bonds) are typically used to construct yield curves. There are several reasons for this: Their yields are easily found in financial publications, they have no risk of default, and they are homogeneous with regard to quality and other

FIGURE 9.3
Two Types of Yield Curves

A yield curve relates term-to-maturity to yield-to-maturity at a given point in time. Although yield curves come in many shapes and forms, the most common is the *upward-sloping curve,* which shows that investor returns (yields) increase with longer maturities.

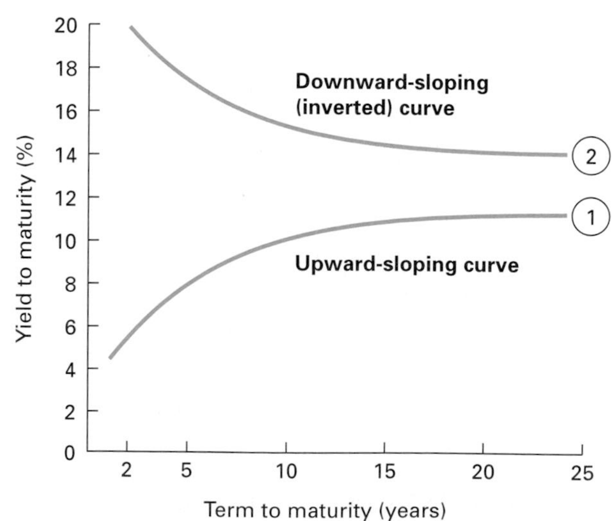

issue characteristics. Investors can also construct yield curves for other classes of debt securities, such as A-rated municipal bonds, Aa-rated corporate bonds, or even certificates of deposit.

Figure 9.4 shows the yield curves for Treasury securities on two dates, October 18, 1994 and November 18, 1997. To draw these curves, you need Treasury quotes from the *Wall Street Journal*—note that actual quoted yields for curve 2 are provided in the boxed information right below the graph. Given the required quotes, select the yields for the Treasury bills, notes, and bonds maturing in approximately 3 months, 6 months, and 1, 2, 5, 10, 20, and 30 years. The yields used for this curve are highlighted. (You could include more points, but they would not have much effect on the general shape of the curve.) Next, plot the points on a graph whose horizontal (x) axis represents time to maturity in years and whose vertical (y) axis represents yield to maturity. Connect the points to create the curves shown in Figure 9.4. Note that in both cases the pattern is upward-sloping, which historically has been the "normal" shape.

Explanations of the Term Structure of Interest Rates

As we noted earlier, the shape of the yield curve changes over time. Three commonly cited theories—the expectations hypothesis, the liquidity preference theory, and the market segmentation theory—explain more fully the reasons for the general shape of the yield curve.

expectations hypothesis
theory that the shape of the yield curve reflects investor expectations of future interest rates.

Expectations Hypothesis The **expectations hypothesis** suggests that the yield curve reflects investor expectations about the future behavior of (short-term) interest rates. The relationship between rates today and rates expected in the future is due primarily to investor expectations regarding inflation. If investors anticipate higher rates of inflation in the future, they will require higher long-term interest rates today, and vice versa. To see how this explanation of the term structure can be applied in practice, consider the behavior of U.S. Treasury securities.

Because Treasury securities are considered essentially risk-free, only two components determine their yield: the real rate of interest and inflation expectations. Because the real interest rate is the same for all maturities, variations in yields are caused by differing inflation expectations associated with different maturities. This hypothesis can be illustrated using the November 18, 1997, yields for four of the Treasury maturities in Figure 9.4. If we assume that the real rate of interest is 3%, then the inflation expectation during the period to maturity is as shown in column 3 of the following table.

Maturity	(1) November 18, 1997 Yield	(2) Real Rate of Interest	(3) Inflation Expectation [(1) − (2)]
3 months	5.24%	3.00%	2.24%
1 year	5.63	3.00	2.63
5 years	5.82	3.00	2.82
30 years	6.15	3.00	3.15

The numbers in column 3 strongly suggest that in mid-November 1997 investors didn't foresee much of a problem with inflation. As a result, the yield curve (in Figure 9.4) was a lot flatter in 1997 than it was in 1994.

FIGURE 9.4
Yield Curves on U.S. Treasury Issues

Here we see two yield curves constructed from actual market data (quotes). Note that although they are about the same in general shape, curve 1 is a lot steeper than curve 2, because there's a wider spread between short- and long-term interest rates.

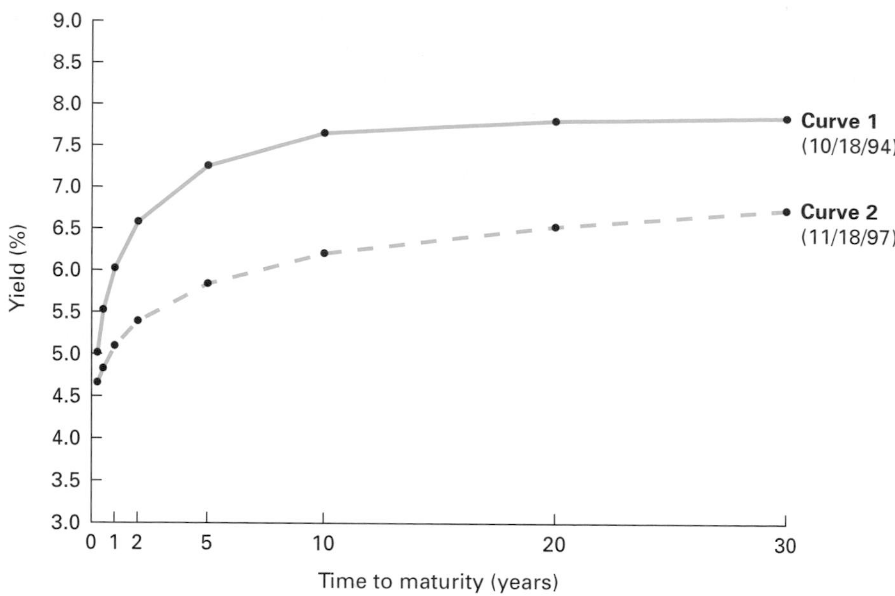

Yield Data for Curve #2
Treasury Issues—Bills, Notes, and Bonds
Tuesday, November 18, 1997

	Maturity	Days to Mat.	Bid	Asked	Chg.	Ask Yld.
	Nov 20 '97	3	4.76	4.72	+0.03	4.79
	Nov 28 '97	11	4.84	4.80	+0.03	4.87
	Dec 04 '97	17	4.76	4.72	−0.03	4.80
	Dec 11 '97	24	4.77	4.73	+0.02	4.81
	Dec 18 '97	31	4.80	4.76	+0.02	4.85
	Dec 26 '97	39	4.92	4.88	+0.02	4.97
	Jan 02 '98	46	5.00	4.96	+0.03	5.06
	Jan 08 '98	52	5.10	5.06	+0.03	5.17
	Jan 15 '98	59	5.10	5.06	+0.03	5.17
	Jan 22 '98	66	5.20	5.18	+0.02	5.30
	Jan 29 '98	73	5.11	5.09	+0.02	5.21
	Feb 05 '98	80	5.14	5.12	+0.02	5.25
	Feb 12 '98	87	5.12	5.11	+0.02	5.25
	Feb 19 '98	94	5.10	5.08	+0.02	5.22
3 Month	Feb 19 '98	94	5.11	5.10	....	5.24
	Feb 26 '98	101	5.11	5.09	+0.02	5.24
	Mar 05 '98	108	5.16	5.14	+0.02	5.29
	Mar 12 '98	115	5.15	5.13	−0.01	5.29
	Mar 19 '98	122	5.14	5.12	+0.01	5.28
	Mar 26 '98	129	4.94	4.92	−0.01	5.08
	Apr 02 '98	136	5.15	5.13	−0.02	5.30
	Apr 09 '98	143	5.15	5.13	−0.02	5.31
	Apr 16 '98	150	5.17	5.15	−0.01	5.34
	Apr 23 '98	157	5.17	5.15	−0.01	5.34
	Apr 30 '98	164	5.18	5.16	−0.01	5.36
	May 07 '98	171	5.12	5.10	+0.01	5.30
	May 14 '98	178	5.15	5.14	+0.01	5.35
6 Month	May 21 '98	185	5.13	5.12	....	5.33
	May 28 '98	192	5.15	5.13	+0.01	5.34
	Jun 25 '98	220	5.16	5.14	+0.01	5.36
	Jul 23 '98	248	5.17	5.15	....	5.38

	Rate	Maturity Mo/Yr	Bid	Asked	Chg.	Ask Yld.
	4¾	Oct 98n	99:04	99:06	....	5.63
	5⅞	Oct 98n	100:05	100:07	....	5.63
	5½	Nov 98n	99:26	99:28	....	5.63
	8⅞	Nov 98n	103:02	103:04	....	5.60
1 Year	5⅛	Nov 98n	99:14	99:16	....	5.63
	5⅝	Nov 98n	99:30	100:00	....	5.62
	5⅛	Dec 98n	99:13	99:15	+ 1	5.62
	5¾	Dec 98n	100:02	100:04	....	5.63
	6⅜	Jan 99n	100:24	100:26	....	5.63
	6⅞	Aug 99n	101:30	102:00	+ 1	5.67
	5¾	Sep 99n	100:03	100:04	+ 1	5.67
	7⅛	Sep 99n	102:16	102:18	+ 1	5.65
	6	Oct 99n	100:19	100:21	+ 1	5.63
	5⅝	Oct 99n	99:29	99:30	+ 1	5.66
	7½	Oct 99n	103:07	103:09	− 1	5.70
2 Year	5⅞	Nov 99n	100:09	100:11	+ 1	5.69
	7⅞	Nov 99n	104:01	104:03	+ 1	5.67
	7¾	Nov 99n	103:27	103:29	+ 1	5.69
	7¾	Dec 99n	104:00	104:02	+ 1	5.68
	6⅜	Jan 00n	101:11	101:13	+ 1	5.67
	7¾	Jan 00n	104:03	104:05	+ 1	5.71
	6	Jul 02n	100:21	100:23	....	5.82
	6⅜	Aug 02n	102:06	102:08	....	5.82
	6¼	Aug 02n	101:21	101:23	+ 1	5.83
	5⅞	Sep 02n	100:06	100:07	− 1	5.82
	5¾	Oct 02n	99:27	99:28	....	5.78
5 Year	11⅝	Nov 02	124:21	124:27	....	5.82
	6¼	Feb 03n	101:26	101:28	....	5.83
	10¾	Feb 03	121:25	121:31	....	5.83
	10¾	May 03	122:19	122:25	....	5.84
	6¾	Aug 03n	99:14	99:16	....	5.85
	11⅛	Aug 03	125:06	125:12	....	5.86
	11⅞	Nov 03	129:26	130:00	....	5.87
	5⅞	Feb 04n	100:02	100:04	....	5.85
	7¼	May 04n	107:09	107:11	....	5.87
	12⅜	May 04	134:15	134:21	....	5.88

	Rate	Maturity Mo/Yr	Bid	Asked	Chg.	Ask Yld.
	6¼	Feb 07n	102:09	102:11	....	5.92
	7⅝	Feb 02-07	106:03	106:05	....	5.96
	6⅝	May 07n	105:04	105:05	+ 2	5.91
10 Year	6⅛	Aug 07n	101:30	101:31	....	5.86
	7⅞	Nov 02-07	108:28	108:30	....	5.79
	8⅜	Aug 03-08	112:04	112:08	....	5.83
	8¾	Nov 03-08	113:20	113:24	....	5.99
	8¾	May 17	128:21	128:27	+ 4	6.18
20 Year	8⅞	Aug 17	130:08	130:14	+ 4	6.18
	9⅛	May 18	133:22	133:28	+ 5	6.19
	9	Nov 18	132:18	132:24	+ 5	6.19
	8⅞	Feb 19	131:07	131:13	+ 4	6.20
	8⅛	Aug 19	122:20	122:26	+ 5	6.20
	8½	Feb 20	127:12	127:18	+ 6	6.20
	8¾	May 20	130:16	130:22	+ 5	6.20
	8¾	Aug 20	130:21	130:27	+ 6	6.20
	7⅞	Feb 21	120:07	120:13	+ 6	6.21
	8⅛	Aug 21	123:15	123:21	+ 6	6.21
	8	Nov 21	122:01	122:07	+ 6	6.21
	7¼	Aug 22	112:31	113:03	+ 6	6.21
	7⅝	Nov 22	117:25	117:29	+ 6	6.21
	7⅛	Feb 23	111:17	111:21	+ 6	6.20
	6¼	Aug 23	100:20	100:22	+ 6	6.20
	7½	Nov 24	116:29	117:01	+ 7	6.19
	7⅝	Feb 25	118:20	118:24	+ 8	6.19
	6⅞	Aug 25	109:00	109:02	+ 8	6.19
	6	Feb 26	97:19	97:21	+ 7	6.18
	6¾	Aug 26	107:24	107:26	+ 8	6.17
	6½	Nov 26	104:17	104:19	+ 8	6.16
30 Year	6⅝	Feb 27	106:10	106:12	+ 8	6.15

Generally, under the expectations hypothesis, an increasing inflation expectation results in an upward-sloping yield curve, a decreasing inflation expectation results in a downward-sloping yield curve, and a stable inflation expectation results in a relatively flat yield curve. Although, as we'll see below, other theories do exist, the observed strong relationship between inflation and interest rates lends considerable credence to this widely accepted theory.

liquidity preference theory
theory that investors tend to prefer the greater liquidity of short-term securities and therefore require a premium to invest in long-term securities.

Liquidity Preference Theory More often than not, yield curves have at least a mild upward slope, just as in 1997. One explanation for the frequency of upward sloping yield curves is the **liquidity preference theory.** This theory states that, intuitively, long-term bond rates should be higher than short-term rates because of the added risks involved with the longer maturities. In other words, because of the risk differential (real or perceived) between long- and short-term debt securities, rational investors prefer the less risky, short-term obligations *unless they can be motivated, via higher interest rates, to invest in the longer bonds.*

Actually, there are a number of reasons why rational investors should prefer short-term securities. To begin with, they are more liquid (more easily converted to cash) and less sensitive to changing market rates, which means there is less risk of loss of principal. For a given change in market rates, the prices of longer-term bonds will show considerably more movement than the prices of short-term bonds. Simply put, uncertainty increases over time, and investors therefore require a premium to invest in long maturities. In addition, just as investors tend to require a premium for tying up funds for longer periods, borrowers will also pay a premium in order to obtain long-term funds. Borrowers thus assure themselves that funds will be available and they can avoid having to roll over short-term debt at unknown and possibly unfavorable rates. All of these preferences and market forces explain why higher rates of interest should be associated with longer maturities and why it's perfectly rational to expect upward-sloping yield curves.

market segmentation theory
theory that the market for debt is segmented on the basis of maturity, that supply and demand within each segment determines the prevailing interest rate, and that the slope of the yield curve depends on the relationship between the prevailing rates in each segment.

Market Segmentation Theory Another often-cited theory, the **market segmentation theory,** suggests that the market for debt is segmented on the basis of maturity preferences of different types of financial institutions and investors. According to this theory, the yield curve changes as the supply and demand for funds within each maturity segment determines its prevailing interest rate. The equilibrium between the financial institutions that supply the funds for short-term maturities (e.g., banks) and the borrowers of those short-term funds (e.g., businesses with seasonal loan requirements) establishes interest rates in the short-term markets. Similarly, the equilibrium between suppliers and demanders in such long-term markets as life insurance and real estate determines the prevailing long-term interest rates. The shape of the yield curve can be either upward- or downward-sloping, as determined by the general relationship between rates in each market segment. When supply outstrips demand for short-term loans, short-term rates are relatively low. If, at the same time, the demand for long-term loans is higher than the available supply of funds, then long-term rates are high, and the yield curve slopes upward. Simply stated, low rates in the short-term segment and high rates in the long-term segment cause an upward-sloping yield curve, and vice versa.

So, Which One Is Right? It is clear that all three theories of the term structure have merit in explaining the shape of the yield curve. From them, we can conclude that at any time, the slope of the yield curve is affected by (1) inflationary expectations, (2) liquidity preferences, and (3) the supply and demand conditions in the short- and long-term market segments. Upward-sloping yield curves result from higher inflation expectations, lender preferences for shorter-maturity loans, and greater supply of short- than of long-term loans relative to the respective demand in each market segment. The opposite behavior, of course, results in a downward-sloping yield curve. At any point in time, the interaction of these forces determines the prevailing slope of the yield curve.

Using the Yield Curve in Investment Decisions

Bond investors often use yield curves in making investment decisions. As noted earlier, yield curves change in accordance with market conditions. Analyzing the changes in yield curves over time provides investors with information about future interest rate movements and how they can affect price behavior and comparative returns. For example, if the yield curve begins to rise sharply, it usually means that inflation is starting to heat up or is expected to do so in the near future; thus investors can expect that interest rates, too, will rise. Under these conditions, most seasoned bond investors turn to short or intermediate (3 to 5 years) maturities, which provide reasonable returns and at the same time minimize exposure to capital loss when interest rates go up (and bond prices fall). A downward-sloping yield curve, though unusual, generally results from actions of the Federal Reserve to reduce inflation. As suggested by the expectations hypothesis, this would signal that rates have peaked and are about to fall.

Another factor to consider is the difference in yields on different maturities at a particular point in time, or the "steepness" of the curve. For example, a steep yield curve—that is, one where long rates are *much higher* than short rates—is often seen as an indication that long-term rates may be near their peak and are about to fall, thereby narrowing the spread between long and short rates. Steep yield curves are generally viewed as a bullish sign. For aggressive bond investors, they could be the signal to start moving into long-term securities. Flatter yield curves, on the other hand, sharply reduce the incentive for going long-term. For example, look at yield curve 2 in Figure 9.4. Note that the difference in yield between the 10- and 30-year maturities is quite small (only about 25 basis points, or about a quarter of 1%). As a result, a lot of investors would tend to favor the 10-year security, because they would not gain enough (only 20 or 30 basis points) to justify the much greater risk of the 30-year maturity. However, if the spread were, say, 75 to 100 basis points, the investor would have to consider his or her own risk tolerance to determine whether this risk premium was sufficient compensation for the additional risk of buying the longer-term security.

CONCEPTS IN REVIEW

9.1 Is there a single market rate of interest applicable to all segments of the bond market, or does a series of market yields exist? Explain and note the investment implication of such a market environment.

9.2 Explain why interest rates are important to both conservative and aggressive bond investors. What causes interest rates to move, and how can you monitor such movements?

9.3 What is the *term structure of interest rates,* and how is it related to the *yield curve?* What information is required to plot a yield curve? Describe an upward-sloping yield curve and explain what it has to say about the behavior of interest rates.

9.4 How might you, as a bond investor, use information on the term structure of interest rates and yield curves when making investment decisions?

http://hepg.aw.com

Interest rate changes are to a large extent due to investors buying and selling fixed-income securities. Investors' inflation expectations are one factor that helps define the shape of the yield curve at any point in time. The following Web page has several features that enable investors to observe and learn about shifts in the yield curve.

www.smartmoney.com/si/tools/onebond/cfm?story=yieldcurve

The Pricing of Bonds

LG 3

If there's one common denominator in the bond market, it's the way bonds are priced. No matter who the issuer is, what kind of bond it is, or whether it's fully taxable or tax-free, all bonds are priced pretty much the same. In particular, all bonds (including *notes* with maturities of more than a year) are priced according to the *present value of their future cash flow* streams. Indeed, once the prevailing or expected market yield is known, the whole process becomes rather mechanical. Even so, this system is very effective, and it is the process through which the market value of a bond is established.

Bond prices are driven by market yields. That's because in the marketplace, the *appropriate yield at which the bond should sell is determined first,* and then that yield is used to find the price (or market value) of the bond. The appropriate yield on a bond is a function of certain market and economic forces (e.g., the risk-free rate of return and inflation), as well as key issue and issuer characteristics—such as the number of years to maturity and the agency rating assigned to the bond. Together, these forces combine to form the *required rate of return,* which is the rate of return the investor would like to earn in order to justify an investment in a given fixed-income security. In the bond market, required return is market driven and is generally considered to be the issue's market yield. That is, the required return defines the yield at which the bond should be trading and serves as the *discount rate* in the bond valuation process.

Basically, bond investors are entitled to two distinct types of cash flows: (1) the periodic receipt of coupon income over the life of the bond and (2) the recovery of principal (or par value) at the end of the bond's life. Thus, in valuing a bond, you're dealing with an *annuity* of coupon payments plus a large *single cash flow,* as represented by the recovery of principal at maturity. These cash flows, along with the required rate of return on the investment, are then used in a present-value-based bond valuation model to find the dollar price of a bond. We'll demonstrate the bond valuation process in two ways. First, we'll use *annual compounding*—that is, because of its computational simplicity, we'll assume we're dealing with coupons that are paid once a year. Second, we'll examine bond valuation under conditions of *semiannual compounding*, which is more like the way most bonds actually pay their coupons. (*Note:* Although we'll use present-value interest factors to illustrate the various bond price measures, it should be clear that all these calculations could just as easily be done on a good hand-held calculator. Even so, before you revert to the regular use of one of these calculators, we encourage you to work through the bond valuation models, at least once or twice, using the procedures outlined below, in order to gain a thorough understanding of what's embedded in a bond price or yield measure.)

Annual Compounding

Along with a table of present-value interest factors (see Appendix A, Tables A.3 and A.4), the following information is needed to value a bond: (1) the size of the annual coupon payment, (2) the bond's par value, and (3) the number of years remaining to maturity. The prevailing market yield (or an estimate of future market rates) is then used as the discount rate to compute the price of a bond as follows:

Equation 9.2

$$\text{Bond price} = \frac{\text{present value of the annuity}}{\text{of annual interest income}} + \frac{\text{present value of the}}{\text{bond's par value}}$$

Equation 9.2a

$$\text{BP} = (I \times PVIFA) + (PV \times PVIF)$$

where

I = amount of annual interest income

$PVIFA$ = present-value interest factor for an *annuity* (Appendix A, Table A.4)

PV = par value of the bond, which is assumed to be \$1,000

$PVIF$ = present-value interest factor for a *single cash flow* (Appendix A, Table A.3)

To illustrate the bond price formula in action, consider a 20-year, 9½% bond that is being priced to yield 10%. From this we know the bond pays an annual coupon of 9½% (or \$95), has 20 years left to maturity, and should be priced to provide a market yield of 10%. As we saw in Chapter 4, the maturity and market yield information is used to find the appropriate present-value interest factors (in Appendix A, Tables A.3 and A.4). Given these interest factors, we can now use Equation 9.2 to find the price of our bond.

$$\begin{aligned}\text{Bond price} &= (\$95 \times PVIFA \text{ for } 10\% \text{ and } 20 \text{ years}) + \\ &\quad (\$1{,}000 \times PVIF \text{ for } 10\% \text{ and } 20 \text{ years}) \\ &= (\$95 \times 8.514) + (\$1{,}000 \times .149) = \underline{\underline{\$957.83}}\end{aligned}$$

Note that because this is a coupon-bearing bond, we have an annuity of coupon payments of \$95 a year for 20 years, plus a single cash flow of \$1,000 that occurs at the end of year 20. Thus, in bond valuation, we first find the present value of the coupon annuity and then add that amount to the present value of the recovery of principal at maturity. In this particular case, around \$958 is what you should be willing to pay for this bond so long as you're satisfied with earning 10% on your money.

Semiannual Compounding

In practice, most (domestic) bonds pay interest every 6 months, so semiannual compounding is used in the valuation of bonds. Although using annual compounding, as we did above, simplifies the valuation process a bit, it's not the way bonds are actually valued in the marketplace. Fortunately, it's relatively easy to go from annual to semiannual compounding: All you need do is cut the annual coupon payment in half and make two minor modifications to the present-value interest factors. Given these changes, finding the price of a bond under conditions of semiannual compounding is much like pricing a bond using annual compounding. That is,

Equation 9.3

$$\text{Bond price (with semiannual compounding)} = \text{present value of an annuity of } \textit{semiannual} \text{ coupon payments} + \text{present value of the bond's par value}$$

Equation 9.3a

$$BP = (I/2 \times PVIFA^*) + (PV \times PVIF^*)$$

where

$PVIFA^*$ = present-value interest factor for an annuity, with required return and years-to-maturity adjusted for *semiannual compounding* (Appendix A, Table A.4)

$PVIF^*$ = present-value interest factor for a single cash flow, with required return and years-to-maturity adjusted for *semiannual compounding* (Appendix A, Table A.3)

I, PV = as described above

Note that in Equation 9.3, the present-value interest factors (both $PVIFA$ and $PVIF$) are adjusted to accommodate semiannual compounding. To do so, *simply cut the required return in half and double the number of years to maturity.* By making those modifications, we are, in effect, dealing with a semiannual measure of return and using the number of 6-month periods to maturity (rather than *years* to maturity). For example, in our bond illustration above, we wanted to price a 20-year bond to yield 10%. With semiannual compounding, we would be dealing with a semiannual return of 10%/2 = 5%, and with 20 × 2 = 40 semiannual periods to maturity. Thus we'd find the present-value interest factors for 5% and 40 periods from Table A.4 (for $PVIFA^*$) and from Table A.3 (for $PVIF^*$). Also note that we adjust the present-value interest factor for the \$1,000 par value, because that too will be subject to semiannual compounding, even though the cash flow will still be received in one lump sum.

INVESTOR FACT

PRICE GO UP, PRICES GO DOWN—We all know that when market rates go up, bond prices go down (and vice versa). But did you know that bond prices don't move up and down at the same speed? That's because bond prices don't move in a straight line. Rather, the relationship between market yields and bond prices is "convex," which means that bond prices will rise at an increasing rate when yields fall and decline at a decreasing rate when yields rise—*that is, bond prices go up faster than they go down.* This is known as *positive convexity,* and it's a property that applies to all noncallable bonds. Thus, for a given change in yield, you stand to make more money when prices go up than you'll lose when prices move down!

To see how this all fits together in the bond valuation process, consider once again the 20-year, 9½% bond, but this time assume it's being priced to yield 10%, *compounded semiannually.* Using Equation 9.3, you'd have:

$$\text{Bond price (with semiannual compounding)} = (\$95/2 \times PVIFA^{*} \text{ for } 5\% \text{ and } 40 \text{ periods}) + (\$1{,}000 \times PVIF^{*} \text{ for } 5\% \text{ and } 40 \text{ periods})$$
$$= (\$47.50 \times 17.159) + (\$1{,}000 \times .142) = \underline{\underline{\$957.02}}$$

The price of the bond in this case ($957.02) is slightly less than the price we obtained with annual compounding ($957.83). Clearly, it doesn't make much difference whether we use annual or semiannual compounding, though the differences do tend to increase a bit with lower coupons and shorter maturities.

CONCEPTS IN REVIEW

9.5 Explain how market yield affects the price of a bond. Could you value (price) a bond without knowing its market yield? Explain.

9.6 Why are bonds generally priced using semiannual compounding? Does it make much difference if you use annual compounding?

Measures of Yield and Return

LG 4

As surprising as it may seem, in the bond market, investment decisions are made more on the basis of a bond's yield than its dollar price. Not only does yield affect the price at which a bond trades, it also serves as an important measure of return. To use yield as a measure of return, we simply *reverse the bond valuation process* described above and solve for the yield on a bond, rather than its price. Actually, there are two widely used measures of yield: current yield and yield-to-maturity. We'll look at both of them here, along with a variation of yield-to-maturity, known as *expected return,* which measures the expected (or actual) rate of return earned over a specific holding period.

Current Yield

current yield
return measure that indicates the amount of current income a bond provides relative to its market price.

Current yield is the simplest of all return measures but also has the most limited application. This measure looks at just one source of return: *a bond's interest income.* In particular, it indicates the amount of current income a bond provides relative to its prevailing market price. It is calculated as follows:

Equation 9.4

$$\text{Current yield} = \frac{\text{annual interest}}{\text{current market price of the bond}}$$

For example, an 8% bond would pay $80 per year in interest for every $1,000 of principal. However, if the bond were currently priced at $800, it would have a current yield of 10% ($80/$800 = 0.10). Current yield is a measure of a bond's annual coupon income, so it would be of interest to investors seeking high levels of current income.

Yield-to-Maturity

yield-to-maturity (YTM) the fully compounded rate of return earned by an investor over the life of a bond, including interest income and price appreciation.

promised yield same as yield-to-maturity.

Yield-to-maturity (YTM) is the most important and widely used bond valuation measure. It evaluates both interest income and price appreciation and considers total cash flow received over the life of an issue. Also known as **promised yield,** it indicates the fully compounded rate of return earned by an investor, *given that the bond is held to maturity and all principal and interest payments are made in a prompt and timely fashion.* This measure of yield is used not only to gauge the return on a single issue but also to track the behavior of the market in general. In other words, market interest rates are basically a reflection of the average promised yields that exist in a given segment of the market. Promised yield provides valuable insight about an issue's investment merits and is used to assess the attractiveness of alternative investment vehicles. Other things being equal, the higher the promised yield of an issue, the more attractive it is.

Although there are a couple of ways to compute promised yield, the best and most accurate procedure is one that is derived directly from the bond valuation model described above. That is, assuming annual compounding, you can use Equation 9.2 to measure the YTM on a bond. The difference is that now, rather than trying to determine the price of the bond, *we know its price and are trying to find the discount rate that will equate the present value of the bond's cash flow (its coupon and principal payments) to its current market price.* This procedure may sound familiar: It's just like the *internal rate of return* measure described in Chapter 4. Indeed, we're basically looking for the internal rate of return on a bond; when we find that, we have the bond's yield-to-maturity.

Unfortunately, unless you have a hand-held calculator or computer software that will do the calculations for you, finding yield-to-maturity is a matter of trial and error. Let's say we want to find the yield-to-maturity on a 7½% ($1,000 par value) bond that has 15 years remaining to maturity and is currently trading in the market at $809.50. From Equation 9.2, we know that

$$\text{Bond price} = (I \times PVIFA) + (PV \times PVIF)$$

As it now stands, we know the current market price of the bond ($809.50), the amount of annual interest/coupon income (7½% = $75), the par value of the bond ($1,000), and the number of years to maturity (15). To compute yield-to-maturity, we need to find the discount rate (in the present-value interest factors) that produces a bond price of $809.50.

Here's what we have so far:

$$\text{Bond price} = (I \times PVIFA) + (PV \times PVIF)$$

$$\$809.50 = (\$75 \times PVIFA \text{ for 15 years and a discount rate of ?\%}) + (\$1{,}000 \times PVIF \text{ for 15 years and a discount rate of ?\%})$$

Right now there's only one thing we know about the yield on this bond—it has to be more than 7½%. (Why? This is a discount bond, so the yield-to-maturity must exceed the coupon rate.) Thus through trial and error, we might start with a discount rate of, say, 8% or 9% (or any number above the bond's coupon). Sooner or later, we'll move to a discount rate of 10%. And look what happens at that point: Using Equation 9.2 to price this bond at a discount rate of 10%, we see that

$$\begin{aligned}\text{Bond price} &= (\$75 \times \textit{PVIFA} \text{ for 15 years and 10\%}) \\ &\quad + (\$1{,}000 \times \textit{PVIFA} \text{ for 15 years and 10\%}) \\ &= (\$75 \times 7.606) + (\$1{,}000 \times 0.239) \\ &= \underline{\underline{\$809.45}}\end{aligned}$$

The computed price of $809.45 is reasonably close to the bond's current market price of $809.50. As a result, the solving rate of 10% represents the yield-to-maturity (or promised yield) on this bond. That is, 10% is the discount rate that leads to a *computed bond price* equal (or very close) to the *current market price* of the bond. In this case, if you were to pay $809.50 for the bond and hold it to maturity, you would expect to earn a yield of 10.0%. Now there's no doubt that promised yield is an important measure of performance. However, as discussed in the accompanying *Investing in Action* box, this measure tells only part of the story.

Using Semiannual Compounding

Given some fairly simple modifications, it's also possible to find yield-to-maturity using semiannual compounding. To do so, we cut the annual coupon in half, double the number of years (periods) to maturity, and use the bond valuation model in Equation 9.3. Returning to our 7½%, 15-year bond, let's see what happens when we try a discount rate of 10%. In this case, with semiannual compounding, we'd use a discount rate of 5% (10% ÷ 2); using this discount rate and 30 six-month periods to maturity (15 × 2) to specify the present-value interest factor, we have

$$\begin{aligned}\text{Bond price} &= (\$75/2 \times \textit{PVIFA}^{*} \text{ for 5\% and 30 periods}) \\ &\quad + (\$1{,}000 \times \textit{PVIFA} \text{ for 5\% and 30 periods}) \\ &= (\$37.50 \times 15.373) + (\$1{,}000 \times 0.231) = \underline{\underline{\$807.49}}\end{aligned}$$

As you can see, a semiannual discount rate of 5% results in a computed bond value that's a bit short of our target price of $809.50. Given the inverse relationship between price and yield, it follows that if we need a higher price, we'll have to try a lower yield (discount rate). Therefore, we know the semiannual yield on this bond has to be something less than 5%. Through interpolation, we find that a semiannual discount rate of 4.90% gives us a computed bond value of $809.50.

At this point, because we're dealing with semiannual cash flows, to be technically accurate we should find the bond's "effective" annual yield. However, that's not the way it's done in practice. Rather, *market convention is to simply state the annual yield as twice the semiannual yield.* This practice produces what the market refers to as the **bond-equivalent yield.** Returning to

bond-equivalent yield
the annual yield on a bond, calculated as twice the semiannual yield.

INVESTING IN ACTION

There's More to Bond Returns Than Yield Alone

When individuals choose bond investments, they usually focus on yields, in the belief that higher yields generate better returns. But yields and returns are two different things, and investors who blindly chase higher yields can end up regretting it.

The fact is that yield is only part of the story: It tells you what you can expect going into an investment, *not* what you'll actually end up earning on the deal. Indeed, yield is often a poor proxy for return, and confusing the two can be damaging to your wealth!

Total return for fixed-income investments is made up of not only the initial yield but also (1) interest on reinvested interest and (2) price change. Only in the case of short-term investments, such as 1-year CDs or Treasury bills, is yield a good gauge of return. For long-term bonds and bonds purchased at prices far above or below face value, other factors often dwarf yield in determining returns. That's true even when the bonds are of triple-A quality and are noncallable.

For instance, interest on interest easily becomes the biggest factor in returns for buy-and-hold investors in long-term bonds, especially if interest rates rise during the life of the bond. If you bought a 30-year Treasury bond yielding 6.0% today and interest rates subsequently rose so that your average reinvestment rate was 8.0% over the life of the bond, more than 75% of your total return at maturity would come from income on reinvested interest. On the other hand, although interest on interest dominates bond returns for long holding periods, price change dominates return for short-term investors. In either case, future interest rate changes are the major concern for investors who want to safeguard their total returns.

The starting yield on a bond becomes a bigger boon or burden to investors the longer the bond's maturity—which makes total returns on longer-term bonds much more sensitive to interest rate swings. For instance, in the 1950s, 1960s, and 1970s, long-term Treasury bonds actually had lower total returns than money market funds, despite their persistently higher yields. Unfortunately, steadily rising interest rates erased an average of 2.5% a year from the value of long-term bond portfolios in the 1950–1980 period, more than wiping out the bonds' yield advantage over T-bills. In the 1980s and 1990s, by contrast, a steady decline in interest rates meant long-term bonds put on a much better showing than yields would have indicated. Rising bond prices, caused by falling market rates, pushed total returns on Treasury bonds up to an average of 12.6% a year, beating T-bill returns by 3.7 percentage points.

Of course, no one really knows where interest rates will go—and trying to predict them has proved a fruitless exercise. But investors can get a handle on the risks they face in the short run by considering how total returns on different investments might react to interest rate changes over, say, the next 12 months. For example, if interest rates were to fall 1 percentage point over the next 12 months, a typical portfolio of long-term bonds (with lives of more than 10 years) would generate an estimated total return of about 13%. But if interest rates were to rise by 1 percentage point, the total return would shrink to about 1%, making a money fund return look good by comparison. Looking at the problem this way tells the investor how much rates would have to rise before the returns on long-term bonds were reduced to the level of, say, bank CDs or some other short-term benchmark. Clearly, the farther rates have to rise, the more cushion you have and the more secure your investments.

The old adage "You can't judge a book by its cover" certainly does apply to the bond market: Just because a bond promises a *yield* of *x* percent doesn't mean that's the *return* you'll actually end up with.

the bond yield problem we started above, we know that the issue has a semi-annual yield of 4.90%. According to the bond-equivalent yield convention, all we have to do now is *double the solving rate in order to obtain the annual rate of return on this bond.* Doing this gives us a yield-to-maturity (or promised yield) of 4.90% × 2 = 9.80%, which is the annual rate of return we'll earn on this bond if we hold it to maturity.

Yield Properties

Actually, in addition to holding the bond to maturity, there are a couple of other critical assumptions embedded in any yield-to-maturity figure. The computed promised yield measure—whether found with annual or semiannual compounding—is based on present-value concepts and therefore contains important reinvestment assumptions. That is, the yield-to-maturity figure itself is the *minimum required reinvestment rate the investor must subsequently earn on each of the interim coupon receipts* to generate a return equal to or greater than promised yield. In essence, the calculated yield-to-maturity figure is the return "promised" only so long as the issuer meets all interest and principal obligations on a timely basis *and* the investor reinvests all coupon income (from the date of receipt to maturity) at an average rate equal to or greater than the computed promised yield. In our example above, the investor would have to reinvest (to maturity) each of the coupons received over the next 15 years at a rate of about 10%. *Failure to do so would result in a realized yield of less than the 10% promised.* In fact, if the worst did occur and the investor made no attempt to reinvest any of the coupons, he or she would earn a realized yield over the 15-year investment horizon of just over 6½%—far short of the 10% promised return. Clearly, unless it's a zero-coupon bond, a significant portion of a bond's total return over time is derived from the *reinvestment of coupons.*

Finding the Yield on a Zero

The same promised-yield procedures described above—Equation 9.2 with annual compounding or Equation 9.3 with semiannual compounding—can also be used to find the yield-to-maturity on a zero-coupon bond. The only difference is that the coupon portion of the equation can be ignored because it will, of course, equal zero. All you have to do to find the promised yield on a zero is to divide the current market price of the bond by $1,000 (the bond's par value) and then look for the computed interest factor in the present-value Table A.3 (in Appendix A).

To illustrate, consider a 15-year zero-coupon issue that can be purchased today for $315. Dividing this amount by the bond's par value of $1,000, we obtain an interest factor of $315/$1,000 = 0.315. Now, using annual compounding, look in Table A.3 (the table of present-value interest factors for single cash flows); go down the first column to year 15 and then look across that row until you find an interest factor that equals (or is very close to) 0.315. Once you've found the factor, look up the column to the "Interest Rate" heading and you've got the promised yield of the issue. Using this approach, we see that the bond in our example has a promised yield of 8%, because that rate gives us the interest factor we're looking for. Had we been using semiannual compounding, we'd do exactly the same thing, except we'd go down to "year 30" and start the process there.

Expected Return

Rather than buying a bond and holding it to maturity (as presumed in the promised-yield formulas), many investors trade in and out of bonds long before they mature. These investors have short anticipated holding periods and really have no intention of holding the bonds to maturity. As a result, yield-to-maturity has relatively little meaning for them, other than providing an indication of the rate of return used to price the bond. These investors obviously need an alternative measure of return that can be used to assess the investment appeal of those bonds they intend to trade. Such an alternative measure is **expected return,** which indicates the rate of return an investor can expect to earn by holding a bond over a period of time that's less (and in many cases, substantially less) than the life of the issue. (Expected return is also known as **realized yield,** because it shows the return an investor would realize by trading in and out of bonds over short holding periods.)

expected return
the rate of return an investor can expect to earn by holding a bond over a period of time that's less than the life of the issue.

realized yield
same as expected return.

Expected return lacks the precision of yield-to-maturity, because the major cash flow variables are largely the product of investor estimates. In particular, going into the investment, both the length of the holding period and the future selling prices of the bond are pure estimates and therefore subject to varying degrees of uncertainty. Even so, we can use pretty much the same procedure to find expected/realized yield as we did to find promised yield. That is, with some simple modifications to the standard bond-pricing formula, we can use the following equation to find the expected return on a bond.

Equation 9.5

$$\text{Bond price} = \begin{array}{c}\text{present value of the bond's}\\ \text{annual interest income}\\ \text{over the holding period}\end{array} + \begin{array}{c}\text{present value of the bond's}\\ \text{future price at the}\\ \text{end of the holding period}\end{array}$$

Equation 9.5a

$$BP = (I \times PVIFA) + (FV \times PVIF)$$

where

the present-value interest factors (for both $PVIFA$ and $PVIF$) are for the length of the expected holding period only, not for the term to maturity

FV = the expected future price of the bond

Note that in this case, the *expected future price* of the bond is used in place of par value ($1,000), and the *length of the holding period* is used in place of term to maturity. As indicated above, we must determine the *future price* of the bond when computing expected realized yield; this is done by using the standard bond price formula, as described above. The most difficult part of deriving a reliable future price is, of course, coming up with future market interest rates that you feel will exist when the bond is sold. Thus, by evaluating current and expected market interest rate conditions, *the investor estimates a promised yield that the issue is expected to carry at the date of sale and then uses that yield to calculate the bond's future price.*

To illustrate, take one more look at our 7½%, 15-year bond. This time, let's assume that the investor feels the price of the bond, which is now trading at a discount, will rise sharply as interest rates fall over the next few years. In particular, assume the bond is currently priced at $810 (to yield 10%) and that the investor anticipates holding the bond for 3 years. Over that time, she expects market rates to drop so that the price of the bond should rise to around $960 by the end of the 3-year holding period. (Actually, we found the future price of the bond—$960—by assuming interest rates would fall to 8% in 3 years; we then used the standard bond price formula—in this case Equation 9.2—to find the value of a 7½%, 12-year obligation, which is how many years to maturity a 15-year bond will have at the end of a 3-year holding period.) Thus we are assuming that an investor will buy the bond today at a market price of $810 and sell the issue 3 years later—after interest rates have

INVESTOR FACT

SEARCHING FOR YIELDS IN THE FIELDS OF NICARAGUA —Investors in bonds have often looked overseas to get higher yields than those available in the United States. But even the boldest investors might find Nicaragua bonds a bit scary. These bonds were issued to Nicaraguan farmers whose property was seized when the Sandinistas ruled the country in the 1980s. They yield 17%, and the Nicaraguan government has never missed an interest payment. What's the catch? To collect interest, you must present your bond certificates to the Finance Ministry in Managua. And instead of being traded by computer, the bonds are traded hand to hand. And, oh yes, most of the farmers who own these bonds travel heavily armed—to ward off thieves.

declined to 8%—at a price of $960. Given these assumptions, the expected return (realized yield) on this bond is 14.6%, which is the discount rate in the following equation that will produce a current market price of $810.

$$\text{Bond price} = (\$75 \times \textit{PVIFA} \text{ for 3 years and } 14.6\%) + (\$960 \times \textit{PVIF} \text{ for 3 years and } 14.6\%)$$

$$= (\$75 \times 2.301) + (\$960 \times 0.664) = \underline{\underline{\$810.02}}$$

The better than 14½% return on this investment is fairly substantial, but keep in mind that this is a measure of *expected return* only. It is, of course, subject to variation if things do not turn out as anticipated, particularly with regard to the market yield expected to prevail at the end of the holding period. (*Note:* This illustration uses annual compounding, but you could just as easily have used *semiannual compounding,* which, everything else being the same, would have resulted in an expected yield of 14.4% rather than the 14.6% found with annual compounding. Also, if the anticipated horizon is 1 year or less, you would want to use the simple *holding period return (HPR)* measure described in Chapter 4.)

Valuing a Bond

Depending on investor objectives, the value of a bond can be determined by either its promised yield or its expected return. Conservative, income-oriented investors employ *promised yield* to value bonds. Coupon income over extended periods of time is the principal objective of these investors, and promised yield provides a viable measure of return under these circumstances. More aggressive bond traders, on the other hand, use *expected return* to value bonds. The capital gains that can be earned by buying and selling bonds over relatively short holding periods is a chief concern of these investors, and expected return is more important to them than the promised yield that exists at the time the bond is purchased.

In either case, promised or expected yield provides a *measure of return* that can be used to determine the relative attractiveness of fixed-income securities. But to do so, we must evaluate the appropriate measure of return in light of the amount of *risk* involved in the investment. Bonds are no different from stocks in that the amount of promised or expected return should be sufficient to cover the investor's exposure to risk. Thus the greater the amount of perceived risk, the greater the amount of return the bond should generate. If the bond meets this hurdle, it can be compared to other potential investments outlets. If you find it difficult to do better in a risk-return sense, then the bond under evaluation should be given serious consideration as an investment outlet.

CONCEPTS IN REVIEW

9.7 What's the difference between *current yield* and *yield-to-maturity?* Between *promised yield* and *realized yield?*

9.8 Briefly describe the term *bond-equivalent yield.* Is there any real difference between promised yield and bond-equivalent yield? Explain.

9.9 Why is the reinvestment of interest income so important to bond investors?

9.10 According to the *Investing in Action* box on page 359, is there really any difference between a bond's yield and its return? If so, which of these measures is more important? Explain.

http://hepg.aw.com

Calculation of the actual yield-to-maturity requires the use of a calculator, unless of course you have lots of time and prefer the trial-and-error approach. Several Web sites have calculators that will do the work for you. Two of these site addresses follow.

www.financenter.com/invest.htm

www.datachimp.com/articles/finworks/fmbondytm.htm

Duration and Immunization

LG 6

One of the problems with yield-to-maturity (YTM) is that it assumes you can reinvest the bond's periodic coupon payments at the same rate over time. But if you reinvest this interest income at a lower rate (or if you spend it), your real return will be much lower than that indicated by YTM. The assumption that interest rates will remain constant is a key weakness of YTM. Another flaw is that YTM assumes the issuer will make all payments on time and won't call the bonds before maturity, as often happens when interest rates drop. For bonds that are not held to maturity, prices will reflect prevailing interest rates, which are likely to differ from YTM. If rates have moved up since a bond was purchased, the bond will sell at a discount. If interest rates have dropped, it will sell at a premium. The sales price will obviously have a major impact on the total return earned.

The problem with yield-to-maturity, then, is that it fails to take into account the effects of reinvestment risk and price (or market) risk. To see how reinvestment and price risks behave relative to one another, consider a situation in which market interest rates have undergone a sharp decline. Under such conditions, you might be tempted to cash out your holdings and take some gains (i.e., do a little "profit taking"). The fact is that selling before maturity is the only way to take advantage of falling interest rates, because a bond will pay its par value at maturity, regardless of prevailing interest rates. But there's a downside to falling rates: When interest rates fall, so do opportunities to invest at high rates. Therefore, although you gain on the price side, you lose on the reinvestment side. Even if you don't sell out, you are faced with increased reinvestment risk, because in order to earn the YTM promised on your bonds, you have to be able to reinvest each coupon payment at the same YTM rate. Obviously, as rates fall, you'll find it increasingly difficult to reinvest the stream of coupon payments at or above the YTM rate. When market rates rise, just the opposite happens: The price of the bond falls, but your reinvestment opportunities improve.

duration
a measure of bond price volatility, which captures both price and reinvestment risks and which is used to indicate how a bond will react to different interest rate environments.

What is needed is a yardstick, or measure of performance, that overcomes these deficiencies and takes into account both price and reinvestment risks. Such a yardstick is provided by something called **duration**, which captures in a single measure the extent to which the price of a bond will react to different interest rate environments. Because duration gauges the price volatility of a bond, it gives you a better idea of how likely you are to earn the return (YTM) you expect. That in turn will help you tailor your holdings to your expectations of interest rate movements.

The Concept of Duration

The concept of duration was first developed in 1938 by actuary Frederick Macaulay to help insurance companies match their cash inflows with payments. When applied to bonds, duration recognizes that the amount and frequency of the interest payments, yield-to-maturity, and time to maturity all affect the "time dimension" of a bond. The time to maturity is important because it influences how much a bond's price rises or falls as interest rates change. In general, when rates move, bonds with longer maturities fluctuate more than shorter-term issues. However, maturity alone isn't a sufficient measure of the time dimension of bonds. Maturity tells you only when the last payment will be made; it doesn't say anything about interim payments. The amount of reinvestment risk is also directly related to the size of a bond's coupons: Bonds that pay high coupons have greater reinvestment risk simply because there's more to reinvest.

Any change in interest rates will cause price risk and reinvestment risk to push and pull bonds in opposite directions. An increase in rates will produce a drop in price but will lessen reinvestment risk by making it easier to reinvest coupon payments at or above the YTM rate. Declining rates, in contrast, will boost prices but increase reinvestment risk. At some point in time, these two forces should exactly offset each other. *That point in time is the bond's duration.*

In general, bond duration possesses the following properties:

- Higher coupons result in shorter durations.
- Longer maturities mean longer durations.
- Higher yields (YTMs) lead to shorter durations.

A bond's coupon, maturity, and yield interact to produce the issue's measure of duration. Knowing a bond's duration is helpful because it combines price and reinvestment risks in such a way that it captures the underlying *volatility* of a bond. *A bond's duration and volatility are directly related: The shorter the duration, the less volatility there is in bond prices.*

Measuring Duration

Duration is a measure of the effective, as opposed to actual, maturity of a fixed-income security. As we will see, only those bonds promising a single payment to be received at maturity (zero-coupon bonds) have durations equal to their actual years to maturity. For all others, *duration measures are always less than their actual maturities.*

Although a bond's term to maturity is a useful concept, it falls short of being a reliable measure of a bond's effective life, because it does not consider all the bond's cash flows or the time value of money. Duration is a far superior measure of the effective timing of a bond's cash flows; it explicitly considers both the time value of money and the bond's coupon and principal payments. Duration may be thought of as the *weighted-average life of a bond,* where the weights are the relative future cash flows of the bond, all of which are discounted to their present values. Mathematically, we can find the duration of a bond as follows:

Equation 9.6

$$\text{Duration} = \sum_{t=1}^{T}\left[\frac{PV(C_t)}{P_{\text{bond}}} \times t\right]$$

where

$PV(C_t)$ = present value of a future coupon or principal payment

P_{bond} = current market price of the bond

t = year in which the cash flow (coupon or principal) payment is received

T = remaining life of the bond, in years

The duration measure obtained from Equation 9.6 is often referred to as *Macaulay duration*—named after the actuary who developed the concept.

Although duration can be (and often is) computed using semiannual compounding, Equation 9.6 uses *annual coupons and annual compounding* in order to keep the ensuing discussion and calculations as simple as possible. But even so, the formula looks more formidable than it actually is. If you just follow the basic steps noted below, you'll find that duration is not tough to calculate after all. Here are the steps involved:

Step 1. Find the present value of each annual coupon or principal payment [$PV(C_t)$]. *Use the prevailing YTM on the bond as the discount rate.*

Step 2. Divide this present value by the current market price of the bond (P_{bond}).

Step 3. Multiply this relative value by the year in which the cash flow is to be received (t).

Step 4. Repeat steps 1 through 3 for each year in the life of the bond, and then *add up* the values computed in step 3.

Duration for a Single Bond Table 9.1 illustrates the four-step procedure for calculating the duration of a 7½%, 15-year bond priced (at $957) to yield 8%. Note that this particular 15-year bond has a duration of less than 9½ years—9.36 years, to be exact. Here's how we found that value: Along with the current market price of the bond ($957), the first three columns of Table 9.1 provide the basic input data: Column (1) is the year (t) of the cash flow, column (2) is the amount of the annual cash flows (from coupons and principal), and column (3) lists the appropriate present-value interest factors, given an 8% discount rate (which is equal to the prevailing YTM on the bond). The first thing we do—step 1—is find the present value of each of the annual cash flows (column 4), and then—step 2—we divide each of these present values by the current market price of the bond (column 5). Multiplying the relative cash flows from column (5) by the year (t) in which the cash flow occurs—step 3—results in a time-weighted value for each of the annual cash flow streams (column 6). Adding up all the values in column (6)—step 4—yields the duration of the bond. As you can see, the duration of this bond is a lot less than its

TABLE 9.1 Duration Calculation for a 7½%, 15-year Bond Priced to Yield 8%

(1) Year (t)	(2) Annual Cash Flow (C_t)	(3) PVIF (at 8%)	(4) Present Value of Annual Cash Flows [$PV(C_t)$] (2) × (3)	(5) $PV(C_t)$ Divided by Current Market Price of the Bond* (4) ÷ $957	(6) Time-Weighted Relative Cash Flow (1) × (5)
1	$ 75	.926	$ 69.45	.0726	.0726
2	75	.857	64.27	.0672	.1343
3	75	.794	59.55	.0622	.1867
4	75	.735	55.12	.0576	.2304
5	75	.681	51.08	.0534	.2668
6	75	.630	47.25	.0494	.2962
7	75	.583	43.72	.0457	.3198
8	75	.540	40.50	.0423	.3386
9	75	.500	37.50	.0392	.3527
10	75	.463	34.72	.0363	.3628
11	75	.429	32.18	.0336	.3698
12	75	.397	29.78	.0311	.3734
13	75	.368	27.60	.0288	.3749
14	75	.340	25.50	.0266	.3730
15	1075	.315	338.62	.3538	5.3076
					Duration: 9.36 yrs.

*If this bond is priced to yield 8%, it will be quoted in the market at $957.

maturity—a condition that would exist with any coupon-bearing bond. In addition, keep in mind that *the duration on any bond will change over time* as YTM and term to maturity change. For example, the duration on this 7½%, 15-year bond will fall as the bond nears maturity and/or as the market yield (YTM) on the bond increases.

INVESTOR FACT

DIFFERENT BONDS, SAME DURATIONS—Sometimes, you really can't judge a book—or a bond, for that matter—by its cover. Here are three bonds that, on the surface, appear to be totally different:

- An 8-year, zero-coupon bond priced to yield 6%.
- A 12-year, 8¾% bond that trades at a yield of 8%.
- An 18-year, 10½% bond priced to yield 13%.

Although these three bonds have different coupons and different maturities, they have one thing in common: They all have *identical durations* of 8 years. Thus if interest rates went up or down by 50 to 100 basis points, the market prices of these bonds would all behave pretty much the same!

Duration for a Portfolio of Bonds The concept of duration is not applied merely to single securities; it can also be applied to whole portfolios of fixed-income securities. The duration of an entire portfolio is actually fairly easy to calculate—all we need are the durations of the individual securities in the portfolio and the proportion that each security contributes to the overall value of the portfolio. Given this, *the duration of a portfolio is simply the weighted average of the durations of the individual securities in the portfolio*, where the weights are the wealth proportions of each of the individual securities. For example, consider a five-bond portfolio made up as follows:

Bond	Amount Invested*	Weight	×	Bond Duration	=	Portfolio Duration
Government bonds	$ 270,000	0.15		6.25		0.9375
Aaa corporates	180,000	0.10		8.90		0.8900
Aa utilities	450,000	0.25		10.61		2.6525
Agency issues	360,000	0.20		11.03		2.2060
Baa industrials	540,000	0.30		12.55		3.7650
	$1,800,000	1.00				10.4510

*Amount invested = current market price times the par value of the bonds. That is, if the government bonds are quoted at 90 and the investor holds $300,000 in these bonds, then 0.90 × $300,000 = $270,000.

In this case, the \$1.8 million bond *portfolio* has an average duration of approximately 10.5 years. Obviously, if you want to change the duration of the portfolio, you can do so by either (1) changing the asset mix of the portfolio (shift the weight of the portfolio to longer- or shorter-duration bonds, as desired) and/or (2) adding new bonds to the portfolio with the desired duration characteristics. As we will see below, such information is used in a bond portfolio strategy known as *bond immunization*.

Bond Duration and Price Volatility

A bond's price volatility is, in part, a function of its term to maturity and, in part, a function of its coupon yield. Unfortunately, there is no exact relationship between bond maturities and bond price volatilities with respect to interest rate changes. There is, however, a fairly close relationship between bond duration and price volatility—at least, so long as the market doesn't experience wide swings in yield. That is, duration can be used as a viable predictor of price volatility *so long as the yield swings are relatively small* (no more than 100 basis points or so). The problem is that because the price-yield relationship of a bond is convex in form (but duration is not), when the market (or bond) undergoes a *big change* in yield, duration will *understate* the appreciation in price when rates fall and *overstate* the price decline when rates rise. Assuming that's not the case (i.e., we're dealing with relatively small changes in market yield), then multiplying a bond's duration value by −1 results in its price elasticity with respect to interest rate changes. Thus, by calculating a bond's duration, we can obtain a fairly accurate measure of how much its price will change relative to a given (reasonably small) change in market interest rates.

The mathematical link between bond price and interest rate changes involves the concept of *modified duration*. To find modified duration, we simply take the (Macaulay) duration for a bond—as found from Equation 9.6—and adjust it for the bond's yield to maturity.

Equation 9.7

$$\text{Modified duration} = \frac{\text{(Macaulay) duration in years}}{1 + \text{yield to maturity}}$$

Thus the modified duration for the 15-year bond discussed above is

$$\text{Modified duration} = \frac{9.36}{1 + 0.08} = \underline{\underline{8.67}}$$

Note that here we use the bond's computed (Macaulay) duration of 9.36 years and the same YTM we used to compute duration in Equation 9.6; in this case, the bond was priced to yield 8%, so we use a yield-to-maturity of 8%.

To determine, in percentage terms, how much the price of this bond would change as market interest rates increased from, say, 8% to 8½%, we multiply the modified duration value calculated above first by −1 (because of the inverse relationship between bond prices and interest rates) and then by the change in the level of the market interest rates. That is,

Equation 9.8

$$\text{Percent change in bond price} = -1 \times \text{modified duration} \times \text{change in interest rates}$$

$$= -1 \times 8.67 \times 0.5\% = \underline{\underline{-4.33\%}}$$

Thus a 50-basis-point (or ½ of 1%) change in market interest rates will lead to an almost 4½% drop in the price of this 15-year bond. Such information is useful to bond investors seeking—or trying to avoid—price volatility.

Uses of Bond Duration Measures

Bond investors have learned to use duration analysis in many ways. For example, as we saw above, you could use modified duration to measure the potential price volatility of a particular issue. Another, perhaps more important use of duration is in the *structuring of bond portfolios*. That is, if you thought that interest rates were about to increase, you could calculate the expected percentage decrease in the value of the portfolio, given a certain change in market interest rates, and then reduce the overall duration of the portfolio by selling higher-duration bonds and buying those of shorter duration. Such a strategy would prove profitable, because short-duration instruments do not decline in value to the same degree as longer bonds. Of course, if you felt that interest rates were about to decrease, the opposite strategy would be appropriate.

Although active, short-term investors frequently use duration analysis in their day-to-day operations, longer-term investors have also employed duration analysis in planning their investment decisions. Indeed, a strategy known as *bond portfolio immunization* represents one of the most important uses of duration.

Bond Immunization

Some investors hold portfolios of bonds not for the purpose of "beating the market" but, rather, to accumulate a specified level of wealth by the end of a given investment horizon. For these investors, bond portfolio immunization often proves to be of great value. Immunization allows an investor to derive a specified rate of return from bond investments over a given investment interval *regardless of what happens to market interest rates over the course of the holding period*. In essence, an investor is able to "immunize" his or her portfolio from the effects of changes in market interest rates over a given investment horizon.

To understand how and why bond portfolio immunization is possible, you need to understand that changes in market interest rates lead to two distinct and opposite changes in bond valuation: The first effect, known as the *price effect,* results in portfolio valuation changes when interest rates change before the end of the desired investment horizon. This is true because interest rate decreases lead to bond price increases, and vice versa. The second effect, known as the *reinvestment effect,* arises because the yield-to-maturity calculation assumes that all of a bond's coupon payments will be reinvested at the yield-to-maturity rate that existed when the bond was purchased. If interest rates increase, however, the coupons may be reinvested at a higher rate than that expected by the investor, leading to increases in investor wealth. Of course, the opposite is true when interest rates decrease. Thus, whereas an increase in rates has a negative effect on a bond's price, it has a positive effect on the reinvestment of coupons: Therefore, when interest rate changes do occur, the price and reinvestment effects work against each other from the standpoint of the investor's wealth.

When do these counteracting effects exactly offset each other and leave the investor's wealth position unchanged? You guessed it: when the average duration of the portfolio just equals your investment horizon. This should not come as much of a surprise, because such a property is already embedded in the measure of duration itself. Accordingly, if it applies to a single bond, it should also apply to the *weighted-average duration of a bond portfolio*. When such a condition (of offsetting price and reinvestment effects) exists, *a bond portfolio is said to be immunized.* More specifically, your wealth position is immunized from the effects of interest rate changes *when the weighted-average duration of the bond portfolio exactly equals your desired investment horizon.* Table 9.2 provides an example of bond immunization using a 10-year, 8% coupon bond with a duration of 8 years; here, we assume the investor's desired investment horizon is also 8 years in length.

The example provided in Table 9.2 assumes that you, as the investor, originally purchased the 8% coupon bond at par. It further assumes that market interest rates for bonds of this quality drop from 8% to 6% at the end of the fifth year. Now, because you had an investment horizon of exactly 8 years and desire to lock in an interest rate return of exactly 8%, it follows that you expect to have a terminal value of $1,850.90 [i.e., $1,000 invested at 8% for 8 years = $1,000 × (1.08)^8 = $1,850.90], regardless of interest rate changes in the interim. As can be seen from the bottom-line results presented in Table 9.2, the immunization strategy netted you a total of $1,850.31—just 59 cents short of your desired goal. Note that in this case, although reinvestment opportunities

TABLE 9.2 Bond Immunization

Year	Cash Flow from Bond						Terminal Value of Reinvested Cash Flow
1	$80	×	$(1.08)^4$	×	$(1.06)^3$	=	$ 129.63
2	80	×	$(1.08)^3$	×	$(1.06)^3$	=	120.03
3	80	×	$(1.08)^2$	×	$(1.06)^3$	=	111.14
4	80	×	(1.08)	×	$(1.06)^3$	=	102.90
5	80	×	$(1.06)^3$			=	95.28
6	80	×	$(1.06)^2$			=	89.89
7	80	×	(1.06)			=	84.80
8	80					=	80.00
8	$1,036.64*					=	1,036.64
			Total				$1,850.31
			Investor's required wealth at 8%				$1,850.90
			Difference				$ .59

*The bond could be sold at a market price of $1,036.64, which is the value of an 8% bond with 2 years to maturity that is priced to yield 6%.

Note: Bond interest coupons are assumed to be paid at year-end. Therefore, there are 4 years of reinvestment at 8% and 3 years at 6% for the first year's $80 coupon.

declined in years 5, 6, and 7 (when market interest rates dropped to 6%), that same lower rate led to a higher market price for the bond, which in turn provided just about enough capital gains to offset the loss in reinvested income. This remarkable result clearly demonstrates the power of bond immunization and the versatility of bond duration. Even though the table uses a single bond for purposes of illustration, the same results—that is, achieving a desired terminal value/rate of return—can be obtained from a bond *portfolio* that is maintained at the *proper weighted-average duration.*

Although bond immunization is a powerful investment tool, it is clearly not a passive investment strategy. Maintaining a fully immunized portfolio requires *continual portfolio rebalancing* on the part of the investor. Indeed, every time interest rates change, the duration of a portfolio changes. Because effective immunization requires that the portfolio have a duration value equal in length to the investor's *remaining investment horizon,* the composition of the investor's portfolio must be rebalanced each time interest rates change. Further, even in the absence of interest rate changes, a bond's duration declines more slowly than its term to maturity. This, of course, means that the mere passage of time will dictate changes in portfolio composition. Such changes will ensure that the duration of the portfolio continues to match the remaining time in the investment horizon. In summary, portfolio immunization strategies can be extremely effective, but it is important to realize that immunization is not a passive strategy and is not without potential problems, the most notable of which are associated with portfolio rebalancing.

CONCEPTS IN REVIEW

9.11 What does the term *duration* mean to bond investors, and how does the duration on a bond differ from its maturity? What is *modified duration,* and how is it used?

9.12 Describe the process of *bond portfolio immunization* and explain why an investor would want to immunize a portfolio. Would you consider portfolio immunization a passive investment strategy comparable to, say, a buy-and-hold approach? Explain.

http://hepg.aw.com

Some investors have trouble understanding the idea of duration. This risk measure is too important for anyone who invests in bonds *not* to have a clear understanding of its meaning and use. The following Web page has a short but clearly written paper on duration.

www.iix.com/clu/sections/FC109401.htm

Bond Investment Strategies

LG 6

Generally, bond investors tend to follow one of three kinds of investment programs. First, there are those who live off the income: the conservative, quality-conscious, income-oriented investors who seek to maximize current income. Then there are the speculators (bond traders), who have a considerably different investment objective: to maximize capital gains, often within a short time span. This investment approach requires considerable expertise, because it is based almost entirely on estimates of the future course of interest rates. Finally, there are the serious long-term investors, whose objective is to maximize *total return*—from both current income and capital gains—over fairly long holding periods.

In order to achieve the objectives of any one of these three programs, you need to adopt a strategy that is compatible with your goals. Professional money managers use a variety of techniques to manage the multi-million-dollar bond portfolios under their direction. These vary from passive approaches, to semiactive strategies, to active, fully managed strategies using interest rate forecasting and yield spread analysis. Most of these strategies are fairly complex and require substantial computer support. Even so, we can look briefly at some of the more basic strategies to gain an appreciation of the different ways in which fixed-income securities can be used to reach different investment objectives.

Passive Strategies

The bond immunization strategies we have discussed are considered to be primarily *passive* in nature; investors using these tools typically are *not* attempting to beat the market. Rather, these investors immunize their portfolios in an effort to lock in specified rates of return (or terminal values) that they deem acceptable, given the risks involved. Generally speaking, passive investment strategies are characterized by a lack of input regarding investor expectations of changes in interest rate and/or bond price. Further, these strategies typically do not generate significant transaction costs. A *buy-and-hold* strategy is perhaps the most passive of all investment strategies: All that is required is that the investor replace bonds that have deteriorating credit ratings, have matured, or have been called. Although buy-and-hold investors restrict their ability to earn above-average returns, they also minimize the dead-weight losses that transaction costs represent.

bond ladders
an investment strategy wherein equal amounts of money are invested in a series of bonds with staggered maturities.

One approach that is a bit more active than buy-and-hold and is popular with many individual and institutional investors is the use of so-called **bond ladders.** In this strategy, equal amounts are invested in a *series* of bonds with staggered maturities. Here's how a bond ladder works: Suppose you want to confine your investing to fixed-income securities with maturities of 10 years or less; given that maturity constraint, you could set up a ladder by investing in (roughly) equal amounts of, say, 3-, 5-, 7-, and 10-year issues. Then, when the 3-year issue matures, the money from it (along with any new capital) would be put into a new 10-year note. The process would continue rolling over like this so that eventually you would hold a full ladder of staggered 10-year notes. By rolling into new 10-year issues every 2 or 3 years, you can do a kind of dollar-cost averaging and thereby lessen the impact of swings in market rates. Actually, the laddered approach is a safe, simple, and almost automatic way of investing for the long haul—indeed, once the ladder is set up, it should be followed in a fairly routine manner. A key ingredient of this or any other passive strategy is, of course, the use of high-quality investment vehicles that possess attractive features, maturities, and yields. Bond ladders, however, are just part of the story. As noted in the accompanying *Investing in Action* box, there

INVESTING IN ACTION

Pondering Bond Ladders and Barbells

U.S. government bonds will never default, and that's why investors around the world buy them. But as for all bonds, interest rate risk is ever-present. Buying a 30-year Treasury bond with a 6% coupon is a bad investment if interest rates rise. But buying a 2-year Treasury security with a 5% coupon means lost opportunity if interest rates fall.

Unfortunately, no one can predict on a consistent basis the direction of interest rates. But there are some strategies that bond investors use to cope with interest rate volatility. One is a *ladder* investment strategy, which is an easy way to immunize a portfolio against interest rate risk. Take $100,000 and buy ten $10,000 Treasury bonds, the first maturing in 1 year, the second in 2 years, and so on. Let a year go by, and then take the $10,000 from the bond maturing in 1 year and buy a 10-year bond with it. By having lots of positions across the yield curve, you're diversified in the event that yields move differently in one part of the curve than in another. "To me, a ladder portfolio structure is the best way to diversify a fixed-income portfolio," says Alan Koepplin, head of fixed-income investments for Cowen Asset Management.

Another good approach is a *barbell* strategy, which consists of buying a mixture of very short and very long bonds. As on a barbell, the weights are on each end of the bar. The drawback is that "it subjects you to the greatest amount of yield curve risk," says Koepplin. "If interest rates on 30-year bonds go up 200 basis points, then half your portfolio would go down sharply in value." On the other hand, a barbell approach was perfect in late 1997, just before the Asian economic crisis hit. A flight to quality bonds ensued, boosting prices on U.S. Treasury bonds. Yields fell sharply from 6.2% to 5.6%, and bond investors with half their money in 30-year bonds were rewarded handsomely. Meanwhile, the other half of the barbell was invested in short-term investments. The Federal Reserve Board, which controls short-term interest rates, decided to maintain a stable monetary policy, and short-term rates remained unchanged at 5.50%. "A barbell is a more aggressive strategy than a ladder because you're saying 'I want to benefit from the decline in rates,'" says Koepplin. "By the same token, you're softening your bet on interest rates by keeping half your money close to home."

Just a year earlier, the yield curve was quite a bit steeper. The Fed had just raised short-term interest rates from 5.25% to 5.50%. The 30-year Treasury was yielding about 7.1%, the highest it had been in a few years. Yet inflation was running only between 2% and 3%. Many bond managers employed a barbell strategy with this yield curve. Hence half the money went to buy the long bond at 7.1% to lock in the high yield. If interest rates fell, the investor would achieve maximum capital appreciation from half of the portfolio. If the less likely outcome occurred—that is, if interest rates rose further—then the short end of the portfolio would be reinvested immediately at the higher rates.

is another way of setting up a portfolio of bonds: *Instead of using a ladder, you could use a barbell.*

Trading on Forecasted Interest Rate Behavior

The *forecasted interest rate* approach to bond investing is highly risky, because it relies on the imperfect forecast of future interest rates. It seeks attractive capital gains when interest rates are expected to decline and the preservation of capital when an increase in interest rates is anticipated. The idea is to increase the return on a bond portfolio by making strategic moves in anticipation of interest rate changes. Such a strategy is essentially *market timing,* so it carries definite risks and costs. An unusual feature of this tactic is that most of the trading is done with *investment-grade securities,* because a high degree of interest rate sensitivity is required to capture the maximum amount of price behavior.

Once interest rate expectations have been specified, this strategy rests largely on technical matters. For example, when a decline in rates is anticipated, aggressive bond investors often seek to lengthen the maturity (or duration) of their bonds (or bond portfolios). The reason: Longer-term bonds rise more in price in response to a given drop in rates than their shorter-term counterparts do. At the same time, investors look for low-coupon and/or moderately discounted bonds, which will add to duration and increase the amount of potential price volatility. These interest swings are usually short-lived, so bond traders try to earn as much as possible in as short a time as possible. (Margin trading—the use of borrowed money to buy bonds—is also used as a way of magnifying returns when rate declines are expected.) When rates start to level off and move up, these investors begin to shift their money out of long, discounted bonds and into high-yielding issues with short maturities. In other words, they do a complete reversal. During those periods when bond prices are dropping, investors are more concerned about preservation of capital, so they take steps to protect their money from capital losses. Thus they tend to use such short-term obligations as Treasury bills, money funds, short-term (2 to 5 years) notes, or even variable-rate notes.

Bond Swaps

bond swap
an investment strategy wherein an investor liquidates one bond holding and simultaneously buys a different issue in its place.

In a **bond swap,** an investor simply liquidates one position and simultaneously buys a different issue in its place. Swaps can be executed to increase current yield or yield-to-maturity, to take advantage of shifts in interest rates, to improve the quality of a portfolio, or for tax purposes. Although some swaps are highly sophisticated, most are fairly simple transactions. They go by a variety of colorful names, such as "profit takeout," "substitution swap," and "tax swap," but they are all used for one basic reason: *to seek portfolio improvement.* We will briefly review two types of bond swaps that are fairly simple and hold considerable appeal for investors: the yield pickup swap and the tax swap.

yield pickup swap
replacement of a low-coupon bond for a comparable higher-coupon bond in order to realize an increase in current yield and yield-to-maturity.

In a **yield pickup swap,** an investor switches out of a low-coupon bond into a comparable higher-coupon issue in order to realize an automatic and instantaneous pickup of current yield and yield-to-maturity. For example, you would be executing a yield pickup swap if you sold the 20-year, A-rated, 6½% bonds you held (which were yielding 8% at the time) and replaced them with an equal amount of 20-year, A-rated, 7% bonds that were priced to yield 8½%. By executing the swap, you would improve your current yield (your coupon income would increase from $65 a year to $70 a year) as well as your yield-to-maturity (from 8 to 8½%). Basically, such swap opportunities arise because of the *yield spreads* that normally exist between, say, industrial and public utility bonds. The mechanics are fairly simple, and you can execute such swaps simply by watching for swap candidates and/or asking your broker to do so. In fact, the only thing you have to be careful of is that commissions and transaction costs do not eat up all the profits.

tax swap
replacement of a bond that has a capital loss for a similar security; used to offset a gain generated in another part of an investor's portfolio.

The other type of swap that's popular with many investors is the **tax swap,** which is also relatively simple and involves few risks. The technique can be used whenever an investor has a substantial tax liability that has come about as a result of selling some security holdings at a profit. The objective is to execute a bond swap in such a way that the tax liability accompanying the capital gains can be *eliminated* or *substantially reduced.* This is done by selling an issue that has undergone capital *loss* and replacing it with a comparable obligation. For example, assume that you had $10,000 worth or corporate bonds that you sold (in the current year) for $15,000, resulting in a capital gain of $5,000. You can eliminate the tax liability accompanying the capital gain by selling securities that have capital losses of $5,000. Let's assume you find you hold a 20-year, 4¾% municipal bond that (strictly by coincidence, of course) has undergone a $5,000 drop in value. Thus you have the required tax shield in your portfolio, and all you have to do is find a viable swap candidate. Suppose you find a comparable 20-year, 5% municipal issue currently trading at about the same price as the issue being sold. By selling the 4¾s and simultaneously buying a comparable amount of the 5s, you will not only increase your tax-free yields (from 4¾% to 5%) but also eliminate the capital gains tax liability. The only precaution is that *identical issues cannot be used* in such swap transactions, because the IRS would consider that a "wash sale" (see Chapter 3) and therefore disallow the loss. Moreover, the capital loss must occur in the same taxable year as the capital gain. This limitation explains why the technique is so popular with knowledgeable investors, particularly at year-end, when tax loss sales and tax swaps multiply as investors hurry to establish capital losses.

CONCEPTS IN REVIEW

9.13 Briefly describe a *bond ladder* and note how and why an investor would use this investment strategy. What is a *tax swap,* and why would it be used?

9.14 According to the *Investing in Action* box on page 372, what is the difference between the *barbell* and *ladder* strategies? Under what conditions would you rather have a bond barbell than a bond ladder? Explain.

9.15 What strategy would you expect an aggressive bond investor (someone who's looking for capital gains) to employ?

9.16 Why is interest sensitivity so important to bond speculators? Does the need for interest sensitivity explain why active bond traders tend to use high-grade issues? Explain.

http://hepg.aw.com

Successful active bond management strategies require the investor to make consistently accurate predictions of interest rate movements. Information about past rates is sometimes helpful for forecasting future rate movement. The following Web page has links to historical information on a large variety of fixed-income securities.

www.mes.com/~tyrhardz/tmp55.html#55FirstSection

Summary

LG 1 **Explain the behavior of market interest rates and identify the forces that cause interest rates to move.** The behavior of interest rates is the single most important force in the bond market, because it determines not only the amount of current income an investor will receive but also the amount of the investor's capital gains (or losses). Indeed, changes in market interest rates can have a dramatic impact on the total returns actually obtained from bonds over time.

LG 2 **Describe the term structure of interest rates and note how these so-called yield curves can be used by investors.** Many forces drive the behavior of interest rates over time, including inflation, the cost and availability of funds, the size of the federal deficit, and the level of interest rates in major foreign markets. One force that's particularly important is the term structure of interest rates, which relates yield-to-maturity to term-to-maturity.

LG 3 **Gain an understanding of how bonds are valued in the marketplace.** Bonds are valued (priced) in the marketplace on the basis of their required rates of return (or market yields). The whole process of pricing a bond begins with the yield it should provide. Once that piece of information is known (or estimated), a standard, present-value-based model is used to find the dollar price of a bond.

LG 4 **Describe the various measures of yield and return, and explain how these standards of performance are used in the bond valuation process.** Three types of yields are important to investors: current yield, promised yield, and expected yield (or return). Promised yield (also known as yield-to-maturity) is the most important and widely used bond valuation measure and captures both the current income and the price appreciation of an issue. Expected return, in contrast, is a valuation measure that's used by aggressive bond traders to show the total return that can be earned from trading in and out of a bond long before it matures.

LG 5 **Understand the basic concept of duration, how it can be measured, and its use in the management of bond portfolios.** Bond duration is one of the most important concepts in bond valuation and investing. Duration takes into account the effects of both reinvestment and price (or market) risks. It captures, in a single measure, the extent to which the price of a bond will react to different interest rate environments. Equally important, duration can be used to immunize whole bond portfolios from the often devastating forces of changing market interest rates.

LG 6 **Discuss various bond investment strategies and the different ways these securities can be used by investors.** As investment vehicles, bonds can be used as a source of income, as a way to seek capital gains by speculating on the movement in interest rates, or as a way to earn attractive long-term returns. To achieve these objectives, investors often employ one or more of the following bond investment strategies: passive strategies such as buy-and-hold, bond ladders, and portfolio immunization; bond trading based on forecasted interest rate behavior; and bond swaps.

Discussion Questions

LG 2 Q9.1. Briefly describe each of the following theories of the term structure of interest rates.

a. Expectations hypothesis
b. Liquidity preference theory
c. Market segmentation theory

According to these theories, what conditions would result in a downward-sloping yield curve? What conditions would result in an upward-sloping yield curve? Which theory do you think is most valid, and why?

LG 2 Q9.2. Using a recent copy of the *Wall Street Journal* or *Barron's*, find bond yields for Treasury securities with the following maturities: 3 months, 6 months, 1 year, 3 years, 5 years, 10 years, 15 years, 20 years, and 30 years. Construct a yield curve based on these reported yields, putting term-to-maturity on the horizontal (x) axis and yield-to-maturity on the vertical (y) axis. Briefly discuss the general shape of your yield curve. What conclusions might you draw about interest rate movements from this yield curve?

LG 5 Q9.3. Briefly explain what will happen to a bond's duration measure if each of the following events occur.

a. The yield-to-maturity on the bond falls from 8½% to 8%.
b. The bond gets 1 year closer to its maturity.
c. Market interest rates go from 8% to 9%.
d. The bond's *modified* duration falls by half a year.

LG 6 Q9.4. Assume that an investor comes to you looking for investment advice. She has $200,000 to invest and wants to put it all into bonds.

a. If she considers herself a fairly aggressive investor who is willing to take the risks necessary to generate the big returns, what kind of investment strategy (or strategies) will you suggest? Be specific.
b. What kind of investment strategies would you recommend if your client were a very conservative investor, who could not tolerate market losses?
c. What kind of investor do you think is most likely to use:
   (1) An immunized bond portfolio?
   (2) A yield pickup swap?
   (3) A bond ladder?
   (4) A long-term zero-coupon bond when interest rates fall?

LG 4 LG 5 Q9.5. Using the resources available at your campus or public library, select any six bonds you like, consisting of *two* Treasury bonds, *two* corporate bonds, and *two* agency issues. Determine the latest current yield and promised yield for each. (For promised yield, use annual compounding.) In addition, find the duration and modified duration for each bond.

a. Now, assuming that you put an equal amount into each of the six bonds you selected, find the duration for this six-bond portfolio.
b. What would happen to your bond portfolio if market interest rates fell by 100 basis points?
c. Assuming that you have $100,000 to invest, use at least four of these bonds to develop a bond portfolio that emphasizes either the potential for capital gains or the preservation of capital. Briefly explain your logic.

Problems

LG 3 P9.1. Two bonds have par values of $1,000; one is a 5%, 15-year bond priced to yield 8%, and the other is a 7½%, 20-year bond priced to yield 6%. Which of these two has the lower price? (Assume annual compounding in both cases.)

LG 3 P9.2. Using semiannual compounding, find the prices of the following bonds:

a. A 10½%, 15-year bond priced to yield 8%
b. A 7%, 10-year bond priced to yield 8%
c. A 12%, 20-year bond priced at 10%

Repeat the problem using annual compounding. Then comment on the differences you found in the prices of the bonds.

LG 3 P9.3. An investor is considering the purchase of an 8%, 18-year corporate bond that's being priced to yield 10%. She thinks that in a year, this same bond will be priced

in the market to yield 9%. Using annual compounding, find the price of the bond today and in 1 year. Next, find the holding period return on this investment, assuming that the investor's expectations are borne out. (If necessary, see Chapter 4 for the holding period return formula.)

 LG 4

P9.4. Compute the current yield of a 10%, 25-year bond that is currently priced in the market at $1,200. Use annual compounding to find the promised yield on this bond. Repeat the promised yield calculation, but this time use semiannual compounding to find yield-to-maturity.

 LG 4

P9.5. A 25-year, zero-coupon bond was recently being quoted at 11⅝. Find the current yield *and* the promised yield of this issue, given that the bond has a par value of $1,000. Using annual compounding, determine how much an investor would have to pay for this bond if it were priced to yield 12%.

 LG 4

P9.6. Assume that an investor pays $800 for a long-term bond that carries an 8% coupon. In 3 years, she hopes to sell the issue for $850. If her expectations come true, what realized yield will this investor earn? What would her holding period return be if she were able to sell the bond (at $850) after only 6 months?

 LG 4

P9.7. Using annual compounding, find the yield-to-maturity for each of the following bonds.

a. A 9½%, 20-year bond priced at $957.43
b. A 16%, 15-year bond priced at $1,684.76
c. A 5½%, 18-year bond priced at $510.65

 LG 5

P9.8. Find the Macaulay duration and the modified duration of a 20-year, 10% corporate bond that's being priced to yield 8%. According to the modified duration of this bond, how much of a price change would this bond incur if market yields rose to 9% in 1 year? Using annual compounding, calculate the price of this bond in 1 year if rates do rise to 9%. How does this price change compare to that predicted by the modified duration? Explain the difference.

 LG 5

P9.9. Which *one* of the following bonds would you select if you thought market interest rates were going to fall by 50 basis points over the next 6 months?

a. A bond with a Macaulay duration of 8.46 years that's currently being priced to yield 7½%
b. A bond with a Macaulay duration of 9.30 years that's priced to yield 10%
c. A bond with a Macaulay duration of 8.75 years that's priced to yield 5¾%

 LG 5 LG 6

P9.10. Ella Hollohan is an aggressive bond trader who likes to speculate on interest rate swings. Market interest rates are presently at 9%, but she expects them to fall to 7% within a year. As a result, Ella is thinking about buying either a 25-year, zero-coupon bond or a 20-year, 7½% bond. (Both bonds have $1,000 par values and carry the same agency rating.) Assuming that Ella wants to maximize capital gains, which of the two issues should she select? What if she wants to maximize the total return (interest income and capital gains) from her investment? Why did one issue provide better capital gains than the other? Based on the duration of each bond, which one should be more price volatile?

 LG 5 LG 6

P9.11. Saul Newman is a 35-year-old bank executive who has just inherited a large sum of money. Having spent several years in the bank's investments department, he's well aware of the concept of duration and decides to apply it to his bond portfolio. In particular, Saul intends to use $1 million of his inheritance to purchase four U.S. Treasury bonds:

1. An 8½%, 13-year bond that's priced at $1,045 to yield 7.47%
2. A 7⅞%, 15-year bond that's priced at $1,020 to yield 7.60%
3. A 20-year stripped Treasury that's priced at $202 to yield 8.22%
4. A 24-year, 7½% bond that's priced at $955 to yield 7.90%

a. Find the duration and the modified duration of each bond.
b. Find the duration of the whole bond portfolio if Saul puts $250,000 into each of the four U.S. Treasury bonds.
c. Find the duration of the portfolio if Saul puts $360,000 each into bonds 1 and 3 and $140,000 each into bonds 2 and 4.
d. Which portfolio—(b) or (c)—should Saul select if he thinks rates are about to head up and wants to avoid as much price volatility as possible? Explain. From which portfolio does he stand to make more in annual interest income? Which portfolio would you recommend, and why?

Case Problem 9.1 *The Bond Investment Decisions of Rob and Kathy Jobst*

Rob and Kathy Jobst live in the Boston area, where Rob has a successful orthodontics practice. The Jobsts have built up a sizable investment portfolio and have always had a major portion of their investments in fixed-income securities. They adhere to a fairly aggressive investment posture and actively go after both attractive current income and substantial capital gains. Assume that it is now 1998 and Rob is currently evaluating two investment decisions: One involves an addition to their portfolio, the other a revision to it.

The Jobsts' first investment decision involves a short-term trading opportunity. In particular, Rob has a chance to buy a 7½%, 25-year bond that is currently priced at $852 to yield 9%; he feels that in 2 years the promised yield of the issue should drop to 8%.

The second is a bond swap; the Jobsts hold some Beta Corporation 7%, 2013 bonds that are currently priced at $785. They want to improve both current income and yield-to-maturity, and they are considering one of three issues as a possible swap candidate: (a) Dental Floss, Inc., 7½%, 2013, currently priced at $780; (b) Root Canal Products of America, 6½%, 2011, selling at $885; and (c) Kansas City Dental Insurance, 8%, 2015, priced at $950. All of the swap candidates are of comparable quality and have comparable issue characteristics.

QUESTIONS

a. Regarding the short-term trading opportunity:
   1. What basic trading principle is involved in this situation?
   2. If Rob's expectations are correct, what will the price of this bond be in 2 years?
   3. What is the expected return on this investment?
   4. Should this investment be made? Why?

b. Regarding the bond swap opportunity:
   1. Compute the current yield and the promised yield (use semiannual compounding) for the bond the Jobsts currently hold and for each of the three swap candidates.
   2. Do any of the three swap candidates provide better current income and/or current yield than the Beta Corporation bonds the Jobsts now hold? If so, which one(s)?

3. Do you see any reason why Rob should switch from his present bond holding into one of the other three issues? If so, which swap candidate would be the best choice? Why?

Case Problem 9.2 Stacy Decides to Immunize Her Portfolio

LG 4 LG 5 LG 6

Stacy Wong is the owner of an extremely successful dress boutique in midtown Manhattan. Although high fashion is Stacy's first love, she's also interested in investments, particularly bonds and other fixed-income securities. She actively manages her own investments and over time has built up a substantial portfolio of securities. She's well versed on the latest investment techniques and is not afraid to apply those procedures to her own investments.

Stacy has been playing with the idea of trying to immunize a big chunk of her bond portfolio. She'd like to cash out this part of her portfolio in 7 years and use the proceeds to buy a vacation home on the South Carolina seashore. To do this, she intends to use the $200,000 she now has invested in the following four corporate bonds (she currently has $50,000 invested in each one).

1. A 12-year, 7½% bond that's currently priced at $895
2. A 10-year, zero-coupon bond priced at $405
3. A 10-year, 10% bond priced at $1,080
4. A 15-year, 9¼% bond priced at $980

(*Note:* These are all noncallable, investment-grade, nonconvertible/straight bonds.)

QUESTIONS

a. Given the information provided, find the current yield and the promised yield for each bond in the portfolio. (Use annual compounding.)

b. Calculate the Macaulay and modified durations of each bond in the portfolio, and indicate how the price of each bond would change if interest rates were to rise by 75 basis points. How would the price change if interest rates were to fall by 75 basis points?

c. Find the duration of the current four-bond portfolio. Given the 7-year target that Stacy has, would you consider this an immunized portfolio? Explain.

d. How could you lengthen or shorten the duration of this portfolio? What's the shortest portfolio duration you can achieve? What's the longest?

e. Using one or more of the four bonds described above, is it possible to come up with a $200,000 bond portfolio that will exhibit the duration characteristics Stacy is looking for? Explain.

f. Using one or more of the four bonds, put together a $200,000 immunized portfolio for Stacy. Because this portfolio will now be immunized, will Stacy be able to treat it as a buy-and-hold portfolio—one she can put away and forget about? Explain.

Home Page Exercises

http://hepg.aw.com **Keyword: Invest**

When the word *investment* is mentioned, most investors immediately think of common stocks. This response is not surprising, given the daily publicity that these assets receive. Many investors are surprised to learn that there are more bond issues outstanding than stock issues. The limited attention given to bonds is one reason why the Web does not generate as many sites dedicated to bonds as can be found for stocks. However, the sites listed here provide good information on bond investments.

Web Address	*Primary Investment Focus*
www.bondsonline.com	A site dedicated to fixed-income securities
www.aaii.org/fxdincme	This American Association of Individual Investors site has some interesting articles on fixed-income investments
www.smartmoney.com	A wealth of information about bonds, including interactive bond yield and asset allocation tools
www.moneypages.com/syndicate	Bond information and links to related sites, with a glossary of municipal bond terms
www.netspace.org/users/david/finance.html	A large number of links to sites that offer information on bonds

W9.1. When it comes to pricing investment assets, bonds are the easiest to do. Some basic time-value-of-money calculations lead to the current value of a bond's future cash flow, and thus the bond's fair market price. The Web page listed here gives daily closing prices for some widely traded bond issues for major corporations. Select one of the bonds listed. Using the information provided, calculate the present value of the interest payments and the present value of the maturity value. Do you obtain the same bond value as that shown in the quote?

www.dbc.com/cgi-bin/htx.exe/newsroom/bel_corp.html

W9.2. General interest rate movements are reflected by changes in the yield curve. The Web page cited here has an interactive segment that allows investors to observe current and historical yield curves. Write the approximate yield that existed or exists for 1-, 5-, 10-, and 20-year bonds for the month of November in 1980, 1988, 1992, 1996, and the current year. How have interest rates changed over these periods? What do these changes imply for bond investments?

www.smartmoney.com/si/tools/onebond/index.cfm?story=yieldcurve

W9.3. Interest rates, bond prices, and movements in the yield curve are driven by changes in expectations of the economy. On the Web page listed, click on the four yield curves—normal, steep, inverted, and flat—to read about the economic conditions that existed when each shape occurred in the economy. Write a brief discussion of the economic conditions that caused the yield curve to assume each shape.

www.smartmoney.com/si/tools/onebond/index.cfm?story=yieldcurve

Preferred Stocks and Convertible Securities

Chapter 10

Alaska Airlines

Fare wars . . . cut-throat competition . . . airline mergers . . . labor unrest . . . bankruptcies. The airline industry has had its share of stress during the 1990s, and not surprisingly, the industry has been notoriously turbulent as an investment. Sensitive to oil prices and the strength of the economy, airline securities were not very popular in the early part of the 1990s. As a result, many had to issue securities with special features to attract attention. Convertible bonds became a popular financing vehicle to provide investors with income while they awaited rising stock prices.

Alaska Air Group, parent of Alaska Airlines, was one such airline. As it cut costs and focused on its niche of serving the West Coast, the airline's common stock and convertible bonds soared. In 1997 the stock rose 85%. Its 6.5% convertible senior debentures due in 2005 rose from a low of 112 to a high of 184 during 1997, an increase of 64%.

In this chapter, you will learn about these creative forms of financing, as well as the advantages that each offers to both investor and issuer.

Learning Goals

After studying this chapter, you should be able to:

LG 1 Describe the basic features of preferred stock, including sources of value and exposure to risk.

LG 2 Discuss the rights and claims of preferred stockholders and note some of the popular issue characteristics that are often found with these securities.

LG 3 Understand the various measures of investment worth and identify several investment strategies that can be used with preferred stocks.

LG 4 Identify the fundamental characteristics of convertible securities and explain the nature of the underlying conversion privilege.

LG 5 Describe the advantages and disadvantages of investing in convertible securities, including their risk and return attributes.

LG 6 Measure the value of a convertible security and explain how these securities can be used to meet different investment objectives.

Preferred Stocks

LG 1 LG 2

What would you think of a stock that promised to pay you a fixed annual dividend for life—nothing more, nothing less? If you're an income-oriented investor, the offer might sound pretty good. But where would you find such an investment? Right on the NYSE or AMEX, where hundreds of these securities trade every day, in the form of *preferred stock*—a type of security that looks like a stock but doesn't behave like one. In the first two sections of this chapter we will look at preferred stock as an investment vehicle. In the third and fourth sections of the chapter we will turn to another type of corporate security called *convertible debentures*—securities originally issued as bonds that later can be converted into shares of the issuing firm's common stock. Both of these investment vehicles—preferred stock and convertibles—are forms of *fixed-income* corporate securities. As you'll see in the chapter, both are also *hybrid securities,* meaning they contain elements of both debt and equity. Let's first take a close look at preferred stocks.

preferred stock
a stock that has a prior claim (ahead of common) on the income and assets of the issuing firm.

Preferred stocks carry fixed dividends that are paid quarterly and are expressed either in dollar terms or as a percentage of the stock's par (or stated) value. They're used by companies that need money but don't want to raise debt to get it; in effect, preferred stocks are widely viewed by issuers as an alternative to debt. Companies like to issue preferreds because they don't count as common stock (and, therefore, don't affect EPS). However, being a form of equity, they don't count as debt, either—and therefore don't add to the company's debt load. There are today about a thousand OTC and listed preferred stocks outstanding, many of which are issued by public utilities, although the number of industrial, financial, and insurance issues is rapidly increasing.

Preferred Stocks as Investment Vehicles

Preferred stocks are available in a wide range of quality ratings, from investment-grade issues to highly speculative stocks. Table 10.1 provides a representative sample of some actively traded preferred stocks. It shows the types

TABLE 10.1 A Sample of Some High-Yielding Preferred Stock

S&P Rating	Issuer	Annual Dividend	Market Price	Dividend Yield
A−	Citicorp	$6.00	$99.62	6.02%
AA	Dupont	4.50	83.00	5.42
BBB+	GM	2.28	28.50	8.00
A−	Merrill Lynch	2.25	31.25	7.20
BBB+	Public Service G&E	2.00	25.80	7.75
BBB−	Arizona Public Service	1.81	25.55	7.08
A−	Cadburry Schwepps	2.16	27.10	7.97
BB−	USX	2.19	25.50	8.59
BBB	Bear Sterns	1.97	25.75	7.65
AA−	J.P. Morgan	3.31	55.10	6.01
BBB	PECO Energy	2.25	25.88	8.69
BB−	Digital Equipment	2.22	26.10	8.50

Note: All of these issues are straight (nonconvertible) preferred stocks traded on the NYSE. All the information that appears in this table was obtained in December 1997.

of annual dividends and dividend yields that these securities were providing in December 1997. Note especially the variety of different types of issuers and how the market price of a preferred tends to vary with the size of the annual dividend.

Advantages and Disadvantages

Investors are attracted to preferred stocks because of the current income they provide. Moreover, such dividend income is highly predictable, even though it can, under certain circumstances, be temporarily discontinued. Figure 10.1 illustrates the average yields on preferred stocks, from 1975 through 1997, and shows how they compare to high-grade bond returns. Note the tendency for preferreds to generate yields that are slightly *less* than those on high-grade bonds. This is due to the fact that 70 percent of the preferred dividends *received by a corporation* are exempt from federal income taxes; and since corporations are big investors in preferred stock, the net effect of this favorable tax treatment is reduced preferred dividend yields. Another reason for investing in preferreds is the level of safety they offer investors.That is, despite a few well-publicized incidents, *high-grade* preferred stocks have an excellent record of meeting dividend payments in a prompt and timely manner. A final advantage of preferred stocks is the low unit cost ($25 to $50 per share) of many of the issues, which gives even small investors the opportunity to actively participate in preferreds.

A major disadvantage of preferred stocks is their susceptibility to inflation and high interest rates. Like many other fixed-income securities, preferred stocks simply have not proved to be satisfactory long-term hedges against inflation. Another disadvantage is that preferred dividends may be suspended, or "passed," if the earnings of the corporate issuer drop off. Thus, unlike coupon payments on a bond, dividends on preferreds have no legal backing, and failure to pay them does not lead to default. Still another drawback is that most preferreds lack substantial capital gains potential. Although it is possible to enjoy fairly attractive capital gains from preferred stocks when interest rates decline dramatically, these amounts generally do not match the price performance of common stocks. But perhaps the biggest disadvantage of preferreds is the *yield give-up* they incur relative to bonds. In essence, there is virtually

FIGURE 10.1
Average High-Grade Preferred Stock Yields Versus Average Market Yields on AA-Rated Corporate Bonds

Note that preferred stock yields tend to move in concert with the market behavior of bond returns—and that they tend to stay *below* bond yields. (Source: Standard & Poor's *Trade and Securities Statistics.)*

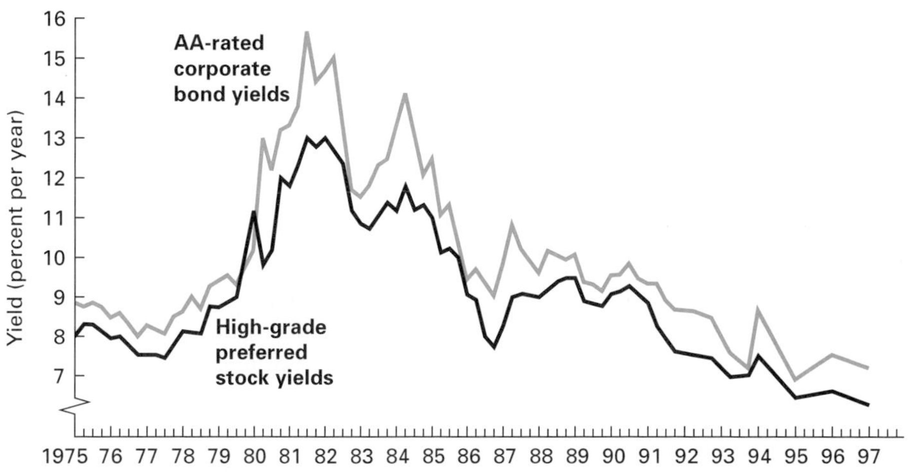

nothing a preferred has to offer that can't be obtained from a comparably rated corporate bond—and *at less risk and more return than can be earned from a preferred.*

Sources of Value

With the exception of convertible preferreds, the value of high-grade preferred stocks is a function of the dividend yields they provide. More specifically, the value (or market price) of a preferred stock is closely related to prevailing market rates: Thus, as the general level of interest rates moves up, so do the yields on preferreds, and their prices decline accordingly. When interest rates drift downward, so do the yields on preferreds, as their prices rise. Just like bond prices, therefore, *the price behavior of a high-grade preferred stock is inversely related to market interest rates.* Moreover, its price is directly linked to the issue's level of income. That is, other things being equal, the higher the dividend payment, the higher the market price of an issue. Thus the price of a preferred stock can be defined as follows:

Equation 10.1

$$\text{Price of a preferred stock} = \frac{\text{annual dividend income}}{\text{prevailing market yield}}$$

This equation is simply a variation of the standard dividend yield formula, but here we solve for the price of the issue. (You might also detect a similarity between this formula and the zero-growth dividend valuation model introduced in Chapter 7.) Equation 10.1 is used to price preferred stocks and to compute the future price of a preferred, given an estimate of expected market interest yields. For example, a \$2.50 preferred stock (the stock pays a dividend of \$2.50 per year) would be priced at \$20.83 if the prevailing market yield were 12%:

$$\text{Price} = \frac{\$2.50}{0.12} = \underline{\underline{\$20.83}}$$

Note that higher prices are obtained with this formula by decreasing the market yield, thus giving you the inverse relationship between price and yield.

The yield that a preferred stock offers—and therefore its market value—is a function not only of market interest rates but also of the issue's credit quality: That is, *the lower the quality of a preferred, the higher its yield.* Such behavior is, of course, compatible with the risk-return tradeoffs that usually exist in the marketplace. Fortunately, preferred stocks are rated, much like bonds, by Moody's and Standard & Poor's. Finally, the value of a preferred is affected by issue characteristics such as call features and sinking-fund provisions. For example, freely callable preferreds normally provide higher yields than noncallable issues because of the greater call risk inherent in the former type of security. Quality and issue features, however, have only slight effects on price behavior over time, and they certainly do not compare in importance with the movement of market yields.

Risk Exposure

Preferred stock investors are exposed to both business and interest rate risks. *Business risk* is important with preferreds, because these securities are a form of equity ownership and, as such, lack many of the legal protections of bonds. Annual operating costs and corporate financial strength, therefore, are of concern to preferred stockholders. Preferred stock ratings (discussed later in this chapter) can be used to assess the amount of business risk embedded in an issue; higher-quality/higher-rated issues are believed to possess less business risk. Because of the fixed-income nature of these securities and the way they're valued in the market, *interest rate risk* is also important to preferred stockholders. That is, when market interest rates move up, the value of these securities (like that of bonds) falls. Indeed, such risk exposure can be very damaging if interest rates move against you in a big way.

Market Transactions

Preferred stocks are subject to the same transaction costs—brokerage fees and transfer taxes—as shares of common stock. In addition, preferred investors use the same types of orders (market, limit, and stop-loss) and operate under the same margin requirements. And, as you can see in Figure 10.2, even the quotes of preferred stock are commingled with those of common. Fortunately, preferreds are easy to pick out in the financial pages; simply look for the letters *pf* or *pr* after the name of the company. (Technically, the *pf* denotes *regular preferred stock,* and the *pr* stands for *prior preferred,* or *preference,* shares. The differences are explained below.)

Quotes for preferred stock are interpreted exactly like those for common stock, except that the price/earnings ratios are not listed. Note also that preferreds are sometimes (but not always) listed right after the company's

FIGURE 10.2 Published Quotes for Preferred Stocks

Preferred stocks are listed right along with the company's common stock. They are identified by the two-letter symbol *pf* or *pr* that appears after the name of the company. (Source: *Wall Street Journal,* December 8, 1997.)

52 Weeks Hi	52 Weeks Lo	Stock	Sym	Div	Yld %	PE	Vol 100s	Hi	Lo	Close	Net Chg
▲ 30⅛	21½	OcciPete	OXY	1.00	3.3	18	13934	30¾	29⅝	30¼	+ 7/16
107⅜	58	OcciPete pf		3.00	3.6	...	12	83⅝	83¼	83⅝	+ ⅝
70 9/16	38	♣OceanEngy	OEI		...	31	645	56⅞	54 11/16	56⅞	+2
s 27 5/16	13¾	Oceanrglnt	OII		...	22	621	21⅜	19⅞	21⅜	+1 3/16
s 28 13/16	12⅝	OcwenFnl	OCN		...	17	384	25¾	25	25⅝	+ ⅜
23 11/16	12	OffcDepot	ODP		...	25	7073	23⅛	22 11/16	23	+ ⅜
16 5/16	9⅞	OfficeMax	OMX		...	23	3731	14 15/16	14 11/16	14⅞	...
▲ 27⅜	18⅜	Ogden	OG	1.25	4.6	19	716	27 7/16	26¾	27 7/16	+ 9/16
▲ 58	48	OhioEd pfA		3.90	6.8	...	z660	58½	56½	57	−1
▲ 63	54½	OhioEd pfC		4.44	6.6	...	z160	67	64½	67	+4¼
▲ 66½	56¼	OhioEd pfD		4.56	6.6	...	z560	68¾	66½	68¾	+2¼
26	23⅞	OhioEd pfM		1.94	7.6	...	50	25½	25½	25½	− ⅛
n 25¾	23⅜	OhioPwr pfB	OJA	1.98	7.7	...	35	25⅝	25 7/16	25⅝	+ 3/16
18 7/16	14⅛	♣OilDriAmer	ODC	.32	2.0	16	41	16¾	16¼	16 5/16	− ⅜
40 3/16	24⅝	OldRepublic	ORI	.52	1.4	13	881	37⅝	37⅛	37¼	− ⅜
s 51⅜	35 45/128	♣Olin	OLN	1.20	2.4	10	913	50 3/16	49⅞	50⅛	+ 3/16
23	13½	OlstenCp	OLS	.28	1.8	14	2855	15½	15 1/16	15½	+ 3/16
38 5/16	30¼	OmegaHlthcr	OHI	2.58	7.1	17	1046	36⅝	36¼	36 5/16	− 5/16
n 27¼	24¾	OmegaHlthcr pfA		2.31	8.7	...	50	26 9/16	26⅛	26 9/16	+ 1/16
34 9/16	22⅜	Omnicare	OCR	.07	.2	46	12920	30⅜	29⅞	30 5/16	+ 5/16

Ohio Edison's preferred stocks

common stock—that's done with the Occidental Petroleum and Omega Health Care stocks, but *not* with Ohio Edison. In the quotes in Figure 10.2, we see that there are four issues of preferred stocks listed for Ohio Edison (OhioEd). Actually, the company could have other issues outstanding, but if they did not trade on the day of the quotes, they would not be listed. These preferreds pay annual dividends of anywhere from $1.94 to $4.56 per share. (Note that the higher the annual dividend, the higher the price of the stock.) At quoted market prices, these preferreds were providing current yields of 6.6% to 7.6%. Observe also the relatively low unit cost of the stock: One of the preferreds is priced at around $25 a share, another is priced in the mid-fifties ($57 a share), and the other two are moderately priced at around $65 to $70 a share.

Issue Characteristics

conversion feature
allows the holder of a convertible preferred to convert to a specified number of shares of the issuing company's common stock.

Preferred stocks possess features that not only distinguish them from other types of securities but also help differentiate one preferred from another. For example, preferred stocks may be issued as convertible or nonconvertible, although the majority fall into the nonconvertible category. A **conversion feature** allows the holder to convert the preferred stock into a specified number of shares of the issuing company's common stock. Because convertible preferreds are, for all intents and purposes, very much like convertible bonds, they will be discussed later in this chapter. At this point, we'll concentrate on *nonconvertible issues,* although many of the features we are about to discuss apply equally to convertible preferreds. In addition to convertibility, investors should be aware of several other important features of preferred stocks; they include the rights of preferred stockholders and the special provisions (such as those pertaining to passed dividends or call features) that are built into preferred stock issues.

Rights of Preferred Stockholders

adjustable-rate (floating-rate) preferreds
preferred stock whose dividends are adjusted periodically in line with yields on certain Treasury issues.

The contractual agreement of a preferred stock specifies the rights and privileges of preferred stockholders. The most important of these deal with the level of annual dividends, the claim on income, voting rights, and the claim on assets. The issuing company agrees that it will pay preferred stockholders a (minimum) fixed level of quarterly dividends and that such payments *will take priority over common stock dividends.* The only condition is that the firm generate income sufficient to meet the preferred dividend requirements. However, the firm is not legally bound to pay dividends. Of course, it cannot pass dividends on preferred stock and then pay dividends on common stock, because that would violate the preferreds' prior claim on income. Although most preferred stocks are issued with dividend rates that remain fixed for the life of the issue, in the early 1980s some preferreds began to appear with floating dividend rates. Known as **adjustable-rate** (or **floating-rate**) **preferreds,** these issues adjust dividends periodically in line with yields on specific Treasury issues, although minimum and maximum dividend rates are usually established as a safeguard for investors.

Even though they hold an ownership position in the firm, preferred stockholders normally have no voting rights. However, if conditions deteriorate to the point where the firm needs to pass one or more consecutive quarterly dividends, preferred shareholders are usually given the right to elect a certain number of corporate directors so that their views can be represented. And if liquidation becomes necessary, the holders of preferreds are given a prior claim on assets. These preferred claims, limited to the par or stated value of the stock, must be satisfied before the claims of the common stockholders. Of course, this obligation does not always mean that the full par or stated value of the preferred will be recovered, because the claims of senior securities, like bonds, must be met first. That is, all bonds—including convertible bonds—have a higher claim on assets (and income) than preferred stock, whereas preferreds have a higher claim than common stock. Thus preferred shareholders have a claim that's somewhere between that of bondholders and common stockholders.

preference (prior preferred) stock
a type of preferred stock that has seniority over other preferred stock in its right to receive dividends and in its claim on assets.

Finally, when a company has more than one issue of preferred stock outstanding, it sometimes issues **preference** (or **prior preferred**) **stock.** Essentially, this stock has seniority over other preferred stock in its right to receive dividends and in its claim on assets in the event of liquidation. Therefore, preference stocks should be viewed as senior preferreds. They're usually easy to pick out in the financial pages because they use the letters *pr* instead of *pf* in their quotes.

Preferred Stock Provisions

There are three preferred stock provisions that investors should be well aware of *before* making an investment in a preferred security. Especially important is the obligation of the issuer in case any dividends are missed. In addition, the investor should determine whether the stock has a call feature and/or a sinking fund provision. Let's start by looking at how passed dividends are handled, which depends on whether the preferred stock is issued on a cumulative or a noncumulative basis.

cumulative provision
a provision requiring that any preferred dividends that have been passed must be paid in full before dividends can be restored to common stockholders.

in arrears
having outstanding unfulfilled preferred dividend obligations.

Fortunately for investors, most preferred stocks are issued on a **cumulative** basis. This means that any preferred dividends that have been passed *must be made up in full* before dividends can be restored to common stockholders. As long as dividends on preferred stocks remain **in arrears**—which means that there are outstanding unfulfilled preferred dividend obligations—a corporation is not able to make dividend payments on common shares. Assume, for example, that a firm normally pays a $1 quarterly dividend on its preferred stock but has missed the dividend for three quarters in a row. In this case, the firm has preferred dividends in arrears of $3 a share, which it is obligated to meet, along with the next quarterly dividend payment, before it can pay dividends to common shareholders. The firm could fulfill this obligation by paying, say, $2 per share to the preferred stockholders at the next quarterly dividend date and $3 per share at the following one (with the $3 covering the remaining $2 in arrears and the current $1 quarterly payment). If the preferred stock had carried a **noncumulative provision,** the issuing company would have been under no obligation to make up any of the passed dividends. Of course, the firm could not make dividend payments on common stock either, but all it would have to do to resume such payments would be to meet the next quarterly preferred dividend. Other things being equal, a cumulative preferred stock should be more highly valued than an issue without such a provision—that is, the cumulative feature should increase the price (and in so doing, lower the yield) of these issues.

noncumulative provision
a provision found on some preferred stocks excusing the issuing firm from having to make up any passed dividends.

INVESTOR FACT

HOW TO HIDE FROM RISING RATES—One of the biggest fears of fixed-income investors (including preferred stock investors) is rising interest rates. To hedge against rising rates, investors often turn to *adjustable-rate preferreds,* whose cash dividends are adjusted quarterly to reflect market conditions. The dividends on adjustable preferreds usually have a floor and a ceiling, but that still leaves plenty of room to move up or down with market rates. Thus when rates move up, rather than the price of the issue going down, the dividend payment goes up instead. Bottom line: There's far less price volatility with adjustables than with fixed-rate preferreds.

Since the early 1970s, it has become increasingly popular to issue preferred stocks with call features. Today, a large number of preferreds carry this provision, which gives the firm the right to call the preferred for retirement. Callable preferreds are usually issued on a *deferred-call basis,* which means they cannot be retired for a certain number of years after the date of issue. After the deferral period, which often extends for 5 to 7 years, the preferreds become freely callable. Of course, such issues are then susceptible to call if the market rate for preferreds declines dramatically, which explains why the yields on freely callable preferreds should be higher than those on noncallable issues. As with bonds, the call price of a preferred is made up of the par value of the issue and a call premium that may amount to as much as 1 year's dividends.

Another preferred stock feature that has become popular in the past 10 years is the *sinking-fund provision,* which denotes how all or a part of an issue will be paid off—amortized—over time. Such sinking-fund preferreds actually have *implied* maturity dates. They are used by firms to reduce the cost of financing, because sinking-fund issues generally have *lower* yields than nonsinking-fund preferreds. A typical sinking-fund preferred might require the firm to retire half the issue over a 10-year period by retiring, say, 5% of the issue each year. Unfortunately, the investor has no control over which shares are called for sinking-fund purposes.

CONCEPTS IN REVIEW

10.1 Define a *preferred stock.* What types of prior claims do preferred stockholders enjoy?

10.2 In what ways is a preferred stock like equity? In what ways is it like a bond?

10.3 What are the advantages and the disadvantages of investing in preferreds?

10.4 Distinguish a *cumulative* preferred from a *callable* preferred. Do cumulative dividend provisions and call features affect the investment merits of preferred issues? Explain.

http://hepg.aw.com

Terms such as *participating, cumulative,* and *dividend in arrears* are unique to the investment asset known as preferred stock. You should have a clear understanding of these and other terms before you consider investing in preferred stock. The following Web site has comprehensive definitions of these and other investment terms.

www.investorwords.com/glossary.htm

Valuing and Investing in Preferreds

LG 3

As we just saw, although preferred stocks may be a form of equity, they behave in the market more like a bond than a stock. Therefore, it seems logical that preferreds should be *valued* much like bonds, with market interest rates and investment quality playing key roles. Similarly, when it comes to investing in preferreds, you would expect interest rates—that is, either the level of market interest rates or the movements therein—to play key roles in preferred stock investment strategies. In fact, that's exactly what you find: The two most widely used preferred investment strategies involve either going after high levels of current income or seeking capital gains when market rates are falling.

Putting a Value on Preferreds

Evaluating the investment suitability of preferreds involves assessing comparative return opportunities. Let's look now at some of the return measures that are important to preferred stockholders, and then at the role that agency ratings play in the valuation process.

Dividend Yield: A Key Measure of Value

Dividend yield is the critical variable in determining the price and return behavior of most preferred stocks. It is computed according to the following simple formula:

Equation 10.2

$$\text{Dividend yield} = \frac{\text{annual dividend income}}{\text{current market price of the preferred stock}}$$

dividend yield
a measure of the amount of return earned on annual dividends.

Dividend yield is a measure of the amount of return earned on annual dividends, and is the basis on which comparative preferred investment opportunities are evaluated. (It is basically the same as the *dividend yield* used in Chapter 6 with common stocks and is comparable to the *current yield* measure used with bonds, as described in Chapter 9.)

Here is how dividend yield works: Suppose an 8% preferred stock has a par value of $25 and is currently trading at a price of $27.50 per share. The annual dividend on this stock is $2—that is, for preferreds whose dividends are denoted as a percent of par (or stated) value, the dollar value of the annual dividend is found by multiplying the dividend rate (in this case, 8%) by the par value (here it's $25). Therefore, the dividend yield in this example is

$$\text{Dividend yield} = \frac{\$2}{\$27.50} = \underline{\underline{7.27\%}}$$

As you can see, at $27.50 a share, this particular preferred is yielding about 7.3% to investors. If the price of this preferred moves down (to say, $21 a share), the dividend yield increases (in this case, to about 9½%). In practice, we would expect investors to compute or have available a current dividend yield measure for each preferred under consideration and then to make a choice by comparing the yields on the alternative preferreds—along with, of course, the risk and issue characteristics of each.

Whereas long-term investors may consider dividend yield a key factor in their investment decisions, that's not necessarily the case with the short-term traders. Instead, these traders generally focus on anticipated price behavior and the expected return from buying and selling an issue over a short period of time. Thus the expected future price of a preferred is important to short-term traders. It is found by first forecasting future market interest rates and then using that information to determine expected future price. To illustrate, suppose a preferred stock pays $3 in dividends and its yield is expected to decline to 6% within the next 3 years. If such market rates prevail, then 3 years from now, the issue will have a market price of $50 (using Equation 10.1, annual dividend ÷ yield = $3 ÷ 0.06 = $50). This forecasted price, along with the current market price and level of annual dividends, would then be used in either the expected return or the holding period return formula to assess the return potential of the investment.

To continue with our example, if the stock were currently priced at $28 a share, it would have an *expected return* (over the 3-year investment horizon) of a very attractive 30.3%. This can be found by using *the IRR approach* we first introduced in Chapter 4 and then applied (as a measure of expected return) to common stocks in Chapter 7 and to bonds in Chapter 9. Basically, you'd want to find the discount rate, in the present-value-based yield formula, that equates the expected future cash flows from this preferred (the $50 price in 3 years, plus the annual dividends of $3 a share over each of the next 3 years) to its current market price of $28 a share. As it turns out, that discount rate equals 30.3%; at that rate, the present value of the future cash flows amounts to $28 a share. You now have a measure of the relative attractiveness of this preferred stock. Of course, other things (like risk) being equal, the higher the expected return, the more appealing the investment. (Note that if the above performance had occurred over a period of 6 months, rather than 3 years, you would use the *holding period return* measure to assess the potential return of this preferred. See Chapter 4 for details.)

Book Value

book value (net asset value)
a measure of the amount of debt-free assets supporting each share of preferred stock.

The **book value** (or **net asset value**) of a preferred stock is simply a measure of the amount of debt-free assets supporting each share of preferred stock. Book value per share is found by subtracting all the liabilities of the firm from its total assets and dividing the difference by the number of preferred shares outstanding. It reflects the quality of an issue with regard to the preferred's *claim on assets.* Obviously, a preferred with a book value of $150 per share enjoys generous asset support and more than adequately secures a par value of, say, $25 a share. Net asset value is most relevant when it is used relative to an issue's par, or stated, value. Other things being equal, *the quality of an issue improves as the margin by which book value exceeds par value increases.*

Fixed Charge Coverage

fixed charge coverage
a measure of how well a firm is able to cover its preferred stock dividends.

Fixed charge coverage is a measure of how well a firm is able to cover its preferred dividends; attention centers on the firm's ability to service the dividends on its preferred stock and live up to the preferred's preferential *claim on income.* Therefore, fixed charge coverage is an important ingredient in determining the quality of a preferred stock. Fixed charge coverage is computed as follows:

Equation 10.3

$$\text{Fixed charge coverage} = \frac{\text{earnings before interest and taxes (EBIT)}}{\text{interest expense} + \dfrac{\text{preferred dividends}}{0.65}}$$

Note in this equation that preferred dividends are adjusted by a factor of 0.65 to take into account the fact that *a company pays dividends from the earnings that are left after taxes.* The adjustment factor (0.65) implies a corporate tax rate of 35%, which is a reasonable rate to use for our purposes here. By making the indicated adjustment, you essentially place preferred dividends on the same basis as interest paid on bonds, which is a tax-deductible expense. *Normally, the higher the fixed charge coverage, the greater the margin of safety.* A ratio of 1.0 means the company is generating just enough earnings to meet its preferred dividend payments—not a very healthy situation. A coverage ratio of 0.7 suggests the potential for some real problems, whereas a coverage of, say, 7.0 indicates that the preferred dividends are fairly secure.

Agency Ratings

Standard & Poor's has long rated the investment quality of preferred stocks, and since 1973, so has Moody's. S&P uses basically the same rating system as it does for bonds; Moody's uses a slightly different system. For both agencies, the greater the likelihood that the issuer will be able to pay dividends promptly, the higher the rating. Much like bonds, the top four ratings designate *investment-grade* (high-quality) preferreds. Although preferreds come in a full range of agency ratings, most tend to fall in the medium-grade categories (a and baa) or lower. Generally speaking, higher agency ratings reduce the market yield of an issue and increase its interest sensitivity. Agency ratings not only eliminate much of the need for fundamental analysis, but also help investors get a handle on the yield and potential price behavior of an issue.

Investment Strategies

There are several investment strategies that preferred stockholders can follow. Each is useful in meeting a different investment objective, and each offers a different level of return and exposure to risk.

Looking for Yields

This strategy represents perhaps the most popular use of preferred stocks and is ideally suited for serious long-term investors. High current income is the objective, and the procedure basically involves seeking out those preferreds with the most attractive yields. Of course, consideration must also be given to such features as the quality of the issue, whether the dividends are cumulative, and the existence of any call or sinking-fund provisions.

Certainty of income and safety are important in this strategy, because yields are attractive only as long as dividends are paid. Some investors may never buy anything but the highest-quality preferreds. Others may sacrifice quality in return for higher yields when the economy is strong and use higher-quality issues only during periods of economic distress. Whenever you leave one of the top four agency ratings, you should recognize the speculative position you are assuming and the implications it holds for your investment portfolio. This is especially so with preferreds; after all, their dividends lack legal enforcement. Individual investors should also keep in mind that this investment strategy is likely to involve a yield give-up relative to what could be obtained from comparably rated corporate bonds: As noted earlier, preferreds usually generate somewhat lower yields than bonds, even though they are less secure and may be subject to a bit more risk.

monthly income preferred stock (MIPS)
a type of preferred stock that offers attractive tax provisions to the issuers, and attractive *monthly* returns to investors.

There is, however, a way to get around that yield give-up and earn *monthly income* to boot. That is to consider investing in a type of hybrid security known as **monthly income preferred stock** (**MIPS,** for short). But as the accompanying *Investing in Action* box explains, although these securities do, indeed, offer attractive yields, they are a very unusual type of investment vehicle. You should learn as much as you can about MIPS before investing in them.

Trading on Interest Rate Swings

Rather than assuming a "safe" buy-and-hold position, the investor who trades on movements in interest rates adopts an aggressive short-term trading posture. This is done for one major reason: *capital gains*. Of course, although a high level of return is possible with this approach, it is not without the burden of higher risk exposure. Because preferreds are fixed-income securities, the market behavior of *investment-grade issues* is closely linked to movements in interest rates. If market interest rates are expected to decline substantially, attractive capital gains opportunities may be realized from preferred stocks. Indeed, this is precisely what happened in the mid-1980s, and again in the early 90s (1991 through 1993), when market interest rates dropped sharply. During this period, it was not uncommon to find preferreds generating *annual* returns of 20% to 30%, or more.

As is probably clear by now, this strategy is identical to that used by bond investors. In fact, many of the same principles used with bonds apply equally well to preferred stocks. For example, it is important to select high-grade preferred stocks, because interest sensitivity is an essential ingredient of this investment strategy. Moreover, margin trading is often used as a way to magnify short-term holding period returns. A basic difference is that the very high leverage rates of bonds are not available with preferreds, because they fall under the same, less generous margin requirements as common stocks. The investment selection process is simplified somewhat as well, because neither maturity nor the size of the annual preferred dividend (which is equivalent to a bond's coupon) has an effect on the *rate of price volatility.* That is, a $2 preferred will appreciate just as much (in percentage terms) as an $8 preferred for a given change in market yields.

Speculating on Turnarounds

This speculative investment strategy can prove profitable if you're nimble enough to catch a trading opportunity before everyone else does. The idea is to find preferred stocks whose dividends have gone into arrears and whose rating has tumbled to one of the speculative categories. The price of the issue, of course, would be depressed to reflect the corporate problems of the issuer. There is more to this strategy, however, than simply finding a speculative-grade preferred stock. The difficult part is to uncover a speculative issue whose fortunes, for one reason or another, *are about to undergo a substantial turnaround*. This strategy requires a good deal of fundamental analysis and is, in many respects, akin to investing in speculative common stock.

In essence, the investor is betting that the firm will undergo a turnaround and will once again be able to service its preferred dividend obligations easily—a set of conditions that obviously involves a fair amount of risk. Unfortunately, although the rewards from this kind of high-risk investing can be substantial, they are somewhat limited. For example, if the turnaround can-

INVESTING IN ACTION

MIPS: There's More to Them Than Monthly Income and Higher Yields

In 1993 Goldman Sachs & Co., a leading investment banking firm, invented *monthly income preferred stock,* or MIPS, which looks like a win–win arrangement: Everyone seems to benefit. The issuer gets a tax deduction. The investor gets high *monthly* income, as well as the upside potential inherent in a stock. By 1995, 70% of all preferred stock issued by corporations were MIPS. Here's how they work: XYZ Corporation creates a new entity called a limited-life company (LLC) that sells MIPS to the public and lends the proceeds to the parent corporation. The parent pays interest to the LLC on the loan, which in turn is paid to MIPS holders in the form of monthly dividends.

From the issuer's point of view, MIPS are attractive because the payments are tax deductible, even though MIPS are not considered straight debt and thus do not raise the corporation's debt ratio. That's good, because credit rating agencies don't like to see debt ratios rise. MIPS are typically listed on the New York Stock Exchange, like many preferred stocks. Issuers have included such household names as Aetna, Texaco, GTE, and Corning. From the investor's point of view, MIPS offer higher yields than certificates of deposit and money market funds. They also provide higher yields than corporate bonds and conventional preferred stock. And the payments are made monthly, whereas bonds pay interest every 6 months and stocks pay dividends quarterly.

The yield on conventional preferred stock tends to be driven down by corporate investors, who can deduct up to 70% of the dividend payments from their corporate income tax. Individual investors don't get that tax break, so conventional preferreds haven't been marketed heavily to individuals. But MIPS have gotten their attention.

Not everyone thinks MIPS are great. The first drawback is that despite the term *preferred* in their name, MIPS are quite low on the issuing corporation's list of obligations. If an issuer gets into financial trouble, MIPS holders have to stand toward the end of the repayment line. The second drawback is lack of call protection. If interest rates fall, the issuer can redeem the securities at par without paying a penalty. That leaves the investor stuck with cash to reinvest at lower rates. The third drawback has to do with your taxes. Corporations set up partnerships to issue these securities, which means that you get a K-1 instead of a Form 1099 at the end of the year. In contrast to 1099s, which are sent out at the end of January, most K-1s aren't sent out until mid-March. And they're a more complicated document. That means you'll spend more time on your taxes—or your accountant will, which means a higher bill to you. Indeed, a high accounting fee could even wipe out the higher yields that MIPS offer.

didate is expected to recover to a single-a rating, we would expect its capital gains potential to be limited by the price level of other a-rated preferreds. This condition is depicted in Figure 10.3. As the figure shows, although price performance may be somewhat limited, it is still substantial and can readily amount to holding period returns of 50% or more. However, in view of the substantial risks involved, such returns are certainly not out of line.

Investing in Convertible Preferreds

The investor following this strategy uses the conversion feature to go after speculative opportunities and the chance for attractive returns. The use of *convertible preferreds* is based on their link to the company's common stock and on the belief that they will provide generous price appreciation. Convertibles will be reviewed in detail below; at this point, suffice it to say that as the price

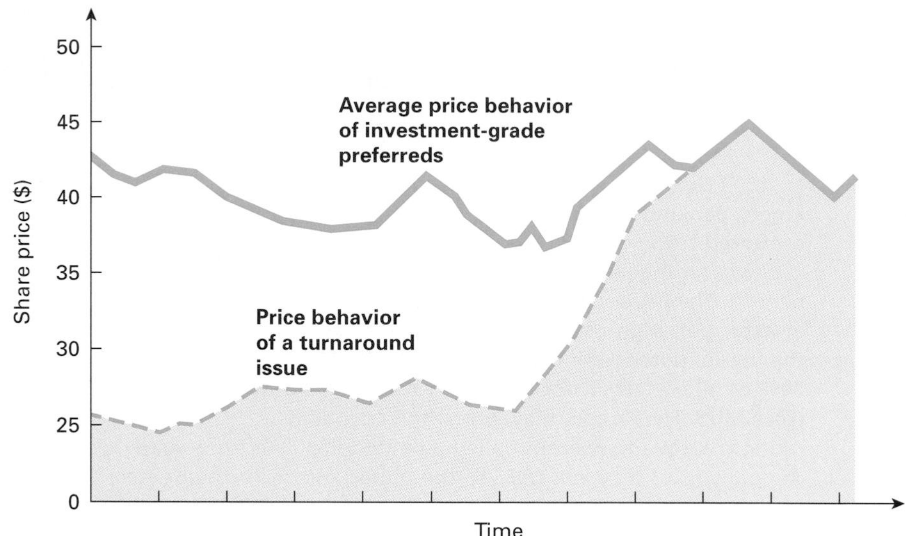

FIGURE 10.3
Price Pattern of a Hypothetical Preferred Turnaround Candidate

Although a turnaround issue seeks the price level of other preferreds of comparable quality and dividend payout, this level also acts as a type of price cap and clearly limits capital appreciation.

of the underlying common stock appreciates, so does the market price of a convertible preferred. This strategy can offer handsome returns, but remember that investors who employ it are actually speculating on the common stock dimension of the security. Therefore, it is the equity position of the issue that should be subjected to scrutiny. The idea is to look for equity situations that hold considerable promise for appreciation, and then, rather than buying the common stock of the firm, purchase its convertible preferred instead.

CONCEPTS IN REVIEW

10.5 Describe how high-grade preferred stocks are priced in the market. What role does dividend yield play in the valuation of preferred stocks? Could you use the zero-growth dividend valuation model to value a preferred stock? Explain.

10.6 Discuss why dividend yield is critical in evaluating the investment merits of high-grade preferred stocks during periods when market yields are expected to decline.

10.7 The *Investing in Action* box on page 393 discussed *monthly income preferred stock.* Briefly describe these securities, and note why investors might be interested in buying them. Do these securities have any noteworthy features? Are there any unusual risks associated with them? Explain.

10.8 Identify several investment uses of preferred stocks. Would preferreds be suitable for both conservative and aggressive investors? Explain.

convertible securities
fixed-income obligations that have a feature permitting the holder to convert the security into a specified number of shares of the issuing company's common stock.

Convertible Securities

LG 4 LG 5

Convertible securities, more popularly known simply as convertibles, represent still another type of fixed-income security. Usually issued as debenture bonds, these securities are subsequently convertible into shares of the issuing firm's common stock. Although it possesses the features and performance characteristics of both a fixed-income security and equity, a convertible should be viewed primarily *as a form of equity.* That's because most investors commit their capital to such obligations not for the attractive yields they provide but, rather, for the potential price performance of the stock side of the issue. In fact, it is always a good idea *to determine whether a corporation has convertible issues outstanding whenever you are considering a common stock investment.* In some circumstances, the convertible may be a better investment than the firm's common stock.

Convertibles as Investment Outlets

equity kicker
another name for the conversion feature, giving the holder of a convertible security a deferred claim on the issuer's common stock.

deferred equity
securities issued in one form and later redeemed or converted into shares of common stock.

Convertible securities are popular with investors because of their **equity kicker**—that is, the right of the holder/investor to convert his or her bonds into the company's common stock. Because of this feature, the market price of the convertible has a tendency to behave very much like the price of the underlying common stock. They are used by all types of companies and are issued either as convertible *bonds* (by far the most common type) or as convertible *preferreds.* Companies like to issue convertibles principally because *they enable firms to raise equity capital at fairly attractive prices.* That is, when a company issues stock in the normal way (by simply selling more shares in the company), it does so by setting a price on the stock that's *below* prevailing market prices. For example, it might be able to get $25 for a stock that's currently priced in the market at, say, $30 a share. In contrast, when it issues the stock indirectly through a convertible issue, a firm can set a price that's *above* the prevailing market—that is, it might be able to get $35 for the same stock. As a result, the company can raise the *same amount of money* by issuing a lot less stock through a convertible than by selling it directly in the market. Thus companies issue convertibles *not* as a way of raising debt capital but as a way of raising equity. Because they are supposed to be converted eventually into shares of the issuing company's common stock, convertible securities are usually viewed as a form of **deferred equity.**

Not surprisingly, whenever the stock market is strong, convertibles tend to perform well, but when the market softens, so does interest in convertibles. Convertible bonds and convertible preferreds are both linked to the equity position of the firm, so they are usually considered interchangeable for investment purposes. Except for a few peculiarities (e.g., the fact that preferreds pay dividends rather than interest and do so on a quarterly basis rather than semi-annually), convertible bonds and convertible preferreds are evaluated in much the same way. The discussion that follows, therefore, will be couched largely in terms of bonds, but the information and implications apply equally well to convertible preferreds.

INVESTOR FACT

TIME WARNER'S CONVERTIBLE STORE—If you want a wide selection of convertible bonds at varying interest rates, maturities, and structures, take a look at Time Warner, the entertainment and publishing conglomerate. The company, which a few years ago merged with Turner Broadcasting System, had a total of $12 billion in debt on its books at the end of 1996. This included a billion dollars worth of zero-coupon convertible notes due in 2013.

With all this debt, the company is constantly refinancing, trying to reduce its reliance on convertibles. The reason: The convertibles were issued at very high yields when the company's finances were shaky.

Convertible Bonds

Convertible bonds are usually issued as debentures (long-term, unsecured corporate debt), but they carry the provision that within a stipulated time period, *the bond may be converted into a certain number of shares of the issuing company's common stock.* Generally, there is little or no cash involved at the time of conversion; the investor merely trades in the convertible bond for a stipulated number of shares of common stock. Figure 10.4 provides some specifics about a convertible bond recently issued by Systems & Computer Technology

FIGURE 10.4 A New Convertible Bond Issue

Holders of this SCT (Systems & Computer Technology Corp.) bond can convert it into the company's common stock at the stated price of $52.75 per share. As a result, they would receive 18.96 shares of stock for each $1,000 convertible bond owned. Prior to conversion, the bondholder will receive annual interest income of $50 for each bond—which, in the context of 1997 market interest rates, clearly makes this a very low-yielding corporate debt security. (Source: *Wall Street Journal,* November 6, 1997.)

This announcement is neither an offer to sell nor a solicitation of an offer to buy these securities. The offer is made only by the Prospectus.

October 17, 1997

$74,750,000

Systems & Computer Technology Corporation

5% Convertible Subordinated Debentures Due 2004

The Debentures are convertible at any time prior to maturity, unless previously redeemed, into Common Stock at a conversion price of $52.75 per share, subject to adjustment in certain events.

Price 100%

Plus accrued interest, if any, from October 22, 1997

Copies of the Prospectus may be obtained in any State in which this announcement is circulated only from such of the undersigned as may legally offer these securities in such State.

C.E. UNTERBERG, TOWBIN

JANNEY MONTGOMERY SCOTT INC.

Corporation. Note that this obligation originally was issued as a 5% subordinated debenture. The reason the bond carried such a low coupon (compared to prevailing market rates of 7½% or 8%) is, of course, the fact that it offers an attractive conversion feature—in particular, each $1,000 bond can be converted into SCT stock at $52.75 a share. Thus, *regardless of what happens to the market price of the stock,* the convertible investor can redeem each bond for 18.96 shares of the company's stock (i.e., $1,000 ÷ $52.75 = 18.96

shares). If at the time of conversion, SCT stock is trading in the market at, say, $95 a share, then the investor would have just converted a $1,000 bond into $1,801.20 worth of stock (18.96 × $95 = $1,801.20).

forced conversion
the calling in of convertible bonds by the issuing firm.

The *bondholder* has the right to convert the bond at any time, but more commonly, the issuing firm initiates conversion by calling the bonds—a practice known as **forced conversion.** To provide the corporation with the flexibility to retire the debt and force conversion, most convertibles come out as freely callable issues, or they carry very short call deferment periods. To force conversion, the corporation would call for the retirement of the bond and give the bondholder one of two options: Either convert the bond into common stock or redeem it for cash at the stipulated call price (which, in the case of convertibles, contains very little call premium). So long as the convertible is called when the market value of the stock exceeds the call price of the bond (which is almost always the case), seasoned investors would never choose the second option. Instead, they would opt to convert the bond, as the firm wants them to. Then they can hold the stocks if they wanted to, or if they didn't, they could always sell their new shares in the market (and end up with a lot more cash than they would have received by taking the call price). After the conversion is complete, the bonds no longer exist; instead, there is additional common stock in their place.

Conversion Privilege

conversion privilege
the conditions and specific nature of the conversion feature on convertible securities.

conversion period
the time period during which a convertible issue can be converted.

The key element of any convertible is its **conversion privilege,** which stipulates the conditions and specific nature of the conversion feature. To begin with, it states exactly when the debenture can be converted. With some issues, there may be an initial waiting period of 6 months to perhaps 2 years after the date of issue, during which time the security cannot be converted. The **conversion period** then begins, and the issue can be converted at any time. Although the conversion period typically extends for the remaining life of the debenture, it may exist for only a certain number of years. This is done to give the issuing firm more control over its capital structure. If the issue has not been converted by the end of its conversion period, it reverts to a straight-debt issue with no conversion privileges.

conversion ratio
the number of shares of common stock into which a convertible issue can be converted.

conversion price
the stated price per share at which common stock will be delivered to the investor in exchange for a convertible issue.

From the investor's point of view, the most important piece of information is the *conversion price* or the *conversion ratio.* These terms are used interchangeably and specify the number of shares into which the bond can be converted. **Conversion ratio** denotes the number of common shares into which the bond can be converted; **conversion price** indicates the stated value per share at which the common stock will be delivered to the investor in exchange for the bond. When you stop to think about these two measures, it becomes clear that a given conversion ratio implies a certain conversion price, and vice versa. For example, a $1,000 convertible bond might stipulate a conversion ratio of 20, which means that the bond can be converted into 20 shares of common stock. This same privilege could also be stated in terms of a conversion price—that the $1,000 bond may be used to acquire stock in the corporation at a "price" of $50 per share (here, the conversion ratio of 20 signifies a conversion price of $50). Note that the SCT convertible depicted in Figure 10.4 uses just the conversion price ($52.75 a share) to describe its conversion feature. Even so, that stated conversion price still carries an implied conversion ratio—in this

INVESTOR FACT

HERE'S A SECURITY THAT ONLY THE HEALTHY COULD LOVE—Convertible preferred stocks outperformed the S&P 500 Index for a good chunk of the 1990s. The Salomon Brothers index of convertible preferred stocks generated a 79% return from January 1992 to June 1995—nearly double the S&P 500 Index's performance.

But performance does not necessarily tell you anything about risk. Sometimes, issuing convertible preferreds is the only way a company can raise money. A case in point: Cytogen Corp, a Princeton, New Jersey–based biotechnology company. The company's common stock plummeted 71% in 1997, a year in which the S&P 500 Index rose 31%. And yet, on December 9, 1997, Cytogen announced that it had arranged $20 million of 6% convertible preferred stock financing. The chairman of the company said that the proceeds would be used to support the marketing efforts for its new therapies. It's not a security for the faint of heart. For the 9 months ended September 30, 1997, the company reported a $26 million net loss on revenues of just $10 million. But if the company turns around, investors could get a great return. And at least they'll get 6% on their money while they wait and hope.

case, 18.96 shares of stock. (One basic difference between a convertible debenture and a convertible preferred is that whereas the conversion ratio of a debenture generally deals with large multiples of common stock, such as 15, 20, or 30 shares, the conversion ratio of a preferred is generally very small, often less than 1 share of common and seldom more than 3 or 4 shares.)

The conversion ratio is generally fixed over the conversion period, although some convertibles are issued with variable ratios/prices. In such cases, the conversion ratio decreases (while the conversion price increases) over the life of the conversion period, to reflect the supposedly higher value of the equity. The conversion ratio is also normally adjusted for stock splits and significant stock dividends, to maintain the conversion rights of the investor. As a result, if a firm declares, say, a 2-for-1 stock split, the conversion ratio of any of its outstanding convertible issues also doubles. And when the ratio includes a fraction, such as 33½ shares of common, the conversion privilege specifies how any fractional shares are to be handled. Usually, the investor can either put up the additional funds necessary to purchase another full share of stock at the conversion price or receive the cash equivalent of the fractional share (at the conversion price). Table 10.2 lists some basic features for a number of actively traded convertible bonds and preferreds and reveals a variety of conversion privileges.

PERCs and LYONs

Wall Street is notorious for taking a basic investment product and turning it into a new investment vehicle. Certainly that's the case with two very special types of convertible securities known as PERCs and LYONs. Unlike conventional convertibles, these securities have certain features and characteristics that separate them from the rest of the pack. **PERCs,** which stands for **preferred equity redemption cumulative stock,** is a type of convertible preferred that offers not only an equity kicker but an attractive dividend yield to boot. There is a catch, however, and that's the cap placed on the capital appreciation potential of these securities. Whereas a regular convertible stipulates (or implies) a certain number of shares of stock into which the security can be converted, regardless of the market value of the stock, a PERC stipulates a certain *dollar amount of the underlying common stock that will be received on the stipulated maturity date of the PERC.* Such a conversion privilege sets a cap on the amount of capital gains you can earn. For example, a conversion price of $50 a share defines the most you can receive. If the underlying stock is trading at $50 or less on the maturity date of the PERC, you'll receive one share of stock; but if it's trading at more than $50 a share, you'll receive less than a full share of stock. Thus, if the stock is at $75, you'll receive 2/3 of a share, or $50 worth of stock. This is the price you pay to have both the equity kicker and an attractive dividend yield. In essence, in return for the relatively high dividend yield, you have to be willing to accept limits on the equity kicker. As an investor, you have to decide which is more important to you: full participation in the equity kicker or an attractive dividend yield.

PERC
preferred equity redemption cumulative stock; preferred securities that carry conversion privileges and offer attractive dividend returns.

LYON
liquid yield option note; a zero-coupon bond that carries both a conversion feature and a put option.

In contrast, a **LYON,** which stands for **liquid yield option note,** is a type of convertible bond that's anything but conventional. Basically, a LYON is a *zero-coupon bond* that carries both *a conversion feature* and *a put option.* These bonds are convertible, at a fixed conversion ratio, for the life of the

TABLE 10.2 Convertible Preferred Stocks and Bonds

Convertible Preferreds	S&P Rating	Conversion Ratio	Market Price	Yield*	Conversion Premium	Exchange
AMC Entertainment $1.75 pfd	B−	1.7240	$38.50	4.5%	0.37%	AM
Battle Mountain Gold $3.25 pfd	B+	4.7820	45.00	7.2	64.34%	NYSE
Chiquita Brands $2.875 pfd	B	2.6316	51.19	5.6	19.26%	NYSE
McDermott Intl. $2.20 pfd	BB+	1.0000	38.00	5.8	3.74%	NYSE
Bowmar Instrument $3.00 pfd	NR	13.3300	36.75	8.2	4.83%	AM
Unisys Corp. $3.75 pfd	B−	1.6700	45.06	8.3	94.41%	NYSE
WNX Corp. $3.25 pfd	B	3.1686	45.75	7.1	20.32%	NYSE
Convertible Bonds						
Chock Full O'Nuts 8.09% 2006	B−	126.04	$1035.00	7.7%	15.48%	AM
Hilton 5.00% 2006	BBB	30.98	1095	4.6	18.81%	NY
Men's Warehouse 5.25% 2003	B	29.30	1120	4.7	10.00%	OTC
Oryx Energy 7.50% 2014	BB−	25.58	1010	7.4	54.96%	NY
Pennzoil 4.75% 2004	BBB	17.00	1340	3.5	18.95%	NY
Home Depot 3.25% 2001	NR	21.70	1340	2.4	4.89%	NY
Nova Care 5.50% 2000	B	37.52	950	5.8	92.91%	NY

*Yield-to-maturity for convertible bonds; current yield for convertible preferreds; all prices and yields as of December 1997.

issue. Thus they give you the built-in increase in value over time that accompanies any zero-coupon bond (as it moves toward its par value at maturity) and full participation in the equity side of the issue via the equity kicker. Unlike a PERC, there's no current income with a LYON (because it is a zero-coupon bond), but there's no limit on capital gains either. In addition, the option feature enables you to "put" the bonds back to the issuer (at specified values). That is, *the put option gives bondholders the right to redeem their bonds periodically at prespecified prices.* Thus you know you can get out of these securities, at set prices, if things move against you. Although it may appear that LYONs provide the best of all worlds, there are some negatives. True, LYONs provide downside protection (via the put option feature) and full participation in the equity kicker. But being zero-coupon bonds, they don't generate any current income. And you have to watch out for the put option: Depending on the type of put option, the payout doesn't have to be in cash—it can be in stocks or bonds/notes. One other thing: Because the conversion ratio on the LYON is fixed while the underlying value of the zero-coupon bond keeps increasing (as it moves to maturity), *the conversion price on the stock keeps getting higher over time.* Thus the market price of the stock had better go up by more than the rate of appreciation of the bond, or you'll never be able to convert your LYON.

Sources of Value

Because convertibles—even PERCs and LYONs—are fixed-income securities linked to the equity position of the firm, they are normally valued in terms of *both the stock and the bond dimensions* of the issue. In fact, it is ultimately the stock and the bond (or fixed-income) dimensions that give the convertible its value. This, of course, explains why it is so important to analyze the underlying common stock *and* to formulate interest rate expectations when considering convertibles as an investment outlet. Let's look first at the stock dimension.

Convertible securities trade much like common stock—in effect, they will derive their values from the common stock—whenever the market price of the stock starts getting close to, or exceeds, the stated conversion price. This means that whenever a convertible trades near its par value ($1,000) or above, it exhibits price behavior that closely matches that of the underlying common stock: If the stock goes up in price, so does the convertible, and vice versa. In fact, the price change of the convertible exceeds that of the common, because the conversion ratio defines the convertible's rate of price change. For example, if a convertible carries a conversion ratio of, say, 20, then for every point the common stock goes up (or down) in price, the price of the convertible moves *in the same direction* by roughly that same multiple (in this case, 20). In essence, whenever a convertible trades as a stock, its market price approximates a multiple of the share price of the common, the size of the multiple being defined by the conversion ratio. Indeed, as more fully explained in the accompanying *Investing in Action* box, convertibles have a tendency to behave so much like their underlying common stocks that it is often difficult to detect any real differences in their comparative returns.

When the price of the common is depressed, so that its trading price is well below the conversion price, the convertible loses its tie to the underlying common stock and begins to trade as a bond. The issue should then trade according to prevailing bond yields. At that point, an investor should focus attention on *market rates of interest*. However, because of the equity kicker and their relatively low agency ratings, *convertibles generally do not possess high interest rate sensitivity*. Gaining more than a rough idea of what the prevailing yield of the convertible obligation ought to be is often difficult. For example, if the issue is rated Baa and the market rate for this quality range is 9%, then the convertible should be priced to yield *something around* 9%, plus or minus perhaps as much as half a percentage point. The bond feature will also establish a *price floor* for the convertible, which tends to parallel interest rates and is independent of the behavior of common share prices.

Advantages and Disadvantages of Investing in Convertibles

The major advantage of a convertible issue is that it reduces downside risk (via the issue's bond value or price floor) and at the same time provides an upward price potential comparable to that of the firm's common stock. This two-sided feature is critical with convertibles and is impossible to match with straight common stock or straight debt. Another benefit is that the current income from bond interest normally exceeds the income from the dividends that would be paid with a *comparable investment* in the underlying common stock. For example, let's say you had the choice of investing $1,000 in a new 8% convertible or investing the same amount in the company's common stock, currently trading at $42.50 a share. (As is customary with new convertibles, the stock price is a bit *below* the bond's conversion price—of $50 a share.) Under these circumstances, you could buy *one* convertible or *23½ shares* of common stock ($1,000/$42.50 = 23.5). If the stock paid $2 a share in annual dividends, a $1,000 investment in the stocks would yield $47 a year

INVESTING IN ACTION

Convertibles: Bonds That Pay Off Like Stocks

During the Great Bull Market of the 1980s and 1990s, stocks have been the place to be. But a close second would be convertible bonds. It's not hard to understand why. A convertible bond pays you interest income every 6 months just like any bond. And when you convert it into a stock, you enjoy the appreciation of the stock market. Thus you get income while you own a bond and appreciation when you convert it to a stock—the best of both worlds.

According to Froley, Revy Investment Co., a Los Angeles–based money management firm, convertible bonds did almost as well as the Standard & Poor's 500 Index from March 1975, through March 1997. Over that 22-year period, the S&P 500 produced an average annual return of 15.87%. During the same period, the firm's index of convertible bonds produced a total return of 14.87%. In comparison, the Lehman Brothers Government/Corporate Index, which tracks regular government and corporate bonds, returned 9.63%.

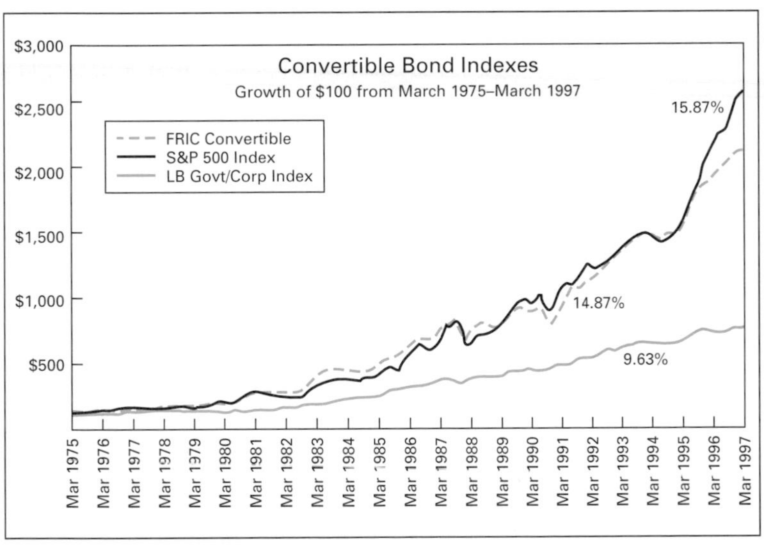

Convertible bonds are issued by a wide range of companies throughout the economy. As of July 31, 1997, Pacific Alliance Capital Management created a convertible securities portfolio on behalf of its clients. A variety of industries, coupon rates, and due dates were included. Coupon interest payments offered to investors ranged from as low as 2% and 3% to as high as 10.25%. Typically, a company that had a lower credit rating upon issuance had to pay a higher interest rate. Another reason for the high interest rate might be that the bond was issued in the late 1980s when interest rates were higher. Most of the convertibles included, though, paid in the range of 5%. Due dates ranged from 2 to 10 years, though most bonds were due within 4 to 6 years. The total value of the convertible bond portfolio was close to $16 million. (The complete portfolio is listed on our Home Page at **hepg.aw.com.**)

As one would expect, this convertible bond portfolio produced a 27% return—somewhere in between the returns yielded by stocks and bonds in fiscal 1997. During the same period, the average bond portfolio as measured by Lipper Analytical Services, Inc., rose about 15%, while the S&P 500 stock index soared 52%. Using these numbers, it doesn't look like convertible bonds produced returns halfway between stocks and bonds. However, remember that most convertible bonds are issued by smaller companies. The mid-1990s was an unusual period in which large blue-chip stocks outperformed small-cap stocks by a wide margin. Indeed, during the fiscal 1997 period in question, the Russell 2000 Index, a benchmark for small-cap stocks, was up a less spectacular 25%. Using the Russell 2000 as an index for stocks would seem to be fairer—and it makes the convertible bond portfolio's performance look much better by comparison.

in dividends. In contrast, you could collect substantially more by putting the same amount into the company's convertible bond, where you would receive $80 a year in interest income. Thus it is possible with convertibles to reap the advantages of common stock (in the form of potential upward price appreciation) and yet generate improved current income.

On the negative side, buying the convertible instead of directly owning the underlying common stock means you have to give up some potential profits. Consider the example in the preceding paragraph: Put $1,000 directly into the common stock and you can buy 23½ shares; put the same $1,000 into the company's convertible bond and you end up with a claim on only 20 shares of stock. Thus the convertible bond investor is left with a *shortfall* of 3½ shares of stock—which represents potential price appreciation the convertible investor will never enjoy. In effect, it's a *give-up* that you have to take in exchange for the convertible's higher current income and safety. Looked at from another angle, this is basically what **conversion premium** is all about. That is, unless the market price of the stock is very high and exceeds the conversion price by a wide margin, a convertible almost always trades at a price that is above its true value. The amount of this excess price is conversion premium, and it has the unfortunate side effect of diluting the price appreciation potential of a convertible. What's more, an investor who truly wants to hold bonds can almost certainly find better current and promised yields from straight-debt obligations.

conversion premium
the amount by which the market price of a convertible exceeds its conversion value.

If improved returns are normally available from the direct investment in either straight debt and/or straight equity, why buy a convertible? The answer is simple: Convertibles provide a great way to achieve attractive risk–return tradeoffs. In particular, by combining the characteristics of both stocks and bonds into one security, convertibles offer some risk protection and at the same time considerable—though perhaps not maximum—upward price potential. Thus, although the return may not be the most in absolute terms, neither is the risk.

Executing Trades

Convertible bonds are subject to the same brokerage fees and transfer taxes as straight corporate debt, and convertible preferreds trade at the same costs as straight preferreds and common stock. Any market or limit order that can be used with bonds or stocks can also be used with convertibles.

Convertible debentures are listed along with corporate bonds; they are distinguished from straight-debt issues by the letters *cv* in the "Cur Yld" column of the bond quotes, as illustrated in Figure 10.5. Note that it's not unusual for some convertibles (e.g., the Home Depot 3¼% issue of 2001) to trade at fairly high prices. These situations are justified by the correspondingly high values attained by the underlying common stock. Convertible preferreds, in contrast, normally are not isolated from other preferreds. They are listed with a *pf* annotation, but they carry no other distinguishing symbols. As a result, the investor must turn to some other source to find out whether a preferred is convertible. One national business newspaper, *Investor's Business Daily,* provides a separate list of preferred stocks traded on the NYSE and the AMEX and uses boldface type to highlight the convertible issues.

FIGURE 10.5
Listed Quotes for Convertible Bonds

Convertible bonds (of which there are five in this figure) are listed right along with other corporate issues and are identified by the letters *cv* in the "Cur Yld" column. Except for this distinguishing feature, they are quoted like any other corporate bond. (Source: *Wall Street Journal,* December 11, 1997.)

Bonds	Cur Yld	Vol	Close	Net Chg.
FedDs 10s01	9.2	50	109⅛	...
FidNtl zr09	...	3	69	+1
Fldcst 6s12	cv	120	82¾	+ ¾
FFnMgt 5cld	cv	5	124	−1
FstRep 8s09	8.0	10	100	+ ¼
FUnRE 8⅞03	8.7	10	102	−1⅛
Florsh 12¾02	11.5	5	111	+1⅛
FordCr 6⅜08	6.5	20	98¼	−1
GHost 11½02	11.1	40	104	−1¼
GHost 8s02	cv	10	99¾	...
GMA 5¼01	5.7	10	96½	− ¾
GMA 7s02	6.8	30	102⅜	+ ⅛
GMA zr12	...	45	371¾	+ ¾
GMA zr15	...	37	315⅞	+2⅞
GrandCas 10⅛03	9.4	30	107½	...
Hlthso 9½01	9.1	45	104⅞	− ¼
Hills 12½03	15.8	196	79	+ ⅛
Hilton 5s06	cv	23	106	+ ½
Hollngr 9¼06	8.9	100	104⅜	− ⅛
HomeDpt 3¼01	cv	16	133½	−1½
ITT Cp 7⅜15	7.7	20	95¼	+1¼
ITT Cp 7¾25	8.1	270	95¾	+ ⅜

Home Depot convertible bond

CONCEPTS IN REVIEW

10.9 What is a *convertible debenture*? How does a *convertible bond* differ from a *convertible preferred?*

10.10 Identify the *equity kicker* of a convertible security and explain how it affects the value and price behavior of convertibles.

10.11 According to the *Investing in Action* box on page 401, how does the return performance of convertible bonds compare to that of common stock? How does their performance stack up to that of bonds?

10.12 Explain why it is necessary to examine both the bond and the stock properties of a convertible debenture when determining its investment appeal.

10.13 What are the investment attributes of convertible debentures? What are the disadvantages of such vehicles?

http://hepg.aw.com

Convertible bonds also have a vocabulary all their own. You need to understand such terms as *conversion value* and *conversion parity* before you consider including convertibles in a portfolio. The following Web site has comprehensive definitions of these and other investment terms.

www.investorwords.com/glossary.htm

Valuing and Investing in Convertibles

LG 6

Basically, investing in convertibles can take two different forms: Either you use convertibles as a type of deferred equity investment, in which case you're looking at the stock side of the security, or you use convertibles as a high-yield, fixed-income investment, where it's the bond value that's important. Regardless of which approach you follow, to get the most from your investment program, you need a good understanding of the normal price and investment behavior of convertible securities. Of course, you also have to know how to value a convertible. Let's take a look at the valuation concepts used with convertible bonds and then at a couple of convertible bond investment strategies.

Measuring the Value of a Convertible

In order to evaluate the investment merits of convertible securities, you must consider both the bond and the stock dimensions of the issue. Fundamental security analysis of the equity position is, of course, especially important in light of the key role the equity kicker plays in defining the price behavior of a convertible. In contrast, agency ratings are helpful and are widely used in evaluating the bond side of the issue. And just as is done with other types of bonds, yield-to-maturity and current yield are important measures of return. But there's more: In addition to analyzing the bond and stock dimensions of the issue, it is also essential to evaluate the conversion feature itself. The two critical areas in this regard are conversion value and investment value. These measures have a vital bearing on a convertible's price behavior and therefore can have a dramatic effect on an issue's holding period return.

Conversion Value

conversion value
an indication of what a convertible issue would trade for if it were priced to sell on the basis of its stock value.

In essence, **conversion value** indicates what a convertible issue would trade for if it were priced to sell on the basis of its stock value. Conversion value is easy to find:

Equation 10.4

$$\text{Conversion value} = \text{conversion ratio} \times \text{current market price of the stock}$$

conversion equivalent (conversion parity)
the price at which the common stock would have to sell in order to make the convertible security worth its present market price.

For example, a convertible that carries a conversion ratio of 20 would have a conversion value of $1,200 if the firm's stock traded at a current market price of $60 per share (20 × $60 = $1,200). Sometimes an alternative measure is used, and the **conversion equivalent,** or what is also known as **conversion parity,** may be computed. The conversion equivalent indicates the price at which the common stock would have to sell in order to make the convertible security worth its present market price. Conversion equivalent is calculated as follows:

Equation 10.5

$$\text{Conversion equivalent} = \frac{\text{current market price of the convertible bond}}{\text{conversion ratio}}$$

Thus, if a convertible were trading at $1,400 and had a conversion ratio of 20, the conversion equivalent of the common stock would be $70 per share ($1,400 ÷ 20 = $70). In effect, you would expect the current market price of the common stock in this example to be at or near \$70 per share in order to support a convertible trading at \$1,400.

Conversion Premium Unfortunately, convertible issues *seldom* trade precisely at their conversion values. Rather, as noted earlier, they trade at a conversion premium. The absolute size of an issue's conversion premium is determined by taking the difference between the convertible's market price and its conversion value (per Equation 10.4). To place the premium on a relative basis, simply divide the dollar amount of the conversion premium by the issue's conversion value. That is,

Equation 10.6

$$\text{Conversion premium (in \$)} = \begin{array}{c}\text{current market price}\\ \text{of the convertible bond}\end{array} - \begin{array}{c}\text{conversion}\\ \text{value}\end{array}$$

where conversion value is found according to Equation 10.4. Then

Equation 10.7

$$\text{Conversion premium (in \%)} = \frac{\text{conversion premium (in \$)}}{\text{conversion value}}$$

To illustrate, if a convertible trades at \$1,400 and its conversion value equals \$1,200, it has a conversion premium of \$200 (\$1,400 – \$1,200 = \$200). In relation to what the convertible should be trading at, this \$200 differential would amount to a conversion premium of 16.7% (\$200/\$1,200 = 0.167). Conversion premiums are common in the market (see Table 10.2) and can often amount to as much as 25% to 30% (or more) of an issue's true conversion value.

Investors are willing to pay a premium primarily because of the added current income a convertible provides relative to the underlying common stock. An investor can recover this premium either through the added current income the convertible provides or by subsequently selling the issue at a premium equal to or greater than that which existed at the time of purchase. Unfortunately, the latter source of recovery is tough to come by, because conversion premiums tend to fade away as the price of the convertible goes up. Thus if a convertible is bought for its potential price appreciation (which many are), all or a major portion of this price premium will probably disappear as the convertible appreciates and moves closer to its true conversion value.

payback period
the length of time it takes for the buyer of a convertible to recover the conversion premium from the extra current income earned on the convertible.

Payback Period The size of the conversion premium can obviously have a major impact on investor return, so when picking convertibles, one of the major questions you should ask is whether the premium is justified. One way to assess conversion premium is to compute the issue's **payback period,** a measure of the length of time it takes for the buyer to recover the conversion premium from the *extra* interest income earned on the convertible. Because this added income is a principal reason for the conversion premium, it makes sense to use it to assess the premium. The payback period can be found as follows:

Equation 10.8

$$\text{Payback period} = \frac{\text{conversion premium (in \$)}}{\begin{array}{c}\text{annual interest}\\ \text{income from convertible}\\ \text{bond}\end{array} - \begin{array}{c}\text{annual dividend}\\ \text{income from underlying}\\ \text{common stocks}\end{array}}$$

where *annual dividends are found by multiplying the stock's latest annual dividends per share by the bond's conversion ratio.*

For example, in the foregoing illustration, the bond had a conversion premium of $200. Now let's say this bond (which carries a conversion ratio of 20) has an 8% coupon and the underlying stock paid dividends this past year of 50 cents a share. Given this information, we can use Equation 10.8 to find the payback period.

$$\text{Payback period} = \frac{\$200}{\$85 - (20 \times \$0.50)}$$

$$= \frac{\$200}{\$85 - (\$10.00)} = \underline{\underline{2.7 \text{ years}}}$$

In essence, the investor in this case will recover the premium in 2.7 years (a fairly decent payback period). As a rule, everything else being equal, *the shorter the payback period, the better.* Also, watch out for excessively high premiums (of 50% or more); you may have real difficulty ever recovering such astronomical premiums. Indeed, to avoid such premiums, most experts recommend sticking to convertibles that have payback periods of 4 years or less. In order to get the most from these investments, take the time to evaluate a bond's conversion premium fully before investing.

Investment Value

The price floor of a convertible is defined by its bond properties and is the object of the investment value measure. It's the point within the valuation process where attention focuses on current and expected market interest rates. **Investment value** is the price at which the bond would trade if it were nonconvertible and if it were priced at or near the prevailing market yields of comparable nonconvertible bonds. The same bond price formula given in Chapter 9 is used to compute investment value—see Equation 9.2. Because the coupon and maturity are known, the only additional piece of information needed is the market yield-to-maturity of comparably rated issues. For example, if comparable nonconvertible bonds were trading at 9% yields and if a particular 20-year convertible carried a 6% coupon, its investment value would be roughly $725. (*Note:* This value was calculated using techniques discussed in Chapter 9.) This figure indicates how far the convertible will have to fall before it hits its price floor and begins trading as a straight-debt instrument. Other things being equal, the greater the distance between the current market price of a convertible and its investment value, the farther the issue can fall in price before it hits its bond floor, and (as a result) the greater the downside risk exposure.

investment value
the price at which a convertible would trade if it were nonconvertible and priced at or near the prevailing market yields of comparable nonconvertible issues.

An Overview of Price and Investment Behavior

The price behavior of a convertible security is influenced by both the equity and the fixed-income elements of the obligation. The variables that play key roles in defining the market value of a typical convertible therefore include: (1) the potential price behavior of the underlying common stock and (2) expectations regarding the pattern of future market yields and interest rates.

The typical price behavior of a convertible issue is depicted in Figure 10.6. In the top panel are the three market elements of a convertible bond: the bond value, or price floor; the stock (conversion) value of the issue; and the actual market price of the convertible. The figure reveals the customary relationship among these three important elements and shows that conversion premium is a common occurrence with these securities. Note especially that the conversion premium tends to diminish as the price of the stock increases. The top panel of Figure 10.6 is somewhat simplified, however, because of the steady price floor (which unrealistically assumes no variation in market interest rates) and the steady upswing in the stock's value. The lower panel of the figure relaxes these conditions, although for simplicity we ignore conversion premium. The figure illustrates how the market value of a convertible approximates the price behavior of the underlying stock *so long as stock value is greater than bond value.* When the stock value drops below the bond value floor, as it does in the shaded areas of the illustration, the market value of the convertible becomes linked to the bond portion of the obligation, and it continues to move as a debt security until the price of the underlying stock picks up again and approaches or equals this price floor.

FIGURE 10.6
Typical Price Behavior of a Convertible Bond

The price behavior of a convertible security is tied to the stock or the bond dimension of the issue. When the price of the underlying stock is up, the convertible trades much like the stock; when the price of the stock falls, the bond value acts as a price floor for the convertible.

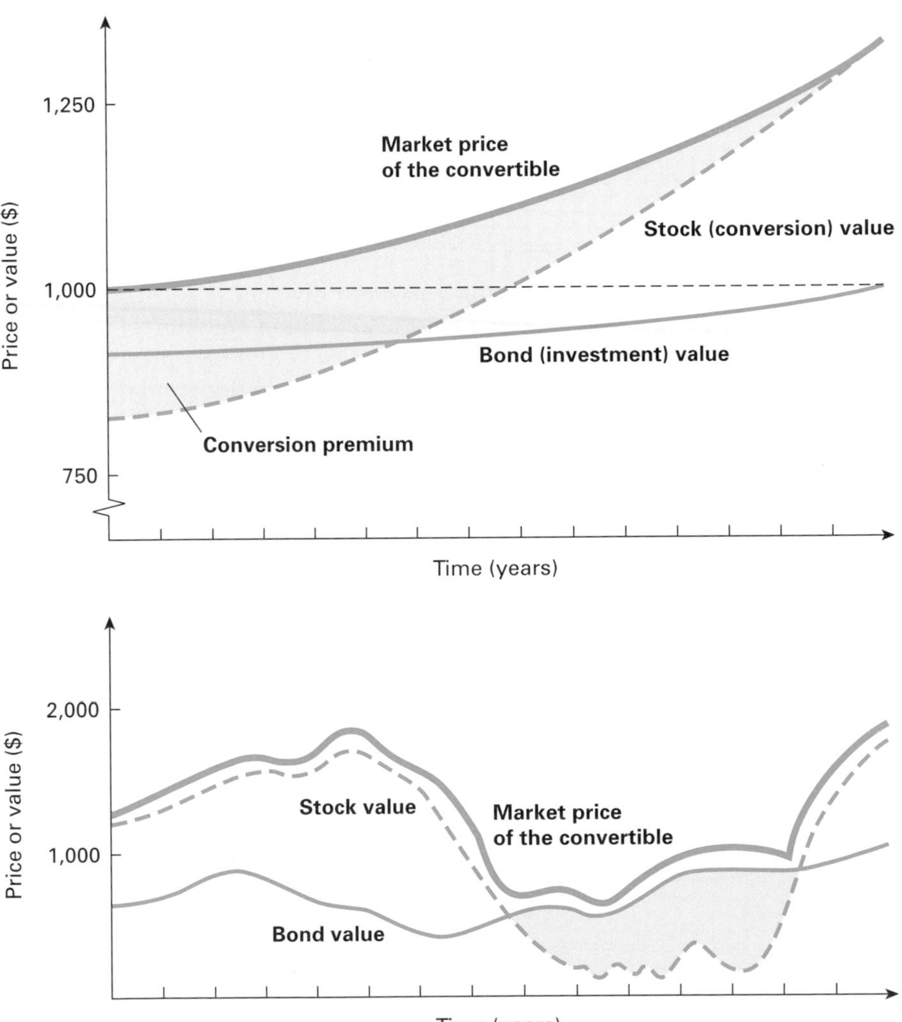

Investment Strategies

Convertibles can be used to generate attractive returns from either the stock or the bond side of the issue. That is, for stock investors, convertibles can serve as a form of deferred equity, where the investor is more concerned with capital gains than with current income. This, of course, represents a fairly aggressive use of convertibles. But for the more conservative investor, who is looking for current income as a key source of return, convertibles can also be used as a form of high-yielding fixed-income security. Let's now take a look at both of these investment strategies.

Convertibles as Deferred Equity Investments

Convertible securities—even zero-coupon convertibles—are purchased most often because of their *equity attributes*. Using convertibles as an alternative to a company's common stock, investors may be able to match (or even exceed) the return from the common, but with less exposure to risk. Also, convertibles generally offer better current income than stocks. Convertibles can be profitably used as alternative equity investments whenever you feel that the underlying stock offers desired capital gains opportunities. In order to achieve maximum price appreciation under such circumstances, you want assurance that the convertible is trading in concert with its stock value and that it does not have an inordinate amount of conversion premium. If these necessary conditions exist, then you can begin to focus on the potential market behavior of the underlying stock. To assess such behavior, it is necessary to evaluate both current and expected conversion value.

For example, assume a 7% convertible bond carries a conversion ratio of 25 and is currently trading in the market at $900. In addition, assume the stock (which pays no dividends) is currently trading at $32 and the convertible is trading at a conversion premium of $100, or 12.5%. The formulation of future interest rates also comes into play with this trading strategy, as you will want to assess the bond price floor and the extent of downward risk exposure: Using the approach discussed in Chapter 9, you will try to get a handle on future interest rates, which can then be used to determine the possible bond price behavior of the issue. Generally speaking, a drop in interest rates is viewed positively by convertible bond investors, because such behavior signals a rise in the price floor of the convertible issue and therefore a reduction in downside risk exposure. That is, should the common stock not perform as expected, the price of the convertible could still go up as the (bond) price floor rises—or at the least, it would reduce any drop in the price of the convertible issue.

But most of the attention is centered not on the bond price floor but on the anticipated behavior of the common stock and the conversion premium. To continue our example, assume that you expect the price of the stock to rise to $60 per share within the next 2 years. A conversion ratio of 25 would then yield a future conversion value of $1,500. If an expected conversion premium of 6% to 7% (or about $100) is added on, it means the market price of the convertible should rise to about $1,600 by the end of the 2-year investment horizon. This expected future price of the convertible, along with its annual coupon payment and current market price, is then used to determine the issue's expected return. That is, using the internal rate of return (IRR) procedure, you want to find the discount rate that equates the annual coupon payments ($70 a year) over the next 2 years, plus the expected future price of the convertible ($1,600), to the current market price ($900) of the issue. Putting all this into a formula (see Equation 9.2), you end up with something like this:

$$\$900 = (\$70 \times PVIFA_{2yrs,?\%}) + (\$1,600 \times PVIF_{2yrs,?\%})$$

Using annual compounding to solve this equation, you'll find that the present-value discount rate that equates the future cash flow of the convertible to its current price is 40.2%—which, of course, is the expected yield on this investment.

Although this 40.2% rate of return may indeed appear attractive, you should be sure of several points before committing capital to this security—in particular, you should be certain that this approach is in fact superior to a direct investment in the issuer's common stock (at least from a risk–return point of view) and that there is no better rate of return (with commensurate risk exposure) available from some other investment vehicle. To the extent that these conditions are met, investing in a convertible may be a suitable course of action, especially if (1) the price of the underlying common stock is under strong upward pressure, (2) bond interest rates are falling off sharply, and (3) there is little or no conversion premium in the price of the convertible. The first attribute means that conversion value should move up, leading to appreciation in the price of the convertible. The second means that the bond value (price floor) should also move up, thereby reducing exposure to risk. And the third feature means that the investor should be able to capture all or most of the price appreciation of the underlying common stock rather than losing a chunk of it to the inevitable drop in conversion premium. Although it would be nice if all three of these attributes were available with a single security, very rarely is that the case. Thus investors normally have to settle for only one or two of these features and then assess the effect of the missing attribute(s) on potential returns. The bottom line may reveal that the convertible is still an attractive investment vehicle.

Convertibles as High-Yield Fixed-Income Investments

Another common use of convertibles is to buy them for the attractive fixed-income returns they offer. The key element in this strategy is the issue's bond dimension. Many convertible securities provide current yields and yields-to-maturity that are safe and highly competitive with straight debt obligations. Investors should make certain, however, that the high yields are not a function of low (speculative) ratings. Normally, such investors would seek discount issues, particularly those that are trading close to their bond price floor. Otherwise, the issue would be trading at a premium price, which would certainly involve a yield give-up, and perhaps a substantial one. Most investors who use this strategy view convertibles as ideal for locking in high rates of return. They are not widely used for speculating on interest rates, however, because even investment-grade convertibles often lack the needed interest sensitivity (because of the equity kicker of the issue). Yet for those who use convertibles to seek high, safe yields, the equity kicker can provide an added source of return if the underlying stock does indeed take off. The investor then has a bond that offers a handsome rate of return and an equity kicker to boot.

CONCEPTS IN REVIEW

10.14 What is the difference between *conversion parity* and *conversion value?* How would you describe the *payback period* on a convertible? What is the bond *investment value* of a convertible, and what does it reveal?

10.15 Discuss the alternative investment uses of convertible debentures. What are the three major attributes that investors should look for when using convertibles as deferred equity investments?

Summary

LG 1 **Describe the basic features of preferred stock, including sources of value and exposure to risk.** Preferred stocks are hybrid securities—combining features of both debt and equity—that offer potentially rewarding investment opportunities. Preferred stocks are considered senior to common because they have a higher claim on the income and assets of the issuing company; among other things, this means that preferred dividends have to be paid before the company can pay dividends to its common stockholders. As investment vehicles, preferreds provide attractive dividend yields, and when interest rates decline, they produce capital gains as well.

LG 2 **Discuss the rights and claims of preferred stockholders and note some of the popular issue characteristics that are often found with these securities.** Preferreds are considered less risky than common stock because their shareholders enjoy a senior position with regard to dividend payments and asset claims. The most important feature of a preferred stock is its preferential claim on dividends. Investors should also be aware of several other preferred stock provisions: the obligations of the issuer in case any dividends are missed (i.e., whether the stock is cumulative or noncumulative), whether it is callable, and whether it carries sinking-fund provisions.

LG 3 **Understand the various measures of investment worth and identify several investment strategies that can be used with preferred stocks.** Except for convertible preferreds, the value of a preferred is generally linked to the dividend yield it provides to investors. Indeed, the price behavior of a preferred stock is inversely related to market interest rates. The principal reason for holding preferreds is their yield, but they can also be held for capital gains purposes by investors willing to trade on interest rates or on turnaround situations.

LG 4 **Identify the fundamental characteristics of convertible securities and explain the nature of the underlying conversion privilege.** Convertible securities are initially issued as bonds (or preferreds), but they can subsequently be converted into shares of common stock. These securities offer investors a generous stream of fixed income (in the form of annual coupon payments), plus an equity kicker.

LG 5 **Describe the advantages and disadvantages of investing in convertible securities, including their risk and return attributes.** From an investment perspective, convertibles provide a combination of both good upside potential (from the equity feature of the issue) and good downside protection (through the fixed-income characteristics of the issue). This risk–return tradeoff, combined with the relatively high current income of convertibles, is unmatched by any other type of security.

LG 6 **Measure the value of a convertible security and explain how these securities can be used to meet different investment objectives.** The value of a convertible depends largely on the price behavior of the underlying common stock. This is captured in the security's conversion value, which represents the worth of a convertible if it were converted into common stock. Investors use convertible securities primarily as a form of deferred equity, where the investment is made as a way to capture the capital gains potential of the underlying common stock. In addition, convertibles are sometimes used as high-yielding fixed-income securities; here the investor principally goes after the higher current income of the bond (and the equity kicker is viewed as little more than a pleasant by-product).

Discussion Questions

LG 2 LG 3

Q10.1. Briefly describe each of the following, and note how each differs from a conventional preferred stock.

a. Convertible preferreds
b. Floating-rate preferreds
c. Prior preferred stocks
d. MIPS

As an investor, why would you choose a *convertible preferred* over a straight preferred? Why would you choose a *floating rate preferred* over a (fixed rate) preferred? Finally, instead of investing in a conventional preferred, why not just invest in a common stock?

LG 2

Q10.2. Is it possible for a firm to pass (miss) dividends on preferred stocks, even if it earns enough to pay them? Explain. What usually happens when a company passes (misses) a dividend on a cumulative preferred stock? Are common stock dividends affected in any way?

LG 1 LG 4

Q10.3. Why do companies like to issue convertible securities—i.e., what's in it for them? What about preferred stocks—why do companies like to issue them?

LG 4

Q10.4. Describe *PERCs* and *LYONs,* noting especially the unusual features and characteristics of each. How does each of these differ from conventional convertibles? Are there any similarities between these securities and conventional convertibles? Explain. What kind of investor might be attracted to a PERC? To a LYON?

LG 6

Q10.5. Using the resources available at your campus or public library, find the information requested below.

a. Select any two *convertible debentures* and determine the conversion ratio, conversion parity, conversion value, conversion premium, and payback period for each.
b. Select any two *convertible preferreds* and determine the conversion ratio, conversion parity, conversion value, conversion premium, and payback period for each.
c. In what way(s) are the two convertible bonds and the two convertible preferreds you selected similar to one another? Are there any differences? Explain.

Problems

LG 3

P10.1. An adjustable-rate preferred is currently selling at a dividend yield of 9%; assume that the dividend rate on the stock is adjusted once a year and that it is currently paying an annual dividend of $5.40 a share. Because of major changes that have occurred in the market, it's anticipated that annual dividends will drop to $4.50 a share on the next dividend adjustment date, which is just around the corner. What will the new dividend yield on this issue be if its market price does not change? What will the new market price on the issue be if the stock's dividend yield holds at 9%? What will it be if the yield drops to 7%?

LG 3

P10.2. The Danzer Company has 500,000 shares of $2 preferred stock outstanding; it generates an EBIT of $40 million and has annual interest payments of $2 million. Given this information, determine the fixed charge coverage of the preferred stock.

 LG 3

P10.3. Select one of the preferred stocks listed in Table 10.1. Using the resources available at your campus or public library, determine

a. The latest market price
b. The dividend yield
c. The fixed charge coverage
d. The book value per share
e. The stated par value

Now comment briefly on the issue's yield and the quality of its claim on income and assets.

 LG 1

P10.4. The Fazio Co. has a preferred stock outstanding that pays annual dividends of \$3.50 a share. At what price would this stock be trading if market yields were 7½%? Use one of the dividend valuation models (from Chapter 7) to price this stock, assuming you have a 7½% required rate of return. Are there any similarities between the two prices? Explain.

 LG 3

P10.5. Charlene Weaver likes to speculate with preferred stock by trading on movements in market interest rates. Right now, she believes the market is poised for a big drop in rates. Accordingly, she is thinking seriously about investing in a certain preferred stock that pays \$7 in annual dividends and is currently trading at \$75 a share. What rate of return will she realize on this investment if the market yield on the preferred drops to 6½% within 2 years? What if the drop in rates takes place in 1 year?

 LG 6

P10.6. A certain 6% annual pay convertible bond (maturing in 20 years) is convertible at the holder's option into 20 shares of common stock. The bond is currently trading at \$800, and the stock (which pays 75¢ a share in annual dividends) is currently priced in the market at \$35 a share.

a. What is the current yield of the convertible bond?
b. What is the conversion price?
c. What is the conversion ratio?
d. What is the conversion value of this issue? What is its conversion parity?
e. What is the conversion premium, in dollars and as a percentage?
f. What is the bond's payback period?
g. What is the yield-to-maturity of the convertible bond?
h. If comparably rated nonconvertible bonds sell to yield 8%, what is the investment value of the convertible?

 LG 6

P10.7. An 8% convertible bond carries a par value of \$1,000 and a conversion ratio of 20. Assume that an investor has \$5,000 to invest and that the convertible sells at a price of \$1,000 (which includes a 25% conversion premium). How much total income (coupon plus capital gains) will this investment offer if, over the course of the next 12 months, the price of the stock moves to \$75 per share and the convertible trades at a price that includes a conversion premium of 10%? What is the holding period return on this investment? Finally, given the information in the problem, determine what the underlying common stock is currently selling for.

 LG 6

P10.8. Assume you just paid \$1,200 for a convertible bond that carries a 7½% coupon and has 15 years to maturity. The bond can be converted into 24 shares of stock, which are now trading at \$50 a share. Find the bond investment value of this issue, given that comparable nonconvertible bonds are currently selling to yield 9%.

 LG 6

P10.9. Find the conversion value of a *convertible preferred stock* that carries a conversion ratio of 1.8, given that the market price of the underlying common stock is \$40 a share. Would there be any conversion premium if the convertible preferred were selling at \$90 a share? If so, how much (in dollar and percentage terms)? Also, explain the concept of conversion parity, and then find the conversion parity of this issue, given that the preferred trades at \$90 per share.

Case Problem 10.1 *Penni Shows a Preference for Preferreds*

LG 1 LG 2

Kathleen "Penni" Jock is a young career woman who has built up a substantial investment portfolio. Most of her holdings are preferred stocks—a situation she does not want to change. Penni is now considering the purchase of $4,800 worth of LaRamie Mine's $5 preferred, which is currently trading at $48 a share. Penni's stockbroker has told her that he feels the market yield on preferreds like LaRamie should drop to 7% within the next 3 years and that these preferreds would make a sound investment. Instead of buying the LaRamie preferred, Penni could choose an alternative investment (with comparable risk exposure) that she is confident can produce earnings of about 10% over each of the next 3 years.

QUESTIONS

a. If preferred yields behave as Penni's stockbroker thinks they will, what will be the price of the LaRamie $5 preferred in 3 years?

b. What return will this investment offer over the 3-year holding period if all the expectations about it come true (particularly with regard to the price it is supposed to reach)? How much profit (in dollars) will Penni make from her investment?

c. Would you recommend that she buy the LaRamie preferred? Why?

d. What are the investment merits of this transaction? What are its risks?

Case Problem 10.2 *Dave and Marlene Consider Convertibles*

LG 5 LG 6

Dave and Marlene Jenkins live in Irvine, California, where she manages a bridal shop and he runs an industrial supply firm. Their annual income is usually in the middle to upper nineties; they have no children and maintain a "comfortable" lifestyle. Recently, they came into some money and are eager to invest it in a high-yielding fixed-income security. Though they are not aggressive investors, they like to maximize the return on every investment dollar they have. For this reason, they like the high yields and added equity kicker of convertible bonds and are now looking at such an issue as a way to invest their recent windfall. In particular, Dave and Marlene have their eye on the convertible debentures of Maria Pottery, Inc. They have heard that the price of the stock is on the way up, and after some in-depth analysis of their own, they feel the company's prospects are indeed bright. They've also looked at market interest rates, and on the basis of economic reports obtained from their broker, they expect interest rates to decline sharply.

The details on the convertible they're looking at are as follows: It's a 20-year, $1,000 par value issue that carries a 7½% annual-pay coupon and is at present trading at $800. The issue is convertible into 15 shares of stock, and the stock, which pays no dividends, was recently quoted at $49.50 per share.

QUESTIONS

a. Ignoring conversion premium, find the price of the convertible if the stock goes up to $66.67 per share in 2 years. What if it goes up to $75 per share? To $100 per share? Repeat the computations, assuming that the convertible will trade at a 5% conversion premium.

b. Find the promised yield of the convertible. (*Hint:* Use annual compounding and the same approach that we used with straight bonds in Chapter 9.)

1. Now find the bond value of the convertible if, within 2 years, interest rates drop to 8%. (*Remember:* In 2 years, the security will have only 18 years remaining to maturity.) What if interest rates drop to 6%?
2. What implication does the drop in interest rates hold as far as the investment appeal of the convertible is concerned?

c. Given expected future stock prices and interest rate levels (as stated above), find the minimum and maximum expected yield that this investment offers over the 2-year holding period. (Assume a zero conversion premium in both cases.)

1. What is the worst return Dave and Marlene can expect over their 2-year holding period if the price of the stock drops to $40 per share and interest rates drop to 9%?
2. What if the price of the stock drops to $40 and interest rates rise to 11%?

d. Should Dave and Marlene invest in the Maria convertibles? Discuss the pros and cons of the investment.

Home Page Exercises

http://hepg.aw.com **Keyword: Invest**

Preferred stock and convertible bonds both offer unique blends of debt and equity investing in a single security. Their unique features make them attractive to many investors, but this uniqueness may also intimidate the average investor. The result is limited interest in these securities in spite of their attractive features. This limited appeal is reflected in the quantity and quality of Web sources that address these securities. Most of what is available is redundant and merely descriptive, but here are a couple of interesting sites:

Web Address	*Primary Investment Focus*
www.worth.com/articles/B01.html	*Worth* magazine article on the benefits of convertible securities
www.fed.fil.com/convertibles/glossary.htm	Definitions of terms related to convertible bonds plus links to current bond market news and events

W10.1. Calculating the market value of a convertible bond is a little different from calculating the value of a nonconvertible bond. The option component for the ability to convert the bond to stock changes the inputs into the valuation process. At the Web page given here, click on the *Convertible Bond Calculator* link. Look up a convertible bond in the *Wall Street Journal,* or other source, and provide the required inputs for the interactive bond calculator. Discuss how the conversion value, the actual market value, the theoretical market value, and the straight bond value differ.

stocks.miningco.com/library/weekly/aa112497.htm

W10.2. Firms in the utility industry are among the most frequent users of preferred stock. Go to Duke Energy's financial statements, found through the Web address here. Use the latest year-end financial statements, including the accompanying notes to the statements, to locate (a) the number of preferred stock issues, (b) the par value of each issue, (c) the total dollar amount of each issue, and (d) the dividends per share of each issue. Are any of the preferred stock issues convertible?

www.duke-energy.com/investor.htm

Part Four

Derivative Securities

Chapter 11
Options: Puts, Calls, and Warrants

Chapter 12
Commodities and Financial Futures

CHAPTER 11

OPTIONS: PUTS, CALLS, AND WARRANTS

LEARNING GOALS

After studying this chapter, you should be able to:

LG 1 Discuss the basic nature of options in general and puts and calls in particular, and understand how these investment vehicles work.

LG 2 Describe the options market, and note key options provisions, including strike prices and expiration dates.

LG 3 Explain how put and call options are valued and the forces that drive options prices in the marketplace.

LG 4 Describe the profit potential of puts and calls, and note some of the more popular put and call investment strategies.

LG 5 Describe market index options, puts and calls on foreign currencies, and LEAPS, and show how these securities can be used by investors.

LG 6 Discuss the investment characteristics of stock warrants, and describe the trading strategies that can be used to gain maximum benefits from this investment vehicle.

Dow Jones Index Options

The big institutional investors have always had fancy ways to buy and sell the overall stock market. Now there's a way for the "little guys" to buy and sell the market as well. In 1997 the Chicago Board Options Exchange (CBOE) created options on the Dow Jones Industrial Average. With "DJX" options, you can trade on the overall direction of the market, whether it rises or falls. This is done through two types of options: calls and puts.

What's the advantage of this? Sometimes, investors don't want to buy individual stocks. Rather, they want to invest in the market as a whole. DJX options offer a way to do that without buying every stock in the Dow Jones Industrial Average. They trade exclusively at the CBOE, home to more than 90% of all index options. In 1983 the CBOE created the S&P 100 Index, the world's first index options product. Known as OEX, this product is the most actively traded index options contract in the world.

Options are playing an increasingly important role in the investment landscape. This chapter will explain their essential characteristics and demonstrate how they can be used in investment programs.

Put and Call Options

LG 1 LG 2

When investors buy shares of common or preferred stock, they become the registered owners of these securities and are entitled to all the rights and privileges of ownership. Investors who acquire bonds or convertibles issues are also entitled to the benefits of ownership. Stocks, bonds, and convertibles are all examples of *financial assets*. They represent financial claims on the issuing corporation or organization.

option
a security that gives the holder the right to buy or sell a certain amount of an underlying financial asset at a specified price for a specified period of time.

In contrast, investors who buy options acquire nothing more than the right subsequently to buy or sell other, related securities. That is, an **option** gives the holder the right to buy or sell a certain amount of an underlying security at a specified price over a specified period of time. Options are *contractual instruments,* whereby two parties enter into an agreement (a contract) to give something of value to the other. The option *buyer* has the right to buy or sell an underlying asset for a given period of time, at a price that was fixed at the time of the contract. The option *seller,* on the other hand, stands ready to buy or sell the underlying asset according to the terms of the contract—for which the seller has been paid a certain amount of money.

We'll look at two basic kinds of options in this chapter: (1) puts and calls and (2) warrants. Another kind of option that is occasionally found in the market, but is not covered in this text, is the *stock right.* Rights are like short-term call options that originate when corporations raise money by issuing new shares of common stocks. Essentially, the rights enable stockholders to buy shares of the new issue at a specified price for a specified, fairly short period of time. But because their life span is so short—usually no more than a few weeks—stock rights hold very little investment appeal for the average individual investor. (For a more extensive discussion of rights, including their basic characteristics and investment attributes, see this textbook's Web site, at **hepg.aw.com.**) Puts and calls enjoy considerable popularity today as attractive trading vehicles, and so, to a lesser extent, do warrants. These securities are a bit unusual, however, and their use requires special investor know-how.

Definitions and Characteristics

One of the market phenomena of the 1970s was the remarkable performance and investment popularity of stock options, particularly puts and calls on common stock. By the early 1980s, the interest in options spilled over to other kinds of financial assets, and today, investors can trade puts and calls on

- Common stock
- Stock indexes
- Debt instruments
- Foreign currencies
- Commodities and financial futures

As we will see, although the underlying financial assets may vary, the basic features and behavioral characteristics of these securities are pretty much the same. Regardless of the type of option, much of the popularity of options stems from the fact that investors can buy a lot of price action with a limited amount of capital, while nearly always enjoying limited exposure to risk.

A Negotiable Contract

put
a negotiable instrument that enables the holder to sell the underlying security at a specified price over a set period of time.

call
a negotiable instrument that gives the holder the right to buy securities at a stated price within a certain time period.

Puts and calls are negotiable instruments, issued in bearer form, that allow the holder to buy or sell a specified amount of a specified security at a specified price. For example, a put or a call on common stock covers 100 shares of stock in a specific company. A **put** enables the holder to sell the underlying security at the specified price (known as the *exercise* or *strike* price) over a set period of time. A **call**, in contrast, gives the holder the right to buy the securities at the stated (strike) price within a certain time period. As with any option, there are no voting rights, no privileges of ownership, and no interest or dividend income. Instead, *puts and calls possess value to the extent that they allow the holder to participate in the price behavior of the underlying financial asset.*

derivative securities
securities, such as puts, calls, and other options, that derive their value from the price behavior of an underlying real or financial asset.

Because puts and calls derive their value from the price behavior of some other real or financial asset, they are known as **derivative securities.** Rights and warrants, as well as futures contracts (which we'll study in Chapter 12), are also derivative securities; they too derive their value from an underlying security or asset. The fact is that many different types of derivative securities are available in the market today, from puts and calls to structured CDs to exotic debt instruments such as collateralized mortgage obligations (CMOs). Although certain segments of this market are for big institutional investors only, there's still ample room for the individual investor, because many of these securities—especially those on listed exchanges—are readily available to, and are actively traded by, individuals as well as institutions.

leverage
the ability to obtain a given equity position at a reduced capital investment, thereby magnifying returns.

One of the key features of puts and calls (and of many other types of derivative securities) is the very attractive **leverage** opportunities they offer investors. Such opportunities exist because of the low prices these options carry relative to the market prices of the underlying financial assets—but here's the real kicker, the lower cost in no way affects the payoff or capital appreciation potential of your investment! To illustrate, consider a call on a common stock that gives the holder the right to buy 100 shares of a $50 stock at a (strike) price of $45 a share. The stock, of course, would be priced at $50, but the call would trade at an effective price of only $5 a share (or the difference between the market price of the common and the price at which it can be purchased as specified on the call). However, because a single stock option always involves 100 shares of stock, the actual market price of our $5 call would be $500 (i.e., $5 × 100 shares = $500). Even so, for $500 you get (just about) all the capital gains potential of a $5,000 investment—or at least the part that occurs over the life of the call option.

Maker Versus Buyer

option maker (writer)
the individual or institution that writes/creates put and call options.

Puts and calls are a unique type of security because they are *not* issued by the organizations that issue the underlying stock or financial asset. Instead, puts and calls *are created by investors.* It works like this: Suppose an individual wants to sell to another the right to buy 100 shares of common stock. This individual would "write a call." The individual (or institution) writing the option is known as the **option maker** or **writer.** Thus it's the option writer who sells the option in the market and so is entitled to receive the price paid for the put or call (less modest commissions and other transaction costs). The put or call option is now a full-fledged financial asset and trades in the open market much like any other security.

Puts and calls are both written (sold) and purchased through security brokers and dealers, and they are actively bought and sold in the secondary market. The writer stands behind the option, because it is the *writer* who must buy or deliver the stocks or other financial assets according to the terms of the option. (*Note:* Unlike the buyers of put or call options, the writers of these securities *do have a legally binding obligation* to stand behind the terms of the contracts they have written. The buyer can just walk away from the deal if it turns sour; the writer cannot.) Puts and calls are written for a variety of reasons, most of which we will explore below. At this point, suffice it to say that writing options can be a viable investment strategy and can be a profitable course of action because, more often than not, *options expire worthless.*

How Puts and Calls Work

Taking the *buyer's* point of view, let us now briefly examine how puts and calls work and how they derive their value. To understand the mechanics of puts and calls, it is best to look at their profit-making potential. For example, using stock options as a basis of discussion, consider a stock currently priced at $50 a share. Assume you can buy a call on the stock for $500, which enables you to purchase 100 shares of the stock at a fixed price of $50 each. A rise in the price of the underlying security (in this case, common stock) is what you, as an investor, hope for. What is the profit potential from this transaction if the price of the stock does indeed move up to, say, $75 by the expiration date on the call?

The answer is that you will earn $25 ($75 − $50) on each of the 100 shares of stock in the call, for a total gross profit of some $2,500—and all from a $500 investment. This is because you can buy 100 shares of the stock—from the option writer—at a price of $50 each and immediately turn around and sell them in the market for $75 a share. You could have made the same ($2,500) profit by investing directly in the common stock, but because you would have had to invest $5,000 (100 shares × $50 per share), your rate of return would have been much lower. Obviously, there is considerable difference between the return potential of common stocks and calls, and it is this difference that attracts investors and speculators to calls whenever the price outlook for the underlying financial asset is positive. Such differential returns, of course, are the direct result of *leverage,* which rests on the principle of reducing the level of required capital in a given investment position *without materially affecting the dollar amount of the payoff or capital appreciation from that investment.* (Note that although our illustration is couched in terms of common stock, this same valuation principle applies to any of the other financial assets that may underlie call options, such as market indexes, foreign currencies, and futures contracts.)

A similar situation can also be worked out for puts. Assume that for the same $50 stock you could pay $500 and buy a put to sell 100 shares of the stock at a strike price of $50 each. As the buyer of a put, you want the price of the stock to *drop*. Assume that your expectations are correct and the price of the stock does indeed drop, to $25 a share. Here again, you realize a gross profit of $25 for each of the 100 shares in the put. You can do this by going to the market and buying 100 shares of the stock at a price of $25 a share and then immediately selling them to the writer of the put at a price of $50 per share.

Fortunately, put and call investors do *not* have to exercise their options and make simultaneous buy and sell transactions in order to receive their profit.

That's because *the options themselves have value and therefore can be traded in the secondary market.* In fact, the value of both puts and calls is directly linked to the market price of the underlying financial asset. That is, the *value of a call* increases as the market price of the underlying security *rises,* whereas the *value of a put* increases as the price of the security *declines.* Thus *investors can get their money out of options by selling them in the open market,* just as with any other security.

Advantages and Disadvantages

The major advantage of investing in puts and calls is the leverage they offer. This feature also carries the advantage of limiting the investor's exposure to risk, because only a set amount of money (the purchase price of the option) can be lost. Also appealing is the fact that puts and calls can be used profitably when the price of the underlying security goes up *or* down.

A major disadvantage of puts and calls is that the holder enjoys neither interest or dividend income nor any other ownership benefit. Moreover, because the instruments have limited lives, the investor has a limited time frame in which to capture desired price behavior. Another disadvantage is that puts and calls themselves are a bit unusual, and many of their trading strategies are complex. Thus investors must possess special knowledge and must fully understand the subtleties of this trading vehicle.

Options Markets

Although the concept of options can be traced back to the writings of Aristotle, options trading in the United States did not begin until the late 1700s. And even then, up to the early seventies, this market remained fairly small, largely unorganized, and the almost private domain of a handful of specialists and traders. All of this changed, however, on April 26, 1973, when a new securities market was created with the opening of the Chicago Board Options Exchange (CBOE).

Conventional Options

Prior to the creation of the CBOE, put and call options trading was conducted in the over-the-counter market through a handful of specialized dealers. Investors who wished to purchase puts and calls dealt with these options dealers via their own brokers, and the dealers would find individuals (or institutions) willing to write the options. If the buyer wished to exercise an option, he or she did so with the writer and no one else—a system that largely prohibited any secondary trading. On the other hand, there were virtually no limits to what could be written, so long as the buyer was willing to pay the price. Put and call options were written on New York and American stocks, as well as on regional and over-the-counter securities, for as short a time as 30 days and for as long as a year. Over-the-counter options, known today as **conventional options,** were initially hit hard by the CBOE and other options exchanges. However, the conventional (OTC) market has since bounced back and is today every bit as big as the listed market, though it is used almost exclusively by big institutional investors. Accordingly, our attention in this chapter will focus on listed markets, like the CBOE, where individual investors do most of their options trading.

conventional options
put and call options sold over the counter.

Listed Options

listed options
put and call options listed and traded on organized securities exchanges, such as the CBOE.

The creation of the CBOE signaled the birth of so-called **listed options,** a term used to describe put and call options traded on organized exchanges rather than over the counter. The CBOE launched trading in calls on just 16 firms. From these rather humble beginnings, there evolved in a relatively short time a large and active market for listed options. Today, trading in listed options is done in both puts and calls and takes place on four exchanges, the largest of which is the CBOE. Options are also traded on the AMEX, the Philadelphia Exchange, and the Pacific Stock Exchange. In total, *put and call options are now traded on over 2,000 different stocks.* (Actually, over 3,000 options were listed on all four exchanges in 1997, but many of the more actively traded options are listed on more than one exchange.) Although many of the options are written on large, well-known NYSE companies, the list also includes a number of AMEX and OTC stocks both large and small. In addition to stocks, listed options are available on stock indexes, debt securities, foreign currencies, and even commodities and financial futures.

Listed options not only provided a convenient market for the trading of puts and calls but also standardized the expiration dates and exercise prices. The listed options exchanges created a clearinghouse organization that eliminated direct ties between buyers and writers of options and reduced the cost of executing put and call transactions. They also developed an active secondary market, with wide distribution of price information. As a result, it is now as easy to trade a listed option as a listed stock.

Stock Options

The advent of the CBOE and other listed option exchanges had a quick and dramatic impact on the trading volume of puts and calls. Indeed, the level of activity in listed stock options grew so rapidly that it took only 8 years for the annual volume of contracts traded to pass the 100 million mark. Although contract volume fell off after 1987, it started back up again, and today well over 200 million listed options contracts are traded each year.

INVESTOR FACT

DERIVATIVES CAN TURN UP IN THE MOST UNLIKELY PLACES—You'll find them in government bond funds, and now, even in bank CDs. These New Age CDs are powered by derivatives linked to a market index, like the S&P 500. Here's how they work: You buy a 5-year, $25,000 CD from the bank. The bank uses part of that money to buy a call option on a market index—say, the S&P 500—which will capture any gain on the S&P over the life of the CD. The rest of the deposit funds a discounted, zero-coupon bond whose value will rise to $25,000 over the same period, so that if the S&P takes a dive, at least you'll get your money back.

The creation and continued expansion of listed options exchanges have unquestionably given the field of investments a whole new dimension. In order to avoid serious (and possibly expensive) mistakes with these securities, however, investors must fully understand their basic features. In the sections that follow, we will look closely at the investment attributes and trading strategies that can be used with stock options. Later, we'll explore stock-index options and then briefly look at other types of puts and calls, including interest rate and currency options, and long-term options. (Futures options will be taken up in Chapter 12, after we study futures contracts.)

Stock Option Provisions

Because of their low unit cost, stock options (or *equity options,* as they're also called) are very popular with individual investors. Except for the underlying financial asset, they are like any other type of put or call, subject to the same kinds of contract provisions and market forces. As far as options contracts are concerned, there are two provisions that are especially important and to which investors should pay particular attention: (1) the price—known as the *strike price*—at which the stock (or other financial asset) can be bought or sold, and (2) the amount of time remaining until expiration. As we'll see below, both the strike price and the time remaining to expiration have a significant bearing on the valuation and pricing of options.

strike price
the price contract between the buyer of an option and the writer; the stated price at which you can buy a security with a call or sell a security with a put.

Strike Price The **strike price,** as specified on the option, represents the price contract between the buyer of the option and the writer. For a call, the strike price specifies the price at which each of the 100 shares of stock can be bought. For a put, it represents the price at which the stock can be sold to the writer. With conventional (OTC) options, there are no constraints on the strike price, although it is usually specified at or near the prevailing market price of the stock at the time the option is written. With listed options, however, strike prices are *standardized:* Stocks selling for less than $25 per share carry strike prices that are set in 2½ dollar increments ($7½, $10, $12½, $15, etc.). The increment jumps to $5 for stocks selling between $25 and $200 per share. Finally, for stocks that trade at more than $200 a share, the strike price is set in $10 increments. And, of course, the strike price is adjusted for substantial stock dividends and stock splits.

expiration date
the date at which an option expires.

Expiration Date The **expiration date** is also an important provision, because it specifies the life of the option, just as the maturity date indicates the life of a bond. The expiration date, in effect, specifies the length of the contract between the holder and the writer of the option. Thus if you hold a 6-month call on Sears, that option gives you the right to buy 100 shares of Sears common stock at a strike price of, say, $40 per share at any time over the next 6 months. Now, *no matter what happens to the market price of the stock,* you can use your call option to buy 100 shares of Sears at $40 a share for the next 6 months. If the price of the stock moves up, you stand to make money; if it goes down, you'll be out the cost of the option.

Expiration dates for options in the conventional market can fall on any working day of the month. In contrast, expiration dates are standardized in the *listed* options market. The exchanges initially created three expiration cycles for all listed options, and each issue was (and still is) assigned to one of these three cycles. One cycle is January, April, July, and October; another is February, May, August, and November; the third is March, June, September, and December. This system has been modified a bit to include both the current month and the following month, plus the next two months in the regular expiration cycle. The exchanges still use the same three expiration cycles, but they've been altered so that investors are always able to trade in the two near-term months plus the next two closest months in the option's regular expiration cycle. For reasons that are pretty obvious, this is sometimes referred to as a *two-plus-two* schedule.

Take, for example, the January cycle. The following options are available in January: January, February, April, and July. These are the two current months (January and February) and the next two months in the cycle (April and July). In February, the available contracts would be February, March, April, and July, and so on, as the expiration dates continue rolling over during the course of the year. Given the month of expiration, the actual day of expiration is always the same: the Saturday following the third Friday of each expiration month. Thus, for all practical purposes, *listed options always expire on the third Friday of the month of expiration.*

Put and Call Transactions

Option traders are subject to commission and transaction costs whenever they buy or sell an option or whenever an option is written. The writing of puts and calls is subject to normal transaction costs, because it effectively represents remuneration to the broker or dealer for *selling* the option. Listed options have their own marketplace and quotation system. Finding the price (or *premium*, as it's called) of a listed stock option is fairly easy, as the options quotations in Figure 11.1 indicate. Note that quotes are provided for calls and puts separately and that for each option, quotes are listed for various combinations

FIGURE 11.1 Listed Options Quotations

The quotes for puts and calls are listed side by side. In addition to the closing price of the option, the latest price of the underlying security is shown, along with the strike price on the option. (Source: *Wall Street Journal,* December 17, 1997.)

Option/Strike		Exp.	– Call – Vol.	– Call – Last	– Put – Vol.	– Put – Last
HelmP	65	Jan	...	...	1250	2⅝
67⅜	75	Dec	...	...	1250	7¼
67⅜	85	Mar	1250	1½	...	...
67⅜	95	Mar	1250	¾	...	...
Hewlet	65	Dec	246	¼	799	2⅜
63⅜	65	Jan	253	1¾	73	3½
Intel	50	Jan	444	21⅜	...	...
71 3/16	55	Jan	10	18⅝	2575	5/16
71 3/16	60	Jan	4053	13¾	285	9/16
71 3/16	65	Dec	182	6½	436	¼
71 3/16	65	Jan	2060	7⅞	3388	1⅜
71 3/16	65	Apr	30	12¾	2137	3⅜
71 3/16	67½	Jan	13	7⅜	1240	2
71 3/16	70	Dec	2462	2¼	9155	15/16
71 3/16	70	Jan	7080	4½	2666	3
71 3/16	70	Apr	4065	7¾	5264	5¼
71 3/16	72½	Jan	187	3	228	4¼
71 3/16	75	Dec	7059	¼	2865	4⅛
71 3/16	75	Jan	1989	2⅛	3549	5⅝
71 3/16	75	Apr	270	5⅝	179	8⅛
71 3/16	80	Dec	517	1/16	399	9
71 3/16	80	Jan	1183	1	225	9¾
71 3/16	80	Apr	242	3⅞	192	11¼
71 3/16	85	Dec	57	1/16	233	14
71 3/16	85	Jan	713	⅜	226	14⅝
71 3/16	87½	Jan	498	5/16	26	16¾
71 3/16	90	Jan	1202	¼	41	17
71 3/16	90	Apr	232	1¾	61	19¾
71 3/16	95	Apr	319	1¼	10	23⅞
71 3/16	100	Jan	282	1/16	...	...
71 3/16	100	Apr	728	¾	29	29¼
71 3/16	102½	Jan	542	1/16	...	...
IBM	80	Apr	2	26⅝	602	1½
103 9/16	85	Jan	21	20	202	½
103 9/16	90	Dec	21	15	702	1/16
103 9/16	90	Jan	36	15¾	268	15/16

Call option quotes
Put option quotes
Name of the company
Price of a January call that carries a strike price of 60
Strike price on the option
Month of expiration
Number of January puts traded (with a strike price of 70)
Number of December calls traded (with a strike price of 75)
Price of a January put that carries a strike price of 80
Latest market price of the underlying common stock

of strike prices and expiration dates. Because there are so many options and a substantial number of them are rarely traded, financial publications like the *Wall Street Journal* list quotes only for the most actively traded options. Also, the quotes listed are only for the options that actually traded on the day in question. For example, in Figure 11.1, there may be many other options available on Intel, but only the ones that actually traded (on Wednesday, December 16, 1997) are listed.

The quotes are standardized: The name of the company and the closing price of the underlying stock are listed first; note that Intel stock closed at 71 3/16. The strike price is listed next, followed by the expiration date (or month in which the option expires); then the closing prices of the call (and/or put) options are quoted relative to their strike prices and expiration dates. For example, an Intel January *call* with a strike price of $60 is quoted at 13 3/4 (which translates into a dollar price of $1,375 because stock options trade in 100-share lots). In contrast, an Intel *put* with an $80 strike price and a January expiration date is trading at 9 3/4 (or $975).

CONCEPTS IN REVIEW

11.1 Describe *put* and *call* options. Are they issued like other corporate securities? Explain.

11.2 What are *listed options,* and how do they differ from *conventional options?*

11.3 What are the main investment attractions of put and call options? What are the risks?

11.4 What is a *stock option?* What is the difference between a stock option and a *derivative security?* Describe a derivative security and give several examples.

11.5 What is a *strike price?* How does it differ from the market price of the stock? Do both puts and calls have strike prices? Explain.

11.6 Why do put and call options have expiration dates? Is there a market for options that have passed their expiration dates? Explain.

http://hepg.aw.com

Equity options obtain their value from the underlying common stock. Investors in options always have the choice of purchasing the stock directly. The differences and similarities between equity options and common stock are discussed in a brochure at the following Web address.

www.optionscentral.com/resource/brochure/usochap2.html

Options Pricing and Trading

LG 3 LG 4

The value of a put or call depends to a large extent on the market behavior of the financial asset that underlies the option. Getting a firm grip on the current and expected future value of a put or call is extremely important to options traders and investors. Similarly, to get the most from any options trading program, it is imperative that investors understand how options are priced in the market. *Continuing to use stock options as a basis of discussion,* let's look now at the basic principles of options valuation and pricing, starting with a brief review of how profits are derived from puts and calls. Then we'll take a look at several ways in which investors can use these options.

The Profit Potential of Puts and Calls

Although the quoted market price of a put or call is affected by such factors as time to expiration, stock volatility, and market interest rates, by far the most important variable is the *price behavior of the underlying common stock.* This is the variable that drives any significant moves in the price of the option and that in turn determines the option's profit (return) potential. Thus, when the underlying stock moves *up* in price, *calls do well;* when the price of the underlying stock *drops, puts do well.* Such performance also explains why it's important to get a good handle on the expected future price behavior of a stock *before* buying or selling (writing) an option.

The typical price behavior of an option is illustrated graphically in Figure 11.2. The diagram on the left depicts a call, the one on the right a put. The *call* diagram is constructed assuming you pay $500 for a call that carries a strike price of $50; likewise, the *put* diagram assumes you can buy a put for $500 and obtain the right to sell the underlying stock at $50 a share. With the call, the diagram shows what happens to the value of the option when the price of the stock increases; with the put, it shows what happens when the price of the stock falls. Observe that a call does not gain in value until the price of the stock *advances past the stated exercise price* ($50). Also, because it costs $500 to buy the call, the stock has to move up another 5 points (from $50 to $55) in order for you to recover the premium and thereby reach a break-even point. So long as the stock continues to rise in price, everything from there on out is profit. Once the premium is recouped, the profit from the call position is limited only by the extent to which the stock price increases over the remaining life of the contract.

The value of a put is also derived from the price of the underlying stock, except that their respective market prices move in opposite directions. Note in Figure 11.2 that the value of the put remains constant until the market price of the corresponding stock *drops to the exercise price* ($50) on the put. Then, as the price of the stock continues to fall, the value of the option increases accordingly. Again, note that because the put cost $500, you don't start making money on the investment until the price of the stock drops below the break-even point of $45 a share. Beyond that point, the profit from the put is defined by the extent to which the price of the underlying stock continues to fall over the remaining life of the option.

INVESTOR FACT

WHERE THE ACTION IS—During 1997, there were, on average, more than a million stock option contracts traded each day on the four U.S. listed options markets. The most active of the bunch: **Intel,** with an average daily volume of over 57,000 contracts. Here's a list of the five most actively traded stock options in 1997:

Stock Option	Avg. Daily Volume
Intel	57,111 contracts
IBM	32,608 contracts
Teletron	22,369 contracts
Microsoft	21,987 contracts
Compaq	20,687 contracts

Note that four out of the top five are technology issues (indeed, eight of the top ten are high-tech stocks); together, these five options accounted for nearly 15% of all trades on the U.S. equity options markets.

Fundamental Value

As we have seen, the fundamental value of a put or call depends ultimately on the exercise price stated on the option, as well as on the prevailing market price of the underlying common stock. More specifically, the *value of a call* is determined according to the following simple formula:

FIGURE 11.2 The Valuation Properties of Put and Call Options

The value of a put or call reflects the price behavior of its underlying common stock (or other financial asset). Therefore, once the cost of the option has been recovered (which occurs when the option passes its break-even point), the profit potential of a put or call is limited only by the price behavior of the underlying asset, and by the length of time to the expiration of the option.

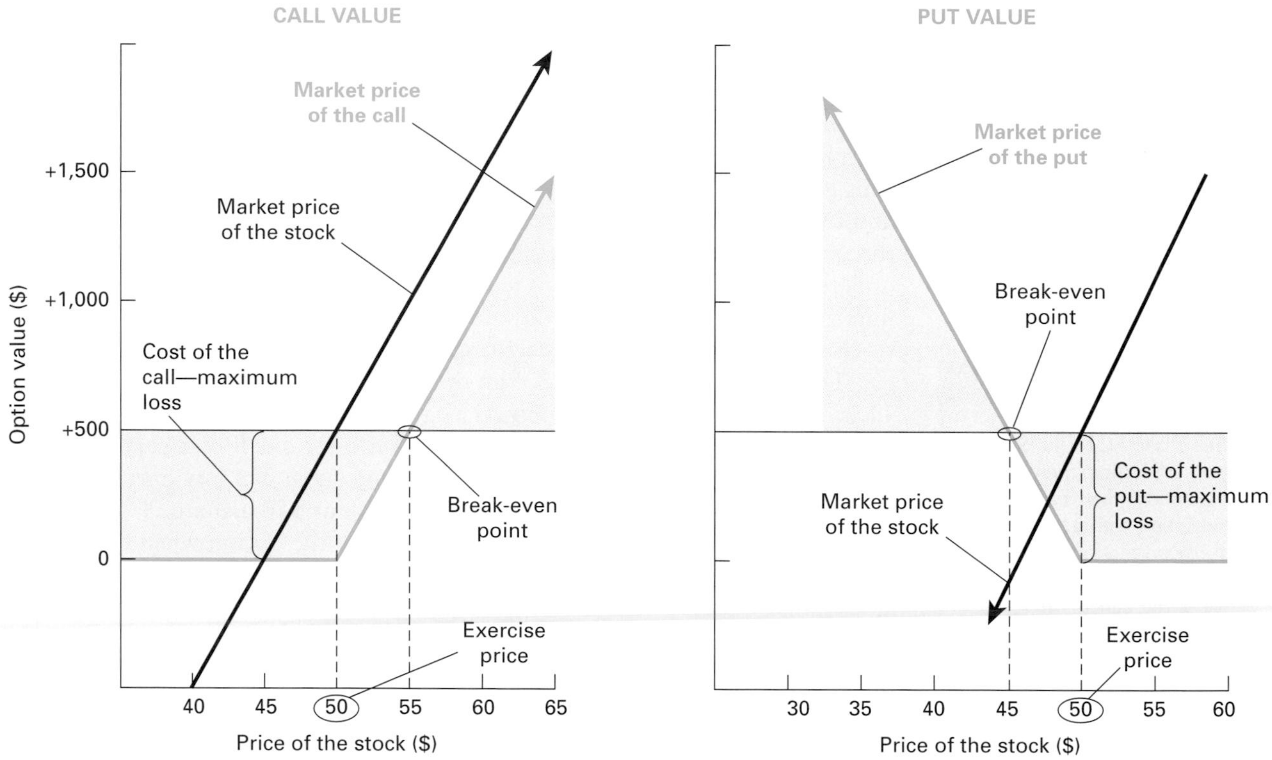

Equation 11.1

$$\text{Fundamental value of a call} = \left(\begin{array}{c}\text{market price of}\\ \text{underlying}\\ \text{common stock}\end{array} - \begin{array}{c}\text{strike price}\\ \text{on}\\ \text{the call}\end{array}\right) \times 100$$

$$V = (MP - SPC) \times 100$$

In other words, the fundamental or intrinsic value of a call is nothing more than the difference between market price and strike price. As implied in Equation 11.1, a call has an intrinsic value whenever the market price of the underlying stock (or financial asset) exceeds the strike price stipulated on the call. A simple illustration will show that a call carrying a strike price of \$50 on a stock currently trading at \$60 has a value of \$1,000; that is, (\$60 − \$50) × 100 = \$10 × 100 = \$1,000.

A put, on the other hand, cannot be valued in the same way, because puts and calls allow the holder to do different things. To find the *value of a put,* we simply change the order of the equation a bit:

Equation 11.2

$$\text{Fundamental value of a put} = \left(\begin{array}{c}\text{strike price}\\ \text{on}\\ \text{the put}\end{array} - \begin{array}{c}\text{market price of}\\ \text{underlying}\\ \text{common stock}\end{array}\right) \times 100$$

$$V = (SPP - MP) \times 100$$

In this case, a put has value so long as the market price of the underlying stock (or financial asset) *is less than* the strike price stipulated on the put.

In-the-Money/Out-of-the-Money

in-the-money
a call option with a strike price less than the market price of the underlying security; a put option whose strike price is greater than the market price of the underlying security.

out-of-the-money
a call option with no real value because the strike price exceeds the market price of the stock; a put option whose market price exceeds the strike price.

When written, options do not necessarily have to carry strike prices at the prevailing market prices of the underlying common stocks. Also, as an option subsequently trades on the listed exchanges, the price of the option will move in response to moves in the price of the underlying common stock. When a call has a strike price that is less than the market price of the underlying common stock, it has a positive intrinsic value and is known as an **in-the-money** option. A major portion of the option price in this case is based on (or derived from) the fundamental or intrinsic value of the call. When the strike price exceeds the market price of the stock, the call has no "real" value and is known as an **out-of-the-money** option. Because the option has no intrinsic value, its price is made up solely of investment premium. As you might expect, the situation is reversed for put options. That is, a put is considered in-the-money when its strike price is greater than the market price of the stock, and it's considered out-of-the-money when the market price of the stock exceeds the strike price. These terms are much more than convenient, exotic names given to options. As we will see, they characterize the investment behavior of options and can affect return and risk.

Option Prices and Premiums

option premium
the quoted price the investor pays to buy a listed put or call option.

Put and call values, as found according to Equations 11.1 and 11.2, denote what the options *should* be valued and trading at. This rarely occurs, however; these securities almost always trade at prices that exceed their intrinsic or fundamental values, especially for options that still have a long time to run. That is, puts and calls nearly always trade at premium prices. Therefore, the term **option premium** is used to describe the market price of listed put and call options. Technically, the option premium is the (quoted) price the buyer pays for the *right* to buy or sell a certain amount of the underlying common stock (or other financial asset) at a specified price for a specified period of time. The option seller, on the other hand, receives the premium and gets to keep it whether or not the option is exercised. To the option seller, the option premium represents compensation for agreeing to fulfill certain *obligations* of the contract.

As we'll see below, the term *premium* is also used to denote the extent to which the market price of an option exceeds its fundamental or intrinsic value. Thus, to avoid confusion and keep matters as simple as possible, we'll use the word *price* in the usual way: to describe the amount it takes to buy an option in the market.

What Drives Options Prices?

time premium
the amount by which the option price exceeds the option's fundamental value.

Option prices can be reduced to two separate components. The first is the *fundamental* (or *intrinsic*) value of the option, which is driven by the current market price of the underlying common stock. That is, as we saw in Equations 11.1 and 11.2, the greater the difference between the market price of the stock and the strike price on the option, the greater the value of the put or call. The second component of an option price is customarily referred to as the **time premium,** which represents, in effect, the excess value embedded in the option price. That is, time premium is *the amount by which the option price exceeds the option's fundamental value.* Table 11.1 lists some quoted prices for an actively traded call option. These quoted prices (panel A) are then separated into fundamental value (panel B) and time premium (panel C). Note that three strike prices are used—$65, $70, and $75. Relative to the market price of the stock ($71.75), one strike price ($65) is well below market; this is an in-the-money call. One ($70) is fairly near the market. The third ($75) is well above the market; this is an out-of-the-money call. Note the considerable difference in the makeup of the options prices as we move from an in-the-money call to an out-of-the-money call.

Panel B in the table lists the fundamental values of the call options, as determined by Equation 11.1. For example, note that although the March 65 call (the call with the March expiration date and $65 strike price) is trading at 7¾, its intrinsic value is only 6¾. The intrinsic or fundamental value (of 6¾), in effect, represents the extent to which the option is trading in-the-money. But observe that although most of the price of the March 65 call is made up of fundamental value, not all of it is. Now take a look at the calls with the $75 strike price. None of these has any fundamental value; they're all out-of-the-money, because their prices are made up solely of time premium. Basically, the value of these options is determined entirely by the *belief* that the price of the underlying stock could rise to over $75 a share before the options expire.

TABLE 11.1 Option Price Components for an Actively Traded Call Option

Stock Price	Strike Price	Expiration Months		
		February	March	June
Panel A: Quoted Options Prices				
71¾	65	—	7¾	9¾
71¾	70	2¼	3⅞	6¾
71¾	75	3/16	1½	3⅞
Panel B: Underlying Fundamental Values				
71¾	65	—	6¾	6¾
71¾	70	1¾	1¾	1¾
71¾	75	neg.	neg.	neg.
Panel C: Time Premiums				
71¾	65	—	1	3
71¾	70	½	2⅛	5
71¾	75	3/16	1½	3⅞

Note: neg. = Options have negative intrinsic/fundamental values.

Panel C shows the amount of time premium embedded in the call prices, which represents the difference between the quoted call price (panel A) and the call's fundamental value (panel B). It shows that the price of (just about) every traded option contains at least some premium. Indeed, unless the options are about to expire, you'd expect them to be trading at a premium. Also, note that with all three strike prices, *the longer the time to expiration, the greater the size of the premium.*

As you might expect, *time to expiration* is an important element in explaining the size of the price premium in panel C. However, a couple of other variables also have a bearing on the behavior of this premium. One is the *price volatility of the underlying common stock.* Other things being equal, the more volatile the stock, the more it enhances the speculative appeal of the option—and therefore the bigger the time premium. In addition, the size of the premium is *directly related to the level of interest rates.* That is, the amount of premium imbedded in a call option generally increases along with interest rates. Less important variables include the dividend yield on the underlying common stock, the trading volume of the option, and the exchange on which the option is listed. For the most part, however, four major forces drive the price of an option. They are, in descending order of importance, (1) the price behavior of the underlying common stock (or other financial asset), (2) the amount of time remaining to expiration, (3) the amount of price volatility in the underlying financial asset, and (4) the general level of interest rates.

Option-Pricing Models

Some fairly sophisticated option-pricing models have been developed, notably by Professor Myron Scholes and the late Fisher Black, to value call options (and, with minor modifications, put options). Many active options traders use these formulas to identify and trade over- and undervalued options. Not surprisingly, these models are based on the same variables we identified above. For example, the five parameters used in the Black-Scholes option-pricing model are (1) the risk-free rate of interest, (2) the price volatility of the underlying stock, (3) the current price of the underlying stock, (4) the strike price of the option, and (5) the option's time to expiration. (A more detailed discussion of the Black-Scholes option-pricing model, including the basic equations used in the model, can be found on this textbook's Web site, at **hepg.aw.com.**)

Trading Strategies

For the most part, stock options can be used in three types of trading strategies: (1) buying puts and calls for speculation, (2) hedging with puts and calls, and (3) option writing and spreading.

Buying for Speculation

Buying for speculation is the simplest and most straightforward use of puts and calls. Basically, it is just like buying stock ("buy low, sell high") and, in fact, represents an alternative to investing in stock. For example, if you feel the market price of a particular stock is going to move up, one way of capturing that price appreciation is to buy a call on the stock. In contrast, if you feel the stock is about to drop in price, a put could convert the price decline into a profitable situation. In essence, investors buy options rather than stock whenever the options are likely to yield a greater return. The principle here, of course, is to get the biggest return from your investment dollar—something that can often be done with puts and calls because of the added leverage they offer. Furthermore, options offer downside protection—the most you can lose is the cost of the option, which is always less than the cost of the underlying stock. Thus, by using options as a vehicle for speculation, you can put a cap on losses and still get almost as much profit potential as with the underlying stock.

Speculating with Calls To illustrate the essentials of speculating with options, imagine that you have uncovered a stock you feel will move up in price over the next 6 months. What you would like to find out at this point is what would happen if you were to buy a call on this stock rather than investing directly in the firm's common. To find out, let's see what the numbers show. The price of the stock is now $49, and you anticipate that within 6 months, it will rise to about $65. In order to determine the relative merits of your investment alternatives, you need to determine the expected return associated with each course of action. Because call options have short lives, holding period return can be used to measure yield (see Chapter 4). Thus, if your expectations about the stock are correct, it should go up by $16 a share and, in so doing, provide stockholders with a 33% holding period return [($65 − $49) ÷ $49 = $16 ÷ $49 = 0.33].

But there are also some listed options available on this stock; let's see how they would do. For illustrative purposes, we will use two 6-month calls that carry a $40 and a $50 strike price, respectively. A recap of these two call alternatives, relative to the behavior of the underlying common stock, is summarized in Table 11.2. Clearly, from a holding period return perspective, either call option represents an investment superior to buying the stock itself. The dollar amount of profit may be a bit more with the stock, but note that the size of the required investment ($4,900) is a lot more too—so it has the lowest HPR.

TABLE 11.2 Speculating with Call Options

	100 Shares of Underlying Common Stock	6-Month Call Options on the Stock	
		$40 Strike Price	$50 Strike Price
Today			
Market value of stock (at $49/share)	$4,900		
Market price of calls*		$1,100	$ 400
6 Months Later			
Expected value of stock (at $65/share)	$6,500		
Expected price of calls*		$2,500	$1,500
Profit	$1,600	$1,400	$1,100
Holding period return**	**33%**	**127%**	**275%**

*The price of the calls was computed according to Equation 11.1. It includes some investment premium in the purchase price but none in the expected sales price.

**Holding period return (HPR) = (ending price of the stock or option − beginning price of the stock or option)/beginning price of the stock or option.

Observe that one of the calls is an in-the-money option (the one with the $40 strike price) and the other is out-of-the-money. The difference in returns generated by these calls is rather typical; that is, investors are usually able to generate much better rates of return with lower-priced (out-of-the-money) options and also enjoy less exposure to loss. Of course, the major drawback of out-of-the-money options is that their price is made up solely of investment premium—a sunk cost that will be lost if the stock does not move in price.

Speculating with Puts To see how you can speculate in puts, consider the following situation. The price of your stock is now $51, but you anticipate a drop in price to about $35 per share within the next 6 months. If that occurs, you could sell the stock short and make a profit of $16 per share. (See Chapter 2 for a discussion of short selling.) Alternatively, an out-of-the-money put (with a strike price of $50) can be purchased for, say, $300. Again, if the price of the underlying stock does indeed drop, you will make money with the put. The profit and rate of return on the put are summarized below, along with the comparative returns from short selling the stock.

Comparative Performance Given Price of Stock Moves from $51 to $35/Share Over a 6-Month Period:	Buy 1 Put ($50 strike price)	Sell Short 100 Shares of Stock
Purchase price (today)	$ 300	
Selling price (6 months later)	1,500*	
Short sell (today)		$5,100
Cover (6 months later)		3,500
Profit	$1,200	$1,600
Holding period return	**400%**	**63%****

*The price of the put was computed according to Equation 11.2 and does not include any investment premium.
**Assumes the short sale was made with a required margin deposit of 50%.

Once again, in terms of holding period return, the stock option is the superior investment vehicle by a wide margin.

Of course, not all option investments perform as well as the ones in our examples; success in this strategy rests on picking the right underlying common stock. Thus *security analysis and proper stock selection are critical dimensions of this technique.* It is a highly risky investment strategy, but it may be well suited for the more speculatively inclined investor.

Hedging

hedge
a combination of two or more securities into a single investment position for the purpose of reducing or eliminating risk.

A **hedge** is simply a combination of two or more securities into a single investment position for the purpose of reducing risk. This strategy might involve buying stock and simultaneously buying a put on that same stock, or it might consist of selling some stock short and then buying a call. There are many types of hedges, some of which are very sophisticated and others very simple. They are all used for the same basic reason: to earn or protect a profit without exposing the investor to excessive loss.

An options hedge may be appropriate if you have generated a profit from an earlier common stock investment and wish to protect that profit. Or it may be appropriate if you are about to enter into a common stock investment and wish to protect your money by limiting potential capital loss. If you hold a stock that has gone up in price, the purchase of a put would provide the type of downside protection you need; the purchase of a call, in contrast, would provide protection to a short seller of common stock. Thus option hedging always involves two transactions: (1) the initial common stock position (long or short) and (2) the simultaneous or subsequent purchase of the option.

Let's examine a simple options hedge in which a put is used to limit capital loss or protect profit. Assume that you want to buy 100 shares of stock. Being a bit apprehensive about the stock's outlook, you decide to use an option hedge to protect your capital against loss. Therefore, you simultaneously buy the stock and a put on the stock (which fully covers the 100 shares owned). This type of hedge is known as a *protective put*. Preferably, the put would be a low-priced option with a strike price at or near the current market price of the stock. Suppose you purchase the common at $25 and pay $150 for a put with a $25 strike price. Now, no matter what happens to the price of the stock over the life of the put, you can lose no more than $150; at the same time, there's no limit on the gains. If the stock does not move, you will be out the cost of a put. If it drops in price, then whatever is lost on the stock will be made up with the put. The bottom line? The most you can lose is the cost of the put ($150, in this case). However, if the price of the stock goes up (as hoped), the put becomes useless, and you will earn the capital gains on the stock (less the cost of the put, of course).

The essentials of this option hedge are shown in Table 11.3. The $150 paid for the put is sunk cost, and that's lost no matter what happens to the price of the stock. In effect, it is the price paid for the hedge. Moreover, this hedge is good only for the life of the put. When this put expires, you will have to replace it with another put or forget about hedging your capital.

TABLE 11.3 Limiting Capital Loss with a Put Hedge

		Stock	Put*
Today			
Purchase price of the stock		$25	
Purchase price of the put			$ 1½
Sometime Later			
A. Price of common goes *up* to:		**$50**	
Value of put			$ 0
Profit:			
100 shares of stock ($50 − $25)	$2,500		
Less: Cost of put	− 150		
Profit:	$2,350		
B. Price of common goes *down* to:		**$10**	
Value of put**			$15
Profit:			
100 shares of stock (loss: $10 − $25)	−$1,500		
Value of put (profit)	+ 1,500		
Less: Cost of put	− 150		
Loss:	$ 150		

*The put is purchased simultaneously and carries a strike price of $25.
**See Equation 11.2.

The other basic use of an option hedge involves entering into the options position *after* a profit has been made on the underlying stock. This could be done because of investment uncertainty or for tax purposes (to carry over a profit to the next taxable year). For example, if you bought 100 shares of a stock at $35 and it moved to $75, there would be a profit of $40 per share to protect. You could protect the profit with an option hedge by buying a put; assume you decide to put such a hedge in place and you do so by buying a 3-month put with a $75 strike price at a cost of $250. Now, regardless of what happens to the stock over the life of the put, you are guaranteed a minimum profit of $3,750 (the $4,000 profit in the stock made so far, less the $250 cost of the put). This can be seen in Table 11.4. Note that if the price of the stock should fall, the worst that can happen is a guaranteed minimum profit of $3,750. And there is still *no limit on how much profit can be made:* As long as the stock continues to go up, you will reap the benefits. (*Note:* Although this discussion pertains to put hedges, it should be clear that call hedges can also be set up to limit the loss or protect a profit on a short sale. For example, when a stock is sold short, a call can be purchased to protect the short seller against a rise in the price of the stock—with the same basic results as outlined above.)

Option Writing and Spreading

The advent of listed options has led to many intriguing options-trading strategies. Yet, despite the appeal of these techniques, there is one important point that all the experts agree on: *Such specialized trading strategies should be left*

TABLE 11.4 Protecting Profits with a Put Hedge

		Stock	3-Month Put with a $75 Strike Price
Purchase price of the stock		$ 35	
Today			
Market price of the stock		$ 75	
Market price of the put			$ 2½
3 Months Later			
A. Price of common goes *up* to:		**$100**	
Value of put			$ 0
Profit:			
100 shares of stock ($500 − $35)	$6,500		
Less: Cost of put	− 250		
Profit:	$6,250		
B. Price of common goes *down* to:		**$ 50**	
Value of put*			$25
Profit:			
100 shares of stock ($50 − $35)	$1,500		
Value of put (profit)	2,500		
Less: Cost of put	− 250		
Profit:	$3,750		

*See Equation 11.2.

to experienced investors who fully understand their subtleties. Our goal at this point is not to master these specialized strategies but to explain in general terms what they are and how they operate. There are two types of specialized options strategies: (1) writing options and (2) spreading options.

Writing Options Generally, investors write options because they believe the price of the underlying stock is going to move in their favor. That is, it is not going to rise as much as the buyer of a call expects, nor will it fall as much as the buyer of a put hopes. *And, more often than not, the option writer is right;* that is, he or she makes money far more often than the buyer of the put or call. Such favorable odds explain, in part, the underlying economic motivation for writing put and call options. Options writing represents an investment transaction to the writers, because they receive the full option premium (less normal transaction costs, of course) in exchange for agreeing to live up to the terms of the option.

naked options
options written on securities not owned by the writer.

Investors can write options in one of two ways. One is to write **naked options,** which involves writing options on stock not owned by the writer. You simply write the put or call, collect the option premium, and hope the price of the underlying stock does not move against you. If successful, naked writing can be highly profitable because of the modest amount of capital required. One thing to keep in mind, however, is that the amount of return to the writer is always limited to the amount of option premium received. On the other hand, there is really *no limit to loss exposure.* And that's the catch: The price of the underlying stock can rise or fall by just about any amount over the life of the option and, in so doing, can deal a real blow to the writer of the naked put or call.

covered options
options written against stock owned (or short sold) by the writer.

Such risk exposure can be partially offset by writing **covered options,** in which case the options are written against stocks the investor (writer) already owns or has a position in. For example, you could write a call against stock you own or write a put against stock you have short sold. In this way, you can use the long or short position to meet the terms of the option. Such a strategy represents a fairly conservative way to generate attractive rates of return. The object is to write a slightly out-of-the-money option, pocket the option premium, and hope the price of the underlying stock will move up or down to (but not exceed) the option's strike price. In effect, what you are doing is adding option premium to the other usual sources of return that accompany stock ownership or short sales (dividends and/or capital gains). But there's more: While the option premium adds to the return, it also reduces risk, because it can be used to cushion a loss if the price of the stock moves against the investor.

There is a hitch to all this, of course, and it is that the amount of return the covered option investor can realize is limited. For once the price of the underlying common stock begins to exceed the strike price on the option, the option becomes valuable. When that happens, you start *to lose* money on the options. From this point on, for every dollar you make on the stock position, you lose an equal amount on the option position. That's a major risk of writing covered call options—if the price of the underlying stock takes off, you'll miss out on the added profits.

To illustrate the ins and outs of covered call writing, let's assume you own 100 shares of PFP, Inc.—an actively traded, high-yielding common stock. The stock is currently trading at 73½ and pays *quarterly* dividends of $1 a share. You decide to write a 3-month call on PFP, giving the buyer the right to take the stock off your hands at $80 a share (i.e., the call carries a strike price of

80). Such options are trading in the market at 2½, so you receive $250 for writing the call. Now, if you're like most covered call writers, you fully intend to hold on to the stock, so you'd like to see the price of PFP stock rise to no more than 80 by the expiration date on the call. If that happens, not only do you earn the dividends and capital gains on the stock, but you also get to pocket the $250 you received when you wrote the call, because it (the call option) will expire worthless. Basically, you've just *added* $250 to the quarterly return on your stock.

Table 11.5 summarizes the profit and loss characteristics of this covered call position. Note that the maximum profit on this transaction occurs *when*

TABLE 11.5 Covered Call Writing

		Stock		3-Month Call with an $80 Strike Price
Current market price of the stock		$73½		
Current market price of the put				$ 2½
3 Months Later				
A. Price of the stock is *unchanged:*		**$73½**		
Value of the call				$ 0
Profit:				
Quarterly dividends received	$ 100			
Proceeds from sale of call	250			
Total profit:	$ 350			
B. Price of the stock goes *up* to:		**$80**	←	Price Where Maximum Profit Occurs
Value of the call				$ 0
Profit:				
Quarterly dividends received	$ 100			
Proceeds from sale of call	250			
Capital gains on stock ($80 – $73½)	650			
Total profit:	$1,000			
C. Price of the stock goes *up* to:		**$90**		
Value of the call*				$10
Profit:				
Quarterly dividends received	$ 100			
Proceeds from sale of call	250			
Capital gains on stock ($90 – $73½)	$1,650			
Less: Loss on call	($1,000)			
Net profit:	$1,000			
D. Price of the stock *drops* to:		**$71**	←	Break-even Price
Value of the call*				$ 0
Profit:				
Capital loss on stock ($71 – $73½)	($ 250) } $0 profit or loss			
Proceeds from sale of call	250			
Quarterly dividends	100			
Net profit:	$ 100			

*See Equation 11.1.

the market price of the stock equals the strike price on the call. If the price of the stock keeps going up, you miss out on the added profits. Even so, the $1,000 profit that's earned at a stock price of 80 or above translates into a (3-month) holding period return of a very respectable 13.6% ($1,000/$7,350)—which represents an *annualized* return of nearly 55%! With this kind of return potential, it's not difficult to see why covered call writing is so popular. Moreover, as *situation D* in the table illustrates, covered call writing adds a little cushion to losses: The price of the stock has to drop more than 2½ points (which is what you received when you wrote/sold the call) before you start losing money.

Besides covered calls and protective puts, there are many different ways of combining options with other types of securities to achieve a given investment objective. Probably none is more unusual than the creation of so-called *synthetic securities.* A case in point: Say you want to buy a convertible bond on a certain company, but that company doesn't have any convertibles outstanding. That's really not a big problem, for as explained in the accompanying *Investing in Action* box, you can create your own customized convertible by combining a straight (nonconvertible) bond with a listed call option on your targeted company.

option spreading
combining two or more options with different strike prices and/or expiration dates into a single transaction.

Spreading Options **Option spreading** is nothing more than the combination of two or more options into a single transaction. You could create an options spread, for example, by simultaneously buying and writing options on the same underlying stock. These cannot be identical options, however; they must differ with respect to strike price and/or expiration date. Spreads are a very popular use of listed options, and they account for a substantial amount of the trading activity on the listed options exchanges. These spreads go by a variety of exotic names, such as *bull spreads, bear spreads, money spreads, vertical spreads,* and *butterfly spreads.* Each is different, constructed to meet a certain type of investment goal.

Consider, for example, a *vertical spread,* which would be set up by *buying* a call at one strike price and then *writing* a call (on the same stock and for the same expiration date) at a different—higher—strike price. For instance, you could buy a February call on XYZ at a strike price of, say, 30 and simultaneously sell (write) a February call on XYZ at a strike price of 35. Strange as it may sound, such a position would generate a hefty return if the price of the underlying stock went up by just a few points. Other spreads are used to profit from a falling market, and still others try to make money when the price of the underlying stock moves either way, up *or* down.

Whatever the objective, most spreads are created to take advantage of differences in prevailing option prices and premiums. The payoff from spreading is usually substantial, but *so is the risk.* In fact, some spreads that seem to involve almost no risk may end up with devastating results if the market and the "spread" (or difference) between option premiums move against the investor.

option straddle
the simultaneous purchase (or sale) of a put and a call on the same underlying common stock (or financial asset).

A variation on this theme involves an **option straddle;** the simultaneous purchase (or sale) of *both* a put *and* a call on the same underlying common stock. Unlike spreads, straddles normally involve the same strike price and expiration date. Here, the object is to earn a profit from *either* a big or a small swing in the price of the underlying common stock. For example, you make money on a *long straddle* (where you *buy* an equal number of the puts and calls) when the underlying stock goes through a big change in price—either up

INVESTING IN ACTION

Customized Convertibles: Do-It-Yourself Investing

It would be nice if every company offered a convertible bond. That way, you could buy the bonds, collect the income, and have the option of participating in capital appreciation if the company's stock went up. But the fact is that most companies *don't* offer convertible bonds to their shareholders. One reason is that convertible bonds are a very expensive way to raise capital. The company has to pay interest on the bond, and when a bondholder converts the bond to shares of stock, then the other shareholders' interests are diluted. Most financing instruments entail one cost or another, but not both. Typically, it's the company with the low credit rating and the shaky financial condition that issues such a win–win security for the investor.

Most companies don't issue convertible bonds, so what's the investor to do? That's the beauty of so-called synthetic securities. These are do-it-yourself, customized convertibles that *you* design. You create a type of convertible bond by investing in a mixture of interest-bearing securities and call options. It's not perfect, but it has many advantages. A popular method is known as the 90/10 strategy. This strategy involves placing 10% of your money in call options and the other 90% in an interest-bearing instrument such as a money market instrument held until the option's expiration. The options provide leverage, and the money market funds provide limited risk. Your downside: the amount of the call premium minus interest earned on the money market funds.

Here's an example of how these customized convertibles work. Assume that XYZ Corp. is currently trading at $60 per share. The purchase of 100 shares of XYZ would require an investment of $6,000, all of which would be exposed to the risk of a price decline. Instead, to employ the 90/10 strategy, you would buy a 6-month XYZ 60 call. Assuming a call premium of 6, the cost of the option would be $600, leaving you with $5,400 to invest in a money market fund for 6 months. Assuming an interest rate of 5%, the $5,400 would earn interest of $135 over the 6-month period, effectively reducing the cost of the option to $465 ($600 − $135). If the price of XYZ Corp. rises by more than $4.65 per share, then at expiration your call will realize appreciation equivalent to a long position in 100 shares of XYZ. However, you will have less capital invested in the option than would have been invested in the 100 shares of stock. That means you'll realize a higher return on capital employed with the option ($600) than with the stock ($6,000).

If the stock price increases by less than $4.65, or if it falls, then your loss will be limited to the price you paid for the option ($600) minus interest earned on your money market fund ($135). Your net cost of $465 could be further offset by any proceeds you receive from closing out your position by selling the option. Creating your own customized convertible bond can be done with any company for which options trade. Unlike buying a real convertible bond issued by a company, creating your own isn't free. The option premium minus interest is an out-of-pocket cost to you. But no "free" convertible bond can offer you 10 times the normal return on capital employed if the stock price soars.

or down, it doesn't make any difference. That is, if the price of the stock shoots way up, you make money on the call side of the straddle but are out the cost of the puts. In contrast, if the price of the stock plummets, you make money on the puts, but the calls are useless. In either case, so long as you make more money on one side than the cost of the options for the other side, you're ahead of the game! In a similar fashion, you make money with a *short straddle* (where you *sell/write* an equal number of puts and calls) when the price of the underlying stock goes nowhere—that is, when it moves sideways. In effect, you get to keep all or most of the option premiums you collected when you wrote the options.

Except for obvious structural differences, the principles that underlie the creation of straddles are much like those for spreads: to build an investment position through the combination of options that will enable an investor to capture the benefits of certain types of stock price behavior. But keep in mind that if the prices of the underlying stock and/or the option premiums do not behave in the anticipated manner, the investor loses. *Spreads and straddles are extremely tricky and should be used only by knowledgeable investors.*

CONCEPTS IN REVIEW

11.7 Briefly explain how you would make money on (a) a call option and (b) a put option. Do you have to exercise the option to capture the profit? Explain.

11.8 How do you find the intrinsic value of a call? Of a put? Does an *out-of-the-money option* have intrinsic value? Explain.

11.9 Name at least four variables that affect the price behavior of listed options, and briefly explain how each affects prices. How important are fundamental (intrinsic) value and time value to in-the-money options? To out-of-the-money options?

11.10 Describe at least three different ways in which investors can use stock options.

11.11 What's the most that can be made from writing calls? Why would an investor want to write *covered calls?* Can you reduce the risk on the underlying common stock by writing covered calls? Explain.

11.12 According to the *Investing in Action* box on page 437, what is a *synthetic security?* Briefly describe how you'd create a synthetic convertible for a company, say, like Intel.

http://hepg.aw.com

The popularity of trading in options is greatly enhanced by the Option Clearing Corporation (OCC). The OCC stands behind the credit quality of every listed option. The home page of the OCC offers resources to help you learn more about this vital link in the success of the options market.

www.optionsclearing.com

Stock-Index and Other Types of Options

LG 5

Imagine being able to buy or sell a major stock market index like the S&P 500—and at a reasonable cost. Think of what you could do: If you felt the market was heading up, you could invest in a security that tracks the price behavior of the S&P 500 index and make money when the market goes up. No longer would you have to go through the often haphazard process of selecting specific stocks that you hope will capture the market's performance. Rather, you could play the *market as a whole*. That's exactly what you can do with *stock-index options*—puts and calls that are written on major stock market indexes. Index options have been around since 1983 and have become immensely popular with both individual and institutional investors. Let's now take a closer look at these popular and often highly profitable investment vehicles.

Stock-Index Options: Contract Provisions

stock-index option
a put or call option written on a specific stock market index, such as the S&P 500.

Basically, a **stock-index option** is nothing more than a put or call written on a specific stock market index. The underlying security in this case is the specific market index. Thus, when the market index moves in one direction or another, the value of the index option moves accordingly. Because there are no stocks or other financial assets backing these options, settlement is defined in terms of cash. Specifically, the cash value of an *index option* is equal to 100 times the published market index that underlies the option. For example, if the S&P 500 is at 975, then the cash value of an S&P 500 index option will be $100 × 975 = $97,500. If the underlying index moves up or down in the market, so will the cash value of the option.

In late 1997, put and call options were available on 35 market measures of performance, including options on just about every major U.S. stock market index or average (such as the Dow Jones Industrial Average, the S&P 500, the Russell 2000, and the S&P MidCap 400), options on a handful of foreign markets (e.g., Mexico and Japan), and options on different segments of the market (pharmaceuticals, oil services, semiconductors, bank, utility indexes, etc.). Many of these options, however, are very thinly traded and really don't amount to much of a market. Actually, the following six indexes dominate the stock-index options market and account for the vast majority of trading activity:

- The S&P 500 Index (traded on the CBOE)
- The S&P 100 Index (CBOE)
- The Dow Jones Industrial Average (CBOE)
- The Institutional Index (AMEX)
- The Nasdaq 100 Index (CBOE)
- The Russell 2000 Index (CBOE)

Among these six actively traded index options, you'll find contracts not only on the S&P 500 (a widely used index that captures the market behavior of large-cap stocks) but also on the S&P 100 (another large-cap index composed of 100 stocks, drawn from the S&P 500, that have actively traded stock options). And after many years of waiting, there are now options available on the most popular index of all—the DJIA. Trading in this measure of the blue-chip segment of the market began in October 1997, and within a matter of weeks, it became one of the most actively traded index options. There's even an index of the 75 stocks that are most favored by big institutional investors (the Institutional Index) and an index (the Russell 2000) that tracks the behavior of small-cap stocks. Of all these index options, the S&P 500, the S&P 100, and the DJIA are far the most popular. In fact, there's more trading in these three contracts than in all the 32 other index options combined! Indeed, these are three of *the most actively traded of all listed options, regardless of type.*

Both puts and calls are available on index options. They are valued and have issue characteristics like any other put or call. That is, a put lets a holder profit from a drop in the market (when the underlying market index goes down, the value of a put goes up); a call enables the holder to profit from a market that's going up. As seen in Figure 11.3, these options even have a quotation system that is very similar to that used for puts and calls on stocks. (Actually, there is one small difference between the *Wall Street Journal* quotes

INVESTOR FACT

HERE'S A SPIDER YOU CAN HOLD—No, not the hairy, eight-legged kind. These spiders don't bite, but they do pack a wallop. These "spiders" are really *SPDRs,* which is shorthand for *S*tandard & *P*oor's (stock index) *D*epositary *R*eceipts. They represent an interest in a trust holding shares of all the stocks in the S&P 500 Index and, like stock-index options, enable investors to track the performance of the market as a whole. They're listed on the AMEX and trade at about one-tenth the moment-to-moment value of the S&P 500; thus, if the S&P 500 is at 985, SPDRs trade at about 98½. Unlike stock-index options, SPDRs also pay dividends. The dividends paid on the 500 stocks held in trust are passed on to investors quarterly (less a small handling fee). The AMEX also offers MidCap SPDRs, based on the S&P MidCap 400 index, and recently added options based on the DJIA—which are known as "Diamonds."

FIGURE 11.3
Quotations on Index Options

The quotation system used with index options is a lot like that used with stock options: Strike prices and expiration dates are shown along with closing option prices. The biggest differences are that put (p) and call (c) quotes are mixed together and the closing values for the *underlying indexes* are shown separately. (Source: *Wall Street Journal,* December 18, 1997.)

CHICAGO

Strike		Vol.	Last	Net Chg.	Open In.
DJ INDUS AVG(DJX)					
Mar	74p	10	1 5/8	− 1/8	2,452
Dec	75c	2	5	+ 1 1/8	14,829
Dec	76c	4	3 3/4	− 1/4	19,369
Dec	76p	420	1/16	...	21,530
Jan	76c	352	4 7/8	− 3/8	1,181
Jan	76p	50	1 5/16	...	1,948
Mar	76p	23	2 5/16	− 1/16	6,450
Dec	77c	80	2 7/16	− 13/16	4,129
Dec	77p	20	1/16	− 1/16	4,928
Jan	77p	53	1 1/4	− 1/8	623
Dec	78**c**	38	1 7/8	− 1/16	8,321
Dec	78p	464	3/16	...	8,924
Jan	78c	655	3 1/8	− 3/8	1,145
Jan	78p	992	1 9/16	+ 1/4	4,843
Mar	78**p**	3	2 11/16	− 3/16	899
Dec	79c	1,013	7/8	− 1/4	8,308
Dec	79p	1,028	7/16	− 1/16	8,683
Jan	79c	83	2 11/16	− 1/16	5,249
Jan	79p	7	1 13/16	+ 1/4	5,269
Dec	80c	1,542	1/4	− 5/16	5,317
Dec	80p	10,382	7/8	+ 1/8	12,098
Jan	80c	10,218	1 7/8	− 5/16	4,459
Jan	80p	10,152	2 1/4	+ 1/8	5,479
Mar	80c	10	3 1/2	− 1/2	8,405
Mar	80p	11	3 1/2	+ 3/8	12,263
Jun	80p	3	4 3/8	+ 1/8	4,437
Dec	81c	402	1/8	− 1/16	2,909
Dec	81p	53	1 11/16	+ 1/4	1,894
Jan	81c	57	1 3/8	− 1/4	398
Jan	81p	47	2 11/16	+ 1/16	124
Dec	82c	24	1/16	...	**24,366**
Dec	82p	109	2 1/16	− 5/16	16,190
Jan	82c	175	1	− 3/16	1,526
Jan	82p	19	2 7/8	− 1/8	413
Mar	82c	19	2 3/4	− 1/8	19,711
Mar	82p	3	4	...	1,047
Dec	83p	70	3	− 5/8	251
Jan	84c	45	3/8	− 3/16	1,113
Jan	84p	3	4	− 1/2	194
Mar	84c	5	2	+ 1/4	2,642
Mar	84p	2	5 1/8	− 1 1/8	8
Jun	88c	6	2 1/8	− 1/8	212
Call vol.......... 24,758			Open In........ 186,516		
Put vol. 24,555			Open In........ 304,106		
S&P 100 INDEX(OEX)					
Dec	450c	744	11	− 3 1/2	9,640
Dec	450p	5,667	1 3/8	+ 1/16	20,228
Jan	460c	131	20	− 2 3/8	6,571
Jan	450p	752	8 1/2	+ 1/2	11,528
Feb	450p	70	11 5/8	− 1/8	2,965
Mar	450p	3	14 3/4	− 1/4	230
Dec	455c	1,778	6 7/8	− 2 7/8	10,521
Dec	455p	5,024	2 1/8	+ 5/16	12,706
Jan	**455**c	101	**17 1/2**	− 3/4	4,115
Jan	455p	298	10	+ 1 1/8	3,655
Dec	460c	13,287	3 1/2	− 2 3/4	20,706

Closing values for the underlying indexes:

- Russell 2000 79.57
- S&P 100 460.50

Name of market index

Month of expiration

c: call option

p: put option

Open interest: number of contracts outstanding on this one (Dec-82-call) option

Strike price

Price of a January call with a strike price of 455

for stock options and those for index options. The closing value for the underlying index is not listed with the rest of the quote; instead, these values are listed separately in a table that accompanies the quotes.)

Putting a Value on Stock-Index Options

Like equity options, the market price of index options is a function of the difference between the strike price on the option (which is stated in terms of the underlying index) and the latest published stock market index. To illustrate, consider the highly popular S&P 100 Index, traded on the CBOE. As the index option quotes in Figure 11.3 reveal, this index recently closed at 460.50 (see the highlighted "closing values for the underlying indexes" at the bottom of the exhibit); at the same time, there was a January call on this index that carried a strike price of 455. Given that a stock-index *call* will have a value so long as the underlying index exceeds the index strike price (just the opposite for puts), the intrinsic value of this call would be 460.50 − 455 = 5.50. As you can see in the quotes (Figure 11.3), this call was trading at 17½, some 12 points *above* the call's underlying fundamental value. This difference, of course, was the *time premium*. For just like stock options, the amount of premium in an index option tends to *increase with longer options* and with *more volatile market conditions*.

If the S&P 100 Index in our example were to go up to, say 480 by late January (the expiration date on the call), this option would be quoted at 480 − 455 = 25; now, because index options (like equity options) are valued in multiples of $100, this contract would be worth $2,500. If you had purchased this option when it was trading at 17½, it would have cost you $1,750 and, in less than 2 months, would have generated a profit of $2,500 − $1,750 = $750. That translates into a holding period return of more than 40%. This example illustrates several points. First, it's not the value of the underlying index that drives the market price of the option, but, rather, the difference between the prevailing value of the underlying index and the strike price of the option. Second, because index options are valued just like equity options, Equations 11.1 and 11.2 are used to value calls and puts, respectively, on index options. Finally, because they're a form of derivative security, stock-index options are valued according to how the market (i.e., the market index) performs. Thus *calls should be more highly valued if the market is expected to go up in the future*, whereas *puts should be more highly valued in falling markets*.

Whereas most index options use the full market value of the underlying index for purposes of options trading and valuation, that's not the case with two of the Dow Jones measures. In particular, the option on the *Dow Jones Industrial Averages is based on 1% (or 1/100) of the actual Industrial Average*, and *the D.J. Utility Average option is based on 10% (or 1/10) of the actual average*. For example, if the DJIA is at 8,950.75, the index option would use 1% of that amount—or 89.50. Thus the cash value of this option is not $100 times the underlying DJIA, but instead is $100 times 1% of the DJIA, which equals the Dow Jones Industrial Average itself—i.e., $100 × 89.50 = $8,950. Fortunately, the option strike prices are also based on the same 1% of the Dow, so this really has no effect on option valuation: It's still the difference between the strike price on the option and (1% of) the DJIA that matters. For instance, note in Figure 11.3 that the DJIA option index closed at 79.57 (the actual Dow was at 7,957); note also that there was a January call option available on this index with a strike price of 76, which was trading at 4⅞—that is, it was trading at 4⅞ × $100 = $487.50. Using Equation 11.1, you can see that this in-the-money option had an intrinsic value of 79.57 − 76.00 = 3.57 (or $357); the rest was time premium.

Except for this little twist, Dow Jones index options are valued like any other. Indeed, the greatest impact of this pricing mechanism is the *number of options necessary to establish a given position*. For example, look once more at Figure 11.3. Note that whereas the S&P 100 index option has a cash value of around $46,000, the DJIA option is worth less than $8,000. Thus it would take nearly six Dow options to give you the same $46,000 position as one S&P 100 index option. Hence the low quoted Dow index option prices are a bit misleading when you consider that it would take a lot more of them to give you approximately the same coverage/position as one S&P 100 index option.

Investment Uses

Although index options, like equity options, can be used in spreads, straddles, or even covered calls, they are perhaps used most often for speculating or for hedging. When used as a speculative vehicle, index options give investors an opportunity to play the market with a relatively small amount of capital. Like any other put or call, *index options provide attractive leverage opportunities and at the same time limit exposure to loss to the price paid for the option.*

Index options are equally effective as *hedging vehicles.* In fact, hedging is a major use of index options and accounts for a good deal of the trading in these securities. To see how these options can be used for hedging, consider an investor who holds a diversified portfolio of common stocks. One way to protect the whole portfolio against an adverse market is to buy puts on one of the market indexes. If you hold a portfolio of, say, a dozen different stocks and you think the market is heading down, you can protect your capital by selling all of your stocks. However, that could become expensive, especially if you plan to get back into the market after it drops, and it could lead to a good deal of unnecessary taxes. Fortunately, there is a way to "have your cake and eat it too," and that is to hedge your stock portfolio with a stock index put. In this way, if the market does go down, you'll make money on your puts, which can then be used to buy more stocks at the lower, "bargain" prices. On the other hand, if the market continues to go up, you'll be out *only the cost of the puts*—which could well be recovered from the increased value of your stock holdings. The principles of hedging with stock-index options are exactly the same as those for hedging with stock options; the only difference is that with stock-index options, you're trying to protect a *whole portfolio* of stocks rather than *individual* stocks.

There is one important consideration to keep in mind, however: The amount of profit you make or the protection you obtain depends in large part on how closely the behavior of your stock portfolio is matched by the behavior of the stock-index option you employ in the hedge. *There is no guarantee that the two will behave in the same way.* You should therefore select an index option that closely reflects the nature of the stocks in your portfolio. If, for example, you hold a number of small-cap stocks, you might be well advised to select something like the Russell 2000 index option as the hedging vehicle. If, on the other hand, you hold mostly blue chips, you might choose the DJIA index option. You probably can't get dollar-for-dollar portfolio protection, but you should try to get as close a match as possible. Another factor that's important in portfolio hedging is the cost of the underlying hedge vehicle itself. This and other considerations are discussed in the accompanying *Investing in Action* box, which deals with the use of index options in portfolio hedging.

Given their effectiveness for either speculating or hedging the entire market, it's little wonder that index options have become so popular with investors. But a word of caution is in order: Although trading index options appears simple and seems to provide high rates of return, these vehicles involve

INVESTING IN ACTION

Using Index Options to Protect a Whole Portfolio

When the stock market heads down, investors begin to worry about protecting the value of their portfolios. But simply liquidating their stock holdings and putting the proceeds into a money market fund is too drastic a step for most people. Not only would they incur substantial brokerage commissions and capital gains taxes, but they would also lose out if the market rallies. A far less drastic—and less costly—way for investors to shield their portfolios from the possibility of a sustained sell-off is to buy "insurance" in the form of stock-index put options.

These options offer a simple method of insuring the value of an entire portfolio with a single trade. That can be especially helpful because many issues in an investor's portfolio may not have individual put options traded on them. Such portfolio protection is similar to any other kind of insurance. The more protection investors want and the less risk they are willing to bear, the more the insurance costs. For example, suppose an investor wants to hedge a $100,000 stock portfolio and, after examining the characteristics of the major stock indexes, concludes that the S&P 100 best matches the portfolio. With the S&P 100 Index standing at, say, 509 in March, the market value of the S&P 100 Index would be $50,900. So the investor would buy two puts to approximate the $100,000 portfolio value.

The investor might buy two "June 480" puts that expire in 3 months (i.e., in June) with a strike price of 480 and a price of about 10. To turn that into dollars, an investor multiplies by 100; the puts would cost about $1,000 each—$2,000 for both—or 2% of the $100,000 portfolio. If the market retreats about 15% from current levels, bringing the S&P 100 down to about 433, each June 480 put would be worth a minimum of 47 points (480 − 433), or $4,700. After paying their cost, the investor would have a profit on the puts of $7,400 ($4,700 − $1,000 = $3,700 × 2), offsetting a substantial portion of the $15,000 the portfolio would have lost in a 15% decline.

By purchasing puts with strike prices that are 19 points below the current level of the S&P Index, the investor effectively insures the portfolio against any losses that occur *after* the market has fallen 29 points, or 56.7%, to 480. An investor willing to bear more market risk could reduce the insurance cost even further by purchasing puts with even lower strike prices. On the other hand, to be fully insured, an investor might have bought puts with a higher strike price, but that would have raised the cost of the insurance. June 500 puts, for instance, would have cost 14½, or $1,450 each. Harrison Roth, an options strategist, says the basic question for investors is "Do you want to hedge against any and all declines, or do you simply want protection against catastrophic moves?" He believes most investors are in the second camp.

Even with relatively low-cost puts such as the June 480s, the cost of put option hedges can add up if the insurance goes unused. Buying 3-month puts like these four times a year would cost the equivalent of 8% of a $100,000 portfolio. One way to reduce the cost is to sell the put options before they expire. Put options lose most of their value in the final few weeks before their expiration if they have strike prices below the current price of the underlying securities. For this reason, some market advisers recommend that investors hold their options for only a month, sell them, and then buy the next month out. This strategy recovers most of the options' value, significantly reducing the cost to hedge, even after the higher commissions.

high risk and are subject to considerable price volatility. They should not be used by amateurs. True, there's only so much you can lose with these options; the trouble is that it's very easy to lose that amount. Attractive profits are indeed available from these securities, but they're not investments you can buy and then forget about until they expire. With the wide market swings that are so common today, *these securities must be closely monitored on a daily basis.*

Other Types of Options

Although options on stocks and stock indexes account for most of the market activity in listed options, put and call options can also be obtained on debt instruments and foreign currencies. In addition to these securities, you can also buy puts and calls with extended expiration dates—these options are known as *LEAPS*. Let's now take a brief look at these other kinds of options, starting with interest rate options.

Interest Rate Options

interest rate options
put and call options written on fixed-income (debt) securities.

Puts and calls on fixed-income (debt) securities are known as **interest rate options.** At the present time, interest rate options are written only on U.S. Treasury securities; there are four maturities used: 30-year T-bonds, 10-year and 5-year T-notes, and short-term T-bills. These options are a bit unusual because they are *yield-based* rather than price-based, which means they track the yield behavior (rather than the price behavior) of the underlying Treasury security. That is, other types of options—like equity or index options—are set up so that they react to movements in the price (or value) of the underlying asset; interest rate options, in contrast, are set up to react to *the yield of the underlying Treasury security.* Thus, when yields rise, the value of a call goes up, and when yields fall, puts go up in value. In effect, because bond prices and yields move in opposite directions, the value of an interest rate call option goes up at the very time that the price (or value) of the underlying debt security is going down (and vice versa for puts). This unusual behavioral characteristic may help explain why the market for interest rate options has never taken hold and remains very small to this day. Most professional investors simply don't care for interest rate options but instead prefer to use interest rate futures contracts or options on these futures contracts (both of which will be examined in Chapter 12) for hedging or other investment purposes.

Currency Options

currency options
put and call options written on foreign currencies.

Foreign exchange options, or just **currency options** as they're more commonly called, provide a way for investors to speculate on foreign exchange rates or to hedge foreign currency or foreign security holdings. Currency options are available on the currencies of most of the countries with which the U.S. has strong trading ties. These options are traded on the Philadelphia Exchange and include the following currencies:

- British pound
- Swiss franc
- German mark
- Canadian dollar
- Japanese yen
- Australian dollar

In essence, puts and calls on these currencies give the holders the right to sell or buy large amounts of the specified foreign currency. However, in contrast to the standardized contracts used with stock and stock-index options, the specific unit of trading in this market varies with the particular underlying currency, the details of which are spelled out in Table 11.6. Currency options are traded in full or fractional cents per unit of the underlying currency, relative to the amount of foreign currency involved. Thus, if a put or call on the British pound were quoted at, say, 6.40 (which is read as "6.4 cents"),

TABLE 11.6 Foreign Currency Option Contracts on the Philadelphia Exchange

Underlying Currency*	Size of Contracts	Underlying Currency*	Size of Contracts
British pound	31,250 pounds	Canadian dollar	50,000 dollars
Swiss franc	62,500 francs	Japanese yen	6,250,000 yen
German mark	62,500 marks	Australian dollar	50,000 dollars

*The British pound, Swiss franc, German mark, Canadian dollar, and Australian dollar are all quoted in full cents; the Japanese yen is quoted in hundredths of a cent.

it would be valued at $2,000, because 31,250 British pounds underlie this option—that is, 31,250 × .064 = $2,000.

The value of a currency option is linked to the exchange rate between the U.S. dollar and the underlying foreign currency. For example, if the Canadian dollar becomes stronger *relative to the U.S. dollar,* causing the exchange rates to go up, the price of a *call* option on the Canadian dollar will increase, and the price of a *put* will decline. [*Note:* Some cross-currency options are available in the market, but such options/trading techniques are beyond the scope of this book; thus our discussion will focus solely on foreign currency options (or futures) that are linked to U.S. dollars.]

To understand how you can make money with currency options, consider a situation in which an investor wants to speculate on exchange rates. The strike price of a currency option is stated in terms of *exchange rates.* Thus a strike price of 150 implies that each unit of the foreign currency (such as one British pound) is worth 150 cents, or $1.50, in U.S. money. If you held a 150 call on this foreign currency, you would make money if *the foreign currency strengthened relative to the U.S. dollar* so that the exchange rate rose—say, to 155. In contrast, if you held a 150 put, you would profit from a decline in the exchange rate—say, to 145. Success in forecasting movements in foreign exchange rates is obviously essential to a profitable foreign currency options program.

LEAPS

LEAPS long-term options.

They look like regular puts and calls, they behave pretty much like regular puts and calls, but they're not—they're different. We're talking about **LEAPS,** which are puts and calls with lengthy expiration dates. Basically, LEAPS are long-term options. Whereas standard options have maturities of 8 months or less, LEAPS have expiration dates that extend out as far as 2 years. Known formally as *Long-term Equity AnticiPation Securities,* they are listed on all four of the major options exchanges. LEAPS are available on over 100 different stocks and several stock indexes, including the S&P 100, the S&P 500, and the DJIA.

Aside from their time frame, LEAPS work like any other equity or index option. For example, a single (equity) LEAPS contract gives the holder the right to buy or sell 100 shares of stock at a predetermined price on or before the specified expiration date. LEAPS give investors more time to be right about their bets on the direction of a stock or stock index, and they give hedgers more time to protect their positions. But there's a price for all this extra time:

You can expect to pay a lot more for a LEAPS than you would for a regular (short-term) option. For example, in late 1997, a 4-month, out-of-the-money call on Intel (with a strike price of 100) was trading at 3/8 of a point; the same call with a 2-year expiration date was trading at 9⅛. The difference should come as no surprise, because LEAPS, being nothing more than long-term options, are loaded with *time premium.* And as we saw earlier in this chapter, other things being equal, *the more time an option has to expiration, the higher the quoted price.*

CONCEPTS IN REVIEW

11.13 Briefly describe the differences and similarities between *stock-index options* and *stock options.* Do the same for *foreign currency options* and stock options.

11.14 Identify and briefly discuss two different ways to use stock-index options. Do the same for foreign currency options. Explain how index options can be used by investors to hedge or protect a whole portfolio of stocks.

11.15 Why would an investor want to use index options to hedge a portfolio of common stock? If the investor thinks the market is in for a fall, why not just sell the stock?

11.16 What are *LEAPS?* Why would an investor want to use a LEAPS option rather than a regular listed option?

http://hepg.aw.com

The American Stock Exchange trades options on over 25 equity indexes. These indexes are divided into (1) broad-based indexes, (2) international indexes, and (3) sector indexes. Visit this site and learn more about these three index groups; follow the *Options and Derivatives* and the *Index Options* choices.

www.amex.com/cge-bin/WebObjects/AmexWeb

Warrants

LG 6

warrant
a long-lived option that gives the holder the right to buy stock in a company at a price specified on the warrant.

A **warrant** is a type of long-term option that enables the holder to acquire common stock. And like most options, warrants are found in the corporate sector of the market. Occasionally, warrants can be used to purchase preferred stock or even bonds, but common stock is the leading redemption vehicle.

General Attributes

Of the various types of options, warrants normally have the longest lives, with maturities that extend to 5, 10, or even 20 years or more. Indeed, some warrants have no maturity date at all. Warrants have no voting rights, pay no dividends, and have no claim on the assets of the company. What they do offer, however, is a chance to participate indirectly in the market behavior of the issuing firm's common stock and, in so doing, to generate capital gains.

Warrants are perhaps most closely related to *call LEAPS,* or long-term *call* options, although there are important differences. First, whereas call LEAPS cover 100 shares of stock, a warrant usually covers just one or two shares of the underlying stock (or some fraction thereof). The second big difference involves the issuer of the instruments: Whereas warrants are issued by the same company that issues the underlying stock, LEAPS are not—they can be written by anybody or any institution.

Warrants are created as "sweeteners" to bond issues. To make a bond more attractive, the issuing corporation sometimes attaches warrants, which give the holder the right to purchase a stipulated number of stocks at a stipulated price anytime within a stipulated period. A single warrant usually allows the holder to buy one full share of stock, although some involve more than one share per warrant and a few involve fractional shares. The life of a warrant is specified by its *expiration date,* and the stock purchase price stipulated on the warrant is known as the *exercise price.*

Because warrants are a type of equity issue, they can be margined at the same rate as common stock. They are purchased through brokers and are subject to commission and transaction costs similar to those for common stock. Warrants are usually listed with the common stock of the issuer, but their quotes are easy to pick out, because the letters *wt* appear next to the name of the company. For example, the quote for the America West Airlines warrant is highlighted in Figure 11.4. Note that the market information for warrants is just like that for any other common stock, except, of course, there's no dividend, dividend yield, or price/earnings ratio.

Advantages and Disadvantages

Warrants offer investors several advantages, one of which is their tendency to exhibit price behavior much like the common stock to which they are linked—which is just what you'd expect from a type of (call) option. Warrants thus provide the investor with an alternative way of achieving capital gains from an equity issue; that is, instead of buying the stock, you can purchase warrants on

FIGURE 11.4 Stock Quotations Showing Market Information for a Warrant

Warrants are listed right along with common stocks, but they're easy to pick out—just look for the letters *wt* behind the company name. (Source: *Wall Street Journal,* December 22, 1997.)

52 Weeks Hi	Lo	Stock	Sym	Div	Yld %	PE	Vol 100s	Hi	Lo	Close	Net Chg
27½	21¼	AmcastInd	AIZ	.56	2.5	15	125	22¾	22⅜	22⅜	– ⅛
64½	47⅜	AmerHess	AHC	.60	1.2	25	5527	51	49 5/16	50¾	– ½
26 13/16	24¼	Amerco pfA		2.13	8.0		760	26½	26¼	26½	+ ⅛
91⅛	31¾	AmOnline	AOL		...	dd	21835	85 9/16	81½	84¾	+ 1
8½	3¾	AmWestAir wt			...	...	385	6¾	5 15/16	6⅜	– ⅜
18 13/16	12	AmWest B	AWA		...	11	2866	17 7/16	16¼	17	– ½
27⅛	25	AmAnnuity TOPrS		2.32	8.8	...	19	26½	26½	26½	...
23⅞	13¾	AmAnnuity	AAG	.10f	.5	14	211	21 7/16	20 15/16	21⅜	+ 3/16
43 7/16	23 11/16	AmBkrsIns	ABI	.44	1.0	18	1261	44¼	42⅛	44¼	+ 1¾

the stock. Indeed, such a tactic may even be more rewarding than investing directly in the stock.

Another advantage is the relatively low unit cost of warrants and the attractive leverage potential that accompanies this low unit cost. That is, you can use warrants to obtain a given equity position at a substantially reduced capital investment. And in so doing, you can *magnify returns,* because the warrant provides roughly the same capital appreciation potential as the more costly common stock. For example, note in Figure 11.4 that the America West warrants are trading at 6⅜, whereas shares of the common are trading at 17.

A final advantage of warrants is that their low unit cost leads to reduced downside risk exposure. In essence, the lower unit cost simply means there is less to lose if the investment goes sour. For example, a $50 stock can drop to $25 if the market falls, but there is no way that the same company's $10 warrants can drop by the same amount.

However, warrants do have some *disadvantages.* For one thing, warrants pay no dividends, which means that investors sacrifice current income. Second, because these issues usually carry an expiration date, there is only a certain period of time during which you can capture the type of price behavior sought. Although this may not be much of a problem with long-term warrants, it can be a burden for those issues with fairly short lives (of 1 to 2 years, or less).

Putting a Value on Warrants

A warrant, like any option, is a type of *derivative security;* it derives its value from some underlying stock (or other financial asset). For example, the America West warrants noted above are directly linked to the price behavior of the AWA common stock. Thus, under the right conditions, when America West stock goes up (or down) in price, the warrants will too. Actually, warrants possess value whenever the market price of the underlying common equals or exceeds the exercise price on the warrant. This so-called *fundamental value* is determined as follows:

Equation 11.3

$$\text{Fundamental value of a warrant} = (M - E) \times N$$

where

M = prevailing market price of the common stock

E = exercise price stipulated on the warrant

N = number of shares of stock that can be acquired with one warrant (if one warrant entitles the holder to buy one share of stock, $N = 1$; however, if two warrants are necessary to buy one share of stock, $N = 0.5$, etc.)

The formula shows fundamental value and therefore what the market value of a warrant *should be,* given the respective market and exercise prices of the common and the number of shares of stock that can be acquired with one warrant. As an example, consider a warrant that carries an exercise price of $40 per share and enables the holder to purchase one share of stock per warrant. If the common stock has a current market price of $50 a share, then the warrants would be valued at $10 each:

Fundamental value of a warrant = ($50 − $40) × 1 = ($10) × 1 = $10

Obviously, the greater the spread between the market and exercise prices, the greater the fundamental value of a warrant. *So long as the market price of the stock equals or exceeds the exercise price of the warrant*, and the redemption provision carries a 1-to-1 ratio (which means that one share of common can be bought with each warrant), the value of a warrant will be closely linked to the price behavior of the common stock.

Premium Prices

warrant premium
the difference between the true value of a warrant and its market price.

Equation 11.3 indicates how warrants should be valued, but they are seldom priced exactly that way in the marketplace. Instead, the market price of a warrant usually *exceeds* its fundamental value. This happens when warrants with negative values trade at prices greater than zero. It also occurs when warrants with positive fundamental values trade at even higher market prices (e.g., when a warrant that's valued at $10 trades at $15). This discrepancy is known as **warrant premium,** and it exists because warrants possess speculative value. As a rule, the amount of premium embedded in the market price of a warrant is directly related to the option's time to expiration and the volatility of the underlying common stock. On the other hand, the amount of premium does tend to diminish as the underlying (fundamental) value of a warrant increases. This can be seen in Figure 11.5, which shows the typical behavior of warrant premiums.

The premium on a warrant is easy to measure: Just take the difference between the value of a warrant (as computed according to Equation 11.3) and its market price. For instance, a warrant has $5 in premium if it has a value of $10 but is trading at $15. The amount of premium can also be expressed on a relative (percentage) basis by dividing the dollar premium by the warrant's fundamental value. For example, there is a 50% premium embedded in the price of that $15 warrant (the dollar premium ÷ the fundamental value of the

FIGURE 11.5
The Normal Price Behavior of Warrant Premiums

Observe that as the price of the underlying common stock increases, the amount of premium in the market price of the warrant tends to decrease—though it never totally disappears.

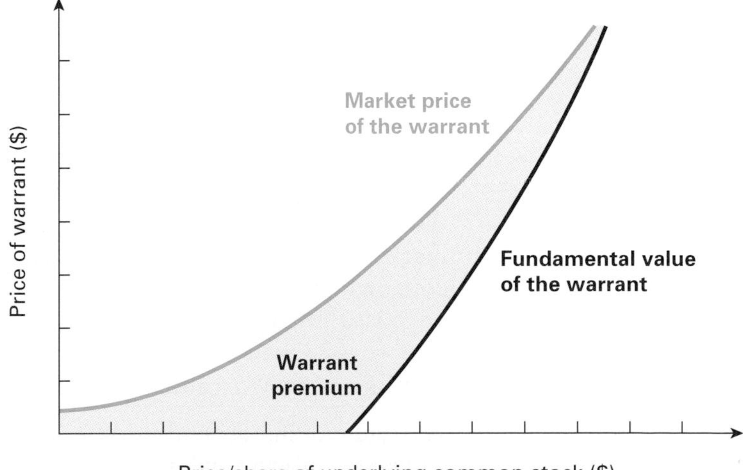

warrant = \$5 ÷ \$10 = 0.50). Premiums on warrants can at times become fairly substantial. Indeed, premiums of 20% to 30% or more are not at all uncommon.

Trading Strategies

Because their attraction to investors rests primarily with the capital gains opportunities they provide, warrants are used chiefly as alternatives to common stock investments. Let's now look at some warrant-trading strategies and the basic ways in which these securities can be profitably employed by investors.

The Basic Price Behavior of Warrants

Because warrants carry relatively low unit costs, they possess much greater *price volatility* and the potential for generating substantially higher *rates of return* than a direct investment in the underlying common stock. Consider the following illustration, which involves the common shares and warrants of the same company. Assume the price of the common is now \$50 per share and the warrant, which carries a one-to-one redemption provision, has a \$40 exercise price. (We will ignore premium in this illustration.) Observe what happens when the price of the stock increases by \$10:

	Common Stock	Warrant
Issue price *before* increase	\$50	\$10
Increase in price of common	\$10	—
Issue price *after* increase	\$60	\$20
Increase in market value	\$10	\$10
Holding period return	**20%**	**100%**
(increase in value/beginning issue price)		

The reason the warrants provide a rate of return five times greater than the common stock is, of course, the fact that the two issues move parallel to one another, even though the warrant carries a much lower unit cost.

As in our illustration above, the holding period return formula is used to assess the payoff when the investment horizon equals 1 year or less. In contrast, the standard expected return (IRR) measure is used when the investment horizon amounts to more than a year. For example, given our illustration above, if we felt the warrant should go from a price of \$10 to \$20 over a 3-year period of time, it would have an expected return of around 24%. Note that in this case, because we can ignore dividends, all we need do is find the discount rate that equates the price of \$20 in 3 years to the warrant's current market price of \$10. This is pretty much like finding the yield on a zero-coupon bond. That is, because there are no dividends on warrants, the returns are based solely on the capital gains produced by the investment.

Trading with Warrants

Warrant trading generally follows one of two approaches: (1) The leverage embedded in warrants is used to magnify dollar returns, or (2) their low unit cost is used to reduce the amount of invested capital and limit losses. The first approach is the more aggressive, and the second has considerable merit as a conservative strategy.

Our comparative illustration (where the price of the stock goes from $50 to $60 a share) can be used to demonstrate the first technique, which seeks to magnify returns. If you want to make a $5,000 equity investment and if price appreciation is the main objective, you would be better off committing such a sum to the warrants. The reason is that a $5,000 investment in the common stock will buy 100 shares of stock ($5,000 ÷ $50 = 100 shares), which will generate only $1,000 in capital gains ($10 profits per share × 100 shares). That same $5,000 invested in the lower-priced warrants will buy 500 of these securities ($5,000 ÷ $10 = 500 warrants) and will result in $5,000 in profits ($10 in profits per warrant × 500 warrants). The common stock thus provides a 20% HPR, whereas the warrants yield 100 percent. The biggest risk in this investment is the potential loss exposure. Observe that if the price of the stock in our example decreases by $10, your warrant investment is virtually wiped out. (Actually, the warrant will probably retain some value greater than zero, but not much.) In contrast, the price of the stock drops to "only" $40, and, as a stockholder, you will still have $4,000 in capital left.

One way to limit this exposure to loss is to follow the second, more conservative trading approach. In this strategy, you buy only enough warrants to realize the level of capital gains available from the common stock. In our illustration, because we are dealing with options that carry one-to-one redemption provisions, you would need to acquire only 100 warrants to obtain the same price behavior as that of 100 shares of stock. Thus, rather than buying $5,000 worth of stock, you would purchase only $1,000 worth of the warrants to realize the same capital gains. If the stock performs as expected, you will realize a 100% return by generating the same amount of capital gains as the stock—$1,000. But this will be done with substantially less capital, so the yield with the warrants will be greater *and* the loss exposure will be less. In this case, if the price of the stock drops by 10 points, the most the warrant holder can lose is $1,000. On the other hand, if the price of the stock drops by *more* than $10 a share, the warrant holder still will lose no more than $1,000, whereas the stockholder can lose a lot more, depending on the extent of the drop in share price.

CONCEPTS IN REVIEW

11.17 What is a *warrant* and what is its chief attraction? Describe the leverage features of a warrant and note why leverage is so attractive to investors.

11.18 What factors are important in determining the investment appeal of warrants? Why is the price of the warrant itself so important in the investment decision?

http://hepg.aw.com

The Web site that follows provides a calculator to calculate the value of a warrant. The specific Web page listed explains the variables that go into the valuation model. Understanding these inputs should be helpful in getting a better grasp of the warrant valuation process.

www.numa.com/derivs/ref/calculator/warrant/calc-wtb.htm#top

Summary

LG 1 **Discuss the basic nature of options in general and puts and calls in particular, and understand how these investment vehicles work.** An option gives the holder the right to buy or sell a certain amount of some real or financial asset at a set price for a set period of time. Puts and calls are by far the most widely used type of option; these derivative securities offer attractive value and considerable leverage potential. A put enables the holder to *sell* a certain amount of a specified security at a specified price over a specified time period. A call gives the holder the right to *buy* the same security at a specified price over a specified period of time.

LG 2 **Describe the options market and note key options provisions, including strike prices and expiration dates.** The options market is made up of conventional (OTC) options, which are used predominantly by institutional investors, and listed options, which are traded on organized exchanges such as the CBOE and the AMEX. The creation of listed options exchanges led to the use of standardized options features and opened the way for widespread use of options by individual investors. Among the provisions stipulated on options are the strike price (which is the stipulated price at which the underlying asset can be bought or sold) and the expiration date (which stipulates when the contract expires).

LG 3 **Explain how put and call options are valued and the forces that drive options prices in the marketplace.** The value of a call is measured as the market price of the underlying security less the strike price designated on the call. The value of a put is its strike price less the market price of the security. Although the value of an option is driven by the current market price of the underlying asset, most puts and calls sell at premium prices. The size of the premium depends on the length of the option contract (the so-called time premium), the speculative appeal and amount of price volatility in the underlying financial asset, and the general level of interest rates.

LG 4 **Describe the profit potential of puts and calls, and note some of the more popular put and call investment strategies.** Investors who hold puts make money when the value of the underlying asset goes down over time; in contrast, call investors make money when the underlying asset moves up in price. Aggressive investors will use puts and calls either for speculation or in highly specialized writing and spreading programs. Conservative investors are attracted to puts and calls because of their low unit costs and the limited risk they offer in absolute dollar terms. Conservative investors often use options in covered call writing programs or to form hedge positions in combination with other securities.

LG 5 **Describe market index options, puts and calls on foreign currencies, and LEAPS, and show how these securities can be used by investors.** In addition to listed stock options, standardized put and call options are also available on stock-market indexes, like the S&P 500 (index options), and on a number of foreign currencies (currency options). Also available are LEAPS, which are listed options that carry lengthy expiration dates. Although these securities can be used just like stock options, the index and currency options tend to be used primarily for speculation or to develop hedge positions.

LG 6 **Discuss the investment characteristics of stock warrants and describe the trading strategies that can be used to gain maximum benefits from this investment vehicle.** A warrant is similar to a call option, but its maturity is much longer. Attached to bond issues as "sweeteners," warrants allow the holder to purchase common stock at a set exercise price on or before a stipulated expiration date. Trading in warrants is done primarily as a substitute for common stock investing and is based on the magnified capital gains that warrants offer. The value of a warrant changes directly with, and by approximately the same amount as, the underlying common stock, but because a warrant's unit cost is often much lower than that of the common stock, the same dollar change in price represents a considerably larger percentage yield.

Discussion Questions

LG 2 LG 5

Q11.1. Using the stock or index option quotations in Figures 11.1 and 11.3, respectively, find the option premium, the time premium, and the stock or index break-even point for the following puts and calls.

a. The April Intel *call* with the $65 strike price
b. The January IBM *put* with the $115 strike price
c. The December Heinz *call* with the strike price of 50
d. The December S&P 100 *call* with the strike price of 455
e. The March DJIA *put* with the strike price of 82

LG 3

Q11.2. Prepare a schedule similar to the one in Table 11.1 for the December, January, and February S&P 100 *calls* listed in Figure 11.3. (Use the ones with strike prices of 455, 460, and 465.) Do the same for the December, January, and February S&P 100 *puts* (using the same three strike prices). Briefly explain your findings.

LG 5

Q11.3. Assume you hold a well-balanced portfolio of common stocks. Under what conditions might you want to use a stock-index option to hedge the portfolio?

a. Briefly explain how such options could be used to hedge a portfolio against a drop in the market.
b. Discuss what happens if the market does, in fact, go down.
c. What happens if the market instead goes up?

LG 3 LG 4

Q11.4. Using the resources available at your campus or public library, complete each of the following tasks. (*Note:* Show your work for all calculations.)

a. Find an *in-the-money call* (select an *equity option* that is at least $5 in the money) that has 2 or 3 months to expiration. What's the fundamental value of this option, and how much premium is it carrying? Using the current market price of the underlying stock (the one listed with the option), determine what kind of dollar and percentage return the option would generate if the underlying stock goes up 10%. How about if the stock goes down 10%?
b. Repeat part (a), but this time use an *in-the-money put* (an equity option that's at least $5 in the money and has 2 or 3 months to expiration). Answer the same questions as above.
c. Repeat once more the exercise in part (a), but this time use an *out-of-the-money call* (an equity option, at least $5 out of the money, 2 or 3 months to expiration). Answer the same questions.
d. Compare the valuation properties and performance characteristics of in-the-money calls and out-of-the-money calls [from parts (a) and (c)]. Note some of the advantages and disadvantages of each.

Problems

 LG 3

P11.1. A 6-month call on a certain common stock carries a strike price of $60; it can be purchased at a cost of $600. Assume that the underlying stock rises to $75 per share by the expiration date of the option. How much profit would this option generate over the 6-month holding period, and (using HPR) what is its rate of return?

 LG 5

P11.2. Dorothy McBride does a lot of investing in the stock market and is a frequent user of stock-index options. She is convinced that the market is about to undergo a broad retreat and has decided to buy a put on the S&P 100 Index. The put carries a strike price of 490 and is quoted in the financial press at 4½. Although the S&P Index of 100 stocks is currently at 486.45, Dorothy thinks it will drop to 465 by the expiration date on the option. How much profit will she make, and what will be her holding period return if she is right? How much will she lose if the S&P 100 goes up (rather than down) by 25 points and reaches 515 by the date of expiration?

 LG 3 LG 4

P11.3. Bill Polaski holds 600 shares of Lubbock Gas and Light. He bought the stock several years ago at 48½, and the shares are now trading at 75. Bill is concerned that the market is beginning to soften; he doesn't want to sell the stock, but he would like to be able to protect the profit he's made. He decides to hedge his position by buying 6 puts on Lubbock G&L; the 3-month puts carry a strike price of 75 and are currently trading at 2½.

a. How much profit or loss will Bill make on this deal if the price of Lubbock G&L does indeed drop—to $60 a share—by the expiration date on the puts?
b. How would he do if the stock kept going up in price and reached $90 a share by the expiration date?
c. What do you see as the major advantages of using puts as hedge vehicles?
d. Would Bill have been better off using in-the-money puts—that is, puts with an $85 strike price that are trading at 10½? How about using out-of-the-money puts—say, those with a $70 strike price, trading at 1? Explain.

LG 4 LG 5

P11.4. C. F. Wong holds a well-diversified portfolio of high-quality, large-cap stocks. The current value of Wong's portfolio is $475,000, but he is concerned that the market is heading for a big fall (perhaps as much as 20%) over the next 3 to 6 months. He doesn't want to sell all his stocks because he feels they all have good long-term potential and should perform nicely once stock prices have bottomed out. As a result, he decides to look into the possibility of using index options to hedge his portfolio. Assume that the S&P 500 currently stands at 970 and among the many put options available on this index are two that have caught his eye: (1) a 6-month put with a strike price of 950 that's trading at 26, and (2) a 6-month put with an 890 strike price that's quoted at 12.

a. How many S&P 500 puts would Wong have to buy to protect his $475,000 stock portfolio? How much would it cost him to buy the necessary number of 950 puts? How much would it cost to buy the 890 puts?
b. Now, considering the performance of both the put options and the Wong portfolio, determine how much *net* profit (or loss) Wong will earn from each of these put hedges if both the market (as measured by the S&P 500) and the Wong portfolio fall by 15% over the next 6 months? What if the market and the Wong portfolio fall by only 5%? What if they go up by 10%?
c. Do you think Wong should set up the put hedge and, if so, using which put option? Explain.
d. Finally, assume that the DJIA is currently at 7,950 and that a 6-month put option on the Dow is available with a strike price of 78 (which would be roughly equivalent to the S&P 950 put, above); the Dow option is currently trading at 2½. How many of these puts would Wong have to buy to protect his portfolio, and what would they cost? Would Wong be better off with the Dow options or the S&P 950 puts? Briefly explain.

 LG 3 LG 4

P11.5. Angelo Martino just purchased 500 shares of AT&E at 61½, and he has decided to write covered calls against these stocks. Accordingly, he sells 5 AT&E calls at their current market price of 5¾; the calls have 3 months to expiration and carry a strike price of 65. The stock pays a quarterly dividend of 80 cents a share.

a. Determine the total profit and holding period return Angelo will generate if the stock rises to $65 a share by the expiration date on the calls.
b. What happens to Angelo's profit (and return) if the price of the stock rises to more than $65 a share?
c. Does this covered call position offer any protection (or cushion) against a drop in the price of the stock? Explain.

LG 4 LG 5

P11.6. Here's your chance to try your hand at setting up an index-option *straddle*. Use the quotes for the DJIA index options listed in Figure 11.3. Assume that the market, as measured by the DJIA, stands at 8,000 and you decide to set up a *long straddle* on the Dow by buying 100 March 80 calls and an equal number of March 80 puts. (Ignore transaction costs.)
a. What will it cost you to set up the straddle, and how much profit (or loss) do you stand to make if the market falls by 554 points by the expiration dates on the options? What if it goes up by 554 points by expiration? What if it stays at 8,000?
b. Repeat part (a), but this time assume that you set up a *short straddle* by selling/writing 100 March 80 puts and calls.
c. What do you think of the use of option straddles as an investment strategy? What are the risks, and what are the rewards?

LG 6

P11.7. Assume that 1 warrant gives the holder the right to buy 2½ shares of stock at an exercise price of $40.
a. What is the value of this warrant if the current market price of the stock is $44? At what premium (in dollars and as a percentage) would the warrants be trading if they were quoted in the market at a price of $12.50?
b. Rework this problem given that 1 warrant gives the holder the right to buy just 1 share of stock at the stipulated exercise price. (In this case, assume that the warrants are currently trading in the market at a price of $5 each.)

LG 6

P11.8. A warrant carries an exercise price of $20; assume it takes 3 warrants to buy 1 share of stock. At what price would the warrant be trading if it sold at a 20% premium and the market price of the stock was $35 per share? What holding period return will an investor make if he or she buys these warrants (at a 20% premium) when the stock is trading at $35 and sells them sometime later, when the stock is at $48½ and the premium on the warrants has dropped to 15%?

Case Problem 11.1 *The Escobars' Investment Options*

LG 3 LG 4 LG 6

Phil Escobar is a successful businessman in Atlanta. The box-manufacturing firm he and his wife, Judy, founded several years ago has prospered. Because he is self-employed, Phil is building his own retirement fund. So far, he has accumulated a substantial sum in his investment account, mostly by following an aggressive investment posture; he does this because, as he puts it, "In this business, you never know when the bottom's gonna fall out." Phil has been following the stock of Rembrandt Paper Products (RPP), and after conducting extensive analysis, he feels the stock is about ready to move. Specifically, he believes that within the next 6 months, RPP could go to about $80 per share, from its current level of $57.50. The stock pays annual dividends of $2.40 per share, and Phil figures he would receive two quarterly dividend payments over his 6-month investment horizon.

In studying the company, Phil has learned that it has some warrants outstanding (they mature in 8 years and carry an exercise price of $45); also, it has 6-month call options (with $50 and $60 strike prices) listed on the CBOE. Each warrant is good for

1 share of stock, and they are currently trading at $15; the CBOE calls are quoted at $8 for the options with $50 strike prices and at $5 for the $60 options.

QUESTIONS

a. How many alternative investment vehicles does Phil have if he wants to invest in RPP for no more than 6 months? What if he has a 2-year investment horizon?

b. Using a 6-month holding period and assuming the stock does indeed rise to $80 over this time frame:

1. Find the market price of the warrants at the end of the holding period, given that they then trade at a premium of 10%.
2. Find the value of both calls, given that at the end of the holding period neither contains any investment premium.
3. Determine the holding period return for each of the four investment alternatives open to Phil Escobar.

c. Which course of action would you recommend if Phil simply wants to maximize profit? Would your answer change if other factors (e.g., comparative risk exposure) were considered along with return? Explain.

Case Problem 11.2 *Fred's Quandary: To Hedge or Not to Hedge*

LG 3 LG 4

A little more than 10 months ago, Fred Weaver, a mortgage banker in Phoenix, bought 300 shares of stock at $40 per share. Since then, the price of the stock has risen to $75 per share. It is now near the end of the year, and the market is starting to weaken; Fred feels there is still plenty of play left in the stock but is afraid the tone of the market will be detrimental to his position. His wife, Denise, is taking an adult education course on the stock market and has just learned about put and call hedges. She suggests that he use puts to hedge his position. Fred is intrigued by the idea, which he discusses with his broker—who advises him that the needed puts are indeed available on his stock. Specifically, he can buy 3-month puts, with $75 strike prices, at a cost of $550 each (quoted at 5½).

QUESTIONS

a. Given the circumstances surrounding Fred's current investment position, what benefits could be derived from using the puts as a hedge device? What would be the major drawback?

b. What will Fred's minimum profit be if he buys three puts at the indicated option price? How much would he make if he did not hedge but instead sold his stock immediately at a price of $75 per share?

c. Assuming Fred uses three puts to hedge his position, indicate the amount of profit he will generate if the stock moves to $100 by the expiration date of the puts. What if the stock drops to $50 per share?

d. Should Fred use the puts as a hedge? Explain. Under what conditions would you urge him *not* to use the puts as a hedge?

Home Page Exercises

http://hepg.aw.com **Keyword: Invest**

The use of put and call options has increased in recent years. These investment instruments are increasingly being used for both speculation and hedging. Individual investors and businesses have an interest in these instruments. The growth in the use of options is paralleled by the growth in related Web sites. The main thrust of many of these sites is to educate the investor on the risks and rewards of investing in options.

Web Address	*Primary Investment Focus*
www.cboe.com	The home page for the Chicago Board Options Exchange (CBOE)
www.options-iri.com/options/basic/basic.htm	An excellent comprehensive site for learning about options
www.adtrading.com	*Applied Derivatives Trading* magazine has articles on options and other derivatives; its *Beginners Corner* is for new investors
www.pacificex.com/options	Good information on specific options, such as LEAPS and index options
www.optionscentral.com	Both education and trading material, as well as links to other option sites

W11.1. Like common stock, equity option orders require the use of a ticker symbol to place and execute an order properly. The exact ticker symbol depends on the underlying stock, on whether the option is a put or a call, on the expiration month, and on the strike price. Find two call and two put option quotations in the *Wall Street Journal.* Go to the Web address shown and write out the full ticker symbol for these options.

www.options-iri.com/options/basic/read.htm

W11.2. The CBOE has an interactive calculator that allows investors to view the theoretical value of put and call options. Access this calculator at the following site. At this site, click on the *Education* button and then on the *Option Calculator* choice. Insert the strike price, stock price, and expiration month from an option listed in the *Wall Street Journal.* Change each of the following five variables one at a time: (a) strike price, (b) volatility, (c) annual interest rate, (d) annual dividend yield, and (e) expiration month. Observe and discuss what happens to the value of the options when each variable is changed.

www.cboe.com

CHAPTER 12 COMMODITIES AND FINANCIAL FUTURES

LEARNING GOALS

After studying this chapter, you should be able to:

LG 1 Describe the essential features of a futures contract and explain how the futures market operates.

LG 2 Explain the role that hedgers and speculators play in the futures market, including how profits are made and lost.

LG 3 Describe the commodities segment of the futures market and the basic characteristics of these investment vehicles.

LG 4 Discuss the various trading strategies investors can use with commodities, and explain how investment returns are measured.

LG 5 Explain the difference between a physical commodity and a financial future, and discuss the growing role of financial futures in the market today.

LG 6 Discuss the trading techniques that can be used with financial futures, and note how these securities can be used in conjunction with other investment vehicles.

Bear Stearns

It's not the biggest. It's not the most "buttoned-down." But in terms of sheer profitability, few Wall Street firms can match Bear Stearns. In 1997 the company earned $613 million on $3.53 billion in revenues. Like most Wall Street investment banks, Bear Stearns conducts futures and options activity. Its Futures Department advises clients on the use of exchange-traded futures and options in their global trading and hedging strategies. The firm's emphasis is on financial futures, principally interest rates, stock indexes, and foreign currencies. Specialists within the department also actively trade in the energy and tropical commodities (cocoa, coffee, and sugar) markets. Bear Stearns's Derivatives Department is an active trader of various derivative securities, such as interest rate swaps, equity swaps, and equity options, which can be combined with fixed-income securities, stocks, foreign exchange, and entire portfolios to create a wide array of risk management solutions.

The use of futures contracts for commodities and financial instruments is a very important tool to control risk. You'll see in this chapter how these investment vehicles work and how individual investors can use them.

The Futures Market

LG 1 LG 2

Psst, wanna buy some copper? How about some coffee, or pork bellies, or propane? Maybe the Japanese yen or Swiss franc strikes your fancy. Sound a bit unusual? Perhaps, but these items have one thing in common: They all represent investment vehicles. This is the more exotic side of investing—the market for commodities and financial futures—and it often involves a considerable amount of speculation. In fact, the risks are enormous, but with a little luck, the payoffs can be phenomenal, too. Even more important than luck, however, is the need for patience and know-how. Indeed, *these are specialized investment products that require specialized investor skills.*

The amount of futures trading in the United States has mushroomed over the past 25 years as an increasing number of investors have turned to futures trading as a way to earn attractive, highly competitive rates of return. But it's *not* the traditional commodities contracts that have drawn many of these investors; rather, it's the new investment vehicles that are being offered. That is, a major reason behind the growth in the volume of futures trading has been *the big jump in the number and variety of contracts available for trading.* Today, in addition to the traditional primary commodities, such as grains and metals, markets also exist for live animals, processed commodities, crude oil and gasoline, foreign currencies, money market securities, U.S. Treasury notes and bonds, Eurodollar securities, and common stocks (via stock market indexes). You can even buy listed put and call *options* on just about any actively traded futures contract. All these commodities and financial assets are traded in what is known as the *futures market.*

Market Structure

cash market
a market where a product or commodity changes hands in exchange for a cash price paid when the transaction is completed.

futures market
the organized market for the trading of futures contracts.

When a bushel of wheat is sold, the transaction takes place in the **cash market;** in other words, the bushel changes hands in exchange for a cash price paid to the seller. The transaction occurs at that point in time and for all practical purposes is completed then and there. Most traditional securities are traded in this type of market. However, a bushel of wheat could also be sold in the **futures market,** the organized market for the trading of futures contracts. In this market, the seller would not actually deliver the wheat until some mutually agreed-upon date in the future. As a result, the transaction would not be completed for some time: The seller would receive partial payment for the bushel of wheat at the time the agreement was entered into and the balance on delivery. The buyer, in turn, would own a highly liquid futures contract that could be held (and presented for delivery of the bushel of wheat) or traded in the futures market. No matter what the buyer does with the contract, as long as it is outstanding, the seller has a *legally binding obligation to make delivery* of the stated quantity of wheat on a specified date in the future, and the buyer/holder has a similar *obligation to take delivery* of the underlying commodity.

Futures Contracts

futures contract
a commitment to deliver a certain amount of some specified item at some specified date in the future.

delivery month
the time when a commodity must be delivered; defines the life of a futures contract.

A **futures contract** is a commitment to deliver a certain amount of a specified item at a specified date at a price agreed upon at the time the contract is sold. Each market establishes its own contract specifications, which include not only the quantity and quality of the item but also the delivery procedure and delivery month. The **delivery month** for a futures contract is much like the expiration date used on put and call options; it specifies when the commodity or item must be delivered and thus defines the life of the contract. For example, the Chicago Board of Trade specifies that each of its soybean contracts will involve 5,000 bushels of USDA Grade 2 yellow soybeans; delivery months are January, March, May, July, August, September, and November. In addition, futures contracts have *their own trading hours*. Unlike listed stocks and bonds, which begin and end trading at the same time, normal trading hours for commodities and financial futures vary widely. For example, oats trade from 9:30 A.M. to 1:15 P.M. (Central); silver, from 7:25 A.M. to 1:40 P.M.; live cattle, from 9:05 A.M. to 1:15 P.M.; U.S. Treasury bills, from 7:20 A.M. to 2:15 P.M.; and S&P 500 stock-index contracts, from 8:30 A.M. to 3:15 P.M. It may sound a bit confusing, but it seems to work.

Table 12.1 lists a cross section of 12 different commodities and financial futures. As you can see, the typical futures contract covers a large quantity of the underlying product or financial instrument. However, although the value of a single contract is normally quite large, the actual amount of investor capital required to deal in these vehicles is relatively small, because *all trading in this market is done on a margin basis.*

Options Versus Futures Contracts In many respects, futures contracts are closely related to the call options we studied in Chapter 11. Both involve the future delivery of an item at an agreed-upon price. But there is a *significant difference* between a futures contract and an options contract: A futures contract *obligates* a person to buy or sell a specified amount of a given commodity on or before a stated date, unless the contract is canceled or liquidated before it expires. In contrast, an option gives the holder the *right* to buy or sell a specific amount of a real or financial asset at a specific price over a specified period of time. In addition, whereas *price* (i.e., strike price) is one of the specified variables on a call option, it is *not* stated anywhere on a futures contract. Instead, the price on a futures contract is established through trading on the floor of a commodities exchange, which means that the delivery price is set by

TABLE 12.1 Futures Contract Dimensions

Contract	Size of a Contract*	Recent Market Value of a Single Contract**
Corn	5,000 bu	$ 12,962
Wheat	5,000 bu	17,150
Live cattle	40,000 lb	26,480
Pork bellies	40,000 lb	22,840
Coffee	37,500 lb	63,000
Cotton	50,000 lb	33,050
Gold	100 troy oz	28,340
Copper	25,000 lb	19,462
Japanese yen	12.5 million yen	97,500
Treasury bills	$1 million	949,300
Treasury bonds	$100,000	120,280
S&P 500 Stock Index	$250 times the index	242,375

*The size of some contracts may vary by exchange.
**Contract values are representative of those that existed in late 1997.

supply and demand at whatever price the contract sells for. Equally important, the risk of loss with an option is limited to the price paid for it, whereas a futures contract has *no such limit on exposure to loss.*

Major Exchanges

Futures contracts in this country got their start in the agricultural segment of the economy over 150 years ago, when individuals who produced, owned, and/or processed foodstuffs sought a way to protect themselves against adverse price movements. Later, futures contracts came to be traded by individuals who were not necessarily connected with agriculture but who wanted to make money with commodities by speculating on their price swings.

The first organized commodities exchange in this country was the Chicago Board of Trade, which opened its doors in 1848. Over time, additional markets opened, and at one time there were more than a dozen U.S. exchanges that dealt in listed futures contracts. However, like a lot of other industries, this market has gone through a recent period of consolidation, and there are now just eight commodities exchanges left in operation in this country. The Chicago Board of Trade (CBT) is the largest and most active U.S. exchange. (In fact, it's the largest commodities exchange in the world.) The CBT is followed in size by the Chicago Mercantile Exchange (CME), and the New York Mercantile Exchange (NYMerc). Together, these three exchanges account for more than 90 percent of all the trading conducted on American futures exchanges.

open outcry auction
in futures trading, an auction in which trading is done through a series of shouts, body motions, and hand signals.

hedgers
producers and processors who use futures contracts to protect their interest in an underlying commodity or financial instrument.

INVESTOR FACT

DRIVING THE DESK—Across the farm belt, rural women are organizing commodity clubs to plot hedging strategies on futures exchanges. As the U.S. government phases out crop subsidies, growers are looking for ways to get more income from their crops. One way to do that is to stop selling crops at harvest prices, usually the year's lowest, and instead use the futures market to lock in higher prices. The number of farmers using futures is growing quickly. More than 100,000 farms are already wired to get futures prices over a PC or dedicated terminal. Because many farm wives handle the family's bookkeeping, they are the ones attending futures trading seminars, subscribing to trading-advisory services, and accessing market information on the Internet. Besides, adds one farm wife, "Getting a farmer to do paperwork is like nailing butter to a wall . . . So I drive the desk."

Most exchanges deal in a number of different commodities or financial assets, and many commodities and financial futures are traded on more than one exchange. Although the exchanges are highly efficient and annual volume has surpassed the trillion-dollar mark, futures trading is still conducted by **open outcry auction:** As shown in Figure 12.1, actual trading on the floors of these exchanges is conducted through a series of shouts, body motions, and hand signals.

Trading in the Futures Market

Basically, the futures market contains two types of traders: hedgers and speculators. The market simply could not exist and operate efficiently without either one. The **hedgers** are commodities producers and processors (which today include financial institutions and corporate money managers) who use futures contracts as a way to protect their interest in the underlying commodity or financial instrument. For example, if a rancher thinks the price of cattle will drop in the near future, he will hedge his position by selling a futures contract on cattle in the hope of locking in as high a price as possible for his herd. In effect, the hedgers provide the underlying strength of the futures market and represent the very reason for its existence. *Speculators,* in contrast, give the market liquidity; they are the ones who trade futures contracts simply to earn a profit on expected swings in the price of a futures contract. They are the risk takers, the investors who have no inherent interest in any aspect of the commodity or financial future other than the price action and potential capital gains it can produce.

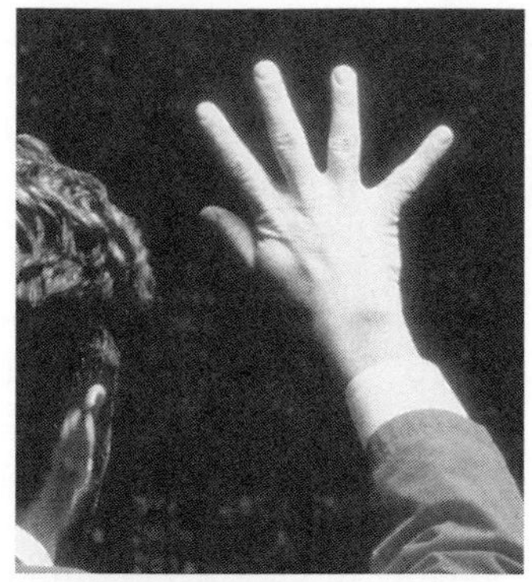

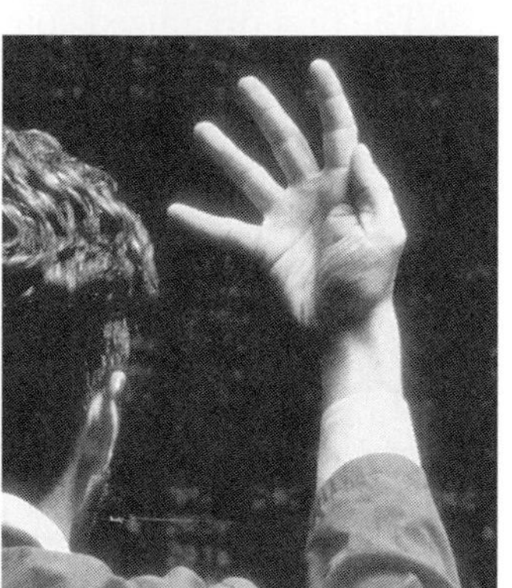

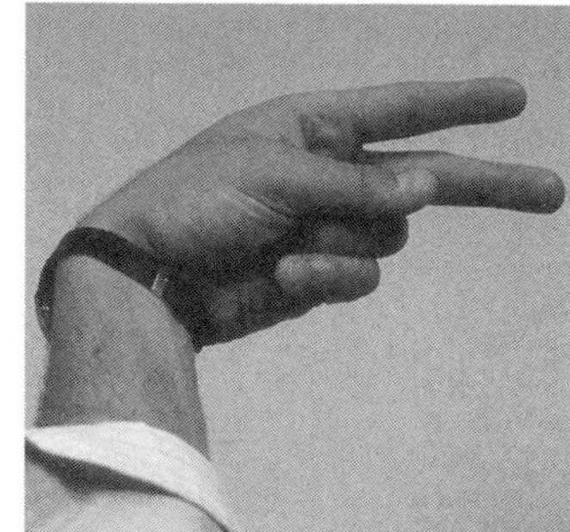

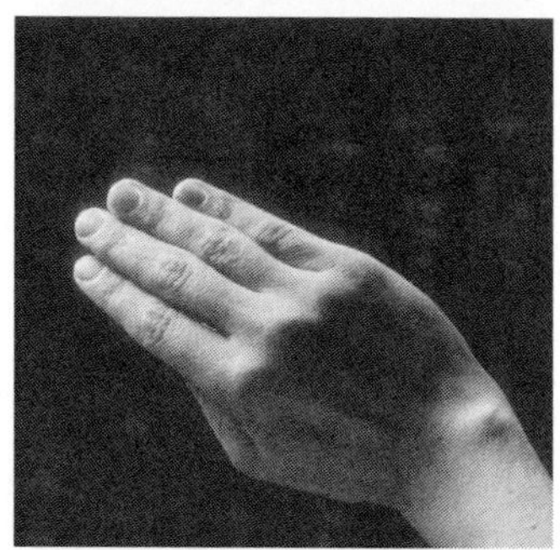

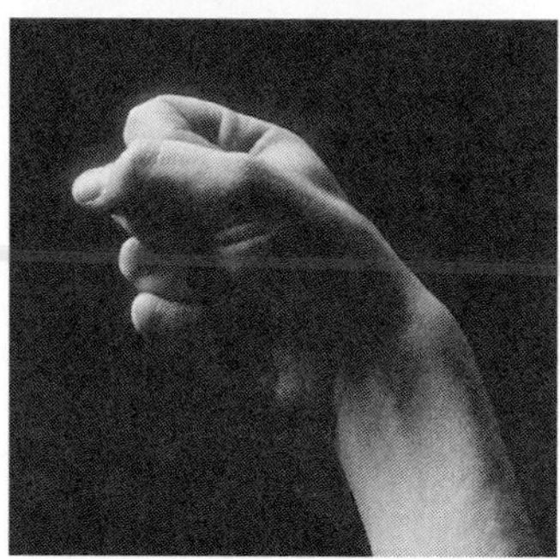

FIGURE 12.1 The Auction Market at Work on the Floor of the Chicago Board of Trade

Traders employ a system of open outcry and hand signals to indicate whether they wish to buy or sell and the price at which they wish to do so. Fingers held *vertically* indicate the number of contracts a trader wants to buy or sell. Fingers held *horizontally* indicate the fraction of a cent above or below the last traded full-cent price at which the trader will buy or sell. (Source: Chicago Board of Trade.)

Trading Mechanics

Once futures contracts are created, they can readily be traded in the market. Like common stocks and other traditional investment vehicles, futures contracts are bought and sold through local brokerage offices. Most firms have at least one or two people in each office who specialize in futures contracts. In addition, a number of commodity firms that deal only in futures contracts stand ready to help individuals with their investment needs. Except for setting up a special commodities trading account, there is really no difference between trading futures and dealing in stocks or bonds. The same types of orders are used, and the use of margin is the standard way of trading futures. Any investor can buy or sell any contract, with any delivery month, at any time, so long as it is currently being traded on one of the exchanges.

Buying a contract is referred to as taking a *long position,* whereas selling one is termed taking a *short position.* It is exactly like going long or short with stocks and has the same connotation: The investor who is long wants the price to rise, and the short seller wants it to drop. Both long and short positions can be liquidated simply by executing an offsetting transaction. The short seller,

round-trip commissions
the commission costs on both ends (buying and selling) of a securities transaction.

margin deposit
amount deposited with a broker to cover any loss in the market value of a futures contract that may result from adverse price movements.

initial deposit
the amount of investor capital that must be deposited with a broker at the time of a commodity transaction.

maintenance deposit
the minimum amount of margin that must be kept in a margin account at all times.

mark-to-the-market
a daily check of an investor's margin position, determined at the end of each session, at which time the broker debits or credits the account as needed.

for example, would cover his or her position by buying an equal amount of the contract. In general, less than 1% of all futures contracts are settled by delivery; the rest are offset prior to the delivery month. All trades are subject to normal transaction costs, which include **round-trip commissions** of about $60 to $90 for each contract traded. (A round-trip commission includes the commission costs on both ends of the transaction—to buy and to sell a contract.) The exact size of the commission depends on the number and type of contracts being traded.

Margin Trading

Buying on margin means putting up only a fraction of the total price in cash; margin, in effect, is the *amount of equity* that goes into the deal. Margin trading plays a crucial role in futures transactions because *all futures contracts are traded on a margin basis*. The margin required usually ranges from about 2% to 10% of the value of the contract, which is very low when compared to the margin required for stocks and most other types of securities. Furthermore, there is *no borrowing* required on the part of the investor to finance the balance of the contract; the margin, or **margin deposit,** as it is called with futures, exists simply as a way to guarantee fulfillment of the contract. The margin deposit is not a partial payment for the commodity or financial instrument, nor is it in any way related to the value of the product or item underlying the contract. Rather, it represents security to cover any loss in the market value of the contract that may result from adverse price movements.

The size of the required margin deposit is specified as a dollar amount. It varies according to the type of contract (i.e., the amount of price volatility in the underlying commodity or financial asset) and, in some cases, the exchange on which the commodity is traded. Table 12.2 gives the margin requirements for the same 12 commodities and financial instruments listed in Table 12.1 on page 460. Compared to the size and value of futures contracts, margin requirements are very low. The **initial deposit** noted in Table 12.2 is the amount of investor capital that must be deposited with the broker when the transaction is initiated and represents the amount of money required to make a given investment.

After the investment is made, the market value of a contract will, of course, rise and fall as the quoted price of the underlying commodity or financial instrument goes up or down. Such market behavior will cause the amount of margin on deposit to change. To be sure that an adequate margin is always on hand, investors are required to meet a second type of margin requirement, the **maintenance deposit.** This deposit is slightly less than the initial deposit and establishes the minimum amount of margin that must be kept in the account at all times. For instance, if the initial deposit on a commodity is $1,000 per contract, its maintenance margin might be $750. So long as the market value of the contract does not fall by more than $250 (the difference between the contract's initial and maintenance margins), the investor has no problem. But if the market moves against the investor and the value of the contract drops by more than the allowed amount, the investor will receive a *margin call.* He or she must then immediately deposit enough cash to bring the position back to the initial margin level.

An investor's margin position is checked daily via a procedure known as **mark-to-the-market.** That is, the gain or loss in a contract's value is determined at the end of each session, at which time the broker debits or credits the trader's account accordingly. In a falling market, an investor may receive a

TABLE 12.2 Margin Requirements for a Sample of Commodities and Financial Futures

	Initial Margin Deposit	Maintenance Margin Deposit
Corn	$ 1,000	$ 750
Wheat	1,000	750
Live cattle	1,000	750
Pork bellies	1,000	750
Coffee	2,500	1,875
Cotton	1,000	750
Gold	900	675
Copper	1,000	750
Japanese yen	2,500	1,900
Treasury bills	1,000	750
Treasury bonds	2,700	2,000
S&P 500 Stock Index	10,500	8,750

Note: These margin requirements were specified by a major full-service brokerage firm in late 1997; they may exceed the minimums established by the various exchanges. They are meant to be typical of the ongoing requirements that customers are expected to live up to. Depending on the volatility of the market, exchange-minimum margin requirements are changed frequently, and thus the requirements in this table are also subject to change on short notice.

number of margin calls and be required to make additional margin payments in order to keep the position above the maintenance margin level. Failure to do so will mean that the broker has no choice but to close out the position—that is, to sell the contract.

CONCEPTS IN REVIEW

12.1 What is a *futures contract?* Briefly explain how it is used as an investment vehicle.

12.2 Discuss the difference between a *cash market* and a *futures market.*

12.3 What is the major source of return to commodities speculators? How important to these investors is current income from dividends and interest?

12.4 Why are both hedgers and speculators important to the efficient operation of a futures market?

12.5 Explain how margin trading is conducted in the futures market.
a. What is the difference between an *initial deposit* and a *maintenance deposit?*
b. Are investors ever required to put up additional margin? If so, when?

http://hepg.aw.com

The largest exchange for trading futures contracts is the Chicago Board of Trade (CBT). The history of the CBT is very much the history of the futures markets. The following CBT page provides links both to a history of the exchange and to a comprehensive glossary of futures trading terms.

www.cbot.com/visitor/visitors.htm

Commodities

LG 3 LG 4

Physical commodities like grains, metals, wood, and meat make up a major portion of the futures market. They have been actively traded in this country for well over a century and still account for a good deal of the trading activity. The material that follows focuses on *commodities trading* and begins with a review of the basic characteristics and investment merits of these vehicles.

Basic Characteristics

Various types of physical commodities are found on nearly all of the U.S. futures exchanges (in fact, three of them deal only in commodities). The market for commodity contracts is divided into four major segments: grains and oilseeds, livestock and meat, food and fiber, and metals and petroleum. Such segmentation does not affect trading mechanics and procedures but provides a convenient way of categorizing commodities into groups based on similar underlying characteristics. Table 12.3 shows the diversity of the commodities market and the variety of contracts available. Although the list changes yearly, we can see from the table that investors had nearly three dozen different commodities to choose from in 1998, and a number of these (e.g., soybeans, wheat, and sugar) are available in several different forms or grades.

A Commodities Contract

Every commodity has its own specifications regarding the amounts and quality of the product being traded. Figure 12.2 is an excerpt from the "Futures Prices" section of the *Wall Street Journal* and shows the contract and quotation system used with commodities. Each commodity quote is made up of the same five parts, and all prices are quoted in an identical fashion. In particular, every commodities contract or quote specifies (1) the product; (2) the exchange on which

TABLE 12.3 Major Classes of Commodities

Grains and Oilseeds	*Metals and Petroleum*
Corn	Electricity
Oats	Copper
Soybeans	Gold
Soybean meal	Platinum
Soybean oil	Silver
Wheat	Palladium
Barley	Gasoline
Canola	Heating oil
Flaxseed	Crude oil
Rice	Gas oil
	Propane
	Natural gas
Livestock and Meat	*Food and Fiber*
Cattle—live	Cocoa
Cattle—feeder	Coffee
Hogs	Cotton
Pork bellies	Orange juice
	Sugar

FIGURE 12.2 Quotations on Actively Traded Commodity Futures Contracts

These quotes reveal at a glance key information about the various commodities, including the latest high, low, and closing ("settle") prices, as well as the lifetime high and low prices for each contract. (Source: *Wall Street Journal,* December 17, 1997.)

Tuesday, December 16, 1997

Open Interest Reflects Previous Trading Day

GRAINS AND OILSEEDS

CORN (CBT) 5,000 bu.; cents per bu.

	Open	High	Low	Settle	Change	Lifetime High	Lifetime Low	Open Interest
Dec	261¾	262	259	259¼	– ½	310	227½	5,118
Mr98	271¾	273½	270¾	271	– ¾	305	236	176,182
May	279	280¾	278¼	278½	– ½	310	241¾	45,960
July	284½	286¼	283½	284	– ½	315½	245	56,965
Sept	281	281½	279¾	279¾	– ¾	301	244	5,624
Dec	281¾	283	281	281¼	– ½	299½	247	33,439
Mr99	288	288	286½	286½	– ½	305	286½	989
July	295	295	294	294	– ½	312	256¼	320
Dec	277¾	277¾	276	276	– ¼	291½	265	665

Est vol na; vol Mon 63,413; open int 325,262, –6,324.

OATS (CBT) 5,000 bu.; cents per bu.

	Open	High	Low	Settle	Change	Lifetime High	Lifetime Low	Open Interest
Dec	150½	150½	147	147	– 2¾	183	143	10
Mr98	157	158½	154½	154¾	– 2¾	180	148¼	8,113
May	162	162	159	159	– 2	182½	151	1,578
July	164	164	163½	163½	– ¾	184	153	571
Sept	164	166½	164	164½	– 1	177	155	290
Dec	167	167	167	167	....	177½	163	116

Est vol na; vol Mon 448; open int 10,678, –104.

SOYBEANS (CBT) 5,000 bu.; cents per bu.

	Open	High	Low	Settle	Change	Lifetime High	Lifetime Low	Open Interest
Jan	689¾	693½	685½	686	– 2¾	752	583	56,415
Mar	690	694	686	686½	– 2½	749½	593	37,765
May	692	697½	691	691½	– 1¼	752	601	24,035
July	699	701	695	695½	– 1	753	611½	25,261
Aug	697	698	693	693	+ [illegible]	745	631	3,232
Sept	680	681½	677	677	+ 3½	723	637	185
Nov	670	672	667	667	+ ¼	717	597	9,979

Est vol na; vol Mon 61,694; open int 156,981, –198.

SOYBEAN MEAL (CBT) 100 tons; $ per ton.

	Open	High	Low	Settle	Change	Lifetime High	Lifetime Low	Open Interest
Dec	217.60	218.70	215.80	216.10	– 1.60	246.20	186.00	5,549
Ja98	212.20	213.50	210.50	210.70	– 1.40	239.50	185.50	27,266
Mar	209.50	210.30	207.60	207.70	– 1.10	234.40	184.50	34,803
May	207.00	208.50	206.30	206.30	– .40	231.00	185.50	22,680
July	208.00	209.50	207.50	207.60	+ .40	231.50	188.50	15,827
Aug	208.50	209.70	207.50	207.60	+ .10	231.50	189.00	4,553
Sept	208.50	209.00	207.50	207.70	+ .70	231.50	192.00	3,453
Oct	207.00	207.00	205.70	205.70	+ .40	226.00	190.00	748
Dec	207.00	207.20	205.50	205.50	+ .50	231.00	193.00	3,254

Est vol na; vol Mon 34,769; open int 118,142, –1,126.

SOYBEAN OIL (CBT) 60,000 lbs.; cents per lb.

	Open	High	Low	Settle	Change	Lifetime High	Lifetime Low	Open Interest
Dec	24.60	24.72	24.52	24.53	....	27.50	21.72	685
Ja98	24.70	24.90	24.68	24.69	+ .01	27.45	21.98	36,615
Mar	25.19	25.27	25.04	25.06	+ .02	27.50	22.20	38,072
May	25.35	25.40	25.23	25.27	+ .06	27.55	22.35	14,606
July	25.45	25.55	25.35	25.40	+ .08	27.40	22.40	12,112
Aug	25.40	25.50	25.30	25.30	+ .08	26.70	22.72	3,372
Sept	25.40	25.40	25.15	25.16	+ .09	26.15	22.90	1,048
Oct	25.35	25.35	24.85	24.95	+ .05	26.20	22.80	468
Dec	25.20	25.20	24.97	25.00	+ .03	26.30	23.00	1,161

Est vol na; vol Mon 21,915; open int 108,139, +3,350.

WHEAT (CBT) 5,000 bu.; cents per bu.

	Open	High	Low	Settle	Change	Lifetime High	Lifetime Low	Open Interest
Dec	332	332½	330½	331½	+ 2½	473½	327	112
Mr98	343¼	345¾	342¾	343	+ ½	470	340¾	55,142
May	351½	353	342	350¾	+ 1¼	439½	342	11,764
July	357	358	355¾	356¾	+ 1¼	425	333	19,077
Sept	362	363	362	362¾	+ 2¼	403	359	458
Dec	370	372¼	370	371	+ 1½	417	368	2,880

Est vol na; vol Mon 16,707; open int 89,490, +500.

WHEAT (KC) 5,000 bu., cents per bu.

	Open	High	Low	Settle	Change	Lifetime High	Lifetime Low	Open Interest
Dec	343	343	343	343	+ 1	498	340	335
Mr98	354	356½	351	351½	– ¼	491	350	28,410
May	360½	363½	358	358¼	– ¾	450	350	6,171
July	366	370½	365½	366	+ 1¼	408½	333	7,665
Sept	....	....	....	369½	+ ½	410	335	335
Dec	381	381	378	378	....	418½	377	465

Est vol na; vol Mon 7,919; open int 43,386, –136.

WHEAT (MPLS) 5,000 bu.; cents per bu.

	Open	High	Low	Settle	Change	Lifetime High	Lifetime Low	Open Interest
Dec	369	369	369	369	+ 3½	479	349	7
Mr98	377	380¾	375½	376	+ ½	469	361	14,525
May	383	385¼	380½	381	– ¼	440	363	3,094
July	389	391½	388¾	387	+ 1	416	368	1,030
Sept	394	395	391½	391	+ ½	418	360	627

Est vol na; vol Mon 2,557; open int 19,380, +10.

CANOLA (WPG) 20 metric tons; Can. $ per ton

	Open	High	Low	Settle	Change	Lifetime High	Lifetime Low	Open Interest
Jan	381.60	382.00	379.50	380.40	+ 1.00	407.00	337.00	19,003
Mar	387.20	388.00	385.30	386.20	+ .40	412.30	339.00	21,579
May	390.90	391.50	389.90	390.80	+ 1.00	416.40	341.00	2,942
July	395.00	395.00	395.00	395.00	+ 1.50	417.40	366.00	429
Sept	390.00	391.00	390.00	391.00	– 1.50	391.00	363.50	208
Nov	366.50	368.50	366.50	368.50	+ 5.00	384.00	365.00	457

Est vol 5,415; vol Mn 9,117; open int 44,678, –963.

	Open	High	Low	Settle	Change	Lifetime High	Lifetime Low	Open Interest
July	582.0	596.5	582.0	596.0	+ 6.0	700.0	438.0	6,409
Sept		....	....	595.7	+ 6.0	592.5	453.0	808
Dec	592.0	596.0	591.0	595.3	+ 6.0	734.0	448.5	5,647
Mr99		....	....	594.9	+ 6.0	550.0	473.0	1,119
July		....	....	593.7	+ 6.0	660.0	472.0	1,257
Dec		....	....	591.5	+ 6.0	720.0	484.0	1,484
Jl00		....	....	591.5	+ 6.0	590.0	538.0	905
Dec		....	....	591.5	+ 6.0	585.0	537.0	436

Est vol 17,000; vol Mn 11,170; open int 92,941, +697.

CRUDE OIL, Light Sweet (NYM) 1,000 bbls.; $ per bbl.

	Open	High	Low	Settle	Change	Lifetime High	Lifetime Low	Open Interest
Jan	18.17	18.25	17.97	18.17	....	22.65	17.04	64,875
Feb	18.44	18.45	18.20	18.37	+ 0.02	22.30	17.15	101,969
Mar	18.54	18.62	18.40	18.56	+ 0.02	22.05	17.30	41,197
Apr	18.60	18.78	18.60	18.74	+ 0.02	21.75	17.38	24,637
May	18.85	18.91	18.75	18.88	+ 0.02	21.59	17.39	20,606
June	18.85	18.99	18.84	18.96	+ 0.03	21.35	17.17	34,433
July	18.92	19.06	18.90	19.01	+ 0.04	21.05	17.60	15,675
Aug	18.97	19.09	18.97	19.04	+ 0.05	21.12	18.80	15,963
Sept	19.00	19.10	18.95	19.06	+ 0.05	20.82	17.94	8,430
Oct	19.14	19.14	19.11	19.08	+ 0.05	20.75	17.75	6,445
Nov	19.15	19.15	19.02	19.10	+ 0.05	20.63	18.95	4,300
Dec	19.05	19.15	19.04	19.12	+ 0.05	20.74	17.05	18,960
Ja99	19.00	19.15	19.00	19.12	+ 0.05	20.30	17.85	9,828
Feb	19.03	19.09	19.02	19.11	+ 0.05	20.32	18.90	7,237
Mar	19.07	19.07	19.07	19.09	+ 0.05	20.20	18.70	4,408
Apr	....	....	....	19.08	+ 0.06	20.27	19.00	3,824
May	19.05	19.05	19.00	19.07	+ 0.06	20.29	19.00	1,160
June	19.05	19.05	19.00	19.07	+ 0.07	20.47	17.80	8,509
July	....	....	....	19.06	+ 0.07	20.14	18.93	1,621
Aug	19.04	19.04	19.04	19.05	+ 0.06	19.47	19.04	335
Sept	19.03	19.03	19.03	19.04	+ 0.06	20.10	19.03	753
Oct	....	....	....	19.03	+ 0.06	20.14	19.21	1,608
Nov	18.97	18.97	18.97	19.01	+ 0.06	19.90	18.97	566
Dec	18.95	18.96	18.95	18.99	+ 0.06	20.75	17.62	12,665
Dc00	....	....	....	18.97	+ 0.06	20.75	18.80	5,797
Jan	18.96	18.96	18.96	18.98	+ 0.06	19.15	18.96	2,093
Feb	....	....	....	18.97	+ 0.06	20.16	19.16	733
Mar	....	....	....	18.97	+ 0.06	20.10	19.16	218
June	....	....	....	18.97	+ 0.06	20.10	18.90	5,200
Dc01	....	....	....	18.97	+ 0.06	20.98	18.80	4,866
Dc02	....	....	....	18.97	+ 0.06	21.38	19.10	5,445
Dc03	....	....	....	19.01	+ 0.06	22.00	18.91	3,888
Dc04	....	....	....	19.05	+ 0.06	19.07	19.07	3

Est vol 101,486; vol Fri 81,552; open int 438,470, –8,445.

HEATING OIL NO. 2 (NYM) 42,000 gal.; $ per gal.

	Open	High	Low	Settle	Change	Lifetime High	Lifetime Low	Open Interest
Jan	.5160	.5220	.5110	.5159	+ .0008	.6375	.5110	42,966
Feb	.5225	.5245	.5165	.5206	– .0003	.6360	.5165	39,296
Mar	.5240	.5260	.5190	.5221	– .0003	.6240	.5190	16,870
Apr	.5180	.5205	.5160	.5181	– .0003	.6050	.5160	9,787
May	.5140	.5155	.5130	.5131	– .0003	.5880	.5130	8,065
June	.5130	.5150	.5125	.5111	– .0008	.5755	.5125	10,346
July	.5150	.5175	.5150	.5131	– .0003	.5720	.5145	4,131
Aug	.5220	.5220	.5220	.5186	– .0003	.5750	.5220	3,875
Sept	.5300	.5305	.5295	.5266	– .0003	.5840	.5290	4,251
Oct	.5375	.5375	.5375	.5341	– .0003	.5850	.5370	1,423
Nov	.5440	.5475	.5440	.5416	– .0003	.5905	.5440	1,070
Dec	.5525	.5545	.5525	.5491	– .0003	.5900	.5515	2,638
Ja99	.5580	.5580	.5580	.5521	– .0003	.5950	.5540	1,362
Feb	.5570	.5570	.5570	.5506	– .0003	.5850	.5520	446
Mar	.5500	.5500	.5500	.5431	– .0003	.5830	.5489	426
Apr	.5350	.5350	.5350	.5286	– .0003	.5900	.5315	172

Est vol 38,926; vol Fri 21,597; 147,214, –1,068.

GASOLINE-NY Unleaded (NYM)) 42,000 gal.; $ per gal.

	Open	High	Low	Settle	Change	Lifetime High	Lifetime Low	Open Interest
Jan	.5495	.5560	.5455	.5551	+ .0067	.6330	.5330	27,008
Feb	.5505	.5585	.5490	.5574	+ .0042	.6300	.5375	28,054
Mar	.5570	.5635	.5555	.5629	+ .0037	.6300	.5500	12,101
Apr	.5835	.5890	.5835	.5889	+ .0027	.6530	.5820	10,355
May	.5830	.5885	.5830	.5871	+ .0024	.6510	.5800	10,671
June	.5785	.5820	.5775	.5821	+ .0024	.6270	.5775	7,814
July	.5720	.5720	.5720	.5756	+ .0022	.6345	.5720	6,687
Aug	....	....	....	.5671	+ .0022	.6110	.5680	3,347
Sept	.5590	.5590	.5590	.5581	+ .0022	.6150	.5560	3,699
Oct	....	....	....	.5441	+ .0022	.5780	.5650	151

Est vol 35,476; vol Fri 20,818; open int 110,003, –667.

NATURAL GAS, (NYM) 10,000 MMBtu.; $ per MMBtu's

	Open	High	Low	Settle	Change	Lifetime High	Lifetime Low	Open Interest
Jan	2.309	2.415	2.305	2.409	+ .102	3.740	2.075	41,338
Feb	2.273	2.370	2.270	2.369	+ .096	3.215	2.010	35,353
Mar	2.225	2.305	2.225	2.299	+ .066	2.820	1.930	24,257
Apr	2.178	2.220	2.178	2.220	+ .042	2.460	1.825	11,843
May	2.170	2.195	2.170	2.192	+ .027	2.350	1.830	9,359
June	2.185	2.185	2.170	2.185	+ .020	2.330	1.745	8,770
July	2.175	2.185	2.170	2.185	+ .020	2.325	1.852	9,485
Aug	2.185	2.190	2.175	2.185	+ .018	2.325	1.845	9,234
Sept	2.190	2.190	2.180	2.195	+ .018	2.320	1.850	6,544
Oct	2.225	2.235	2.215	2.230	+ .018	2.350	1.840	6,018
Nov	2.355	2.355	2.340	2.352	+ .016	2.480	1.915	4,150
Dec	2.485	2.490	2.480	2.483	+ .014	2.615	1.950	7,302

the contract is traded; (3) the size of the contract (in bushels, pounds, tons, etc.); (4) the method of valuing the contract, or pricing unit (e.g., cents per pound or dollars per ton); and (5) the delivery month. Using a corn contract as an illustration, we can see each of these parts in the following illustration:

KEY
1 the product
2 the exchange
3 the size of the contract
4 the pricing unit
5 the delivery months

	Open	High	Low	Settle	Change	Lifetime High	Lifetime Low	Open Interest
1 2 3 4								
Corn (CBT)—5,000 bu.; cents per bu.								
May	253½	253¾	252¼	252½	−1¾	286½	230½	42,796
July	258	258	256½	256¾	−1¾	288	233	60,477
5 Sept.	260	260½	259	259	−1½	263	236	7,760
Dec.	263½	264	262½	263	−1¼	267¼	244	41,638
Mar. 99	271¾	272	270½	271	−1¼	276	254¾	11,098
May	277¼	278	276¼	277	−1	281	273¼	1,326

settle price
the closing price (last price of the day) for commodities and financial futures.

open interest
the number of contracts currently outstanding on a commodity or financial future.

The quotation system used for commodities is based on the size of the contract and the pricing unit. The financial media generally report the open, high, low, and closing prices for each delivery month. With commodities, the last price of the day, or the closing price, is known as the **settle price.** Also reported, at least by the *Wall Street Journal,* is the amount of **open interest** in each contract—that is, the number of contracts currently outstanding. Note in the above illustration that the settle price for May corn was 252½. The pricing system is cents per bushel, so this means that the contract was being traded at $2.52½ per bushel and that the market value of the contract was $12,625 (each contract involves 5,000 bushels and each bushel is worth $2.52½; thus 5,000 × $2.525 = $12,625).

Price Behavior

Commodity prices react to a unique set of economic, political, and international pressures—as well as to the weather. Although the explanation of *why* commodity prices change is beyond the scope of this book, it should be clear that they do move up and down just like any other investment vehicle, which is precisely what speculators want. However, because we are dealing in such large trading units (5,000 bushels of this or 40,000 pounds of that), even a modest price change can have an enormous impact on the market value of a contract and therefore on investor returns or losses. For example, if the price of corn goes up or down by just 20 cents per bushel, the value of a *single contract* will change by $1,000. A corn contract can be bought with a $750 initial margin deposit, so it is easy to see the effect this kind of price behavior can have on investor return.

But do commodity prices really move all that much? Judge for yourself: The price change columns in Figure 12.2 show some excellent examples of sizable price changes that occur from one day to the next. Note, for example, that December oats fell $137.50, December soybean meal fell $160, December wheat rose $175, and the January natural gas contract went up a whopping $1,020. Now, keep in mind that these are *daily* price swings that occurred on *single* contracts. These are sizable changes, even by themselves; but when you look at them relative to the (very small) original investment required (sometimes as low as $1,000), they quickly add up to serious returns (or losses)! And they occur not because of the volatility of the underlying prices but because of the sheer magnitude of the commodities contracts themselves.

Clearly, this kind of price behavior is one of the magnets that draws investors to commodities. The exchanges recognize the volatile nature of commodities contracts and try to put lids on price fluctuations by imposing daily price limits and maximum daily price ranges. (Similar limits are also put on financial futures.) The **daily price limit** restricts the interday change in the price of the underlying commodity. For example, the price of corn can change by no more than 10 cents per bushel from one day to the next, and the daily limit on copper is 3 cents per pound. Such limits, however, still leave plenty of room to turn a quick profit. For example, the daily limits on corn and copper translate into per-day changes of $500 for one corn contract and $750 for a copper contract. The **maximum daily price range,** in contrast, limits the amount the price can change *during* the day and is usually equal to twice the daily limit restrictions. For example, the daily price limit on corn is 10 cents per bushel and its maximum daily range is 20 cents per bushel.

daily price limit
restriction on the day-to-day change in the price of an underlying commodity.

maximum daily price range
the amount a commodity price can change during the day; usually equal to twice the daily price limit.

Return on Invested Capital

Futures contracts have only one source of return: the capital gains that can be earned when prices move in a favorable direction. There is no current income of any kind. The volatile price behavior of futures contracts is one reason why high returns are possible; the other is leverage. That is, because all futures trading is done on margin, it takes only a small amount of money to control a large investment position and to participate in the price swings that accompany many futures contracts. Of course, the use of leverage also means that it is possible for an investment to be wiped out with just one or two bad days.

Investment return can be measured by calculating **return on invested capital.** This is simply a variation of the standard holding period return formula, where return is based on the *amount of money actually invested in the contract,* rather than on the value of the contract itself. It is used because of the generous amount of leverage (margin) used in commodities trading. The return on invested capital for a commodities position can be determined according to the following simple formula:

return on invested capital
return to investors based on the amount of money actually invested in a security, rather than the value of the contract itself.

Equation 12.1

$$\text{Return on invested capital} = \frac{\text{selling price of commodity contract} - \text{purchase price of commodity contract}}{\text{amount of margin deposit}}$$

Equation 12.1 can be used for both long and short transactions. To see how it works, assume you just bought two September corn contracts at 280 ($2.80 per bushel) by depositing the required initial margin of $2,000 ($1,000 for each contract). Your investment amounts to only $2,000, but you control 10,000 bushels of corn worth $28,000 at the time they were purchased. Now, assume that September corn has just closed at 294, so you decide to sell out and take your profit. Your return on invested capital is

$$\text{Return on invested capital} = \frac{\$29{,}400 - \$28{,}000}{\$2{,}000}$$

$$= \frac{\$1{,}400}{\$2{,}000} = \underline{\underline{70.0\%}}$$

Clearly, this high rate of return was due not only to an increase in the price of the commodity but also—and perhaps more crucially—to the fact that you were using very low margin. (The initial margin in this particular transaction equaled just 7% of the underlying value of the contract.)

Trading Commodities

Investing in commodities takes one of three forms. The first, *speculating*, involves using commodities as a way to generate capital gains. In essence, speculators try to capitalize on the wide price swings that are characteristic of so many commodities. Figure 12.3 provides daily futures prices (in cents per bushel) for corn contracts over the 12-month period ending February 1998, and graphically illustrates the volatile behavior of commodity prices. Although such price movements appeal to speculators, they frighten many other investors. As a result, some of these more cautious investors turn to *spreading*, the second form of commodities investing. Futures investors use this trading technique much like the spreading that's done with put and call options, as a way to capture some of the benefits of volatile commodities prices but without all the exposure to loss.

Finally, commodities futures can be used as *hedging* vehicles. A hedge in the commodities market is more of a technical strategy and is used almost exclusively by producers and processors to protect a position in a product or commodity. For example, a producer or grower would use a commodity hedge to obtain as *high a price* as possible for the goods he or she sells. The processor or manufacturer who uses the commodity, however, would use a hedge for the opposite reason: to obtain the goods at as *low a price* as possible. A successful hedge, in effect, means added income to producers and lower costs to processors. Let's now look briefly at the two trading strategies that are most used by individual investors—speculating and spreading—to see not only what they are, but also to gain a better understanding of how commodities can be used as investment vehicles.

INVESTOR FACT

CALL IT THE FORREST GUMP FUTURES CONTRACT— We're talking about one of the futures contracts listed on the Minneapolis Grain Exchange, and it has nothing to do with grain and even less to do with Minneapolis. This commodities exchange is the only one in the world where *shrimp futures contracts* are traded. The exchange began trading white shrimp futures in July 1993 and in late 1994 added futures contracts on black tiger shrimp. For example, each black tiger shrimp contract covers 5,000 pounds of the tiny creatures and, using early 1995 prices (of $6.45 per pound), was valued at about $32,000. All of which makes you wonder: Would Bubba have considered this another use for shrimp?

Speculating

Speculators are in the market for one reason: They expect the price of a commodity to go up or down, and they hope to capitalize on it by going long or short. To see why a speculator would go long when prices are expected to rise, consider an individual who buys a March silver contract at 595½ (i.e., $5.95½ an ounce) by depositing the required initial margin of $1,300. One silver contract involves 5,000 troy ounces, so it has a market value of $29,775. If silver goes up, the investor makes money. Assume that it does and that by February (1 month before the contract expires), the price of the contract rises to 614. The speculator then liquidates the contract and makes a profit of 18½ cents per ounce (614 − 595½). That means a $925 profit from an investment of just $1,300—which translates into a return on invested capital of 71.2%.

Of course, instead of rising, the price of silver could have dropped by 18½ cents per ounce. In this case, the investor would have lost most of his original investment ($1,300 − $925 leaves only $375, out of which would have to come a round-trip commission of $60 or $70). But the drop in price would be just what a *short seller* is after. Here's why: You sell "short" the March silver

FIGURE 12.3 The Behavior of Commodity Prices over Time

This graph shows the volatile nature of commodity prices and underscores the investor's need for know-how when dealing in commodities. (Source: Courtesy of *Commodity Price Charts,* Cedar Falls, Iowa, 800-635-3931.)

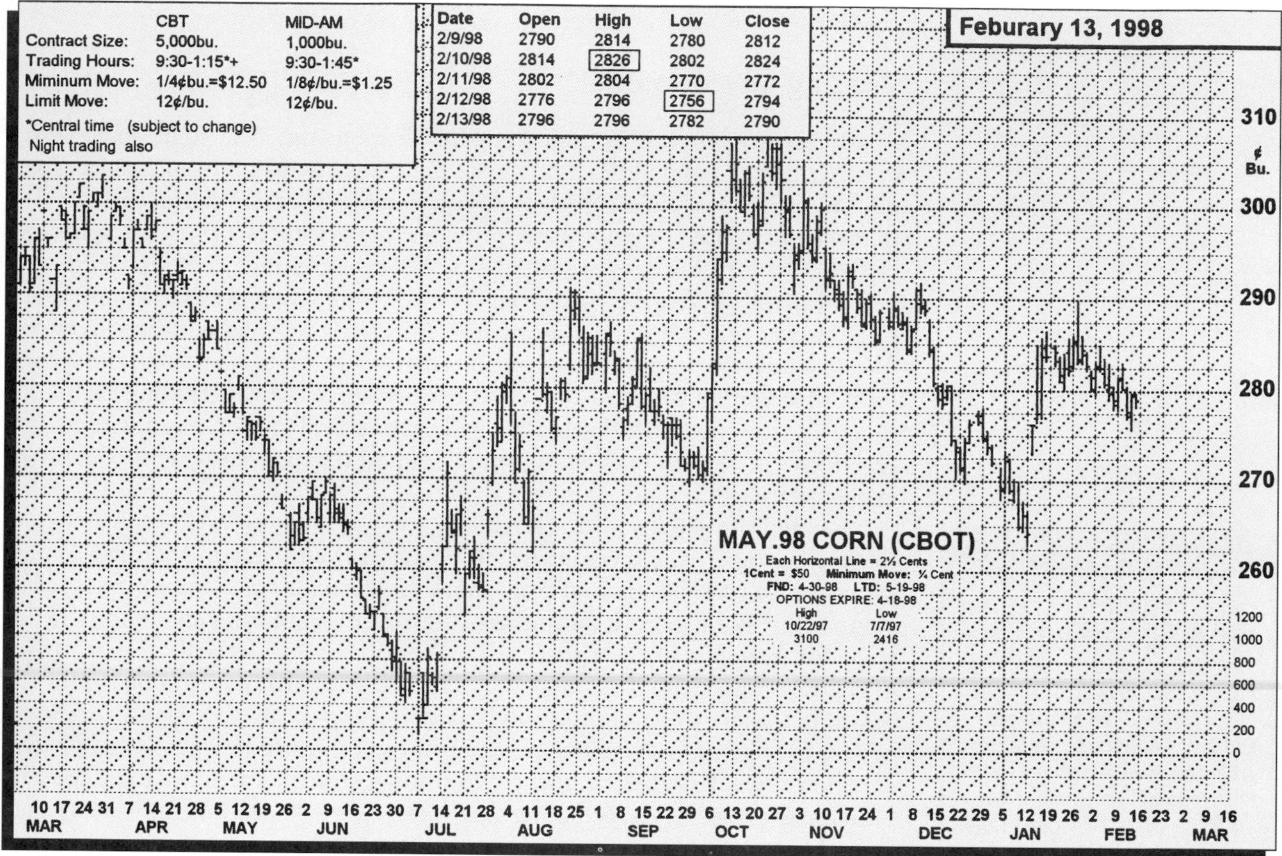

at 595½ and buy it back sometime later at 577. Clearly, the difference between the selling price and the purchase price is the same 18½ cents, but in this case it is *profit,* because the selling price exceeds the purchase price. (See Chapter 2 for a review of short selling.)

Spreading

Instead of attempting to speculate on the price behavior of a futures contract, you might choose to follow the more conservative tactic of *spreading.* Much like spreading with put and call options, the idea is to combine two or more different contracts into one investment position that offers the potential for generating a modest amount of profit while restricting your exposure to loss. One very important reason for spreading in the commodities market is that, unlike options, *there is no limit to the amount of loss that can occur with a futures contract.* You set up a spread by buying one contract and simultaneously selling another. Although one side of the transaction will lead to a loss, you hope that the profit earned from the other side will more than offset the loss, and that the net result will be at least a modest amount of profit. And if you're wrong, the spread will serve to limit (but not eliminate) any losses. Here is a simple example of how a spread might work: Suppose you buy contract A at 533½ and at the same time short sell contract B for 575½. Sometime later, you close out your interest in contract A by selling it at 542 and simultaneously cover your short position in B by purchasing a contract at 579. Although you made a profit of 8½ points on the long position, contract A (542 − 533½), you lost 3½ points on the contract you shorted, B (575½ − 579). The net effect, however, is a profit of 5 points, which, if you were dealing in cents per pound, would mean a profit of $250 on a 5,000-pound contract. All sorts of commodity spreads can be set up for almost any type of investment situation. Most of them, however, are highly sophisticated and require specialized skills.

Commodities and the Individual Investor

Commodities appeal to investors because of the high rates of return they offer and their ability to act as inflation hedges during periods of rapidly rising consumer prices. More often than not, in periods of high inflation investors lose more in purchasing power than they gain from after-tax returns. Under such conditions, investors can be expected to seek outlets that provide better protection against inflation, which explains why the interest in commodities tends to pick up with inflation.

Commodities can play an important role in your portfolio so long *as you understand the risks involved and are well versed in the principles and mechanics of commodities trading*. Making money in the commodities market is extremely difficult. It may look easy—perhaps too easy—but very few investors (even the most experienced) are able to earn big returns consistently by trading futures. Indeed, for most people, the quickest way to lose money in commodities is to jump in without knowing what they are doing. Because there is the potential for a lot of price volatility and because commodity trading is done on a very low margin, the potential for loss is enormous. Accordingly, most experts recommend that only a portion of your investment capital be committed to commodities. The specific amount would, of course, be a function of your aversion to risk and the amount of resources you have available. You have to be prepared mentally and should be in a position financially to absorb losses—perhaps a number of them. And not only should an adequate cash reserve be kept on hand (to absorb losses or to meet margin calls), but it's also a good idea to maintain a diversified holding of commodities in order to spread your risks.

If you decide to try your hand at commodities, keep in mind there are several different ways of investing. You can invest directly in the commodities market by trading futures contracts on your own, or, to reduce your risk exposure a bit, you might want to trade put and call options on some of the more actively traded futures contracts. Alternatively, you can invest in limited partnership *commodity pools*. These pools, which are a lot like mutual funds, might be used by individuals who wish to invest in the commodities market but lack the time or expertise to manage their own investments. Still another alternative is to consider investing in *commodities-oriented futures funds.* These are essentially mutual funds that pool investors' money and actively trade futures contracts. Most of these funds invest only about 20% to 25% of their money in margined futures contracts and then keep the rest in interest-earning assets such as T-bills or bonds. These funds may offer investors a way to gain some exposure to the commodities market, but they do have a downside: Not only can their performance be highly volatile, but their costs can also be quite high, sometimes running to as much as 20% of assets under management. All of which should come as no surprise, because in this market, there's no easy way to make money!

CONCEPTS IN REVIEW

12.6 List and briefly define the five essential parts of a commodity contract. Which parts have a direct bearing on the price behavior of the contract?

12.7 Briefly define each of the following:
- a. Settle price
- b. Daily price limit
- c. Open interest
- d. Maximum daily price range
- e. Delivery month

12.8 What is the one source of return on futures contracts? What measure is used to calculate the return on a commodity contract?

12.9 Note several approaches to investing in commodities and explain the investment objectives of each.

12.10 Explain why you should be well versed in the behavior and investment characteristics of commodities futures when investing in this market. Why should futures holdings be well diversified?

http://hepg.aw.com

Understanding how the market for commodities works is the key to understanding how money can be made by investing in commodity futures. The Web site listed has an electronic course entitled "A Short Course Introducing Commodity Market & Futures Trading."

tfc-charts.w2d.com/tafm/

Financial Futures

LG 5 LG 6

financial futures
a type of futures contract in which the underlying "commodity" is a financial asset, such as debt securities, foreign currencies, or market baskets of common stocks.

Another dimension of the futures market is **financial futures,** a segment of the market in which futures contracts are traded on a variety of financial instruments. Actually, financial futures are little more than an extension of the commodities concept. They were created for much the same reason as commodity futures, they are traded in the same market, their prices behave a lot like commodities, and they have similar investment merits. Yet despite all these similarities, financial futures are a unique type of investment vehicle. Let's now look more closely at these instruments and how investors can use them.

The Financial Futures Market

Even though the financial futures market has been around for only 25 years or so, it is today a dominant force in the whole futures market. Indeed, the level of trading today in the financial futures market far surpasses that of the traditional commodities market. Much of the interest in financial futures is due to hedgers and big institutional investors who use these contracts as portfolio- and debt-management tools. But individual investors can also find plenty of opportunities here. For example, financial futures offer yet another way to speculate on the behavior of interest rates. And they can also be used to speculate in the stock market. They even offer a convenient way to speculate in the highly specialized, and often highly profitable, foreign currency markets.

The financial futures market was established in response to the economic turmoil the United States experienced during the 1970s. The dollar had become unstable on the world market and was causing serious problems for multinational firms. Closer to home, interest rates had begun to behave in a volatile manner, which caused severe difficulties for corporate treasurers, financial institutions, and money managers in general. All these parties needed a way to protect themselves from the ravages of wide fluctuations in the value of the dollar and interest rates, so a market for financial futures was born. Hedging provided the economic rationale for the market in financial futures, but speculators were quick to respond as they found the price volatility of these instruments attractive and at times highly profitable. At present, most of the financial futures trading in this country occurs on just three exchanges—the Chicago Board of Trade, the MidAmerica Commodity Exchange, and the Chicago Mercantile Exchange—as well as on several foreign exchanges, the most noteworthy of which is the London International Financial Futures Exchanges. The three basic types of financial futures include foreign currencies, debt securities, and stock indexes.

Foreign Currencies, Interest Rates, and Stock Indexes

currency futures
futures contracts on foreign currencies, traded much like commodities.

The financial futures market started rather inconspicuously in May 1972, with the listing of a handful of foreign currency contracts. Known as **currency futures,** they have become a major hedging vehicle as international trade to and from this country has mushroomed. Most of the currency trading today is conducted in the following seven foreign currencies:

- British pound
- German mark
- Swiss franc
- Mexican peso
- Canadian dollar
- Japanese yen
- Australian dollar

All of these currencies involve countries with which the United States has strong international trade and exchange ties.

interest rate futures
futures contracts on debt securities.

In October 1975, the first futures contract on debt securities, or **interest rate futures,** as they are more commonly known, was established when trading started in GNMA pass-through certificates (a special type of mortgage-backed bond issued by an agency of the U.S. government). In time, other issues were added, and today trading is carried out in a variety of U.S. and foreign debt securities and interest rates, including:

- U.S. Treasury bills
- U.S. Treasury notes
- U.S. Treasury bonds
- Municipal bonds (via a muni bond index)
- Various 30-day interest rate contracts (e.g., 30-day Federal Funds)
- 90-day Euromarket deposits (e.g., Eurodollar deposits, Euromark deposits, etc.)
- Various foreign government bonds (e.g., bonds issued by the British, German, and Canadian governments)

Interest rate futures were immediately successful, and their popularity continues to grow today.

stock-index futures
futures contracts written on broad-based measures of stock market performance (e.g., the S&P 500 Stock Index), allowing investors to participate in the general movements of the stock market.

In February 1982, a new trading vehicle was introduced: the stock-index futures contract. **Stock-index futures,** as they are called, are contracts pegged to broad-based measures of stock market performance. At present, trading is done in seven U.S. stock-index futures:

- The Dow Jones Industrial Average
- The S&P 500 Index
- The S&P MidCap 400 Index
- The NYSE Composite Index
- The Value Line Composite Stock Index
- The Nasdaq 100 Index
- The Russell 2000 Index

In addition to these U.S. indexes, investors can also trade stock-index futures contracts based on the London, Tokyo, Paris, Sydney, and Toronto stock exchanges. Stock-index futures, which are similar to the stock-index options we discussed in Chapter 11, allow investors to participate in the general movements of the entire stock market. These index futures (and other futures contracts) represent a type of *derivative security* because they, like options, derive their value from the price behavior of the assets that underlie them. In the case of stock-index futures, they are supposed to reflect the general performance of the stock market as a whole, as measured by a particular index like the S&P 500. Thus, when the market, as measured by the S&P 500, goes up, the value of an S&P 500 futures contract should go up as well. Accordingly, investors can use stock-index futures as a way to buy the market—or a reasonable proxy thereof—and thereby participate in broad market moves.

Contract Specifications

In principle, financial futures contracts are like commodities contracts. They control large sums of the underlying financial instrument and are issued with a variety of delivery months. All this can be seen in Figure 12.4, which lists quotes for several foreign currency, interest rate, and stock-index futures contracts. Looking first at currency futures, we see that the contracts entitle the holders to a certain position in a specified foreign currency; in effect, the owner of a currency future holds a claim on a certain amount of foreign money. The precise amount ranges from 62,500 British pounds to 12.5 million Japanese yen. Similarly, holders of interest rate futures have a claim on a certain amount of the underlying debt security. This claim is also quite large; it amounts to $100,000 worth of Treasury notes and bonds, $1 million worth of Eurodollar deposits and Treasury bills, and $5 million in 30-day Federal Funds contracts.

Stock-index futures, however, are a bit different because the seller of one of these contracts is *not* obligated to deliver the *underlying stocks* at the expiration date. Instead, ultimate delivery is in the form of cash (which is fortunate, because it would indeed be a task to make delivery of the 2,000 small-cap stocks that are in the Russell 2000 Index or of the 500 issues in the S&P Index). The commodity underlying stock-index futures, therefore, is *cash*. Basically, the amount of underlying cash is set at a certain multiple of the value of the underlying stock index. In particular,

Index	*Multiple*
DJIA	$10 × index
S&P 500	$250 × index
Nasdaq 100	$100 × index
Value Line	$100 × index
S&P 400	$500 × index
NYSE Composite	$500 × index
Russell 2000	$500 × index

Thus, if the S&P 500 stood at 1050, then the amount of cash underlying a single S&P 500 stock-index futures contract would be $250 × 1,050 = $262,500. Again, the amount is substantial. In terms of delivery months, the lives of financial futures contracts run from about 12 months or less for most stock-index and currency futures to about 5 years or less for interest rate instruments.

INVESTOR FACT

THE HOTTEST FUTURES MARKETS—The top five futures contracts in fiscal 1997 were

Contract (Exchange)	*Volume of Contracts*
U.S. Treasury bonds (CBOT)	93,422,575
Eurodollars (CME)	91,206,281
Crude oil (NYMEX/COMEX)	23,925,489
10-year Treasury notes (CBOT)	22,661,759
S&P 500 Index (CME)	19,633,885

As you can see, four of the top five are financial futures contracts. Only one is energy-related and none are agricultural. Corn futures contracts, which had appeared on the 1996 top-five list with a volume of 20,335,842 that year, dropped off the top-five list in 1997 at 16,659,122 contracts.

Volume of contracts tells only part of the story. In terms of notional value—the value of assets underlying these agreements—financial futures contracts are even more dominant. For example, there's $100,000 in Treasury bonds underlying each CBOT T-bond contract; thus, the 93 million T-bond futures contracts traded in 1997 translates into $9.3 *trillion* worth of underlying Treasury bonds. Now, that's a lot of money!

Prices and Profits

There are three basic types of financial futures, and not surprisingly, the price of each type of contract is quoted somewhat differently.

- *Foreign currency futures.* All currency futures are quoted in dollars or cents per unit of the underlying foreign currency (e.g., in dollars per British pound or cents per Japanese yen). Thus, according to the closing ("settle") prices in Figure 12.4, one March British pound contract was worth $101,850 (62,500 pounds × $1.6296), and a June Japanese yen contract was valued at $98,275 (because a quote of 0.7862 cents per yen equals less than a penny a yen, we have 12,500,000 yen × $0.007862).

- *Interest rate futures.* Except for the quotes on Treasury bills and other short-term securities, which we'll examine in the next section, interest rate futures contracts are priced as a percentage of the par value of the underlying debt instrument (e.g., Treasury notes or Treasury bonds). Because these instruments are quoted in increments of 1/32 of 1%, a quote of 120-04 for the settle price of the March (1998) Treasury bonds (in Figure 12.4) translates into 120-4/32, which converts to a quote of 120⅛ on 120.125% of par. Applying this rate to the par value of the underlying security, we see that this March Treasury bond contract is worth $120,125 (i.e., $1,000,000 × 1.20125).

FIGURE 12.4
Quotations on Selected Actively Traded Financial Futures

The trading exchange, size of the trading unit, pricing unit, and delivery months are all vital pieces of information included as part of the quotation system used with financial futures. (Source: *Wall Street Journal*, December 17, 1997.)

CURRENCY

JAPAN YEN (CME)-12.5 million yen; $ per yen (.00)

	Open	High	Low	Settle	Change	Lifetime High	Lifetime Low	Open Interest
Mr98	.7755	.7760	.7726	.7755	− .0002	.9375	.7708	97,714
June	.7860	.7866	.7842	.7862	− .0004	.9090	.7842	1,663
Sept	....	....	....	.7967	− .0010	.8695	.7900	1,270

Est vol 9,501; vol Mn 25,512; open int 152,143, +1,866.

DEUTSCHEMARK (CME)-125,000 marks; $ per mark

	Open	High	Low	Settle	Change	Lifetime High	Lifetime Low	Open Interest
Mr98	.5664	.5669	.5630	.5643	− .0023	.6160	.5383	62,129
June	....	....	....	.5671	− .0023	.5995	.5490	4,392
Sept	....	....	....	.5696	− .0023	.5944	.5670	140

Est vol 11,065; vol Mn 25,195; open int 94,706, −3,219.

CANADIAN DOLLAR (CME)-100,000 dlrs.; $ per Can $

	Open	High	Low	Settle	Change	Lifetime High	Lifetime Low	Open Interest
Dec	.7035	.7045	.7027	.7029	− .0013	.7685	.6995	25,783
Mr98	.7066	.7066	.7039	.7041	− .0025	.7670	.7024	55,787
June	.7070	.7070	.7054	.7055	− .0029	.7470	.7040	3,165
Sept	.7080	.7080	.7070	.7065	− .0033	.7463	.7070	783
Dec	.7100	.7100	.7090	.7074	− .0037	.7400	.7090	404

Est vol 8,915; vol Mn 14,447; open int 85,973, −2,563.

BRITISH POUND (CME)-62,500 pds.; $ per pound

	Open	High	Low	Settle	Change	Lifetime High	Lifetime Low	Open Interest
Mr98	1.6264	1.6310	1.6202	1.6296	+ .0048	1.7020	1.5680	33,893
June		....	....	1.6226	+ .0048	1.6940	1.5610	1,265

Est vol 9,140; vol Mn 23,502; open int 56,622, +3,182.

INTEREST RATE

TREASURY BONDS (CBT)-$100,000; pts. 32nds of 100%

	Open	High	Low	Settle	Change	Lifetime High	Lifetime Low	Open Interest
Dec	120-03	120-13	119-31	120-09	+ 6	120-24	100-08	76,657
Mr98	119-27	120-10	119-25	120-04	+ 6	120-20	104-21	650,921
June	119-23	119-27	119-15	119-26	+ 6	120-05	104-03	27,683
Sept	119-12	119-18	119-09	119-17	+ 6	119-25	103-22	4,171
Dec	....	....	....	119-09	+ 6	119-17	103-13	4,758

Est vol 250,000; vol Mon 319,721; open int 764,346, +6,035.

TREASURY BONDS (MCE)-$50,000; pts. 32nds of 100%

	Open	High	Low	Settle	Change	Lifetime High	Lifetime Low	Open Interest
Dec	120-10	120-10	120-09	120-08	+ 4	120-20	105-20	1,036
Mr98	120-03	120-11	119-25	120-03	+ 4	120-15	111-27	10,441

Est vol 4,000; vol Mon 4,895; open int 11,481, +267.

TREASURY NOTES (CBT)-$100,000; pts. 32nds of 100%

	Open	High	Low	Settle	Change	Lifetime High	Lifetime Low	Open Interest
Dec	112-08	112-10	112-02	112-07	+ 1	112-17	104-10	25,886
Mr98	111-31	112-04	111-26	112-00	+ 1	112-12	105-24	343,657
June	111-27	111-31	111-27	111-31	+ 1	112-05	106-26	2,314

Est vol 66,996; vol Mon 113,715; open int 371,857, −1,104.

5 YR TREAS NOTES (CBT)-$100,000; pts. 32nds of 100%

	Open	High	Low	Settle	Change	Lifetime High	Lifetime Low	Open Interest
Dec	08-175	108-18	08-135	08-165	....	109-06	04-005	24,520
Mr98	08-175	108-18	08-125	08-165	+ .5	108-27	106-07	240,094

Est vol 31,000; vol Mon 44,813; open int 264,770, −1,113.

2 YR TREAS NOTES (CBT)-$200,000, pts. 32nds of 100%

	Open	High	Low	Settle	Change	Lifetime High	Lifetime Low	Open Interest
Dec	03-285	03-285	103-26	03-272	− 1.2	104-09	02-265	2,244
Mr98	03-275	03-277	103-25	03-267	− .5	03-302	103-08	30,886

Est vol 2,500; vol Mon 2,666; open int 33,150, −344.

30-DAY FEDERAL FUNDS (CBT)-$5 million; pts. of 100%

	Open	High	Low	Settle	Change	Lifetime High	Lifetime Low	Open Interest
Dec	94.410	94.420	94.410	94.415	+ .005	94.480	93.780	4,960
Ja98	94.41	94.42	94.40	94.42	+ .01	94.47	93.97	5,942
Feb	94.41	94.42	94.41	94.42	+ .01	94.48	93.84	7,054
Mar	94.37	94.38	94.36	94.37	....	95.30	94.13	1,431
May	94.37	94.38	94.37	94.38	....	94.43	94.15	429

Est vol 3,333; vol Mon 2,114; open int 20,237, +663.

TREASURY BILLS (CME)-$1 mil.; pts. of 100%

	Open	High	Low	Settle	Chg	Discount Settle	Discount Chg	Open Interest
Dec	....	....	....	94.93	− .01	5.07	+ .01	3,059
Mr98	95.07	95.07	95.04	95.07	....	4.93	....	7,058
June	95.09	95.10	95.06	95.07	− .01	4.93	+ .01	1,070

Est vol 298; vol Fri 817; open int 11,210, +197.

INDEX

DJ INDUSTRIAL AVERAGE (CBOT) $10 times average

	Open	High	Low	Settle	Chg	High	Low	Open Interest
Dec	7970.0	8030.0	7965.0	7986.0	+ 59.0	8252.0	6870.0	9,783
Mr98	8035.0	8108.0	8035.0	8065.0	+ 60.0	8335.0	6970.0	9,271
June	8182.0	8182.0	8140.0	8146.0	+ 61.0	8346.0	7070.0	581
Sept	8265.0	8265.0	8224.0	8231.0	+ 61.0	8455.0	7150.0	90

Est vol 11,000; vol Mn 13,278; open int 19,733, +593.
The index: High 8019.82; Low 7924.34; Close 7976.31+53.72

S&P 500 INDEX (CME) $250 times index

	Open	High	Low	Settle	Chg	High	Low	Open Interest
Dec	968.00	974.30	965.70	969.50	+ 6.20	992.25	753.00	155,922
Mr98	973.90	985.50	973.30	980.40	+ 6.20	100260	854.40	283,045
June	990.70	995.00	986.00	990.50	+ 6.40	101200	864.25	7,493
Sept		....	....	100050	+ 6.40	102295	884.00	1,675
Dec		....	....	101160	+ 6.50	103625	895.00	685
Ju99	103150	103890	103140	103420	+ 5.80	106115	959.35	196

Est vol 178,069; vol Mn 235,439; open int 449,155, +9,056.
Indx prelim High 973.00; Low 963.39; Close 968.04+4.65

- *Stock-index futures.* Stock-index futures are quoted in terms of the actual underlying index, but, as noted above, they carry a face value of anywhere from \$10 to \$500 times the index. Thus, according to the settle price in Figure 12.4, the March 1998 DJIA contract would be worth \$80,650, because the value of this particular futures contract is equal to \$10 times the (settle) price of the index (or, 8065.0 × \$10).

The value of an interest rate futures contract responds to interest rates exactly as the debt instrument that underlies the contract does. That is, when interest rates go up, the value of an interest rate futures contract goes down, and vice versa. However, the quote system for interest rate as well as currency and stock-index futures is set up to reflect the *market value of the contract* itself. Thus, when the price or quote of a financial futures contract increases, the investor who is long makes money. In contrast, when the price decreases, the short seller makes money.

Price behavior is the only source of return to speculators, for even though stocks and debt securities are involved in some financial futures, such contracts have no claim on the dividend and interest income of the underlying issues. Even so, huge profits (or losses) are possible with financial futures because of the equally large size of the contracts. For instance, if the price of Swiss francs goes up by just 2 cents against the dollar, the investor is ahead \$2,500. Likewise, a 3-point drop in the NYSE Composite Index means a \$1,500 loss to an investor (3 × \$500). When related to the relatively small initial margin deposit required to make transactions in the financial futures markets, such price activity can mean very high rates of return—or very high risk of a total wipeout.

Pricing Futures on Treasury Bills and Other Short-Term Securities

index price
technique used to price T-bill and other short-term securities futures contracts, by subtracting current yield from an index of 100.

Because Treasury bills and other short-term securities are normally traded in the money market on what is known as a discount basis, it was necessary to devise a special pricing system that would reflect the actual price movements of these futures contracts. To accomplish this, an **index price** system was developed whereby the yield is subtracted from an index of 100. Thus when the yield on an underlying security, such as a Treasury bill or Eurodollar deposit, is 5.25%, the contract would be quoted at an index of 94.75 (100.00 − 5.25). Under such a system, when someone buys, say, a T-bill future and the index goes up, that individual has made money; when the index goes down, a short seller has made money. Note also that 30-day interest rate futures, as well as 90-day T-bill and Eurodollar/Euromarket contracts, are all quoted in *basis points,* where 1 basis point equals 1/100 of 1%. Thus a quote of 95.07 (which was the settle price on the March 1998 T-bill contract in Figure 12.4) translates into a T-bill yield of 4.93% (i.e., 100.00 − 95.07).

The index price system traces only the price behavior of the futures contract. To find the *actual price* or *value* of a 90-day T-bill or Eurodollar contract (two of the more actively traded short-term contracts), we use the formula

Equation 12.2

$$\text{Price of a 90-day futures contract} = \$1{,}000{,}000 - \left(\frac{\text{security's yield} \times 90 \times \$10{,}000}{360}\right)$$

A similar formula would be used to find the price of a 30-day interest rate contract, except a value of 30 would be used in place of the 90 in the formula's numerator.

Note that this price formula is based not on the quoted price index but on the *yield of the security itself,* which can be determined by subtracting the price index quote from 100. To see how it works, consider the 90-day T-bill futures contract quoted at 95.07; recall that this T-bill futures contract is priced to yield 4.93%. Now, using Equation 12.2, we can see that the price (or value) of this futures contract is

$$\text{Price of a 90-day futures contract} = \$1{,}000{,}000 - \left(\frac{4.93 \times 90 \times \$10{,}000}{360}\right)$$
$$= \$1{,}000{,}000 - \$12{,}325$$
$$= \underline{\underline{\$987{,}675}}$$

A handy shortcut for *tracking the price behavior* of T-bill or Eurodollar/Euromarket futures contracts is to remember that the price of a 90-day contract will change by $25 for every basis point change in yield. Thus, when the yield on the underlying 90-day security moves from 4.93% to 5.08%, it goes up by 15 basis points and causes the price of the futures contract to drop by 15 × $25 = $375.

Trading Techniques

Like commodities, financial futures can be used for hedging, spreading, and speculating. Multinational companies and firms that are active in international trade might consider *hedging* with currency or Euromarket futures, whereas various financial institutions and corporate money managers often use interest rate futures for hedging purposes. In either case, the objective is the same: to lock in the best monetary exchange or interest rate possible. In addition, individual investors and portfolio managers use stock-index futures for hedging purposes to protect their security holdings against temporary market declines. Financial futures can also be used for *spreading.* This tactic is popular with investors who adopt strategies of simultaneously buying and selling combinations of two or more contracts to form a desired investment position. One type of futures spread is described in the accompanying *Investing in Action* box; note in this case that the spread is set up to capture profits from the "January effect" in the stock market. Finally, financial futures are widely used for *speculation.*

Although investors can employ any one of the three trading strategies noted above, we will focus primarily on the use of financial futures by speculators and hedgers. (The *Investing in Action* box on page 479 is our only look at the use of financial futures for spreading.) We will first examine speculating in currency and interest rate futures and then look at how these contracts can be used to hedge investments in stocks, bonds, and foreign securities.

Speculating in Financial Futures

Speculators are especially interested in financial futures because of the size of the contracts. For instance, in early 1998, Canadian dollar contracts were worth over $70,000, Treasury notes were going for over $100,000, and Treasury bill contracts were being quoted at close to $1 million. With con-

INVESTING IN ACTION

Playing the "January Effect" with Stock-Index Futures

In an efficient market, an investor should not be able to outperform the market consistently. Yet we know that certain market anomalies do exist, and that knowledgeable investors can take advantage of unusual price patterns that seem to appear with some degree of regularity. One of the most widely known market anomalies is the so-called *January effect,* in which small stocks typically begin to rally each December, outpacing big stocks, in a phenomenon that extends into January. This rally occurs after tax-related selling beats prices to bargain-basement levels. But trying to profit from the January effect is dicey at best. That's because playing this price pattern in the most obvious ways (buying and selling small stocks) isn't always easy. For example, if investors buy just a few small stocks, they may select ones that perform poorly. Also, they frequently pay the highest going price, the "asked price," when they buy, and receive the lower "bid price" when they sell. Obviously, this bid-ask penalty can put a real dent in January-effect profits. Throw in commissions, and investors are lucky if there's any profit left.

One way small investors can play the January effect and minimize transaction costs is to use the futures markets to create a *spread*. The Value Line futures contract on the Kansas City Board of Trade is based on an index of approximately 1,650 stocks; of these, about 33% have a market value of less than $1 billion. In contrast, less than 2% of the stocks in the Standard & Poor's 500 Stock Index have market values below $1 billion. Other indexes top-weighted with big stocks are the New York Stock Exchange Composite Index and, of course, the DJIA. The difference in composition means the January effect can be exploited by buying Value Line futures and simultaneously selling futures contracts based on an index with more big stocks, such as the S&P 500. This kind of futures trade is known as a *spread.*

For instance, if the market does rally and the January effect works, the Value Line contracts should move up more than the S&P 500 contracts. If the market falls, the Value Line contracts should fall less than the big stock index futures. Either scenario would produce a profit for investors holding a spread that consisted of long, or purchased, Value Line futures and short positions in futures based on a big stock index. (With a spread, if the market goes up, you'll make money on the long position but lose on the short—the object, of course, is to net out more profit than loss.)

Since 1982, when stock-index futures started trading, the use of spread where the Value Line contract was used as a proxy for small stocks and the S&P 500 represented big stocks, has produced a theoretical profit in every year but one—in 1997, this spread, for the first time, did result in a loss. In each case, it was assumed that the trade was initiated, using March futures contracts, on December 15 and was closed out on the following January 15. The largest profit was $6,000 per spread closed out in January 1993, and the smallest was $275 for a trade closed in 1989. The median profit was about $1,800. That's not bad—especially when you consider that the capital needed to execute this spread is only about $9,500. With commissions at a discount broker of only $30 to $50, plenty of profit is left. Of course, there's no guarantee that the January effect will occur each year. But it's clear that the futures spread described here puts you in a pretty good position to make a nice profit when it does.

tracts of this size, it obviously doesn't take much movement in the underlying asset to produce big price swings—and therefore big profits. Currency or interest rate futures are popular with investors, and can be used for just about any speculative purpose. For example, if you expect the dollar to be devalued relative to the German mark, you would buy mark currency futures, because the contracts should go up in value. In a similar fashion, if you anticipate a rise in interest rates, you might consider going short (selling) interest rate futures, because they should go down in value. Because margin is used and financial futures have the same source of return as commodities (appreciation in the price of the futures contract), return on invested capital (Equation 12.1) is used to measure the profitability of financial futures.

Going Long a Foreign Currency Contract Suppose you believe that the Swiss franc is about to appreciate in value relative to the dollar. As a result, you decide to go long (buy) three September S-franc contracts at 0.7055—i.e., at a quote of just over 70 cents a franc. Each contract would be worth \$88,187.50 (125,000 S-francs × 0.7055), and the total underlying value of the three contracts would be \$264,562.50. Even so, given an initial margin requirement of, say, \$2,500 per contract, you would have to deposit only \$7,500 to acquire this position. Now, if Swiss francs move up just a few pennies—say, from 0.7055 to 0.75 (or 75 cents a franc)—the value of the three contracts will rise to \$281,250, and in a matter of months, you will have made a profit of \$16,687.50. Using Equation 12.1 for return on invested capital, we find that such a profit translates into an unbelievable 222% rate of return. Of course, an even smaller fractional change in the other direction would have wiped out this investment, so it should be clear that these *high returns are not without equally high risk.*

Going Short an Interest Rate Contract Let's assume that you're anticipating a sharp rise in long-term rates. Because a rise in rates means that interest rate futures will drop in value, you decide to short sell two June T-bond contracts at 115-00, which means that the contracts are trading at 115% of par. Thus the two contracts are worth \$230,000 (\$100,000 × 1.15 × 2), but the amount of money required to make the investment is only \$5,400 (the initial margin deposit is \$2,700 per contract). Assume that interest rates do, in fact, move up and that as a result, the price on Treasury bond contracts drops to 106-16 (or 106½). Under such circumstances, you would buy back the two June T-bond contracts (in order to cover the short position) and in the process make a profit of \$17,000. (Remember, you originally sold the two contracts at \$230,000 and then bought them back sometime later at \$213,000; as with any investment, such a difference between what you pay for a security and what you sell it for is profit.) In this case, the return on invested capital amounts to 315%. Again, however, this kind of return is due in no small part to the *enormous risk of loss* the investor assumes.

Trading Stock-Index Futures

Most investors use stock-index futures for speculation or hedging. (Stock-index futures are similar to the *index options* introduced in Chapter 11; therefore, much of the discussion that follows also applies to index options.) Whether speculating or hedging, the key to success is *predicting the future course of the stock market.* Because you are "buying the market" with stock-index futures, it is important to get a handle on the future direction of the market via technical analysis (as discussed in Chapter 7) or some other technique. Once you have a feel for the market's direction, you can formulate a stock-index futures trading or hedging strategy. For example, if you feel strongly that the market is headed up, you would want to go long (buy stock-index futures); in contrast, if your analysis of the market suggests a sharp drop in equity values, you could make money by going short (selling stock-index futures).

Assume, for instance, that you believe the market is undervalued and a move up is imminent. You can try to identify one or a handful of stocks that should go up with the market (and assume the stock selection risks that go along with this approach), or you can buy an S&P 500 stock-index future currently trading at, say, 974.45. To execute this speculative transaction, you would need to deposit an initial margin of only $10,500. Now, if your expectations are correct and the market does rise so that the S&P 500 Index moves to 990.95 by the expiration of the futures contract, you will earn a profit of $4,125—i.e., (990.95 − 974.45) × $250 = $4,125. Given that this was earned on a $10,500 investment, your return on invested capital would amount to a very respectable 39.3%. Of course, keep in mind that if the market drops by 42 points (or just 4.3 percent), the investment will be a *total loss*.

Hedging with Stock-Index Futures Stock-index futures also make excellent hedging vehicles in that they provide investors with a highly effective way of protecting stock holdings in a declining market. Although this tactic is not perfect, it does enable investors to obtain desired protection against a decline in market value without disturbing their equity holdings. Here's how a so-called *short hedge* would work: Assume that an investor holds a total of 2,000 shares of stock in a dozen different companies and that the market value of this portfolio is around $235,000. If the investor thinks the market is about to undergo a temporary sharp decline, she can do one of two things: sell all of her shares or buy puts on each of the stocks. Clearly, these alternatives are cumbersome and/or costly and therefore undesirable for protecting a widely diversified portfolio. The desired results could also be achieved, however, by *short selling stock-index futures*. (Note that basically the same protection can be obtained in this hedging situation by turning to options and buying a *stock-index put.*)

Suppose the investor short sells one NYSE stock-index futures contract at 468.75. Such a contract would provide a close match to the current value of the investor's portfolio (it would be valued at 468.75 × $500 = $234,375), and yet the stock-index futures contract would require an initial margin deposit of only $5,000. (Margin deposits are lower for hedgers than for speculators.) Now, if the NYSE Composite Index drops to 448.00, the investor will make a profit from the short-sale transaction of some $10,000. That is, because the index fell 20.75 points (468.75 − 448.00), the total profit will be $10,375 (20.75 × $500). Ignoring taxes, this profit can be added to the portfolio (additional shares of stock can be purchased at their new lower prices), the net result being a new portfolio position that will approximate the one that existed prior to the decline in the market.

How well the "before" and "after" portfolio positions match will depend on how far the portfolio dropped in value. If the average price dropped about $5 per share in our example, the positions will closely match. However, this does not always happen; the price of some stocks will change more than others, so the amount of protection provided by this type of short hedge depends on how sensitive the stock portfolio is to movements in the market. Thus what types of stocks are held in the portfolio is an important consideration in structuring the stock-index short hedge. For the investor who keeps that caveat in mind, hedging with stock-index futures can be a low-cost yet

INVESTING IN ACTION

Triple Witching Day

There's an unusually volatile day on Wall Street on the third Friday in March, June, September, and December, and the volatility has nothing to do with the U.S. economy, corporate profits, interest rates, inflation, or other factors that are normally associated with stock market performance. It's the *Triple Witching Day,* when stock options, stock-index options, and stock-index futures all expire more or less simultaneously.

Here's why the volatility occurs: Let's say you manage an index fund for individual investors, who merely expect you to keep up with the Standard & Poor's 500 Index. Suddenly, there's pessimism in the marketplace, and the S&P 500 Index futures contract is trading at a 2% discount to its fair value. So you sell the 500 stocks and buy the futures contract, thereby guaranteeing that you will beat the S&P 500 by 2% (less transaction costs) between the date of the transaction and the expiration of the futures contract. By making this trade, you will beat the market by 2%, whether the market goes up or down. On the contract's expiration day, however, you must go out and buy the exact stocks that are in the index; otherwise you're not performing the job you were hired to do. If enough people attempt to make this trade at the same time, then there will be an order imbalance: Buyers won't care what price they pay because it's the same exact price at which the futures contracts are settled.

The other side of the trade could occur when market sentiment is "frothy" and the futures contract is overvalued. In this situation, as the index fund manager you would sell the futures contract and buy the stocks, again locking in the difference. On expiration day, you must sell the stocks to have the cash to settle the futures contract. Again, this can cause an order imbalance, pushing stock prices downward.

All this may seem like a free lunch, and it was for a number of years. When stock-index futures contracts were in their infancy, they were much more inefficiently priced than they are today. For example, during the stock market crash of 1987, General Motors sold billions of dollars worth of stocks in its pension plan and bought futures contracts. On the day of the crash, the Dow Jones Industrial Average fell from about 2,200 to 1,700, and at the end of the day, the futures contract was priced at the equivalent of 1,200, indicating the extreme bearishness that gripped the market that day. GM pension managers reasoned that if the market stayed at 1,700, then they would profit by 500 DJIA points merely by switching from stocks to futures.

However, the ability to make money in this transaction has diminished over the years, and so the triple witching volatility has decreased some in recent years. Today, there are many more players in the market, making the available profits much thinner, and that is one reason the volatility has diminished. Another reason for the diminished volatility is that the exchanges have spread the expirations over a longer period. Although options on individual stocks and on the S&P 100 Index still expire at the close on Friday, S&P 500 Index options and futures now settle at the beginning of that business day. (They used to expire within a single hour.) By spreading out the expiration times, the exchanges have diluted the impact of the Triple Witching Day. But it's still enough to cause extra volatility in the stock market, and nervousness on Wall Street four times a year.

effective way of obtaining protection against loss in a declining stock market. For an unusual aspect relating to the timing of investments in stock-index futures, see the nearby *Investing in Action* box.

Hedging Other Securities

Just as stock-index futures can be used to hedge stock portfolios, *interest rate futures* can be used to hedge bond portfolios, and *foreign currency futures* can be used with foreign securities as a way to protect against foreign exchange risk. *Let's consider an interest rate hedge:* If you held a substantial portfolio of bonds, the last thing you would want to see is a big jump in interest rates, which could cause a sharp decline in the value of your portfolio. Assume you hold around $300,000 worth of Treasury and agency issues, with an average (approximate) maturity of about 18 years. If you strongly believed that market rates are headed up, you could hedge your bond portfolio by short selling three U.S. Treasury bond futures contracts (each T-bond futures contract is worth about $100,000, so it would take three of them to cover a $300,000 portfolio). Now, if rates do head up, the portfolio will be protected against loss—though, as we noted with stocks above, the exact amount of protection will depend on how well the T-bond futures contracts parallel the price behavior of this particular bond portfolio.

There is, of course, a downside to all this: *If market interest rates go down,* rather than up, *you will miss out on potential profits as long as the short hedge position remains in place.* This is so because all or most of the profits being made in the portfolio will be offset by losses from the futures contracts. Actually, this will occur with any type of portfolio (stocks, bonds, or anything else) that's tied to an offsetting short hedge, because when the short hedge is created, it essentially *locks in a position at that point.* Although you don't lose anything when the market falls, you also don't make anything when the market goes up. In either case, the profits you make from one position are offset by losses from the other.

Hedging Foreign Currency Exposure To see how futures contracts can be used to hedge foreign exchange risk, let's assume that an investor has just purchased $150,000 worth of German government 1-year notes. (The investor did this because higher yields were available on the German notes than on comparable U.S. Treasury securities.) Because these notes are denominated in *marks,* this investment is subject to loss if currency exchange rates move against the investor (i.e., if the value of the dollar rises relative to the mark). If all the investor wanted was the higher yield offered by the German note, he or she could eliminate most of the currency exchange risk by setting up a currency hedge. Here's how it's done: Let's say that at the current exchange rate, one U.S. dollar will "buy" 1.65 marks, which means that marks are worth about 60 cents ($1/1.65 marks = $0.60). If currency contracts on German marks were trading at around $0.60 a mark, our investor would have to *sell* two contracts in order to protect the $150,000 investment. Each mark contract covers 125,000 marks, so if they're being quoted at 0.6000, then each contract is worth $0.60 × 125,000 = $75,000.

Assume that 1 year later, the value of the dollar has increased, relative to the mark, so that one U.S. dollar will now "buy" 1.725 marks. Under such conditions, a German mark futures contract would be quoted at around 0.5800 (i.e., $1/1.725 = $0.58). At this price, each futures contract would be worth $72,500 (125,000 × $0.58). Each contract, in effect, would be worth $2,500 less than it was a year ago, but because the contract was sold short when the hedge was set up, the hedger will make a profit of $2,500 per contract—for a total profit of $5,000 on the two contracts. Unfortunately, that's not *net profit,* because this profit will offset the loss the investor will incur on the German note investment. In very simple terms, when the investor sent $150,000 overseas to buy the German notes, the money was worth 250,000 marks; however, when the investor brought the money back a year later, those 250,000 marks purchased only 145,000 American dollars. Thus the investor is out $5,000 on his or her original investment. Were it not for the currency hedge, the investor would be out the full $5,000, and the return on this investment would be a lot lower. But the hedge covered the loss, and the net effect was that the investor was able to enjoy the added yield of the German note without having to worry about any potential loss from currency exchange rates.

Financial Futures and the Individual Investor

Financial futures can play an important role in your portfolio so long as you (1) thoroughly understand these investment vehicles, (2) clearly recognize the tremendous risk exposure of such vehicles, and (3) are fully prepared (financially and emotionally) to absorb some losses. Financial futures are highly volatile securities that have enormous potential for profit and for loss. For instance, in 1997, during a 9-month period, the December S&P 500 futures contract fluctuated in price from a low of 753.0 to a high of 992.25. This range of over 239 points for a single contract translates into a *potential* profit—or loss—of some $59,800, and all from an initial investment of only $10,500. Investment diversification is obviously essential as a means of reducing the potentially devastating impact of price volatility. Financial futures are exotic investment vehicles, but, if properly used, they can provide generous returns.

Options on Futures

futures options
options that give the holders the right to buy or sell a single standardized futures contract for a specified period of time at a specified strike price.

The evolution that began with listed stock options and financial futures spread, over time, to interest rate options and stock-index futures. Eventually, it led to the merger of options and futures and to the creation of the ultimate leverage vehicle: *options on futures contracts.* **Futures options** represent listed puts and calls on actively traded futures contracts. In essence, they give the holders the right to buy (with calls) or sell (with puts) a single standardized futures contract for a specific period of time at a specified strike price. Table 12.4 lists the futures options available in early 1998; note that such options are available on both commodities and financial futures. For the most part, these puts and calls cover the same amount of assets as the underlying futures contracts—for example, 112,000 pounds of sugar, 100 ounces of gold, 62,500 British pounds, or $100,000 in Treasury bonds. Accordingly, they also involve the same amount of price activity as is normally found with commodities and financial futures.

Futures options have the same standardized strike prices, expiration dates, and quotation system as other listed options. Depending on the strike price on the option and the market value of the underlying futures contract, these options can also be in-the-money or out-of-the-money. Futures options are valued like other puts and calls—by the difference between the option's strike price and the market price of the underlying futures contract (see Chapter 11). Moreover, they can also be used like any other listed option—that is, for speculating or hedging, in options writing programs, or for spreading. The biggest

TABLE 12.4 Futures Options: Puts and Calls on Futures Contracts

Commodities			
Corn	Sugar	Cocoa	Copper
Soybeans	Live cattle	Coffee	Gold
Soybean meal	Live hogs	Wheat	Silver
Soybean oil	Feeder cattle	Oats	Crude oil
Heating oil	Lumber	Rice	Natural gas
Gasoline	Orange juice	Platinum	Gas oil
Cotton			

Financial Futures		
British pound	U.S. dollar Index	British government bonds
German mark	Eurodollar deposits	German government bonds
Swiss franc	Euromark deposits	NYSE Composite Index
Japanese yen	Treasury bills	S&P 500 Stock Index
Canadian dollar	Treasury notes	Dow Jones Industrial Average
Brazilian real	Treasury bonds	Nasdaq 100 Index
Mexican peso	Muni bond index	

difference between a futures option and a futures contract is that *the option limits the loss exposure* to the price of the option. The most you can lose is the price paid for the put or call, whereas there is no real limit to the amount of loss a futures investor can incur.

To see how futures options work, assume that you want to trade some gold contracts. You believe that the price of gold will increase over the next 4 or 5 months from its present level of $285 an ounce to around $330 an ounce. You can buy a futures contract at 288.10 by depositing the required initial margin of $1,300, or you can buy a futures call option with a $280 strike price that is currently being quoted at 10.90. (Because the underlying futures contract covers 100 ounces of gold, the total cost of this option would be $10.90 × 100 = $1,090.) The call is an in-the-money option, because the market price of gold exceeds the exercise price on the option. The figures that follow summarize what happens to both investments if the price of gold reaches $330 an ounce by the expiration date and also what happens if the price of gold drops by $45 to $240 an ounce.

	Futures Contract		Futures Option	
	Dollar Profit (or Loss)	Return on Invested Capital	Dollar Profit (or Loss)	Return on Invested Capital
If price of gold *increases* by $45 an ounce	$4,190	322.3%	$3,910	358.7%
If price of gold *decreases* by $45 an ounce	($4,810)	—	($1,090)	—

Clearly, the futures option provides not only a competitive rate of return (in this case, it's even a bit higher), but also a reduced exposure to loss. Futures options offer interesting investment opportunities, but, as always, they *should be used only by knowledgeable commodities and financial futures investors.*

CONCEPTS IN REVIEW

12.11 What is the difference between physical *commodities* and *financial futures?* What are their similarities?

12.12 Describe a *currency future* and contrast it with an *interest rate future.* What is a *stock-index future,* and how can it be used by investors?

12.13 Discuss how stock-index futures can be used for speculation and for hedging. What advantages are there to speculating with stock-index futures rather than specific issues of common stock?

12.14 Briefly describe the January effect discussed in the *Investing in Action* box on page 479 and explain how the futures spread described there works.

12.15 What are *futures options?* Explain how they can be used by speculators. Why would an investor want to use an option on an interest rate futures contract rather than the futures contract itself?

12.16 The *Investing in Action* box on page 482 describes a market phenomenon known as the "triple witching day." Why do they call it that and what are the implications for investors?

http://hepg.aw.com

The most widely traded equity index futures contract is for the S&P 500 Index. Learn more about this contract and the index at the following site.

futurestrading.com/sp50077.htlm

Summary

LG 1 **Describe the essential features of a futures contract, and explain how the futures market operates.** Commodities and financial futures are traded in futures markets. Today, there are eight U.S. exchanges that deal in futures contracts, which are commitments to make (or take) delivery of a certain amount of some real or financial asset at a specified date in the future.

LG 2 **Explain the role that hedgers and speculators play in the futures market, including how profits are made and lost.** Futures contracts control large amounts of the underlying commodity or financial instrument and, as a result, can produce wide price swings and very attractive rates of return (or very unattractive losses). Such returns (or losses) are further magnified because all trading in the futures market is done on margin. Whereas a speculator's profit is derived directly from the wide price fluctuations that occur in the market, hedgers derive their profit from the protection they gain against adverse price movements.

LG 3 **Describe the commodities segment of the futures market and the basic characteristics of these investment vehicles.** Commodities like grains, metals, and meat make up the traditional (commodities) segment of the futures market. Although a large portion of this market is concentrated in the agricultural segment of our economy, there's also a very active market for various metals and petroleum products. As the prices of commodities go up and down in the market, the respective futures contracts behave in much the same way; thus, if the price of corn goes up, the value of corn futures contracts rises as well.

LG 4 **Discuss the various trading strategies that investors can use with commodities, and explain how investment returns are measured.** A variety of trading strategies can be used with commodities contracts, including speculating, spreading, and hedging. Regardless of whether investors are in a long or a short position, they have only one source of return from commodities and financial futures: appreciation (or depreciation) in the price of the contract. Rate of return on invested capital is used to assess the actual or potential profitability of a futures transaction.

LG 5 **Explain the difference between a physical commodity and a financial future, and discuss the growing role of financial futures in the market today.** Whereas commodities deal with physical assets, financial futures deal with financial assets, such as stocks, bonds, and currencies. Even though the nature of the underlying assets may differ, both are traded in the same place: the futures market. Financial futures are the newcomers, but this segment of the market has grown to the point where the volume of trading in financial futures now far exceeds that of commodities.

LG 6 **Discuss the trading techniques that can be used with financial futures, and note how these securities can be used in conjunction with other investment vehicles.** There are three types of financial futures: currency futures, interest rate futures, and stock-index futures. The first type deals in different kinds of foreign currencies. Interest rate futures, in contrast, involve various types of short- and long-term debt instruments. Stock-index futures are pegged to broad movements in the stock market, as measured by such indexes as the S&P 500 and the NYSE Composite Index. These securities can be used for speculating, spreading, or hedging. They hold a special appeal to investors who use them to hedge other security positions. For example, interest rate futures contracts are used to protect bond portfolios against a big jump in market interest rates, and currency futures are used to hedge the foreign currency exposure that accompanies investments in foreign securities.

Discussion Questions

LG 1 Q12.1. Three of the biggest U.S. commodities exchanges—the CBT, CME, and NYMerc—were identified in this chapter. Other U.S. exchanges and several foreign commodities exchanges are also closely followed here in the United States. Obtain a recent copy of the *Wall Street Journal* and look in the "Futures Prices" section of the paper for the futures quotes. As noted in this chapter, futures quotes include the name of the exchange on which a particular contract is traded.

a. Using these quotes, how many more *U.S. commodities exchanges* can you identify? List them.
b. Are quotes from *foreign exchanges* listed in the *Wall Street Journal*? If so, list them, too.
c. For each U.S. and foreign exchange you found in parts (a) and (b), give an example of one or two contracts traded on that exchange. For example: CBT—Chicago Board of Trade: oats and Treasury bonds.

LG 3 LG 5 Q12.2. Using settle prices from Figures 12.2 and 12.4, find the value of the following commodity and financial futures contracts.

a. July soybean oil
b. May 1998 corn
c. September heating oil
d. June deutsche mark
e. March 1998 5-year Treasury notes
f. June S&P 500 Index

LG 4 LG 6 Q12.3. Listed below are a variety of futures transactions. On the basis of the information provided, indicate how much profit or loss you would make in each of the transactions. (*Hint:* You might want to refer to Figures 12.2 and 12.4 for the size of the contract, pricing unit, etc.)

a. You buy three yen contracts at a quote of 1.0180 and sell them a few months later at 1.0365.
b. The price of wheat goes up 60 cents a bushel, and you hold three contracts.
c. You short sell two crude oil contracts at $18.75 a barrel, and the price of crude oil drops to $14.10 a barrel.
d. You recently purchased a 90-day Treasury bill contract at 94.15, and T-bill interest rates rise to 6.60%.
e. You short sell S&P 500 contracts when the index is at 996.55 and cover when the index moves to 971.95.
f. You short three corn contracts at $2.34 a bushel, and the price of corn goes to $2.49½ a bushel.

Problems

LG 3 LG 4

P12.1. Kirk O'Malley considers himself a shrewd commodities investor. Not long ago he bought one July cotton contract at 54 cents a pound, and he recently sold it at 58 cents a pound. How much profit did he make? What was his return on invested capital if he had to put up a $1,500 initial deposit?

LG 4

P12.2. Shirley Ledbetter is a regular commodities speculator; she is currently considering a short position in July oats, which are now trading at 148. Her analysis suggests that July oats should be trading at about 140 in a couple of months. Assuming that her expectations hold up, what kind of return on invested capital will she make if she shorts three July oats contracts (with each contract covering 5,000 bushels of oats) by depositing an initial margin of $500 per contract?

LG 5 LG 6

P12.3. Marc Lato is thinking about doing some speculating in interest rates; he thinks rates will fall and, in response, the price of Treasury bond futures should move from 92–15, their present quote, to a level of about 98. Given a required margin deposit of $2,000 per contract, what would Marc's return on invested capital be if prices behave as he expects?

LG 5 LG 6

P12.4. Annie Ryan has been an avid stock market investor for years; she manages her portfolio fairly aggressively and likes to short sell whenever the opportunity presents itself. Recently, she has become fascinated with stock-index futures, especially the idea of being able to play the market as a whole. At the present time, Annie thinks the market is headed down, and she decides to short sell some NYSE Composite stock-index futures. Assume she shorts three contracts at 587.95 and has to make a margin deposit of $6,000 for each contract. How much profit will she make, and what will her return on invested capital be if the market does indeed drop so that the NYSE contracts are trading at 565.00 by the time they expire?

LG 6

P12.5. A wealthy investor holds $500,000 worth of U.S. Treasury bonds; these bonds are currently being quoted at a little over par—i.e., at 105% of par. The investor is concerned, however, that rates are headed up over the next 6 months, and he would like to do something to protect this bond portfolio. His broker advises him to set up a hedge using T-bond futures contracts; assume these contracts are now trading at 111–06.
a. Briefly describe how the investor would set up this hedge. Would he go long or short, and how many contracts would he need?
b. It's now 6 months later, and rates have indeed gone up. The investor's Treasury bonds are now being quoted at 93½, and the T-bond futures contracts used in the hedge are now trading at 98–00. Show what has happened to the value of the bond portfolio and the profit (or loss) made on the futures hedge.
c. Was this a successful hedge? Explain.

LG 6

P12.6. Not long ago, Vanessa Garcia sold the company she founded for several million dollars (after taxes); she took some of that money and put it into the stock market. Today, Vanessa's portfolio of blue-chip stocks is worth $2.3 million. Vanessa wants to keep her portfolio intact, but she's concerned about a developing weakness in the market for blue chips. She decides, therefore, to hedge her position with 6-month futures contracts on the Dow Jones Industrial Average (DJIA), which are currently trading at 7960.

a. Why would she choose to hedge her portfolio with the DJIA rather than the S&P 500?
b. Given that Vanessa wants to cover the full $2.3 million in her portfolio, describe how she would go about setting up this hedge.
c. If each contract required a margin deposit of $1,000, how much money would she need to set up this hedge?
d. Assume that over the next 6 months stock prices do fall, and the value of Vanessa's portfolio drops to $2.0 million. If DJIA futures contracts are trading at 6960, how much will she make (or lose) on the futures hedge? Is it enough to offset the loss in her portfolio? That is, what is her net profit or loss on the hedge?
e. Will she now get her margin deposit back, or is that a "sunk cost"—gone forever?

LG 6

P12.7. An American currency speculator feels strongly that the value of the Canadian dollar is going to fall relative to the U.S. dollar over the short run. If he wants to profit from these expectations, what kind of position (long or short) should he take in Canadian dollar futures contracts? How much money would he make from each contract if Canadian dollar futures contracts moved from an initial quote of 0.7775 to an ending quote of 0.7250?

LG 6

P12.8. With regard to futures options, how much profit would an investor make if she bought a call option on gold at 7.20 when gold was trading at $482 an ounce, given that the price of gold went up to $525 an ounce by the expiration date on the call? (*Note:* Assume the call carried a strike price of 480.)

Case Problem 12.1 *T.J.'s Fast Track Investments: Interest Rate Futures*

LG 5 LG 6

T.J. Patrick is a young, successful industrial designer in Portland, Oregon, who enjoys the excitement of commodities speculation. T.J. has been dabbling in commodities since he was a teenager—he was introduced to this market by his dad, who is a grain buyer for one of the leading food processors. T.J. recognizes the enormous risks involved in commodities speculating but feels that because he's still single, now is the perfect time to take chances. And he can well afford to: As a principal in a thriving industrial design firm, T.J. earns more than $100,000 a year. He follows a well-disciplined investment program and annually adds $15,000 to $20,000 to his portfolio.

Recently, T.J. has started playing with financial futures—interest rate futures, to be exact. He admits he is no expert in interest rates, but he likes the price action these investment vehicles offer. This all started several months ago, when T.J. met Vinnie Banano, a broker who specializes in financial futures, at a party. T.J. liked what Vinnie had to say (mostly how you couldn't go wrong with interest-rate futures) and soon set up a trading account with Vinnie's firm, Banano's of Portland.

The other day, Vinnie called T.J. and suggested he get into T-bill futures. As Vinnie saw it, interest rates were going to continue to head up at a brisk pace, and T.J. should short sell some 90-day T-bill futures. In particular, he thinks that rates on T-bills should go up by another half-point (moving from about 5½% up to 6%), and he recommends that T.J. short four contracts. This would be a $4,000 investment, because each contract requires an initial margin deposit of $1,000.

QUESTIONS

a. Assume 90-day T-bill futures are now being quoted at 94.35.
   1. Determine the current price (underlying value) of this T-bill futures contract.
   2. What would this futures contract be quoted at if Vinnie is right and the yield goes up by ½ of 1%?

b. How much profit will T.J. make if he shorts four contracts at 94.35 and T-bill yields do go up by ½ of 1%—that is, if T.J. covers his short position when T-bill futures contracts are quoted at 93.85? Also, calculate the return on invested capital from this transaction.

c. What happens if rates go down? For example, how much will T. J. make if the yield on T-bill futures goes down by just ¼ of 1%?

d. What risks do you see in the recommended short-sale transaction? What is your assessment of T. J.'s new interest in financial futures? How do you think it compares to his established commodities investment program?

Case Problem 12.2 *Jim and Polly Parker Try Hedging with Stock-Index Futures*

LG 5 LG 6

Jim Parker and his wife, Polly, live in Birmingham, Alabama. Like many young couples today, the Parkers are a two-income family; Jim and Polly are both college graduates and hold well-paying jobs. Jim has been an avid investor in the stock market for a number of years and over time has built up a portfolio that is currently worth nearly $175,000. The Parkers' portfolio is well diversified, although it is heavily weighted in high-quality, mid-cap growth stocks. The Parkers reinvest all dividends and regularly add investment capital to their portfolio. Up to now, they have avoided short selling and do only a modest amount of margin trading.

Their portfolio has undergone a substantial amount of capital appreciation in the last 18 months or so, and Jim is eager to protect the profit they have earned. And that's the problem, because Jim feels the market has pretty much run its course and is about to enter a period of decline. He has studied the market and economic news very carefully and does not believe the retreat will be of major magnitude or cover an especially long period of time. He feels fairly certain, however, that most, if not all, of the stocks in his portfolio will be adversely affected by these market conditions—though they certainly won't all be affected to the same degree (some will drop more in price than others). Jim has been following stock-index futures for some time and believes he knows the ins and outs of these securities pretty well. After careful deliberation, Jim and Polly decide to use stock-index futures—in particular, the S&P MidCap 400 futures contract—as a way to protect (hedge) their portfolio of common stocks.

QUESTIONS

a. Explain why the Parkers would want to use stock-index futures to hedge their stock portfolio, and note how they would go about setting up such a hedge. Be specific.
   1. What alternatives do Jim and Polly have to protect the capital value of their portfolio?
   2. What are the benefits and risks of using stock-index futures for such purposes (as hedging vehicles)?

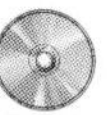

b. Assume that S&P MidCap 400 futures contracts are currently being quoted at 325.60. How many contracts would the Parkers have to buy (or sell) to set up the hedge?

1. Say the value of the Parker portfolio dropped 12% over the course of the market retreat. To what price must the stock-index futures contract move in order to cover that loss?
2. Given that a $6,000 margin deposit is required to buy or sell a single S&P 400 futures contract, what would be the Parkers' return on invested capital if the price of the futures contract changed by the amount computed in part (b1)?

c. Assume that the value of the Parker portfolio declined by $32,000, while the price of an S&P 400 futures contract moved from 325.60 to 277.60. (Assume that Jim and Polly short sold one futures contract to set up the hedge.)

1. Add the profit from the hedge transaction to the new (depreciated) value of the stock portfolio. How does this amount compare to the $175,000 portfolio that existed just before the market started its retreat?
2. Why did the stock-index futures hedge fail to give complete protection to the Parker portfolio? Is it possible to obtain *perfect* (dollar-for-dollar) protection from these types of hedges? Explain.

d. What if, instead of hedging with futures contracts, the Parkers decide to set up the hedge by using *futures options?* Unfortunately, no futures options are currently available on the S&P MidCap 400 Index, but let's say there are. (Assume that these future options, like their underlying futures contracts, are valued/priced at $500 times the premiums.) Now, suppose a put on the S&P MidCap 400 futures contract (strike price = 325) is currently quoted at 5.80, and a comparable call is quoted at 2.35. Use the same portfolio and futures price conditions as set out in part (c) to determine how well the portfolio would be protected. (*Hint:* Add the net profit from the hedge to the new depreciated value of the stock portfolio.) What are the advantages and disadvantages of using futures options, rather than the stock-index futures contract itself, to hedge a stock portfolio?

Home Page Exercises

http://hepg.aw.com **Keyword: Invest**

Commodity and financial futures allow investors to speculate on or hedge the direction of interest rates and stock markets, the prices of agricultural products such as wheat, or the price of other commodities such as lumber. These assets are not for the "faint of heart" or the uninformed. Keeping up with the specific trading characteristics and daily prices of these contracts is a must for the serious investor. Up-to-the-minute information usually has a cost, but it is essential for investors in financial futures. The Web sites listed here provide free educational material. Some of these sites also offer—again, for a fee—the real-time price information that futures investors need.

Web Address	*Primary Investment Focus*
www.worldlinkfutures.com/trad.htm	Provides an electronic course on futures and options for beginners
www.eftc.gov/cftc_information.html	This Commodity Trading Futures Corporation site has information on the regulation and trading of futures
www.ahandyguide.com/cat1/f/f263.htm	Provides multiple links to a variety of Web sites on futures trading
www.margil.com/mrgl101.htm	Educational resources and links on futures trading
www.kcbt.com	The home page for the Kansas City Board of Trade
www.cbot.com	The home page for the Chicago Board of Trade

W12.1. Each commodity futures contract is unique in many ways. At the Coffee, Sugar, and Cocoa Exchange home page, whose address is shown here, access *Contract Specs* for the coffee and for the milk commodities. Record, for each contract, (a) the units of trading, (b) the hours for trading, (c) the latest price quote, (d) the available delivery months, and (e) the date of the last day the nearest contract can be traded.

www.csce.com

W12.2. Commodity prices are subject to rapid and dramatic short-term price movements. The Web page provided here allows free access to historical closing prices for commodity and financial futures. Record the closing prices and the change in the closing price for the past 7 trading days for both the 30-year Treasury bond futures and the S&P 500 Index futures. For each of the 7 days, calculate the closing value of each contract and the amount of money made or lost by a buyer of each contract.

www.teleport.com/~rpotts/prices/prices.html

Part Five

Other Popular Investment Vehicles

CHAPTER 13 MUTUAL FUNDS: AN INDIRECT ROUTE TO THE MARKET

LEARNING GOALS

After studying this chapter, you should be able to:

LG 1 Describe the basic features of mutual funds, and note what they have to offer as investment vehicles.

LG 2 Differentiate between open- and closed-end mutual funds, and discuss the various types of fund loads, fees, and charges.

LG 3 Discuss the types of funds available and the variety of investment objectives these funds seek to fulfill.

LG 4 Identify and discuss the investor services offered by mutual funds and how these services can fit into an investment program.

LG 5 Gain an appreciation of the investor uses of mutual funds, along with the variables that one should consider when assessing and selecting funds for investment purposes.

LG 6 Identify the sources of return and compute the rate of return earned on an investment in a mutual fund.

The Vanguard Group

In just 25 years, The Vanguard Group of mutual funds has become one of the largest mutual funds in a booming industry. Its competitive weapon: the lowest operating expenses in the industry. Why should mutual fund customers care about a mutual fund's operating expenses? Because those expenses are deducted from their returns. The average equity mutual fund levies annual fees of about 1.5% of total assets. These fees essentially wipe out most, if not all, of the dividends earned on a fund's holdings, given that the yield on the average stock is just 1.7%. By contrast, Vanguard's flagship fund, the Vanguard Index 500, charges investors a fee of just 0.20% annually.

As you'll see in this chapter, investing in mutual funds is a good way for individual investors to accomplish objectives that they couldn't achieve otherwise. From index funds that reflect the movement of the S&P 500 to emerging markets funds that buy stocks in remote areas of the world, the mutual fund industry is an increasingly important factor in the investor's toolbox.

The Mutual Fund Phenomenon

LG 1 LG 2

Questions of which stock or bond to select, when to buy, and when to sell have plagued investors for as long as there have been organized capital markets. Such concerns lie at the very heart of the mutual fund concept and in large part explain the growth that mutual funds have experienced. Many investors lack the time, know-how, or commitment to manage their own portfolios, so they turn to professional fund managers and simply let them decide which securities to buy and when to sell.

mutual fund
an investment company that invests its shareholders' money in a diversified portfolio of securities.

Basically, a **mutual fund** is a type of financial services organization that receives money from its shareholders and then invests those funds on their behalf in a diversified portfolio of securities. Mutual funds have been a part of our investment landscape for nearly 75 years. The first one was started in Boston in 1924—and it's still in business today. By 1940 the number of mutual funds had grown to 68, and by 1980 there were 564. But that was only the beginning: The next 17 years saw unprecedented growth in the mutual fund industry, as assets under management grew from less than $100 billion in 1980 to *over $4 trillion* in 1997. Indeed, by 1997 *there were more than 8,500 publicly traded mutual funds.* To put that number in perspective, *there are more mutual funds in existence today than there are stocks listed on the New York and American exchanges combined!* The fund industry has grown so much that it is now *the largest financial intermediary* in this country—ahead of even banks. Finally, though we tend to think of mutual funds as an American phenomenon, the fact is that mutual funds, in one form or another, are found in all the major markets of the world, and the amount under management in these funds rivals that held in U.S. funds.

An Overview of Mutual Funds

Mutual fund investors come from all walks of life and all income levels. They range from highly inexperienced to highly experienced investors who all share a common view: Each has decided, for one reason or another, to turn over at least a part of his or her investment management activities to professionals.

> **INVESTOR FACT**
>
> WHO OWNS THE FUNDS?—U.S. households own the majority of the mutual fund industry's $4 trillion in assets. As of December 31, 1996, they held $2.6 trillion, or 74%, of mutual fund assets. Institutional investors held the balance. The average mutual fund investor is a member of the middle class, is 44 years old, has financial assets of $50,000, and is married and employed.
>
> Generation Xers are also very much interested in mutual fund investing. This group of shareholders has the lowest level of household assets yet has the second highest portion of its assets in mutual funds, second only to those aged 50 to 70.

Pooled Diversification

An investment in a mutual fund really represents *an ownership position in a professionally managed portfolio of securities.* When you buy shares in a mutual fund, you become a part owner of a portfolio of securities. That's because a mutual fund combines the investment capital of many people who have similar investment goals and invests the funds for those individuals in a wide variety of securities. In an abstract sense, think of a mutual fund as the *financial product* that's sold to the public by an investment company. That is, the investment company builds and manages a portfolio of securities and sells ownership interests—shares of stock—in that portfolio through a vehicle known as a mutual fund.

Investors in mutual funds are able to enjoy much wider investment diversification than they could otherwise achieve. To appreciate the extent of such diversification, take a look at Figure 13.1. It provides a partial list of the securities held in the portfolio of a major mutual fund (it is one page of a 6-page list of security holdings). Observe that in June 1997, this fund owned anywhere from 1,000 shares of two companies (Abacus Direct and Sandisk Corp.) to nearly *4 million shares* of another (Microchip Technology). Furthermore,

FIGURE 13.1 A Partial List of Portfolio Holdings

This list represents just *one page* of security holdings for this particular fund; the total list of holdings goes on for six full pages and includes stocks in hundreds of different companies. Certainly, this is far more diversification than most individual investors could ever hope to achieve. (Source: The Kaufman Fund.)

Common Stocks – continued

	Shares	Value (000s)
COMPUTER SOFTWARE (continued)		
Simulation Sciences, Inc.	445,000	$ 6,786
Sterling Software, Inc.	357,400	11,169
Synopsys, Inc.	700,000	25,725
Tecnomatix Technologies Ltd.	100,000	3,250
Transaction System Architects, Inc. - Class A	650,000	22,425
Unison Software, Inc.	300,000	2,100
Veritas Software Corporation	600,000	30,150
Walsh International, Inc.	1,258,400	10,539
		332,554
COMPUTER SERVICES – 4.6%		
Abacus Direct Corporation	1,000	32
Affiliated Computer Services, Inc.	1,400,000	39,200
American Business Information, Inc.	400,000	8,700
Billing Information Concepts	950,000	33,131
CCC Information Services Group.	930,000	18,135
Computer Services Corporation	400,000	28,850
Concord EFS, Inc.	1,100,000	28,463
CSG Systems International, Inc.	400,000	12,350
DecisionOne Corporation	410,000	9,327
ECsoft Group plc	250,000	3,500
Gemstar International Group Limited	10,000	184
Intelligroup, Inc.	500,000	4,813
Lightbridge, Inc.	400,000	3,050
Metromail Corporation	406,200	10,053
Ovid Technologies, Inc.	200,000	2,125
Quick Response Services, Inc.	700,000	25,375
Sterling Commerce, Inc.	602,000	19,791
USCS International, Inc.	100,000	3,275
		250,354
ELECTRONIC COMPONENTS – 1.3%		
LeCroy Corporation	350,000	$ 12,906
Richey Electronics, Inc.	575,000	4,815
Smartflex Systems, Inc.	281,400	2,744
Vicor Corporation	2,304,000	51,840
		72,306
SEMICONDUCTOR & EQUIPMENT – 7.4%		
Alliance Semiconductor Corporation	200,000	1,637
Altera Corporation	3,600,000	181,800
Cypress Semiconductor Corporation	100,000	1,450
DuPont Photomasks, Inc.	500,000	27,000
Etec Systems, Inc.	600,000	25,725
FEI Company	23,000	362
Information Storage Devices, Inc.	700,000	4,988
Lam Research Corporation	150,000	5,559
LSI Logic Corporation	300,000	9,600
Microchip Technology, Inc.	3,900,000	116,025
NeoMagic Corporation	10,000	224
Photronics, Inc.	150,000	7,163
RF Micro Devices, Inc.	75,000	1,434
Sandisk Corporation	1,000	15
Sawtek Inc.	80,000	2,700
Supertex, Inc.	255,000	2,837
Vitesse Semiconductor Corpoation	405,000	13,238
Xilinx, Inc.	100,000	4,906
		406,663

note that within each industry segment, the fund diversified its holdings across a number of different stocks. Clearly, this is far more diversification than most investors could ever hope to attain. Yet each investor who owns shares in this fund is, in effect, a part owner of this diversified portfolio of securities.

Of course, not all funds are as big or as widely diversified as the one depicted in Figure 13.1. But whatever the size of the fund, as the securities held by it move up and down in price, the market value of the mutual fund shares moves accordingly. And when dividend and interest payments are received by the fund, they too are passed on to the mutual fund shareholders and distributed on the basis of prorated ownership. For example, if you own 1,000 shares of stock in a mutual fund and that represents 1% of all shares outstanding, you will receive 1% of the dividends paid by the fund. When a security held by the fund is sold for a profit, the capital gain is also passed on to fund shareholders. The whole mutual fund idea, in fact, rests on the concept of **pooled diversification**, which works very much like health insurance, whereby individuals pool their resources for the collective benefit of all the contributors.

pooled diversification
a process whereby investors buy into a diversified portfolio of securities for the collective benefit of the individual investors.

Attractions and Drawbacks of Mutual Fund Ownership

The attractions of mutual fund ownership are numerous. One of the most important is *diversification;* it benefits mutual fund shareholders by spreading out holdings over a wide variety of industries and companies, thus reducing the risk inherent in any one investment. Another appeal of mutual funds is *full-time professional management,* which relieves investors of many day-to-day management and record-keeping chores. What's more, the fund may be able to offer better investment talents than individual investors can provide. Still another advantage is that most mutual fund investments can be started with a *modest capital outlay.* Sometimes no minimum investment is required, and after the initial investment has been made, additional shares can usually be purchased in small amounts. The *services that mutual funds offer* also make them appealing to many investors: These include automatic reinvestment of dividends, withdrawal plans, and exchange privileges. Finally, mutual funds offer *convenience.* They are relatively easy to acquire; the funds handle the paperwork and record keeping; their prices are widely quoted; and it is possible to deal in fractional shares.

There are, of course, some major drawbacks to mutual fund ownership. One of the biggest disadvantages is that mutual funds in general *can be costly* and involve substantial transaction costs. Many funds carry sizable commission charges ("load charges"). In addition, a **management fee** is levied annually for the professional services provided, and it is deducted right off the top, regardless of whether the fund has had a good or a bad year. Yet, even in spite of all the professional management and advice, it seems that *mutual fund performance* over the long haul is at best about equal to what you would expect from the market as a whole. There are some notable exceptions, but most funds do little more than keep up with the market—and in many cases, they don't even do that.

management fee
a fee levied annually for professional mutual fund services provided; paid regardless of the performance of the portfolio.

Figure 13.2 shows the investment performance for ten different types of equity (or equity-oriented) funds over the 5-year period from 1993 to 1997. The reported returns are average, fully compounded annual rates of return, and they assume that all dividends and capital gains distributions are reinvested into additional shares of stock. Note that when compared to the S&P 500, only *two* fund categories outperformed the market, whereas several of them fell far short of the mark. The message is clear: *Consistently beating the market is no easy task,* even for professional money managers. Although a handful of funds have given investors above-average and even spectacular rates of return, most mutual funds simply do not meet those levels of performance. This is not to say that the long-term returns from mutual funds are substandard or that they fail to equal what you could achieve by putting your money in, say, a savings account or some other risk-free investment outlet. Quite the contrary: The long-term returns from mutual funds have been substantial (and perhaps even better than what a lot of individual investors could have achieved on their own), but most of these returns can be traced to strong market conditions and/or to the reinvestment of dividends and capital gains.

How Mutual Funds Are Organized and Run

Although it's tempting to think of a mutual fund as a single large entity, that view is not really accurate. Various functions—investing, record keeping, safekeeping, and others—are split among two or more companies. To begin with,

FIGURE 13.2
The Comparative Performance of Mutual Funds Versus the Market

Even with the services of professional money managers, it's tough to outperform the market. In this case, the average performance of eight out of the ten fund categories failed to meet the market's standard of return. (Source: *Morningstar,* December 1997.)

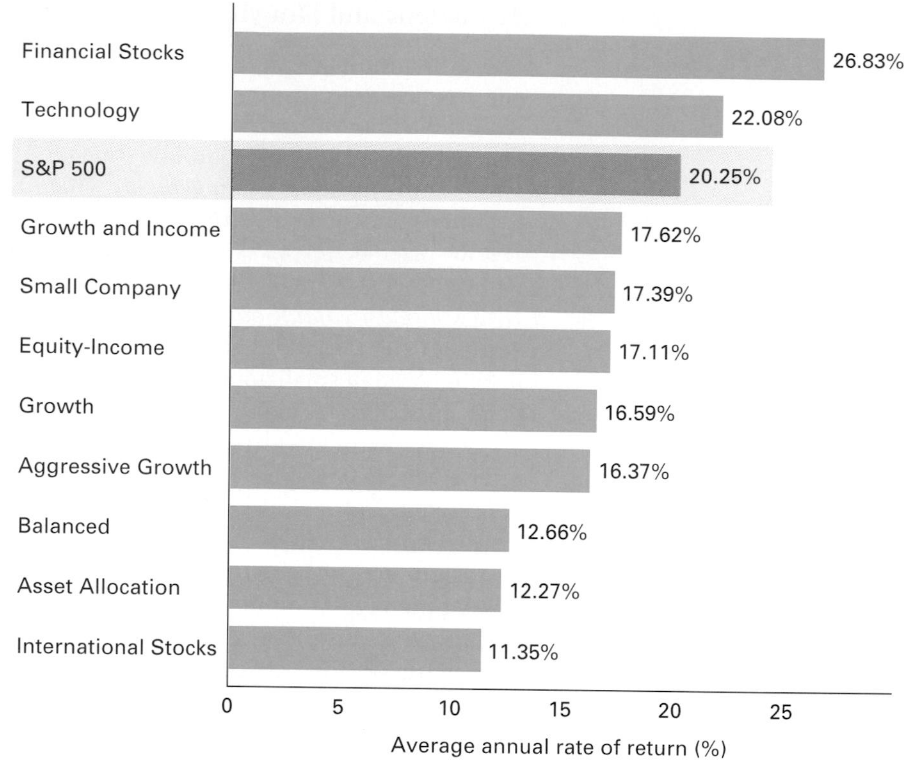

there's the fund itself, which is organized as a separate corporation or trust and is owned by the shareholders, not by the firm that runs it. In addition, there are several other main players:

- The *management company* runs the fund's daily operations. Management companies are the firms we know as Fidelity, Vanguard, T. Rowe Price, American Century, and Dreyfus; they are the ones that create the funds in the first place. Usually, the management firm also serves as investment adviser.

- The *investment adviser* buys and sells stocks or bonds and otherwise oversees the portfolio. Usually, three parties participate in this phase of the operation: (1) the *money manager,* who actually runs the portfolio and makes the buy and sell decisions; (2) *securities analysts,* who analyze securities and look for viable investment candidates; and (3) *traders,* who buy and sell big blocks of securities at the best possible price.

- The *distributor* sells fund shares, either directly to the public or through authorized dealers (like major brokerage houses and commercial banks). When you request a prospectus and sales literature, you deal with the distributor.

- The *custodian* physically safeguards the securities and other assets of the fund, without taking a role in the investment decisions. To discourage foul play, an independent party (usually a bank) serves in this capacity.

- The *transfer agent* keeps track of purchase and redemption requests from shareholders and maintains other shareholder records.

All this separation of duties is designed to protect the mutual fund investor/shareholder. Obviously, as a mutual fund investor, you will lose money if your fund's stock or bond holdings go down in value. But that's really the only risk of loss you face, because the chance of your ever losing money *from fraud, scandal, or a mutual fund collapse* is almost nonexistent. Here's why: In addition to the separation of duties we have noted, the only formal link between the mutual fund and the company that manages it (the management company) is a contract that must be renewed—and approved by shareholders—on a regular basis. One of the provisions of this contractual arrangement is that the fund's assets—stocks, bonds, cash, or other securities in the portfolio—can *never be in the hands of the management company.* As still another safeguard, each fund must have a board of directors, or trustees, who are elected by shareholders and are charged with keeping tabs on the management company and renewing its contract. The bottom line is that in over 70 years there has never been a major crisis or scandal in the mutual fund industry. Nor, given all the tight regulations and structural firewalls in place, is there likely to be one.

Mutual Fund Regulations

We discussed securities regulations in Chapter 2, but it might be helpful to briefly review some of the major regulatory provisions that apply to mutual funds. To begin with, the *Securities Act of 1933* requires the filing of full information about a mutual fund with the SEC. This act also requires the fund to provide potential investors with a fund profile or current prospectus, disclosing the fund's management, its investment policies and objectives, and other essential data. In addition, the purchase and sale of mutual fund shares are subject to the antifraud provisions of the *Securities Exchange Act of 1934*, and the *Investment Advisers Act of 1940* regulates the activities of the investment advisers that work for mutual funds. Most important, in order to qualify for investment company status, a fund must comply with the provisions of the *Investment Company Act of 1940.* That comprehensive piece of legislation provides the foundation for the regulation of the mutual fund industry and, among other things, establishes standards of income distribution, fee structures, and diversification of assets.

From a tax perspective, a mutual fund can be treated as an essentially tax-exempt organization (and thereby avoid the double taxation of dividends and income) so long as it qualifies under *Subchapter M* of the Internal Revenue Code of 1954. Briefly, to operate as a regulated investment company and enjoy the attendant tax benefits, a fund must annually distribute to its shareholders all of its realized capital gains and at least 90% of its interest and dividend income. That way, the fund will pay *no* taxes on any of its earnings, whether they're derived from current income or capital gains.

Essential Characteristics

Although investing in mutual funds has been made as simple as possible, investors nevertheless should have a clear understanding of what they're getting into. For starters, it's essential that you be aware of the many different types of mutual funds available. In addition, you should become familiar with the differences in organizational structures, as well as with the wide array of fees and charges that you might encounter when investing in mutual funds.

Open-End Investment Companies

open-end investment company
a type of investment company in which investors buy shares from, and sell them back to, the mutual fund itself, with no limit on the number of shares the fund can issue.

The term *mutual fund* is commonly used to describe an open-end investment company. In an **open-end investment company,** investors buy their shares from, and sell them back to, the mutual fund itself. When an investor buys shares in an open-end fund, the fund issues new shares of stock and fills the purchase order with those new shares. There is no limit, other than investor demand, to the number of shares the fund can issue. (Occasionally, funds *temporarily* close themselves to new investors—they won't open any new accounts—in an attempt to keep fund growth in check.) All open-end mutual funds stand behind their shares and buy them back when investors decide to sell. Thus there is never any trading between individuals. Open-end mutual funds are the dominant type of investment company and account for well over 90% of the assets under management. Many of these funds are very large and hold *billions* of dollars' worth of securities. Indeed, in 1997, the typical stock or bond fund held an average portfolio of some $500 million, and there were more than 400 billion-dollar funds.

Both buy and sell transactions in (open-end) mutual funds are carried out at prices based on the current market value of all the securities held in the fund's portfolio. (Technically, this would also include the book value of any other assets, such as cash and receivables from securities transactions, that the fund might hold at the time, though for all practical purposes, these other assets generally account for only a tiny fraction of the fund's total portfolio.) Known as the fund's **net asset value (NAV),** this current market value is calculated at least once a day and represents the underlying value of a share of stock in a particular mutual fund. NAV is found by taking the total market value of all securities (and other assets) held by the fund, less any liabilities, and dividing this amount by the number of fund shares outstanding. For example, if the market value of all the securities (and other assets) held by the XYZ mutual fund on a given day equaled $10 million, and if XYZ on that particular day had 500,000 shares outstanding, the fund's net asset value per share would amount to $20 ($10,000,000 ÷ 500,000 = $20). This figure, as we will see, is then used to derive the price at which the fund shares are bought and sold.

net asset value (NAV)
the underlying value of a share of stock in a particular mutual fund.

Closed-End Investment Companies

Whereas the term *mutual fund* is supposed to be used only with open-end funds, it is also commonly used to refer to closed-end investment companies. **Closed-end investment companies** operate with a fixed number of shares outstanding and do not regularly issue new shares of stock. In effect, they have a capital structure like that of any other corporation, except that the corporation's business happens to be investing in marketable securities. Shares in closed-end investment companies, like those of any other common stock, are actively traded in the secondary market. But unlike open-end funds, *all trading in closed-end funds is done between investors in the open market.* The fund itself plays no role in either buy or sell transactions; once the shares are issued, the fund is out of the picture. By far, most closed-end investment companies

closed-end investment companies
a type of investment company that operates with a fixed number of shares outstanding.

are traded on the New York Stock Exchange, a few are traded on the American Exchange, and occasionally some are traded in the OTC market or on some other exchange. As Figure 13.3 shows, the shares of closed-end companies are listed right along with shares of other common stocks. In this case, Adams Express (one of the larger closed-end investment companies) is quoted on the NYSE.

Many of the investment advisers that run closed-end funds (like Putnam, Kemper, Nuveen, MFS, and Franklin-Templeton) also manage open-end funds, often with similar investment objectives. They offer both closed- and open-end funds because they are really *two different investment products*. For although it may not appear so at first glance, there are some major differences between these two types of funds. To begin with, because closed-end funds have a fixed amount of capital to work with, they don't have to worry about stock redemptions or new money coming into the fund. Therefore, they don't have to be concerned about keeping cash on hand (or readily available) to meet redemptions. Equally important, because there is no pressure on portfolio managers to cash in these securities at inopportune times, they can be more aggressive in their investment styles by investing in obscure yet attractive securities that may not be actively traded. And, of course, because they don't have new money flowing in all the time, portfolio managers don't have to worry about finding new investments but, instead, can concentrate on a set portfolio of securities.

Of course, this also puts added pressures on the money managers, since their investment styles and fund portfolios are closely monitored and judged

FIGURE 13.3 Stock Quotations for Closed-End Investment Companies

The quotes for closed-end investment companies are listed right along with those of other common stocks. Except for the lack of a P/E ratio, their quotes are pretty much the same. (Source: *Wall Street Journal,* December 16, 1997.)

	52 Weeks Hi	Lo	Stock	Sym	Div	Yld %	PE	Vol 100s	Hi	Lo	Close	Net Chg
	36 1/8	12 1/2	Abercrombie A	ANF		...	...	2379	32 1/8	29 7/8	30 3/8	−2 3/8
	21	12 1/2	Abitibi g	ABY	.40	...	...	1745	12 7/8	12 5/8	12 13/16	+ 3/16
	28 5/8	17 3/4♣	AcceptIns	AIF		...	12	167	25 5/16	25 1/16	25 1/16	− 1/4
	32	15 3/4	AccuStaff	ASI		...	39	1881	27 3/8	27	27 1/4	+ 1/16
	101 1/16	55 3/4	ACE Ltd	ACL	.96f	1.0	11	1467	93	92	92 5/16	+ 5/16
	18 1/2	10	AckrlyGrp	AK	.02	.1	26	236	16 1/2	16 1/16	16 1/4	+ 1/4
	10 3/8	5	AcmeElec	ACE		...	86	409	5 5/16	5	5 3/16	− 1/16
	20 3/8	9 5/8	AcmeMetals	AMI		...	dd	267	10 1/4	9 7/8	9 5/16	...
	24 5/8	14	ACNielsen	ART		...	41	739	22 9/16	22 1/4	22 5/16	− 1/16
	29 3/4	16 3/4	Acuson	ACN		...	40	512	17 7/16	17 3/32	17 1/4	...
	25 1/2	19 3/8	AdamsExp	ADX	1.96e	8.5	...	310	23 3/8	23 1/16	23 3/16	+ 1/4
n	26 1/2	13 3/4	Administaff	ASF		...	...	56	23 1/4	22 5/8	23 1/4	+ 7/8
▼	48 1/2	17 7/8♣	AdvMicro	AMD		...	dd	19318	18 1/2	17 1/2	18 7/16	+ 1/4
	27 1/2	10 1/8	Advest	ADV	.16f	.7	14	257	23	21 3/4	22 15/16	+ 15/16
	23 5/8	11	Advo	AD		...	20	409	21 9/16	21 7/16	21 1/2	...
	12 15/16	7 ♣	Advocat	AVC		...	10	271	8	7 3/4	7 15/16	− 1/4
	88 15/16	54 1/8♣	AEGON	AEG	1.52e	1.7	23	118	88 1/4	87 7/8	88 1/8	+1 5/8
	12 1/2	3 1/8♣	Aeroflex	ARX		...	21	541	8 1/4	7 3/4	7 3/4	...
	57 1/2	32 5/8	AeroVick	ANV	.80	1.6	15	944	49	48 1/2	48 9/16	− 3/16

by the market. That is, the share prices of closed-end companies are determined not only by their net asset values but also by general supply and demand conditions in the stock market. As a result, depending on the market outlook and investor expectations, closed-end companies generally trade at a discount or premium to NAV (they almost never trade at net asset value). Share price discounts and premiums can at times become quite large. For example, it's not unusual for such spreads to amount to as much as 25% to 30% of net asset value—occasionally more—depending on market judgments and expectations. Figure 13.4 lists some actively traded closed-end funds, along with prevailing premiums (+) and discounts (−).

Unit Investment Trusts

unit investment trust (UIT) a type of investment vehicle whereby the trust sponsors put together a fixed/unmanaged portfolio of securities and then sell ownership units in the portfolio to individual investors.

A **unit investment trust** (UIT) represents little more than an interest in an *unmanaged* pool of investments. UITs are like mutual funds to the extent that both involve portfolios of securities. But that's where the similarity ends, because once a portfolio of securities is put together for a UIT, it is simply held in safekeeping for investors under conditions set down in a trust agreement. Traditionally, these portfolios were made up of various types of *fixed-income securities*, with long-term municipal bonds being the most popular by far. There is no trading in the portfolios, so the returns, or yields, are fixed and fairly predictable—at least for the short term. Not surprisingly, these unit investment

FIGURE 13.4
Some Actively Traded Closed-End Mutual Funds

As can be seen here, the market prices of closed-end mutual funds often exceed or fall short of the funds' NAV—all of which results in the funds' premiums or discounts. (Source: *Wall Street Journal,* December 15, 1997.)

Fund Name	Stock Exch	NAV	Market Price	Prem /Disc	52-week Market Return
		General Equity Funds			
Adams Express (ADX)	N	28.00	22 15/16	− 18.1	27.5
Alliance All-Mkt (AMO)	N	32.31	30 15/16	− 4.2	64.1
Avalon Capital (MIST)	O	14.78	12	− 18.8	9.1
Baker Fentress (BKF)	N	21.33	17 5/8	− 17.4	22.7
Bergstrom Cap (BEM)	A	159.18	144	− 9.5	31.7
Blue Chip Value (BLU)	N	10.36	11 1/4	+ 8.6	34.3
Central Secs (CET)	A	27.59	30 1/8	+ 9.2	37.0
Corp Renaissance (CREN)-c	O	7.90	5 5/8	− 28.8	− 28.6
Engex (EGX)	A	N/A	N/A	N/A	N/A
Equus II (EQS)	A	29.35	23	− 21.6	50.4
Gabelli Equity (GAB)	N	11.53	11 5/8	+ 0.8	32.9
General American (GAM)	N	28.72	25 7/8	− 9.9	40.5
		Specialized Equity Funds			
C&S Realty (RIF)	A	12.18	12 3/8	+ 1.6	19.2
C&S Total Rtn (RFI)-a	N	18.81	18 1/2	− 1.6	22.9
Centrl Fd Canada (CEF)-c	A	4.28	3 5/8	− 15.3	− 17.9
Delaware Gr Div (DDF)-a	N	17.95	18 5/8	+ 3.8	25.8
Delaware Grp Gl (DGF)	N	N/A	N/A	N/A	N/A
Duff&Ph Util Inc (DNP)	N	9.48	10 1/16	+ 6.1	25.5
Emer Mkts Infra (EMG)	N	14.11	11 3/16	− 20.7	6.1
Emer Mkts Tel (ETF)	N	19.03	15 13/16	− 16.9	11.9
First Financial (FF)	N	16.23	17 13/16	+ 9.8	50.5
Gabelli Gl Media (GGT)	N	10.36	8 5/8	− 16.7	30.9

trusts appeal mainly to income-oriented investors looking for a safe, steady stream of income.

In the early 1990s, brokerage firms began aggressively marketing a new type of investment product, the *stock-oriented UIT.* These new equity trusts caught on quickly with investors seeking capital gains and attractive returns. The most popular equity trusts are those based on the "dogs of the Dow" (see Chapter 5), although growth stock, high dividend yield, and market index trusts also do well. Stock trusts are normally offered with terms that range from 1-year (typical of the Dow dogs products) to 5 years (found on many stock index trusts). Except for the shorter terms (1 to 5 years for equity trusts vs. 15 to 30 years for fixed-income products), these trusts are really no different from the traditional bond-oriented UITs: Once the portfolios are put together, they usually remain untouched for the life of the trust.

Various sponsoring brokerage houses put together these pools of securities and then sell units of the pool to investors (each unit being like a share in a mutual fund). For example, a brokerage house might put together a diversified pool of corporate securities that amounts to, say, $100 million. The sponsoring firm would then sell units in this pool to the investing public at anywhere from $250 (for many equity trusts) to $1,000 per unit (common for fixed-income products). The sponsoring organization does little more than routine recordkeeping, and it services the investments by collecting coupons or dividends and distributing the income (often on a monthly basis) to the holders of the trust units. There is a dark side to UITs, however. *They tend to be very costly.* These products can have not only substantial up-front transaction costs but also hefty annual fees. For example, many equity UITs assess load charges of 1% to 3% and then another 1½% to 2½% in annual fees—both of which are well above what you'd pay for a typical equity mutual fund. Brokers argue that they earn those fat fees by removing fear and greed from the investment process and by enabling investors to build a well-diversified portfolio at a reasonable cost.

Load and No-Load Funds

The question of whether a fund is "load" or "no-load" is a matter of concern only to investors in *open-end* funds. The load charge on an open-end fund is the commission the investor pays when buying shares in a fund. (Recall from our discussion above that closed-end funds trade on listed or OTC markets and thus are subject to the same commission and transactions costs as any other share of common stock.) Generally speaking, the term **load fund** is used to describe a mutual fund that charges a commission when shares are bought (such charges are also known as *front-end loads*). In a **no-load fund** no sales charges are levied. Load charges can be fairly substantial and can amount to as much as 8½% of the *purchase price* of the shares (though only a handful of funds today charge this maximum front-end load).

load fund
a mutual fund that charges a commission when shares are bought; also known as a *front-end load fund.*

no-load fund
a mutual fund that does not charge a commission when shares are bought.

Although there may be little or no difference in the performance of load and no-load funds, *the cost savings with no-load funds tend to give investors a head start in achieving superior rates of return.* Unfortunately, the true no-load fund is becoming harder to find, as more and more no-loads are becoming *12(b)-1 funds.* Although such funds do not directly charge commissions at the time of purchase, they assess what are known as 12(b)-1 charges *annually* to make up for any lost commissions (these charges are more fully described below). Overall, less than 30% of the funds sold today are pure no-loads; the rest charge some type of load or fee.

Fortunately, you can use the mutual fund quotes (at least those in the *Wall Street Journal*) to separate the no-load from the load funds. That is, all open-end mutual funds are priced according to their net asset values, which—as you can see in the first column in Figure 13.5—are part of standard mutual fund quotations. The "NAV" (net asset value) column is the price the mutual fund will pay to buy back the fund shares (or, from the investor's point of view, the price at which the shares can be sold); it's also the price you pay when you buy *no-load* funds. The price you would have to pay to buy *load* funds, however, is not included in the *Wall Street Journal* quotes. To find the so-called *offer price* of a fund—the price you pay to *buy shares*—you'd have to either call the fund itself to get a quote or estimate it using the NAV price.

To estimate the offer price from the NAV, simply factor in the initial load charge (which is listed in the next-to-last column in Figure 13.5—see the column headed "Maximum Initial Charge"). That is, if you take the quoted NAV and multiply it by *one plus the initial load charge,* you'll end up with a fairly close approximation to the load fund's offer price (it's an approximation because the load charge is stated relative to the fund's offer price, not the lower net asset value). Thus, for the FPA Paramount Fund, which has a quoted NAV in Figure 13.5 of $11.88 and an initial load charge of 6.5%, you'd have an *approximate offer price* of $11.88 × 1.065 = $12.65 (the actual offer price was $12.70). The difference between the NAV and the offer price represents the front-end load charge. For the FPA Paramount Fund, the stated load charge of 6½% is *relative to the fund's offer price.* However, the load rate is actually *more* when the commission is related to a more appropriate base—the NAV of the fund. When stated as a percentage of NAV, the load charge for this fund is closer to 7%. Relative to what it costs to buy and sell common stocks, that's a pretty hefty charge, even after taking into account the fact that you normally don't have to pay a commission on the *sale* of most funds. Although the *maximum* load charge allowable is 8½% of the purchase price, very few funds charge the maximum. Rather, many funds charge commissions of only 2% or 3%—such funds are known as **low-load funds.** There is a commission to pay on low-load funds, but it's relatively small.

low-load fund
a mutual fund that charges a small commission (2% to 3%) when shares are bought.

back-end load
a commission charged on the *sale* of shares in a mutual fund.

Occasionally, a fund will have a **back-end load,** which means commissions are levied when shares are sold. These loads may amount to as much as 7¼% of the value of the shares sold, although back-end loads tend to decline over time and usually disappear altogether after 5 or 6 years. The stated purpose of back-end loads is to enhance fund stability by discouraging investors from trading in and out of the funds over short investment horizons. In addition, a substantial (and growing) number of funds charge something called a **12(b)-1 fee** that's assessed annually for as long as you own the fund. Known appropriately as *hidden loads,*, these fees are designed to help funds (particularly the no-loads) cover their distribution and marketing costs. They can amount to as much as 1% per year of assets under management. In good markets and bad, these fees are paid right off the top, and that can take its toll. Consider, for instance, $10,000 in a fund that charges a 1% 12(b)-1 fee. That translates into a charge of $100 a year—certainly not an insignificant amount of money.

12(b)-1 fee
a fee levied annually by some mutual funds to cover management and other operating costs; amounts to as much as 1% of the average net assets.

The latest trend in mutual fund fees is the so-called *multiple-class sales charge.* You'll find such arrangements at firms like American Capital, Dreyfus,

FIGURE 13.5 Mutual Fund Quotes

Open-end mutual funds are listed separately from other securities, and they have their own quotation system, as shown in these *Wall Street Journal* quotes. For one thing, these securities are quoted in dollars and cents (most other securities are listed in eighths, sixteenths, or thirty-seconds). Also, the type of load charge, if any, as well as the annual expense ratio, is indicated as part of these *monthly* quotes. Note that the quotes shown here appear once a month (usually on the first Monday of the month), whereas the rest of the time, the quotes will normally contain just three pieces of information: the NAV, net change, and year-to-date returns. (Source: *Wall Street Journal*, January 16, 1998.)

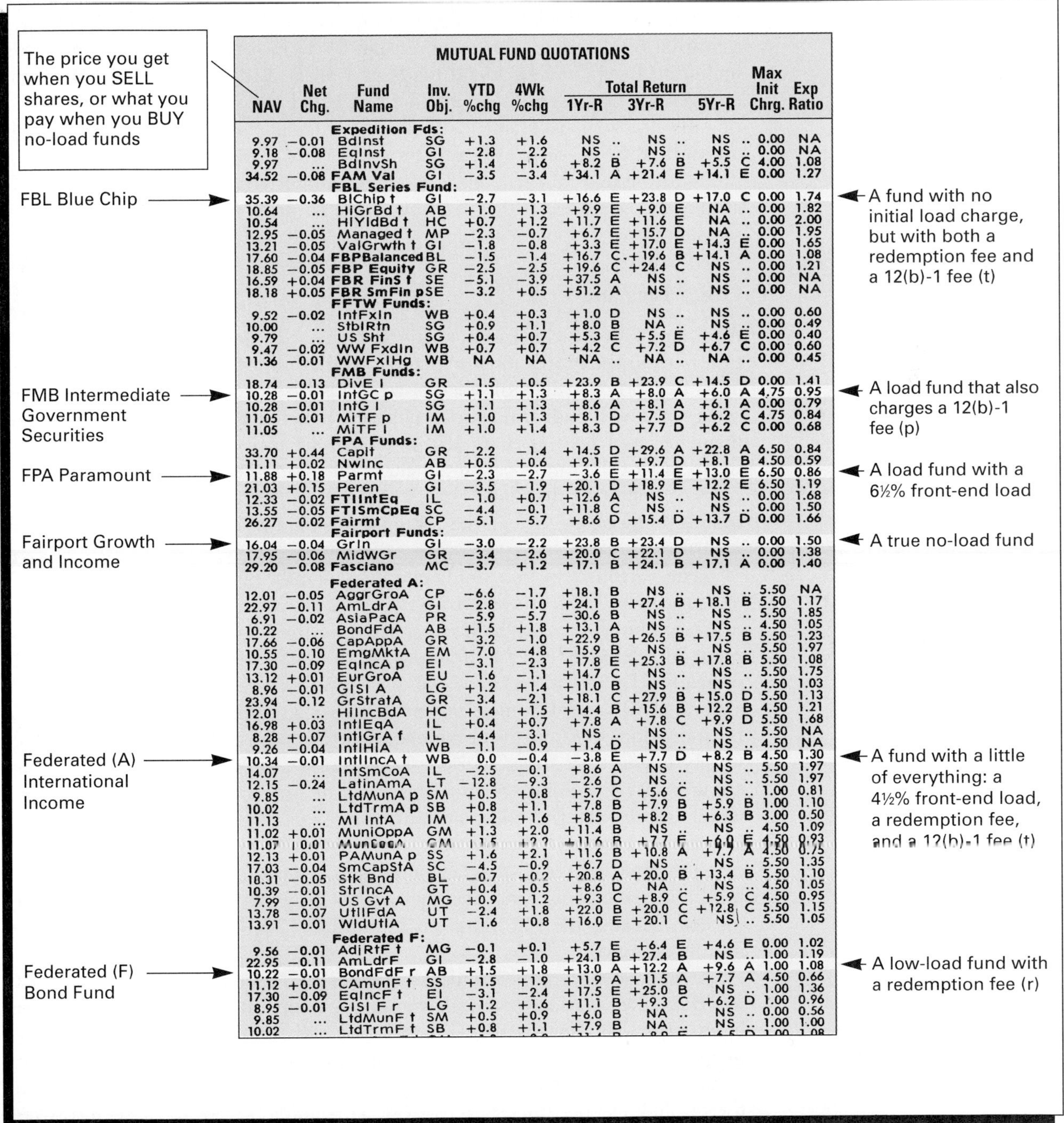

MUTUAL FUND QUOTATIONS

NAV	Net Chg.	Fund Name	Inv. Obj.	YTD %chg	4Wk %chg	Total Return 1Yr-R		3Yr-R		5Yr-R		Max Init Chrg.	Exp Ratio
		Expedition Fds:											
9.97	−0.01	BdInst	SG	+1.3	+1.6	NS	..	NS	..	NS	..	0.00	NA
9.18	−0.08	EqInst	GI	−2.8	−2.2	NS	..	NS	..	NS	..	0.00	NA
9.97	...	BdInvSh	SG	+1.4	+1.6	+8.2	B	+7.6	B	+5.5	C	4.00	1.08
34.52	−0.08	**FAM Val**	GI	−3.5	−3.4	+34.1	A	+21.4	E	+14.1	E	0.00	1.27
		FBL Series Fund:											
35.39	−0.36	BlChip t	GI	−2.7	−3.1	+16.6	E	+23.8	D	+17.0	C	0.00	1.74
10.64	...	HiGrBd t	AB	+1.0	+1.3	+9.9	E	+9.0	E	NA	..	0.00	1.82
10.54	...	HIYldBd t	HC	+0.7	+1.2	+11.7	E	+11.6	E	NA	..	0.00	2.00
12.95	−0.05	Managed t	MP	−2.3	−0.7	+6.7	E	+15.7	D	NA	..	0.00	1.95
13.21	−0.05	ValGrwth t	GI	−1.8	−0.8	+3.3	E	+17.0	E	+14.3	E	0.00	1.65
17.60	−0.04	**FBPBalanced**	BL	−1.5	−1.4	+16.7	C	+19.6	B	+14.1	A	0.00	1.08
18.85	−0.05	**FBP Equity**	GR	−2.5	−2.5	+19.6	C	+24.4	C	NS	..	0.00	1.21
16.59	+0.04	**FBR FinS t**	SE	−5.1	−3.9	+37.5	A	NS	..	NS	..	0.00	NA
18.18	+0.05	**FBR SmFin p**	SE	−3.2	+0.5	+51.2	A	NS	..	NS	..	0.00	NA
		FFTW Funds:											
9.52	−0.02	IntFxIn	WB	+0.4	+0.3	+1.0	D	NS	..	NS	..	0.00	0.60
10.00	...	StbIRtn	SG	+0.9	+1.1	+8.0	B	NA	..	NS	..	0.00	0.49
9.79	...	US Sht	SG	+0.4	+0.7	+5.3	E	+5.5	E	+4.6	E	0.00	0.40
9.47	−0.02	WW FxdIn	WB	+0.7	+0.7	+4.2	C	+7.2	D	+6.7	C	0.00	0.60
11.36	−0.01	WWFxIHg	WB	NA	NA	NA	..	NA	..	NA	..	0.00	0.45
		FMB Funds:											
18.74	−0.13	DivE I	GR	−1.5	+0.5	+23.9	B	+23.9	C	+14.5	D	0.00	1.41
10.28	−0.01	IntGC p	SG	+1.1	+1.3	+8.3	A	+8.0	A	+6.0	A	4.75	0.95
10.28	−0.01	IntG I	SG	+1.1	+1.3	+8.6	A	+8.1	A	+6.1	A	0.00	0.79
11.05	−0.01	MiTF p	IM	+1.0	+1.3	+8.1	D	+7.5	D	+6.2	C	4.75	0.84
11.05	...	MiTF I	IM	+1.0	+1.4	+8.3	D	+7.7	D	+6.2	C	0.00	0.68
		FPA Funds:											
33.70	+0.44	Caplt	GR	−2.2	−1.4	+14.5	D	+29.6	A	+22.8	A	6.50	0.84
11.11	+0.02	NwInc	AB	+0.5	+0.6	+9.1	E	+9.7	D	+8.1	B	4.50	0.59
11.88	+0.18	Parmt	GI	−2.3	−2.7	−3.6	E	+11.4	E	+13.0	E	6.50	0.86
21.03	+0.15	Peren	GI	−3.5	−1.9	+20.1	D	+18.9	E	+12.2	E	6.50	1.19
12.33	−0.02	**FTIIntEq**	IL	−1.0	+0.7	+12.6	A	NS	..	NS	..	0.00	1.68
13.55	−0.05	**FTISmCpEq**	SC	−4.4	−0.1	+11.8	C	NS	..	NS	..	0.00	1.50
26.27	−0.02	**Fairmt**	CP	−5.1	−5.7	+8.6	D	+15.4	D	+13.7	D	0.00	1.66
		Fairport Funds:											
16.04	−0.04	GrIn	GI	−3.0	−2.2	+23.8	B	+23.4	D	NS	..	0.00	1.50
17.95	−0.06	MidWGr	GR	−3.4	−2.6	+20.0	C	+22.1	D	NS	..	0.00	1.38
29.20	−0.08	**Fasciano**	MC	−3.7	+1.2	+17.1	B	+24.1	B	+17.1	A	0.00	1.40
		Federated A:											
12.01	−0.05	AggrGroA	CP	−6.6	−1.7	+18.1	B	NS	..	NS	..	5.50	NA
22.97	−0.11	AmLdrA	GI	−2.8	−1.0	+24.1	B	+27.4	B	+18.1	B	5.50	1.17
6.91	−0.02	AsiaPacA	PR	−5.9	−5.7	−30.6	B	NS	..	NS	..	5.50	1.85
10.22	...	BondFdA	AB	+1.5	+1.8	+13.1	A	NS	..	NS	..	4.50	1.05
17.66	−0.06	CapAppA	GR	−3.2	−1.0	+22.9	B	+26.5	B	+17.5	B	5.50	1.23
10.55	−0.10	EmgMktA	EM	−7.0	−4.8	−15.9	B	NS	..	NS	..	5.50	1.97
17.30	−0.09	EqIncA p	EI	−3.1	−2.3	+17.8	E	+25.3	B	+17.8	B	5.50	1.08
13.12	+0.01	EurGroA	EU	−1.6	−1.1	+14.7	C	NS	..	NS	..	5.50	1.75
8.96	−0.01	GISI A	LG	+1.2	+1.4	+11.0	B	NS	..	NS	..	4.50	1.03
23.94	−0.12	GrStratA	GR	−3.4	−2.1	+18.1	C	+27.9	B	+15.0	D	5.50	1.13
12.01	...	HiIncBdA	HC	+1.4	+1.5	+14.4	B	+15.6	B	+12.2	B	4.50	1.21
16.98	+0.03	IntlEqA	IL	+0.4	+0.7	+7.8	A	+7.8	C	+9.9	D	5.50	1.68
8.28	+0.07	IntlGrA f	IL	−4.4	−3.1	NS	..	NS	..	NS	..	5.50	NA
9.26	−0.04	IntlHiA	WB	−1.1	−0.9	+1.4	D	NS	..	NS	..	4.50	NA
10.34	−0.01	IntlIncA t	WB	0.0	−0.4	−3.8	E	+7.7	D	+8.2	B	4.50	1.30
14.07	...	IntSmCoA	IL	−2.5	−0.1	+8.6	A	NS	..	NS	..	5.50	1.97
12.15	−0.24	LatinAmA	LT	−12.8	−9.3	−2.6	D	NS	..	NS	..	5.50	1.97
9.85	...	LtdMunA p	SM	+0.5	+0.8	+5.7	C	+5.6	C	NS	..	1.00	0.81
10.02	...	LtdTrmA p	SB	+0.8	+1.1	+7.8	B	+7.9	B	+5.9	B	1.00	1.10
11.13	...	MI IntA	IM	+1.2	+1.6	+8.5	D	+8.2	B	+6.3	B	3.00	0.50
11.02	+0.01	MuniOppA	GM	+1.3	+2.0	+11.4	B	NS	..	NS	..	4.50	1.09
11.07	+0.01	MunSecA	GM	+1.5	+2.2	+11.6	B	+7.7	E	+6.0	E	4.50	0.93
12.13	+0.01	PAMunA p	SS	+1.6	+2.1	+11.6	B	+10.8	A	+7.7	A	4.50	0.75
17.03	−0.04	SmCapStA	SC	−4.5	−0.9	+6.7	D	NS	..	NS	..	5.50	1.35
18.31	−0.05	Stk Bnd	BL	−0.7	+0.2	+20.8	A	+20.0	B	+13.4	B	5.50	1.10
10.39	−0.01	StrIncA	GT	+0.4	+0.5	+8.6	D	NA	..	NS	..	4.50	1.05
7.99	−0.01	US Gvt A	MG	+0.9	+1.2	+9.3	C	+8.9	C	+5.9	C	4.50	0.95
13.78	−0.07	UtilFdA	UT	−2.4	+1.8	+22.0	B	+20.0	C	+12.8	C	5.50	1.15
13.91	−0.01	WldUtlA	UT	−1.6	+0.8	+16.0	E	+20.1	C	NS	..	5.50	1.05
		Federated F:											
9.56	−0.01	AdjRtF t	MG	−0.1	+0.1	+5.7	E	+6.4	E	+4.6	E	0.00	1.02
22.95	−0.11	AmLdrF	GI	−2.8	−1.0	+24.1	B	+27.4	B	NS	..	1.00	1.19
10.22	−0.01	BondFdF r	AB	+1.5	+1.8	+13.0	A	+12.2	A	+9.6	A	1.00	1.08
11.12	+0.01	CAmunF t	SS	+1.5	+1.9	+11.9	A	+11.5	A	+7.7	A	4.50	0.66
17.30	−0.09	EqIncF t	EI	−3.1	−2.4	+17.5	E	+25.0	B	NS	..	1.00	1.36
8.95	−0.01	GISI F r	LG	+1.2	+1.6	+11.1	B	+9.3	C	+6.2	D	1.00	0.96
9.85	...	LtdMunF t	SM	+0.5	+0.9	+6.0	B	NA	..	NS	..	0.00	0.56
10.02	...	LtdTrmF t	SB	+0.8	+1.1	+7.9	B	NA	..	NS	..	1.00	1.00

Merrill Lynch, MFS, Keystone, Smith Barney, and Prudential. The mutual fund issues different classes of stocks on the same fund or portfolio of securities, each class having a different fee structure. For example, class A shares might have normal (relatively high) front-end loads; class B shares might have no front-end loads but substantial back-end loads along with a modest annual 12(b)-1 fee; and class C shares might carry maximum 12(b)-1 fees and nothing else. In other words, you choose your own poison.

To try to bring some semblance of order to fund charges and fees, in 1992 the SEC instituted a series of caps on mutual fund fees. Under the 1992 rules, a mutual fund cannot charge more than 8½% in *total sales charges and fees,* including front- and back-end loads as well as 12(b)-1 fees. Thus, if a fund charges a 5% front-end load and a 1% 12(b)-1 fee, it can charge a maximum of only 2½% in back-end load charges without violating the 8½% cap. In addition, the SEC set a 1% cap on annual 12(b)-1 fees and, perhaps more significantly, stated that true no-load funds cannot charge more than 0.25% in annual 12(b)-1 fees. If they do, they have to drop the no-load label in their sales and promotional material.

Other Fees and Costs

Another cost of owning mutual funds is the *management fee,* the compensation paid to the professional managers who administer the fund's portfolio. It must be paid regardless of whether a fund is load or no-load and whether it is open- or closed-end. Unlike load charges, which are one-time costs, management fees and 12(b)-1 charges, if imposed, are levied annually; they are paid regardless of the fund's performance. In addition, there are the administrative costs of operating the fund. These are fairly modest and represent the normal cost of doing business (e.g., the commissions paid when the fund buys and sells securities).

The various fees that funds charge generally range from less than 0.5% to as much as 2.5% of average assets under management. Total expense ratios bear watching, because high expenses take their toll on performance. As a point of reference, in 1997 domestic stock funds had average expense ratios of around 1.45%, foreign stock funds of around 1.85%, stock index funds of around 0.30%, and domestic bond funds of around 1.00%. Expense ratios for individual funds are quite easy to monitor because they are published each Friday in the *Wall Street Journal.* Take another look at Figure 13.5. The last column in the exhibit, "Exp Ratio," shows the fund's total expense ratio, which represents the latest administrative, management, and 12(b)-1 fees levied by the fund in question. Note that FBL Blue Chip had an annual expense ratio of 1.74% of assets under management, whereas FPA Paramount fund had an expense ratio of only 0.86%. Why the big difference? Probably, in part, because the FBL fund has an annual 12(b)-1 charge, and FPA Paramount does not.

A final cost of mutual funds is the taxes paid on securities transactions. To avoid double taxation, nearly all mutual funds operate as *regulated investment companies.* This means that all (or nearly all) of the dividend and interest income is passed on to the investor, as are any capital gains realized when securities are sold. The mutual fund therefore pays no taxes but instead passes the tax liability on to its shareholders. This holds true whether such distributions are reinvested in the company (in the form of additional mutual fund shares) or paid out in cash. Mutual funds annually provide each stockholder with a summary report on the amount of dividends and capital gains received and the amount of taxable income earned (and to be reported to the IRS) by the fund shareholder.

Keeping Track of Fund Fees and Loads

Critics of the mutual fund industry have come down hard on the proliferation of fund fees and charges. Indeed, some argue that the different charges and fees are really meant to do one thing: confuse the investor. A lot of funds were going to great lengths—lowering a cost here, tacking on a fee there, hiding a charge somewhere else—to make themselves look like something they weren't. The funds were following the letter of the law, and indeed they were fully disclosing all their expenses and fees. The trouble was that the funds were able to hide all but the most conspicuous charges in a bunch of "legalese." Fortunately, steps have been taken to bring fund fees and loads out into the open.

For one thing, fund charges are now more fully reported by the financial press. You don't have to look any further than the mutual fund quotations found in the *Wall Street Journal* and most other major papers. For example, refer to the quotations in Figure 13.5; note the use of the letters *r, p,* and *t* behind the name of the fund. An *r* behind a fund's name means that the fund charges some type of redemption fee, or back-end load, when you sell your shares. This is the case, for example, with the Federated (F) Bond Fund. A *p* in the quotes means that the fund levies a 12(b)-1 fee, which you'll have to pay, for example, if you invest in the FMB Intermediate Government Securities Fund. Finally, a *t* indicates funds that charge both redemption fees and 12(b)-1 fees. Note, for example, that the Federated (A) International Income Fund is one such fund. The point is this: Don't be surprised to find load funds that also charge redemption and/or 12(b)-1 fees. The same goes for no-load funds, which are allowed to charge annual 12(b)-1 fees of 0.25% and still call themselves "no-load" funds. The quotations, of course, tell you only the *kinds* of fees charged by the funds; they do not tell you how much is charged. To get the specifics on the amount charged, you'll have to turn to the fund itself.

All (open-end) mutual funds are required *to disclose fully* all of their expenses in a standardized, easy-to-understand format. Every fund profile or prospectus must contain, up front, a fairly detailed *fee table,* much like the one illustrated in Table 13.1. Note that this table has three parts. The first specifies all *shareholder transaction costs.* In effect, this tells you what it's going to cost to buy and sell shares in the mutual fund. The next section lists the *annual operating expenses* of the fund. Showing these expenses as a percentage of average net assets, the fund must break out management fees, those elusive 12(b)-1 fees, and any other expenses. The third section provides a rundown of the *total cost over time* of buying, selling, and owning the fund. This part of the table contains both transaction and operating expenses and shows what the total costs would be over hypothetical 1-, 3-, 5-, and 10-year holding periods. To ensure consistency and comparability, the funds must follow a rigid set of guidelines when constructing the illustrative costs.

TABLE 13.1 Mutual Fund Expense Disclosure Table

Expenses and Costs of Investing in the Fund

The following information is provided in order to assist investors in understanding the transaction costs and annual expenses associated with investing in the Fund.

A. Shareholder Transaction Costs

Sales load on purchases	2%
Sales load on reinvested dividends	None
Redemption fees or deferred sales charges	None
Exchange (or conversion) fees	None

B. Annual Fund Operating Expenses (as a percentage of average net assets)

Management fees	0.40%
12(b)-1 fees	None
Other expenses (estimated)	0.32%

C. Example of Fund Expenses over Time

You would pay the following total expenses over time on a $1,000 investment assuming a 5% annual return, and a complete redemption of the investment at the end of each indicated time period:

1 year	3 years	5 years	10 years
$27	$43	$59	$108

CONCEPTS IN REVIEW

13.1 What is a *mutual fund?* Discuss the mutual fund concept, including the importance of diversification and professional management.

13.2 What are the attractions and drawbacks of mutual fund ownership?

13.3 Briefly describe how a mutual fund is organized. Who are the key players in a typical mutual fund organization?

13.4 Define each of the following:
   a. Open-end investment company
   b. Closed-end investment company
   c. Unit investment trust

13.5 What is the difference between a *load fund* and a *no-load fund?* What are the advantages of each type? What is a 12(b)-1 fund? Can such a fund operate as a no-load fund?

13.6 Describe a *back-end load,* a *low load,* and a *hidden load.* How can you tell what kind of fees and charges a fund has?

http://hepg.aw.com

Investing in mutual funds can be a relatively simple task for most investors. To make it easy, you must understand what mutual funds are, their risk and return features, and how a particular fund fits into your overall investment strategy. The Mutual Fund Investor's Center provides a good set of Web-based material to educate investors of all levels on mutual funds.

www.mfea.com/educidx.html

Types of Funds and Services

LG 3 LG 4

Some mutual funds specialize in stocks, others in bonds. Some have maximum capital gains as an investment objective, and some high current income. Some funds appeal to speculators, while others are of inerest primarily to income-oriented investors. Every fund has a particular investment objective, and each fund is expected to do its best to conform to its stated investment policy and objective. Categorizing funds according to their investment policies and objectives is a common practice in the mutual fund industry, because doing so reflects similarities not only in how the funds manage their money, but also in their risk and return characteristics. Some of the more popular types of mutual funds are growth, aggressive growth, equity-income, balanced, growth-and-income, bond, money market, index, sector, socially responsible, asset allocation, and international funds. Let's look now at these various types of mutual funds to see what they are and how they operate.

Types of Mutual Funds

Growth Funds

growth fund
a mutual fund whose primary goals are capital gains and long-term growth.

The objective of a **growth fund** is simple: capital appreciation. Long-term growth and capital gains are the primary goals of such funds. Therefore, growth funds invest principally in well-established, large- or mid-cap companies that have above-average growth potential, although they may offer little (if anything) in the way of dividends and current income. Because of the uncertain nature of their investment income, growth funds may involve a fair amount of risk exposure. They are usually viewed as long-term investment vehicles most suitable for the more aggressive investor who wants to build up capital and has little interest in current income.

Aggressive Growth Funds

aggressive growth fund
a highly speculative mutual fund that seeks large profits from capital gains

Aggressive growth funds are the so-called performance funds that tend to increase in popularity when markets heat up. **Aggressive growth funds** are highly speculative investment vehicles that seek large profits from capital gains. Also known as *capital appreciation* or *small-cap* funds, many are fairly small, and their portfolios consist mainly of high-flying common stocks. These funds often buy stocks of small, unseasoned companies; stocks with relatively high price/earnings multiples; and common stocks whose prices are highly volatile. They seem to be especially fond of turnaround situations and may even use leverage in their portfolios (i.e., buy stocks on margin); they also use options fairly aggressively, various hedging techniques, and perhaps even short selling. These techniques are designed, of course, to yield big returns. But aggressive funds are also highly speculative and are among the most volatile of all mutual funds. When the markets are good, aggressive growth funds do well; when the markets are bad, these funds often experience substantial losses.

Equity-Income Funds

equity-income fund
a mutual fund that emphasizes current income and capital preservation and invests primarily in high-yielding common stocks.

Equity-income funds emphasize current income by investing primarily in high-yielding common stocks. Capital preservation is also important, and so are capital gains, although capital appreciation is not a primary objective of equity-income funds. These funds invest heavily in high-grade common stocks, some convertible securities and preferred stocks, and occasionally even junk bonds or certain types of high-grade foreign bonds. As far as their stock holdings are concerned, they lean heavily toward blue chips (including perhaps even "baby blues"), public utilities, and financial shares. They like securities that generate hefty dividend yields but also consider potential price appreciation over the longer haul. In general, because of their emphasis on dividends and current income, these funds tend to hold higher-quality securities that are subject to less price volatility than the market as a whole. They're generally viewed as a fairly low-risk way of investing in stocks.

Balanced Funds

balanced fund
a mutual fund whose objective is to generate a balanced return of both current income and long-term capital gains.

Balanced funds tend to hold a balanced portfolio of both stocks and bonds for the purpose of generating a well-balanced return of both current income and long-term capital gains. In many respects, they're much like equity-income funds, but balanced funds usually put more into fixed-income securities; generally, they keep at least 25% to 50% of their portfolios in bonds. The bonds are used principally to provide current income, and stocks are selected mainly for their long-term growth potential.

The funds can, of course, shift the emphasis in their security holdings one way or the other. Clearly, the more the fund leans toward fixed-income securities, the more income-oriented it will be. For the most part, balanced funds tend to confine their investing to high-grade securities, including growth-oriented blue-chip stocks, high-quality income shares, and high-yielding investment-grade bonds. Therefore, they're usually considered a relatively safe form of investing, in which you can earn a competitive rate of return without having to endure a lot of price volatility.

Growth-and-Income Funds

growth-and-income fund
a mutual fund that seeks both long-term growth and current income, with primary emphasis on capital gains.

Growth-and-income funds also seek a balanced return made up of both current income and long-term capital gains, but they place a greater emphasis on growth of capital. Moreover, unlike balanced funds, growth-and-income funds put most of their money into equities. Indeed, it's not unusual for these funds to have 80% to 90% of their capital in common stocks. They tend to confine most of their investing to quality issues, so growth-oriented blue-chip stocks appear in their portfolios, along with a fair amount of high-quality income stocks. Part of the appeal of these funds is the fairly substantial returns many of them have generated over the long haul. Of course, these funds involve a fair amount of risk, if for no other reason than the emphasis they place on stocks and capital gains. Thus growth-and-income funds are most suitable for those investors who can tolerate the risk and price volatility.

Bond Funds

bond fund
a mutual fund that invests in various kinds and grades of bonds, with income as the primary objective.

As the name implies, **bond funds** invest exclusively in various types and grades of bonds—from Treasury and agency bonds to corporates and municipals. Income is the primary investment objective, although capital gains is not ignored. There are three important advantages of buying shares in bond funds rather than investing directly in bonds. First, the bond funds are generally more liquid than direct investments in bonds. Second, they offer a cost-effective way of achieving a high degree of diversification in an otherwise expensive investment vehicle (most bonds carry minimum denominations of $1,000 to $5,000). Third, bond funds will automatically reinvest interest and other income, thereby allowing the investor to earn fully compounded rates of return.

Bond funds, generally considered to be a fairly conservative form of investment, are not without risk, because *the prices of the bonds held in the fund's portfolio fluctuate with changing interest rates.* Many bond funds are managed pretty conservatively, but a growing number are becoming increasingly aggressive. In fact, much of the growth that bond funds have experienced recently can be attributed to a more aggressive investment attitude. In today's market, investors can find everything from high-grade government bond funds to highly speculative funds that invest in nothing but junk bonds or even in highly volatile derivative securities. Indeed, exotic derivative securities became a real problem in 1993–1994, when many of the bond funds that had large positions in derivatives experienced eye-popping losses. These losses taught investors a valuable lesson: Watch out for funds with heavy exposure to exotic derivative securities, or at least recognize that if the fund is heavily invested in such securities, you may be in for a very bumpy ride.

Bond funds today remain a sound investment and continue to be popular with investors who seek a relatively conservative investment outlet. Here's a list of the different types of bond funds available to investors:

- *Government bond funds,* which invest in U.S. Treasury and agency securities.

- *Mortgage-backed bond funds,* which put their money into various types of mortgage-backed securities of the U.S. government (e.g., GNMA issues). These funds appeal to investors for several reasons: (1) They provide diversification, (2) they are an affordable way to get into mortgage-backed securities, and (3) they allow investors (if they so choose) to reinvest the principal portion of the monthly cash flow, thereby enabling them to preserve rather than consume their capital.

- *High-grade corporate bond funds,* which invest chiefly in investment-grade securities rated triple-B or better.

- *High-yield corporate bond funds,* which are risky investments that buy junk bonds for the yields they offer.

- *Convertible bond funds,* which invest primarily in securities (domestic and possibly foreign) that can be converted or exchanged into common stocks. These funds offer investors some of the price stability of bonds, along with the capital appreciation potential of stocks.

- *Municipal bond funds,* which invest in tax-exempt securities and are suitable for investors who seek tax-free income. Like their corporate counterparts, municipals can come out as either high-grade or high-yield funds. A special type of municipal bond fund is the so-called *single-state fund,* which invests in the municipal issues of only one state, thus producing (for residents of that state) interest income that is *fully exempt* from both federal and state taxes (and possibly even local/city taxes as well).

- *Intermediate-term bond funds,* which invest in bonds with maturities of 7 to 10 years or less and offer not only attractive yields but relatively low price volatility as well. Shorter (2- to 5-year) funds are also available and are often used as substitutes for money market investments by investors looking for higher returns on their money, especially when short-term rates are way down.

Clearly, no matter what you're looking for in a fixed-income security, you're likely to find a bond fund that fits the bill. The number and variety of such funds have skyrocketed in the past 15 years, and by 1997, there were roughly 3,500 publicly traded bond funds that together had more than *$1 trillion* worth of bonds under management.

Money Market Funds

money market mutual fund (money fund)
a mutual fund that pools the capital of investors and uses it to invest in short-term money market instruments.

The first **money market mutual fund,** or **money fund** for short, was set up in November 1972 with just $100,000 in total assets. It was a new idea that applied the mutual fund concept to the buying and selling of short-term money market instruments—bank certificates of deposit, U.S. Treasury bills, and the like. For the first time, investors with modest amounts of capital were given access to the high-yielding money market, where many instruments require minimum investments of $100,000 or more. (Money funds, along with other short-term investment vehicles, were discussed in detail in Chapter 3.) The idea caught on quickly, and the growth in money funds was nothing short of phenomenal. That growth temporarily peaked in 1982, when the introduction of money market deposit accounts by banks and S&Ls caused money fund assets to level off and eventually decline. It didn't take long for the industry to recover, however, and by 1997, there were some 1,300 money funds that together held nearly $1.1 *trillion* in assets.

There are several different kinds of money market mutual funds:

- *General-purpose money funds,* which invest in any and all types of money market investment vehicles, from Treasury bills and bank CDs to corporate commercial paper. The vast majority of money funds are of this type. They invest their money wherever they can find attractive short-term yields.

- *Government securities money funds,* which were established as a way to meet investor concerns for safety. They effectively eliminate any risk of default by confining their investments to Treasury bills and other short-term securities of the U.S. government or its agencies.

- *Tax-exempt money funds*, which limit their investing to very short (30-day to 90-day) tax-exempt municipal securities. Because their income is free from federal income taxes, they appeal predominantly to investors in high tax brackets. The yields on these funds are about 35% to 40% below the returns on other types of money funds, so you need to be in a high enough tax bracket to produce a competitive after-tax return. Some tax-exempt funds confine their investing to the securities of a single state so that residents of high-tax states can enjoy income that's free from both federal and state taxes.

Just about every major brokerage firm has at least four or five money funds of its own, and hundreds more are sold by independent fund distributors. Most require minimum investments of $1,000 (although $2,500 to $5,000 minimum requirements are not uncommon). Because the maximum average maturity of fund holdings cannot exceed 90 days, money funds are highly liquid investment vehicles. They're also very low in risk and virtually immune to capital loss, because at least 95% of the fund's assets must be invested in top-rated/prime-grade securities. Because the interest income produced tends to follow general interest rate conditions, the returns to shareholders are subject to the ups and downs of market interest rates. Even so, the yields on money funds are highly competitive with those of other short-term securities. And with the check-writing privileges they offer, money funds are just as liquid as checking or savings accounts. They are viewed by many investors as a convenient, safe, and profitable way to accumulate capital and temporarily store idle funds.

Index Funds

index fund
a mutual fund that buys and holds a portfolio of stocks (or bonds) equivalent to those in a specific market index.

"If you can't beat 'em, join 'em." That saying pretty much describes the idea behind index funds. Essentially, an **index fund** is a type of mutual fund that buys and holds a portfolio of stocks (or bonds) equivalent to those in a market index like the S&P 500. An index fund that's trying to match the S&P 500, for example, would hold the same 500 stocks that are held in that index, in exactly (or very nearly) the same proportions. Rather than trying to beat the market, as most actively managed funds do, *index funds simply try to match the market*—that is, to match the performance of the index on which the fund is based. They do this through low-cost investment management; in fact, in most cases, the whole portfolio is run almost entirely by a computer that matches the fund's holdings with those of the targeted index.

The approach of index funds is strictly buy-and-hold. Indeed, about the only time an index-fund portfolio changes is when the targeted market index alters its "market basket" of securities. (Occasionally an index will drop a few securities and replace them with new ones.) A pleasant by-product of this buy-and-hold approach is that the funds have extremely low portfolio turnover rates and, therefore, very little in *realized* capital gains. As a result, aside from a modest amount of dividend income, these funds produce very little taxable income from year to year, which causes some high-income investors to view them as a type of tax-sheltered investment.

In addition to their tax shelter, these funds provide something else: By simply trying to match the market, index funds actually produce *highly competitive returns* to investors! It's very tough to outperform the market, whether you are a professional money manager or a seasoned individual investor. Index funds readily acknowledge this fact and don't even try to outperform the market; all they try to do is match market returns. Surprisingly, the net result of this strategy, combined with a *very low cost structure,* is that most index funds readily outperform the vast majority of all other types of stock funds. Indeed, historical data show that only about 20% to 25% of stock funds outperform the market. Because a (true) index fund pretty much matches the market, these funds tend to produce better returns than 75% to 80% of competing stock funds.

Besides the S&P 500, which is the most popular index, a number of other market indexes are used, including the S&P Midcap 400, the Russell 2000 Small Stock, and the Wilshire 5000 indexes, as well as value-stock indexes, growth-stock indexes, international-stock indexes, and even bond indexes. When picking index funds, be sure to avoid high-cost funds; such fees significantly *reduce* the chance that the fund will be able to match the market. Also, avoid index funds that use gimmicks as a way to "enhance" yields: That is, rather than follow the index, these funds will "tilt" their portfolios in an attempt to outperform the market. Your best bet is to buy a *true* index fund—one that has no added "bells and whistles"—and a low-cost one at that.

Sector Funds

sector fund
a mutual fund that restricts its investments to a particular segment of the market.

One of the hottest products on Wall Street is the so-called **sector fund,** a mutual fund that restricts its investments to a particular sector, or segment, of the market. These funds concentrate their investment holdings in one or more industries that make up the sector being aimed at. For example, a health care sector fund would focus on such industries as drug companies, hospital management firms, medical suppliers, and biotech concerns. The portfolio of a sector fund would then consist of promising growth stocks from these particular industries. Among the more popular sector funds are those that concentrate their investments in real estate, technology, financial services, gold and precious metals, leisure and entertainment, natural resources, electronics, chemicals, computers, telecommunications, utilities, and, of course, health care—all the "glamour" industries.

The overriding investment objective of a sector fund is *capital gains.* A sector fund is similar to a growth fund in many respects and should be considered speculative. The sector fund concept is based on the belief that the really attractive returns come from small segments of the market; so rather than diversifying your portfolio across the market, put your money where the action is! It's an interesting notion that may warrant consideration by investors willing to take on the added risks that often accompany these funds.

Socially Responsible Funds

For some, investing is far more than just cranking out financial ratios and calculating investment results. To these investors, the security selection process doesn't end with bottom lines, P/E ratios, growth rates, and betas. Rather, it also includes the *active, explicit consideration of moral, ethical, and environmental issues.* The idea is that social concerns should play just as big a role in investment decisions as do profits and other financial matters. Not surprisingly, there are a number of funds that cater to such investors: Known as **socially responsible funds,** they actively and directly incorporate ethics and morality into the investment decision. Their investment decisions revolve around *both* morality and profitability.

socially responsible fund
a mutual fund that actively and directly incorporates ethics and morality into the investment decision.

Socially responsible funds consider only certain companies for inclusion in their portfolios; if a company doesn't meet the fund's moral, ethical, or environmental tests, fund managers simply won't consider buying the stock, no matter how good the bottom line looks. Generally speaking, these funds refrain from investing in companies that derive revenues from tobacco, alcohol, or gambling; that are weapons contractors; or that operate nuclear power plants. In addition, the funds tend to favor firms that produce "responsible" products or services, that have strong employee relations and positive environmental records, and that are socially responsive to the communities in which they operate. Although these screens may seem to eliminate a lot of stocks from consideration, these funds (most of which are fairly small) still have plenty of securities to choose from, so it's not difficult for them to keep their portfolios fully invested.

As far as performance is concerned, the general perception is that there's a price to pay, in the form of lower average returns, for socially responsible investing. That's not too surprising, however, for whenever you add more investment hurdles, you're likely to reduce return potential. But to those who truly believe in socially responsible investing, the sacrifice apparently is worth it.

Asset Allocation Funds

Studies have shown that the most important decision an investor can make is where to allocate his or her investment assets. *Asset allocation* involves deciding how you're going to divide up your investments among different types of securities. For example, what portion of your money do you want to devote to money market securities, what portion to stocks, and what portion to bonds? Asset allocation deals in broad terms (types of securities) and does not address individual security selection. Strange as it may seem, asset allocation has been found to be a far more important determinant of total returns on a portfolio than individual security selection.

asset allocation fund
a mutual fund that spreads investors' money across stocks, bonds, and money market securities.

Because many individual investors have a tough time making asset allocation decisions, the mutual fund industry has created a product to do the job for them. Known as **asset allocation funds,** these funds spread investors' money across different types of markets. That is, whereas most mutual funds concentrate on one type of investment—whether stocks, bonds, or money market securities—asset allocation funds put money into all these markets. Many of them also include foreign securities in the asset allocation scheme, and some even include inflation-resistant investments, such as gold or real estate. In 1997 there were over 225 asset allocation funds in existence, all designed for people who want to hire fund managers not only to select individual securities for them but also to decide how to allocate money among the various markets.

Here's how a typical asset allocation fund works. The money manger establishes a desired allocation mix, which might look something like this: 50% of the portfolio goes to U.S. stocks, 30% to bonds, 10% to foreign securities, and 10% to money market securities. Securities are then purchased for the fund in these proportions, and the overall portfolio maintains the desired mix. Actually, each segment of the fund is managed almost as a separate portfolio. Thus securities within, say, the stock portion are bought, sold, and held as the market dictates. What really separates asset allocation funds from the rest of the pack is that *as market conditions change over time, the asset allocation mix changes as well.* For example, if the U.S. stock market starts to soften, funds will be moved out of stocks to some other area; as a result, the stock portion of the portfolio might drop to, say, 35% and the foreign securities portion might increase to 25%. Of course, there's no assurance that the money manager will make the right moves at the right time, but the expectation with these funds is that he or she will. (It's interesting to note that *balanced funds* are really a form of asset allocation fund, except that they tend to follow a *fixed-mix* approach to asset allocation—putting, say, 60% of their portfolio into stocks and 40% into bonds—and then pretty much stick to that mix, no matter what the markets are doing.)

Asset allocation funds are supposed to provide investors with one-stop shopping. That is, you just find an asset allocation fund that fits your needs and invest in it, rather than buying a couple of stock funds, a couple of bond funds, and so on. The success of these funds rests not only on how well the money manager picks securities but also on how well he or she times the market and moves funds among different segments of the market. Mutual funds are considered by many to be the ultimate asset allocation vehicle, a fact that has led a number of fund companies to develop what some suggest is the ultimate mutual fund product: *mutual funds that invest in other mutual funds.* Take a look at the accompanying *Investing in Action* box—it describes these so-called funds-of-funds, and explains how they work and what's in it for you.

International Funds

international fund
a mutual fund that does all or most of its investing in foreign securities.

In their search for higher yields and better returns, U.S. investors have shown a growing interest in foreign securities. Sensing an opportunity, the mutual fund industry was quick to respond with a proliferation of so-called **international funds**—a type of mutual fund that does all or most of its investing in foreign securities. Just compare the number of international funds around today with those in existence a few years ago: In 1985 there were only about 40 of these funds; by 1997, the number had grown to over 1,200. The fact is that a lot of people would like to invest in foreign securities but simply don't have the experience or know-how to do so. International funds may be just the vehicle for such investors, *provided they have at least a basic appreciation of international economics.* Because these funds deal with the international economy, balance-of-trade positions, and currency valuations, investors should have a fundamental understanding of what these issues are and how they can affect fund returns.

Technically, the term *international fund* describes a type of fund that invests *exclusively in foreign securities,* often confining its activities to specific geographic regions (e.g., Mexico, Australia, Europe, or the Pacific Rim). In addition, international funds known as *global funds,* invest not only in foreign securities but also in U.S. companies—usually multinational firms. As a rule, global funds provide more diversity and, with access to both foreign and domestic markets, can go wherever the action is.

Regardless of whether they're global or international (we'll use the term *international* to apply to both), you'll find just about any type of fund you could possibly want in the international sector. There are international stock funds, international bond funds, even international money market funds. There are aggressive growth funds, balanced funds, long-term growth funds, high-grade bond funds, and so forth. There are funds that confine their investing to large, established markets (Japan, Germany, Australia, etc.) and others that stick to the more exotic (and risky) emerging markets (e.g., such as Thailand, Mexico, Chile, and even former Communist countries like Poland). No matter what your investment philosophy or objective, you're likely to find what you're looking for in the international area.

INVESTOR FACT

WEAVING A WEB OF FOREIGN INVESTMENTS— Want to invest in one specific country? Try a World Equity Benchmark Share (WEBS). These single-country index stocks, which trade on the American Stock Exchange, allow you to buy most of the publicly traded companies within a single country. At last count, WEBS were available on 17 countries, including Australia, Canada, Hong Kong, Mexico, Singapore, Switzerland, and the United Kingdom. As index-based stocks, WEBS track the Morgan Stanley Capital International indexes for their 17 nations. The most striking thing about WEBS: these index stocks consistently outperform single-country mutual funds where portfolio managers try to pick stocks.

Basically, these funds attempt to take advantage of international economic developments in two ways: (1) by capitalizing on changing market conditions and (2) by positioning themselves to benefit from devaluation of the dollar. They do so because they can make money either from rising share prices in a foreign market or, perhaps just as important, from a falling dollar

INVESTING IN ACTION

Funds of Funds: They Won't Put All Your Eggs in One Basket

Some people invest in individual stocks. Others invest in mutual funds to get professional management and diversification. Still others like the "belt-and-suspenders" approach: *They invest in mutual funds that invest in other mutual funds.* There are nearly 100 of these so-called "funds of funds" today. For example, Vanguard has a fund of funds, the Vanguard Star, that owns shares of six Vanguard equity funds, two Vanguard fixed-income funds, and one Vanguard money market fund. Vanguard Star maintains a target weighting of about 62.5% equities, 25% bonds, and 12.5% money market funds. Buying these investments separately at Vanguard's average $3,000 minimum would require an investment of $27,000 for nine funds. And sometimes these funds are closed to new accounts. But using Star, you can get them all for a $500 minimum investment!

Is this taking diversification to extremes? It depends on your tolerance for risk. To be sure, greater diversification means less risk and means greater downside protection in a bear market. In 1994 the average domestic mutual fund lost 8%. In contrast, the average fund of funds lost just 4%. But the lower volatility also produces below-average performance in up markets. Another drawback of these funds of funds tends to be high fees. Many charge investors two layers of fees: one for the underlying funds' loads and one for the umbrella fund. Two layers of fees often smother performance. The one exception is fund families that invest only in their own mutual funds. They don't usually charge you twice.

Funds of funds have a troubled past. The concept's inventor, the late Bernie Cornfeld, was charged with violating federal securities law after his fund of funds collapsed in the early 1970s. He wound up serving prison time in Switzerland. Congress cracked down by generally prohibiting funds from owning more than 3% of another fund's assets. But time heals old wounds, and those regulations have since been liberalized. With some 8,500 mutual funds in existence today, it's tempting to buy a mutual fund that picks mutual funds. That's especially true if you don't have much money to invest. If you have less than $10,000 to invest, then you may not be able to afford separate funds for stocks, bonds, foreign stocks, and so on. A fund of funds allows you to achieve diversification on a budget. That's assuming that the fees don't get to you first.

(which in itself produces capital gains for American investors in international funds). Many of these funds, however, attempt to protect their investors from currency exchange risks by using various types of *hedging strategies*. That is, by using foreign currency options and futures (or some other type of derivative product), the fund tries to eliminate (or reduce) the effects of fluctuating currency exchange rates. Some funds, in fact, do this on a permanent basis: In essence, these funds hedge away exchange risk so that they can concentrate on the higher returns offered by the foreign securities themselves. Others are only occasional users of currency hedges and employ them only when they feel there's a real chance of a substantial swing in currency values. But even with currency hedging, international funds are still considered fairly high-risk investments and should be used only by investors who understand and are able to tolerate such risks. This warning is especially true for funds that invest narrowly in *a single developing country* (like Thailand or Indonesia), where diversification is so limited that if something goes wrong in the host country (as it did in both Thailand and Indonesia in 1997–1998), the whole fund suffers—often in a big way.

Investor Services

Ask most investors why they buy a particular mutual fund and they'll probably tell you that the fund provides the kind of income and return they're looking for. Now, no one would question the importance of return in the investment decision, but there are some other important reasons for investing in mutual funds, not the least of which are the valuable services they provide. Some of the most sought-after *mutual fund services* are automatic investment and reinvestment plans, regular income programs, conversion and phone-switching privileges, and retirement programs.

Automatic Investment Plans

automatic investment plan
a mutual fund service that allows shareholders to send fixed amounts of money from their paychecks or bank accounts automatically into the fund.

It takes money to make money, and for an investor, that means being able to accumulate the capital to put into the market. Unfortunately, that's not always easy. Enter mutual funds, which have come up with a program that makes savings and capital accumulation as painless as possible. The program is the **automatic investment plan,** which allows fund shareholders to automatically funnel fixed amounts of money *from their paychecks or bank accounts* into a mutual fund. It's much like a payroll deduction plan, where investments to your mutual fund are automatically deducted from your paycheck or bank account.

This fund service has become very popular, because it enables shareholders to invest on a regular basis without having to think about it. Just about every fund group offers some kind of automatic investment plan for virtually all of its stock and bond funds. To enroll, you simply fill out a form authorizing the fund to siphon a set amount (usually a minimum of $25 to $100 per period) from your bank account or paycheck at regular intervals, such as monthly or quarterly. Once enrolled, you'll be buying more shares in the fund(s) of your choice every month or quarter (most funds deal in fractional shares). Of course, if it's a load fund, you'll still have to pay normal sales charges on your periodic investments. To remain diversified, you can divide your money among as many funds (within a given fund family) as you like. Finally, you can get out of the program any time you like, without penalty, by simply calling the fund. Although convenience is perhaps the chief advantage of automatic investment plans, they also make solid investment sense: One of the best ways of building up a sizable amount of capital is to add funds to your investment program systematically over time. The importance of making regular contributions to your investment program cannot be overstated; it ranks right up there with compound interest.

Automatic Reinvestment Plans

automatic reinvestment plan
a mutual fund service that enables shareholders automatically to buy additional shares in the fund through reinvestment of dividends and capital gains income.

An automatic reinvestment plan is one of the real draws of mutual funds and is a service offered by just about every open-ended fund. Whereas automatic investment plans deal with money the shareholder is putting into a fund, automatic *re*investment plans deal with the dividends the funds pay to their shareholders. Much like the dividend reinvestment plans we looked at with stocks (in Chapter 5), the **automatic reinvestment plans** of mutual funds enable you to keep your capital fully employed. Through this service, dividend and/or capital gains income is automatically used to buy additional shares in the fund. Most funds deal in fractional shares, and such purchases are often commission-free. Keep in mind, however, that even though an investor may reinvest all dividends and capital gains distributions, the IRS still treats them as cash receipts and taxes them as investment income in the year in which they were received.

Automatic reinvestment plans are especially attractive because they enable investors to earn fully compounded rates of return. That is, by plowing back profits, the investor can essentially put his or her profits to work in generating even more earnings. Indeed, the effects of these plans on total accumulated capital over the long run can be substantial. Figure 13.6 shows the long-term impact of one such plan. (These are the actual performance numbers for a *real* mutual fund, Fidelity Contrafund.) In the illustration, we assume the investor starts with $10,000 and, except for the reinvestment of dividends and capital gains, *adds no new capital over time*. Even so, note that the initial investment of $10,000 grew to $149,000 over a 15-year period (which amounts to a compounded rate of return of almost 19¾%). Of course, not all periods will match this performance, nor will all mutual funds be able to perform as well, even in strong markets. The point is that as long as care is taken in selecting an appropriate fund, *attractive benefits can be derived from the systematic accumulation of capital offered by automatic reinvestment plans.*.

FIGURE 13.6 The Effects of Reinvesting Income

Reinvesting dividends or capital gains can have a tremendous impact on one's investment position. This graph shows the results of a hypothetical investor who initially invested $10,000 and, for a period of 15 years, reinvested all dividends and capital gains distributions in additional fund shares. (No adjustment has been made for any income taxes payable by the shareholder, which is appropriate so long as the fund was held in an IRA or Keogh account.) (Source: *Morningstar Principia.*)

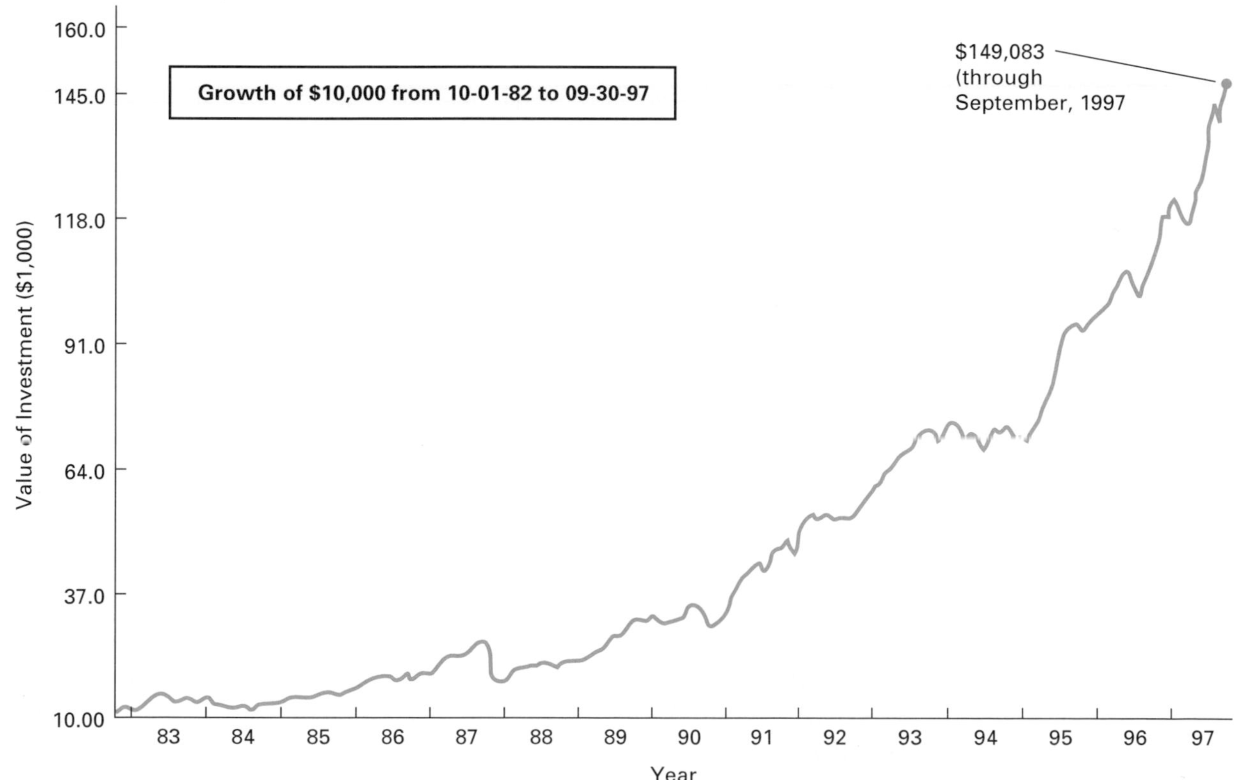

Regular Income

systematic withdrawal plan
a mutual fund service that enables shareholders automatically to receive a predetermined amount of money every month or quarter.

Although automatic investment and reinvestment plans are great for the long-term investor, what about the investor who's looking for a steady stream of income? Once again, mutual funds have a service to meet this kind of need. It's called a **systematic withdrawal plan,** and it's offered by most open-ended funds. Once enrolled in one of these plans, an investor automatically receives a predetermined amount of money every month or quarter. Most funds require a minimum investment of $5,000 or more in order for the investor to participate, and the size of the minimum payment must normally be $50 or more per period (with no limit on the maximum). The funds will pay out the monthly or quarterly income first from dividends and realized capital gains. If this source proves to be inadequate and the shareholder so authorizes, the fund can then tap the principal or original paid-in capital in the account to meet the required periodic payments.

Conversion Privileges and Phone Switching

conversion (exchange) privilege
feature of a mutual fund that allows shareholders to move money from one fund to another, within the same family of funds.

fund families
different kinds of mutual funds offered by a single investment management company.

Sometimes investors find it necessary to switch out of one fund and into another. For example, the investor's investment objectives or the investment climate itself may have changed. **Conversion** (or **exchange**) **privileges** were devised to meet the needs of such investors in a convenient and economical manner. Investment management companies that offer a number of different funds—known as **fund families**—often provide conversion privileges that enable shareholders to move easily from one fund to another, usually by phone. Indeed, with *phone switching* you simply pick up the phone to move money among funds—the only constraint being that the switches must be confined to the same *family* of funds. For example, you can switch from a Dreyfus growth fund to a Dreyfus money fund, a Dreyfus income fund, or any other fund managed by Dreyfus. With some fund families, the alternatives open to investors seem almost without limit; indeed, some of the larger families offer 40 or 50 funds. One investment company (Fidelity) has over 200 different funds in its family: everything from high-performance stock funds to bond funds, tax-exempt funds, a couple dozen sector funds, and a couple dozen money funds. More than 100 fund families are in operation today. They all provide low-cost conversion/phone-switching privileges, and some even provide these privileges free, although most families that offer free exchanges have limits on the number of times such switches can occur each year. Fifteen of the largest fund families are listed in Table 13.2. Note that together these 15 families have nearly $1.3 *trillion* in assets under management and offer more than 1,450 different mutual funds to the investing public.

Conversion privileges are usually considered beneficial from the shareholder's point of view, because they allow investors to meet their ever-changing long-term investment goals. In addition, they permit investors to manage their mutual fund holdings more aggressively by allowing them to move in and out of funds as the investment environment changes. Unfortunately, there is one major drawback: For tax purposes, the exchange of shares from one fund to another is regarded as a sale transaction followed by a subsequent purchase of a new security. As a result, if any capital gains exist at the time of the exchange, the investor is liable for the taxes on that profit, even though the holdings were not truly liquidated.

TABLE 13.2 Fifteen of the Biggest Fund Families

Fund Families	Total Number of Funds Available	Total Amount of Assets Under Management ($ billions)
Fidelity	225	$325.7
Morgan Stanley/Dean Witter	173	61.4
Dreyfus	138	33.5
Merrill Lynch	133	69.2
Franklin/Templeton	127	135.6
Vanguard	86	202.1
Putnam Financial Services	75	106.9
T. Rowe Price	71	60.0
Van Kamp./Amer. Capital	69	28.0
Smith Barney	68	33.6
Scudder	64	33.0
Massachusetts Financial Services (MFS)	62	32.3
American Century	57	43.4
American Express/IDS	53	54.7
Oppenheimer	52	45.3

Note: Number of funds in existence as of late 1997; assets under management for stock-and-bond-funds only.

Source: Mutual Funds, February 1998; *Smart Money*, March 1997.

Retirement Programs

As a result of government legislation, self-employed individuals are permitted to divert a portion of their pretax income into self-directed retirement plans. And all working Americans, whether or not they are self-employed, are allowed to establish individual retirement arrangements (IRAs). Indeed, with the legislation passed in 1997, *qualified investors* can now choose between deductible and nondeductible (Roth) IRAs, and even those who make too much to qualify for one of these programs can set up special nondeductible IRAs. The details of these various IRA programs are spelled out in Chapter 15. Today all mutual funds provide a special service that allows individuals to set up tax-deferred retirement programs as either IRA or Keogh accounts—or, through their place of employment, to participate in a qualified tax-sheltered retirement plan, such as a 401(k). The funds set up the plans and handle all the administrative details so that the shareholder can easily take full advantage of available tax savings.

CONCEPTS IN REVIEW

13.7 Briefly describe each of the following types of mutual funds:

a. Aggressive growth funds
b. Equity-income funds
c. Growth-and-income funds
d. Bond funds
e. Sector funds
f. Socially responsible funds

13.8 What is an *asset allocation fund,* and how does it differ from other types of mutual funds? According to the *Investing in Action* box on page 517, what is a *fund of funds* and how does this type of fund differ from a normal mutual fund?

13.9 If growth, income, and capital preservation are the primary objectives of mutual funds, why do we bother to categorize them by type? Do you think such classifications are helpful in the fund selection process? Explain.

13.10 What are *fund families?* What advantages do fund families offer investors? Are there any disadvantages?

13.11 Briefly describe some of the investor services provided by mutual funds. What are *automatic reinvestment plans,* and how do they differ from *automatic investment plans?* What is phone switching, and why would an investor want to use this type of service?

http://hepg.aw.com

Matching your investment objectives and those of a particular mutual fund is vital if you are to be comfortable with your portfolio and to meet your investment goal. Most mutual fund families that have home pages on the Web list their funds, which enables you to look at fund objectives and other criteria. The following site is for the Green Line family of funds, which groups its funds by objective.

www.tdbank.com/tdbank/mutual/product/

Investing in Mutual Funds

LG 5 LG 6

Suppose you are confronted with the following situation: You have money to invest and are trying to select the right place to put it. You obviously want to pick a security that meets your idea of acceptable risk and will generate an attractive rate of return. The problem is that you have to make the selection from a list of over 8,500 securities. Sound like a "mission impossible"? Well, that's basically what you are up against when trying to select a suitable mutual fund. However, if the problem is approached systematically, it may not be so formidable a task. As we will see, it is possible to whittle down the list of alternatives by matching your investment needs with the investment objectives of the funds. Before doing that, though, it might be helpful to examine more closely the various investor uses of mutual funds. With this background, we can then look at the selection process and at several measures of return that can be used to assess performance.

Investor Uses of Mutual Funds

Mutual funds can be used by individual investors in a variety of ways. For instance, performance funds can serve as a vehicle for capital appreciation, whereas bond funds can provide current income. Regardless of the kind of income a mutual fund provides, individuals tend to use these investment vehicles for one of three reasons: (1) as a way to accumulate wealth, (2) as a storehouse of value, and (3) as a speculative vehicle for achieving high rates of return.

Accumulation of Wealth

Accumulation of wealth is probably the most common reason for using mutual funds. Basically, the investor uses mutual funds over the long haul to build up investment capital. Depending on the investor's personality, a modest amount of risk may be acceptable, but usually preservation of capital and capital stability are considered important. The whole idea is to form a "partnership" with the mutual fund in building up as big a capital pool as possible: You provide the capital by systematically investing and reinvesting in the fund, and the fund provides the return by doing its best to invest your resources wisely.

Storehouse of Value

Investors may also use mutual funds as a storehouse of value. The idea here is to find a place where investment capital can be fairly secure and relatively free from deterioration yet still generate a relatively attractive rate of return. Short- and intermediate-term bond funds are logical choices for such purposes, and so are money funds. Capital preservation and income over the long term are very important to some investors, whereas others might seek storage of value only for the short term, using money funds as a place to "sit it out" until a more attractive opportunity comes along.

INVESTOR FACT

WHAT'LL THEY THINK OF NEXT?—Want a really long-term investment? The Pauze Tombstone Fund is a mutual fund that invests in funeral companies. It may sound grim, but death is a booming business, explains Phillip Pauze, president and founder of Pauze Swanson Management Co. and the son of a casket maker. The fund is taking advantage of a huge demographic trend: the aging of baby boomers, who will increasingly require the services of a funeral director over the next 20 years. Stocks eligible for the fund include Service Corp. International, a major funeral company; Hillenbrand Industries Inc., a casket manufacturer; and funeral company Stewart Enterprises.

Speculation and Short-Term Trading

Speculation is not a common use of mutual funds; the reason, of course, is that most mutual funds are long-term in nature and thus not meant to be used as aggressive trading vehicles. However, a growing number of funds (e.g., sector funds) now cater to speculators, and some investors find that mutual funds are, in fact, attractive outlets for speculation and short-term trading.

One way to do this is to trade in and out of funds aggressively as the investment climate changes. Load charges can be avoided (or reduced) by dealing in families of funds offering low-cost conversion privileges and/or by dealing only in no-load funds. Other investors might choose to invest in funds for the long run but still seek high rates of return by investing in aggressive mutual funds. A number of funds follow very aggressive trading strategies, which may well appeal to investors who are willing to accept substantial risk exposure. These are usually the fairly specialized, smaller funds: Sophisticated enhanced-yield funds, leverage funds, option funds, emerging-market funds, small-cap aggressive growth funds, and sector funds are examples. In essence, such investors are simply applying the basic mutual fund concept to their investment needs by letting professional money managers handle their accounts in a way they would like to see them handled: *aggressively.*

The Selection Process

When it comes to mutual funds, there is one question every investor has to answer: Why invest in a mutual fund to begin with—why not just go it alone by buying individual stocks and bonds directly? For beginning investors and investors with little capital, the answer is pretty simple: With mutual funds, investors are able to achieve far more diversification than they could ever get on their own, and they get the help of professional money managers at a very reasonable cost. For more seasoned, wealthier investors, the answers are probably a bit more involved. Certainly, diversification and professional money management come into play, but there are other reasons as well. The competitive returns offered by mutual funds are a factor with many investors, as are the services they provide. Many well-to-do investors have simply decided they can get better returns over the long haul by carefully selecting mutual funds than by investing on their own. As a result, they put all or a big chunk of their money into funds. Some of these investors use part of their capital to buy and sell individual securities on their own and use the rest *to buy mutual funds that invest in areas they don't fully understand or don't feel well informed about.* For example, they'll use mutual funds to get into foreign markets, to buy mortgage-backed securities, to buy junk bonds (where diversification is so very important), or to buy value funds (because that's such a tricky and time-consuming way to invest).

Once you have decided to use mutual funds, you have to decide which fund(s) to buy. In many respects, the selection process is critical in determining how much success you will have with mutual funds. It means putting into action all you know about funds, in order to gain as much return as possible from an acceptable level of risk. The selection process begins with an assessment of your own investment needs, which sets the tone of the investment program. Obviously, what you want to do is select from those 8,500 or so funds the one or two (or three or four) that will best meet your total investment needs.

Objectives and Motives for Using Funds

Selecting the right investment means finding those funds that are most suitable to your investment needs. The place to start is with your own investment objectives. In other words, why do you want to invest in a mutual fund, and what are you looking for in a fund? Obviously, an attractive rate of return would be desirable, but there is also the matter of a tolerable amount of risk exposure. Face it: Some investors are more willing to take risks than others. Probably, when you look at your own risk temperament in relation to the various types of mutual funds available, you will discover that certain types of funds are more appealing to you than others. For instance, aggressive growth or sector funds are usually *not* attractive to individuals who wish to avoid high exposure to risk.

Another important factor in the selection process is the intended use of the mutual fund. That is, do you want to invest in mutual funds as a means of accumulating wealth, as a storehouse of value, or to speculate for high rates of return? This information puts into clearer focus the question of exactly what you are trying to do with your investment dollars. Finally, there is the matter of the types of services provided by the fund. If you are particularly interested in certain services, you should be sure to look for them in the funds you select. Having assessed what you are looking for in a fund, you are ready to look at what the funds have to offer.

What the Funds Offer

Just as each individual has a set of investment needs, each fund has its own *investment objective,* its own *manner of operation,* and its own *range of services.* These three parameters are useful in helping you to assess investment alternatives. But where do you find such information? One obvious place is the fund's *profile,* or its prospectus (or "Statement of Additional Information"), which supplies information on investment objectives, portfolio composition, management, and past performance. Publications such as the *Wall Street Journal, Barron's, Money, Fortune,* and *Forbes* also offer useful information about mutual funds. These sources provide a wealth of operating and performance statistics in a convenient and easy-to-read format. For instance, each year *Forbes* rates over 1,800 mutual funds, and every quarter *Barron's* publishes an extensive mutual fund performance report.

There are also a number of reporting services that provide background information and assessments on a wide range of funds. Among the best in this category are *Morningstar Mutual Funds* (an excerpt of which is shown in Figure 13.7), Wiesenberger's *Investment Companies* (an annual publication with quarterly updates), Standard & Poor's/Lipper Analytical's *Mutual Fund ProFiles* (a publication that comes out in four quarterly editions), and *Value Line Mutual Fund Survey* (which produces a mutual fund report similar to its stock report). In addition, all sorts of performance statistics are available on disks and on the Internet for easy use on home computers. For example, quarterly or annually updated software is available, at very low cost, from Morningstar or from the American Association of Individual Investors (AAII). Using sources like these, investors can obtain information on such things as investment objectives, load charges and annual expense rates, summary portfolio analyses, services offered, historical statistics, and reviews of past performance. Or, you can look to the publications put out by the funds themselves, as explained in the *Investing in Action* box on page 527.

Whittling Down the Alternatives

At this point, the fund selection becomes a process of elimination as investor needs are weighed against the types of funds available. A large number of funds can be eliminated from consideration simply because they fail to meet stated needs. Some funds may be too risky; others may be unsuitable as a storehouse of value. Thus, rather than trying to evaluate 8,500 different funds, you can narrow down the list to two or three *types* of funds that best match your investment needs. From here, you can whittle down the list a bit more by introducing other constraints. For example, because of cost considerations, you may want to deal only in no-load or low-load funds (more on this topic below), or you may be seeking certain services that are important to your investment goals.

Now we introduce the final (but certainly not the least important) element in the selection process: *the fund's investment performance.* Useful information includes (1) how the fund has performed over the past 5 to 7 years, (2) the type of return it has generated in good markets as well as bad, (3) the level of dividend and capital gains distributions, and (4) the type of investment stability the fund has enjoyed over time (or put another way, the amount of volatility/risk in the fund's return). By evaluating such information, you can identify some of the more successful mutual funds—the ones that not only offer the investment objectives and services you seek but also provide the best payoffs. And while you're looking at performance, it probably wouldn't hurt to check out the fund's *fee structure.* Be on guard for funds that charge abnormally high management fees; they can really hurt returns over time.

Note that in this decision process, considerable weight is given to *past performance.* As a rule, the past is given little or no attention in the investment decision—after all, it's the future that matters. Although the *future performance* of a mutual fund is still the variable that holds the key to success, investors should look carefully at past investment results to see how successful the fund's investment managers have been. In essence, the success of a mutual fund rests in large part on the *investment skills of the fund managers.* Therefore, when investing in a mutual fund, look for consistently good performance,

INVESTOR FACT

SOME MUTUAL FUND FACTS EVERY INVESTOR SHOULD KNOW . . .

- Even bad funds sometimes rank as top performers.
- Stock funds that get hit hard in market crashes aren't necessarily bad investments.
- Even great funds have bad years now and then.
- Most stock (and bond) funds fail to beat the market.
- You don't need a broker to buy mutual funds.
- A fund that doesn't charge a sales commission isn't necessarily a no-load fund.
- If you own more than a dozen different funds, you probably own too many.

FIGURE 13.7 Some Relevant Information About Specific Mutual Funds

Investors who want in-depth information about the operating characteristics, investment holdings, and market behavior of specific mutual funds, such as this one for the Brandywine fund, can usually find what they're looking for in publications like *Morningstar Mutual Funds* or, as shown here, from computer-based information sources like *Morningstar's Principia.* (Source: Morningstar, Inc., *Principia,* release date: 9/30/97.)

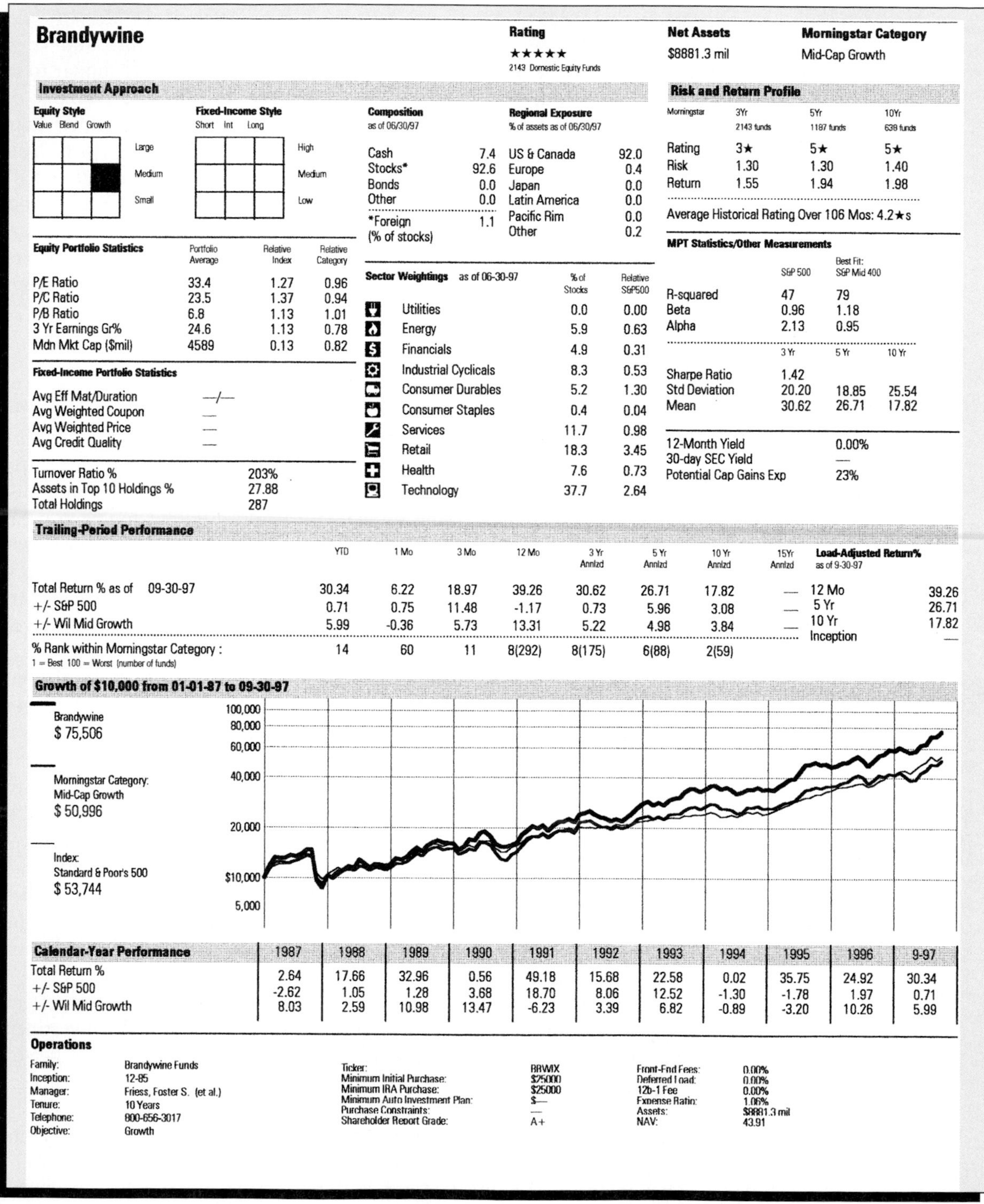

Brandywine

Rating ★★★★★ 2143 Domestic Equity Funds

Net Assets $8881.3 mil

Morningstar Category Mid-Cap Growth

Investment Approach

Equity Style: Value Blend Growth / Large Medium Small

Fixed-Income Style: Short Int Long / High Medium Low

Composition as of 06/30/97

Cash	7.4
Stocks*	92.6
Bonds	0.0
Other	0.0
*Foreign (% of stocks)	1.1

Regional Exposure % of assets as of 06/30/97

US & Canada	92.0
Europe	0.4
Japan	0.0
Latin America	0.0
Pacific Rim	0.0
Other	0.2

Equity Portfolio Statistics

	Portfolio Average	Relative Index	Relative Category
P/E Ratio	33.4	1.27	0.96
P/C Ratio	23.5	1.37	0.94
P/B Ratio	6.8	1.13	1.01
3 Yr Earnings Gr%	24.6	1.13	0.78
Mdn Mkt Cap ($mil)	4589	0.13	0.82

Fixed-Income Portfolio Statistics

Avg Eff Mat/Duration	—/—
Avg Weighted Coupon	—
Avg Weighted Price	—
Avg Credit Quality	—

Turnover Ratio %	203%
Assets in Top 10 Holdings %	27.88
Total Holdings	287

Sector Weightings as of 06-30-97

	% of Stocks	Relative S&P500
Utilities	0.0	0.00
Energy	5.9	0.63
Financials	4.9	0.31
Industrial Cyclicals	8.3	0.53
Consumer Durables	5.2	1.30
Consumer Staples	0.4	0.04
Services	11.7	0.98
Retail	18.3	3.45
Health	7.6	0.73
Technology	37.7	2.64

Risk and Return Profile

Morningstar	3Yr 2143 funds	5Yr 1187 funds	10Yr 639 funds
Rating	3★	5★	5★
Risk	1.30	1.30	1.40
Return	1.55	1.94	1.98

Average Historical Rating Over 106 Mos: 4.2★s

MPT Statistics/Other Measurements

	S&P 500	Best Fit: S&P Mid 400
R-squared	47	79
Beta	0.96	1.18
Alpha	2.13	0.95

	3 Yr	5 Yr	10 Yr
Sharpe Ratio	1.42		
Std Deviation	20.20	18.85	25.54
Mean	30.62	26.71	17.82

12-Month Yield	0.00%
30-day SEC Yield	—
Potential Cap Gains Exp	23%

Trailing-Period Performance

	YTD	1 Mo	3 Mo	12 Mo	3 Yr Annlzd	5 Yr Annlzd	10 Yr Annlzd	15Yr Annlzd
Total Return % as of 09-30-97	30.34	6.22	18.97	39.26	30.62	26.71	17.82	—
+/- S&P 500	0.71	0.75	11.48	-1.17	0.73	5.96	3.08	—
+/- Wil Mid Growth	5.99	-0.36	5.73	13.31	5.22	4.98	3.84	—
% Rank within Morningstar Category: 1 = Best 100 = Worst (number of funds)	14	60	11	8(292)	8(175)	6(88)	2(59)	

Load-Adjusted Return% as of 9-30-97

12 Mo	39.26
5 Yr	26.71
10 Yr	17.82
Inception	—

Growth of $10,000 from 01-01-87 to 09-30-97

Calendar-Year Performance

	1987	1988	1989	1990	1991	1992	1993	1994	1995	1996	9-97
Total Return %	2.64	17.66	32.96	0.56	49.18	15.68	22.58	0.02	35.75	24.92	30.34
+/- S&P 500	-2.62	1.05	1.28	3.68	18.70	8.06	12.52	-1.30	-1.78	1.97	0.71
+/- Wil Mid Growth	8.03	2.59	10.98	13.47	-6.23	3.39	6.82	-0.89	-3.20	10.26	5.99

Operations

Family:	Brandywine Funds
Inception:	12-85
Manager:	Friess, Foster S. (et al.)
Tenure:	10 Years
Telephone:	800-656-3017
Objective:	Growth

Ticker:	BRWIX
Minimum Initial Purchase:	$25000
Minimum IRA Purchase:	$25000
Minimum Auto Investment Plan:	$—
Purchase Constraints:	—
Shareholder Report Grade:	A+

Front-End Fees:	0.00%
Deferred Load:	0.00%
12b-1 Fee	0.00%
Expense Ratio:	1.06%
Assets:	$8881.3 mil
NAV:	43.91

INVESTING IN ACTION

Knowing Where to Look Is Half the Battle

Only a lawyer could love a mutual fund prospectus. So many words, so little meaning. No wonder half of the investing public ignores the admonition to "read the prospectus before you invest." But the prospectus really does contain a wealth of information if you know how to separate the wheat from the chaff. Among the most important data are the mutual fund's *expenses.* The Expenses section explains whether the fund has a sales load and how much it is; it also breaks out management and marketing fees for your approval or disapproval.

The Investment Objective section will tell you about the fund's *investment style*—whether it seeks value, growth, income, or whatever. You might get some real detail here, such as the information that the fund buys small stocks with market values between $100 million and $500 million. Then there's the discussion of *risk.* A good prospectus alerts you to specific risks that pertain to your portfolio. For example, the prospectus could tell you that the fund's bias toward high-dividend stocks could limit its potential for capital appreciation. In contrast, a poorly prepared prospectus provides general risk information that applies to all mutual funds. Such general information can go on for pages, and it probably protects the mutual fund company in the event of a lawsuit. Unfortunately, it doesn't help the investor make a prudent investment decision.

Most funds list long-term *total returns* in the prospectus. You might discover that the fund's returns are very volatile and not to your liking. If the prospectus does not list total returns, it may be because the results aren't very good.

A prospectus also gives you a biography of the portfolio manager. Why is this important information? If the manager is brand new, then the total return is irrelevant because the current manager didn't compile it.

Still, reading a prospectus has not always been something that most people like to do. But now, at long last, things are beginning to change. That is, according to rules recently adopted by the SEC, investors now have the choice of buying into a mutual fund on the basis of a brief (2 to 6 page), concise, readable document called a *fund profile,* or requesting a more detailed *prospectus* from the fund company. The fund profile is designed to tell you (in plain English and in a standardized format) the most important things you need to know about a fund (e.g., its investment objectives, principle risks, fees and expenses, etc.) without overwhelming you in a bunch of unnecessary legalese. Likewise, the fund prospectuses are now far more user-friendly, as they too must be simplified and downsized (by removing all the irrelevant "boiler-plate"); and they must be written in plain English, as well.

Should you want even more information than provided in either the profile or prospectus, you can always ask for a copy of the fund's *Statement of Additional Information,* which provides detailed information on the fund's investment objectives, portfolio composition, management, and past performance. Or, ask to see the fund company's last annual or semiannual report. That document usually has a lot to say about a fund's performance, what the portfolio includes, and the portfolio managers' outlook for the future.

in up as well as down markets, over *extended* periods of time (5 years or more). Most important, check whether the same key people are still running the fund. Although past success is certainly no guarantee of future performance, a strong team of money managers can have a significant bearing on the level of fund returns.

Stick with No-Loads or Low-Loads

There's a long-standing "debate" in the mutual fund industry regarding load funds and no-load funds. Do load funds add value? And if not, then why pay the load charges? As it turns out, the results generally don't support the idea that load funds provide added value. Indeed, load fund returns, in general, don't seem to be any better than the returns from no-load funds. In fact, in many cases, the funds with abnormally high loads and 12(b)-1 charges often produce returns that are far less than what you can get from no-load funds. In addition, because of compounding, the differential returns tend to widen with longer holding periods. But that should come as no surprise, because big load charges and/or 12(b)-1 fees reduce your investable capital—and therefore reduce the amount of money you have working for you. In fact, the only way a load fund can overcome this handicap is to produce *superior returns*—which is no easy thing to do, year in and year out. Granted, a handful of load funds have produced very attractive returns over extended periods of time, but they are the exception rather than the rule.

Obviously, it's in your best interest to pay close attention to load charges (and other fees) whenever you consider investing in a mutual fund. As a rule, to maximize returns, you should *seriously consider sticking to no-load funds or to low-loads* (funds that have total load charges, including 12(b)-1 fees, of 3% or less). At the very minimum, you should consider a more expensive load fund *only* if it has a much better performance record (and offers more return potential) than a less expensive fund. There may well be times when the higher costs are justified, but far more often than not, you're better off trying to minimize load charges. That shouldn't be difficult to do. There are thousands of no-load and low-load funds to choose from, and they come in all different types and sizes. What's more, most of the top-performing funds are found in the universe of no-loads or low-loads. So why would you even want to look anywhere else?

Investing in Closed-End Funds

A closed-end fund is, in many respects, both a common stock and an investment company. As the original form of investment company, closed-end funds have enjoyed a long, though not always illustrious, history that dates back to nineteenth-century England and Scotland. In the United States, closed-end funds were actively traded during the 1920s bull market, when they far outnumbered their open-end relatives. During that freewheeling era, however, they were highly leveraged and consequently were hit hard during the Crash of 1929, earning a bad reputation with investors. They remained something of an oddity for decades afterward, and it wasn't until the bull market that began in the early 1980s that closed-end funds came back into fashion.

Today, the assets of closed-end funds (CEFs) represent only a fraction of the more than $4 trillion invested in open-end funds. Indeed, as we can see in Table 13.3, at the end of the 1997, there were more than 500 CEFs, which together held total net assets of less than $300 billion. Like open-end funds, CEFs come in a variety of different types and styles, including funds that specialize in municipal bonds, taxable bonds, various types of equity securities, and international securities, as well as regional and single-country funds. Both taxable and tax-free bonds dominate the CEF universe—in fact, municipal bonds alone account for 44% of CEF assets. In addition to bonds, many closed-end funds target foreign stock markets. For example, regional funds focus on a group of countries within a broad geographic area, such as Europe or Latin America. In contrast, *single-country funds* target either *emerging*

TABLE 13.3 The Closed-End Fund Universe

Fund Category	Number of Funds*	Total Net Assets* ($ in billions)
Municipal Bond	196	$ 61.0
Taxable Bond	144	41.7
Hybrid[1]	18	2.7
Domestic Equity	32	19.1
World Equity	5	177.7 mil
Foreign Equity	6	613.4 mil
International Regional Equity[2]	71	13.9
Total	472	$139.2

*As of April 1998.
[1]Hybrid includes Domestic hybrid, International hybrid and Convertibles.
[2]Includes regional and single-country funds.
Source: Morningstar, Inc.

markets, such as Brazil, China, the Czech Republic, India, Indonesia, Mexico, the Philippines, and Turkey, or *developed markets,* such as France, Germany, Japan, and the United Kingdom.

Some Key Differences Between Closed-End and Open-End Funds

Because closed-end funds trade like stocks, you must deal with a broker to buy or sell shares, and the usual brokerage commissions apply. Open-end funds, in contrast, are bought from and sold to the fund operators themselves. Another important difference between open- and closed-end funds is their liquidity. You can buy and sell relatively large dollar amounts of an open-end mutual fund at its NAV without worrying about affecting the price. However, a relatively large buy or sell order for a CEF could easily bump your price up or down. Thus the greater liquidity of open-end funds gives them a distinct advantage. Just like open-end funds, most CEFs offer dividend reinvestment plans, but in many cases, that's about it. CEFs simply don't provide the full range of services that mutual fund investors are accustomed to.

All things considered, probably the most important difference (because it *directly affects* investor costs and returns) is the way these funds are priced in the marketplace. Whereas open-end funds can be bought and sold at NAV (plus any front-end load or minus any redemption charge), CEFs have *two values*— a market value, or stock price, and net asset value (NAV). The two are rarely the same, because CEFs typically trade at either a premium or a discount. Premiums and discounts are reported weekly in *Barron's,* the *Wall Street Journal,* and other newspapers. The premium or discount is calculated as follows:

Equation 13.1

$$\text{Premium (or discount)} = (\text{share price} - \text{NAV}) / \text{NAV}$$

Suppose Fund A has a NAV of $10. If its share price is $8, it will sell at a 20% discount. That is,

$$\begin{aligned}\text{Premium (or discount)} &= (\$8 - \$10)/\$10 \\ &= -\$2/\$10 = -.20 = \underline{\underline{-20\%}}\end{aligned}$$

Because this answer is negative, the fund is trading at a *discount*. On the other hand, if this same fund were priced at $12 per share, it would be trading at a *premium* of 20%—that is, ($12 − $10) / $10 = $2/$10 = 0.20. Because the value is positive, the fund is trading at a premium.

What to Look for in a Closed-End Fund

If you know what to look for and your timing and selection are good, you may find that some *deeply discounted CEFs* provide a great way to earn attractive returns. For example, if a fund trades at a 20% discount, you pay only 80 cents for each dollar's worth of assets. At certain times, the market offers the opportunity to pick up funds at attractive prices—which could well be the case when double-digit discounts exist. At other times, discounts may be too narrow to represent any special value. If you can buy a fund at an abnormally wide discount and sell it when the discount narrows or turns to a premium, you can enhance your overall return. In fact, even if the discount does not narrow, your return will be improved, because the yield on your investment is higher than it would be with an otherwise equivalent open-end fund. The reason: You're investing less money. Here's a simple example. Suppose a CEF trades at $8, a 20% discount from its NAV of $10. If the fund distributed $1 in dividends for the year, it would yield 12.5% ($1 divided by its $8 price). However, if it was a no-load, open-end fund, it would be trading at its higher NAV and therefore would yield only 10% ($1 divided by its $10 NAV). Thus, when investing in CEFs, be sure to pay close attention to the size of the premium and discount; in particular, keep your eyes open for funds trading at deep discounts, because that feature alone can enhance potential returns.

For the most part, except for the premium or discount, a CEF should be analyzed just like any other mutual fund. That is, pay close attention to the expense ratio, portfolio turnover rate, past performance, cash position, and so on. In addition, study the history of the discount. Information on closed-end funds can be found in such publications as *Morningstar Closed-End Funds,* Standard & Poor's *Stock Reports,* and *Value Line Investment Survey.* Also, keep in mind that with CEFs, you probably won't get a prospectus (as you might with an open-end fund), because they do not continuously offer new shares to investors.

One final point to keep in mind when developing a closed-end fund investment program: Stay clear of new issues (IPOs) of closed-end funds and funds that sell at steep *premiums.* Never buy new CEFs when they are brought to the market as IPOs. Why? IPOs are always brought to the market at *hefty premiums,* and the investor therefore faces the almost inevitable risk of losing money as the shares fall to a discount within a month or two. This drop in price occurs because the IPO funds have to be offered at a premium just to cover the amount of the underwriting spread. You also want to avoid funds that are trading at premiums—especially at steep premiums, such as volatile single-country portfolios. That too can lead to built-in losses when, if sentiment sours, these premiums quickly turn to discounts.

Measuring Performance

As in any investment decision, return performance is a major dimension in the mutual fund selection process. The level of dividends paid by the fund, its capital gains, and its growth in capital are all important aspects of return. Such return information enables the investor to judge the investment behavior of a fund and to appraise its performance in relation to other funds and investment vehicles. Here, we will look at different measures that mutual fund investors use to assess return. Also, because risk is so important in defining the investment behavior of a fund, we will examine mutual fund risk as well.

Sources of Return

An open-end mutual fund has three potential sources of return: (1) dividend income, (2) capital gains distribution, and (3) change in the price (or net asset value) of the fund. Depending on the type of fund, some mutual funds derive more income from one source than another. For example, we would normally expect income-oriented funds to have much higher dividend income than capital gains distributions. Open-end mutual funds regularly publish reports that recap investment performance. One such report is the *Summary of Income and Capital Changes,* an example of which is provided in Table 13.4. This statement, which is found in the fund's profile or prospectus, gives a brief overview of the fund's investment activity, including expense ratios and portfolio turnover rates. Of interest here is the top part of the report (which runs from "Investment income" to "NAV at the end of the year"—lines 1 to 9). This part reveals the amount of dividend income and capital gains distributed to the shareholders, along with any change in the fund's net asset value.

TABLE 13.4 A Report of Mutual Fund Income and Capital Changes
(For a share outstanding throughout the year)

		1998	1997	1996
	Income and Expenses			
	1. Investment income	$ .76	$ .88	$ .67
	2. Less expenses	.16	.22	.17
	3. Net investment income	$ .60	$ .66	$ .50
Dividend Income→	4. Dividends from net investment income	(.55)	(.64)	(.50)
	Capital Changes			
	5. Net realized and unrealized gains (or losses) on security transactions	6.37	(1.74)	3.79
Capital Gains Distribution→	6. Distributions from realized gains	(1.75)	(.84)	(1.02)
Change in NAV→	7. Net increase (decrease) in NAV*	$ 4.67	($ 2.56)	$ 2.77
	8. NAV at beginning of year	24.47	27.03	24.26
	9. NAV at end of year	$29.14	$24.47	$27.03
	10. Ratio of operating expenses to average net assets	1.04%	0.85%	0.94%
	11. Ratio of net investment income to average net assets	1.47%	2.56%	2.39%
	12. Portfolio turnover rate**	85%	144%	74%
	13. Shares outstanding at end of year (000s omitted)	10,568	6,268	4,029

**Net increase (decrease) in NAV,* line 7 = line 3 − line 4 + line 5 − line 6. For example, the 1998 net increase in NAV was found as $.60 − .55 + 6.37 − 1.75 = $4.67.

***Portfolio turnover rate* relates the number of shares bought and sold by the fund to the total number of shares held in the fund's portfolio. A high turnover rate (in excess of 100%) would mean the fund has been doing a lot of trading.

dividend income
income derived from the dividend and interest income earned on the security holdings of a mutual fund.

capital gains distributions
payments made to mutual fund shareholders that come from the profits that a fund makes from the sale of its securities.

unrealized capital gains (paper profits)
a capital gain made only "on paper" —that is, not realized until the fund's holdings are sold.

Dividend income is derived from the dividend and interest income earned on the security holdings of the mutual fund. It is paid out of the *net investment income* that's left after all operating expenses have been met. When the fund receives dividend or interest payments, it passes these on to shareholders in the form of dividend payments. The fund accumulates all of the current income it has received for the period and then pays it out on a prorated basis. If a fund earned, say, $2 million in dividends and interest in a given year and if that fund had 1 million shares outstanding, each share would receive an annual dividend payment of $2. **Capital gains distributions** work on the same principle, except that these payments are derived from the capital gains earned by the fund. It works like this: Suppose the fund bought some stock a year ago for $50 and sold that stock in the current period for $75 per share. Clearly, the fund has achieved capital gains of $25 per share. If it held 50,000 shares of this stock, it would have realized a total capital gain of $1,250,000 ($25 × 50,000 = $1,250,000). Given that the fund has 1 million shares outstanding, each share is entitled to $1.25 in the form of a capital gains distribution. Note that this capital gains distribution applies only to *realized* capital gains—that is, the security holdings were actually sold and the capital gains actually earned.

Unrealized capital gains (or **paper profits**) are what make up the third and final element of a mutual fund's return. When the fund's holdings go up or down in price, the net asset value of the fund moves accordingly. Suppose an investor buys into a fund at $10 per share and sometime later the fund is quoted at $12.50. The difference of $2.50 per share is the unrealized capital gains contained in the fund's security holdings. It represents the profit that shareholders would receive (and are entitled to) if the fund were to sell its holdings. (Actually, as Table 13.4 shows, some of the change in net asset value can also be made up of *undistributed dividends*.)

The return on *closed-end* investment companies is derived from the same three sources as that of open-end funds and from a *fourth source* as well: changes in price discounts or premiums. But because discount or premium is already embedded in the share price of a fund, it follows that, for a closed-end fund, the third element of return—change in share price—is made up not only of change in net asset value but also of change in price discount or premium.

What About Future Performance?

There's no doubt that a statement like the one in Table 13.4 provides a convenient recap of a fund's past behavior. Looking at past performance is useful, but it doesn't tell you what the future will be. Ideally, you want an indication of what the same three elements of return—dividend income, capital gains distribution, and change in NAV—*will be.* The trouble is that when it comes to the future performance of a mutual fund, it's extremely difficult—if not impossible—to get a firm grip on what the future holds in dividends, capital gains, and NAV. This is because a mutual fund's future investment performance is directly linked to the *future make-up of the securities it holds in its portfolio,* something that is next to impossible to get a clear reading on. It's not like evaluating the expected performance of a share of stock, in which case you're keying in on one company. With mutual funds, investment performance depends on the behavior of many different stocks and bonds.

Where, then, do you look for insight on future performance? Most market observers suggest that the first place to look is the market itself. In particular, try to get a fix on the future direction of *the market as a whole*. This is important because the behavior of a well-diversified mutual fund tends to reflect the general tone of the market. Thus, if the feeling is that the market is going to be drifting up, so should the investment performance of mutual funds. Also spend some time evaluating the *track records* of potential mutual fund investments; past performance has a lot to say about the investment skills of the fund's money managers. In essence, look for funds that you think will be able to capture the best of what the future market environment holds.

Measures of Return

A simple but effective measure of performance is to describe mutual fund return in terms of the three major sources noted above: dividends earned, capital gains distributions received, and change in price. When dealing with investment horizons of 1 year or less, we can easily convert these fund payoffs into a return figure by using the standard holding period return (HPR) formula. The computations necessary are illustrated below using the 1998 figures from Table 13.4. Referring to the exhibit, we can see that in 1998, this hypothetical no-load, open-end fund paid 55 cents per share in dividends and another $1.75 in capital gains distributions; it had a price at the beginning of the year of $24.47 that rose to $29.14 by the end of the year. Thus, summarizing this investment performance, we have

Price (NAV) at the *beginning* of the year	$24.47
Price (NAV) at the *end* of the year	29.14
Net increase	$ 4.67
Return for the year:	
Dividends received	$ .55
Capital gains distributions	1.75
Net increase in price (NAV)	4.67
Total return	$ 6.97
Holding period return (HPR)	**28.5%**
(Total return/beginning price)	

This HPR measure not only captures all the important elements of mutual fund return but also provides a handy indication of yield. Note that the fund had a total dollar return of $6.97 and, on the basis of a beginning investment of $24.47 (the initial share price of the fund), was able to produce an annual return of 28.5%.

HPR with Reinvested Dividends and Capital Gains Many, if not most, mutual fund investors have their dividends and/or capital gains distributions reinvested in the fund. How do you obtain a measure of return when you receive your (dividend/capital gains) payout in additional shares of stock rather than cash? With slight modifications, you can continue to use holding period return; the only difference is that you have to keep track of the number of shares acquired through reinvestment. To illustrate, let's continue with the example above and assume that the investor initially bought 200 shares in the mutual fund. Assume also that you were able to acquire shares through the fund's reinvestment program at an average price of $26.50 a share. Thus the $460 in dividends and capital gains distributions [($.55 + $1.75) × 200] provided you with another 17.36 shares in the fund ($460/$26.50). Holding period return under these circumstances would relate the market value of the stock holdings at the beginning of the period with holdings at the end:

Equation 13.2

$$\text{Holding period return} = \frac{\left(\begin{array}{c}\text{number of}\\ \text{shares at } \textit{end}\\ \text{of period}\end{array} \times \begin{array}{c}\text{ending}\\ \text{price}\end{array}\right) - \left(\begin{array}{c}\text{number of}\\ \text{shares at } \textit{beginning}\\ \text{of period}\end{array} \times \begin{array}{c}\text{initial}\\ \text{price}\end{array}\right)}{\begin{array}{c}\text{number of shares}\\ \text{at } \textit{beginning} \text{ of period}\end{array} \times \begin{array}{c}\text{initial}\\ \text{price}\end{array}}$$

Thus the holding period return would be

$$\text{Holding period return} = \frac{(217.36 \times \$29.14) - (200 \times \$24.47)}{(200 \times \$24.47)}$$

$$= \frac{(\$6{,}333.87) - (\$4{,}894.00)}{\$4{,}894.00} = \underline{\underline{29.4\%}}$$

This holding period return, like the preceding one, provides a rate-of-return measure that can now be used to compare the performance of this fund to those of other funds and investment vehicles.

Measuring Long-Term Returns Rather than using 1-year holding periods, it is sometimes necessary to assess the performance of mutual funds over extended periods of time. In these cases, it would be inappropriate to employ holding period return as a measure of performance. But that's no problem, because when faced with multiple-year investment horizons, we can use the present-value-based *internal rate of return* (IRR) procedure to determine the fund's average annual compound rate of return. To illustrate, refer to Table 13.4, but assume that this time we want to find the annual rate of return over the full 3-year period (1996 through 1998). In this case, we see that the mutual fund had the following annual dividends and capital gains distribution.

	1998	1997	1996
Annual dividends paid	$ .55	$ .64	$ .50
Annual capital gains distributed	$1.75	$ .84	$1.02
Total distributions	$2.30	$1.48	$1.52

Now, given that the fund had a price of $24.26 at the beginning of the period (1/1/96) and was trading at $29.14 at the end of 1998 (3 years later), we have the following time line of cash flows:

Initial Cash Flows	Subsequent Cash Flows		
	Year 1	Year 2	Year 3
$24.26 (Beginning Price)	$2.30 (Distributions)	$1.48 (Distributions)	$1.52 + $29.14 (Distributions + Ending Price)

The idea is to find the discount rate that will equate the annual dividends/capital gains distributions *and* the ending price in year 3 to the beginning (1996) price of the fund ($24.26).

Using standard present-value techniques, we find that the mutual fund in Table 13.4 provided its investors with an annual rate of return of 13.3% over the 3-year period from 1996 through 1998—that is, at 13.3%, the present values of the cash flows in years 1, 2, and 3 equal the beginning price of the fund ($24.26). Such information is helpful in assessing fund performance and in comparing the return performance of one fund to other funds and investment vehicles. According to SEC regulations, mutual funds must report historical return behavior in a standardized format that employs fully compounded, total-return figures similar to those obtained from the approximate-yield measure. Although the funds are not required to report such information, if they do cite performance in their promotional material, they must follow a full-disclosure manner of presentation that takes into account not only dividends and capital gains distributions but also any increases or decreases in the fund's NAV that have occurred over the past 1-, 5-, and ten-year periods.

Actually, a great place to find the latest total-return numbers for open-end funds is in the *Wall Street Journal.* Each day, the quotes provide year-to-date returns for each of the several thousand funds listed in the *Journal.* Then, on Fridays, they also provide returns over different investment horizons ranging from 4 weeks to 1 year, 3 years, and 5 years (see Figure 13.5). Also on Fridays, each fund is *ranked* relative to other funds with the same investment objectives according to their average annual return performance—a fund gets an A if it's in the top 20% of its group, a B if it's in the next 20%, and so on. By using these quotes, an investor can stay up to date not only on the fund's current market price but also on the total returns it is generating.

Returns on Closed-End Funds Generally speaking, the returns of CEFs are customarily reported on the basis of their NAVs—that is, *price premiums and discounts are ignored when computing various return measures.* At the same time, it's becoming increasingly common to see return performance expressed in terms of actual market prices, a practice that captures the impact of changing market premiums or discounts on holding period returns. As you might expect, the greater the premiums or discounts and the greater the changes in these values over time, the greater their impact on reported returns. That is, it's not at all uncommon for CEFs to have totally different market-based and NAV-based holding period returns. When NAVs are used, you find the returns on CEFs in exactly the same way as you do the returns on open-end funds. In contrast, when market values are used to measure return, all you need do is *substitute the market price of the fund* (with its embedded premium or discount) *for the corresponding NAV in the holding period or internal rate of return* measure. Some CEF investors like to run *both* NAV-based and market-based measures of return to see how changing premiums (or discounts) have added to or hurt the returns on their mutual fund holdings. Even so, as a rule, NAV-based return numbers are generally viewed as the preferred measures of performance, because the fund managers often have little or no control over changes in premium or discounts. Thus NAV-based measures are felt to give a truer picture of the performance of the fund itself.

The Matter of Risk

Because most mutual funds are so diversified, their investors are largely immune to the business and financial risks normally present with individual securities. Even with extensive diversification, however, the investment behavior of most funds is still exposed to a considerable amount of *market risk*. In fact, because mutual fund portfolios are so well diversified, they often reflect the behavior of the marketplace itself and, as we have noted, tend to perform very much like the market. Although a few funds, like gold funds, tend to be defensive (or countercyclical), market risk is an important behavioral ingredient in a large number of mutual funds, both open- and closed-end. When formulating a mutual fund investment program, investors should be aware of the effect the general market has on the investment performance of a fund. For example, if the market is trending downward and you anticipate a continuation of such a trend, it might be best to place any new investment capital into something like a money fund until the market reverses itself. At that time, you can make a more long-term commitment.

Another important risk consideration revolves around the management practices of the fund itself. If the portfolio is managed conservatively, the risk of a loss in capital is likely to be much less than for aggressively managed funds. Obviously, the more speculative the investment goals of the fund, the greater the risk of instability in the net asset value. On the other hand, a conservatively managed portfolio does not necessarily eliminate all price volatility, because the securities in the portfolio are still subject to inflation, interest rate, and general market risks. However, these risks are generally reduced or minimized as the investment objectives and portfolio management practices of the funds become more conservative.

CONCEPTS IN REVIEW

13.12 How important is the general behavior of the market in affecting the price performance of mutual funds? Explain. Why is a fund's past performance important to the mutual fund selection process? Does the future behavior of the market matter in the selection process? Explain.

13.13 The *Investing in Action* box on the use of a *fund prospectus* (page 527) suggested six things you should do to get the most from these fund documents. List and briefly discuss each of these six points.

13.14 What are the major types of closed-end mutual funds? What is the difference between regional funds and single-country funds? How do CEFs differ from open-end funds?

13.15 Identify three potential sources of return to mutual fund investors and briefly discuss how each could affect total return to shareholders. Explain how the discount or premium of a closed-end fund can also be treated as a return to investors.

13.16 Discuss the various types of risk to which mutual fund shareholders are exposed. What is the major risk exposure of mutual funds? Are all funds subject to the same level of risk? Explain.

http://hepg.aw.com

Morningstar provides one of the most popular sources of information for the selection of mutual funds. Morningstar's style box, which is widely used, offers a quick summary of the broad selection criteria of the fund manager.

At the Web page listed here, find the article titled *Recipe for Morningstar StyleBox* to learn more about interpreting this valuable indicator.

text.morningstar.net/Cover/LearnArchive.html

Summary

LG 1 **Describe the basic features of mutual funds, and note what they have to offer as investment vehicles.** Mutual fund shares represent ownership in a diversified, professionally managed portfolio of securities; many investors who lack the time, know-how, or commitment to manage their own money turn to mutual funds as an investment outlet. By investing in mutual funds, shareholders benefit from a level of diversification and investment performance they might otherwise find difficult to achieve. In addition, they can establish an investment program with a limited amount of capital and obtain a variety of investor services not available elsewhere.

LG 2 **Differentiate between open- and closed-end mutual funds, and discuss the various types of fund loads, fees, and charges.** Investors can buy either open-end funds, which have no limit on the number of shares they may issue, or closed-end funds, which have a fixed number of shares outstanding and trade in the secondary markets like any other share of common stock. There is a cost, however, to investing in mutual funds. That is, mutual fund investors face an array of loads, fees, and charges, including front-end loads, back-end loads, annual 12(b)-1 charges, and annual management fees. Some of these costs are one-time charges (e.g., front-end loads), but others are paid annually [e.g., 12(b)-1 and management fees]. Investors should have a good handle on fund costs, which can be a real drag on fund performance and return.

LG 3 **Discuss the types of funds available and the variety of investment objectives these funds seek to fulfill.** Each fund has an established investment objective that determines its investment policy and identifies it as a certain type of fund. Some of the more popular types of funds are growth funds, aggressive growth funds, equity-income funds, balanced funds, growth-and-income funds, asset allocation funds, index funds, bond funds, money funds, sector funds, socially responsible funds, and international funds. The different categories of funds have different risk-return characteristics and are important variables in the fund selection process.

LG 4 **Identify and discuss the investor services offered by mutual funds and how these services can fit into an investment program.** In addition to investment returns, mutual funds also offer special services, such as automatic investment and reinvestment plans, systematic withdrawal programs, low-cost conversion and phone-switching privileges, and retirement programs.

LG 5 **Gain an appreciation of the investor uses of mutual funds, along with the variables that one should consider when assessing and selecting funds for investment purposes.** Mutual funds can be used to accumulate wealth, as a storehouse of value, or as a vehicle for speculation and short-term trading. The fund selection process generally starts by assessing the investor's needs and wants. The next step is to consider what the funds have to offer, particularly with regard to investment objectives, risk exposure, and investor services. The investor then narrows down the alternatives by aligning his or her needs with the types of funds available and, from this short list of funds, applies the final selection tests: fund performance and cost.

LG 6 **Identify the sources of return and compute the rate of return earned on an investment in a mutual fund.** The payoff from investing in a mutual fund includes dividend income, distribution of realized capital gains, growth in capital (unrealized capital gains), and—for closed-end funds—the change in premium or discount. Various measures of return recognize these elements and provide simple yet effective ways of gauging the annual rate of return from a mutual fund. Return is important to mutual fund investors, but so is risk. Although a fund's extensive diversification may protect investors from business and financial risks, considerable market risk still remains because most funds tend to perform much like the market, or at least like that segment of the market in which they specialize.

Discussion Questions

LG 1 LG 2

Q13.1. Contrast *mutual fund ownership* with *direct investment in stocks and bonds.* Assume your class is going to debate the merits of investing through mutual funds versus investing directly in stocks and bonds. Develop some arguments on each side of this debate and be prepared to discuss them in class. If you had to choose one side to be on, which would it be? Why?

LG 2

Q13.2. Using the mutual fund quotes in Figure 13.5, answer the questions listed below for each of the following 5 funds:

(1) Fairmont Fund (Fairmt)
(2) FPA Capital Fund (Capit)
(3) Federated Ohio Municipal Bond Fund-F (OHmunF)
(4) Federated Utility Fund-A (UtilFdA)
(5) FBL High Yield Bond Fund (HiYldBd)

a. How much would you have to pay to buy each of the funds?
b. How much would you pay (in dollars and percentage) in front-end load charges with each of the funds?
c. How much would you receive for each if you were selling the funds?
d. Which of the five listed funds have 12(b)-1 fees?
e. Which funds have redemption fees?
f. Are any of the funds no-loads?
g. Which fund has the highest year-to-date return? Which has the lowest?
h. Which fund has the highest expense ratio? Which has the lowest?

LG 3

Q13.3. For each pair of funds listed below, select the one that is likely to be the *less* risky. Briefly explain your answer.

a. Growth versus growth-and-income funds
b. Equity-income versus high-grade corporate bond funds
c. Balanced versus sector funds
d. Global versus aggressive growth funds
e. Intermediate-term bonds versus high-yield municipal bond funds

LG 3 LG 5

Q13.4. Imagine that you've just inherited $20,000 from a rich relative. Now you're faced with the "problem" of how to spend it. You could make a down payment on a condo, or you could buy that sports car you've always wanted. Or you could build a mutual fund portfolio. After some soul-searching, you decide to do the latter: to build a $20,000 mutual fund portfolio. Using actual mutual funds and actual quoted prices, come up with a plan to invest as much of the $20,000 as you can in a portfolio of mutual funds. Be specific! Briefly describe your planned portfolio, including the investment objectives you are trying to achieve.

Problems

LG 6

P13.1. A year ago, an investor bought 200 shares of a mutual fund at $8.50 per share; over the past year, the fund has paid dividends of 90 cents per share and had a capital gains distribution of 75 cents per share.

a. Find the investor's holding period return, given that this no-load fund now has a net asset value of $9.10.

b. Find the holding period return, assuming all the dividends and capital gains distributions are reinvested into additional shares of the fund at an average price of $8.75 per share.

 LG 6

P13.2. A year ago, the Really Big Growth Fund was being quoted at a NAV of $21.50 and an offer price of $23.35; today it's being quoted at $23.04 (NAV) and $25.04 (offer). What is the holding period return on this load fund, given that it was purchased a year ago and that its dividends and capital gains distributions over the year have totaled $1.05 per share?

 LG 6

P13.3. The All State Mutual Fund has the following 5-year record of performance.

	1998	1997	1996	1995	1994
Net investment income	$ .98	$ .85	$ .84	$ .75	$ .64
Dividends from net investment income	(.95)	(.85)	(.85)	(.75)	(.60)
Net realized and unrealized gains (or losses) on security transactions	4.22	5.08	(2.18)	2.65	(1.05)
Distributions from realized gains	(1.05)	(1.00)	—	(1.00)	—
Net increase (decrease) in NAV	$ 3.20	$ 4.08	($ 2.19)	$ 1.65	($ 1.01)
NAV at beginning of year	12.53	8.45	10.64	.99	10.00
NAV at end of year	$15.73	$12.53	$ 8.45	$10.64	$ 8.99

Find this no-load fund's 5-year (1994–1998) average annual compound rate of return; also find its 3-year (1996–1998) average annual compound rate of return. If an investor bought the fund in 1994 at $10.00 a share and sold it 5 years later (in 1998) at $15.73, how much total profit per share would she have made over the 5-year holding period?

 LG 6

P13.4. You've uncovered the following per-share information about a certain mutual fund.

	1996	1997	1998
Ending share prices:			
Offer	$46.20	$64.68	$61.78
NAV	43.20	60.47	57.75
Dividend income	2.10	2.84	2.61
Capital gains distribution	1.83	6.26	4.32
Beginning share prices:			
Offer	55.00	46.20	64.68
NAV	51.42	43.20	60.47

On the basis of this information, find the fund's holding period return for 1996, 1997, and 1998. (In all three cases, assume you buy the fund at the beginning of the year and sell it at the end of each year.) In addition, find the fund's average annual compound rate of return over the 3-year period, 1996–1998. What would the 1997 holding period return have been if the investor had initially bought 500 shares of stock and reinvested both dividends and capital gains distributions into additional shares of the fund at an average price of $52.50 per share?

 LG 2 LG 6

P13.5. Listed on the next page is the 10-year, per-share performance record of Larry, Moe, & Curly's Growth Fund, as obtained from the fund's May 30, 1998, prospectus.

	Years Ended March 31									
	1998	1997	1996	1995	1994	1993	1992	1991	1990	1989
1. Investment income	$ 1.98	$ 1.90	$ 1.64	$ 1.17	$ .81	$ .76	$1.11	$ .63	$ .44	$ .61
2. Expenses	.59	.55	.55	.54	.39	.27	.32	.26	.11	.23
3. Investment income—net	$ 1.39	$ 1.35	$ 1.09	$ .63	$ .42	$ .49	$ .79	$ .37	$ .33	$ .38
4. Dividends from investment income—net	(.83)	(1.24)	(.90)	(.72)	(.46)	(.65)	(.37)	(.26)	(.33)	(.58)
5. Realized and unrealized gain (loss) on investments—net	8.10	9.39	8.63	(6.64)	11.39	19.59	5.75	2.73	15.80	(.02)
6. Distributions from realized gain on investments—net	(2.42)	(3.82)	—	(9.02)	(6.84)	(1.78)	(3.69)	(1.88)	(1.23)	(9.92)
7. Net increase (decrease) in net asset value	$ 6.24	$ 5.68	$ 8.82	($15.75)	$ 4.51	$17.65	$ 2.48	$ .96	$14.57	($10.14)
Net asset value:										
8. Beginning of year	58.60	52.92	44.10	59.85	55.34	37.69	35.21	34.25	19.68	29.82
9. End of year	$64.84	$58.60	$52.92	$44.10	$59.85	$55.34	$37.69	$35.21	$34.25	$19.68

Use this information to find LM&C's holding period return in 1998 and 1995. Also find the fund's rate of return over the 5-year period 1994–1998, and the 10-year period 1989–1998. Finally, rework the four return figures assuming the LM&C fund has a front-end load charge of 3% (of NAV). Comment on the impact of load charges on the return behavior of mutual funds.

LG 3 LG 6

P13.6. Using the resources available at your campus or public library, select five mutual funds—a growth fund, an equity-income fund, an international (stock) fund, a sector fund, and a high-yield corporate bond fund—that you feel would make good investments. Briefly explain why you selected these funds. List the funds' holding period returns for the past year and their annual compound rates of return for the past 3 years. (Use a schedule like the one in Table 13.4 to show relevant performance figures.)

LG 6

P13.7. One year ago, Super Star Closed-End Fund had a NAV of $10.40 and was selling at an 18% discount; today its NAV is $11.69 and it is priced at a 4% premium. During the year, Super Star paid dividends of 40 cents and had a capital gains distribution of 95 cents. On the basis of the above information, calculate each of the following:

a. Super Star's NAV-based holding period return for the year
b. Super Star's market-based holding period return for the year. Did the market premium/discount hurt or add value to the investor's return? Explain.
c. Repeat the market-based holding period return calculation, except this time assume the fund started the year at an 18% *premium* and ended it at a 4% *discount*. (Assume the beginning and ending NAVs remain at $10.40 and $11.69, respectively.) Is there any change in this measure of return? Why?

Case Problem 13.1 *Reverend Robin Ponders Mutual Funds*

LG 3 LG 5

Reverend Robin is the minister of a church in the San Antonio area. He is married, has one young child, and earns a "modest income." Because religious organizations are not notorious for their generous retirement programs, the reverend has decided he should do some investing on his own. He would like to set up a program that enables him to supplement the church's retirement program and at the same time provide some funds for his child's college education (which is still some 12 years away). He is not out to break any investment records but feels he needs some backup in order to provide for the long-run needs of his family.

Although his income is meager, Reverend Robin feels that, with careful planning, he can probably invest about $250 a quarter (and, with luck, increase this amount over time). He currently has about $15,000 in a passbook savings account that he would be willing to use to begin this program. In view of his investment objectives, he is not interested in taking a lot of risk. Because his knowledge of investments extends to savings accounts, Series EE savings bonds, and a little bit about mutual funds, he approaches you for some investment advice.

QUESTIONS

a. In light of Reverend Robin's long-term investment goals, do you think mutual funds are an appropriate investment vehicle for him?

b. Do you think he should use his $15,000 savings to start a mutual fund investment program?

c. What type of mutual fund investment program would you set up for the reverend? Include in your answer some discussion of the types of funds you would consider, the investment objectives you would set, and any investment services (e.g., withdrawal plans) you would seek. Would taxes be an important consideration in your investment advice? Explain.

Case Problem 13.2 *Tom Lasnicka Seeks the Good Life*

LG 3 LG 4 LG 5 LG 6

Tom Lasnicka is a widower who recently retired after a long career with a major midwestern manufacturer. Beginning as a skilled craftsman, he worked his way up to the level of shop supervisor over a period of more than 30 years with the firm. Tom receives Social Security benefits and a generous company pension; together, these two sources amount to over $3,500 per month (part of which is tax-free). The Lasnickas had no children, so he lives alone. Tom owns a two-bedroom rental house that is next to his home, and the rental income from it covers the mortgage payments for both the rental house and his house.

Over the years, Tom and his late wife Camille always tried to put a little money aside each month. The results have been nothing short of phenomenal; the value of Tom's liquid investments (all held in bank CDs and passbook savings accounts) runs well into the six figures. Up to now, Tom has just let his money grow and has not used any of his savings to supplement his Social Security, pension, and rental income. But things are about to change. Tom has decided, "What the heck, it's time I start living the good life!" Tom wants to travel and, in effect, start reaping the benefits of his labors. He has therefore decided to move $100,000 from one of his savings accounts to one or two high-yielding mutual funds. He would like to receive $1,000–$1,500 a month from the fund(s) for as long as possible, because he plans to be around for a long time.

QUESTIONS

a. Given Tom's financial resources and investment objectives, what kinds of mutual funds do you think he should consider?

b. What factors in Tom's situation should be taken into consideration in the fund selection process? How might these affect Tom's course of action?

c. What types of services do you think he should look for in a mutual fund?

d. Assume Tom invests in a mutual fund that earns about 12% annually from dividend income and capital gains. Given that Tom wants to receive $1,000 to $1,500 a month from his mutual fund, what would be the size of his investment account 5 years from now? How large would the account be if the fund earned 16% on average and everything else remained the same? How important is the fund's rate of return to Tom's investment situation? Explain.

Home Page Exercises

http://hepg.aw.com **Keyword: Invest**

The proliferation of mutual funds as an investment outlet for individual investors has been phenomenal. Individuals have approximately $4 trillion invested through mutual funds, so naturally the World Wide Web provides a plethora of sites that offer information on this topic. These sites can tell you just about anything you want to know about mutual funds. A few interesting sites are listed here.

Web Address	*Primary Investment Focus*
www.stocksmart.com mutualfundspro.html	Basic data on all funds sorted by fund family
www.fundsinteractive.com/ newbie.html	Educational material for beginning mutual fund investors
www.morningstar.net	Home page for the premier mutual fund reporting company. Fund profiles are available
www.schwab.com/ SchwabNOW/Snlibrary/ SNnlib014/SN014.html	Very good fund profiles by Charles Schwab
www.mfea.com	Mutual Fund Investor's Center has a variety of educational and historical information and data on funds

W13.1. One of the most important factors in the selection of an appropriate mutual fund is finding one that has a good long-run performance record. The Quicken site given here is a great source for information on historical returns. On this Quicken page, select *Top 25 Funds.* Find the top 25 funds for the Large Value Morningstar Category for the 1-year, 5-year, and 10-year periods. Print out the results so that you can compare the lists. How many firms do you see on all three lists? On the basis of what you observe, which time horizon(s) do you believe investors should use to evaluate fund performance?

www.quicken.com/investments/mutualfunds/

W13.2. Annual expenses of mutual funds are one of the most important factors in determining real fund returns for the investor. The Mutual Fund Investor's Center provides interactive screening of funds based on various fund objectives and expenses. Use this screen to find all no-load Growth and Income (GI) funds with no 12b-1 fee, expense ratios and management fees of 1% or less, and a $2,500 minimum investment. Apply the same criteria for Fixed Income (FI) funds. How many funds did you find with each screen? Why do you think the numbers of funds differ?

www.mfea.com/fundcntr.html

Real Estate and Other Tangible Investments

CHAPTER 14

Starwood Lodging

It is fitting that Starwood Lodging trades on the New York Stock Exchange under the symbol "HOT." During the period 1995 through 1997, Starwood provided its shareholders with annual returns in excess of 75%. Based in Phoenix, Arizona, Starwood Lodging is the nation's largest hotel company, with names like Ritz-Carlton, Westin, Marriott, and Sheraton on its register. Its strategy is to acquire upscale, full-service hotels at prices below the cost of building the property from scratch. As of early 1998, the company owned 650 hotels and resorts in 70 countries.

Actually, Starwood is a special kind of public company. It is a real estate investment trust (REIT)—a professionally managed company that invests in various types of real estate and typically offers investors a high level of income in addition to the appreciation potential. REITs, originally signed into law by President Eisenhower in the 1950s to enable the "little guy" to invest in big-time real estate, also enjoy special tax advantages.

As you will see in this chapter, real estate is an important part of an investment portfolio, whether the investment is made through a REIT or through direct purchase of property.

Learning Goals

After studying this chapter, you should be able to:

LG 1 Describe how real estate investment objectives are set, how the features of real estate are analyzed, and what determines real estate value.

LG 2 Discuss the valuation techniques commonly used to estimate the market value of real estate.

LG 3 Understand the procedures involved in performing real estate investment analysis.

LG 4 Demonstrate the framework used to value a prospective real estate investment, and evaluate results in light of the stated investment objectives.

LG 5 Describe the structure and investment appeal of real estate investment trusts and real estate limited partnerships.

LG 6 Understand the investment characteristics of tangibles such as gold and other precious metals, gemstones, and collectibles, and review the suitability of investing in them.

Investing in Real Estate

LG 1

real estate
entities such as residential homes, raw land, and income property.

tangibles
investment assets, other than real estate, that can be seen and touched.

What do warehouses, gold ingots, and Pez containers have in common? They are all investment vehicles—yes, even the Pez containers—chosen by investors who want to put their money in something that can be seen and felt. Real estate and other tangible investments, such as gold, gemstones, and collectibles, offer attractive ways to diversify a portfolio. As noted in Chapter 1, **real estate** includes entities such as residential homes, raw land, and a variety of forms of income property, including warehouses, office and apartment buildings, and condominiums. **Tangibles** are investment assets, other than real estate, that can be seen and touched. Ownership of real estate and tangibles differs from ownership of security investments in one primary way: It involves an asset you can see and touch rather than a security that evidences a financial claim. Particularly appealing are the favorable risk–return tradeoffs resulting from the uniqueness of real estate and other tangible assets and the relatively inefficient markets in which they are traded. In addition, certain types of real estate investments offer attractive tax benefits that may enhance their returns. In this chapter we first consider the important aspects of real estate investment.

In addition to the fact that real estate is a tangible asset, it differs from security investments in yet another way: Managerial decisions about real estate greatly affect the returns earned from investing in it. In real estate, you must answer unique questions: What rents should be charged? How much should be spent on maintenance and repairs? What purchase, lease, or sales contract provisions should be used to transfer certain rights to the property? Along with market forces, answers to such questions determine whether you will earn the desired return on a real estate investment.

Like other investment markets, the real estate market changes over time. For example, the national real estate market was generally strong through the 1970s and 1980s. The strong market during this period was driven by generally prosperous economic times, including high income growth; it was also supported by the demand of large numbers of foreign investors, particularly from Japan and Europe, for U.S. commercial and residential real estate. But in 1989 the real estate market declined, and it remained weak through the early 1990s. This market sag resulted from a variety of factors, including changes in tax law that eliminated important tax benefits for investments in real estate, the collapse of oil prices, a slowing economy, the S&L crisis, and an excessive inventory of commercial real estate. Last to recover from the real estate collapse in the late 1980s were markets whose regional economies had been hit particularly hard: specifically, the "oil patch"—Texas, Oklahoma, Louisiana, and Colorado—New England, and California. In the mid-1990s a resurgence in the real estate market began, and by early 1998 the market nationally had returned nearly to pre-1989 levels. Today real estate values in most areas of the country are steadily rising as a result of the growing demand occasioned by economic growth, low unemployment, low interest rates, and a depleted inventory of available properties. For today's real estate investors, the lessons are clear: Macro issues such as the economic outlook, interest rate levels, the demand for new space, the current supply of space, and regional considerations are of major importance.

As recent history demonstrates, investing in real estate means more than just "buying right" or "selling right." It also means choosing the right properties for your investment needs and managing them well. Here we begin by considering investor objectives, analysis of important features, and determinants of real estate value.

Investor Objectives

Setting objectives involves two steps: First, you should consider differences in the investment characteristics of real estate. Second, you should establish investment constraints and goals.

Investment Characteristics

Individual real estate investments differ in their characteristics even more than individual people differ in theirs. Just as you wouldn't marry without thinking long and hard about the type of person you'd be happy with, you shouldn't select an investment property without some feeling for whether it is the right one for you. To select wisely, you need to consider the available types of properties and whether you want an equity or a debt position.

In this chapter we discuss real estate investment primarily from the standpoint of equity. Individuals can also invest in instruments of real estate debt, such as mortgages and deeds of trust. Usually, these instruments provide a fairly safe rate of return if the borrowers are required to maintain at least a 20% equity position in the mortgaged property (no more than an 80% loan-to-value ratio). This equity position gives the real estate lender a margin of safety if foreclosure has to be initiated.

income property
leased-out residential or commercial real estate that is expected to provide returns primarily from periodic rental income.

speculative property
raw land and real estate investment properties that are expected to provide returns primarily from appreciation in value.

We can classify real estate into two investment categories: income properties and speculative properties. **Income property** includes residential and commercial properties that are leased out and expected to provide returns primarily from periodic rental income. *Residential properties* include single-family properties (houses, condominiums, cooperatives, and townhouses) and multifamily properties (apartment complexes and buildings). *Commercial properties* include office buildings, shopping centers, warehouses, and factories. **Speculative property** typically includes raw land and investment properties that are expected to provide returns primarily from appreciation in value due to location, scarcity, and so forth, rather than from periodic rental income.

Income properties are subject to a number of sources of risk and return. Losses can result from tenant carelessness, excessive supply of competing rental units, or poor management. On the profit side, however, income properties can provide increasing rental incomes, appreciation in the value of the property, and possibly even some shelter from taxes.

Speculative properties, as the name implies, give their owners a chance to make a financial killing but carry also the risk of heavy loss. For instance, rumors may start that a new multimillion-dollar plant is going to be built on the edge of town. Land buyers would jump into the market, and prices soon would be bid up. The right buy–sell timing could yield returns of several hundred percent or more. But people who bought into the market late or those who failed to sell before the market turned might lose the major part of their investment. Before investing in real estate, you should determine the risks that various types of properties present and then decide which risks you will accept and can afford.

Constraints and Goals

When setting your real estate investment objectives, you also need to set both financial and nonfinancial constraints and goals. One financial constraint is the risk–return relationship you find acceptable. In addition, you must consider how much money you want to allocate to the real estate portion of your portfolio, and you should define a quantifiable financial objective. Often this financial goal is stated in terms of *discounted cash flow* (also referred to as *net present value*) or *yield*. Later in this chapter we will show how various constraints and goals can be applied to real estate investing.

Although you probably will want to invest in real estate for its financial rewards, you also need to consider how your technical skills, temperament, repair skills, and managerial talents fit a potential investment. Do you want a prestigious, trouble-free property? Or would you prefer a fix-up special on which you can release your imagination and workmanship? Would you enjoy living in the same building as your tenants, or would you prefer as little contact with them as possible? Just as you wouldn't choose a career just for the money, neither should you buy a property solely on that basis.

Analysis of Important Features

The analytical framework suggested in this chapter can guide you in estimating a property's investment potential. Yet first you must consider four general features related to real estate investment.

1. *Physical property.* When buying real estate, make sure you are getting both the quantity and the quality of property you think you are. Problems can arise if you fail to obtain a site survey, an accurate square-footage measurement of the buildings, or an inspection for building or site defects. When signing a contract to buy a property, make sure it accurately identifies the real estate and lists all items of personal property (such as refrigerator and curtains) that you expect to receive.

2. *Property rights.* Strange as it may seem, what you buy when you buy real estate is a bundle of legal rights that fall under concepts in law such as deeds, titles, easements, liens, and encumbrances. When investing in real estate, make sure that along with various physical inspections, you get a legal inspection from a qualified attorney. Real estate sale and lease agreements should not be the work of amateurs.

3. *Time horizon.* Like a roller coaster, real estate prices go up and down. Sometimes market forces pull them up slowly but surely; in other periods, prices can fall so fast that they take an investor's breath away. Before judging whether a prospective real estate investment will appreciate or depreciate, you must decide what time period is relevant. The short-term investor might count on a quick drop in mortgage interest rates and buoyant market expectations, whereas the long-term investor might look more closely at population growth potential.

4. *Geographic area.* Real estate is a spatial commodity, which means that its value is directly linked to what is going on around it. For some properties, the area of greatest concern consists of a few blocks; for others, an area of hundreds of square miles serves as the relevant market area. You must decide what spatial boundaries are important for your investment before you can productively analyze real estate demand and supply.

Determinants of Value

In the analysis of a real estate investment, value generally serves as the central concept. Will a property increase in value? Will it produce increasing amounts of cash flows? To address these questions, you need to evaluate four major determinants: demand, supply, the property, and the property transfer process.

Demand

demand
in real estate, people's desire to buy or rent a given property.

In the valuing of real estate, **demand** refers to people's desire to buy or rent a given property. In part, demand stems from a market area's economic base. In most real estate markets, the source of buying power comes from jobs. Property values follow an upward path when employment is increasing, and values typically fall when employers begin to lay off workers. Therefore, these are the first questions you should ask about demand: What is the outlook for jobs in the relevant market area? Are schools, colleges, and universities gaining enrollment? Are major companies planning expansion? Are wholesalers, retailers, and financial institutions increasing their sales and services? Upward trends in these indicators often signal a rising demand for real estate.

demographics
measurable characteristics of an area's population, such as household size, age structure, occupation, gender, and marital status.

psychographics
characteristics that describe people's mental dispositions, such as personality, lifestyle, and self-concept.

Population characteristics also influence demand. To analyze demand for a specific property, you should look at an area's population demographics and psychographics. **Demographics** refers to measurable characteristics, such as household size, age structure, occupation, gender, and marital status. **Psychographics** includes characteristics that describe people's mental dispositions, such as personality, lifestyle, and self-concept. By comparing demographic and psychographic trends to the features of a property, you can judge whether it is likely to gain or lose favor among potential buyers or tenants. For example, if an area's population is made up of a large number of sports-minded, highly social 25- to 35-year-old singles, the presence of nearby or on-site health club facilities may be important to a property's success.

Mortgage financing is also a key factor. Tight money can choke off the demand for real estate. As investors saw in the early 1980s, rising interest rates and the relative unavailability of mortgages caused inventories of unsold properties to grow and real estate prices to fall. Conversely, as mortgage interest rates fell, beginning in late 1982 and early 1983 and continuing through 1988, real estate sales and refinancing activity in many cities throughout the United States rapidly expanded. Although interest rates rose slightly in 1989 and 1990, their steady decline through 1994 failed to stimulate real estate activity because of generally poor economic conditions and a large surplus of investment properties. In spite of the fact that interest rates rose slightly between 1994 and early 1997, the rapidly improving economy and shrinking property inventory during this time began to drive up prices and returns. The declining mortgage rates in 1997 further stimulated the recovery and growth in real estate activity and values that continue today.

Supply

supply
in real estate, the potential competitors available in the market.

Analyzing **supply** means sizing up the competition. Nobody wants to pay you more for a property than the price he or she can pay your competitor; nor when you're buying (or renting) should you pay more than the prices asked for other, similar properties. As a result, you should identify sources of potential competition and inventory them by price and features. In general, people in real estate think of competitors in terms of similar properties. If you are trying to sell a house, for example, your competition is other, similar houses for sale in the same area.

principle of substitution
the principle that people do not buy or rent real estate per se but, instead, judge properties as different sets of benefits and costs.

For longer-term investment decisions, however, you should expand your concept of supply and identify competitors through the **principle of substitution.** This principle holds that people do not buy or rent real estate per se but, instead, judge properties as different sets of benefits and costs. Properties fill people's needs, and it is these needs that create demand. Thus potential competitors are not just geographically and physically similar properties. In some markets, for example, low-priced single-family houses might compete with condominium units, manufactured homes ("mobile homes"), and even rental apartments. Before investing in any property, you should decide what market that property appeals to and then define its competitors as other properties that its buyers or tenants might also typically choose. After identifying all relevant competitors, look for the relative pros and cons of each property in terms of features and respective prices.

INVESTOR FACT

IT EVEN HAS A KITCHEN—Here's the new use for some types of investment real estate—housing for business travelers. As shortages of hotel rooms in large cities drive up costs of business travel, Bridge-Street Accommodations has an alternative: The company leases scattered-site furnished apartments from property managers and rents them out nightly, weekly, or monthly. Bridge-Street's clientele is mostly business travelers sent out of town on temporary assignments or those being relocated, although there is also a growing leisure travel market for the properties. The average price is "in the $70-a-night range." Information is available on the Internet at **www.bridgest.com**. BridgeStreet Accommodations has found a novel way to apply the principles of supply and demand in the real estate market.

The Property

We've seen that a property's value is influenced by demand and supply. The price people will pay is governed by their needs and the relative prices of the properties available to meet those needs. Yet in real estate, the property itself is also a key ingredient. To try to develop a property's competitive edge, an investor should consider five items: (1) restrictions on use, (2) location, (3) site, (4) improvements, and (5) property management.

Restrictions on Use In today's highly regulated society, both state and local laws and private contracts limit the rights of all property owners. Government restrictions derive from zoning laws, building and occupancy codes, and health and sanitation requirements. Private restrictions include deeds, leases, and condominium bylaws and operating rules. You should not invest in a property until you or your lawyer determines that what you want to do with the property *fits within* applicable laws, rules, and contract provisions.

Location You may have heard the adage "The three most important factors in real estate value are location, location, and location." Of course, location is not the only factor that affects value, yet a good location unquestionably increases a property's investment potential. With that said, how can you tell a bad location from a good one? A good location rates high on two key dimensions: convenience and environment.

convenience
in real estate, the accessibility of a property to the places the people in a target market frequently need to go.

Convenience refers to how accessible a property is to the places the people in a target market frequently need to go. Any residential or commercial market segment has a set of preferred places its tenants or buyers will want to be close to. Another element of convenience is transportation facilities. Proximity to highways, buses, subways, and commuter trains is of concern to both tenants and buyers of commercial and residential property. Commercial properties need to be readily accessible to their customers, and the customers also value such accessibility.

environment
in real estate, the natural as well as aesthetic, socioeconomic, legal, and fiscal surroundings of a property.

In the analysis of real estate, the term **environment** has broader meaning than trees, rivers, lakes, and air quality. When you invest in real estate, even more important than its natural surroundings are its aesthetic, socioeconomic, legal, and fiscal surroundings. Neighborhoods with an *aesthetic environment* are those where buildings and landscaping are well executed and well maintained. Intrusion of noise, sight, and air pollution is minimal, and encroaching unharmonious land uses are not evident. The *socioeconomic environment* consists of the demographics and lifestyles of the people who live or work in nearby properties. The *legal environment* relates to the restrictions on use that apply to nearby properties. And last, you need to consider a property's *fiscal environment:* the amount of property taxes and municipal assessments you will be required to pay and the government services you will be entitled to receive (police, fire, schools, parks, water, sewer, trash collection, libraries). Property taxes are a two-sided coin. On the one hand, they impose a cost, but on the other, they provide services that may be of substantial benefit.

Site One of the most important features of a property site is its size. For residential properties, some people want a large yard for a garden or for children to play in; others may prefer no yard at all. For commercial properties, such as office buildings and shopping centers, adequate parking space is necessary. Also, with respect to site size, if you are planning a later addition of space, make sure the site can accommodate it, both physically and legally. Site quality as reflected in soil fertility, topography, elevation, and drainage is also important. For example, sites with relatively low elevation may be subject to flooding.

improvements
in real estate, the additions to a site, such as buildings, sidewalks, and various on-site amenities.

Improvements In real estate, the term **improvements** refers to the additions to a site, such as buildings, sidewalks, and various on-site amenities. Typically, building size is measured and expressed in terms of square footage. Because square footage is so important in building and unit comparison, you should get accurate square-footage measures on any properties you consider investing in.

Another measure of building size is room count and floor plan. For example, a well-designed 750-square-foot apartment unit might in fact be more livable, and therefore easier to rent even at a higher price, than a poorly designed one of 850 square feet. You should make sure that floor plans are logical; that traffic flows through a building will pose no inconveniences; that there is sufficient closet, cabinet, and other storage space; and that the right mix of rooms exists. For example, in an office building you should not have to cross through other offices to get to the building's only restroom facilities, and small merchants in a shopping center should be located where they receive the pedestrian traffic generated by the larger (anchor) tenants.

Attention should also be given to amenities, style, and construction quality. Amenities such as air conditioning, swimming pools, and elevators can significantly affect the value of investment property. In addition, the architectural style and quality of construction materials and workmanship are important factors influencing property value.

Property Management In recent years, real estate owners and investors have increasingly recognized that investment properties (apartments, office buildings, shopping centers, and the like) do not earn maximum cash flows by themselves. They need to be guided toward that objective, and skilled property management can help. Without effective property management, no real estate investment can produce maximum benefits for its users and owners.

Today, property management requires you or a hired manager to run the entire operation as well as to perform day-to-day chores. The property manager will segment buyers, improve a property's site and structure, keep tabs on competitors, and develop a marketing campaign. The property manager also assumes responsibility for the maintenance and repair of buildings and their physical systems (electrical, heating, air conditioning, and plumbing) and for the keeping of revenue and expense records. In addition, property managers decide the best ways to protect properties against loss from perils such as fire, flood, theft, storms, and negligence. In its broadest sense, **property management** means finding the optimal level of benefits for a property and providing them at the lowest costs. Of course, for speculative investments such as raw land, the managerial task is not so pronounced and the manager has less control over the profit picture.

property management
in real estate, finding the optimal level of benefits for a property and providing them at the lowest costs.

Property Transfer Process

In Chapter 7 we introduced the concept of an *efficient market,* in which information flows so quickly among buyers and sellers that it is virtually impossible for an investor to outperform the average systematically. As soon as something good (an exciting new product) or something bad (a multimillion-dollar product liability suit) occurs, the price of the affected company's stock adjusts to reflect its current potential for earnings or losses. Some people accept the premise that securities markets are efficient; others do not. But one thing is sure: *No one believes real estate markets are efficient.* What this means is that skillfully conducted real estate analysis can help you beat the averages.

The reason why real estate markets differ from securities markets is that no good system exists for complete information exchange among buyers and sellers and among tenants and lessors. There is no central marketplace, like the NYSE, where transactions are conveniently made by equally well-informed investors who share similar objectives. Instead, real estate is traded in generally *illiquid markets* that are regional or local in nature and where transactions are made to achieve investors' often unique investment objectives.

property transfer process
the process of promotion and negotiation of real estate, which can significantly influence the cash flows a property will earn.

In the **property transfer process** itself, the inefficiency of the market means that how you collect and disseminate information affects your results. The cash flows that a property earns can be influenced significantly through promotion and negotiation. *Promotion* is the task of getting information about a property to its buyer segment. You can't sell or rent a property quickly or for top dollar unless you can reach the people you want to reach in a cost-effective way. Among the major ways to promote a property are advertising, publicity, sales gimmicks, and personal selling. *Negotiation* of price is just as important. Seldom does the minimum price a seller is willing to accept just equal the maximum price a buyer is willing to pay; often some overlap occurs. In real estate, the asking price for a property may be anywhere from 5% to 60% *above* the price that a seller (or lessor) will actually accept. Therefore, the negotiating skills of each party determine the final transaction price.

CONCEPTS IN REVIEW

14.1 Define and differentiate between *real estate* and *tangibles.* Give examples of each of these forms of investment.

14.2 How does real estate investment differ from securities investment? Why might adding real estate to your investment portfolio decrease your overall risk? Explain.

14.3 Define and differentiate between *income property* and *speculative property*. Differentiate between and give examples of *residential* and *commercial* income properties.

14.4 Briefly describe the following important features to consider when making a real estate investment.
  a. Physical property b. Property rights
  c. Time horizon d. Geographic area

14.5 What role do demand and supply play in determining the value of real estate? What are *demographics* and *psychographics,* and how are they related to demand? How does the *principle of substitution* affect the analysis of supply?

14.6 How do restrictions on use, location, site, improvements, and property management affect a property's competitive edge?

14.7 Are real estate markets *efficient?* Why or why not? How does the efficiency or inefficiency of these markets affect both promotion and negotiation as parts of the property transfer process?

http://hepg.aw.com

Real estate, like most areas of investing, has its own jargon. No matter what type of real estate transactions you may be engaged in, you must understand the jargon of this business. This Web site has a comprehensive glossary of real estate terms.

www.interest.com/terms.html

Real Estate Valuation

LG 2 LG 3

market value
in real estate, the actual worth of a property; indicates the price at which it would sell under current market conditions.

In real estate, **market value** is a property's actual worth, which indicates the price at which it would sell under current market conditions. This concept is interpreted differently from its meaning in stocks and bonds. The difference arises for a number of reasons: (1) Each property is unique; (2) terms and conditions of sale may vary widely; (3) market information is imperfect; (4) properties may need substantial time for market exposure, time that may not be available to any given seller; and (5) buyers too sometimes need to act quickly. All these factors mean that no one can tell for sure what a property's "true" market value is. As a result, many properties sell for prices significantly above or below their estimated market values. To offset such inequities, many real estate investors forecast investment returns to evaluate potential property investments. Here we first look at procedures for estimating the market value of a piece of real estate and then consider the role and procedures used to perform investment analysis.

Estimating Market Value

appraisal
in real estate, the process for estimating the current market value of a piece of property.

In real estate, estimating the current market value of a piece of property is done through a process known as a real estate **appraisal.** Using certain techniques, an appraiser determines what he or she feels is the current market value of the property. Even so, you should interpret the appraised market value a little skeptically. Because of both technical and informational shortcomings, this estimate is subject to substantial error.

Although you can arrive at the market values of frequently traded stocks simply by looking at current quotes, in real estate, appraisers and investors typically must use three complex, and imperfect, techniques and then correlate the results to come up with one best estimate. These three approaches to real estate market value are (1) the cost approach, (2) the comparative sales approach, and (3) the income approach.

The Cost Approach

cost approach
a real estate valuation approach based on the idea that an investor should not pay more for a property than it would cost to rebuild it at today's prices.

The **cost approach** is based on the idea that an investor should not pay more for a property than it would cost to rebuild it at today's prices for land, labor, and construction materials. This approach to estimating value generally works well for new or relatively new buildings. The cost approach is more difficult to apply to older properties, however. To value older properties, you would have to subtract from the replacement cost estimates some amount for physical and functional depreciation. Most experts agree that the cost approach is a good method to use as a check against a price estimate, but rarely should it be used exclusively.

The Comparative Sales Approach

comparative sales approach
a real estate valuation approach that uses as the basic input the sales prices of properties that are similar to the subject property.

The **comparative sales approach** uses as the basic input the sales prices of properties that are similar to the subject property. This method is based on the idea that the value of a given property is about the same as the prices for which other, similar properties have recently sold. Of course, the catch here is that all properties are unique in some respect. Therefore, the price that a subject property could be expected to bring must be adjusted upward or downward to reflect its superiority or inferiority to comparable properties.

Nevertheless, because the comparable sales approach is based on *selling* prices, not asking prices, it can give a good feel for the market. As a practical matter, if you can find at least one sold property slightly better than the one you're looking at, and one slightly worse, their recent sales prices can serve to bracket an estimated market value for the property you have your eye on.

The Income Approach

income approach
a real estate valuation approach that calculates a property's value as the present value of all its future income.

net operating income (NOI)
the amount left after subtracting vacancy and collection losses and property operating expenses from an income property's *gross potential* rental income.

Under the **income approach,** a property's value is viewed as the present value of all its future income. The most popular income approach is called *direct capitalization*. This approach is represented by the formula in Equation 14.1. It is similar in logic and form to the zero-growth dividend valuation model presented in Chapter 7 for common stock (see Equation 7.7 on page 265).

Equation 14.1

$$\text{Market value} = \frac{\text{annual net operating income}}{\text{market capitalization rate}}$$

Equation 14.1a

$$V = \frac{\text{NOI}}{R}$$

Annual **net operating income** (**NOI**) is calculated by subtracting vacancy and collection losses and property operating expenses, including property insur-

market capitalization rate
the rate used to convert an income stream to a present value; used to estimate the value of real estate under the *income approach*.

ance and property taxes, from an income property's *gross potential* rental income. An estimated **market capitalization rate** is obtained by looking at recent market sales figures to determine the rate of return currently required by investors. Technically, the market capitalization rate means the rate used to convert an income stream to a present value. By dividing the annual net operating income by the appropriate market capitalization rate, you get an income property's estimated market value. An example of the application of the income approach is shown in Table 14.1.

Using an Expert

Real estate valuation is a complex and technical procedure. It requires reliable information about the features of comparable properties, their selling prices, and terms of financing. It also involves some subjective judgments, as was the case in the example in Table 14.1. Rather than relying exclusively on their own judgment, many investors hire a real estate agent or a professional real estate appraiser to advise them about the market value of a property. As a form of insurance against overpaying, the use of an expert can be well worth the cost.

Performing Investment Analysis

investment analysis
approach to real estate valuation that not only considers what similar properties have sold for but also looks at the underlying determinants of value.

Estimates of market value play an integral role in real estate decision making. Yet today, more and more investors supplement their market value appraisals with **investment analysis.** This form of real estate valuation not only considers what similar properties have sold for but also looks at the underlying determinants of value. It is an extension of the traditional valuation approaches

TABLE 14.1 Applying the Income Approach

Comparable Property	(1) NOI	(2) Sale Price	(3) (1) ÷ (2) Market Capitalization Rate (*R*)
2301 Maple Avenue	$16,250	$182,500	.0890
4037 Armstrong Street	15,400	167,600	.0919
8240 Ludwell Street	19,200	198,430	.0968
7392 Grant Boulevard	17,930	189,750	.0945
Subject property	$18,480	?	?

From this market-derived information, an appraiser would work through Equation 14.1a to determine the subject property's value as follows:

$$V = \frac{\text{NOI}}{R}$$

$$V = \frac{\$18{,}480}{R}$$

$$V = \frac{\$18{,}480}{.093^*}$$

$$V = \underline{\underline{\$198{,}710}}$$

*Based on an analysis of the relative similarities of the comparables and the subject property, the appraiser decided that the appropriate *R* equals .093.

(cost, comparative sales, and income) that gives investors a better picture of whether a selected property is likely to satisfy their investment objectives.

Market Value versus Investment Analysis

The concept of market value differs from investment analysis in four important ways: (1) retrospective versus prospective, (2) impersonal versus personal, (3) unleveraged versus leveraged, and (4) net operating income (NOI) versus after-tax cash flows.

Retrospective versus Prospective Market value appraisals look backward; they attempt to estimate the price a property will sell for by looking at the sales prices of similar properties in the recent past. Under static market conditions, such a technique can be reasonable. But if, say, interest rates, population, or buyer expectations are changing rapidly, past sales prices may not accurately indicate a property's current value or its future value. An investment analysis tries to incorporate in the valuation process such factors as economic base, population demographics and psychographics, cost of mortgage financing, and potential sources of competition.

Impersonal versus Personal A market value estimate represents the price a property will sell for under certain specified conditions—in other words, a sort of market average. But in fact, every buyer and seller has a unique set of needs, and each real estate transaction can be structured to meet those needs. Thus an investment analysis looks beyond what may constitute a "typical" transaction and attempts to evaluate a subject property's terms and conditions of sale (or rent) as they correspond to a given investor's constraints and goals.

For example, a market value appraisal might show that with normal financing and conditions of sale, a property is worth $180,000. Yet because of personal tax consequences, it might be better for a seller to ask a higher price for the property and offer owner financing at a below-market interest rate.

Unleveraged versus Leveraged The returns a real estate investment offers will be influenced by the amount of the purchase price that is financed with debt. But simple income capitalization [$V = (\text{NOI}/R)$] does not incorporate alternative financing plans that might be available. It assumes either a cash or an unleveraged purchase.

leverage
in real estate, the use of debt financing to purchase a piece of property and thereby affect its risk–return parameters.

positive leverage
a position in which, if a property's return is in excess of its debt cost, the investor's return is increased to a level well above what could have been earned from an all-cash deal.

negative leverage
a position in which, if a property's return is below its debt cost, the investor's return is less than from an all-cash deal.

The use of debt financing, or **leverage,** gives differing risk–return parameters to a real estate investment. Leverage automatically increases investment risk because borrowed funds must be repaid. Failure to repay a mortgage loan results in foreclosure and possible property loss. Alternatively, leverage may also increase return. If a property can earn a return in excess of the cost of the borrowed funds (that is, debt cost), the investor's return is increased to a level well above what could have been earned from an all-cash deal. This is known as **positive leverage.** Conversely, if the return is below the debt cost, the return on invested equity is less than from an all-cash deal. This is called **negative leverage.** The following example both shows how leverage affects return and provides insight into the possible associated risks.

Assume you purchase a parcel of land for $20,000. You have two financing choices: Choice A is all cash; that is, no leverage is employed. Choice B involves 80% financing (20% down payment) at 12% interest. With leverage

TABLE 14.2 The Effect of Positive Leverage on Return: An Example*

Purchase price: $20,000
Sale price: $30,000
Holding period: 1 year

Item Number	Item	Choice A No Leverage	Choice B 80% Financing
1	Initial equity	$20,000	$ 4,000
2	Loan principal	0	16,000
3	Sale price	30,000	30,000
4	Capital gain [(3) − (1) − (2)]	10,000	10,000
5	Interest cost [0.12 × (2)]	0	1,920
6	Net return [(4) − (5)]	10,000	8,080
	Return on investor's equity [(6) ÷ (1)]	$\frac{\$10,000}{\$20,000} = +50\%$	$\frac{\$8,080}{\$4,000} = +202\%$

*To simplify this example, all values are presented on a *before-tax* basis. To get the true return, one would consider taxes on the capital gain and the interest expense.

(choice B), you sign a $16,000 note (0.80 × $20,000) at 12% interest, with the entire principal balance due and payable at the end of 1 year. Now suppose the land appreciates during the year to $30,000. (A comparative analysis of this occurrence is presented in Table 14.2.) Had you chosen the all-cash deal, the 1-year return on your initial equity would have been 50%. The use of leverage magnifies that return, no matter how much the property appreciated. The leveraged alternative (choice B) involved only a $4,000 investment in personal initial equity, with the balance financed by borrowing at 12% interest. The property sells for $30,000, of which $4,000 represents recovery of the initial equity investment, $16,000 goes to repay the principal balance on the debt, and another $1,920 of gain is used to pay interest ($16,000 × 0.12). The balance of the proceeds, $8,080, represents your return. The return on your initial equity is 202%—over four times that provided by the no-leverage alternative, choice A.

We used 12% in this example, but the cost of money has surprisingly little effect on comparative (leveraged versus unleveraged) returns. For example, using 6% interest, the return on equity rises to 226%, still way above the unleveraged alternative. Granted, using a lower interest cost does improve return, but other things being equal, what really drives return on equity is the *amount* of leverage.

There is another side to the coin, however. No matter what the eventual outcome, risk is *always* inherent in leverage; it can easily turn a bad deal into a disaster. Suppose the $20,000 property discussed above dropped in value by 25% during the 1-year holding period. The comparative results are presented in Table 14.3. The unleveraged investment would have resulted in a negative return of 25%. This is not large, however, compared to the leveraged position, in which you would lose not only the entire initial investment of $4,000 but an additional $2,920 ($1,000 additional principal on the debt + $1,920 interest). The total loss of $6,920 on the original $4,000 of equity results in a (negative) return of 173%. Thus the loss in the leverage case is nearly seven times the loss experienced in the unleveraged situation.

TABLE 14.3 The Effect of Negative Leverage on Return: An Example*

Purchase price: $20,000
Sale price: $30,000
Holding period: 1 year

Item Number	Item	Choice A No Leverage	Choice B 80% Financing
1	Initial equity	$20,000	$ 4,000
2	Loan principal	0	16,000
3	Sale price	15,000	15,000
4	Capital loss [(3) − (1) − (2)]	5,000	5,000
5	Interest cost [0.12 × (2)]	0	1,920
6	Net loss [(4) − (5)]	5,000	6,920
	Return on investor's equity [(6) ÷ (1)]	$\frac{-\$5,000}{\$20,000} = -25\%$	$\frac{-\$6,920}{\$4,000} = -173\%$

*To simplify this example, all values are presented on a *before-tax* basis. To get the true return, one would consider taxes on the capital loss and the interest expense.

NOI versus After-Tax Cash Flows Recall that to estimate market value, the income approach capitalizes net operating income (NOI). To most investors, though, the NOI figure holds little meaning. This is because the majority of real estate investors finance their purchases. In addition, few investors today can ignore the effect of federal income tax law on their investment decisions. Investors want to know how much cash they will be required to put into a transaction and how much cash they are likely to get out. The concept of NOI does not address these questions. Thus we instead use **after-tax cash flows** (ATCFs), which are the annual cash flows earned on a real estate investment, net of all expenses, debt payments, and taxes. To them we apply the familiar finance measure of investment return—discounted cash flow—as a prime criterion for selecting real estate investments. (Sometimes yield is used instead to assess the suitability of a prospective real estate investment.)

after-tax cash flows (ATCFs)
the annual cash flows earned on a real estate investment, net of all expenses, debt payments, and taxes.

Calculating Discounted Cash Flow

discounted cash flow
use of present-value techniques to find *net present value (NPV).*

net present value (NPV)
the difference between the present value of the cash flows and the amount of equity necessary to make an investment.

Calculating **discounted cash flow** involves the techniques of present value we discussed in Chapter 4; in addition, you need to learn how to calculate annual after-tax cash flows and the after-tax net proceeds of sale. You then can discount the cash flows an investment is expected to earn over a specified holding period. This figure in turn gives you the present value of the cash flows. Next, you find the **net present value** (NPV)—the difference between the present value of the cash flows and the amount of equity necessary to make the investment. The resulting difference tells you whether the proposed investment looks good (a positive net present value) or bad (a negative net present value).

This process of discounting cash flows to calculate the net present value (NPV) of an investment can be represented by the following equation:

Equation 14.2

$$NPV = \left[\frac{CF_1}{(1+r)^1} + \frac{CF_2}{(1+r)^2} + \cdots + \frac{CF_{n-1}}{(1+r)^{n-1}} + \frac{CF_n + CF_{R_n}}{(1+r)^n}\right] - I_0$$

where:

I_0 = the original required investment

CF_i = annual after-tax cash flow for year i

CF_{R_n} = the after-tax net proceeds from sale (reversionary after-tax cash flow) occurring in year n

r = the discount rate and $[1/(1 + r)^i]$ is the present-value interest factor for \$1 received in year i using an r percent discount rate

In this equation, the annual after-tax cash flows, *CF*s, may be either inflows to investors or outflows from them. Inflows are preceded by a plus (+) sign, outflows by a minus (−) sign.

Calculating Yield

An alternative way to assess investment suitability is to calculate the *yield*, which was first presented in Chapter 4. It is the discount rate that causes the present value of the cash flows just to equal the amount of equity, or, alternatively, it is the discount rate that causes net present value (NPV) just to equal \$0. Setting the NPV in Equation 14.2 equal to zero, we can rewrite the equation as follows:

Equation 14.3

$$\left[\frac{CF_1}{(1+r)^1} + \frac{CF_2}{(1+r)^2} + \cdots + \frac{CF_{n-1}}{(1+r)^{n-1}} + \frac{CF_n + CF_{R_n}}{(1+r)^n}\right] = I_0$$

Because estimates of the cash flows (CF_i), including the sale proceeds (CF_{R_n}), and the equity investment (I_0) are known, the yield is the unknown discount rate (r) that solves Equation 14.3. It represents the compounded annual rate of return actually earned by the investment.

Unfortunately, the yield is often difficult to calculate without the use of the sophisticated routine found on most financial business calculators or, alternatively, the use of a properly programmed personal computer. For our purposes, we will use the following three-step procedure to estimate yield to the nearest whole percent (1%).

Step 1: Calculate the investment's net present value (NPV) using its required return.

Step 2: *If the NPV found in step 1 is positive (> \$0),* raise the discount rate (typically 1% to 5%) and recalculate the NPV using the increased rate.

If the NPV found in step 1 is negative (< \$0), lower the discount rate (typically 1% to 5%) and recalculate the NPV using the decreased rate.

Step 3: *If the NPV found in step 2 is very close to \$0,* the resulting discount rate is a good estimate of the investment's yield to the nearest whole percent.

If the NPV is still not close to \$0, repeat step 2.

If the calculated yield is greater than the discount rate appropriate for the given investment, the investment is acceptable. In that case, the net present value would be positive.

When consistently applied, the net present value and yield approaches give the same recommendation for accepting or rejecting a proposed real estate investment. The next section shows how all the elements discussed so far in this chapter can be applied to a real estate investment decision.

CONCEPTS IN REVIEW

14.8 What is the *market value* of a property? What is real estate *appraisal?* Comment on the following statement: "Market value is always the price at which a property sells."

14.9 Briefly describe each of the following approaches to real estate market value:

a. Cost approach
b. Comparative sales approach
c. Income approach

14.10 What is real estate *investment analysis?* How does it differ from the concept of market value?

14.11 What is *leverage,* and what role does it play in real estate investment? How does it affect the risk–return parameters of a real estate investment?

14.12 What is *net operating income (NOI)?* What are *after-tax cash flows (ATCFs)?* Why do real estate investors prefer to use ATCFs?

14.13 What is the *net present value (NPV)?* What is the *yield?* How are the NPV and yield used to make real estate investment decisions?

http://hepg.aw.com

The valuation of real estate requires a thorough and detailed understanding of all the variables that are involved in the valuation process. The following Web page provides multiple links to articles that deal with real estate investing and valuation.

www.investorhome.com/re.htm

An Example of Real Estate Valuation

LG 4

Assume that Jack Wilson is deciding whether to buy the Academic Arms Apartments. To improve his real estate investment decision making, Jack follows a systematic procedure. He designs a schematic framework of analysis that corresponds closely to the topics we've discussed. Following this framework (shown in Figure 14.1), Jack follows a five-step procedure. He (1) sets out his investment objectives, (2) analyzes important features of the property, (3) collects data on the determinants of the property's value, (4) performs valuation and investment analysis, and (5) synthesizes and interprets the results of his analysis.

FIGURE 14.1 Framework for Real Estate Investment Analysis

This framework depicts a logical five-step procedure for analyzing potential investment properties to assess whether they are acceptable investments that might be included in one's investment portfolio. (Source: Adapted from Gary W. Eldred, *Real Estate: Analysis and Strategy,* New York: Harper & Row, 1987, p. 18.)

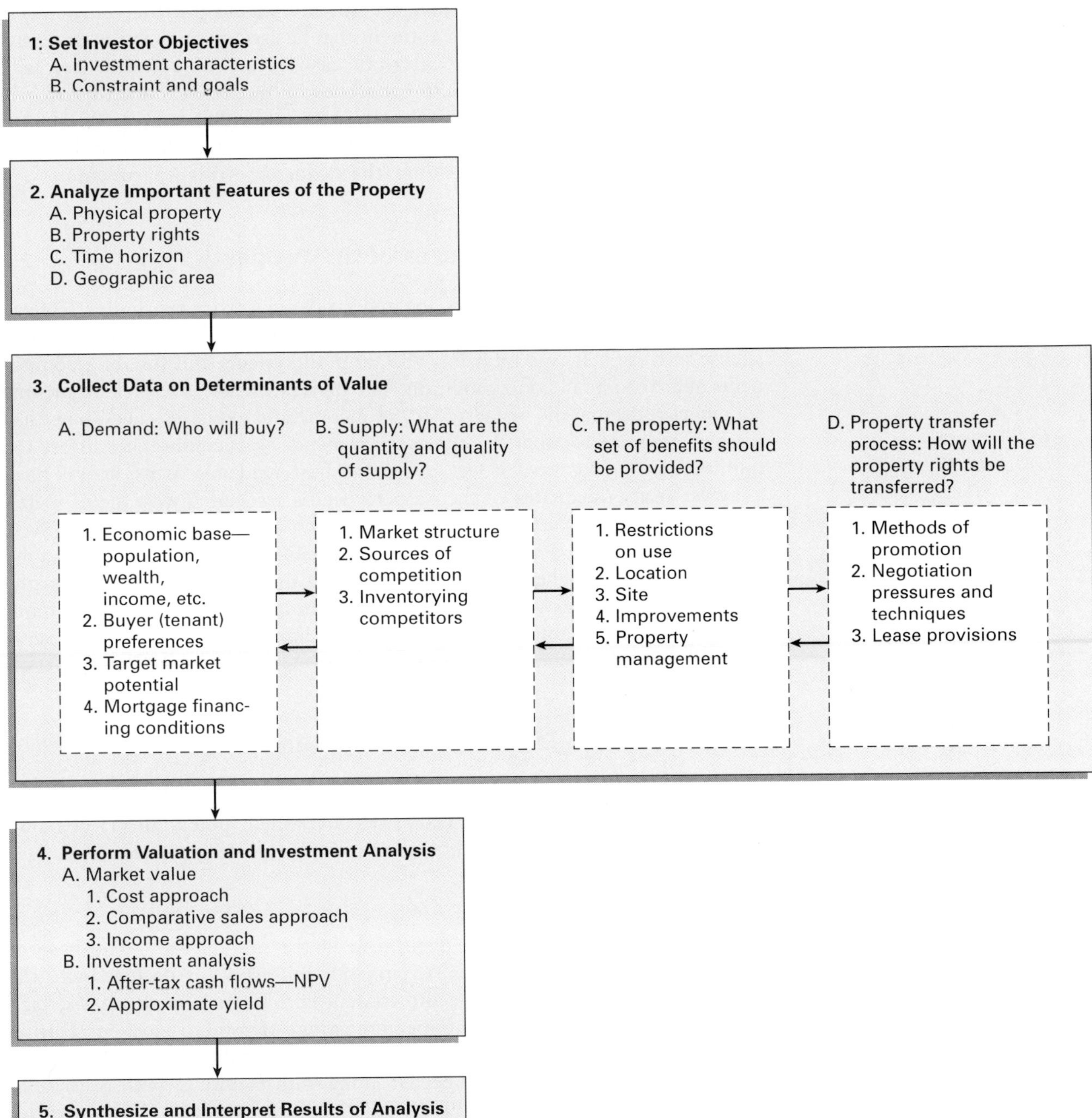

Set Investor Objectives

Jack is a tenured associate professor of management at Finley College. He's single, age 40, and earns an income of $85,000 per year from salary, consulting fees, stock dividends, and book royalties. His applicable tax rate on ordinary income is 31%. Jack wants to diversify his investment portfolio further. He would like to add a real estate investment that has good appreciation potential and provides a positive yearly after-tax cash flow. For convenience, Jack requires the property to be close to his office, and he feels his talents and personality are suited to the ownership of apartments. Jack has $60,000 of cash to invest. On this amount, he would like to earn a 13% rate of return. Jack has his eye on a small apartment building, the Academic Arms Apartments.

Analyze Important Features of the Property

The Academic Arms building is located six blocks from the Finley College Student Union. The building contains eight 2-bedroom, 2-bath units of 1,100 square feet each. It was built in 1983, and all systems and building components appear to be in good condition. The present owner gave Jack an income statement reflecting the property's 1998 income and expenses. The owner has further assured Jack that no adverse easements or encumbrances affect the building's title. Of course, if Jack decides to buy Academic Arms, he will have a lawyer verify the quality of the property rights associated with the property. For now, though, he accepts the owner's word.

Jack considers a 5-year holding period reasonable. At present, he's happy at Finley and thinks he will stay there at least until age 45. Jack defines the market for the property as a 1-mile radius from campus. He reasons that students who walk to campus (the target market) limit their choice of apartments to those that fall within that geographic area.

Collect Data on Determinants of Value

Once Jack has analyzed the important features, he next thinks about the factors that will determine the property's investment potential: (1) demand, (2) supply, (3) the property, and (4) the property transfer process.

Demand

Finley College is the lifeblood institution in the market area. The base of demand for the Academic Arms Apartments will grow (or decline) with the size of the college's employment and student enrollment. On this basis, Jack judges the prospects for the area to be in the range of good to excellent. During the coming 5 years, major funding (due to a $25 million gift) will increase Finley's faculty by 15%, and expected along with faculty growth is a rise in the student population from 3,200 to 3,700 full-time students. Jack estimates that 70% of the *new* students will live away from home. In the past, Finley largely served the local market, but with its new affluence—and the resources this affluence can buy—the college will draw students from a wider geographic area. Furthermore, because Finley is a private college with relatively high tuition, the majority of students come from upper-middle-income families.

Parental support can thus be expected to heighten students' ability to pay. Overall, then, Jack believes the major indicators of demand for the market area look promising.

Supply

Jack realizes that even strong demand cannot yield profits if a market suffers from oversupply. Fortunately, Jack thinks that Academic Arms is well insulated from competing units. Most important is the fact that the designated market area is fully built up, and as much as 80% of the area is zoned single-family residential. Any efforts to change the zoning would be strongly opposed by neighborhood residents. The only potential problem Jack sees is that the college might build more student housing on campus. Though the school administration has discussed this possibility, no funds have yet been allocated to such a project. In sum, Jack concludes that the risk of oversupply in the Academic Arms market area is low—especially during the next 5 years.

The Property

Now the question is whether the Academic Arms Apartments will appeal to the desired market segment? On this issue, Jack concludes the answer is yes. The property already is zoned multifamily, and its present (and intended) use complies with all pertinent ordinances and housing codes. Of major importance, though, is the property's location. Not only does the site have good accessibility to the campus, but it is also three blocks from the Campus Town shopping district. In addition, the aesthetic, socioeconomic, legal, and fiscal environments of the property are compatible with student preferences.

On the negative side, the on-site parking has space for only six cars. Still, the building itself is attractive, and the relatively large two-bedroom, two-bath units are ideal for roommates. Although Jack has no experience managing apartments, he feels that if he studies several books on property management and applies his formal business education, he can succeed.

Property Transfer Process

As noted earlier, real estate markets are *not efficient*. Thus, before a property's sale price or rental income can reach its potential, an effective means to get information to buyers or tenants must be developed. Here, of course, Jack has a great advantage. Notices on campus bulletin boards and an occasional ad in the school newspaper should be all he needs to keep the property rented. Although he might experience some vacancy during the summer months, Jack feels he can overcome this problem by requiring 12-month leases but then granting tenants the right to sublet as long as the sublessees meet his tenant-selection criteria.

Perform Valuation and Investment Analysis

Real estate cash flows depend on the underlying characteristics of the property and the market. That is why we have devoted so much attention to analyzing the determinants of value. Often real estate investors lose money because they "run the numbers" without sufficient research. Jack decided to use the determinants of value to perform an investment analysis, which should allow him

TABLE 14.4 Income Statement, Academic Arms Apartments, 1998

Gross rental income		
(8 × $335 × 12)		$32,160
Operating expenses:		
Utilities	$2,830	
Trash collection	675	
Repairs and maintenance	500	
Promotion and advertising	150	
Property insurance	840	
Property taxes	3,200	
Less: Total operating expenses		8,195
Net operating income (NOI)		$23,965

to assess the property's value relative to his investment objectives. He may later use an appraisal of market value as confirmation. As we go through Jack's investment analysis calculations, remember that the numbers coming out will be only as accurate as the numbers going in.

The Numbers

At present, Mrs. Bowker, the owner of Academic Arms Apartments, is asking $260,000 for the property. To assist in the sale, she is willing to offer owner financing to a qualified buyer. The terms would be 20% down, 11.5% interest, and full amortization of the outstanding mortgage balance over 30 years. The owner's income statement for 1998 is shown in Table 14.4. After talking with Mrs. Bowker, Jack believes she would probably accept an offer of $60,000 down, a price of $245,000, and a 30-year mortgage at 11%. On this basis, Jack prepares his investment calculations.

Cash Flow Analysis

As a first step in cash flow analysis, Jack projects the owner's income statement for 1999 (as shown in Table 14.5). This projection reflects higher rent levels, higher expenses, and a lower net operating income. Jack believes that because of poor owner management and deferred maintenance, Mrs. Bowker is not getting as much in rents as the market could support. In addition, how-

TABLE 14.5 Projected Income Statement, Academic Arms Apartments, 1999

Gross potential rental income	$37,800	
Less: Vacancy and collection losses at 4%	1,512	
Effective gross income (EGI)		$36,288
Operating expenses:		
Management at 5% of EGI	$ 1,814	
Utilities	3,100	
Trash collection	750	
Repairs and maintenance	2,400	
Promotion and advertising	150	
Property insurance	960	
Property taxes	4,292	
Less: Total operating expenses		13,466
Net operating income (NOI)		$22,822

ever, her expenses understate those he is likely to incur. For one thing, a management expense should be deducted. Jack wants to separate what is rightfully a return on labor from his return on capital. Also, once the property is sold, a higher property tax assessment will be levied against it. Except for promotion and advertising, other expenses have been increased to adjust for inflation and a more extensive maintenance program. With these adjustments, the NOI for Academic Arms during 1999 is estimated at $22,822.

To move from NOI to after-tax cash flows (ATCFs), we need to perform the calculations shown in Table 14.6. This table shows that to calculate ATCF, Jack must first compute the income tax savings or income taxes he would incur as a result of property ownership. In this case, potential tax savings accrue during the first 3 years because the allowable tax deductions of interest and depreciation exceed the property's net operating income; in the final 2 years, income exceeds deductions, so taxes are due.

depreciation
in real estate investing, a tax deduction based on the original cost of a building and used to reflect its declining economic life.

The "magic" of simultaneously losing and making money is caused by **depreciation.** Tax statutes incorporate this tax deduction, which is based on the original cost of the building, to reflect its declining economic life. However, because this deduction does not actually require a current cash outflow by the property owner, it acts as a *noncash expenditure* that reduces taxes and increases cash flow. In other words, in the 1999–2001 period, the property ownership provides Jack with a tax shelter; that is, Jack uses the income tax losses sustained on the property to offset the taxable income he receives from salary, consulting fees, stock dividends, and book royalties. (We'll consider tax shelters in more detail in Chapter 15.)

Once the amount of tax savings (or taxes) is known, it is added to (or subtracted from) the before-tax cash flow. Because Jack qualifies as an "active manager" of the property (an important provision of the Tax Reform Act of 1986, discussed more fully in Chapter 15) and because his income is low enough (also discussed in Chapter 15), he can use the real estate losses to reduce his other income. It is important to recognize that under the Tax

TABLE 14.6 Cash Flow Analysis, Academic Arms Apartments, 1999–2003

	1999	2000	2001	2002	2003
Income Tax Computations					
NOI	$22,822	$24,419	$26,128	$27,957	$29,914
– Interest*	20,350	20,259	20,146	20,022	19,877
– Depreciation**	6,545	6,545	6,545	6,545	6,545
Taxable income (loss)	($ 4,073)	($ 2,385)	($ 563)	$ 1,390	$ 3,492
Marginal tax rate	0.31	0.31	0.31	0.31	0.31
Tax savings (+) or taxes (–)	+$ 1,263	+$ 739	+$ 175	–$ 431	–$ 1,083
After-Tax Cash Flow (ATCF) Computations					
NOI	$22,822	$24,419	$26,128	$27,957	$29,914
– Mortgage payment	21,280	21,280	21,280	21,280	21,280
Before-tax cash flow	$ 1,542	$ 3,139	$ 4,848	$ 6,677	$ 8,634
Tax savings (+) or taxes (–)	+ 1,263	+ 739	+ 175	– 431	– 1,083
After-tax cash flow (ATCF)	$ 2,805	$ 3,878	$ 5,023	$ 6,246	$ 7,551

*Based on a $185,000 mortgage at 11%, compounded annually. Some rounding has been used.
**Based on straight-line depreciation over 27.5 years and a depreciable basis of $180,000. Land value is assumed to equal $65,000.

Reform Act of 1986, the amount of tax losses that can be applied to other taxable income is limited. *It is therefore important to consult a tax expert about the tax consequences of expected income tax losses when calculating ATCFs from real estate investments.*

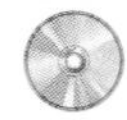

Proceeds from Sale

Jack must now estimate the net proceeds he will receive when he sells the property. For purposes of this analysis, Jack has assumed a 5-year holding period. Now he must forecast a selling price for the property. From that amount he will subtract selling expenses, the outstanding balance on the mortgage, and applicable federal income taxes. The remainder equals Jack's after-tax net proceeds from sale. These calculations are shown in Table 14.7. (Note that although Jack's ordinary income is subject to a 31% tax rate, because he would have held the property for more than 18 months, the maximum rate of 20% applies to the capital gain expected on the sale of the property.)

Jack wants to estimate his net proceeds from sale conservatively. He believes that at a minimum, market forces will push up the selling price of the property at the rate of 5% per year beyond his assumed purchase price of $245,000. Thus he estimates that the selling price in 5 years will be $312,620. (He obtained this amount by multiplying the $245,000 purchase price by the future-value interest factor of 1.276 from Appendix A, Table A.1, for 5% and 5 years—that is, $245,000 × 1.276 = $312,620.) Making the indicated deductions from the forecasted selling price, Jack computes after-tax net proceeds from the sale equal to $95,791.

Discounted Cash Flow

In this step, Jack discounts the projected cash flows to find their present value, and he subtracts the amount of his equity investment from their total to get net present value (NPV). In making this calculation (see Table 14.8), Jack finds

TABLE 14.7 Estimated After-Tax Net Proceeds from Sale, Academic Arms Apartments, 2003

Income Tax Computations	
Forecasted selling price (at 5% annual appreciation)	$312,620
− Selling expenses at 7%	21,883
− Book value (purchase price less accumulated depreciation)	212,275
Gain on sale	$ 78,462
× Tax rate on gain*	20%
Taxes payable	$ 15,692
Computation of After-Tax Net Proceeds	
Forecasted selling price	$312,620
− Selling expenses	21,883
− Mortgage balance outstanding	179,254
Net proceeds before taxes	$111,483
− Taxes payable (calculated above)	15,692
After-tax net proceeds from sale (CF_{R2003})	$ 95,791

*Although Jack's ordinary income is taxed at a 31% rate, under the *Taxpayer Relief Act of 1997*, this gain would be taxed at the 20% maximum rate applicable to capital gains.

TABLE 14.8 Net Present Value, Academic Arms Apartments*

$$NPV = \left[\frac{CF_1}{(1+r)^1} + \frac{CF_2}{(1+r)^2} + \frac{CF_3}{(1+r)^3} + \frac{CF_4}{(1+r)^4} + \frac{CF_5 + CF_{R5}}{(1+r)^5}\right] - I_0$$

$$NPV = \left[\frac{\$2,805}{(1+0.13)^1} + \frac{\$3,878}{(1+0.13)^2} + \frac{\$5,023}{(1+0.13)^3} + \frac{\$6,246}{(1+0.13)^4} + \frac{\$103,342^{**}}{(1+0.13)^5}\right] - 60,000$$

NPV = \$2,483 + \$3,037 + \$3,481 + \$3,829 + \$56,115 − \$60,000***

NPV = \$68,945 − \$60,000

NPV = +\$8,945

*All inflows are assumed to be end-of-year receipts.

**Includes both the fifth-year annual after-tax cash flow of \$7,551 and the after-tax net proceeds from sale of \$95,791.

***Calculated using present-value interest factors from Appendix A, Table A.3.

that at his required rate of return of 13%, the NPV of these flows equals \$8,945. Looked at another way, the present value of the amounts Jack forecasts he will receive exceeds the amount of his initial equity investment by about \$8,900. The investment therefore meets (and exceeds) his acceptance criterion.

Yield

Alternatively, Jack could estimate the yield by using the initial equity, I_0, of \$60,000, along with the after-tax cash flow, CF_i, for each year i (shown at the bottom of Table 14.6) and the after-tax net proceeds from sale, CF_{R2003}, of \$95,791 (calculated in Table 14.7). The future cash flows associated with Jack's proposed investment in Academic Arms Apartments are summarized in column 1 of Table 14.9. Using these data along with the planned \$60,000 equity investment, we can apply the three-step procedure described earlier in this chapter to estimate the yield.

Step 1: The investment's NPV at the 13% discount rate is \$8,495, as shown in Table 14.8.

Step 2: Because the NPV in step 1 is positive, we decide to recalculate the NPV using a 15% discount rate as shown in columns 2 and 3 of Table 14.9. As shown at the bottom of column 3, the NPV at the 15% discount rate is \$3,612.

Step 3: Because the NPV of \$3,612 calculated in step 2 is well above \$0, we repeat step 2.

Step 2: We decide to raise the discount rate to 17% and recalculate the NPV as shown in columns 4 and 5 of Table 14.9. As shown at the bottom of column 5, the NPV at the 17% discount rate is –\$1,172.

Step 3: Because the NPV of –\$1,172 calculated in our first repetition of step 2 is below \$0, we again repeat step 2.

Step 2: We now decide to lower the rate by 1%, to 16%, and recalculate the NPV as shown in columns 6 and 7 of Table 14.9. As shown at the bottom of column 7, the NPV is \$1,159.

TABLE 14.9 Yield Estimation, Academic Arms Apartments

		NPV at 15%		NPV at 17%		NPV at 16%	
End of Year	(1) After-Tax Cash Flow*	(2) 15% PVIF**	(3) (1) × (2) Present Value	(4) 17% PVIF**	(5) (1) × (4) Present Value	(6) 16% PVIF**	(7) (1) × (6) Present Value
1	$ 2,805	.870	$ 2,441	.855	$ 2,398	.862	$ 2,418
2	3,878	.756	2,932	.731	2,835	.743	2,882
3	5,023	.658	3,305	.624	3,135	.641	3,220
4	6,246	.572	3,573	.534	3,336	.552	3,448
5	103,342***	.497	51,361	.456	47,124	.476	49,191
Present value of cash flows			$63,612		$58,828		$61,159
− Initial equity			60,000		60,000		60,000
Net present value (NPV)			$ 3,612		−$ 1,172		$ 1,159

*Cash flows derived in Tables 14.6 and 14.7 and summarized in the numerators of terms to the right of the equals sign in the second equation in Table 14.8.

**PVIF represents the present-value interest factors found in Appendix A, Table A.3.

***Includes the fifth-year annual after-tax cash flow of $7,551 and the after-tax net proceeds from sale of $95,791.

Step 3: It is now clear that the yield is somewhere between 16% and 17%, because the NPV would equal $0 in that range. The better estimate to the nearest whole percent is *16%*, because the NPV at this rate is closer to $0 ($1,159) than that at the 17% rate (–$1,172).

Because the yield is estimated (to the nearest whole percent) to be *16%*, which is greater than Jack's required rate of return of 13%, the investment meets—and exceeds—his acceptance criterion. Though it yields merely an estimate, when consistently applied this technique should always result in the same conclusion about acceptability as that obtained using net present value.

Synthesize and Interpret Results of Analysis

Now Jack reviews his work. He evaluates his analysis for important features and determinants of the property's value, checks all the facts and figures in the investment analysis calculations, and then evaluates the results in light of his stated investment objectives. He asks himself, "All things considered, is the expected payoff worth the risk?" In this case, he decides it is.

Even a positive finding, however, does not necessarily mean Jack should buy this property. He might still want to shop around to see if he can locate an even better investment. Furthermore, he might be wise to hire a real estate appraiser to confirm that the price he is willing to pay seems reasonable with respect to the recent sales prices of similar properties in the market area.

Nevertheless, Jack realizes that any problem can be studied to death; no one can ever obtain all the information that will bear on a decision. He gives himself a week to investigate other properties and talk to a professional appraiser. If nothing turns up to cause him to have second thoughts, he will offer to buy the Academic Arms Apartments. On the terms presented, he is willing to pay up to a maximum price of $245,000.

CONCEPTS IN REVIEW

14.14 List and briefly describe the five steps in the framework for real estate investment analysis shown in Figure 14.1.

14.15 Define *depreciation* from a tax viewpoint. Explain why it is said to offer tax shelter potential. What real estate investments provide this benefit? Explain.

14.16 Explain why, despite its being acceptable on the basis of NPV or of yield, a real estate investment still might not be acceptable to a given investor.

Real Estate Investment Securities

LG 5

The most popular ways to invest in real estate are through individual ownership (as we've just seen), real estate investment trusts (REITs), and real estate limited partnerships (RELPs). Individual ownership of investment real estate is most common among wealthy individuals, professional real estate investors, and financial institutions. The strongest advantage of individual ownership is personal control, and the strongest drawback is that it requires a relatively large amount of capital. Although thus far we have emphasized active, individual real estate investment, it is likely that most individuals will invest in real estate by purchasing shares of either a real estate investment trust (such as Starwood Lodging, which was discussed at the beginning of the chapter) or a limited partnership. Here we will examine each of these investment alternatives.

Real Estate Investment Trusts (REITs)

real estate investment trust (REIT) a type of closed-end investment company that sells shares to investors and invests the proceeds in various types of real estate and real estate mortgages.

A **real estate investment trust** (**REIT**) is a type of closed-end investment company (see Chapter 13) that invests money, obtained through the sale of its shares to investors, in various types of real estate and real estate mortgages. REITs were established with the passage of the Real Estate Investment Trust Act of 1960, which set forth requirements for forming a REIT, as well as rules and procedures for making investments and distributing income. The appeal of REITs lies in their ability to allow small investors to receive both the capital appreciation and the income returns of real estate ownership without the headaches of property management.

REITs were quite popular until the mid-1970s, when the bottom fell out of the real estate market as a result of many bad loans and an excess supply of property. In the early 1980s, however, both the real estate market and REITs began to make a comeback. Indeed, by 1998 there were about 210 such investment companies. The recent high interest in REITs has been attributed to a strong economy, rising real estate values, generally low mortgage interest rates, and the greatly diminished appeal of real estate limited partnerships (described later) that has resulted from changes in the tax laws. REITs are again popular forms of real estate investment that at times have earned attractive annual rates of return of 10% to 20% or more.

Basic Structure

REITs sell shares of stock to the investing public and use the proceeds, along with borrowed funds, to invest in a portfolio of real estate investments. The

> **INVESTOR FACT**
>
> REIT INDUSTRY PROFILE—Some REITs invest in a variety of property types, such as shopping centers, apartments, warehouses, office buildings, and hotels. Other REITs specialize in one property type. For example, health care REITs might specialize in hospitals, medical office buildings, nursing homes, or assisted living centers. Some REITs invest throughout the country. Others specialize in one region. Here is a profile of the REIT industry's property investment strategy in late 1997:
>
> Retail, 22.4%
> Residential, 21.0%
> Industrial/office, 20.8%
> Health care, 10.3%
> Specialty, 10.1%
> Self-storage, 5.4%
> Mortgage-backed, 5.1%
> Diversified, 4.9%

investor therefore owns part of the real estate portfolio held by the real estate investment trust. Typically, REITs yield a return at least 1 to 2 percentage points above money market funds and about the same return as high-grade corporate bonds. REITs are required by law to pay out 95% of their income as dividends, which leaves little to invest in new acquisitions. Furthermore, they must keep at least 75% of their assets in real estate investments, earn at least 75% of their income from real estate, and hold each investment for at least 4 years.

Like any investment fund, each REIT has certain stated investment objectives, which should be carefully considered before acquiring shares. There are three basic types of REITs:

- *Equity REITs.* These invest in properties such as apartments, office buildings, shopping centers, and hotels.
- *Mortgage REITs.* These make both construction and mortgage loans to real estate investors.
- *Hybrid REITs.* These invest both in properties and in construction and real estate mortgage loans.

Equity REITs are by far the most common type. The shares of REITs are traded on organized exchanges such as the NYSE and the AMEX as well as in the over-the-counter (OTC) market.

Investing in REITs

REITs provide an attractive mechanism for real estate investment by individual investors. They also provide professional management. In addition, because their shares can be traded in the securities markets, investors can purchase and sell shares conveniently with the assistance of a full-service, discount, or online broker. Investors in REITs can reap tax benefits by placing their shares in a Keogh plan, an individual retirement arrangement (IRA), or some other tax-deferring vehicle.

The most direct way to investigate REITs before you buy is to get the names of those that interest you and then call or write the headquarters of each for information on the properties and/or mortgages it holds, its management, its future plans, and its track record. Additional information on REIT investments can be obtained from the National Association of Real Estate Investment Trusts, 1129 Twentieth Street NW, Suite 305, Washington, DC 20036 (202–785–8717).

The evaluation process will, of course, depend on the type of REIT you are considering. Equity REITs tend to be most popular because they share directly in real estate growth. If a property's rent goes up, so will the dividend distribution, and share prices may also rise to reflect property appreciation. Equity REITs can be analyzed by applying the same basic procedures described in Chapters 6 and 7 for common stock valuation. Because mortgage REITs earn most of their income as interest on real estate loans, they tend to trade like bonds; therefore, many of the techniques for analyzing bond investments presented in Chapters 8 and 9 can be used to evaluate them. Hybrid REITs have the characteristics of both property and mortgages and should therefore be evaluated accordingly.

Regardless of type, you should review the REIT's investment objective and performance as you would those of a mutual fund (see Chapter 13). Carefully check the types of properties and/or mortgages held by the REIT. Be sure to look at the REIT's dividend yield and capital gain potential. Above all, as with any investment, select the REIT that is consistent with your investment risk and return objectives. The *Investing in Action* box on page 570 discusses REITs that have captured recent investor interest and offers guidelines for selecting a REIT that's right for you.

Real Estate Limited Partnerships (RELPs)

real estate limited partnership (RELP)
a professionally managed real estate syndicate that invests in various types of real estate; the managers take the role of general partner, with unlimited liability, and other investors are limited partners, with liability limited to the amount of their investment.

A **real estate limited partnership** (RELP) is a professionally managed real estate syndicate that invests in various types of real estate. Some RELPs are set up to speculate in raw land; others invest in such income-producing properties as apartments, office buildings, and shopping centers; and still others invest in various types of mortgages (the so-called *debt partnerships,* as opposed to the *equity partnerships* that own land and buildings). Managers of RELPs assume the role of general partner, which means their liability is unlimited, and other investors are limited partners, which means they are legally liable for only the amount of their investment. Most limited partnerships require a minimum investment of between $2,500 and $10,000. Because of the limited liability, along with the potentially high returns provided by these arrangements, they often appeal to individual investors who wish to buy real estate. (A detailed discussion of the structure and operation of limited partnerships is presented in Chapter 15.) Investment in a limited partnership can be made directly through ads in the financial news, through stockbrokers or financial planners, or with the assistance of a commercial real estate broker.

Types of Syndicates

single-property syndicate
a type of RELP established to raise money to purchase a specific property (or properties).

There are two basic types of real estate limited partnerships: single-property and blind pool syndicates. The **single-property syndicate** is established to raise money to purchase a specific property (or properties). For example, 50 units of a partnership can be sold at $7,500 each to buy a piece of property for $1 million. A "unit" in a limited partnership is like a share of stock in a company and represents an ownership position in the partnership. In this case, a total of $375,000 (50 units × $7,500) would come from the partners, and the remaining $625,000 would be borrowed.

blind pool syndicate
a type of RELP formed by a syndicator to raise a given amount of money to be invested at the syndicator's discretion.

The **blind pool syndicate,** on the other hand, is formed by a syndicator to raise a given amount of money to be invested at his or her discretion, though the general partner often has some or all of the properties already picked out. The blind pool syndicator takes a specified percentage of all income generated as a management fee. Large, typically well-known, real estate management firms commonly arrange these types of syndicates.

Investing in RELPs

Prior to the Tax Reform Act of 1986, much of the appeal of real estate limited partnerships came from the tax-sheltered income these investments provided. However, that is no longer the case. Now these limited partnerships are

INVESTING IN ACTION

Real Estate Rides Again

Want to own a golf course? Or would a factory outlet shopping center be more your style? The new breed of real estate investment trusts (REITs) makes it easy to choose. Unlike earlier REITs that bought a variety of properties and made speculative loans on new construction, today's REITs are niche players that typically focus on one geographic area and specialize in one property type—apartments, factory outlet malls, shopping centers, office buildings, mobile home parks, even golf courses. This investment strategy has paid off: According to a 10-year study by Kemper Securities, specialized REITs averaged returns of 19% per year, compared to 3% for broadly diversified REITs.

The popularity of REITs waxes and wanes depending on economic conditions and the returns on other investments. For example, investors flocked to REITs in 1994 when the stock and bond markets faltered. This capital influx doubled the REIT market to an estimated $40 billion in about 18 months. REIT share prices fell as these new offerings created a glut on the market. Today, individual investors are the main source of real estate capital, replacing institutional investors who cut back on real estate investments after the real estate market collapsed in the early 1990s. By the end of 1997, the total amount invested in REITs exceeded $100 billion.

Many financial advisers recommend putting 5% to 10% of your portfolio in real estate. If you find REITs attractive, advisers recommend buying several types of them to diversify both geographically and in terms of property type, because each type of REIT performs differently.

Choosing an REIT can be difficult. For one thing, the accounting is different from that for the typical public company. Instead of reading about earnings per share, you'll have to analyze the REIT's funds from operations (FFO). The main difference between FFO and EPS is that FFO adds back depreciation. The reason for the new term: Historically, real estate has not depreciated to the same extent as machinery, computers, and other personal property used in traditional businesses. In addition, you must evaluate not only the types and merits of property owned, plus regional and local economic factors, but also the structure of the REIT itself (ownership, management, debt, etc.). Finally, you must take general stock market dynamics into account. Study the prospectus carefully, concentrating on the following areas:

- ***Management.*** Look for a track record of 5 or more years of buying, selling, and managing properties before going public. Management should also own 10% to 15% of the REIT; thus you can be confident that its interests are the same as yours.
- ***Leverage.*** This should be under 40% and should be largely fixed-rate, amortized, long-term debt rather than short-term, variable-rate debt, which leaves the REIT vulnerable to changes in interest rates.
- ***Assets.*** Analyze the quality of assets, consistency by geographic region or type of asset, and demographic and economic characteristics of the locations.

Still confused about which REITs to buy? Then buy shares in a real estate mutual fund that invests in REITs and let professional managers choose the best REITs.

considered *passive* investments like other forms of real estate, so the amount of write-offs that can be taken on them is limited to the amount of income generated from passive activities. This means that such write-offs cannot be used to shelter ordinary income from taxes.

Although limited partnerships have lost some of their appeal, they remain a popular way to invest in real estate, especially for those with limited investment capital. Today, rather than emphasizing the tax-sheltered nature of their income, many of the real estate limited partnerships are less leveraged (some use no debt at all) and are structured to provide attractive current income (from rents, etc.) and/or capital gains. In essence, they are now being promoted for their underlying investment merits and not on the basis of some artificial tax motive. Certainly, for an individual with as little as $2,500 to $5,000 to invest, a carefully selected limited partnership may be a sensible way to invest in real estate.

master limited partnerships (MLPs) limited partnerships that are publicly traded on major stock exchanges.

One of the key drawbacks of RELPs is that it's always been difficult to get out of them, because there is no organized market for limited partnership units. A number of years ago, it appeared that **master limited partnerships (MLPs)**—partnerships that are publicly traded on major stock exchanges—would improve partnership liquidity. However, recent changes in tax laws have greatly reduced their attractiveness.

The annual return on RELPs *in the past* typically ranged between 5% and 15% of the amount invested. (There is, of course, *no* insurance that such returns will continue in the future.) The emphasis with respect to the type of return generated differs from one syndicate to another. Most real estate limited partnerships today place major emphasis on producing attractive levels of current income for their investors; some, however, still emphasize capital gains. Information useful in analyzing RELPs can be obtained from the syndicator in the form of a *prospectus*. Of course, you should carefully evaluate the goals of the syndicate, the quality of its management, and the specific properties involved *before* purchasing, in order to estimate the expected risk and return and to make sure that it is the best vehicle for meeting your investment objectives.

CONCEPTS IN REVIEW

14.17 Briefly describe the basic structure and investment considerations associated with a *real estate investment trust (REIT).* What are the three basic types of REITs?

14.18 According to the *Investing in Action* box on page 570, what measure should you look for in evaluating a REIT that differs from the accounting measure you'd consider for a typical public company? What role does the concept of diversification play with regard to investments in REITs?

14.19 Briefly describe the basic structure and investment considerations associated with a *real estate limited partnership (RELP).* Differentiate between a *single-property syndicate* and a *blind pool syndicate.* What is a *master limited partnership (MLP)?*

http://hepg.aw.com

One of the most popular ways for individuals to invest in real estate, without becoming real estate experts, is through the REIT. Price and trading information on REITs is not as readily available in print publications as is information on other financial assets. This site deals with REIT investments, including price quotations and other information links.

www.inrealty.com/restocks/mort.htm

Other Tangible Investments

LG 6

Although real estate investing is much more popular, some individuals find *tangibles*—investment assets, other than real estate, that can be seen and touched—to be attractive investment vehicles. Common types of tangibles (which we'll refer to as "other tangible investments" because real estate itself is a tangible asset) include precious metals, gemstones, coins, stamps, artwork, antiques, and other so-called *hard assets.* During the 1970s, tangibles soared in popularity, for several reasons. First, double-digit inflation rates made investors nervous about holding cash or securities like stocks, bonds, and mutual funds. Their nervousness was heightened by the poor returns securities offered in those years. As a result, they turned to investments offering returns that exceeded the rate of inflation—in other words, tangibles.

In 1981 and 1982, things began to change, however, as interest in tangibles waned and their prices underwent substantial declines. For example, in the 12-month period from June 1981 to June 1982, the price of gold dropped 34%, silver plunged 45%, and U.S. coins fell almost 30% in value. With a few exceptions, the investment returns on tangibles continued at a substandard pace through the rest of the 1980s and through the 1990s. Such performance, of course, is precisely what you would have expected: These investment vehicles tend to perform nicely during periods of high inflation, but they don't do nearly so well when inflation drops off—as it has since 1982. Indeed, as Table 14.10 reveals, the investment performance of tangibles from 1972 to 1982 stands in stark contrast to the returns on these same investments from 1982 to 1992. Note especially how stocks and bonds performed in the latest period compared to the decade of the 1970s. There's no doubt that securities today are more lucrative investments than most tangibles. Even so, because there's still a lot of interest in tangibles as investment vehicles, we'll take a brief look at these unusual and at times highly profitable investment vehicles.

Tangibles as Investment Outlets

You can hold a gold coin, look at a work of art, or sit in an antique car. Some tangibles, such as gold and diamonds, are easily transported and stored; others, such as art and antiques, usually are not. These differences can affect the price behavior of tangibles. Art and antiques, for example, tend to appreciate fairly rapidly during periods of high inflation and relatively stable international conditions. Gold, on the other hand, is preferred during periods of unstable international conditions, in part because it is portable. Investors appear to believe that if international conditions deteriorate past the crisis point, at least they can "take their gold and run."

The market for tangibles varies widely, and therefore so does the *liquidity* of these investments. On the one hand are gold and silver, which can be purchased in a variety of forms and which are generally viewed as being fairly liquid because they're relatively easy to buy and sell. (To a degree, platinum also falls into this category.) On the other hand are all the other forms of tangibles, which are highly *illiquid:* They are bought and sold in rather fragmented markets, where transaction costs are high and where selling an item is often a time-consuming and laborious process.

The tangibles market is dominated by three forms of investments:

- Gold and other precious metals (silver and platinum)

TABLE 14.10 Comparative Rates of Return for Various Investment Vehicles

10 Years, 6/72–6/82		10 Years, 6/82–6/92	
Vehicle	Return*	Vehicle	Return*
Stamps	21.9%	Stocks	18.4%
Gold	18.6	Bonds	15.2
Chinese ceramics	15.3	Old Master paintings	13.3
Silver	13.6	Chinese ceramics	8.5
Diamonds	13.3	3-month Treasury bills	7.6
Real estate	9.9	Diamonds	6.4
Old Master paintings	9.0	Foreign exchange	4.5
Stocks	3.8	Housing	4.0
Bonds	3.6	Gold	0.6

*Investment returns are measured in terms of average annual fully compounded rates of return. They represent the effective annual yields from these investments; annual returns do not include taxes or transaction costs.

Source: Salomon Bros., Inc.

- Gemstones (diamonds, rubies, emeralds, sapphires)
- Collectibles (everything from coins and stamps to artworks and antiques)

As the *Investing in Action* box on page 574 indicates, interest in collectibles has exploded lately as our consumer culture has churned out even more products deemed collectible.

Investment Merits

The only source of return from investing in tangibles comes in the form of *appreciation in value*—capital gains, in other words. No current income (interest or dividends) accrues from holding tangibles. Instead, if their tangibles do not appreciate rapidly in value, investors may be facing substantial *opportunity costs* in the form of lost income that could have been earned on the capital. Another factor to consider is that most tangibles have *storage* and/or *insurance costs* that require regular cash outlays.

The future prices and therefore the potential returns on tangibles tend to be affected by one or more of the following key factors:

- Rate of inflation
- Scarcity (supply–demand relationship) of the assets
- Domestic and international instability

Because future prices are linked to inflation as well as to the changing supply–demand relationship of these assets, investments in tangibles tend to be somewhat risky. A slowdown in inflation or a sizable increase in the supply of the asset relative to the demand for it can unfavorably affect its market price. On the other hand, increasing inflation and continued scarcity can favorably influence the return. Another factor that tends to affect the market value—and therefore the return—of tangible investments, especially precious metals and gemstones, is the domestic and/or international political environment. In favorable times, these forms of investing are not especially popular, whereas in times of turmoil, demand for them tends to rise because of their tangible (and portable) nature.

INVESTING IN ACTION

Treasure or Trash?

No longer is the world of collectibles the exclusive domain of the rich, cultured, and famous. Today's collectors are as likely to save comic books, snow domes, a Soviet space suit, and autographed baseballs as Old Master paintings, rare books, and antiques. "Miscellany"—ranging from costly jewelry, vintage clothes, and sports and entertainment memorabilia to mundane things like comic books and Pez candy dispensers—is now a major category at leading auction houses.

Collecting has captured the fancy of "baby boomers" (those born between 1946 and 1964) and of "Generation Xers" (the children of the baby boomers), whose eclectic tastes are changing the collectibles markets. Popular culture reigns supreme; a first edition of Dashiell Hammett's *Maltese Falcon* now outprices a rarer seventeenth-century first edition of Milton's *Paradise Lost.* Experts predict that the new treasures will be relics of the twentieth-century technology revolution—old televisions and computers—and things boomers and busters remember from childhood—Barbie and G.I. Joe dolls, comic books, typed manuscripts, Princess telephones, and entertainment memorabilia from favorite TV shows and movies.

What's behind the broadened popularity of collecting? Many like the sheer fun and the thrill of the hunt. There's always the chance you'll find hidden treasure, but it's rare that anyone makes a killing in "junk collectibles." Figuring out what will become next year's hottest collectible is difficult. Karen Keane, managing director of Skinner, Inc., a Boston auction house, recommends things that represent their time period. Who could guess that a 1900-era electric fan would sell for $13,200 or a Barbie no. 1 doll would fetch $4,000? Also, collectibles run in cycles, and today's fad may be out tomorrow. For example, the market for old computers didn't exist in 1989 but was hot in 1994; baseball cards were hot in the early 1990s but cooled off during the prolonged 1994–1995 baseball strike.

To identify future prize collectibles, look for museum demand for a certain historical period, a cultlike group of collectors (*Star Trek* fans, for example), an oversold market, and limited availability. Don't expect mass-market items or manufactured collectibles such as Hummels and so-called limited-edition collector's plates and coins to appreciate much. Veteran collectors advise novices to pick a field that interests them so that they also get pleasure from what they own. The Internet is bursting with collectibles. Just type in the word *collectibles* in any search engine and you'll find a marketplace of buyers and sellers. Consider Andy's Zippo Page (**http://www.4thave.com/zipposale.html**), for instance. That site promises to beat by 5% any prices posted on the Web for eclectic baby boomer items ranging from Beatles memorabilia to James Bond and the Three Stooges.

What's ahead for collectors? Some possible collectibles for the late 1990s and beyond are psychedelic 1960s record album covers, cigarette memorabilia, fast-food premiums like Happy Meal favors, old PCs, Vietnam memorabilia, slide rules, and metal roller skates. Only time will tell, however, whether these become treasure or trash.

Investing in Tangibles

To some extent, investing in tangibles is no different from investing in securities. Selection and timing are important in both cases and play a key role in determining the rate of return on invested capital. Yet when investing in tangibles, you have to be careful to separate the economics of the decision from the pleasure of owning these assets. Let's face it, many people gain a lot of pleasure from wearing a diamond, owning a piece of fine art, or driving a rare automobile. There's certainly nothing wrong with that, but when you're buying tangible assets for their *investment merits,* there's only one thing that matters—the economic payoff from the investment.

As a serious investor in tangibles, you must consider expected price appreciation, anticipated holding period, and potential sources of risk. In addition, you should carefully weigh the insurance and storage costs of holding such assets, as well as the potential impact that a lack of a good resale market can have on return. Perhaps most important, *don't start a serious tangibles investment program until you really know what you're doing.* Know what to look for when buying gems, a rare coin, or a piece of fine art, and know what separates the good gems, rare coins, or artwork from the rest. In the material that follows, we look at tangibles strictly as *investment vehicles.*

Gold and Other Precious Metals

precious metals
tangibles—like gold, silver, and platinum—that concentrate a great deal of value in a small amount of weight and volume.

Precious metals are tangibles that concentrate a great deal of value in a small amount of weight and volume. In other words, just a small piece of a precious metal is worth a lot of money. Three kinds of precious metals command the most investor attention: gold, silver, and platinum. Of these three, silver (at about $5.70 per ounce in early 1998) is the cheapest. It is far less expensive than either gold (about $300.00 per ounce) or platinum (about $390.00 per ounce), which were also priced in early 1998. Gold is by far the most popular, so we'll use gold here to discuss precious metals.

For thousands of years, people have been fascinated with gold. Records from the age of the pharaohs in Egypt show a desire to own gold. Today, ownership of gold is still regarded as a necessity by many investors, although its price has dropped considerably since the January 1980 peak of $875 per ounce. Actually, Americans are relatively recent gold investors because of the legal prohibition on gold ownership, except in jewelry form, that existed from the mid-1930s until January 1, 1975. Like other forms of precious metals, gold is a highly speculative investment vehicle whose price has fluctuated widely in recent years (see Figure 14.2). Many investors hold at least a part—and at times, a substantial part—of their portfolios in gold as a hedge against inflation or a world economic or political disaster.

Gold can be purchased as coins, bullion, or jewelry (all of which can be physically held); it can also be purchased through gold-mining stocks and mutual funds, gold futures (and futures options), and gold certificates. Here's a brief rundown of the different ways gold can be held as a form of investing:

- *Gold coins.* Gold coins have little or no collector value; rather, their value is determined primarily by the quality and amount of gold in the coins. Popular gold coins include the American Eagle, the Canadian Maple Leaf, the Mexican 50-Peso, and the Chinese Panda.

- *Gold bullion.* Gold bullion is gold in its basic ingot (bar) form. Bullion ranges in weight from 5- to 400-gram bars; the kilo bar (which weighs 32.15 troy ounces) is probably the most popular size.

- *Gold jewelry.* Jewelry is a popular way to own gold, but it's not a very good way to invest in gold, because gold jewelry usually sells for a substantial premium over its underlying gold value (to reflect artisan costs, retail markups, and other factors). Moreover, most jewelry is not pure 24-carat gold but a 14- or 18-carat *blend* of gold and other, nonprecious metals.

FIGURE 14.2
The Price of Gold, 1974–1998

The price of gold is highly volatile and can pave the way to big returns or, just as easily, subject the investor to large losses.

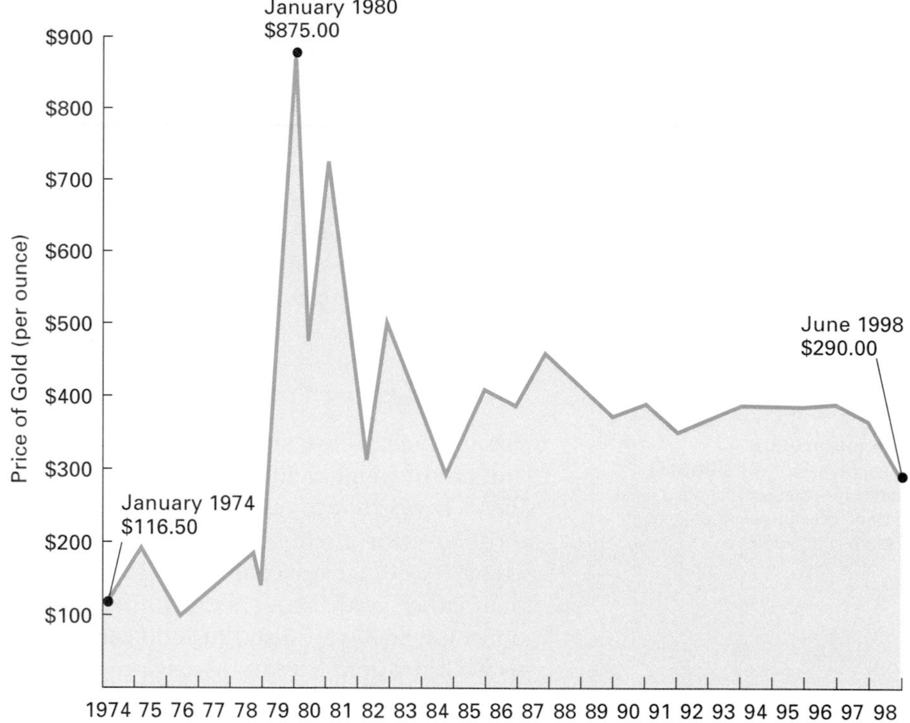

- *Gold stocks and mutual funds.* Many investors prefer to purchase shares of gold-mining companies or mutual funds that invest in *gold stocks.* The prices of gold-mining stocks tend to move in direct relationship to the price of gold. Thus, when gold rises in value, these stocks usually move up too. It is also possible to purchase shares in mutual funds that invest primarily in gold-mining stocks. Gold funds offer professional management and a much higher level of portfolio diversification; the shares of gold-oriented mutual funds also tend to fluctuate along with the price of gold.

- *Gold futures.* A popular way of investing in the short-term price volatility of gold is through futures contracts or futures options.

- *Gold certificates.* A convenient and safe way to own gold is to purchase a gold certificate through a bank or broker. The certificate represents ownership of a specific quantity of gold that is stored in a bank vault. In this way, you do not have to be concerned about the safety that taking physical possession of gold entails; also, by purchasing gold certificates, you can avoid state sales taxes (which may be imposed on coin or bullion purchases).

Like gold, silver and platinum can be bought in a variety of forms. Silver can be purchased as bags of silver coins, bars or ingots, silver-mining stocks, futures contracts, or futures options. Similarly, platinum can be bought in the form of coins, plates and ingots, platinum-mining stocks, or futures contracts.

Transaction costs in precious metals vary widely, depending on the investment form chosen. At one extreme, an investor buying one Canadian Maple Leaf coin might pay 5% commission, 7% dealer markup, and 4% gross excise tax (sales tax). In contrast, the purchase of a gold certificate would entail only a 2% total commission and markup, with no sales tax. Storage costs vary as well. Gold coins and bars can easily be stored in a safe-deposit box that costs perhaps $25 per year. Gold purchased via gold certificates usually is subject to a storage fee of less than 1% per year. Gold coins, bullion, and jewelry can be easily stolen, so it is imperative that these items be stored in a safe-deposit box at a bank or other depository. Except for transaction costs, the expenses of buying and holding gold can be avoided when investments are made in gold-mining stocks and mutual funds and in gold futures.

Gemstones

gemstones
diamonds and colored precious stones (rubies, sapphires, and emeralds).

By definition, **gemstones** consist of diamonds and the so-called colored precious stones (rubies, sapphires, and emeralds). Precious stones offer their owners beauty and are often purchased for aesthetic pleasure. However, diamonds and colored stones also serve as a viable form of investing. Along with gold, they are among the oldest of investment vehicles, providing a source of real wealth, as well as a hedge against political and economic uncertainties. However, diamonds and colored stones are very much a specialist's domain. Generally, standards of value are fully appreciated only by experienced personnel at fine stores, dealers, cutters, and an occasional connoisseur-collector. In diamonds, the value depends on the whiteness of the stone and the purity of crystallization. A key factor, therefore, is for the purchaser to understand the determinants of quality. Precious stones vary enormously in price, depending on how close they come to gem color and purity.

Investment diamonds and colored stones can be purchased through registered gem dealers. Depending on quality and grade, commissions and dealer markups can range from 20% to 100%. Because of the difficulty in valuing gemstones, it is imperative to select only dealers with impeccable reputations. As investment vehicles, diamonds and colored stones offer no current income, but their prices are *highly* susceptible to changing market conditions. For example, the peak price of the best-quality, flawless 1-carat diamond, a popular investment diamond, was about $60,000 in early 1980. By late 1982, this stone was worth only about $20,000—a drop of 67% in just over 2 years. Since then, prices have fluctuated a bit but still remain at about $20,000 in early 1998.

The big difficulty in precious stone investments, aside from the expertise needed in deciding what is in fact gem quality, is the relative *illiquidity* of the stones. As a rule, gemstones should be purchased only by investors who can hold them for at least 2 years; high transaction costs usually mean that profitable resale is not possible after shorter periods. Furthermore, gemstones can be difficult to resell, and sellers often wait a month or more for a sale. Diamonds and colored stones also require secure storage, and there are no payoffs prior to sale.

Collectibles

collectibles
items that have value because of their attractiveness to collectors and because of their beauty, scarcity, historical significance, or age.

Collectibles represent a broad range of items—from coins and stamps to posters and cars—that are desirable for any number of reasons, such as beauty, scarcity, historical significance, or age. **Collectibles** have value because of their attractiveness to collectors. During the 1970s, many collectibles shot up in value, but since the early 1980s, most have either fallen in value or have appreciated at a much lower rate than inflation. There are some exceptions, of course, but they remain just that—the exception rather than the rule. Some

INVESTOR FACT

ESTATES OF THE RICH AND FAMOUS—On April 23, 1996, the estate of Jacqueline Kennedy was auctioned at Sotheby's in New York City. Here's one item that set the tone: A 19-inch pearl necklace valued at $500 was sold for $211,500. The auction proved the power of "Camelot," that magical time in the early 1960s when President and Mrs. Kennedy occupied the White House. More than a year later, a similar result was obtained with the sale, during her lifetime, of gowns worn by Diana, Princess of Wales. Celebrities whose estates have been posthumously auctioned include Leonard Bernstein, Marlene Dietrich, Pamela Harriman, Albert Einstein, Timothy Leary, John Lennon, Jimi Hendrix, and Janis Joplin. What motivates the buyers may or may not have anything to do with getting a good return on their investment, but the sheer priceless pleasure of owning the collectible plays a major part.

examples of collectibles that did well in the 1980s are paintings, exotic automobiles and early "muscle cars," cartoon celluloids, and baseball cards.

An investment-grade collectible is an item that is relatively scarce as well as historically significant within the context of the collectible genre itself and, preferably, within the larger context of the culture that produced it. Further, it should be in excellent condition and attractive to display. Although there are almost no bounds to what can be collected (beer cans, fishing tackle, magazines, sheet music), the major categories of collectibles that tend to offer the greatest investment potential include:

- Rare coins (*numismatics*)
- Rare stamps (*philately*)
- Artwork (the paintings, prints, sculpture, and crafts of recognized artists)
- Antiques (cars, furniture, etc.)
- Baseball cards
- Books
- Games, toys, and comic books
- Posters
- Movie memorabilia
- Historical letters

In general, collectibles are *not* very liquid. Their resale markets are poor, and transaction costs can be high. Artwork, for example, commonly has a 100% dealer markup, and sales tax is added to the retail price. (Works sold on consignment to dealers have much lower costs—generally, a commission of "only" 25%—but they can take months to sell.) In addition, investing in collectibles can be hazardous unless you understand the intricacies of the market. In this area of investing, *you are well advised to become a knowledgeable collector before even attempting to be a serious investor in collectibles.*

Although certain psychic income may be realized in the form of aesthetic pleasure, the financial return, if any, is realized only when the item is sold. On a strictly financial basis, items that have a good market and are likely to appreciate in value are the ones to collect. If an item under consideration is expensive, *its value and authenticity should always be confirmed by an expert prior to purchase.* (There are many unscrupulous dealers in collectible items.) After purchase, you should make certain to store collectibles in a safe place and adequately insure them against all relevant perils. Despite these obstacles, collectibles can provide highly competitive rates of return and can be good inflation hedges during periods of abnormally high inflation.

CONCEPTS IN REVIEW

14.20 What are *tangibles?* Briefly describe the conditions that tend to cause tangibles to rise in price.

14.21 What are the three basic forms of tangible investments? Briefly discuss the investment merits of tangibles. Be sure to note the key factors that affect the future prices of tangibles.

14.22 Why, according to the *Investing in Action* box on page 574, do experienced collectors advise novices to pick a field of collecting that particularly interests them?

14.23 Describe the different ways in which one can hold gold and other precious metals as a form of investing. Discuss gemstone investments in terms of quality, commissions, and liquidity.

14.24 What are some popular types of collectibles? What important variables should be taken into account when investing in them?

http://hepg.aw.com

Investing in tangible assets requires specialized knowledge. The following Web site presents some details on investing in and collecting U.S. currency. Many people say they invest in coins. But are they truly *investing* in coins, or are they just collectors?

www.pueblo/gsa.gov/press/nfcpubs/uscurenc.txt

Summary

LG 1 **Describe how real estate investment objectives are set, how the features of real estate are analyzed, and what determines real estate value.** The starting point for investing in real estate is setting objectives. Investment real estate includes income properties, which can be residential or commercial, and speculative properties, such as raw land, which are expected to provide returns from appreciation in value rather than from periodic rental income. The investor also needs to analyze important features such as the physical property, the rights that owning it entails, the relevant time horizon, and the geographic area of concern.

The four determinants of real estate value are demand, supply, the property, and the property transfer process. *Demand* refers to people's willingness to buy or rent, and *supply* includes all those properties from which potential buyers or tenants can choose. To analyze a property, one should evaluate restrictions on its use, location, site, improvements, and property management. The transfer process involves promotion and negotiation of a property.

LG 2 **Discuss the valuation techniques commonly used to estimate the market value of real estate.** A market value appraisal can be used to estimate real estate value. The three imperfect approaches to real estate valuation are the cost approach, the comparative sales approach, and the income approach. The cost approach estimates replacement cost. The comparative sales approach bases value on the prices at which similar properties recently sold. The income approach measures value as the present value of all the property's future income.

LG 3 **Understand the procedures involved in performing real estate investment analysis.** Real estate investment analysis considers the underlying determinants of a property's value. It involves forecasting a property's cash flows and then calculating either their net present value or the yield to evaluate the proposed investment relative to the investor's objectives. Risk and return parameters vary depending on the degree of leverage employed in financing a real estate investment. Any quantitative analysis of real estate value and returns must be integrated with various subjective and market considerations.

LG 4 **Demonstrate the framework used to value a prospective real estate investment, and evaluate results in light of the stated investment objectives.** The framework for analyzing a potential real estate investment involves five steps: (1) set investor objectives; (2) analyze important features of the property; (3) collect data on determinants of value; (4) perform valuation and investment analysis, which involves forecasting the property's cash flows and either applying discounted cash flow techniques to find the net present value (NPV) or estimating the yield; (5) synthesize and interpret results of analysis.

LG 5 **Describe the structure and investment appeal of real estate investment trusts and real estate limited partnerships.** An alternative to active real estate ownership is real estate investment securities—real estate investment trusts (REITs) and real estate limited partnerships (RELPs). REITs allow investors to buy publicly traded ownership shares in a professionally managed portfolio of real estate properties, mortgages, or both. The risk–return characteristics of REITs can be analyzed much like stocks, bonds, and mutual funds. RELPs provide a vehicle for buying shares in professionally managed real estate syndicates that invest in specified types of properties and/or mortgages. They offer attractive current income and/or capital gains rather than tax shelter advantages. A major drawback of RELPs is their general lack of liquidity.

LG 6 **Understand the investment characteristics of tangibles such as gold and other precious metals, gemstones, and collectibles, and review the suitability of investing in them.** Tangibles represent a non–real-estate investment vehicle that can be seen and touched and that has an actual form and substance. The three basic types of tangibles are gold and other precious metals, gemstones, and collectibles. Some tangibles, particularly precious metals, can be held in a variety of forms. Tangibles generally provide substantial returns during periods of high inflation.

Discussion Questions

LG 1 Q14.1. Assume you have inherited a large sum of money and wish to use part of it to make a real estate investment.

a. Would you invest in income property or speculative property? Why? Describe the key characteristics of the income or speculative property on which you would focus your search.
b. Describe the financial and nonfinancial goals you would establish prior to initiating a search for suitable property.
c. What time horizon would you establish for your analysis? What geographic area would you isolate for your property search?

LG 1 Q14.2. Imagine that you have been hired by a wealthy out-of-town investor to find him a residential income property investment with five to ten units located within a 5-mile radius of the college or university you attend.

a. Search the defined area to find three suitable properties. You may want to use a real estate agent to isolate suitable properties more quickly.
b. Research the area to assess the demand for the properties you've isolated. Be sure to consider both the demographics and the psychographics of the area's population. Also assess mortgage market conditions as they would relate to financing 75% of each property's purchase price.
c. Assess the supply of competitive properties in the geographic area you've isolated. Identify the key competitive properties by using the principle of substitution.
d. Compare the competitive positions of the properties, and isolate the best property on the basis of the following five features: (1) restrictions on use, (2) location, (3) site, (4) improvements, and (5) property management.

LG 2 LG 3 LG 4 Q14.3. Contact a local commercial realtor and obtain a copy of a valuation he or she has performed on an investment property in your immediate general geographic area.

a. Review the analysis and critically evaluate the realtor's work. Specifically review the cost approach, the comparative sales approach, and the income approach.
b. Drive by the property and assess the demand for and supply of competitive properties in the area.

c. On the basis of your review of the realtor's professional analysis and your own assessment of the property, make a list of your questions and comments on the professional analysis.
d. Make an appointment with the realtor who provided you with the analysis, and in your meeting with him or her, go over your list of questions and comments.

LG 5

Q14.4. Contact a stockbroker and obtain a copy of a prospectus for a currently popular real estate investment trust (REIT) and one for a currently popular real estate limited partnership (RELP). Study each prospectus.
a. Indicate what type of REIT (equity, mortgage, or hybrid) and RELP (single-property or blind pool) each represents.
b. Evaluate the quality of the properties held by each of them.
c. Assess the financial and management track record of each.
d. Choose which of the two forms of real estate investment you would prefer, and explain why.

LG 6

Q14.5. Assume you're interested in investing in gold to protect against an expected significant decline in consumer confidence and securities values.
a. Isolate and evaluate the various alternatives for investing in gold coins, gold stocks, gold futures, and gold certificates.
b. Prepare a comparative grid of the costs, ease of purchase and sale, commissions (if any), and potential returns from each of these alternative ways to invest in gold.
c. Choose and justify your choice of the best of these alternative investments in gold. Discuss the risks you associate with this investment.
d. What alternative forms of tangible investment (excluding real estate) would you consider as potential substitutes for gold?

Problems

LG 2 LG 3

P14.1. Charles Cook, an investor, is considering two alternative financing plans for purchasing a parcel of real estate costing $50,000. Alternative X involves paying cash; alternative Y involves obtaining 80% financing at 10.5% interest. If the parcel of real estate appreciates in value by $7,500 in 1 year, calculate (a) Charles's net return and (b) his return on equity for each alternative. If the value dropped by $7,500, what effect would this have on your answers to parts (a) and (b)?

LG 4

P14.2. In the coming year, the Sandbergs expect a potential rental property investment costing $120,000 to have gross potential rental income of $20,000, vacancy and collection losses equaling 5% of gross income, and operating expenses of $10,000. The mortgage on the property is expected to require annual payments of $8,500. The interest portion of the mortgage payments and the depreciation are given below for each of the next 3 years. The Sandbergs are in the 28% marginal tax bracket.

Year	Interest	Depreciation
1	$8,300	$4,500
2	8,200	4,500
3	8,100	4,500

The net operating income is expected to increase by 6% each year beyond the first year.
a. Calculate the net operating income (NOI) for each of the next 3 years.
b. Calculate the after-tax cash flow (ATCF) for each of the next 3 years.

LG 4

P14.3. Walt Hubble is contemplating selling rental property that originally cost $200,000. He believes that it has appreciated in value at an annual rate of 6% over its 4-year holding period. He will have to pay a commission equal to 5% of the sale price to sell the property. Currently, the property has a book value of $137,000. The mortgage balance outstanding at the time of sale currently is $155,000. Walt will have to pay a 20% tax on any capital gains.

a. Calculate the tax payable on the proposed sale.
b. Calculate the after-tax net proceeds associated with the proposed sale, CF_R.

LG 4

P14.4. Bezie Foster has estimated the annual after-tax cash flows (ATCFs) and after-tax net proceeds from sale (CF_R) of a proposed real estate investment as noted below for the planned 4-year ownership period.

Year	ATCF	CF_R
1	$6,200	
2	8,000	
3	8,300	
4	8,500	$59,000

The initial required investment in the property is $55,000. Bezie must earn at least 14% on the investment.

a. Calculate the net present value (NPV) of the proposed investment.
b. Estimate the yield (to the nearest whole percent) from the investment.
c. From your findings in parts (a) and (b), what recommendation would you give Bezie? Explain.

Case Problem 14.1 *Gary Sofer's Appraisal of the Wabash Oaks Apartments*

LG 1 LG 2 LG 3 LG 4

Gary Sofer wants to estimate the market value of the Wabash Oaks Apartments, an 18-unit building with 9 one-bedroom units and 9 two-bedroom units. The present owner of Wabash Oaks provided Gary with the following annual income statement. Today's date is March 1, 1999.

Owner's Income Statement
Wabash Oaks Apartments, 1998

Gross income		$65,880
Less: Expenses		
Utilities	$14,260	
Property insurance	2,730	
Repairs and maintenance	1,390	
Property taxes	4,790	
Mortgage payments	18,380	
Total expenses		41,550
Net income		$24,330

Current rental rates of properties similar to Wabash Oaks typically run from $300 to $315 per month for one-bedroom units and $340 to $360 per month for two-bedroom units. From a study of the market, Gary determined that a reasonable required rate of return for Wabash Oaks would be 9.62% and that vacancy rates for comparable apartment buildings are running around 4%.

QUESTIONS

a. Using Figure 14.1 as a guide, discuss how you might go about evaluating the features of this property.

b. Gary has studied economics and knows about demand and supply, yet he doesn't understand how to apply them to an investment analysis. Advise Gary in a practical way how he might incorporate demand and supply into an investment analysis of the Wabash Oaks Apartments.

c. Should Gary accept the owner's income statement as the basis for an income appraisal of Wabash Oaks? Why or why not?

d. In your opinion, what is a reasonable estimate of the market value for the Wabash Oaks?

e. If Gary could buy Wabash Oaks for $10,000 less than its market value, would it be a good investment for him? Explain.

Case Problem 14.2 *Analyzing Dr. Davis's Proposed Real Estate Investment*

LG 2 LG 3 LG 4

Dr. Marilyn Davis, a single, 34-year-old heart specialist, is considering the purchase of a small office building. She wants to add some diversity to her investment portfolio, which now contains only corporate bonds and preferred stocks. In addition, because of her high federal tax bracket of 36%, Marilyn wants an investment that produces a good after-tax rate of return.

A real estate market and financial consultant has estimated that Marilyn could buy the office building for $200,000. In addition, this consultant analyzed the property's rental potential with respect to trends in demand and supply. He discussed the following items with Marilyn: (1) The office building was occupied by two tenants, who had 3 years each remaining on their leases, and (2) it was only 4 years old, was in excellent condition, and was located near a number of major thoroughfares. For her purposes, Marilyn decided the building should be analyzed on the basis of a 3-year holding period. The gross rents in the most recent year were $32,000, and operating expenses were $15,000. The consultant pointed out that the leases had built-in 10% per year rent escalation clauses and that he expected operating expenses to increase by 8% per year. He further expected no vacancy or collection loss, because both tenants were excellent credit risks.

Marilyn's accountant estimated that annual tax depreciation would be $5,100 in each of the next 3 years. To finance the purchase of the building, Marilyn has considered a variety of alternatives, one of which would involve assuming the existing $120,000 mortgage. On the advice of a close friend, a finance professor at the local university, Marilyn decided to arrange a $150,000, 10.5%, 25-year mortgage from the bank at which she maintains her business account. The annual loan payment would total $17,000. Of this, the following breakdown between interest and principal would apply in each of the first 3 years:

Year	Interest	Principal	Total
1	$15,750	$1,250	$17,000
2	15,620	1,380	17,000
3	15,470	1,530	17,000

The loan balance at the end of the 3 years would be $145,840. The consultant expects the property to appreciate by about 9% per year to $260,000 at the end of 3 years. Marilyn would incur a 5% sales commission expense on this assumed sale price. The building's book value at the end of 3 years would be $184,700. The net proceeds on the sale would be taxed at Marilyn's capital gains tax rate of 20%.

QUESTIONS

a. What is the expected annual after-tax cash flow (ATCF) for each of the 3 years (assuming Marilyn has other passive income that can be used to offset any losses from this property)?

b. At a 15% required rate of return, will this investment produce a positive net present value?

c. What is the estimated yield for this proposed investment?

d. Could Marilyn increase her returns by assuming the existing mortgage at a 9.75% interest rate rather than arranging a new loan? What measure of return do you believe Marilyn should use to make this comparison?

e. Do you believe Marilyn has thought about her real estate investment objectives enough? Why or why not?

Home Page Exercises

http://hepg.aw.com **Keyword: Invest**

Real estate and tangible assets are very specialized areas of investing. No one who does not understand the unique nature of these assets should have either of them in her or his investment portfolio. When it comes to the Web, there is a bias toward the area of residential real estate (home purchasing). Most sites are intent on educating homebuyers and helping them obtain information on making this purchase. The market for investing in commercial real estate and tangible assets receives little attention on the Web, which is not surprising because a relatively limited number of individuals are interested in making these types of investments.

Web Address	*Primary Investment Focus*
www.ccim.com	The Commerical Real Estate Network has general information about the real estate market and certain professional certifications
www.101percent.com/education/business/investing/realestate.html	Information primarily on personal real estate purchasing, including access to amortization and other interactive calculators
www.austincoins.com/srv08.htm	Information on collecting old coins
www.nareit.com	The National Association of Real Estate Investment Trusts has a variety of information on REITS and a screening model for selection of REITs
www.wealthnetwork.com	Dedicated to providing a variety of information on real estate

W14.1. One way for investors to put their money into real estate is to invest in mutual funds that hold real estate as their major asset. One such fund is the Seneca Real Estate Securities Fund. Gather information on this fund from the following Web site. Using the pie chart under *portfolio characteristics* and the line chart under *historical performance*, discuss the benefits of investing in this type of fund. How well has the fund performed?

www.senecafunds.com/real_h.htm

W14.2. Stan Simpson is considering the purchase of a house as an investment. To make the purchase, he will need to finance $100,000 of the cost. The house is large, and Stan believes he will be able to rent it to several local university students for a combined rent of $1,000 per month. The following Web site has a mortgage calculator that you can run with interest rate and financing scenarios. If Stan can finance the house at an 8% annual rate for 30 years, what will be the monthly mortgage payment? What is the total cost of the house, including principal and interest, over the life of the mortgage? (Ignore taxes.) If Stan finances the house for 15 years at the same rate, how much interest will he save? When you get to this Web page, click on *Karl Jeacle's Mortgage Calculator* to access the interactive calculator.

www.101percent.com/education/business/investing/realestate.html

CHAPTER 15 TAX-ADVANTAGED INVESTMENTS

LEARNING GOALS

After studying this chapter, you should be able to:

LG 1 Understand what taxable income is and how to calculate it.

LG 2 Define tax avoidance and tax deferral and cite the characteristics of tax shelters.

LG 3 Explain the basic strategies by which investors can earn tax-favored income.

LG 4 Summarize the characteristics of deferred annuities and single-premium life insurance.

LG 5 Describe the tax status of limited partnerships and explain how they work.

LG 6 Discuss popular forms of limited partnerships, partnership structure, and the essential investment considerations of these vehicles.

Microsoft

One of the best tax-advantaged investments is a growth stock that appreciates in value but doesn't pay dividends. The reason: The taxation of capital gains is much more favorable than the taxation of dividends, which are taxed at ordinary income tax rates. A great example of such an investment is Microsoft, which dominates the world of computer software. In the 3-year period ending June 30, 1997, Microsoft shares rose from about $23 per share to $135, a six-fold increase. During fiscal 1997, Microsoft earned $2.63 per share, up from $0.94 per share in fiscal 1994. But like many growth companies, particularly in technology, Microsoft doesn't pay dividends. An investor in the 28% tax bracket or above who bought Microsoft in 1994 and sold it late in 1997 would pay a 20% federal tax on the capital gain. In contrast, an investor in an oil company or a utility, companies that typically pay high dividends, could have paid tax on dividends at a rate approaching 40%.

As you'll see in this chapter, taxation often plays a decisive role in the investment process. An awareness of the vehicles and strategies for legally reducing one's tax liability can help investors shelter their investment profits.

Tax Fundamentals

LG 1

tax planning
the formulation of strategies that will exclude, defer, or reduce the taxes to be paid.

tax-advantaged investments
vehicles and strategies for legally reducing one's tax liability.

It is often said that the necessities of life include food, clothing, and shelter. Shelter protects us from the elements—rain, wind, snow, extreme heat or cold—in the physical environment. Similarly, investors need shelter from the taxes charged on income; without adequate protection, investors' returns can be greatly reduced by the ravages of the tax code. Thus, in making investment decisions, we must assess not only risk and return but also the tax effects associated with a given investment vehicle or strategy. Because tax effects depend on one's "tax bracket," it is important to choose investment vehicles that provide the maximum after-tax return for a given risk. Making such choices is part of **tax planning,** which involves the formation of strategies that will exclude, defer, or reduce the taxes to be paid.

You should make tax planning an essential part of your investment strategy. An awareness of **tax-advantaged investments,** which are vehicles and strategies for legally reducing one's tax liability, and an understanding of the role they can play in a portfolio are fundamental to obtaining the highest after-tax returns for a given level of risk. We begin this chapter by looking at tax fundamentals.

As currently structured, federal income tax law imposes a higher tax burden on higher taxable income. This is done through a progressive rate structure that taxes income at one of five rates: 15, 28, 31, 36, or 39.6%. As we saw in Chapter 3, taxpayers filing *individual* returns must follow one tax rate structure and those filing *joint* returns must follow another. Table 15.1 shows the tax rates and income brackets for these two major filing categories. Note that you pay not only more taxes as your taxable income increases but also *progressively* more if your taxable income rises into a higher bracket.

Taxable Income

taxable income
the income to which tax rates are applied; equals adjusted gross income minus itemized deductions and exemptions.

Taxable income is the income to which tax rates are applied. From an investments perspective, this includes such items as cash dividends, interest, profits from a sole proprietorship or share in a partnership, and gains from the sale of securities or other assets. Federal tax law makes an important distinction between ordinary income and capital gains (and losses).

To review, *ordinary income* broadly refers to any compensation received for labor services (active income) or from invested capital (portfolio or passive income). The form in which the income is received is immaterial. For example, if you owe a debt to someone and that person forgives the debt (excuses you from repaying it), the amount could wind up as income taxable to you,

TABLE 15.1 Tax Rates and Income Brackets for Individual and Joint Returns (1997)

	Taxable Income	
Tax Rates	Individual Returns	Joint Returns
15%	$0 to $24,650	$0 to $41,200
28%	$24,651 to $59,750	$41,201 to $99,600
31%	$59,751 to $124,650	$99,601 to $151,750
36%	$124,651 to $271,050	$151,751 to $271,050
39.6%	Over $271,050	Over $271,050

depending on how the debt was initially created and treated for tax purposes in previous periods. As a general rule, *any event that increases your net worth is income, and unless it is specifically excluded from taxable income or considered a capital gain, it is ordinary income.*

The tax law as revised by the *Taxpayer Relief Act of 1997* treats gains or losses resulting from the sale of capital assets differently from ordinary income. A **capital asset** is defined as anything you own and use for personal reasons, pleasure, or investment. A house and a car are capital assets; so are shares of common stock, bonds, and even stamp collections. Your **basis** in a capital asset usually means what you paid for it, including commissions and other costs related to the purchase. If an asset is sold for a price greater than its basis, a *capital gain* is the result; if the reverse is true, then you have a *capital loss*. Depending on how long the capital asset was held, the capital gain may be taxed at a lower rate than that applicable to ordinary income. (*Note:* The tax rates applicable to capital gains were described in Chapter 3 and are also discussed in the following section.) As for capital losses, a maximum of $3,000 of losses in excess of capital gains can be claimed in any 1 year. Any losses that cannot be applied in the current year can be carried forward to future years and then deducted. (Timing the sale of securities to optimize the tax treatment of capital gains and losses, which is an important part of tax planning, is treated more thoroughly later in this chapter.)

capital asset
anything owned and used for personal reasons, pleasure, or investment.

basis
the amount paid for a capital asset, including commissions and other costs related to the purchase.

Determining Taxable Income

Determining taxable income involves a series of steps. Because these are illustrated more clearly with an example, let us consider the 1997 income tax situation of the Edward and Martha Meyer family, a family of three. In 1997, the family had the following income items:

1. Wages and salaries	
Edward	$40,000
Martha	15,000
2. Interest on tax-free municipal bonds	400
3. Interest on savings accounts	900
4. Dividends on common stock (owned jointly)	600
5. Capital gains on securities (all held for less than 1 year)	1,500

The family also had the following deductions in 1997:

1. Deductible contribution to IRA account	$ 1,800
2. Interest on home mortgage	10,500
3. Charitable contributions	1,000

The Meyers' income tax due for 1997 was $5,513, as determined in Table 15.2 and explained below.

Gross Income

Gross income begins with all includable income but then allows certain exclusions that are provided in the tax law. Table 15.2 shows that in the Meyers' case, all income is included except interest on the tax-free municipal bonds,

gross income
all includable income for federal income tax purposes.

TABLE 15.2 Determining 1997 Federal Income Tax Due for the Edward and Martha Meyer Family

I. GROSS INCOME	
1. Wages and salaries ($40,000 + $15,000)	$55,000
2. Interest on savings accounts	900
3. Dividends	600
4. Capital gains	1,500
Gross income	$58,000
II. ADJUSTMENTS TO GROSS INCOME	
Deductible IRA contribution	$ 1,800
III. ADJUSTED GROSS INCOME (I − II) = ($58,000 − $1,800)	$56,200
IV. ITEMIZED DEDUCTIONS	
1. Mortgage interest	$10,500
2. Charitable contributions	1,000
Total itemized deductions	$11,500
V. EXEMPTIONS	
Edward, Martha, and one child (3 × $2,650)	$ 7,950
VI. TAXABLE INCOME (III − IV − V) = ($56,200 − $11,500 − $7,950)	$36,750
VII. FEDERAL INCOME TAX (per rate schedule, Table 15.1) (0.15 × $36,750)	$ 5,513
VIII. TAX CREDITS	$ 0
IX. TAX DUE (VII − VIII) = ($5,513 − $0)	$ 5,513

which is not subject to federal income tax. Note that interest on savings accounts and dividend income *is* included. In addition, all capital gains are included in gross income because the securities on which they were realized had been held for 1 year or less. Recall from Chapter 3 that *for assets held for 1 year or less,* the amount of the capital gain realized is added to other sources of income and taxed as ordinary income. The maximum tax rate on a capital gain is 28% *for assets held for more than 1 year but not over 18 months,* and 20% (or 10% if the taxpayer is in the 15% tax bracket) *for assets held more than 18 months.*

Adjustments to Gross Income

Adjustments to gross income reflect the intent of Congress to favor certain activities. The only one shown for the Meyers is their allowable IRA contribution (discussed later) of $1,800. You should note the tax-sheltering quality of the IRA; without it, the Meyers would have paid taxes on an additional $1,800 of income in 1997.

Adjusted Gross Income

adjusted gross income gross income less the total allowable adjustments for tax purposes.

Subtracting the adjustments from gross income yields **adjusted gross income.** This figure is necessary in calculating certain deductions (e.g, medical and dental expenses, charitable contributions, job and other expenses, and the amount of allowable real estate losses) not illustrated in our example. The Meyers' adjusted gross income is $56,200.

Itemized Deductions

standard deduction
an amount, indexed to the cost of living, that taxpayers can elect to deduct from adjusted gross income without itemizing.

itemized deductions
personal living and family expenses that can be deducted from adjusted gross income.

Taxpayers can elect to take a **standard deduction,** which is indexed to the cost of living. The standard deduction for 1997 ranged from $3,450 to $10,100, depending on filing status, age, and vision. (There are specific deductions for taxpayers who are age 65 or older and/or blind.) The standard deduction for the Meyers, if they choose to take it, is $6,900.

If they don't wish to take the standard deduction, taxpayers can choose to *itemize deductions.* Taxpayers with itemized deductions in excess of the applicable standard deduction will prefer to itemize. This group typically includes those individuals who own a mortgaged primary and/or second home. Such was the case for the Meyers, because their itemized deductions of $11,500 exceeded the $6,900 standard deduction.

A number of personal living and family expenses qualify as **itemized deductions;** the most common are residential mortgage interest, charitable contributions, and medical and dental expenses (in excess of 7.5% of adjusted gross income). All other things being equal, there is a tax advantage to ownership of a principal (and even of a second) residence, because interest on the associated mortgage loans is tax-deductible. Consumer interest (such as interest paid on credit card accounts) is *not* tax-deductible, whereas investment interest—interest paid on funds borrowed for personal investment purposes—is deductible, subject to certain limitations. Clearly, tax deductibility reduces the cost of allowable interest charges.

INVESTOR FACT

A CHECKLIST OF DEDUCTIBLE INVESTMENT EXPENSES—The following investment expenses are deductible as miscellaneous itemized deductions subject to the 2% adjusted gross income (AGI) floor.

- Accounting and tax fees for keeping records of investment income
- Bank and brokerage fees
- Fees for a safe-deposit box to hold securities
- Investment management or financial planning fees
- Employee salaries to keep track of your investment income
- Travel costs to look after investments or to confer with your attorney, accountant, or investment counsel

Let's say you pay investment management fees of $3,500, a tax preparation fee of $500, and a safe-deposit box fee of $50. Your AGI is $100,000. Your deduction is figured as follows:

Investment management fees	$3,500
Tax preparation fees	500
Safe-deposit box fee	50
Less: 2% of AGI (0.02 × $100,000)	(2,000)
Total deductible investment expenses	$2,050

Exemptions

exemption
a deduction from adjusted gross income for each qualifying dependent of a federal taxpayer.

The tax law allows a deduction, called an **exemption,** for each qualifying dependent. It was $2,650 in 1997 ($2,700 in 1998). When taxpayers have adjusted gross income above specified values, their allowable exemptions are reduced by formula. Specific rules determine who qualifies as a dependent. These should be reviewed if the potential dependent is not your child or an immediate member of your family residing in your home. Table 15.2 shows that the Meyers claimed three exemptions.

Taxable Income

Subtracting itemized deductions and exemptions from adjusted gross income leaves *taxable income;* in the Meyers' case, this amount is $36,750. Although the Meyers have none, certain *miscellaneous expenses,* which include union dues, safe-deposit box rent, investment advice, membership dues for professional organizations, and the cost of business publications, generally can be deducted only to the extent that they exceed 2% of adjusted gross income. In addition, certain *unreimbursed employee expenses,* such as 50% of entertainment bills, 100% of travel expenses, and 50% of meal expenses, are deductible if substantiated by receipts.

marginal tax rate
the tax rate on additional income.

You can use Table 15.1 to calculate the tax due for the Meyers. Their taxable income of $36,750 puts them in the 15% income bracket. Thus their tax, as calculated in the table, is $5,513. The Meyers pay a 15% **marginal tax rate,** which means the tax rate on additional income up to $41,200 is 15%. *It is the marginal tax rate that should be considered when evaluating the tax implications of an investment strategy.*

average tax rate
taxes due divided by taxable income; different from the *marginal tax rate.*

By all means, do not confuse the marginal rate with the average rate. The **average tax rate** is simply taxes due divided by taxable income. In the Meyers' case, because they are in the lower tax bracket, this rate also equals 15% ($5,513 ÷ $36,750). For taxpayers in the 28, 31, 36, or 39.6% tax brackets, the marginal rate will exceed the average tax rate. The average tax rate has absolutely no relevance to the Meyers' investment decision making.

Tax Credits

tax credits
tax reductions allowed by the IRS on a dollar-for-dollar basis under certain specified conditions.

A number of **tax credits** are available. These are particularly attractive because they reduce taxes on a dollar-for-dollar basis, in contrast to a *deduction,* which reduces taxes only by an amount determined by the marginal tax rate. A frequently used tax credit is for expenses incurred for child and dependent care. Other common tax credits include the credit for the elderly or disabled, foreign tax credit, minimum tax credit, mortgage interest credit, and electric vehicle credit. The Meyers, as is true for most taxpayers under the Tax Reform Act of 1986, were not eligible for any tax credits.

Taxes Due or Refundable

The final amount of tax due is determined by subtracting any tax credits from the income tax. The Meyers' tax due is $5,513. They now compare this amount to the total of tax withheld (indicated on their year-end withholding statements) and any estimated taxes they paid during 1997. If these two add up to more than $5,513, then they are entitled to a refund of the difference; if the total is less than $5,513, they must pay the difference when they file their 1997 federal income tax return.

The Alternative Minimum Tax

alternative minimum tax (AMT)
a tax passed by Congress to ensure that all individuals pay at least some federal income tax.

As a result of many taxpayers effectively using tax shelters (tax-favored investments) to reduce their taxable incomes to near zero, Congress in 1978 introduced the **alternative minimum tax** (AMT). The purpose of this law is to raise additional revenue by making sure that all individuals pay at least some tax. The AMT rate is 26% of the first $175,000 of the alternative minimum tax base and 28% of the excess. The AMT base is determined by making adjustments to the individual's regular taxable income. The procedures for determining the alternative minimum tax base and the alternative minimum tax are quite complicated. You should consult a tax expert if you think the alternative minimum tax might apply in your situation.

CONCEPTS IN REVIEW

15.1 What is *tax planning?* Describe the current tax rate structure and explain why it is considered progressive.

15.2 What is a *capital asset?* Explain how capital asset transactions are taxed, and compare their treatment to that of ordinary income.

15.3 Describe the steps involved in calculating a person's taxable income. How do any tax credits differ from tax deductions?

http://hepg.aw.com

Making out their tax return is probably near the top of the list of things people do not like to do. Unfortunately, taxes are a must for virtually every American adult. The majority of taxpayers have similar difficulties in preparing their returns. A variety of Web sites offer help on the most commonly asked questions. The following site addresses some general-interest personal tax topics.

www.investorguide.com/ATaxes.htm

Tax Strategies

LG 2

A comprehensive tax strategy attempts to maximize the total after-tax income of an investor over his or her lifetime. The goal is either to avoid taxable income altogether or to defer it to another period when it may receive more favorable tax treatment. Even when deferral does not reduce one's taxes, it still gives the investor the use of saved tax dollars during the deferral period.

Tax Avoidance and Tax Deferral

tax evasion
illegal activities designed to avoid paying taxes by omitting income or overstating deductions.

tax avoidance
reducing or eliminating taxes in *legal ways.*

Tax avoidance is quite different from **tax evasion,** which consists of illegal activities such as omitting income or overstating deductions. **Tax avoidance** is concerned with *legal ways* of reducing or eliminating taxes. As we have already noted in the Meyers example, the most popular form of tax avoidance is investing in securities that offer tax-favored income (to be explained in greater detail in the next section). Another broad approach to avoiding taxes is to distribute income-producing assets to family members (usually children) who either pay no taxes at all or pay them at much lower rates. Because this is also a highly specialized area of the tax law, we do not pursue it further in this text. Again, you should seek professional counsel whenever you contemplate a tax strategy of this type.

tax deferral
the strategy of delaying taxes by shifting income subject to tax into a later period.

Tax deferral deals with means of delaying taxes and can be accomplished in a number of ways. Frequently, taxes are deferred for only 1 year as part of a year-end tax strategy to shift income from one year to the next when it is known that taxable income or tax rates will be lower. A simple way to defer taxes is to use vehicles specifically designed to accomplish this objective—401(k)s, Keoghs, and IRAs—and annuities. The role of each of these vehicles is described later in this chapter.

Tax Shelters

tax shelter
an investment vehicle that offers potential reductions of taxable income.

A **tax shelter** is any investment vehicle that offers potential reductions of taxable income. Usually, you must own the vehicle directly, rather than indirectly. For example, if the Meyers had had a tax-deductible loss of $1,000 on investment property directly owned by them, it could have provided a tax shelter. Had they instead set up a corporation to own this property, the net loss of $1,000 would have been the corporation's, not theirs. Thus they could not have claimed that tax deduction and the related tax savings on their individual tax return. Similarly, when publicly owned corporations show huge losses, those losses are of no immediate tax benefit to the shareholders. Although the market price of the stock probably falls, which means you could sell it at a tax loss, such a capital loss is limited to $3,000 a year (in excess of capital gains). If you owned a large amount of stock, your loss might be many times that amount and yet be of no immediate use in reducing your taxes.

Thus there is a tax advantage in organizing certain activities as sole proprietorships or partnerships, and even more specifically, as limited partnerships. The majority of these business forms can pass on losses resulting from certain deductions—depreciation, depletion, and amortization—directly to individual owners. The amount, if any, of such losses that can be deducted when calculating taxable income is currently limited by law. The few remaining tax shelters and the structure of the limited partnerships that are commonly used to organize them are explained later in this chapter. Now, however, let us turn our attention to those vehicles that offer tax-favored income.

CONCEPTS IN REVIEW

15.4 How does *tax avoidance* differ from *tax deferral*? Explain whether either of these is a form of *tax evasion*.

15.5 What is a *tax shelter*? What is the tax advantage of organizing certain business activities as a sole proprietorship or a partnership rather than as a corporation?

Tax-Favored Income

LG 3

tax-favored income
an investment return that is not taxable, is taxed at a rate less than that on other, similar investments, defers the payment of tax to a later period, or trades current income for capital gains.

An investment is said to offer **tax-favored income** if it has any of the following results:

1. Offers a return that is not taxable
2. Offers a return that is taxed at a rate less than that on other, similar investments
3. Defers the payment of tax to a later period—typically to the next year or to retirement
4. Trades current income for capital gain income

These tax "favors" have been written into the tax law to foster or promote certain activities as well as to provide convenient tax-reporting procedures. So far in this book, we have examined in detail how real estate can provide shelter from taxes for certain investors (see Chapter 14). Here, we briefly examine a number of other noteworthy tax-sheltered vehicles and strategies; later in the chapter, we'll look at two other vehicles: deferred annuities and single-premium life insurance.

Income Excluded from Taxation

Some items are simply *excluded from taxation,* either totally or partially. These include interest earned on tax-free municipals and on Treasury and government agency issues, as well as certain proceeds from the sale of a personal residence. Tax exclusion was written into the tax code for these vehicles in order to encourage investment in them. (If Congress so decided, the tax exclusions on these investment vehicles could be removed.)

Tax-Free Municipal Bond Interest

Municipal bonds were described in Chapter 8. All interest received from the most common form—tax-free municipals—is free of federal income tax. In fact, this income is not even reported on the return. However, any gains or losses resulting from the sale of municipal bonds must be included as capital gains or losses. In addition, interest paid on money borrowed to purchase municipal bonds is *not* tax-deductible.

Treasury and Government Agency Issues

Treasury and government agency issues were also discussed in Chapter 8. Although interest on these securities is included as income on the federal tax return, for most issues it is excluded for state and local income tax purposes. The reason why states and localities are prohibited from taxing interest income derived from federal government debt is to make it easier and less expensive for the federal government to borrow to finance its operations. Because combined state and local income tax rates can be as high as 20%, individuals in high tax brackets may find such exclusions worthwhile.

Sale of Personal Residence

A capital gain results if you sell your personal residence for a price greater than its basis (the price originally paid for it). However, a tax provision aimed at stimulating home ownership softens the tax impact and actually makes investment in a home an excellent tax shelter. On individual returns, a taxpayer who has owned and used a property as a principal residence for at least 2 years can exclude up to $250,000 of the gain from its sale. On a joint return, the exclusion applies to as much as $500,000. Under the right conditions, this exclusion can be used as frequently as every 2 years, and a partial exclusion may be available under special circumstances described in the tax code.

Strategies That Defer Tax Liabilities to the Next Year

Very often, an investor may enjoy sizable gains in a security's value within a relatively short period of time. Suppose you bought 100 shares of XYZ common stock in early 1998 at $30 a share and by year-end 1999 your investment has increased in value by 50%, to around $45 a share. Assume that at year-end 1999, after 21 months of ownership, you believe the stock price has just about peaked and you wish to sell it and invest the $4,500 elsewhere. In such a case, you would be taxed on a capital gain of $1,500 ($4,500 sale price − $3,000 cost). Assuming a 28% tax bracket, you would qualify for a 20% tax rate on the capital gain because the stock was held for more than 18 months. You therefore owe income taxes for 1999 of $300 on the sale. However, because you believe tax rates may be lower next year, or merely to benefit from the time value of money, you wish to defer the tax on this transaction to the following year (2000). Two available strategies for preserving a gain while deferring tax to the following year are (1) a put hedge and (2) a deep-in-the-money call option.

Put Hedge

put hedge
the purchase of a put option on shares currently owned, to lock in a profit and defer taxes on the profit to the next tax year.

The put hedge can be used to lock in a profit and defer the taxes on the profit to the next tax year, without losing the potential for additional price appreciation. Essentially, a **put hedge** involves buying a *put*, which, as noted in Chapter 11, is an *option* that enables its holder to sell the underlying security at a specified price over a set period of time, on shares currently owned. (Options were discussed in Chapter 11.) If the price of the stock falls, your losses on the shares are offset by the profit on the put option. For example, suppose that when XYZ was trading at $45, you purchased for $150 a 6-month put option with a contractual sale price of $45. By doing this, you locked in a price of $45: If the price fell to, say, $40 a share, your $500 loss on the stock would be offset exactly by a $500 profit on the option. However, you would still be out the $150 cost of the option. At a closing price of $40 and a 28% tax rate, your ending after-tax position would be

1. Initial cost of 100 shares		$3,000
2. Profit on 100 shares [100 × ($40 − $30)]		1,000
3. Profit on the put option	$ 500	
4. Cost of the put option	− 150	
5. Taxable gain on put option [(3) − (4)]		350
6. Total tax on transaction		
Profit on stock (2)	$1,000	
Plus taxable gain on put (5)	+ 350	
Total gain	$1,350	
Times tax rate	× .28	
Total tax		378
7. After-tax position [(1) + (2) + (5) − (6)]		$3,972

The final after-tax position in this example is about the same as if you had simply held the stock while its price declined to around $43.50 a share. However, keep in mind two important points: (1) The put hedge locks in this position regardless of how low the price might fall, whereas simply holding the stock does not, and (2) any price appreciation will be enjoyed with either approach.

Deep-in-the-Money Call Option

deep-in-the-money call option
a tax-deferral strategy that involves selling a call option on shares currently owned, thus locking in a price equal to the amount received from the sale of the call option but giving up future price appreciation.

Selling a **deep-in-the-money call option** is a strategy similar to the put hedge, but with important differences: In this case, you give up any potential future price increases, and you lock in a price only to the extent of the amount you receive from the sale of the *call*, which, as noted in Chapter 11, is an *option* that gives its holder the right to buy the underlying security at a specified price over a set period of time.

To illustrate, suppose that call options on XYZ with a $40 contractual buy price and 6-month maturity were traded at $600 ($6 per share) when XYZ was selling for $45. If 6 months later XYZ closed at $40, it would result in this ending after-tax position:

1. Initial cost of 100 shares		$3,000
2. Profit on 100 shares [100 × ($40 − $30)]		1,000
3. Profit on the sale of the option; because the stock closed at the contractual buy price of $40, profit is the total amount received		600
4. Total tax on transaction		
Profit on stock (2)	$1,000	
Plus profit on option (3)	+ 600	
Total gain	$1,600	
Times tax rate	× .28	
Total tax		448
5. After-tax position [(1) + (2) + (3) − (4)]		$4,152

This final after-tax position is better than with the put hedge, but it closes off any price appreciation. In effect, when you sell the call option, you are agreeing to deliver your shares at the option's contractual buy price. If the price of XYZ increases to, say, $50 or beyond, you do not benefit, because you have agreed to sell your shares at $40. Furthermore, your downside protection extends only to the amount received for the option—$6 per share. Therefore, if XYZ's price went to $35, you would lose $4 a share before taxes [$45 − ($35 + $6)].

Summary of the Strategies

As you can see, deferring tax liabilities to the next year is a potentially rewarding activity requiring the analysis of a number of available techniques. The choice can be simplified by considering which method works best given one's expectation of the future price behavior of the stock. Table 15.3 summarizes how each strategy performs under different expectations of future price behavior.

To complete the analysis, you would have to consider commission costs—something we have omitted. Although these costs can be somewhat high in absolute dollars, they are usually a minor part of the total dollars involved if the potential savings is as large as the ones we have been considering in our examples. However, if the savings is relatively small—say, under $500—then commissions may be disproportionately large in relation to the tax savings and/or deferral. Clearly, you need to work out the specific figures for each situation.

TABLE 15.3 Ranking of Strategies to Defer Tax Liabilities to the Next Year Given Different Expectations About the Future Price of the Stock

Strategy	Price Will Vary by a Small Amount Above or Below Current Price	Price Will Vary by a Large Amount Above or Below Current Price	Future Price Will Be Higher than Current Price	Future Price Will Be Lower Than Current Price
Do nothing—hold into next tax year	2	4	1	4
Put hedge	3+	1	2	2
Sell deep-in-the-money call option	1	2+	3	3

Note: Ranking: 1, best; 4, worst.

Programs That Defer Tax Liabilities to Retirement

As noted in Chapter 3, accumulating funds for retirement is the *single most important reason for investing.* A large part of the retirement income of many people comes from Social Security and basic employer-sponsored programs. Such programs may be totally funded by the employer, may require employee contributions, or may involve a combination of employer and employee contributions. Here we focus on arrangements that give the employee (or self-employed person) an option to contribute to a retirement program that provides tax shelter by deferring taxes to retirement. The three programs are 401(k) plans, Keogh plans, and individual retirement arrangements (IRAs).

401(k) Plans

401(k) plans
retirement programs that allow employees to divert a portion of salary or wages to a company-sponsored tax-sheltered savings account, thus deferring taxes until the funds are withdrawn.

Many employers offer their employees *salary reduction plans* known as **401(k) plans.** (*Note:* Although our discussion here will center on 401(k) plans, similar programs are also available for employees of public, nonprofit organizations; known as *403(b) plans,* they offer many of the same features and tax shelter provisions as 401(k) plans.) Basically, a 401(k) plan gives you, as an employee, the option to divert a portion of your salary or wages to a company-sponsored tax-sheltered savings account. Taxes on both the salary (wages) placed in the savings plan and the investment earnings accumulated are deferred until the funds are withdrawn.

Generally, participants in 401(k) plans are offered several options for investing their contributions—typically, a money market fund, company stock, one or more equity funds, or a guaranteed investment contract (GIC). About 45% of all 401(k) plan investments are made in **guaranteed investment contracts (GICs),** which are portfolios of fixed-income securities with guaranteed competitive rates of return that are backed and sold by insurance companies. A firm's pension plan manager buys large GIC contracts and invests employees' 401(k) contributions in them.

guaranteed investment contracts (GICs)
portfolios of fixed-income securities with guaranteed competitive rates of return that are backed and sold by insurance companies.

Of course, *taxes will have to be paid on 401(k) funds eventually, but not until you start drawing down the account at retirement.* At that point, presumably, you will be in a lower tax bracket. A special attraction of most 401(k) plans is that the firms offering them often "sweeten the pot" by matching all or part of your contribution (up to a set limit). Currently, about 85% of the companies that offer 401(k) plans have some type of matching contribution program, often putting up 50 cents (or more) for each $1 contributed by the employee. Such matching programs provide both tax and savings incentives to individuals and clearly enhance the appeal of 401(k) plans.

In 1998, an individual employee could put as much as $10,000 (depending on salary level) into a tax-deferred 401(k) plan. The annual dollar cap increases yearly, because it is indexed to the rate of inflation. (*Note:* The contribution limits for 403(b) plans are now also set at a maximum of $10,000 per year and indexed to the rate of inflation.) To encourage savings for retirement, such contributions are "locked up" until the employee turns 59½ or leaves the company. A major exception to this rule lets employees tap their accounts, without penalty, in the event of any of a number of clearly defined "financial hardships."

To see how such tax-deferred plans work, assume you earned $50,000 in 1998 and want to contribute the maximum allowable ($10,000) to the 401(k) plan where you work. Doing so would reduce your taxable income to $40,000 and enable you to lower your federal tax bill (assuming you're in the 28% bracket) by $2,800 (0.28 × $10,000). Such tax savings will offset a good portion of your contribution. In effect, you will add $10,000 to your retirement program with only $7,200 of your own money; the rest will come from the IRS via a reduced tax bill. What's more, *all the earnings* on your contribution will accumulate tax-free. Remember, the taxes on both the earnings placed in the 401(k) plan and the investment earnings accumulated on them are deferred until retirement. The *Investing in Action* box on page 599 provides some tips from professionals on managing your 401(k) plan.

Keogh Plans

Keogh plans
programs that allow *self-employed individuals* to establish self-directed, tax-deferred retirement plans for themselves and their employees.

Keogh plans allow *self-employed individuals* to establish self-directed, tax-deferred retirement plans for themselves and their employees. Like contributions to 401(k) plans, payments to Keogh accounts may be taken as deductions from taxable income, to reduce the tax bill of self-employed individuals. The maximum contribution to this tax-deferred retirement plan is $30,000 per year (indexed to the rate of inflation) or 20% of earned income, whichever is less. Any individual who is self-employed, either full- or part-time, is eligible to set up a Keogh account. Keoghs can be used not only by the self-employed businessperson or professional but also by individuals who hold full-time jobs *and* "moonlight" on a part-time basis—for example, the engineer who has a small consulting business on the side and the accountant who does tax returns in the evenings and on weekends. Take the engineer, for example. If he earns $10,000 a year from his part-time consulting business, he can contribute 20% of that income ($2,000) to his Keogh account and in so doing reduce both his taxable income and the amount he pays in taxes. Also, he is eligible to receive full retirement benefits from his full-time job.

Keogh accounts can be opened at banks, insurance companies, brokerage firms, mutual funds, and other financial institutions. Annual contributions must be made by the time the respective tax return is filed, or by April 15 of the following calendar year (you have until April 15, 1999, to make the contribution to your Keogh for 1998). A designated financial institution acts as custodian of all the funds held in a Keogh account, but *the actual investments held in the account are under the complete direction of the individual contributor.* Unlike 401(k) plans, these are self-directed retirement programs: The *individual* decides which investments to buy and sell (subject to a few basic restrictions). The income earned from the investments in a Keogh plan must be plowed back into the account, and it too accrues tax-free.

All Keogh contributions and investment earnings must remain in the account until the individual turns 59½, unless the individual becomes seriously ill or disabled. However, you are *not required* to start withdrawing the funds at age 59½. Rather, they can stay in the account and continue to earn tax-free income until you turn 70½, at which time you have the remainder of your life to liquidate the account. In fact, as long as the self-employment income continues, an individual can continue to make tax-deferred contributions to a Keogh account, up to the maximum age of 70½. Of course, once an individual starts withdrawing funds from a Keogh account (at age 59½ or after), all such withdrawals are treated as active income and are subject to the payment of ordinary income taxes. *Thus the taxes on all contributions to and*

INVESTING IN ACTION

Don't Ignore Your 401(k) Plan

Traditional pension plans—funded by employers and managed by professionals—are on the decline. Therefore, chances are that you'll have to manage your own defined-contribution plan—401(k)s at private firms and the similar 403(b)s for public, nonprofit employees. How much retirement money you'll have depends on how much you invest and how well you manage the funds.

Until recently, the average 401(k) plan offered limited options—perhaps a guaranteed investment contract (GIC), the company's stock, and a mutual fund. But new regulations protect companies against lawsuits over poor 401(k) performance if they meet certain conditions: They must offer at least three different investment options in addition to company stock, provide information about investment options so that participants can assess risk–return features, report performance frequently, and allow more frequent changes to employees' plans. Having more fund choices is good news, in a way, except that as investment choices increase, so does confusion about selecting the right investments.

A trap many fall into, according to investment advisers, is being too conservative with their 401(k) investments. The average 401(k) investor chooses GICs and low-yielding money market funds, focusing more on the safety of capital than on the way inflation erodes returns. Jonathan Pond, president of Financial Planning Information of Boston, notes that a *professional* pension fund manager who invested this way would be grossly negligent of his or her responsibilities; the typical pension plan holds about 60% equities for dividend growth, capital appreciation, and an inflation hedge. Another common mistake of those who manage their own pension plans is buying too much company stock. It's too risky to invest in one stock, especially when you also work for the company. Advisers typically suggest limiting company stock to 10% to 25% of your 401(k).

What do financial planning experts suggest as an ideal 401(k) plan? They recommend following the lead of the pension funds and investing heavily in common stock; the percentage and type of equities should change as you move through life cycle stages. You should also coordinate your 401(k) plan with your other investments so that you have an appropriate balance overall. Are you now in your twenties? Start your plan now and save whatever you can—especially if your employer matches contributions—even if you can't contribute the maximum. Concentrate on growth-oriented equities, up to 100% of your plan, while you're young. As you move through your thirties, diversify into international equities and move a portion—say, 30%—into fixed-income investments. During your forties and fifties, shift into more conservative equity and fixed-income investments as you near retirement. Many advisers recommend keeping a reasonably high portion in equities to hedge against inflation even after you retire, because today's longer life expectancy means you'll probably live for quite a while past 65.

The new Roth IRA, described in the next section of the chapter, is the first serious challenge to the 401(k) plan. The reason is that the Roth IRA allows you to accumulate savings on a tax-free basis. In contrast, the 401(k) is a tax-deferred investment that is ultimately taxed when the money is withdrawn at retirement. However, the 401(k) plan has one big advantage: You can save up to $10,000 per year, whereas with the Roth IRA, you're limited to $2,000 ($4,000 on a joint tax return).

earnings from a Keogh account are deferred to retirement, when they will have to be paid.

A program that's similar in many respects to the Keogh account is something called a *Simplified Employee Pension Plan (SEP-IRA).* It's aimed at small-business owners, particularly those with *no employees,* who want a plan that is simple to set up and administer. SEP-IRAs *can be used in place of Keoghs.* Although they are simpler to administer and have the same annual dollar contribution cap ($30,000), their contribution *rate* is less generous: You can put in only 15% of earned income for a SEP-IRA, versus 20% for a Keogh.

Individual Retirement Arrangements (IRAs)

individual retirement arrangements (IRAs) self-directed, tax-deferred retirement programs *available to any gainfully employed individual,* who can make up to a specified maximum annual contribution.

Individual retirement arrangements (**IRAs**) are virtually the same as any other investment account you open with a bank, savings and loan, credit union, stockbroker, mutual fund, or insurance company, with one exception: IRAs are self-directed, tax-deferred retirement programs that are *available to any gainfully employed individual.* The form you complete to open the account designates the account as an IRA and makes the institution its trustee. The *Taxpayer Relief Act of 1997* added some new twists to IRAs. For a *traditional deductible IRA,* the maximum deductible contribution is $2,000 for an individual and up to $4,000 for an individual and spouse. The following conditions determine the extent to which your annual IRA contributions are tax-deductible.

1. *Work and Company-Sponsored Plan Participation*
   - If you and your spouse (if filing a joint return) work and are both covered by a company-sponsored pension plan, *you cannot use any deduction.*
   - If your spouse (if filing a joint return) works and is covered by a company-sponsored pension plan, *you can deduct up to a full $2,000 contribution,* provided that adjusted gross income (AGI) on the joint return is less than $150,000. (*Note:* The amount that is deductible is phased out with AGI over $150,000; full phase-out occurs at $160,000.)
   - If neither of you (if filing a joint return) has a company-sponsored pension plan and one of you has earned income, *you can each deduct up to $2,000 (a total of $4,000).*
2. Your adjusted gross income (in 1998) must be less than $50,000 (rising to $80,000 in 2007) for married couples and $30,000 (rising to $50,000 in 2005) for singles.

Translated, this means your IRA contributions *would fully qualify* as a tax deduction if you were covered by a company-sponsored pension plan but your adjusted gross income fell below the specified amounts ($50,000 for joint filers or $30,000 for singles) *or* if you (and/or your spouse) work and are not (or, if filing jointly, neither of you is) covered by a company-sponsored pension plan, no matter how much your adjusted gross income. [*Note:* The income ceilings are phased out, so that people with adjusted gross incomes (in 1998) of $50,000 to $60,000 (or $30,000 to $40,000) who are covered by employer pension plans are still entitled to prorated *partial deductions.*] If the contributions qualify as tax deductions (per the two conditions noted above), then the amount of the IRA contributions can be shown on the tax return as a deduction from taxable income—which, of course, reduces the amount of taxes that have to be paid. As with 401(k) and Keogh plans, the taxes on all the *earnings* from an IRA account are deferred until you start drawing down the funds.

In addition to the traditional deductible IRA described above, there are two other types of IRAs: the *Roth IRA* and the *nondeductible IRA.* In addition, a special type of IRA—the *Education IRA*—is available to certain taxpayers. Before describing the benefits of deductible IRAs, we describe the characteristics of these other forms of IRAs.

Roth IRA
an IRA that allows a worker and spouse with earnings from employment to, subject to certain limits, each contribute up to $2,000 annually. Contributions are nondeductible, but the earnings are not taxable when withdrawn in accordance with certain requirements.

Roth IRA A **Roth IRA** allows a worker and spouse with earnings from employment each to contribute up to $2,000 annually, whether or not they participate in company-sponsored pension plans. The $2,000 annual limit is reduced by any contributions made to other IRAs. In addition, a phase out of the $2,000 limit begins for couples filing jointly with adjusted gross income in excess of $150,000 (for singles, in excess of $95,000), and the opportunity to contribute is completely eliminated at $160,000 (for singles, at $110,000).

The contributions to a Roth IRA are *nondeductible*—you will have already paid taxes on the money you put into it. But as long as you are age 59½ or older and the account is at least 5 years old, withdrawals are tax-free. Otherwise, the earnings are taxed and you may be subject to a 10% penalty. Clearly, the tax-free accumulation in a Roth IRA makes it an attractive vehicle for tax deferral.

nondeductible IRA
an IRA with contribution limits and penalties similar to those of a traditional deductible IRA, available to taxpayers who fail to meet income cutoffs for a traditional deductible IRA or a Roth IRA. Contributions are nondeductible, earnings are deferred, and taxes are due on withdrawals.

Nondeductible IRA A **nondeductible IRA** allows taxpayers who fail to meet the income cutoffs for the traditional deductible IRA or Roth IRA to obtain the benefit of tax-deferred earnings. Like a traditional IRA, the earnings in this IRA accumulate tax-free until you withdraw funds. This IRA offers less tax advantage than the other types of IRAs: As in a Roth IRA, contributions *are not tax-deductible,* but it is unlike the Roth IRA in that withdrawals *are taxable.* Contribution limits and penalties on nondeductible IRAs are similar to those on the traditional deductible IRA except that there is no income cutoff.

All three of the IRAs described so far allow the withdrawal of cash without the 10% early withdrawal tax penalty if the proceeds are used to (1) buy a first home (subject to a $10,000 limit), (2) fund a college education for you, your spouse, or your children or grandchildren (no income limit), or (3) pay medical expenses in excess of 7.5% of your adjusted gross income. All three of these IRAs allow penalty-free withdrawals for any reason starting at age 59½. But the Roth IRA, unlike the traditional and nondeductible IRAs, which *require* withdrawal to start by age 70½, allows you to leave your money in the account for as long as you wish. The Roth IRA allows contributions (not accumulated earnings) to be withdrawn at any time without penalty or taxes; the other IRAs do not permit penalty-free withdrawal until age 59½.

Education IRA
an IRA that allows the taxpayer, subject to income limits, to contribute a *nondeductible* $500 per year for each child under age 18 into an account in which earnings accumulate tax-free and distributions are tax-exempt if they are used to pay higher-education (college) expenses for the child for whom the account exists.

Education IRA An **Education IRA** can be used to save for the future educational expenses of a child under age 18. In 1998 the maximum annual contribution per beneficiary was set at $500, but an increase to $2,000 was then under consideration by the Senate Finance Committee. The contribution is phased out for couples filing jointly with modified adjusted gross income in excess of $150,000 (for singles, in excess of $95,000) and is completely eliminated at $160,000 (for singles, at $110,000). The contributions to these IRAs are *nondeductible,* but earnings accumulate tax-free, and withdrawals to pay college expenses of the child for whom the account exists are tax-exempt. (*Note:* Although in 1998 these accounts could be used only to pay college expenses, the Senate Finance Committee was considering allowing tax-free withdrawals for spending on elementary and secondary education.)

INVESTOR FACT

EDUCATION IRA—TAX BREAK OR HEADACHE?—Are Education IRAs worthwhile tax breaks or just another record-keeping headache? Let's say you open an Education IRA when your child is born in 1998, making the $500 maximum annual contribution each year for 17 years. Assuming an annual rate of return of 12%, you will have nearly $25,000 in the account in the year 2015.

Some financial planners think the limit of $500 per year is too low to make the Education IRA worthwhile, especially because many mutual funds impose annual fees to manage them. Others disagree, arguing that the $500 per year is a good start toward saving for college. What do you think?

An individual's contributions to an Education IRA are separate from, and in addition to, contributions to an individual's own IRA.

IRAs are *self-directed accounts*—that is, you are free, within limits, to make whatever investment decisions you wish with the capital in your IRA. Of course, your investment options are limited by the products offered by financial institutions. Banks and thrift institutions push savings vehicles, insurance companies have annuities, and brokerage houses offer everything from mutual funds to stocks, bonds, and annuities. Except for the limited exceptions noted earlier, any withdrawals from an IRA prior to age 59½ are subject to a 10% penalty on top of the regular tax on the withdrawal itself.

Bear in mind that deductible IRAs, along with all other retirement plans that permit contributions on a pretax basis, *defer* but do not *eliminate* taxes. When you receive the income (contributions and investment earnings) in retirement, it is taxed at the then-prevailing tax rates. Even so, the impact of tax deferral is substantial. Table 15.4 compares the results of investments in a traditional deductible IRA and a non-IRA account, both of which earn an annual rate of return of 8%. This example assumes that you invest $1,000 of earned income each year. If you choose the traditional deductible IRA, you shelter from taxes both the $1,000 initial investment and its subsequent earnings, so that at the end of the first year, for example, you have accumulated $1,080. If you select the same investment vehicle but do not make it an IRA, you must first pay $280 in taxes (assuming a 28% tax rate), leaving only $720 to invest. The subsequent earnings of $58 (0.08 × $720) are also taxed at 28%, leaving after-tax income of only $42 [$58 − (0.28 × $58) = $58 − $16 = $42]. Thus the first-year accumulation is just $762. As the table indicates, after about 25 years, accumulated funds in the IRA are about twice as great as for the non-IRA; after 45 years, the funds are nearly 2.6 times as great ($417,417 vs. $159,502). The power of compounding is even greater when earnings are not taxable, as the *Investing in Action* box on Roth IRAs on page 603 demonstrates.

Funding Keoghs and IRAs

As with any investment, an individual can be conservative or aggressive when choosing securities for a Keogh or IRA, though the nature of these retirement programs generally favors a more conservative approach. In fact, conventional wisdom favors funding your Keogh and IRA with *income-producing assets.* This strategy would also suggest that if you are looking for capital gains, it is best to do so *outside of* your retirement account. The reasons for this are

TABLE 15.4 Accumulated Funds from a $1,000-a-Year Investment in a Traditional Deductible IRA and from a Fully Taxable (Non-IRA) Account*

Years Held	IRA	Non-IRA	Years Held	IRA	Non-IRA
1	$ 1,080	$ 762	25	$ 78,951	$ 40,471
5	6,335	4,272	30	122,341	57,821
10	15,645	9,926	35	186,097	80,778
15	29,323	17,405	40	279,774	111,153
20	49,421	27,359	45	417,417	159,502

*Contributions and earnings are taxed at 28% in the non-IRA account but are tax-free in the traditional deductible IRA; an annual rate of return of 8% is assumed in both cases.

INVESTING IN ACTION

You're Never Too Young to Start That IRA

You're working your way through college at the campus bookstore. At the end of the year, you look at your pay stub and it says you earned $3,000, which you use to pay for entertainment and transportation expenses. Because you have earned income, you're eligible to contribute to an IRA, although you haven't really thought about it because retirement is so far away. However, your grandparents are impressed with your hard work and want to make a gift to you, so they open a Roth IRA in your name and plunk $2,000 into a mutual fund. They figure that if that mutual fund earns an average annual return of 12%, the $2,000 account will be worth nearly $600,000 in the year 2048 when you retire at age 70. If the account earns an average annual return of 15%, then the account will be worth about $2.2 million. All from a single $2,000 deposit!

They're also planning on making additional $2,000 annual contributions to your IRA as long as you're in school. Using future value tables, they figure that an annual $2,000 contribution to a Roth IRA for the next 50 years would be worth nearly $5 million if the account earned 12% and nearly $14.5 million if it earned 15%. You're duly impressed, and you pledge to them that you will make the annual $2,000 contribution as long as you're gainfully employed.

Because there is no minimum age requirement for IRAs, many youngsters who have earnings can get into the game. A 4-year-old who earns money modeling clothes for a local retailer's sales catalog, a 12-year-old with income from baby-sitting or a paper route, a teen who bags groceries or flips burgers, and a college student who works at the bookstore are all eligible. Even if children don't have an outside job, they can work for their parents, getting paid for doing chores around the house.

If an IRA is set up for a minor, then the parent or other adult must serve as custodian, making investment decisions and controlling the funds until the child comes of age. The practice is likely to proliferate as the Roth IRA, started in 1998, picks up steam.

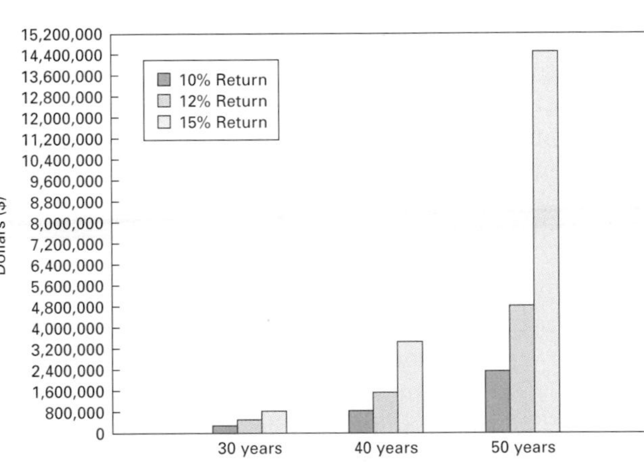

twofold: (1) Growth-oriented securities are by nature *more risky,* and (2) you cannot write off losses from the sale of securities held in a Keogh or IRA account. This does *not* mean it would be altogether inappropriate to place a good-quality growth stock or mutual fund in a Keogh or IRA. In the end, *it is how much you have in your retirement account that matters, rather than how your earnings were made along the way.*

Although very few types of investments are prohibited outright, some should be avoided simply because they are inappropriate for such accounts. For example, with tax-free municipal securities, the tax shelter from a Keogh or IRA would be redundant because their income is tax-exempt anyway. In addition to most long-term securities, money market accounts—both bank deposits (MMDAs) and mutual funds (MMMFs)—also appeal to Keogh and

IRA investors, especially those who view short-term securities as one way to capture volatile market interest rates. Not surprisingly, as the size of an account begins to build up, an investor often uses more than one kind of security to diversify the portfolio.

Remember that although Keoghs and IRAs offer tax advantages, they in no way affect the underlying risks of the securities held in these accounts. Also, though the specific investment vehicles may (and probably should) be changed occasionally, once money is put into a Keogh or IRA, it's meant to stay there for the long haul.

Strategies That Trade Current Income for Capital Gains

Whereas ordinary income is taxed in the year it's received, capital gains are not taxed until they are actually realized. This means that *unrealized* capital gains are not taxed. For example, the receipt of \$100 in cash dividends on a stock in the current year would be taxed at your assumed 28% rate, leaving \$72 of after-tax income. On the other hand, if the price of a stock that pays no dividend rises by \$100 during the current year, *no tax is due until the stock is actually sold.* Sooner or later, you'll pay taxes on your income, but at least with capital gains, you defer the taxes until the profit is actually realized, which could be years away. Therefore, if the market price of the stock is stable or increasing, earning capital gains may achieve a tax-deferred buildup of funds. From a strict tax viewpoint, investment vehicles that provide such a tax-deferred buildup of value may be more attractive than those that provide annual taxable income. Some of the more common methods for trading current income for capital gains are described below.

Growth Versus Income Stocks

Choosing growth rather than income stocks or mutual funds is a simple yet basic way to earn capital gains income. Companies and funds that pay out a low percentage of earnings as dividends usually reinvest the retained earnings to take advantage of growth opportunities. During the bull market of the 1990s, index funds (discussed in Chapter 13) were very effective in this regard. They earn market returns and pay out very low dividends, thereby providing capital gains nearly equivalent to the rate of appreciation of the market portfolio of stocks.

If you select a company that pays dividends amounting to a 10% current return on your investment, your after-tax return will be 7.2%, assuming you are in the 28% tax bracket. In comparison, a company or fund that pays no dividends but is expected to experience 10% annual growth in its share price from reinvestment of earnings also offers an after-tax rate of return of 7.2% $[(1.00 - 0.28) \times 0.10]$, but in this case the taxes will not have to be paid until the stock or fund is actually sold and the gain realized. At that point, the hope is that you will be in a lower tax bracket or that the tax rate will be lower. If neither, at least in the interim you've been able to keep invested the funds that you otherwise would have paid out in taxes. The deferral of tax payment is, of course, appealing as long as the stock or fund price continues to increase.

Deep-Discount Bonds

deep-discount bond
a bond selling at a price far below its par value.

Purchasing a **deep-discount bond**—one that is selling at a price far below its par value—also offers a capital gains opportunity. To illustrate, suppose you have the choice of buying two different bonds: ABC's bond, which has a coupon rate of 5% and is selling for $700 in the market, or DEF's bond, with a coupon of 10% and selling at par. Which would you prefer if both mature to a $1,000 par value at the end of 10 years? With the ABC bond, you will earn interest of $50 a year taxed as ordinary income. At the end of 10 years, you will have a $300 capital gain, which will be taxed at the lower capital gains tax rate. With the DEF bond, all of your return—that is, the $100 you receive each year—is ordinary income. From a strict tax perspective, the ABC bond is clearly the better of the two, *because the portion of the return represented by the capital gain is not taxed until it is realized at maturity, and the rate at which it is taxed is below that applicable to ordinary income.* Remember, though, that the higher-coupon bond is giving you a higher return earlier, and that adds to its attractiveness.

To choose between the two bonds, you could perform a rate-of-return analysis. Assuming you have $7,000 to invest, you could purchase 10 ABC bonds or 7 DEF bonds. Total annual interest on the ABC bonds would be $500; on the DEF bonds, it would be $700. Assuming you are in the 28% tax bracket, the after-tax advantage of the DEF bonds is $144 (0.72 × $200) a year. However, the ABC bonds will be worth $10,000 at maturity, whereas the DEF bonds will be worth only their current value of $7,000. Assuming a 20% capital gains tax rate, on an after-tax basis, the additional $3,000 is worth $2,400 [$3,000 − (0.20 × $3,000)].

The choice boils down to whether you prefer $144 of additional income each year for the next 10 years or an additional $2,400 at the *end* of 10 years. Using the future value techniques developed in Chapter 4, you would arrive at the conclusion that it would take about an 11% rate of return to make you indifferent between the two bonds. That is, if you invest $144 a year for 10 years at 11%, it accumulates to around $2,400 at the end of 10 years. Interpreting this answer, if you can invest at an after-tax rate greater than 11%, you should select the DEF bonds; if you feel your after-tax reinvestment rate will be lower, then you should select the ABC bonds.

Income Property Depreciation

Federal tax law, as noted in Chapter 14, permits the *depreciation* of income property such as apartment houses and similar structures. Essentially, a specified amount of annual depreciation can be deducted from ordinary pretax income. The depreciable life of residential rental property (apartments) is 27.5 years. Nonresidential property (office buildings and shopping centers) placed in service after May 13, 1993, has a depreciable life of 39 years. In both cases, straight-line depreciation is used. When a property is sold, any amount received in excess of its book value is treated as a capital gain and is taxed at the applicable capital gains rate.

To see the tax effects of depreciation, assume you buy a four-unit apartment building for $100,000 and hold it for 3 years, taking $2,900 in depreciation each year. Now suppose that at the end of the third year you sell it for its original $100,000 purchase price. The depreciation you took reduced ordinary income each year by $2,900 and was worth, assuming a 28% tax bracket, $812 (0.28 × $2,900). Your gain on the sale is $8,700 (3 years × $2,900 per year), which results in a tax of $2,436 (0.28 × $8,700). There is no tax savings in this situation; however, you received a tax *deferral* because the tax savings of $812 in each of the first 3 years did not have to be paid back until the property was sold at the end of the third year. (Of course, if the property were sold for less than its original purchase price, full repayment would not occur.)

The use of the depreciation deduction (which does not involve any actual cash payment) results in a type of interest-free loan. The deduction reduces taxes during the property's holding period and delays the repayment of those taxes until the property is sold. *This tax deferral is the primary tax benefit provided by depreciation.* In our example, the tax deferral of $812 in each of the first 3 years (3 × $812 = $2,436), which is repaid as $2,436 of taxes at the end of the third year, represents a loan at a 0% rate of interest. However, very restrictive limits on the use of tax losses resulting from real estate investments, established by the Tax Reform Act of 1986, may severely limit an investor's ability to take advantage of these depreciation tax benefits. As a result, as noted in Chapter 14, the appeal of real estate investment no longer lies in its potential value as a tax shelter but in its ability to earn a profit from annual rents and/or price appreciation.

Tax Swaps: A Strategy That Reduces or Eliminates a Tax Liability

Thus far we have considered several short-term strategies aimed at affecting an investor's tax liability: (1) ways to exclude income from taxation, (2) ways to defer taxes from one tax year to the next, (3) programs that defer tax liabilities to retirement, and (4) techniques that trade current income for capital gains. We will now look at a strategy that essentially reduces or eliminates a tax liability altogether. This procedure, called a tax swap, is extremely popular at year-end among knowledgeable stock and bond investors.

tax swap
selling one security that has a capital loss and replacing it with another, similar security to offset, partially or fully, a capital gain that has been *realized* in another part of the portfolio.

A **tax swap** is simply the replacement of one security that has a capital loss with another, similar security to offset, partially or fully, a capital gain that has been *realized* in another part of the portfolio. Of course, because the aim is to offset a gain, the security that is sold in the tax swap should be one that has *lost* money for the investor. Because you are selling one security that has experienced a capital loss and replacing it with another, similar security, your stock or bond position remains essentially unchanged, although your tax liability has been reduced—and perhaps substantially so.

A tax swap works like this: Suppose that during the current year you realized a capital gain of $1,100 on the sale of bonds. Assume that in your portfolio you held 100 shares of International Oil Corporation common stock, purchased 20 months earlier for $38 per share and currently selling for $28 per share. Although you wish to maintain an oil stock in your portfolio, it does not matter to you whether you hold International Oil or one of the other multinational oils. To realize the capital loss of $10 per share on International Oil while not altering your portfolio, you sell the 100 shares of International Oil and buy 100 shares of World Petroleum, which is also selling for $28 per share. The result is a *realized* capital loss of $1,000 [100 × ($28 − $38)], which can be used to offset all but $100 of the $1,100 capital gain realized on the earlier bond sale.

Swaps of common stock are an important part of year-end tax planning. Even more popular are bond swaps, because it is usually far easier to find a substitute bond for the one held. Most full-service brokerage houses publish a list of recommended year-end swaps for both stocks and bonds. You might wonder why it wouldn't make sense just to sell the security for tax purposes and then immediately buy it back. This procedure, which is called a **wash sale,** is disallowed under the tax law. A sold security cannot be repurchased within 30 days before or after its sale *without losing the tax deduction.*

wash sale
the procedure of selling securities on which capital losses can be realized and then immediately buying them back; disallowed under the tax law.

CONCEPTS IN REVIEW

15.6 What is *tax-favored income?* Briefly describe the following forms of income excluded from taxation.
   a. Tax-free municipal bond interest
   b. Treasury and government agency issues
   c. Sale of a personal residence

15.7 Explain conditions that favor the following strategies for deferring tax liabilities to the next year.
   a. A put hedge
   b. Selling a deep-in-the-money call option
When is it best simply to hold the stock and do nothing?

15.8 Briefly describe each of the following programs for deferring taxes to retirement.
   a. 401(k) plans
   b. Keogh plans
   c. Individual retirement arrangements (IRAs)

15.9 According to the *Investing in Action* box on page 599, how will the percentages and types of equities change as you move through life cycle stages in an ideal 401(k) plan?

15.10 Describe and compare the key features of each of the following types of individual retirement arrangements (IRAs).
   a. Traditional deductible IRA   b. Roth IRA
   c. Nondeductible IRA   d. Education IRA

15.11 According to the example in the *Investing in Action* box on page 603, what advantage does a Roth IRA offer that traditional and nondeductible IRAs do not?

15.12 What are *guaranteed investment contracts (GICs),* and what role do they play in 401(k) plans? What investment vehicles might be suitable for funding a Keogh or IRA?

15.13 Briefly describe each of the following strategies that trade current for capital gains income.
   a. Growth stocks
   b. Deep-discount bonds
   c. Income property depreciation

15.14 Describe how a *tax swap* can be used to reduce or eliminate a tax liability without significantly altering the composition of one's portfolio.

http://hepg.aw.com

Two investments often chosen by investors who wish to avoid paying taxes are municipal bonds and U.S. Treasury issues. These investments serve the needs of some investors better than those of others. The Web page listed here provides a profile of the typical municipal bond investor. The secondary market for "munis" is also discussed.

www.cpa.Texas.gov/localinf/debtguide/Ch1.html

Deferred Annuities and Single-Premium Life Insurance

LG 4

Effective tax strategy seeks to defer taxable income for extended periods of time. The earnings on investment are therefore available for reinvestment during the period of deferment. The additional earnings resulting from investment of pretax rather than after-tax dollars over long periods of time can be large. Put in proper perspective, a tax-deferred annuity may be worth more to an individual investor than any other single tax strategy. That is why it is important to understand the topic thoroughly. A somewhat similar, but generally less attractive, product is single-premium life insurance.

Annuities: An Overview

An **annuity** is a contract issued by an insurance company that guarantees a series of payments for a number of years or over a lifetime. The two types of annuities are classified by their purchase provisions: The **single-premium annuity** is purchased with a single lump-sum payment. The purchaser pays a certain amount and receives a series of payments that begins either immediately or at some future date. The second type of annuity, the **installment annuity,** is acquired by making payments over time; at a specified future date, the installment payments, plus interest earned on them, are used to purchase an annuity. The person to whom the future payments are directed is called the **annuitant.** Annuities of many types are issued by hundreds of insurance companies.

The period of time between when payments are made to the insurance company and when payments to the annuitant begin is the **accumulation period.** All interest earned on the accumulated payments during this period is tax-deferred: Because no payment is made to the purchaser, no tax liability is created. The period of time over which payments are made to the annuitant is the **distribution period.** Earnings on the annuity during the accumulation and distribution periods become taxable to the annuitant when received.

An **immediate annuity** is one under which payments to the annuitant begin as soon as it is purchased. The amount of the payment is based on statistical analyses performed by the insurance company and depends on the annuitant's gender and age; the payment is a function of how long the insurance company expects the annuitant to live. A **deferred annuity,** in contrast, is one in which the payments to the annuitant begin at some future date. The date is specified in the contract or at the annuitant's option. The amount the annuitant will periodically receive depends on his or her contributions, the interest earned on them, the annuitant's gender, and the annuitant's age when payments begin.

annuity
a contract issued by an insurance company that guarantees a series of payments for a number of years or over a lifetime.

single-premium annuity
an annuity purchased with a single lump-sum payment.

installment annuity
an annuity acquired by making payments over time; at a specified future date, the installment payments, plus interest earned on them, are used to purchase an annuity.

annuitant
the person to whom the future payments on an annuity are directed.

accumulation period
under an annuity, the period of time between when payments are made to the insurance company and when payments to the annuitant begin.

distribution period
under an annuity, the period of time over which payments are made to the annuitant.

immediate annuity
an annuity under which payments to the annuitant begin as soon as it is purchased.

deferred annuity
an annuity in which the payments to the annuitant begin at some future date.

Characteristics of Deferred Annuities

current interest rate
for an annuity contract, the yearly return the insurance company pays on accumulated deposits.

Deferred annuities generally pay market-competitive interest rates. An annuity contract's **current interest rate** is the yearly return the insurance company pays on accumulated deposits. The current interest rate fluctuates with market rates over time and is not guaranteed by the insurance company. However, some contracts have a "bailout" provision that allows an annuity holder to withdraw the contract value—principal and all earned interest—if the insurance company fails to pay a specified minimum return. The minimum is typically a return that is 1% or more below the initial rate.

minimum guaranteed interest rate
for a deferred annuity purchase contract, the minimum interest rate on contributions, which the insurance company guarantees over the full accumulation period.

The deferred annuity purchase contract specifies a **minimum guaranteed interest rate** on contributions, which the insurance company guarantees over the full accumulation period. The minimum rate is usually substantially less than the current interest rate. You should study a prospectus or contract and remember that *the minimum rate is all you are guaranteed.* (Very often, the promotional literature provided by the company emphasizes the high *current* interest rate.)

Special Tax Features

Deferred annuities, both single-premium and installment, have several advantageous tax shelter features. First, interest earned on the purchaser's contributions is not subject to income tax until it is actually paid by the insurance company. Suppose you invest $10,000 in a 7% single-premium deferred annuity. During the first year the contract is in effect, the account earns $700 in interest. If none of this interest is withdrawn, no income tax is due. Thus, if you are in the 28% tax bracket, your first year's tax savings is $196. The tax-deferral privilege permits you to accumulate substantial sums of compound interest that can be used to help provide a comfortable retirement income. However, note that the Tax Reform Act of 1986 provides that this tax-favored treatment is available only on annuity contracts held by individuals, trusts, or other entities (such as a decedent's estate, a qualified employer plan, a qualified annuity plan, or an IRA). In all other cases, the income on the annuity is taxed when earned.

tax-sheltered annuity
an annuity that allows employees of certain institutions to make a *tax-free contribution* from current income to purchase a deferred annuity.

Certain employees of institutions such as schools, universities, governments, and not-for-profit organizations may qualify for a **tax-sheltered annuity.** A special provision in the income tax laws allows these employees to make a *tax-free contribution* from current income to purchase a deferred annuity. The interest earned on these contributions is tax-deferred as well. The maximum amount that can be contributed is limited. Purchasers of these annuities do not have to pay any income tax on contributions or on interest earnings until they actually receive annuity payments in future years. The expectation is that, if timed to coincide with retirement, the deferred income will be taxed at a lower rate than current income would be.

Investment Payout

payout
the investment return provided by an annuity; it is realized when the distribution period begins.

straight annuity
an annuity that provides for a series of payments for the rest of the annuitant's life.

The investment return, or **payout,** provided by an annuity is realized when the distribution period begins. The annuitant can choose a **straight annuity,** which is a series of payments for the rest of his or her life. Most companies also offer other payout options, such as a contract specifying payments for both annuitant and spouse for the rest of both their lives, as well as a contract specifying rapid payout of accumulated payments with interest over a short period of time.

The amount an annuitant receives depends on the amount accumulated in the account and on the payout plan chosen. It is important to choose the program that provides the highest return for the desired payout plan. Such a plan will probably have a relatively high interest rate and relatively low (or no) sales charges and administration fees.

Deferred Annuities and Retirement Plans

Many investors tie the purchase of deferred annuities to their overall retirement plans. Because Keogh plans and IRAs are somewhat similar to deferred annuities, they should be evaluated with them. If you are not fully using any allowable deductible IRA exclusion each year, you may prefer adding to it as a part of your retirement plan, rather than purchasing a tax-deferred annuity. Far greater benefit results from deducting from taxable income the full amount of the allowable IRA payment. With an annuity, unless you're in one of the qualified professional fields noted above, you cannot deduct its purchase price but can only defer earned income.

Although both IRA (except for contributions to a Roth IRA) and deferred annuity withdrawals prior to age 59½ are subject to a 10% additional tax, it is important to recognize that income withdrawn from a deferred annuity will be taxed in the year it is withdrawn. Moreover, any annuity withdrawal is first viewed for tax purposes as income; once all income is withdrawn, subsequent withdrawals are treated as a return of principal, so any partial withdrawal is likely to be fully taxable.

Fixed versus Variable Annuity

fixed annuity
an annuity that pays an unchanging amount of monthly income during the distribution period.

variable annuity
an annuity that adjusts the monthly income it pays during the distribution period according to the investment experience (and sometimes the mortality experience) of the insurer.

The annuity payout during the distribution period can be either fixed or variable. Most contracts are written as **fixed annuities:** Once a payment schedule is selected, the amount of monthly income does not change. In contrast, a growing number of annuity plans adjust the monthly income according to the actual investment experience (and sometimes the mortality experience) of the insurer. These latter contracts are called **variable annuities.** The advantage of a fixed annuity is that the dollar amount of monthly income is guaranteed regardless of how poorly or well the insurer's investments perform. A major disadvantage, however, is that in periods of inflation, the purchasing power of the dollar erodes. For example, with a 5% annual inflation rate, $1 of purchasing power is reduced to 78 cents in just 5 years.

The variable annuity was developed to overcome the lack of inflation protection provided by fixed-dollar annuities. With this plan, annuitants face a different risk, however. They cannot be certain how well the insurer's investments—which may consist of common stocks, bonds, or money market funds—will do. Annuitants therefore take a chance that they will receive an even lower monthly income, in absolute dollars, than a fixed-dollar contract would provide. Most people who participate in variable annuity plans, of course, anticipate that they will be able at least to keep up with the cost of living. Unfortunately, variable annuity values and inflation, often measured by the consumer price index (CPI), do not always perform the same.

Some people invest in a variable annuity during the accumulation period and then switch to a fixed annuity at retirement. In this manner, they participate in the growth of the economy over their working careers but guard against short-term recessions that may occur during their retirement years.

Annuities as Investment Vehicles

Annuities have several potential uses in an investment program. An immediate annuity can provide a safe and predictable source of income for the balance of one's life. A deferred annuity offers tax shelter and safety features and in addition can provide a convenient method for accumulating funds. When considering the purchase of a deferred annuity, you need to assess its investment suitability and understand the purchase procedures.

Investment Suitability

The principal positive feature of deferred annuities is that they allow you to accumulate tax-deferred earnings. The tax-deferral feature allows interest to accumulate more quickly than would be the case if earnings were taxed. For those who qualify for a tax-sheltered annuity, current income tax on premium payments can be deferred as well. Furthermore, annuities are a low-risk type of investment.

On the negative side, deferred annuities have two disadvantages: (1) lack of inflation protection and (2) high sales charges and administration fees. Most variable annuities, despite providing a fluctuating interest rate during the accumulation period, do not provide an annual interest rate in excess of the rate of inflation. Thus they are not an inflation hedge. The second disadvantage—relatively high charges and fees—is due largely to the fact that sales commissions are generous. In addition, insurance companies have high overheads that must be met from annuity proceeds.

In general, then, although annuities can play an important role in an investment portfolio, they should not be the only vehicle held. Other vehicles providing higher returns (and probably carrying higher risk) are available.

Buying Annuities

Annuities are sold by licensed salespersons and many stockbrokers. There are probably 50 or more annuity plans available through these outlets in a given community. Before you invest in a particular annuity, you should obtain a prospectus and any other available literature on a number of them. Then carefully compare these materials. The annuity you choose should be one that contains features consistent with your investment objectives and also offers the highest actual return on investment after all charges and fees are deducted.

Many annuities are sold by salespersons who must be compensated for their services. Some annuities, called "no-load," have no sales charges paid by the purchaser; in this case, the insurance company pays the salesperson directly. Other annuities require the purchaser to pay commissions of up to 10%. Administration fees for management, yearly maintenance, and one-time "setup charges" may also be levied.

Also, because *the annuity is only as good as the insurance company that stands behind it,* check to see how the company is rated in *Best's Insurance Reports*. These ratings are much like those found in the bond market and reflect the *financial strength* of the insurance company. Letter grades (ranging from A+ down to C) are assigned on the principle that the stronger the company, the lower the risk of loss. Accordingly, if security is important to you, stick with insurers that carry A+ or A ratings. If you're considering a *variable annuity,* go over it in much the same way as you would a traditional mutual fund: Look for superior past performance, proven management talents, moderate expenses, and the availability of attractive investment alternatives that you can switch in and out of.

Single-Premium Life Insurance

Since 1982, tax legislation has reduced the tax shelter appeal of single-premium deferred annuities (SPDAs). Currently, a 10% federal tax penalty is charged on withdrawals made prior to age 59½, regardless of how long the annuity has been held. In addition, most insurers charge withdrawal penalties—typically, on withdrawals of 10% or more during the first 7 to 10 years. Clearly, these restrictions limit the tax shelter appeal of SPDAs.

single-premium life insurance (SPLI) policy
an investment vehicle for which the policyholder purchases a whole life insurance policy that provides a stated death benefit and earns interest on the cash value buildup, which occurs over time on a tax-free basis.

As a result of the limitations placed on single-premium deferred annuities by the tax laws, the **single-premium life insurance (SPLI) policy** emerged as a popular alternative investment vehicle. These policies, in addition to offering the features of SPDAs, provided a mechanism for making tax-sheltered withdrawals prior to age 59½. Generally, the policyholder paid a large premium, often $15,000 or more, to purchase *whole life insurance.* (See the text's Web site—**hepg.aw.com**—for discussion of life insurance.) Whole life provided a stated death benefit (which is passed tax-free to beneficiaries) and earned a competitive interest rate on the cash value buildup, which occurred over time on a tax-free basis. As with any whole life policy, the policyholder could cancel the policy and withdraw its cash value. In such a case, taxes would be due on any gains above the amount originally invested.

The most attractive feature of SPLI policies was the ability they afforded the policyholder to *make tax-free cash withdrawals at any time, using a policy loan.* However, in 1988 Congress closed the loophole in the tax law that allowed tax-free policy loans. Today's SPLI policies preserve the principal and usually guarantee returns for the first year or so. After that, rates of return are changed periodically to reflect prevailing money market rates; however, rates normally cannot fall below a certain minimum level (usually around 4% to 6%), as specified in the policy. Single-premium *variable life insurance* policies (see the Web site—www.hepg.awl.com—noted above) let policyholders put their money in a number of investment choices, ranging from stocks and bonds to mutual funds and money market instruments. However, these policies *do not guarantee preservation of principal or a minimum return.* Substantial investment losses can result.

The rate of return on investment in SPLI policies is frequently below the return on tax-exempt municipal bonds, and the value of SPLI as life insurance is not as great as that available from term insurance. Like all forms of whole life insurance, SPLIs' only tax shelter appeals are the tax-free buildup of value and the tax-free passage of death benefits to beneficiaries. Because

SPDAs are vehicles for retirement, whereas SPLI policies provide greatest benefits when held until death, interest rates on SPDAs are usually half a percentage point higher than on SPLIs. Despite the aggressive and often tempting sales pitches, today most experts agree that this product is *not* well suited for young, moderate-income families, because it is neither an especially attractive tax-sheltered investment nor a very effective form of life insurance.

CONCEPTS IN REVIEW

15.15 Define an *annuity,* explain the role it might play in an investment portfolio, and differentiate between:

a. Single-premium and installment annuities
b. Immediate and deferred annuities
c. Fixed and variable annuities

15.16 Define the following terms as they are related to deferred annuities.

a. Current interest rate
b. Minimum guaranteed interest rate
c. Payout

15.17 Explain how a deferred annuity works as a tax shelter. How does a *tax-sheltered annuity* work, and who is eligible to purchase one? Discuss whether a deferred annuity is a better tax shelter than an IRA.

15.18 Discuss the investment suitability of a deferred annuity, particularly its positive and negative features. Briefly describe the procedures for buying annuities.

15.19 What is a *single-premium life insurance (SPLI) policy?* Describe the basic features of an SPLI policy, compare it to the single-premium deferred annuity (SPDA), and explain why the popularity of SPLI policies has diminished since 1988.

http://hepg.aw.com

Deferred annuities are among the most popular investment alternatives for retirement planning. They are also among the most controversial. The better you understand the pros and cons of deferred annuities, the more likely you are to make the right investment decision for your goals. A good presentation on both fixed and variable annuities can be found at the following Web site.

www.savingsnet.com/annuity.htm

limited partnership (LP)
vehicle in which the investor can passively invest with limited liability, receive the benefit of active professional management, and apply the resulting profit or loss (subject to limits) to his or her tax liability.

Limited Partnerships

LG 5 LG 6

passive activity
an investment in which the investor does not "materially participate" in its management or activity.

The **limited partnership** (LP) is a vehicle in which you can passively invest with limited liability, receive the benefit of active professional management, and apply the resulting profit or loss (subject to limits) to your tax liability. The Tax Reform Act of 1986 in effect eliminated the tax-sheltering appeal of LPs. It limited the tax deductions for net losses generated by passive activities to the amount of net income earned by the taxpayer on all passive activities. Generally, a **passive activity** is one in which the investor does not "materially participate" in its management or activity. Rental investments involving real estate, equipment, and other property are treated as passive activities regardless of whether or not the taxpayer materially participates.

An important exception exists for taxpayers actively participating in real estate rental activities. If more than half of an investor's personal service and at least 750 hours in a year are spent in active participation in a real estate rental activity, the passive loss restrictions do *not* apply. Investors who actively participate, but at lower levels, may deduct up to $25,000 of net losses if their adjusted gross income (AGI) is less than $100,000. The deduction is gradually phased out for AGI between $100,000 and $150,000; taxpayers with AGI above $150,000 cannot apply such losses. Another exception applies to oil and gas properties if the form of ownership does *not* limit the taxpayer's liability.

Although the value of LPs for tax shelters is no longer significant, this form of ownership is widely used to structure profit-making, cash-flow-generating investments. Like any investment, limited partnerships should be purchased *on their investment merits* only, after considering both risk and return. It is therefore important to first understand why LPs are used and how they work.

Pooling of Capital and Sharing of Risks

syndicate
a joint venture—general partnership, corporation, or limited partnership—in which investors pool their resources.

corporation
a form of organization that provides a limited-liability benefit to shareholder investors and that has an indefinite life.

In an effort to obtain economies of scale and diversify risk, investors often pool their resources and form joint ventures. These joint ventures, frequently called **syndicates,** can take several forms: corporations, general partnerships, or limited partnerships.

The corporate form of syndication—that is, a **corporation**—provides a limited-liability benefit to shareholder investors. Additionally, corporations have an indefinite life and do not cease to exist if a stockholder dies (whereas a partnership could end if a general partner dies). However, the corporate form has a significant disadvantage: Its profits and losses cannot be passed directly to its stockholders.

general partnership
a joint venture in which all partners have management rights, and all assume unlimited liability for any debts or obligations the partnership incurs.

The partnership form of syndication, on the other hand, provides for the flow-through of profits and losses. In a **general partnership,** all partners have management rights, and all assume unlimited liability for any debts or obligations the partnership incurs. Obviously, the unlimited-liability feature can be disadvantageous to passive investors (those who do not wish to participate actively in the partnership's operation). The *limited partnership* combines the favorable investment features of both the corporation and the general partnership: It provides an investor with a limited-liability vehicle that allows profits and losses to flow through to each partner's tax return.

How Limited Partnerships Work

Legal Structure

A limited partnership (LP) is a legal arrangement governed principally by state law. Though state laws vary, they typically require that written documents be filed with a county or state official prior to the commencement of the limited partnership's business. Additionally, the limited partnership is normally structured to conform to IRS regulations; this is done to ensure that any tax benefits generated can be used by the partners. Limited partnerships can be utilized to invest in many types of assets, and their size and scope vary widely. However, all must have at least one general partner and at least one limited partner.

general partner
the managing partner who assumes unlimited liability and uses her or his expertise to run the business.

Figure 15.1 illustrates a typical limited-partnership arrangement. The **general partner**—the active manager of the operation—runs the business and assumes unlimited liability. (Often, to mitigate the unlimited liability, the general partner is a corporation.) The general partner's major contribution is frequently in the form of management expertise, not capital. Most of the capital is usually supplied by the limited partners, who do little else. They cannot participate in the management of the enterprise or they will lose their limited-liability protection. Furthermore, a limited partner's liability normally does not exceed his or her capital contribution, an amount specified in the partnership agreement. **Limited partners,** then, are the suppliers of capital whose role in the venture is passive. Usually, the only power limited partners have is to fire the general partner and/or to sell their partnership investment. A person considering investment in a limited partnership should carefully analyze the general partner's management capabilities, because the success of the partnership depends on them.

limited partners
the passive investors in a partnership, who supply most of the capital and accept liability limited to the amount of their investment.

Return to Investors

Investors can realize a return from a limited-partnership investment in two ways—through cash flow and through price appreciation. Investors in a limited partnership receive periodic cash payments as the investment generates income. These periodic returns are the partnership's *cash flow.* Limited partners receive a share of this cash flow, prorated to the size of their investment. Cash distributions may be made monthly, quarterly, or yearly, and these returns are taxable to the limited partners as ordinary income. The general partner's management fee is normally paid prior to the distribution of cash flow. However, frequently the general partner takes only a small fee until the limited partners have fully recovered their initial investment. Then the general partner's share of additional cash distributions becomes commensurately larger.

The other source of investment return for limited partners is *price appreciation,* resulting from an increase in the value of the investment. The general partner may earn a portion of the realized price appreciation as well. Investments, such as real estate, that increase in value as a result of inflation and other factors are often sources of appreciated value for limited-partnership investors.

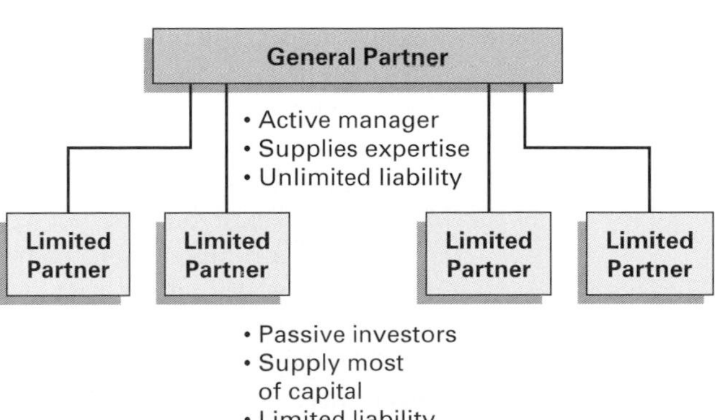

FIGURE 15.1
The Limited-Partnership Structure

In a limited partnership, the general partner is an active manager who typically provides management expertise and assumes unlimited liability. The limited partners are passive investors who supply most of the capital and accept liability limited to the amount of their investment.

Like the appreciation experienced on any investment vehicle, this form of return may be realized or unrealized (as an actual return of dollars or as a "paper" return). Of course, realized capital gains are taxable to the partners.

Popular Forms of Limited Partnerships

Limited partnerships are most often formed to invest in opportunities that require sizable outlays and professional management. Limited partnerships vary in risk, from a conservative one formed to own a fully rented office building with long-term leases, to a risky one formed to own the sperm bank of a famous thoroughbred horse that has never sired a winning offspring. Here we focus on three principal areas: real estate, energy resources, and equipment leasing. Other popular areas include livestock feeding or breeding programs, research and development programs, major movie or play production programs, cable TV programs, and real estate mortgage programs.

Real Estate

Depending on property type, limited partnerships in real estate may produce a periodic cash flow, price appreciation, and/or a tax shelter. Raw land is normally purchased for its price appreciation potential. Apartment buildings, shopping centers, office buildings, and the like can provide cash flow as well as price appreciation. The typical real estate limited partnership consists of a general partner who manages the investment and the limited partners who provide most or all of the capital. As noted earlier, limited tax shelter may be available only to those *actively* participating in real estate investment.

There are two major types of real estate syndicates. The *blind pool syndicate* is formed by a syndicator to raise a given amount of money to be invested at his or her discretion, though the general partner often has some or all of the properties already picked out. The *single-property syndicate,* on the other hand, is established to raise money to purchase specific properties. Very often, the large, multiproperty limited-partnership syndicates with many investors are blind pools. Single-property syndicates are generally smaller in scope.

Energy Resources

The United States depends heavily on energy for its economic well-being, so the federal government has provided tax incentives to encourage people to invest in the search for energy. Limited partnerships are a popular vehicle with which to finance exploration for oil, natural gas, coal, and geothermal steam. The most popular energy-related limited partnerships are oil and gas investments.

There are three basic types of oil and gas limited partnerships. *Exploratory programs,* also known as "wildcats," drill in areas where oil or gas is believed to exist but has not yet been discovered. *Developmental programs* finance the drilling of wells in areas of known and proven oil and gas reserves. (They often drill wells that are near already-producing oil or gas finds.) *Income programs* buy existing wells with proven reserves.

The oil and gas business is risky because of the high degree of uncertainty associated with it. Even the most knowledgeable geologists and petroleum engineers cannot be sure how much oil or gas is in a particular well or field.

Oil and gas limited-partnership investments are therefore risky. The degree of risk, of course, depends on the type of program an investor purchases. Exploratory programs carry the highest risk of the three types and, correspondingly, offer the highest potential return.

Equipment Leasing

Another popular limited-partnership investment deals with various types of leasable property: airplanes, railroad cars, machinery, computers, trucks, and automobiles. The limited partnership buys the equipment, such as a computer, and then leases it to another party. As the lessor of the equipment, the partnership can depreciate the item. Additionally, the partnership may use borrowed capital to increase potential return. The business of leasing property requires a great deal of knowledge and skill. The key to investment success in leasing is a competent general partner. Computers and various types of industrial machinery, for example, often have a high obsolescence risk.

Partnership Structure: Private or Public

The size and scope of limited partnerships vary considerably. For example, three friends might establish a limited partnership to buy a six-unit apartment building. In contrast, large partnerships involving thousands of investors and tens of millions of dollars are frequently formed to acquire producing oil and gas properties. There are two distinct types of limited partnerships: private and public. State and federal laws regulate offerings of all limited-partnership programs.

Private Partnerships

private partnership
a limited partnership that has a limited number of investors and is not registered with a public agency.

The **private partnership** has a limited number of investors and is not registered with a public agency such as a state securities commission or the SEC. Private limited partnerships are often assembled by a local real estate broker or an attorney. Often the investors know one another personally. Potential investors in the partnership are commonly given a *private placement memorandum*, a document that describes the property to be purchased, management fees, and other financial details. It usually also contains the limited-partnership agreement. Private partnerships tend to *take more risks* than public partnerships.

Private partnerships have several advantages. Because they do not have to be registered with a public agency, they usually carry lower transaction and legal costs than public partnerships. It also may be easier to obtain firsthand knowledge about the general partner in a private partnership. A good source of information on a general partner is other limited partners who have previously invested in his or her partnerships.

Public Partnerships

public partnership
a limited partnership that is registered with the appropriate state and/or federal regulators and usually has 35 or more investors.

The **public partnership** is registered with the appropriate state and/or federal regulators and usually has 35 or more investors. Interstate sales of limited-partnership interests must comply with federal as well as state laws. Offerings sold only within one state, however, need comply only with that state's laws. Public partnerships are sold by stockbrokers and other licensed securities dealers, and transaction costs are high. The brokerage commission on a typical oil and gas limited partnership is about 8%.

A potential buyer of a public limited partnership must be given a *prospectus,* a detailed statement that contains the financial data, management information, and transaction and legal costs associated with the offering. Most public partnerships are large in scope and usually contain over $5 million in assets. An investor in a public partnership may find that his or her shares represent an investment in a *diversified* portfolio of real estate or energy resource properties. Geographic diversity may be easier to obtain by investing in public partnerships.

Essential Investment Considerations

Limited-partnership promoters sometimes concoct unbelievable schemes for earning significant returns. They advertise that you can earn a sizable return on an investment as a result of the general partner's unique situation or expertise. Although this is possible, it is certainly not without risk, and generally the actual amount earned, if any, is far less than the amount suggested. For each potential investment in a limited partnership, you should review its leverage, its risk and return, and its investment suitability.

Leverage

In limited partnerships the presence of *leverage* indicates that the underlying business activity utilizes borrowed funds—perhaps in substantial amounts. An equipment-leasing venture, for example, might involve 80% to 90% of debt financing. This means your initial investment dollar buys more assets than would be the case were leverage not used. For example, suppose a limited partnership raises $100,000, borrows $900,000 for which the partners have shared liability, and then buys computer equipment for $1,000,000 to lease to a business over a 10-year period. Suppose further that the partnership earns $50,000 in the first year. If you own 5% of the partnership (you invested $5,000, i.e., 0.05 × $100,000), in the first year your earnings are $2,500. Your total first-year recovery is therefore equal to 50% of your total investment. Had the partnership not used leverage, you would have had to invest $50,000 to own 5% (0.05 × $1,000,000) of the investment. In such a case, your return would have been only 5% on your initial investment ($2,500 ÷ $50,000). Clearly, the use of leverage enhances your return.

However, you must also bear in mind that you are legally liable for your share of the loan, which is $45,000 (0.05 × $900,000). If the loan is with some type of captive finance company that is willing to forgive the debt if the partnership goes under, or if you do not have legal liability for your portion of the debt, the whole deal may (except in the case of real estate partnerships) be considered a sham by the Internal Revenue Service. In such a case, you could be subject to tax penalties. Remember that leverage can increase returns but almost always carries more risk.

Risk and Return

Evaluating the risk and return of a limited-partnership investment depends on the property involved. There are two general factors to consider: First, you should carefully *study the general partner.* Again, read the private placement memorandum or prospectus carefully. Find out how much the promoters (general partner and associates) are taking off the top in commissions, legal fees, and management fees. The more they take, the less of your money is invested in the project and the less likely it is that you will receive a high return.

A second factor to recognize is that *most limited partnerships are not very liquid.* In fact, depending on state law, they may not be salable prior to their disbandment. In other words, your interest may be difficult or impossible to resell.

Two vehicles are available for enhancing the marketability of LP shares. One is the *master limited partnership (MLP),* which is a limited partnership that is publicly traded on a major stock exchange. The stock represents a marketable claim on a group of limited-partnership interests that are acquired by the MLP. Although MLPs were engineered to improve partnership liquidity, subsequent tax-law changes have greatly diminished their attractiveness. The second outlet for LP shares is the emerging secondary market for them. For better-known public limited partnerships, established market makers provide quotes. Private deals and smaller public deals remain quite illiquid, however. Of course, sizable commissions must be paid on these LP transactions, and the general lack of LP liquidity tends to increase the risk associated with investment in them.

Investment Suitability

As you have probably concluded by now, limited partnerships tend to be risky and illiquid, and thus they are usually not suitable for conservative investors primarily interested in the preservation of capital. A private placement memorandum or prospectus often contains a statement limiting purchase to investors with a minimum net worth (e.g., $100,000) and in the 31, 36, or 39.6% federal tax bracket. This rule excluding certain types of investors is called a **suitability rule.** Its purpose is to allow only investors who can bear a high amount of risk to participate. Additionally, there may be a statement in the prospectus that says, "The securities offered herewith are very high-risk." Believe this statement: *If the regulatory authorities require it, it must be a high-risk investment.* Suitability rules vary, depending on applicable state and federal laws. The rules are intended to prevent the sale of high-risk projects to investors who cannot sustain the loss financially. Suitability rules are also usually fairly rigid for public limited partnerships (offerings registered with securities regulators).

suitability rule
a rule excluding investors who cannot bear a high amount of risk from buying limited-partnership interests.

CONCEPTS IN REVIEW

15.20 How does a *limited partnership (LP)* differ from a *corporation* and a *general partnership?* What are the functions of the general and limited partners? How did the Tax Reform Act of 1986 affect the popularity of LPs as tax shelters?

15.21 In what two ways can an investor earn a return from a limited partnership?

15.22 What are the popular forms of limited partnerships? Differentiate between *private partnerships* and *public partnerships.*

15.23 How does leverage affect the return and risk of a limited partnership? Why must *suitability rules* be applied to limited-partnership investors?

Summary

LG 1 **Understand what taxable income is and how to calculate it.** As taxable income increases, so do tax burdens imposed by federal tax law. Taxable income can be either ordinary income—active, portfolio, or passive—or capital gains. The tax rates applicable to capital gains realized on assets held for at least certain periods of time are lower than the rates applicable to a taxpayer's ordinary income. Taxable income is calculated first by finding gross income, which includes most forms of income; then subtracting certain adjustments to gross income, to get adjusted gross income; and finally subtracting standard (or itemized) deductions and exemptions. Federal income taxes are calculated on the taxable income. Taxes due are found by subtracting any eligible tax credits from the federal income tax.

LG 2 **Define tax avoidance and tax deferral and cite the characteristics of tax shelters.** Tax-avoidance strategies attempt to earn tax-favored income—income not subject to taxes. Tax-deferral strategies attempt to defer taxes from current periods to later periods. A tax shelter is an investment vehicle that earns a portion of its return by offering potential offsets to the investor's other taxable income.

LG 3 **Explain the basic strategies by which investors can earn tax-favored income.** Strategies for earning tax-favored income include excluding income from taxation, deferring tax liabilities to the next year, deferring tax liabilities to retirement through retirement programs, trading current income for capital gains, and tax swaps. Tax-favored income excluded from taxation includes tax-free municipal bond interest, Treasury and government agency issues (free of state and local income taxes), and the sale of a personal residence. Strategies that defer tax liabilities to the next year include a put hedge and selling a deep-in-the-money call option. Each strategy has relative advantages and disadvantages, depending on the assumed future movement of the stock's price.

Programs that defer tax liabilities to retirement include 401(k) plans, Keogh plans, and individual retirement arrangements (IRAs). The four types of IRAs are the traditional deductible IRA, the Roth IRA, the nondeductible IRA, and the Education IRA. Popular strategies that trade current income for capital gains include buying growth rather than income stocks, buying deep-discount bonds, and investing in income property. Tax swaps are a strategy that can be used to reduce or eliminate a tax liability without altering the basic portfolio.

LG 4 **Summarize the characteristics of deferred annuities and single-premium life insurance.** Because they pay relatively high market rates of interest and allow for tax-free reinvestment, deferred annuities have some appeal as a tax-deferral vehicle. Employees of certain institutions can purchase tax-sheltered annuities by making limited tax-free contributions from current income. Annuity payouts can be either fixed or variable; the payouts on variable annuities depend on the insurer's actual investment performance.

Deferred annuities are relatively low-risk vehicles that may not produce earnings on a par with inflation rates. The single-premium life insurance policy, in the past a popular alternative to the deferred annuity, has diminished in popularity because of tax-law changes that virtually eliminated the ability to use policy loans to make tax-free withdrawals.

LG 5 **Describe the tax status of limited partnerships and explain how they work.** A limited partnership is an organizational form that allows an individual to invest with limited liability, receive the benefit of professional management, and apply the resulting profit or loss (subject to limits) when calculating his or her tax liability. The general partner actively runs the business, whereas the limited partners supply the capital and take a passive role in the venture. The return from a limited partnership comes from either cash flow or price appreciation.

LG 6

Discuss popular forms of limited partnerships, partnership structure, and the essential investment considerations of these vehicles. Limited partnerships have been formed to acquire many different kinds of assets; the most common are real estate, energy resources, and equipment for leasing purposes. Limited partnerships can be structured as private or public partnerships. Leverage can increase the potential earnings as well as the risk in a limited partnership. Investors should study the limited partnership's private placement memorandum or prospectus to determine the investment's risk–return characteristics and its suitability. Often investors themselves must meet certain suitability rules prior to investing in a limited partnership.

Discussion Questions

LG 1

Q15.1. Obtain a copy of the most recent year's Form 1040 (*U.S. Individual Income Tax Return*), along with Schedules A (*Itemized Deductions*), B (*Interest and Dividend Income*), and D (*Capital Gains and Losses*) and instructions for preparing the return. Use your actual (or forecast) data to prepare your return for the most recent year. If you earn no or very low income, use data provided by a family member.

a. Discuss the exemptions claimed and their effect on taxable income.
b. Study Schedule A and discuss how each of the following are treated:
   (1) Medical and dental expenses
   (2) Mortgage interest
   (3) Job expenses
c. Discuss the key factor affecting whether to itemize deductions or take the standard deduction.
d. Describe how the total tax was calculated. What top tax bracket applied?
e. What, if any, recommendation would you give with regard to actions that might be advantageous from a tax standpoint?

LG 3

Q15.2. Assume you have a sizable gain on 200 shares of stock that you bought 2 years ago for $22 per share and that is now (December 15) selling for $50 per share. Given a just-announced tax rate cut, effective next calendar year, you want to delay realizing the gain until next year, but you are concerned that the stock's price might decline in the interim. To defer the tax liability to next year, you are considering either using a put hedge, or selling deep-in-the-money call options.

a. Contact a stockbroker and obtain the approximate cost of implementing each of these strategies.
b. Compare and contrast the brokerage costs associated with these strategies. Which strategy is cheaper in terms of these costs?
c. What, if any, impact should the brokerage costs have on the selection of the better strategy? (Be sure to measure these costs on a *per-share* basis.)
d. For the cheaper strategy, by approximately how much will the brokerage costs reduce the unrealized gain on the stock?

LG 3

Q15.3. Imagine that, given your current age and marital status, you have decided to make the maximum contribution to an individual retirement arrangement (IRA) each year from now until age 65. (Assume that the current maximum contribution rate will remain unchanged over this period.) You expect to earn a 10% annual rate of return on IRA investments and are subject to a 30% tax rate.

a. Determine how much you will have in the IRA account at age 65 if you can earn 10% on IRA investments and IRA contributions are:
   (1) Deductible
   (2) Nondeductible
b. How much better off would you be as a result of having a traditional deductible IRA rather than a nondeductible IRA? What, if any, tax benefit does a nondeductible IRA offer?

c. Describe and justify the overall investment strategy you would employ on your IRA investments.
d. What specific types of vehicles would you include in your IRA investment portfolio? Justify your choices.
e. Compare and contrast the traditional deductible IRA to (1) a 401(k) plan and (2) a Keogh plan. If you could contribute to only one of these plans, which would be preferable? Why?

LG 4 Q15.4. Obtain from a licensed salesperson or stockbroker a prospectus and any other literature available on a popular deferred annuity. Analyze the terms, and answer the following questions.

a. What is the *current interest rate?* How does it compare to T-bill rates? To AAA bond yields?
b. What is the *minimum guaranteed interest rate* on contributions? How does it compare to T-bill rates? To AAA bond yields?
c. What, if any, *tax benefit* does it offer the investor?
d. What *payout options* does it offer? Is it a *fixed* or *variable annuity?* Which payout option do you find most appealing?
e. What sales charges and administrative fees are levied on this annuity? How does it compare to other annuities?
f. What is the rating of the financial strength of the insurer given in *Best's Insurance Reports?*
g. What are the pros and cons of purchasing this annuity?

LG 6 Q15.5. Ask a stockbroker for the prospectus of a currently popular public limited-partnership real estate investment. Carefully analyze the prospectus, and answer the following questions.

a. What are the *suitability rules* for investing in this partnership?
b. What is the partnership's investment objective? Does it seem achievable?
c. Is this partnership a *blind pool* or a *single-property syndicate*? In general, what kind of properties are being acquired?
d. What is the background of the general partner? Does it seem appropriate/acceptable?
e. Is *leverage* being used by the partnership? What effect does it have on risk?
f. What are the potential risk–return factors of this investment? What other important factors should be considered when evaluating this partnership? Would you recommend investing in this partnership?

Problems

LG 1 P15.1. Using Table 15.1, calculate Ed Robinson's income tax due on his $35,000 taxable income, assuming that he files as a single taxpayer. After you make the calculation, explain to Ed what his marginal tax rate is and why it is important in making investment decisions.

LG 1 P15.2. During the year just ended, Jean Sanchez's taxable income of $48,000 was twice as large as her younger sister Rachel's taxable income of $24,000. Use the tax rate schedule in Table 15.1 to answer the following questions with regard to the Sanchez sisters, who are both single.

a. Calculate each sister's tax liability.
b. Determine (1) the marginal tax rate and (2) the average tax rate for each sister.

c. Do your findings in part (b) demonstrate the progressive nature of income taxes? Explain.

LG 1

P15.3. Sheila and Jim Mendez reported the following income tax items in 1999:

Salaries and wages	$46,000
Interest on bonds	1,100*
Dividends (jointly owned stocks)	1,000
Capital gains on securities (all held for more than 18 months)	1,500
Deductible IRA contribution	2,000
Itemized deductions	12,000

*$400 of this total was received from tax-free municipal bonds.

If Sheila and Jim claim three dependents and file a joint return for 1999, calculate their income tax due. (Use Table 15.1 and assume an exemption of $2,650 for each qualifying dependent.)

LG 1

P15.4. The Akais just finished calculating their taxable income for their 1999 joint federal income tax return. It totaled $68,750 and showed no tax credits. Just prior to filing their return, the Akais realized that they had treated a $2,000 outlay as an itemized deduction, rather than correctly treating it as a $2,000 tax credit.

a. Use the tax rate schedule in Table 15.1 to calculate the Akais' tax liability and tax due on the basis of their original $68,750 estimate of taxable income.
b. How much taxable income will the Akais have if they correctly treat the $2,000 as a tax credit rather than a tax deduction?
c. Use your finding in part (a) to calculate the Akais' tax liability and tax due after converting the $2,000 tax deduction to a tax credit.
d. Compare and contrast your findings in parts (a) and (c). Which would you prefer, a tax deduction or an equal-dollar-amount tax credit? Why?

LG 3

P15.5. Shawn Healy bought 300 shares of Apple Computer common stock at $32 a share. Fifteen months later, in December, Apple was up to $47 a share and Shawn was considering selling her shares, because she believed Apple's price could drop as low as $42 within the next several months. What advice would you offer Shawn for locking in the gain and deferring the tax to the following year? Explain.

LG 3

P15.6. Karen Jones purchased 200 shares of Mex Inc. common stock for $10 per share exactly 2 years ago, in December 1997. Today, December 15, 1999, the stock is selling for $18 per share. Because Karen strongly believes that the stock is fully valued in the market, she wishes to sell it and invest the proceeds in the stock of an attractive emerging company. Karen, who is in the 28% tax bracket, realizes that if she sells the stock prior to year-end, the capital gain of $1,600 [200 shares × ($18 sale price − $10 purchase price)] will result in taxes for 1999 of $320 (.20 × $1,600). Because Karen would like to lock in her $1,600 profit but defer the tax on it until 2000, she plans to investigate the strategies available for accomplishing this objective.

a. If Karen can purchase two put options on Mex Inc.'s stock at a contractual sale price of $18 for a total cost of $180 ($90 per 100-share option), what will her after-tax position be if the stock price declines to $16 per share? Will Karen be able to benefit from any future increases in Mex Inc.'s stock price using this put hedge strategy?
b. If Karen can sell two call options on Mex Inc.'s stock with a $16 contractual buy price and 6-month maturity for $480 ($240 per 100-share option)

when the stock is selling for $18 per share, what will her after-tax position be if the stock price declines to $16 per share? Will Karen be able to benefit from any future increases in Mex Inc.'s stock price using this deep-in-the-money call option strategy? Is the price of $18 fully locked in using this strategy?

c. Use your findings in parts (a) and (b) to compare and contrast the two strategies. Then recommend a strategy to Karen, assuming the stock price *does* drop below the current price.

LG 3

P15.7. Juan Gonzalez, a single person working for Harla, Inc., earned $48,000 in 1999 and is considering contributing $7,000 to the firm's 401(k) plan. If Juan is in the 28% tax bracket, what will his taxable income be? How much tax savings will result, and how much will it cost Juan, on an after-tax basis, to make the $7,000 contribution?

Case Problem 15.1 *Tax Planning for the Wilsons*

LG 1 LG 3

Hal and Terri Wilson had most of their funds invested in common stock in the spring of 1998. The Wilsons didn't really do very much investment planning, and they had practically no background or understanding of how income taxes might affect their investment decisions. Their holdings consisted exclusively of common stocks, selected primarily on the advice of their stockbroker, Sid Nichols. Despite a relatively lackluster market, they did experience some nice capital gains, even though several of their holdings showed losses from their original purchase prices. A summary of their holdings on December 20, 1998, follows.

Stock	Date Purchased	Original Cost	Current Market Value
Consolidated Power and Light	2/10/96	$10,000	$16,000
Cargon Industries	7/7/98	3,000	8,000
PYT Corporation	6/29/98	7,000	6,000
Amalgamated Iron & Steel	8/9/97	8,000	5,000
Jones Building Supplies	3/6/94	4,500	4,700

Hal feels this might be a good time to revise their portfolio. He favors selling all their holdings and reinvesting the funds in several growth-oriented mutual funds and perhaps several real estate limited partnerships. Terri agrees that their portfolio could use some revision, but she is reluctant to sell everything. For one thing, she is concerned that federal income taxes might take a sizable share of their profits. In addition, she strongly believes Amalgamated Iron & Steel will make a significant recovery, as will all steel stocks, in 1999.

After some discussion, the Wilsons decided to consult their friend, Elaine Byer, who was a CPA for a major public accounting firm. Byer indicated that she was not an expert in the investment field and therefore couldn't tell the Wilsons which securities to buy or sell from that perspective. From a tax point of view, however, she did not recommend selling everything in the 1998 tax year. Instead, she said that Consolidated Power and Light, PYT Corporation, Amalgamated Iron & Steel, and Jones Building Supplies should be sold in December 1998 but that Cargon Industries should be carried into 1999 and sold then—if that was what the Wilsons wanted to do.

Hal and Terri were grateful for Byer's advice, but they had two major concerns. First, they were concerned about waiting to sell Cargon Industries, because it had showed such a sizable gain and they were afraid its price might decline sharply in a stock market sell-off. Second, they were reluctant to sell Amalgamated Iron & Steel despite the benefit of its tax loss, because they wanted to remain invested in the steel industry over the long run. As a final step, they contacted Nichols, their stockbroker, who agreed with Byer's advice; he said not to worry about the Cargon situation. The stock was selling at $80 a share, and he would sell a deep-in-the-money call option on Cargon, which would enable them to deliver the shares sometime early in 1999. He also explained that they could use a tax swap to get the tax benefit of the loss on Amalgamated Iron & Steel while staying invested in the steel industry. He suggested United States Iron as a swap candidate, because it was selling for about the same price as Amalgamated.

QUESTIONS

a. Assuming the Wilsons are in the 28% ordinary income tax bracket, calculate the resulting federal income tax (1) if they sold all their securities in 1998 at their current market values, and (2) if they sold Consolidated Power and Light, PYT Corporation, Amalgamated Iron & Steel, and Jones Building Supplies at their respective market values in 1998 and then sold Cargon Industries at its current market value on January 2, 1999. What do you conclude from your calculations?

b. As noted, Nichols suggested selling a deep-in-the-money call option on Cargon. Explain his reasoning about the future price of this stock.

c. Suppose you thought Cargon had a good possibility for further price increases in 1999, but you were equally concerned that its price could fall sharply. Would you then agree with the strategy Nichols recommended, or would you prefer a different strategy? Explain your answer.

d. Discuss the tax swap suggested by Nichols. Does this strategy allow the Wilsons to minimize taxes while retaining their position in the steel industry? Explain.

e. What overall strategies would you recommend to the Wilsons, given their investment objectives and tax status? Explain.

Case Problem 15.2 *Do Oil and Fred Cranston Mix?*

LG 5 LG 6

Fred Cranston, age 36, is the West Coast marketing manager and vice-president of a major auto parts supply firm. His salary reflects his success in his job: $90,000 per year. Additionally, his firm provides him with a car, an excellent pension and profit-sharing plan, superior life and medical insurance coverage, and company stock options. Fred owns his home, which is located in the exclusive Marin County, California, area.

In addition to Fred's house and his pension and profit-sharing plans, he has a stock portfolio worth about $75,000, a tax-free municipal bond portfolio valued at $150,000, and about $100,000 in a highly liquid money market mutual fund. Fred would like to make more risky investments to increase his returns. He is considering taking $50,000 out of the money market mutual fund and investing in some limited partnerships. His broker, Marie Bell, has proposed that he invest $50,000 among five oil and gas limited partnerships. Marie's specific recommendation is to buy two developmental and three income programs, each for $10,000. She explained to Fred that this $50,000 investment could potentially increase his income by $20,000 per year. Marie has also pointed out that if the expected rise in oil prices occurs, Fred could expect to receive even larger cash returns in future years. Fred meets the suitability rules required for such investments as prescribed by the securities commission of California. Being a relatively conservative individual, he is trying to assess the reasonableness of his broker's recommendations.

QUESTIONS

a. What do you think of Marie Bell's investment recommendations for Fred? Are developmental programs too risky? Should Fred buy five different oil and gas programs, or should he invest the entire $50,000 in one program? Explain.

b. How would you describe to Fred the legal structure of a limited partnership? What should Fred know about the general partner in each of these programs?

c. In general, does investment in oil and gas development and income programs make sense to you? Why or why not?

d. What other forms of limited partnerships might you suggest that Fred consider? Discuss the leverage and risk–return tradeoffs involved in them.

Home Page Exercises

http://hepg.aw.com **Keyword: Invest**

Investors love to hate taxes. When it comes to investments, there is strong justification for wanting to avoid or defer tax obligations. Money paid in taxes is not available to earn a return and increase an investor's wealth. The financial services community is happy to provide information about financial assets that offer tax deferral. You can read about 401(k) and IRA plans at a large number of sites, although most offer the same information. When it comes to limited partnerships and more complicated tax-deferral strategies, the availability of Web sites drops off the chart. These latter alternatives require so much specialized training and knowledge that offering general information about them does not justify the time and expense of maintaining a detailed Web site.

Web Address	*Primary Investment Focus*
www.irs.ustrea.gov/prod/cover.html	The home page for the Internal Revenue Service
www.401k.com/401k/	Fidelity Investments information on 401(k) plans
www.investorguide.com/Retirement.htm#IRAs	Provides multiple links to information sources about 401(k) and IRA plans, including links to interactive retirement planning calculators

W15.1. Bart Ierland expects to invest $2,000 annually in a deductible IRA and is trying to decide whether a Roth or a traditional IRA is best for him. Bart is 35 years old and is currently in the 31% marginal tax bracket, but he expects to be in the 15% tax bracket when he retires. His risk tolerance allows him to accept a level of risk that should provide an average annual return of 10% during his working years. When he retires at age 65 he will reduce his risk and cut his expected return to 6%. Bart has a life expectancy of 20 years after retirement. Which alternative will maximize Bart's retirement income and by how much? Bart wants to have the same question answered for his twin brother, Burt. The same information applies to both Burt and Bart, except that Burt is currently earning a higher income and has a 39.6% marginal tax rate. Use the Roth-versus-traditional calculator at the following Web address to derive the figures needed to answer this question.

www.etrade.com/advantage/ira/calc/contri_index.html

W15.2. Problem W15.1 investigated the choice between a Roth and a traditional IRA, given differences in current marginal tax rates. One element that significantly affects the amount of money available during retirement is whether the contribution to the traditional IRA is deductible. Repeat your calculations for Problem W15.1, changing the deductibility of the traditional IRA from 100% to 75%, 50%, and 0%. What changes occurred in the results?

www.etrade.com/advantage/ira/calc/contri_index.html

Part Six

Investment Administration

Chapter 16
Portfolio Construction

Chapter 17
Portfolio Management and Control

CHAPTER 16 PORTFOLIO CONSTRUCTION

LEARNING GOALS

After studying this chapter, you should be able to:

LG 1 Understand the objectives of portfolio management and the procedures used to calculate the return and standard deviation of a portfolio.

LG 2 Discuss the concepts of correlation and diversification, their impact on portfolio risk and return, and the effectiveness, methods, and benefits of international diversification.

LG 3 Review the two basic approaches to portfolio management—traditional and modern—and reconcile them.

LG 4 Describe the role of investor characteristics and objectives and of portfolio objectives and policies in constructing an investment portfolio.

LG 5 Summarize why and how investors use an asset allocation scheme to construct an investment portfolio.

LG 6 Relate investor objectives to the asset allocations and risk–return profiles reflected in various types of portfolios.

Travelers Group Inc.

In early 1998, the largest merger in corporate history, between Citicorp and Travelers Group Inc., created the world's largest financial-services concern. Like most mergers, this one proposed to combine two companies that operate in the same business. Both Citicorp and Travelers have extensive money management divisions, where professional investment analysts and portfolio managers invest their clients' money. Travelers' asset management division is Salomon Smith Barney Asset Management, itself the product of a merger of Salomon Bros. and Smith Barney in 1997.

Like other money management firms, Salomon Smith Barney Asset Management hires college graduates and MBAs who begin their careers as investment analysts. After a few years of experience analyzing an industry or a group of stocks or bonds, analysts become assistant portfolio managers, working as part of a team. The principles they use to assemble and manage portfolios are based on complex mathematical concepts, many of which are beyond the scope of an introductory investments textbook. But the research that professional portfolio managers do and the basic strategies they employ can be put to use by individual investors in planning their own portfolios. In this chapter, we will study the basics of portfolio construction.

Principles of Portfolio Planning

LG 1 LG 2

growth-oriented portfolio
a portfolio whose primary goal is long-term price appreciation.

income-oriented portfolio
a portfolio that stresses current dividend and interest returns.

Investors benefit from holding portfolios of investments rather than single investment vehicles. *Without sacrificing returns, investors who hold portfolios can reduce risk, often to a level below that of any of the investments held in isolation.* In other words, when it comes to risk, $1 + 1 < 1$.

As defined in Chapter 1, a *portfolio* is a collection of investment vehicles assembled to meet a common investment goal. Of course, different investors will have different objectives for their portfolios: The primary goal of a **growth-oriented portfolio** is long-term price appreciation. An **income-oriented portfolio** stresses current dividend and interest returns.

Portfolio Objectives

Setting portfolio objectives involves definite tradeoffs: tradeoffs between risk and return, between potential price appreciation and current income, and between varying risk levels in the portfolio. These will depend on your income tax bracket, current income needs, and ability to bear risk. The key point is that the portfolio objectives must be established *before* beginning to invest.

efficient portfolio
a portfolio that provides the highest return for a given level of risk or that has the lowest risk for a given level of return.

The ultimate goal of an investor is an **efficient portfolio,** one that provides the highest return for a given level of risk or that has the lowest risk for a given level of return. Thus, when confronted with the choice between two equally risky investments offering different returns, the investor would be expected to choose the alternative with the higher return. Likewise, given two investment vehicles offering the same returns but differing in risk, the *risk-averse* investor would prefer the vehicle with the lower risk. In trying to create an efficient portfolio, you should be able to put together the best portfolio possible given your disposition toward risk and the alternative investment vehicles available. Such portfolios aren't necessarily obvious: Investors usually must search out investment alternatives to get the best combinations of risk and return.

Portfolio Return and Standard Deviation

The *return on a portfolio* is calculated as a weighted average of returns on the assets (investment vehicles) from which it is formed. The portfolio return, r_p, can be found by using Equation 16.1:

Equation 16.1

$$\text{Return on portfolio} = \left(\begin{array}{c}\text{proportion of}\\ \text{portfolio's total}\\ \text{dollar value}\\ \text{represented by}\\ \text{asset 1}\end{array} \times \begin{array}{c}\text{return}\\ \text{on asset}\\ 1\end{array}\right) + \left(\begin{array}{c}\text{proportion of}\\ \text{portfolio's total}\\ \text{dollar value}\\ \text{represented by}\\ \text{asset 2}\end{array} \times \begin{array}{c}\text{return}\\ \text{on asset}\\ 2\end{array}\right) + \cdots + \left(\begin{array}{c}\text{proportion of}\\ \text{portfolio's total}\\ \text{dollar value}\\ \text{represented by}\\ \text{asset } n\end{array} \times \begin{array}{c}\text{return}\\ \text{on asset}\\ n\end{array}\right) = \sum_{j=1}^{n}\left(\begin{array}{c}\text{proportion of}\\ \text{portfolio's total}\\ \text{dollar value}\\ \text{represented by}\\ \text{asset } j\end{array} \times \begin{array}{c}\text{return}\\ \text{on asset}\\ j\end{array}\right)$$

Equation 16.1a

$$r_p = (w_1 \times r_1) + (w_2 \times r_2) + \cdots + (w_n \times r_n) = \sum_{j=1}^{n} (w_j \times r_j)$$

Of course, $\sum_{j=1}^{n} w_j = 1$, which means that 100% of the portfolio's assets must be included in this computation.

The *standard deviation of a portfolio's returns* is found by applying Equation 4.11, the formula we used in Chapter 4 to find the standard deviation of a single asset. Assume that we wish to determine the return and standard deviation of returns for Portfolio XY, created by combining equal portions (50%) of assets X and Y. The expected returns of assets X and Y for each of the next 5 years (2000–2004) are given in columns 1 and 2, respectively, in part A of Table 16.1. In columns 3 and 4, the weights of 50% for both assets X and Y, along with their respective returns from columns 1 and 2, are substituted into Equation 16.1 to get an expected portfolio return of 12% for each year, 2000 to 2004. Furthermore, as shown in part B of Table 16.1, the average expected portfolio return, $\bar{r}_p$, over the 5-year period is also 12%. Substituting into Equation 4.11, Portfolio XY's standard deviation, s_p, of 0% is calculated in part C of Table 16.1. This value should not be surprising, because the expected return each year is the same, 12%. Therefore, no variability is exhibited in the expected returns from year to year shown in column 4 of part A of the table.

TABLE 16.1 Expected Return, Average Return, and Standard Deviation of Returns for Portfolio XY

A. Expected Portfolio Returns

	(1)	(2)	(3)	(4)
	Expected Return			Expected Portfolio
Year	Asset X	Asset Y	Portfolio Return Calculation*	Return, r_p
2000	8%	16%	(.50 × 8%) + (.50 × 16%) =	12%
2001	10	14	(.50 × 10) + (.50 × 14) =	12
2002	12	12	(.50 × 12) + (.50 × 12) =	12
2003	14	10	(.50 × 14) + (.50 × 10) =	12
2004	16	8	(.50 × 16) + (.50 × 8) =	12

B. Average Expected Portfolio Return, 2000–2004

$$\bar{r}_p = \frac{12\% + 12\% + 12\% + 12\% + 12\%}{5} = \frac{60\%}{5} = \underline{\underline{12\%}}$$

C. Standard Deviation of Expected Portfolio Returns**

$$s_p = \sqrt{\frac{(12\% - 12\%)^2 + (12\% - 12\%)^2 + (12\% - 12\%)^2 + (12\% - 12\%)^2 + (12\% - 12\%)^2}{5 - 1}}$$

$$= \sqrt{\frac{0\% + 0\% + 0\% + 0\% + 0\%}{4}} = \sqrt{\frac{0\%}{4}} = \underline{\underline{0\%}}$$

*Using Equation 16.1.

**Using Equation 4.11 presented in Chapter 4.

Correlation and Diversification

As noted in Chapter 1, *diversification* involves the inclusion of a number of different investment vehicles in a portfolio. It is an important aspect of creating an efficient portfolio. Underlying the intuitive appeal of diversification is the statistical concept of *correlation*. For effective portfolio planning, you need to understand the concepts of correlation and diversification and their relationship to a portfolio's total risk and return. Here we take a closer look at these key concepts and their interrelationships.

Correlation

correlation
a statistical measure of the relationship, if any, between series of numbers representing data of any kind.

positively correlated
describes two series that move in the same direction.

negatively correlated
describes two series that move in opposite directions.

correlation coefficient
a measure of the degree of correlation between two series.

perfectly positively correlated
describes two positively correlated series that have a correlation coefficient of +1.

perfectly negatively correlated
describes two negatively correlated series that have a correlation coefficient of −1.

Correlation is a statistical measure of the relationship, if any, between series of numbers representing data of any kind. If two series move in the same direction, they are **positively correlated.** If the series move in opposite directions, they are **negatively correlated.**

The degree of correlation—whether positive or negative—is measured by the **correlation coefficient.** The coefficient ranges from +1 for **perfectly positively correlated** series to −1 for **perfectly negatively correlated** series. These two extremes are depicted in Figure 16.1 for Series M and N. The perfectly positively correlated series move exactly together, whereas the perfectly negatively correlated series move in exactly opposite directions.

Diversification

To reduce overall risk in a portfolio, it is best to combine assets that have a negative (or a low-positive) correlation. Combining negatively correlated assets can reduce the overall variability of returns, *s*, or risk. Figure 16.2 shows that a portfolio containing the negatively correlated assets F and G, both having the same average expected return, $\bar{r}$, also has the same return, $\bar{r}$, but has less risk (variability) than either of the individual assets. Even if assets are not negatively correlated, the lower the positive correlation between them, the lower the resulting risk.

uncorrelated
describes two series that lack any relationship or interaction and therefore have a correlation coefficient close to zero.

Some assets are **uncorrelated:** They are completely unrelated, with no interaction between their returns. Combining uncorrelated assets can reduce risk—not as effectively as combining negatively correlated assets, but more effectively than combining positively correlated assets. The correlation coefficient for uncorrelated assets is close to zero and acts as the midpoint between perfect positive and perfect negative correlation.

FIGURE 16.1
The Correlation Between Series M and N

The perfectly positively correlated series M and N in the graph on the left move exactly together. The perfectly negatively correlated series M and N in the graph on the right move in exactly opposite directions.

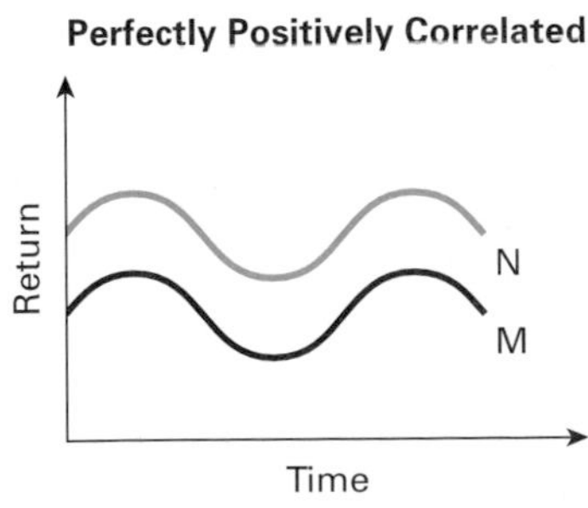

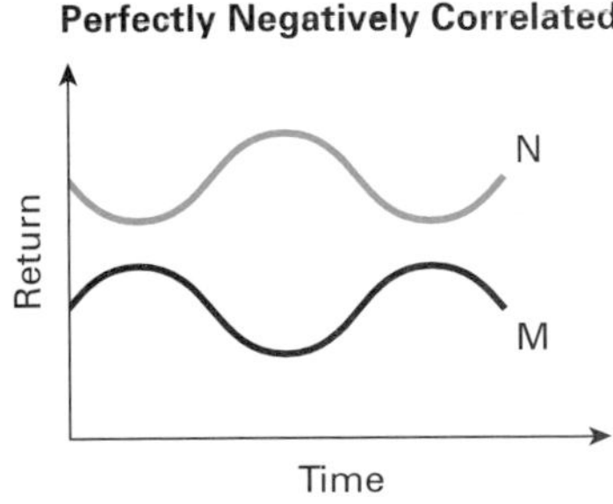

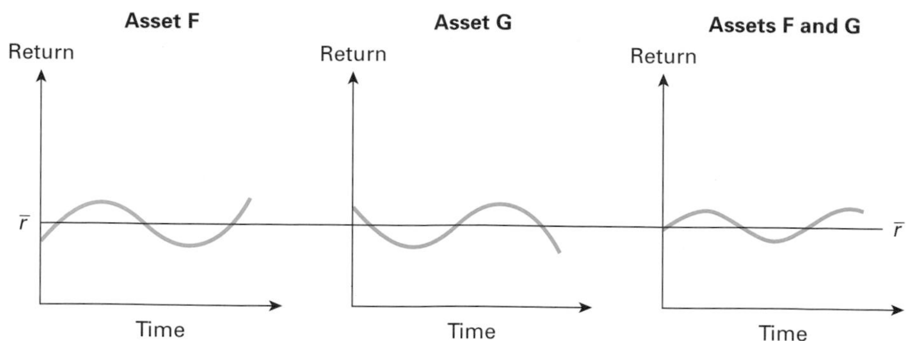

FIGURE 16.2
Combining Negatively Correlated Assets to Diversify Risk

The risks or variability of returns, resulting from combining negatively correlated assets F and G, both having the same expected return, $\bar{r}$, results in a portfolio (shown in the rightmost graph) with the same level of expected return but less risk.

Correlation is important to reducing risk, but it can do only so much. A portfolio of two assets that have perfectly positively correlated returns *cannot* reduce the portfolio's overall risk below the risk of the least risky asset. However, a portfolio combining two assets with less than perfectly positive correlation *can* reduce total risk to a level below that of either of the components, which in certain situations may be zero.

For example, assume you own the stock of a machine tool manufacturer that is very *cyclical,* having high earnings when the economy is expanding and low earnings during a recession. If you bought stock in another machine tool company, which would have earnings positively correlated with those of the stock you already own, the combined earnings would continue to be cyclical. As a result, risk would remain the same. As an alternative, however, you could buy stock in a sewing machine manufacturer, which is *countercyclical,* having low earnings during economic expansion and high earnings during recession (because consumers are more likely to make their own clothes and clothing repairs at such a time). Combining the machine tool stock and the sewing machine stock, which have negatively correlated earnings, should reduce risk: The low machine tool earnings during a recession would be balanced out by high sewing machine earnings, and vice versa.

A numeric example will provide a better understanding of the role of correlation in the diversification process. Table 16.2 presents the expected returns from three different assets—X, Y, and Z—over the next 5 years (2000–2004), along with their average returns and standard deviations. Each of the assets has an expected value of return of 12% and a standard deviation of 3.16%. The assets therefore have equal return and equal risk, although their return patterns are not necessarily identical. Comparing the return patterns of assets X and Y, we see that they are perfectly negatively correlated, because they move in exactly opposite directions over time. On the other hand, assets X and Z are perfectly positively correlated: They move in precisely the same direction. (Note that the returns for X and Z are identical, although it is not necessary for return streams to be identical in order for them to be perfectly positively correlated.)

Portfolio XY (shown in Table 16.2) is created by combining equal portions of assets X and Y—the perfectly negatively correlated assets. Calculation of portfolio XY's annual expected returns, average expected return, and the standard deviation of expected portfolio returns is demonstrated in Table 16.1. The risk of the portfolio created by this combination, as reflected in the standard deviation, is reduced to 0%, while its average return remains at 12%. Because both assets have the same average return, are combined in the

TABLE 16.2 Expected Returns, Average Returns, and Standard Deviations for Assets X, Y, and Z and Portfolios XY and XZ

	Assets			Portfolios	
				XY*	XZ**
Year	X	Y	Z	(50%X + 50%Y)	(50%X + 50%Z)
2000	8%	16%	8%	12%	8%
2001	10	14	10	12	10
2002	12	12	12	12	12
2003	14	10	14	12	14
2004	16	8	16	12	16
Statistics:					
Average return†	12%	12%	12%	12%	12%
Standard deviation‡	3.16%	3.16%	3.16%	0%	3.16%

*Portfolio XY illustrates *perfect negative correlation,* because these two return streams behave in completely opposite fashion over the 5-year period. The return values shown here were calculated in part A of Table 16.1.

**Portfolio XZ illustrates *perfect positive correlation,* because these two return streams behave identically over the 5-year period. These return values were calculated using the same method demonstrated for Portfolio XY in part A of Table 16.1.

†The average return for each asset is calculated as the arithmetic average found by dividing the sum of the returns for the years 2000–2004 by 5, the number of years considered.

‡Equation 4.11 was used to calculate the standard deviation. Calculation of the average return and standard deviation for portfolio XY is demonstrated in parts B and C, respectively, of Table 16.1. The portfolio standard deviation can be directly calculated from the standard deviation of the component assets using the following formula:

$$s_p = \sqrt{w_1^2 s_1^2 + w_2^2 s_2^2 + 2w_1 w_2 p_{1,2} s_1 s_2}$$

where w_1 and w_2 are the proportions of the component assets 1 and 2; s_1 and s_2 are the standard deviations of the component assets 1 and 2; and $p_{1,2}$ is the correlation coefficient between the returns of component assets 1 and 2.

optimum proportions (a 50–50 mix in this case), and are perfectly negatively correlated, the combination results in the complete elimination of risk. Whenever assets are perfectly negatively correlated, an optimum combination (similar to the 50–50 mix in the case of assets X and Y) exists for which the resulting standard deviation will equal 0.

Portfolio XZ (shown in Table 16.2) is created by combining equal portions of Assets X and Z—the perfectly positively correlated assets. The risk of this portfolio, reflected by its standard deviation, which remains at 3.16%, is unaffected by this combination, and the average return remains at 12%. Whenever perfectly positively correlated assets such as X and Z are combined, the standard deviation of the resulting portfolio cannot be reduced below that of the least risky asset; the maximum portfolio standard deviation will be that of the riskiest asset. Because assets X and Z have the same standard deviation (3.16%), the minimum and maximum standard deviations are both 3.16%, which is the only value that could be taken on by a combination of these assets.

Impact on Risk and Return

In general, the lower (less positive and more negative) the correlation between asset returns, the greater the potential diversification of risk. For each pair of assets, there is a combination that will result in the lowest risk (standard deviation) possible. *The amount of potential risk reduction for this combination depends on the degree of correlation of the two assets.* This concept is a bit difficult to grasp, because many potential combinations could be made, given the expected return for each of two assets, the standard deviation for each

INVESTOR FACT

THE ROARING NINETIES—It took nearly 75 years for the Dow Jones Industrial Average to get to 1000, which it reached on November 14, 1972, immediately following Richard Nixon's re-election to the U.S. presidency. It took the Dow another 15 years to hit 2000, which it did on January 8, 1987, the year of the stock market crash. Four years later, on April 17, 1991, stocks hit 3000, as the U.S. won the Persian Gulf War. Less than four years later, the Dow hit 4000, on February 23, 1995.

Since then the milestones have come fast and furious: The Dow crossed 5000 on November 21, 1995; 6000 on October 14, 1996; 7000 on February 13, 1997; 8000 on July 16, 1997; and 9000 on April 6, 1998. The big questions for investors now are these: How high can the market go, and how risky is the market, with price-earnings ratios at all-time highs?

asset, and the correlation coefficient. However, *only one combination* of the infinite number of possibilities will minimize risk.

Three possible correlations—perfect positive, uncorrelated, and perfect negative—illustrate the effect of correlation on the diversification of risk and return. Table 16.3 summarizes the impact of correlation on the range of return and risk for various two-asset portfolio combinations. The table shows that as we move from perfect positive correlation to uncorrelated assets to perfect negative correlation, the ability to reduce risk is improved. Note that in no case will creating portfolios of assets result in risk greater than that of the riskiest asset included in the portfolio. To demonstrate, assume that a firm has carefully calculated the average return, $\bar{r}$, and risk, s, for each of two assets—A and B—as summarized below:

Asset	Average Return, $\bar{r}$	Risk (Standard Deviation), s
A	6%	3%
B	8%	8%

From these data, we can see that asset A is clearly a lower-risk, lower-return asset than asset B.

To evaluate possible combinations, let's consider three possible correlations: perfect positive, uncorrelated, and perfect negative. The results of the analysis are shown in Figure 16.3. The ranges of return and risk exhibited are consistent with those noted in Table 16.3. In all cases, the return will range between the 6% return of A and the 8% return of B. The risk, on the other hand, ranges between the individual risks of A and B (from 3% to 8%) in the case of perfect positive correlation; from below 3% (the risk of A), but greater than 0%, to 8% (the risk of B) in the uncorrelated case; and between 0% and 8% (the risk of B) in the perfectly negatively correlated case. Note that *only in the case of perfect negative correlation can the risk be reduced to 0%*. As the correlation becomes less positive and more negative (moving from the top of the figure down), the ability to reduce risk improves. Keep in mind that the amount of risk reduction achieved also depends on the proportions in which the assets are combined. Although determining the risk-minimizing combination is beyond the scope of this discussion, you should know that it is an important issue in developing portfolios of assets.

TABLE 16.3 Correlation, Return, and Risk for Various Two-Asset Portfolio Combinations

Correlation Coefficient	Range of Return	Range of Risk
+1 (perfect positive)	Between returns of two assets held in isolation	Between risk of two assets held in isolation
0 (uncorrelated)	Between returns of two assets held in isolation	Between risk of most risky asset and less than risk of least risky asset, but greater than 0
−1 (perfect negative)	Between returns of two assets held in isolation	Between risk of most risky asset and 0

FIGURE 16.3 Range of Portfolio Return and Risk for Combinations of Assets A and B for Various Correlation Coefficients

The range of a portfolio's return (r_p) is between that of the lowest and highest component asset returns and is unaffected by the degree of asset correlation. Portfolio risk (s_p), on the other hand, can be reduced below the risk of the least risky asset as the asset correlation moves from perfectly positive to uncorrelated to perfectly negative, where it can be reduced to zero by combining assets in the proper proportion.

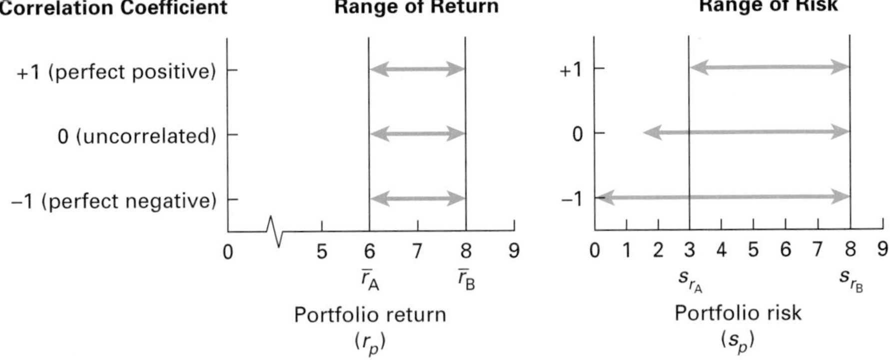

International Diversification

Diversification is clearly a primary consideration when constructing an investment portfolio for the risk-averse investor. Thus far, our focus and examples have been basically domestic. However, as noted in several earlier discussions in this book, numerous opportunities for international diversification are now available to investors. Here we consider three aspects of international diversification: effectiveness, methods, and benefits.

Effectiveness of International Diversification

Investing internationally obviously offers greater diversification than investing only domestically. That is true for U.S. investors. It is even truer for investors from countries with capital markets that offer much more limited diversification opportunities than are available in the United States.

However, does the diversification that international investment offers actually reduce risk, particularly the variability of rates of return? Two recent studies overwhelmingly support the argument that well-structured international diversification does indeed reduce the variability (risk) of a portfolio and increase the return on portfolios of comparable risk. One study looked at diversification across 12 European countries in 7 different industries between 1978 and 1992. It demonstrated that an investor could actually reduce the risk of a portfolio much more by diversifying internationally *in the same industry* than by diversifying across industries within one country. If the investor diversified both across countries and across industries, the opportunities for risk reduction would be even greater.

Another study examined the risk–return performance between January 1984 and November 1994 of diversified stock portfolios: the S&P 500 in the United States and Morgan Stanley's Europe/Australia/Far East (EAFE) Index. It found that a 100% EAFE portfolio offered a much greater return than a

100% S&P 500 portfolio did—but at much greater risk. However, by creating a portfolio composed of various combinations of the two indexes, an investor would have realized both lower risk and a higher return than for the 100% S&P 500 portfolio, and less risk and a moderately lower return than for the 100% EAFE portfolio. For the U.S. investor, a portfolio consisting of 70% S&P 500 coupled with 30% EAFE would have reduced risk by about 5% and increased return by about 7% (from around 14% to more than 15%). Or, for the same degree of risk, an investor could have increased return by about 18% (from around 14% to more than 16.5%).

Methods of International Diversification

In earlier chapters we examined a wide range of alternatives for international portfolio diversification. Investments in bond and other debt instruments can be made abroad in U.S. dollars in the Euromarket or in foreign currencies—either directly or via foreign mutual funds. Foreign currency investment, however, brings the risk (and potential benefit) of changing currency exchange rates. This risk can be hedged using various contracts, most commonly currency forwards, futures, and options.

Investing abroad, even if there is little or no currency exchange risk, is generally less convenient, more expensive, and riskier than investing domestically. When making direct investments abroad, you must know what you're doing: You should have a clear idea of the benefits being sought and should have the time to monitor foreign markets.

International diversification can also be achieved domestically in the United States. Several hundred foreign companies list and sell their stocks on U.S. exchanges or over the counter; most of them are Canadian companies. Also, many foreign issuers, both corporate and government, sell their bonds (called *Yankee bonds*) in the United States. The stocks of about 400 foreign companies, from about 30 countries, trade in the United States in the form of American Depositary Receipts. Finally, country, global, and other international mutual funds (such as the Fidelity Japan Fund and the Prudential Global Fund) provide investors with a broad range of foreign investment opportunities. These domestic alternatives offer the advantages of convenience and low cost, often with less risk than investments made directly abroad.

> **INVESTOR FACT**
>
> A FALL FROM GRACE—In 1989 Japan's stock market was the largest in the world, with a total market capitalization of nearly $5 trillion. The United States was second at about $4 trillion, the United Kingdom far behind at about $1 trillion. By early 1998, Japan had sunk to number 3, behind the U.K. and far behind the U.S. While Japan and the U.K. jockey for position at about $3 trillion, the total value of the U.S. stock market has soared to roughly $13 trillion. One reason for London's good fortune: Like the rest of Europe, the U.K. stock market has surged, aided by favorable economic reports on inflation and corporate profits. In contrast, Japan's economy has actually shrunk. What does this mean for the individual investor? The benefit of international diversification results from its ability to balance the poor or average performance in certain markets with the exceptional performance in others.

Benefits of International Diversification

Can greater returns be found overseas than in the United States? Yes! Can a portfolio's risk be reduced by including foreign investments? Yes! Is international diversification desirable for you? We don't know! A successful global investment strategy depends on many things, just as a purely domestic strategy does. Included are factors such as your resources, goals, sophistication, and psychology.

In general, you should avoid investing directly in foreign-currency-denominated instruments. Unless the magnitude of each foreign investment is in hundreds of thousands of dollars, the transactions costs will tend to be high—not just when you are buying and selling, but especially when dividends or interest are paid. Therefore, for most investors who are sophisticated enough to seek international diversification, the optimal vehicles are available in the United States. International mutual funds are available for those who seek diversified foreign investments, coupled with the professional investment expertise of fund managers. ADRs can be used by those who want to make foreign investments in individual stocks. With either mutual funds or ADRs, the investment offers low cost, convenience, transactions in U.S. dollars, protection under U.S. security laws, and (usually) attractive markets (although some ADRs have thin markets).

CONCEPTS IN REVIEW

16.1 What is an *efficient portfolio,* and what role should such a portfolio play in investing?

16.2 How can the return and standard deviation of a portfolio be determined? Compare the portfolio standard deviation calculation to that used for a single asset.

16.3 What is *correlation,* and why is it important with respect to asset returns? Describe the characteristics of returns that are (a) positively correlated, (b) negatively correlated, and (c) uncorrelated. Define and differentiate between *perfect positive correlation* and *perfect negative correlation.*

16.4 What is *diversification?* How does the diversification of risk affect the risk of the portfolio compared to the risk of the individual assets it contains?

16.5 Discuss how the correlation between asset returns affects the risk and return behavior of the resulting portfolio. Describe the potential range of risk and return when the correlation between two assets is (a) perfectly positive, (b) uncorrelated, and (c) perfectly negative.

16.6 What benefit, if any, does international diversification offer the individual investor? Compare and contrast the methods of achieving international diversification by investing abroad versus investing domestically.

http://hepg.aw.com

A fundamental principle of portfolio construction is that investors must diversify. Some investors are led to believe that ownership of one mutual fund is adequate diversification, because most funds hold large numbers of stocks. However, adequate diversification often requires the purchase of shares in more than one mutual fund. Read the article on the following Web page to get one firm's opinion on how many funds to own.

www.investorama.com/features/piazza3.shtml

Traditional versus Modern Portfolio Theory

LG 3

Two approaches are currently used by portfolio managers to plan and construct their portfolios. The *traditional approach* refers to the less quantitative methods that money managers have been using since the evolution of the public securities markets. *Modern portfolio theory (MPT)* is a more recent, more mathematical development that continues to grow in popularity and acceptance. Some MPT concepts are indirectly used by practitioners of the traditional approach, yet there are major differences between the two.

The Traditional Approach

traditional portfolio management an approach to portfolio management that emphasizes "balancing" the portfolio by assembling a wide variety of stocks and/or bonds of companies from a broad range of industries.

Traditional portfolio management emphasizes "balancing" the portfolio by assembling a wide variety of stocks and/or bonds. The typical emphasis is *interindustry diversification,* which produces a portfolio that contains securities of companies from a broad range of industries. Traditional portfolios are constructed using the security analysis techniques discussed in Chapters 6 and 7.

Table 16.4 presents the industry groupings and the percentages invested in them by a typical mutual fund that is managed by professionals using the traditional approach. This fund, the Zweig Appreciation Fund, is an open-end mutual fund with a 5.5% maximum initial load. The portfolio's value at December 31, 1997, was approximately $567 million. Its objective is to provide investors with long-term capital appreciation through investment primarily in small-company stocks, consistent with preservation of capital and reduction of portfolio exposure to market risk. The Zweig Appreciation Fund holds shares of 527 different stocks from 54 industries, as well as short-term obligations, repurchase agreements, and other assets.

Analyzing the stock portion of the Zweig Appreciation Fund, which accounts for about 96% of the fund's total assets, we can observe the traditional approach to portfolio management at work. This fund holds numerous stocks from a diverse cross section of the total universe of available stocks, although its stocks represent only small companies. By far the largest industry group is oil and gas, with 10.15% of the total portfolio. The fund's largest individual holding is MacDermid, Inc., a developer and producer of specialty chemicals, which accounts for only 1.06% of the total portfolio. Comdisco, Inc., a computer equipment dealer and service company, ranks second, at 0.82%. The third largest holding—0.81%—is Columbia Gas System, Inc., a major natural gas company. Although most of the fund's 527 stocks are those of small companies, it does include the stocks of some major companies, such as Dow Chemical, K-Mart, and Raytheon.

Traditional portfolio managers want to invest in well-known companies for three reasons. First, because these companies have been and probably will continue to be successful business enterprises, investing in them is perceived as less risky than investing in lesser-known firms. Second, professional managers prefer to invest in large companies because the securities of these firms are more liquid and are available in large quantities. Managers of large portfolios invest substantial sums of money and need to acquire securities in large quantities to achieve an efficient order size. Third, traditional portfolio managers also prefer successful well-known companies because it is easier to convince clients to invest in them. Called *window dressing,* this practice of loading up a portfolio, particularly at the end of a reporting period, with successful well-known stocks makes it easier for investment managers to sell their services.

Modern Portfolio Theory

modern portfolio theory (MPT) an approach to portfolio management that uses several basic statistical measures to develop a portfolio plan.

During the 1950s, Harry Markowitz, a trained mathematician, first developed the theories that form the basis of modern portfolio theory. Many other scholars and investment experts have contributed to the theory in the intervening years. **Modern portfolio theory** (**MPT**) utilizes several basic statistical measures to develop a portfolio plan. Included are *expected returns* and *stand-*

TABLE 16.4 Portfolio of Zweig Appreciation Fund, December 31, 1997

The Zweig Appreciation Fund appears to adhere to the traditional approach to portfolio management. Its total portfolio value is about $567 million, of which over 95% ($544 million) is common stock, including 527 different stocks in 54 industry groupings, plus about 2% ($13 million) in short-term obligations, about 1% ($7 million) in repurchase agreements, and about 1% ($3 million) in other assets.

Zweig Appreciation Fund
Investments by Industry Group
as of December 31, 1997

Industry Group	Percentage	Industry Group	Percentage
Common Stocks	**95.86%**	Insurance	6.84%
Aerospace	.92	Investment banking and brokerage	3.73
Air freight	.87	Investment management	.00
Airlines	3.48	Manufacturing	4.50
Apparel and textiles	.61	Metal fabrication	2.57
Automobiles	2.01	Metals and mining	1.60
Automobile parts and equipment	2.08	Oil and gas	10.15
Banks	3.12	Pollution control equipment	.06
Building materials and products	4.25	Printing and forms	.75
Chemicals	2.49	Publishing	.14
Commercial services	.27	Railroads	.20
Communications equipment	1.07	Recreational products	.15
Computers and software	2.67	Restaurants	.74
Conglomerates	.18	Retail trade	4.78
Construction equipment	.99	Savings and loan associations	3.59
Consumer products and services	.15	Shipping	.40
Containers and packaging	.12	Shoes	.07
Electrical products	1.15	Steel	2.51
Electronics	2.70	Supermarket chains	.22
Engineering	.21	Telecommunications	1.08
Entertainment	.05	Tobacco	.97
Farm equipment	.47	Transportation	.04
Finance	4.19	Trucking	1.85
Food and beverages	.63	Utilities	8.34
Forest and paper products	.33	Waste management	.01
Healthcare facilities and products	1.28	Wholesale distributors	.62
Homebuilding and land development	1.16	**Short-Term Obligations**	**2.29**
Household furnishings and products	1.13	**Repurchase Agreements**	**1.32**
Industrial products, services, and machinery	1.37	**Other Assets (net)**	**.53**

Source: Zweig Series Trust, *1997 Annual Report,* December 31, 1997, pp. 18–23.

ard deviations of returns for both securities and portfolios and the *correlation* between returns. According to MPT, diversification is achieved by combining securities in a portfolio *in such a way that individual securities have negative (or low-positive) correlations between each other's rates of return.* Thus the statistical diversification is the deciding factor in choosing securities for an MPT portfolio. Two important aspects of MPT are the *efficient frontier* and *beta.* As we'll soon see, the efficient frontier is a more theoretical but less practical tool than beta.

The Efficient Frontier

At any point in time, you are faced with virtually hundreds of investment vehicles from which to choose. Using some or all of these vehicles, you can form a large number of possible portfolios. In fact, using only, say, 10 of the vehicles, hundreds of portfolios could be created by changing the weights, w_j, that represent the proportion of the portfolio's dollar value represented by each asset j.

If we were to create all possible portfolios, calculate the return and risk of each, and plot each risk–return combination on a set of risk–return axes, we would have the *feasible* or *attainable set* of all possible portfolios. This set is represented by the shaded area in Figure 16.4. It is the area bounded by ABYOZCDEF. As defined earlier, an *efficient portfolio* is a portfolio that provides the highest return for a given level of risk or provides minimum risk for a given level of return. For example, let's compare portfolio T to portfolios B and Y depicted in Figure 16.4. It appears that portfolio Y is preferable to portfolio T because it has a higher return for the same level of risk. Portfolio B also "dominates" portfolio T because it has lower risk for the same level of return.

efficient frontier
the leftmost boundary of the feasible (attainable) set of portfolios that includes all efficient portfolios—those providing the best attainable tradeoff between risk (measured by the standard deviation) and return.

The boundary BYOZC of the feasible or attainable set of portfolios, called the **efficient frontier,** represents *all efficient portfolios*—those that provide the best tradeoff between risk and return. *All portfolios on the efficient frontier are preferable to all other portfolios in the feasible or attainable set.* Any portfolios that would fall to the left of the efficient frontier are *not available* for investment, because they fall outside of the feasible or attainable set. Portfolios that fall to the right of the efficient frontier are *not desirable,* because their risk–return tradeoffs are inferior to those of portfolios on the efficient frontier.

The efficient frontier can, in theory, be used to find the highest level of satisfaction the investor can achieve given the available set of portfolios. To do this, we would plot on the risk–return axes an *investor's utility function* or

FIGURE 16.4
The Feasible or Attainable Set and the Efficient Frontier

The *feasible* or *attainable set* (shaded area) represents the risk–return combinations attainable with all possible portfolios; the *efficient frontier* is the locus of all efficient portfolios. The point O where the investor's highest possible indifference curve is tangent to the efficient frontier is the optimal portfolio. It represents the highest level of satisfaction the investor can achieve given the available set of portfolios.

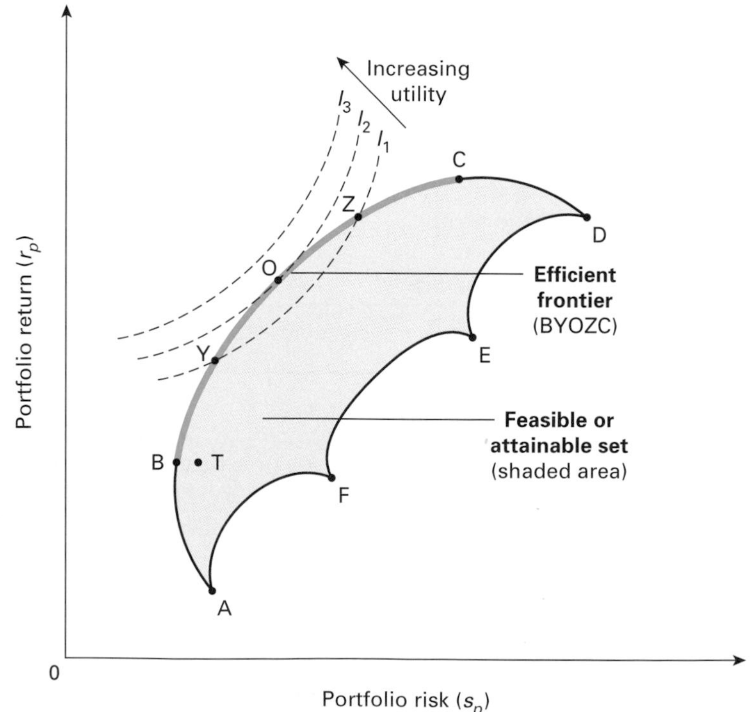

risk-indifference curves, which indicate, for a given level of utility (satisfaction), the set of risk–return combinations among which an investor would be indifferent. These curves, labeled I_1, I_2, and I_3 in Figure 16.4, reflect increasing utility (satisfaction) as we move from I_1 to I_2 to I_3. The optimal portfolio, O, is the point at which indifference curve I_2 meets the efficient frontier. The higher utility provided by I_3 cannot be achieved given the best available portfolios represented by the efficient frontier.

When coupled with a risk-free asset, the efficient frontier can be used to develop the *capital asset pricing model* (introduced in Chapter 4) in terms of portfolio risk (measured by the standard deviation, s_p) and return (r_p). Rather than focus further on theory, we will shift our attention to the more practical aspects of the efficient frontier and its extensions. To do so, we revisit *beta,* the risk measure introduced in Chapter 4, and consider its use in a portfolio context.

Portfolio Betas

As we have noted, investors strive to diversify their portfolios by including a variety of noncomplementary investment vehicles, in order to reduce risk while meeting return objectives. Remember from Chapter 4 that investment vehicles embody two basic types of risk: (1) *diversifiable risk,* the risk unique to a particular investment vehicle, and (2) *nondiversifiable risk,* the risk possessed by every investment vehicle.

A great deal of research has been conducted on the topic of risk as it is related to security investments. As noted in Chapter 4, the results show that in general, *to earn more return, one must bear more risk.* More startling, however, are research results showing that only with nondiversifiable risk is there a positive risk–return relationship. High levels of *diversifiable risk* do not result in correspondingly high levels of return. Because there is no reward for bearing diversifiable risk, investors should minimize this form of risk by diversifying the portfolio so that only nondiversifiable risk remains.

Risk Diversification As we've seen, diversification minimizes diversifiable risk by offsetting the poor return on one vehicle with the good return on another. Minimizing diversifiable risk through careful selection of investment vehicles requires that the vehicles chosen for the portfolio come from a wide range of industries.

To understand better the effect of diversification on the basic types of risk, let's consider what happens when we begin with a single asset (security) in a portfolio and then expand the portfolio by randomly selecting additional securities from, say, the population of all actively traded securities. Using the standard deviation, s_p, to measure the portfolio's *total risk,* we can depict the behavior of the total portfolio risk as more securities are added, as done in Figure 16.5. As securities are added (x-axis) the total portfolio risk (y-axis) declines because of the effects of diversification (explained earlier), and it tends to approach a limit. Research has shown that, on average, most of the benefits of diversification, in terms of risk reduction, can be gained by forming portfolios containing 8 to 15 randomly selected securities. Unfortunately, because an investor holds but one of a large number of possible x-security portfolios, it is unlikely that he or she will experience the average outcome. As a consequence, some researchers suggest that the individual investor needs to hold about 40

FIGURE 16.5
Portfolio Risk and Diversification

As randomly selected securities are combined to create a portfolio, the total risk of the portfolio (measured by its standard deviation, s_p) declines. The portion of the risk eliminated is the *diversifiable risk;* the remaining portion is the *nondiversifiable* or *relevant risk.* On average, most of the benefits of diversification result from forming portfolios that contain 8 to 15 randomly selected securities.

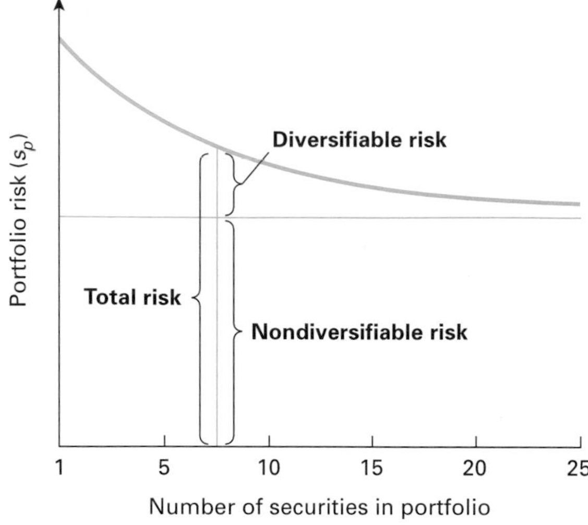

different stocks to achieve efficient diversification. This suggestion tends to support the popularity of investment in mutual funds.

relevant risk
risk that is nondiversifiable.

Because any investor can create a portfolio of assets that will eliminate all, or virtually all, diversifiable risk, the only **relevant risk** is that which is nondiversifiable. You must therefore be concerned solely with nondiversifiable risk, which reflects the contribution of an asset to the risk of the portfolio. The measurement of nondiversifiable risk is thus of primary importance in selecting those assets that possess the most desired risk–return characteristics.

Calculating Portfolio Betas The *nondiversifiable* or *relevant risk* of a security can be measured using *beta*, a measure we studied in Chapter 4. Betas can be positive (return changes in the same direction as the market) or negative (return changes in the opposite direction from the market). Most betas are positive. The beta for the market is equal to 1.0. Securities with betas greater than 1.0 are more risky than the market, and those with betas below 1.0 are less risky than the market. The beta for the risk-free asset is 0.0. Betas for a broad range of securities can be readily obtained from brokerage firms and subscription services such as *Value Line*.

portfolio beta, b_p
the beta of a portfolio; calculated as the weighted average of the betas of the individual assets the portfolio includes.

The **portfolio beta,** b_p, is merely the weighted average of the betas of the individual assets it includes. It can be easily estimated using the betas of the component assets. To find the portfolio beta, b_p, we can use Equation 16.2:

Equation 16.2

$$\text{Portfolio beta} = \left(\begin{array}{c}\text{proportion of}\\ \text{portfolio's total}\\ \text{dollar value}\\ \text{represented by}\\ \text{asset 1}\end{array} \times \begin{array}{c}\text{beta}\\ \text{for}\\ \text{asset 1}\end{array}\right) + \left(\begin{array}{c}\text{proportion of}\\ \text{portfolio's total}\\ \text{dollar value}\\ \text{represented by}\\ \text{asset 2}\end{array} \times \begin{array}{c}\text{beta}\\ \text{for}\\ \text{asset 2}\end{array}\right) + \cdots +$$

$$\left(\begin{array}{c}\text{proportion of}\\ \text{portfolio's total}\\ \text{dollar value}\\ \text{represented by}\\ \text{asset } n\end{array} \times \begin{array}{c}\text{beta}\\ \text{for}\\ \text{asset } n\end{array}\right) = \sum_{j=1}^{n} \left(\begin{array}{c}\text{proportion of}\\ \text{portfolio's total}\\ \text{dollar value}\\ \text{represented by}\\ \text{asset } j\end{array} \times \begin{array}{c}\text{beta}\\ \text{for}\\ \text{asset } j\end{array}\right)$$

Equation 16.2a

$$b_p = (w_1 \times b_1) + (w_2 \times b_2) + \cdots + (w_n \times b_n) = \sum_{j=1}^{n} (w_j \times b_j)$$

Of course, $\sum_{j=1}^{n} w_j = 1$, which means that 100% of the portfolio's assets must be included in this computation.

Portfolio betas are interpreted in exactly the same way as individual asset betas. They indicate the degree of responsiveness of the portfolio's return to changes in the market return. For example, when the market return increases by 10%, a portfolio with a beta of .75 will experience a 7.5% increase in its return (0.75 × 10%). A portfolio with a beta of 1.25 will experience a 12.5% increase in its return (1.25 × 10%). Low-beta portfolios are less responsive, and therefore less risky, than high-beta portfolios. Clearly, a portfolio containing mostly low-beta assets will have a low beta, and vice versa.

To demonstrate, consider the Austin Fund, a large investment company that wishes to assess the risk of two portfolios, V and W. Both portfolios contain five assets, with the proportions and betas shown in Table 16.5. The betas for portfolios V and W, b_v and b_w, can be calculated by substituting the appropriate data from the table into Equation 16.2, as follows:

$$b_v = (.10 \times 1.65) + (.30 \times 1.00) + (.20 \times 1.30) + (.20 \times 1.10) + (.20 \times 1.25)$$
$$= .165 + .300 + .260 + .220 + .250 = 1.195 \approx \underline{\underline{1.20}}$$
$$b_w = (.10 \times .80) + (.10 \times 1.00) + (.20 \times .65) + (.10 \times .75) + (.50 \times 1.05)$$
$$= .080 + .100 + .130 + .075 + .525 = \underline{\underline{.91}}$$

Portfolio V's beta is 1.20, and portfolio W's is .91. These values make sense because portfolio V contains relatively high-beta assets and portfolio W contains relatively low-beta assets. Clearly, portfolio V's returns are more responsive to changes in market returns—and therefore more risky—than portfolio W's.

Using Portfolio Betas The usefulness of beta depends on how well it explains relative return fluctuations. The *coefficient of determination (R^2)* can statistically evaluate a beta coefficient. That is, it indicates the percentage of the change in the return on an individual security that is explained by its relationship with the market return. R^2 can range from 0 to 1.0. If a regression equation has an R^2 of 0, then none (0%) of the variation in the security's

TABLE 16.5 Austin Fund's Portfolios V and W

	Portfolio V		Portfolio W	
Asset	Proportion	Beta	Proportion	Beta
1	.10	1.65	.10	.80
2	.30	1.00	.10	1.00
3	.20	1.30	.20	.65
4	.20	1.10	.10	.75
5	.20	1.25	.50	1.05
Total	1.00		1.00	

return is explained by its relationship with the market. An R^2 of 1.0 indicates the existence of perfect correlation (100%) between a security and the market.

Beta is much more useful in explaining a portfolio's return fluctuations than a security's return fluctuations. A well-diversified stock portfolio will have a beta equation R^2 of around .90. This means that 90% of the stock portfolio's fluctuations are related to changes in the stock market as a whole. Individual security betas have a wide range of R^2s but tend to be in the .20 to .50 range. Other factors (diversifiable risk, in particular) also cause individual security prices to fluctuate. When securities are combined in a well-diversified portfolio, most of the fluctuation in that portfolio's return is caused by the movement of the entire stock market.

Interpreting Portfolio Betas If a portfolio has a beta of +1.0, the portfolio experiences changes in its rate of return equal to changes in the market's rate of return. This means the +1.0 beta portfolio would tend to experience a 10% increase in return if the stock market as a whole experienced a 10% increase in return. Conversely, if the market return fell by 6%, the return on the +1.0 beta portfolio would also fall by 6%.

Table 16.6 lists the expected returns for three portfolio betas in two situations: an increase in market return of 10% and a decrease in market return of 10%. The 2.0 beta portfolio is twice as volatile as the market. When the market return increases by 10%, the portfolio return increases by 20%. Conversely, the portfolio's return will fall by 20% when the market return declines 10%. This portfolio would be considered a high-risk, high-return portfolio. The middle, .5 beta portfolio is considered a low-risk, low-return portfolio—a conservative portfolio for investors who wish to maintain a low-risk investment posture. The .5 beta portfolio is half as volatile as the market. A portfolio with a beta of −1.0 moves in the opposite direction from the market. A bearish investor would probably want to own a negative-beta portfolio, because this type of investment tends to rise in value when the stock market declines, and vice versa. Finding securities with negative betas is difficult, however. Most securities have positive betas, because they tend to experience return movements in the same direction as changes in the stock market.

The Risk–Return Tradeoff: Some Closing Comments

Another valuable outgrowth of modern portfolio theory is the specific link between nondiversifiable risk and investment return. The basic premise is that an investor must have a portfolio of relatively risky investments to earn a rel-

TABLE 16.6 Portfolio Betas and Associated Changes in Returns

Portfolio Beta	Change in Market Return	Change in Expected Portfolio Return
+2.0	+10.0% −10.0	+20.0% −20.0
+ .5	+10.0 −10.0	+ 5.0 − 5.0
−1.0	+10.0 −10.0	−10.0 +10.0

risk–return tradeoff
the positive relationship between the risk associated with a given investment and its expected return.

risk-free rate, R_F
the return an investor can earn on a risk-free investment such as a U.S. Treasury bill or an insured money market deposit account.

atively high rate of return. That relationship is illustrated in Figure 16.6. The upward-sloping line shows the **risk–return tradeoff.** The point where the risk–return line crosses the return axis is called the **risk–free rate, R_F.** This is the return an investor can earn on a risk-free investment such as a U.S. Treasury bill or an insured money market deposit account. As we proceed upward along the line, portfolios of risky investments appear. For example, four investment portfolios, A through D, are depicted. Portfolios A and B are investment opportunities that provide a level of return commensurate with their respective risk levels. Portfolio C provides a high return at a relatively low risk level—and therefore would be an excellent investment. Portfolio D, in contrast, offers high risk but low return—an investment to avoid.

Reconciling the Traditional Approach and MPT

We have reviewed two fairly different approaches to portfolio management: the traditional approach and MPT. The question that naturally arises is which technique should you use. There is no definite answer; the question must be resolved by the judgment of each investor. However, we can offer a few useful ideas. The average individual investor does not have the resources, computers, and mathematical acumen to implement a total MPT portfolio strategy. But most individual investors can extract and use ideas from *both* the traditional and MPT approaches. The traditional approach stresses security selection using fundamental and technical analysis. It also emphasizes diversification of the portfolio across industry lines. MPT stresses negative correlations between rates of return for the securities within the portfolio. This approach calls for diversification, to minimize diversifiable risk. Thus diversification must be accomplished to ensure satisfactory performance with either strategy. Also, beta is a useful tool for determining the level of a portfolio's nondiversifiable risk and should be part of the decision-making process.

We recommend the following portfolio management policy, which uses aspects of both approaches:

- Determine how much risk you are willing to bear.
- Seek diversification among different types of securities and across industry lines, and pay attention to how the return from one security is related to that from another.

FIGURE 16.6
The Portfolio Risk–Return Tradeoff

As the risk of an investment portfolio increases from zero, the return provided should increase above the risk-free rate, R_F. Portfolios A and B offer returns commensurate with their risk, portfolio C provides a high return at a low-risk level, and portfolio D provides a low return for high risk. Portfolio C is highly desirable; Portfolio D should be avoided.

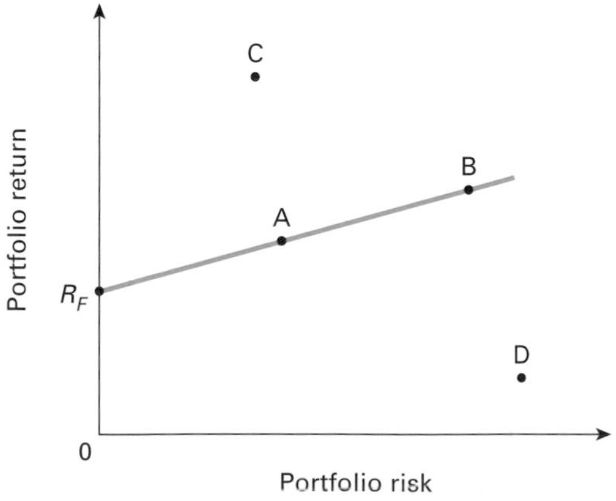

- Consider how a security responds to the market, and use beta in diversifying your portfolio as a way to keep the portfolio in line with your acceptable level of risk.
- Evaluate alternative portfolios to make sure that the portfolio selected provides the highest return for the given level of acceptable risk.

CONCEPTS IN REVIEW

16.7 Describe *traditional portfolio management.* Give three reasons why traditional portfolio managers like to invest in well-established companies. Explain each reason.

16.8 What is *modern portfolio theory (MPT)?* What is the feasible or attainable set of all possible portfolios? How is it derived for a given group of investment vehicles?

16.9 What is the *efficient frontier?* How is it related to the feasible or attainable set of all possible portfolios? How can it be used with an investor's utility function or risk-indifference curves to find the optimal portfolio?

16.10 Define and differentiate among the diversifiable, nondiversifiable, and total risk of a portfolio. Which is considered the *relevant risk*? How is it measured?

16.11 Define *beta.* How can you find the beta of a portfolio when you know the beta for each of the assets included within it?

16.12 What does the coefficient of determination (R^2) for the regression equation used to derive a beta coefficient indicate? Would this statistic indicate that beta is more useful in explaining the return fluctuations of individual assets than of portfolios?

16.13 Explain how traditional and modern portfolio approaches can be reconciled.

http://hepg.aw.com

Modern portfolio theory relies on an understanding of the distinction between diversifiable and nondiversifiable risk. The following Web page gives a brief explanation of systematic (nondiversifiable) risk and its importance in a diversified portfolio.

finance.wat.ch/cbt/options/00004980.html

Constructing a Portfolio Using an Asset Allocation Scheme

LG 4 LG 5

In this section we will examine the criteria that can be used to construct a portfolio: investor characteristics and objectives and portfolio objectives and policies. We then will use these factors to develop a plan for allocating assets in various investment categories. This plan provides a basic, useful framework for selecting individual investment vehicles for the portfolio. In attempting to weave the concepts of risk and diversification into a solid portfolio policy, we will rely on both traditional and modern approaches.

Investor Characteristics and Objectives

Your financial and family situations are important inputs in determining portfolio policy. The following are vital determinants: level and stability of income, family factors, net worth, investor experience and age, and disposition toward risk. Your portfolio strategy obviously must be tailored to meet your needs. The types of investments in the portfolio depend on relative income needs and ability to bear risk. Simply stated, *your risk exposure should not exceed your ability to bear risk.*

The size of your income and the certainty of your employment also bear on portfolio strategy. An investor with a secure job is more likely to embark on a risk-oriented investment program than one who has a less secure position. Income taxes bear on the investment decision as well. The higher your income, the more important the tax ramifications of an investment program become. Your investment experience also influences the appropriate investment strategy. It normally is best to "get one's feet wet" in the investment market by slipping into it gradually rather than leaping in headfirst. Very often, investors who make risky initial investments suffer heavy losses, damaging the long-run potential of their entire investment program. A cautiously developed investment program is likely to provide more favorable long-run results than an impulsive, risky one.

Once you have developed a personal financial profile, the next question is "What do I want from my portfolio?" You must generally choose between earning a high current income from an investment portfolio or obtaining significant capital appreciation from it. It is difficult to have both. The price of having high appreciation potential in the portfolio is often low potential for current income.

The investor's needs may determine which avenue is chosen. For instance, a retired investor whose income depends on his or her portfolio will probably choose a lower-risk, current-income-oriented approach. In contrast, a high-income, financially secure investor (such as a physician) may be much more willing to take on risky investments in the hope of improving net worth. Thus it should be clear that a portfolio must be built around the individual's needs, which depend on income, responsibilities, financial resources, age, retirement plans, and ability to bear risk.

Portfolio Objectives and Policies

Constructing a portfolio is a logical activity and is best done after careful analysis of your needs and of the available investment vehicles. You should consider the following objectives when planning and constructing a portfolio: current income needs, capital preservation, capital growth, tax considerations, and risk.

Any one or more of these factors will play an influential role in defining the desirable type of portfolio. For convenience, these factors can be tied together as follows: The first two items—current income and capital preservation—are portfolio objectives synonymous with a low-risk, conservative investment strategy. Normally, a portfolio with this orientation contains low-beta (low-risk) securities. A capital growth objective (the third item) implies increased risk and a reduced level of current income. Higher-risk growth stocks, options, futures, real estate, gold, and other more speculative investments may be suitable for this investor. An investor's tax bracket (the fourth item) will influence investment strategy. A high-income investor probably wishes to defer taxes and earn investment returns in the form of capital gains. This implies a strategy of higher-risk investments and a longer holding period. Lower-bracket investors are less concerned with how they earn the income, and they may wish to invest in higher-current-income vehicles. The most important item, finally, is risk. The risk–return tradeoff should be considered *in all investment decisions.*

Developing an Asset Allocation Scheme

asset allocation
a scheme that involves dividing one's portfolio into various asset classes to preserve capital by protecting against negative developments while taking advantage of positive ones.

Once your needs are converted into specific portfolio objectives, you can construct a portfolio designed to achieve these goals. Before buying any investment vehicles, however, you must develop an *asset allocation scheme.* **Asset allocation** involves dividing one's portfolio into various asset classes, such as U.S. stocks, U.S. bonds, foreign securities, short-term securities, and other vehicles like tangibles (especially gold) and real estate. The emphasis of asset allocation is on *preservation of capital*—protecting against negative developments while taking advantage of positive developments. Asset allocation, although similar to diversification in its objective, is a bit different: Its focus is on *investment in various asset classes,* whereas diversification tends to focus more on investing in various vehicles *within* an asset class.

Asset allocation is based on the belief that the total return of a portfolio is influenced more by the division of investments into asset classes than by the actual investments. In fact, studies have shown that as much as 90% or more of a portfolio's *return* comes from asset allocation. Therefore, less than 10% can be attributed to the actual selection of securities. Furthermore, researchers have found that asset allocation has a much greater impact on reducing *total risk* than does selecting the best investment vehicle in any single asset category. Clearly, asset allocation is an important aspect of portfolio management.

Approaches to Asset Allocation

There are three basic approaches to asset allocation. The first two, fixed weightings and flexible weightings, differ with respect to the proportions of each asset category maintained in the portfolio. The third, tactical asset allocation, is a more exotic technique frequently used by sophisticated institutional portfolio managers.

fixed-weightings approach
asset allocation plan in which a fixed percentage of the portfolio is allocated to each asset category.

Fixed Weightings The **fixed-weightings approach** allocates a fixed percentage of the portfolio to each of the asset categories, of which there typically are three to five. Assuming four categories—common stocks, bonds, foreign securities, and short-term securities—a fixed allocation might be

Category	Allocation
Common stock	30%
Bonds	50
Foreign securities	15
Short-term securities	5
Total portfolio	100%

Generally, the fixed weightings do not change over time. Because of shifting market values, the portfolio may have to be adjusted annually or after major market moves to maintain the desired fixed-percentage allocations.

Fixed weights may or may not represent equal percentage allocations to each category. One could, for example, allocate 25% to each of the four categories above. Research has shown that over a long period (1967–1988) equal (20%) allocations to U.S. stocks, foreign stocks, long-term bonds, cash, and real estate resulted in a portfolio that outperformed the S&P 500 in terms of both return and risk. These findings add further support to the importance of even a somewhat naive "buy and hold" asset allocation strategy.

flexible-weightings approach asset allocation plan in which weights for each asset category are adjusted periodically based on market analysis or technical analysis.

Flexible Weightings The **flexible-weightings approach** involves periodic adjustment of the weights for each asset category on the basis of either market analysis or technical analysis (market timing). The use of a flexible weighting scheme is often called *strategic asset allocation*. For example, the initial and new allocation based on a flexible weighting scheme may be

Category	Initial Allocation	New Allocation
Common stock	30%	45%
Bonds	40	40
Foreign securities	15	10
Short-term securities	15	5
Total portfolio	100%	100%

A change from the initial to the new allocation would be triggered by shifts in market or technical indicators. For example, the new allocation shown above may have resulted from an anticipated decline in inflation, which would be expected to result in increased domestic stock and bond prices and a decline in foreign and short-term security returns. The weightings were therefore changed to capture greater returns in a changing market.

tactical asset allocation asset allocation plan that uses stock-index futures and bond futures to change a portfolio's asset allocation.

Tactical Asset Allocation The third approach, **tactical asset allocation,** uses stock-index futures and bond futures (see Chapter 12) to change a portfolio's asset allocation. When stocks seem less attractive than bonds, this strategy involves selling stock-index futures and buying bond futures. Conversely, when bonds seem less attractive than stocks, the strategy results in buying stock-index futures and selling bond futures. Because this sophisticated technique relies on a large portfolio and the use of quantitative models for cues, it is generally appropriate only for large institutional investors.

Asset Allocation Alternatives

Assuming the use of a fixed-weight asset allocation plan and using, say, four asset categories—common stock, bonds, foreign securities, and short-term securities—we can demonstrate three asset allocations. Table 16.7 shows allocations in each of the categories for a conservative (low-return–low-risk), a moderate (average-return–average-risk), and an aggressive (high-return–high-risk) portfolio: The conservative allocation relies heavily on bonds and short-term securities to provide predictable returns. The moderate allocation consists largely of common stock and bonds and includes more foreign securities and fewer short-term securities than the conservative allocation. Its moderate risk–return behavior reflects a move away from safe, short-term securities to a

INVESTING IN ACTION

Portfolio-Building Tips for the Novice Investor

You've managed to squirrel away a few thousand dollars and you're ready to invest it. Where do you start?

Before you spend a penny, be sure you have a cash reserve fund for emergencies and other liquidity needs. That's typically 3 months' salary, which should be available in the event that you lose your job or have some kind of medical emergency. Leave the money in a money market fund for liquidity and safety—and perhaps 4% interest.

Once you've satisfied this emergency reserve requirement, develop a long-term investment strategy, with a mix of assets geared to your overall goals. Stick to this framework as you build your portfolio; otherwise, you could end up with investments that don't fit your needs. With limited funds, you can't fully implement your game plan right away, but you can work toward it. Start with your largest asset category and add to the others as you have more funds to invest.

Fortunately, a small investor can take many routes to build a portfolio. One conservative approach that appeals to many novices starts with a balanced or asset allocation mutual fund that invests in stocks, bonds, and cash. Many mutual fund families offer balanced funds or asset allocation funds. The big advantage of such a fund is that it provides you with instant diversification across a number of asset classes. With just a few thousand dollars, that would be difficult for you to accomplish outside a mutual fund environment. You can add to this type of fund regularly until you build up enough money—and investment confidence—to move into specific fund categories or individual stocks.

Another alternative is to plunge right into an equity mutual fund, bypassing bonds and cash. The logic: You've already got your cash reserve fund for emergencies, and stocks offer greater returns than bonds. If you're many years away from retirement, the disadvantage of stocks—volatility—becomes less of a problem as your time horizon lengthens. Because there are thousands of mutual funds to choose from, you might decide to invest in a stock-index fund that promises to match the Standard & Poor's 500 Stock Composite Index, a broad index of large-capitalization stocks. You need a greater risk tolerance to focus on stocks, but an index fund is a conservative way to do it. Then, once you build up a nice balance in your stock-index fund, you might want to diversify into bonds. Or you might decide to diversify into small-cap stocks or international investments.

Building a portfolio of individual stocks takes more time and discipline than buying a fund. However, there are advantages. For one thing, buying stocks and holding them minimizes your income tax liability. In contrast, mutual funds generate tax liability every year in the form of capital-gains distributions. In addition, mutual funds have operating expenses, which reduce your returns. Buying individual stocks *does* involve paying a commission to a broker, but brokerage commissions have come down considerably since the advent of discount and online brokers. Another way to minimize your commissions is to have your dividends automatically reinvested. Most major companies offer DRIPs, or dividend reinvestment plans. Those that do tend to be larger, slower-growing companies, such as financial service and utility companies.

Whether you invest in individual stocks or buy mutual funds, the key to investing is to come up with a plan and stick with it. Invest regularly—every month or pay period, if possible—and be patient. Plan to hold your investments for a long time. Otherwise, transaction costs and taxes will eat up your returns.

larger dose of common stock and foreign securities than under the conservative allocation. Finally, in the aggressive portfolio, more dollars are allocated to common stock, fewer to bonds, and more to foreign securities, thereby generally increasing the expected portfolio return and risk. The *Investing in Action* box above offers some basic portfolio-building tips for the novice investor.

TABLE 16.7 Alternative Asset Allocations

	Allocation Alternative		
Category	Conservative (low-return–low-risk)	Moderate (average-return–average-risk)	Aggressive (high-return–high-risk)
Common stock	15%	30%	40%
Bonds	45	40	30
Foreign securities	5	15	25
Short-term securities	35	15	5
Total portfolio	100%	100%	100%

Applying Asset Allocation

An asset allocation plan should consider the economic outlook and your investments, savings and spending patterns, tax situation, return expectations, risk tolerance, and so forth. Such plans must be formulated for the long run, must stress capital preservation, and must provide for periodic revision to maintain consistency with changing investment goals. Generally, to decide on the appropriate asset mix, you must evaluate each asset category in terms of current return, growth potential, safety, liquidity, transaction costs (brokerage fees), and potential tax savings.

Many investors use mutual funds (see Chapter 13) as part of their asset allocation activities, to diversify within each asset category. As an alternative to constructing your own portfolio, however, you can buy shares in an **asset allocation fund**—a mutual fund that seeks to reduce variability of returns by investing in the right assets at the right time. These funds, like all asset allocation schemes, emphasize diversification and perform at a relatively consistent level by passing up the potential for spectacular gains in favor of predictability. Some asset allocation funds use fixed weightings, whereas others have flexible weights that change within prescribed limits. As a rule, investors with more than about $50,000 to invest and adequate time can justify do-it-yourself asset allocation; those with between $5,000 and $50,000 and adequate time can use mutual funds to create a workable asset allocation; and those with less than $5,000 or with limited time may find asset allocation funds most attractive.

asset allocation fund
a mutual fund that seeks to reduce the variability of returns by investing in the right assets at the right time; emphasizes diversification and relatively consistent performance rather than the potential for spectacular gains.

Most important, you should recognize that to be effective, an asset allocation scheme *must be designed for the long haul.* Develop an asset allocation scheme you can live with for at least 7 to 10 years, and perhaps longer. Once you have it set, stick with it. The key to success is remaining faithful to your asset allocation; that means fighting the temptation to wander.

CONCEPTS IN REVIEW

16.14 What role, if any, do an investor's personal characteristics play in determining portfolio policy? Explain.

16.15 What role do an investor's portfolio objectives play in constructing a portfolio?

16.16 What is *asset allocation?* How does it differ from diversification? What role does asset allocation play in constructing an investment portfolio?

16.17 Briefly describe the three basic approaches to asset allocation: (a) fixed weightings, (b) flexible weightings, and (c) tactical asset allocation.

16.18 What role could an *asset allocation fund* play in this process? What makes an asset allocation scheme effective?

16.19 Based on the *Investing in Action* box on page 652, what steps might the conservative small investor take to build an investment portfolio? What role does a cash reserve fund for emergencies play in this process?

http://hepg.aw.com

The asset allocation decision is of vital importance to an investor. In addition to being a major factor in portfolio returns, the mix of asset classes selected must also be consistent with the portfolio management and risk preferences of the investor. The following site has several excellent online articles that address the matching of asset allocation with the successful investor.

www.bondtrades.com/essent/

Portfolio Planning in Action

LG 6

In this section we will analyze four portfolios that have been developed to meet four different investment objectives. The principles and ideas discussed throughout this book will be applied to these four situations.

In each of the analyses that follow, the objectives and the portfolios are real, although the investors' and securities' names are fictitious. When possible, asset allocation weights are given. The specific reasons why a stock or bond is included in the portfolio are also given. As a useful exercise, you might want to consider each situation and develop your own recommendations using current investment information. The *Investing in Action* box on page 655 emphasizes the importance of keeping good records of transactions as your portfolio grows over time.

The four cases have different risk–return profiles because the investors for whom the portfolios are designed have different incomes and lifestyles. Each portfolio relies heavily on the *traditional approach*, with the following exceptions: First, the number of securities in each portfolio is *below the normal number* the traditional portfolio manager would be likely to recommend. In line with MPT, it is assumed that the proper interindustry diversification can be achieved with the careful selection of 8 to 12 securities in a $100,000 portfolio. A larger portfolio might have more securities, but it would probably also have fewer securities than a traditionalist might recommend. Second, beta is utilized to quantify risk in the all-equity portfolios. Thus these examples blend elements of modern portfolio theory (MPT) with the traditional approach to portfolio management.

Dara Yasakawa: Woman Wonder

At age 28, Dara Yasakawa has done well for herself. She has built a $300,000 investment portfolio consisting of investment real estate in Honolulu, Hawaii, with a current market value of $240,000, and $60,000 in short-term securi-

INVESTING IN ACTION

Taming the Portfolio Monster

As your portfolio grows in number and type of investments, it's easy to become overwhelmed and confused by the paperwork you accumulate. Before long, you might lose control of your investments or lose track of important details, such as why you bought that stock in the first place. "People tend to build portfolios the way they pick up seashells on the beach," says Roger Gibson, author of *Asset Allocation: Balancing Financial Risk.* As a result, many investors don't know whether the parts of their portfolio make sense when taken together.

How do you get an overall view of your portfolio? A good place to start is by doing a thorough housecleaning of your financial assets. That means sorting through stacks of paper: mutual fund "welcome" kits, prospectuses, annual and quarterly reports, brokerage firm and mutual fund statements. Take all the paperwork from each brokerage firm and mutual fund and put it in one pile, organized by date, with the most recent mailing on top. You can throw out items you no longer need, such as welcome kits, old annual reports, and monthly or quarterly statements whose information is included in the annual statement. Then file each set of documents in an individual file folder.

Next, list all of your assets categorized by asset categories. Across the top, make columns for cash, domestic bonds, international bonds, domestic stocks, international stocks, real estate, and so on. Use the rows for the source, such as ABC mutual fund or XYZ brokerage firm. If one investment falls into two or more categories, such as a 401(k) retirement plan with both bond and stock investments, then divide it accordingly. Add up all of your assets by category, and calculate the percentage of your portfolio for each asset category.

You may discover that you have many small, similar investments that can be consolidated to simplify your portfolio while still achieving your objectives. For example, do you really need three stockbrokers, or can you combine your accounts at one firm? The same goes for mutual funds. You may want to concentrate on one or two large fund families with many fund choices. Consolidating brokerage firms and mutual funds will certainly cut down on the blizzard of paperwork.

Having organized records also will be a major benefit at tax time. Your records will provide you with the necessary details about securities you sold during the year—such as the purchase and sale dates, the number of shares you bought or sold, and the purchase and sale prices. But most important, having neat files and summary tables will make it easy for you to make informed investment decisions that fit your life circumstances.

ties. Her current asset allocation is therefore 80% real estate ($240,000 ÷ $300,000) and 20% short-term securities ($60,000 ÷ $300,000). Ms. Yasakawa is currently employed as the controller of Kamehameha Management, a real estate management firm in Honolulu. She is a CPA, and her income from salary and property rentals is $75,000 per year, putting her in a 35% marginal income tax bracket (federal and Hawaii state income tax combined). Ms. Yasakawa is single, and her only debts are secured by her properties.

Dara Yasakawa has decided to diversify her portfolio, to reduce her risk exposure and increase her overall investment return. Most of her net worth consists of rental condominiums located in the Waikiki area of Honolulu. The Hawaii real estate market is somewhat unpredictable, and Ms. Yasakawa wishes to lessen her risk exposure in that market. She asked her investment adviser, Marjorie Wong, to help her diversify into common stock. Marjorie recommended selling one of Dara's properties for $60,000 and selling $15,000

INVESTOR FACT

MUTUAL FUNDS FOR LESS— If you want to buy mutual funds for your portfolio but don't have the $2,500 or more minimum initial investment that some funds require, don't despair. Look around for funds with minimums of $500 or less, such as AARP Growth & Income, AIM Funds, and Alliance Capital, to name a few. (Just make sure you don't get them mixed up with ARK Funds, where the minimum investment on most funds is $100,000.) Of course, minimums aren't the only consideration—don't forget about the loads. Some funds charge as much as 5.75% of your investment. To provide an overview of the mutual fund industry, the *Wall Street Journal*, *Barron's*, and *Business Week* produce quarterly performance reports on most funds, including minimum investments, total assets under management, loads, expense ratios, and quarterly, 1-year, 3-year, and 5-year performance.

of her short-term securities to obtain $75,000 to invest in common stock. The resulting asset allocation would be 60% real estate ($180,000 ÷ $300,000), 25% common stock ($75,000 ÷ $300,000), and 15% short-term securities ($45,000 ÷ $300,000). Because of her relatively young age and her strong future earning capacity, Ms. Yasakawa can bear the risks of a speculative investment program. Her portfolio of stocks will emphasize issues that have a strong price appreciation potential.

Ms. Yasakawa's common stock portfolio is presented in Table 16.8. It consists of eight stocks, all of which have above-average risk–return potential. The betas of the issues range from 1.13 to 2.31; the portfolio's beta (calculated using Equation 16.2) is approximately 1.59, indicating an above-average risk exposure. The portfolio is diversified across industry lines, with a fairly wide mix of securities. All are selected for their above-average price appreciation potential. Altuna Airlines, an interisland carrier in Hawaii, was chosen because of the expected increase in the number of visitors to Hawaii. Betta Computer is a fast-growing personal computer manufacturer. Easy Work, Inc., is a growing retailer that services the do-it-yourself home improvement market. Gomez Industries is a rapidly expanding glass manufacturer and photo processor. Hercules is a growing brewer. Jama Motor, based in Japan, provides a measure of international diversification for the portfolio. Karl Lewis Enterprises is an expanding fast-food operator based in California. Ranch Petroleum is a small oil company with refining and oil-production interests.

Most of the securities Ms. Wong selected for Ms. Yasakawa are not "household names." Rather, they are firms with exciting growth potential. Given the portfolio's beta, Dara's holdings should fluctuate in value at a rate approximately 1.6 times greater than the stock market as a whole. The dividend yield on the portfolio is a relatively low 0.6%. Most of the return Ms. Yasakawa anticipates from this portfolio is in the form of price appreciation. She plans to hold the stocks for at least 3 to 5 years to realize this anticipated appreciation. Given Ms. Yasakawa's relatively high marginal income tax bracket, it seems preferable for her to defer taxes and earn returns in the form of capital gains.

TABLE 16.8 Dara Yasakawa's Common Stock Portfolio

Objective: Speculative Growth (High Risk, Potential for High Return)

Number of Shares	Company	Dividend per Share	Dividend Income	Price per Share	Total Cost (including commission)	Beta	Dividend Yield
1,200	Altuna Airlines	$ —	$ —	$ 7	$ 8,480	1.75	—%
300	Betta Computer	—	—	30	9,090	1.87	—
400	Easy Work, Inc.	—	—	25	10,090	1.59	—
300	Gomez Industries	0.36	108	30	9,090	1.19	1.2
300	Hercules Brewing	0.80	240	32	9,700	1.27	2.5
300	Jama Motor ADR	0.35	105	33	10,000	1.13	1.1
500	Karl Lewis Enterprises	—	—	20	10,100	1.79	—
1,300	Ranch Petroleum	—	—	6	7,880	2.31	—
	Total		$453		$74,430		0.6%

Portfolio beta = 1.59

Bob and Gail Weiss: Lottery Winners

Bob Weiss, a professor of political science at the University of West Bay City in Michigan, and his wife, Gail, are lucky people. Professor Weiss bought a $1 Michigan State Lottery ticket and won $300,000! After paying income taxes on the prize and spending a small amount for personal needs, Bob and Gail had $210,000 left. Because of their philosophy of saving any windfalls and not spending accumulated capital on day-to-day living expenses, they chose to invest these funds (in contrast with many lottery winners, who simply blow their winnings on fast living).

The Weisses have two young children. Bob Weiss is 37 years of age and has a secure teaching position. His salary is approximately $70,000 per year. In addition, he earns approximately $20,000 per year from book publishing royalties and from several other small sources. Professor Weiss's tax bracket (federal and state) is approximately 33%. His life insurance protection of approximately $90,000 is provided by the university. Bob's wife is a librarian. She currently is at home with their children and is not expected to be a source of steady income for another several years. The Weiss family owns (free and clear) their home in Bay City. In addition, they have about $40,000 in a money market mutual fund. Therefore, their asset allocation prior to the lottery windfall was 100% money funds ($40,000 ÷ $40,000). They have no outstanding debts.

Professor Weiss asked his investment adviser, Gene Bowles, to develop an investment portfolio for them. Together, they decided on the following strategy: First, the professor and his wife tend to be somewhat risk-averse; that is, they do not wish to bear inordinate amounts of risk of loss. In addition, the Weisses indicated they would welcome some increase in spendable income. Given these facts, Mr. Bowles suggested the portfolio presented in Table 16.9. With this portfolio their asset allocation would become about 84% common stock ($210,000 ÷ $250,000) and 16% money funds ($40,000 ÷ $250,000). The emphasis in the portfolio is long-term growth at an average risk level, with a moderate dividend return. The portfolio consists of nine issues; this

TABLE 16.9 Bob and Gail Weiss's Common Stock Portfolio

Objective: Long-term Growth (Average Risk, Moderate Dividends)

Number of Shares	Company	Dividend per Share	Dividend Income	Price per Share	Total Cost (including commission)	Beta	Dividend Yield
1,000	Bancorp West, Inc.	$1.20	$ 1,200	$22	$ 22,200	.86	5.4%
600	BST, Inc.	2.80	1,680	40	24,200	1.00	6.9
1,000	Florida Southcoast Banks	1.20	1,200	23	23,200	.84	5.2
1,000	Kings	1.60	1,600	25	25,300	.88	6.3
500	Light Newspapers	0.92	460	46	23,200	1.12	2.0
600	Miller Foods	1.88	1,128	37	22,400	1.07	5.0
800	State Oil of California	1.00	800	27	21,800	1.30	3.7
600	Vornox	2.28	1,368	40	24,200	1.04	5.7
600	Woodstock	1.30	780	36	21,800	1.32	3.6
	Total		$10,216		$208,300		4.9%

Portfolio beta = 1.04

appears to be sufficient diversification. The portfolio's beta is 1.04, indicating a level of nondiversifiable risk that approximately equals that of the stock market as a whole. The portfolio's dividend yield is about 4.9%, which approximates the average dividend return for the entire stock market. The betas of individual securities in the portfolio vary somewhat. However, the portfolio's overall risk is moderate.

The Weiss portfolio consists of stocks from a wide range of American business. All the companies have above-average growth potential, and none is engaged in high-risk businesses that could face technological obsolescence or heavy foreign competition. Two banking stocks are included: Bancorp West, Inc., and Florida Southcoast Banks. The former is a well-managed bank holding company that owns the largest bank in California. The latter is a growing bank holding company located on the south coast of Florida. Both regions are experiencing rapid economic growth and population increases. BST, Inc., appears to be well positioned in the growing communications industry. Kings is a food processor with a solid future. Light Newspapers is a large chain with many Sunbelt papers. Miller Foods is expanding as well, helped by its 1998 acquisition of Denton Companies, a superbly managed supermarket chain. The portfolio has two natural resource stocks, State Oil of California and Woodstock. These companies are well positioned in their respective industries. Vornox is a major drug firm that should benefit from America's aging demographic mix. All of the stocks in the Weisses' portfolio are securities of well-managed companies. With this portfolio, the Weisses will have potential price appreciation coupled with a steady dividend income.

Julio and Gina Vitello: Retirees

Having just sold their family business and liquidated their real estate investment property, Julio and Gina Vitello are eager to begin their retirement. At age 60, both have worked hard for 35 years building the successful business they recently sold. In addition, they have made some successful real estate investments over the years. The sale of their business and real estate holdings has netted them \$600,000 after taxes. They wish to invest these funds and have asked their investment adviser, Jane Tuttle, to develop a portfolio for them. The relevant financial information about the Vitellos is as follows: They own their home free and clear and have a \$300,000 bond portfolio that yields yearly income of \$30,000. In addition, they have \$100,000 in short-term securities that they wish to hold as a ready cash reserve. Their most recent asset allocation is therefore 60% business and real estate investments (\$600,000 ÷ \$1,000,000), 30% bonds (\$300,000 ÷ \$1,000,000), and 10% short-term securities (\$100,000 ÷ \$1,000,000). Mr. Vitello has a \$200,000 whole-life insurance policy on his life, with Mrs. Vitello the designated beneficiary.

Now that they are retired, neither of the Vitellos plans to seek employment. They do have a small pension plan that will begin paying an income of \$6,000 per year in 5 years. However, their main source of income will be their investment portfolio. During their last few working years, their combined yearly income was approximately \$85,000. Their standard of living is rather high, and they do not wish to change their lifestyle significantly. They do not plan to spend any of their investment capital on living expenses, because they want to keep their estate intact for their two children. Thus the Vitellos' basic investment objective is current income with some capital appreciation potential. The Vitellos do not wish to reinvest in real estate but, rather, have asked Ms. Tuttle to develop a $600,000 securities portfolio for them. (They will leave their $300,000 bond portfolio and $100,000 in short-term securities undisturbed.) Their resulting asset allocation would shift to 60% common stock, 30% bonds, and 10% short-term securities.

The portfolio developed for the Vitellos is shown in Table 16.10. It contains nine stocks with approximately $65,000 invested in each issue. The emphasis is on quality, with low-risk–high-yield issues, and diversification. The portfolio's beta is approximately .80—a risk level that is below that of the general stock market. It is expected that a large portion of the portfolio's total return (dividends plus price appreciation) will be in the form of dividend income. The portfolio has a current dividend yield of approximately 8.7%, an above-average dividend yield. Dividend income totals over $52,000, which, added to the bond income and the short-term securities' interest, will provide the Vitellos with a gross income of about $85,000. The Vitellos' after-tax income will equal their working years' income, so they will not have to alter their lifestyle.

Analyzing the individual issues in the Vitellos' portfolio, we can see that four public utility stocks are included. Utility stocks are often suitable for low-risk, current-income-oriented portfolios. High-quality electric and natural gas concerns tend to have moderate growth in earnings and dividends. The four issues in the portfolio—Findly Power and Light, Gulf Gas and Electric, Public Power Company, and Southwest Utilities—have growing service areas and records of increases in profits and dividends. The stocks of two large American companies, Energon and Smith, Roberts & Company, are included in the portfolio. Energon is a large U.S. energy company that offers a high dividend yield. Smith, Roberts is one of the largest retailers, and the company is now diversifying into information services. Two bank holding company stocks were also selected: Alaska Bancorp and Dallas National. Alaska Bancorp offers a top-quality vehicle to participate in Alaska's growth. Dallas National was selected because of its above-average dividend yield and because the firm

TABLE 16.10 Julio and Gina Vitello's Common Stock Portfolio

Objective: Current Income (Low Risk, High Yield)

Number of Shares	Company	Dividend per Share	Dividend Income	Price per Share	Total Cost (including commission)	Beta	Dividend Yield
3,000	Alaska Bancorp, Inc.	$1.20	$ 3,600	$22	$ 66,600	.86	5.4%
2,000	Dallas National Corporation	2.40	4,800	30	60,600	.81	7.9
2,500	Energon	3.00	7,500	27	68,100	1.01	11.0
2,000	Findly Power and Light	3.36	6,720	32	64,600	.63	10.4
2,000	Geoco	2.80	5,600	35	70,700	1.13	7.9
2,500	Gulf Gas and Electric	3.00	7,500	28	70,700	.53	10.6
4,000	Public Power Company	1.76	7,040	16	64,600	.72	10.9
2,500	Smith, Roberts & Company	1.36	3,400	27	68,100	.92	5.0
3,000	Southwest Utilities	2.04	6,120	21	63,600	.60	9.6
	Total		$52,280		$597,600		8.7%

Portfolio beta = .80

is well positioned in the Dallas market. Additionally, the company has raised its dividend several times in recent years, and future dividend increases are expected. Geoco is a large company with chemical and other diversified operations. All the issues in the Vitellos' portfolio are well-known, relatively large corporations. Stability, low risk, and a relatively high dividend yield with some potential for increased share values characterize the stocks in this portfolio.

Lucille Hatch: Widow

Most retirees have less money to invest than the Vitellos in the preceding example. Lucille Hatch, age 70, was recently widowed. Between the estate of her late husband, her personal assets, and their jointly owned assets, Lucille has approximately $485,000 in liquid assets, all of it in savings and money market accounts (short-term investments). Her current asset allocation is therefore 100% short-term investments ($485,000 ÷ $485,000). Lucille owns her home free and clear. Other than the interest on her savings, her income consists of $900 per month from Social Security. Unfortunately, her husband's employer did not have a pension plan. She has turned to her investment adviser, Charles Puckett, to discuss strategy and develop an investment policy.

Between Social Security and interest earned on her short-term investments, Mrs. Hatch's current income is approximately $35,000 annually. She wishes to increase that income, if possible, while only minimally raising her risk exposure. Mr. Puckett recommended the investment portfolio presented in Table 16.11. The portfolio's objective is to maximize current income while keeping risk at a low level. All of the money was invested in fixed-income securities, with approximately $415,000 going to high-quality corporate bonds and the balance ($70,000) retained in short-term investments to provide a substantial contingency reserve. The resulting asset allocation is about

TABLE 16.11 Lucille Hatch's Bond Portfolio

Objective: Maximize Current Income (Minimal Risk)

Par Value	Issue	Standard & Poor's Bond Rating	Interest Income	Quoted Price	Total Cost	Yield to Maturity	Current Yield
$70,000	Boise Northern 8⅞% due 2020	A	$ 6,212.50	100	$ 70,000	8.875%	8.875%
70,000	Dalston Company 7½% due 2004	A	5,250.00	98	68,600	8.000	7.650
70,000	Maryland-Pacific 6.70% due 2002	A	4,690.00	97	67,900	7.860	6.900
70,000	Pacific Utilities 8⅞% due 2028	AA	6,212.50	100	70,000	8.875	8.875
70,000	Trans-States Telephone 8.70% due 2034	A	6,090.00	97	67,900	8.980	8.970
70,000	Urban Life 8½% due 2005	AA	5,950.00	100	70,000	8.500	8.500
	Total		$34,405.00		$414,400	8.340%	8.300%

86% bonds ($415,000 ÷ $485,000) and 14% short-term investments ($70,000 ÷ $485,000). Investing in the bond portfolio will increase Mrs. Hatch's yearly income from approximately $35,000 to about $48,700 ($10,800 Social Security, $3,500 earnings on short-term investments, and $34,400 bond interest). This puts Mrs. Hatch in a 30% marginal tax bracket (federal and state tax combined). Taxable corporate bonds were recommended over tax-free municipal bonds because her after-tax rate of return would be greater with the former.

Turning to the portfolio, we see that there are six corporate bond issues that cost about $70,000 each. Each issuer is a high-quality company with a low risk of default. Mrs. Hatch's portfolio is diversified in several ways: First, it contains a mix of industrial, utility, railroad, and financial issues. The two utility bond issues are Pacific Utilities and Trans-States Telephone. Both companies are large and financially secure. The two industrial concerns, Dalston and Maryland-Pacific, are large as well. Boise Northern is a financially solid railroad, and Urban Life is a large, secure insurance company. A second added measure of diversification is attained by staggering the bonds' maturities. They mature in six different years: 2002, 2004, 2005, 2020, 2028, and 2034. The shorter-term bonds will provide ready cash when they mature, and they generally will fluctuate less in price than the longer-term bonds. The portfolio has been diversified to keep the risk of loss low. By switching funds out of her short-term investments into bonds, Mrs. Hatch was able to increase her current income substantially while experiencing only a small increase in risk.

CONCEPTS IN REVIEW

16.20 Evaluate the effective system for keeping track of your portfolio records that was described in the *Investing in Action* box on page 655. How might this system help you consolidate your portfolio?

16.21 Describe and contrast the expected portfolios for each of the following investors:

a. A retired investor in need of income
b. A high-income, financially secure investor
c. A young investor with a secure job and no dependents

Summary

LG 1 **Understand the objectives of portfolio management and the procedures used to calculate the return and standard deviation of a portfolio.** A portfolio is a collection of investment vehicles assembled to achieve a common investment goal. It involves a tradeoff between risk and return, potential price appreciation and current income, and varying risk levels in the portfolio. The return on a portfolio is calculated as a weighted average of the returns of the assets from which it is formed. The standard deviation of a portfolio's returns is found by applying the same formula that is used to find the standard deviation of a single asset.

LG 2 **Discuss the concepts of correlation and diversification, their impact on portfolio risk and return, and the effectiveness, methods, and benefits of international diversification.** Correlation is a statistic used to measure the relationship, if any, between the returns on assets. To diversify, it is best to add assets with negatively correlated returns. In general, the less positive and more negative the correlation between asset returns, the more effectively a portfolio can be diversified to reduce its risk. Through diversification, the risk (standard deviation) of a portfolio can be reduced below the risk of the least risky asset (sometimes to zero); however, the return of the resulting portfolio will be no lower than the smallest return of its component assets. International diversification may allow an investor to reduce portfolio risk without experiencing a corresponding reduction in return. It can be achieved by investing abroad or through domestic investment in foreign companies or funds. The use of ADRs or international mutual funds available in the United States is generally preferable.

LG 3 **Review the two basic approaches to portfolio management—traditional and modern—and reconcile them.** Under the traditional approach, portfolios are constructed by combining a large number of securities issued by companies from a broad cross section of industries. Modern portfolio theory (MPT) uses statistical diversification to develop efficient portfolios. Theoretically, to determine the optimal portfolio, MPT finds the efficient frontier and couples it with an investor's utility function or risk-indifference curves. In practice, portfolio betas can be used to develop efficient portfolios consistent with the investor's risk–return preferences. Generally, investors use elements of both the traditional approach and MPT to create portfolios.

LG 4 **Describe the role of investor characteristics and objectives and of portfolio objectives and policies in constructing an investment portfolio.** To construct a portfolio, the investor should consider characteristics such as level and stability of income, family factors, net worth, experience and age, and disposition toward risk. He or she should specify objectives and should plan and construct a portfolio consistent with them. Commonly considered portfolio objectives include current income, capital preservation, capital growth, tax considerations, and level of risk.

LG 5 **Summarize why and how investors use an asset allocation scheme to construct an investment portfolio.** Asset allocation involves dividing one's portfolio into various asset classes in order to preserve capital. Like diversification, asset allocation aims to protect against negative developments while taking advantage of positive developments. The basic approaches to asset allocation involve the use of fixed weightings, flexible weightings, or tactical asset allocation—a sophisticated approach that uses futures contracts. Asset allocation can be achieved on a do-it-yourself basis, with the use of mutual funds, or by merely buying shares in an asset allocation fund.

LG 6 **Relate investor objectives to the asset allocations and risk–return profiles reflected in various types of portfolios.** An investor's objectives determine the asset allocations and risk–return profile for his or her portfolio. A single investor who wants to build wealth quickly will tend to allocate funds to more risky assets that have high growth potential; a retired couple who needs income to meet their living expenses will allocate funds to conservative, low-risk investment vehicles that provide periodic income in the form of dividends or interest.

Discussion Questions

LG 1 Q16.1. State your portfolio objectives. Then construct a 10-stock portfolio (of companies that have been public for at least 5 years) that you feel is consistent with your objectives. Obtain annual dividend and price data on the stocks you've chosen for each of the past 5 years.

a. Calculate the historical return for each stock for each year.
b. Calculate the historical portfolio return for each of the 5 years, using your findings in part (a).
c. Use your findings in part (b) to calculate the average portfolio return over the 5 years.

d. Use your findings in parts (b) and (c) to find the standard deviation of the portfolio's returns over the 5-year period.
e. Use the historical average return from part (c) and the standard deviation from part (d) to evaluate the portfolio's return and risk in light of your stated portfolio objectives.

LG 2

Q16.2. Choose, according to the following guidelines, the stocks—A, B, and C—of three firms that have been public for at least 10 years. Stock A should be one you are interested in buying. Stock B should be a stock, possibly in the same line of business or industry, that you feel will have high positive return correlation with stock A. Finally, stock C should be one you feel will have high negative return correlation with stock A.

a. Calculate the annual rates of return for each of the past 10 years for each stock.
b. Plot the 10 annual return values for each stock on the same set of axes, where the x-axis is the year and the y-axis is the annual return in percentage terms.
c. Join the points for the returns for each stock on the graph. Evaluate and describe the returns of stocks A and B in the graph. Do they exhibit the expected positive correlation? Why or why not?
d. Evaluate and describe the relationship between the returns of stocks A and C in the graph. Do they exhibit the expected negative correlation? Why or why not?
e. Compare and contrast your findings in parts (c) and (d) to the expected relationships among stocks A, B, and C. Discuss your findings.

LG 2 LG 3

Q16.3. Obtain a prospectus and an annual report for a major mutual fund that includes some international securities. Carefully read the prospectus and annual report and study the portfolio's composition in light of the fund's stated objectives.

a. Assess the fund manager's investment approach. Does the fund use a traditional approach, modern portfolio theory (MPT), or a combination of the two?
b. Evaluate the amount of diversification and the types of industries and companies held. Is the portfolio well diversified?
c. Assess the degree of international diversification achieved. Does management consciously include international securities to improve the fund's risk–return outcome?
d. Overall, how well does management seem to be managing the portfolio in light of the fund's stated objectives with regard to diversification?

LG 3

Q16.4. Use *Value Line* or some other source to select six stocks with betas ranging from about .5 to 1.5. Record the current market prices of each of these stocks. Assume you wish to create a portfolio that combines all six stocks in such a way that the resulting portfolio beta is about 1.1.

a. Through trial and error, use all six stocks to create a portfolio with the target beta of 1.1.
b. If you have $100,000 to invest in this portfolio, on the basis of the weightings determined in part (a), how much in dollars would you invest in each stock?
c. Approximately how many shares of each of the six stocks would you buy, given the dollar amounts calculated in part (b)?
d. Repeat parts (a), (b), and (c) with a different set of weightings that still result in a portfolio beta of 1.1. Can only one unique portfolio with a given beta be created from a given set of stocks?
e. Why might the use of beta to measure the risk of the portfolios created in parts (a) and (d) not be an accurate measure of risk in this case? Explain.

LG 4 LG 5 LG 6

Q16.5. List your personal characteristics and then state your investment objectives in light of them. Use these objectives as a basis for developing and stating your portfolio objectives and policies. Assume that you plan to create a portfolio aimed at achieving your stated objectives. The portfolio will be constructed by allocating your money to any of the following asset classes: common stock, bonds, foreign securities, short-term securities, and real estate.

a. Determine and justify an asset allocation to these five classes in light of your stated portfolio objectives and policies.
b. Describe the types of investments you would choose for each of the asset classes.
c. Assume that after making the asset allocations specified in part (a), you receive a sizable inheritance that causes your portfolio objectives to change to a much more aggressive posture. Describe the changes from your answer to part (a) that you would make in your asset allocations.
d. Describe other asset classes you might consider when developing your asset allocation scheme.

Problems

LG 1 LG 2

P16.1. Assume you are considering a portfolio containing two assets, L and M. Asset L will represent 40% of the dollar value of the portfolio, and asset M will account for the other 60%. The expected returns over the next 6 years, 2000–2005, for each of these assets are summarized in the following table.

	Expected Return (%)	
Year	Asset L	Asset M
2000	14	20
2001	14	18
2002	16	16
2003	17	14
2004	17	12
2005	19	10

a. Calculate the expected portfolio return, r_p, for each of the 6 years.
b. Calculate the average expected portfolio return, $\bar{r}_p$, over the 6-year period.
c. Calculate the standard deviation of expected portfolio returns, s_p, over the 6-year period.
d. How would you characterize the correlation of returns of the two assets L and M?
e. Discuss any benefits of diversification achieved through creation of the portfolio.

LG 1 LG 2

P16.2. You have been given the following return data on three assets—F, G, and H—over the period 2000–2003.

	Expected Return (%)		
Year	Asset F	Asset G	Asset H
2000	16	17	14
2001	17	16	15
2002	18	15	16
2003	19	14	17

Using these assets, you have isolated three investment alternatives:

Alternative	Investment
1	100% of asset F
2	50% of asset F and 50% of asset G
3	50% of asset F and 50% of asset H

a. Calculate the portfolio return over the 4-year period for each of the three alternatives.
b. Calculate the standard deviation of returns over the 4-year period for each of the three alternatives.
c. On the basis of your findings in parts (a) and (b), which of the three investment alternatives would you recommend? Why?

LG 1 LG 2

P16.3. You have been asked for your advice in selecting a portfolio of assets and have been supplied with the following data:

	Expected Return (%)		
Year	Asset A	Asset B	Asset C
2000	12	16	12
2001	14	14	14
2002	16	12	16

You have been told that you can create two portfolios—one consisting of assets A and B and the other consisting of assets A and C—by investing equal proportions (50%) in each of the two component assets.

a. What is the average expected return, $\bar{r}$, for each asset over the 3-year period?
b. What is the standard deviation, s, for each asset's expected return?
c. What is the average expected return, $\bar{r}_p$, for each of the two portfolios?
d. How would you characterize the correlations of returns of the two assets making up each of the two portfolios identified in part (c)?
e. What is the standard deviation of expected returns, s_p, for each portfolio?
f. Which portfolio do you recommend? Why?

LG 1 LG 2

P16.4. Assume you wish to evaluate the risk and return behaviors associated with various combinations of assets V and W under three assumed degrees of correlation: perfect positive, uncorrelated, and perfect negative. The following average return and risk values were calculated for these assets:

Asset	Average Return, $\bar{r}$ (%)	Risk (Standard Deviation), s (%)
V	8	5
W	13	10

a. If the returns of assets V and W are *perfectly positively correlated* (correlation coefficient = +1), describe the *range* of (1) return and (2) risk associated with all possible portfolio combinations.
b. If the returns of assets V and W are *uncorrelated* (correlation coefficient = 0), describe the *approximate range* of (1) return and (2) risk associated with all possible portfolio combinations.
c. If the returns of assets V and W are *perfectly negatively correlated* (correlation coefficient = −1), describe the *range* of (1) return and (2) risk associated with all possible portfolio combinations.

LG 3

P16.5. Portfolios A through J, which are listed in the following table along with their returns (r_p) and risk (measured by the standard deviation, s_p), represent all currently available portfolios in the feasible or attainable set.

Portfolio	Return (r_p)	Risk (s_p)
A	9%	8%
B	3	3
C	14	10
D	12	14
E	7	11
F	11	6
G	10	12
H	16	16
I	5	7
J	8	4

a. Plot the *feasible or attainable set* represented by these data on a set of portfolio risk, s_p(x-axis)–portfolio return, r_p (y-axis) axes.
b. Draw the *efficient frontier* on the graph in part (a).
c. Which portfolios lie on the efficient frontier? Why do these portfolios dominate all others in the feasible or attainable set?
d. How would an investor's *utility function* or *risk-indifference curves* be used with the efficient frontier to find the optimal portfolio?

LG 3

P16.6. For his portfolio, David Finney randomly selected securities from all those listed on the New York Stock Exchange. He began with one security and added securities one by one until a total of 20 securities were held in the portfolio. After each security was added, David calculated the portfolio standard deviation, s_p. The calculated values follow.

Number of Securities	Portfolio Risk, s_p (%)	Number of Securities	Portfolio Risk, s_p (%)
1	14.50	11	7.00
2	13.30	12	6.80
3	12.20	13	6.70
4	11.20	14	6.65
5	10.30	15	6.60
6	9.50	16	6.56
7	8.80	17	6.52
8	8.20	18	6.50
9	7.70	19	6.48
10	7.30	20	6.47

a. On a set of axes showing number of securities in portfolio (x-axis) and portfolio risk, s_p (y-axis), plot the portfolio risk data given in the preceding table.
b. Divide the total portfolio risk in the graph into its *nondiversifiable* and *diversifiable* risk components, and label each of these on the graph.
c. Describe which of the two risk components is the *relevant risk,* and explain why it is relevant. How much of this risk exists in David Finney's portfolio?

LG 3

P16.7. If portfolio A has a beta of +1.5 and portfolio Z has a beta of −1.5, what do the two values indicate? If the return on the market rises by 20%, what impact, if any, would this have on the returns from portfolios A and Z? Explain.

LG 3

P16.8. Stock A has a beta of 0.80, stock B has a beta of 1.40, and stock C has a beta of −0.30.

a. Rank these stocks from the most risky to the least risky.
b. If the return on the market portfolio increases by 12%, what change in the return for each of the stocks would you expect?
c. If the return on the market portfolio declines by 5%, what change in the return for each of the stocks would you expect?
d. If you felt the stock market was about to experience a significant decline, which stock would you be most likely to add to your portfolio? Why?
e. If you anticipated a major stock market rally, which stock would you be most likely to add to your portfolio? Why?

LG 3

P16.9. Rose Berry is attempting to evaluate two possible portfolios consisting of the same five assets but held in different proportions. She is particularly interested in using beta to compare the risk of the portfolios and, in this regard, has gathered the following data:

		Portfolio Weights (%)	
Asset	Asset Beta	Portfolio A	Portfolio B
1	1.30	10	30
2	.70	30	10
3	1.25	10	20
4	1.10	10	20
5	.90	40	20
	Total	100	100

a. Calculate the betas for portfolios A and B.
b. Compare the risk of each portfolio to the market as well as to each other. Which portfolio is more risky?

Case Problem 16.1 *Traditional versus Modern Portfolio Theory: Who's Right?*

LG 3

Walt Davies and Shane O'Brien are district managers for Lee, Inc. Over the years, as they moved through the firm's sales organization, they became (and they still remain) close friends. Walt, who is 33 years old, currently lives in Princeton, New Jersey; Shane, who is 35, lives in Houston, Texas. Recently, at the national sales meeting, they were discussing various company matters, as well as bringing each other up to date on their families, when the subject of investments came up. Each of them had always been fascinated by the stock market, and now that they had achieved some degree of financial success, they had begun actively investing. As they discussed their investments, Walt indicated that he felt the only way an individual who does not have hundreds of thousands of dollars can invest safely is to buy mutual fund shares. He emphasized that to be safe, a person needs to hold a broadly diversified portfolio and that only those with a lot of money and time can achieve independently the diversification that can be readily obtained by purchasing mutual fund shares.

Shane totally disagreed. He said, "Diversification! Who needs it?" He felt that what one must do is look carefully at stocks possessing desired risk–return characteristics and then invest all one's money in the single best stock. Walt told him he was crazy. He said, "There is no way to measure risk conveniently—you're just gambling." Shane disagreed. He explained how his stockbroker had acquainted him with beta, which is a measure of risk. Shane said that the higher the beta, the more risky the stock, and therefore the higher its return. By looking up the betas for potential stock investments in his broker's beta book, he can pick stocks that have an acceptable risk level for him. Shane explained that with beta, one does not need to diversify; one merely needs to be willing to accept the risk reflected by beta and then hope for the best. The conversation continued, with Walt indicating that although he knew nothing about beta, he didn't believe one could safely invest in a single stock. Shane continued to argue that his broker had explained to him that betas can be calculated not just for a single stock but also for a portfolio of stocks, such as a mutual fund. He said, "What's the difference between a stock with a beta of, say, 1.20 and a mutual fund with a beta of 1.20? They both have the same risk and should therefore provide similar returns."

As Walt and Shane continued to discuss their differing opinions relative to investment strategy, they began to get angry with each other. Neither was able to convince the other that he was right. The level of their voices now raised, they attracted the attention of the company vice-president of finance, Elinor Green, who was standing nearby. She came over and indicated she had overheard their argument about investments and thought that, given her expertise on financial matters, she might be able to resolve their disagreement. She asked them to explain the crux of their disagreement, and each reviewed his own viewpoint. After hearing their views, Elinor responded, "I have some good news and some bad news for each of you. There is some validity to what each of you says, but there also are some errors in each of your explanations. Walt tends to support the traditional approach to portfolio management; Shane's views are more supportive of modern portfolio theory." Just then, the company president interrupted them, needing to talk to Elinor immediately. Elinor apologized for having to leave and offered to continue their discussion later that evening.

QUESTIONS

a. Analyze Walt's argument and explain why a mutual fund investment may be over-diversified. Also explain why one does not necessarily have to have hundreds of thousands of dollars to diversify adequately.

b. Analyze Shane's argument and explain the major error in his logic relative to the use of beta as a substitute for diversification. Explain the key assumption underlying the use of beta as a risk measure.

c. Briefly describe the traditional approach to portfolio management and relate it to the approaches supported by Walt and Shane.

d. Briefly describe modern portfolio theory (MPT) and relate it to the approaches supported by Walt and Shane. Be sure to mention diversifiable risk, nondiversifiable risk, and total risk, along with the role of beta.

e. Explain how the traditional approach and modern portfolio theory can be blended into an approach to portfolio management that might prove useful to the individual investor. Relate this to reconciling Walt's and Shane's differing points of view.

Case Problem 16.2 *Susan Lussier's Inherited Portfolio: Does It Meet Her Needs?*

LG 3 LG 4 LG 5

Susan Lussier is a 35-year-old divorcée currently employed as a tax attorney for a major oil and gas exploration company. She has no children and earns nearly $90,000 per year from her salary and from participation in the company's drilling activities. Divorced only a year, Susan has found being single quite exciting. An expert on oil and gas taxation, she is not worried about job security—she is content with her income and finds it adequate to allow her to buy and do whatever she wishes. Her current philosophy is to live each day to its fullest, not concerning herself with retirement, which is too far in the future to require her current attention.

A month ago, Susan's only surviving parent, her father, was killed in a sailing accident. He had retired in La Jolla, California, 2 years earlier and had spent most of his time sailing. Prior to retirement, he owned a children's clothing manufacturing firm in South Carolina. Upon retirement he sold the firm and invested the proceeds in a security portfolio that provided him with retirement income of over $30,000 per year. In his will, which incidentally had been drafted by Susan a number of years earlier, he left his entire estate to her. The estate was structured in such a way that in addition to a few family heirlooms, Susan received a security portfolio having a market value of nearly $350,000 and about $10,000 in cash. The portfolio contained 10 securities: 5 bonds, 2 common stocks, and 3 mutual funds. The accompanying table lists the securities and their key characteristics. The common stocks were issued by large, mature, well-known firms that had exhibited continuing patterns of dividend payment over the past 5 years. The stocks offered only moderate growth potential—probably no more than 2% to 3% appreciation per year. The mutual funds in the portfolio were income funds invested in diversified portfolios of income-oriented stocks and bonds. They provided stable streams of dividend income but offered little opportunity for capital appreciation.

Case 16.2 The Securities Portfolio That Susan Lussier Inherited

			Bonds				
Par Value	**Issue**	**S&P Rating**	**Interest Income**	**Quoted Price**	**Total Cost**		**Current Yield**
$40,000	Delta Power and Light 10⅛% due 2017	AA	$ 4,050	98	$ 39,200		10.33%
30,000	Mountain Water 9¾% due 2009	A	2,925	102	30,600		9.56
50,000	California Gas 9½% due 2004	AAA	4,750	97	48,500		9.79
20,000	Trans-Pacific Gas 10% due 2015	AAA	2,000	99	19,800		10.10
20,000	Public Service 9⅞% due 2005	AA	1,975	100	20,000		9.88
			Common Stocks				
Number of Shares	**Company**	**Dividend per Share**	**Dividend Income**	**Price per Share**	**Total Cost**	**Beta**	**Dividend Yield**
2,000	International Supply	$2.40	$ 4,800	$ 22	$ 44,900	.97	10.91%
3,000	Black Motor	1.50	4,500	17	52,000	.85	8.82
			Mutual Funds				
Number of Shares	**Fund**	**Dividend per Share**	**Dividend Income**	**Price per Share**	**Total Cost**	**Beta**	**Dividend Yield**
2,000	International Capital Income A Fund	$ .80	$ 1,600	$ 10	$ 20,000	1.02	8.00%
1,000	Grimner Special Income Fund	2.00	2,000	15	15,000	1.10	7.50
4,000	Ellis Diversified Income Fund	1.20	4,800	12	48,800	.90	10.00
		Total annual income:	$33,400	Portfolio value:	$338,000	Portfolio current yield:	9.88%

Now that Susan owns the portfolio, she wishes to determine whether it is suitable for her situation. She realizes that the high level of income provided by the portfolio will be taxed at a rate (federal plus state) in excess of 35%. Because she does not currently need it, Susan plans to invest the after-tax income in tax-deferred real estate, oil and gas partnerships, and/or common stocks offering high capital gain potential. She clearly needs to shelter taxable income. (Susan is already paying out a sizable portion of her current income in taxes.) She feels fortunate to have received the portfolio and wants to make certain it provides her with the maximum benefits, given her financial situation. The $10,000 cash left to her will be especially useful in paying broker's commissions associated with making portfolio adjustments.

QUESTIONS

a. Briefly assess Susan's financial situation and develop a portfolio objective for her that is consistent with her needs.

b. Evaluate the portfolio left to Susan by her father. Assess its apparent objective and evaluate how well it may be doing in fulfilling this objective. Use the total cost values to describe the asset allocation scheme reflected in the portfolio. Comment on the risk, return, and tax implications of this portfolio.

c. If Susan decided to invest in a security portfolio consistent with her needs—indicated in response to question (a)—describe the nature and mix, if any, of securities you would recommend she purchase. What asset allocation scheme would result from your recommendation? Discuss the risk, return, and tax implications of such a portfolio.

d. Compare the nature of the security portfolio inherited by Susan [from the response to question (b)] with what you believe would be an appropriate security portfolio for her [from the response to question (c)].

e. What recommendations would you give Susan about the inherited portfolio? Explain the steps she should take to adjust the portfolio to her needs.

Home Page Exercises

http://hepg.aw.com **Keyword: Invest**

Putting together a portfolio of assets can be an intimidating experience for the novice investor. The thousands of assets available make the selection process challenging at best. The Web offers sites that assist individual investors with the topic of asset allocation. Discussion of modern portfolio theory is less readily available on the Web. Most information on modern portfolio theory is from academic sites that provide relatively complicated treatment of the topic.

Web Address	*Primary Investment Focus*
mail.coos.or.us/~wbern/eff/index.shtm	A journal dealing exclusively with efficient asset allocation using modern portfolio theory techniques
www.columbiafunds.com maximizing_return.html#1	A useful article on matching investor objectives with asset allocation
www.healthwealthsolutions.com/globaltrading/	A good site on the need for and approach to global investing
www.wellsfargo.com/investing/assetall	A Wells Fargo Bank Web address with pages on portfolio planning and asset allocation

W16.1. Barbara Jolly has $2,000 that she wishes to invest. Barbara has talked with her friends about the need for diversification between asset classes and within each class to reduce the risk of an investor's portfolio. She understands that investing in a mutual fund provides some diversification. Barbara read that the Fidelity family of mutual funds is one of the largest families available. Her friends have mentioned that they own shares in Fidelity's Air Transportation Portfolio and its Growth and Income Portfolio. Access these two portfolios at the Fidelity Web site given here, and select the *Fidelity Select Portfolios* or the *Growth and Income* option from the menu to find the specific portfolios Barbara is considering. Review the major market sectors and the top 10 holdings for both funds, and then answer the questions that follow.

personal32.fidelity.com/products/funds/fidelityindex.html

a. What asset classes and sectors does each fund invest in?
b. What are the top 10 holdings and what portion of the total portfolio do they represent?
c. What information would you provide Barbara about the degree of diversification she would achieve by investing in each fund?

W16.2. Hank and Harriet Hathaway have completed questionnaires about risk tolerance and find that they are able to accept a moderate to moderately conservative amount of risk. After reading the *Wall Street Journal* over several months, they have found six companies whose stock they may want to buy. At the Morningstar Web site listed here, click on *Quicktake Reports,* and then enter the appropriate ticker symbols to obtain the individual company reports. Under the Valuation section, access the Morningstar style box. If you are unfamiliar with the Morningstar style boxes or need to review their meaning, read the article titled "Recipe for the Morningstar Style Box" at *www.morningstar.net/Cover/LearnArchive.html.*

www.morningstar.net

a. Which, if any, of these six stocks appear(s) to be consistent with Hank and Harriet's risk preference?
   (1) Dole Food (DOL)
   (2) Dow Chemical (DOW)
   (3) First Union (FTU)
   (4) Compaq Computer (CPQ)
   (5) Kimberly Clark (KMB)
   (6) Hitachi (HIT)

CHAPTER 17

PORTFOLIO MANAGEMENT AND CONTROL

LEARNING GOALS

After studying this chapter, you should be able to:

LG 1 Discuss sources of needed data and the indexes commonly used to evaluate the performance of investments.

LG 2 Describe the techniques used to measure the performance of individual investment vehicles, and compare performance to investment goals.

LG 3 Understand the techniques used to measure income, capital gains, and total portfolio return relative to the amount of money invested in a portfolio.

LG 4 Use the Sharpe, Treynor, and Jensen measures to compare a portfolio's return with a risk-adjusted, market-adjusted rate of return, and discuss portfolio revision.

LG 5 Describe the role of formula plans and the logic of dollar-cost averaging, constant-dollar plans, constant-ratio plans, and variable-ratio plans.

LG 6 Explain the role of limit and stop-loss orders in investment timing, the warehousing of liquidity, and the key factors in timing investment sales to achieve investment goals.

Berkshire Hathaway Inc.

He's known as the "Oracle of Omaha" for his stock-picking common sense. As chairman of Berkshire Hathaway Inc., Warren Buffet has multiplied his investors' money by a factor of 1,000 over the past three decades. The Omaha-based company is really a publicly held investment firm, with major holdings in American Express, Coca-Cola, Disney, GEICO insurance, McDonald's, The Washington Post, Wells Fargo, and others. Berkshire Hathaway stock doesn't come cheap: In mid-1998, it was selling for roughly \$71,000 per share. Over the last 32 years, the company's per share book value has grown from \$19 to \$19,000. Buffet's claim to fame has been his ability to buy businesses at prices far below what he calls their "intrinsic" value, which includes such intangibles as quality of management and the power of superior brand names. He's also known for his "aw-shucks" demeanor, displayed in his annual letter to shareholders—which you can find at **www.berkshirehathaway.com** on the Internet.

As you'll see in this chapter, which describes portfolio management and control, investing is a process of analysis, followed by action, followed by still more analysis. What has made Buffet so successful is his long-term horizon and his patience—a trait that is often in short supply on Wall Street. You may not be the next Warren Buffet (or maybe you will!), but understanding the techniques for evaluating portfolio performances will put you on the right track.

Evaluating the Performance of Individual Investments

LG 1 LG 2

Imagine that one of your most important personal goals is to have accumulated $15,000 of savings 3 years from now in order to make the down payment on your first house. You project that the desired house will cost $100,000 and that the $15,000 will be sufficient to make a 10% down payment and pay the associated closing costs. Your calculations indicate that this goal can be achieved by investing existing savings plus an additional $200 per month over the next 3 years in a vehicle earning 12% per year. Projections of your earnings over the 3-year period indicate that you should just be able to set aside the needed $200 per month. You consult with an investment adviser, Cliff Orbit, who leads you to believe that under his management, the 12% return can be achieved.

It seems simple: Give Cliff your existing savings, send him $200 each month over the next 36 months, and at the end of that period, you will have the $15,000 needed to purchase the house. Unfortunately, there are many uncertainties involved. What if you don't set aside $200 each month? What if Cliff fails to earn the needed 12% annual return? What if in 3 years the desired house costs more than $100,000? Clearly, you must do more than simply devise what appears to be a feasible plan for achieving a future goal. You must also periodically assess your progress toward the goal. As actual outcomes occur, you must compare them to the *planned* outcomes and make any necessary alterations in your plans—or in your goals. Knowing how to measure investment performance is therefore crucial. Here we will emphasize measures suitable for analyzing investment performance. We begin with sources of data.

Obtaining Needed Data

The first step in analyzing investment returns is gathering data that reflect the actual performance of each investment. As pointed out in Chapter 3, many sources of investment information are available. The *Wall Street Journal* and *Barron's,* for example, contain numerous items of information useful in assessing the performance of securities. The same type of information that is used to *make* an investment decision is used to *evaluate* the performance of investments. Two key areas to stay informed about are (1) returns on owned investments and (2) economic and market activity.

Return Data

The basic ingredient in analyzing investment returns is current market information, such as daily price quotations for stocks and bonds. Investors often maintain logs that contain the cost of each investment, as well as dividends, interest, and other sources of income received. By regularly recording price and return data, you can create an ongoing record of price fluctuations and cumulative returns. You should also monitor corporate earnings and dividends, which will affect a company's stock price. The two sources of investment return—current income and capital gains—must of course be combined to determine total return. Combining return components using the techniques presented in Chapter 4 will be illustrated for some of the more popular investment vehicles later in this chapter.

Economic and Market Activity

Changes in the economy and market will affect returns—both the level of current income and the market value of an investment vehicle. The astute investor keeps abreast of international, national, and local economic and market developments. By following economic and market changes, you should be able to assess their potential impact on returns. As economic and market conditions change, you must be prepared to make revisions in the portfolio. In essence, being a knowledgeable investor will improve your chances of generating a profit (or avoiding a loss).

Indexes of Investment Performance

In measuring investment performance, it is often worthwhile to compare your returns with appropriate, broad-based market measures. Indexes useful for the analysis of common stock include the Dow Jones Industrial Average (DJIA), the Standard & Poor's 500 stock composite index (S&P 500), and the New York Stock Exchange composite index (NYSE index). (Detailed discussions of these averages and indexes can be found in Chapter 3.) Although the DJIA is widely cited by the news media, it is *not* considered the most appropriate comparative gauge of stock price movement; this is because of its narrow coverage and its exclusion of many types of stocks. If your portfolio is composed of a broad range of common stocks, the NYSE composite index is probably a more appropriate tool.

A number of indicators are also available for assessing the general behavior of the bond markets. These indicators consider either bond price behavior or bond yield. The Dow Jones composite bond average, based on the closing prices of 10 utility and 10 industrial bonds, is a popular measure of bond price behavior. Like bond quotations, this average reflects the average percentage of face value at which the bonds sell. Also available are bond yield data, which reflect the rate of return one would earn on a bond purchased today and held to maturity. Popular sources of these data include the *Wall Street Journal, Barron's,* Standard & Poor's, Moody's Investor Services, and the Federal Reserve. Indexes of bond price and bond yield performance can be obtained for specific types of bonds (industrial, utility, and municipal), as well as on a composite basis. In addition, these and other indexes are sometimes reported in terms of *total returns*—that is, dividend/interest income is combined with price behavior (capital gain or loss) to reflect total return. Such indexes are available for both stocks and bonds.

A few other indexes cover listed options and futures. There are no widely publicized indexes/averages for mutual funds or tangibles. Nor is there a broad index of real estate returns, because such returns tend to be localized. Thus real estate investors should compare their returns with those earned by other local real estate investors. In addition, it might be wise to compare your real estate returns with the consumer price index and with the NYSE composite index. The former will serve as a useful comparative measure of real estate's effectiveness as an inflation hedge. The latter is useful in comparing the relative return on a diversified stock portfolio with that from real estate investment. Similar approaches can be used in assessing other forms of property investment.

Measuring the Performance of Investment Vehicles

Reliable techniques for consistently measuring the performance of each investment vehicle are needed to monitor an investment portfolio. In particular, the holding period return (HPR) measure, first presented in Chapter 4, can be used to determine *actual* return performance. Investment holdings need to be evaluated periodically over time—at least once a year. HPR is an excellent way to assess actual return behavior, because it captures *total return* performance; it is most appropriate for holding or assessment periods of 1 year or less. Total return, in this context, includes the periodic cash income from the investment as well as price appreciation or loss, whether realized or unrealized. The calculation of returns for periods of more than a year should be made using *yield* (internal rate of return), because it recognizes the time value of money; yield can be estimated using the techniques described in Chapter 4 (see pages 133–135). Because the following discussions center on the annual assessment of return, HPR will be used as the measure of return.

The formula for HPR, presented in Chapter 4 (Equation 4.8) and applied throughout this chapter, is restated in Equation 17.1:

Equation 17.1

$$\text{Holding period return} = \frac{\begin{matrix}\text{current income} \\ \text{during period}\end{matrix} + \begin{matrix}\text{capital gain (or loss)} \\ \text{during period}\end{matrix}}{\text{beginning investment value}}$$

Equation 17.1a

$$\text{HPR} = \frac{C + CG}{V_0}$$

where

Equation 17.2

$$\begin{matrix}\text{Capital gain (or loss)} \\ \text{during period}\end{matrix} = \begin{matrix}\text{ending investment} \\ \text{value}\end{matrix} - \begin{matrix}\text{beginning investment} \\ \text{value}\end{matrix}$$

Equation 17.2a

$$CG = V_n - V_0$$

Stocks and Bonds

There are several measures of investment return for stocks and bonds. *Dividend yield,* discussed in Chapter 5, measures the current yearly dividend return earned from a stock investment. It is calculated by dividing a stock's yearly cash dividend by its price. The *current yield* and *promised yield* (yield-to-maturity) for bonds, analyzed in Chapter 9, capture various components of return but do not reflect actual total return. The *holding period return* method *measures the total return (income plus change in value) actually earned on an investment over a given investment period.* We will use HPR, with a holding period of approximately 1 year, in the illustrations that follow.

Stocks The HPR for common and preferred stocks includes both cash dividends received and any price change in the security during the period of ownership. Table 17.1 illustrates the HPR calculation as applied to the actual performance of a common stock. Assume you purchased 1,000 shares of Dallas National Corporation in May 1998 at a cost of $27,312 (including commissions). After holding the stock for just over 1 year, you sold the stock,

TABLE 17.1 Calculation of Pretax HPR on a Common Stock

Security: Dallas National Corporation common stock
Date of purchase: May 1, 1998
Purchase cost: $27,312
Date of sale: May 7, 1999
Sale proceeds: $32,040
Dividends received (May 1998 to May 1999): $2,000

$$\text{Holding period return} = \frac{\$2{,}000 + (\$32{,}040 - \$27{,}312)}{\$27{,}312}$$

$$= +24.63\%$$

reaping proceeds of $32,040. You also received $2,000 in cash dividends during the period of ownership and realized a $4,728 capital gain on the sale. Thus the calculated HPR is 24.63%.

This HPR was calculated without consideration for income taxes paid on the dividends and capital gain. Because many investors are concerned with both pretax and after-tax rates of return, it is useful to calculate an after-tax HPR. We assume, for simplicity in this example, that you are in the 30% tax bracket (federal and state combined); we also assume that, for federal and state tax purposes, capital gains for holding periods of 12 to 18 months are taxed at the same 30% rate. Thus your dividend and capital gain income is taxed at a 30% rate. Income taxes reduce the after-tax dividend income to $1,400 [(1 − 0.30) × $2,000] and the after-tax capital gain to $3,310 [(1 − 0.30) × ($32,040 − $27,312)]. The after-tax HPR is therefore 17.25% [($1,400 + $3,310) ÷ $27,312], a reduction of 7.38 percentage points. It should be clear that both pretax HPR and after-tax HPR are useful gauges of return.

Bonds The HPR for a bond investment is similar to that for stocks. The calculation holds for both straight debt and convertible issues. It includes the two components of a bond investor's return: interest income and capital gain or loss. Calculation of the HPR on a bond investment is illustrated in Table 17.2. Assume you purchased the Phoenix Brewing Company bonds for $10,000, held them for just over 1 year, and then realized $9,704 at sale. In addition, you earned $1,000 in interest during the period of ownership. Thus the HPR of this investment is 7.04%. The HPR is lower than the bond's current yield

TABLE 17.2 Calculation of Pretax HPR on a Bond

Security: Phoenix Brewing Company 10% bonds
Date of purchase: June 2, 1998
Purchase cost: $10,000
Date of sale: June 5, 1999
Sale proceeds: $9,704
Interest earned (June 1998 to June 1999): $1,000

$$\text{Holding period return} = \frac{\$1{,}000 + (\$9{,}704 - \$10{,}000)}{\$10{,}000}$$

$$= +7.04\%$$

of 10% (\$1,000 interest ÷ \$10,000 purchase price) because the bonds were sold at a capital loss. Assuming a 30% tax bracket, the after-tax HPR is 4.93%: {[(1 − 0.30) × \$1,000] + [(1 − 0.30) × (\$9,704 − \$10,000)]} ÷ \$10,000—about 2 percentage points less than the pretax HPR.

Mutual Funds

There are two basic components of return from a mutual fund investment: dividend income (including any capital gains distribution) and change in value. The basic HPR equation for mutual funds is identical to that for stocks. Table 17.3 presents a holding period return calculation for a no-load mutual fund. Assume you purchased 1,000 shares of the fund in July 1998 at a NAV of \$10.40 per share. Because it is a no-load fund, no commission was charged, so your cost was \$10,400. During the 1-year period of ownership, the Pebble Falls Mutual Fund distributed investment income dividends totaling \$270 and capital gains dividends of \$320. You redeemed (sold) this fund at a NAV of \$10.79 per share, thereby realizing \$10,790. As seen in Table 17.3, the pretax holding period return on this investment is 9.42%. Assuming a 30% tax bracket, the after-tax HPR for the fund is 6.60%: {[(1 − 0.30) × (\$270 + \$320)] + [(1 − 0.30) × (\$10,790 − \$10,400)]} ÷ \$10,400—nearly 3 percentage points below the pretax return.

Real Estate

The two basic components of return from real estate are the yearly after-tax cash flow and the change in property value that is likely to occur.

An investor who purchases raw land is interested only in capital appreciation because there is normally no positive cash flow from such an investment. Carrying costs associated with a raw land investment may include property taxes, special assessments, and interest costs if financing is used. An investor's return from a raw land investment is normally realized when the land is sold. **Reversion,** the after-tax net proceeds received upon disposition of real property, is calculated by subtracting from the property's realized selling price all selling costs (commissions plus closing costs), any mortgage principal balances that are paid upon sale, and all income taxes paid on realized capital gains from the sale. Reversion, then, represents the after-tax dollars an investor puts in her or his pocket when the property is sold.

reversion
the after-tax net proceeds received upon disposition of real property.

TABLE 17.3 Calculation of Pretax HPR on a Mutual Fund

Security: Pebble Falls Mutual Fund
Date of purchase: July 1, 1998
Purchase cost: \$10,400
Date of redemption: July 3, 1999
Sale proceeds: \$10,790
Distributions received (July 1998 to July 1999)
  Investment income dividends: \$270
  Capital gains dividends: \$320

$$\text{Holding period return} = \frac{(\$270 + \$320) + (\$10{,}790 - \$10{,}400)}{\$10{,}400}$$

$$= +9.42\%$$

An income property investment provides return in two forms: yearly after-tax cash flow and reversion. A property's yearly after-tax cash flow is basically its rental income minus operating expenses, mortgage payments, and income taxes. In other words, after-tax cash flow is the yearly net cash return an investor receives from rental properties. Both yearly after-tax cash flow and reversion are included when calculating an investor's total return from a rental property.

To provide some insight into the calculation of real estate investment returns, we demonstrate in Table 17.4 the calculation of the after-tax holding period return on an apartment property. (*Note:* Because of the complex nature of real estate taxation, only the after-tax HPR calculation is illustrated.) Assume you acquired the Maitland Apartments 1 year ago with a $100,000 equity investment. If you sold the property today, you would realize reversion of $110,000 after all sales expenses, mortgage repayments, and taxes (at a tax rate of 30%). The holding period return analysis in Table 17.4 contains the proper real estate cash flow statement, your income tax statement for the past year of ownership, and the HPR calculation. You received $6,750 in after-tax cash flow plus $10,000 ($110,000 − $100,000) in after-tax capital appreciation, resulting in an after-tax HPR of 16.75%. An investor seeking to compare the return on a security with the return on real estate or other property investments should find the HPR calculation illustrated in Table 17.4 a useful analytical tool.

Other Investment Vehicles

The only source of return on other investment vehicles (such as options, futures, and tangibles) is capital gains. To calculate a holding period return for an investment in gold, for instance, the basic HPR formula is used (but cur-

TABLE 17.4 Cash Flow, Tax Statement, and After-Tax HPR Calculation for Maitland Apartments (Past year)

Real Estate Cash Flow Statement	
Gross potential rental income	$51,000
Less: Vacancy and collection losses	−1,500
Effective gross income (EGI)	$49,500
Less: Total operating expenses	−20,000
Net operating income (NOI)	$29,500
Less: Mortgage payment	−20,500
Before-tax cash flow	$ 9,000
Less: Your income tax (from below)	−2,250
After-tax cash flow (ATCF)	$ 6,750
Your Income Tax Statement	
Net operating income	$29,500
Less: Interest	−17,000
Less: Depreciation	−5,000
Taxable income	$ 7,500
Your income tax (tax rate = 0.30)	$ 2,250

After-Tax HPR Calculation

$$\text{After-Tax HPR} = \frac{\$6{,}750 + (\$110{,}000 - \$100{,}000)}{\$100{,}000}$$

$$= +16.75\%$$

rent income is set equal to zero). If you purchased 10 ounces of gold for $325 per ounce and sold the gold 1 year later for $385 per ounce, the pretax holding period return would be 18.46%. This is simply sales proceeds ($3,850) minus cost ($3,250) divided by cost. Assuming a 30 percent tax rate, the after-tax HPR would be 12.92 percent, which is the after-tax gain of $420 [$600 − (0.30 × $600)] divided by cost ($3,250). The HPRs of options and futures are calculated in a similar fashion. Because the return is in the form of capital gains only, the HPR analysis can be applied to any investment on a pretax or an after-tax basis. (The same basic procedure is used for securities that are sold short.)

Comparing Performance to Investment Goals

After computing an HPR (or yield) on an investment, you must compare it to your investment goal. Keeping track of an investment's performance by periodically computing its return will help you decide which investments you should continue to hold and which have become possible candidates for sale. Clearly, an investment would be a candidate for sale if (1) it failed to perform up to expectations and no real change in performance is anticipated, (2) it has met the original investment objective, or (3) more attractive uses of your funds (better investment outlets) are currently available.

INVESTOR FACT

NO GOLD IN ASIA?—It's a sign of the times. The worst-performing mutual funds for the 12 months ending March 31, 1998, were funds that invested in Asia and funds that invested in gold. In the fall of 1997, the Asian economic crisis led to a series of currency devaluations in the Far East, as well as hard times for anyone doing business in places like Malaysia, Korea, and Japan. Investing in gold didn't work either, because inflation was under 2% in 1997. According to the *Wall Street Journal,* the worst 10 funds for the 12-month period were

1. Citifunds Emerging Asia, −61.30%
2. WEBS: Malaysia, −57.35%
3. US Global: Gold Shares, −55.24%
4. Midas Fund, −51.88%
5. Bull & Bear Gold Investors, −47.04%
6. Merrill Emerging Tigers, −46.61%
7. INVESCO Strategic Gold, −45.94%
8. Morgan Stanley Asia, −45.64%
9. Lexington Strategic Investments, −44.70%
10. Mathews International: Korea, −44.25%

Of course, this situation can easily change as Asia's economy improves or if the specter of inflation returns.

Comparing Risk and Return

In this book, we have frequently discussed the basic tradeoff between investment risk and return. The relationship is fundamentally as follows: To earn more return, you must take more risk. In analyzing an investment, the key question is "Am I getting the proper return for the amount of investment risk I am taking?"

Nongovernment security and property investments are by nature riskier than U.S. government bonds or insured money market deposit accounts. This implies that *a rational investor should invest in these riskier vehicles only when the expected rate of return is well in excess of what could have been earned from a low-risk investment.* Thus one benchmark against which to compare investment returns is the rate of return on low-risk investments. If one's risky investments are outperforming low-risk investments, they are obtaining extra return for taking extra risk. If they are not outperforming low-risk investments, you should carefully examine your investment strategy.

Isolating Problem Investments

A *problem investment* is one that has not lived up to expectations. It may be a loss situation or an investment that has provided a return less than you expected. Many investors try to forget about problem investments, hoping the problem will go away or the investment will turn itself around. This is obviously a mistake: Problem investments require immediate attention, not neglect. In studying a problem investment, the key question is "Should I take my loss and get out, or should I hang on and hope it turns around?"

It is best to analyze each investment in a portfolio periodically. For each, two questions should be considered. First, has it performed in a manner that could reasonably be expected? Second, if you didn't currently own it, would you buy it today? If the answers to both are negative, then the investment probably should be sold. A negative answer to one of the questions qualifies the investment for the "problem list." It should then be watched closely. In general, maintaining a portfolio of investments requires constant attention and analysis to ensure the best chance of satisfactory returns. Problem investments need special attention and work.

CONCEPTS IN REVIEW

17.1 Why is it important to continuously manage and control your portfolio?

17.2 What role does current market information play in analyzing investment returns? How do changes in economic and market activity affect investment returns? Explain.

17.3 Which indexes can you use to compare your investment performance to general market returns? Briefly explain each of these indexes.

17.4 What are indicators of bond market behavior, and how are they different from stock market indicators? Name three sources of bond yield data.

17.5 Aside from comparing returns on real estate investment with those of local real estate investors, why would a real estate investor also compare returns with the consumer price index and with the New York Stock Exchange composite index?

17.6 Briefly discuss *holding period return (HPR)* and *yield* as measures of investment return. Are they equivalent? Explain.

17.7 Distinguish between the types of dividend distributions that mutual funds make. Are these dividends the only source of return for a mutual fund investor? Explain.

17.8 What are the two basic components of return from real estate investment? What is *reversion,* and how is it calculated?

17.9 Under what three conditions would an investment holding be a candidate for sale? What must be true about the expected return on a risky investment, when compared with the return on a low-risk investment, to cause a rational investor to acquire the risky investment? Explain.

17.10 What is a *problem investment?* What two questions should one consider when analyzing an investment portfolio?

http://hepg.aw.com

To evaluate portfolio performance, investors must compare the return on the portfolio with equivalent-risk market indexes. The index must replicate the investor's portfolio risk as closely as possible to achieve a fair comparison. There are many equity indexes available. The Web site listed here offers a look at the variety of indexes provided by Frank Russell Company.

www.russell.com

Assessing Portfolio Performance

LG 3 LG 4

active portfolio management
building a portfolio using traditional and modern approaches and managing and controlling it to achieve its objectives; a worthwhile activity that can result in superior returns.

A portfolio can be either passively or actively built and managed. A *passive portfolio* results from buying and holding a well-diversified portfolio over the given investment horizon. An *active portfolio* is built using the traditional and modern approaches presented in Chapter 16 and is managed and controlled to achieve its stated objectives. Although passive portfolios may outperform equally risky active portfolios, evidence suggests that **active portfolio management** is a worthwhile activity that can result in superior returns. Many of the ideas presented in this text are consistent with the belief that active portfolio management will improve your chance of earning superior returns.

Once a portfolio is built, the first step in active portfolio management is to assess performance on a regular basis and use that information to revise the portfolio. Calculating the portfolio return can be tricky, as discussed in the *Investing in Action* box on page 682. The procedures used to assess portfolio performance are based on many of the concepts presented earlier in this chapter. Here we will demonstrate how to assess portfolio performance, using a hypothetical securities portfolio over a 1-year holding period. We will examine each of three measures that can be used to compare a portfolio's return with a risk-adjusted, market-adjusted rate of return.

Measuring Portfolio Return

Table 17.5 presents the investment portfolio, as of January 1, 1999, of Bob Hathaway. He is a 50-year-old widower, whose children are married. His income is $60,000 per year. His primary investment objective is long-term growth with a moderate dividend return. He selects stocks with two criteria in mind: quality and growth potential. On January 1, 1999, his portfolio consisted of 10 issues, all of good quality. Hathaway has been fortunate in his selection process: He has approximately $74,000 in unrealized price appreciation in his portfolio. During 1999, he decided to make a change in the portfolio. On May 7 he sold 1,000 shares of Dallas National Corporation for

TABLE 17.5 Bob Hathaway's Portfolio (January 1, 1999)

Number of Shares	Company	Date Acquired	Total Cost (including commission)	Cost per Share	Current Price per Share	Current Value
1,000	Bancorp West, Inc.	1/16/97	$ 21,610	$21.61	$30	$ 30,000
1,000	Dallas National Corporation	5/ 1/98	27,312	27.31	29	29,000
1,000	Dator Companies, Inc.	4/13/93	13,704	13.70	27	27,000
500	Excelsior Industries	8/16/96	40,571	81.14	54	27,000
1,000	Florida Southcoast Banks	12/16/96	17,460	17.46	30	30,000
1,000	Maryland-Pacific	9/27/96	22,540	22.54	26	26,000
1,000	Moronson	2/27/96	19,100	19.10	47	47,000
500	Northwest Mining and Mfg.	4/17/97	25,504	51.00	62	31,000
1,000	Rawland Petroleum	3/12/97	24,903	24.90	30	30,000
1,000	Vornox	4/16/97	37,120	37.12	47	47,000
	Total		$249,824			$324,000

INVESTING IN ACTION

Portfolio Return Is Tough to Calculate

The Beardstown Ladies is an investment club of 14 older women from Beardstown, Illinois, who became famous for supposedly whipping most hot-shot Wall Street investors. The Ladies wrote a best-selling book that touted an average annual return of 23.4% on their investment portfolio for the decade ending 1993. But in 1998 the club was forced to concede that it had made a mistake in its performance calculations. Indeed, an audit by the accounting firm of Price Waterhouse showed an average annual return of just 9.1% during that period.

Most investors have a pretty good idea of how major market benchmarks like the S&P 500 Stock Composite Index did during the year, because the results are published in newspapers. But when it comes to their own performance, most people have only a rough idea. And there aren't many easy answers in year-end brokerage and mutual fund statements. Why don't they provide this information? For one thing, it would be a lot of work and a lot of computer programming effort. Another reason could be that if the results are poor, it might reflect badly on the broker.

True, if all you have is one brokerage account with a $50,000 balance, if you don't add any funds during the year, and if you don't withdraw any funds, it's pretty easy to calculate your total return. Let's say your ending balance is $60,000; that means your total return is $10,000, or $10,000/$50,000 = 20%.

Now, to make the calculation a little bit more complicated, let's say you begin the year with a $100,000 portfolio and end it with $125,000. During the year, your additions to the portfolio less your withdrawals totaled $5,000. You began the year with $100,000 and ended it with $125,000, so you can make the assumption that your average balance during the year was $112,500. Your total gain during the year would be your ending balance minus your beginning balance minus your additions to the portfolio, or $20,000 ($125,000 − $100,000 − $5,000). Your total return percentage is $20,000 divided by $112,500, or roughly 18% before taxes.

The next step would be to compare your results against the appropriate benchmark: the S&P 500 Stock Composite Index for large domestic stocks, the Morgan Stanley EAFE (Europe, Australia, and Far East) Index for international stocks, or the Russell 2000 Index for small U.S. stocks. If it's a bond portfolio, then you might compare your results against the Lehman Brothers Government/Corporate Bond Index.

If you want to compute your precise rate of return, you would need software like Quicken Deluxe or the portfolio tracker available free on *Money* magazine's Web site (**www.money.com**). You would also need to know the exact timing of any additions or withdrawals you made during the year. It's a lot of work to come up with these numbers, and it may not be worth the effort to be that precise, unless, like the Beardstown Ladies, you plan to advertise your results in the media.

$32,040. Hathaway's holding period return for that issue was discussed earlier in this chapter (see Table 17.1). Using funds from the Dallas National sale, he acquired an additional 1,000 shares of Florida Southcoast Banks on May 10, because he liked the prospects for the Florida bank. Florida Southcoast is based in one of the fastest-growing counties in the country.

Measuring the Amount Invested

Every investor would be well advised to list his or her holdings periodically, as is done in Table 17.5. The table shows number of shares, acquisition date, cost, and current value for each issue. These data aid in continually formulating strategy decisions; the cost data, for example, are used to determine the amount invested. Hathaway's portfolio does not utilize the leverage of a margin account. Were leverage present, all return calculations would be based on the investor's *equity* in the account. (Recall from Chapter 2 that an investor's equity in a margin account equals the total value of all the securities in the account minus any margin debt.)

To measure Hathaway's return on his invested capital, we need to perform a 1-year holding period return analysis. His invested capital as of January 1, 1999, is $324,000. No new additions of capital were made in the portfolio during 1999, although he sold one stock, Dallas National, and used the proceeds to buy another, Florida Southcoast Banks.

INVESTOR FACT

WHO NEEDS DIVIDENDS?—Apparently not investors in U.S. stocks. As of late 1997, the stock market's average dividend yield—dividends divided by stock price—was about 1.5%, less than half the yield in the early 1980s. High-technology stocks, among the most popular sectors in the 1990s, typically pay no dividends at all.

If you paid $100 for a stock, would you be satisfied with no dividend? You would be if the value of the stock increased to $130 within 1 year. If you need income, you can always sell some shares. Another reason to avoid dividends is taxes. If you're in the highest tax bracket, you pay a nearly 40% federal income tax on dividends. On the other hand, if you hold your stock for at least 18 months, you pay only a 20% tax on the stock's appreciation in price when you sell your shares.

Measuring Income

There are two sources of return from a portfolio of common stocks: income and capital gains. Current income is realized from dividends or, for a portfolio of bonds, is earned in the form of interest. Investors must report taxable dividends and interest on federal and state income tax returns. Companies are required to furnish income reports (Form 1099-DIV for dividends and Form 1099-INT for interest) to stockholders and bondholders. Many investors maintain logs to keep track of dividend and interest income as it is received.

Table 17.6 lists Hathaway's dividends for 1999. He received two quarterly dividends of 45 cents per share before he sold the Dallas National stock, and he received two 32-cent-per-share quarterly dividends on the additional Florida Southcoast Banks shares he acquired. His total dividend income for 1999 was $10,935.

Measuring Capital Gains

Table 17.7 shows the unrealized gains in value for each of the issues in the Hathaway portfolio. The January 1, 1999, and December 31, 1999, values are listed for each issue except the additional shares of Florida Southcoast Banks. The amounts listed for Florida Southcoast Banks reflect the fact that 1,000 additional shares of the stock were acquired on May 10, 1999, at a cost of

TABLE 17.6 Dividend Income on Hathaway's Portfolio (Calendar year 1999)

Number of Shares	Company	Annual Dividend per Share	Dividends Received
1,000	Bancorp West, Inc.	$1.20	$ 1,200
1,000	Dallas National Corporation*	1.80	900
1,000	Dator Companies, Inc.	1.12	1,120
500	Excelsior Industries	2.00	1,000
2,000	Florida Southcoast Banks**	1.28	1,920
1,000	Maryland-Pacific	1.10	1,100
1,000	Moronson	—	—
500	Northwest Mining and Mfg.	2.05	1,025
1,000	Rawland Petroleum	1.20	1,200
1,000	Vornox	1.47	1,470
	Total		$10,935

*Sold May 7, 1999.
**1,000 shares acquired on May 10, 1999.

TABLE 17.7 Unrealized Gains in Value of Hathaway's Portfolio (January 1, 1999, to December 31, 1999)

Number of Shares	Company	Market Value (1/1/99)	Market Price (12/31/99)	Market Value (12/31/99)	Unrealized Gain (Loss)	Percentage Change
1,000	Bancorp West, Inc.	$ 30,000	$27	$ 27,000	($ 3,000)	−10.0%
1,000	Dator Companies, Inc.	27,000	36	36,000	9,000	+33.3
500	Excelsior Industries	27,000	66	33,000	6,000	+22.2
2,000	Florida Southcoast Banks*	62,040	35	70,000	7,960	+12.8
1,000	Maryland-Pacific	26,000	26	26,000	—	—
1,000	Moronson	47,000	55	55,000	8,000	+17.0
500	Northwest Mining and Mfg.	31,000	60	30,000	(1,000)	− 3.2
1,000	Rawland Petroleum	30,000	36	36,000	6,000	+20.0
1,000	Vornox	47,000	43	43,000	(4,000)	− 8.5
	Total	$327,040**		$356,000	$28,960	+ 8.9%

*1,000 additional shares acquired on May 10, 1999, at a cost of $32,040. The value listed is the cost plus the market value of the previously owned shares as of January 1, 1999.

**This total includes the $324,000 market value of the portfolio on January 1, 1999 (from Table 17.5) plus the $3,040 *realized* gain on the sale of the Dallas National Corporation stock on May 7, 1999. The inclusion of the realized gain in this total is necessary to calculate the *unrealized* gain on the portfolio during 1999.

$32,040. Hathaway's current holdings had beginning-of-the-year values of $327,040 (including the additional Florida Southcoast Banks shares at the date of purchase) and are worth $356,000 at year-end.

During 1999, the portfolio increased in value by 8.9%, or $28,960, in unrealized capital gains. In addition, Hathaway realized a capital gain in 1999 by selling his Dallas National holding. From January 1, 1999, until its sale on May 7, 1999, the Dallas National holding rose in value from $29,000 to $32,040. This was the only sale in 1999, so the total *realized* gain was $3,040. During 1999, the portfolio had both a realized gain of $3,040 and an unrealized gain of $28,960. The total gain in value equals the sum of the two: $32,000. Put another way, because no capital was added to or withdrawn from the portfolio over the year, the total capital gain is simply the difference between the year-end market value (of $356,000, from Table 17.7) and the value on January 1 (of $324,000, from Table 17.5). This, of course, amounts to $32,000, of which, for tax purposes, only $3,040 is considered realized.

Measuring the Portfolio's Holding Period Return

We use the holding period return (HPR) to measure the total return on the Hathaway portfolio during 1999. The basic 1-year HPR formula for portfolios is

Equation 17.3

$$\text{Holding period return for a portfolio} = \frac{\text{dividends and interest received} + \text{realized gain} + \text{unrealized gain}}{\text{initial equity investment} + \left(\text{new funds} \times \dfrac{\text{number of months in portfolio}}{12}\right) - \left(\text{withdrawn funds} \times \dfrac{\text{number of months withdrawn from portfolio}}{12}\right)}$$

Equation 17.3a

$$\text{HPR}_p = \frac{C + RG + UG}{E_0 + \left(NF \times \frac{ip}{12}\right) - \left(WF \times \frac{wp}{12}\right)}$$

This formula includes both the realized gains (income plus capital gains) and the unrealized yearly gains of the portfolio. Portfolio additions and deletions are time-weighted for the number of months they are in the portfolio.

Table 17.7 lays out in detail the portfolio's change in value: All the issues that are in the portfolio as of December 31, 1999, are listed, and the unrealized gain during the year is calculated. The beginning and year-end values are included for comparison purposes. The crux of the analysis is the HPR calculation for the year, presented in Table 17.8. All the elements of a portfolio's return are included. Dividends total $10,935 (from Table 17.6). The realized gain of $3,040 represents the increment in value of the Dallas National holding from January 1, 1999, until its sale. During 1999 the portfolio had a $28,960 unrealized gain (from Table 17.7). There were no additions of new funds, and no funds were withdrawn. Utilizing Equation 17.3 for HPR, we find that the portfolio had a total return of 13.25% in 1999.

Comparison of Return with Overall Market Measures

Bob Hathaway can compare the HPR figure for his portfolio with market measures such as stock indexes. This comparison will show how Hathaway's portfolio is doing in relation to the stock market as a whole. The S&P 500 stock composite index and the NYSE composite index are acceptable indexes for this type of analysis, because they are broadly based and so can be said to represent the stock market as a whole. Assume that during 1999, the return on the S&P 500 index was +10.75% (including both dividends and capital gains). The return from Hathaway's portfolio was +13.25%, which compares very favorably with the broadly based index: The Hathaway portfolio performed about 23% better than the broad indicator of stock market return.

TABLE 17.8 Holding Period Return Calculation on Hathaway's Portfolio (January 1, 1999, to December 31, 1999, holding period)

Data	
Portfolio value (1/1/99):	$324,000
Portfolio value (12/31/99):	$356,000
Realized appreciation (1/1/99 to 5/7/99 when Dallas National was sold):	$ 3,040
Unrealized appreciation (1/1/99 to 12/31/99):	$ 28,960
Dividends received:	$ 10,935
New funds invested or withdrawn:	None

Portfolio HPR Calculation

$$\text{HPR}_p = \frac{\$10{,}935 + \$3{,}040 + \$28{,}960}{\$324{,}000}$$

$$= +13.25\%$$

Although such a comparison tends to factor out the influences of general market movements, *it fails to consider risk*. Clearly, a raw return figure, such as this +13.25%, requires further analysis. A number of risk-adjusted, market-adjusted rate-of-return measures are available for use in assessing portfolio performance. Here we'll discuss three of the most popular—Sharpe's measure, Treynor's measure, and Jensen's measure—and demonstrate their application to Hathaway's portfolio.

Sharpe's Measure

Sharpe's measure
a measure of portfolio performance that gives the *risk premium per unit of total risk,* which is measured by the portfolio's standard deviation of return.

Sharpe's measure of portfolio performance, developed by William F. Sharpe, compares the risk premium on a portfolio to the portfolio's standard deviation of return. The risk premium on a portfolio is the total portfolio return minus the risk-free rate. Sharpe's measure can be expressed as the following formula:

Equation 17.4

$$\text{Sharpe's measure} = \frac{\text{total portfolio return} - \text{risk-free rate}}{\text{portfolio standard deviation}}$$

Equation 17.4a

$$SM = \frac{r_p - R_F}{s_p}$$

This measure allows the investor to assess the *risk premium per unit of total risk,* which is measured by the portfolio standard deviation. Assume the risk-free rate, R_F, is 7.50% and the standard deviation of Hathaway's portfolio, s_p, is 16%. The total portfolio return, r_p, which is the HPR for Hathaway's portfolio calculated in Table 17.8, is 13.25%. Substituting those values into Equation 17.4, we get Sharpe's measure, SM.

$$SM = \frac{13.25\% - 7.50\%}{16\%} = \frac{5.75\%}{16\%} = \underline{\underline{0.36}}$$

Sharpe's measure is meaningful when compared either to other portfolios or to the market. In general, the higher Sharpe's measure, the better—the higher the risk premium per unit of risk. If we assume that the market return, r_m, is currently 10.75% and the standard deviation for the market portfolio, s_{p_m}, is 11.25%, Sharpe's measure for the market, SM_m, is

$$SM_m = \frac{10.75\% - 7.50\%}{11.25\%} = \frac{3.25\%}{11.25\%} = \underline{\underline{0.29}}$$

Because Sharpe's measure of 0.36 for Hathaway's portfolio is greater than the measure of 0.29 for the market portfolio, Hathaway's portfolio exhibits superior performance: Its risk premium per unit of risk is above that of the market. Of course, had Sharpe's measure for Hathaway's portfolio been below that of the market (below 0.29), the portfolio's performance would be considered inferior to the market performance.

Treynor's measure
a measure of portfolio performance that gives the *risk premium per unit of nondiversifiable risk,* which is measured by the portfolio's beta.

Treynor's Measure

Jack L. Treynor developed a portfolio performance measure similar to Sharpe's measure. **Treynor's measure** uses the portfolio beta to measure the portfolio's risk. Treynor therefore focuses only on *nondiversifiable risk,* assuming that the portfolio has been built in a manner that diversifies away all diversifiable risk. In contrast, Sharpe focuses on *total risk* measured by the standard deviation. Treynor's measure is calculated as shown in Equation 17.5.

Equation 17.5

$$\text{Treynor's measure} = \frac{\text{total portfolio return} - \text{risk-free rate}}{\text{portfolio beta}}$$

Equation 17.5a

$$TM = \frac{r_p - R_F}{b_p}$$

This measure gives *the risk premium per unit of nondiversifiable risk,* which is measured by the portfolio beta. Using the data for the Hathaway portfolio presented earlier and assuming that the beta for Hathaway's portfolio, b_p, is 1.20, we can substitute into Equation 17.5 to get Treynor's measure, *TM,* for Hathaway's portfolio.

$$TM = \frac{13.25\% - 7.50\%}{1.20} = \frac{5.75\%}{1.20} = \underline{\underline{4.79\%}}$$

Treynor's measure, like Sharpe's, is useful when compared either to other portfolios or to the market. Generally, the higher the value of Treynor's measure, the better—the greater the risk premium per unit of nondiversifiable risk. Again assuming that the market return, r_m, is 10.75%, and recognizing that, by definition, the beta for the market portfolio, b_{p_m}, is 1.00, we can use Equation 17.5 to find Treynor's measure for the market, TM_m.

$$TM_m = \frac{10.75\% - 7.50\%}{1.00} = \frac{3.25\%}{1.00} = \underline{\underline{3.25\%}}$$

The fact that Treynor's measure of 4.79% for Hathaway's portfolio is greater than the measure of 3.25% for the market portfolio indicates that Hathaway's portfolio exhibits superior performance: Its risk premium per unit of nondiversifiable risk is above that of the market. Conversely, had Treynor's measure for Hathaway's portfolio been below that of the market (below 3.25%), the portfolio's performance would be viewed as inferior to that of the market.

Jensen's Measure (Jensen's Alpha)

Jensen's measure (Jensen's alpha) a measure of portfolio performance that uses the portfolio's beta and CAPM to calculate its *excess return,* which may be positive, zero, or negative.

Michael C. Jensen developed a portfolio performance measure that seems quite different from the measures of Sharpe and Treynor yet is theoretically consistent with Treynor's measure. **Jensen's measure,** also called **Jensen's alpha,** is based on the *capital asset pricing model (CAPM),* which was developed in Chapter 4 (see Equation 4.13). It calculates the portfolio's *excess return*—the amount by which the portfolio's actual return deviates from its required return, which is determined using its beta and CAPM. The value of the excess return may be positive, zero, or negative. Like Treynor's measure, Jensen's measure focuses only on the *nondiversifiable,* or *relevant, risk* by using beta and CAPM; it assumes that the portfolio has been adequately diversified. Jensen's measure is calculated as shown in Equation 17.6.

Equation 17.6

Jensen's measure = (total portfolio return − risk-free rate) − [portfolio beta × (market return − risk-free rate)]

Equation 17.6a

$$JM = (r_p - R_F) - [b_p \times (r_m - R_F)]$$

Jensen's measure indicates the difference between the portfolio's actual return and its required return. Positive values are preferred; they indicate that the portfolio earned a return in excess of its risk-adjusted, market-adjusted required return. A value of zero indicates that the portfolio earned *exactly* its required return; negative values indicate the portfolio failed to earn its required return.

Using the data for Hathaway's portfolio presented earlier, we can substitute into Equation 17.6 to get Jensen's measure, *JM*, for Hathaway's portfolio.

$$JM = (13.25\% - 7.50\%) - [1.20 \times (10.75\% - 7.50\%)]$$
$$= 5.75\% - (1.20 \times 3.25\%) = 5.75\% - 3.90\% = \underline{\underline{1.85\%}}$$

The 1.85% value for Jensen's measure indicates that Hathaway's portfolio earned an *excess return* 1.85 percentage points above its required return, given its nondiversifiable risk as measured by beta. Clearly, Hathaway's portfolio has outperformed the market on a risk-adjusted basis.

Note that unlike the Sharpe and Treynor measures, Jensen's measure, through its use of CAPM, automatically adjusts for the market return. Therefore, there is no need to make a separate market comparison. In general, the higher Jensen's measure, the better the portfolio has performed; only those portfolios with positive Jensen measures have outperformed the market on a risk-adjusted basis. Because of its computational simplicity, its reliance only on nondiversifiable risk, and its inclusion of both risk and market adjustments, Jensen's measure (alpha) tends to be preferred over those of Sharpe and Treynor for assessing portfolio performance.

INVESTOR FACT

TIME TO REVISE YOUR PORTFOLIO?—Over time, you will need to review your portfolio to ensure that it reflects the right risk–return characteristics for your goals and needs. Here are four good reasons to perform this task:

- A major life event—marriage, birth of a child, job loss, illness, loss of a spouse, a child's finishing college—changes your investment objectives.
- The proportion of one asset class increases or decreases substantially.
- You expect to reach a specific goal within 2 years.
- The percentage in an asset class varies from your original allocation by 10% or more.

Portfolio Revision

In the Hathaway portfolio we have been discussing, one transaction occurred during 1999. The reason for this transaction was that Hathaway believed the Florida Southcoast Banks stock had more return potential than the Dallas National stock. You should periodically analyze your portfolio with one basic question in mind: "Does this portfolio continue to meet my needs?" In other words, does the portfolio contain those issues that are best suited to your risk–return needs? Investors who systematically study the issues in their portfolios will occasionally find a need to sell certain issues and purchase new securities to replace them. This process is commonly called **portfolio revision.** As the economy evolves, certain industries and stocks become either less or more attractive as investments. In today's stock market, timeliness is the essence of profitability.

portfolio revision
the process of selling certain issues in a portfolio and purchasing new securities to replace them.

Given the dynamics of the investment world, periodic reallocation and rebalancing of the portfolio are a necessity. Many circumstances require such changes. In Chapter 16 we noted that as an investor nears retirement, the portfolio's emphasis normally evolves from a strategy that stresses growth/capital appreciation to one that seeks to preserve capital. Changing a portfolio's emphasis normally occurs as an evolutionary process rather than an overnight switch. Individual issues in the portfolio often change in risk–return characteristics. As this occurs, you would be wise to eliminate those issues that do not meet your objectives. In addition, the need for diversification is constant. As issues rise or fall in value, their diversification effect may be lessened. Thus portfolio revision may be needed to maintain diversification in the portfolio.

CONCEPTS IN REVIEW

17.11 What is *active portfolio management?* Will it result in superior returns? Explain.

17.12 Describe the steps involved in measuring portfolio return. Explain the role of the portfolio's HPR in this process, and explain why one must differentiate between realized and unrealized gains.

17.13 According to the *Investing in Action* box on page 682, why don't year-end brokerage and mutual fund statements provide performance data? How should you calculate your portfolio's return, and against what benchmarks should you compare it?

17.14 Why is comparing a portfolio's return to the return on a broad market index generally inadequate? Explain.

17.15 Briefly describe each of the following risk-adjusted, market-adjusted return measures available for assessing portfolio performance, and explain how they are used.

a. Sharpe's measure
b. Treynor's measure
c. Jensen's measure (Jensen's alpha)

17.16 Why is Jensen's measure (alpha) generally preferred over the measures of Sharpe and Treynor for assessing portfolio performance? Explain.

17.17 Explain the role of *portfolio revision* in the process of managing a portfolio.

http://hepg.aw.com

There are several ways of measuring the relative performance of portfolio returns. The methods discussed in this section are also of interest to investors who use the Web to obtain information. Use the Web site given here to link to discussions of HPR and the Sharpe, Treynor, and Jensen measures.

www.finplan.com/invest/invtools.htm

Timing Transactions

LG 5 LG 6

The essence of timing is to "buy low and sell high." This is the dream of all investors. Although there is no tried-and-true way to achieve such a goal, there are several methods you can utilize to time purchases and sales. First, there are formula plans; a discussion of these follows. Investors can also use limit and stop-loss orders as a timing aid, can follow procedures for warehousing liquidity, and can take into consideration other aspects of timing when selling their investments.

Formula Plans

formula plans
mechanical methods of portfolio management that try to take advantage of price changes in securities that result from cyclical price movements.

Formula plans are mechanical methods of portfolio management that try to take advantage of price changes in securities that result from cyclical price movements. Formula plans are not set up to provide unusually high returns; rather, they are conservative strategies employed by investors who do not wish to bear a high level of risk. Four popular formula plans are discussed here: dollar-cost averaging, the constant-dollar plan, the constant-ratio plan, and the variable-ratio plan.

Dollar-Cost Averaging

dollar-cost averaging
a formula plan for timing investment transactions, in which a fixed dollar amount is invested in a security at fixed intervals.

Dollar-cost averaging is a formula plan in which a fixed dollar amount is invested in a security at fixed intervals. In this passive buy-and-hold strategy, the periodic dollar investment is held constant. To make the plan work, you must have the discipline to invest on a regular basis. The goal of a dollar-cost averaging program is growth in the value of the security to which the funds are allocated. The price of the investment security will probably fluctuate over time. If the price declines, more shares are purchased per period; conversely, if the price rises, fewer shares are purchased per period.

Look at the example of dollar-cost averaging in Table 17.9, which shows investment of $500 per month in the Wolverine Mutual Fund, a growth-oriented, no-load mutual fund. During 1 year's time, the investor has placed $6,000 in the mutual fund shares. Because this is a no-load fund, shares are purchased at net asset value. Purchases were made at NAVs ranging from a low of $24.16 to a high of $30.19. At year-end, the investor's holdings in the fund were valued at slightly less than $6,900. Dollar-cost averaging is a passive strategy; other formula plans are more active.

TABLE 17.9 Dollar-Cost Averaging
($500 per month, Wolverine Mutual Fund shares)

Transactions

Month	Net Asset Value (NAV) Month-End	Number of Shares Purchased
January	$26.00	19.23
February	27.46	18.21
March	27.02	18.50
April	24.19	20.67
May	26.99	18.53
June	25.63	19.51
July	24.70	20.24
August	24.16	20.70
September	25.27	19.79
October	26.15	19.12
November	29.60	16.89
December	30.19	16.56

Annual Summary

Total investment: $6,000.00
Total number of shares purchased: 227.95
Average cost per share: $26.32
Year-end portfolio value: $6,881.81

Constant-Dollar Plan

constant-dollar plan
a formula plan for timing investment transactions, in which the investor establishes a target dollar amount for the speculative portion of the portfolio and establishes trigger points at which funds are transferred to or from the conservative portion as needed to maintain the target dollar amount.

A **constant-dollar plan** consists of a portfolio that is divided into two parts, speculative and conservative. The speculative portion is invested in securities that have high promise of capital gains. The conservative portion consists of low-risk investments such as bonds or a money market account. The target dollar amount for the speculative portion is constant, and the investor establishes trigger points (upward or downward movement in the speculative portion) at which funds are removed from or added to that portion. The constant-dollar plan basically skims off profits from the speculative portion of the portfolio if it rises a certain percentage or amount in value and adds these funds to the conservative portion of the portfolio. If the speculative portion of the portfolio declines by a specific percentage or amount, funds are added to it from the conservative portion.

Table 17.10 illustrates a constant-dollar plan over time. The beginning $20,000 portfolio consists of $10,000 invested in a high-beta, no-load mutual fund and $10,000 deposited in a money market account. The investor has decided to rebalance the portfolio every time the speculative portion is worth $2,000 more or $2,000 less than its initial value of $10,000: If the speculative portion of the portfolio equals or exceeds $12,000, sufficient shares of the fund are sold to bring its value down to $10,000. The proceeds from the sale are added to the conservative portion. If the speculative portion declines in value to $8,000 or less, funds are taken from the conservative portion and used to purchase sufficient shares to raise the value of the speculative portion to $10,000.

Two portfolio-rebalancing actions are taken in the time sequence illustrated in Table 17.10. Initially, $10,000 is allocated to each portion of the portfolio. When the mutual fund's NAV rises to $12.00, at which point the speculative portion is worth $12,000, the investor sells 166.67 shares valued at $2,000, and the proceeds are added to the money market account. Later, the mutual fund's NAV declines to $9.50 per share, causing the value of the speculative portion to drop below $8,000. This change triggers the purchase of sufficient shares to raise the value of the speculative portion to $10,000. Over the long run, if the speculative investment of the constant-dollar plan rises in value, the conservative component of the portfolio will increase in dollar value as profits are transferred into it.

TABLE 17.10 Constant-Dollar Plan

Mutual Fund NAV	Value of Speculative Portion	Value of Conservative Portion	Total Portfolio Value	Transactions	Number of Shares in Speculative Portion
$10.00	$10,000.00	$10,000.00	$20,000.00		1,000
11.00	11,000.00	10,000.00	21,000.00		1,000
12.00	12,000.00	10,000.00	22,000.00		1,000
→ 12.00	10,000.00	12,000.00	22,000.00	Sold 166.67 shares	833.33
11.00	9,166.63	12,000.00	21,166.63		833.33
9.50	7,916.64	12,000.00	19,916.64		833.33
→ 9.50	10,000.00	9,916.64	19,916.64	Purchased 219.30 shares	1,052.63
10.00	10,526.30	9,916.64	20,442.94		1,052.63

Constant-Ratio Plan

constant-ratio plan
a formula plan for timing investment transactions, in which a desired fixed *ratio* of the speculative portion to the conservative portion of the portfolio is established; when the actual ratio differs by a predetermined amount from the desired ratio, transactions are made to rebalance the portfolio to achieve the desired ratio.

The **constant-ratio plan** is similar to the constant-dollar plan except that it establishes a desired fixed *ratio* of the speculative portion to the conservative portion of the portfolio. When the actual ratio of the two differs by a predetermined amount from the desired ratio, rebalancing occurs. At that point, transactions are made to bring the actual ratio back to the desired ratio. An investor who uses the constant-ratio plan must decide on the appropriate apportionment of the portfolio between speculative and conservative investments. Then a decision must be made regarding the ratio trigger point at which transactions occur.

A constant-ratio plan for an initial portfolio of $20,000 is illustrated in Table 17.11. The investor has decided to allocate 50% of the portfolio to the speculative, high-beta mutual fund and 50% to a money market account. Rebalancing will occur when the ratio of the speculative portion to the conservative portion is greater than or equal to 1.20 or less than or equal to 0.80. A sequence of changes in net asset value is listed in Table 17.11. Initially, $10,000 is allocated to each portion of the portfolio. When the fund NAV reaches $12, the 1.20 ratio triggers the sale of 83.33 shares. Then the portfolio is back to its desired 50–50 ratio. Later, the fund NAV declines to $9, lowering the value of the speculative portion to $8,250. The ratio of the speculative portion to the conservative portion is then 0.75, which is below the 0.80 trigger point. A total of 152.78 shares is purchased to bring the desired ratio back up to the 50–50 level.

variable-ratio plan
a formula plan for timing investment transactions, in which the ratio of the speculative portion to the total portfolio value varies depending on the movement in value of the speculative securities; when the ratio rises or falls by a predetermined amount, the amount committed to the speculative portion of the portfolio is reduced or increased, respectively.

The long-run expectation under a constant-ratio plan is that the speculative securities will rise in value. When this occurs, sales of the securities will be undertaken to reapportion the portfolio and increase the value of the conservative portion. This philosophy is similar to the constant-dollar plan, except that a *ratio* is utilized as a trigger point.

Variable-Ratio Plan

The **variable-ratio plan** is the most aggressive of these four fairly passive formula plans. It attempts to turn stock market movements to the investor's

TABLE 17.11 Constant-Ratio Plan

Mutual Fund NAV	Value of Speculative Portion	Value of Conservative Portion	Total Portfolio Value	Ratio of Speculative Portion to Conservative Portion	Transactions	Number of Shares in Speculative Portion
$10.00	$10,000.00	$10,000.00	$20,000.00	1.000		1,000
11.00	11,000.00	10,000.00	21,000.00	1.100		1,000
12.00	12,000.00	10,000.00	22,000.00	1.200		1,000
→ 12.00	11,000.00	11,000.00	22,000.00	1.000	Sold 83.33 shares	916.67
11.00	10,083.00	11,000.00	21,083.00	0.917		916.67
10.00	9,166.70	11,000.00	20,166.70	0.833		916.67
9.00	8,250.00	11,000.00	19,250.00	0.750		916.67
→ 9.00	9,625.00	9,625.00	19,250.00	1.000	Purchased 152.78 shares	1,069.44
10.00	10,694.40	9,625.00	20,319.40	1.110		1,069.44

advantage by timing the market; that is, it tries to "buy low and sell high." The ratio of the speculative portion to the total portfolio value varies depending on the movement in value of the speculative securities. When the ratio rises a certain predetermined amount, the amount committed to the speculative portion of the portfolio is reduced. Conversely, if the value of the speculative portion declines so that it drops significantly in proportion to the total portfolio value, the amount committed to the speculative portion of the portfolio is increased.

When implementing the variable-ratio plan, you have several decisions to make. First, you must determine the initial allocation between the speculative and conservative portions of the portfolio. Next, you must choose trigger points to initiate buy or sell activity. These points are a function of the ratio between the value of the speculative portion and the value of the total portfolio. Finally, you must set adjustments in that ratio at each trigger point.

An example of a variable-ratio plan is shown in Table 17.12. Initially, the portfolio is divided equally between the speculative and the conservative portions. The former consists of a high-beta (around 2.0) mutual fund, and the latter is a money market account. The investor decided that when the speculative portion reached 60% of the total portfolio, its proportion will be reduced to 45%. If the speculative portion of the portfolio dropped to 40% of the total portfolio, then its proportion would be raised to 55%. The logic behind this strategy is an attempt to time the cyclical movements in the mutual fund's value. When the fund moves up in value, profits are taken, and the proportion invested in the no-risk money market account is increased. When the fund declines markedly in value, the proportion of capital committed to it is increased.

A sequence of transactions is depicted in Table 17.12. When the fund NAV climbs to $15, the 60% ratio trigger point is reached, and 250 shares of the fund are sold. The proceeds are placed in the money market account, which causes the speculative portion then to represent 45% of the value of the portfolio. Later the fund NAV declines to $10, causing the speculative portion of the portfolio to drop to 35%. This triggers a portfolio rebalancing, and 418.75 shares are purchased, moving the speculative portion to 55%. When the fund NAV then moves to $12, the total portfolio is worth in excess of $23,500. In comparison, had the initial investment of $20,000 been allocated equally and had no rebalancing been done between the mutual fund and the

TABLE 17.12 Variable-Ratio Plan

Mutual Fund NAV	Value of Speculative Portion	Value of Conservative Portion	Total Portfolio Value	Ratio of Speculative Portion to Total Portfolio Value	Transactions	Number of Shares in Speculative Portion
$10.00	$10,000.00	$10,000.00	$20,000.00	0.50		1,000
15.00	15,000.00	10,000.00	25,000.00	0.60		1,000
→ 15.00	11,250.00	13,750.00	25,000.00	0.45	Sold 250 shares	750
10.00	7,500.00	13,750.00	21,250.00	0.35		750
→ 10.00	11,687.50	9,562.50	21,250.00	0.55	Purchased 418.75 shares	1,168.75
12.00	14,025.00	9,562.50	23,587.50	0.59		1,168.75

money market account, the total portfolio value at this time would have been only $22,000 ($12 × 1,000 = $12,000 in the speculative portion plus $10,000 in the money market account).

Using Limit and Stop-Loss Orders

In Chapter 2 we discussed the market order, the limit order, and the stop-loss order. (See pages 41–43 for a review of these types of orders.) Here we will see how the limit and stop-loss orders can be employed to rebalance a portfolio. These types of security orders, if properly used, can increase an investor's return by lowering transaction costs.

Limit Orders

There are many ways investors can use limit orders when securities are bought or sold. For instance, if you have decided to add a stock to the portfolio, a limit order to buy will ensure that you buy only at the desired purchase price or below. A limit *good-'til-canceled (GTC)* order to buy instructs the broker to buy stock until the entire order is filled. The primary risk in using limit instead of market orders is that the order may not be executed. For example, if you placed a GTC order to buy 100 shares of State Oil of California at $27 per share and the stock never traded at $27 per share or less, the order would never be executed. Thus you must weigh the need for immediate execution (market order) against the possibility of a better price with a limit order.

Limit orders, of course, can increase your return if they enable you to buy a security at a lower cost or sell it at a higher price. During a typical trading day, a stock will fluctuate up and down over a normal trading range. For example, suppose the common shares of Jama Motor traded ten times in the following sequence: 36, 35⅞, 35¾, 35 15/16, 35½, 35⅝, 35 13/16, 36, 36⅛, 36. A market order to sell could have been executed at somewhere between 35½ (the low) and 36⅛ (the high). A limit order to sell at 36 would have been executed at 36. Thus a half-point per share (50 cents) might have been gained by using a limit order.

Stop-Loss Orders

Stop-loss orders can be used to limit the downside loss exposure of an investment. For example, assume you purchase 500 shares of Easy Work at 26 and have set a specific goal to sell the stock if it reaches 32 or drops to 23. To implement this goal, you would enter a GTC stop order to sell with a price limit of 32 and another stop order at a price of 23. If the issue trades at 23 or less, the stop-loss order becomes a market order, and the stock is sold at the best price available. Conversely, if the issue trades at 32 or higher, the broker will sell the stock. In the first situation, you are trying to reduce your losses, in the second, to protect a profit.

whipsawing
the situation where a stock temporarily drops in price and then bounces back upward.

The principal risk in using stop-loss orders is **whipsawing**—a situation where a stock temporarily drops in price and then bounces back upward. If Easy Work dropped to 23, then 22 9/16, and then rallied back to 26, you would have been sold out at a price between 23 and 22 9/16. For this reason, limit orders, including stop-loss orders, require careful analysis before they are placed. You must consider the stock's probable fluctuations as well as the need to purchase or sell the stock when choosing among market, limit, and stop-loss orders.

Warehousing Liquidity

Investing in risky stocks or in property offers probable returns in excess of money market deposit accounts or bonds. However, stocks and property are risky investments. One recommendation for an efficient portfolio is to keep a portion of it in a low-risk, highly liquid investment to protect against total loss. The low-risk asset acts as a buffer against possible investment adversity. A second reason for maintaining funds in a low-risk asset is the possibility of future opportunities. When opportunity strikes, an investor who has extra cash available will be able to take advantage of the situation. If you have set aside funds in a highly liquid investment, you need not disturb the existing portfolio.

There are two primary media for warehousing liquidity: money market deposit accounts at financial institutions and money market mutual funds. The money market accounts at savings institutions provide relatively easy access to funds and furnish returns competitive with (but somewhat lower than) money market mutual funds. Over time, the products offered by financial institutions are expected to become more competitive with those offered by mutual funds and stock brokerage firms. (See Chapter 3 for a detailed discussion of the vehicles available for warehousing liquidity.)

INVESTOR FACT

ENRICHING SHAREHOLDERS—Microsoft has made many of its shareholders and employees rich. In a 3-year period ending June 30, 1997, Microsoft shares rose from about $23 per share to $135, a six-fold increase. During fiscal 1997, Microsoft earned $2.63 per share, up from $0.94 per share in fiscal 1994. During these 3 years, many Wall Street analysts insisted that Microsoft stock was too expensive. After all, its price/earnings ratio had risen from 25 to 50. The debate on Wall Street ensued: Did Microsoft deserve a P/E multiple of 50?

The naysayers argued that Microsoft stock would drop sharply if the company stumbled in its introduction of Windows 95 and then Office 97, two of its main software products. Microsoft was also playing catch-up on the Internet. The company was also facing scrutiny from the federal government over its business practices. But in fact, the new Windows products proved to be a big success. Its Internet Explorer software came from behind and beat back its most serious competitor, Netscape. The company's domination of software and the Internet convinced the investment community that the government scrutiny would be a minor issue for the company. Investors who had tried to time the sale of Microsoft shares were generally sorry; since the end of fiscal '97, the stock had risen another 50%.

Timing Investment Sales

Knowing when to sell a stock is as important as deciding which stock to buy. The *Investing in Action* box on page 696 offers some tips on knowing when and what to sell. Periodically, you should review your portfolio and consider possible sales and new purchases. Here we discuss two items relevant to the sale decision: tax consequences and achieving investment goals.

Tax Consequences

Taxes affect nearly all investment actions. All investors can and should understand certain basics. The treatment of capital losses is important: *A maximum of $3,000 of losses in excess of capital gains can be written off against other income in any one year.* If you have a loss position in an investment and have concluded that it would be wise to sell it, the best time to sell is when a capital gain is available against which the loss can be applied. Clearly, one should carefully consider the tax consequences of investment sales prior to taking action.

Achieving Investment Goals

Every investor would enjoy buying an investment at its lowest price and selling it at its top price. At a more realistic level, an investment should be sold when it no longer meets the needs of the portfolio's owner. In particular, if an investment has become either more or less risky than is desired, or if it has not met

INVESTING IN ACTION

Knowing When to Hold and When to Fold

One of your stocks is up 20% in value and another is down 15%. Should you sell either one? Selling a winner is a tough call because it may go even higher. Nor is it easy to admit you made a mistake and dump a loser. It may bounce back. Then again, it may not. Investors in Boston Chicken watched the stock fall from $50 to $10 during 1996–1997. Those who didn't sell were still waiting for a bounce-back as of early 1998.

Or maybe you need the cash for a new car or your child's college tuition, and you feel that you have to sell. But selling the wrong securities can throw your whole portfolio out of balance or increase your taxes. In truth, the money you have in the stock market should be for long-term purposes so that you're not forced to sell at a point in time when the market is down.

As a result, you probably should be selling some securities throughout the year to generate cash to meet your short-term needs. To do so, you'll need a selling strategy. If you have such a strategy, then you won't make emotional decisions at an inopportune time. For example, you may create a selling discipline such that you'll sell when the stock reaches a certain price goal, when its price/earnings ratio hits a certain level, or when the company is no longer pursuing goals that you find attractive.

Your criteria should reflect your investing style. If you're a *value investor,* then set a target price at a certain percentage over the purchase price. When it reaches that price, re-evaluate the stock to see whether you would be willing to buy the stock today at that price. If not, sell. Another strategy is to sell the stock when it reaches the market price/earnings multiple. That means it's no longer cheap or a good value.

On the other hand, if you're a *growth investor,* you are probably willing to hold your stocks when they trade at a price/earnings multiple that equals or exceeds the company's growth rate. Prior to the 1990s bull market, a growth investor might have sold when the company's price/earnings ratio exceeded the growth rate. That formula doesn't work very well in 1998, however, because many growth companies, such as Coca-Cola, are selling at double their growth rates. Coke was recently selling at 40 times earnings, even though the company isn't even increasing its earnings at 20% per year.

Another sell discipline involves asset or sector allocation. Many institutional money managers lock themselves into a portfolio that mirrors the S&P 500 in terms of industry concentration. When stocks in a certain industry begin to outperform other industries represented in the portfolio, the total assets in that industry become overweighted. The money manager must sell the top performers, even though he or she still likes the company. In another case, a single stock may do fabulously well and then represent too large a chunk of an overall portfolio. For diversification reasons, many pros say that no single holding can represent more than 5% of their portfolio.

Yet another issue is the length of your investment horizon. If your goals are long-term in nature, then you should emphasize growth stocks. They're more volatile in the short run, but they also tend to excel over a 10-year horizon. If you're approaching retirement, then you might want to lighten up on growth stocks and begin to focus on income.

Finally, taxes are a consideration. You might sell the stock that generates the least taxes. If you've held the stock longer than 18 months, then your federal capital gains tax is just 20%. If you've held it less than a year, then you might pay nearly double that rate.

its return objective, it should be sold. The tax consequences mentioned above help to determine the appropriate time to sell. However, *taxes are not the foremost consideration in a sale decision:* The dual concepts of risk and return should be the overriding concerns.

Each investment should be examined periodically in light of its return performance and relative risk. You should sell any investment that no longer belongs in the portfolio and should buy vehicles that are more suitable. Finally, you should not hold out for every nickel of profit. Very often, those who hold out for the top price watch the value of their holdings plummet. If an investment looks ripe to sell, sell it, take the profit, reinvest it in an appropriate vehicle, and enjoy your good fortune.

CONCEPTS IN REVIEW

17.18 Explain the role that *formula plans* can play in the timing of security transactions. Describe the logic underlying the use of these plans.

17.19 Briefly describe each of the following plans and differentiate among them.
- a. Dollar-cost averaging
- b. Constant-dollar plan
- c. Constant-ratio plan
- d. Variable-ratio plan

17.20 Describe how a limit order can be used when securities are bought or sold. How can a stop-loss order be used to reduce losses? To protect profit?

17.21 Give two reasons why an investor might want to maintain funds in a low-risk, highly liquid investment.

17.22 Describe some of the popular selling strategies discussed in the *Investing in Action* box on page 696. How should your selling criteria relate to your investing style?

17.23 Describe the two items an investor should consider before reaching a decision to sell an investment vehicle.

http://hepg.aw.com

Dollar-cost averaging is a formula investing technique that is encouraged by many investment advisors and followed by many investors. The Vanguard fund site has a detailed presentation on how dollar-cost averaging works under various economic scenarios.

www/vanguard.com/educ/lib/plain/dca.html

Summary

LG 1 **Discuss sources of needed data and the indexes commonly used to evaluate the performance of investments.** To analyze the performance of individual investments, the investor must gather current market information and stay abreast of international, national, and local economic and market developments. Indexes of investment performance such as the Dow Jones Industrial Average (DJIA) and bond market indicators are available for use in assessing market behavior.

LG 2 **Describe the techniques used to measure the performance of individual investment vehicles, and compare performance to investment goals.** The performance of individual investment vehicles, including stocks, bonds, mutual funds, real estate, and other investment vehicles, can be measured on both a pretax and an after-tax basis by using the holding period return. HPR measures the total return (income plus change in value) actually earned on the investment during the investment period. HPR can be compared to investment goals to assess whether the proper return is being earned for the risk involved and to identify any problem investments.

LG 3

Understand the techniques used to measure income, capital gains, and total portfolio return relative to the amount of money invested in a portfolio. To measure portfolio return, the investor must estimate the amount invested, the income earned, and any capital gains—both realized and unrealized—over the relevant current time period. Using these values, along with information about any new funds added or funds withdrawn during the period, the investor can calculate the portfolio's holding period return (HPR) by dividing the total returns by the amount of investment during the period. Comparison of the portfolio's HPR to overall market measures can provide some insight with regard to the portfolio's performance relative to the market.

LG 4

Use the Sharpe, Treynor, and Jensen measures to compare a portfolio's return with a risk-adjusted, market-adjusted rate of return, and discuss portfolio revision. A risk-adjusted, market-adjusted comparison of a portfolio's return can be made using Sharpe's measure, Treynor's measure, or Jensen's measure. Sharpe's and Treynor's measures find the risk premium per unit of risk, which can be compared with similar market measures to assess the portfolio's performance relative to the market. Jensen's measure, which is theoretically consistent with Treynor's, calculates the portfolio's excess return using beta and CAPM. Because it is relatively easy to calculate and directly makes both risk and market adjustments, Jensen's measure tends to be preferred over Sharpe's and Treynor's. Portfolio revision—selling certain issues and purchasing new ones to replace them—should take place when returns are unacceptable or when the portfolio fails to meet the investor's objectives.

LG 5

Describe the role of formula plans and the logic of dollar-cost averaging, constant-dollar plans, constant-ratio plans, and variable-ratio plans. Formula plans are used to time purchase and sale decisions to take advantage of price changes that result from cyclical price movements. The four commonly used formula plans are dollar-cost averaging, the constant-dollar plan, the constant-ratio plan, and the variable-ratio plan. All of them have certain decision rules or triggers that signal a purchase and/or sale action.

LG 6

Explain the role of limit and stop-loss orders in investment timing, the warehousing of liquidity, and the key factors in timing investment sales to achieve investment goals. Limit and stop-loss orders can be used to trigger the rebalancing of a portfolio to contribute to improved portfolio returns. Low-risk, highly liquid investment vehicles such as money market deposit accounts and money market mutual funds can warehouse liquidity. Such liquidity can protect against total loss and allow the investor to seize quickly any attractive opportunities that occur. Investment sales should be timed to obtain maximum tax benefits (or minimum tax consequences) and to contribute to the achievement of the investor's goals.

Discussion Questions

LG 1 LG 2

Q17.1. Choose an established local (or nearby) company whose stock is listed and actively traded on a major exchange. Find the stock's closing price at the end of each of the preceding 6 years and the amount of dividends paid in each of the preceding 5 years. Also, obtain the value of the Dow Jones Industrial Average (DJIA) at the end of each of the preceding 6 years.

a. Use Equation 17.1 to calculate the pretax holding period return (HPR) on the stock for each of the preceding 5 years.
b. Study the international, national, and local economic and market developments that occurred during the preceding 5 years.
c. Compare the stock's returns to the DJIA for each year over the 5-year period of concern.

d. Discuss the stock's returns in light of the economic and market developments noted in part (b) and the behavior of the DJIA as noted in part (c) over the 5 preceding years. How well did the stock perform in light of these factors?

LG 2

Q17.2. Assume that you are in the 35% tax bracket (federal and state combined). Select a major stock, bond, and mutual fund in which you are interested in investing. For each of them, gather data for each of the past 3 years on the annual dividends or interest paid and the capital gain (or loss) that would have resulted had they been purchased at the start of each year and sold at the end of each year. For the mutual fund, be sure to separate any dividends paid into investment income dividends and capital gains dividends.

a. For each of the three investment vehicles, calculate the pretax and after-tax HPR for each of the 3 years.
b. Use your annual HPR findings in part (a) to calculate the average after-tax HPR for each of the investment vehicles over the 3-year period.
c. Compare the average returns found in part (b) for each of the investment vehicles. Discuss the relative risks in view of these returns and the characteristics of each vehicle.

LG 3

Q17.3. Choose six actively traded stocks for inclusion in your investment portfolio. Assume the portfolio was created 3 years earlier by purchasing 200 shares of each of the six stocks. Find the acquisition price of each stock, the annual dividend paid by each stock, and the year-end prices for the 3 calendar years. Record for each stock its total cost, cost per share, current price per share, and total current value at the end of each of the 3 calendar years.

a. For each of the 3 years, find the amount invested in the portfolio.
b. For each of the 3 years, measure the annual income from the portfolio.
c. For each of the 3 years, determine the unrealized capital gains from the portfolio.
d. For each of the 3 years, calculate, using the values in parts (a), (b), and (c), the portfolio's HPR.
e. Use your findings in part (d) to calculate the average HPR for the portfolio over the 3-year period. Discuss your finding.

LG 4

Q17.4. Find five actively traded stocks and record their prices at the start and the end of the most recent calendar year. Also, find the amount of dividends paid on each stock during that year and each stock's beta at the end of the year. Assume that the five stocks were held during the year in an equal-dollar-weighted portfolio (20% in each stock) created at the start of the year. Also find the current risk-free rate, R_F, and the market return, r_m, for the given year. Assume that the standard deviation for the portfolio of the five stocks is 14.25% and that the standard deviation for the market portfolio is 10.80%.

a. Use the formula presented in Chapter 16 (Equation 16.1) to find the portfolio return, r_p, for the year under consideration.
b. Calculate Sharpe's measure for both the portfolio and the market. Compare and discuss these values. On the basis of this measure, is the portfolio's performance inferior or superior? Explain.
c. Calculate Treynor's measure for both the portfolio and the market. Compare and discuss these values. On the basis of this measure, is the portfolio's performance inferior or superior? Explain.
d. Calculate Jensen's measure (Jensen's alpha) for both the portfolio and the market. Compare and discuss these values. On the basis of this measure, is the portfolio's performance inferior or superior? Explain.
e. Compare, contrast, and discuss your analysis using the three measures in parts (b), (c), and (d). Is the portfolio a good one?

LG 5

Q17.5. Choose a high-growth mutual fund and a money market mutual fund. Find and record their closing net asset values (NAVs) at the end of each *week* for the immediate past year. Assume that you wish to invest $10,400.

a. If you use dollar-cost averaging to buy shares in both the high-growth and the money market funds by purchasing $100 of each of them at the end of each week—a total investment of $10,400 (52 weeks × $200/week)—how many shares would you have purchased in each fund by year-end? What are the total number of shares, the average cost per share, and the year-end portfolio value of each fund? Total the year-end fund values and compare them to the total that would have resulted from investing $5,200 in each fund at the end of the first week.

b. Assume you use a constant-dollar plan with 50% invested in the high-growth fund (speculative portion) and 50% invested in the money market fund (conservative portion). If the portfolio is rebalanced every time the speculative portion is worth $500 more or $500 less than its initial value of $5,200, what would be the total portfolio value and the number of shares in the speculative portion at year-end?

c. Assume that, as in part (b), you initially invest 50% in the speculative portion and 50% in the conservative portion. But in this case you use a constant-ratio plan under which rebalancing to the 50–50 mix occurs whenever the ratio of the speculative to the conservative portion is greater than or equal to 1.25 or less than or equal to 0.75. What would be the total portfolio value and the number of shares in the speculative portion at year-end?

d. Compare and contrast the year-end values of the total portfolio under each of the plans in parts (a), (b), and (c). Which plan would have been best in light of these findings? Explain.

Problems

LG 1 LG 2

P17.1. Mark Smith purchased 100 shares of the Tomco Corporation in December 1998, at a total cost of $1,762. He held the shares for 15 months and then sold them, netting $2,500. During the period he held the stock, the company paid him $200 in cash dividends. How much, if any, was the capital gain realized upon the sale of stock? Calculate Mark's pretax HPR.

LG 1 LG 2

P17.2. Jill Clark invested $25,000 in the bonds of Industrial Aromatics, Inc. She held them for 13 months, at the end of which she sold them for $26,746. During the period of ownership, she earned $2,000 interest. Calculate the pretax and after-tax HPR on Jill's investment. Assume she is in the 31% tax bracket (federal and state combined).

LG 1 LG 2

P17.3. Charlotte Smidt bought 2,000 shares of the balanced no-load LaJolla Fund exactly 1 year ago for a NAV of $8.60 per share. During the year, the fund distributed investment income dividends of 32 cents per share and capital gains dividends of 38 cents per share. At the end of the year, Charlotte, who is in the 35% tax bracket (federal and state combined), realized $8.75 per share on the sale of all 2,000 shares. Calculate Charlotte's pretax and after-tax HPR on this transaction.

LG 1 LG 2

P17.4. Peter Hancock bought a parcel of land in Red Woods 1 year ago for $55,000. He sold the property this year for $63,000, and his reversion from the sale was $61,000 after deducting $2,000 in closing costs and income taxes. Estimate Peter's after-tax holding period return on the investment.

LG 1 LG 2

P17.5. Marilyn Gore, who is in a 33% tax bracket (federal and state combined), purchased 10 ounces of gold for $4,000 exactly 1 year ago. Because of the release of a large amount of gold onto the market by a major South African mining company,

Marilyn netted only $370 per ounce upon the sale of her 10 ounces of gold today. What are Marilyn's pretax and after-tax HPRs on this transaction?

LG 3 LG 4

P17.6. On January 1, 1999, Simon Love's portfolio of 15 common stocks, completely equity-financed, had a market value of $264,000. At the end of May 1999, Simon sold one of the stocks, which had a beginning-of-year value of $26,300, for $31,500. He did not reinvest those or any other funds in the portfolio during the year. He received total dividends from stocks in his portfolio of $12,500 during the year. On December 31, 1999, Simon's portfolio had a market value of $250,000. Find the HPR on Simon's portfolio during the year ended December 31, 1999. (Measure the amount of withdrawn funds at their beginning-of-year value.)

LG 3 LG 4

P17.7. Niki Malone's portfolio earned a return of 11.8% during the year just ended. The portfolio's standard deviation of return was 14.1%. The risk-free rate is currently 6.2%. During the year, the return on the market portfolio was 9.0% and its standard deviation was 9.4%.

a. Calculate Sharpe's measure for Niki Malone's portfolio for the year just ended.
b. Compare the performance of Niki's portfolio found in part (a) to that of Hector Smith's portfolio, which has a Sharpe's measure of 0.43. Which portfolio performed better? Why?
c. Calculate Sharpe's measure for the market portfolio for the year just ended.
d. Use your findings in parts (a) and (c) to discuss the performance of Niki's portfolio relative to the market during the year just ended.

LG 3 LG 4

P17.8. During the year just ended, Anna Schultz's portfolio, which has a beta of 0.90, earned a return of 8.6%. The risk-free rate is currently 7.3%, and the return on the market portfolio during the year just ended was 9.2%.

a. Calculate Treynor's measure for Anna's portfolio for the year just ended.
b. Compare the performance of Anna's portfolio found in part (a) to that of Stacey Quant's portfolio, which has a Treynor's measure of 1.25%. Which portfolio performed better? Explain.
c. Calculate Treynor's measure for the market portfolio for the year just ended.
d. Use your findings in parts (a) and (c) to discuss the performance of Anna's portfolio relative to the market during the year just ended.

LG 3 LG 4

P17.9. Chee Chew's portfolio has a beta of 1.3 and earned a return of 12.9% during the year just ended. The risk-free rate is currently 7.8%, and the return on the market portfolio during the year just ended was 11.0%.

a. Calculate Jensen's measure (Jensen's alpha) for Chee's portfolio for the year just ended.
b. Compare the performance of Chee's portfolio found in part (a) to that of Carri Uhl's portfolio, which has a Jensen's measure of −0.24. Which portfolio performed better? Explain.
c. Use your findings in part (a) to discuss the performance of Chee's portfolio relative to the market during the period just ended.

LG 3 LG 4

P17.10. The risk-free rate is currently 8.1%. Use the data in the accompanying table for the Fio family's portfolio and the market portfolio during the year just ended to answer the questions that follow.

Data Item	Fios' Portfolio	Market Portfolio
Rate of return	12.8%	11.2%
Standard deviation of return	13.5%	9.6%
Beta	1.10	1.00

a. Calculate Sharpe's measure for the portfolio and the market, compare them, and assess the performance of the Fios' portfolio during the year just ended.
b. Calculate Treynor's measure for the portfolio and the market, compare them, and assess the performance of the Fios' portfolio during the year just ended.
c. Calculate Jensen's measure (Jensen's alpha), and use it to assess the performance of the Fios' portfolio during the year just ended.
d. On the basis of your findings in parts (a), (b), and (c), assess the performance of the Fios' portfolio during the year just ended.

LG 5 LG 6

P17.11. Over the past 2 years, Jonas Cone has used a dollar-cost averaging formula to purchase $300 worth of FCI common stock each month. The price per share paid each month over the 2 years is given in the following table. Assume that Jonas paid no brokerage commissions on these transactions.

	Price per Share of FCI	
Month	Year 1	Year 2
January	11⅝	11⅜
February	11½	11¾
March	11½	12
April	11	12
May	11¾	12⅛
June	12	12½
July	12⅜	12¾
August	12½	13
September	12¼	13¼
October	12½	13
November	11⅞	13⅜
December	11½	13½

a. How much was Jonas's total investment over the 2-year period?
b. How many shares did Jonas purchase over the 2-year period?
c. Use your findings in parts (a) and (b) to calculate Jonas's average cost per share of FCI.
d. What was the value of Jonas's holdings in FCI at the end of the second year?

Case Problem 17.1 *Assessing the Stalchecks' Portfolio Performance*

LG 1 LG 2 LG 3 LG 4

The Stalchecks, Mary and Nick, have an investment portfolio containing four vehicles. It was developed to provide them with a balance between current income and capital appreciation. Rather than acquire mutual fund shares or diversify within a given class of investment vehicle, they developed their portfolio with the idea of diversifying across various types of vehicles. The portfolio currently contains common stock, industrial bonds, mutual fund shares, and a real estate investment. They acquired each of these vehicles during the past 3 years, and they plan to invest in gold and other vehicles sometime in the future.

Currently, the Stalchecks are interested in measuring the return on their investment and assessing how well they have done relative to the market. They hope that the return earned over the past calendar year is in excess of what they would have earned by investing in a portfolio consisting of the S&P 500 stock composite index. Their investigation has indicated that the risk-free rate was 7.2% and that the (before-tax) return on the S&P stock portfolio was 10.1% during the past year. With the aid of a friend, they have been able to estimate the beta of their portfolio, which was 1.20. In their analysis, they have planned to ignore taxes, because they feel their earnings have been adequately sheltered. Because they did not make any portfolio transactions during the past year, the Stalchecks would have to consider only unrealized capital gains, if any. To make the necessary calculations, the Stalchecks have gathered the following information on each of the four vehicles in their portfolio.

Common stock. They own 400 shares of KJ Enterprises common stock. KJ is a diversified manufacturer of metal pipe and is known for its unbroken stream of dividends. Over the past few years, it has entered new markets and, as a result, has offered moderate capital appreciation potential. Its share price has risen from 17¼ at the start of the last calendar year to 18¾ at the end of the year. During the year, quarterly cash dividends of 20, 20, 25, and 25 cents were paid.

Industrial bonds. The Stalchecks own eight Cal Industries bonds. The bonds have a $1,000 par value, have a 9¾% coupon, and are due in 2009. They are A-rated by Moody's. The bond was quoted at 97 at the beginning of the year and ended the calendar year at 96⅜.

Mutual fund. The Stalchecks hold 500 shares in the Holt Fund, a balanced, no-load mutual fund. The dividend distributions on the fund during the year consisted of 60 cents in investment income and 50 cents in capital gains. The fund's NAV at the beginning of the calendar year was $19.45, and it ended the year at $20.02.

Real estate. The Stalchecks own a parcel of raw land that had an appraised value of $26,000 at the beginning of the calendar year. Although they did not have it appraised at year-end, they were offered $30,500 for it at that time. Because the offer was made through a realtor, they would have had to pay nearly $1,500 in sales commissions and fees to make the sale at that price.

QUESTIONS

a. Calculate the holding period return on a before-tax basis for each of these four investment vehicles.

b. Assuming that the Stalchecks' ordinary income is currently being taxed at a combined (state and federal) tax rate of 38%, determine the after-tax HPR for each of their four investment vehicles.

c. Recognizing that all gains on the Stalchecks' investments were unrealized, calculate the before-tax portfolio HPR for their four-vehicle portfolio during the past calendar year. Evaluate this return relative to its current income and capital gain components.

d. Use the HPR calculated in question (c) to compute Jensen's measure (Jensen's alpha) to analyze the performance of the Stalchecks' portfolio on a risk-adjusted, market-adjusted basis. Comment on your finding. Is it reasonable to use Jensen's measure to evaluate a four-vehicle portfolio? Why or why not?

e. On the basis of your analysis in questions (a), (c), and (d), what, if any, recommendations might you offer the Stalchecks relative to the revision of their portfolio? Explain your recommendations.

Case Problem 17.2 *Evaluating Formula Plans: Charles Spurge's Approach*

LG 5 LG 6

Charles Spurge, a mathematician with Ansco Petroleum Company, wishes to develop a rational basis for timing his portfolio transactions. He currently holds a security portfolio with a market value of nearly $100,000, divided equally between a very conservative, low-beta common stock, ConCam United, and a highly speculative, high-beta stock, Fleck Enterprises. On the basis of his reading of the investments literature, Charles does not believe it is necessary to diversify one's portfolio across 8 to 15 securities. His own feeling, based on his independent mathematical analysis, is that one can achieve the same results by holding a 2-security portfolio in which one security is very conservative and the other is highly speculative. His feelings on this point will not be altered; he plans to continue to hold such a 2-security portfolio until he finds that his theory does not work. During the past couple of years, he has earned a rate of return in excess of the risk-adjusted, market-adjusted rate expected on such a portfolio.

Charles's current interest centers on investigating and possibly developing his own formula plan for timing portfolio transactions. The current stage of his analysis focuses on the evaluation of four commonly used formula plans in order to isolate the desirable features of each. The four plans being considered are (1) dollar-cost averaging, (2) the constant-dollar plan, (3) the constant-ratio plan, and (4) the variable-ratio plan. Charles's analysis of the plans will involve the use of two types of data. Because dollar-cost averaging is a passive buy-and-hold strategy in which the periodic investment is held constant, whereas the other plans are more active in that they involve periodic purchases and sales within the portfolio, differing data are needed to evaluate each of them.

For evaluating the dollar-cost averaging plan, Charles decided he would assume an investment of $500 at the end of each 45-day period. He chose to use 45-day time intervals to achieve certain brokerage fee savings that would be available by making larger transactions. The $500 per 45 days totaled $4,000 for the year and equaled the total amount Charles invested during the past year. (*Note:* For convenience, the returns earned on the portions of the $4,000 that remain uninvested during the year are ignored.) In evaluating this plan, he would assume that half ($250) was invested in the conservative stock (ConCam United) and the other half in the speculative stock (Fleck Enterprises). The share prices for each of the stocks at the end of the eight 45-day periods when purchases were to be made are given in the accompanying table.

	Price per Share	
Period	ConCam	Fleck
1	22⅛	22⅛
2	21⅞	24½
3	21⅞	25⅜
4	22	28½
5	22¼	21⅞
6	22⅛	19¼
7	22	21½
8	22¼	23⅝

To evaluate the three other plans, Charles decided to begin with a $4,000 portfolio evenly split between the 2 stocks. He chose to use $4,000, because that amount would correspond to the total amount invested in the 2 stocks over 1 year using dollar-cost averaging. He planned to use the same eight points in time given earlier to assess the portfolio and make transfers within it if required. For each of the three plans evaluated using these data, he established the following triggering points.

Constant-dollar plan. Each time the speculative portion of the portfolio is worth 13% more or less than its initial value of $2,000, the portfolio is rebalanced to bring the speculative portion back to its initial $2,000 value.

Constant-ratio plan. Each time the ratio of the value of the speculative portion of the portfolio to the value of the conservative portion is (1) greater than or equal to 1.15 or (2) less than or equal to 0.84, the portfolio is rebalanced through sale or purchase, respectively, to bring the ratio back to its initial value of 1.0.

Variable-ratio plan. Each time the value of the speculative portion of the portfolio rises above 54% of the total value of the portfolio, its proportion is reduced to 46%. Each time the value of the speculative portion of the portfolio drops below 38% of the total value of the portfolio, its proportion is raised to 50%.

QUESTIONS

a. Under the dollar-cost averaging plan, determine the total number of shares purchased, the average cost per share, and the year-end portfolio value expressed both in dollars and as a percentage of the amount invested for (1) the conservative stock, (2) the speculative stock, and (3) the total portfolio.

b. Using the constant-dollar plan, determine the year-end portfolio value expressed both in dollars and as a percentage of the amount initially invested for (1) the conservative portion, (2) the speculative portion, and (3) the total portfolio.

c. Repeat question (b) for the constant-ratio plan. Be sure to answer all parts.

d. Repeat question (b) for the variable-ratio plan. Be sure to answer all parts.

e. Compare and contrast your results from questions (a) through (d). You may want to summarize them in tabular form. Which plan would appear to have been most beneficial in timing Charles's portfolio activities during the past year? Explain.

Home Page Exercises

http://hepg.aw.com **Keyword: Invest**

For many of the topics covered in this textbook, we have found companion information on the Web. There are numerous sites offering advice on *how* and *where* to invest. The quantity and variety of such information are overwhelming. But once you have made some investments, you need to determine how well your portfolio is performing. Although the Web provides some historical performance information, primarily on mutual funds, if you want to know how your particular portfolio is doing, you will find little help. The one exception is that you can register for a portfolio-tracking program that updates prices regularly. The Yahoo! and Infoseek search engines provide free portfolio monitoring.

Web Address	*Primary Investment Focus*
www.slu.edu:80/department/finance/363class.htm	Provides links to many useful sources of investment information; very good links to the specific assets included in over 40 market indexes
www.aol.com/finlist/perform	Discusses the Sharpe, Treynor, and Jensen performance measures
www.investools.com/cgi-bin/f/1	Register for free portfolio monitoring

W17.1. Phil Billsworth owns a portfolio of four common stocks. He is getting ready to measure the return performance of his portfolio against an appropriate market index. Phil has equal dollar amounts invested in Ethan Allen Interiors (ETH), Borg Warner (BOR), Digital Equipment Corporation (DEC), and Mobil Oil (MOB). At the Morningstar Web site, click on *Quicktake Reports* and then enter the appropriate ticker symbols to obtain the individual company reports. Under the Stock Performance section, select *CalendarYearReturns* to find yearly capital gains, dividends, and total returns. Calculate Phil's portfolio return for the latest full year and for the year to date.

www.morningstar.net

W17.2. Becky Eakin owns a portfolio of three stocks. Becky has 40% of her portfolio in Boeing Aircraft (BA), 25% in H & R Block (HR), and 35% in Wal-Mart (WMT). Calculate the holding period return on each of the three stocks over the 12 months just ended. Calculate Becky's return on her portfolio over this same 12-month holding period. At the Web page listed here, go to each company's detailed company report by entering the appropriate ticker symbol. You can obtain the prices needed to calculate any capital gains by clicking on the appropriate month in the graph provided. The dividends paid can be found in the accompanying table.

www.rapidresearch.com

APPENDIX A

FINANCIAL TABLES

TABLE A.1 Future-Value Interest Factors for One Dollar, *FVIF*

Period	1%	2%	3%	4%	5%	6%	7%	8%	9%	10%	11%	12%	13%	14%	15%	16%	17%	18%	19%	20%
1	1.010	1.020	1.030	1.040	1.050	1.060	1.070	1.080	1.090	1.100	1.110	1.120	1.130	1.140	1.150	1.160	1.170	1.180	1.190	1.200
2	1.020	1.040	1.061	1.082	1.102	1.124	1.145	1.166	1.188	1.210	1.232	1.254	1.277	1.300	1.322	1.346	1.369	1.392	1.416	1.440
3	1.030	1.061	1.093	1.125	1.158	1.191	1.225	1.260	1.295	1.331	1.368	1.405	1.443	1.482	1.521	1.561	1.602	1.643	1.685	1.728
4	1.041	1.082	1.126	1.170	1.216	1.262	1.311	1.360	1.412	1.464	1.518	1.574	1.630	1.689	1.749	1.811	1.874	1.939	2.005	2.074
5	1.051	1.104	1.159	1.217	1.276	1.338	1.403	1.469	1.539	1.611	1.685	1.762	1.842	1.925	2.011	2.100	2.192	2.288	2.386	2.488
6	1.062	1.126	1.194	1.265	1.340	1.419	1.501	1.587	1.677	1.772	1.870	1.974	2.082	2.195	2.313	2.436	2.565	2.700	2.840	2.986
7	1.072	1.149	1.230	1.316	1.407	1.504	1.606	1.714	1.828	1.949	2.076	2.211	2.353	2.502	2.660	2.826	3.001	3.185	3.379	3.583
8	1.083	1.172	1.267	1.369	1.477	1.594	1.718	1.851	1.993	2.144	2.305	2.476	2.658	2.853	3.059	3.278	3.511	3.759	4.021	4.300
9	1.094	1.195	1.305	1.423	1.551	1.689	1.838	1.999	2.172	2.358	2.558	2.773	3.004	3.252	3.518	3.803	4.108	4.435	4.785	5.160
10	1.105	1.219	1.344	1.480	1.629	1.791	1.967	2.159	2.367	2.594	2.839	3.106	3.395	3.707	4.046	4.411	4.807	5.234	5.695	6.192
11	1.116	1.243	1.384	1.539	1.710	1.898	2.105	2.332	2.580	2.853	3.152	3.479	3.836	4.226	4.652	5.117	5.624	6.176	6.777	7.430
12	1.127	1.268	1.426	1.601	1.796	2.012	2.252	2.518	2.813	3.138	3.498	3.896	4.334	4.818	5.350	5.936	6.580	7.288	8.064	8.916
13	1.138	1.294	1.469	1.665	1.886	2.133	2.410	2.720	3.066	3.452	3.883	4.363	4.898	5.492	6.153	6.886	7.699	8.599	9.596	10.699
14	1.149	1.319	1.513	1.732	1.980	2.261	2.579	2.937	3.342	3.797	4.310	4.887	5.535	6.261	7.076	7.987	9.007	10.147	11.420	12.839
15	1.161	1.346	1.558	1.801	2.079	2.397	2.759	3.172	3.642	4.177	4.785	5.474	6.254	7.138	8.137	9.265	10.539	11.974	13.589	15.407
16	1.173	1.373	1.605	1.873	2.183	2.540	2.952	3.426	3.970	4.595	5.311	6.130	7.067	8.137	9.358	10.748	12.330	14.129	16.171	18.488
17	1.184	1.400	1.653	1.948	2.292	2.693	3.159	3.700	4.328	5.054	5.895	6.866	7.986	9.276	10.761	12.468	14.426	16.672	19.244	22.186
18	1.196	1.428	1.702	2.026	2.407	2.854	3.380	3.996	4.717	5.560	6.543	7.690	9.024	10.575	12.375	14.462	16.879	19.673	22.900	26.623
19	1.208	1.457	1.753	2.107	2.527	3.026	3.616	4.316	5.142	6.116	7.263	8.613	10.197	12.055	14.232	16.776	19.748	23.214	27.251	31.948
20	1.220	1.486	1.806	2.191	2.653	3.207	3.870	4.661	5.604	6.727	8.062	9.646	11.523	13.743	16.366	19.461	23.105	27.393	32.429	38.337
21	1.232	1.516	1.860	2.279	2.786	3.399	4.140	5.034	6.109	7.400	8.949	10.804	13.021	15.667	18.821	22.574	27.033	32.323	38.591	46.005
22	1.245	1.546	1.916	2.370	2.925	3.603	4.430	5.436	6.658	8.140	9.933	12.100	14.713	17.861	21.644	26.186	31.629	38.141	45.923	55.205
23	1.257	1.577	1.974	2.465	3.071	3.820	4.740	5.871	7.258	8.954	11.026	13.552	16.626	20.361	24.891	30.376	37.005	45.007	54.648	66.247
24	1.270	1.608	2.033	2.563	3.225	4.049	5.072	6.341	7.911	9.850	12.239	15.178	18.788	23.212	28.625	35.236	43.296	53.108	65.031	79.496
25	1.282	1.641	2.094	2.666	3.386	4.292	5.427	6.848	8.623	10.834	13.585	17.000	21.230	26.461	32.918	40.874	50.656	62.667	77.387	95.395
30	1.348	1.811	2.427	3.243	4.322	5.743	7.612	10.062	13.267	17.449	22.892	29.960	39.115	50.949	66.210	85.849	111.061	143.367	184.672	237.373
35	1.417	2.000	2.814	3.946	5.516	7.686	10.676	14.785	20.413	28.102	38.574	52.799	72.066	98.097	133.172	180.311	243.495	327.988	440.691	590.657
40	1.489	2.208	3.262	4.801	7.040	10.285	14.974	21.724	31.408	45.258	64.999	93.049	132.776	188.876	267.856	378.715	533.846	750.353	1051.642	1469.740
45	1.565	2.438	3.781	5.841	8.985	13.764	21.002	31.920	48.325	72.888	109.527	163.985	244.629	363.662	538.752	795.429	1170.425	1716.619	2509.583	3657.176
50	1.645	2.691	4.384	7.106	11.467	18.419	29.456	46.900	74.354	117.386	184.559	288.996	450.711	700.197	1083.619	1670.669	2566.080	3927.189	5988.730	9100.191

Using the Calculator to Compute the Future Value of a Single Amount

Before you begin, clear the memory, ensure that you are in the *end mode* and that your calculator is set for *one payment per year*, and set the number of decimal places that you want (usually two for dollar-related accuracy).

Sample Problem

You place $800 in a savings account at 6% compounded annually. What is your account balance at the end of 5 years?

Hewlett-Packard HP 12C, 17 BII, and 19 BII[a]

Inputs:	800	5	6	
Functions:	PV	N	I%YR	FV
Outputs:				1070.58[b]

[a] For the 12C, you would use the n key instead of the N key, and the i key instead of the I%YR key.

[b] The minus sign that precedes the output should be ignored.

TABLE A.1 (Continued)

Period	21%	22%	23%	24%	25%	26%	27%	28%	29%	30%	31%	32%	33%	34%	35%	40%	45%	50%
1	1.210	1.220	1.230	1.240	1.250	1.260	1.270	1.280	1.290	1.300	1.310	1.320	1.330	1.340	1.350	1.400	1.450	1.500
2	1.464	1.488	1.513	1.538	1.562	1.588	1.613	1.638	1.664	1.690	1.716	1.742	1.769	1.796	1.822	1.960	2.102	2.250
3	1.772	1.816	1.861	1.907	1.953	2.000	2.048	2.097	2.147	2.197	2.248	2.300	2.353	2.406	2.460	2.744	3.049	3.375
4	2.144	2.215	2.289	2.364	2.441	2.520	2.601	2.684	2.769	2.856	2.945	3.036	3.129	3.224	3.321	3.842	4.421	5.063
5	2.594	2.703	2.815	2.932	3.052	3.176	3.304	3.436	3.572	3.713	3.858	4.007	4.162	4.320	4.484	5.378	6.410	7.594
6	3.138	3.297	3.463	3.635	3.815	4.001	4.196	4.398	4.608	4.827	5.054	5.290	5.535	5.789	6.053	7.530	9.294	11.391
7	3.797	4.023	4.259	4.508	4.768	5.042	5.329	5.629	5.945	6.275	6.621	6.983	7.361	7.758	8.172	10.541	13.476	17.086
8	4.595	4.908	5.239	5.589	5.960	6.353	6.767	7.206	7.669	8.157	8.673	9.217	9.791	10.395	11.032	14.758	19.541	25.629
9	5.560	5.987	6.444	6.931	7.451	8.004	8.595	9.223	9.893	10.604	11.362	12.166	13.022	13.930	14.894	20.661	28.334	38.443
10	6.727	7.305	7.926	8.594	9.313	10.086	10.915	11.806	12.761	13.786	14.884	16.060	17.319	18.666	20.106	28.925	41.085	57.665
11	8.140	8.912	9.749	10.657	11.642	12.708	13.862	15.112	16.462	17.921	19.498	21.199	23.034	25.012	27.144	40.495	59.573	86.498
12	9.850	10.872	11.991	13.215	14.552	16.012	17.605	19.343	21.236	23.298	25.542	27.982	30.635	33.516	36.644	56.694	86.380	129.746
13	11.918	13.264	14.749	16.386	18.190	20.175	22.359	24.759	27.395	30.287	33.460	36.937	40.745	44.912	49.469	79.371	125.251	194.620
14	14.421	16.182	18.141	20.319	22.737	25.420	28.395	31.691	35.339	39.373	43.832	48.756	54.190	60.181	66.784	111.119	181.614	291.929
15	17.449	19.742	22.314	25.195	28.422	32.030	36.062	40.565	45.587	51.185	57.420	64.358	72.073	80.643	90.158	155.567	263.341	437.894
16	21.113	24.085	27.446	31.242	35.527	40.357	45.799	51.923	58.808	66.541	75.220	84.953	95.857	108.061	121.713	217.793	381.844	656.841
17	25.547	29.384	33.758	38.740	44.409	50.850	58.165	66.461	75.862	86.503	98.539	112.138	127.490	144.802	164.312	304.911	553.674	985.261
18	30.912	35.848	41.523	48.038	55.511	64.071	73.869	85.070	97.862	112.454	129.086	148.022	169.561	194.035	221.822	426.875	802.826	1477.892
19	37.404	43.735	51.073	59.567	69.389	80.730	93.813	108.890	126.242	146.190	169.102	195.389	225.517	260.006	299.459	597.625	1164.098	2216.838
20	45.258	53.357	62.820	73.863	86.736	101.720	119.143	139.379	162.852	190.047	221.523	257.913	299.937	348.408	404.270	836.674	1687.942	3325.257
21	54.762	65.095	77.268	91.591	108.420	128.167	151.312	178.405	210.079	247.061	290.196	340.446	398.916	466.867	545.764	1171.343	2447.515	4987.883
22	66.262	79.416	95.040	113.572	135.525	161.490	192.165	228.358	271.002	321.178	380.156	449.388	530.558	625.601	736.781	1639.878	3548.896	7481.824
23	80.178	96.887	116.899	140.829	169.407	203.477	244.050	292.298	349.592	417.531	498.004	593.192	705.642	838.305	994.653	2295.829	5145.898	11222.738
24	97.015	118.203	143.786	174.628	211.758	256.381	309.943	374.141	450.974	542.791	652.385	783.013	938.504	1123.328	1342.781	3214.158	7461.547	16834.109
25	117.388	144.207	176.857	216.539	264.698	323.040	393.628	478.901	581.756	705.627	854.623	1033.577	1248.210	1505.258	1812.754	4499.816	10819.242	25251.164
30	304.471	389.748	497.904	634.810	807.793	1025.904	1300.477	1645.488	2078.208	2619.936	3297.081	4142.008	5194.516	6503.285	8128.426	24201.043	69348.375	191751.000
35	789.716	1053.370	1401.749	1861.020	2465.189	3258.053	4296.547	5653.840	7423.988	9727.598	12719.918	16598.906	21617.363	28096.695	36448.051	130158.687	*	*
40	2048.309	2846.941	3946.340	5455.797	7523.156	10346.879	14195.051	19426.418	26520.723	36117.754	49072.621	66519.313	89962.188	121388.437	163433.875	700022.688	*	*
45	5312.758	7694.418	11110.121	15994.316	22958.844	32859.457	46897.973	66748.500	94739.937	134102.187	*	*	*	*	*	*	*	*
50	13779.844	20795.680	31278.301	46889.207	70064.812	104354.562	154942.687	229345.875	338440.000	497910.125	*	*	*	*	*	*	*	*

*Not shown because of space limitations.

Texas Instruments BA-35, BAII, BAII Plus[c]

Inputs:	800	5	6		
Functions:	PV	N	%i	CPT	FV
Outputs:					1070.58[d]

[c] For the Texas Instruments BAII, you would use the 2nd key instead of the CPT key; for the Texas Instruments BAII Plus, you would use the I/Y key instead of the %i key.

[d] If a minus sign precedes the output, it should be ignored.

TABLE A.2 Future-Value Interest Factors for a One-Dollar Annuity, *FVIFA*

Period	1%	2%	3%	4%	5%	6%	7%	8%	9%	10%	11%	12%	13%	14%	15%	16%	17%	18%	19%	20%
1	1.000	1.000	1.000	1.000	1.000	1.000	1.000	1.000	1.000	1.000	1.000	1.000	1.000	1.000	1.000	1.000	1.000	1.000	1.000	1.000
2	2.010	2.020	2.030	2.040	2.050	2.060	2.070	2.080	2.090	2.100	2.110	2.120	2.130	2.140	2.150	2.160	2.170	2.180	2.190	2.200
3	3.030	3.060	3.091	3.122	3.152	3.184	3.215	3.246	3.278	3.310	3.342	3.374	3.407	3.440	3.472	3.506	3.539	3.572	3.606	3.640
4	4.060	4.122	4.184	4.246	4.310	4.375	4.440	4.506	4.573	4.641	4.710	4.779	4.850	4.921	4.993	5.066	5.141	5.215	5.291	5.368
5	5.101	5.204	5.309	5.416	5.526	5.637	5.751	5.867	5.985	6.105	6.228	6.353	6.480	6.610	6.742	6.877	7.014	7.154	7.297	7.442
6	6.152	6.308	6.468	6.633	6.802	6.975	7.153	7.336	7.523	7.716	7.913	8.115	8.323	8.535	8.754	8.977	9.207	9.442	9.683	9.930
7	7.214	7.434	7.662	7.898	8.142	8.394	8.654	8.923	9.200	9.487	9.783	10.089	10.405	10.730	11.067	11.414	11.772	12.141	12.523	12.916
8	8.286	8.583	8.892	9.214	9.549	9.897	10.260	10.637	11.028	11.436	11.859	12.300	12.757	13.233	13.727	14.240	14.773	15.327	15.902	16.499
9	9.368	9.755	10.159	10.583	11.027	11.491	11.978	12.488	13.021	13.579	14.164	14.776	15.416	16.085	16.786	17.518	18.285	19.086	19.923	20.799
10	10.462	10.950	11.464	12.006	12.578	13.181	13.816	14.487	15.193	15.937	16.722	17.549	18.420	19.337	20.304	21.321	22.393	23.521	24.709	25.959
11	11.567	12.169	12.808	13.486	14.207	14.972	15.784	16.645	17.560	18.531	19.561	20.655	21.814	23.044	24.349	25.733	27.200	28.755	30.403	32.150
12	12.682	13.412	14.192	15.026	15.917	16.870	17.888	18.977	20.141	21.384	22.713	24.133	25.650	27.271	29.001	30.850	32.824	34.931	37.180	39.580
13	13.809	14.680	15.618	16.627	17.713	18.882	20.141	21.495	22.953	24.523	26.211	28.029	29.984	32.088	34.352	36.786	39.404	42.218	45.244	48.496
14	14.947	15.974	17.086	18.292	19.598	21.015	22.550	24.215	26.019	27.975	30.095	32.392	34.882	37.581	40.504	43.672	47.102	50.818	54.841	59.196
15	16.097	17.293	18.599	20.023	21.578	23.276	25.129	27.152	29.361	31.772	34.405	37.280	40.417	43.842	47.580	51.659	56.109	60.965	66.260	72.035
16	17.258	18.639	20.157	21.824	23.657	25.672	27.888	30.324	33.003	35.949	39.190	42.753	46.671	50.980	55.717	60.925	66.648	72.938	79.850	87.442
17	18.430	20.012	21.761	23.697	25.840	28.213	30.840	33.750	36.973	40.544	44.500	48.883	53.738	59.117	65.075	71.673	78.978	87.067	96.021	105.930
18	19.614	21.412	23.414	25.645	28.132	30.905	33.999	37.450	41.301	45.599	50.396	55.749	61.724	68.393	75.836	84.140	93.404	103.739	115.265	128.116
19	20.811	22.840	25.117	27.671	30.539	33.760	37.379	41.446	46.018	51.158	56.939	63.439	70.748	78.968	88.211	98.603	110.283	123.412	138.165	154.739
20	22.019	24.297	26.870	29.778	33.066	36.785	40.995	45.762	51.159	57.274	64.202	72.052	80.946	91.024	102.443	115.379	130.031	146.626	165.417	186.687
21	23.239	25.783	28.676	31.969	35.719	39.992	44.865	50.422	56.764	64.002	72.264	81.698	92.468	104.767	118.809	134.840	153.136	174.019	197.846	225.024
22	24.471	27.299	30.536	34.248	38.505	43.392	49.005	55.456	62.872	71.402	81.213	92.502	105.489	120.434	137.630	157.414	180.169	206.342	236.436	271.028
23	25.716	28.845	32.452	36.618	41.430	46.995	53.435	60.893	69.531	79.542	91.147	104.602	120.203	138.295	159.274	183.600	211.798	244.483	282.359	326.234
24	26.973	30.421	34.426	39.082	44.501	50.815	58.176	66.764	76.789	88.496	102.173	118.154	136.829	158.656	184.166	213.976	248.803	289.490	337.007	392.480
25	28.243	32.030	36.459	41.645	47.726	54.864	63.248	73.105	84.699	98.346	114.412	133.333	155.616	181.867	212.790	249.212	292.099	342.598	402.038	471.976
30	34.784	40.567	47.575	56.084	66.438	79.057	94.459	113.282	136.305	164.491	199.018	241.330	293.192	356.778	434.738	530.306	647.423	790.932	966.698	1181.865
35	41.659	49.994	60.461	73.651	90.318	111.432	138.234	172.314	215.705	271.018	341.583	431.658	546.663	693.552	881.152	1120.699	1426.448	1816.607	2314.173	2948.294
40	48.885	60.401	75.400	95.024	120.797	154.758	199.630	259.052	337.872	442.580	581.812	767.080	1013.667	1341.979	1779.048	2360.724	3134.412	4163.094	5529.711	7343.715
45	56.479	71.891	92.718	121.027	159.695	212.737	285.741	386.497	525.840	718.881	986.613	1358.208	1874.086	2590.464	3585.031	4965.191	6879.008	9531.258	13203.105	18280.914
50	64.461	84.577	112.794	152.664	209.341	290.325	406.516	573.756	815.051	1163.865	1668.723	2399.975	3459.344	4994.301	7217.488	10435.449	15088.805	21812.273	31514.492	45496.094

Using the Calculator to Compute the Future Value of an Annuity

Before you begin, clear the memory, ensure that you are in the *end mode* and that your calculator is set for *one payment per year*, and set the number of decimal places that you want (usually two for dollar-related accuracy).

Sample Problem

You want to know what the future value will be at the end of 5 years if you place five end-of-year deposits of $1,000 in an account paying 7% annually. What is your account balance at the end of 5 years?

Hewlett-Packard HP 12C, 17 BII, and 19 BII[a]

Inputs:	1000	5	7	
Functions:	PMT	N	I%YR	FV
Outputs:				5750.74[b]

[a] For the 12C, you would use the n key instead of the N key, and the i key instead of the I%YR key.

[b] The minus sign that precedes the output should be ignored.

TABLE A.2 (Continued)

Period	21%	22%	23%	24%	25%	26%	27%	28%	29%	30%	31%	32%	33%	34%	35%	40%	45%	50%
1	1.000	1.000	1.000	1.000	1.000	1.000	1.000	1.000	1.000	1.000	1.000	1.000	1.000	1.000	1.000	1.000	1.000	1.000
2	2.210	2.220	2.230	2.240	2.250	2.260	2.270	2.280	2.290	2.300	2.310	2.320	2.330	2.340	2.350	2.400	2.450	2.500
3	3.674	3.708	3.743	3.778	3.813	3.848	3.883	3.918	3.954	3.990	4.026	4.062	4.099	4.136	4.172	4.360	4.552	4.750
4	5.446	5.524	5.604	5.684	5.766	5.848	5.931	6.016	6.101	6.187	6.274	6.362	6.452	6.542	6.633	7.104	7.601	8.125
5	7.589	7.740	7.893	8.048	8.207	8.368	8.533	8.700	8.870	9.043	9.219	9.398	9.581	9.766	9.954	10.946	12.022	13.188
6	10.183	10.442	10.708	10.980	11.259	11.544	11.837	12.136	12.442	12.756	13.077	13.406	13.742	14.086	14.438	16.324	18.431	20.781
7	13.321	13.740	14.171	14.615	15.073	15.546	16.032	16.534	17.051	17.583	18.131	18.696	19.277	19.876	20.492	23.853	27.725	32.172
8	17.119	17.762	18.430	19.123	19.842	20.588	21.361	22.163	22.995	23.858	24.752	25.678	26.638	27.633	28.664	34.395	41.202	49.258
9	21.714	22.670	23.669	24.712	25.802	26.940	28.129	29.369	30.664	32.015	33.425	34.895	36.429	38.028	39.696	49.152	60.743	74.887
10	27.274	28.657	30.113	31.643	33.253	34.945	36.723	38.592	40.556	42.619	44.786	47.062	49.451	51.958	54.590	69.813	89.077	113.330
11	34.001	35.962	38.039	40.238	42.566	45.030	47.639	50.398	53.318	56.405	59.670	63.121	66.769	70.624	74.696	98.739	130.161	170.995
12	42.141	44.873	47.787	50.895	54.208	57.738	61.501	65.510	69.780	74.326	79.167	84.320	89.803	95.636	101.840	139.234	189.734	257.493
13	51.991	55.745	59.778	64.109	68.760	73.750	79.106	84.853	91.016	97.624	104.709	112.302	120.438	129.152	138.484	195.928	276.114	387.239
14	63.909	69.009	74.528	80.496	86.949	93.925	101.465	109.611	118.411	127.912	138.169	149.239	161.183	174.063	187.953	275.299	401.365	581.858
15	78.330	85.191	92.669	100.815	109.687	119.346	129.860	141.302	153.750	167.285	182.001	197.996	215.373	234.245	254.737	386.418	582.980	873.788
16	95.779	104.933	114.983	126.010	138.109	151.375	165.922	181.867	199.337	218.470	239.421	262.354	287.446	314.888	344.895	541.985	846.321	1311.681
17	116.892	129.019	142.428	157.252	173.636	191.733	211.721	233.790	258.145	285.011	314.642	347.307	383.303	422.949	466.608	759.778	1228.165	1968.522
18	142.439	158.403	176.187	195.993	218.045	242.583	269.885	300.250	334.006	371.514	413.180	459.445	510.792	567.751	630.920	1064.689	1781.838	2953.783
19	173.351	194.251	217.710	244.031	273.556	306.654	343.754	385.321	431.868	483.968	542.266	607.467	680.354	761.786	852.741	1491.563	2584.665	4431.672
20	210.755	237.986	268.783	303.598	342.945	387.384	437.568	494.210	558.110	630.157	711.368	802.856	905.870	1021.792	1152.200	2089.188	3748.763	6648.508
21	256.013	291.343	331.603	377.461	429.681	489.104	556.710	633.589	720.962	820.204	932.891	1060.769	1205.807	1370.201	1556.470	2925.862	5436.703	9973.762
22	310.775	356.438	408.871	469.052	538.101	617.270	708.022	811.993	931.040	1067.265	1223.087	1401.215	1604.724	1837.068	2102.234	4097.203	7884.215	14961.645
23	377.038	435.854	503.911	582.624	673.626	778.760	900.187	1040.351	1202.042	1388.443	1603.243	1850.603	2135.282	2462.669	2839.014	5737.078	11433.109	22443.469
24	457.215	532.741	620.810	723.453	843.032	982.237	1144.237	1332.649	1551.634	1805.975	2101.247	2443.795	2840.924	3300.974	3833.667	8032.906	16579.008	33666.207
25	554.230	650.944	764.596	898.082	1054.791	1238.617	1454.180	1706.790	2002.608	2348.765	2753.631	3226.808	3779.428	4424.301	5176.445	11247.062	24040.555	50500.316
30	1445.111	1767.044	2160.459	2640.881	3227.172	3941.953	4812.891	5873.172	7162.785	8729.805	10632.543	12940.672	15737.945	19124.434	23221.258	60500.207	154105.313	383500.000
35	3755.814	4783.520	6090.227	7750.094	9856.746	12527.160	15909.480	20188.742	25596.512	32422.090	41028.887	51868.563	65504.199	82634.625	104134.500	325394.688	*	*
40	9749.141	12936.141	17153.691	22728.367	30088.621	39791.957	52570.707	69376.562	91447.375	120389.375	*	*	*	*	*	*	*	*
45	25294.223	34970.230	48300.660	66638.937	91831.312	126378.937	173692.875	238384.312	326686.375	447005.062	*	*	*	*	*	*	*	*

*Not shown because of space limitations.

Texas Instruments BA-35, BAII, BAII Plus[c]

Inputs:	1000	5	7		
Functions:	PMT	N	%i	CPT	FV
Outputs:					5750.74[d]

[c] For the Texas Instruments BAII, you would use the 2nd key instead of the CPT key; for the Texas Instruments BAII Plus, you would use the I/Y key instead of the %i key.

[d] If a minus sign precedes the output, it should be ignored.

TABLE A.3 Present-Value Interest Factors for One Dollar, *PVIF*

Period	1%	2%	3%	4%	5%	6%	7%	8%	9%	10%	11%	12%	13%	14%	15%	16%	17%	18%	19%	20%
1	.990	.980	.971	.962	.952	.943	.935	.926	.917	.909	.901	.893	.885	.877	.870	.862	.855	.847	.840	.833
2	.980	.961	.943	.925	.907	.890	.873	.857	.842	.826	.812	.797	.783	.769	.756	.743	.731	.718	.706	.694
3	.971	.942	.915	.889	.864	.840	.816	.794	.772	.751	.731	.712	.693	.675	.658	.641	.624	.609	.593	.579
4	.961	.924	.888	.855	.823	.792	.763	.735	.708	.683	.659	.636	.613	.592	.572	.552	.534	.516	.499	.482
5	.951	.906	.863	.822	.784	.747	.713	.681	.650	.621	.593	.567	.543	.519	.497	.476	.456	.437	.419	.402
6	.942	.888	.837	.790	.746	.705	.666	.630	.596	.564	.535	.507	.480	.456	.432	.410	.390	.370	.352	.335
7	.933	.871	.813	.760	.711	.665	.623	.583	.547	.513	.482	.452	.425	.400	.376	.354	.333	.314	.296	.279
8	.923	.853	.789	.731	.677	.627	.582	.540	.502	.467	.434	.404	.376	.351	.327	.305	.285	.266	.249	.233
9	.914	.837	.766	.703	.645	.592	.544	.500	.460	.424	.391	.361	.333	.308	.284	.263	.243	.225	.209	.194
10	.905	.820	.744	.676	.614	.558	.508	.463	.422	.386	.352	.322	.295	.270	.247	.227	.208	.191	.176	.162
11	.896	.804	.722	.650	.585	.527	.475	.429	.388	.350	.317	.287	.261	.237	.215	.195	.178	.162	.148	.135
12	.887	.789	.701	.625	.557	.497	.444	.397	.356	.319	.286	.257	.231	.208	.187	.168	.152	.137	.124	.112
13	.879	.773	.681	.601	.530	.469	.415	.368	.326	.290	.258	.229	.204	.182	.163	.145	.130	.116	.104	.093
14	.870	.758	.661	.577	.505	.442	.388	.340	.299	.263	.232	.205	.181	.160	.141	.125	.111	.099	.088	.078
15	.861	.743	.642	.555	.481	.417	.362	.315	.275	.239	.209	.183	.160	.140	.123	.108	.095	.084	.074	.065
16	.853	.728	.623	.534	.458	.394	.339	.292	.252	.218	.188	.163	.141	.123	.107	.093	.081	.071	.062	.054
17	.844	.714	.605	.513	.436	.371	.317	.270	.231	.198	.170	.146	.125	.108	.093	.080	.069	.060	.052	.045
18	.836	.700	.587	.494	.416	.350	.296	.250	.212	.180	.153	.130	.111	.095	.081	.069	.059	.051	.044	.038
19	.828	.686	.570	.475	.396	.331	.277	.232	.194	.164	.138	.116	.098	.083	.070	.060	.051	.043	.037	.031
20	.820	.673	.554	.456	.377	.312	.258	.215	.178	.149	.124	.104	.087	.073	.061	.051	.043	.037	.031	.026
21	.811	.660	.538	.439	.359	.294	.242	.199	.164	.135	.112	.093	.077	.064	.053	.044	.037	.031	.026	.022
22	.803	.647	.522	.422	.342	.278	.226	.184	.150	.123	.101	.083	.068	.056	.046	.038	.032	.026	.022	.018
23	.795	.634	.507	.406	.326	.262	.211	.170	.138	.112	.091	.074	.060	.049	.040	.033	.027	.022	.018	.015
24	.788	.622	.492	.390	.310	.247	.197	.158	.126	.102	.082	.066	.053	.043	.035	.028	.023	.019	.015	.013
25	.780	.610	.478	.375	.295	.233	.184	.146	.116	.092	.074	.059	.047	.038	.030	.024	.020	.016	.013	.010
30	.742	.552	.412	.308	.231	.174	.131	.099	.075	.057	.044	.033	.026	.020	.015	.012	.009	.007	.005	.004
35	.706	.500	.355	.253	.181	.130	.094	.068	.049	.036	.026	.019	.014	.010	.008	.006	.004	.003	.002	.002
40	.672	.453	.307	.208	.142	.097	.067	.046	.032	.022	.015	.011	.008	.005	.004	.003	.002	.001	.001	.001
45	.639	.410	.264	.171	.111	.073	.048	.031	.021	.014	.009	.006	.004	.003	.002	.001	.001	.001	*	*
50	.608	.372	.228	.141	.087	.054	.034	.021	.013	.009	.005	.003	.002	.001	.001	.001	*	*	*	*

* *PVIF* is zero to three decimal places.

Using the Calculator to Compute the Present Value of a Single Amount

Before you begin, clear the memory, ensure that you are in the *end mode* and that your calculator is set for *one payment per year*, and set the number of decimal places that you want (usually two for dollar-related accuracy).

Sample Problem

You want to know the present value of $1,700 to be received at the end of 8 years, assuming an 8% discount rate.

Hewlett-Packard HP 12C, 17 BII, and 19 BII[a]

Inputs:	1700	8	8	
Functions:	FV	N	I%YR	PV
Outputs:				918.46[b]

[a] For the 12C, you would use the n key instead of the N key, and the i key instead of the I%YR key.

[b] The minus sign that precedes the output should be ignored.

TABLE A.3 (Continued)

Period	21%	22%	23%	24%	25%	26%	27%	28%	29%	30%	31%	32%	33%	34%	35%	40%	45%	50%
1	.826	.820	.813	.806	.800	.794	.787	.781	.775	.769	.763	.758	.752	.746	.741	.714	.690	.667
2	.683	.672	.661	.650	.640	.630	.620	.610	.601	.592	.583	.574	.565	.557	.549	.510	.476	.444
3	.564	.551	.537	.524	.512	.500	.488	.477	.466	.455	.445	.435	.425	.416	.406	.364	.328	.296
4	.467	.451	.437	.423	.410	.397	.384	.373	.361	.350	.340	.329	.320	.310	.301	.260	.226	.198
5	.386	.370	.355	.341	.328	.315	.303	.291	.280	.269	.259	.250	.240	.231	.223	.186	.156	.132
6	.319	.303	.289	.275	.262	.250	.238	.227	.217	.207	.198	.189	.181	.173	.165	.133	.108	088
7	.263	.249	.235	.222	.210	.198	.188	.178	.168	.159	.151	.143	.136	.129	.122	.095	.074	.059
8	.218	.204	.191	.179	.168	.157	.148	.139	.130	.123	.115	.108	.102	.096	.091	.068	.051	.039
9	.180	.167	.155	.144	.134	.125	.116	.108	.101	.094	.088	.082	.077	.072	.067	.048	.035	.026
10	.149	.137	.126	.116	.107	.099	.092	.085	.078	.073	.067	.062	.058	.054	.050	.035	.024	.017
11	.123	.112	.103	.094	.086	.079	.072	.066	.061	.056	.051	.047	.043	.040	.037	.025	.017	.012
12	.102	.092	.083	.076	.069	.062	.057	.052	.047	.043	.039	.036	.033	.030	.027	.018	.012	.008
13	.084	.075	.068	.061	.055	.050	.045	.040	.037	.033	.030	.027	.025	.022	.020	.013	.008	.005
14	.069	.062	.055	.049	.044	.039	.035	.032	.028	.025	.023	.021	.018	.017	.015	.009	.006	.003
15	.057	.051	.045	.040	.035	.031	.028	.025	.022	.020	.017	.016	.014	.012	.011	.006	.004	.002
16	.047	.042	.036	.032	.028	.025	.022	.019	.017	.015	.013	.012	.010	.009	.008	.005	.003	.002
17	.039	.034	.030	.026	.023	.020	.017	.015	.013	.012	.010	.009	.008	.007	.006	.003	.002	.001
18	.032	.028	.024	.021	.018	.016	.014	.012	.010	.009	.008	.007	.006	.005	.005	.002	.001	.001
19	.027	.023	.020	.017	.014	.012	.011	.009	.008	.007	.006	.005	.004	.004	.003	.002	.001	*
20	.022	.019	.016	.014	.012	.010	.008	.007	.006	.005	.005	.004	.003	.003	.002	.001	.001	*
21	.018	.015	.013	.011	.009	.008	.007	.006	.005	.004	.003	.003	.003	.002	.002	.001	*	*
22	.015	.013	.011	.009	.007	.006	.005	.004	.004	.003	.003	.002	.002	.002	.001	.001	*	*
23	.012	.010	.009	.007	.006	.005	.004	.003	.003	.002	.002	.002	.001	.001	.001	*	*	*
24	.010	.008	.007	.006	.005	.004	.003	.003	.002	.002	.002	.001	.001	.001	.001	*	*	*
25	.009	.007	.006	.005	.004	.003	.003	.002	.002	.001	.001	.001	.001	.001	.001	*	*	*
30	.003	.003	.002	.002	.001	.001	.001	.001	*	*	*	*	*	*	*	*	*	*
35	.001	.001	.001	.001	*	*	*	*	*	*	*	*	*	*	*	*	*	*
40	*	*	*	*	*	*	*	*	*	*	*	*	*	*	*	*	*	*
45	*	*	*	*	*	*	*	*	*	*	*	*	*	*	*	*	*	*
50	*	*	*	*	*	*	*	*	*	*	*	*	*	*	*	*	*	*

* *PVIF* is zero to three decimal places.

Texas Instruments BA-35, BAII, BAII Plus[c]

Inputs:	1700	8	8		
Functions:	FV	N	%i	CPT	PV
Outputs:					918.46[d]

[c] For the Texas Instruments BAII, you would use the 2nd key instead of the CPT key; for the Texas Instruments BAII Plus, you would use the I/Y key instead of the %i key.

[d] If a minus sign precedes the output, it should be ignored.

TABLE A.4 Present-Value Interest Factors for a One-Dollar Annuity, *PVIFA*

Period	1%	2%	3%	4%	5%	6%	7%	8%	9%	10%	11%	12%	13%	14%	15%	16%	17%	18%	19%	20%
1	.990	.980	.971	.962	.952	.943	.935	.926	.917	.909	.901	.893	.885	.877	.870	.862	.855	.847	.840	.833
2	1.970	1.942	1.913	1.886	1.859	1.833	1.808	1.783	1.759	1.736	1.713	1.690	1.668	1.647	1.626	1.605	1.585	1.566	1.547	1.528
3	2.941	2.884	2.829	2.775	2.723	2.673	2.624	2.577	2.531	2.487	2.444	2.402	2.361	2.322	2.283	2.246	2.210	2.174	2.140	2.106
4	3.902	3.808	3.717	3.630	3.546	3.465	3.387	3.312	3.240	3.170	3.102	3.037	2.974	2.914	2.855	2.798	2.743	2.690	2.639	2.589
5	4.853	4.713	4.580	4.452	4.329	4.212	4.100	3.993	3.890	3.791	3.696	3.605	3.517	3.433	3.352	3.274	3.199	3.127	3.058	2.991
6	5.795	5.601	5.417	5.242	5.076	4.917	4.767	4.623	4.486	4.355	4.231	4.111	3.998	3.889	3.784	3.685	3.589	3.498	3.410	3.326
7	6.728	6.472	6.230	6.002	5.786	5.582	5.389	5.206	5.033	4.868	4.712	4.564	4.423	4.288	4.160	4.039	3.922	3.812	3.706	3.605
8	7.652	7.326	7.020	6.733	6.463	6.210	5.971	5.747	5.535	5.335	5.146	4.968	4.799	4.639	4.487	4.344	4.207	4.078	3.954	3.837
9	8.566	8.162	7.786	7.435	7.108	6.802	6.515	6.247	5.995	5.759	5.537	5.328	5.132	4.946	4.772	4.607	4.451	4.303	4.163	4.031
10	9.471	8.983	8.530	8.111	7.722	7.360	7.024	6.710	6.418	6.145	5.889	5.650	5.426	5.216	5.019	4.833	4.659	4.494	4.339	4.192
11	10.368	9.787	9.253	8.760	8.306	7.887	7.499	7.139	6.805	6.495	6.207	5.938	5.687	5.453	5.234	5.029	4.836	4.656	4.486	4.327
12	11.255	10.575	9.954	9.385	8.863	8.384	7.943	7.536	7.161	6.814	6.492	6.194	5.918	5.660	5.421	5.197	4.988	4.793	4.611	4.439
13	12.134	11.348	10.635	9.986	9.394	8.853	8.358	7.904	7.487	7.013	6.750	6.424	6.122	5.842	5.583	5.342	5.118	4.910	4.715	4.533
14	13.004	12.106	11.296	10.563	9.899	9.295	8.745	8.244	7.786	7.367	6.982	6.628	6.302	6.002	5.724	5.468	5.229	5.008	4.802	4.611
15	13.865	12.849	11.938	11.118	10.380	9.712	9.108	8.560	8.061	7.606	7.191	6.811	6.462	6.142	5.847	5.575	5.324	5.092	4.876	4.675
16	14.718	13.578	12.561	11.652	10.838	10.106	9.447	8.851	8.313	7.824	7.379	6.974	6.604	6.265	5.954	5.668	5.405	5.162	4.938	4.730
17	15.562	14.292	13.166	12.166	11.274	10.477	9.763	9.122	8.544	8.022	7.549	7.120	6.729	6.373	6.047	5.749	5.475	5.222	4.990	4.775
18	16.398	14.992	13.754	12.659	11.690	10.828	10.059	9.372	8.756	8.201	7.702	7.250	6.840	6.467	6.128	5.818	5.534	5.273	5.033	4.812
19	17.226	15.679	14.324	13.134	12.085	11.158	10.336	9.604	8.950	8.365	7.839	7.366	6.938	6.550	6.198	5.877	5.584	5.316	5.070	4.843
20	18.046	16.352	14.878	13.590	12.462	11.470	10.594	9.818	9.129	8.514	7.963	7.469	7.025	6.623	6.259	5.929	5.628	5.353	5.101	4.870
21	18.857	17.011	15.415	14.029	12.821	11.764	10.836	10.017	9.292	8.649	8.075	7.562	7.102	6.687	6.312	5.973	5.665	5.384	5.127	4.891
22	19.661	17.658	15.937	14.451	13.163	12.042	11.061	10.201	9.442	8.772	8.176	7.645	7.170	6.743	6.359	6.011	5.696	5.410	5.149	4.909
23	20.456	18.292	16.444	14.857	13.489	12.303	11.272	10.371	9.580	8.883	8.266	7.718	7.230	6.792	6.399	6.044	5.723	5.432	5.167	4.925
24	21.244	18.914	16.936	15.247	13.799	12.550	11.469	10.529	9.707	8.985	8.348	7.784	7.283	6.835	6.434	6.073	5.746	5.451	5.182	4.937
25	22.023	19.524	17.413	15.622	14.094	12.783	11.654	10.675	9.823	9.077	8.422	7.843	7.330	6.873	6.464	6.097	5.766	5.467	5.195	4.948
30	25.808	22.396	19.601	17.292	15.373	13.765	12.409	11.258	10.274	9.427	8.694	8.055	7.496	7.003	6.566	6.177	5.829	5.517	5.235	4.979
35	29.409	24.999	21.487	18.665	16.374	14.498	12.948	11.655	10.567	9.644	8.855	8.176	7.586	7.070	6.617	6.215	5.858	5.539	5.251	4.992
40	32.835	27.356	23.115	19.793	17.159	15.046	13.332	11.925	10.757	9.779	8.951	8.244	7.634	7.105	6.642	6.233	5.871	5.548	5.258	4.997
45	36.095	29.490	24.519	20.720	17.774	15.456	13.606	12.108	10.881	9.863	9.008	8.283	7.661	7.123	6.654	6.242	5.877	5.552	5.261	4.999
50	39.196	31.424	25.730	21.482	18.256	15.762	13.801	12.233	10.962	9.915	9.042	8.304	7.675	7.133	6.661	6.246	5.880	5.554	5.262	4.999

Using the Calculator to Compute the Present Value of an Annuity

Before you begin, clear the memory, ensure that you are in the *end mode* and that your calculator is set for *one payment per year*, and set the number of decimal places that you want (usually two for dollar-related accuracy).

Sample Problem

You want to know what the present value of an annuity of $700 per year received at the end of each year for 5 years will be, given a discount rate of 8%.

Hewlett-Packard HP 12C, 17 BII, and 19 BII[a]

Inputs:	700	5	8	
Functions:	PMT	N	I%YR	PV
Outputs:				2794.90[b]

[a] For the 12C, you would use the n key instead of the N key, and the i key instead of the I%YR key.

[b] The minus sign that precedes the output should be ignored.

TABLE A.4 (Continued)

Period	21%	22%	23%	24%	25%	26%	27%	28%	29%	30%	31%	32%	33%	34%	35%	40%	45%	50%
1	.826	.820	.813	.806	.800	.794	.787	.781	.775	.769	.763	.758	.752	.746	.741	.714	.690	.667
2	1.509	1.492	1.474	1.457	1.440	1.424	1.407	1.392	1.376	1.361	1.346	1.331	1.317	1.303	1.289	1.224	1.165	1.111
3	2.074	2.042	2.011	1.981	1.952	1.923	1.896	1.868	1.842	1.816	1.791	1.766	1.742	1.719	1.696	1.589	1.493	1.407
4	2.540	2.494	2.448	2.404	2.362	2.320	2.280	2.241	2.203	2.166	2.130	2.096	2.062	2.029	1.997	1.849	1.720	1.605
5	2.926	2.864	2.803	2.745	2.689	2.635	2.583	2.532	2.483	2.436	2.390	2.345	2.302	2.260	2.220	2.035	1.876	1.737
6	3.245	3.167	3.092	3.020	2.951	2.885	2.821	2.759	2.700	2.643	2.588	2.534	2.483	2.433	2.385	2.168	1.983	1.824
7	3.508	3.416	3.327	3.242	3.161	3.083	3.009	2.937	2.868	2.802	2.739	2.677	2.619	2.562	2.508	2.263	2.057	1.883
8	3.726	3.619	3.518	3.421	3.329	3.241	3.156	3.076	2.999	2.925	2.854	2.786	2.721	2.658	2.598	2.331	2.109	1.922
9	3.905	3.786	3.673	3.566	3.463	3.366	3.273	3.184	3.100	3.019	2.942	2.868	2.798	2.730	2.665	2.379	2.144	1.948
10	4.054	3.923	3.799	3.682	3.570	3.465	3.364	3.269	3.178	3.092	3.009	2.930	2.855	2.784	2.715	2.414	2.168	1.965
11	4.177	4.035	3.902	3.776	3.656	3.544	3.437	3.335	3.239	3.147	3.060	2.978	2.899	2.824	2.752	2.438	2.185	1.977
12	4.278	4.127	3.985	3.851	3.725	3.606	3.493	3.387	3.286	3.190	3.100	3.013	2.931	2.853	2.779	2.456	2.196	1.985
13	4.362	4.203	4.053	3.912	3.780	3.656	3.538	3.427	3.322	3.223	3.129	3.040	2.956	2.876	2.799	2.469	2.204	1.990
14	4.432	4.265	4.108	3.962	3.824	3.695	3.573	3.459	3.351	3.249	3.152	3.061	2.974	2.892	2.814	2.478	2.210	1.993
15	4.489	4.315	4.153	4.001	3.859	3.726	3.601	3.483	3.373	3.268	3.170	3.076	2.988	2.905	2.825	2.484	2.214	1.995
16	4.536	4.357	4.189	4.033	3.887	3.751	3.623	3.503	3.390	3.283	3.183	3.088	2.999	2.914	2.834	2.489	2.216	1.997
17	4.576	4.391	4.219	4.059	3.910	3.771	3.640	3.518	3.403	3.295	3.193	3.097	3.007	2.921	2.840	2.492	2.218	1.998
18	4.608	4.419	4.243	4.080	3.928	3.786	3.654	3.529	3.413	3.304	3.201	3.104	3.012	2.926	2.844	2.494	2.219	1.999
19	4.635	4.442	4.263	4.097	3.942	3.799	3.664	3.539	3.421	3.311	3.207	3.109	3.017	2.930	2.848	2.496	2.220	1.999
20	4.657	4.460	4.279	4.110	3.954	3.808	3.673	3.546	3.427	3.316	3.211	3.113	3.020	2.933	2.850	2.497	2.221	1.999
21	4.675	4.476	4.292	4.121	3.963	3.816	3.679	3.551	3.432	3.320	3.215	3.116	3.023	2.935	2.852	2.498	2.221	2.000
22	4.690	4.488	4.302	4.130	3.970	3.822	3.684	3.556	3.436	3.323	3.217	3.118	3.025	2.936	2.853	2.498	2.222	2.000
23	4.703	4.499	4.311	4.137	3.976	3.827	3.689	3.559	3.438	3.325	3.219	3.120	3.026	2.938	2.854	2.499	2.222	2.000
24	4.713	4.507	4.318	4.143	3.981	3.831	3.692	3.562	3.441	3.327	3.221	3.121	3.027	2.939	2.855	2.499	2.222	2.000
25	4.721	4.514	4.323	4.147	3.985	3.834	3.694	3.564	3.442	3.329	3.222	3.122	3.028	2.939	2.856	2.499	2.222	2.000
30	4.746	4.534	4.339	4.160	3.995	3.842	3.701	3.569	3.447	3.332	3.225	3.124	3.030	2.941	2.857	2.500	2.222	2.000
35	4.756	4.541	4.345	4.164	3.998	3.845	3.703	3.571	3.448	3.333	3.226	3.125	3.030	2.941	2.857	2.500	2.222	2.000
40	4.760	4.544	4.347	4.166	3.999	3.846	3.703	3.571	3.448	3.333	3.226	3.125	3.030	2.941	2.857	2.500	2.222	2.000
45	4.761	4.545	4.347	4.166	4.000	3.846	3.704	3.571	3.448	3.333	3.226	3.125	3.030	2.941	2.857	2.500	2.222	2.000
50	4.762	4.545	4.348	4.167	4.000	3.846	3.704	3.571	3.448	3.333	3.226	3.125	3.030	2.941	2.857	2.500	2.222	2.000

Texas Instruments BA-35, BAII, BAII Plus[c]

Inputs:	700	5	8		
Functions:	PMT	N	%i	CPT	FV
Outputs:					2794.90[d]

[c] For the Texas Instruments BAII, you would use the 2nd key instead of the CPT key; for the Texas Instruments BAII Plus, you would use the I/Y key instead of the %i key.

[d] If a minus sign precedes the output, it should be ignored.

Credits

Page 4, Investing in Action: Adapted from "Seeing the Sites," *Barron's,* October 27, 1997. Page 7, Investor Fact: From Investment Company Institute. Page 9, Investing in Action: Adapted from "Generation $ Is More Like It," *Business Week,* November 3, 1997. Page 13, Investor Fact: From Investment Company Institute. Page 20, Investor Fact: From *Wall Street Journal,* October 9, 1997, p. A1. Page 24, Investor Fact: From *Wall Street Journal,* January 2, 1998, p. R4. Page 26, Investing in Action: Adapted from "The Booming Big Board," *Business Week,* August 4, 1997. Page 28, Figure 2.2: Reprinted by permission of Playtex Products, Inc., April 23, 1998, p. 1. Page 29, Investor Fact: From *New York Times,* December 28, 1997, p. BU8. Page 35, Investing in Action: Adapted from "Capitalism with a Vengeance," *The New York Times,* October 5, 1997. Page 38, Investor Fact: From *Wall Street Journal,* January 17, 1997. Page 70, Investor Fact: From American Century Family of Funds. Page 82, Figure 3.3: Reprinted by permission of *The Wall Street Journal,* © 1994 Dow Jones & Company, Inc. All Rights Reserved Worldwide. Page 86, Figure 3.4: Copyright 1998 by *Value Line Publishing, Inc.* Reprinted By Permission. All Rights Reserved. Page 90, Figure 3.5: Reprinted by permission of Hewlett-Packard. Page 97; Investing in Action: From NAIC, *New York Times,* April 21, 1996. Page 99, Figure 3.6: Reprinted by permission of *The Wall Street Journal,* © 1994 Dow Jones & Company, Inc. All Rights Reserved Worldwide. Page 100, Figure 3.7: Reprinted by permission of *The Wall Street Journal,* © 1994 Dow Jones & Company, Inc. All Rights Reserved Worldwide. Page 119, Investing in Action: From *Business Week,* November 10, 1997; *The Arizona Republic,* October 5, 1997; *Washington Post,* September 7, 1997. Page 122, Investor Fact: From *S&P Outlook,* November 5, 1997. Page 146, Investor Fact: From *Investor's Business Daily,* December 11, 1997, p. B1. Page 149, Investor Fact: From *Wall Street Journal,* January 8, 1998, p. R3. Page 152, Investing in Action: Maria Crawford Scott, "Life-Cycle Investing: Investment Decisions and Your Personal Investment Profile," *AAII Journal,* March 1993, pp. 16–19 (downloaded from America Online); and Ann Perry, "Putting Stock in the Market," *San Diego Union-Tribune,* July 18, 1993, pp. 11–12. Page 169, Investor Fact: From *Wall Street Journal,* April 7, 1997, p. C1. Page 176, Figure 5.3: Reprinted by permission of Donaldson, Lufkin & Jenrette. Page 177, Investing in Action: From "Why Catch a Knife?" *Barron's,* October 6, 1997, p. 17; "Why Spin-offs Work For Investors," *Fortune,* October 16, 1995, p. 90; "Free at Last," *Worth* magazine, July/August 1995, p. 27. Page 180, Figure 5.4: Reprinted by permission of *The Wall Street Journal,* © 1997 Dow Jones & Company, Inc. All Rights Reserved Worldwide. Page 185, Figure 5.5: Reprinted by permission of *The Wall Street Journal,* © 1997 Dow Jones & Company, Inc. All Rights Reserved Worldwide. Page 190, Wal-Mart Stock Report: Reprinted by permission of Standard & Poor's, a division of the McGraw-Hill Companies. Page 191, Intel Stock Report: Reprinted by permission of Standard & Poor's, a division of the McGraw-Hill Companies. Page 193, Wendy's Stock Report: Reprinted by permission of Standard & Poor's, a division of the McGraw-Hill Companies. Page 194, Alaska Air Group Stock Report: Reprinted by permission of Standard & Poor's, a division of the McGraw-Hill Companies. Page 197, Investing in Action: From "Are the Best Global Values Right Here at Home?" *Smart Money,* May 1996, p. 42; *Wall Street Journal,* June 26, 1997, p. R16. Page 198, Investor Fact: From *Bloomberg Personal,* 1997. Page 216, Investing in Action: From *Investor's Business Daily,* November 10, 1997, p. A-6; *Business Week,* November 17, 1997, p. 35. Page 222, Figure 6.1: Reprinted by permission of Standard & Poor's, a division of the McGraw-Hill Companies. Page 230, Investing in Action: Based on William H. Beaver, "Ten Commandments of Financial Statement Analysis," *Financial Analysts Journal,* January/February 1991, pp. 9, 18. Page 237, Investor Fact: From *Forbes,* September 8, 1997, p. 78. Page 240, Figure 6.2: Reprinted by permission of Standard & Poor's, a division of the McGraw-Hill Companies. Page 254, Investor Fact: From *Wall Street Journal,* June 26, 1997, p. R16. Page 255, Table 7.1: Reprinted by permission of Standard & Poor's, a division of the McGraw-Hill Companies. Page 278, Figure 7.1: Reprinted by permission of *The Wall Street Journal,* © 1997 Dow Jones & Company, Inc. All Rights Reserved Worldwide. Page 280, Figure 7.2: Reprinted by permission of *The Wall Street Journal,* © 1997 Dow Jones & Company, Inc. All Rights Reserved Worldwide. Page 281, Investing in Action: From *Wall Street Journal,* October 28, 1997, p. C1. Page 283, Figure 7.3: Reprinted by permission of Daily Graphs, Inc., 12655 Beatrice Street, Los Angeles, CA 90066, 800-472-7479. Page 288, Investor Fact: From "Market Timing Can be Painful," *Fidelity Focus,* Winter 1996. Page 311, Figure 8.2: Reprinted by permission of Bear Stearns Company. Page 312, Investor Fact: From "On the Frontier of Creative Finance," *Fortune,* April 28, 1997, p. 50. Page 315, Figure 8.4: Reprinted by permission of *The Wall Street Journal,* © 1997 Dow Jones & Company, Inc. All Rights Reserved Worldwide. Page 316, Investing in Action: From Burton Malkiel, "Hot Tips?" *Bloomberg Personal,* September 1997, p. 39; "When Does a 3.5% Bond Yield Beat 6.5%? *Kiplinger's Personal Finance Magazine,* April 1997, p. 16; Tom Herman, "How to Decide What to Do Next Week When Inflation-Indexed Bonds Debut," *Wall Street Journal,* January 24, 1997, p. C-1; Maria Fiorini Ramirez, "The New Bond on the Block," *Bloomberg Personal,* November/December 1996, p. 54. Page 318, Investor Fact: From Duff McDonald, "Consider Investing in Taxable Municipal Bonds," *Money,* December 1995, p. 19. Page 325, Investing in Action: From Kim Clark, "How Wall Street Can Securitize Anything," *Fortune,* April 28, 1997, p. 50; Cecile Gutscher, "Banks Are Getting Rid of Low-Margin Loans by Bundling Them as New Bonds Called CLOs," *Wall Street Journal,* September 9, 1997, p. C19; Gregory Zuckerman, "Asset-Backed Bonds Boosted by Equity Loans," *Wall Street Journal,* September 29, 1997, p. C1. Page 332, Investor Fact: From Suzanne McGee, "Crossover Bonds Meet Strong Demand from Investors in Search of Better Yields, *Wall Street Journal,* June 6, 1996, p. C1. Reprinted by permission of *The Wall Street Journal,* © 1997 Dow Jones & Company, Inc. All Rights Reserved Worldwide. Page 334, Figure 8.5: Reprinted by permission of *The Wall Street Journal,* © 1997 Dow Jones & Company, Inc. All Rights Reserved Worldwide. Page 346, Figure 9.1: Reprinted by permission of *The Wall Street Journal,* © 1997 Dow Jones & Company, Inc All Rights Reserved Worldwide. Page 350, Figure 9.4: Reprinted by permission of *The Wall Street Journal,* © 1997 Dow Jones & Company, Inc. All Rights Reserved Worldwide. Page 359, Investing in Action: Adapted from Barbara Donnelly, "Bond Investors Who Fixate Too Much on Yields Risk Missing the Big Picture," *Wall Street Journal,* March 13, 1992, p. C1. Page 361, Investor Fact: From Pamela Druckerman, "Bond Traders Hunt for Yields in the Fields of Nicaragua," *Wall Street Journal,* September 16, 1997, p. A14. Reprinted by permission of *The Wall Street Journal ,* © 1997 Dow Jones & Company, Inc. All Rights Reserved Worldwide. Page 372, Investing in Action: From Christopher Graja, "Ladders, Barbells, and Bullets," *Bloomberg Personal,* November 1997, p. 25; Clint Willis, "Build Fiscal Fitness with Barbells," *Worth,* October 1995, p. 74 Page 381, Vignette: From *Wall Street Journal,* January 2, 1998, P. R37. Page 383, Figure 10.1: Reprinted by permission of Standard & Poor's, a division of the McGraw-Hill Companies. Page 385, Figure 10.2: Reprinted by permission of *The Wall Street Journal,* © 1997 Dow Jones & Company, Inc. All Rights Reserved Worldwide. Page 393, Investing in Action: From Robert T. Kleiman and Anandi P. Sahu, "Hybrid Securities: A Basic Look at Monthly Income Preferred Stock," *AAII Journal,* July

1997, p. 14; James A. Anderson, "Not New and Improved," *Smart Money,* July 1995, p. 44. Page 394, Figure 10.3: Moody's Investor Services. Reprinted with permission. Page 396, Figure 10.4: Source: C.E. Unterberg, Towbin, Janney Montgomery Scott Inc. Reprinted with permission. Page 398, Investor Fact: From *Fortune,* September 18, 1995, p. 240; http://www.cytogen.com; *Wall Street Journal,* January 2, 1998, p. R25. Page 401, Investing in Action: From Jersey Gilbert, "Yes It's a Bond, But It Pays Off Like a Stock," *Smart Money,* June 1996, p. 42; Richard D. Hylton, "Convertible Preferred Stock Strategies," *Fortune,* September 18, 1995, p. 240; http://www.froleyrevy.com; Pacific Alliance Capital Management, a division of Union Bank of California. Page 403, Figure 10.5: Reprinted by permission of *The Wall Street Journal,* © 1997 Dow Jones & Company, Inc. All Rights Reserved Worldwide. Page 421, Investor Fact: From "Souped-Up Certificates of Deposit," *Business Week,* August 8, 1993, p. 55. Page 423, Figure 11.1: Reprinted by permission of *The Wall Street Journal,* © 1997 Dow Jones & Company, Inc. All Rights Reserved Worldwide. Page 425, Investor Fact: From The Options Clearing Corp. Page 437, Investing in Action: From Witold Sames, "Up, Down, or Sideways," *Bloomberg Personal,* October 1997, p. 30; "Understanding Stock Options," *The Chicago Board Options Exchange,* http://www.cboe.com/intro/undstopt.html. Page 440, Figure 11.3: Reprinted by permission of *The Wall Street Journal,* © 1997 Dow Jones & Company, Inc. All Rights Reserved Worldwide. Page 443, Investing in Action: Adapted and updated from Stanley W. Angrist, "Put Options Can Help Protect Portfolios," *Wall Street Journal,* February 28, 1989, p. C1. Page 447, Figure 11.4: Reprinted by permission of *The Wall Street Journal,* © 1997 Dow Jones & Company, Inc. All Rights Reserved Worldwide. Page 458, Vignette: From Bear Stearns 1997 Annual Report. Page 461, Investor Fact: From Scott Kilman, "Farm Wives Step Into Futures, As Brokerage Firms Woo Them," *Wall Street Journal,* February 11, 1998, p. C1. Page 462, All photos: Copyright © Chicago Board of Trade. Reprinted with permission. Page 466, Figure 12.2: Reprinted by permission of *The Wall Street Journal,* © 1997 Dow Jones & Company, Inc. All Rights Reserved Worldwide. Page 469, Investor Fact: From Minneapolis Grain Exchange. Page 470, Figure 12.3: Reprinted with permission of Commodity Price Charts, published by Futures Communications Company, Chicago, Illinois. Page 475, Investor Fact: From CFTC Annual Report 1997. Page 476, Figure 12.4: Reprinted by permission of *The Wall Street Journal,* © 1997 Dow Jones & Company, Inc. All Rights Reserved Worldwide. Page 479, Investing in Action: Adapted from Stanley W. Angrist, "Futures Offer Cheap Play on Small Stocks' Annual Rally," *Wall Street Journal,* December 13, 1990, p. C1. Page 482, Investing in Action: From "Stocks Lower Early on Triple Witching Day," *Reuters,* September 19, 1997; Interview with Robert N. Gordon, President and Founder, Twenty-First Securities Corporation, New York. Page 494, Vignette: From Andrew Bary, "Bigger Isn't Better," *Barron's,* November 17, 1997, p. 25; http://www.vanguard.com. Page 495, Investor Fact: From *1997 Mutual Fund Fact Book,* Ch. 5. Page 496, Figure 13.1: Reprinted by permission of the Kaufmann Fund. Page 498, Figure 13.2: Reprinted by permission of Morningstar. Page 501, Figure 13.3: Reprinted by permission of *The Wall Street Journal,* © 1997 Dow Jones & Company, Inc. All Rights Reserved Worldwide. Page 502, Figure 13.4: Reprinted by permission of *The Wall Street Journal,* © 1997 Dow Jones & Company, Inc. All Rights Reserved Worldwide. Page 505, Figure 13.5: Reprinted by permission of *The Wall Street Journal,* © 1998 Dow Jones & Company, Inc. All Rights Reserved Worldwide. Page 516, Investor Fact: From Eric Uhlfelder, "Country Baskets," *Mutual Funds,* September 1996, p. 45. Page 517, Investing in Action: From Christopher Williams, "Funds of Funds," *Mutual Funds,* April 1997, p. 57; Mary Beth Grover, "House Blends," *Forbes,* August 25, 1997, p. 158; Johnathan Burton, "Let a Pro Pick Your Funds," *Mutual Funds,* February 1996, p. 47; Deborah Lohse, "The Diet Spread," *Wall Street Journal,* December 8, 1995, p. R9. Page 519, Figure 13.6: Reprinted by permission of Morningstar. Page 521, Table 13.2: Mutual Funds Magazine. Reprinted by permission. Page 523, Investor Fact: From David Franecki, "Buried Treasures: Houston Firm Takes Grave View of Profits," *Wall Street Journal,* May 23, 1997, p. B8C. Page 526, Figure 13.7: Reprinted by permission of Morningstar. Page 527, Investing in Action: From Steven Kaufman, "Breaking the Code," *Individual Investor,* December 1997, p. 125; Dan Moreau, "Prospectuses Are Getting Easier to Read," *Investor's Business Daily,* December 15, 1997, p. B1; Ruth Simon, "Invest Smarter by Ferreting Out the Secrets in Fund Prospectuses," *Money,* October 1997, p. 41; Barbara Whelehan, "Prospectusphobia," *Mutual Funds,* November 1995, p. 45. Page 529, Table 13.3: Reprinted by permission of Morningstar. Page 543, Vignette: From http://www.starwood-logdging.com; Frequently Asked Questions About REITS, National Association of Real Estate Investment Trusts. Page 548, Investor Fact: From Michael Conlon, "Away on Business," Reuters News Service, as published in the *St. Louis Post-Dispatch,* December 29, 1997, p. P14. Page 568, Investor Fact: National Association of Real Estate Investment Trusts, 1997. Page 570, Investing in Action: Adapted from Lynn Asinoff, "REITs: A Smart Investment or a Sucker's Bet?" *Wall Street Journal,* June 3, 1994, p. C1; Jack Egan, "Best Real Estate Deal on the Block?" *U.S. News & World Report,* November 21, 1994, p. 98; Stephanie Anderson Forest, "Now Dividend Hunters Are Stalking REITs," *Business Week,* June 6, 1994, pp. 120–21; Gordon Williams, "They're Baaaaaaack," *Financial World,* May 24, 1994, pp. 80–83; and National Association of Real Estate Investment Trusts. Page 574, Investing in Action: Adapted from Edward Baig, "Collectibles: How Do You Tell Trash from Treasure?" *Business Week,* June 27, 1994, pp. 106, E2–E4; Christie Brown, "Revenge of the Philistines," *Forbes,* December 6, 1993, pp. 149–54; and Alexandra Peers, "Keep Everything," *Wall Street Journal,* December 9, 1994, p. R8. Page 578, Investor Fact: From http://www.sothebys.com; http://www.christies.com. Page 586, Vignette: From Microsoft, *1997 Annual Report.* Page 599, Investing in Action: From Jane Bryant Quinn, "Is Your 401(k) OK?" *Newsweek,* September 19, 1994, pp. 44–45; Ruth Simon, "We Have Some Bad News About Your 401(k)," *Money,* May 1994, pp. 94–102; Penelope Wang, "ABC's of 401(k) Investing," *Money,* February 1995, pp. 144–45; and Gordon Williams, "Fiddling with 401(k)s," *Financial World,* February 1, 1994, pp. 64–68. Page 602, Investor Fact: From Carole Gould, "Education IRA's Are Already Getting Low Marks," *New York Times,* January 18, 1998, p. 7 BU; 1997 Tax Law Summary, Ernst & Young. Page 603, Investing in Action: From Ingrid Eisenstadter, "Retirement Foresight from the Younger Set," *New York Times,* February 22, 1998, p. 6 BU; "To Roth or Not to Roth," *IAI Advisor* newsletter, Winter 1998, p. 6. Page 630, Vignette: From Timothy L. O'Brien & Joseph B. Treaster, "In Largest Deal Ever, Citicorp Plans Merger with Travelers Group," *New York Times,* April 7, 1998, p. A1; Travelers Group 1997 Annual Report. Page 636, Investor Fact: From Michael Santoli, "Nearly 9000," *Barron's,* April 6, 1998. Page 638, Investor Fact: From Jathon Sapsford and Sara Webb, "Tokyo Market's Current Slogan: We Are No. 3," *Wall Street Journal,* March 31, 1998, p. C1. Page 656, Investor Fact: From *Wall Street Journal,* April 6, 1998, Section R. Page 679, Investor Fact: From Quarterly Mutual Fund Review, *Wall Street Journal,* April 6, 1998, p. R7. Page 682, Investing in Action: From Karen Slater, "Portfolio Return Is Tough Figure to Find," *Wall Street Journal,* January 22, 1990, p. C1; "How Did You Do in 1997?" *Money* magazine, Forecast 1998, p. 24A; Karen Hube, "How to Sidestep a 'Beardstown Blunder' When Calculating Portfolio Performance," *Wall Street Journal,* March 25, 1998, p. C1. Page 695, Investor Fact: From Microsoft 1997 Annual Report.

INDEX

FUNDAMENTALS OF INVESTING (FOI) CD-ROM SOFTWARE USER'S GUIDE

SYSTEM REQUIREMENTS

- IBM or IBM Compatible PC
- Microsoft® Windows 95 Operating System
- CD-ROM Drive

USING THE FUNDAMENTALS OF INVESTING SOFTWARE

1. Insert the Fundamentals of Investing CD-ROM into your CD-ROM drive.
2. Click the Windows 95 Start button.
3. Select Run, type **D:\FunInvest.exe** (or the letter of your CD-ROM drive).
4. Copy FunInvest.exe to your hard drive to speed up loading of the application.
5. For ease of use, it is preferable to set the screen resolution to 800 by 600 pixels using "Small Fonts".

Please be sure to store the CD-ROM in a safe place.

ABOUT THIS PROGRAM

The Fundamentals of Investing (FOI) software is composed of a set of pull-down menus with topics correlated to the 7th edition of the Fundamentals of Investing textbook. The topics covered in the software are shown below with the top level of the menu bar shown in bold print.

- **Analysis**
  - How an Investment Grows
  - Finding a Lump Sum Investment
  - Making a Series of Investments over Time
  - Margin Trading
  - Treasury Bill Yields
  - Holding Period Return (HPR)
  - Measuring Risk
  - Estimating Return
  - Time Value of Money

- **Securities**
  - Stock Valuations
    - Key Financial Ratios – Corporate Measures
    - Key Financial Ratios – Common Stock Measures
    - Estimating Future Stock Prices & Dividends
    - Stock Valuation Models

  - Bond Valuations
    - Bond Prices and Yields
    - Expected Return
    - Taxable Equivalent Yields
    - Bond Duration

  - Convertibles
    - Conversion Measures
    - Yields
    - Expected Return on a Convertible

- **Securities (continued)**
  - Preferreds
    - Pricing Preferreds
    - Valuing Preferreds
    - Expected Return on a Preferred

  - Options & Futures Valuations
    - Options Valuation
    - Warrant Valuation
    - Futures Contracts

  - Returns on Foreign Securities

- **Mutual Funds**
  - Holding Period Returns
  - Long Term Returns

- **Real Estate**
  - Market Value
  - Net Present Value
  - Yield
  - After-Tax Cash Flows
  - After-Tax Net Proceeds from Sale

- **Portfolio Measures**
  - Portfolio Performance
  - HPR for a Portfolio
  - Stock Beta
  - Portfolio Beta